Atlas Obscura

AN
EXPLORER'S
GUIDE TO
THE WORLD'S
HIDDEN
WONDERS

Joshua Foer, Dylan Thuras & Ella Morton

WORKMAN PUBLISHING · NEW YORK

An Important Note to Readers

Though the publisher and authors have taken reasonable steps to ensure the accuracy and timeliness of the information contained in the book, readers are strongly encouraged to confirm details before making any travel plans. Location and direction information may change; GPS coordinates are approximations and should be treated as such. If you discover any out-of-date or incorrect information in the book, please let us know via book@atlasobscura.com.

Atlas Obscura was written in the spirit of adventure, and readers are cautioned to travel at their own risk and to obey all local laws. Some of the places described in this book are not open to the public and are not meant to be visited without appropriate permissions. Neither the authors nor the publisher shall be liable or responsible for any loss, injury, or damage allegedly arising from any information or suggestions contained in this book.

....

The beginning of our happiness lies in the understanding that life without wonder is not worth living.

—Abraham Joshua Heschel

CONTENTS

More than 350 feet below the surface, rowboats bob on a lake inside Romania's Turda Salt Mine. Now an underground amusement park, the mine produced table salt continuously from the 11th century until the 1930s. Page 88.

INTRODUCTION

When we launched Atlas Obscura in 2009, our goal was to create a catalog of all the places, people, and things that inspire our sense of wonder. One of us had recently spent two months driving all over the United States searching out tiny museums and eccentric outsider art projects. The other was about to set off for a year of travels in Eastern Europe. We wanted a way of finding the curious, out-of-the-way places that don't often make it into traditional guidebooks—the kinds of destinations that expand our sense of what is possible, but which we would never be able to find without a tip from someone in the know. Over the years, thousands of people from all over the world have joined us in this collaborative project by contributing entries to the Atlas. This book represents just a tiny fraction of what our community has unearthed. Every one of you out there who added a place to the Atlas, made an edit, or sent in a photo: You are all our coauthors. Thank you.

This revised second edition has been updated to include over 100 incredible new places that members of our community have shared with us since the first edition of this book was published in 2016. We've also added a foldout map depicting our idea of the world's most amazing (and longest) road trip. Though Atlas Obscura may have the trappings of a travel guide, it is in truth something else. The site, and this book, are a kind of wunderkammer of places, a cabinet of curiosities that is meant to inspire wonderlust as much as wanderlust. In fact, many of the places in this book are in no way "tourist sites" and should not be treated as such. Others are so out of the way, so treacherously situated, or (in at least one case) so deep beneath the surface, that few readers will ever be able to visit them. But here they are, sharing this marvelously strange planet with us.

This book would never exist without the incomparable and indefatigable Ella Morton, or our ace project manager, Marc Haeringer, who guided this book from beginning to end. Though we have tried to check the accuracy of every fact in these pages, please don't book any plane tickets without first doing your own independent research. Or do! Just be ready for an adventure.

We often ask ourselves just how large a truly comprehensive compendium of the world's wonders and curiosities could ultimately be. The economics of printing and the dimensions of the page set limits on what could be included in this book. But even our website, which faces no such constraints, can never be complete. There is an Atlas Obscura yet to be written that is as comprehensive as the world itself, for wonder can be found wherever we are open to searching for it.

Joshua Foer and Dylan Thuras
cofounders of Atlas Obscura

Europe

Great Britain and Ireland

ENGLAND · IRELAND · NORTHERN IRELAND
SCOTLAND

Western Europe

AUSTRIA · BELGIUM · FRANCE · GERMANY · GREECE
CYPRUS · ITALY · NETHERLANDS · PORTUGAL
SPAIN · SWITZERLAND

Eastern Europe

BULGARIA · CROATIA · CZECH REPUBLIC
ESTONIA · HUNGARY · LATVIA · LITHUANIA · MACEDONIA
POLAND · ROMANIA · RUSSIA · SERBIA · SLOVAKIA · UKRAINE

Scandinavia

DENMARK · FINLAND · ICELAND
NORWAY · SWEDEN

-10°
Miles
0
50
100
0
50
100
Kilometers
N
SCOTLAND
NORTH SEA
Fingal's Cave
ATLANTIC OCEAN
The Poison Garden
Giant's Causeway
Garden of Cosmic Speculation
Vanishing Lake
55°
55°
NORTHERN IRELAND
The Silver Swan
IRISH SEA
The Crypts at Christ Church
DUBLIN
MV Plassey
Leviathan of Parsonstown
Victor's Way
ENGLAND
IRELAND
The Chained Books of Hereford Cathedral
WALES
Skellig Michael
LONDON
Irish Sky Garden
River Thames
Maunsell Sea Forts
Mechanical Clock at Salisbury Cathedral
Witley Underwater Ballroom
Sound Mirrors
GREAT BRITAIN AND IRELAND
The Tempest Prognosticator
No Man's Land Luxury Sea Fort
CELTIC SEA
ENGLISH CHANNEL
50°
-10°
5°
0°
50°
0°

ENGLAND

The Silver Swan

NEWGATE, DURHAM

This uncannily lifelike musical automaton mimics a full-size swan floating on a pond of spun-glass rods. Created in the 1770s, it uses three clockwork mechanisms to perform a 40-second routine set to calming bell-like music. When wound, the swan moves its neck from side to side to preen its feathers before dipping its beak into the pond and snatching up a tiny fish.

First displayed in British jeweler James Cox's Mechanical Museum, the swan was purchased by collector John Bowes in 1872 and is now housed in the Bowes Museum—a French chateau in the north of England.

Bowes Museum, Newgate. A museum curator demonstrates the swan at 2 p.m. daily. The Bowes Museum is 17 miles (27.4 km) from Darlington railway station, which is a 2.5-hour train trip from London. Buses run from the station to the museum.
Ⓝ 54.542142 Ⓦ 1.915462 ➻

➡ Walking, Eating, Moving Machines

Automatons—mechanical figures that move in an eerily lifelike manner—have existed for centuries, but their heyday was during the 18th and 19th centuries.

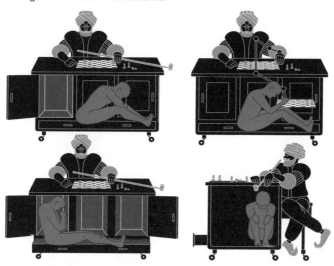

The Turk had a human microcontroller.

The Turk, built in 1770, was one of the most impressive: It consisted of a mechanical man in a turban who played chess against anyone willing to take him on. The machine toured the world, battling opponents like Napoleon Bonaparte and Benjamin Franklin. During the early 19th century, the Turk's apparent intelligence and skill dazzled audiences and frustrated skeptics, who suspected a trick.

In the end, eagle-eyed observers, including Edgar Allan Poe, who encountered the Turk in Virginia in 1835, discovered the secret: a hidden human. The cabinet beneath the chess board held a squashed chess master who made every move by candlelight, pulling levers to operate the Turk's arm and keeping track of the moves on his or her own board. The Turk was nothing but an elaborate hoax.

While the Turk was frustrating its opponents, genuine automatons delighted onlookers with their realistic movements. The Digesting Duck, the 1739 creation of Jacques de Vaucanson, flapped its wings, moved its head, ate grains, and shortly afterward defecated. The digestion process was not authentic— the duck's backside housed a reservoir of droppings that would fall in response to the amount of grains being "eaten"—but it was the first step toward what de Vaucanson hoped would eventually be a genuine eating machine.

Pierre Jaquet-Droz and his two sons spent six years starting in 1768 crafting The Musician, The Draftsman, and The Writer, a trio of dolls now housed in Switzerland's Museum of Art and History. The female musician plays an organ, her chest rising and falling to mimic breathing and her body moving in the manner of an impassioned pianist. The draftsman and writer are dressed identically in lacy shirts, gold satin breeches, and red velvet robes, and each sits at a desk. While the draftsman draws one of four programmed images, including portraits of Louis XV and a dog, the writer dips a goose feather in ink and can write custom text of up to 40 characters.

Steam Men were all the rage in the late 1800s, beginning with 22-year-old New Jersey resident Zadoc Dederick's 1868 model: a 7-foot-9-inch (236 cm) man in a top hat who pulled a carriage. His bulky torso housed a boiler that generated enough power to propel him forward, one footstep at a time.

Canadian George Moore's 1893 version, unattached to a carriage, measured 6 feet (2 m) tall and resembled a medieval knight. An exhaust pipe emerged from his nostril, making him appear to have steamy breath whenever he walked. His movement was limited by one crucial factor: Since he was attached to a horizontal stabilizing arm, he could only walk in circles.

Tipu's Tiger, a tidy representation of the enmity between the residents of India and their 18th-century British colonizers, is an Indian-made, crank-operated toy located in the Victoria & Albert Museum. It depicts a tiger mauling a helpless British officer. Turning the handle makes the man's left hand rise weakly in an attempt to shield his face from the attack. As the hand moves up and down, air rushes through two pairs of bellows. The resulting sounds—beastly growls and the cries of a man in his death throes— leave no ambiguity as to who wins the tussle.

Tipu's Tiger, immortalized mid-meal.

THE POISON GARDEN

ALNWICK, NORTHUMBERLAND

To enter the poison garden of Alnwick, you must first fetch a guide to unlock the black iron gates, which are decorated with a white skull and crossbones and a worrying message: *"These plants can kill."*

Inspired by the poison gardens in 16th-century Padua where the Medicis plotted the frothing ends of their royal enemies, the Duchess of Northumberland created this garden in 2005, dedicating it entirely to poisonous or narcotic flora.

The duchess, Jane Percy, is an unlikely patron. In 1995, her husband unexpectedly became the twelfth Duke of Northumberland following his brother's death, and Alnwick Castle fell into their family's care. Roaming the elaborate gardens, the newly minted duchess decided to transform an overgrown, neglected section into something that was at once both traditional and dangerous. The poison garden now sits nestled among 14 acres of greenery dotted with water sculptures, a cherry orchard, a bamboo labyrinth, and an enormous tree house.

This carefully curated garden contains about 100 plants that have the power to stimulate, intoxicate, sicken, or kill. Guides detail their dangerous properties while enforcing the strict "No touching; no smelling" rules. Poppies, cannabis, hallucinogenic mushrooms, and deadly strychnine are among the innocent-looking greenery. Because of the danger posed by the flora (some can kill or sicken just through touch), some plants are caged, and the garden is secured under a 24-hour security watch.

Denwick Lane, Alnwick. The garden is open from March to October.
Ⓝ 55.414098 Ⓦ 1.700515

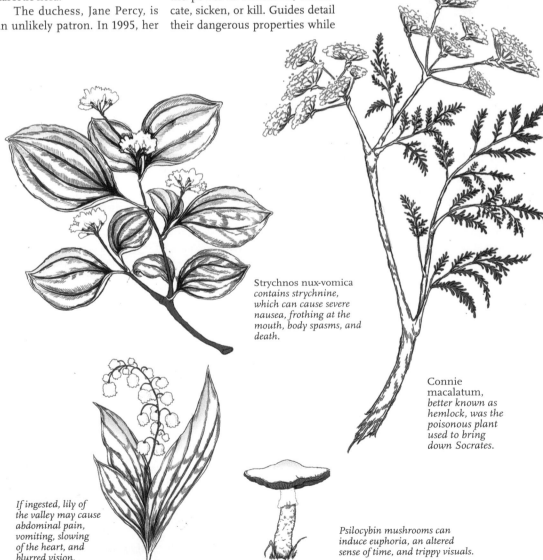

Strychnos nux-vomica contains strychnine, which can cause severe nausea, frothing at the mouth, body spasms, and death.

Connie macalatum, better known as hemlock, was the poisonous plant used to bring down Socrates.

If ingested, lily of the valley may cause abdominal pain, vomiting, slowing of the heart, and blurred vision.

Psilocybin mushrooms can induce euphoria, an altered sense of time, and trippy visuals.

THE CHAINED BOOKS OF HEREFORD CATHEDRAL

HEREFORD, HEREFORDSHIRE

This cathedral contains two medieval marvels: a chained library of rare books and one of the earliest maps of the world.

In the Middle Ages, before the availability of the printing press, volumes on law and religion were quite rare and valuable. To protect against theft, the books at Hereford Cathedral were chained to desks, pulpits, and study tables.

The chained library was created in 1611 when a collection of hand-transcribed, hand-bound books was moved into the Lady Chapel. Most of the volumes in the collection are acquisitions dating back to the 1100s, although the oldest book in the collection, the *Hereford Gospels*, dates to about the year 800.

The medieval world map stored at Hereford Cathedral depicts three continents: Europe, Asia, and Africa. On the as-yet-unexplored periphery of these lands roam fire-breathing dragons, dog-faced men, people who survive on only the scent of apples, and the Monocoli, a race of mythical beings who take shade under their giant feet when the sun becomes too bright.

The 5 x 4.5-foot map (1.5 x 1.4 m), created around 1300, is part geography, part history, and part religious teaching aid. A lack of confirmed information on Asian and African geography presented no obstacle for the mapmaker, who used hearsay, mythology, and imagination to fill in the gaps—which explains the four-eyed Ethiopians.

5 College Cloisters, Cathedral Close, Hereford. The cathedral is a 3.5-hour train trip from London and a 15-minute walk from Hereford railway station. Ⓝ 52.053613 Ⓦ 2.714945

ALSO IN NORTHERN ENGLAND

Steetley Magnesite

Hartlepool · This derelict chemical plant on the North Sea is a photogenic industrial ruin.

Beverley Sanctuary Stones

Beverley · A haven for criminals of all stripes, these stones mark a sacred area where the medieval church provided asylum to thieves and brigands.

MECHANICAL CLOCK AT SALISBURY CATHEDRAL

SALISBURY, WILTSHIRE

The mechanical clock at Salisbury Cathedral is old, but just *how* old is the subject of ongoing debate. The exact date is a matter of importance, for if it was built in 1386, as many horologists believe, it is the oldest working clock in the world.

The faceless clock introduced Salisbury to the new concept of standardized hours, which would replace the season-based increments of the sundial era. It chimed hourly, reminding townspeople to attend church services, and provided a reliable structure for each day.

In 1928, following its rediscovery in the cathedral tower, the clock was disassembled and restored. Although it no longer chimes, today the clock functions in much the same way as it did more than 600 years ago, striking away the hours in the north aisle of the nave.

Salisbury Cathedral, 33 The Close, Salisbury. Trains from London (Waterloo) take 90 minutes. The cathedral is a 10-minute walk from Salisbury station. Ⓝ 51.064933 Ⓦ 1.797677

Salisbury's 600-year-old timepiece may be the oldest working clock in the world.

George Merryweather's carousel of weather-predicting leeches was more charming than accurate.

THE TEMPEST PROGNOSTICATOR

OKEHAMPTON, DEVON

Surgeon George Merryweather had a passion for leeches. According to Merryweather, the creepy worms possessed humanlike instincts, experienced the hollow ache of loneliness, and were capable of forecasting weather. All this gave him an idea for a machine that he believed could transform meteorology.

In 1851, Merryweather unveiled his "tempest prognosticator" at the Great Exhibition in London. Having witnessed the agitation of freshwater leeches during the lead-up to a heavy storm, the doctor concluded he could build a leech-powered weather forecasting device. The contraption resembled a miniature merry-go-round, but in place of the usual ponies were a dozen glass bottles, each containing a single leech. Should a storm approach, the creatures would make their way to the top of the glass, triggering a wire connected to a central bell.

Though certainly novel, Merryweather's invention did not catch on. His vision of the British government deploying tempest prognosticators nationwide remained mere fantasy, but his invention lives on in the form of a reconstructed version prominently displayed in the Barometer World Exhibition museum in Devon. (Another can be found in the Whitby Museum in North Yorkshire.)

Quicksilver Barn, Merton, Okehampton. The museum is open by appointment. Ⓝ 50.891854 Ⓦ 4.095316

ALSO IN SOUTHWEST ENGLAND

The World's Largest Greenhouse

St Austell · Huge inflated domes at the Eden Project contain artificial biomes with over one million types of plants.

Lost Gardens of Heligan

St Austell · A 400-year-old garden with fantastical sculptures that has been restored to beauty after years of neglect.

The Museum of Witchcraft and Magic

Boscastle · The world's largest collection of occult- and witchcraft-related artifacts includes dried cats.

The House That Moved

Exeter · A 21-ton Tudor home built in the 1500s and moved 230 feet (70 m) down the street on thick iron rails in 1961 to make way for a new road.

The Cheddar Man and Cannibals Museum

Cheddar · A museum about life, death, and cannibalism in prehistoric Britain.

WITLEY UNDERWATER BALLROOM

GODALMING

The 9,000-acre Victorian estate of James Whitaker Wright was extravagant in every way. With the fortune he made from years of financial fraud, Wright built a 32-room mansion set on lavishly landscaped grounds that included three artificial lakes. Hidden underneath one of the lakes is his most spectacular creation of all: the underwater ballroom.

Built just below the surface of the water, this glorious submerged room has a domed, glass-paneled aquarium roof crowned with an epic statue that rises above the lake as if it's floating on the water. Called a "ballroom" due to its round shape and overall grandeur, the room was actually a smoking room where Wright would entertain his lucky guests. It was splendid, and like everything else on Wright's estate, it was ultimately doomed.

Wright built his palatial home with the money he made from swindling investors out of millions of dollars. In 1904, he was caught, convicted of fraud, and sentenced to seven years in prison. But Wright would never serve time. In a court anteroom, he took his own life by swallowing a cyanide pill immediately after the sentencing. After his death, the estate was purchased by Irish shipbuilder William Pirrie (of SS *Titanic* fame). The mansion was destroyed in a fire in 1952, but the now ancient-looking ballroom is still there, algae-covered and rusting away beneath the lake.

Witley Park is a private property, and while permission is occasionally granted to view the ballroom, it isn't open to the public. Ⓝ 51.147834 Ⓦ 0.683197

A statue of Neptune floats atop this subterranean smoking room.

NO MAN'S LAND LUXURY SEA FORT

GOSPORT, HAMPSHIRE

On maps, it registers as a tiny, nameless speck in the Solent strait between mainland England and the Isle of Wight, but No Man's Land Fort has a dramatic history that belies its cartographic insignificance.

Built in the late 1800s to protect the English coast against a French invasion that never happened, No Man's Land could accommodate 80 soldiers and 49 cannons.

The 200-foot-wide (61 m) fort sat idle for decades, and the Ministry of Defense decommissioned No Man's Land in the 1950s. When the government

Now available for laser-themed birthdays.

tried to sell it in 1963, no buyers came forward. In the 1990s, the abandoned fort was transformed into a luxury hotel, complete with two helipads, 21 bedrooms, a roof garden, and restaurants. The submerged center was glassed in as an atrium for the heated pool. Despite its creature comforts and promise of privacy, the hotel never took off.

In 2004, developer Harmesh Pooni bought No Man's Land for £6 million (about $9 million at the time) with the intention of renting it out for special occasions. Unfortunately, contaminated water in the hotel pool caused an outbreak of Legionnaires' disease. Faced with financial ruin and the possibility of losing the island, Pooni took an extreme approach: He covered the helipads with upturned tables, grabbed his keys, and barricaded himself inside the fortress. After a protracted standoff, he was finally evicted in early 2009.

No Man's Land sold for the bargain price of £910,000 (around $1.36 million) in March 2009 to Gibraltar-based Swanmore Estates Ltd. The fort has since been transformed into a venue for weddings and corporate retreats. Standout features include a sauna, a cabaret club, and a laser tag arena located in the former gunpowder storage area.

The Solent is 1.4 miles (2.3 km) north of the Isle of Wight. Ⓝ 50.739546 Ⓦ 1.094995

Before radar, huge concrete "ears" were built to listen for incoming enemy aircraft.

GREATSTONE SOUND MIRRORS

GREATSTONE, KENT

As part of its national defense strategy after World War I, Britain built three massive concrete acoustic mirrors on the southeast coast of England to detect the sound of distant airplane engines in the sky. Working much like giant ears, the trio of reflectors could provide a 15-minute warning of an air invasion by magnifying the sound waves over the English Channel and directing them at microphones. An operator sitting in a nearby booth listened to the transmitted signal through headphones that resembled a stethoscope.

The Greatstone site features three different reflectors, including a 200-foot-long (61 m) curved wall, a 30-foot-tall (9 m) parabolic dish, and a 20-foot-tall (6 m) shallow dish.

Dungeness National Nature Reserve, off Dungeness Road, Romney Marsh. Ⓝ 50.956111 Ⓔ 0.953889

ALSO IN SOUTHEAST ENGLAND

The Little Chapel

Guernsey · One of the smallest chapels in the world, intricately decorated with stones, pebbles, broken china, and glass.

The Margate Shell Grotto

Margate · Discovered in 1835, this mysterious subterranean passageway of unknown age is covered with mystical designs made entirely from seashells.

MAUNSELL ARMY SEA FORTS

THAMES ESTUARY, OFF THE EAST COAST OF ENGLAND

Rising from the water like robotic sentinels on stilts, the Maunsell Army Sea Forts in the Thames Estuary east of London are rusting reminders of World War II's darkest days. Part of the Thames Estuary defense network, the anti-aircraft tower-forts were constructed in 1942 to deter German air raids. Each of the three original forts consisted of a cluster of seven buildings on stilts surrounding a central command tower. Two remain: the Red Sands Fort and the Shivering Sands Fort.

After their wartime career the forts were decommissioned. In the 1960s, pirate-radio broadcasters moved in and established unauthorized stations in the remaining forts. In 1966, Reginald Calvert, manager of the Radio City pirate station, died in a fight with rival Radio Caroline station owner Oliver Smedley. The next year, the British government passed legislation making offshore broadcasting illegal, driving out the pirates and leaving the forts abandoned.

Attempting to enter the decaying forts is not advised. They can be seen by boat or, on a clear day, from Shoeburyness East Beach. Ⓝ 51.361047 Ⓔ 1.024256

An overhead plan of the forts, which were once connected by bridges.

Attention, H. G. Wells:
Your rusty invaders have arrived.

A millennium-long piece of music composed for Tibetan singing bowls will be playing at Trinity Buoy Wharf through 2999.

LONGPLAYER

LONDON

If you miss hearing Longplayer on your next trip to London, you'll get the chance to catch it again—the musical composition will be playing in the old lighthouse at Trinity Buoy Wharf for the next 1,000 years. Longplayer consists of six short recorded pieces written for Tibetan singing bowls that are transposed and combined in such a way that the variations will never repeat during the song's millennium-long run.

It began playing on December 31, 1999, and is scheduled to end in the dying seconds of 2999.

Custodians of the project have established the Longplayer Trust to devise ways of keeping the music alive in the face of the inevitable technological and social changes that will occur over the next ten centuries.

64 Orchard Place, London. Open on weekends. The nearest Tube stop is Canning Town. You can also listen to a livestream of the composition on longplayer.org. Ⓝ 51.508514 Ⓔ 0.008079

ALSO IN LONDON

Clapham North Deep-Level Air Raid Shelter

London · An abandoned World War II bomb shelter, it is the only one of eight deep-level air raid shelters that sits unused.

The Lost River Fleet

London · The largest of London's subterranean rivers now flows through its sewers. The Fleet can be heard flowing through a grate in front of the Coach and Horse pub on Ray Street, Clerkenwell.

The Churchill War Rooms

Westminster · These perfectly preserved underground rooms are where Winston Churchill and his cabinet toiled as they waged war against Hitler's Germany.

Lilliputian Police Station

Trafalgar Square · Now a glorified broom closet, in its heyday London's smallest police station was staffed with eagle-eyed bobbies to keep rowdy Trafalgar Square protesters under control.

The Old Operating Theatre Museum and Herb Garret

Southwark · Sharing the attic of St. Thomas Church with some dusty cobwebs and specimens that seem to be molting, Europe's oldest operating theater looks a lot like it probably did in 1822, minus the screaming, bloody patients.

CITY GUIDE: More to Explore in London

The Hardy Tree

Camden Town • Inside the walls of Saint Pancras Churchyard is an ash tree with scores of gravestones encircling the trunk. The scalloped rows were formed by novelist Thomas Hardy when he was just a moody young architecture student enlisted to care for the churchyard.

Masonic Lodge of the Andaz Hotel

East London • Forgotten behind a wall for decades, this sumptuous Masonic lodge was rediscovered during renovations, and looks like something out of an Agatha Christie novel.

The Last Tuesday Society's Viktor Wynd Museum of Curiosities, Fine Art & Natural History

Dalston • This reinterpretation of a 17th-century *Wunderkabinett* is a museum, cafe, and art gallery—one part retro-Victorian curiosity shop, two parts dusty horror show, with a jigger or two waiting for you at the bar upstairs.

Wellcome Collection & Library

Bloomsbury • The medical curios of an American pharmacist, collector, and philanthropist run the gamut from Napoleon's toothbrush to a re-creation of a 16th-century barber-surgeon workshop.

Grant Museum of Zoology and Comparative Anatomy

Bloomsbury • With more than 60,000 creatures, including a few that are long extinct and a micrarium of teeny-tiny ones, this is the last of London's zoological museums still open to the public.

Lullaby Factory

Bloomsbury • Wedged between two buildings at the Great Ormond Street Hospital is a secret lullaby-music machine, a network of instruments made of pipes, horns, and pieces of an old hospital boiler.

Novelty Automation

Holborn • These arcade games and satiric automata cover a range of experiences such as "How to practice money laundering," "Buy a house before you get too old," and "Operate a nuclear reactor."

Sir John Soane's Museum

Holborn • A treasure trove of a museum, Soane's is topped with a glass dome and well stacked with tens of thousands of sculptures, paintings, antiquities, and artifacts.

Hunterian Museum

Holborn • John Hunter may have been a bit of a mad scientist, but this anatomical museum befits the unconventional doctor, scientist, and collector of all bodily things, including half of mathematician Charles Babbage's brain and the seven-and-a-half-foot skeleton of Charles Byrne, the 18th-century "Irish Giant" (Hunter may have bribed the undertaker to get that one).

Polly at Ye Olde Cheshire Cheese

Holborn • The taxidermied remains of this beloved parrot still swing in a cage at this 17th-century pub, a former hangout for literary types like Dickens, Tennyson, Twain, and Sir Arthur Conan Doyle.

The First Public Drinking Fountain

Holborn • We can thank the Metropolitan Drinking Fountain and Cattle Trough Association for this 1859 public water fountain, London's very first and an instant hit.

Memorial to Self-Sacrifice

City of London • Slipped into a quiet jewel of a park is a poignant wall of tiled memorials to the bravery of policemen, firemen, and

Headstones arranged by Thomas Hardy.

ordinary Londoners who gave their lives to save others.

Whispering Gallery at St. Paul's Cathedral

City of London • The acoustics of St. Paul's Cathedral Dome, designed by the great Christopher Wren, have a hushed and hidden secret: Speak across the span, all 137 feet (42 m) of glorious light and air, and every word is crystal clear, like a secret whispered in your ear.

Temple of Mithras

City of London • Just blocks from the financial heart of the City of London is a reminder of the city of Londinium: the reassembled remnants of a temple to the Roman god Mithras, whose mystery cult has fueled conspiracy theories for centuries.

London's Original and All-Inspiring Coffee House

City of London • The site of London's first coffee house is still serving drinks of one kind or another, as it has for more than 360 years.

Tomb of the Unknown London Girl

City of London • The 1,600-year-old remains of a Roman girl are reinterred and memorialized at the base of the "Gherkin," a modern architectural landmark.

Shackleton's Crow's Nest

City of London • The lookout from Sir Ernest Shackleton's last ship is inside the crypt of All Hallows-by-the-Tower, one of London's oldest churches.

Houseboats of Regent's Canal

Limehouse • A group of artists and entrepreneurs has built a bohemian community of colorful houseboats along the 8 miles from Little Venice to Limehouse.

Hyde Park Pet Cemetery

Hyde Park • Here lie Dolly, Rex, and Pupsey, in a cemetery devoted to more than 300 Victorian-era furry companions, inside one of the city's largest parks.

Seven Noses of Soho

Soho • Originally numbering 35, it's a challenge to find all the surviving schnoz sculptures (no one really has an exact count) scattered around Soho by artist Rick Buckley—his protest against the proliferation of too many nosy "Big Brother" CCTV cameras. On Bateman Street, Meard Street, D'Arblay Street, Great Windmill Street, Shaftesbury Avenue, Endell Street, and Floral Street.

JEREMY BENTHAM'S AUTO ICON

LONDON

Jeremy Bentham has been sitting in a corridor at University College London since 1850.

The moral philosopher, whose advocacy of animal welfare, prison reform, universal suffrage, and gay rights was far ahead of his time, left a will with specific instructions on the treatment of his corpse. He decreed that his mummified head and skeleton be clad in a black suit, seated upright on a chair in a wooden cabinet, under a placard reading "Auto Icon." He also suggested that his corpse could preside over regular meetings of followers of his utilitarian philosophy.

Bentham's plans for his remains became something of an obsession. For 10 years prior to his death, he reportedly carried a pair of glass eyes in his pocket so that embalmers could easily implant them after his death. Unfortunately, when the time came, something went wrong in the preservation process. Bentham's head took on a mottled, hollow-cheeked look, its leathery skin sagging under a pair of intensely blue glass eyes. In order to create a less grotesque display, preservers created a wax bust of Bentham and screwed it onto the skeleton. They placed the real head between Bentham's feet.

There it sat, undisturbed, until 1975, when a group of mischievous students kidnapped it and demanded a £100 ransom be donated to charity. The university made a counteroffer of £10, and the students caved, returning Bentham's head to its rightful place between his legs. After a few more pranks, including one in which the skull was apparently used as a football, university administrators decided to remove the head from public display. It now sits in the Conservation Safe in the Institute of Archaeology and is removed only for special occasions.

On Gower Street, between Grafton Way and University Street, enter the university grounds at Porter's Lodge. Find the ramp entrance to the South Cloisters, Wilkins Building. Jeremy Bentham is just inside.
Ⓝ 51.524686 Ⓦ 0.134025

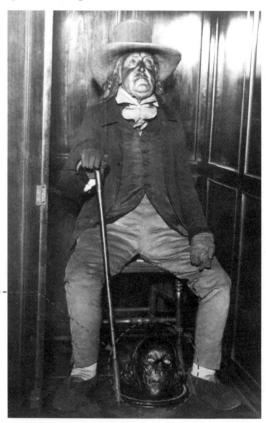

Seated in a hallway at University College London, the long-dead utilitarian philosopher guards his own head from those who might souvenir it.

ARCHIE THE GIANT SQUID

LONDON

The giant squid is often depicted as a sea monster. In Jules Verne's *20,000 Leagues Under the Sea*, a giant squid attacks a boat and devours one of its crew. The kraken of Norse mythology—an enormous creature whose tentacles could supposedly wrap around the tallest of ship masts and rip whole vessels asunder—likely arose from a combination of giant squid sightings, imagination, and exaggeration.

The deep-sea-dwelling giant squid's notorious elusiveness only fueled tall tales. Though records show they have been sighted sporadically since the 16th century, it wasn't until 2002 that photographers were able to capture an image of a live giant squid in its natural habitat—which makes the Natural History Museum's 28-foot (8.5 m) specimen a rare delight. Caught off the coast of the Falkland Islands in 2004 and named Archie in recognition of its species name, *Architeuthis dux*, the giant squid is preserved in a custom-made acrylic tank.

Natural History Museum, Cromwell Road, London. Archie is in the Darwin Spirit Collection of the museum, accessible on special guided tours. Ⓝ 51.495983 Ⓦ 0.176372

HIGHGATE CEMETERY

LONDON

Opened in 1839, Highgate is one of London's most famous cemeteries. Its residents include Karl Marx (his memorial recognizable by the glowering bearded bust), sci-fi author Douglas Adams, and Adam Worth, the possible inspiration for Sherlock Holmes's nemesis, Professor Moriarty. In the Victorian era, anyone who was anyone wanted to be buried in London's fashionable Highgate Cemetery.

But fashion is fickle. By the 1940s, the Victorian cemetery was in a state of neglect, its once-coveted burial plots covered in vines. In 1970, members of a group interested in the occult claimed to have seen supernatural creatures lurking in the graveyard. Initial reports of ghosts gave way to talk that a vampire—a Transylvanian prince brought to the cemetery in the 1800s—was hiding out in Highgate.

Seán Manchester and David Farrant, self-described magicians and rival monster hunters, vowed to track down and kill the beast. Each proclaimed the other to be a charlatan incapable of finding the vampire. They took their feud to the media—capitalizing on an interest in the occult fueled by the recent release of *The*

Could there be a vampire lurking behind the trees?

Exorcist—and announced an official vampire hunt would take place on Friday the 13th of March, 1970. That night, a mob overpowered police and broke into Highgate wielding stakes, garlic, crosses, and holy water. Chaos ensued. No vampires were sighted.

Manchester and Farrant continued to visit the cemetery over the next few years, determined to drive a stake into the heart of the Highgate Vampire. Though neither magician ever found the supposed vampire, real graves were ransacked and real corpses staked and beheaded during the search. In 1974, Farrant received a jail sentence for vandalizing memorials and interfering with human remains in the cemetery.

Debate between Farrant and Manchester continues to this day, while the cemetery remains a popular location for occult, paranormal, and vampire enthusiasts. **Swain's Lane. The cemetery is a 20-minute walk up Highgate Hill and through Waterlow Park.**
Ⓝ **51.566927** Ⓦ **0.147071**

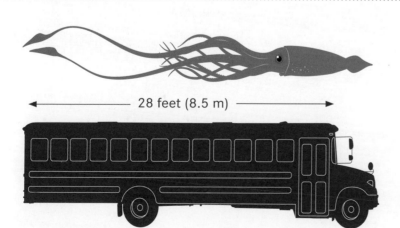
28 feet (8.5 m)

Caught in 2004 and now kept at the Natural History Museum, Archie the Giant Squid is as long as a school bus.

DIFFERENCE ENGINE #2

LONDON

There was almost a Victorian computer. Charles Babbage came achingly close with his 1822 "Difference Engine," a design for a hulking gadget with cranks and gears capable of generating mathematical tables.

The machine offered a well-thought-out solution to the problem of human error in complex calculations, but it proved too large, complicated, and expensive to construct. Government grants allowed Babbage to hire a machinist, Joseph Clement, but after 10 years and much quarreling over prices, Clement had built just a small portion of the prototype.

Undeterred by practical constraints and workplace unpleasantness, Babbage moved on to plans for Difference Engine #2.

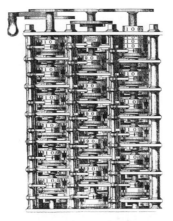

Now functional: Charles Babbage's Victorian computer.

This would be a more streamlined version: 5 tons, 5,000 parts, and 11 feet long (3.4 m). It, too, never progressed to a working model. Babbage died in 1871, leaving reams of notes and sketches for machines that were beyond the era's construction capabilities.

In 1985, more than a century after Babbage's death, London's Science Museum announced plans to investigate the feasibility of his designs by building a difference engine based on the blueprints—and 19th-century materials—devised for Engine #2. The construction team finished the calculating section in 1991, just in time to commemorate the 200th anniversary of Babbage's birth. It functioned flawlessly, confirming Babbage's rightful place in the annals of computing history.

The engine, which features a printing apparatus added in 2002, is now on display at the museum, along with half of Babbage's brain. (The other half is housed at the Hunterian Museum, also in London.)

Science Museum, Exhibition Road, London. Ⓝ 51.498190 Ⓦ 0.173972

IRELAND

VICTOR'S WAY INDIAN SCULPTURE PARK

ROUNDWOOD, WICKLOW

Covering 22 acres, this park includes sculptures of an emaciated Buddha, an enormous disembodied finger, and *The Split Man*, a figure ripping itself in two, representing "the mental state of the dysfunctional human." Victor Langheld established the park in 1989 after traveling to India in search of spiritual enlightenment. The series of sculptures, carved in stone by craftsmen in the south Indian state of Tamil Nadu, represent spiritual progression, from *Awakening* (a child emerging from a decaying fist) to *The Ferryman's End* (a cadaverous old man in a sinking boat, half-submerged in a lake).

Roundwood. The park is a 45-minute drive from Dublin. It's open from May through September. Dress for the damp. Ⓝ 53.085765 Ⓦ 6.219654

The emaciated ferryman invites visitors to contemplate mortality at Victor's Way Sculpture Park.

RUINS OF THE MV *PLASSEY*

INISHEER, GALWAY

More rust than metal at this point, the creaky shell of the steam trawler MV *Plassey* has been sitting on a bed of rocks on the shore of Inisheer Island for over half a century.

Early in the morning of March 8, 1960, the cargo ship was transporting yarn, stained glass, and whiskey across the Atlantic when it got caught in a terrible storm. Fierce winds blew the vessel toward Inisheer, tearing a hole in the bottom and causing water to rush into the engine room.

Using a breeches buoy—a rocket-fired rescue device similar to a zip line—islanders managed to save all 11 members of the crew from the icy sea. No sooner had they warmed up and calmed down with a few shots of local whiskey than another storm hit, delivering the MV *Plassey* to the rocky coast of Inisheer. Locals salvaged wool, lumber, and doors for construction, and made off with a stash of Black & White scotch hidden in the hold.

Today, the bronze-colored wreck, riddled with holes and stripped of all its assets, looks oddly beautiful against the gray rocks, green grass, and blue sky. **The wreck is on the east coast of Inisheer, just south of Killagoola. Ferries from the mainland leave from Doolin. Ⓝ 53.055816 Ⓦ 9.503730**

With its flaking hull full of holes, the MV *Plassey* is slightly less than seaworthy.

LEVIATHAN OF PARSONSTOWN

BIRR, OFFALY

William Parsons, the third earl of Rosse, built this 58-foot (17.7 m) telescope in the 1840s to investigate the space phenomena he knew as "nebulae." At the time, telescopes were not powerful enough to show that these so-called nebulae were actually an assortment of different objects ranging from star clusters and galaxies to clouds of gas and dust. Parsons's 6-foot-wide (2 m) telescope lens exposed the solar system in greater detail than ever before—though it was not until the 1920s that Edwin Hubble discovered that some of the fuzzy objects were in fact galaxies.

Dubbed "the Leviathan of Parsonstown," Parsons's reflecting telescope remained the largest in the world for over 75 years. However, following the death of the earl of Rosse—and that of his son, who tended to the instrument in his absence—the telescope fell into disuse in 1878 and was dismantled in 1908. Thanks to the seventh and current earl, the telescope was reconstructed in the late 1990s with a new mirror and motors. You can now see the restored Leviathan and learn about its workings in the attached science center.

Birr Castle, Birr. Two hours from Dublin by car and about one hour from Shannon Airport and Galway city. Ⓝ 53.097123 Ⓦ 7.913780

The Leviathan may look like a cannon, but it was made for stargazing.

IRISH SKY GARDEN

SKIBBEREEN, IRELAND

Designed by American James Turrell in 1992, this magical knoll is an unparalleled piece of public art. The enormous grassy crater features a central stone plinth reminiscent of ancient Celtic and Egyptian altars. The plinth rises up at an angle, and a stone footrest on each end allows the viewer to lie down and see up and out toward the edge of the crater above. All that is visible from this vantage point is the green grass and sky, creating a uniquely serene experience that invokes past rituals and ancient rites.

The Sky Garden is set in the natural landscape of the Liss Ard ("High Fort" in Gaelic) estate, which is situated on an ancient Celtic ring fort. So even though the sky garden is a contemporary piece of art with a strikingly postmodern shape and aesthetic, it is the perfect complement to a place that is already a bridge between two worlds.

Liss Ard Estate, Castletownshend Road Skibbereen, County Cork. The garden is open on certain days during May and June. You'll need to get a key from reception and pay a small entrance fee.
Ⓝ 51.528405 Ⓦ 9.254247

SKELLIG MICHAEL

THE SKELLIGS, KERRY

The dozen monks who sequestered themselves on this rocky island in the 7th century were a hardy lot.

Skellig Michael—*skellig* is derived from the Irish word *sceillic*, meaning "steep rock"—lies 8 miles (13 km) from the coast of County Kerry. It is beset by wind and rain, which make the ascent to its 714-foot-high (217.6 m) peak extra treacherous.

Despite these harsh conditions, a group of determined Irish Christians established a monastic outpost on the island that remains largely intact 1,400 years later. Using stones, the monks built hundreds of stairs leading up to Skellig Michael's summit, where they erected six beehive-shaped stone huts and a small chapel. They survived on a diet of fish, seabirds, and vegetables grown in the monastery garden. Withstanding multiple Viking raids during the 9th century, the monks occupied Skellig Michael until the late 12th century, when frequent storms sent them back to the mainland.

Climbing the 670 uneven, steep steps to the top presents both a physical and mental challenge, but at the summit, you'll be able to enter the monastic huts and imagine the grueling life of a 7th-century ascetic.

Boats leave from Portmagee (a 90-minute trip) from April to September, weather permitting.
Ⓝ 51.772080 Ⓦ 10.538858

Beehive-shaped monastic cells, built by medieval monks, top the rocky island of Skellig Michael.

The largest crypt in Ireland is known for its mummified cat and rat, known locally as "Tom & Jerry."

THE CRYPTS AT CHRIST CHURCH CATHEDRAL

DUBLIN

In 1030, the Viking rulers of Dublin built the original Christ Church Cathedral out of wood. When the Normans invaded in 1171, they tore the cathedral down and built one of stone, adding an enormous crypt.

Laurence O'Toole, the archbishop of Dublin, oversaw the rebuilding process. After O'Toole was canonized as the patron saint of Dublin in 1225, his heart was preserved in a heart-shaped reliquary and kept in the cathedral inside an iron cage.

The saintly heart remained in an alcove until March 2012, when two men pried open the cage and stole the icon. Six years later the heart was recovered by police and restored to its proper place.

Other fascinating relics worth seeing are a set of stocks made in 1670 that were once used outdoors to punish criminals publicly and a marble monument depicting Nathaniel Sneyd, an Irish politician who died in 1833. Text beside the sculpture states that he "perished by the indiscriminating violence of an unhappy maniac"—in other words, he was shot.

The most unusual objects in the crypt are the mummified cat and rat, whose poses suggest they died mid-chase. According to church lore, the cat pursued the rat into a pipe of the church organ during the 1850s, and both became stuck. James Joyce used both cat and rat as a simile in *Finnegan's Wake* when he described someone as being "as stuck as that cat to that mouse in that tube of that christchurch organ."

Christchurch Place, Dublin. Ⓝ 53.343517 Ⓦ 6.271057

ALSO IN IRELAND

The Calendar Sundial

Galway · A modern sundial uses ancient methods to tell time and date perfectly.

St. Michan's Mummies

Dublin · Down a set of dimly lit narrow stone steps, a vault underneath the church holds dozens of mummified remains, including an 800-year-old "Crusader" whose finger you are allowed to touch.

Wallabies of Lambay

Lambay Island · Despite being 10,000 miles (16,000 km) from their native Australia, a group of wallabies has made Lambay Island home for the last 25 years after being relocated by the Dublin Zoo.

NORTHERN IRELAND
THE VANISHING LAKE

BALLYCASTLE, ANTRIM

East of the seaside town of Ballycastle, on the side of the coastal road, is a lake—sometimes. When you get there, it may be gone. But it will come back.

Loughareema, also known as "the vanishing lake," sits on a bed of porous limestone with a "plug hole" that attracts peat. When enough peat accumulates in the hole, it prevents drainage, causing the water level to rise. When the peat dislodges, the lake empties—sometimes disappearing in a matter of hours.

Loughareema Road (by Ballypatrick Forest), Ballycastle. The lake is a 2-hour bus ride from Belfast. Be prepared for a dry chalk bed, an expansive lake, or anything in between. Ⓝ 55.157084 Ⓦ 6.108058

The vanishing lake of Ballycastle in its unvanished state.

THE GIANT'S CAUSEWAY

BUSHMILLS, ANTRIM

With its thousands of interlocking hexagonal columns that rise vertically like steps, the Giant's Causeway is a geological oddity that looks distinctly man-made.

Volcanic activity created the unusual formation near the start of the Paleogene period (23–65 million years ago) when molten basalt came into contact with chalk beds and formed a lava plateau. When the lava cooled quickly, the plateau contracted and cracked, forming 40,000 columns of varying heights that look like giant stepping stones. The largest stand almost 36 feet tall (11 m).

According to legend, an Irish giant by the name of Fionn mac Cumhaill constructed the causeway so he could skip over to Scotland to defeat his Scottish counterpart, Benandonner. While in transit to Scotland, Fionn fell asleep, and Benandonner decided to cross the causeway to look for his competitor. To protect her slumbering husband, Fionn's wife gathered him up and wrapped him up in cloth to disguise him as a baby. When Benandonner made it to Northern Ireland, he saw the large infant and could only imagine how big Fionn must be. Frightened, Benandonner fled back to Scotland—but the causeway remained.

44 Causeway Road, Bushmills. The causeway is an hour by car from Belfast or 3 hours by bus, which runs along a scenic route. Ⓝ 55.240807 Ⓦ 6.511555

ALSO IN NORTHERN IRELAND

Skate 56 at the Belfry

Newcastle · A church turned indoor skate park.

Peace Maze

Castlewellan · One of the world's largest hedge mazes celebrates peace in Northern Ireland.

The hexagonal basalt columns of the Giant's Causeway are the stuff of Celtic legend.

SCOTLAND
FINGAL'S CAVE

OBAN, ARGYLL AND BUTE

Like something out of an epic fantasy novel, Scotland's Fingal's Cave is a 270-foot-deep, 72-foot-tall (82 x 22 m) sea cave with walls of perfectly hexagonal columns. Celtic legends held that the cave was once part of a bridge across the sea, built by giants to fight one another. Science says it was formed by enormous masses of lava that cooled so slowly that they broke into long hexagonal pillars, like mud cracking under the hot sun.

When naturalist Sir Joseph Banks rediscovered the cave in 1772, it quickly captured people's imagination and inspired the work of artists, writers, and musicians. Composer Felix Mendelssohn wrote an overture about the cave in 1830, the same year painter J. M. W. Turner depicted it on canvas. Thus was born a Romantic-era tourist site that is just as entrancing today.

Get a train from Glasgow to Oban, where you can take a ferry to Craignure, located on the Isle of Mull. A bus will take you to Fionnphort for a boat tour to Staffa.
Ⓝ 56.433889 Ⓦ 6.336111

The cave's contours have provided artistic inspiration for everyone from Jules Verne to Pink Floyd.

ALSO IN SCOTLAND

The Ruins of St. Peter's

Cardross · This hulking skeleton of a modernist seminary was completed in 1966 and abandoned in the 1980s.

Yester Castle

Gifford, East Lothian · A castle that opens into a subterranean vaulted "goblin hall" from the 13th century.

The Dunmore Pineapple

Dunmore Park · This house with a top shaped like a giant pineapple, a symbol of hospitality and affluence, was built in the late 1700s and is now available as a vacation rental.

Dog Cemetery at Edinburgh Castle

Edinburgh · The final resting place of mascots and Scottish guards' loyal canine companions.

Greyfriars Cemetery Mortsafes

Edinburgh · Cages built over 19th-century burial sites to protect the dead from being disinterred by opportunistic body snatchers.

Holyrood Abbey Ruins

Edinburgh · A ruined 11th-century abbey built by King David I.

Britannia Panopticon Music Hall

Glasgow · The world's oldest surviving music hall.

Cultybraggan Camp

Perth · Built to hold the worst of the worst of Nazi war criminals.

Scotland's Secret Bunker

St. Andrews · A bunker that was built to shelter the politicians and "essential" people of Scotland in the event of nuclear attack.

Within these gardens are the keys to life and the universe.

GARDEN OF COSMIC SPECULATION

HOLYWOOD, DUMFRIES AND GALLOWAY

Among the daffodils and daisies of the Garden of Cosmic Speculation are black holes, Fibonacci sequences, fractals, and DNA double helixes.

Architectural theorist Charles Jencks and his late wife, Maggie Keswick, designed the 30-acre garden for their own property. Its aesthetic is guided by the fundamentals of modern physics, reflecting the shapes and patterns of the unfolding universe. Begun in 1988, the garden took almost 20 years to build, during which time Keswick succumbed to cancer. Jencks continued the project in her memory, occasionally altering designs in response to shifts and breakthroughs in scientific knowledge. (The Human Genome Project inspired the DNA Garden section, with its plant-threaded double helix.)

Holywood, 5 miles (8 km) north of Dumfries. The garden is open to the public one day a year, during the first week of May. Managed by the Scotland's Gardens Scheme, the yearly event helps raise money for Maggie's Centers, a cancer foundation named after Jencks's late wife. Ⓝ 55.129780 Ⓦ 3.665830

AMSTERDAM

- Electric Ladyland Museum of Fluorescent Art
- Micropia

VIENNA

- Kugelmugel
- Esperanto Museum

ROME

- Passetto Di Borgo
- Vatican City
- Pope Leo's Bathroom
- Museum of Holy Souls

DNK

RUS

POL

ENG

- The Impaled Stork
- Eisinga Planetarium
- Giethoorn
- Teufelsberg Spy Station
- Thousand-Year Rose

AMSTERDAM

BERLIN

- Teylers Museum

THE HAGUE ★ **NETHERLANDS**

- The Externsteine
- Castle of Wewelsburg

BRUSSELS

GERMANY

- Tower of Eben-Ezer
- The Mundaneum
- Folx-les-Caves

BELGIUM

CZE

LUX

- Kaspar Hauser

SVK

- Hollow at La Meauffe

PARIS

- René de Chalon
- Optical Telegraph
- Space Travel Museum
- Eisbachwelle
- Saint Munditia
- Gallery of Beauties

VIENNA

- Hellbrunn Palace
- World of Ice Giants

AUSTRIA

HUN

- Bruno Weber Skulpturenpark
- The Rat King
- Astronomical Clock
- Abbey Library of Saint Gall

BERN

- Le Musée des Grenouilles
- Child-Eater of Bern

SVN

FRANCE

SWITZERLAND

- Villa de Vecchi

- Oradour-sur-Glane

- Poveglia
- Le Palais Idéal
- Temples of Damanhur
- Wooden Books

ITALY

- Solar Furnace

AND

- La Specola
- Galileo's Middle Finger

SPA

- Civita di Bagnoregio

ADRIATIC SEA

- Park of the Monsters

ROME ★

Corsica

MEDITERRANEAN SEA

- Secret Cabinet of Erotica

TYRRHENIAN SEA

Sardinia

N

Miles
100   200

0   100   200
Kilometers

- Capuchin Catacombs

Sicily

IONIAN SEA

WESTERN EUROPE

Greece and Cyprus, *see page 48*
Portugal and Spain, *see page 66*

TUN

MLT

DZA

The interior of this spherical state houses a museum on the history of the micronation.

AUSTRIA

REPUBLIC OF KUGELMUGEL

VIENNA

The Republic of Kugelmugel is one of many "micronations." These independent states, often established as art projects, social experiments, or simply for personal amusement, are not recognized by international governments.

When creative urges compelled artist Edwin Lipburger and his son to build a spherical studio on their farm in 1970, they didn't realize that local laws prohibited the building of spherical structures. In an attempt to protect their creation from demolition, the Lipburgers created their own Kugelmugel township, complete with self-made street signs around the building. Later, as the legal dispute escalated, Edwin Lipburger attempted to declare the structure its own federal state—the Republic of Kugelmugel—even going as far as to issue his own stamps and currency and refusing to pay taxes. The elder Lipburger was eventually sent to jail for 10 weeks in 1979 (he was later pardoned by the Austrian president).

In the early 1980s, Austria's culture minister suggested Kugelmugel be moved to the Vienna Prater amusement park. The Lipburgers went along with the idea, having been promised access to tap water, electricity, and sewers. But these facilities

The micronation of Kugelmugel was founded to protect an artist's space from demolition.

were never provided, which resulted in an ongoing dispute with the city of Vienna.

Edwin Lipburger died in 2015 and his son took over the presidency. The building now serves as an art gallery and is open for special exhibitions and performances. A proud "micronation," it counts about 600 people as citizens, though not all citizens can fit in the space at once.

2 Antifaschismusplatz, Vienna. Get a bus to Venediger Au. Kugelmugel is located in Vienna's famous Prater park, depicted in Carol Reed's classic film _The Third Man_, and is found at the western edge of the park in the shadow of a roller coaster. Ⓝ 48.216234 Ⓔ 16.396221 ➻

➽ Other Micronations

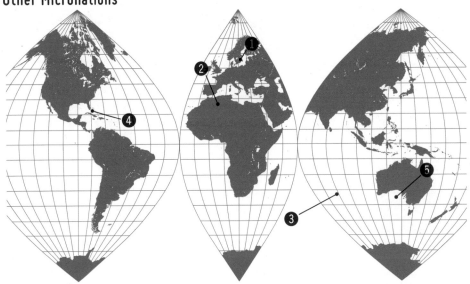

1 NIMIS, LADONIA
Nimis, a mountainous, multi-towered sculpture made of 70 tons of driftwood planks, is the main attraction of the micronation of Ladonia. It is also the only reason Ladonia exists at all. The ersatz country—two-thirds of a square mile (1.7 square km) in size, located on a Swedish peninsula protruding into the Kattegat—was established in 1996 following a long court battle between artist Lars Vilks and the Swedish government. Vilks began building Nimis in secret in 1980. Far from civilization and only fully visible from the water, it went unnoticed by Swedish authorities for two years until they discovered it and declared it would have to be destroyed. (The land is part of a nature reserve, where it is forbidden to build structures.) Goaded, Vilks ignored the announcement, sold Nimis to the artist Cristo, built a similarly sized stone-and-concrete sculpture called Arx, and decided to take control of the area and secede from Sweden. The nation of Ladonia was born.

Today, Ladonia claims over 15,000 citizens, all of whom reside outside its borders in accordance with the nation's nomadic lifestyle policy. Citizenship is free and requires an online application, but if you would like to become part of Ladonia's nobility, you will need to pay $12 and send an email informing the administrators of your preferred title.

The Ladonian flag is green, with a faint white outline of the Nordic cross—a design chosen because it is what the blue-and-yellow Swedish flag would look like if it was boiled. Taxes are payable, but money is not accepted. Instead, citizens must contribute some of their creativity. The citizenship application process caused confusion among 3,000 Pakistanis who applied for immigrant status with the intent to live in Ladonia, only to be told it was not possible to move there.

Though residing in Ladonia is prohibited, visiting is not.

The micronation of Ladonia is known for its artisanal wooden towers.

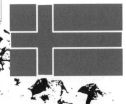

2 THE PRINCIPALITY OF SEALAND

Sealand came into being in 1967, when Roy Bates commandeered a former military sea fort off the east coast of England with plans to broadcast a pirate radio station. When members of the British Royal Marines approached the fort, Roy's 14-year-old son Michael fired warning shots at their boat. The Bates duo appeared in court on firearms charges, where the judge ruled the case invalid due to the army fort being outside British jurisdiction. The father and son returned to Sealand, where Roy dubbed himself prince of the fledgling micronation.

In 1978, Bates the elder and his wife were in England when Alexander Achenbach, self-described prime minister of Sealand, assembled a team to storm the fort by air and sea to attempt a coup. He captured the prince Michael Bates and held him hostage, only for Roy to return later—with armed assistants, in a helicopter piloted by a former James Bond–franchise stuntman—and capture Achenbach and his crew. Roy charged Achenbach with treason, keeping him captive for several weeks until Germany sent a diplomat to Sealand to negotiate Achenbach's release. Achenbach has since established a remote rebel government in exile: a micro-micronation.

3 PRINCIPALITY OF HUTT RIVER

When the Australian government imposed a restrictive wheat crop production quota in late 1969, wheat farmer Leonard Casley was infuriated. With fields full of wheat waiting to be harvested and nowhere to send the sizable yield, he fought to change the government's new agricultural policy. The government was unmoved. Casley then took the next logical step: secession.

The Principality of Hutt River was founded in April 1970, when Casley informed authorities that he and his family would no longer be under Australia's jurisdiction. His one-page letter name-checked the Magna Carta, English common law, the Atlantic Treaty, and the Charter of the United Nations.

During the 1970s, relations between Hutt River and Western Australia were strained. The national postal service refused to deliver to the area, and the Australian Tax Office repeatedly demanded the Casleys pay taxes, prompting the self-proclaimed Prince Leonard I to declare war on Australia in 1977. A few days later, the prince sent official notification that the war was over. There were no deaths, no injuries, and no acknowledgment from Australia that the conflict ever existed.

Conch Republic passports are not valid for international travel.

4 THE CONCH REPUBLIC

"We seceded where others failed" is the motto of this micronation in Key West, Florida, formed in 1982 in response to a new border patrol checkpoint that inconvenienced residents and slowed tourism. Soon after seceding, the Conch Republic engaged in a one-minute war with the United States, during which newly proclaimed Prime Minister Dennis Wardlow thwacked a man in a naval uniform on the head with a stale loaf of bread. The PM then surrendered and immediately sought a billion dollars in foreign aid from the US. He has yet to receive it.

Although Conch Republic passports are not valid for international travel, the micronation's website claims a Conch citizen traveling in Guatemala avoided certain death by showing his Conch passport to armed revolutionaries instead of his American one. Supposedly, the rebels dropped their weapons and treated the visitor to several rounds of tequila.

5 REPUBLIC OF MINERVA

Las Vegas real estate mogul Michael Oliver dreamed of an island utopia: a tax-free, welfare-free, government-intervention-free haven for 30,000 people, supported by fishing, tourism, and other "unspecified activities."

Oliver targeted two unclaimed submerged atolls south of Fiji and Tonga as the location for the new state. International law states that islands can only be claimed if they are a foot (.3 m) above the high tide point. The atolls became submerged at high tide, therefore no one owned them. In 1971, Oliver shipped in barges of sand, dumped them on the reefs, and staked his claim, naming it the Republic of Minerva.

This bold colonization soon caught the attention of Tongan king Taufa'ahau Tupou IV, who set sail for Minerva accompanied by nobles, cabinet ministers, soldiers, police, and a brass band. Upon arrival, the motley crew tore down the Minervan flag and claimed the land in the name of Tonga.

ESPERANTO MUSEUM

VIENNA

When Ludwig Lazarus Zamenhof invented the Esperanto language in the 1870s, his goal was to ease communication between people of different nationalities. Esperanto, a hybrid of Romance, Germanic, and Slavic languages, is documented and studied at this museum, along with around 500 other constructed languages, or "conlangs."

On display is an impressive array of Esperanto objects: sodas and toothpaste containers with Esperanto labels; novels written in Esperanto; language manuals; and 19th-century photographs of "planned-language" pioneers. At its peak, Esperanto had as many as two million speakers.

On the eve of WWI, Esperantists still dreamed of uniting the world behind a common language.

Esperanto ranks among the top 200 most-spoken languages out of over 6,000 left on the planet. There are estimated to be a thousand native Esperanto speakers, who learned the language as children; among them is the American financier George Soros.

If the museum piques your interest in learning Esperanto, take note that becoming conversant in the language entitles you to join the Esperantist passport service, a worldwide directory of people willing to host Esperanto speakers in their homes free of charge.

Herrengasse 9, Vienna. Take the U-Bahn to Herrengasse. Ⓝ 48.209474 Ⓔ 16.365771 ➻

➻ How to Say "Crazy" in Toki Pona

More than 900 constructed languages have been invented since the 13th century. Some, like Esperanto and Volapük, were created with the ambitious goal of becoming a universal lingua franca. Others are meant to test the contentious Sapir-Whorf hypothesis, which holds that a person's worldview is shaped by the vocabulary and syntax available in his or her language.

Kala

Kasi

Toki Pona, created by Canadian linguist Sonja Elen Kisa in 2001, is a language for minimalists. Consisting of just 123 words, the language is meant to reflect a Zen outlook on life. Toki Pona combines simple words to create complex ones—such as joining the words for "crazy" and "water" to create the word for "alcohol." The language's two main features—a restricted vocabulary and the linking of root words—also occur in Newspeak, the fictional language used in George Orwell's dystopian novel *1984*.

Láadan Is American science-fiction writer Suzette Haden Elgin's experimental answer to the feminist hypothesis that existing languages are inadequate for conveying the breadth of female experience. The language, created in 1982, includes words like *radiidin*, defined as "a time [that is] allegedly a holiday but actually so much a burden because of work and preparations that it is a dreaded occasion; especially when there are too many guests and none of them help."

French author and musician François Sudre began working on Solresol in the 1820s. The language is based on the seven syllables that correspond to sounds on a musical scale: *do, re, mi, fa, sol, la,* and *si*. Every word is composed of one or

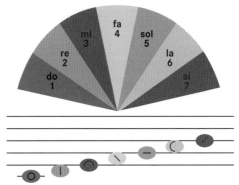

Sentences in Solresol can be performed on a violin, spoken as a series of numbers, or communicated using the colors of the rainbow.

more of those sounds—for example, *si* means "yes" while *dofalado* means "sincerity." There are 2,668 words in all.

Since the base sounds correspond to musical notes, Solresol messages can be communicated through musical instruments. Each of the seven base sounds also corresponds to a color of the rainbow. In his 1902 book on Solresol grammar, Boleslas Gajewski suggested messages be relayed "at night, by shooting rockets of each of the seven colors . . . always separating every syllable as needed, then pausing briefly between every word."

Listen for the archbishop ghost's cackling on the wind as water bursts from his old prank fountains.

TRICK FOUNTAINS OF HELLBRUNN PALACE

SALZBURG

The Prince-Archbishop Markus Sittikus von Hohenems was quite the prankster. When building Hellbrunn Palace, his summer home, the 17th-century Salzburg monarch booby-trapped its gardens with trick fountains that would spray unsuspecting guests as they toured the grounds. At each spot was a patch that remained dry—that is where the prince would stand while his visitors got soaked.

Nearly 400 years later, the palace remains almost completely unchanged, except for the 1750 addition of the mechanical theater, a water-powered diorama of a Baroque town with 200 miniature townspeople moving to organ music.

Fürstenweg 37, Salzburg. Hellbrunn is open from April to early November. Dress appropriately—you will get wet. Ⓝ 47.763132 Ⓔ 13.061121

ALSO IN AUSTRIA

Eggenburg Charnel

Eggenburg · Artfully arranged skeletons sit at the bottom of this 14th-century pit.

Fucking, Austria

Fucking · American soldiers discovered Europe's best one-liner at the end of World War II. Since then, the Fuckingers, as residents of the town are called, have had to deal with hordes of visitors posing in front of their street signs.

House of Artists

Gugging · In this home for the mentally ill, the walls are open canvases for patients to paint their frustrations, fears, and hopes.

Franz Gsellmann's Weltmaschine

Kam · This behemoth of whirring, spinning, turning parts includes toy gondolas, a xylophone, miniature windmills, a spaceship, and an oxygen tank—created by an untrained farmer.

Minimundus

Klagenfurt · A park filled with famous buildings from around the world built on a 1:25 scale.

Kremsmunster Observatory

Kremsmunster · Founded as a monastery in the 8th century and upgraded to a five-story "mathematical tower" in the 1750s, this weather observatory has been operational for over 250 years.

Dom Museum's Kunst und Wunderkammer

Salzburg · This lovingly re-created and restored collection of curiosities once belonged to the Archbishop Wolf Dietrich.

Starkenberger Beer Resort

Starkenberg · Lager lovers can literally immerse themselves in one of seven 13-foot (4 m) pools of warm beer, each containing some 42,000 pints. Cold beer is provided for drinking.

WORLD OF THE ICE GIANTS

WERFEN, SALZBURG

At 26 miles (42 km) long, Eisriesenwelt, or "World of the Ice Giants," is the largest ice cave in the world. It is filled with naturally formed sheets of dripping, curving ice, the result of melting snow from the surface flowing into the cave through cracks and crevices and solidifying when it meets the freezing temperatures. Bright magnesium lights illuminate the ice formations, making the scene even more dramatic.

Getreidegasse 21, Werfen. Eisriesenwelt is 25 miles (40.3 km) south of Salzburg. The cave is open to visitors from May to October. Bring warm clothing; the caves are below freezing, even in summer. Ⓝ 47.50778 Ⓔ 13.189722

Handheld lamps illuminate the dripping formations in the world's largest ice cave.

BELGIUM

TOWER OF EBEN-EZER

BASSENGE, LIÈGE

This seven-story stone tower—topped with a bull, a lion, an eagle, and a sphinx—looks medieval, but harks from a more recent time. Beginning in 1951, Robert Garcet spent over a decade building the Tower of Eben-Ezer by hand, as a totem to peace and the pursuit of knowledge.

A devotee of the Bible, numerology, and ancient civilizations, Garcet used symbolic dimensions when designing the building. The tower is 33 meters tall (to represent Jesus's age when he died) and topped with a quartet of statues (matching the four horsemen of the apocalypse). Each floor measures 12 by 12 meters—12 being the number of Jesus's disciples.

The interior walls are filled with Garcet's artwork, which depicts scenes from the apocalypse, biblical quotes, and Cretaceous dinosaurs. Climb the spiral staircase to the rooftop and you'll emerge from under a winged lion to see panoramic views of the Belgian countryside.

4690 Eben-Emael, Bassenge. A train from Brussels takes about 2 hours. Ⓝ 50.793317 Ⓔ 5.665638

The hand-built turreted Eben-Ezer Tower was inspired by the Bible and ancient civilizations.

THE MUNDANEUM

MONS, HAINAUT

The Mundaneum was, to put it mildly, an ambitious undertaking. Belgian lawyer Paul Otlet and Nobel Peace Prize winner Henri LaFontaine established the project in 1910 with the aim of compiling the entirety of human knowledge on 3 × 5-inch index cards. The collection was to be the centerpiece of a "world city" designed by architect Le Corbusier, forming a nucleus of knowledge that would inspire the world with its libraries, museums, and universities.

To address the daunting task of arranging bits of paper into a coherent compendium of world history, Otlet developed a system called Universal Decimal Classification. Over the next few decades, a growing staff created and catalogued over 12 million cards summarizing the contents of books and periodicals. Having assembled this wealth of knowledge, Otlet began offering a fee-based research service. Queries came in by mail and telegraph from around the globe at the rate of 1,500 per year.

With the paper-based system becoming cumbersome by 1934, Otlet hoped to move on to another system: a mechanical data cache accessible via a global network of what he termed "electric telescopes." To his dismay, the Belgian government had little enthusiasm for the idea. With World War II looming and priorities elsewhere, the Mundaneum moved to a smaller site, eventually ceasing operations after years of financial instability. The final blow came during the Nazi invasion of Belgium, when soldiers destroyed thousands of boxes filled with index cards and hung Third Reich artwork on the walls.

Otlet died in 1944, his Mundaneum and world city mere memories. He is now regarded as one of the forefathers of information science—his vision of a globally searchable network of interlinked documents anticipated the World Wide Web.

The remains of the Mundaneum—books, posters, planning documents, and drawers with original index cards—are now on display at the Musée Mundaneum in Mons.

76, rue de Nimy, Mons. The Mundaneum is a 15-minute walk from the Mons train station.
Ⓝ 50.457674 Ⓔ 3.955428

The Mundaneum, with its 12 million info-packed index cards, was the early-20th-century version of the internet.

THE GROTTOES OF FOLX-LES-CAVES

ORP-JAUCHE, WALLOON BRABANT

Down a narrow staircase, 50 feet below the small town of Folx-les-Caves, are nearly 15 acres of human-made caves. Carved from tuff, or compressed volcanic ash, they were probably dug during the Roman era or the Middle Ages. In 1886, farmers began growing mushrooms in the cold, dark grottoes—the fungi grow there to this day.

Prior to the mushroom era, the cave served as a refuge for bandits on the lam. Words and names chiseled into the stone—graffiti from a pre–spray can age—provide evidence of its past inhabitants. One of the most famous was Pierre Colon, an 18th-century thief who robbed passing merchants and shared his spoils with the poor. Colon was sent to jail, but escaped after his wife pulled the now-cliché move of sneaking him a metal file inside a cake. The legend of Colon is celebrated at Folx-les-Caves every year in early October with a festival of music, dance, and food.

35, rue Auguste Baccus, Orp-Jauche. Orp-Jauche is about an hour east of Brussels. Ⓝ 50.669216 Ⓔ 4.941959

ALSO IN BELGIUM

Caves of Remouchamps	Plantin-Moretus Museum of Printing	The Atomium	The Musical Instrument Museum	Dr. Guislain Museum
Aywaille · Take a 90-minute boat ride along the world's longest subterranean river. If you're lucky, you'll spot a translucent shrimp.	*Antwerp* · A 16th-century publishing house–cum–museum features two of the oldest printing presses, a Gutenberg Bible, and the world's only copy of the original Garamond punches and matrices.	*Brussels* · Enjoy the view from the top of an iron crystal structure magnified to 165 billion times its size, built for the 1958 Brussels World's Fair.	*Brussels* · A three-floor wonderland displays over 1,500 instruments of all shapes and sizes. Check out the componium, the first automatic instrument capable of improvisation.	*Ghent* · Housed within an operating mental institution, this museum mixes art and education in its mission to educate the public about psychiatric care.

FRANCE

HOLLOW AT LA MEAUFFE

LA MEAUFFE, NORMANDY

Holloways, which appear like deep trenches dragged into the earth, are centuries-old thoroughfares worn down by the traffic of time. In Europe, most of these sunken lanes go back to Roman times, or as early as the Iron Age.

These deep-recessed roads were naturally tunneled into the soft ground by years of footsteps, cart wheels, and animal hooves. Water flowing through the embankments like a gully further molded the paths into rounded ditches that have sunk as much as 20 feet lower than the land on either side. In some cases, trees rise up from the banks flanking the narrow path and reach toward each other to form a canopy over the road, making the holloway look like a tunnel running through the thick greenery.

Holloways are especially common in the *bocage*, or "hedgerow," landscape around Normandy, where the countryside is divided into small fields enclosed by sunken lanes and high hedges. Like many sunken roads, the trench-like holloway in La Meauffe was used as a shelter during times of war. During World War II, the La Meauffe hollow was a defensive strongpoint for the German army, providing perfect cover from the advancing American troops. The limited visibility of the terrain caused the Americans to suffer heavy losses during the attack, leading US soldiers to call the road in La Meauffe "Death Valley Road."

The holloway in La Meauffe is located off the main road on the southern edge of town. Ⓝ 49.174619 Ⓦ 1.112959

Many who walk through holloways don't realize they are retracing ancient steps.

ORADOUR-SUR-GLANE

ORADOUR-SUR-GLANE, LIMOUSIN

The village of Oradour-sur-Glane has stood in ruins since 1944. Among the scorched, crumbling buildings are the possessions of people who lived here over 70 years ago: burned shells of cars; sewing machines; bed frames; the skeleton of a stroller. All sit quietly, at the mercy of nothing but weather and time.

On June 10, 1944, in response to suspected Resistance activity in the region, the Nazi SS stormed Oradour-sur-Glane and ordered every resident to assemble in the village square. The unit then led the men to barns and sheds, where they had set up machine guns. They locked the women and children in the church, and set the

The burned-out remains of a village left untouched for 70 years.

building on fire. Anyone who tried to escape through a window was met with a hail of gunfire.

Within hours, the Waffen-SS had murdered 642 residents of Oradour-sur-Glane. Satisfied, they left, but not before torching every structure in the village.

When World War II ended, French president Charles de Gaulle declared that while a new Oradour-sur-Glane would be built next to the original, the old one must be kept in ruins as a reminder of the atrocities of war. Apart from the addition of signs, plaques, and a museum, the ghost village is untouched. A sign above the entrance reads *Souviens-Toi*: "Remember."

Oradour-sur-Glane is a 30-minute drive west of Limoges. On June 10, wreaths are laid in the village's ruined church to mark the anniversary of the attack.
Ⓝ 45.931233 Ⓔ 1.035125

THE CHAPPE OPTICAL TELEGRAPH

SAVERNE, BAS-RHIN

Messages needed to travel swiftly across the country during the French Revolution, and Claude Chappe's optical telegraph was just the device for the job.

In 1791, Chappe debuted his chain of stone towers—topped with 10-foot (3 m) poles and 14-foot (4.3 m) pivoting crossbeams, and spaced as far apart as the eye could see—on the Champs-Élysées. He also created a language of 9,999 words, each represented by a different position of the swinging arms. When operated by well-trained optical telegraphers, the system allowed messages to be transmitted up to 150 miles (241.4 km) in two minutes.

The French military saw the value of Chappe's invention and built lines of his towers from Paris to Dunkirk and Strasbourg. Within a decade, a network of optical telegraph lines crisscrossed the

nation. When Napoleon seized power in 1799, he used the optical telegraph to dispatch the message "Paris is quiet and the good citizens are content."

Renovated in 1998, the optical telegraph next to the Rohan Castle in Saverne functioned as part of the Strasbourg line from 1798 until 1852. It is one of several remaining

relay points in the system that can still be visited today.
Rohan Castle, place du Général de Gaulle, Saverne. The castle is a 5-minute walk from the Saverne train station. Ⓝ 48.742222 Ⓔ 7.363333

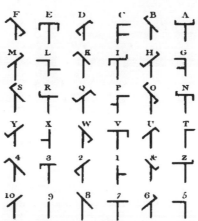

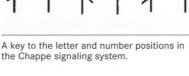

A key to the letter and number positions in the Chappe signaling system.

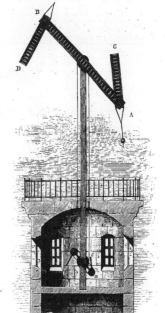

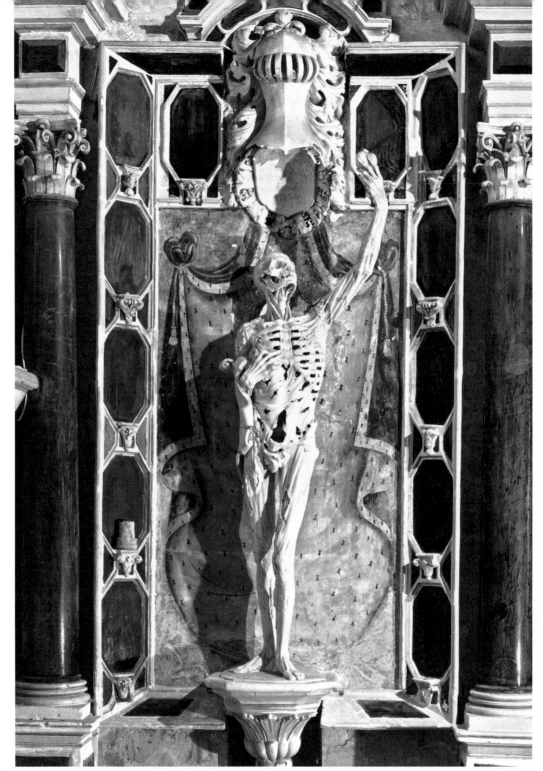

The postmortem statue of René de Chalon once held the man's own dried heart.

THE ROTTING BODY OF RENÉ DE CHALON

BAR-LE-DUC, LORRAINE

Saint-Étienne church, in the city of Bar-le-Duc, is home to a statue of a rotting corpse. Visible musculature and skin hang in flaps over the hollow carcass. The exposed skull looks toward a raised left hand, which once held the dried heart of René de Chalon, the 16th-century prince the statue depicts. (The heart is believed to have gone missing sometime around the French Revolution.)

The life-size sculpture by Ligier Richier is part of the "transi" Renaissance art form—stone sculptures of rotting bodies that served as a reminder of temporary flesh and eternal afterlife.

Saint-Étienne church, place Saint-Pierre, Bar-le-Duc. The train ride from Paris to Bar-le-Duc takes two and a half hours. Ⓝ 48.768206 Ⓔ 5.159390

The many dials of what may be the most complicated horological device ever constructed.

THE ASTRONOMICAL CLOCK OF BESANÇON CATHEDRAL

BESANÇON, FRANCHE-COMTÉ

Besançon Cathedral, located in the center of France's 19th-century clock-making capital, is home to a 19-foot-tall (5.8 m) clock with 30,000 pieces. It is one of the most complicated horological devices ever made. Installed in 1860, the clock shows the local time in 17 places around the world, as well as the time and height of the tides in eight French ports, a perpetual calendar with leap-year cycles, and the times of sunrise and sunset.

Besançon Cathedral, rue du Chapitre, Besançon. The cathedral is a leisurely stroll from the main train station.

Ⓝ 47.237829 Ⓔ 6.024054

ALSO IN FRANCE

The Chapel Oak

Allouville-Bellefosse · A tiny chapel built inside the trunk of the oldest known tree in France.

Mechanical Dragon Clock

Blois · A huge golden mechanical dragon emerges from a villa at regular intervals like a cuckoo clock—a homage to magician and automaton creator Jean Eugène Robert-Houdin.

La Maison Picassiette

Chartres · A home covered top to bottom in mosaics, made by a frustrated grave sweeper.

Douaumont Ossuary

Douaumont · The remains of nearly 130,000 soldiers fill this World War I memorial.

Secret Passages of Mont Sainte-Odile

Ottrott · An ancient fortified monastery contains hidden passages and has a history of mysterious book thefts.

Collégiale de Saint-Bonnet-le-Château

Saint-Bonnet-le-Château · Thirty mummified bodies, believed to be Catholic nobles killed by a Protestant leader in 1562, were rediscovered in 1837, when one of the vaults of this church was opened.

MUSÉE DE LA CHASSE ET DE LA NATURE

PARIS

Housed in the 17th-century Hôtel de Guénégaud, the Museum of Hunting and Nature displays stuffed animals, the decorated vintage weapons that killed them, and artwork depicting the chase.

One room features a large wooden cabinet dedicated to a variety of hunted animals. Concealed in the cabinet drawers are bronze casts of each animal's footprints and droppings, depictions of its natural habitat, and a poem dedicated to the creature. A room on the second floor has a ceiling entirely covered in the feathers and heads of five owls.

In the dramatic room packed with taxidermy specimens from around the world, look out for one item that's not like the others: a wall-mounted, animatronic moving albino boar head that speaks perfect French. **62, rue des Archives, Paris. Take the Métro to Rambuteau.** Ⓝ 48.857127 Ⓔ 2.354125

Graffiti, moss, and abandoned train tracks form a loop around Paris's outer arrondissements.

THE PETITE CEINTURE

PARIS

The "little belt" railway ringing central Paris served urban travelers from 1862 to 1934, connecting five main stations owned by five different rail companies. The 20th-century expansion of Paris and the Métro eventually made the circular railway obsolete.

Stretches of the track now exhibit a quirky blend of idyllic nature and gritty urban life—plants and flowers grow between the rails against a backdrop of vivid graffiti and street art. Bridges, tunnels, and the original tracks remain mostly untouched, hidden just beyond the streets and neighborhoods of the outer arrondissements.

The Petite Ceinture is still owned by SNCF, France's national railway company, so a walk along the rails is considered trespassing. That said, an innocent bit of urban exploration is unlikely to land you in trouble. If you're strictly by the book, visit the section between the Porte d'Auteuil and the Gare de la Muette—in 2008, the area was classified as a nature trail open to pedestrians.

There are multiple points of entry to the Petite Ceinture. For the most scenic walks, access the track from the Balard, Porte de Vincennes, Porte Dorée, or Buttes Chaumont Métro stop. Ⓝ 48.821375 Ⓔ 2.342287

RUINS OF LE JARDIN D'AGRONOMIE TROPICALE

PARIS

In 1907, as part of the city's Colonial Exposition, a set of pavilions and artificial villages went on display on the edge of the Bois de Vincennes. Each pavilion exhibited indigenous food, plants, products, and resources from colonies of the French empire. Each village mimicked its Asian or African original. Visitors didn't even need to imagine the actual people who lived in these far-off lands—as with the plants, Paris imported them and put them on display.

Throughout the summer, Indochinese, Malagasy, Congolese, Sudanese, and Tuareg people lived in recreated "typical" environments in the park. They wore costumes, sang, and danced for curious audiences. French visitors swarmed to the garden to observe the human zoo.

When cooler weather set in, the residents returned to their homes in the colonies, and the site began to decay. The land, owned by the French state, remained closed to the public until the city of Paris purchased it and reopened the site in 2007.

The five villages are still there, but the buildings—today fenced off from visitors—have almost completely collapsed. Most have trees and other vegetation growing from within. The plants inside the greenhouses have been left to rot. A few key pieces of architecture, such as a Chinese gate, are the only hints of the garden's former role as a tribute to the "glories" of colonial expansion.

45, avenue de la Belle-Gabrielle, Paris. The garden is a 10-minute walk from the Nogent-sur-Marne train station. Ⓝ 48.841007 Ⓔ 2.465697 ➤➤

➤➤ Humans on Display

Visitors to New York's Bronx Zoo in September 1906 were surprised to see a new mammal on display at the Monkey House. Imported from the Belgian Congo, he stood just under 5 feet (1.5 m), weighed 103 pounds (46.7 kg), and went by the name Ota Benga. Crowds jostled to watch him bare his sharp teeth and play with his cagemates: a parrot and an orangutan. The zoo had never displayed a member of his species before; Ota Benga was a human being.

The public exhibition of people was once a way for the world's colonizers to show off the "exotic" inhabitants of the countries they owned. Plucked from their homes like living souvenirs, indigenous people performed a counterfeit version of their daily lives at world's fairs, carnivals, and, most outlandishly, in zoos.

The producers of these shows showed little regard for the indigenous culture of the performers, preferring to create a version that would shock, amaze, and sell tickets. In 1882, Canadian theater agent Robert Cunningham visited Australia to recruit for a P. T. Barnum tour of "savage tribes." Cunningham selected nine Aboriginal men

and women from seven separate communities. Each community spoke a different traditional language, and only two of the nine spoke English.

Promotional posters described the performers as "tattooed cannibal black trackers and boomerang throwers." They danced, sang, and engaged in mock fights at exhibitions across America and Europe. Within two years, five of the nine were dead.

The case of Saartjie Baartman is a particularly unsettling example of 19th-century Europe's fascination with so-called primitives. In 1810, the young Khoisan woman was living in South Africa when William Dunlop, a visiting British doctor, persuaded Baartman to accompany

him to London. There, he exhibited her naked in a cage, demanding she walk, sit, or stand so that onlookers could get a better view of her large buttocks and genitalia. Anthropologists used her physical proportions as evidence that the white race ranked highest. Known as the Hottentot Venus, Baartman died at the age of 26.

As for Ota Benga, a flurry of complaints, particularly from African American ministers, brought about his release from the zoo. Freedom from the animal cage, however, did not mean happiness. After a stay at an orphanage, Benga had his teeth capped, went to school, and was working at a tobacco factory when World War I destroyed his

Ota Benga

dreams of returning to the Congo. Miserable at the thought of never going home, Benga chipped the caps off his teeth and fatally shot himself. He was 32.

DEYROLLE TAXIDERMY

PARIS

Exotic taxidermy, entomology, and natural history collections displayed in antique wooden cases and glass bell jars have made this store a destination for Parisians ever since it opened in 1881.

In 2007, many of the animals were reduced to blackened fragments after a fire tore through the store. With the help of artists and collectors worldwide, the shop is back in business, and today houses everything from stuffed house cats to polar bears among its 19th-century decor. Though some of the more exotic animals are not for sale, you can always borrow a lion for a party—almost everything in the store is available for rent.

46, rue du Bac, Paris. Take the Métro to rue du Bac. Ⓝ 48.856444 Ⓔ 2.326564

A motionless menagerie with representatives from every corner of the animal kingdom.

Argonaute Submarine

19th Arr. • It was the dawn of the Space Age, but in 1958 the pride of the French military was one of the most modern submarines of any fleet, silently cruising the briny dark.

The "I Love You" Wall

Clignancourt • Covered in 612 cobalt-blue lava tiles and sprinkled with the red of a few broken hearts, this Montmartre wall expresses love via 250 languages.

Le Louxor Palais du Cinéma

10th Arr. • This stylish Egyptian Revival theater, inspired by Theda Bara's 1917 *Cleopatra*, is perhaps the oldest surviving movie palace in Paris, abandoned for decades and restored in 2013 to its former glory.

Parc Monceau

L'Europe • The ruins of the Duke of Chartres's 18th-century bucolic fantasy, where camels once roamed alongside faux Dutch windmills and Italianate vineyards, lend the landscape of this scruffy royal folly an airy charm.

UCJG and the World's Oldest Basketball Court

9th Arr. • Most weekend b-ballers who bang the backboards in the basement of this UCJG youth hostel (the French YMCA) have no idea that they are playing on the oldest basketball court in the world. Built in 1892, it is an almost exact copy of the Springfield, Massachusetts, court (long gone), where the game was invented.

Museum of Vampires and Legendary Creatures

Les Lilas • An eccentric scholar of the undead, and a rabid collector of their trappings, has assembled this macabre collection that includes Dracula toys, a vampire-killing kit, and a merry clutter of vampiric books, art, and literature.

A Parisian guide to the language of love.

Museum of Arts and Crafts

3rd Arr. • One of the world's great collections of mechanical instruments was founded by anti-cleric French revolutionaries, so it is no small irony that these engineering wonders and contraptions are now partly housed in the former abbey church of Saint Martin des Champs.

Medici Column

Les Halles • Standing extra tall yet supporting nothing, the nine-story Medici Column in front of the Paris Commodities Exchange hides a secret spiral staircase that runs to a viewing platform at the top, originally built so Catherine de Medici's personal astrologer could contemplate the stars.

The Duluc Detective Agency

Les Halles • Noirish green neon marks the location of one of France's oldest private detective agencies, a favorite spot for film directors and fans of gumshoe novels alike, with a Prussian-blue door and an engraved plain brass plaque that reads: DULUC. INVESTIGATIONS. 1ST FLOOR.

The Relic Crypt of St. Helena at Église Saint-Leu-Saint-Gilles

Les Halles • Forgotten by most Parisian Catholics but venerated by the Russian Orthodox community, this little-known reliquary holds stolen pieces of Constantine's mother, who helped spread Christianity throughout the Roman Empire in the 4th century, even as most of her body still rests in Rome.

House of Nicolas Flamel

Le Marais • This former home of the legendary 15th-century alchemist dates to 1407, making it the oldest stone house in Paris. Covered in strange and arcane symbols of magical transformation, it may hold the secret of turning tin into gold.

Paris Sewer Museum

Rive Gauche • What Victor Hugo described as "fetid, wild, fierce" has been a tourist destination since 1889, when the tangled labyrinth under the streets of Paris was first opened to the public to show off a marvel of French engineering.

Gustave Eiffel's Secret Apartment

Faubourg St-Germain • At the top of the city's iconic tower is a jewel box of an apartment built by Eiffel to entertain the elite science community of Paris—and to make everyone else jealous.

Bird Market

Île de la Cité • Every Sunday, when most of the flower vendors take their one day off, stacks of cages fill the market square on Île de la Cité near Notre-Dame, with pets and livestock of the chirping, squeaking, and flapping varieties.

Chapelle de Saint Vincent de Paul

7th Arr. • Behind the stark facade of a chapel near the Luxembourg Gardens at the top of a carved double staircase guarded by marble statuary, the robed bones and waxy remains of the 18th-century Saint Vincent de Paul rest in a glass-fronted solid silver reliquary, looking like he was just caught napping.

Arènes de Lutèce

St. Victor • Paris is the city of Notre-Dame, of Hemingway and Harry's Bar, of la Belle Époque and Marie Antoinette, but the Roman past of Paris is often overlooked. To wit, the quiet remnant of an ancient Lutetian amphitheater that has no guard, no entry fee, and few tourists.

Louis XIV's Globes

Quartier de la Gare • Created during the 17th-century reign of the Sun King, the golden age of French art, literature, and geographical exploration, two exquisite globes—the Earth and the cosmos—each 20 feet (6 m) in diameter, glow overhead at the National Library.

MUSÉE FRAGONARD

PARIS

At the Musée Fragonard, human fetuses dance a jig alongside a ten-legged sheep while a skinless horseman of the apocalypse looks on.

Founded in 1766 as a veterinary school with a private collection, the museum has rooms devoted to anatomy, physical abnormalities, articulated animal skeletons, and disease. However, by far the most striking room is the collection of écorchés, or "flayed figures," created by Honoré Fragonard.

Louis XV appointed Fragonard as a professor at the first veterinary school in Lyon, and it was there that he began skinning and preserving animal and, later, human corpses. Though he intended for his écorchés to be used as educational

A deceased rider flogging a dead horse.

tools, Fragonard arranged many of his figures into theatrical poses, creating eerie posthumous narratives. The horseman of the apocalypse, inspired by Albrecht Dürer's painting, is the most notable example. A skinless corpse with dried, varnished muscles and unnerving glass eyes sits astride a similarly preserved horse caught mid-gallop, the thick arteries of its neck filled with red wax. Reins loop from the animal's mouth and over the rigid sinew of the rider's hands.

Fragonard worked in Lyon for six years before his flayed figures began frightening the townspeople. He was dismissed from the institution amid accusations of insanity. The public would not see the flayed figures until the Fragonard museum opened in 1991.

7, avenue de Général de Gaulle, Maisons-Alfort. Located in a suburb of Paris, you can take the Métro to École Veterinaire de Maisons-Alfoet. Ⓝ 48.812714 Ⓔ 2.422311

ALSO IN AND NEAR PARIS

Dans le Noir?

Paris · Dine in complete darkness at this restaurant chain, staffed by vision-impaired waiters.

Eyewear Museum

Paris · A tiny museum filled with hundreds of famous spectacles.

The French Freemasonry Museum

Paris · Peek into the private world of a secret society.

Musée de la Contrefaçon

Paris · A museum dedicated to French counterfeits, from pens to pants.

Musée de la Magie

Paris · A museum documenting the history of magic in what was once the basement home of the Marquis de Sade.

Musée d'Anatomie Delmas-Orfila-Rouvière

Paris · France's largest collection of human anatomy specimens sits hidden from the public.

Musée des Arts et Métiers

Paris · The national museum of scientific and industrial instruments is home to Foucault's actual pendulum.

The Dog Cemetery

Asniéres-sur-Seine · Pay your respects at a pet graveyard dating back to the late 1800s.

Absinthe Museum

Auvers-sur-Oise · Learn about the history of the delicious beverage called the "green fairy"— purported to cause wild hallucinations and insanity, and banned in Europe and the US for nearly 100 years.

Musée Mondial de l'Aérostation

Balleroy · The top floor of this chateau is dedicated to the sport of ballooning.

Heart of the Dauphin

Saint-Denis · A crystal jar in the Basilica of Saint-Denis holds Louis XVI's small, withered heart.

THE RAT KING

NANTES, PAYS DE LA LOIRE

Tucked away in the Natural History Museum among the beautiful taxidermy birds, sparkling minerals, and mammal skeletons is a very rare and possibly forged specimen: a rat king. Folklore holds that rat kings are formed when a group of rats get their tails inextricably entangled. Thus trapped, the creatures spend the rest of their lives intertwined and unable to move, relying on other rats to bring them food.

The Nantes rat king specimen, found in 1986, consists of nine conjoined rodents preserved in alcohol. It is one of only a handful of cases ever found, though scientific consensus considers its natural occurrence unlikely.

12, rue Voltaire, Nantes. Take the tram to Médiathèque. Ⓝ 47.212446 Ⓦ 1.564685

Le Palais Idéal

HAUTERIVES, RHÔNE-ALPES

It all began with a postman and a pebble. Walking on his usual mail delivery route in 1879, Ferdinand Cheval tripped on a rock, took note of its peculiar shape, and had a sudden vision of a grand palace made of irregular stones. For the next 33 years, he worked diligently to transfer the palace from his imagination into reality, collecting rocks in a wheelbarrow while delivering letters. An oil lamp guided his hands as he worked on the palace alone at night. Not once did he ask for, or receive, help.

Cheval had little formal education and no architectural experience. His stone, cement, and wire creation was inspired by different styles and eras, incorporating Chinese, Algerian, and Northern European designs. The final castle (the Ideal Palace) is a magnificent tangle of grottoes, flying buttresses, and animal statues. A shrine holds the wooden wheelbarrow that carried the rocks.

When French authorities denied Cheval's wish to be buried within his palace, he was undeterred. Over the next eight years, the 80-year-old self-made architect built his own magnificent vault in the local cemetery, in a style closely resembling that of Le Palais Idéal. He died a year after its completion.

8, rue du Palais, Hauterives. The palace is 30 miles (48.3 km) south of Lyon, just off D538. The nearest train station is St. Vallier sur Rhône, a 45-minute ride from Lyon. Ⓝ 45.255889 Ⓔ 5.027794

"Everything you can see, passer-by, is the work of one peasant" is inscribed on the wall of this postman's castle.

The Odeillo solar furnace benefits from southern France's 2,400 hours of sunshine per year.

WORLD'S LARGEST SOLAR FURNACE

ODEILLO, LANGUEDOC-ROUSSILLON

A solar furnace uses a large concave surface of mirrors to reflect sunlight onto a focal point the size of a cooking pot. The temperature at this point may reach above 6,000°F (3,315°C), enough to generate electricity, melt metal, or produce hydrogen fuel.

The world's largest solar furnace is located in Font-Romeu-Odeillo-Via, a commune in the sunny Pyrenees mountains on the French-Spanish border. Operational since 1970, it uses a field of 10,000 ground-mounted mirrors to bounce the sun's rays onto a large concave mirror that shows a distorted, upside-down reflection of the countryside. Tours of the site include workshops and demonstrations on renewable energy and the solar system. **Grand Four Solaire d'Odeillo, 7, rue du Four Solaire, Font-Romeu-Odeillo-Via. The Odeillo station, a 15-minute walk from the furnace, is a stop on the scenic Little Yellow Train route. The train, which has two open-air carriages, offers splendid views of valleys, mountains, and Villefranche-de-Conflent, a fortified medieval town. Ⓝ 42.494916 Ⓔ 2.035357**

ALSO IN SOUTHERN FRANCE

Bugarach Mountain

Bugarach · New Agers believe this mountain spaceship is home to aliens who will rescue them in the apocalypse. It was the site of much hubbub around the Mayan Doomsday predictions of 2012.

Nude City

Cap d'Adge · Nudity is legal and common at this family-style resort. Roughly 40,000 daily visitors dine, shop, and stroll naked.

Carriolu Miniature Village

Carriolu · French cheese maker Jean-Claude Marchi has built a meticulously detailed mini village out of pebbles.

FRANCE / GERMANY / 41

GERMANY
SPACE TRAVEL MUSEUM

FEUCHT, BAVARIA

Dedicated to space technology, the Hermann Oberth Space Travel Museum celebrates the zeal and inventiveness of its namesake—one of the forgotten founding fathers of rocketry and modern astronautics.

Born in 1894, Hermann Oberth was interested in astronomy from a young age. After reading Jules Verne's *From the Earth to the Moon* at 11, Oberth began sketching designs for rockets. By the time he was 14, Oberth designed plans for a recoil rocket that could propel itself through space by expelling exhaust gases from its base. (This was quite the achievement for an adolescent, considering rockets meant for manned spaceflight would not exist for another 50 years.)

After studying physics, aerodynamics, and medicine at universities in Munich, Heidelberg, and Göttingen, Oberth published a 429-page tome in 1929 titled *The Rocket into Interplanetary Space*. The book had a global impact. It would have been a banner year for the newly esteemed scientist if not for the fact that he lost vision in his left eye while building a flying rocket model for Fritz Lang's sci-fi film *Woman in the Moon*.

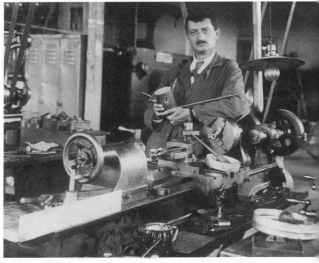

Hermann Oberth, the father of space travel, surrounded by his tools of the trade.

Exhibits inside the museum include a Cirrus rocket and a Kumulus rocket developed in the 1960s and launched outside of Cuxhaven, Germany. A Swiss Zenit sounding rocket is also on display. **Pfinzingstraße 12-14, Feucht. Feucht is a short S-Bahn ride from Nuremberg. Ⓝ 48.136607 Ⓔ 11.577085**

THE GALLERY OF BEAUTIES

MUNICH, BAVARIA

Though married at 24, 19th-century Bavarian King Ludwig I kept 36 beautiful young women in his palace. Whenever he became enamored with a female acquaintance's good looks, a portrait of her placid face would soon appear in the Schönheitgalerie, his Gallery of Beauties, a room in the south pavilion of Nymphenburg Palace—literally, Nymph Castle. The women are captured in their late teenage years or early twenties, milk-skinned and serene.

The standout work of the collection is Helene Sedlmayr, a doe-eyed, dark-haired shoemaker's daughter who gave toys to Ludwig's children. Her beauty was particularly appreciated by the king's valet, Hermes Miller, with whom she went on to bear 10 children.

Included in this collection are portraits of the adventurous aristocrat Jane Digby and Irish performer Lola Montez.

Schloss Nymphenburg, Eingang 19, Munich. The vast palace is 20 minutes via tram from central Munich toward Amalienburgstraße. Ⓝ 48.136607 Ⓔ 11.577085

Saint Munditia's bejeweled right hand holds a glass container filled with dried blood.

Jeweled Skeleton of Saint Munditia

MUNICH, BAVARIA

St. Peter's Church, or "Alter Peter," as locals call it, is Munich's oldest church, dating from before the city's founding in 1158. A quarter of the way down the aisle is a glass coffin bearing the skeleton of Saint Munditia, who met her end courtesy of a hatchet beheading in 310 CE. Once kept hidden in a wooden box, she was carefully adorned and put on display in 1883. Glass eyes stare out from the sockets of her sepia-stained skull. Jewels conceal her rotted teeth. And her skeleton, covered in gold and gemstones, has been reunited with her skull.

St. Peter's Church, Rindermarkt 1, Munich. St. Munditia's feast day, November 17, is celebrated with a candle procession at the church.
N 48.136497 E 11.575672 ➻

➻ Jeweled Saints: Adorned and Adored

The practice of adorning the skeletons of saints with gold and jewels began after the rediscovery of the Roman catacombs in 1578. It was a tumultuous time for the Catholic Church—Protestant reformers had revolted against Catholic practices perceived as corrupt. In addition to criticizing papal authority, transubstantiation, purgatory, and confession, they also found the Church's excessive veneration of saints and their relics to be contrary to the teachings of scripture.

In response to the Protestant Reformation, a meeting of Catholic cardinals known as the Council of Trent set out to restore the Church's image. One way of doing that was to double down on the spiritual power of saints and their relics. The Church took the skeletons of supposed saints from the Roman catacombs and displayed them dressed in the elaborately embellished clothing of the time. This practice continued until the mid-1700s, and the jeweled skeletons found their final resting places in churches around Europe.

Waldsassen Basilica, a Bavarian church near the Czech border, has the largest collection of jeweled saints: There are 10 of them lining the aisles, each one in a glass case. Known as the Holy Bodies, the skeletons, many of whom have their teeth intact, seem to smile beatifically.

EISBACHWELLE

MUNICH, BAVARIA

If you're riding the Munich subway in the dead of winter and see someone carrying a surfboard, chances are they're headed for the Eisbach, the artificial stream that runs through Munich's biggest park, the English Gardens. A 1.5-foot (.5 m) stationary wave at a spot beneath a bridge was once an occasional sight, until local surfers funneled it into a more forceful, permanent swell by installing planks of wood on the sides of the river. Now the site attracts wave riders who brave the cold water—39°F in winter, 60°F in summer—to surf the stream in front of a crowd of onlookers.

So popular is the site that queues of surfers form on both sides of the narrow river. Those who pioneered the permanent wave have become disgruntled by the mass influx of newcomers, but their real ire is reserved for beginner surfers who lack the skills to conquer the wave.

Surf's up at the English Gardens, where there's an artificial wave beneath the bridge.

Englischer Garten, Munich. Get the U-Bahn to Lehel. The surf spot is at a river bridge in the English Gardens, just north of the Haus der Kunst art museum. There are three stationary waves in Munich, some better suited to beginners. Ⓝ 48.173644 Ⓔ 11.613079

THE EXTERNSTEINE

HORN-BAD MEINBERG, NORTH RHINE-WESTPHALIA

The Externsteine, translated variously as "stones of the ridge" or the "Star Stones," are a collection of limestone formations that jut up from the ground in

Between neo-pagans and neo-Nazis, the Star Stones have drawn quite the curious cult following.

a forest south of Detmold. There is scant evidence of the site's historical significance, but among the few known facts is that Christian monks carved stairs and reliefs into the stones during the late 8th century.

The Externsteine were a blank slate for Heinrich Himmler and his Third Reich comrades. Himmler was the head of the Nazi's occult division, *Ahnenerbe*, a pseudo-scientific think tank devoted to finding or—in many cases—fabricating an honorable and far-reaching Germanic history. The society identified the Externsteine as an important location of ancient Teutonic activity.

Today, the site remains a pilgrimage spot for both neo-pagans and neo-Nazis. Visit on the summer solstice, or on the celebration of Walpurgisnacht, and you will encounter a motley crew of pagans, hippies, mystics, and skinheads—each group celebrating for different reasons.

Externsteine Strasse, Horn-Bad Meinberg. Walpurgisnacht is April 30. Ⓝ 51.867376 Ⓔ 8.918495

ALSO IN SOUTHERN GERMANY

German Butcher Museum

Böblingen · Learn about the development and history of animal butchery. A strong stomach is recommended.

Heidelberg Thingstätte

Heidelberg · A Nazi-built stone amphitheater sits on a hill littered with ancient burial grounds.

Nördlingen

Nördlingen · A town centered in a 15-million-year-old meteor crater in the Bavarian countryside.

European Asparagus Museum

Schrobenhausen · A museum dedicated to Germany's favorite "royal vegetable."

The Pig Museum

Stuttgart · An old slaughterhouse turned museum with 25 themed rooms dedicated to pig paraphernalia.

Thousand-Year Rose

HILDESHEIM, LOWER SAXONY

The wild shrub that sprawls up a wall of Hildesheim Cathedral is believed to be the oldest living rose bush in the world.

Local tradition says that in 815, Louis the Pious, King of the Franks, was on a hunting trip in Hildesheim and stopped to observe Mass. After departing the area, he realized he had left behind a relic of the Blessed Virgin Mary. When he returned to retrieve it, he discovered the relic caught in a dog rose bush that refused to let it go. Taking this as a sign of the divine, Louis had a chapel built around the rose bush. In the 11th century, the chapel was expanded into what became Hildesheim Cathedral.

Even if the rose bush isn't as old as its legend, it has certainly proven its resilience. In March 1945, Allied bombs leveled the cathedral. Somehow, out of the burning rubble, the rose bush flourished once more. It now covers a courtyard-facing outer wall of the cathedral, which was rebuilt between 1950 and 1960.

Domhof 17, Hildesheim. To see the roses in bloom, visit at the end of May. Ⓝ 52.148889 Ⓔ 9.947222

The man at left represents an adult Kaspar, while the boy on the right is Kaspar as a "feral child."

Kaspar Hauser Monument

ANSBACH, BAVARIA

On a quiet street in the small city of Ansbach stand two statues depicting the same person, one as a boy and the other as a young man. They are both the mysterious Kaspar Hauser. The odd, unresolved story of Kaspar Hauser began on a May afternoon in 1828, when a stumbling, squinting teenage boy appeared on the streets of Nuremberg. The 4-foot-9-inch (1.4 m) Hauser had pale, soft skin, spoke few words, and seemed ill at ease among people. He carried two letters: The first, dated 1828, detailed the hardships that forced the author—apparently the boy's caretaker—to give him up. It ended with an ultimatum: Take care of Kaspar or, if you cannot, kill him. The second letter, dated 1812, was written by Kaspar's mother. She stated that she could not afford to raise him, and wished for him to join the Sixth Cavalry regiment at Nuremberg when he turned 17. A close examination of the letters revealed they were likely written by the same person in a single session.

The mystery deepened when Kaspar began talking. He claimed he spent his childhood locked in a small, dark cell, never seeing another person and waking up each day to a meal of bread and water. His only human contact, he said, was with a man who arrived shortly before his release and taught him to say the phrase, "I want to be a cavalryman like my father."

Frederich Daumer, a professor, took Kaspar into his home and taught him to speak German, ride horses, and draw. The boy began to adapt to his environment, but his highly attuned senses and inexplicable sensitivity to magnets and metal caused him anguish. One day in October 1829, Kaspar appeared with a bleeding wound on his forehead, claiming he had been attacked by a hooded man while using the bathroom. The man was never found, and the wound may have been self-inflicted. A few months later, a gunshot rang out from Kaspar's room. Again he was discovered with a wound to the head, this time declaring he had knocked a pistol to the ground, where it accidentally went off.

Kaspar's strange life ended in 1833, when he sustained a fatal stab to the chest at the palace gardens in Ansbach. He said a man had lured him there and lunged at him. He even provided a note from the assailant.

Platenstrasse, Ansbach. Kaspar Hauser is also remembered at Ansbach's Markgrafenmuseum, which exhibits the bloodstained clothes he was found in, the two letters, and some of his personal belongings. Ⓝ 49.302248 Ⓔ 10.570951

CASTLE OF WEWELSBURG

WEWELSBURG, NORTH RHINE-WESTPHALIA

SS leader Heinrich Himmler had grand, horrifying plans for the triangular Renaissance castle in Wewelsburg. In 1934, undeterred by its dilapidated state, he signed a 100-year lease on the property. His mission was to turn the castle into an SS training center, where young Aryan minds could study Nazi-skewed versions of history, archaeology, astronomy, and art.

The SS redesigned the castle, incorporating swastikas and occult symbols, and used slave laborers from the nearby Niederhagen and Sachsenhausen concentration camps to bring the plans to life. Nazi-approved artwork and historical objects decorated the halls. The focal point of the redesign was a circular chamber known as "the crypt," which featured an eternal flame at the center of the room surrounded by 12 seats—an allusion to the Knights of the Round Table. On the ceiling was a large swastika.

As construction continued, Himmler expanded his vision for the town of Wewelsburg. From 1941, he began to view it as the future center of the new world order, with the castle anchoring a village populated exclusively by SS leaders. But in spite of all the plans, SS training never took place at Wewelsburg. The SS did conduct meetings there, and it functioned as a venue for SS officer marriage consecrations—although prospective spouses had to provide genealogical documentation proving their Aryan heritage before the ceremony could take place.

After Germany's 1943 defeat at Stalingrad—regarded as the beginning of the end for the Nazis—construction at Wewelsburg halted. On March 30, 1945, a month before Hitler's suicide, Himmler ordered SS major Heinz Macher to destroy the castle. The US Third Infantry Division arrived the next day to discover the castle interior in ashes. Only the outside walls remained.

Today, Wewelsburg is one of Germany's largest youth hostels, offering 204-bed accommodations and team-building programs for schoolchildren. A museum at the entrance presents the history of the SS and pays tribute to its victims.

From Nazi indoctrination center to youth hostel.

Burgwall 19, Büren. From the Paderborn train station, take a half-hour bus ride to Büren-Wewelsburg. The castle is a three-minute walk from the Schule/ Kreismuseum stop. Ⓝ 51.606991 Ⓔ 8.651241

THE IMPALED STORK

ROSTOCK, MECKLENBURG-VORPOMMERN

Until the 19th century, the annual disappearance of white storks each fall puzzled European birdwatchers. Aristotle thought the storks went into hibernation with the other disappearing avian species, perhaps at the bottom of the sea. Other hypotheses argued that the disappearing birds flew to the moon to escape the cold weather.

In 1822, a stunning piece of evidence proved key to solving the mystery of the disappearing birds. A white stork, shot on the Bothmer Estate near Mecklenburg, was discovered with a 2.5-foot-long (80 cm) Central African spear embedded in its neck. Remarkably, the stork had flown all the way from its equatorial wintering grounds in this impaled state.

The stork now sits alongside the 60,000 other specimens of water animals, mollusks, birds, and insects of the University of Rostock's Zoological Collection. **Universitätsplatz 2, Rostock. Get a bus or tram to Lange Straße and walk two blocks south.** Ⓝ 54.087436 Ⓔ 12.134371

ALSO IN NORTHWESTERN GERMANY

Wunderland Kalkar

North Rhine-Westphalia · An amusement park built on the grounds of an unused nuclear reactor.

The Wuppertal Suspension Railway

Wuppertal · The name of the world's oldest monorail system translates as "floating railway."

TEUFELSBERG SPY STATION

BERLIN

Atop a mountain in Grunewald forest, about six miles (9.7 km) west of central Berlin, are two sphere-topped cylindrical towers wrapped in shredded white canvas. During the Cold War, these buildings were part of Field Station Berlin, an NSA listening post where spies could tune in to Soviet radio frequencies.

The spy station was constructed on top of a Nazi military college complex built in 1937. Intended to be part of Hitler's World Capital Germania—a revitalized National Socialist version of Berlin—the college was abandoned at the start of World War II.

Postwar, the rubble of bombed-out Berlin was trucked to Grunewald and dumped on top of the college in a pile that topped 37 stories and became known as Teufelsberg: German for "Devil's Mountain." In 1963, the NSA station began operating in newly constructed buildings at the top of Teufelsberg, its satellite antennae positioned in prime hilltop spots concealed by the canvas-covered spheres.

The station became a key surveillance post for American and British intelligence officers studying the goings-on in East Germany. After the fall of the Berlin Wall, the station was abandoned. In 1996 the site was sold to property developers Hartmut Gruhl and Hanfried Schütte, who envisioned a bold transformation involving luxury apartments, a hotel, and a restaurant. Those plans, however, have not materialized.

The former NSA station is still at Teufelsberg, and has attracted artists looking to make their mark on its abandoned walls and, eventually, establish an official residency. **From Berlin, get a train to the Heerstrasse S-bahn stop and walk to Teufelsberg via the Teufelsseestrasse. You may encounter tour guides at the gate asking you for a fee to visit the site.** Ⓝ 52.497992 Ⓔ 13.241283

The tattered mountaintop remains of an NSA listening post, built atop a Nazi military college.

CITY GUIDE: More to Explore in Berlin

Subterranean Berlin

Brunnenstraße • A tour of the subterranean city meanders through abandoned tunnels, old hospitals, secret bunkers, World War II munitions storage, and Cold War–era passages used by dissenters to escape from East Germany.

Spandau Citadel

Spandau • Since the 12th century, a strategic island at the convergence of the Havel and Spree Rivers has been the site of a protective citadel, including the 13th-century Julius Tower (Berlin's oldest building) and 16th-century fortifications. Today it is the site of tours, concerts, and festivals.

Gardens of the World

Marzahn-Hellersdorf • Once an austere East Berlin park, it was transformed in 1987 into Gardens of the World, 50 acres of lush gardens: Chinese, Japanese, Italian, some even biblical and fairy-tale themed.

Tieranatomisches Theater

Mitte • Within this elegant anatomical theater built in 1789, with its airy dome and pastoral murals, live the ghosts of thousands of animals dissected under the orders of King Frederick William II, who thought the four-legged citizens of Berlin needed a dedicated veterinary school.

Designpanoptikum

Mitte • A shrine to the art of repurposing, recycling, and reengineering, the Surrealist Museum of Industrial Objects is a disorienting trip through an inspired world of retro machinery, strange medical devices, and a few interesting things stolen from the salvage yard.

Tajikistan Tearoom

Mitte • A little taste of Tajikistan dropped into a central Berlin courtyard, this classic Central Asian–style tearoom is plush with

These murals embody Berlin's hopes for a brighter future.

Persian carpets, pillows, and tapestries, and beckons you to lounge on the floor to enjoy a traditional tea service.

Hall of Mirrors, Clarchens Ballhaus

Mitte • Off to the side of Clarchens Ballhaus, an ornate dance hall that predates World War I, there is a mirrored ballroom that still carries the spirit of Wilhelmine Germany, moody and evocative, and mostly undiscovered, even by locals.

Monsterkabinett

Mitte • A design and robotics studio is the creation of the curiously named Dead Pigeon Collective, where unnerving human-androids turn dreams into nightmares and nightmares into eerie performance art.

Hohenzollern Crypt

Mitte • Beneath the Baroque cathedral in the center of the city is the world's largest collection of dead Prussian royals, sent into the afterlife in gorgeous gilded style.

DDR Museum

Mitte • An interactive museum of life in Deutsche Demokratische Republik (East Germany), including a cafeteria that serves up Soviet bloc cuisine, televisions that play crusty old state-run programming, and telephones that are very likely recording your conversations.

Hatch Sticker Museum

Friedrichshain • Opened in 2008 as a side venture for Oliver Baudach and his skate-cult sticker company, this small museum pulls mostly from Baudach's own bottomless pile of vintage street slicks.

Hansa Studios

Mitte • A magnificent recording studio, with glowing chandeliers, gleaming parquet floors, and original 1913 architectural detail, where some of the all-time greats have laid down tracks—from Iggy Pop to David Bowie to R.E.M.

Museum of Things

Friedrichshain • Brimming with more than 35,000 vintage and unique pieces, this collection, including kitchenware, advertisements, packaging, and children's toys, honors the beauty and simplicity found in 20th-century design.

East Side Gallery

Friedrichshain • An open-air art gallery of more than a hundred murals, these reclaimed vestiges of the Berlin Wall have been transformed by a cadre of international artists from the once-impenetrable symbol of suppression into a stark reminder of the fragility of freedom.

Ramones Museum

Friedrichshain • Blitzkrieg bop your way through a collection of more than 500 pieces of memorabilia, including posters, signed photos, ticket stubs, and pants worn by actual Ramones.

Schwerbelastungskörper

Tempelhof • Originally built in the early 1940s to test some Nazi theories of construction, this enormous concrete cylinder—now sunk into Berlin's cushy soil—is too massive to demolish. Visitors can tour its interior rooms.

Tempelhof Field

Tempelhof • The city's oldest airfield hasn't seen a plane come or go for nearly a decade, but its new life as a public park raises hopes of preserving the airport's old Art Deco–style buildings, a throwback to a time when air travel was still in its glamorous youth.

Peacock Island

Berlin-Wannsee • Sitting within the rush of the River Havel, this quiet oasis is scattered with abandoned buildings, flocks of wild peacocks, and the facade of a fairy-tale castle built by a Prussian king.

GREECE
MARKOPOULO SNAKE FESTIVAL

CEPHALONIA, MARKOPOULO

For Orthodox Christians, August 15 commemorates the Assumption of the Virgin Mary into Heaven. At the small hamlet of Markopoulo, on the island of Cephalonia, villagers celebrate by collecting snakes in bags and bringing them to the church, where they slither over feet, flick their tongues at a portrait of Mary and Jesus, and are placed on children's heads for good luck.

The combination of Jesus's mother and snakes—a Biblical symbol for evil and corruption—may seem incongruous, but the basis for the tradition is a miracle said to have taken place on the island in 1705. That year, the story goes, nuns in the village convent escaped a gang of attacking pirates when the Virgin answered their prayers to be transformed into snakes.

The serpents—a small, non-threatening species known as the European Cat Snake—now make an annual appearance at the Church of Virgin Mary, where the faithful and the curious gather to handle them. According to locals, the snakes only emerge in the days leading up to the festival, and cannot be found on the island during the rest of the year. **Markopoulo is a one-hour flight west of Athens. Ⓝ 38.080451 Ⓔ 20.732007**

GREECE AND CYPRUS

MKD

GREECE

● Mount Athos

AEGEAN SEA

Easter Rocket War ●

ATHENS ★

Antikythera Mechanism

● Snake Festival

IONIAN SEA

TUR

TUR

Miles
0   50   100
0   50   100
Kilometers

N

CYPRUS

NICOSIA ★   Varosha Beach Resort ●

SEA OF CRETE

MEDITERRANEAN SEA

Crete

Festival snakes are non-poisonous and defanged prior to church service.

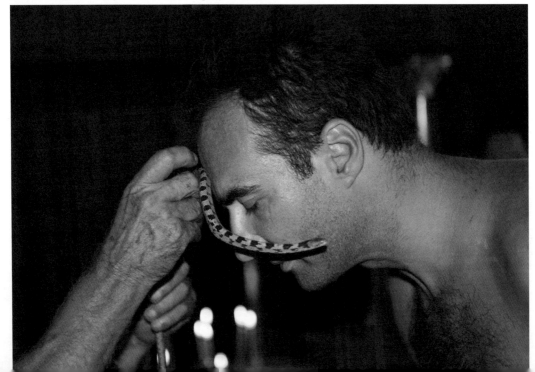

ANTIKYTHERA MECHANISM

ATHENS

An ancient geared computer that uses technology lost in antiquity.

This corroded lump of bronze with a dial on top doesn't look like much, but its discovery forced a complete reevaluation of ancient Greek engineering.

The Antikythera mechanism was part of a shipwreck that lay in the Mediterranean for over 2,000 years. In 1900, sponge divers happened upon the fragmented vessel and hauled the mechanism from the depths. It sat in a museum for 50 years before historians took a serious look at it. They discovered a device of unprecedented complexity.

The machine was built between 150 and 100 BCE, and with over 30 gears hidden behind its dials, it is easily the most advanced technological artifact of the pre–Common Era. Regarded as the first known analog computer, the mechanism can make precise calculations based on astronomical and mathematical principles developed by the ancient Greeks.

Although its builder's identity and its purpose on the ship remain unknown, after a century, scientists are beginning to understand how the device worked. To use the instrument, you would simply enter a date using a crank, and, when the gears stopped spinning, a wealth of information would appear at your fingertips: the positions of the sun, moon, planets, and stars, the lunar phase, the dates of upcoming solar eclipses, the speed of the moon through the sky, and even the dates of the ancient Olympic games. The mechanism's calendar dial could compensate for the extra quarter day in the astronomical year by turning the scale back one day every four years—impressive, given that the Julian calendar, which was the first in the region to include leap years, was not introduced until decades after the instrument was built.

Today, the Antikythera mechanism is housed in the Bronze Collection of the National Archaeological Museum of Athens. The device continues to reveal its secrets to the researchers of the Antikythera Mechanism Research Project, an international effort supported by various universities and technology companies.

National Archaeological Museum, 44 Patission Street, Athens.
Ⓝ 37.989906 Ⓔ 23.731005

THE EASTER ROCKET WAR

VRONTADOS, CHIOS

Since the 19th century, a pair of rival parishes on the Greek island of Chios have celebrated Easter not with bunnies or eggs, but by launching thousands of flaming projectiles at each other's churches while congregants observe Mass inside. When the sun sets on the eve of Orthodox Easter Sunday, members of the Angios Marcos and Panaghia Ereithiani churches—wearing bandanas over their faces to filter out the sulfur-scented smoke—launch the cigar-size rockets from ramps. They blaze across the sky in quick succession, leaving trails of vapor and providing a cacophonous accompaniment to the solemn Easter services taking place within the churches. (Wire mesh protects the windows from damage.)

On the island of Chios, Easter is a time of rebirth, renewal, and shooting rockets at churches.

The origin of this Orthodox yet unorthodox tradition is uncertain, but likely began as an act of defiance against Ottoman occupiers during the 19th century. (There are two versions of the story: In the first, the islanders launched rockets after the Turks confiscated their cannons. In the second, locals fired rockets at each other's churches to keep the Turks away during Easter services.)

The aim of the proceedings is to hit the opposing church's bell tower, but this goal is largely irrelevant given the general chaos of the evening—neither side is declared the victor of the "war," and an annual rematch is assured.

Orthodox Easter is in April or early May. From Athens, the island of Chios is a 45-minute flight or 7-hour ferry ride.
Ⓝ 38.370981 Ⓔ 26.136346

MOUNT ATHOS MONASTERY

MOUNT ATHOS

On a mist-shrouded peninsula east of Thessaloniki is a place where time has stalled and the rules of the modern world do not apply. Mount Athos, known to Greeks as the "holy mountain," is the home of Eastern Orthodox monasticism. Self-governed, and running on Byzantine time—in which the day begins at sunset—Mount Athos accommodates 1,500 monks within its monasteries, most of which were built during the 10th century. The monks' sole purpose in life is to become closer to God.

The monks believe that achieving complete oneness with Jesus Christ is only possible after death, but preparations are made throughout life. Every waking hour is spent praying or reflecting in silence. Monks, who wear long black robes to signify their death from the surrounding world, live in one of 20 communes, or, for those who prefer greater solitude, in cloisters or cells. There are eight hours of church services every day, beginning at 3 a.m. When not at church, monks pray individually, their lips moving silently under their long beards.

Women are forbidden from visiting or living on Mount Athos in accordance with the belief that a female presence would alter the social dynamics and impede the monks' journey toward spiritual enlightenment. The absence of women, according to the monks, also makes it easier to live a life of celibacy. Finally, there is the consideration for the Virgin Mary. According to Athonite tradition, Mary was blown off course during her journey to Cyprus and landed on Mount Athos, where she converted its pagan tribes to Christianity. Banning women from the peninsula allows the Virgin to be revered as the only female influence.

Male visitors to Mount Athos are permitted to attend church services, dine with the monks, and stay overnight in one of the monasteries. A calm, pious demeanor is expected, as most travelers are Orthodox pilgrims seeking spiritual refuge and community. **To visit Mount Athos, you'll need to obtain written permission from the Holy Executive Bureau in Thessaloniki. The office issues about 10 permits per day to non-Orthodox travelers, and 100 to Greek Orthodox travelers—contact them six months in advance to avoid disappointment. From Thessaloniki, get a bus to the small village of Ouranoupolis, where a ferry will transport you to Mount Athos. Female travelers may view the verdant hills and ancient monasteries from a distance on a boat tour. Ⓝ 40.157222 Ⓔ 24.326389**

Built on the side of a cliff, this isolated sanctuary is home to 1,500 monks.

CYPRUS

VAROSHA BEACH RESORT

FAMAGUSTA

Turquoise water, golden beaches, and signs illustrated with a gun-toting soldier that read "Forbidden Zone"—this is the resort town of Varosha.

Since 1974, the northern and southern parts of Cyprus have been divided by the "Green Line," a UN buffer zone that splits the country into the Greek-controlled south and the Turkish-controlled north. The division happened amid much violence: After the Greek military junta backed a coup against the Cypriot government, Turkey invaded Cyprus from the north, forcibly expelling hundreds of thousands of Greek Cypriots and driving them south. Turkish Cypriots in the south abandoned their homes and headed north.

In the early '70s, Famagusta, a town 2 miles north of the Green Line, was the top tourist destination in Cyprus. Its beachside

Varosha quarter, dotted with high-rise hotels, played host to moneyed movie stars like Elizabeth Taylor and Brigitte Bardot. In the wake of the Turkish invasion, its 39,000 residents fled, and Varosha became a ghost town. It has remained enclosed in barbed wire, uninhabited, and under the control of the Turkish military ever since. Left unmaintained for decades, buildings are slowly collapsing.

Just a few feet north of the fenced-off zone is the Arkin Palm Beach Hotel, a newly renovated resort where visitors can sip Caribbean-inspired cocktails beside the lagoon-shaped pool while gazing at the crumbling balconies of the decayed resort next door.

Varosha is closed to the public but visible through barbed-wire fences from the Arkin Palm Beach Hotel area. Photographing the town is forbidden, and soldiers will stop you if they suspect you are carrying a camera. ① 35.116534 ② 33.958992

ITALY

VILLA DE VECCHI

CORTENOVA

Just east of Lake Como, at the foot of the forested mountains of Cortenova, sits a house that's said to be haunted. Villa de Vecchi, also called the Red House, Ghost Mansion, and Casa delle Streghe (House of the Witches), was built between 1854 and 1857 as a summer residence for Count Felix de Vecchi. Within a few short years of its completion, the house witnessed an inexplicable string of tragedies that would forever cement its gothic legacy.

De Vecchi, head of the Italian National Guard and a decorated hero, set out to build a dream retreat for his family with the help of architect Alessandro Sidoli. A year before the villa was complete, Sidoli died. Many would later view this as the first ill omen. Nevertheless, the count and his family made Villa de Vecchi their home during the spring and summer months, and by most accounts lead an idyllic—if brief—existence.

The great mansion boasted a blend of Baroque and classical Eastern styles and was outfitted with all the modern conveniences of the time, including indoor heating pipes and painstakingly detailed frescoes and friezes. A larger-than-life fireplace presided over the main parlor, where a grand piano stood at the ready. Extensive gardens, promenades, and an equally impressive staff house rounded out the already picturesque surroundings.

Legend has it that in 1862 the count returned home to find his wife murdered and daughter missing. The count commandeered a lengthy, unsuccessful search for his daughter before dying by suicide that same year. The house made the rounds of owners and prospective buyers, but by the 1960s was left permanently uninhabited.

While the natural elements began their assault early on, the majority of the abandoned house's irreversible damage has been done by humans. Graffiti covers the walls, and anything capable of

This decaying mansion may be Italy's most haunted house.

being vandalized has been given its due makeover. The grand piano, once said to be played at night by a ghostly entity, has since been smashed to pieces, though some locals claim that music can still be heard coming from the house.

Note that if you enter the house, you are trespassing. An upper floor has collapsed, the stairs are rapidly deteriorating, and bits of ceiling regularly rain down. For safety's sake—not to mention law-abidance—it's best to admire from afar. ① 46.003464 ② 9.387661

UNDERGROUND TEMPLES OF DAMANHUR

BALDISSERO CANAVESE, PIEDMONT

From 1978 to 1992, members of the Damanhur commune dug into the mountain where they lived, tapping into what they believed were energy lines connecting the Earth to the cosmos. Their excavations were done in secret: Having neglected to secure planning approval, they had to conceal their work from authorities. But the world would eventually find out.

Led by philosopher, writer, and painter Oberto Airaudi, the "eco-society" of Damanhur began in 1975 with about 24 members. Billing itself as a "laboratory for the future of humanity," Damanhur is based on neo-pagan and New Age beliefs with emphasis on creative expression, meditation, and spiritual healing. Residents adopt animal and plant names (such as "Sparrow Pinecone") and live in "nucleo-communities" of 20 people in the foothills of the Alps, 30 miles (50 km) north of Turin.

Some former members have railed against Damanhur's sunny-spirited collective, describing it as a cult. It was an ex-Damanhurian who tipped off police about the unauthorized underground construction. When three officers and a public prosecutor arrived to conduct an early-morning raid, they were astonished. Beneath a humble farmhouse, behind a secret door, was a collection of temples spanning five levels.

Damanhur citizens had spent a decade and a half working around the clock in shifts to excavate 8,500 cubic meters of earth and rock. They decorated each hall and hallway in a different theme, with murals, stained-glass windows, mirrors, and mosaics. The New Age, 1970s-style artwork depicts everything from the history of the universe to a forest of endangered animals to the International Space

Minimalism is frowned upon among the interior decorators of Damanhur. Above, the Hall of Earth; below, a section map of the underground temple.

Station. The perimeter of one of the circular rooms is cluttered with sculptures, due to the directive that each member of the community must carve a statue in their own likeness.

Boggled by the unexpected beauty of the subterranean halls, Italian police granted a retroactive construction permit. The eco-society, which currently numbers around 1,000 members, now welcomes visitors to its temples.
Via Pramarzo, 3 Baldissero Canavese.
Ⓝ 45.417763 Ⓔ 7.748451

1. Hall of Mirrors
2. Hall of Spheres
3. Hall of Metals
4. Earth Hall
5. Water Hall
6. Blue Temple
7. Labyrinth

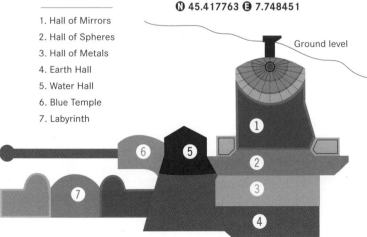

POVEGLIA ISLAND

VENICE, VENETO

The first challenge to visiting Poveglia is finding someone to take you there. It won't be easy. Poveglia, an island just south of Venice, is strictly off-limits for both locals and tourists. Given the island's history, you'll understand why.

For much of its history, Poveglia was a dumping ground for the diseased, the dying, and the mentally ill. In the early 15th century, it functioned as a quarantine island. Those afflicted by one of the many Black Death plagues over the years were taken to the island, along with disease-ridden corpses. The living shivered and vomited blood while the hundreds of dead were thrown into plague pits and burned. The remains of an estimated 160,000 people are mixed into the island's soil.

In 1922, a psychiatric hospital opened on the island. Legend holds that one of the doctors, a sadistic man fond of experimenting on his patients, threw himself off the bell tower after being haunted by the spirits of those who had died on the island. (In some versions of the story, he is thrown off the tower, presumably by a vengeful patient.)

The hospital building, which closed in 1968, is still on Poveglia, covered in scaffolding and colonized by trees. Rusting bed frames, rotting wood beams, and pieces of the ceiling litter the floors. In the bushes surrounding the hospital are the rectangular metal grates that were once fastened to every window to keep patients trapped in their rooms.

Officially, Poveglia is off-limits to visitors. Unofficially, you might find a Venetian boat operator to take you—especially if you're willing to offer a heap of euros.
Ⓝ 45.381879 Ⓔ 12.331196

Poveglia, also known as Plague Island, is guarded by an octagonal fort.

WOODEN BOOKS OF PADUA UNIVERSITY

SAN VITO DI CADORE, VENETO

Each book in this 56-volume collection tells the story of a particular tree—not in words or illustrations, but with parts of the tree itself.

The wooden books of Padua University date from the late 1700s and early 1800s. While most books are made from wood—pulped into paper—these are different: The back and front covers are made from the tree's wood, its spine made of the tree's bark. Inside are samples of the tree's leaves, twigs, flowers, seeds, and roots. Each book is accompanied by a handwritten piece of parchment with a key explaining the contents.

41 Via Ferdinando Ossi, San Vito Di Cadore. Ⓝ 46.453240 Ⓔ 12.213190

LA SPECOLA

FLORENCE, TUSCANY

In 18th-century Florence, artists created wax anatomical models to show medical students what lay beneath the skin of the human body. The model-making process was labor-intensive and began with an artist pressing plaster against the individual organs of a recently dissected cadaver to create a cast. Wax was poured into the molds and each organ painted and varnished. All the body parts were then assembled into a wax torso and overlaid with muscles and membranes, which were either simulated with thread or painted on.

The works were so uncannily realistic—red, glistening muscles lying taut against knobby bones, encased in an intricate web of veins—that it was felt the artistry deserved a wider audience. In 1775, the figures were put on display at La Specola, a natural history and zoology museum established by the Medici family. Over several

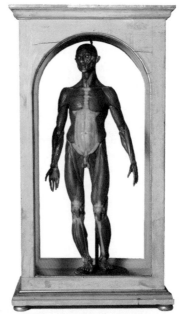

The exhibits at La Specola show what's under the skin.

generations, the Medicis amassed a vast quantity of fossils, minerals, animals, and plants. When

La Specola opened, it became the first publicly accessible science museum in Europe. It featured consistent hours of operation, tour guides, and guards.

Today, La Specola contains 34 rooms filled with human and animal wax models, zoological specimen taxidermy, and medical instruments. Particularly compelling are the wax anatomical Venuses—naked women posed in demure but erotic poses, with their abdominal skin removed and rib cages pulled open to expose the organs underneath. The Marquis de Sade, who harbored a taste for sexual violence, had a particular fondness for these sensuous, gutted female forms.

Via Romana, 17, Florence. Get a bus to San Felice. For a picturesque chaser, visit the Pitti Palace and the Boboli Gardens afterward—they're right next door. ⓝ 43.764487 ⓔ 11.246972 ➡

GALILEO'S MIDDLE FINGER

FLORENCE, TUSCANY

It's hard to think of a more fitting tribute to the ever-defiant Galileo than displaying his middle finger in a goblet accented with gold.

Ninety-five years after Galileo's death in 1642, Anton Francesco Gori, a Florentine priest and scholar, pocketed the astronomer's finger while transporting his remains from their humble original grave to a monumental tomb. The relic was exhibited at Florence's Laurentian Library until 1841, when the town's Natural History Museum—also home to the anatomical and zoological museum La Specola—snatched it up for display.

In 1927, the finger landed at its current resting place—a museum devoted to scientific instruments that was renamed the Galileo Museum in 2010. The middle digit is the

only human fragment among the institution's telescopes, meteorological instruments, and mathematical models. It is mounted vertically in a goblet on a column with a commemorative inscription:

This is the finger, belonging to the illustrious hand that ran through the skies, pointing at the immense spaces, and singling out new stars.

Whether the middle finger points upward to the sky, where Galileo glimpsed the glory of the universe and saw God in mathematics, or if it sits eternally defiant to the church that condemned him is for the viewer to decide.

Galileo Museum, Piazza dei Giudici 1, Florence. ⓝ 43.767734 ⓔ 11.255903

➺ Other Medical Museums of Europe

JOSEPHINUM
VIENNA
Established in 1785, the Josephinum contains over 1,000 wax models, including anatomical Venuses and a heart seemingly floating under a glass dome.

THE NARRENTURM
VIENNA
The Narrenturm, or Fool's Tower, was built in 1784 to house psychiatric patients suffering from such maladies as ecstasy, melancholy, and delirium tremens. Now the circular building, nicknamed the "pound cake" by locals, is an anatomy and pathology museum.

MUSEUM BOERHAAVE
LEIDEN, NETHERLANDS
In one jar, a child's arm protrudes from a lacy sleeve, its fingers suspending the vascular tissue of an eye as though it were a yo-yo. In another jar nearby, a lily-white pig with a deformed head floats. Walking through this museum's exhibit halls filled with artifacts from the anatomical, medical, and scientific history of the Netherlands, visitors are pointedly reminded of their mortality.

To hammer the point home, articulated skeletons even carry flags inscribed with Latin phrases: *pulvis et umbra sumus* ("we are but dust and shadow"), *vita brevis* ("life is short"), and *homo bulla* ("man is a soap bubble"). An old operating theater, antique scientific instruments, and anatomical models of animals complete the experience.

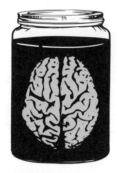

There are plenty of jarred human specimens at Museum Vrolik.

MUSEUM VROLIK
AMSTERDAM
During their many years as anatomy professors in the 1800s, father-and-son team Gerardus and Willem Vrolik amassed a formidable assortment of human abnormalities. Their specimens form the core collection of this museum. Willem focused largely on congenital anomalies such as conjoined twins and cycloptic fetuses. The infant specimens float, gently and ghostlike, in glass jars.

MUSEUM OF MEDICINE
BRUSSELS
Located beside the Museum of Cocoa and Chocolate, the Museum of Medicine features an entire wall of wax reproductive organs ravaged by sexually transmitted diseases.

MUSÉE DES MOULAGES
PARIS
Dedicated to "moulages"—wax models of body parts afflicted with disease—this warehouse of a museum has two spectacular floors of pus-filled, boil-covered, rash-afflicted skin.

MUSÉE DUPUYTREN
PARIS
After running out of money and being forced to close, this collection of thousands of anatomical wax models, pathological models, and abnormal physiological specimens sat neglected for 30 years before reopening in 1967.

HUNTERIAN MUSEUM
LONDON
The Hunterian Museum's collection includes half the brain of mathematician Charles Babbage, Winston Churchill's dentures, and the skeleton of a famed Irish giant.

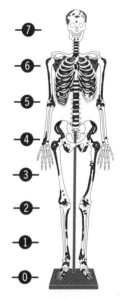

The 7'7" skeleton of Charles Byrne is on view at the Hunterian Museum.

POPE LEO'S BATHROOM

HOLY SEE, ROME

In 1516, Cardinal Bibbiena, a longtime friend and confidant to Pope Leo X, decided to redecorate the bathroom within the Vatican's Papal Apartments. Bibbiena's predilection for the ribald and the risqué inspired him to commission a series of erotic frescoes by another close friend, the artist Raphael. The panels depict Venus, Cupid, nymphs, and satyrs, all cavorting naked in the wild.

The ensuing centuries have brought censorship to the Stufetta del Cardinal Bibbiena (translated as "small heated room of Cardinal Bibbiena"). Scandalized residents of the Papal Apartments painted over sections of the artwork. A few of the panels remaining depict the naked Venus swimming, looking at herself in a mirror, and reclining between the legs of Adonis.

Though it wouldn't be sanctioned by today's Papal Apartment decorators, Raphael's erotic artwork was tame compared to the famed licentiousness of the Renaissance popes. Pope Alexander VI's Banquet of Chestnuts, which took place in the papal palace in 1501, is an example of the behavior that occurred within the Vatican walls. During the event, the pope brought in 50 women, auctioned off their clothing, and made them crawl naked on the floor to pick up chestnuts he and his guests had thrown. Members of the clergy and party guests were then encouraged to have sex with the women. The man who carried out the most "conquests" received a prize of clothing and jewels.

A bathroom in the Vatican's Papal Apartments was customized for 16th-century Cardinal Bibbiena, who had a penchant for the erotic arts.

Viale Vaticano, Rome. Get the Rome metro to Ottaviano–San Pietro–Musei Vaticani. Tours of the Stufetta del Bibbiena are rarely granted—now is the time to exploit any Vatican connections. As an alternative, visit the Borgia Apartments, the scene of Alexander VI's aforementioned banquet. Ⓝ 41.903531 Ⓔ 12.456170

The pope's secret escape route runs along a stone wall in Rome.

PARK OF THE MONSTERS

BOMARZO, LAZIO

The stone sculptures in the Parco dei Mostri emerged from the tormented mind of 16th-century Italian prince Pier Francesco Orsini. Pier endured a brutal war, saw his friend killed, was held for ransom for years, and returned home only to have his beloved wife die. Seeking a way to express his grief, Orsini hired architect Pirro Ligorio to create a park that would shock and frighten its visitors.

The park exhibits the 16th-century Mannerist style—an artistic approach that rejected the Renaissance's elegance and harmony in favor of exaggerated, often tortured expressions and a mishmash of mythological, classical, and religious influences. Its wretched sculptures—including a war elephant attacking a Roman soldier, a monstrous fish head, a giant tearing another giant in half, and a house built on a tilt to disorient the viewer—caught the attention of Salvador Dalí, who visited in 1948 and found much to inspire his surrealist artwork.

The Parco dei Mostri is the monster-filled garden of a grief-stricken prince.

A trip to the park is not complete without a walk up the stone stairs leading into the "Mouth of Hell"—the face of an ogre captured midscream. Walk into its gaping maw, inscribed with "all reason departs," and you'll find a picnic table with benches. **Localita Giardino, Bomarzo. From Rome take a train to Orte Scalo, where you can switch to a bus to the gardens.** Ⓝ 42.491633 Ⓔ 12.247575

PASSETTO DI BORGO

ROME

To the casual eye, the Passetto di Borgo looks like a plain old fortification, but its stone walls hide a passageway that several popes have used as an emergency escape route. Construction of the wall dates back to 850, with Pope Nicholas III overseeing the creation of its current form in 1277. Pope Alexander VI finished the wall in 1492—and just in the nick of time. He used it to flee the invading French only two years later.

The most recent papal escape was in 1527, when Clement VII evaded the 20,000 mutinous troops of Charles V, who murdered most of the Swiss Guard on the steps of St. Peter's Basilica. Since then, the Passetto had languished in declining condition, closed to visitors but available to the reigning pope in case of a crisis. But in 2000, in honor of the pope's Jubilee year, the Passetto was renovated. It now opens to visitors for a limited time each summer.

Borgo Pio, 62, Rome. Take a tram to Risorgimento/ San Pietro. Ⓝ 41.903817 Ⓔ 12.460230

ALSO IN ROME

The Criminology Museum

First assembled in 1837, this collection of prison paraphernalia, torture devices, and items showing the history of criminal anthropology only opened to the public in 1994.

Torre Argentina Cat Sanctuary

Hundreds of stray cats haunt the ruins of the famous Theater of Pompey, where the Roman emperor Julius Caesar was assassinated.

Vigna Randanini

This Jewish catacomb, used in the 3rd and 4th century CE, is one of only two open to the public.

THE MUSEUM OF HOLY SOULS IN PURGATORY

ROME

This small collection of hand-shaped burns imprinted onto prayer books, bed-sheets, and clothing offers purported proof of communication between the dead and the living.

According to Catholic doctrine, the souls of the dead are stranded in purgatory until they atone for their sins. Their ascent to heaven can be hastened, however, through the prayers of the friends and family they've left behind.

Victor Jouet, founder of Rome's Church of the Sacred Heart, was supposedly inspired to build this purgatorial museum after a fire destroyed a portion of the church in 1898, leaving behind the scorched image of a face that he believed to be a trapped soul.

The collection of hand marks, which mostly date from the 18th and 19th centuries, are presented as the earthly manifestations of trapped souls reaching out from purgatory, pleading that their loved ones pray harder.

Lungotevere Prati 12, Rome. The museum is a 15-minute walk from the Lepanto metro stop. Ⓝ 41.903663 Ⓔ 12.472009

ALSO IN SOUTHERN ITALY

Manna of St. Nicholas	**Blue Grotto**	**The Anatomical Machines of Cappella Sansevero**	**Catacombs of San Gennaro**	**Il Castello Incantato**
Bari · The remains of St. Nicholas are said to excrete a sweet-smelling liquid known as manna. Every year on May 9, manna is collected in vials and sold to the public.	*Capri* · Once the personal swimming hole of Roman emperor Tiberius, this sea cave has an unearthly blue glow.	*Naples* · Anatomical models built on top of real human skeletons are just a part of the strange collection of mysterious 18th-century prince Raimondo di Sangro.	*Naples* · An underground proto-Christian burial site comprised of three adjacent cemeteries dating back to the third century CE.	*Sciacca* · Containing over 1,000 carved heads, the life's work of "village madman" Filippo Bentivegna can be found in this small garden.

THE SECRET CABINET OF EROTICA

NAPLES, CAMPANIA

Citizens of Pompeii and Herculaneum believed phalluses provided protection, prosperity, and good luck, and incorporated them into everything from furniture to oil lamps. Frescoes on the walls of homes depicted erotic encounters between wood nymphs and satyrs. Erotica was everywhere.

After the excavation of Pompeii and Herculaneum in the 19th century, the sexy *objets* were put on display in the National Archaeological Museum of Naples. But when the future king of the two Sicilies, Francis I, visited with his wife and young daughter in 1819, he was shocked by all the erotica. He ordered all the explicit items removed from view and locked in a secret cabinet, where access could be restricted to mature gentlemen of high moral standing.

All of this fuss only served to make the collection more famous. The whispered-about secret collection became a must-see for gentlemen during their grand tours of Europe. It remained off-limits to women, children, and the general public.

For a century and a half, the Gabinetto Segreto stayed out of sight, on view only during brief liberal periods under radical 19th-century general Giuseppe Garibaldi and again in the 1960s. The Gabinetto Segreto was finally opened to the public in 2000 and moved into a separate gallery in 2005.

Among dozens of stone penises, phallic wind chimes, and naughty mosaics, one item became the most notorious: *The Satyr and the Goat*. It is a detailed carving of a satyr in flagrante delicto with a female goat, her cloven feet pressed up against his chest as she gazes at him demurely.

19 Piazza Museo, Naples. Take the train to Museo. Ⓝ 40.852828 Ⓔ 14.249750

Sculptures of a more carnal nature are kept in a secret room at the National Archaeological Museum of Naples.

CIVITA DI BAGNOREGIO

CIVITA

The small town of Civita di Bagnoregio has survived for centuries clinging to its high perch, but as the soft clay on the edges of town erodes, its architecture is being lost.

Etruscans first built the tiny town on a tall column of volcanic rock over 2,500 years ago. Civita was accessible via a slim donkey path that led to the arch marking its only entrance. Over the centuries, the borders of the circular town became flush with the edges of the plateau as the tightly packed architecture filled the limited space atop the column. All the while, natural disasters weakened the clay foundations, which were already prone to erosion.

In the 20th century, many of Civita's thousands of residents began to move to more stable areas. Today, the donkey path has finally eroded away, and the only way to get to the village is via a steep footbridge. Supplies only make it up there via moped or three-wheeled *apès*, or "bees," tiny motorized pickup trucks. The population reaches about 100 during the summer months and drops into the single digits during winter. In 2013, the town began charging visitors an entry fee. Tourism has been profitable for the towns-people, but regular landslides continue to reduce the town's borders.

Buses runs from Orvieto, taking about an hour to reach Civita. Come in June or September to catch the wild donkey races. ⓝ 42.627815 ⓔ 12.114002

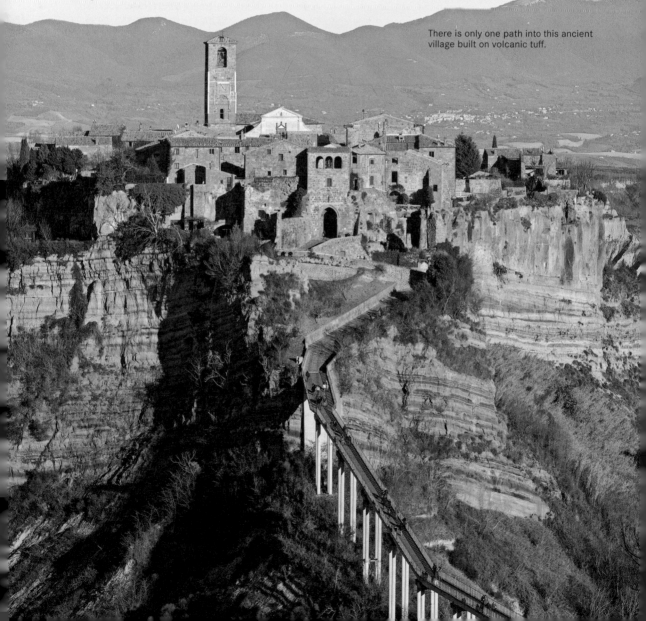

There is only one path into this ancient village built on volcanic tuff.

CAPUCHIN CATACOMBS

PALERMO, SICILY

Eight thousand corpses in various states of decay inhabit the musty, ill-lit Capuchin catacombs of Palermo. Originally intended exclusively for monks, the passageways were expanded over time to make room for prominent locals who paid to be buried in the holy vaults. Separated according to age, sex, occupation, and social status, the mummified bodies are arranged in open coffins, hung from the walls in narrow corridors, and piled on shelves.

In the "Chapel of the Virgins," girls whose families declared them virgins are displayed in faded and tattered white dresses under the inscription: "We follow the lamb wherever he goes; we are virgins."

They wear their best clothes, but their appearance is marred by caved-in noses, empty eye sockets, and sunken cheeks. Many have wide-open mouths—due to a combination of decomposing facial ligaments and gravity—making them look as though they are silently screaming.

The particularly dry atmosphere of the catacombs facilitated the natural mummification of the bodies. Priests would lay the dead on shelves and allow them to drip until they were completely depleted of bodily fluids. When a year had passed, they would rinse the dried-out corpses with vinegar before re-dressing them in their best attire and sending them to their designated eternal room.

The oldest corpse in the collection is that of Silvestro da Gubbio, a friar who passed in 1599. The most recent, Rosalia Lombardo,

was only two years old when she was embalmed in 1920 after dying of pneumonia. The embalming procedure has kept Rosalia looking so well preserved that she has been dubbed "Sleeping Beauty."

The catacombs also serve as a macabre history-of-fashion museum, charting the rise and fall of Palermo high style from the 1600s to the 1920s. Though the mummies once sported glass eyes, they disappeared during World War II when American GIs came through town and plucked them out as souvenirs.

1 Piazza Cappuccini, Palermo. The monastery is a 25-minute walk from Palermo's central railway station.
ℕ 38.116191 Ⓔ 13.362122 ➡

You're always in the company of monks in the halls of the Capuchin catacombs.

➺ Other European Ossuaries

**CHURCH OF
ST. URSULA
COLOGNE**
The Golden Chamber of
this church is filled with
the bones of hundreds of
virgin martyrs—or so the
story goes.

**SANTA MARIA
DELLA CONCEZIONE
DEI CAPPUCCINI
ROME**
A stunning memento mori,
this 6-room crypt is full
of intricate wall frescoes,
arches, and ceiling
decorations made entirely
from human bones—the
remains of some 4,000
Capuchin friars who died
between 1528 and 1870.

**CHURCH OF
ST. PETER AND
PAUL MELNÍK,
CZECH REPUBLIC**
When a plague epidemic
swept through Melník in
the 1520s, creating a huge
demand for additional
burial ground, the remains
of 15,000 people laid to
rest in the surrounding
cemeteries were
disinterred, cleaned, and
dumped into this church
vault.
    In the 1780s, when
ossuaries were declared
a health risk, the vault
was bricked up and
forgotten about until
1913, when Czech
anthropologist Jindřich
Matiegka reopened the

entrance to the crypt
and began arranging the
bones into orderly piles
and decorative patterns.
Thousands of bones form
a large cross adorned
with a palm frond, while
skulls are arranged into
heart shapes. A long, deep
tunnel made mostly of leg
bones represents Christ's
resurrection.

**SEDLEC OSSUARY
KUTNÀ HORA,
CZECH REPUBLIC**
Sedlec Ossuary, also
known as the Bone
Church, has a stunning
centerpiece: a chandelier
made from every bone in
the body.

**SAN BERNARDINO
ALLE OSSA MILAN**
This ossuary was built
in 1210 after the local
graveyard became
overfilled with deceased
patients from the nearest
hospital.

**FONTANELLE
CEMETERY CAVES
NAPLES**
In the early 20th century,
a cult emerged around the
skulls at this crypt. Visitors
brought them flowers and
offerings, made wishes,
and asked for luck—the
most sought-after skulls
were those with a gift for
predicting the winning
lottery numbers.

Artwork, artifacts, and fossils are displayed in beautiful old glass cases and bell jars.

NETHERLANDS

TEYLERS MUSEUM

HAARLEM, NORTH HOLLAND

Lit only by sunlight since it opened in 1784, Teylers Museum is the first and oldest museum in the Netherlands. Its core collection of fossils, paintings, and scientific instruments was originally a "Cabinet of Curiosities" belonging to Pieter Teyler van der Hulst, a Haarlem banker and silk manufacturer. In his will, the Enlightenment-era thinker decreed that his money be used to establish a foundation for science and the arts. This museum is the glorious result.

The current collection includes 25 Michelangelo artworks, drawings by Rembrandt, fossils, beautifully illustrated 18th-century natural history books, coins from the 1600s, and the world's largest electrostatic generator. Its main building—an airy, oval-shaped room with lofty glass-vaulted ceilings—is as eye-catching as the curiosities within.

Spaarne 16, Haarlem, Noord Holland. Buses stop in front of the museum. Ⓝ 52.380256 Ⓔ 4.640391

EISINGA PLANETARIUM

FRANEKER, FRIESLAND

Dutch priest Eelco Alta induced mass panic in 1774 when he predicted that an upcoming alignment of the moon, Mercury, Venus, Mars, and Jupiter would send Earth hurtling into the sun. To calm the widespread fear and demonstrate the varying speeds of the solar system's orbits, amateur astronomer Eise Eisinga installed a planetarium in his living room ceiling. It has been operating ever since, making it the oldest functional planetarium in the world.

Construction took seven years. Eisinga carved the era's six known planets—Mercury, Venus, Earth, Mars, Jupiter, and Saturn—out of wood, painted them gold, and suspended them from the ceiling. A pendulum sends the planets traveling, in real time, in concentric orbits around a painted sun. The ceiling is painted cerulean blue to represent the sky, and shows zodiac constellations and the points at which each planet is farthest from the sun. Hidden in the roof space above the ceiling are 60 wheels and gears that keep the whole thing moving.

Just as Eisinga was putting the finishing touches on his planetarium in 1781, scientists made a discovery: Uranus. But the astronomer did not alter his creation, as adding the planet would have destroyed the planetarium's 1:1012 scale.

Eise Eisingastraat 3, 8801 KE Franeker. Get a bus to Theresia. Ⓝ 53.187335 Ⓔ 5.543735

The world's oldest functional planetarium packs our whole solar system into a cozy-looking Dutch house.

GIETHOORN

GIETHOORN, OVERIJSSEL

With its thatched cottages, narrow canals, and 180 wooden bridges, the village of Giethoorn (population 2,600) is a tiny, bucolic version of Venice.

The village got its canals during the 16th century, when the inhabitants began digging troughs to extract peat for fuel. The resulting four miles of waterways, along with the adjacent footpaths, constitute Giethoorn's transport network—the village has no roads, so all travel is via boat or bike or on foot. The preferred way to ride along the canals is by "whisper boats," whose motors are quiet enough to maintain the tranquil atmosphere.

Giethoorn is a 90-minute drive from Amsterdam. To sightsee around the village, join a boat tour or rent your own flat-bottomed vessel. Ⓝ 52.740178 Ⓔ 6.077331

Bask in the glow of the Summer of Love between Electric Ladyland's fluorescent walls.

ELECTRIC LADYLAND MUSEUM OF FLUORESCENT ART

AMSTERDAM

In a small, dark basement just a five-minute walk from the Anne Frank house is a museum as psychedelic as the Jimi Hendrix album of the same name. The Electric Ladyland Museum of Fluorescent Art begins with a walk through a neon-accented "participatory environment," where the walls glow when the lights go off. Then comes the cabinet of fluorescent minerals. These gray lumps of rock turn brilliant colors when viewed under an ultraviolet bulb.

Museum founder Nick Padalino will gladly talk you through the many kinds of fluorescence being demonstrated under the varying wavelengths of light. Most surprising is the display of common items, such as coconuts, seashells, Depression-era glass, and lentils, rendered in glowing fluorescent hues.

Tweede Leliedwarsstraat 5, Amsterdam. For maximum psychedelic effect, listen to Hendrix's "All Along the Watchtower" while exploring the curves and contours of the immersive environment. Ⓝ 52.375602 Ⓔ 4.882301

Micropia museum makes the invisible observable.

MICROPIA

AMSTERDAM

Micropia is a zoo with a small difference: The creatures it keeps are invisible to the naked eye. Established in 2014, Micropia sheds light on the molds, yeasts, bacteria, viruses, and other microorganisms that are ever-present but go largely unnoticed.

The "Meet Your Microbes" exhibit highlights a few of the 100 trillion microorganisms living in and around your body, while the kissing exhibit ratchets up the romance by illustrating the massive exchange of bacteria that occurs when two people make out. **Artisplein, Plantage Kerklaan 36–38, Amsterdam. Eat something before visiting the museum—the animal feces exhibit has a tendency to quell the appetite.** Ⓝ 52.367668 Ⓔ 4.912447

ALSO IN THE NETHERLANDS

Bijbels Museum

Amsterdam · A collection of biblical memorabilia that includes an exact copy of a Dead Sea scroll. If the Bibles bore you, you can also check out the best-preserved 17th-century kitchen in the Netherlands.

The Hash, Marihuana, Hemp Museum

Amsterdam · Learn about old tools and implements for turning hemp into rope, paper, and clothing, as well as a variety of ancient and not-so-ancient smoking devices.

The Torture Museum

Amsterdam · Inspect torture methods and devices from the past, including the rack, the skull cracker, and the heretic fork.

The Three-Country Labyrinth

Vaals · Seventeen thousand hornbeam shrubs constitute Europe's largest outdoor shrub maze, located where the Netherlands, Belgium, and Germany meet.

Cigar Band House

Volendam · Mosaics created from 11 million cigar bands cover the walls of this house.

ATLANTIC OCEAN

PORTUGAL

SPAIN

● Baby Jumping Festival

★ Don Justo's
Self-Built Cathedral
MADRID

● Boulders of Monsanto

● Mafra Palace Library
Quinta da Regaleira
★ **LISBON**
Preserved
Head of
Diogo Alves

Balearic
Islands

Miles
0   50   100

0   50   100
Kilometers

N

MEDITERRANEAN
SEA

● El Caminito del Rey
Ronda ●

ATLANTIC
OCEAN

CANARY ISLANDS

The Whistling Island

Miles
0   5

0   5
Kilometers

PORTUGAL AND SPAIN

PORTUGAL
THE BOULDERS OF MONSANTO

MONSANTO, IDANHA-A-NOVA

The hillside medieval village of Monsanto was built around a pile of massive granite boulders. The placement of the rocks determined the shapes of the winding streets and the architecture of the stone houses—instead of trying to move the boulders, the villagers used them as walls, floors, and even roofs. From a distance, some of the houses look like they've been crushed by giant falling rocks.

Other than the odd plastic chair and air-conditioning unit, Monsanto has retained its medieval appearance. It is now home to about 800 people. There are no cars—the preferred mode of transport through the narrow cobbled streets is donkey. **Trains run from Lisbon to Castelo Branco. From there, it's a short bus ride northeast to Monsanto.**
Ⓝ 40.031970 Ⓦ 7.0713570

Residents of Monsanto literally live under a rock.

Masonic initiations are rumored to have taken place in this 88-foot-deep well.

QUINTA DA REGALEIRA

SINTRA, GRANDE LISBOA

Eccentric millionaire António Augusto Carvalho Monteiro designed this palace in 1904 as a monument to his diverse interests and secret affiliations. The five-story hilltop mansion mixes Roman, Gothic, Renaissance, and Manueline styles. Its surrounding gardens are a fantasy land of grottoes, fountains, statues, ponds, underground tunnels, and a deep, moss-covered "Initiation Well," believed to be the former site of Masonic rituals. The architecture hides shapes and symbols relating to alchemy, Masonry, the Knights Templar, and the Rosicrucians. A Roman Catholic chapel in front of the palace depicts Catholic saints, but also pentagrams, which are often used in occult religions. **Avenida Barbosa du Bocage 5, Sintra. Make sure to bring a flashlight. Ⓝ 38.812878 Ⓦ 9.369541**

ALSO IN PORTUGAL

Carmo Convent Ruins	Bone Chapel	Drowned Village	Bussaco Palace Hotel
Lisbon · The legacy of a massive earthquake that nearly wiped Lisbon off the face of the earth in 1755.	*Faro* · A small chapel built out of human bones and decorated with a golden skeleton.	*Vilarinho da Furna* · A submerged village appears when the water levels drop at a nearby dam.	*Luso* · A majestic resting place for dreamers nestled in a fairy-tale forest.

MAFRA PALACE LIBRARY

MAFRA

The magnificent library within the 18th-century Palace of Mafra is a national architectural treasure, and it ranks among the finest libraries in Europe. It is also home to a colony of bats that patrol the stacks each night in search of book-eating pests.

The wooden shelves of the rococo-style library are lined with thousands of valuable old volumes. These books are fragile, however, and bookworms, moths, and other insects can wreak havoc on their delicate pages. Most libraries control such pests with more traditional techniques like fumigation or irradiation, but the Mafra Palace Library deploys its own very special force of winged protectors.

During the day, the bats sleep behind the bookcases or out in the palace garden. Then at night, after the library has closed, these tiny flying mammals swoop between the stacks, hunting down book-eating bugs.

This nocturnal feasting has been going on for centuries, perhaps as far back as the creation of the library itself. The bats, however, do come with one disadvantage: the copious covering of droppings they expend upon the floors, shelves, and furniture each and every night. To combat this, library workers cover the furniture before they leave and spend their mornings carefully cleaning the marble floors to erase all evidence of the previous night's excreta. **The Mafra Palace Library is open to researchers and scholars. An appointment is recommended. Because the bats only hunt at night, you're unlikely to see them during visiting hours. To catch a glimpse, stand just outside the library at night and wait for them to make their exit. It's also sometimes possible to hear the bats making sounds from their roosts inside the library on rainy, wet days. Ⓝ 38.936976 Ⓦ 9.325933**

A colony of tiny bats protects the 36,000 volumes of this library.

PRESERVED HEAD OF DIOGO ALVES

LISBON

The head of a 19th-century Portuguese serial killer is alarmingly well preserved in a jar at the University of Lisbon. Upon entering the anatomical theater at the Faculty of Medicine, the first thing you'll notice is the lone pickled head, up on a shelf next to a diaphonized hand. It's yellow, peaceful-looking, and somewhat akin to a potato. It's the head of Diogo Alves, whose claims to fame include being both Portugal's first serial killer and the last man to be hanged.

At least one half of each claim is true. Alves was a serial killer, indeed, but not the first. And he was not the last man to be executed—at least six more followed him to the gallows before Portugal ruled out capital punishment. So why, then, is Alves's head in a jar?

Timing, most likely. Alves was executed in 1841, as phrenology was just beginning to rear its ugly head in Portugal. Today, we recognize phrenology as a pseudoscience but at the time, people believed that personality traits—criminal propensity included—could be felt and measured right on the individual's skull. It's no surprise, then, that a notoriously wicked corpse would draw the attention of Portugal's budding band of phrenologists, who requested Alves's head be severed and preserved for posterity, so the source of his criminal urges could be studied in depth.

This part of the university is only open to students and is not typically accessible by the public.
Ⓝ 38.746963 Ⓦ 9.160439

SPAIN

DON JUSTO'S SELF-BUILT CATHEDRAL

MEJORADA DEL CAMPO, MADRID

Don Justo Gallego Martinez, a former monk with no experience in architecture, construction, or engineering, has been building this cathedral out of recycled and donated materials since 1961. There has never been a formal plan for the building—the design is influenced by St. Peter's Basilica but has changed over the years according to Don Justo's shifting inspirations.

The project began when Don Justo contracted tuberculosis and had to leave the monastic order. With his health in a perilous state, he prayed to the Virgin Mary and vowed to create a shrine in her honor should he survive. Though he never received an official construction permit, the recovered Don Justo devoted himself to building a church that now stands 13 stories tall. Oil drums, paint buckets, scrap metal, and bricks salvaged from a nearby brick factory are all pasted together with thick layers of concrete to form the walls and spires.

Don Justo receives occasional assistance from his nephews and volunteers, but the bulk of the work is done with his own hands. The cathedral is about 10 to 15 years away from completion—a problem, considering its chief builder is in his 90s. The fate of the building is up in the air. As an unapproved construction it could well be razed, eliminating the life's work of a most determined man.

Don Justo, a monk with no formal architectural training, inside his massive cathedral.

Calle del Arquitecto Gaudí, 1, Mejorada del Campo, Madrid. Take a bus from Conde de Casal to Calle de Arquitecto Antoni Gaudí. Ⓝ 40.394561 Ⓦ 3.488481

CLIFF-TOP CITY OF RONDA

RONDA

The city of Ronda is perched high atop the two cliffs of El Tajo Canyon as though a fissure opened and swallowed its center.

Romans established a settlement at Ronda nearly two centuries before the reign of Julius Caesar, and it has since survived through several invading forces. The walls of the canyon are sheer drops to the Guadalevín River over 330 feet (100.6 m) below—that's more than the height of the Statue of Liberty and her pedestal. Ronda's white stone buildings teeter on the very edge of the chasm.

Connecting the two parts of the city are three bridges: the Roman Bridge, the Arab Bridge, and the New Bridge. The first two are so called to recognize the regimes that built them. The (not so) New Bridge was completed in 1793 by the town's Spanish inhabitants. The bridges are impressive feats of stonework with ornate roofs above and massive columns that reach down into the canyon.

Visitors come for the bullfighting, then stay for the view.

Trains from Málaga (2 hours), Madrid (4 hours), or Granada (3 hours) make for a peaceful and scenic path to Ronda. If you're not into bullfighting, skip the popular 18th-century bullring and visit the Arab Baths instead. Ⓝ 36.740529 Ⓦ 5.164396

The devil men of the Baby Jumping Festival can leap four infants in a single bound.

BABY JUMPING FESTIVAL

CASTRILLO DE MURCIA, CASTILE AND LEÓN

Every year, 60 days after Easter, the village of Castrillo de Murcia invites men dressed as devils to leap over some babies.

The annual Baby Jumping Festival takes place in the streets, where infants are laid out on mattresses in rows of two or three. As the babies fidget and squirm in front of an audience gathered on the sidewalks, men dressed in bright yellow suits and devilish masks come charging down the street. They threaten bystanders with whips and act in a menacing manner before jumping over the rows of infants as though they were hurdles on a running track.

Dating back to the 17th century, the festival is intended to absolve infants of evil. Any child born within the last year is eligible to serve as a human hurdle for the devil men.

Castrillo de Murcia. A taxi from Burgos is the best way to reach the tiny town. Ⓝ 42.358769 Ⓦ 4.060704

With its newly upgraded railings and walkway, the path is safer but no less scary.

EL CAMINITO DEL REY

EL CHORRO, MÁLAGA

Until its renovation in 2015, El Caminito del Rey was the most dangerous stroll in Spain. A 3-foot-wide (1 m) concrete path along the steep walls of the El Chorro gorge, 350 feet (107 m) above ground and over a century old, was riddled with large, ragged holes. In some sections the concrete had completely fallen away, leaving only the 3-inch-wide steel supporting beams. Mountain climbers and hikers would come here for the ultimate thrill, inching along the beams in windy conditions and trying not to look down.

The pathway was built in 1901 to provide a faster commute for workers at the nearby hydroelectric plant. Twenty years after the pathway was completed,

King Alfonso XIII crossed it for the inauguration of a new dam. This led to the pathway's modern name, "The King's Little Pathway," or "El Caminito del Rey." Soon after the king's crossing, however, the structure fell into disrepair.

Having recognized the perilous nature of the path—three men fell to their deaths in 2000—the local government began restoring it in 2014, laying down a new trail and adding handrails. Though the pathway no longer presents a potentially lethal challenge to hikers, it is just as thrilling to stand on—especially when the wind picks up.

Trains run infrequently from Alora to El Chorro—a taxi is your best bet for the 8-mile (13 km) journey north. Bring a sturdy harness, and clip onto the wire.
Ⓝ 36.729388 Ⓦ 4.442312

ALSO IN SPAIN

Josep Pujiula Labyrinth

Argelaguer · One man's self-made wonderland, this labyrinth was created from the natural landscape.

Chocolate Museum

Barcelona · Don't miss the chocolate model of the Sagrada Família.

The Hearse Museum

Barcelona · Displaying the finest in cadaver transportation.

Setenil de las Bodegas

Cádiz · This town built into the cliffs, possibly in the first century CE, still has a few thousand inhabitants.

Potty Museum

Ciudad Rodrigo · Thirteen hundred chamber pots are displayed by a single eccentric collector.

World's Biggest Chair

Cordoba · What better place to take a seat?

Castellfollit de la Roca

Girona · A small village situated on a narrow volcanic escarpment.

Los Jameos del Agua

Las Palmas · This partially collapsed lava tube and cave system is complete with concert hall, underground pond, and unique albino crabs.

Cave of the Moon

Madrid · Mysterious Spanish catacombs of unknown origin.

The Gala Dalí Castle

Púbol-la Pera · After buying this medieval castle, Salvador Dalí filled it with sculptures of spindly-legged elephants, busts of Richard Wagner, and a throne for his wife.

San Romà de Sau

Sau · This Romanesque tower appears when water levels drop.

Museo de las Brujas

Zugarramurdi · A museum dedicated to the Spanish occult.

THE WHISTLING ISLAND

LA GOMERA, CANARY ISLANDS

The whistles that echo across the valleys of La Gomera are not mere noise, but conversation. The tiny island's inhabitants speak to one another in Silbo, a wordless language that relies on pitch variation to communicate meaning.

Silbo originates with the Guanches, the first inhabitants of La Gomera, who spoke a tonal language with a simple structure. When Spanish settlers arrived in the 16th century, the Guanches adapted their simple Silbo to the Spanish dialect, creating the more complex version that is used today. To non–Silbo speakers, the sound is like birdsong. More distinctive is the method of speaking: Gomerans insert a finger or a knuckle of one hand into their mouths to make the sounds, while the other hand cups the side of the face to focus sound in the direction of the listener.

Fearing the extinction of the language, Gomerans made Silbo a mandatory part of the island's elementary school curriculum in 1999.

Get a ferry from Los Cristianos in Tenerife to San Sebastian de la Gomera. Ⓝ 28.103304 Ⓦ 17.219358

SWITZERLAND

BRUNO WEBER SKULPTURENPARK

DIETIKON, AARGAU

This park of monsters and mythical creatures is a glimpse into the marvelous mind of Bruno Weber. The Swiss sculptor began building his collection of oversize, exotic animals in 1962 to celebrate the power of imagination in his increasingly modernized hometown of Dietikon. Serpents, winged dogs, caterpillars, and mythological creatures surround a gothic, fairy-tale castle with an 82-foot tower—home to Weber and his wife, Mariann Godon, for decades.

When he was 75, Weber spoke of his plans to build a water garden in the park—a playful place with mosaic-coated sculptures, fountains, and ponds that would provide the finishing touch. Unfortunately, he died in 2011 at the age of 80, unable to complete his final flourish. Picking up his designs, Godon stepped in and finished the garden. It opened to the public six months after Weber's death.

Zur Weinrebe, Dietikon. The park is open on weekends from April to October. Get the train from Zurich to Dietikon, then hop on the bus to Gjuchstrasse. From there, it's a 15-minute walk to the sculpture park. Ⓝ 47.405469 Ⓔ 8.381182

A row of openmouthed, sharp-toothed creatures lines the roof at Bruno Weber Skulpturenpark.

THE CHILD-EATER OF BERN

BERN

Atop a blue and gold column in the middle of Bern sits an ogre, his jaw gaping and teeth bared as he happily eats a baby. He is Kindlifresser—"the Child-Eater"—and hoisting his sack of ready-to-eat-babies, he forms the centerpiece of one of the oldest fountains in the city.

Kindlifresser's origins are contentious. He may represent Kronos, the Titan king who, according to Greek mythology, ate five of his children. Another unfortunate possibility is that the Child-Eater reflects the 16th-century belief that Jews murdered children to use their blood for religious rituals. Kindlifresser's yellow pointed hat is strikingly similar to the headwear that Jews wore at the time.

Whatever the Child-Eater of Bern was originally intended to represent, his wide eyes, grotesque face, and sack of screaming infants makes for a unique city fountain.

Kornhausplatz, Bern. Take a bus to the medieval Zytglogge tower. You'll find the Kindlifresser in the middle of the plaza.
Ⓝ 46.948652 Ⓔ 7.447435

ALSO IN SWITZERLAND

H. R. Giger Museum

Gruyères · The bizarre visions of surrealist artist H. R. Giger are tucked away in a medieval Swiss city.

Collection de l'Art Brut

Lausanne · See artwork by loners, prisoners, and the criminally insane.

St. Maurice's Abbey

Saint Maurice, Valais · An abbey built on the ruins of Roman catacombs.

The Henkermuseum

Sissach · An extensive private collection of authentic medieval devices used for human torture and execution.

Maison d'Ailleurs

Yverdon-les-Bains · A museum of science fiction, utopias, and extraordinary journeys.

Evolver

Zermatt · See the Matterhorn Mountain from another angle on this spiral alpine-view construction.

Medizinhistorisches Museum

Zürich · A museum of medical history featuring Zurich's only authentic 14th-century plague doctor's uniform.

Bern's baby-eater with his sack full of appetizing infants.

Le Musée des Grenouilles

ESTAVAYER-LE-LAC, FRIBOURG

This museum in the medieval town of Estavayer-le-Lac caters to two interests: frogs and guns. During the mid-1800s, eccentric artist François Perrier stuffed over 100 frogs and arranged them into tableaux replicating everyday scenes, including a barber shop, a billiards game, a feast, and a rousing round of dominoes. The taxidermy scenes are in a room attached to an armory that contains firearms and military equipment dating from the Middle Ages through the early 20th century. The relationship between the two rooms, if any, is not clear. **Rue du Musée 13, Estavayer-le-Lac. The museum is near the south shore of Lake Neuchâtel. The train from Fribourg takes around 40 minutes. Ⓝ 47.405469 Ⓔ 8.381182**

Abbey Library of Saint Gall

ST. GALLEN

There are beautiful old libraries, and then there is the Abbey Library of Saint Gall.

Architectural plans for the library attached to the main church date back to the 9th century. As the abbey grew over the years, so did its library, and soon the site became known for its collection of illuminated manuscripts and writings, as well as becoming a leading center for science and Western culture between the 6th and 9th centuries.

In the mid-18th century, the world-renowned collection was moved to a new library space lavishly decorated in rococo style. Elaborate artworks were installed in the ceiling, framed by flowing, curved moldings. The wooden balconies are adorned with flowering shapes and designs.

Today, the library at St. Gall is still considered nearly unrivaled in its beauty. It also holds one of the more important collections in the world, covering 12 centuries. The collection even includes the first example of an architectural plan on parchment. **Klosterhof 6B, St. Gallen. The abbey is a short walk from St. Gallen Spisertor train station. Before touring the library, you'll be given slippers to slide over your shoes to protect the floors. Ⓝ 47.423348 Ⓔ 9.376754**

One of Europe's oldest surviving libraries is also one of its most beautiful.

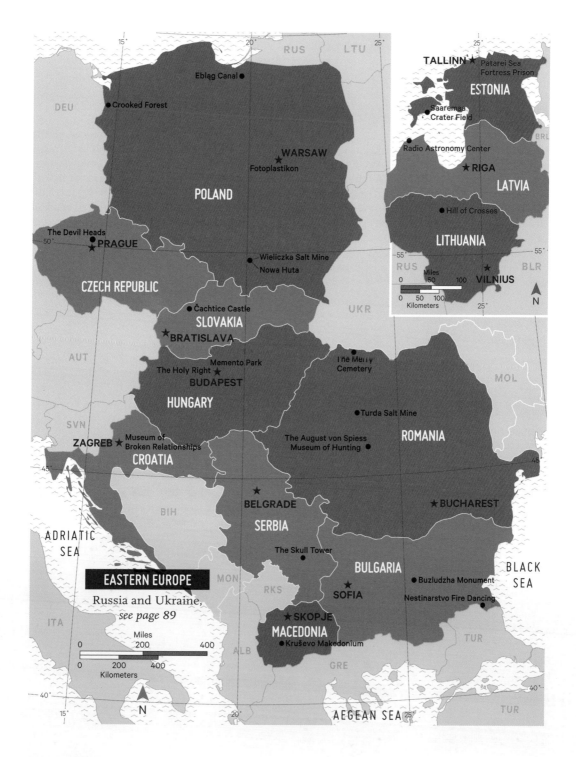

BULGARIA
NESTINARSTVO FIRE DANCING

BALGARI, BURGAS

A tiny village tucked into the southeast corner of Bulgaria, Balgari is the only place in the country where Nestinarstvo, an annual fire-dancing ritual, is performed in its authentic form. The tradition is one in which dancers known as *nestinari* dance barefoot on smoldering embers to encourage fertility and good health.

Nestinarstvo is an amalgam of pagan and Christian practices. Dancers, many of whom enter a trancelike state prior to the ritual, carry icons of the saints as they step onto the circle of embers. Surrounded by an audience of villagers, they walk back and forth to the beat of a drum, shouting prophesies over the sound of bagpipes.

The dance is performed each year on June 3, the feast day of saints Constantine and Helena.

Ⓝ 42.087878 Ⓔ 24.729355

BUZLUDZHA MONUMENT

KZANLAK, STARA ZAGORA

On a remote mountain in Bulgaria sits a smooth, gray, disc-shaped monument that wouldn't look out of place in a schlocky sci-fi film. A red star on the monolith beside it, however, reveals its true origins: In the 1970s, 6,000 workers spent seven years constructing the building as a tribute to Communism. (A compulsory donation from every Bulgarian citizen provided funding for the project.)

When the Bulgarian Communist Party surrendered its political monopoly in 1989, and Bulgaria began the transition toward democracy, the Buzludzha site quickly lost its relevance. Vandals soon attacked the abandoned monument, destroying its interior artwork. The concrete structure remains, but a visit is more likely to inspire anti-communist sentiment than celebrate the wonder of socialism. A message painted in big red letters over the doorway reads: FORGET YOUR PAST.

Approximately 7 miles down a side road from the Shipka Pass in the Balkan Mountains.
Ⓝ **42.735819** Ⓔ **25.393819** ➥

ALSO IN BULGARIA

Belogradchik Rocks

Belogradchik · Bizarrely shaped rock formations are named after equally bizarre legends—the Dervish, the Rebel Velko, the Schoolgirl.

Kaliakra Transmitter

Bulgarevo · A massive, unfinished broadcasting station stands as a monument to the fall of Communism.

Though it looks like a sci-fi movie set, Buzludzha is a homage to the Bulgarian Communist movement.

➠ Other Brutalist Monuments of the Former Yugoslavia

During the 1960s and 1970s, Yugoslavian president Josip Broz "Tito" ordered the construction of these monuments to honor the Communist Party and commemorate the battle sites of World War II. All are made from concrete and designed in the Brutalist style—an imposing architectural movement popular with Socialist countries for its raw, imposing aesthetic.

MRAKOVICA MEMORIAL: MONUMENT TO THE REVOLUTION
Kozara, Bosnia and Herzegovina

KOSOVSKA MITROVICA MONUMENT
Kosovska Mitrovica, Kosovo

KOLAŠIN MONUMENT
Kolašin, Montenegro

MONUMENT TO THE REVOLUTION OF THE PEOPLE OF MOSLAVINA
Podgarić, Croatia

VALLEY OF THE HEROES MONUMENT
Tjentište, Bosnia and Herzegovina

MONUMENT TO THE UPRISING OF THE PEOPLE OF KORDUN AND BANIJA
Petrova Gora, Croatia

JASENOVAC MONUMENT
Jasenovac, Croatia

THE THREE FISTS AT BUBANJ MEMORIAL PARK
Niš, Serbia

The Tjentište War Memorial in Bosnia commemorates World War II's Operation Fall Schwarz.

CROATIA
MUSEUM OF BROKEN RELATIONSHIPS

ZAGREB

When Croatian artists Olinka Vištica and Dražen Grubišić's four-year romance came to an end in 2003, the former couple joked that they would have to set up a museum to display all the objects they had shared. Three years later, they opened the Museum of Broken Relationships.

The institution contains a fascinating gathering of former tokens of affection. Besides the standard teddy bears and letters, the collection also includes a tiny bottle filled with tears, an ax, airsickness bags, and a prosthetic leg. While some of the items are tragic—a woman used the ax to smash her ex-girlfriend's furniture—some are sweet. The airsickness bags are from flights during a long-distance relationship, and the prosthetic leg came from a man who fell in love with his physical therapist.

Ćirilometodska 2, Zagreb. Get the funicular to avoid a steep hill-climb. If you are in the wake of a recently ended relationship, you are welcome to donate an object for exhibition. Ⓝ 45.815019 Ⓔ 15.973434

ALSO IN CROATIA

Goli Otok Prison

Goli Otok · Island gulag shut down in 1988.

Birthplace of Tesla Museum and Memorial Center

Smiljan · Learn about both Nikola Tesla's country upbringing and the scientific discoveries of his adult life.

Sea Organ

Zadar · Random harmonic sounds emerge when the wind and waves hit the tubes of this architectural object.

CZECH REPUBLIC
THE DEVIL HEADS

ŽELÍZY

A disturbing sight awaits hikers exploring the forest above the village of Želízy in Czechia. Looking out over the Kokořínsko nature reserve, two enormous demonic faces carved from the native stone stare back with empty eyes.

Created by the renowned Czech sculptor Václav Levý in the mid-19th century, the nearly 30-foot-tall sandstone heads are known as *Certovy Hlavy*, or "the

Devil Heads," and they have been a local attraction for generations. Now suffering slightly from the ravages of time and weather, the monstrous faces have grown less distinct over time—but no less creepy. **It's possible to see the Devil Heads from the street or by hiking about 0.3 miles up the relatively steep hill to reach the sculpture. There are several other stone works created by Václav Levý in the area, including artificial caves carved into nearby rock faces. Ⓝ 50.420551 Ⓔ 14.464792**

The heads are best explored during the daytime—with a friend.

ALSO IN THE CZECH REPUBLIC

Capuchin Crypt

Brno · The final resting place for 24 perfectly preserved Capuchin monks, arranged in neat rows in front of a large wooden cross.

Křtiny Ossuary

Křtiny · This small-town ossuary features a dozen skulls painted with black laurel leaves.

Alchemy Museum

Kutná Hora · A museum and underground laboratory of modern-day alchemist Michal Pober. Filled with cauldrons, vials, potions, poster board explanations, and life-size dioramas.

Communist Clock

Olomouc · Originally built in the early 15th century, this clock was reconstructed in the Social-Realism style, featuring figures of Communist workers.

Church of St. John of Nepomuk

Žďár nad Sázavou · A Gothic Baroque pilgrimage site containing the incorruptible 14th-century remains of the Czech Republic's national saint.

ESTONIA
SAAREMAA CRATER FIELD

KAALI, SAAREMAA

A 360-foot-wide basin created by a blazing meteorite.

Opinions vary on when it happened, but at some point between 5600 BCE and 600 BCE, a large meteor entered the atmosphere, broke into pieces, and slammed into the forest floor of the island of Saaremaa. The heat of the impact instantly incinerated trees within a 3-mile radius (5 km).

A mythology developed around the nine craters clustered in Saaremaa. Water gathered in the largest cavity—a 360-foot-wide, 72-foot-deep basin (110 x 22 m)—now regarded as a sacred lake. Iron Age inhabitants built a stone wall around it, and the discovery of silver and animal bones during archaeological excavations in the 1970s suggests the lake was a site for animal sacrifice and pagan worship. Some of the site's animal remains were dated to the 1600s, long after the church forbade such rituals.

The crater field now features a meteor museum, souvenir shop, and hotel offering a buffet breakfast and sauna. **Kaali Küla, Pihtla vald, Saaremaa. Ⓝ 58.303309 Ⓔ 22.70604**

PATAREI SEA FORTRESS PRISON

TALLINN, HARJU

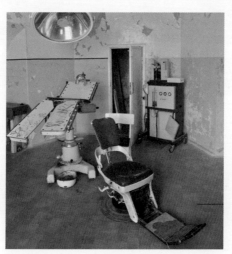

Patarei, a sea fortress built in 1840, housed inmates in its cold, dark confines from 1919 until 2002. The prison has been left virtually untouched since it closed, right down to used cotton swabs in the operating room and pictures of women torn from magazines plastered on the cell walls. Rusting wheelchairs, flaking paint, and dust-covered, neatly made beds provide a creepy atmosphere exceeded only by the musty, dimly lit Hanging Room.

Patarei is available to rent for weddings and parties. **Kalaranna 2, Tallinn. The fortress is open from May to October. Take a bus to Kalamaja. Ⓝ 59.445744 Ⓔ 24.747194**

The walls of the prison's dentistry room are painted a soothing blue.

HUNGARY
MEMENTO PARK

BUDAPEST

When Communism collapsed in Hungary in 1989, the city of Budapest was left with dozens of public monuments that celebrated the fallen regime. Rather than destroy these socialist relics, the city decided to banish them to the suburbs.

Twenty minutes outside the Budapest city center, Memento Park is the final resting place of more than 40 Communist-era statues and plaques. The open-air park displays the outcast monuments in a neutral setting, neither making a mockery of them nor honoring them.

Perhaps the most curious item in the park is a full-scale replica of Stalin's giant boots. A huge 26-foot statue of the Soviet leader once stood at Felvonulási Square in central Budapest, serving as a rallying point and parade route for the Communist regime. On October 23, 1956, Hungarians revolted against the regime and pulled down the huge statue, leaving only Stalin's massive boots behind. Though the revolution was brutally crushed, the replica of the footwear now serves as a memorial to those lost in the uprising—and a reminder of life behind the Iron Curtain.

The park can be reached from Budapest via public transport; the trip is approximately 25 minutes by metro or bus. Ⓝ 47.426346 Ⓝ 18.998732

ALSO IN HUNGARY

Electronic Museum

Budapest · This electric curiosity museum features Tesla coils and a Van de Graaff generator, housed in an old transformer station.

Golden Eagle Pharmacy Museum

Budapest · An alchemy museum that began its life in 1896 as a private collection of pharmaceutical oddities.

Taródi Vár Castle

Sopron · One dedicated family hand-built this 20th-century castle based on a medieval design.

The park encourages visitors to remember the past by confronting its relics.

CITY GUIDE: More to Explore in Budapest

Columbo Statue

Szent István krt • Installed in 2014, TV's iconic rumpled detective, along with his droopy basset hound, is immortalized as a permanent (and puzzling) bronze statue in a glitzy shopping district a couple of blocks from the Danube.

FlipperMuzeum

Józsefvóros • A museum devoted to classic pinball machines in the basement of an unremarkable apartment building, it's packed with rows of rare and vintage machines, including well-worn favorites and an example of the only known Hungarian-made machine.

The Timewheel

Zugló • This art installation in a public park near Vajdahunyad Castle is possibly the world's largest hourglass. It takes an hour to turn it and a complex system of steel cables—a big job for the team of four men who reset it every New Year's Eve.

Vajdahunyad Castle

Zugló • Built in 1896 as part of Hungary's millennial celebration, a temporary exhibition of a Transylvanian-style castle—flimsily glued and nailed together from cardboard and wood—was such a crowd favorite that in 1904 it got an upgrade to real stone.

The Hall of Hunting

Zugló • Inside the mock-Transylvanian Vajdahunyad Castle, to the Agricultural Museum exhibits of forestry, fishing, and taxidermied birds and stags, and up a stately stone staircase is the Hall of Hunting, a cathedral of antlers, horns, and hooves.

Gyermekvasút

Széchenyi-hegy • To say that Gyermekvasút is the world's largest children's railway is true, but it doesn't tell the whole story: Other than the engineer, this 7-mile-long (11.2 km) narrow-gauge rail line is run entirely by children aged 11 to 14.

Shoes on the Danube Promenade

Inner City • A moving place for reflection, this trail of iron footwear is a haunting memorial to the thousands of Jews who were told to remove their shoes before being executed along the river during World War II.

György Ràth Museum

Terézváaros • A wealthy Hungarian optometrist's impressive and charming collection of more than 4,500 Asian curiosities, all collected during the late 19th and early 20th centuries, is a branch of the Museum of Applied Arts, and home to their conservation workshop.

The Hungarian Geological Institute Building

Istvánmező • Home to the Hungarian Geological Institute (the country's oldest scientific research body) and the Geological Museum of Budapest, the building is a glorious example of the homegrown Art Nouveau architectural movement known as *Szecesszió* (Secessionist).

Hospital in the Rock Museum

Castle Hill • Under Buda Castle Hill, squirreled away in the network of tunnels and caverns, there is a museum dedicated to preserving the history (and occasional grisly tableaus) of a secret military hospital, now staffed mostly by stiff-backed uniformed mannequins.

The Castle Hill Funicular

Castle Hill • Built in 1870 at the entrance to the Széchenyi Chain Bridge, the span that originally connected Buda and Pest, this spectacular incline railway was almost lost to relentless shelling during World War II.

Semmelweis Medical History Museum

Castle Hill • With rare wax medical models by Clemente Susini (including a supine Venus), early X-ray machinery, and an array of anatomical curios, this museum (housed in the former childhood home of Ignác Semmelweis, a medical pioneer) spans the history of medicine, surgery, and pharmaceuticals.

Red Ruin

Inner City • The decor of the city's only Communism-themed "ruin bar" takes pride in presenting its own subversive poke in the eye to Cold War propaganda, with plenty of good beer, a whole lot of comic book design, and a tall glass of post-Communism political punditry.

For Sale Pub

Inner City • Covered floor to ceiling in stalactites and stalagmites of cardboard, napkins, and business cards, every possible surface of this cozy bar is available for patrons to post their drawings, notes, photos, and drunken come-ons.

The Garden of Philosophy

Tabán • Up high on Gellért Hill, in a park designed to quiet the mind, somber black statues of the world's most influential religious figures (Abraham, Jesus, Buddha, Lao-tzu, and Akhenaton) convene around a small metal ball under the watchful eyes of Gandhi, Bodhidharma, and Saint Francis of Assisi—representing the confluence and progression of human culture.

The Citadella

Gellérthegy • Occupied by the Austrian army, the Nazis, and then the Soviets, the imposing remains of this fortress have a story as tangled and complex as the city itself. Once a symbol of occupation and oppression, the citadel now represents the city's ability to transform itself.

Zwack Unicum Museum

Ferencváros • Often called the Hungarian national spirit, the Zwack family's eccentric liqueur, Unicum, dates to the late 18th century and gets the full museum treatment next door to their distillery. Exhibits include the 200-year history of the unique herbal concoction, plus Central Europe's largest collection of miniature alcohol bottles.

This installation commemorates Hungary's 2004 inclusion into the European Union.

THE HOLY RIGHT

BUDAPEST

Stephen I, Hungary's first king, died in the 11th century, but a piece of him lives on in Budapest: his right hand.

Talk of healing miracles occurring at Stephen's tomb led to his canonization in 1083. The exhumation of the former king's body revealed an incorruptible right arm—"incorruptible" being the Catholic belief that divine intervention can prevent the posthumous decay of saintly bodies.

Over the ensuing centuries, the king's detached arm passed through multiple countries and owners. During the 13th-century Mongol invasion of Hungary, it was sent to Dubrovnik, Croatia, for safekeeping by the Dominican monks. It was probably at this time that the right hand, or "Holy Right," was severed from the rest of the arm. (Dividing saintly body parts was a common practice at the time. Portions of a relic were often sent to churches in neighboring countries in order to prevent squabbling and political unrest.)

Today, the Holy Right, known to sacrilegious young Hungarians as "the monkey paw," resides in an ornate golden reliquary in Budapest's Basilica of St. Stephen. Drawn into a tight fist and clutching precious jewels, the hand—now shrunken and yellowed—still manages to look strong and defiant. **Szent István Bazilika, Szent István tér 1, Pest.**

Stephen I's desiccated, saintly hand sits in a gilded case at the Budapest basilica named for him.

St. Stephen's Basilica is a block west of the Bajcsy-Zsilinszky stop on the metro. To see the hand, go to the back left of the basilica and put a 100 forint coin in the slot. A light will illuminate the Holy Right for about 30 seconds. Ⓝ 47.500833 Ⓔ 9.053889

LATVIA
RADIO ASTRONOMY CENTER

IRBENE, VENTSPILS

Until 1993, the 105-foot (32 m) radio antenna in the remote forests of Irbene was a top-secret piece of espionage equipment. Members of the Soviet military, who lived in a purpose-built housing complex nearby, used the dish to monitor communications between NATO countries during the Cold War.

Following the restoration of Latvia's independence in 1991, Soviet troops gradually withdrew from the country. Before departing Irbene, soldiers took the time to attack the radio equipment, pouring acid into motors, cutting cables, and hurling pieces of metal into the antenna's mechanisms.

A radio tower once used by spies, now operated by astrophysicists.

Though severely damaged, the big dish—the eighth-largest in the world—survived. In July 1994, the Latvian Academy of Sciences took over the site, spending three years conducting repairs and reconfiguring the antenna to operate as a radio telescope for astronomical studies. The academy's Ventspils International Radio Astronomy Center division now uses the telescope to observe cosmic radiation and debris.

Irbene's Soviet past is evident in its military ghost town, a collection of crumbling concrete blocks filled with the abandoned possessions of its former inhabitants. **Ances Irbene. LV-3612, Ventspils rajons. Irbene is a three-hour bus ride west of Riga, the capital. From there, it's 20 miles (32 km) north to Irbene. The astronomy center offers tours, which include a climb of the telescope. Ⓝ 57.558056 Ⓔ 21.857778**

LITHUANIA
HILL OF CROSSES

MEŠKUIČIAI, ŠIAULIAI

Crosses have been accumulating on this small hill since the 14th century, when Teutonic Knights of the Holy Roman Empire occupied the nearby city of Šiauliai. New crosses tend to appear during periods of occupation or unrest as symbols of Lithuanian independence. This was particularly evident during a peasant uprising against Russian control in 1831, when people began placing crucifixes in remembrance of missing and dead rebels. By 1895, there were 150 large crosses on the site. In 1940, the number had grown to 400.

During the Soviet occupation, which lasted from 1944 to 1991, the Hill of Crosses was bulldozed three times. Each time, locals and pilgrims returned to put up more crosses. The site achieved worldwide fame when Pope John Paul II visited in 1993 to thank Lithuanians for their enduring symbol of faith.

There are now approximately 100,000 crosses on the hill. The faithful are welcome to add their contribution, in whatever form they wish—a crucifix made of Legos recently joined the collection. **The hill is 7 miles (11.3 km) north of Šiauliai, which is reachable by bus or by train from Vilnius. From Šiauliai, catch a bus bound for Joniškis and get off at the Domantai stop. From there, it's a brief walk to the crosses. Ⓝ 56.015278 Ⓔ 23.416668**

ALSO IN LITHUANIA

Witches Hill

Curonian Spit · This outdoor sculpture trail features carvings of 80 Lithuanian folk heroes located at the site of annual midsummer celebrations.

Grūtas Park

Druskininkai · A sort of Soviet theme park and open-air museum, it features re-creations of gulag prison camps complete with barbed wire and guard towers.

Devils' Museum

Kaunas · A collection of 3,000 artworks depicting the devil shows myriad interpretations of the dark lord.

100,000 crosses of all sizes are crammed together on a hill.

MACEDONIA
The Kruševo Makedonium

KRUŠEVO, KRUŠEVO

The space-age spherical building on a hill overlooking the medieval town of Kruševo resembles something between a *Star Wars* set piece and a giant virus. Neither of these remotely relates to the monument's solemn purpose: to commemorate the 1903 Ilinden uprising, when a group of Macedonians revolted against the Ottoman Empire in an attempt to establish an autonomous state. Eight hundred rebels took control of Kruševo on the night of August 2, renaming it the "Kruševo Republic."

The Kruševo Republic lasted 10 days before the Ottomans struck back. An 18,000-strong army stormed the town and quickly recaptured it, burning and plundering as they went. Despite the short life of the Kruševo Republic, Macedonians revere the leaders of the Ilinden Uprising, and August 2 is a national holiday. The Makedonium monument, built in 1973, is held in similar esteem, and it also appears on national currency. It contains stained glass skylights, a centerpiece that resembles an oversize gas burner, and the tomb of the uprisings' leader Nikola Karev.

The Makedonium is a space-age–style tribute to an early-20th-century uprising.

Kruševo is a two-hour drive south of Skopje. The monument is less than a mile from the center of town. Ⓝ 41.377404 Ⓔ 21.248334

POLAND
Elbląg Canal

JELONKI

Due to drastic changes in elevation, the Elbląg Canal is broken up into short strips of water separated by stretches of land. In order to navigate this tricky waterway, an ingenious system of inclined planes was created to transform boats into railroad cars for the troublesome portions of the journey.

Stretching from Lake Drużno to Jeziorak Lake, the narrow course is the longest navigable canal in Poland. Yet it was nearly unusable until the mid-1800s, when the King of Prussia ordered a novel solution. As the canal is too long and steep to use traditional water locks, pairs of rail tracks are laid across the dry stretches. Giant water-powered cradles then lift the boats up out of the water,

A creative engineering feat that combines two modes of transportation.

place them on the tracks, and carry them across the ground to the next bit of sailing territory. The unique amphibious canal has been hailed as one of Europe's most impressive engineering marvels.

Today, the canal is still in use, though mostly as a tourist attraction. Boat tours run the length of the canal, a roughly 11-hour journey. If the entire trip is too lengthy, you can hop off about halfway through, but the full impact of this clever invention might be somewhat derailed. Ⓝ 54.028372 Ⓝ 19.594404

The salt mine's Chapel of St. Kinga features chandeliers made of salt.

WIELICZKA SALT MINE

WIELICZKA, LESSER POLAND

Miners at Wieliczka carved its rock salt deposits without interruption from the 13th century until the 1990s. Over the centuries, workers slowly turned the seven-level subterranean mine into a majestic salt city replete with life-size rock salt sculptures of saints, biblical wall reliefs, and tableaus depicting their daily lives.

In the early 1900s, the workers undertook their most ambitious project: an underground church named after Kinga, the patron saint of salt miners. The 331-foot-deep (101 m) St. Kinga's Chapel features a sculpture of Christ on the cross, depictions of scenes from the New Testament, a wall relief of Da Vinci's *The Last Supper*, and two altars. All are carved from salt. Hanging from the ceiling are five chandeliers that miners crafted by dissolving salt, removing its impurities, and reconstituting it into crystals as clear as glass.

Another memorable sight on the tour is the placid subterranean lake in the Józef Piłsudski Chamber, softly lit and overseen by a statue of Saint John Nepomucene—the patron saint of drowning. Take a moment of reflection before you bundle into a small, dark miners' cage with five other people for the long ascent back to the surface.

Take Danilowicza 10, Wieliczka. Located in a suburb of Kraków, the nearest railway station is Dworzec PKP Wieliczka-Rynek. Ⓝ 48.983039 Ⓔ 20.055731

THE CROOKED FOREST

NOWE CZARNOWO, WEST POMERANIA

At first, Gryfino Forest looks to be a run-of-the-mill field of trees. And then you see it: a group of 400 pines, each with a mysterious, dramatic bend close to the ground.

The trees' unusual but uniform "J" shape is likely the result of human intervention—probably farmers who manipulated the trees with the intention of turning them into curved furniture. The pines, planted in 1930, had around ten years of normal growth before being distorted. An alternative theory holds that regular flooding caused the unusual shapes.

Gryfino is a 30-minute train ride from the city of Szczecin. Ⓝ 53.214827 Ⓔ 14.474695

By hook or by crook, the Gryfino trees flourish.

NOWA HUTA

KRAKÓW

As Soviet occupying forces rolled into Poland toward the end of World War II, they found a country devastated by the ferocious fighting on the Eastern Front. Rebuilding was in order, and Moscow saw the opportunity not only to remake Poland's cities, but also to dramatically reshape Polish society while they were at it.

To achieve this, the Soviets set to work planning and building Nowa Huta, which was to be an ideal city representing a vision of a glorious Communist future. The project was approved in 1947, and construction of the urban experiment in social engineering began in 1949.

One of only two fully planned socialist realist cities ever built (the other being Magnitogorsk, Russia),

A Soviet model for proletarian paradise.

Nowa Huta was created as a bustling working-class enclave. Built on the outskirts of Kraków, for a population of 100,000, Nowa Huta was laid out in a sunburst pattern radiating from a monumental central square (Plac Centralny) and built in a stirring architectural style that combined Renaissance elegance with the grand, overwhelming scale typical of Soviet projects. Wide avenues were designed to halt the spread of fires. Trees lining those avenues were planted to absorb the impact of a nuclear blast.

Most important was Nowa Huta's intended status as a proletarian paradise. To that end, the city was built with a massive steel mill at one end (*Nowa Huta* means "New Steel Mill"). The Lenin Steelworks contained the largest blast furnace in Europe and employed 40,000 people at its height, with the capacity to produce 7 million tons of steel annually. It was an odd location for such a facility, given weak local demand for steel, but in this case—as in many others during the Cold War—the symbolism was more important than the logic.

Ironically, Nowa Huta later turned into an anti-Communist hub and was key in the Solidarity movement of the 1980s. Nevertheless, the city remains to this day one of the best examples of socialist realist architecture and urban planning.

Run to Nowa Huta from Kraków's city center. While you're there, swing by Lord's Ark church. Locals fought for 28 years for permission to build it, after which it became a powerful symbol of Polish resistance to Communist rule. Ⓝ 50.071703 Ⓔ 20.037883

ALSO IN POLAND

Live-in Salt Mine	UFO Memorial	Konstantynów Radio Tower	Skarpa Ski Jump
Bochnia · Poland's oldest salt mine has nearly everything you need to live underground forever, including a gymnasium and a spa.	*Emilcin* · Site of the most famous alleged UFO abduction case in Polish history.	*Płocki* · The shattered remains of what was once, at 2,120 feet (646 m), the tallest structure in the world.	*Warsaw* · Ruins of a late 1950s ski jump ramp can be found in the middle of the city.

FOTOPLASTIKON

WARSAW, MASOVIAN

Before movie theaters and motion pictures, the European public entertained itself with a visit to the "fotoplastikon." Invented in Germany in the late 19th century, the fotoplastikon, or Kaiserpanorama, is a cylindrical wooden structure with multiple viewfinders through which people can view illuminated stereoscopic photographs.

In the first half of the 20th century, there were around 250 fotoplastikon devices across Europe. Visitors sat at one of the pairs of goggles and watched, spellbound, as seemingly three-dimensional scenes from around the globe paraded past. Images of African deserts, American cities, and Arctic expeditions—all the stuff of fantasy in the pre-cinema,

pre-air-travel era—provided an escapist thrill and broadened people's perceptions of the world.

This Warsaw model, built in 1905, is one of only a few left that are still in working condition. It is equipped with 18 viewing stations and sits in the middle of a parlor plastered with old travel posters. **Aleje Jerozolimskie 51, Warsaw. The fotoplastikon parlor is 2 blocks from the Centrum metro station. Ⓝ 52.231374 Ⓔ 21.008064**

ROMANIA
THE MERRY CEMETERY

SĂPÂNȚA, MARAMUREȘ

At the Cimitirul Vesel, or "Merry Cemetery," over 600 colorful wooden crosses bear the life stories, dirty details, and final moments of the bodies that lie below. Displayed in bright, cheery pictures and annotated with limericks are the stories of almost everyone who has died in the town of Săpânța. Illustrated crosses depict soldiers being beheaded and a townsperson being hit by a truck. The epigraphs are surprisingly frank and often funny: "Underneath this heavy cross lies my mother-in-law . . . Try not to wake her up. For if she comes back home, she'll bite my head off."

The cemetery's unique style was created by a local named Stan Ioan Pătraș, who at the age of 14 had already begun carving crosses for the graveyard. By 1935, Pătraș was carving clever and ironic poems—done in a rough local dialect—about the deceased, as well as painting their portraits on the crosses, often depicting the way in which they died.

Pătraș died in 1977, having carved his own cross and leaving his house and business to his most talented apprentice, Dumitru Pop. Pop has spent the last three decades continuing the carving work, and has also turned the house into the Merry Cemetery's workshop-museum. Despite the occasionally darkly comic—or merely dark—tones of the crosses, Pop says no one has ever complained about the work:

It's the real life of a person. If he likes to drink, you say that; if he likes to work, you say that . . . There's no hiding in a small town . . . The families actually want the true life of the person to be represented on the cross.

Church of the Assumption, Săpânța. The cemetery is near the Romanian–Ukrainian border, at the intersection of routes 19 and 183. Ⓝ 47.97131 Ⓔ 23.694948

ALSO IN ROMANIA

Zoological Museum

Cluj-Napoca · The natural history museum housed within the Babes-Bolyai University appears as if it has been untouched for half a century. Scruffy, ratty taxidermy fills glass cases, hangs from the ceiling, and peers down from an off-limits second floor.

Decebal's Head

Orșova · While the 13-story bearded stone face overlooking the Danube River looks like something straight from Middle Earth, it is the recent creation of a Romanian businessman. When the ten-year sculpting process was completed in 2004, the head became the tallest rock sculpture in Europe.

Life and death are celebrated in equal measure at the Merry Cemetery.

THE AUGUST VON SPIESS MUSEUM OF HUNTING

SIBIU, SIBIU

Glass-eyed animal heads cover the dimly lit walls of this museum, a stark reminder of Romania's appeal to hunters. The country's large bear population is due to the policies of the country's last Communist leader, Nicolae Ceaușescu, who, after depleting the bear population in his own private reserve, made bear hunting illegal for everyone but himself and a few handpicked Communist Party members.

The measure protected many bears from slaughter, but Ceaușescu killed more than his fair share. Driven by a desire to hunt the biggest animals, he had bear cubs captured, fed a hearty diet, and then released back into the wild when they had fattened up. But the animals had grown so used to being fed by humans that they died hungry in the wild. Undeterred, Ceaușescu switched methods, ordering that the bears be fed raw meat and beaten with sticks to discourage attachment. The resulting aggressive bears were known to attack hikers and cars.

One of Ceaușescu's largest trophies—the skin and stuffed paws of a huge brown bear—is on display at this museum. The bulk of the trophies, however, hail from the 1,000-strong personal collection of Colonel August von Spiess, a fellow chaser of Carpathian bears and Romania's royal hunt master during the 1920s and '30s.

The dog was killed by the bear; the bear by the dog's owner. Both were mounted: one as trophy, the other as homage.

Strada Școala de Înot, Nr. 4, Sibiu. In the heart of Transylvania, Sibiu is a 5-hour train ride northwest from Bucharest. Ⓝ 45.786634 Ⓔ 24.146900

TURDA SALT MINE

TURDA, CLUJ

This former salt mine, excavated by hand and machine over hundreds of years, is now a subterranean fairground-cum-spa. Operational from the times of the Roman Empire until 1932, the mine closed for 60 years, reopening to the public in 1992. The microclimate—a steady 53°F (11.6°C) year-round, with high humidity and no allergens—is ideal for halotherapy, an alternative health treatment in which people with respiratory problems spend time breathing in the salt-infused air.

The current attractions in the 260 × 130-foot (80 × 40 m) space make it easy to pass the hours. They include a Ferris wheel, mini-golf course, bowling alley, and underground lake with paddle boats. To offset the darkness, bright lights hang vertically on strings from the 16-story ceiling, illuminating dripping stalactites with a blue-tinged glow.

Aleea Durgăului 7, Turda. Ⓝ 46.566280 Ⓔ 23.790640

Yellow rowboats bob on an underground lake, illuminated by hanging lights.

RUSSIA
ALEXANDER GOLOD'S PYRAMIDS

OSTASHKOV, TVER OBLAST

Aggression; osteoporosis; blackheads; dizziness; heartburn; depression; sterility; learning disabilities; arachnophobia: All these ailments and many more can be swiftly cured, according to Russian scientist and defense engineer Alexander Golod. The remedy is simple: pyramids.

Seizing upon a New Age belief that pyramids exude healing energy, Golod has built fiberglass pyramids all over Russia. The largest of the structures is 15 stories tall, and located one hour

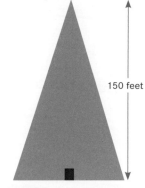

150 feet

Step inside to experience a number of health benefits. (The number likely being zero.)

outside of Moscow. People feeling unwell, run-down, or burdened by life's responsibilities are invited to step inside the pyramid and

experience the musty-smelling tranquility. They are then gently guided to the gift shop, where they may purchase pebbles, mini pyramids—which Golod claims emit a calming, energy-rebalancing force field—and bottled water that has been stored inside the pyramid, where it is said to acquire healing properties.

Despite Golod's claims of miraculous growth and recovery within the pyramids, no scientific body has ever confirmed that the building or its trinkets confer any tangible curative effect.

Ostashkov, Tver. The pyramid is by Lake Seliger, northwest of Moscow.
Ⓝ 57.140268 Ⓔ 33.128516

KUNSTKAMERA

ST. PETERSBURG

Peter the Great, who ruled Russia from 1682 to 1725, was interested in all things modern, scientific, and rational. During his reign—when not busy ordering the interrogation, torture, and death of his own son—Peter collected artwork, scientific books and instruments, fish, reptiles, insects, and human specimens. In 1714, he ordered that his collection form the foundation of a new museum in St. Petersburg. The institution, called the Kunstkamera, was the country's first museum, and aimed to show the world that Russia was a modern, scientific, secular country.

Peter the Great's 300-year-old collection of human body parts

Completed in 1654, the Gottorb Globe was the world's first planetarium.

is displayed on level two of the Kunstkamera. The focus of the collection, established in 1727, is on infant anatomy and disease—malformed fetuses, tumor-ridden stomachs, and jarred children's heads, preserved with care by 17th-century Dutch anatomist Frederik Ruysch.

Also on display is the skeleton of Nikolai Bourgeois, a 7-foot-2-inch (2.2 m) man who was Peter's assistant and a living exhibit at the museum, as well as a stuffed two-headed calf and the preserved fetuses of conjoined twins. The 32 human teeth neatly arranged into a grid were all extracted by Peter the Great, who found dentistry to be a rewarding hobby.

Universitetskaya Embankment, 3, St. Petersburg. Get a bus or trolleybus to Universitetskaya Naberezhnaya. Ⓝ 59.941568 Ⓔ 30.304588

ALSO IN RUSSIA

Kadykchan

Kadykchan · A Siberian ghost town built by gulag prisoners, many of whom later worked in the nearby coal mines.

Manpupuner Rock Formations

Komi · Enormous natural rock formations rise abruptly from the flat landscape surrounding them and tower over the Russian plateau.

Lena's Stone Pillars

Lena River · Evidence of ancient human life and fossils from mammoths, bison, and fleecy rhinos have been found at this remote forest of stone pillars.

Museum of Soviet Arcade Machines

Moscow · Founded by Russian university students in the basement of a technical school, the Museum of Soviet Arcade Machines features over 40 machines from the era, including video games, pinball machines, and collaborative hockey foosball.

House of Evgeny Smolik

Selo Irbeyskoe · Inspired by fairy tales, Evgeny Smolik turned his village home into a surreal palace with intricate wood carvings and fantasy-themed furniture.

Church on Blood in Honor of All Saints Resplendent in the Russian Land

Yekaterinburg · This Russian Orthodox church was built on the site where the last tsar and his family were shot by the Bolsheviks during the Russian Civil War.

TUNGUSKA EVENT EPICENTER

VANAVARA, KRASNOYARSK KRAI

On June 30, 1908, at 7:14 a.m., a powerful explosion shattered windows, knocked people off their feet, and leveled 80 million trees over 830 square miles (2,150 sq. km) of forest around Siberia's Podkamennaya Tunguska River basin. Initial speculation was that a meteorite had hit Earth, but subsequent investigations found no crater in the area.

Naturally, the mysterious nature of the Tunguska Event has given rise to a wealth of conspiracy theories. Among the more far-fetched culprits: a tiny black hole passing through the Earth; a UFO crash; and the testing of Nikola Tesla's secret "death ray." Today, the favored scientific explanation involves the midair explosion of a large meteoroid or comet. Indeed, it is the largest impact event in recent history.

Split, mangled, and felled trees are all still visible around the Tunguska site.

The closest village to the Tunguska Event epicenter is the town of Vanavara, located about 40 miles (65 km) southeast of the epicenter. Ⓝ 60.902539 Ⓔ 101.904508

KOLA SUPERDEEP BOREHOLE

MURMANSK, MURMANSK OBLAST

Until 1970, geologists could only theorize about the composition of the Earth's crust. That was the year Soviet scientists began drilling what would become the deepest hole in the world.

Engaged in a subterranean version of the Space Race, the USSR went all out to beat the US in a journey to the center of the Earth. While American researchers faltered with Project Mohole, a dig off the coast of Mexico that ran out of funding in 1966, their Russian counterparts took a more determined approach. From 1970 to 1994, their drill on the Kola Peninsula burrowed through

Kola hole is the deepest pit ever drilled in the name of science.

layers of rock, reaching an ultimate depth of 7.5 miles (12 km).

The most intriguing discovery made by the Kola borehole researchers was the detection of microscopic life-forms 4 miles (6.7 km) beneath the surface of the Earth. Usually fossils can be found in limestone and silica deposits, but these "microfossils" were encased in organic compounds that remained surprisingly intact despite the extreme pressures and temperatures of the surrounding rock. Drilling at Kola stopped in the early 1990s, but data from the dig is still being analyzed.

The hole is northwest of Murmansk on the Kola Peninsula, a few miles from the Norwegian border.
Ⓝ 69.396219 Ⓔ 30.608667 ➻

➻ World's Deepest Places

DEEPEST CANYON:
11,596 FT/3,534.5 M
Cotahuasi Canyon, Peru

DEEPEST CAVE:
7,208 FT/2,197 M
Krubera Cave, Abkhazia

DEEPEST HOLE:
39,600 FT/12,070 M
Kola Borehole, Russia

DEEPEST MINE:
12,795 FT/3,900 M
TauTona Gold Mine, South Africa

DEEPEST OPEN PIT MINE:
3,937 FT/1,200 M
Bingham Canyon Mine, United States

Bingham Canyon Mine, United States

DEEPEST RAIL TUNNEL:	**DEEPEST POINT UNDER WATER:**	**DEEPEST LAKE:**	**DEEPEST FOUNDATION:**	**DEEPEST MAN-MADE POINT:**
790 FT/240.8 M Seikan Tunnel, Japan	35,838 FT/ 10,923.4 M Mariana Trench, Pacific Ocean	5,314 FT/1,619.7 M Lake Baikal, Russia	394 FT/120 M Petronas Towers, Malaysia	40,502 FT/12,345 M Sakhalin-I Oil Well, Russia

CITY GUIDE: More to Explore in Moscow

Exhibition of Achievements of National Economy

Ostankinsky • Bigger than the principality of Monaco and inspired by the great 19th-century expositions of London, Paris, and Chicago, this open-air market/museum/amusement park works overtime to glorify Russian agriculture, industry, and technology, all on a grand scale.

Monument to the Conquerors of Space

Ostankinsky • Swooping up over the Memorial Museum of Cosmonautics is a 350-foot (107 m) Jetsonian curve of titanium, topped by a rocket blasting into the sky. At the base of the monument are stone bas-relief sculptures of scientists and cosmonauts.

Laika Monument

Airport • It took more than half a century, but in 2008 a monument to a famous space dog was finally unveiled at a space-training facility, where a plaque tells of her bravery and tragic contribution, and her fans can leave flowers and trinkets to say, "Good dog, Laika."

Laika was the first animal to orbit the Earth.

Aquarelle Train on the Moscow Metro

Sokolniki • With stations that look like something out of *Dr. Zhivago*, the Moscow Metro turns public transportation into an art form. Especially nice is the Aquarelle car on the Red Line, wrapped in a floral watercolor skin and with an interior like a museum gallery.

Padlock Tree Park

Yakimanka • In what started as a practical solution to the structural problem often caused by the weight of "love locks" on bridges, the city has installed rows of metal "trees" over Luzhkov Bridge and along the Moscow River, where newlyweds can lock, kiss, and toss their keys into the water to their bursting hearts' content.

Lubyanka

Meshchansky • This Neo-Baroque block of a building was the All-Russia Insurance Company before the KGB filled its long halls. Make an appointment to visit its propaganda-filled museum.

Lenin's Mausoleum

Tverskoy • The world's most famous "modern mummy," the embalmed remains of the leader of the Bolshevik Revolution, can be viewed by small groups inside an oddly stunted pyramid of a tomb.

The Old English Court Museum

Tverskoy • The 16th-century headquarters of the Mystery and Company of Merchant Adventurers, also known as the Muscovy Company, was the conduit for all official trade between England and Russia from 1551 to 1917.

Romanov Palace Chambers in Zaryadye

Tverskoy • Long before they became tsars of the Russian Empire, the Romanovs were just another bunch of aristocrats wrangling for power, and their centuries-old lineage can be traced to this fairly unpretentious family home in the historic Zaryadye district.

Tsar Bell

Tverskoy • It's never actually been rung, but it's still the largest bell in the world. Cast in 1735, the bell rests on some block stone behind the Ivan the Great Bell Tower at Red Square, and is so big it once served as a chapel where parishioners could enter through a "door," which was really a hole caused by the bronze cracking under its own weight.

Miniature Moscow—Capital of the USSR

Dorogomilovo • It's the tallest hotel in Europe, and all 34 stories sparkle and gleam like Stalin ordered, but on the first floor of the historic Hotel Ukraina is a vastly smaller achievement: a 3,200-square-foot (300 m) miniature Moscow, a diorama of the entire city, just as it looked in 1977.

A. N. Scriabin House

Arbat • The innovative and controversial composer Alexander Scriabin's home is reverently preserved and features a working version of his theosophical color keyboard.

Children Are the Victims of Adult Vices

Yakimanka • Along the Moscow River, there is a surreal 13-piece allegorical art installation by Mihail Chemiakin that depicts greed, poverty, and indifference as figurative corrupting influences over two angelic children.

Moscow Cats Theatre

Meshchansky • Be forewarned: This circus of cats and clowns is not without controversy and its wild popularity has brought some well-deserved scrutiny to the felines' welfare, but for anyone curious to see if cats can, in fact, be herded, this may be the place to go.

The Battle of Borodino

Meshchansky • The brutal clash between French and Russian forces at the 1812 Battle of Borodino is masterfully re-created on a 360-degree, 375-foot (115 m) panoramic canvas by artist Franz Roubaud, depicting the more than 250,000 troops and 70,000 casualties.

Fallen Monument Park

Yakimanka • This odd sculpture garden, also called Muzeon Park of Arts, dispassionately displays tossed-aside Soviet sculptural relics like busted-up statues of Stalins, Lenins, and the founder of the KGB, and a Soviet emblem that looks like an old James Bond prop.

State Darwin Museum

Academic • The world's first museum of evolution, its collection dates back to 1907, with dinosaur models (enhanced with a catchy dinosaur soundtrack), dioramas of wildlife from the North Pole to the South, and only slightly moth-eaten taxidermy by master stuffer Filipp Fedulov.

Lenin Hills Museum–Reserve at Gorki Leninskiye

Gorki Leninskiye • Outside of Moscow's city limits is the palatial, very unproletariat final home of Vladimir Lenin, preserved as a museum to his memory, with his Rolls-Royce Silver Ghost (outfitted with tank treads), a reproduction of his Kremlin office, his death mask, and a plaster cast of his stroke-plagued hands.

OYMYAKON

OYMYAKON, SAKHA REPUBLIC

Located just a few hundred miles from the Arctic Circle, the Siberian village of Oymyakon is the coldest permanently inhabited place on Earth.

Every January, the fur-swaddled citizens of Oymyakon endure average daily highs of −47°F (−43.9°C), with nighttime temperatures plummeting to around −60°F (−51.1° C). The lowest temperature ever recorded was −90°F (−67.8°C) in 1933.

Oymyakon's 500 residents live on a diet of mostly reindeer and horse meat because the frozen

Welcome to the coldest town on Earth.

ground makes it difficult to grow crops. Cars are hard to start because the axle grease and fuel tanks freeze, and batteries lose life at an alarming speed.

Summer, however, brings relief. Temperatures can even reach the 70s (20s C) during July. **Trips to Oymyakon start with a flight to Yakutsk, capital of the Sakha Republic and the coldest major city in the world. From there it's about 20 hours of driving to get to Oymyakon. It's best to travel with a local who has a car well-equipped to handle the chill. Ⓝ 63.464263 Ⓔ 142.773770**

TEMPLE OF ALL RELIGIONS

KAZAN

The colorful Temple of All Religions, or Universal Temple, is a mishmash of architectural flourishes culled from most of the major world religions.

Established by philanthropist Ildar Khanov in 1992, the site is not a chapel in the traditional sense, but a center meant to stand as a symbol of religious unity. Khanov, an advocate for rehabilitation services for substance abusers, built the center with the help of patients he met through his work.

The exterior of the temple looks almost like something out of Disneyland's It's a Small World ride, with a Greek Orthodox dome here and a Russian minaret there. There are design influences from Jewish synagogues and Islamic mosques, along with a number of spires and bells. All in all, the temple incorporates architectural influences from 12 religions in a bright cacophony of devotion. **Arakchinskoye Shosse, 4, Kazan. Khanov died in 2013, but his associates continue to work on the temple. You can get there by bus and train from Kazan's railway station. Ⓝ 55.800620 Ⓔ 48.974999**

A colorful symbol of religious unity and rehabilitation.

Kostroma Moose Farm

SUMAROKOVO

In the early 1930s, the USSR set its sights on spreading Communism throughout the world—on mooseback. Large, strong, and agile even through deep snow, the moose seemed to be the perfect animal for the Soviet cavalry. And so began the quest to domesticate the northern moose.

In secret moose husbandries, the wild animals were trained to carry armed riders and not be gunshy. There were attempts to mount pistols and shields to the antlers of the bull moose. In the end, military moose never took off, but these taming efforts did lead to the rise of modern experimental moose farms, where semi-domesticated moose are still raised today.

The early farms were tasked with raising moose for milk, transportation, and to nourish the hungry populace. Despite initial apprehension, it turned out these gentle giants were just as easily milked as cows. However, raising them for meat proved prohibitively expensive, and moose, being clever creatures, wouldn't be led easily to slaughter. Despite years of brutal and bloody experimentation, it was discovered that it's difficult to make a moose do what a moose does not wish to do, and efforts to fully control them were abandoned.

The Kostroma Moose Farm opened in 1963 with a new approach, known as free-range moose ranching. The tamed moose roam the forest but return to the farm by choice, recognizing it as a reliable food source and safe place to give birth. The Kostroma Farm started with just two calves and has since been home to over 800 moose. It's also functioned as a scientific research facility, but today the farm's primary functions are producing moose milk for medical treatments, harvesting antler velvet for pharmaceutical purposes, and providing a place for tourists to visit these fascinating creatures.

The Kostroma Moose Farm is located near the village of Sumarokovo, about 12 miles (20 km) east of the city of Kostroma. The facility is open daily and guided tours can be purchased. The best time to visit is in early spring, when the first calves are born. Ⓝ 57.664955 Ⓝ 41.114243

SERBIA
The Skull Tower

NIŠ, NIŠAVA

The skull tower is the grim product of the 1809 Battle of Čegar, a turning point during the First Serbian Uprising against the Ottoman Empire. Desperate in the face of certain defeat, rebel commander Stevan Sinđelić fired into a gunpowder keg, annihilating his entire army as well as the enemy soldiers who had flooded the trenches.

Angered by Sinđelić's actions, Turkish commander Hurshid Pasha ordered the mutilation of the dead rebels' bodies. Their skins were peeled off their decapitated heads, stuffed with straw, and sent to the imperial court in Istanbul as proof of Turkish victory.

The 952 skulls left behind were used as building blocks for a 15-foot-tall (4.6 m) tower constructed at the entrance of the city. Sinđelić's skull sat at the top. The gruesome construction left a deep scar in the national psyche but did not deter its citizens from fighting for freedom from the Ottoman Empire. The Serbs rebelled again in 1815, this time successfully, driving off the Turks and winning independence in 1830.

In the years immediately following the construction of the tower, the families of deceased rebels chiseled away some of the skulls in order to give them proper funerals. Today, only 58 skulls remain. They are surrounded by hundreds of cavities, each one representing a person who died in battle. A chapel was

A grisly reminder of the sacrifices made for Serbian independence.

built around the tower in 1892 to shield it from the elements.

Dušana Popovića, Niš. Niš is a 3-hour bus ride from Belgrade. Ⓝ 43.311667 Ⓔ 21.923889

Also in Serbia

Devil's Town Rock Formation

Kuršumlija · The 202 bizarre rock spires of Đavolja Varoš are the result of natural soil erosion.

Bridge of Love

Vrnjačka Banja · Young couples have sealed their love by attaching a padlock to this bridge since World War I.

Red Cross Concentration Camp

Niš · A Red Cross memorial museum sits at the site of the Niš concentration camp that operated for four years during World War II. The museum celebrates a daring, 105-person prison escape in February 1942.

SLOVAKIA
ČACHTICE CASTLE RUINS

ČACHTICE

Four hundred years ago, Hungarian countess Elizabeth Báthory died in a closed room inside this castle. Known as the Blood Countess, she was imprisoned for unimaginable acts, which included torturing and killing hundreds of girls, and, if the legends are to be believed, bathing in their blood.

In 1610, after multiple tip-offs from locals that terrible things were happening inside Čachtice Castle, King Matthias II ordered the collection of testimonies and evidence, but Báthory was never convicted. In return for avoiding a trial, the family waived the king's debts. There is no way of knowing how many girls Báthory killed. Estimates of the number of victims ranged from 50 to over 600. Little is left of the building today, but there is enough to evoke the blood-soaked walls and agonized screams of Báthory's torture chambers.

Home of the world's most prolific female serial killer.

The castle is on a hill overlooking Čachtice.
Ⓝ 48.725075 Ⓔ 17.760988

UKRAINE
ODESSA CATACOMBS

ODESSA, ODESSA OBLAST

Rusted mining equipment, World War II grenades, 19th-century wine barrels, and human remains are some of the things you might stumble upon during a journey into the labyrinthine Odessa catacombs.

The estimated 1,500 miles (2,800 km) of passage that weave beneath the streets of the city were mostly dug by limestone miners in the early 1800s. When the mines were abandoned, they quickly became the preferred hideout of rebels, criminals, and eccentrics.

After the Soviets were forced out of Odessa during WWII, dozens of Ukrainian rebel groups stayed, hidden in the tunnels. While waiting for opportunities to strike they attempted to lead normal lives, playing chess and checkers, cooking, and listening to Soviet radio. Meanwhile, the Nazis tossed poison gas canisters into the catacombs and sealed random exits, hoping to trap or smoke out the rebels.

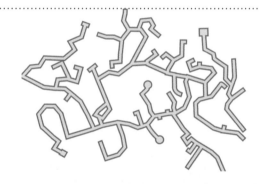

The labyrinthine nature of Odessa's dark and dusty catacomb tunnels has occasionally resulted in tragedy.

Today, only a small portion of the catacombs is open to the public as part of the Museum of Partisan Glory in Nerubayskoye, north of Odessa. The rest of the tunnel system is structurally unstable, partially flooded, and irresistible to urban spelunkers. Groups of explorers spend days underground, bringing headlamps, waders, and backpacks full of food and wine.

Occasionally, the subterranean parties turn deadly. In 2005, a group of Odessa teens spent New Year's Eve partying in the catacombs. In the drunken revelry, one of the girls became separated from the group and got lost in the catacombs. She spent three days wandering in the freezing cold and pitch-black darkness before she died of dehydration. Two years later, police were finally able to locate her body and retrieve it from the depths.

Most catacomb exploration begins in Nerubayskoye, a small town just northwest of downtown Odessa. Exploring the tunnels is not illegal, but it is not encouraged. It would be folly to venture into the catacombs without a guide. Choose carefully—your life is in their hands.
Ⓝ 46.546667 Ⓔ 30.630556 ➤➤

➺ Other Hidden Tunnels

METRO 2

The existence of Metro 2, the informal name of Moscow's alleged secret underground metro system, has never been proven, but KGB defectors, US intelligence, and former Russian ministers all say it's there. The system—said to be larger than Moscow's public metro network—was apparently constructed during Stalin's reign to evacuate leaders during periods of unrest. It continues to operate under the control of the Ministry of Defense, according to everyone except the KGB. In the mid-1990s, urban explorers claimed to have discovered an entrance to the system.

LONDON SEWER SYSTEM

Conditions were pretty grim in 1850s London. Its citizens used the River Thames as an open sewer, resulting in an ever-present stench and waves of cholera epidemics. It was time for the government to build a modern sewer system.

Construction of the 550-mile (885 km) network took place between 1859 and 1865. It incorporated the River Fleet, a major Thames tributary during Roman London that had been

An upside-down medusa head is part of the architecture at the Basilica Cisterns in Istanbul.

gradually forced underground by industrial development.

BASILICA CISTERNS OF ISTANBUL

Beneath Istanbul are hundreds of Byzantine cisterns—underground reservoirs built during the 5th and 6th centuries to store rainwater. The cathedral-like structures have an elegance that belies their utilitarian nature, and contain decorated arches, marble columns, and carvings of Medusa's head.

ANTWERP RUIEN

Antwerp's many natural ditches served as fortifications, trade routes, and open sewers from the 11th to 16th centuries. When the smell became too much to bear, the city asked each citizen to take responsibility for covering the ditches, or *ruien*, on their land. It took citizens 300 years to cover the ditches in a diverse range of materials that reflected their wealth, taste, and competence as builders. The underground ruien functioned as the city's sewers until the 1990s, when they were emptied in favor of a new network of pipes.

UNDERGROUND CITIES OF CAPPADOCIA

Cappadocia, a historic region in Turkey, contains a network of underground, multilevel cities sealed off from the world with large stone doors. Carved from volcanic rock around the 7th or 8th century BCE and connected by tunnels, the cities contained kitchens, wine cellars, wells, staircases, stables, and chapels. Early Christians used the cities as a hiding place to escape Roman persecution.

BALAKLAVA SUBMARINE BASE

BALAKLAVA, CRIMEA

Balaklava was a quiet fishing village until 1957, when the Soviet government suddenly wiped it from official maps in order to establish a secret submarine base. Working under Stalin's orders, military engineers created "Object 825 GTS," a seaside underground complex dedicated to housing and repairing naval submarines, storing weapons and fuel, and acting as a safe bunker in case of nuclear attack.

Moscow subway workers spent long hours gouging out granite to build the rockbound complex. When the four-year construction process finished in 1961, Object 825 GTS boasted a 2,000-foot-long (607 m) canal capable of housing six submarines, a hospital, communication centers, food storehouses,

and an ample arsenal of torpedoes, nuclear warheads, and rockets.

The construction of Object 825 GTS turned Balaklava into a military town with closed borders. Residents—almost all of whom worked at the base—were not even permitted to receive visits from family members.

The submarine base remained secret and operational until 1993, when post-Soviet conditions rendered it unnecessary. In 2004, the base opened to the public as a naval museum. The submarines are gone, but the long stone corridors, dark canals, and a few leftover missiles provide plenty of Cold War atmosphere.

Mramornaya Street, Balaklava. The submarine base turned museum is in Balaklava Bay—get a bus from Sevastopol. Ⓝ 44.515236 Ⓔ 33.560650

PRIPYAT

PRIPYAT, KIEV OBLAST

Pripyat's clocks all read 11:55. That's the moment when, on April 26, 1986, the electricity was cut following a meltdown at the Chernobyl nuclear reactor. A day later, Pripyat residents received the following evacuation announcement:

For the attention of the residents of Pripyat! The city council informs you that due to the accident at Chernobyl Power Station in the city of Pripyat, the radioactive conditions in the vicinity are deteriorating . . . Comrades, leaving your residences temporarily, please make sure you have turned the lights, electrical equipment, and water off, and shut the windows. Please keep calm and orderly in the process of this short-term evacuation.

Today Pripyat is a city of abandoned buildings with paint peeling away from the walls, falling in flakes onto dusty shoes, toys, and Communist propaganda posters. Outside the crumbling City Center Gymnasium, a rusting Ferris wheel sits beside a jumble of bumper cars. They are the lone remains of a carnival that was due to open on May 1, 1986.

This somber, silent city seems an unlikely vacation spot, but it is possible to tour the Chernobyl area. A government-issued day pass is obtainable in Kiev. It is deemed safe to walk around Pripyat for only a few hours at a time, and several precautions must be followed to avoid contamination. Visitors must be accompanied by a tour group and are forbidden from touching structures or placing anything on the ground within the exclusion zone. Arms, legs, and feet must be covered, and the trip ends with everyone being screened for radiation using a Geiger counter.

Visitors are free to take photographs, view the reactor from a distance of 100 meters, and even talk to the few remaining residents of Pripyat who disobeyed orders after the blast and returned to their radiation-contaminated homes.

In the 30 years since Pripyat was abandoned, plants and animals have begun to thrive despite the high levels of radioactivity. Tree roots burst through concrete floors, forests encroach on the roads, and animals, such as beavers, boars, wolves, and bears, long vanished from the area, have returned. Free of human influence, the area has a much greater biodiversity than it did before the disaster.

Guided tours are available and depart by bus from Kiev.
Ⓝ 51.405556 Ⓔ 30.056944

ALSO IN UKRAINE

Underwater Museum

Crimea · Over 50 busts of Communist and Socialist figures from the USSR are lined up on stone shelves underwater.

The Swallow's Nest

Gaspra · A castle-like home perched on the very edge of a cliff overlooks the Crimean Sea.

Monastery of the Caves

Kiev · This 1,000-year-old relic-filled cave also hosts an amazing museum of minuscule portraits, documents, and sculptures that must be viewed through a microscope.

Salo Museum

Lviv · A museum dedicated to one of Eastern Europe's essential ingredients: pure pig fat.

Eternity Restaurant

Truskavets · An eatery, run by the local funeral parlor, features the largest coffin in the world.

Pripyat's creaky Ferris wheel has been still since the Chernobyl meltdown caused the town to be abandoned in 1986.

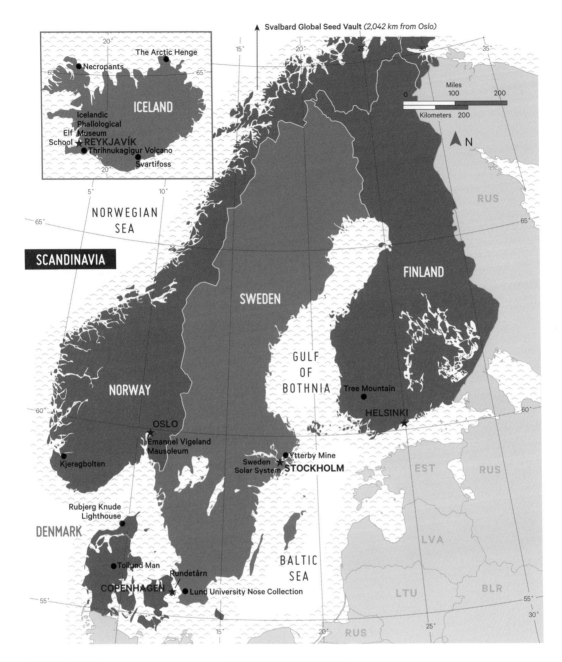

Svalbard Global Seed Vault *(2,042 km from Oslo)*

ICELAND

The Arctic Henge

Necropants

Icelandic
Phallological
Museum
Elf
School ★ REYKJAVÍK
Thrihnukagigur Volcano
Svartifoss

NORWEGIAN
SEA

SCANDINAVIA

NORWAY

Kjeragbolten

OSLO

Emanuel Vigeland
Mausoleum

SWEDEN

GULF
OF
BOTHNIA

FINLAND

Tree Mountain

HELSINKI

Sweden
Solar System STOCKHOLM

Ytterby Mine

RUS

EST

RUS

LVA

Rubjerg Knude
Lighthouse

DENMARK

Tollund Man

COPENHAGEN

Rundetårn

Lund University Nose Collection

BALTIC
SEA

LTU

BLR

RUS

Miles
100   200

Kilometers 200

N

DENMARK
RUBJERG KNUDE LIGHTHOUSE

LØKKEN, HJØRRING

The Rubjerg Knude lighthouse is slowly being swallowed by its suroundings. Built just off the North Sea in 1900, the 75-foot (23 m) tower is now half-buried in sand, the result of coastal erosion, wind, and shifting dunes.

For a few decades, the lighthouse keepers fought against the encroachment. They planted a perimeter of trees and shoveled sand from the courtyard. But it was a losing battle. More sand blew in, hampering views of the sea and forcing the lighthouse to cease

This lighthouse is losing its battle against shifting sands.

operations in 1968. The tower and its surrounding buildings stayed open as a museum and coffee shop until 2002, when the growing dunes threatened to overwhelm the entire operation.

All five of the surrounding buildings are now smothered in sand. The lighthouse, too, will soon be blotted out by the forces of nature. The site is now open for just a few weeks in the summer.

Fyrvejen, Løkken. ⓝ 57.448989 ⓔ 9.777089

RUNDETÅRN

COPENHAGEN

Danish for "round tower," Rundetårn is a cylindrical building, topped with a dome that contains Europe's oldest functioning observatory. Built in 1642—the year of Galileo's death—under the orders of King Christian IV, the tower originally contained a planetarium showing two versions of the solar system: the Galileo-approved, heliocentric model and Danish astronomer Tycho Brahe's geocentric interpretation.

Rundetårn is notable for its internal architecture—it contains no stairs, just a spiral brick path that winds around a central column seven and a half times. The unusual design had a practical purpose: Large, heavy scientific instruments needed to be transported to the top of the tower, and wagons made the job a lot easier.

The Rundetårn observatory operated in conjunction with the University of Copenhagen until 1861, when it was replaced by the new Østervold Observatory, built on the outskirts of town to avoid light pollution.

Rundetårn is now open to the public for stargazing and sightseeing. The tower is also the site of an annual spring unicycle race in which riders pedal up and down the spiral. The current record, set in 1988, is 1:48.7. **Købmagergade 52A, Copenhagen. Take the metro to Nørreport. ❶ 55.681964 ❷ 12.575691**

Come spring, the interior path of Europe's oldest observatory will be filled with unicyclists.

ALSO IN DENMARK

Skeletons of Æbelholt Abbey

Æbelholt · Explore the ruins of a 12th-century abbey and hear the legend of the miracle-working monk who once lived there.

Little Mermaid Statue

Copenhagen · Decapitated, mutilated, and then blown up, this beloved statue and national icon has seen her share of abuse.

Tobacco Museum

Copenhagen · Learn about the long history of tobacco smoking and its assorted paraphernalia and accoutrements.

Hair Jewelry

Frederikshavn · A local-history museum displays examples of the 19th-century fad for jewelry made from human hair.

World Map

Klejtrup Lake · Play mini-golf while traversing a perfect miniature version of the Earth.

Killed in the 4th century BCE and pulled from a peat bog in 1950, the Tollund Man still looks pretty good.

TOLLUND MAN

SILKEBORG, CENTRAL DENMARK

Walking around the Bjældskovdal bog in 1950, brothers Emil and Viggo Højgaard (along with Grethe, Viggo's wife) stumbled upon a body. Believing the man to be the victim of a recent killing, they called the police. Further investigations revealed that he had indeed been murdered—some 2,300 years earlier.

The Tollund Man was found curled in the fetal position with his eyes closed and a serene expression frozen on his face. The cold, acidic, oxygen-starved conditions of the peat bog had kept him remarkably well preserved. His hair, beard stubble, eyelashes, and toenails were all intact, and he was nude, but for a sheepskin cap and wide belt around his waist. A rope was wound tightly around his neck. The Iron Age man had been hanged, likely during a ritual sacrifice.

In 1950, it was not yet known how best to preserve discoveries like Tollund Man. Accordingly, only the head of the original specimen was kept intact. The rest of the body was subjected to various tests to determine his probable age (probably around 40, due to the presence of wisdom teeth and wrinkles) and the conditions surrounding his life and death. Among the details found: Tollund Man was 5 feet 3 inches (1.6 m) tall, his final meal was a gruel made from barley and flaxseed, and his "sacrificers" (read: killers) took the time to close his mouth and eyes after death.

Thousands of "bog bodies" have been discovered in sphagnum swamps across Northern Europe, but the Tollund Man remains the best preserved. His original head and reconstructed body now reside at the Silkeborg Museum. The rope used to end his life is still wrapped around his throat.

Silkeborg Museum, Hovedgårdsvej 7, Silkeborg. A slew of buses stops right in front of the museum.
Ⓝ 56.164444 Ⓔ 9.392778

FINLAND
TREE MOUNTAIN

YLÖJÄRVI, PIRKANMAA

This conical tree-covered hill was not created by nature: It's a planned work of art that was 14 years in the making. Artist Agnes Denes first proposed *Tree Mountain*, a human-made forest on a human-made hill, in 1982. Ten years later, the Finnish government announced that it had approved the project. From 1992 to 1996, 11,000 people each planted a tree on a specially sculpted mound of dirt. Together, the trees form an intricate pattern derived from a combination of the golden ratio and Denes's own pineapple-inspired design.

Each tree belongs to the person who planted it, and their descendants—the site is legally protected for 400 years.

Pinsiönkankaantie 10, Pinsiö. The hill is about a 3-hour drive from Helsinki. Ⓝ 61.571030 Ⓔ 23.477081

ALSO IN FINLAND

Helsinki University Museum

Helsinki · Browse the labyrinthine halls to discover a mid-19th-century Finnish pharmacy, a collection of brass cartography tools, and wax models of infant diseases.

Rock Church

Helsinki · Hidden inside a rocky outcrop is a late-1960s church with rock walls and a wraparound skylight that bathes the space in light. The church has excellent acoustics and hosts concerts.

Veijo Rönkkönen Sculpture Park

Parikkala · See eerie sculptures sporting real human teeth in one of the most important collections of contemporary folk art in Finland.

International Coffee Cup Museum

Posio · Explore worldwide coffee culture through a collection of almost 2,000 cups from over 80 countries.

The Lenin Museum

Tampere · One of the only permanent Lenin museums in the world is located at the Tampere Workers Hall, where Lenin and Stalin met for the first time in 1905.

ICELAND

ICELANDIC PHALLOLOGICAL MUSEUM

REYKJAVÍK

Sigurður Hjartarson began collecting phallic specimens in the 1970s, beginning with a "pizzle"—a whip made from a bull penis. Since then, his phallic collection has grown to enormous proportions.

The museum aims not merely to titillate, but to advance the "ancient science" of phallology, which examines how male genitalia have influenced history, art, psychology, and literature. Devoted to the study and appreciation of mammalian penises, its 280 specimens are drawn from a wide range of animals, including polar bears, badgers, cats, goats, seals, and even a blue whale, whose daunting 5-foot-7-inch (1.7 m) member is the largest in the collection.

The museum also oversees a small collection of *Homo sapiens* specimens, courtesy of men who bequeathed their genitals to the museum. One of the donors, an American, made a cast of his penis—which he dubbed "Elmo"—to be kept in the museum until the real item could be donated. Another, a 95-year-old man from Iceland, decided to contribute his penis so that it might be preserved as an eternal totem of his many youthful indiscretions.

In addition to biological specimens, the museum also features phallic artwork and objects. Following their silver medal win at the 2008 Summer Olympics, 15 members of Iceland's handball team provided casts of their penises. They are painted silver and displayed in a row behind glass—the phallic equivalent of being featured on a cereal box.

Laugavegur 116, 105 Reykjavík. The museum is near the Hlemmur bus station. Ⓝ 64.143033 Ⓦ 21.915643

THE ARCTIC HENGE

RAUFARHÖFN

Located in one of Iceland's most remote northern villages, the Arctic Henge is a colossal piece of stone construction that, when finished, will make Stonehenge look like amateur hour.

Started in 1996, the Arctic Henge project is a monument not only to the country's nordic roots, but also to some of the neo-pagan beliefs that have arisen in certain areas. The piece was inspired by the Eddic poem *Völuspá* (*Prophecy of the Seeress*), taking from it the concept of 72 dwarves who represent the seasons in the world of the poem.

In the Arctic Henge, 72 small blocks, each inscribed with a specific dwarven name, will eventually circle four larger stone monuments, which in turn will surround a central balanced column of massive basalt blocks. Each aspect of the deliberate layout corresponds to some aspect of ancient Norse belief, and when each piece of the monument is installed, visitors will be able to "capture the midnight sun" by viewing it through the various formations at different vantage points depending on the season.

So far, only the imposing central tri-column and one of the four larger gates have been constructed, along with a smattering of the smaller stones.

The Henge is a 90-minute drive from Húsavík, which is a prime spot for whale-watching. Ⓝ 66.462132 Ⓦ 15.962863

The towering Arctic Henge is still a work in progress.

NECROPANTS

HÓLMAVÍK

Some might say it's unseemly to exhume the corpse of a departed friend, flay his skin in one piece from the waist down, and wear that flesh as a pair of leggings. These people do not know about the rich tradition of necropants, a wealth-attracting good-luck garment.

According to the Museum of Icelandic Sorcery and Witchcraft, necropants were a real thing in 17th-century Iceland. The rules were complex. First, you had to get permission from a living man to use his skin after he died. When he kicked the bucket, you would wait around for the burial formalities to conclude, then approach the grave and start digging. Corpse exhumed, you cut around the waist and peeled the skin from the bottom half of the body, making sure to keep it all in one piece.

The next step was to steal a coin from a poor widow. This coin was placed into the scrotum of the necropants, where it would magically attract more money, leaving the wearer with a groin full of coins at all times. Once you'd had enough of the great wealth, or the necropants began to chafe, you would have to find another wearer to step into the magical leggings. In this way, the prosperity was passed down for generations.

A pair of necropants is on view at the museum, in a softly lit alcove, standing on a bed of coins. **Museum of Icelandic Sorcery and Witchcraft, Höfðagata 8-10, Hólmavík. The village of Hólmavík is a 4-hour bus ride from Reykjavík. Ⓝ 65.706546 Ⓦ 21.665667**

SVARTIFOSS

KIRKJUBÆJARKLAUSTUR, SKAFTÁRHREPPUR

Svartifoss, meaning "black fall," is a modest waterfall in terms of height, width, and force, but its backdrop of black hexagonal columns makes for a rare and splendid sight. The columns are basalt crystals, formed from lava flows that cooled over centuries—the same process that created the textured walls of Fingal's Cave in Scotland. Parts of the crystals often break off and plunge into the river, so mind the sharp rocks at the base of the falls.

785 Fagurholsmyri, Skaftafell National Park, Kirkjubæjarklaustur. Bus services to Skaftafell run daily from Reykjavík during the summer months. Svartifoss is an hour-long hike from the Skaftafell National Park visitors' center. Ⓝ 64.020978 Ⓦ 16.981623

ALSO IN ICELAND

Santa's Workshop

Akureyri · The year-round home of Santa Claus—or a very convincing lookalike—is decked out like a gingerbread house.

Bjarnarhöfn Shark Museum

Bjarnarhöfn · Get a taste of Iceland's fishing industry and sample a famous Icelandic delicacy: fermented shark.

Blue Lagoon

Grindavík · A medicinal spa built around the discharge of a geothermal energy plant.

Jökulsárlón

Höfn · Iceland's largest lagoon is home to stunning multicolored icebergs.

Svartifoss: It's fun to say, and even more enchanting to visit.

THRIHNUKAGIGUR VOLCANO

BLUE MOUNTAINS COUNTRY PARK, BLÁFJÖLL

Volcanoes are usually best admired from a safe distance, but Iceland's Thrihnukagigur is so geologically unique, it is possible to go right inside the heart of the volcano. The three calderas of Thrihnukagigur have lain dormant for so long—the last eruption was over 4,000 years ago—brave visitors can actually descend into the volcano's colorful magma chamber.

An open elevator takes you over 600 feet down into the depths of the enormous crater, which is so large it could fit the Statue of Liberty in its entirety. Inside the cavern, you're met with a surreal sight. Rather than the jet-black obsidian you might expect, the craggy walls are covered in a gleaming,

pearlescent rainbow of color that almost makes the cave look like it's composed purely of gems.

This is the only place on Earth where you can take a cable lift into the heart of a volcano, thanks to a strange natural phenomenon. Usually, after an eruption, the roiling magma cools and solidifies in place, effectively plugging the opening. But somehow the fathoms of magma that once boiled inside one of Thrihnukagigur's peaks sank back down into the earth, leaving behind a massive open cavern. **It is a moderate 2-mile hike (about 45 minutes long) through the Icelandic highlands to the Thrihnukagigur summit. Each excursion into the volcano's depths lasts around an hour or two. N 63.998920 W 21.697522**

A cable lift brings visitors to the glittering heart of a volcano.

ICELANDIC ELF SCHOOL

REYKJAVÍK

When Icelandic member of parliament Árni Johnsen escaped unharmed from a car crash in 2010, he knew whom to credit for his survival: elves. After rolling five times, the politician's SUV came to rest beside a 30-ton boulder. Johnsen, believing that multiple generations of elves called that boulder home, concluded that they used their magic to save him. When roadwork later required the removal of the boulder, he claimed it for himself, transporting it to his home to ensure the elves would continue to watch over him.

Johnsen's beliefs are not unusual. According to Icelandic folklore, thousands of elves, fairies, dwarves, and gnomes—collectively known as "hidden people"—live in rocks and trees throughout the country. It is no wonder, then, that the world's only elf school is located in Reykjavík.

Historian Magnús Skarphéðinsson, who has spent decades documenting people's encounters with elves, established the school in 1991. Classes focus on the distinguishing characteristics of Iceland's 13 varieties of hidden people. The school also offers five-hour classes for travelers, which include a tour of Reykjavík's elf habitats. Students receive a diploma in "hidden people research."

Skarphéðinsson has never seen an elf. His knowledge of their appearance and behavior comes from the hundreds of testimonies he has collected from people who claim to have made contact with hidden people.

Though Skarphéðinsson has devoted 30 years to the subject and considers himself the foremost authority on elves, he maintains a sense of humor about it all. At the end of class, he serves homemade coffee and pancakes and tells stories about the people who come up to him to say, "I swear I'm not on drugs, but I saw the strangest thing . . ."

108 Síðumúli, Reykjavík. Buses run on Suðurlandsbraut or Háaleitisbraut. ⓝ 64.133062 ⓦ 21.876143

NORWAY
SVALBARD GLOBAL SEED VAULT

LONGYEARBYEN, SVALBARD

A winter night in Longyearbyen lasts four months. In the ice-covered mountains, the darkness is broken only by a slim concrete building that emits a pale blue glow as it overlooks the 1,000-resident town. The simple structure offers no hint as to what's protected inside: a collection of seeds that could save humanity.

Humanity's genetic safe-deposit box

Due to the loss of genetic diversity among commercially cultivated crops, which tend to be grown from clonal monocultures, many worldwide food crops are at risk of disease. Mutated strains of fungus, or a new bacterium, could potentially wipe out an entire world crop in a matter of months, causing massive food shortages. The Svalbard Global Seed Vault was established by the Norwegian government in 2008 to function as a sort of genetic safe-deposit box.

The facility has the capacity to conserve 4.5 million seed samples. Under the current temperature conditions in the vault, which are similar to those in a kitchen freezer, the seed samples can remain viable to begin new crops for anywhere from 2,000 to 20,000 years.

Svalbard was chosen as the location because it is tectonically stable and its permafrost provides natural refrigeration in case of a power failure. There is no permanent staff at the seed bank, but

it is monitored constantly using electronic surveillance. Access to the vaults, open only to employees, requires passing four locked doors protected by coded access keys.

To get to Longyearbyen, you'll need to fly from Oslo with a stopover in Tromsø. While the seed vaults are off limits, the building itself is a dramatic sight surrounded by banks of snow. Other winter activities in the tiny town include dog sledding and reindeer spotting. ⓝ 78.238166 ⓔ 15.447236

Is the Kjeragbolten stone stable enough to stand on? There's one way to find out.

KJERAGBOLTEN

FORSAND, ROGALAND

Kjeragbolten is a boulder wedged in a mountain crevasse, 3,228 feet (984 m) above the ground. It is a favored spot for BASE jumpers, who hurl themselves from the cliff toward the spectacular fjord below. Visitors without vertigo are welcome to step onto the boulder for a unique photo opportunity—there are no fences restricting access.

Øygardstøl, Forsand. In the summer months, a bus runs from Stavanger to Øygardstøl, where the hike to Kjeragbolten begins. Wear appropriate shoes and be prepared for a steep climb. The journey takes about 3 hours each way. Don't step onto the rock if it's raining or damp. Ⓝ 59.022535 Ⓔ 6.581841

ALSO IN NORWAY

Saltstraumen Maelstrom

Bodø · Behold the world's strongest whirlpool, created by a powerful tidal current.

Hessdalen AMS

Hessdalen · A remote research station devoted to unlocking the mystery behind floating lights seen in a Norwegian valley.

Mølen

Larvik · Found on Norway's largest stone beach, these 230 large man-made rock piles, or *mols*, are in fact an ancient cemetery dating back to 250 BCE.

Steinsdalsfossen Waterfall

Norheimsund · Walk the path behind this 164-foot-high (50 m) waterfall and see it from the other side.

EMANUEL VIGELAND MAUSOLEUM

OSLO

Brother to the more-celebrated Gustav Vigeland, whose eccentric sculptures occupy a prominent park in central Oslo, Emanuel Vigeland will be remembered through his own strange and enchanting artistic work.

The Emanuel Vigeland Museum serves double duty as a mausoleum designed and decorated by Vigeland himself. Visitors enter the building by stooping through a heavy, low iron door. Inside, a large, darkened, barrel-vaulted room is completely covered with paintings that show human life from conception to death in explicitly erotic scenes. The 8,611-square-foot (800 m²) fresco took Vigeland 20 years to finish.

Entering the mausoleum is a solemn, even haunting, experience. Even the quietest footstep echoes across the barrel-vaulted ceiling for up to 14 seconds. A flashlight is needed to reveal the room's dark, painted walls.

Vigeland began construction on the building in 1926 with the intention of later filling it with his paintings and sculptures. Only one wall and the ceiling of the barrel-vaulted room were to be covered by paintings; the rest would be left bare to showcase other works.

Tasked with designing his own mausoleum, Emanuel Vigeland created a room where sounds echo for up to 14 seconds.

When Vigeland decided that the museum would also serve as his mausoleum, he had the windows sealed with bricks, lending the entire building an eerie atmosphere. He completed the fresco, finding inspiration in the burial chambers of antiquity and drawing especially from the dramatic stories of creation and original sin from Christianity. Named *Vita* ("Life"), the fresco focuses on humanity's sexual instinct portrayed by naked bodies captured in an impressive array of intimate acts.

After Vigeland's death, his ashes were put to rest in an urn that sits above the main entrance. Now run by a private foundation, the museum was opened to the public in 1959, more than a decade after Vigeland's death.

Today, the museum is open for only a few hours each week, but it plays host to several concerts (sometimes involving didgeridoos) throughout the year.

Grimelundsveien 8, Oslo. Take the metro to Slemdal. Ⓝ 59.947256 Ⓔ 10.692641

SWEDEN

YTTERBY MINE

STOCKHOLM

39
Y
Yttrium
88.906

Army lieutenant and part-time chemist Carl Axel Arrhenius was excited when, in 1787, he came across a strange, heavy black rock in an old quarry near the Swedish village of Ytterby. Arrhenius named the newly discovered substance ("elements" were not yet recognized) "ytterbite" after the town. A plaque now marks the site.

Also present in the quarry was a crude mineral called yttria, which was the oxidized form of yttrium. Silver yttria contained four rare silvery white elements: ytterbium (now used in electrodes and lasers), terbium (used to make microprocessor chips), erbium (used for medical lasers), and yttrium (used to make phosphors for LEDs), making the site the single richest source of elemental discoveries in the world, and giving the town of Ytterby an outsize presence on the periodic table.

The mine is located in the middle of Ytterby, which is a 40-minute drive from downtown Stockholm. Ⓝ 59.428524 Ⓔ 18.334887

SWEDEN SOLAR SYSTEM

STOCKHOLM

Created at a scale of 1:20 million, this country-spanning model is the world's largest representation of the solar system. It is anchored by Stockholm's spherical Globe Arena building, which represents the sun. The inner planets, all appropriately scaled, are dotted around Stockholm and its suburbs.

Further north are Pluto—still part of the lineup, despite its 2006 reclassification as a dwarf planet—and fellow trans-Neptunian objects Ixion, Sedna, and Eris. A plaque in Sweden's northernmost city of Kiruna, 592 miles (950 km) away, marks the spot for "termination shock," the point at which solar wind slows down and causes changes in the magnetic field.

In 2011, vandals snatched Uranus from the town of Gävle, 100 miles (1,600 km) from Stockholm. But in October 2012, a new model of Uranus appeared a few miles south, in the village of Lövstabruk. (The planet's new location reflects its orbit position when closest to the sun, so the solar system model is still accurate.)

Globentorget 2, Johanneshov, Stockholm. To see the sun, get the subway to Gullmarsplan. To see all the planets, you'll need to plan a road trip.
Ⓝ 59.294167 Ⓔ 18.080816

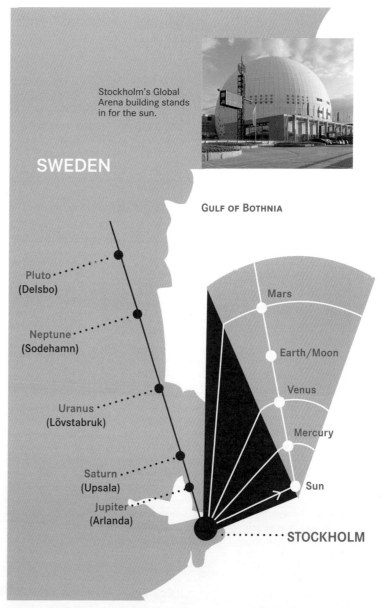

Stockholm's Global Arena building stands in for the sun.

SWEDEN

GULF OF BOTHNIA

Pluto (Delsbo)

Neptune (Sodehamn)

Uranus (Lövstabruk)

Saturn (Upsala)

Jupiter (Arlanda)

Mars

Earth/Moon

Venus

Mercury

Sun

STOCKHOLM

The planets of Earth's solar system are laid out—to scale—throughout the country.

ALSO IN SWEDEN

UFO Memorial

Ängelholm · A memorial dedicated to a Swedish hockey player's supposed encounter with aliens, during which he says he received recipes for natural medical remedies.

Drottningholm Palace Theater

Drottningholm · The royal theater still uses 18th-century levers and pulleys to put on shows, in what they bill as the world's most genuine early opera experience.

Ven Island

Øresund Strat · Explore the site of the first modern observatory, built by Tycho Brahe.

Vasa Museum

Stockholm · The home of the hulking remains of the *Vasa*, a 17th-century warship that was meant to be the greatest vessel of her time—but sank in a matter of minutes on her maiden voyage.

SWEDEN

LUND UNIVERSITY NOSE COLLECTION

LUND, SCANIA

The hundred-strong nose collection at Lund University contains plaster casts of some notable Scandinavian snouts, including a cast of the metal prosthetic famed Danish astronomer Tycho Brahe wore after losing the bridge of his nose during a sword duel.

Lund University, Sandgatan 3, Lund. The noses are in the university's Museum of Student Life, a 10-minute walk from Lund's Central train station. ℕ 55.705673 Ⓔ 13.195374 ⇥

⇥ Post–World War I Facial Prosthetics

Soldiers fighting in World War I had to adapt to a new set of battle rules. Instead of fighting one another at close range, armies dug trenches and spent months living in them under appalling conditions, attempting to slowly destroy the enemy by launching gas grenades and firing machine guns.

A postwar soldier without and with his facial prosthetic.

It was machine guns, a recent addition to the warfare arsenal, that caught so many soldiers off guard. Unaccustomed to rapid-fire weapons, men would poke their heads out of the trench and be attacked by a hail of bullets, one of which would often hit them square in the face.

Injuries that resulted in facial disfigurement made reintegration into civilian life particularly difficult. In addition to bearing the mental scars of war, soldiers would return home looking like grotesque versions of themselves—a hole where an eye should be; a tongue lolling in the absence of a lower jaw; a ragged hole in the cheek that exposed a row of teeth. Mirrors were banned in convalescent hospitals to protect men from the devastation of seeing themselves.

Thousands of British soldiers with facial injuries underwent surgery at the skilled hands of Harold Gillies, a New Zealand–born surgeon who performed an early version of plastic surgery at Queen's Hospital in Sidcup, England. Gillies's groundbreaking reconstructive techniques gave many men the confidence to show themselves in public. For those whose faces could not be healed, there was another option: a mask.

English sculptor Francis Derwent Wood (at the Masks for Facial Disfigurement Department in the Third London General Hospital) and Pennsylvanian sculptor Anna Coleman Ladd (at the American Red Cross Studio for Portrait Masks in Paris) were the two most prominent mask makers, creating customized, hand-painted pieces of galvanized copper to conceal soldiers' wounds. Each mask took weeks to make. The process began with a plaster cast of an injured man's face and ended with the painstaking application of skin-colored paint, a glass eye, and hair or brushstrokes for eyebrows. A pair of wire eyeglasses or a ribbon held each mask against the face.

Plaster casts of injured faces.

Asia

The Middle East
IRAN • IRAQ • ISRAEL • PALESTINE • LEBANON • QATAR
SAUDI ARABIA • SYRIA • UNITED ARAB EMIRATES • YEMEN

South and Central Asia
AFGHANISTAN • BANGLADESH • BHUTAN
INDIA • KAZAKHSTAN • KYRGYZSTAN • PAKISTAN • SRI LANKA
TURKEY • TURKMENISTAN

East Asia
CHINA • HONG KONG • TAIWAN • JAPAN • NORTH KOREA
SOUTH KOREA

Southeast Asia
CAMBODIA • INDONESIA • LAOS • MALAYSIA • MYANMAR
PHILIPPINES • SINGAPORE • THAILAND • VIETNAM

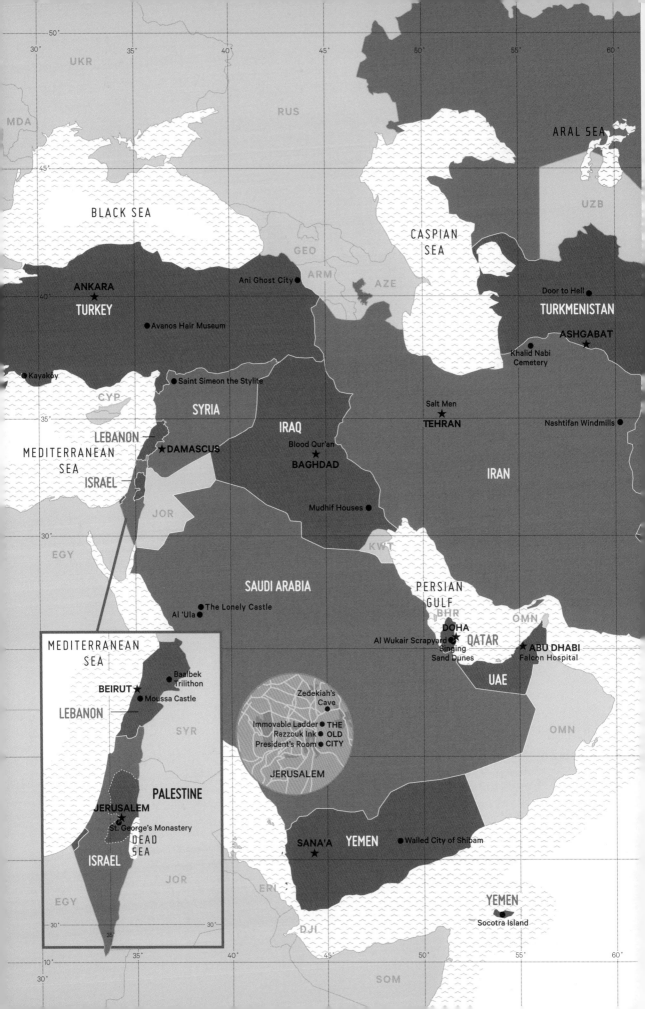

UKR

MDA

BLACK SEA

RUS

ARAL SEA

UZB

CASPIAN
SEA

GEO

ARM

AZE

ANKARA

TURKEY

Ani Ghost City

● Avanos Hair Museum

Door to Hell ●

TURKMENISTAN

ASHGABAT ★

● Kayaköy

CYP

● Saint Simeon the Stylite

SYRIA

Khalid Nabi
Cemetery

LEBANON

MEDITERRANEAN
SEA

★ DAMASCUS

IRAQ

Blood Qur'an
★
BAGHDAD

Salt Men
★
TEHRAN

Nashtifan Windmills ●

ISRAEL

JOR

IRAN

Mudhif Houses ●

KWT

SAUDI ARABIA

PERSIAN
GULF

BHR

● The Lonely Castle

Al 'Ula ●

DOHA
★
Al Wukair Scrapyard ● QATAR
Singing
Sand Dunes

OMN

★ ABU DHABI
Falcon Hospital

MEDITERRANEAN
SEA

UAE

OMN

BEIRUT ★

Baalbek
Trilithon

● Moussa Castle

Zedekiah's
Cave ●

LEBANON

SYR

Immovable Ladder ● ● THE
Razzouk Ink ● ● OLD
President's Room ● ● CITY

PALESTINE

JERUSALEM

JERUSALEM ★
St. George's Monastery

DEAD
SEA

SANA'A
★

YEMEN

● Walled City of Shibam

ISRAEL

JOR

EGY

ERI

EGY

DJI

SOM

YEMEN

● Socotra Island

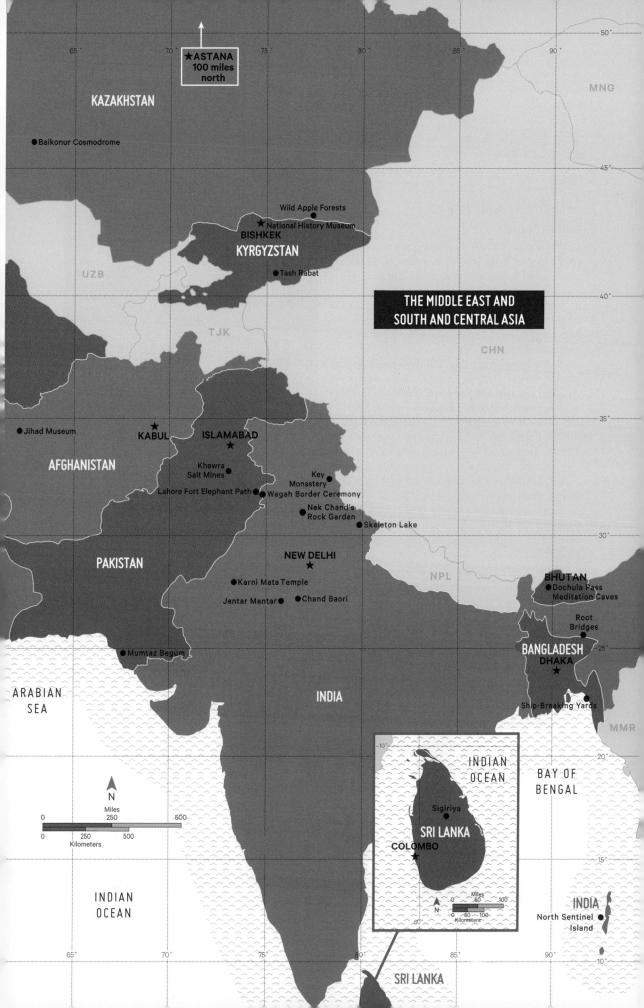

★ASTANA
100 miles
north

KAZAKHSTAN

●Baikonur Cosmodrome

MNG

Wild Apple Forests●
★ ●National History Museum
BISHKEK
KYRGYZSTAN

UZB

●Tash Rabat

TJK

CHN

THE MIDDLE EAST AND
SOUTH AND CENTRAL ASIA

●Jihad Museum

★
KABUL

★ISLAMABAD
★

AFGHANISTAN

Khewra
Salt Mines●
Lahore Fort Elephant Path●
●Wagah Border Ceremony

Key
Monastery●

Nek Chand's●
Rock Garden
●Skeleton Lake

PAKISTAN

NEW DELHI
★

NPL

BHUTAN
●Dochula Pass
Meditation Caves

●Karni Mata Temple

Jantar Mantar● ●Chand Baori

●Root
Bridges

BANGLADESH
DHAKA
★

●Mumtaz Begum

ARABIAN
SEA

INDIA

Ship-Breaking Yards
●

MMR

Miles
0   250   500

N

0   250   500
Kilometers

-10°

INDIAN
OCEAN

BAY OF
BENGAL

●Sigiriya

SRI LANKA

COLOMBO
★

Miles
0   50   100

N

0   50   100
Kilometers

-80°

INDIA

North Sentinel●
Island

INDIAN
OCEAN

SRI LANKA

The Middle East

IRAN
SALT MEN OF CHEHRABAD

HAMZEHLU, ZANJAN

In 1994, workers at the Chehrabad salt mine uncovered a partial body buried in a tunnel. Naturally mummified by the salt, the corpse had long white hair and a beard, and was about 35 years old when he died, sometime around the 4th century. On his single preserved foot was a leather boot. Surrounding him were three iron knives, a rope, some pottery fragments, and a walnut.

Salt mummies are rare, but the surprising find was the first of many at Chehrabad. Between 1994 and 2010, six naturally preserved bodies—all male—were found in the mine. Following careful examination of the specimens, archaeologists estimated that the bodies ranged from 1,400 to 2,400 years old. The six men were likely all salt miners who were crushed and trapped when sections of the mine collapsed. Salt pulled the moisture out of their bodies and naturally mummified them.

The head and left foot of the 1994 mummy are on display at the National Museum of Iran in Tehran. Four of the other bodies were initially exhibited at Rakhtshuikhaneh Museum in Zanjan, but poor display methods resulted in bacterial damage. The

The salt-cured, silver-haired head of an ancient miner.

quartet of bodies is now on display in airtight cases at Zanjan Archaeology Museum.

The sixth mummy remains in the mine, as it is too fragile to be moved. In 2008, Chehrabad's mining permit was revoked, allowing archaeologists to study the area and piece together a portrait of the ancient miners' lives.

National Museum of Iran, 30 Tir Avenue, Emam Khomeini Avenue, Tehran. Ⓝ 35.687044 Ⓔ 51.414611

KHALID NABI CEMETERY

GOLESTAN

In the stunning green hills of northern Iran is a cemetery with headstones distinctly resembling male and female genitalia. Stone phalluses jut out from the ground at odd angles; lower to the ground are the rounded, clover-shaped stones. All told, the cemetery has a total of 600 monuments to sex organs sprawling across the vibrant landscape.

In a country known for its strict religious law, a cemetery dotted with penis-shaped headstones up to 6.5 feet (2 m) tall tends to stand out. Visitors can tell at once that the cemetery was created in a much different era. Due to the cemetery's proximity to the Turkmenistan border,

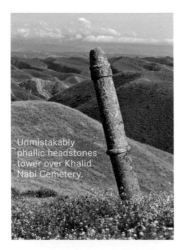

Unmistakably phallic headstones tower over Khalid Nabi Cemetery.

some experts suggest that phallus-worshipping peoples from Central Asia and India created it—although conclusive proof of this does not exist. There has been

little scholarship on the cemetery's origins within Iran because of a strong national embarrassment over the suggestive stones.

Aside from being home to hundreds of penis tombstones, the cemetery also contains the hilltop grave of Khalid Nabi, who was a Christian prophet from Yemen who died in the 4th century. His tomb—which has a conventional, non-anatomical shape—is a pilgrimage site for Turkmens, who place ribbons on his shrine. The combination of pilgrims and curious tourists makes for an odd mix of playful and pious visitors to Khalid Nabi.

The cemetery is about a 2-hour drive north of the city of Gonbad-e Kavus. Ⓝ 37.745472 Ⓔ 55.411236

NASHTIFAN

Located on the arid and wind-swept plains of northeastern Iran, 30 miles (48.3 km) from the Afghan border, the small village of Nashtifan is keeping ancient traditions alive amid the winds of change. The town is home to some of the earliest windmills in the world, and the structures are still in use today.

Nashtifan is known for its uniquely powerful winds. The village's name is derived from words that translate to "storm's sting." Along the southern edge of town, a towering 65-foot-tall (19.8 m) earthen wall shelters residents from abrasive gales. The high wall houses over two dozen vertical axis windmills that date back to ancient Persian times. It's estimated the structures, made of clay, straw, and wood, are around 1,000 years old and were used for milling grain into flour.

During turbulent winter months, the handcrafted wooden blades whirl with a surprising velocity to power grindstones. With periodic repairs, these well-built turbines could continue to function for centuries, so long as there are caretakers willing to maintain them. For now, an amiable custodian named Ali Muhammad Etebari looks after the windmills on a volunteer basis. **The closest international airport is Mashhad. From there it's roughly a 4-hour drive to the windmills.**
Ⓝ **34.431635** Ⓔ **60.174789**

ALSO IN IRAN

Shah Cheragh

Shiraz · Mirrors and glass shards cover every inch of this beautiful mosque.

A thousand years later and still in use, these windmills are a source of local pride.

IRAQ

SADDAM HUSSEIN'S BLOOD QUR'AN

BAGHDAD

On his sixtieth birthday in 1997, Saddam Hussein requested a special gift: a Qur'an written in his own blood. In Islam, blood is considered *najis*, or ritually unclean. A Qur'an written in blood, therefore, is *haraam*—a sinful act of disrespect against the holy book. But none of this concerned Saddam. Over two years, Islamic calligrapher Abbas Shakir Joudi transcribed the holy book's 336,000 words using, if reports are to be believed, a total of 50 pints of blood collected from the dictator at regular donation sessions.

The 605-page "Blood Qur'an" went on display in 2000, housed behind glass in a marble building at the Umm al-Qura mosque complex in Baghdad. It made a fitting addition to the mosque, which was built in Saddam's honor to commemorate the tenth anniversary of the Gulf War.

Then came the 2003 invasion of Iraq and the fall of Saddam. As Baghdad burned and looting ensued, mosque leaders removed the Qur'an from display and hid it in a vault. Since Saddam's execution, the bloodied pages have been in an odd limbo—their very existence is forbidden within Islam, but it is also haraam for a Qur'an to be destroyed.

Umm al-Qura mosque, Baghdad. The Blood Qur'an is not on public display, but at least one journalist has convinced mosque clerics to bring a page out of storage for a quick look. Ⓝ 33.338273 Ⓔ 44.297161

MUDHIF HOUSES

MESOPOTAMIAN MARSHES

For thousands of years, *mudhifs*—large, arched communal huts made from reeds—have served as social and ceremonial hubs for the Marsh Arabs, or Madan, of southern Iraq. Weddings, dispute resolutions, religious celebrations, and community meetings all traditionally take place within the structures.

To build a mudhif, the Madan assemble 30-foot (9 m) lengths of reeds into bunches and bend them into arches. Rows of these arched columns form the basic structure of the house. Woven reed mats and latticed panels fill the gaps, forming the ceiling and walls. Each tribe's sheikh collects tributes from families in order to maintain the mudhif.

After the Gulf War in 1991, Saddam Hussein's regime drained the marshes as an act of revenge against those who had taken refuge there after participating in antigovernment uprisings, transforming the marshes into desert. With their food supply eliminated, about 100,000 Marsh Arabs fled, abandoning their traditional way of life.

With the 2003 defeat of Hussein came the removal of levees and the slow return of water to the marshes. However, droughts, new dams, and upstream irrigation projects have since reduced the levels again. A small number of Madan communities have returned to their old homes and rebuilt their mudhifs, but their ongoing survival in the marshes is far from assured.

The marshes are about 20 miles (32 km) northwest of Basra. Ⓝ 31.040000 Ⓔ 47.025000

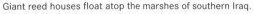

Giant reed houses float atop the marshes of southern Iraq.

ISRAEL
THE IMMOVABLE LADDER AT THE CHURCH OF THE HOLY SEPULCHRE

JERUSALEM

Venerated as the site of the crucifixion, burial, and resurrection of Jesus, the Church of the Holy Sepulchre is perhaps the world's most sacred Christian pilgrimage site. It is also the location of a 150-year-old argument over a ladder.

Under an 1852 mandate, the care of the Church of the Holy Sepulchre is shared by no fewer than six Christian denominations: the Greek Orthodox, Armenian Apostolic, Roman Catholic, Coptic, Ethiopian Orthodox, and Syriac Orthodox churches. Upkeep of the Holy Sepulchre's edifice is carefully divided into sections. While some duties are shared, others belong exclusively to a particular sect. A set of complicated rules governs the transit rights through each section, and some remain hotly disputed. Arguments and fistfights over territory and boundaries are not uncommon.

One such area is a small section of the roof that is disputed between the Copts and Ethiopians. At any given time, at least one Coptic monk sits on a chair placed on a particular spot to express claim to the section. On a stifling summer day in 2002, a monk moved his chair eight inches over, to find shade. This was interpreted as a hostile act and violation of boundaries, and 11 were hospitalized after the fight that ensued.

The Church of the Holy Sepulchre's "immovable ladder" is a centuries-old symbol of this extreme territoriality. During the mid-1700s, a man belonging

Five wooden rungs have caused countless squabbles over the centuries.

to an unknown sect placed the ladder on a ledge against an exterior second-floor wall of the church. With the fear of inciting violence, no one has dared touch it since—except when it disappeared in 1997. A mischievous tourist allegedly plucked it from the ledge and hid it behind an altar, where it remained undiscovered for weeks. The ladder has since been put back into its "appropriate" spot.

Christian Quarter, Old City, Jerusalem. Ⓝ 31.778444 Ⓔ 35.229750

ZEDEKIAH'S CAVE/SOLOMON'S QUARRIES

JERUSALEM

Beneath the Muslim Quarter in Jerusalem's Old City is an underground quarry that goes by two names: Zedekiah's Cave and Solomon's Quarries. The names reflect the two main legends that surround this 750-foot-long (228.6 m) collection of caverns.

The first story is that King Zedekiah fled through the cave to escape from attacking Babylonians around 587 BCE. At the time, the legend goes, the cave extended all the way to Jericho—a distance of about 13 miles (21 km). The Babylonians chased Zedekiah to Jericho, capturing and blinding him. The dripping water in the cave is thus known as Zedekiah's Tears. The second story involves King Solomon, who is fabled to have used stones from the cave to build the First Temple in the 10th century BCE.

There is no archaeological evidence to support either premise. However, chisel markings on the walls suggest Zedekiah's Cave was one of the quarries that supplied limestone for King Herod's Second Temple and Temple Mount expansion. The stones of the Western Wall (also called the Wailing Wall)—Judaism's most sacred prayer site—may indeed have come from this cave.

Sultan Suleiman Street, near Damascus Gate, Jerusalem. Ⓝ 31.768967 Ⓔ 35.213878

President's Room

JERUSALEM

Just south of the Old City on Mount Zion is a building that houses two holy sites. On the ground floor is the Tomb of King David; upstairs is the Upper Room, or Cenacle—the location of the Last Supper.

Less conspicuous is the small domed chamber on the roof, known as the President's Room. From 1948 to 1967, when Jordan controlled East Jerusalem, Jews were prevented from visiting sacred places in the Old City, such as the Western Wall and the Mount of Olives. During this time, Mount Zion was one of the closest vantage points for viewing the forbidden sites. The Ministry of Religious Affairs established the President's Room so that Israel's first head of state, Chaim Weizmann, could keep watch over the Western Wall.

Weizmann never used the room. But his successor, President Yitzhak Ben-Zvi, did. Three times a year, he would ascend the stairs to the dome and look toward the Temple Mount.

Mount Zion, Jerusalem. The building is just southwest of the Zion Gate. Ⓝ 31.771639 Ⓔ 35.229014

ALSO IN ISRAEL

Museum on the Seam

Jerusalem · This collection of contemporary sociopolitical art sits on the border between East and West Jerusalem.

Razzouk Ink

JERUSALEM

As the sole surviving pilgrimage-tattoo business, Razzouk Ink is a place where ancient artifacts meet contemporary machines and rich history intersects with modern technology.

Just inside the Jaffa Gate in Jerusalem's Old City, a big sign above a tiny shop reads TATTOO WITH HERITAGE SINCE 1300. For over 700 years the Razzouk family has been tattooing marks of faith. As Coptic Christians who settled in Jerusalem generations ago, the family had learned the craft in Egypt, where the devout wear similar inked inscriptions. Evidence of such tattoos dates back at least as far as the 8th century in Egypt and the 6th century in the Holy Land, where Procopius of Gaza wrote of tattooed Christians bearing designs of crosses and Christ's name. Early tattoos served as a way for indigenous Christians in the Middle East and Egypt to self-identify. Later, as the faithful came to the Holy Land on pilgrimage, the practice expanded to offer these travelers permanent evidence of their devotion and peregrination.

Razzouk Ink's stone walls and exposed beams lend antique character to the space. A museum-like case holds heirlooms, and an exhibition of pictures on the walls offers glimpses into the family's past. Pilgrims' accounts dating to the late 16th century show how purveyors such as the Razzouks must have tattooed back then, with sewing needles bound to the end of a wooden handle.

13 Greek Catholic Patriarchate St., Old City of Jerusalem Ⓝ 31.777236 Ⓔ 35.228100

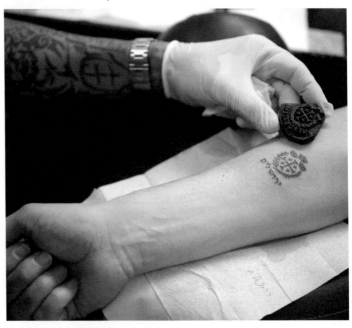

A permanent reminder of one's pilgrimage.

PALESTINE
ST. GEORGE'S MONASTERY

WEST BANK

Clinging to a cliff on the edge of the Wadi Qelt gorge is a Greek Orthodox monastery that's endured many centuries of turmoil and destruction.

The original monastery was founded in the 5th century by a group of cave-dwelling hermits. They chose the site because it was located next to the cave where the prophet Elijah is said to have been fed by ravens during the 9th century BCE.

A Persian invasion in the 7th century drove out the hermits and left the monastery in ruins. Around 500 years later, Crusaders rebuilt St. George's, only to be driven from the site following the Islamic re-conquest of Jerusalem.

The late 19th century saw St. George's restored once again. The monastery is now home to two churches, a small group of Greek Orthodox monks, and the tombs

Monks have been secluding themselves in this cliffside retreat since the 5th century.

of the five hermits who got the whole thing started.

A 15-minute drive from St. George's is the Mount of Temptation—so named because, according to the Bible, it is the place where Jesus was tempted by the devil. This mountain has its own cliffside monastery, established in the 6th century, which has only a single permanent resident. There is also a nearby collection of hermit caves—some of which are said to still occasionally be inhabited by ascetic monks.

Wadi Qelt, West Bank. St. George's is a 20-minute drive from Jerusalem, followed by a 15-minute hike or short camel ride. Ⓝ 31.844452 Ⓔ 35.414085

LEBANON
MOUSSA CASTLE

BEITEDDINE, CHOUF

Moussa al Mamaari's desire to build a castle began in 1945 at the age of 14. Beaten by his teacher and mocked by his schoolyard sweetheart, Moussa vowed to rise above his impoverished origins and live in a castle of his own design.

It took decades of hard work, but Moussa got his wish. After dropping out of school to help his uncle restore old buildings, 20-year-old Moussa used his earnings to buy a plot of land in the Chouf mountains. There, unassisted, he lugged 6,500 stones into place; carved animals, geometric patterns, and plants into them; and slowly assembled the castle's walls.

The three-story Moussa Castle was built by one man over a lifetime.

Moussa Castle, with its medieval ramparts, turrets, moat, and drawbridge, opened to the public in 1967. Moussa filled the castle's three levels with thousands of artfully arranged weapons, mannequins in army uniforms, a two-headed taxidermy lamb, and a wax-figure re-creation of the Last Supper featuring an oddly maniacal-looking Jesus.

As for Moussa's childhood doubters, they receive their own tribute: One room is devoted to a classroom scene in which a wax-figure teacher, face contorted with rage, strikes a cowering student.

Moussa Castle is in the heart of the Chouf mountains between Deir Al Qamar and Beiteddine, south of Beirut. Ⓝ 33.700277 Ⓔ 35.583333

It isn't clear how the Romans moved this 1,000-ton stone.

BAALBEK TRILITHON

BAALBEK, BAALBEK

In 15 BCE, when the city of Baalbek was a Roman settlement by the name of Heliopolis, Emperor Augustus ordered the construction of a grand and mighty temple. Dedicated to the god Jupiter, the temple was built on a layered base of massive foundation stones—so massive that it is unclear how they could have ever been maneuvered into place.

Just six columns are left of the Temple of Jupiter, but its base is mostly intact. On the western side are its three largest stone blocks, collectively known as a trilithon. Each block is 65 feet long, 10 feet wide, and 14 feet deep (20 m × 3 m × 4 m), and weighs in at around 800 tons. They are among the largest monoliths in history—but one mile away, in an ancient quarry, is an even bigger block, known as the Stone of the Pregnant Woman. This stone, weighing approximately 1,000 tons, is half-embedded in the ground, jutting up at an angle like a capsizing ship.

Given that even the largest modern transport equipment would struggle with such hefty stones, the presence of the trilithon and its even heavier quarry counterpart has perplexed archaeologists. A combination of winches, patience, and enormous manpower was surely involved in lifting the stones, but conspiracy theories abound. One hypothesis posits that beneath the temple is a launch pad that extraterrestrials used for their intergalactic spacecraft.

Baalbek is 53 miles (85.3 km) northeast of Beirut. Minibuses depart from the Cola intersection.
Ⓝ 34.006944 Ⓔ 36.203889

....

QATAR
AL WUKAIR SCRAPYARD

QATAR

As the crow flies, the scrapyard in Al Wukair is only 12 miles from the center of Doha, but it could hardly be more different. Leaving behind the city skyline and heading southwest, you encounter the kind of desert that is more akin to *Mad Max* than romantic rolling sand dunes.

It is here you will find the Al Wukair scrapyard, where thousands of unwanted vehicles languish in the desert. At any given time, the gigantic scrapyard accommodates around 20,000 cars, trucks, buses, excavators, bulldozers, cement mixers, and other construction equipment in varying states of neglect and disrepair. Many of the vehicles are burnt beyond recognition.

Walking through the endless rows of dust-covered scrap is an eerie post-apocalyptic experience. But there is also tremendous beauty. Time and sand have worked their magic on these vehicles, and if you're willing to wander amid the wreckage with a camera in hand, you'll be rewarded with gorgeous photographs of industrial decay.

The scrapyard is run under the surveillance of the state police. Visits are not encouraged, but they are not actively discouraged either. At the entrance, there are several bungalow-like offices. It is required that you register yourself with officials upon arriving. An authorized escort accompanies visitors to the scrapyard.

The easiest way to reach the scrapyard is by heading west along Salwa Road, then turning south and following the signs for Mesaieed. Along the way, there is an exit for Al Wukair, which leads directly to the scrapyard. This route is longer than driving through the village of Al Wukair, but it bypasses all the traffic and countless speed bumps.
Ⓝ 25.115668 Ⓔ 51.468979

SINGING SAND DUNES

DOHA

When the air is dry and the wind picks up, a haunting moan rumbles across the sand dunes southwest of Doha. The area is one of dozens of places in the world where the sand sings and the dunes boom.

The sound, which can last for minutes and varies from a hum to a roar to a whistle, occurs when loose sand grains on the top layer of a dune cascade down its slope. The exact means by which this creates the noise are unknown, but researchers at Paris Diderot University have found that the size of the grain determines the pitch of the note.

You can amplify the boom by causing an avalanche—try running along the top of a dune or sliding down one on a homemade sled. Thick cardboard and large trays work well.

The dunes are 25 miles (40 km) southwest of Doha, the capital of Qatar. Avoid going if it has rained recently. Ⓝ 25.038871 Ⓔ 51.405923

SAUDI ARABIA
THE LONELY CASTLE

MADA'IN SALEH

Among the dozens of ruins located in the archaeological playground of Mada'in Saleh, one stands alone. Literally. Carved into a massive boulder is the 1st-century Qasr al-Farid, or "the Lonely Castle."

The "castle" name is misleading, as the grand carving is actually a tomb that was built as part of the ancient Nabataean site of Mada'in Saleh. The Nabataean construction technique was to chisel tombs right out of the rock from the top down. Such is the case with Qasr al-Farid, although the monument appears to never have been completed. The incomplete portion, toward the base of the tomb, is a terrific window into the steps taken by the ancient carvers before the rougher work was polished away.

The castle is at the archaeological site of Mada'in Saleh, 311 miles (500.5 km) southeast of Petra. Ⓝ 26.790694 Ⓔ 37.952000

An unfinished tomb reveals ancient Nabatean carving methods.

The abandoned ruins of a 2,000-year-old village.

AL 'ULA

AL 'ULA

Walking through the narrow corridors of Al 'Ula in northwestern Saudi Arabia is like traversing a maze with ancient history at each turn. Once home to a bustling civilization, these 800 tightly packed mud-brick and stone houses—parts of which are more than 2,000 years old—are now abandoned ruins decaying in the desert sun.

The walled city of Al 'Ula was founded in the 6th century BCE, an oasis in the desert valley, with fertile soil and plenty of water. It was located along "Incense Road," the network of routes that facilitated the trading of spices, silk, and other luxury items through Arabia, Egypt, and India.

Though most of the original houses in the old town were rebuilt over the centuries, there are many remnants of traditional Arab architecture among the ruins. Reconstructed in the 13th century, old town Al 'Ula was inhabited until modern times. When the cramped space and poor infrastructure didn't meet 20th-century standards, residents abandoned Al 'Ula for a new town nearby, called Al-'Ula. The last family left town in 1983, and the last mosque service was held two years later.

Visitors to Al 'Ula often find themselves completely alone in the ruins of an ancient civilization, enjoying the silence and imagining what life in the winding streets would be like when there were hundreds of people living in the mud-brick huts.

Al 'Ula is a 90-minute flight from Riyadh, the Saudi Arabian capital. Ⓝ 26.624967 Ⓔ 37.915600

SYRIA

CHURCH OF SAINT SIMEON THE STYLITE

DEIR SEMAAN, MOUNT SIMEON

The austerities of 5th-century monastic life were simply not strict enough for St. Simeon, who had a penchant for self-inflicted starvation, palm-frond girdles, and sleeping while standing up. After spending a decade at an Aleppo monastery, the ascetic St. Simeon proclaimed that God wanted him to be immobile. He climbed to the top of an abandoned pillar in the desert and remained there for the next 37 years, standing as much as possible, seldom eating, and tying his body upright to a pole to prevent himself from sleeping in a horizontal position.

Simeon died on the pillar in 459 CE, inspiring a rash of copy-cat "stylites"—from the Greek word *stylos*, meaning "pillar"—who spent their days preaching and praying atop columns. The Church of Saint Simeon was built in 491 CE on the site of the original stylite's pillar to honor his devotion. Only a small part of it remains—including the pillar, whittled down to just a few feet from centuries of relic seekers who have carved off shards for themselves.

Saint Simeon spent 37 years balanced on top of a 50-foot pillar. All that remains today is a stub.

The church is a half-hour drive from Aleppo. Ⓝ 36.334166 Ⓔ 36.843888

UNITED ARAB EMIRATES
ABU DHABI FALCON HOSPITAL

ABU DHABI

Located conveniently close to the international airport, Abu Dhabi's Falcon Hospital is where birds of prey go for a talon trim or repair of a broken wing.

When the hospital opened in 1999, it was the first institution in the world to provide veterinary care exclusively for falcons. These days, the services have diversified—there is an on-site pet care center for domestic animals, as well as a shelter for abandoned creatures large and small. The focus, however, is still falcons, over 11,000 of whom come to the hospital each year from the UAE, Saudi Arabia, Qatar, Kuwait, and Bahrain.

Public tours of the Abu Dhabi Falcon Hospital began running in 2007. Visitors encounter an adorable yet confusing sight in the main clinic's waiting room: rows

The most highly prized falcons in the Middle East come for a talon trim or feather transplant.

of falcons sitting on Astroturf perches, some of them wearing hoods that cover their eyes and keep them calm.

In the clinic itself, you may observe a bird getting its talons clipped or getting broken feathers replaced. The room has drawers full of falcon feathers, which are sewed and glued to the injured birds' bodies. Many of the surgical tools used for procedures are modified or improvised versions of what doctors would use on human patients—tools meant for premature babies work well.

Falconry, originally practiced by ancient Bedouin hunters who relied on the birds of prey to gather them food, continues as a sport today. Now trained in a 21st-century way—with the help of drones and radio transmitters attached to their bodies—falcons remain highly prized in the Emirates. An annual falconry festival in Abu Dhabi lures hawks and their trainers from around the world for hunts, parties, and workshops in the desert.
Sweihan Road, Abu Dhabi. Turn right at the last gas station before Abu Dhabi Airport, and you'll end up at the Falcon Hospital. Tours run Sunday through Thursday and must be booked 24 hours in advance.
Ⓝ 24.408265 Ⓔ 54.699379

YEMEN
SOCOTRA ISLAND

SOCOTRA

Describing the flora of Socotra Island is difficult, because it resembles nothing else on Earth. Take the dragon's blood tree, the island's signature specimen, named for its rich red sap. Its silhouette is best explained as that of an umbrella blown inside out. Then there is the desert rose tree—a delicate name that is no match for a bloated, gray trunk that sags beneath thin branches exploding with pink flowers.

These odd-looking organisms are just two of the hundreds of endemic flora and fauna species on this island off the coast of Yemen. The 78 x 28-mile (126 x 45 km) Yemeni territory's biodiversity is the result of long-term isolation—it has been at least 20 million years since the island broke off from Africa, the nearest land mass.

The construction of an airport in 1999 and the introduction of paved roads six years later have resulted in a moderate increase in tourism. That said, you will likely encounter deserted beaches, pristine sand dunes, empty volcanic caves, and shipwreck sites devoid of divers.
Flights to Socotra Island depart from Sana'a. Ⓝ 12.510000 Ⓔ 53.920000

Dragon's blood trees (left and center), and a bottle tree (right) are among the fantastical flora on Socotra Island.

Shibam's city of 16th-century mud high-rises was once a stopping point for traders along the spice route.

WALLED CITY OF SHIBAM

SHIBAM

Like those in New York's borough of Manhattan, the high-rises of Shibam were built on a rectangular grid of streets. Unlike Manhattan's, these "skyscrapers" are made of mud and date back to the 16th century, and the dusty streets are often overrun with goats.

Shibam, in the desert of central Yemen, is home to about 7,000 people. Located at the crossroads of Asia, Africa, and Europe, the small town was once a stopping point for traders traveling along the frankincense and spice routes.

The walled city of skyscrapers was built on a hill in the 1530s after a mighty flood destroyed much of the existing settlement. Its huddled buildings, ranging from five to eight stories high, provided protection against the elements and deterred potential attackers. They continue to shelter the residents of Shibam.

The tower houses, however, are not immune to damage—fresh layers of mud must be applied to the walls regularly to replace sections eroded by wind and rain. A tropical storm in October 2008 brought another disastrous flood, causing some of the buildings to collapse.

Shibam is located 370 miles east of the Yemeni capital of Sana'a. Ⓝ 15.926938 Ⓔ 48.626669

South and Central Asia

AFGHANISTAN

A museum dedicated to overthrowing the Soviets, featuring a diorama of Russians being beaten with shovels.

JIHAD MUSEUM

HERĀT

The Jihad Museum was built in 2010 to pay tribute to the Afghan mujahideen, Islamic guerrillas who fought a bloody war against the Soviets after they invaded Afghanistan in 1979. During the decade-long conflict, the United States provided weapons and funding to the mujahideen to help them resist the USSR. Among the guerrillas fighting on the same side as the USA were Osama bin Laden and key members of the group that would later become Al Qaeda.

The conflict began in 1978, when Afghanistan's Communist party seized the country in a violent coup and began reforming some of its Islamic laws and traditions. In March 1979, armed Afghan rebels revolted in Herāt, killing 100 Soviets who had entered Afghanistan to provide support to the new regime. The Afghan government responded by bombing the city, killing approximately 4,000 people. Uprisings spread across the country, compelling Soviet troops to invade in an attempt to quash rebellion. The ensuing struggle lasted almost a decade. Overpowered by the Afghan resistance, the USSR withdrew the last of its troops in 1989.

The museum's official aim—to educate future generations on Soviet-era jihadist resistance—suggests a restraint that is at odds with its presentation style. Scenes from Herāt are graphically depicted in the museum's central exhibit: a life-size diorama that shows green-tinged corpses lying in bombed-out houses, women in burkas throwing rocks at troops, and bloodied Soviet soldiers slumped in a jeep, as rebels beat them to death with shovels. Surrounding these grim scenes is a 360-degree mural showing Islamist insurgents running through the streets as Russian helicopters bomb the city.

An array of war trophies adds to the sense of triumph—glass cases in the foyer hold Russian rifles, grenades, uniforms, and land mines, while the manicured garden surrounding the circular building contains Soviet tanks, cannons, and a helicopter.

Roodaki Highway, Herāt.
The museum is next to the
US consulate. Ⓝ 34.374166
Ⓔ 62.208888

BANGLADESH
CHITTAGONG SHIP-BREAKING YARDS

CHITTAGONG

The beaches of Chittagong are a massive graveyard for decommissioned ships and tankers. After plowing through the ocean for decades, their battered, rusting hulls sit fully exposed on the sand, waiting for workers in T-shirts, shorts, and flip-flops to tear them apart.

Chittagong is one of the largest ship-breaking yards in the world. Every year, 25,000 employees (down from an estimated 200,000) break down some 250 ships from around the world so their parts can be sold. Since the 1970s, vessels have been brought here to be deconstructed into heaps of steel, cables, generators, nuts, and bolts.

Bangladesh is the port of choice for two reasons: The labor is cheap and the safety standards are poor. Workers, many of whom are children, earn about a dollar a day for pulling apart the hulls by hand, often with little or no safety equipment. The workers inhale noxious fumes and are vulnerable to electrocution, falling debris, and explosions fueled by residual oil.

Organizations such as Greenpeace have been campaigning to impose stricter environmental and health standards at the Chittagong yards, or shift the work to more developed countries. However, mineral-poor Bangladesh is reliant on the steel it gets from the decommissioned ships. For the time being, Bangladesh's ship-breaking yards aren't going anywhere. **The yards, which run for miles along the coast, are not open to visitors, but the massive ships are visible from a distance. As you get closer, you will see bits of metal from the ships being offered for sale in the shops that line the street. Get a bus from Chittagong's railway terminal on Station Road. Ⓝ 22.442400 Ⓔ 91.732000**

Pulling apart colossal steel hulls by hand is one of the world's most dangerous jobs.

BHUTAN
DOCHULA PASS MEDITATION CAVES

DOCHULA

Perched at an altitude of 10,200 feet (3,109 m), Dochula Pass is one of Bhutan's most famous sites. A hidden surprise awaits the few who take the time to venture beyond this well-trodden place.

These curious visitors will discover the meditation caves tucked into the hills just above the pass. These tiny, open-faced caverns are built from stone and painted in colorful detail with Buddhist symbolism. The *druk*, or dragon—Bhutan's long-time national symbol—stretches over the cave entrances, bringing good luck and good tidings.

Meditation is a critical exercise for serious practitioners of Buddhism. To achieve enlightenment, monks and nuns will stay in one location, such as a meditation cave, for three days, three months, and three years. Each period is a trial for the next—if one can manage three days, one proceeds to three months. During this time, one may not speak with or cast eyes on another person. If you make it through three months, it's time to take on three years.

While you may not have three years to spare while visiting these caves, you'd be missing a hidden gem of Dochula Pass if you didn't take the extra ten-minute climb into the forest to explore these carefully constructed meditative retreats that nearly blend into the hills.

There is a café just up the hill from the memorial stupas of Dochula Pass. Head this way and continue upward, following paths built from oval-shaped stone steps. You'll soon encounter the meditation caves. Ⓝ 27.490086 Ⓔ 89.750300

INDIA
NEK CHAND'S ROCK GARDEN

CHANDIGARH, HARYANA/PUNJAB

When Nek Chand became a road inspector in 1951, the city of Chandigarh was in the midst of a dramatic reinvention. Small villages were being demolished to make way for streets, gardens, and sleek modern architecture. As construction continued through the 1950s, piles of debris—pottery fragments, bottles, glass, tiles, and rocks—littered the landscape.

Chand encountered these demolition sites and saw not junk, but potential. He began collecting materials from the scrap heaps and transporting them by bicycle to a forest gorge in Chandigarh's north. It was there that, in 1957, he began work on his own planned city: a sculpture garden, filled with thousands of human and animal figures, all made from recycled debris.

This one-man operation was, by necessity, a secret project. The forest area Chand chose for his garden was a government-designated no-build zone. Authorities remained unaware of Chand's ever-expanding sculpture park until 1975, when they were led there after Chand confided in the city's chief architect. They were astounded to discover 12 acres of statues, courtyards, man-made waterfalls, and pathways.

Despite the illegality of Chand's secret garden—and initial threats of demolition—state authorities allowed the project to expand, even providing Chand with a salary and a crew of 50 workers so he could devote himself to his creation full-time. In 1976, the rock garden opened to the public. It now sprawls over 30 acres, featuring parades of dancing women, gangs of monkeys, and a hillside animal stampede—all rendered in rock, glass, and pieces of colored tile.

Uttar Marg, Sector 1, Chandigarh. The Shatabdi Express—a 3.5-hour ride—runs from New Delhi to Chandigarh twice daily. Buses run from the Chandigarh railway station to Sector 1 in the northern part of the city. Ⓝ 30.760109 Ⓔ 76.801451

Stone sculptures, built secretly and illegally by an eccentric road inspector.

SKELETON LAKE

ROOPKUND, UTTARAKHAND

When park ranger H. K. Madhwal discovered a lake ringed with thousands of human bones while walking in the Uttarakhand Himalayas in 1942, he raised a question that went unanswered for over 60 years: What killed the hundreds of people whose skeletons surrounded the lake? At first, the bones were thought to belong to Japanese soldiers who had stealthily crossed into India during World War II and perished in the high-altitude conditions. But carbon dating during the 1960s showed the estimated death date was wrong—very wrong. A broad range from the "12th to 15th century" was the best possible guess, but no cause of death could be established.

In 2004 the world got an answer to the mystery of Skeleton Lake. Radiocarbon testing at Oxford University narrowed the date of mass death to 850 CE, give or take 30 years. Analysis of skulls showed that, no matter their stature or position, all of the people died in a similar way: from blows to the head. The bodies had wounds only on their heads and shoulders, indicating the blows came from directly above.

After dismissing earlier theories—which included ritual suicide and attacking hordes—the scientists reached an unexpected conclusion: The travelers died from a severe hailstorm.

Hail is rarely lethal. But trapped in a valley without shelter and given no warning of the storm's severity, the 9th-century travelers could not escape the sudden barrage of tennis-ball-size spheres of ice.

Twelve hundred years after the storm, the green-tinged bones of hail victims still ring the lake, preserved alongside skulls and tattered shoes at an altitude of 16,500 feet (5,029 m).

The journey starts at Lohajung, a small pass where you can pick up essential supplies. Hire a guide and bring a mule or porter to help carry your belongings. The best time to go is in May or June, when there is no snow covering the lake and the skeletons are visible. You will need to be physically fit and prepared for high-altitude conditions. Ⓝ 30.262217 Ⓔ 79.731573

KARNI MATA RAT TEMPLE

DESHNOKE, RAJASTHAN

Twenty thousand rats scurry across the checker-board floors of this temple, getting tangled in each other's tails and fighting for access to huge saucers of milk. Far from being regarded as vermin, the rats are venerated as the holy descendants of Karni Mata, who was worshipped as an incarnation of the Hindu goddess Durga during the 15th century.

The story of how Karni Mata's offspring took the form of rodents varies, but the most common version begins with her asking Yama, the god of death, to revive her drowned stepson. After first resisting, Yama gave in, promising that the boy and all of Karni Mata's male descendants would be rein-carnated as rats.

Visitors to the temple are required to remove their shoes before walking inside. When shuffling among the droppings, spilled milk, and scrambling rodents, keep in mind that it is considered lucky for a rat to run across your foot. Another tip is to tread lightly. Temple rules state that if you acciden-tally step on one of the animals and kill it, you must

Visitors must remove their shoes before entering Karni Mata, a temple crawling with thousands of holy rats.

replace it with a rat made of solid gold. **National Highway 89, Deshnoke. Karni Mata is a 30-minute train ride from the larger town of Bikaner. Bring a pair of thick socks that you don't mind throwing out. ⓝ 27.790556 ⓔ 73.340833**

WAGAH BORDER CEREMONY

WAGAH, PUNJAB

The line separating India and Pakistan runs straight through the middle of Wagah, a Punjab village home to the only road joining the two countries that's open to international travelers. It is here that soldiers from each side conduct a precisely choreo-graphed daily border-closing ceremony—a rou-tine that combines flamboyant uniforms, fierce stares, and competitive high kicks.

Multiple wars and an ongoing dispute over Kashmir have fostered hostility between India and Pakistan—a hostility that finds its outlet in the aggressive dance moves of the border soldiers and the patriotic cheering of the daily crowds that come to watch them perform. The atmosphere is akin to a sporting match. Prior to the sunset ceremony, performers and visitors dance to traditional music pumped through loudspeakers on each side. As the anticipa-tion builds, men with microphones rile up the flag-waving spectators in the bleachers.

The ceremony, performed since 1959, begins with a parade of soldiers on both sides of the border. Members of India's Border Security Force wear khaki uniforms with red fanned coxcombs on their turbans, while the Pakistan Rangers wear black uniforms with black coxcombs. In a region where the average male height is 5.5 feet (168 cm), every soldier is over 6 feet tall (183 cm). They march in pairs with synchronized strides, their mustachioed faces dour through all the stomping and high-kicking.

At the border gates, the long-awaited confronta-tion occurs. The guards emerge from each side simultaneously while keeping a stern eye on one another. National flags are lowered—at exactly the same time, so that neither country can be accused of trying to "win"—after which an Indian and a Pakistani guard shake hands rigidly before retreating from the border with more stomps and high kicks. For the hundreds of Indian and Pakistani spectators, the ceremony is a source of national pride and a cathartic expres-sion of built-up tension between the often-clashing countries.

Get a round-trip taxi from Amritsar—the driver will wait while you attend the ceremony. International visitors are entitled to VIP access and seating if they show their passports. Arrive early and travel light, because bags are not allowed. ⓝ 31.604694 ⓔ 74.572916

A dance of aggression, dominance, and coxcomb headgear.

KEY MONASTERY

DHAR LAMA CHUNG CHUNG

Resting snugly within India's Spiti Valley, the Key Monastery (or Ki, or Kye, or Kee) looks like a ramshackle temple of mysticism straight out of a fantasy novel, but this Buddhist training ground is actually the result of repeated attacks by Mongol hordes.

The exact age of the Key Monastery is not known, but it is believed to date back to at least the 11th century. The early structures erected by the original monks would have been built at a lower altitude than the current hilltop huts, which sit at 13,668 feet (4,166 m) above sea level. When Mongol barbarians attacked the monastery, reconstruction efforts then built upon what had gone before, eventually creating the erratic patchwork of rooms, tight hallways, and hidden courtyards that exists today.

Much of the monastery bears a distinct Chinese design influence, dating back to a period in the 14th century when the style came to the area. The interiors are also rich with historic murals and documents precious to the orders that have lived in the ever-changing monastery.

Today Key Monastery is still a fully functioning training ground for lamas, operated by a Gelug sect of Tibetan Buddhist monks. Around 250 monks reside on the site at any given time, training, farming, and generally keeping the thousand-year-old wonder alive. **Between May and October is the best time to visit, taking the roads from Manali via Kaza, as snow makes the (already bumpy and unfinished) route impassable. At the monastery, say yes to the butter tea. Ⓝ 32.297857 Ⓔ 78.011929**

CHAND BAORI STEPWELL

ABHANERI, RAJASTHAN

Built in the 9th century, but reminiscent of an M. C. Escher drawing, Chand Baori is among the largest and most elaborate of India's many stepwells. Locally known as *baori*, stepwells were tiered stone structures used to collect and store rainwater in arid climates. Often accented with arches, columns, sculptures, and geometric patterns, stepwells also served as village gathering places.

The four-sided Chand Baori is 13 stories tall, 100 feet (30.5 m) deep, and lined with 3,500 steps arranged in a spectacular zigzag pattern. Its intricate, multilevel facade overlooks a small pond of bright green water—a reminder of the magnificent structure's

3,500 Escher-esque steps lead down to a pool of stored rainwater.

practical purpose. Other beautiful stepwells worth visiting include Adalaj ki Vav and Rani ki Vav in Gujarat; Agrasen ki Baoli and Rajon ki Baoli in New Delhi; and Raniji ki Baori in Rajasthan. **Chand Baori is a 90-minute drive from Jaipur, on Jaipur-Agra Road. Ⓝ 27.007200 Ⓔ 76.606800**

NORTH SENTINEL ISLAND

ANDAMAN AND NICOBAR ISLANDS

The Stone Age hunter-gatherers who live on North Sentinel Island in the Andaman archipelago east of India may be the world's most isolated people—and they intend to stay that way, despite the increasing encroachment of the industrialized world.

From 1967 through the mid-1990s, Indian anthropologists embarked on periodic "contact expeditions" to North Sentinel Island. Approaching by boat, they attempted to coax out members of the tribe by depositing coconuts, machetes, candy, and, once, a tethered pig onto the beach. The Sentinelese almost always responded to these "gifts" by shooting

arrows, throwing stones, and shouting at the unwelcome visitors.

India discontinued its attempts at peaceful contact in 1997 and ruled that the islanders be left alone, but visits still occur—in 2006, a fishing boat drifted too close to the shore, and Sentinelese archers killed the two men on board. An Indian helicopter was sent to retrieve their bodies, but was also fired upon and could not land. In 2018, an evangelical missionary from the United States was killed while trying to approach the island. Efforts to recover his body were abandoned.

The hostility of the Sentinelese, whose population is estimated at between 100 and 200, is understandable considering the fates of tribes on other Andaman Islands. During British settlement, exposure to newly introduced diseases decimated tribal populations. More recently, roads constructed through forests on these other islands have allowed local sightseeing companies to offer "human safaris," during which travelers try to spot tribe members on their way to other island attractions.

India maintains a 2-mile buffer zone around North Sentinel Island. Access is strictly forbidden, but you can visit other islands in the archipelago. The main port of entry is Port Blair, where flights arrive from Chennai and Kolkata. Ⓝ 11.551782 Ⓔ 92.233350

The Sentinelese may be the most isolated tribe on Earth.

ALSO IN INDIA

New Lucky Restaurant

Ahmedabad · When Krishna Kutti realized there was a burial ground on the land he sought for his new restaurant, he simply incorporated the graves into the dining room decor.

Auroville

Bommayapalayam · This self-proclaimed experimental "city of the future," established by dubious spiritual leaders in 1968, centers around a golden geodesic dome named Mother Temple.

Hampi

Karnakaka · Known as "the last great Hindu Kingdom," Hampi flourished from the 14th to 16th centuries before being ransacked and abandoned. The surviving monuments evoke a grand riverside city.

JANTAR MANTAR ASTRONOMICAL INSTRUMENTS

JAIPUR, RAJASTHAN

Viewed without context, the 90-foot-tall (27 m) Samrat Yantra, or "supreme instrument," is a sand-colored stairway to nowhere. It sits in the middle of what looks like a skateboarder's half-pipe. The stately wooden doors at the base of its stairs and the small pagoda at its apex are merely mysterious. It is only when the Samrat Yantra's purpose is revealed that it becomes impressive: The Samrat Yantra is the world's largest sundial, built in the 18th century and accurate to within two seconds.

Jai Singh II, who became ruler of Amber (now Jaipur) at the tender age of 11, had a great enthusiasm for design, mathematics, and astronomy. Responsible for planning and building the city of Jaipur during the 1720s, Singh also took it upon himself to establish five observatories in North India. The largest, built between 1727 and 1734 in his hometown of Jaipur, is the best preserved.

The Jantar Mantar ("calculation instrument") of Jaipur is a collection of stone buildings used to determine local time, predict eclipses and monsoons, and track the movement of celestial objects. All of the instruments were built according to Hindu and Islamic astronomy and are impressively accurate due to their sizable dimensions.

Jantar Mantar is adjacent to City Palace near Tripolia Bazar. Ⓝ 26.924722 Ⓔ 75.824444

Indian ruler Jai Singh II's quest for scientific data resulted in the largest sundial in the world.

In one of the wettest places on Earth, bridges aren't built—they're grown.

Root Bridges of Cherrapunji

CHERRAPUNJI, MEGHALAYA

To cross the rivers and streams of the Cherrapunji forest, you must put your trust in a tree. There are no standard walkways to be found—instead, the tangled, twisting aerial roots of the rubber trees on the banks stretch across the water, forming a living, ever-growing bridge to the other side.

These organic bridges are the result of a little human guidance and a lot of patience. Members of the local Khasi tribe control their growth by first laying lengths of bamboo or betel nut tree across the water as a guide, then waiting for the roots of the rubber trees to follow along. As the roots grow, the Khasi add handrails made of vines and fill in gaps with mud and stones, creating a solid pathway. It takes up to 20 years for a bridge to become sturdy enough to cross, but once built, it continues to grow and strengthen for up to 500 years.

There are several root bridges in the Cherrapunji region. The most famous is the "Umshiang Double-Decker" root bridge at Nongriat. Its 60- and 80-foot (18 and 24 m) pathways, one atop the other, are made from the roots of the same tree.

The nearest city is Shillong. Bridges are accessible via jungle trek. Reaching the double-decker bridge requires a 6-mile (9.7 km) walk each way. Cherrapunji is one of the wettest places on Earth, so dress appropriately. Ⓝ 25.251513 Ⓔ 91.671963 ➤➤

➤➤ Other Notable Examples of Arbortecture

Arbortecture, or arborsculpture, is the art of shaping a living tree in order to create art or furniture. Using pruning, bending, and grafting, its practitioners spend years guiding each tree into a predetermined design. Arbortecture differs from topiary in that it shapes a tree's trunk or roots, rather than its foliage.

TREE CIRCUS AT GILROY GARDENS, GILROY, CALIFORNIA, USA

In 1947, arborsculpture pioneer Axel Erlandson established a roadside Tree Circus near Santa Cruz, California, to show off his grafted creations. Though the circus closed in 1963, some of his creations, such as a woven Basket Tree and the right-angled Four-Legged Giant, live on at Gilroy Gardens.

Gilroy Gardens

AUERWORLD PALACE, AUERSTEDT, GERMANY

Built by 300 volunteers in 1998, this willow dome is the centerpiece of a yearly summer music festival.

Each spring, a few dozen Auerworld supporters give the dome a ceremonial "haircut," trimming its wildest branches to maintain the mandala-influenced shape.

Auerworld Palace

KAZAKHSTAN
BAIKONUR COSMODROME

BAIKONUR

"Dear friends, known and unknown to me, my dear compatriots and all people of the world! Within minutes from now, a mighty Soviet rocket will boost my ship into the vastness of outer space. What I want to tell you is this. My whole life is now before me as a single breathtaking moment. I feel I can muster up my strength for successfully carrying out what is expected of me."

Those were the words of Yuri Gagarin on April 12, 1961, minutes before the cosmonaut lifted off in the *Vostok 1* spacecraft, becoming the first human to travel into space and enter orbit

around Earth. His journey began at the Baikonur Cosmodrome, the world's oldest and largest space launch facility, set in the desolate desert steppe of Kazakhstan.

The Soviet Union built the cosmodrome in 1955 as a secret missile testing site and space launch facility. Two years later, *Sputnik 1* launched from Baikonur, becoming the first man-made satellite in orbit and igniting the space race between the Soviets and Americans.

The cosmodrome is the world's most active spaceport, with a long list of historic launches. A month after *Sputnik 1*, a stray female dog named Laika hurtled into space aboard *Sputnik 2*, becoming the first animal to enter orbit and paving the way for human spaceflight. (Unfortunately, the canine pioneer's one-way suicide mission

was even shorter than planned—she died of heat exhaustion hours after launch, a detail that was only revealed in 2002.)

Before each launch, a Russian Orthodox priest clad in golden robes blessed the space-bound rocket, spraying holy water in the air and onto the faces of the assembled media.

The only way to see inside the cosmodrome and its space museum is on a guided tour. Since Baikonur is administered by Russia, tours leave from Moscow via a 3.5-hour chartered flight. For the most spectacular experience, time your visit for a launch—planned dates are available online. Be prepared for extreme weather, as Baikonur can reach –40°F (–40°C) in winter and 113°F (45°C) in summer. Ⓝ 45.965000 Ⓔ 63.305000

THE LAST WILD APPLE FORESTS

ALMATY

The common apple has its roots in one specific region of the world: *Malus sieversii*, its ancestor, grows wild in the Tian Shan mountains of Kazakhstan.

In the early 20th century, biologist Nikolai Vavilov first traced the apple genome back to a grove near Almaty, a small town whose wild apples closely resemble the Golden Delicious variety found at grocery stores today. Vavilov visited Almaty and was astounded to find apple trees growing wild, densely entangled and unevenly spaced, a phenomenon found nowhere else in the world.

Scientists believe the Tian Shan apple seeds were first transported out of Kazakhstan by birds and bears long before humans ever cultivated them. By the time humans did begin to grow and trade apples, the *Malus sieversii* had already taken root in Syria. The Romans dispersed the fruit even farther around the world. When modern genome sequencing projects affirmatively linked domestic apples to *Malus sieversii*, Almaty and its surrounding land were officially recognized as the origin of all apples.

The origin of all apples still flourishes.

Almaty means "father of apples," and the town touts its heritage proudly. A fountain in the center of town is apple-shaped, and vendors come out each week to sell their many varieties of domesticated apples at market.

The apple forests exist in patches along the Tian Shan mountain range. There are various protected sections in the Ile-Alatau National Park, but hiring a guide to take you there is recommended, as they are difficult to find. Ⓝ 43.092939 Ⓔ 77.056411

KYRGYZSTAN

TASH RABAT

AT-BASHI, NARYN

During the 15th century, the stone structure of Tash Rabat was a caravansary—a travelers' inn providing refuge for those journeying along the Silk Road. Protected by the high walls of the rectangular courtyard, human and animal travelers took shelter in its stalls to wash, rest, and prepare for the next leg of a long trip.

This desolate part of the trading route was particularly treacherous. Snow covers the ground for eight months of the year, and the area is subject to landslides, flooding, and earthquakes. The difficult conditions persist, which is why, for maximum safety and comfort, you should visit in summer and hire a local guide to drive you. For a fleeting insight into the Silk Road experience, camp in a yurt overnight at Tash Rabat.

Tash Rabat is a 6-hour drive south of the capital of Bishkek. Take precautions against altitude sickness—Tash Rabat is 11,500 feet (3,505 m) above sea level. Ⓝ 40.823150 Ⓔ 75.288766

The domed stone building of Tash Rabat gave weary Silk Road travelers a brief respite from the desert.

KYRGYZ NATIONAL HISTORY MUSEUM

BISHKEK

Kyrgyzstan's National History Museum is probably the only place in the world where you can find a ceiling mural of a naked Nazi in a horned helmet emerging from a wall of flames astride a demonic horse. It is definitely the only place you'll see a mural of Ronald Reagan in a skull mask, American flag T-shirt, and khaki cowboy hat riding a Pershing missile in front of a bunch of anti-nuclear demonstrators.

The museum, established in 1927, contains Kyrgyzstani cultural relics dating back to the Stone Age, such as armor, jewelry, coins, and weapons. The second and third floors became shrines to the legacy of the Soviet Union.

In Kyrgyzstan's time capsule of a museum, the Soviet Union still stands strong.

But images of communist heroes Lenin, Marx, and Engels inspiring the masses are gradually being replaced as the nation moves further away from its Soviet past. The outlandish murals, though, seem destined to stay.

Ala-Too Square, Bishkek. If you're feeling bold, flag down one of the overcrowded minibuses, locally known as *marshrutkas*. For a less stressful option, take a taxi. ℕ 42.876388 Ⓔ 74.603888

PAKISTAN

MUMTAZ BEGUM

KARACHI, SINDH

Resting in a shabby pavilion at Karachi Zoo is a creature by the name of Mumtaz Begum, a lounging fox with the head of a woman who can see the future and provide solid advice.

In reality, Mumtaz Begum is neither a fox nor a woman, but is actually played by performer Murad Ali, who inherited the role from his father. Each day he cakes his face with a thick layer of foundation, drawn-on eyebrows, and bright red lipstick. He then crawls into the box beneath Mumtaz's cage, jutting his head through the hole in the top to make it look as though his head is attached to the lounging fox carcass next to him. A shawl is placed around Ali's head to hide the connection, and then the visitors begin filtering in.

Ali's creature (known as a *kitsune*) is said to be able to see the future. Children and adults alike come to the zoo to ask Mumtaz Begum about everything from exam results to visa approvals. Ali gamely provides advice and peppers the interaction with references to his mysterious African origins.

Visitors coming to see Mumtaz Begum often leave small donations, cake, and juice, like

Pakistan's foremost prognosticating half-woman, half-fox can tell your fortune for a fee.

supplicants to a charlatan prophet. However, in true huckster fashion, anyone wishing to speak with the kitsune will need to pony up for a special ticket into the Mumtaz Mahal.

Karachi Zoo, Nishter Road and Sir Agha Khan III Road, Karachi. Buses, many of them alarmingly overcrowded, run along Nishter Road. ℕ 24.876228 Ⓔ 67.023203

KHEWRA SALT MINES

KHEWRA, PUNJAB

In 326 BCE, Alexander the Great and his army were making their way through present-day Pakistan on horseback when one of Alexander's steeds began voraciously licking the ground. When other horses joined in, soldiers dismounted to investigate, and discovered what is now the second-largest salt mine in the world.

Today, Khewra's 18-story-deep salt mine produces about 350,000 tons of pink Himalayan salt per year, a rate it is projected to maintain for the next 350 years. When salt leaves the mine, it is used for cooking and bathing. Within the mine, a visitors' section contains a mosque, a post office, and a "Palace of Mirrors," all made from salt bricks quarried from the 18 working levels below. The palace, with its illuminated floor of red, brown, and pink tiles, gives off a subterranean disco vibe.

The mine is a 2.5-hour drive south of Islamabad or 3-hour drive northwest of Lahore. Ⓝ 32.647938 Ⓔ 73.008394

ALSO IN PAKISTAN

Derawar Fort

Bahawalpur · In the Cholistan desert stands an enormous square medieval fortress with 98-foot-high (30 m) walls.

LAHORE FORT ELEPHANT PATH

LAHORE

Because it would be a shame to leave one's elephant parked outside the citadel, the magnificent Lahore Fort features a stepped entranceway crafted for an entire pachyderm parade.

As the Mughal Empire expanded across the Indian subcontinent in the 16th century, Lahore became an increasingly important stronghold. The city's fortress was built under the reign of Emperor Akbar between 1566 and 1605 and housed several Mughal and Sikh rulers over the following centuries.

The *Hathi Paer*, or elephant stairs, are part of the private entrance to the royal quarters and effectively allowed royalty to ascend all the way to the doorway before dismounting their enormous animals. In order to accommodate the lumbering creatures, the stairs were designed with wide treads but minimal height. (A balking elephant can really dampen the mood of a procession.) Although it's been centuries since a herd of jewel- and silk-laden elephants traveled several abreast along this sloping corridor, it was once certainly the most magnificent driveway in the world.

The elephant stairs pathway is located at the northwest corner of the Lahore Fort. Ⓝ 31.586606 Ⓔ 74.312300

Elephants in bas-relief line the base of the elephant path.

SRI LANKA

SIGIRIYA

MATALE, CENTRAL PROVINCE

When you've murdered your father and stolen your brother's crown, you need to find yourself a safe, vengeance-proof home. For King Kassapa I, who overthrew his father and buried him alive in the wall of an irrigation tank in 477 CE, that place was Sigiriya.

At the center of Sigiriya is the 650-foot-tall (198 m) hardened magma plug of an extinct volcano. Fearing an attack from his usurped brother Moggallana, Kassapa built a palace for himself

on top of the rock and surrounded it with ramparts, fortifications, fountains, and gardens. A moat around the rock added an extra layer of protection.

Though Kassapa focused on keeping himself safe, he didn't skimp on the design details of Sigiriya. The stone stairway leading up the mountain is flanked by two huge lion paws carved into the rock. At the top of the 1,200 steps originally sat a lion's mouth, which people had to walk through to get to the palace. This explains Sigiriya's alternate name: Lion Rock.

Kassapa sequestered himself in his hilltop palace for 18 years before his greatest fear came to pass. Moggallana, having recruited an army in India, besieged Sigiriya and overpowered Kassapa's soldiers. Facing certain defeat, Kassapa turned his sword on himself and, with his death, granted Moggallana the kingship to which he had always been entitled.

For maximum comfort, go early to avoid the heat. From Colombo, get a bus to Dambulla and switch to a Sigiriya bus. The whole journey takes about 4 hours. ⓝ 7.955154 ⓔ 80.759803

ALSO IN CENTRAL ASIA

ARMENIA

Khor Virap Monastery

Ararat · Visit a hilltop pilgrimage site that once held a saint in its dungeon for 13 years.

AZERBAIJAN

Naftalan Clinic

Naftalan · Bathe in crude oil at this spa devoted to petroleum-induced relaxation.

Mud Volcanoes

Baku · Gurgling volcanoes line the Caspian coast, occasionally erupting in flames.

GEORGIA

Stalin Museum

Gori · Established in 1957, this hometown tribute to the dictator is gradually changing its hagiographic presentation of Soviet history.

KAZAKHSTAN

Aral Sea

Thanks to aggressive irrigation practices, the Aral Sea has gone from being the fourth-largest lake in the world to a toxic desert strewn with rusty fishing vessels.

TURKEY

Cotton Castle

Pamukkale · Once a kind of Roman-era health spa, the spectacular rock formations below the ancient city of Hierapolis form a blindingly white natural cascading fountain.

At the top of Sigiriya, or "Lion Rock," is an ancient fort surrounded by gardens.

TURKEY

KAYAKÖY

KAYAKÖY, MUĞLA

Standing on a hill in the Kaya Valley region of Turkey are the deserted stone buildings of Kayaköy, a small town abandoned abruptly around 1922.

Once known as Levissi, the town was home to around 6,000 people, the vast majority of them Greek Orthodox. Then came World War I and the subsequent Greco-Turkish War, during which Turkey purged the Ottoman Greek people from its lands and Greece sent its Muslim residents to Turkey. In accordance with this population-swap policy, the inhabitants of Kayaköy were exiled to Greece. The Muslim inhabitants who arrived to take their place found Kayaköy's topography unsuited to their agricultural needs. They soon resettled to other parts of Turkey, leaving Kayaköy in the abandoned state that persists today.

There is much to explore, including hundreds of roofless homes and two eerie churches. At the top of the hill you'll get a glorious view down into the valley and out to the sea.

Kayaköy is 45 minutes south of Fethiye. Stay until after dark, when dramatic lights illuminate the crumbling corners of the village. Ⓝ 36.578922 Ⓔ 29.087051

The Greeks abandoned the Turkish town of Kayaköy.

ANI GHOST CITY

OCAKLI KÖYÜ

On the Turkish-Armenian border, scattered in the plains among the wildflowers, are the crumbling remains of a once mighty city. In the 11th century, Ani was home to over 100,000 people. Situated on a number of trade routes, the city became the capital of the Kingdom of Armenia, an independent state established in 961.

Ani was attacked by the Byzantines during the empire's takeover of the Armenian Kingdom in 1045. Two decades later, Seljuk Turkish invaders captured the city, murdered and enslaved its inhabitants, and sold the whole place to a Kurdish dynasty known as the Shaddadids.

The attacks continued in the 13th century, when the Mongols made two attempts—one thwarted, one successful—to capture the city. An earthquake in 1319 caused significant damage to Ani's many 11th-century churches. The city stumbled onward but was much smaller by the mid-17th century and completely abandoned by 1750.

Today Ani is a grand but ruined ghost town. Tensions between Turkey and Armenia have contributed to its neglect—it is an Armenian city but lies within Turkish borders, making conservation and restoration difficult. To visitors, Turkey omits all mentions of Armenia from descriptions of Ani's history and focuses on the city's Turkish and Muslim influences.

Ani is a 45-minute drive from the city of Kars. Bring snacks and water if you plan to spend the day exploring the ruins. Ⓝ 40.507636 Ⓔ 43.572831

Earthquakes, war, and vandalism have weakened the remaining structures of a once-bustling city.

AVANOS HAIR MUSEUM

AVANOS, NEVŞEHIR

 Avanos, a small town in the Cappadocian region, has a millennia-long history of ceramics and pottery. But only one of its potters maintains a cave full of human hair.

In 1979, local potter Galip Korukcu was bidding farewell to a dear friend. When he asked for a memento, she snipped off a lock of her hair. Korukcu stuck the hair on one of the walls of his pottery shop, which is located in a cave. After hearing the story behind the wad of hair on the wall, pottery buyers began contributing their own locks.

The "hair museum" now crams an estimated 16,000 hair samples onto its walls. Visitors are invited to snip off a few strands of hair and attach them to a card with their contact details to add to the display. Pencils, paper, pins, and scissors are provided.

There is an added incentive for contributing to the collection: Twice a year, Korukcu asks a customer to choose 10 hair samples from the walls. The owners of the winning hair receive a free weeklong stay in the connected guest house and workshops with the master potter.
Firin Sokak 24, Avanos. Ⓝ 38.720612 Ⓔ 34.848448

TURKMENISTAN
DOOR TO HELL

DERWEZE, AHAL

When darkness falls, an orange glow illuminates the dusty plains outside of Derweze, a settlement of 350 in the middle of the Karakum Desert. The source of light is the "Door to Hell," a 200-foot-wide (61 m) crater that has been burning for over 45 years.

In 1971, Soviet geologists, looking for natural gas, accidentally burrowed into a huge cavern filled with methane, causing the ground to crumble and their drilling rig to collapse into the huge pit. With the pocket of gas punctured, poisonous fumes began leaking from the hole at an alarming rate. To avoid a potential environmental catastrophe, the geologists set the hole on fire. The crater has been burning ever since.

Following a visit to the Door to Hell in April 2010, Turkmen president Gurbanguly Berdimuhamedow recommended the hole be closed so the area's rich gas reserves could be tapped safely. Thus far the crater remains untouched, but with new pipelines and increased international interest in Turkmen gas reserves, the Door to Hell may not be open for much longer.
The crater is 160 miles (257.5 km) north of the capital city of Ashgabat, where you can hire a guide to drive you to the desert. Ⓝ 40.252777 Ⓔ 58.439444

The 200-foot-wide desert fire pit known as the Door to Hell has been blazing since 1971.

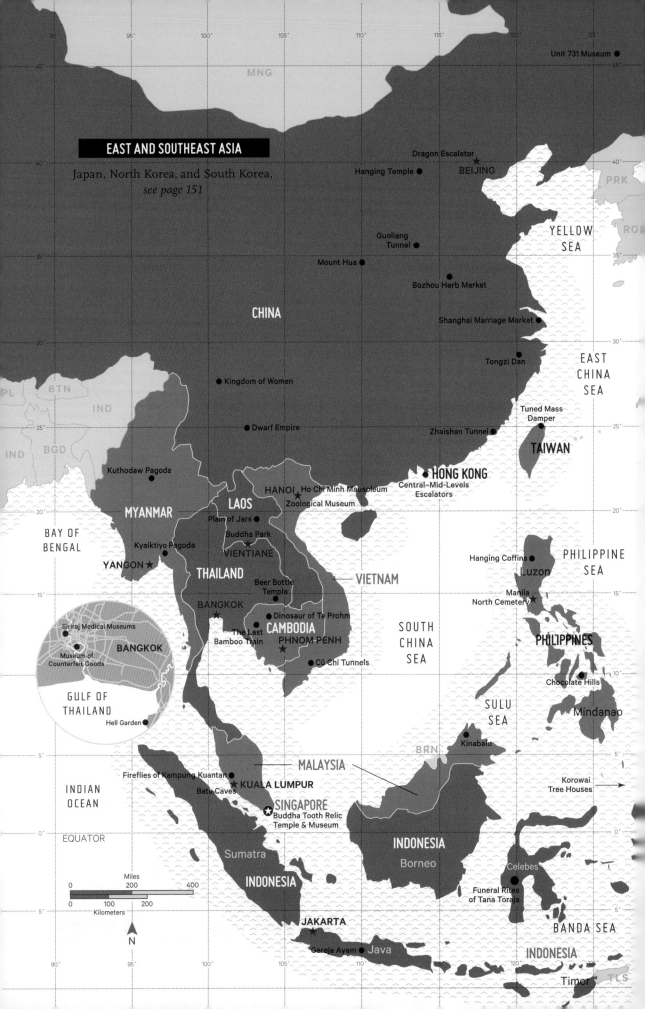

EAST AND SOUTHEAST ASIA

Japan, North Korea, and South Korea,
see page 151

MNG

PRK

ROK

CHINA

Unit 731 Museum •

Dragon Escalator ★
Hanging Temple • BEIJING

YELLOW
SEA

Guoliang
Tunnel •

Mount Hua •

Bozhou Herb Market •

Shanghai Marriage Market •

EAST
CHINA
SEA

Tongzi Dan •

Kingdom of Women •

Dwarf Empire •

Tuned Mass
Damper •

Zhaishan Tunnel •

TAIWAN

PL

BTN

IND

IND

BGD

Kuthodaw Pagoda •

HANOI ★ Ho Chi Minh Mausoleum
Zoological Museum •

LAOS

HONG KONG
Central–Mid-Levels
Escalators

MYANMAR

Plain of Jars •
Buddha Park ★
VIENTIANE

Hanging Coffins •

PHILIPPINE
SEA

Luzon

BAY OF
BENGAL

Kyaiktiyo Pagoda •

YANGON ★

THAILAND

VIETNAM

Beer Bottle
Temple •

BANGKOK ★

Dinosaur of Ta Prohm •
The Last
Bamboo Train • CAMBODIA
PHNOM PENH ★

Cŭ Chi Tunnels •

Manila •
North Cemetery ★

SOUTH
CHINA
SEA

PHILIPPINES

Mindanao

Siriraj Medical Museums •

BANGKOK

Museum of
Counterfeit Goods •

GULF OF
THAILAND

Hell Garden •

Chocolate Hills •

SULU
SEA

Kinabalu •

INDIAN
OCEAN

Fireflies of Kampung Kuantan •
Batu Caves • ★ KUALA LUMPUR

BRN

MALAYSIA

Korowai
Tree Houses →

SINGAPORE
Buddha Tooth Relic
Temple & Museum

Sumatra

INDONESIA

Borneo

Celebes

INDONESIA

EQUATOR

Miles
0   200   400
0   100   200
Kilometers

Funeral Rites
of Tana Toraja •

N

JAKARTA ★

Gereja Ayam • Java

BANDA SEA

INDONESIA

Timor

TLS

Ascending the Longqing Gorge
in serpentine style.

East Asia

CHINA
DRAGON ESCALATOR

BEIJING

Located roughly 53 miles (85.3 km) north of Beijing, Longqing Gorge is a pleasant change of pace from the crowded streets of China's capital. Home to the country's largest dam, the otherwise tranquil surroundings are slashed by a gigantic dragon escalator.

The bright yellow behemoth, which takes riders to the top of the dam, rises 846 feet (257.9 m). At the top you can have even more adventures, including a ride in a cable car or a boat trip on the artificial lake. If a boat ride sounds too slow for you, you can always bungee jump into the gorge.

You can ride the giant escalator as much as you want, but unfortunately, it only goes up. To come down, you can either take the stairs or pay a little extra to ride the toboggan.

Buses run from the Deshengmen bus terminal in Beijing to Gucheng, a short walk from the gorge. The journey takes around an hour. Ⓝ 40.456704 Ⓔ 115.974999

The temple of Hengshan clings to a cliff 246 feet off the ground in apparent defiance of gravity.

HANGING TEMPLE OF HENGSHAN

MOUNT HENG, SHANXI

Two hundred and forty-six feet (75 m) above ground, supported by a few thin wooden stilts driven into the cliff face, the Hanging Temple of Mount Heng dangles in apparent defiance of gravity. Built into the rock during the Northern Wei Dynasty (386–534 CE), the 40-room temple, connected by a dizzying maze of passageways, has survived the erosive effects of wind, sun, and snow due to its protected position.

Unusually, the temple caters to not one but three religions—elements of Confucianism, Taoism, and Buddhism are evident in its 78 statues and carvings. **Mount Heng is 2 hours southeast of Datong, where you can hire a driver to take you there and back.**
Ⓝ 39.673888 Ⓔ 113.735555

UNIT 731 MUSEUM

HARBIN, HEILONGJIANG

Officially, Unit 731 was a lumber mill in Japanese-occupied Manchuria. Its staff received frequent deliveries of *maruta* ("logs"). Black smoke billowed from the chimney day and night.

Unit 731 was not, in fact, a lumber mill. It was a biological weapons research facility in which Japanese scientists conducted torturous, lethal experiments on humans—humans they referred to as "logs." Established in 1936, and operational during the second Sino-Japanese War through World War II, the facility functioned under the approval of Japan's Emperor Hirohito.

The atrocities conducted at Unit 731 consisted of in-house experimentation on predominantly Chinese and Russian individuals. In the laboratories, researchers studied blood loss by performing amputations. They infected patients with diseases such as gonorrhea and syphilis, and then conducted vivisections—removing the organs of living people—to observe their effects on the body. Patients received no anesthetic during these operations.

Planes dropped bombs filled with anthrax, smallpox, typhoid, cholera, and plague-infected fleas on Chinese villages, aiming to maximize death and devastation. On the ground, members of Unit 731 infected hungry children with lethal pathogens by giving them contaminated food and candy.

The secrecy surrounding Unit 731 has made it difficult to estimate how many people died in the experiments. Given the contamination of agricultural crops and water supplies that resulted from the aerial drops, the victims likely numbered in the hundreds of thousands.

In 1945, immediately following Japan's surrender, the members of Unit 731 fled the site, destroying as much evidence as they could on the way out.

Despite the destructive efforts of the departing researchers, portions of Unit 731—including the Frostbite Laboratory (where victims endured exposure to extreme cold), the Yellow Rat breeding room, and the incinerator that cremated the bodies—remain. The site opened as a museum in 1985, offering two floors of exhibits. Graphic photographs, medical instruments, and plaques re-create a period of history that Japan doesn't want to remember, and China will never forget.
23 Xinjiang Street, Pingfang, Harbin. Get a bus from Harbin train station. Ⓝ 45.608244 Ⓔ 126.639633

MOUNT HUA

HUAYIN, SHAANXI

There are two ways to reach the 5,121-foot (1,561 m) North Peak of Mount Hua: an eight-minute cable car ride, or a four-hour climb up narrow staircases carved into the near-vertical cliffs. No matter which option you choose, there is more treachery to come.

The five peaks of Mount Hua, or Huashan, have long been a refuge for determined hermits unfazed by heights. Among the most notable of the hermits was the 10th-century Taoist priest Chen Tuan, who developed a martial art known as "water boxing" while living alone in a secluded high-altitude temple.

In addition to the exhausting stair climbs, the mountain offers hikers an extreme challenge in the form of its most terrifying path: Changkong Zhandao. This one-foot-wide (.3 m) walkway juts out from the cliffs connecting the north and south peaks. It is made of wooden planks—some wobbly, some rotting—that rest on iron bolts driven into the side of the mountain. There is a hand-rail of sorts—a thick chain pinned into the rock at intervals with large nails.

If you opt to walk the planks, your journey will begin with one of the most important purchases of your life: a safety harness, which vendors on the north peak have been renting since 2005. Technically, the harness is optional, but choosing not to attach yourself to the flimsy cable running above the path would be an act of folly.

At the end of Changkong Zhandao is a small shrine with a stunning view of the mountain range—the perfect place to pause and gather your courage before turning around and walking back down.

Trains and buses run from Xi'an, 2 hours southwest. If the idea of scaling a cliff face in the dark sounds fun, climb the mountain at night so you can watch the sunrise from one of the peaks.
Ⓝ 34.478861 Ⓔ 110.069525

A safety harness is recommended for the treacherous journey up Mount Hua.

BOZHOU MEDICINAL HERB MARKET

BOZHOU, ANHUI

Located at the juncture of two key railway lines, the dusty and rusty city of Bozhou is the capital of the Chinese medicinal herb industry. With a population of 3 million people, the city revolves around a massive 85-acre market, where some 6,000 traders come from every corner of southeast Asia to ply the ingredients found in traditional Chinese medicine.

Here you can find barrels of dried human placentas (for fainting sickness), dried fist-size stag beetles (for increased metabolism), dried flying lizards (also for metabolism), cockroaches (a topical anesthetic), crushed pearls to ingest with tea (for influenza), pencil-size millipedes bundled up and bound together in clumps (for a

host of sicknesses), snakes (for arthritis), and a dozen different kinds of ants (for pretty much whatever ails you). Around every corner are hemp sacks overflowing with scorpions, seahorses, turtle shells, antlers, and every kind of root and flower imaginable.

Though the Bozhou herb market feels timeless—and there has indeed been an herbal market on the site for centuries—the market has recently undergone a boom as Westerners have increasingly adopted elements of traditional Chinese medicine. Today, the downtown is ringed with pharmaceutical factories and hotels for visiting traders.

Weiwu Avenue, Bozhou. The overnight train from Shanghai to Bozhou takes about 10 hours.
Ⓝ 33.862205 Ⓔ 115.787453

GUOLIANG TUNNEL

GUOLIANG, HENAN

Located in the Taihang mountains, the village of Guoliang was once accessible only via a treacherous, 720-step cliffside staircase known as the "sky ladder." When its 350 inhabitants needed to stock up on food supplies or get medical attention, they would climb down these 720 steps, built without a railing during the Ming dynasty (1368–1644).

That arrangement changed in 1972, when villager Shen Mingxin and a dozen other men began to dig a road through one of the mountains. Using shovels, spikes, iron hammers, and dynamite that

they purchased by selling livestock, the men spent the next five years hand-carving the tunnel out of rock almost 400 feet (122 m) up the mountain.

On May 1, 1977, the three-quarter-mile Guoliang Tunnel opened to traffic. Illuminated only by sunlight through its 30 rock-hewn windows and measuring under 20 feet (6 m) wide, it requires careful navigation by both vehicles and pedestrians. Drivers use their headlights and honk their horns at regular intervals to help prevent collisions.

From the city of Xinxiang, get a bus to Huixian, then switch to a Nanping-bound bus. The journey takes about 3 hours. Ⓝ 35.731287 Ⓔ 113.603825

Guoliang Tunnel, seen running along the mountain about halfway down the cliff, was dug by hand.

Urine-soaked "boy eggs" make for a pungent street food.

Tongzi Dan

DONGYANG, ZHEJIANG

Every spring, the streets of Dongyang fill up with egg vendors selling a popular seasonal product known as *tongzi dan*. Also called "boy eggs," the traditional delicacy is made by collecting the urine of young boys and using it to hard-boil eggs. After boiling in the steaming urine, the eggs are removed, their shells cracked, and they are placed back into the simmering urine to soak up the robust flavor.

Tongzi dan have been standard street fare in Dongyang in Zhejiang Province for hundreds of years. The smell of steaming urine wafting through the city heralds the arrival of spring. Residents attest to the appetizing taste and medicinal properties of the eggs, believing they increase blood flow and lower internal temperature. Despite these widely held beliefs, doctors in the area do not advocate the consumption of anything boiled in human waste.

The process of acquiring bulk quantities of fresh young urine is surprisingly simple: Local schools line their halls with plastic buckets, which boys under 10 use as toilets when the urge strikes. The receptacles are collected throughout the day and their contents poured into the cooking barrels. In order to keep the process as hygienic as possible, boys who are unwell are asked to refrain from using the buckets.

Dongyang, Zhejiang. Ⓝ 29.289634 Ⓔ 120.241561 ➼

➼ Other Asian Street-Food Eggs

Balut, Philippines

Sold on the streets of the Philippines, *balut* is a boiled duck egg with a difference: It is fertilized. Crack the shell open, and snuggled against the yolk you'll see a veiny pink embryo in its fetal sac. Though recognizably avian, the fetus is too young to have developed a beak, claws, or feathers.

For 17 days, freshly fertilized duck eggs are stored in a warm place to allow the embryo to develop. Then, to prevent further maturation, vendors boil the eggs, killing the fetus and solidifying the yolk. Balut are served warm and salted, often as a snack to accompany beer.

Century Egg, China

The yolk of a century egg is forest-green and smells of sulfur-tinged ammonia. Its surrounding "white" is the color of rust, its texture similar to Jell-O.

The Chinese delicacy earns its pungent odor and distinctive look from a preservation process that raises its pH level. The recipe requires a duck or chicken egg to be encased in a mix of salt, clay, quicklime, ash, and rice hulls for several weeks. Eaten on their own or as a garnish for tofu dishes, century eggs are available at street stalls and in dim sum restaurants, and are often on the menu at birthdays and weddings.

Ōwakudani Black Eggs, Japan

Ōwakudani, or the Great Boiling Valley, is a volcanic zone with hot springs, sulfur vents, and a great view of Mount Fuji. It is also the best place in Japan to eat a black-shelled, longevity-enhancing egg.

The eggs of Ōwakudani turn black when boiled in the thermal pools—the sulfur and minerals in the water react with the eggshell, causing the color change. A gondola lift brings cartons of eggs up the hill for boiling, after which they are sent back down to be sold in packs of five. Due to the presence of hydrogen sulfide and sulfur dioxide in the air, visitors are allowed only a brief look at the cooking process.

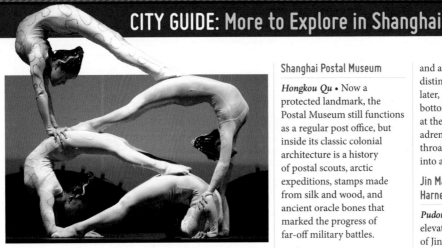

The acrobats at Circus World are among the world's best.

Shanghai Circus World

Zhabei Qu • It's a little out in the suburbs, but you can't miss the giant golden geodesic dome that hosts Circus World, where some of China's most skilled athletic performers and stunt divers combine a modern sensibility with traditional acrobatics, dance, and illusions.

1933 Slaughterhouse

Hongkou Qu • The rivers of cow's blood are long gone from this former slaughterhouse, leaving behind an eerie Escher-esque shell of a building, the last abattoir of its kind: British-designed, pre-communism-built, it is as haunting as it is beautiful.

Jewish Refugees Museum

Hongkou Qu • Shanghai (along with the Dominican Republic) was alone in taking in Jews fleeing Europe during World War II. The turbulent period is remembered at the Jewish Refugees Museum through artifacts, personal documents, photography, and archival copies of the *Shanghai Jewish Chronicle*.

M50 Art District

Putuo Qu • An artist's community dominates the district around an old textile mill on Moganshan Road, with studios open to the public, thought-provoking sculptures and murals, and more than a hundred galleries that show the work of both the well-established and cheeky newcomers.

Shanghai Postal Museum

Hongkou Qu • Now a protected landmark, the Postal Museum still functions as a regular post office, but inside its classic colonial architecture is a history of postal scouts, arctic expeditions, stamps made from silk and wood, and ancient oracle bones that marked the progress of far-off military battles.

Bund Tourist Tunnel

Huangpu Qu • This short underground railway connecting Pudong with the waterfront of the Bund offers a five-minute mind-bending train ride featuring seizure-inducing strobe lights and a psychedelic New Agey soundtrack.

Natural Wild Insect Kingdom

Pudong Xinqu • Billed as an educational science destination, the Insect Kingdom has a butterfly zone, a serpent and python area, beetles, and bugs of all kinds, and it might be the only museum with a Shrimp Appreciation Zone.

Oriental Pearl TV Tower

Pudong Xinqu • When it opened in 1994, this 1,535-foot (468 m) spire was the tallest structure in China, and although it lost that distinction a dozen years later, a trip to the glass-bottom observation deck at the top can still grab adrenaline junkies by the throat—and send acrophobes into a fetal position.

Jin Mao Tower Skywalk Harnessed Observation Deck

Pudong Xinqu • Take the elevator to the 88th floor of Jin Mao Tower, the third tallest building in China, skip the deck, and head for the glass-bottomed ledge called the Skywalk, where you can dangle from a harness over the street below.

Shanghai, circa 2020

Huangpu Qu • The entire city of Shanghai, as it hopes to look in the year 2020, has been scaled down to fit on the third floor of the Urban Planning Museum, over a thousand square feet (93 m²) of perfectly re-created Lego-like neighborhoods, soaring towers, and planned developments.

Shanghai Brush & Ink Museum

Huangpu Qu • The histories of Chinese ink, pens, and brushes are traced at this small museum, including examples of calligraphy from as early as the 4th century up

SHANGHAI MARRIAGE MARKET

SHANGHAI

During weekends, the walkways in the north part of People's Park are filled with middle-aged men and women affixing posters to the ground, the bushes, and lengths of string suspended at eye level. The posters advertise the glowing attributes of the goods they are offering: their marriage-ready sons and daughters.

Traditionally, Chinese marriages begin with parental matchmaking—before a potential couple meets, their parents will discuss the viability of the union, swapping information on looks, interests, and finances. In 21st-century Shanghai, the process can be difficult. Fast-paced lives, busy schedules, and a male-skewed sex ratio resulting from the country's former one-child policy all hinder parents who want to marry their children off before they hit the "crucial" age of 30.

The outdoor marriage bazaar draws hundreds of traders every week, each one clutching a piece of paper listing height, age, educational background, occupation, and spousal preferences. Some mothers and fathers bring a folding chair, settling in for a day of fielding offers from other matchmakers. The success rate is low—there are parents who have been coming every weekend for years—but, given the through colonial occupation, when wealthy merchants underwrote the artists who developed a new and vibrant Shanghai school of painting and calligraphic arts.

Yu Garden Zigzag Bridge

Huangpu Qu • Exquisite pavilions from the Ming Dynasty are all well and good, and Yu Garden certainly has those, but when you need to trick evil spirits, head to the zigzag bridge, because (if legend be believed) evil spirits can only travel in straight lines.

Ballroom Dancing at the Karl Marx and Friedrich Engels Statue

Huangpu Qu • In the French Concession at the northern end of the lush formal gardens of Fuxing Park, couples gather in the morning for some early-bird ballroom dancing under the watchful gaze of a 12-foot statue of Karl Marx and Friedrich Engels.

Waxworks Hall at the First National Congress of the Communist Party Museum

Huangpu Qu • In 1921, when the 13 original delegates of the Chinese Communist Party met for the first time, it was in this small residence in the French Concession. The meeting is re-created with wax figures in the tiny second-floor study.

Dajing Ge Pavilion

Huangpu Qu • The last remaining section of Shanghai's old city wall can be found here. Once more than 3 miles (5 km) of stone fortification, ramparts, and gates, the wall was torn down in 1912, leaving behind only 164 feet (50 m) on the Dajing Road.

Antique Music Box and Gallery

Pudong Xinqu • This collection of miniature and life-size mechanical wonders is as much automata as musical, with more than 200 animatronic birds in cages, twirling dancers, parlor scroll players, and a 1796 "musical device of reduced dimensions"—the world's oldest music box—made by Swiss watchmaker Antoine Favre-Salomon.

Animation & Comics Museum

Pudong Xinqu • Among the familiar Mickey, Jessica Rabbit, and Kung Fu Panda, this story temple to the animated arts celebrates the earliest forms of moving pictures, like sand painting and traditional Chinese shadow puppets.

Tian Zi Fang

DaPuQiao • The open-air Tian Zi Fang is a maze of galleries, trinket stalls, coffee shops, and makeshift craft studios, but it's the traditional Shikumen architecture of this alley bazaar that sets it apart from other stops along the tourist trail—and also what saved it from the redevelopment bulldozers.

Lu Hanbin Typewriter Museum

Yan'an Xi Lu • A temple to the writer's workhorse, this assemblage of more than 300 models and historical displays claims to be the third-largest typewriter museum in the world. With a small sitting area and no admission charge, it's like an internet cafe without the internet.

Propaganda Poster Art Centre

Xuhui • A collection of Chinese propaganda posters spanning a 30-year period from the start of the revolution in 1949 to the reforms of the late 1970s, including examples of idealized military victories and gauzy visions of the model communist life.

Longhua Revolutionary Martyrs Memorial and Cemetery

Xuhui Qu • Once a prison for the pre-Revolutionary Kuomintang party, this vast park of monumental statues and memorials is now a free museum of the Communist struggle, with preserved prison cells and 500 graves of Communist martyrs.

500 Arhats of Longhua Temple

Xuhui Qu • Inside one of the chambers of this Buddhist temple—the biggest and oldest in Shanghai, tracing back to the year 242—there are rows of foot-tall golden Buddhas.

Shanghai Astronomical Museum

Songjiang Qu • In 1900, on a quiet forested hilltop near the Basilica of Our Lady of Sheshan, Jesuit missionaries built China's first astronomical dome, where today there is a museum and public observatory. The original telescope is not only still working but is still one of the largest binocular refracting opticals in the country.

social stigma facing unmarried thirty-somethings, the marriage market has nevertheless thrived.

People's Square, Wusheng Road, Huangpu, Shanghai. Get the Metro to People's Square and walk west into the park.
Ⓝ 31.232229 Ⓔ 121.473163

A son-and-daughter meat market, run by mom and dad.

DWARF EMPIRE

KUNMING, YUNNAN

Before their performances in one of the twice-daily shows, the short-statured performers of Dwarf Empire theme park (also known as the "Kingdom of the Little People") get ready in miniature mushroom-shaped houses with crooked chimneys. Park visitors peer in through the undersized doorways as the actors apply makeup.

Established in 2009 by wealthy real-estate mogul Chen Mingjing, Dwarf Empire is an experience that invites ethical questions. Over a hundred performers, all under 4.5 feet (1.3 m) tall and recruited from around the country, live and work at the park—not in the mushroom houses, but in dormitories customized for their stature. Each day, the performers dance, sing, pose for photos, and sell refreshments to visitors, all while wearing fairy-tale costumes. When the audiences have left for the day, they sweep the park and stack the chairs before retiring to their dorm rooms.

China's treatment of its short-statured population is influenced by a widespread belief that disability is a punishment inflicted on those who have committed past-life sins. Many performers at the park have been ostracized from their families, denied health care or employment, and forced to live on the streets. For them, Dwarf Empire provides support, a steady paycheck, and the chance to display skills such as singing, kung fu, or break dancing.

That said, the park can feel exploitative. Presumably, many visitors are not there to appreciate the performers' skills, but to gawk at the novelty of being in an all-dwarf world. The resulting environment skates uncomfortably close to a human zoo.

Located next to the Butterfly Ecological Park, about 25 miles southwest of Kunming off the G56 Hangrui Expressway. Public buses run from the city center. Ⓝ 24.850411 Ⓔ 102.622266

ALSO IN CHINA

Beichuan Earthquake Memorial	Giant Mao Head	Kissing Dinosaurs	Jade Burial Suits	Hallstatt
Beichuan · Destroyed in the 2008 Sichuan earthquake, the city of Beichuan remains in ruins as a memorial to the thousands who died.	*Changsha* · This massive granite Mao-nument depicts the young Great Leader's windswept, youthful head.	*Erlian* · Two smooching apatosauruses tower over a road near the Mongolian border, their necks creating a tunnel for passing cars.	*Shijiazhuang* · Hebei Provincial Museum displays two intricate suits of armor made from thousands of jade tiles stitched together with gold thread.	*Luoyang* · China has built an exact replica of the Austrian village of Hallstatt to serve as a novelty high-end housing development.

KINGDOM OF WOMEN

LUGU LAKE, YUNNAN

Sitting astride the border of Yunnan and Sichuan provinces, and surrounded by mountains, Lugu Lake is a tranquil place. But most travelers don't come here for the scenery—they arrive tantalized by the promise of a "Kingdom of Women."

The Mosuo, a 50,000-strong Chinese ethnic group with a matriarchal social structure, live in villages around the lake. Women control their multigenerational households and maintain ownership of their homes and land. Children take their mother's surname, and inheritance is distributed through the female line.

An often misunderstood aspect of Mosuo culture is the practice of "walking marriage." When girls turn 13, they attend a coming-of-age ceremony and receive their own private bedroom. From this time onward, girls can receive male "visitors" at night. Visits take place by mutual agreement, and men arrive under cover of darkness, returning to their homes in the morning—the "walking" part of walking marriage. Women may have as many sexual partners as they wish, with no stigma attached, for as long as they desire.

When these trysts result in the birth of a child, the father plays no role in the child's upbringing, beyond occasional gifts and visits. Mothers are responsible for taking care of their children, with the assistance of family members in the household. A father never lives with his children—instead, he stays in the family home in which he grew up, helping to raise the children in that household.

In a country that famously prizes baby boys, the Mosuo are unique for valuing girls and striving for a balance of sexes in the home. If a household becomes skewed in either direction, its matriarch may adopt children of the appropriate sex. These children become equal members of the family.

Lugu Lake is a bumpy 6-hour bus ride from Lijiang, a former Silk Road town that has retained much of its ancient architecture. Ⓝ 27.705719 Ⓔ 100.775127

The Mosuo maintain one of the world's few matrilineal societies.

HONG KONG

CENTRAL–MID-LEVELS ESCALATORS

CENTRAL AND WESTERN DISTRICT

Residents of Hong Kong's affluent, elevated Mid-Levels commute to the city's main business district in a unique way: Instead of hopping on a train, tram, boat, or bus, they spend 20 minutes riding a series of hillside escalators.

Built in 1993 to ease road traffic, the Central–Mid-Levels Escalators comprise the world's longest outdoor covered escalator system. A total of 20 escalators, plus three moving walkways, snake along Cochrane Street and Shelley Street, linking the core urban area of Central to the residential Mid-Levels on Victoria Peak. The total distance covered is 2,600 feet (792 m), with a vertical climb of 443 feet (135 m).

Around 55,000 people use the escalator system every day. From 6 a.m. until 10 a.m., all escalators run downhill. Then it's switchover time—from 10:30 a.m. until

The world's longest outdoor covered escalator system transports commuters across Hong Kong's hilly terrain.

the midnight system shutdown, the mechanical walkways travel uphill. On the moving stairs, you'll glide past the vibrant shops and global restaurants of the bustling SoHo district.

Cochrane Street (between Queen's Road Central and Hollywood Road) and Shelley Street. ⓝ 22.283664 ⓔ 114.154833

ALSO IN HONG KONG

Chungking Mansions

Kowloon · Teeming with illegal goods and services, this towering maze of vice has some of the cheapest accommodation in the city.

TAIWAN

TUNED MASS DAMPER OF TAIPEI 101

TAIPEI

The view of the city from the 89th floor of Taipei 101, one of the world's tallest buildings at 1,667 feet (508 m), is spectacular. But turn your back to the urban panorama and you'll see something equally fascinating: a huge yellow sphere, suspended in the center of the building between floors 88 and 92.

The 728-ton globe is a tuned mass damper, a pendulum-like device designed to counter the effects of wind and seismic activity on high-rises. In strong wind, the upper levels of a skyscraper

will sway a few feet back and forth. The Taipei 101 damper, suspended from eight steel cables, provides a counterforce that offsets the movement and prevents people in the building from feeling unsteady. Given Taiwan's susceptibility to earthquakes—the city sits on the edge of two tectonic plates—the eye-catching damper is an essential architectural feature.

7 Hsin Yi Road, Section 5, Taipei. The building is a 15-minute walk from the Taipei City Hall subway station. You will ride to the observatory level in one of the world's fastest elevators, traveling at 38 miles (61 km) per hour. ⓝ 25.033612 ⓔ 121.564976

ALSO IN TAIWAN

Bei Tou Incinerator

Taipei · Dine in a revolving restaurant at the top of a waste incinerator's chimney.

An enormous pendulum helps keep Taiwan's tallest building from swaying in the wind.

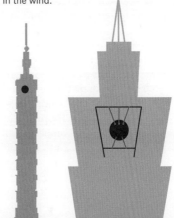

Step through the entrance (left) to this extensive underground tunnel and waterway system and you just might hear some Mozart.

ZHAISHAN TUNNEL

QUANZHOU

Following the Second Taiwan Strait Crisis in 1958, tensions between the People's Republic of China (PRC) and the Republic of China (ROC, now known more commonly as Taiwan) were at breaking point. The Taiwanese island of Kinmen, just a few miles from the mainland, had been shelled relentlessly during the four-week crisis, and a cold war lingered between the two factions.

Faced with potentially devastating artillery bombardments from the Chinese mainland, President Chiang Kai-shek of Taiwan ordered the construction of underground fortifications in the hard granite of Greater Kinmen, a strategically important island just off the coastline. This included the Zhaishan Tunnel, an incredible system of underground tunnels and waterways stretching for 2,592 feet (790 m).

The Zhaishan Tunnel was completed in 1966, comprising two interconnecting A-shaped tunnels. One was an underground waterway built to help protect boats from bombardment and allow for the safe unloading of cargo. It could shelter 42 small naval vessels.

As the cold war tensions gradually lessened, Taiwan went through a period of reform and social change. The Zhaishan Tunnel, meanwhile, was slowly filling up with sand. Maintaining the tunnel would have required money and manpower. With neither available, it was abandoned in 1986.

In the mid-1990s, an increased interest in preserving national historic sites and, more locally, remembering the men and women who fought for Kinmen turned the spotlight back onto the Zhaishan Tunnel. It was handed over to the Kinmen National Park to be restored and preserved. There was, however, one caveat: The Ministry of Defense would always be granted full access and control over the tunnel in times of war and for conducting military exercises.

Alongside its current role as tourist attraction, national historic site, and potential wartime boat shelter, the Zhaishan Tunnel also serves as a concert hall. The annual Tunnel Music Festival shows off the waterway's marvelous acoustics.

Jincheng Township, Kinmen County. Buses run from Jincheng station to the tunnel. Ⓝ 24.394329 Ⓔ 118.320511

Map labels:
CHN
RUS
NORTH KOREA
Friendship Exhibition
PYONGYANG ★
Kijong-dong
Third Tunnel of Aggression
SEOUL ★
SOUTH KOREA
YELLOW SEA
SEA OF JAPAN
Jindo-Modo Land Bridge
Jeju Mermaids
Jeju Glass Castle Theme Park
Battleship Island
EAST CHINA SEA
Wisteria Tunnel
Village of Dolls
Mound of Ears
Mt. Hiei
JAPAN
Firefly Squid
World's Largest Drain
★ TOKYO
Self-Mummifying Monks
PACIFIC OCEAN

TOKYO (inset)
Mushizuka
Ueno Zoo
Meguro Parasitological Museum

N
Miles
0   100   200
0   100   200
Kilometers

JAPAN, NORTH KOREA, AND SOUTH KOREA

JAPAN
MUSHIZUKA, SHRINE TO SLAIN INSECTS

TOKYO

In the garden of Kan'ei-ji Temple is a smooth, engraved boulder—a circa-1821 memorial honoring the slain victims of artist Masuyama Sessai. A man with a sizable conscience, Sessai ordered its construction himself, hoping it would console the spirits of those he killed. The slain were insects killed to serve as anatomy models for an illustrated scientific textbook, but erecting a stone shrine was the least the staunch Buddhist felt he could do. *Mushizuka*, the word engraved on the boulder, means "mound for insects."

1-14-11 Ueno Sakuragi, Taito-ku, Tokyo. Kan'ei-ji Temple is a 5-minute walk from Uguisadani Station's south exit. Ⓝ 35.721453 Ⓔ 139.774204

ALSO IN TOKYO

Kabukicho Robot Restaurant

Tokyo · Neon strobe lights, techno music, drummer women in bikinis, and gyrating cyborgs are but a few notable features of this deeply confusing dining experience.

Nakagin Capsule Tower

Tokyo · This 13-story apartment building is crammed with 144 podlike residences straight out of a dystopian sci-fi novel.

Museum of Kites

Tokyo · This tiny museum hidden above a restaurant houses thousands of modern and traditional kites.

CITY GUIDE: More to Explore in Tokyo

Sogen-ji Kappa-dera Temple

Taitō-ku • This small temple is devoted to the folkloric and sort of cuddly "kappa," turtle-ish goblins who love cucumbers and are known to grab unsuspecting humans from bridges, wrestle with them, and occasionally drown them—so stop by, watch your back, and leave a cucumber.

Ghibli Museum

Shimorenjaku • Experience the wizardry of artist and filmmaker Hayao Miyazaki and explore his world: Play in the animation studio that fostered *My Neighbor Totoro* and *Spirited Away* and watch a short film from the master that can't be seen anywhere else.

Godzilla Head

Shinjuku • The King of the Monsters has stomped his way into a comfortable retirement age, but his giant scaly head still towers over the Toho theater complex, the studio behind the Godzilla franchise.

Pasona Tokyo Headquarters

Chiyoda-ku • Hidden in the Chiyoda district is a sky-scraping urban farm with hydroponic "fields" on the roof, exterior and interior walls, and a genuine rice paddy in the lobby.

Sanrio's indoor theme park boasts over 1 million visitors a year.

Alice in Wonderland Fantasy Dining

Ginza • A rabbit warren of storybook pages, a stack of books to make you feel like a caterpillar, hedges from the Queen's garden, and desserts shaped like the Cheshire cat—this Ginza restaurant will drop you squarely in the Bizarro World of Lewis Carroll.

The Giant Ghibli Clock

Higashishinbashi • Officially called the "NI-Tele Really BIG Clock," four or five times a day this wacked-out symphonic mega-machine spins, dances, whirs, and clanks, and as a side gig tells the time.

Nakagin Capsule Tower

Ginza • While the future of this groundbreaking experiment in modular living is uncertain, you can still experience the mostly unsuccessful—but undeniably thought-provoking—expression of micro-living, designed by famed Japanese "Metabolist" architect Kisho Kurokawa.

Roppongi Hills Garden Pond

Minato-ku • In 2003, these rejuvenated office towers, museums, shops, and hotels were a welcome upgrade for the city, but it's the underwater tenants who might be the most beguiling: little slips of silvery fish called *medaka*, direct descendants of those bred in space aboard the *Columbia* shuttle as part of a series of experiments in extraterrestrial reproduction.

Shakaden Reiyukai

Minato-ku • The temple headquarters of a 20th-century Buddhist off-shoot known as "Inner Trip Reiyukai" is a futuristic black pyramid, where welcoming monks provide free Japanese lessons, and 400 tons of drinking water are held in reserve—because you never know when you might need 400 tons of drinking water.

Gotokuji Temple

Gotokuji • As the birthplace of a kind of 17th-century meme, this Buddhist temple in the Setagaya district is overrun with thousands of porcelain and plastic *maneki-neko*, or good-luck cats, each raising one snowy-white paw to symbolize that this is a place of care and safety.

Lucky Dragon 5 Memorial

Koto Ward • A moving memorial to a little-known nuclear disaster, when the crew members of the trawler *Daigo Fukuryū Maru* (the "Lucky Dragon") unwittingly cruised into the warm and snowy nuclear fallout of a bomb test over a thousand times more powerful than Hiroshima.

Sengaku-ji

Minato-ku • The graves of the 47 Ronin—nearly deified figures of duty, commitment, and honor-bound revenge—are packed in tight rows at a temple befitting their legendary status.

PIGMENT

Higashishinagawa • Like something out of a painter's dreamscape, this Kengo Kuma–designed art-supply store connects ancient principles of Japanese design and ideology to modern aesthetics. Constructed almost entirely of bamboo, the store displays thousands of unmixed tints and hues with names like "Autumn Mystery" and "Luxury Twinkle."

Odaiba Statue of Liberty

Minato-ku • Originally installed as a temporary exhibit, this replica of Lady Liberty may not tower like the original, but it's still four stories tall and so popular, it's the site of dozens of daily photo ops.

Sanrio Puroland

Ochiai • If Hello Kitty was Mickey Mouse, this bright, loud, hyperactive world of pastels and super-morphed feline creatures would be her Disneyland. The blaring candy-colored cartoon world is broken only by the live stage shows and constant fireworks.

Anata No Warehouse

Kawasaki-ku • This faux-seedy video arcade looks like a maze of alleys straight out of a cyberpunk dystopia or a back alley of Hong Kong's Kowloon Walled City.

Ajinomoto MSG Factory Tour

Kawasaki-ku • Just south of Tokyo center at one of the world's largest monosodium glutamate factories, an albino panda named Aji-Kun welcomes you to the factory tour, some handmade MSG goes home with you, and a side-by-side taste test makes a pretty strong case for the often-maligned seasoning.

Aogashima Volcano Island

Aogashima Island • Although it's more than 200 miles (358 km) off the coast, the island of Aogashima—a volcano inside another volcano—is actually part of the city of Tokyo. A quick helicopter ride (or not-as-quick ferry) will take you to five square miles (8.75 km²) of remote and peaceful night skies, volcanic saunas, and the occasional fear-of-eruption twinge.

Meguro Parasitological Museum

TOKYO

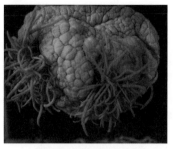

A worm-infested dolphin stomach.

This small but memorable museum, established as a research collection in 1953, pays tribute to the tens of thousands of organisms that thrive at the expense of others. The first floor offers an overview of the parasite-host relationship and life cycle, while the second floor showcases 300 preserved specimens, including a dolphin stomach infected with roundworms, a heartworm-infested dog heart, and a turtle head whose eye sockets are now inhabited by leeches.

For reasons that mystify even museum staff, the institute has become a go-to date spot—young couples hold hands and gaze at the 29-foot (8.8 m) tapeworm extracted from the stomach of a man who ate infected trout.

4-1-1 Shimomeguro, Meguro, Tokyo. The museum is a 15-minute walk from Meguro station. Stop by the gift shop for a preserved parasite key ring. **N** 35.631695 **E** 139.706649 ➤

➤ Parasitic Worms and Their Effects on Humans

GUINEA WORMS (DRACUNCULIASIS)

You won't know you're infected with a guinea worm until a year after it has entered your body. That's when you'll notice a blister on your leg. Within three days, it will rupture, exposing what looks like a piece of white string. That is the guinea worm, and its journey through your body is far from over.

By the time they've spent a year in your connective tissue, where they grow up to 3 feet (1 m) long, guinea worms have generated and stored millions of eggs in their bodies. When a worm emerges from a burst blister, the temptation will be to yank it out. Bad plan. This can result in the worm breaking, causing the remainder of its body—and the eggs it holds—to putrefy and get stuck inside you.

When a worm pokes out of your leg, you must begin winding it around a stick to draw it out. Don't tug. Just wait for it to slither farther out, winding its body around the stick like cotton on a reel. The entire process may take months.

As the worm emerges, you will feel an intense burning sensation around the blister. The temptation to dunk your leg in the nearest pond or river will be overwhelming. Cruelly, this form of relief is how the life cycle of the guinea worm perpetuates: The worm will release larvae into the water. Water fleas eat the larvae. Humans drink water containing the larvae-infested fleas, and the entire process starts anew.

EYE WORM (LOIASIS)

An eye worm, or loa loa, is often asymptomatic, but when the worm makes its presence known, the effect is startling. Loa loa enter your body via the bite of a fly (commonly deer flies or mango flies) that is infected with larvae. Burrowing into your subcutaneous tissue and lungs, and traveling through your circulatory system, loa loa grow to more than 2.5 inches (6.35 cm) long and produce larvae that end up in your spinal fluid, urine, or mucus.

Though the most frequently observed symptom of loiasis is Calabar swellings (itchy red lumps, particularly on the forearms), the first sign of an infection may be a tickle in your eyeball. Loa loa can migrate through the subconjunctival tissues of your eye. In other words, you will be able to watch in a mirror as a worm wriggles beneath the top layer of your eyeball. The sensation will be painful, itchy, and unlike anything you've ever experienced.

TAPEWORMS (TAENIASIS)

Pause before eating pork or beef and check whether it's been properly cooked. Raw or undercooked meat can harbor tapeworm larvae, which, once they reach your intestines, latch on and develop into adults of up to 25 feet (7.6 m) long.

Flat, ribbonlike tapeworms can live inside you for up to 18 years. Their bodies consist of 1,000 to 2,000 proglottids, or individual segments, giving them a ridged look. About 20 percent of the proglottids—the ones toward the rear end—are capable of producing eggs and behaving like individual worms. Segments that break off sometimes crawl out of the anus and down the thighs of their human host. Word is, it tickles.

Most people infected with tapeworms exhibit no symptoms, but a worm that has spent over a decade in your intestines may cause indigestion, abdominal pain, or weight loss. The first sign of an infection will likely be worm segments in the stool. They may be moving.

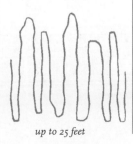

up to 25 feet

UENO ZOO ESCAPED ANIMAL DRILL

TOKYO

Every February, a papier-mâché rhino politely lunges at the staff of Ueno Zoo. The rhino, operated by a pair of zookeepers, is one of the fake creatures used in the zoo's annual Escaped Animal Drill.

Each year, the artificial rhino—along with staff members in furry monkey suits and one dressed as a bipedal tiger—attempts to storm the gates of the zoo and wreak havoc on the streets of Tokyo. Zookeepers band together to capture the "humanimals," encircling them with nets, loading tranquilizer guns, and tapping the ground with sticks. Some zoo staff even feign injury or play dead to heighten the authenticity of the scene. All participants carry out their duties earnestly, never cracking a smile.

The yearly drill is part of Ueno Zoo's emergency preparations for earthquakes and other natural disasters. It has become such a popular attraction in its own right that other Japanese zoos have started to copy the idea.

9-83, Ueno Park, Taito-ku, Tokyo. The Escaped Animal Drill is usually held between February 20–22, but contact the zoo directly to confirm. Ⓝ 35.714070 Ⓔ 139.774081

Once a year, Ueno Zoo's keepers dress as animals and try to break free.

THE WORLD'S LARGEST DRAIN

KASUKABE, SAITAMA

The G-Cans project, more officially known as the Metropolitan Area Outer Underground Discharge Channel, is a massive underground waterway and water storage area built to protect Tokyo from flooding during monsoons.

G-Cans opened in 2009 after 17 years of construction. With its 59 pillars, miles of tunnels, and 83-foot-high (25.3 m) ceilings, the vast space resembles an underground temple. Five 21-story concrete silos collect rainwater, preventing overflow of the city's rivers and waterways. The humongous drainage system can pump over 12,000 tons of water per minute—that's four and a half Olympic-size swimming pools.

There are daily free tours of the drainage system, but you will need to bring your own translator if you can't understand Japanese. This precaution ensures that, in the event of an emergency, you will be able to follow evacuation instructions.

Showa drainage pump, 720 Kamikanasaki, Kasukabe. Free tours of the drainage system are conducted daily in Japanese. The closest train station is Minami-Sakurai (a 40-minute walk), after a one-hour trip from central Tokyo. Ⓝ 35.997417 Ⓔ 139.811454

Tokyo's massive underground waterway is a temple to high-speed drainage.

FIREFLY SQUID OF TOYAMA BAY

TOYAMA BAY, ISHIKAWA AND TOYAMA

The firefly squid is a 3-inch-long (7.6 cm) cephalopod found in the waters surrounding Japan. Its standout feature—a series of photophores that make the squid glow a brilliant blue—is ordinarily concealed by the dark, 1,200-foot-deep (366 m) water it inhabits. But every year, from March to May, millions of firefly squid surface in Toyama to spawn and are swept ashore by the currents of the bowl-shaped bay.

This time of year is also prime fishing season. Nets trawl the predawn waters, hauling up piles of squirming, glowing creatures and turning boats into beacons. The beaches are bathed in a blue glow as the adult squid—who have a one-year life span—lay their eggs and prepare to die. The Japanese government regards the annual light show as a "special natural monument."

While the firefly squid are highly regarded for their magical visual effects, they are also prized for their tasty innards. After basking in the glow of the predawn bioluminescent bay, you can head to a sushi joint and feast on squid served raw, boiled, or turned into tempura.

If you'd like to learn more about the glowing squid before—or instead of—eating them, head to Toyama's Hotaruika Museum, which bills itself as the only firefly squid museum in the world.
Namerikawa fishing port, Toyama Bay. Sightseeing boats depart from the Namerikawa fishing port around 3 a.m. Ⓝ 36.788391 Ⓔ 137.367554

The glowing bodies of bioluminescent squid light up the fishing port of Toyama Bay.

The monks of Shugendo mummified themselves while still alive by drinking tea made from poisonous sap.

SELF-MUMMIFYING MONKS OF SHUGENDO

MOUNT YUDONO, YAMAGATA

The monks of northern Japan who followed Shugendo, an ancient form of esoteric Buddhism, sought to achieve enlightenment through difficult, ritualistic physical and mental challenges. At least two dozen monks successfully enacted an extreme form of self-sacrifice: They brought about their own deaths by slow, excruciating self-mummification.

The entire process took about ten years. During the first of the three stages, the monks spent 1,000 days eating a strict diet of nuts and seeds, while taking part in a regimen of rigorous physical activity that stripped them of their body fat. (Due to its high water content and heat retention, fat accelerates decomposition.)

In stage two, the monks restricted their diet even further, consuming only bark, roots, and a tea made from the toxic sap of the urushi tree—a substance more conventionally used to lacquer wood. This caused vomiting, sweating, and excess urination, achieving the goal of bodily desiccation and insuring that any maggots attempting to feed on the post-mortem flesh would be poisoned.

Finally, a self-mummifying monk would lock himself in a stone tomb 10 feet (3 m) underground, where he would meditate and recite mantras while sitting in the lotus position. His only connection to the outside world was a bamboo air tube and a bell.

Each day, he rang the bell to indicate he was still alive. When the bell stopped ringing, the tube was removed and the tomb sealed.

Hundreds of monks attempted self-mummification; few were successful. A thousand days after the final ringing of the bell, when the tombs were opened, most bodies had decomposed. These monks were resealed in their tombs—respected for their endurance, but not worshipped.

The monk with the most outlandish story is Tetsumonkai, who, according to legend, killed multiple samurai and fell in love with a prostitute before joining the monastery. Newly devoted to a life of self-sacrifice, he castrated himself and then hand-delivered his carefully wrapped testicles to the lovelorn woman. In another incident he cut out his left eye in the hope that it would end the outbreak of ocular disease in Edo. Having decided he needed to leave his body to the world in order to bring salvation to mankind, Tetsumonkai entered his tomb in 1829. His mummy, still in the lotus position, is on display at Churenji temple at Mount Yudono.

From Tokyo, get the Shinkansen (bullet train) to Niigata and switch to an Inaho limited express, getting off at Tsuruoka. This will take about 4 hours. From there, get a Yudono-bound bus to Oami. Churenji and Dainichibo temples are within walking distance.
Ⓝ 38.531952 Ⓔ 139.985089 ➻

➤ Other Mummified Buddhist Monks

LUANG PHO DAENG
After dying during a seated meditation session, 79-year-old Buddhist monk Luang Pho Daeng was encased in a glass coffin at Wat Khunaram temple. That was in 1974. The monk has been on display ever since.

The passage of time has brought remarkably little damage to the body. Besides desiccation and a gradual brown mottling of the white skin, the only visible change is the loss of eyeballs—a development the temple monks dealt with by covering the empty eye sockets with sunglasses.

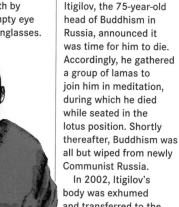

DASHI-DORZHO ITIGILOV
In 1927, Dashi-Dorzho Itigilov, the 75-year-old head of Buddhism in Russia, announced it was time for him to die. Accordingly, he gathered a group of lamas to join him in meditation, during which he died while seated in the lotus position. Shortly thereafter, Buddhism was all but wiped from newly Communist Russia.

In 2002, Itigilov's body was exhumed and transferred to the Ivolginsky Datsan, the most important Buddhist monastery in Russia. Itigilov's mummified remains are still there, sitting in the exact same lotus position as when he died in 1927. Itigilov is exhibited on major Buddhist holidays, during which pilgrims press their foreheads to the silk scarves that flow from Itigilov's hands out through a slot in the glass case.

The mummy of Luang Pho Daeng wears sunglasses so his desiccated eye sockets don't scare visitors.

THE MOUND OF EARS

MIMIZUKA, KYOTO

Tucked among houses on a narrow residential street in suburban Kyoto is a 30-foot-tall (9 m) grassy mound containing the ears and noses of tens of thousands of Koreans.

In 1592, Japanese military commander Hideyoshi Toyotomi led an invasion of Korea with the eventual goal of conquering China. Around 160,000 Japanese troops streamed into Korea with orders to murder indiscriminately.

The amount of respect and remuneration the soldiers received depended on their proving their kill tally. Traditionally, samurai took the severed heads of their victims as war trophies. But given the massive body count, soldiers began removing just the noses, or, less frequently, the ears, of the dead. Estimates vary wildly, but Japanese soldiers took body parts from perhaps as many as 150,000 Koreans. Reportedly, some of the victims were still alive when mutilated and survived the attacks.

Mimizuka literally translates to "mound of ears," despite the fact that it contains mostly noses. When the monument was dedicated in 1597, it was known as Hanazuka, or "mound of noses." The name changed decades later, when it was decided that the image Hanazuka evoked was simply too cruel. Severed ears were somehow more acceptable. **Shomen-dori, Higashiyama, Kyoto. Mimizuka is a short walk north of Shichijō station on the Keihan train line. Ⓝ 34.991389 Ⓔ 135.770278**

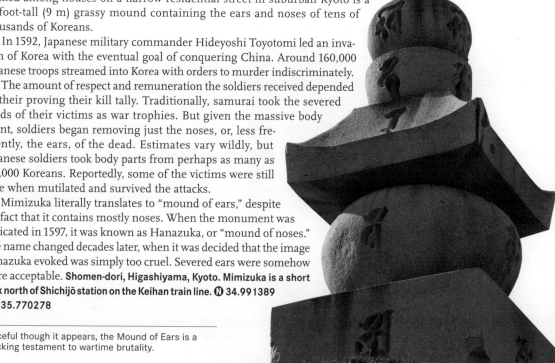

Peaceful though it appears, the Mound of Ears is a shocking testament to wartime brutality.

MARATHON MONKS OF MOUNT HIEI

HONSHU, SHIGA

The circumference of Earth is 24,901 miles (40,075 km). That's 2,000 miles (3,219 km) less than the distance the marathon monks of Mount Hiei must cover, on foot, over a period of seven years.

The marathon monks, or *gyoja*, belong to the Tendai sect of Buddhism, founded at the Enryaku-ji temple on Mount Hiei in the early 9th century. Seeking the status of living sainthood, they elect to undergo the rigors of *kaihogyo*, a seven-year program involving daily long-distance treks on little sleep and meager food rations.

Gyoja are allowed just one week of training before embarking on the first kaihogyo challenge: 100 consecutive days of 25-mile (40 km) walks. During this preparation week, other members of the sect clear the mountainous course of sharp rocks and sticks and weave 80 pairs of straw sandals for each monk to wear. Each pair lasts, at most, a few days.

The monks of Mount Hiei walk daily marathons, in straw sandals, for months on end.

For the next three and a half months, gyoja follow an unwavering daily routine. Each monk wakes at midnight and eats a small meal of rice or noodles before spending an hour in prayer. Then it is time to walk. Wearing a white robe, sandals, and a large rectangular straw hat, the monk follows a strict course, stopping at almost 300 stations along the way to pray and chant. He is forbidden from eating, drinking, or resting. Around his waist is a knife attached to a rope. In the event that the gyoja is unable to complete his kaihogyo, he is honor-bound to commit suicide using either implement.

When the monk completes his daily walk, he bathes, eats another small meal, and participates in chores and Tendai services before going to bed at 9 p.m. At midnight, he wakes and the entire process begins again.

The first three years of the kaihogyo follow the same pattern: one 100-day set of 25-mile (40 km) walks per year. In each of the fourth and fifth years, there are two 100-day sets. The greatest challenge comes on the 700th day, when, in an ordeal known as the *doiri*, the gyoja is denied food, water, and sleep for seven to nine days. The near-death experience, during which the gyoja sits upright in constant prayer, is intended to facilitate the death of the ego and the birth of a transcendent, interconnected being capable of leading others toward enlightenment. Originally, the doiri lasted 10 days, but the zero percent survival rate forced it to be shortened.

In the final two years, the distance of the walks increases—first to 37.5 miles (60 km), then to 52 miles (84 km). Approximately 50 monks have completed the seven-year kaihogyo since 1885. The most recent is Yūsai Sakai, one of three gyoja to have endured the process twice—from 1973 to 1980, and again, after a six-month break, from 1980 to 1987.

Enryaku-ji, the birthplace of Tendai Buddhism, is open to visitors. From Kyoto, take the Keihan Main Line to Demachiyanagi and transfer to an Eizan train to Yase-Hieizanguchi. From here the Eizan Cable Car will take you up Mount Hiei. Ⓝ 35.070556 Ⓔ 135.841111

ALSO IN JAPAN

The Tomb of Jesus

Shingo · According to a faithful few, Jesus died not on a cross on Calvary, but in northern Japan at the age of 106. A grave in the village of Shingo supposedly holds his remains.

Jigokudani Park

Yamanouchi · In the hot springs of snowy Hell's Valley is a spa for macaque monkeys.

WISTERIA TUNNEL

KITAKYUSHU, FUKUOKA

For most of the year, the wisteria tunnel at Kawachi Fuji Gardens is a latticed canopy overlaid with barren, twisting vines. But for a few weeks every spring, the tunnel is in magnificent bloom, its dangling flowers and sweet scent enveloping all those who walk its path.

The private garden is home to around 150 wisteria plants in shades of purple, pink, and white. Visit between late April and mid-May to see the wisteria in bloom—the exact dates vary each year.

2-2-48 Kawachi, Yahata-Higashi-ku, Kitakyushu. A JR train to Yahata Station followed by a bus to Kawachi Shogakko-Mae and a 15-minute walk will get you to the garden. Ⓝ 33.831580 Ⓔ 130.792692

A fragrant pastel passage that blooms for a few glorious weeks each year.

THE VILLAGE OF DOLLS

NAGORO, TOKUSHIMA

The school in the small village of Nagoro has a classroom full of silent students. Staring at an equally silent teacher, they sit motionless day after day, never calling out an answer or rustling their books.

The students and teacher are life-size dolls, created by Nagoro resident Ayano Tsukimi after the school closed due to low enrolment. Tsukimi, who was born in Nagoro, spent decades living in Osaka, Japan's third-largest city. When she returned to her childhood home, the population had dwindled from about 300 to 35 residents.

The dolls began as scarecrows, made to defend Tsukimi's veggie patch. But as Tsukimi created more and more, some in the likeness of deceased friends and relatives, she started placing them around the village in remembrance of the Nagoro residents she once knew. A doll in rain boots and wet-weather gear sits by a creek holding a fishing rod. A couple of elderly cloth people relax side by side on an outdoor bench, watching the world go by. Scenes like this are found all over the village.

Tsukimi estimates she has created 350 dolls, meaning they outnumber Nagoro's human residents 10 to 1.

To visit the village, board a JR train to Awa-Ikeda Station, followed by a bus to Kubo, then a bus to Nagoro. Ⓝ 34.043671 Ⓔ 133.802503

As residents die in the dwindling village of Nagoro, one local artisan is replacing them with cloth dolls.

BATTLESHIP ISLAND

HASHIMA, NAGASAKI

Hashima, an island off the coast of Nagasaki, is known by two nicknames: Gunkanjima ("Battleship Island") and Midori Nashi Shima ("Island Without Green"). The austere brutality conjured by these names is reflected in its appearance—Gunkanjima is a narrow lump of rock covered in the crumbling remains of a crowded concrete village.

The Mitsubishi company purchased the island in 1890 to establish a coal-mining facility for undersea reserves. In 1916, Japan's first concrete highrises sprung up on Gunkanjima—nine-story slabs of gray with cramped rooms and rows of identical balconies overlooking a claustrophobic courtyard. By 1959, over 5,000 coal miners and their families occupied these drab apartments, making the less-than-a-mile-long (1.2 km) island—with a population density of 216,264 people per square mile—the most overcrowded place on Earth.

Residents relied on the mainland for deliveries of food and, until 1957, water, but Gunkanjima was otherwise self-sufficient. Schools, playgrounds, cinemas, shops, a hospital, and even brothels operated in the tiny community. Steep concrete staircases that connected adjoining buildings were the only means of travel to ninth-floor apartments.

In January 1974, Mitsubishi officially closed its mining facility. All residents abandoned their homes for the mainland within two months, and Gunkanjima has been uninhabited ever since. Decades of typhoons, wind, rain, and seawater have caused massive degradation to the monolithic buildings. Wooden planks regularly fall from the disintegrating balcony railings, landing on the piles of crumbled concrete below. Contorted steel beams and rusted iron frames protrude from the walls. Hints of domesticity remain: a teacup; a tricycle; a television manufactured in the 1960s. The only sounds at what was once the world's most crowded place are the whipping wind and crashing waves.

Gunkanjima reopened to visitors in 2009, but official tours provide very limited access due to safety concerns. To actually explore the buildings, you would need to hop aboard an early-morning fishing boat for an unauthorized trip to the island. Official tour boats depart from Nagasaki Port and Tokiwa Terminal.

Ⓝ 32.627833 Ⓔ 129.738588

The lump of rock known as Battleship Island, now a ghost town in the middle of the sea, was once the most over-crowded place on Earth.

NORTH KOREA
KIJONG-DONG

DEMILITARIZED ZONE (DMZ)

Within the 2.5-mile-wide (4 km), 160-mile-long (250 km) heavily guarded demilitarized zone (DMZ) that separates North Korea and South Korea are two villages—one on each side of the border. Built in the 1950s, following the Korean War ceasefire, the northern village of Kijong-dong is a collection of well-appointed, multistory buildings that are home to 200 families. At least, that is the official story according to the North Korean government. In reality, Kijong-dong is an uninhabited propaganda village, built to convince South Koreans peering across the border of the North's economic success.

The apparently populous, well-appointed village of Kijong-dong is not all that it seems.

Viewed from a distance, Kijong-dong—or "Peace Village," as it's called by North Korea—is unremarkable, if a little drab. Look closer, however, and the trickery is revealed. Residential buildings have no glass in their windows. Electric lights—a rare luxury for rural Koreans—operate on an automatic timer. The only people in sight are maintenance workers, occasionally dispatched to sweep the streets to give the impression of ongoing activity.

One mile (1.6 km) from Kijong-dong, on the south side of the border, is the village of Daeseong-dong. Its few hundred residents live in limbo—as residents of the DMZ, they are exempt from taxes and compulsory military service, but these perks come at the price of their freedom. An 11 p.m. curfew is strictly enforced, and relocating is prohibited.

The opposing villages offer a study in the often ridiculous one-upmanship between North and South Korea. In the 1980s, the South Korean government erected a 323-foot-tall (98 m) pole in Daeseong-dong and flew their country's flag. North Korea responded by building a 525-foot (160 m) flagpole—then the tallest in the world—and raised an even larger flag over Kijong-dong.

Sixty endangered species roam around the DMZ, including the Amur leopard, Asiatic black bear, and red-crowned crane. They share their habitat with a million land mines. The Korea Tourism Organization offers nature tours of the DMZ, marketing it as "The Peace and Life Zone."

Entry to either village is not permitted, but both are visible from the UN-controlled Joint Security Area (JSA). You will be asked by the United Nations Command to sign a release form that includes a death waiver.
Ⓝ 37.941761 Ⓔ 126.653430 ➻

➻ Unplanned Nature Reserves

When humans leave, nature thrives. These "involuntary parks," to use a phrase coined by futurist Bruce Sterling, tend to be highly diverse ecosystems populated by species that thrive in the absence of agriculture and development.

EUROPEAN GREEN BELT
The Iron Curtain kept Europe segregated—physically and politically—for over 40 years. During this time, people fled the border regions, and the area between the Soviet-led East and NATO-aligned West became a corridor for wildlife. With the fall of the Iron Curtain came increased development. A grassroots conservation initiative called the European Green Belt aims to preserve and protect the ecological network that runs from the top of Finland to Greece and Turkey.

CYPRUS GREEN LINE
The cease-fire border dividing the Greek and Turkish parts of Cyprus earned its "Green Line" nickname after a peace force commander used a green marker to draw a wobbly line across a map of the country in 1964. Now the zone is verdant with flora and fauna, including the lapwing wading bird, the once-presumed-extinct Cyprus spiny mouse, and the mouflon—a wild sheep with large curled horns.

INTERNATIONAL FRIENDSHIP EXHIBITION

MOUNT MYOHYANG, NORTH PYONGAN

Like all national leaders, former North Korean rulers Kim Jong-il and Kim Il-sung received gifts from international politicians during their reigns. Uniquely, these presents are all on display in a 120-room museum that aims to showcase the world's undying love for the deceased despots.

Many of the gifts, which number around 100,000, are modest tokens of diplomatic etiquette—vases, ashtrays, books, and pens. At the other extreme is the big-ticket bounty received from Communists, terrorists, and despotic leaders keen to curry favor with North Korea. Animal trophies make a popular dictator-to-dictator gift: Fidel Castro handed over a crocodile-skin briefcase, while Nicolae Ceaușescu, the Romanian dictator who was

In order to see Kim Jong-il's bizarre collection of gifts from world leaders, visitors are required to wear white gloves.

overthrown and killed by his own people, proffered a bear head mounted on a red satin pillow.

Former Soviet ruler Joseph Stalin and Chinese chairman Mao Zedong each took a bigger-is-better approach, supplying a bulletproof limousine and armored train car, respectively. (Beyond their extravagance, these gifts show a certain thoughtfulness and sensitivity, given both Kim Jong-il and Kim Il-sung's fear of flying.)

At the end of Madeleine Albright's diplomatic trip to the isolated country in 2000, the US secretary of state presented Kim Jong-il with a basketball signed by Michael Jordan. The ball joins a Sony Walkman, a Casio keyboard, an Apple computer, and a soccer ball signed by Brazilian soccer great Pelé.

Among all the creative gifts, the most perplexing comes from Nicaragua's Sandinista revolutionaries, who donated a stuffed, upright alligator holding a wooden tray of cocktail glasses. **Mount Myohyang is a 2-hour drive from Pyongyang, accessible only by guided tour. You will be provided with fabric covers to wear over your shoes so you do not sully the floors with filth. Photos are prohibited. Ⓝ 40.008831 Ⓔ 126.226469**

SOUTH KOREA
THIRD TUNNEL OF AGGRESSION

PANMUNJOM, GYEONGGI

The demilitarized zone (DMZ) separating North and South Korea is a 160-mile-long (257 km), 2.5-mile-wide (4 km) strip of land where attempts—or perceived attempts—to cross the border result in being shot to death. Two million soldiers patrol the tension-filled buffer, making it the most heavily guarded border on Earth. A stealth ground invasion would be impossible—which is why, following the 1953 ceasefire that ended the Korean War, North Korea began secretly digging tunnels.

South Korea discovered the Third Tunnel of Aggression, named for it being the third one found and its apparent intended function as a conduit for military invasion, in 1978. It is one of at least a dozen rumored tunnels beneath the DMZ, four of which have been found so far. Designed to provide the route for an attack on Seoul, the Third Tunnel measures just over a mile (1.6 km) long, ending 27 miles (43.5 km) from the South Korean city.

At first, North Korea denied digging the 6.5 × 6 foot (2 × 1.8 m) tunnel. Then the story changed: The tunnel was a North Korean coal mine, a statement officials backed up by hurriedly painting its walls black. Refusing to believe the creative explanation, South Korea took control of the passage and blocked the border line with concrete barriers. The tunnel is now open to visitors, who can get within a few feet of the barbed wire and machine guns waiting on the other side of the concrete.

Self-appointed "tunnel hunters" in South Korea continue to search for secret passageways in the DMZ, believing the country won't be safe from a North Korean invasion until all are found. Motivated by deep distrust of their neighbors to the north, some have spent decades poring over maps, searching the ground for clues, and financing fruitless drilling operations. **Tours to the tunnel, located near Panmunjom, in the DMZ, leave from Lotte Hotel in Seoul. Ⓝ 37.956000 Ⓔ 126.677000**

JEJU GLASS CASTLE THEME PARK

JEJU

"Museum" may be a more apt term for the Jeju Glass Castle theme park, since everything is made from shaped glass and is not really conducive to the roughhousing usually associated with a raucous funfair.

The delicate collection is divided into indoor and outdoor sections, each with its own variety of glasswork. The exterior garden features such amazingly naturalistic installations as a glass waterfall, glass flower beds, and a lake made of mirrors, with fish constructed out of used soju bottles. The indoor sights include a towering green glass beanstalk in the center of the exhibition hall, a room full of mirrors where visitors can get lost in their infinite reflections, and even a glass bookshelf with glass books.

Most of the over 200 pieces at the castle are not to be touched, but there are some interactive bits, such as a set of glass drums you can bang on if you dare.

3135-1 Jeoji-ri, Hangyeong-myeon 462, Nokchabunjae-ro, Hangyeong-myeon, Jeju-si. For an extra fee, you can make your own glass creations. Ⓝ 33.314810 Ⓔ 126.273490

ALSO IN SOUTH KOREA

Trick Eye Museum

Seoul · Become part of an optical illusion at this collection of trompe l'oeil paintings that seem to interact with visitors.

The park brims with delicate and unexpected glasswork.

JEJU MERMAIDS

SEOGWIPO, JEJU ISLAND

In the historically patriarchal society in South Korea, some of the small fishing islands off the south coast have flipped the script thanks to the *haenyeo*. Otherwise known as the Jeju Mermaids, these pioneering (and largely elderly) fisherwomen have become the heads of their family units.

The practice began around the 18th century as a way of getting around the high taxes male fishermen had to pay on their meager hauls of shellfish, octopus, and abalone. At the time, women were not taxed at all, so women began exploiting this loophole by taking over fishing duties from their husbands.

As this role reversal persisted, islands such as Jeju saw family units flip power structures almost completely as the women free-dived for sea life in the icy East China Sea. The tradition has survived for hundreds of years, but now the haenyeo are in danger of disappearing as more and more of their daughters are choosing life in bigger mainland cities. Today the majority of haenyeo are women over the age of 50 who still go out and dive as deep as 30 feet (10 meters) to collect their family's main source of income.

Jeju is a beautiful volcanic island the haenyeo call home and is right next to the volcanic crater of Seongsan Ilchulbong. There are also several statues and art pieces in the area devoted to the haenyeo. Ⓝ 33.403554 Ⓔ 126.889611

JINDO–MODO LAND BRIDGE

JINDO, SOUTH JEOLLA

Moses may have parted the Red Sea to rescue the Israelites, but, according to South Korean legend, he is not the only one to achieve such a feat.

Twice a year, the waters separating Jindo and Modo islands recede, creating a causeway almost 2 miles (3 km) long and 120 feet (36.6 m) wide. The traditional explanation for this phenomenon is that a pack of tigers once attacked Jindo, sending its residents fleeing. Everyone escaped except an elderly woman, who prayed to the sea god to split the waters so she could pass safely to Modo. Her wish was granted.

Today, visitors to Jindo and Modo can relive the elderly woman's crossing of the Yellow Sea—once at the beginning of May and once in mid-June. On each of these days, visitors and tourists from each island pull on waterproof boots and walk to the middle of the causeway to meet one another and celebrate. Festivities are fleeting—the land bridge only lasts for about an hour.

Hoedong-ri, Jindo. Jindo is 6 hours from Seoul by bus. From the Jindo bus terminal, get a local bus toward Hoedong-ri. Ⓝ 34.407158 Ⓔ 126.361349

Twice a year, low tides part the Yellow Sea, allowing residents of Jindo and Modo islands to meet in the middle of the ocean.

Southeast Asia

CAMBODIA
DINOSAUR OF TA PROHM

ANGKOR, SIEM REAP

A carving on the wall of the Ta Prohm temple, built in the late 1100s, bears more than a passing resemblance to a stegosaurus. Since a 1997 guidebook first pointed out the strange carving, creationists have held up the Ta Prohm dinosaur as demonstrable "proof" that humans and dinosaurs once coexisted in Cambodia. There is even a replica of the carving on display at the Creation Evidence Museum in Glen Rose, Texas.

While the carved animal does seem to have a row of plates along its spine, it hardly makes a compelling argument for revising the prehistoric timeline. The bas-relief could just as easily be a depiction of a rhino or chameleon, with the "plates" forming a stylized version of foliage.

What's a stegosaurus doing on the wall of a 12th-century temple?

Angkor Thom, Siem Reap. Siem Reap is 6 hours from Phnom Penh by bus, leaving from Sisowath Quay.
Ⓝ 13.435000 Ⓔ 103.889167

THE LAST BAMBOO TRAIN

BATTAMBANG, BATTAMBANG

"Train" is a misleading word for this vehicle. "Queen-size wooden bed frame speeding along a rickety mine track" is a more accurate description. Known to locals as "norries," the bamboo trains of Battambang consist of two axles with welded-on wheels, topped by a 6 × 10-foot (1.8 × 3 m) bamboo platform. A noisy, sputtering engine, stripped from a motorbike or a piece of farming equipment, powers a drive belt that spins the rear axle.

To ride the norry, you simply sit on the platform—observing that your "engineer" is more than likely a child in flip-flops and taking note of the lack of safety rails or means by which to secure yourself—and hope that your balance doesn't betray you as you hurtle along the twisting rails at 30 miles (48 km) per hour.

Bamboo trains, an unregulated, improvised form of public transport, emerged after decades of Khmer Rouge rule decimated

Improvised transport for a region deprived of rail lines.

Cambodia's rail network. Using the poorly maintained tracks the French built in the 1930s, locals began running self-built norries made from scavenged spare parts. A network of norry routes sprang up, allowing people to travel and transport produce or animals.

Now that the restoration of national railway lines is underway, almost all of the norry routes have ceased operation. The sole remaining section runs from the outskirts of Battambang to a small village with a brick factory. Multiple bamboo trains thunder along the tracks in both directions. When two norries meet head-on, the passengers on the vehicle with the smaller load hop off, dismantle the train, and reassemble it once the other train has passed. Reassembly takes about a minute—one of the norry's many charms is that its parts are simply stacked on top of one another, with no nuts or bolts holding them in place. It's a detail you'll remember when you feel the wheels leave the tracks.

Rides on the bamboo train cost about $8 and can be booked through hotels in Battambang.
Ⓝ 13.068816 Ⓔ 103.202205

ALSO IN CAMBODIA

Pangolin Rehabilitation Center

Phnom Penh · This sanctuary, established in 2012, is dedicated to improving the plight of the rare scaly anteater.

Effigies of the dead linger among the living in Tana Toraja.

INDONESIA
Funeral Rites of Tana Toraja

TANA TORAJA, SOUTH SULAWESI

To the 650,000 Torajans of South Sulawesi, death is not the abrupt cessation of life, but a many-stage process that begins with a stopped heart and ends—sometimes years later—with burial.

The funeral rites of Tana Toraja consist of elaborate, multiday public ceremonies involving animal sacrifices, feasting, gift-giving, music, and a procession of village members toward the burial site. Wooden effigies, or *tau tau*, of the deceased are created and placed by the graves.

The cost of organizing and staging these rituals is so high that families may spend weeks, months, or even years raising the necessary funds. During this time, the wrapped corpse, chemically preserved with formalin, is kept in the ancestral home and referred to as "sick" or "asleep" rather than "deceased."

When there is enough money to purchase a herd of sacrificial buffalo, the festivities begin. On the first day, guests form a procession and offer gifts of food, drink, and sacrificial cattle or pigs to the family. The presents are given on an implicit quid pro quo basis—each gift is registered and announced to the crowd, allowing the villagers to keep track of debts paid or incurred.

Later in the week, an animal handler ushers each buffalo to the center of a ring and fastens a rope from its nose ring to a bamboo pole driven into the ground. As adults, children, and family pets look on, the handler raises a machete and drives it into the animal's neck, creating a gaping wound that gushes blood. The buffalo thrashes and writhes, blood spraying more forcefully with each movement. Gradually, the buffalo loses strength and collapses, dying in a pool of blood and mud. This process is repeated with dozens of buffalo and pigs.

According to Toraja belief, animal sacrifices prevent the spirit of the dead from lingering and bringing bad luck—souls travel to the afterlife on the backs of the buffalo. Back in the earthly realm, raw meat from the animal carcasses is distributed to guests, with high-ranking and wealthy people receiving the best cuts.

A week after the sacrificial ceremonies, the entire village parades the coffin to a burial site. The final resting place for a Torajan is usually a carved hole on the side of a cliff. Popular burial cliffs have rows of caskets guarded by tau tau.

The bus from Makassar, capital of South Sulawesi, takes 8 to 10 hours to reach Tana Toraja. Peak funeral season is after the harvest, from July to October. Ceremonies are public, and it is customary for visitors to bring a small gift for the family, such as coffee or cigarettes. Ⓢ 3.075300 Ⓔ 119.742604

GEREJA AYAM

MAGELANG

Should you be trekking through the thick forests of Magelang, Indonesia, try not to be too alarmed if you stumble upon a giant building shaped like a chicken. Known as Gereja Ayam, or the Chicken Church, this massive chapel is an unexpected sight both whimsical and fowl.

While the locals have dubbed it the Chicken Church (and it's easy to see why), the name is a bit of a misnomer since the visionary behind the avian-esque chapel actually intended for it to look like a dove. The architect, Daniel Alamsjah, received a holy vision that inspired him to create the dove-shaped church. He picked a forested hill near Magelang to build his pious tribute and created possibly the most bird-like building in the world, complete with giant, squawking head and ornate decorative tail feathers.

The church opened its doors (or spread its wings, so to speak) in the 1990s. It welcomed worshippers of all religions, and also offered charitable services to the local community. Unfortunately, the project was suspended in 2000 when funding ran out.

Gereja Ayam was vacated and left to the forest, where it continued to rot over time, becoming a bit more ghoulish with each year.

These days, the church has been cleaned up and turned into a proper tourist attraction. Local artists have covered the inner walls with vibrant murals, and there's a small café inside the chicken's rear end that sells traditional, tasty treats. You can even climb up to the top of the bird's head for amazing 360-degree views.

The church is open every day and is often part of the nearby Borobudur Temple tour. There is a small entry fee. ⑤ 7.605706 ⑤ 110.180483

The Chicken Church attracts worshippers of all faiths, locals and tourists alike.

A single notched pole allows access to these elevated houses, strong enough to support up to a dozen people and several animals.

KOROWAI TREE HOUSES

PAPUA

In the thick, remote rain forest of southeastern Papua, the Korowai people lived in total isolation up until the 1970s. Many members of the indigenous tribe still maintain a traditional lifestyle, which centers around a fascinating cultural trait: They are the architects of fantastic treetop homes built as high as 115 feet above the ground.

These unique dwellings protect families from the swarming mosquitoes below, as well as from troublesome neighbors and evil spirits. The tree houses are constructed in clearings with large banyan or wanbom trees selected as the main pole. Most huts are typically between 25 and 40 feet high, though some are built more than 100 feet (30.5 m) above the ground, reached by a single notched pole that serves as a ladder.

The floor is constructed first, then the walls and a sago palm tree roof are added, bound together with raffia. The flooring must be quite strong, as the tree houses often accommodate as many as a dozen people. Whole family groups, along with pets and other domestic animals, may live together in one treetop abode. The larger homes have separate living spaces for the men and women of the family, as well as firepits, and sometimes stairs.

The Korowai inhabit the region that stretches between the villages of Mabul and Yanirumah in the southeastern part of the province of West Papua, near the border of Papua New Guinea. An increasing number of Korowai people are moving away from the traditional nomadic lifestyle into the newly settled villages. To visit the tree houses, you will have to venture a few hours away from the settlements into the jungle. ⑤ 6.593292 ⑥ 140.163599

ALSO IN INDONESIA

Tanah Lot

Bali · The boat-shaped rock island of Tanah Lot holds a temple protected by a holy snake.

LAOS

XIENG KHUAN BUDDHA PARK

VIENTIANE

Though its weathered stone statues of gods, humans, animals, and demons look hundreds of years old, this sculpture park is the 1958 creation of Bunleua Sulilat, an eccentric priest-shaman whose mystic religious philosophies integrated Hinduism and Buddhism.

Sulilat claimed to have acquired his beliefs after falling into a cave and meeting a Hindu-practicing Vietnamese hermit named Keoku. There are 200 concrete sculptures at Xieng Khuan, all built by Sulilat and a few of his followers. They include a 400-foot-long (122 m) reclining Buddha, a Shiva whose eight arms are full of weaponry, and a three-story "Hell, Earth, and Heaven" pumpkin with a demon head inexplicably grafted onto one side. Visitors can enter through the demon's mouth and climb to the pumpkin's upper floors.

Following the Communist revolution in 1975, Sulilat fled across the Mekong River to the Thai city of Nong Khai, where he soon built another Buddha park called Sala Keoku. His mummified body is stored on the third floor of its pavilion.

Thanon Tha Deua, Vientiane. The Buddha Park is a half hour east of Vientiane. A bus from the city's morning market will take you to Friendship Bridge. From there, transfer to a minibus that will bump along uneven gravel roads to the park. ⑩ 17.912289 ⑥ 102.765397

A "spirit city" filled with hundreds of Hindu and Buddhist statues.

400 FEET

350

300

250

200

150

100

50

0 FEET

SPRING TEMPLE BUDDHA
Mount Yao, Henan, China

BUILT: 2008
HEIGHT: 420 feet (128 m)
TOTAL HEIGHT*: 502 feet
(153 m)

The copper Spring Temple
Buddha stands on a 66-
foot (20 m) lotus throne,
which itself is on an
82-foot (25 m) pedestal.
Visitors are welcome to
hug the statue's toes,
which are all taller than
your standard adult
human.

*with pedestal

LAYKYUN SEKKYA
Khatakan Taaung, Myanmar

BUILT: 2008
HEIGHT: 381 feet (116 m)
TOTAL HEIGHT: 427 feet (130 m)

Laykyun Sekkya's golden-
robed Buddha took 12 years
to build. It stands on a 44-foot
(13.5 m) throne, behind
a reclining Buddha that's
equally huge and equally
golden. Both statues gaze
toward the gilded stupa of
the Aung Sakkya Pagoda.

USHIKU DAIBUTSU
Ushiku, Japan

BUILT: 1993
HEIGHT: 393 feet (120 m)
TOTAL HEIGHT: 394 feet
(120 m)

Standing on a lotus
throne atop a pedestal,
the Ushiku Daibutsu is a
bronze standing Buddha
with a four-level museum
inside. New Age music, low
lighting, and incense induce
a state of calm on your way
up to the observation deck,
located in the Buddha's
chest, and with observation
windows built into its chest.

GIANT BUDDHA STATUES OF ASIA

Buddhism is big in South and Southeast Asia—you can tell from the size of the statues. Colossal sculpted Buddhas smile serenely across the region, their imposing forms extending hundreds of feet high. Some are seated, others stand, but all serve as beacons from afar, guiding visitors to the temples and sacred sites they invariably guard.

The five statues drawn to scale below, placed next to a suddenly puny-looking Statue of Liberty, are the biggest Buddhas of them all.

THE GREAT BUDDHA OF THAILAND
Ang Thong, Thailand

BUILT: 2008
TOTAL HEIGHT: 302 feet (92 m)

Thailand's golden seated Great Buddha, the tallest in the country and 18 years in the making, was built on top of a single-story museum. It's made of cement, with a layer of gold painted on top. Stop by the temple's Buddhist hell garden to see sculpted sinners being sawn in half or forced through a meat grinder.

LESHAN GIANT BUDDHA
Sichuan, China

BUILT: 803 CE
HEIGHT: 223 feet (68 m)
TOTAL HEIGHT: 233 feet (71 m)

The Leshan Giant Buddha is carved out of a stone cliff on a tributary of the Yangtze River. Created in the Tang dynasty (7th–10th century), it is the tallest pre-modern statue on Earth.

STATUE OF LIBERTY
New York, USA

BUILT: 1886
HEIGHT: 151 feet (46 m)
TOTAL HEIGHT: 325 feet (93 m)

The thousands of mysterious stone jars left on Xieng Khouang plain may have once stored human remains.

PLAIN OF JARS

PHONSAVAN, XIENG KHOUANG

Ranging from 3 to 10 feet (1 to 3 m) tall, the stone jars scattered across the 500-square-mile (1,295 km²) Xieng Khouang plain in the Laos highlands date back to the Iron Age: 500 BCE to 500 CE. Though their exact purpose is unknown, archaeological surveys of the area during the 1930s uncovered charred human remains, suggesting the jars once functioned as funeral urns. A cave with two man-made holes in its ceiling likely served as a central crematorium.

Many of the vessels bear the marks of more recent history: During the Vietnam War, conflict spilled into Laos, and the Plain of Jars became a valued strategic location. From 1964 to 1973, the U.S. engaged in a "Secret War" in Laos, dropping millions of bombs over the area. Evidence of that war persists in the form of smashed jars, craters, and signs warning of unexploded ordnances (UXOs)—30 percent of bombs dropped did not detonate, and many remain hidden in the landscape despite the consistent work of UXO removal crews.

Phonsavan, at the center of the plain, is an 11-hour bus ride or half-hour flight from the capital of Vientiane. When exploring the sites, pay careful attention to markers left by the Mines Advisory Group, which indicate the areas that have been swept for UXOs. Ⓝ 19.430011 Ⓔ 103.185559

MALAYSIA
SYNCHRONIZED FIREFLIES OF KAMPUNG KUANTAN

KUALA SELANGOR, SELANGOR

As mating rituals go, this one is pretty magical: At night, in the mangrove trees on the banks of the Selangor River, thousands of male fireflies (*Pteroptyx tener*) gather and flash in unison to attract the females of the species. (Scientists haven't determined the exact biological reason for the year-round synchronized flashing, but it's definitely part of courtship.) Viewed from a longboat, the fireflies look like tiny, twinkling string lights.

The Kampung fireflies were once much more numerous, but river pollution and development in their habitat have resulted in declining numbers over the last 10 years. That said, the silence of the boat ride, the pitch darkness, and the surviving clusters of bioluminescent bugs still create an atmosphere of awe.

The Kampung Kuantan Firefly Park is a 45-minute drive from Kuala Lumpur. Boats run from around 8 to 11 p.m. Ⓝ 3.360616 Ⓔ 101.301090

ALSO IN MALAYSIA

Cat Museum

Kuching · Walk through the giant cat mouth to enter a feline-focused world of kitschy figurines, dusty taxidermy, and a mummified furball from ancient Egypt.

BATU CAVES

KUALA LUMPUR

The walk to Batu Caves begins at the feet of Murugan, the Hindu god of war and victory. A 140-foot (43 m) gold-painted statue of the deity greets visitors as they prepare to climb the 272 steps that lead to the trio of large caves. The trip up the stairs would be less challenging if not for the hordes of long-tailed macaque monkeys scampering back and forth.

Long familiar to locals, the caves became more widely known after American naturalist William Hornaday "discovered" them in 1878. When Tamil businessman K. Thamboosamy Pillay visited the caves in 1890, he noticed that the entrance was shaped like the Vel—the spear held by Murugan. This resemblance inspired Pillay to install Hindu shrines and statues in the main Temple Cave, turning the location into a sacred site.

Every year since 1892, Hindus have celebrated the Thaipusam festival at the caves. Occurring in late January or early February, the festival commemorates the occasion when Parvati, goddess of power, gave Murugan his Vel. Participants go on a pilgrimage to the caves, encumbered by a *kavadi*, or "burden." Types of kavadi range from simple tasks (such as carrying a brass jug of milk on their head) to more extreme forms, like piercing their cheeks, chest, back, or tongue with skewers. Dressed in yellow, red, and orange, the kavadi bearers embark on an eight-hour, nine-mile (14 km) procession to the caves, culminating in a climb up the stairs to make offerings to Murugan.

The KTM Komuter train from Kuala Lumpur to Batu Caves takes 25 minutes. Thaipusam occurs on the full moon during the Tamil calendar month of Tai (mid-January to mid-February). Ⓝ 3.237400 Ⓔ 101.683906

During the Hindu festival of Thaipusam, pilgrims whose bodies have been pierced with skewers flock to the Batu caves. The more pain, the more spiritual reward.

PITCHER PLANTS OF KINABALU

SABAH, MALAYSIAN BORNEO

Deep in the forests of Kinabalu Park lurks *Nepenthes rajah*, the largest of the pitcher plants. These carnivorous wonders feature liquid-filled cavities that lure and trap insects.

Ants are the preferred cuisine of the Nepenthes rajah, but the plant has been known to trap much larger organisms in its urn-shaped cavity. Rats, frogs, lizards, and birds have all been found in the rajah's sticky grasp.

Rat-eating plants make for fascinating botanical fodder, but Nepenthes rajah's considerable dimensions—the largest recorded urn can hold almost a gallon of water—probably aren't meant for trapping rodents. In 2011, a team of scientists led by Monash University carnivorous plant expert Dr. Charles Clarke published their findings after studying interactions between tree shrews, rats, and the Nepenthes rajah. The report's main discovery was that these small mammals habitually landed on the rim of the plant and fed on nectar from the lid while defecating into the urn. Nepenthes rajah was their food source and toilet rolled into one. And that suited Nepenthes rajah just fine—the rat and tree shrew feces provided the plant with valuable nitrogen.

As a result of this study, it is now thought that Nepenthes rajah may have evolved to accommodate the feeding and excreting behavior of the tree shrews. The distance from the front rim of the pitcher to the nectar on the lid corresponds to the length of the tree shrew's body, allowing it to dine and defecate simultaneously in comfort. It's a heartwarming example of a plant and animal living in perfect harmony.

The *Nepenthes rajah* plant can swallow small birds, lizards, and frogs.

Kinabalu Park, Sabah. A bus from Padang Merdeka Bus Terminal in the Sabah capital of Kota Kinabalu reaches the park entrance in about 2 hours.
Ⓝ 6.005837 Ⓔ 116.542310

MYANMAR

PAGODA OF THE WORLD'S LARGEST BOOK

MANDALAY

The world's largest book, finished in 1868, is not an oversized bundle of paper pages, but a collection of 729 marble tablets. Each 5-foot-tall (1.5 m) tablet is inscribed with 160 to 200 lines from the Tipitaka—the sacred text of Theravāda Buddhism. The tablets are housed in 728 domed white shrines, arranged in rows around a central 188-foot-high (55 m) golden pagoda. The entire construction is known as Kuthodaw Pagoda.

King Mindon Min, who founded Mandalay in 1857, began the project in 1860. He intended to create a book that would last for five millennia after the Buddha. If Kuthodaw Pagoda remains intact for the next 2,500 years, his wish will be fulfilled.

62nd Street, Mandalay. You can find the pagoda at the bottom of the South East stairway of Mandalay Hill.
Ⓝ 22.004181 Ⓔ 96.113050

KYAIKTIYO BALANCING PAGODA

MOUNT KYAIKTIYO, MON STATE

At 24 feet (7 m) tall, it may not be the biggest pagoda around—but it is certainly one of the most eye-catching. Kyaiktiyo Pagoda sits atop a huge golden boulder balanced precariously on the edge of a cliff. The boulder, painted gold by Buddhist devotees, sits on a natural rock platform but looks as though it's about to tumble down Mount Kyaiktiyo any second.

According to the legend, a Buddhist hermit was given one strand of hair from the Buddha himself, which he then gave to the king. For his gift, the king offered the hermit a stone shaped like his head, and used his magical powers to pull the boulder from the ocean. The king then built the small pagoda atop the rock to enshrine the Buddha's hair for eternity.

Pilgrims have flocked to the site for centuries. The hike uphill takes about 30 minutes—if you are unable or unwilling to make the climb, four porters will carry you in a bamboo sedan chair.

From Yangon, get a bus to Kinpun and then board the open truck that takes you up the mountain to base camp. Be prepared to surrender your personal space—trucks don't depart until they are crammed with people. Ⓝ 17.483583 Ⓔ 97.098428

The precariously perched golden rock defies gravity and inspires pilgrimages.

A golden temple is surrounded by hundreds of stone tablets that together comprise the world's largest book.

The dead outnumber the living ten to one.

PHILIPPINES
MANILA NORTH CEMETERY

MANILA

The largest graveyard in Manila is overflowing with the dead. And the living. Every day, 70 to 80 burials take place in the 133-acre cemetery and while its dead residents number approximately one million, there are an additional 10,000 residents who are very much alive.

Impoverished people who cannot afford more conventional housing often end up living inside their family mausoleums, sleeping on the stone tombs that house their dead relatives. To earn money, adults clean and repair tombs, while children carry coffins at funerals and collect scrap metal to sell. Some enterprising residents maintain shops in the uninhabited mausoleums, selling snacks, candles, and prepaid phone cards. A karaoke machine in one crypt allows visitors to sing pop hits for five pesos per tune.

If a family fails to pay the rent on a deceased relative's tomb for five years, the person's remains are excavated so a new burial can take place. As a result, the unclaimed skulls and bones pile up in the narrow aisles between graves, occasionally becoming toys for the children playing in the cemetery.

Many of the residents were born between tombs and have spent their entire lives in the cemetery. Though living among the dead seems extreme, it is a free, quiet, and—for many—safer alternative to living in Manila's slums.

A. Bonifacio Avenue, Manila. The graveyard is in the Santa Cruz district, next to the Chinese cemetery.
Ⓝ 14.631476 Ⓔ 120.989104

CHOCOLATE HILLS

CARMEN, BOHOL

Chocolate may not be the first image that comes to mind when viewing the field of 1,268 conical, grass-covered hills on Bohol Island. But there is a logical explanation for the name: Each summer, the grass turns brown. Squint and, with a bit of imagination, you'll see a plain of giant chocolate kisses.

The hills, which range from 100 to 400 feet (30 to 122 m) tall, are limestone deposits from an ancient coral reef.

Get a Carmen-bound bus from the Dao terminal in Tagbilaran and ask the driver to let you off at Chocolate Hills, about 2.5 miles (4 km) before the Carmen stop. Ⓝ 9.916667 Ⓔ 124.166667

In Sagada, the dead are suspended from cliff faces for easier access to heaven.

HANGING COFFINS

SAGADA, MOUNTAIN PROVINCE

For 2,000 years, the people of Igorot Sagada have laid their dead to rest by jamming their bodies into compact wooden coffins and hoisting them up onto brackets driven into the side of a cliff. The practice protects the dead from floods and animals, and, according to Sagada beliefs, allows for easier passage to heaven.

Rows of pine caskets, some hundreds of years old, hang from the high bluffs of Echo Valley in Sagada. The Igorots embrace and actively prepare for death—elders, if physically able, carve their own coffins.

In summer, it will take you about 6 hours to travel from Manila to Sagada by bus or private car. During the rainy season, travel time doubles and roads are sometimes closed due to landslides. **N** 17.083333 **E** 120.900000

ALSO IN THE PHILIPPINES

Fire Mummies

Kabayan · In the mountain caves of Kabayan, tucked into hollow logs, are centuries-old mummies preserved via a smoking process.

Waterfalls Restaurant

San Pablo · Dine barefoot in a shallow river, seated beside a waterfall.

People were once mystified by the thousands of Hershey's Kiss–shaped hills on Bohol Island.

An exquisite (and expensive) temple honors an alleged tooth of the Buddha.

SINGAPORE

BUDDHA TOOTH RELIC TEMPLE AND MUSEUM

SINGAPORE

Completed in 2007, this $62 million dollar complex was built to honor a tooth fragment.

That may seem like quite an investment for such a small bit of dental debris, but the tooth purportedly belonged to one of the most famous religious figures in history—the Buddha.

The temple claims that the tooth is a relic recovered in 1980 from a collapsed stupa in Myanmar, but little additional information is provided. Experts have called into question the authenticity of the tooth, saying that it is most likely "the tooth of a cow or water buffalo, but definitely not a human."

The tooth is also only available for viewing during certain hours, but even if you miss the chance to see it, the temple itself is very impressive. It features multiple floors of Buddha statues, nagas (the popular Southeast Asian dragon-snakes that guard sacred relics), and impressive ceremonial venues in which to pray and meditate.

288 South Bridge Road, Singapore. There are a handful of other Asian temples that claim to have Buddha tooth relics, including the Temple of the Sacred Tooth Relic in Kandy, Sri Lanka. ⓝ 1.281519 ⓔ 103.844297

THAILAND
SIRIRAJ MEDICAL MUSEUMS

BANGKOK

A walk through these six museums is a journey into the myriad ways human beings may be horrifically injured, killed, or deformed.

In the pathological museum, you'll see a collection of preserved fetuses and babies with congenital abnormalities, including a baby with cyclopia—a birth defect that results in a face with one malformed central eye, no nose, and no mouth. Next door, the parasitology collection displays multiple human scrota engorged to the size of basketballs due to elephantiasis.

The most gruesome specimens are displayed in the Songkran Niyomsane Forensic Medicine Museum. Shredded limbs that were recovered from car accidents float in glass jars. Photographs of decapitated train crash victims adorn the walls. Inside the cabinets, murder weapons sit beside the body parts they pierced. At the center of the room, standing in an upright glass case that resembles a

Conjoined twins are one of many confounding specimens in the Siriraj collections.

phone booth, is Si Quey. The serial killer and cannibal died at the end of a noose after being sentenced for murdering and eating children during the 1950s. His black, shriveled body leans against one of the cabinet walls.

Adulaydejvigrom Building, Siriraj Hospital, 2 Phrannok Road, Bangkok. The museum is part of the Siriraj Hospital complex. Hop aboard the Chao Phraya Express boat at Bangkok's Central Pier and get off at Thonburi Railway. While the Pathology Museum is somewhat easy to find, it is worth tracking down the beautiful Congdon Anatomical Museum. Photography is not permitted. **ⓃN 13.757925 ⒺE 100.485847**

ALSO IN THAILAND

Goddess Tuptim Shrine

Bangkok · A shrine to a fertility goddess, complete with a forest of phallic offerings, has cropped up in a hotel parking lot.

Wat Samphran

Bangkok · An enormous dragon spirals around the exterior walls of this 17-story cylindrical temple.

MUSEUM OF COUNTERFEIT GOODS

BANGKOK

Knockoff Rolex watches, fake Louis Vuitton handbags, and imitation iPods are found in abundance in the markets of Bangkok—a situation that law firm Tilleke & Gibbins showcases in its Museum of Counterfeit Goods.

After raiding merchants on behalf of clients and seizing their forged goods to use as evidence, the firm ended up with rooms crammed full of counterfeit merchandise. In 1989, Tilleke & Gibbins began displaying 400 fakes in museum exhibits with the goal of educating the public on intellectual property infringement.

The museum's stash of illegal items now numbers over 4,000. T-shirts, perfumes, jewelry, cell phone batteries, and prescription drugs sit alongside their genuine counterparts, the differences often barely noticeable. Accompanying guides examine the societal impacts of counterfeiting—the operations support child labor, human trafficking, and the drug trade, among other ills. Consumer health and safety are also shown to be at risk, due to forged medications, car parts, and baby food that don't meet acceptable standards.

One of the more surprising aspects of the museum is the banality of some of its exhibits—apparently there is a market for counterfeit ballpoint pens, toothpaste, and stationery, along with the usual designer-label luxury goods.

Supalai Grand Tower, 26th floor, 1011 Rama 3 Road, Bangkok. Buses from the Khlong Toei MRT station stop right outside. Make an appointment at least 24 hours in advance. ⓃN 13.683684 ⒺE 100.548534

BEER BOTTLE TEMPLE

KHUN HAN, SISAKET

Every day, the monks of Wat Pa Maha Chedi Kaew Buddhist temple wake up surrounded by empty beer bottles. The order forbids intoxicants, but empty Heineken and Chang bottles are ever present, as they form the walls of the monks' living quarters.

Monks in Sisaket began collecting empty bottles in 1984 to promote recycling and keep the area litter-free. They amassed so many bottles of beer that they began to use them as building blocks for a temple and, eventually, a whole complex.

The main temple is comprised of approximately 1.5 million green Heineken and brown Chang bottles, set in rows. Inside are mosaics, created using pebbles and bottle caps. With the temple built, the monks moved on to new challenges: constructing a crematorium, prayer rooms, water tower, visitor restrooms, and residences—all made from beer bottles.

Construction is ongoing—the more empty bottles people bring, the more the monks will build.
Khun Han, Sisaket. Khun Han is a small village about an hour south of Sisaket. Ⓝ 14.618447 Ⓔ 104.418411

If you're thirsty for spiritual guidance, visit the temple of a million beers.

WANG SAEN SUK HELL GARDEN

CHON BURI

There's an awful lot of blood at Wang Saen Suk. It spurts from the mouths of the people being stabbed, gushes from the torso of the man being sawn in half, and bursts from the abdomen of the woman whose baby is being torn out of her body.

These gruesome scenes are sculptures created to decorate a Buddhist "hell garden" that shows what happens to those who behave badly. Buddhists believe in 16 main hells—eight hot and eight cold, all stacked on top of each other. Each hell is dedicated to specific offenses, and the punishments are tailored to the crimes.

The garden's focal point is an emaciated couple—one male, one female, each 30 feet (9 m) tall with ribs protruding, eyes bulging from exaggerated hollows, and tongues stretched to reach their hips. Surrounding the pair are figures in distress from an array of violent attacks. Some are having their heads eaten by dogs, while others stand helplessly as stern-faced men strip the skin from their bodies, revealing the glistening red layers beneath.

The garden is a popular destination for family day trips.

A depiction of the torture inflicted on those unfortunate souls who end up in Buddhist hell.

Sai 2, Soi 19, Saen Suk, Chon Buri. The garden is about 2 hours southeast of Bangkok. Ⓝ 13.297022 Ⓔ 100.910107

VIETNAM

HO CHI MINH MAUSOLEUM

HANOI

There is always a long line to see the embalmed body of Ho Chi Minh, who died in 1969, during the Vietnam War, at age 79. However, once you're inside the mausoleum, modeled after Stalin's final resting place in Moscow, things move quickly. Guards dressed in white enforce a policy of silence, shuffling people through the dimly lit space and allowing visitors only the briefest of pauses at the glass casket.

The hushed atmosphere reflects the national reverence for "Uncle Ho," who stood at this very spot in 1945 to read his declaration of independence, establishing the Democratic Republic of Vietnam. The need to pay tribute to the Communist revolutionary was strong enough to overpower his own wishes—in his will, Ho Chi Minh requested cremation.

Điên Biên, Ba Dinh District, Hanoi. More than 10 bus lines stop along the streets surrounding the mausoleum. Avoid visiting in October and November, when Ho Chi Minh's body travels to Russia for its annual makeover. Ⓝ 21.036667 Ⓔ 105.834722

ZOOLOGICAL MUSEUM AT VIETNAM NATIONAL UNIVERSITY

HANOI, HOÀN KIÊM

Tucked away atop a staircase and only open by appointment, the zoological museum at Vietnam National University, Hanoi, is a charming, scruffy display of French Colonial taxidermy and preserved animal specimens.

The museum is divided into three rooms: Mammals, Reptiles and Fish, and Birds. The mammal room contains a parade of beasts—big cats, deer, bears, monkeys, and a baby elephant—all frozen midstride in an apparent stampede toward the door. A Komodo dragon, inflated blowfish, and jars full of snakes occupy the Reptiles and Fish room. For moth-eaten charm, you can't beat the Birds room, where eyeless, dust-covered gulls, owls, and pelicans stand or lie in rows, untouched since the early 20th century.

19 Le Thanh Tong, Hanoi. Look for the elephant skeleton at the top of the stairs. It marks the entrance to the little-known museum. Ⓝ 21.020579 Ⓔ 105.858346

CU CHI TUNNELS

HO CHI MINH CITY

Beneath the suburban Cu Chi district of Ho Chi Minh City is a network of tunnels that served as a home, air raid shelter, weapon storage facility, and supply route for the Viet Cong during the Vietnam War. For years, thousands of people effectively lived underground, only emerging after dark to gather supplies. It was a grim existence—the air was stale, the food and water scarce, and malaria spread fast through the claustrophobic, insect- and vermin-infested passages.

Construction on the tunnels began in the 1940s, as Vietnam fought to gain its independence from France. By the 1960s, the network stretched to over 100 miles (161 km). Tiny tunnel entrances, concealed beneath leaves on the jungle floor, required bodily contortion to squeeze into. To guard against enemy infiltration, the tunnel maintainers incorporated traps, such as dead-end passages and revolving floor panels that sent enemies tumbling into pits

of sharpened bamboo. Should a foe make it past these snares and into the underground city, the Viet Cong might respond with a handful of scorpions or a well-aimed snake to the face.

Large sections of the tunnels are gone, having collapsed or been destroyed, but a preserved section, enlarged to fit larger tourist bodies, is open to the public. Visits end with the seemingly inappropriate opportunity to fire AK-47s and M-16s at a shooting range.

Tour buses and public buses make the 90-minute trip from Ho Chi Minh City. Ⓝ 11.143511 Ⓔ 106.464471

ALSO IN VIETNAM

Dragon Bridge

Da Nang · Cross a 6-lane bridge, opened in 2013, dominated by a giant yellow steel dragon that breathes fireballs.

Cao Dai Holy See

Tay Ninh · The lavish temple of the Cao Dai movement is a brightly colored, dragon-infested beauty.

The underground Cu Chi Tunnels, used during the Vietnam War, are a nightmare for the claustrophobic.

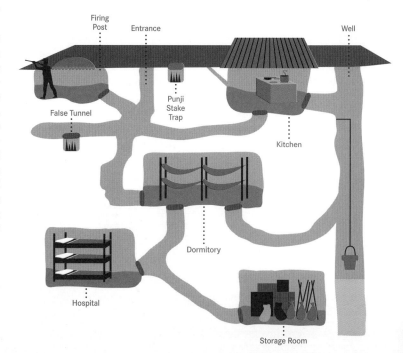

Firing Post · Entrance · Well · False Tunnel · Punji Stake Trap · Kitchen · Dormitory · Hospital · Storage Room

Africa

North Africa

EGYPT · LIBYA · MAURITANIA · MOROCCO · SUDAN · TUNISIA

West Africa

BENIN · BURKINA FASO · CAMEROON · GABON · GHANA · MALI
NIGER · SENEGAL · TOGO

Central Africa

CENTRAL AFRICAN REPUBLIC · CHAD
DEMOCRATIC REPUBLIC OF THE CONGO · REPUBLIC OF THE CONGO

East Africa

ETHIOPIA · SOUTH SUDAN · KENYA · TANZANIA · RWANDA · SOMALIA

Southern Africa

BOTSWANA · MALAWI · MOZAMBIQUE · NAMIBIA · SOUTH AFRICA
SWAZILAND · ZAMBIA · ZIMBABWE

Islands of the Indian and South Atlantic Oceans

MADAGASCAR · SEYCHELLES · SAINT HELENA, ASCENSION,
AND TRISTAN DA CUNHA

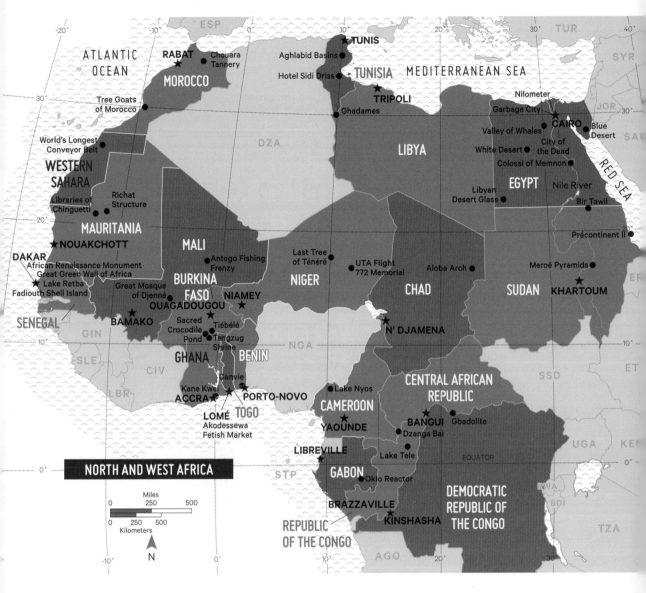

ATLANTIC
OCEAN

RABAT ★   Chouara
Tannery
MOROCCO

Aghlabid Basins
Hotel Sidi Driss

★ TUNIS
TUNISIA   MEDITERRANEAN SEA

TRIPOLI ★

Ghadames

Nilometer
Garbage City
Valley of Whales   CAIRO ★   Blue
White Desert ●   City of   Desert
the Dead
Colossi of Memnon ●

LIBYA

DZA

Tree Goats
of Morocco ●

World's Longest
Conveyor Belt

WESTERN
SAHARA

Libraries of
Chinguetti
Richat
Structure

MAURITANIA
★ NOUAKCHOTT

MALI

EGYPT   Nile River

Libyan
Desert Glass ●
Bir Tawil

RED SEA

SAU

JOR

Précontinent II

DAKAR ★
African Renaissance Monument
Great Green Wall of Africa
Lake Retba
Fadiouth Shell Island

Antogo Fishing
Frenzy
Great Mosque
of Djenné
BURKINA
FASO

Last Tree
of Ténéré

NIGER

UTA Flight
772 Memorial

Aloba Arch ●

Meroë Pyramids ●

ER

CHAD
SUDAN   KHARTOUM ★

SENEGAL

GIN

BAMAKO ★

OUAGADOUGOU ★

NIAMEY ★

Sacred
Crocodile
Pond ●   Tiébélé
● Tengzug
Shrine
GHANA

N' DJAMENA ★

NGA

SSD

BENIN

SLE

CIV
LBR

Kane Kwei
ACCRA ★
LOMÉ ★
Akodessewa
Fetish Market

Ganvie
★ PORTO-NOVO
TOGO

Lake Nyos ●
CAMEROON
★ YAOUNDE

CENTRAL AFRICAN
REPUBLIC

BANGUI ★   Gbadolite
● Dzanga Bai

UGA   KEN

ET

LIBREVILLE ★

GABON

BRAZZAVILLE ★
REPUBLIC
OF THE CONGO

STP

Oklo Reactor ●

Lake Tele ●

EQUATOR

DEMOCRATIC
REPUBLIC OF
THE CONGO

RWA

BDI

KINSHASHA ★

AGO

TZA

NORTH AND WEST AFRICA

Miles
0   250   500

0   250   500
Kilometers

N

North Africa

EGYPT

NILOMETER

CAIRO

Long before the Aswan Dam was constructed to
manage the flooding of the Nile, ancient Egyptians
invented the nilometer to predict the river's behavior. The nilometer on Rhoda (or Rawda) Island in
Cairo is an octagonal marble column held in place by
a wooden beam that spans the width of an ornately
carved well. The massive central column has markings on it that indicated where the river's water level
was at any given time. This information was used to
determine what conditions the future held: drought,
which would mean famine; desirable, which would
mean just enough overflow to leave good soil for
farming; or flood, which could be catastrophic.

Although the behavior of the Nile could mean
life or death for common people, only priests and
rulers were allowed to monitor the nilometer. This
is why many nilometers were built near temples,
where priests would be able to access the mysterious instrument and appear prescient when they
correctly predicted the river's behavior.
**The Rhoda nilometer is on the southern tip of the
island. The three tunnels that once let water into
the stilling well have been filled in, allowing visitors
to walk all the way down to the bottom. Ⓝ 30.007043
Ⓔ 31.224967**

An essential instrument, housed in an elegant well.

BLUE DESERT

SINAI DESERT

When Egypt and Israel signed a peace treaty in 1979, Belgian artist Jean Verame wanted to mark the occa-  sion. Verame journeyed to Egypt's Sinai Desert, near the resort town of Dahab, and created a "line of peace" by painting a stretch of its boulders bright blue. After decades under an unrelenting sun, the rocks are now less vibrant—but still a startling, cartoonish contrast to the beige and gray of the desert.

Verame went through official channels in order to paint the desert. Egypt's then-president Anwar Sadat signed off on the artwork, and the United Nations donated 10 tons of blue paint. The project was completed in 1981, the same year Sadat was assassinated by Islamic fundamentalists who were incensed by his signing of the peace treaty.

Hallawi plateau, between Dahab and St. Catherine.
Ⓝ 28.639722 Ⓔ 34.560833

WHITE DESERT

FARAFRA, WESTERN DESERT

Resembling giant mushrooms, atomic-bomb clouds, and, in one case, a chicken, the limestone rock formations of the White Desert are the heavily eroded remains of a former seabed. During the Cretaceous period, this portion of the desert was underwater, and chalk deposits from the skeletons of marine invertebrates accumulated on the ocean floor. To make a 100-million-year-old story short, the sea dried up, erosion dug odd shapes into the seabed, and now the White Desert is full of weirdly evocative rocks.

The best way to experience the bleached landscape of the White Desert is to camp overnight. As the sun sets and rises, the light on the rock formations changes, and their shadows morph. In the silence you may hear the soft patter of a fennec's paws. These adorably large-eared nocturnal foxes are native to the Sahara.

The White Desert is 25 miles (40 km) north of Farafra, an oasis where you can take a dip in a hot spring.
Ⓝ 27.098254 Ⓔ 27.985839

The eroded remains of a former seabed take the form of clouds, mushrooms, and a chicken.

CITY OF THE DEAD

CAIRO

The narrow, unpaved streets of the City of the Dead wind between densely packed, sand-colored buildings with weathered walls. These buildings are the tombs, family mausoleums, and intricately decorated funerary complexes of a 4-mile-long (6.4 km) Islamic necropolis that lies beneath Mokattam Hills.

The City of the Dead does not just house the deceased. Around half a million people also live there, sleeping, eating, and hanging their laundry in the centuries-old tombs. Many of the residents are families of those laid to rest, but the City of the Dead has also become a refuge for those forced out of Cairo's ever more crowded and expensive urban center. The northern cemetery, with its magnificent Qaitbay mosque, is more populated than the southern cemetery.

The necropolis lies under Mokattam Hills in southeast Cairo. N 30.021667 E 30.303333

The deceased and the living inhabit the same tombs.

Tens of thousands of freelance garbage collectors, known as Zabbaleen, pick up Cairo's trash.

GARBAGE CITY

CAIRO

The south end of the Manshiyat Naser ward in Cairo is better known as Garbage City. This is where the Zabbaleen—"garbage people" in Arabic—bring Cairo's household waste. The narrow streets, blocky apartments, and crammed courtyards are all piled with huge bags of trash waiting to be sorted.

Though the population of greater Cairo exceeds 17 million, the city has no municipal waste collection program. Instead it has tens of thousands of freelance Zabbaleen. For decades, this group has sustained itself by hauling household trash to Manshiyat Naser by truck and donkey-drawn cart. There, they recycle, reuse, and sell the refuse. Plastics and metals are carefully separated by color and composition, then sold as scrap. Pigs eat the organic waste.

This state of affairs shifted in 2003, when the Egyptian government attempted to downgrade the role of the Zabbaleen by bringing in corporations to handle waste disposal. The experiment was not a success—whereas the Zabbaleen received a fee for collecting trash from individual residences, the new system required people to take their garbage to communal collection points on the street. The corporate collectors were less efficient than the Zabbaleen and recycled a much lower percentage of refuse—about 20 percent compared with the Zabbaleen's 80

percent. Further threats to the Zabbaleen's livelihood came in 2009, when the government slaughtered Garbage City's hundreds of thousands of pigs, citing concerns over swine flu.

The vast majority of the Zabbaleen are Coptic Christians, a religious group that has suffered persecution and sectarian violence in the 90 percent Muslim country. Marginalized in the settlement of Garbage City, the Zabbaleen literally carved out safe spaces for themselves in the form of seven churches built into the limestone cliffs of Mokattam.

Garbage City lies at the base of Mokattam Hills in Manshiyat Naser, a ward in southeast Cairo.
Ⓝ 30.036230 Ⓔ 31.278252

ALSO IN EGYPT

Temple of Abu Simbel

Abu Simbel · Completed in 1244 BCE, this temple features four colossal statues of Rameses II, the reigning pharaoh at the time.

Muzawaka Tombs

Dakhla Oasis · See piles of mummies from Egypt's Roman era in these open rock-cut tombs.

Desert Breath

Near Hurghada · Completed in 1997, this giant land-art spiral of dots in the sand is slowly being consumed by the desert.

CITY GUIDE: More to Explore in Cairo

Aquarium Grotto Garden

Zamalek • The Fish Garden, just south of the aquarium on Gezira Island, is a rare spot of green within the chaotic city. Once part of a much larger estate, it was restored in 2000 but still feels like an old curio cabinet—if you can imagine a cabinet packed with sea life.

Agricultural Museum

Dokki • A threadbare remnant of Cairo's colonial past, many of the more decayed buildings in this sprawling complex are closed—but the areas still open are magical, with turn-of-the-20th-century taxidermy and out-of-the-past dioramas depicting early Egyptian daily life.

Lehnert and Landrock Bookshop

Qasar an Nile • The small gallery of glass-plate photographs by the two founders of this nearly 100-year-old shop will bring you back to a historic North Africa that is quickly fading from view.

Oud Shopping on Mohammad Ali Street

Abd el-Aziz • The Khan al-Khalili market is certainly a place to buy an oud, but if you're in need of the real thing from the hands of a true master, the place to go is Mohammad Ali Street, where more than a dozen shops specialize in professional-grade instruments. There they are made, repaired, and shipped to sellers all over the world.

Bayt al-Suhaymi

Qism el-Gamaleya • Once a family home of 17th- and 18th-century Ottoman merchants, this quiet and dignified museum is notable for its streamlined furnishings, elaborately carved wooden screens, and an elegant and organic design of wood and stone that would make Frank Lloyd Wright green with envy.

Bab Zuweila Gate

el-Darb el-Ahmar • One of the three remaining gates of the Old City walls, Bab Zuweila is an elegant example of Fatimid architecture, an Ottoman-era mash-up of Eastern and Western design. Climb up one of its two minarets via a tight spiral staircase.

Mosque of Ibn Tulun

Tolon • This 9th-century mosque in Islamic Cairo is thought to be the oldest in the city, and it's undoubtedly the biggest, with its long double arcades, pointed arches, mesmerizing scrollwork, and a perfectly square fountain holding down the center.

National Military Museum

Qism el-Khalifa • Part of the sprawling citadel on the western edge of the city, the National Military Museum is in a one-time harem palace of Muhammad Ali Pasha al-Mas'ud ibn Agha. The long history of the Egyptian military is captured through ancient armaments, dioramas of famous battles, and more recent materiel like a MiG-21 fighter jet.

The Monastery of Saint Samaan the Tanner

Qism el-Khalifa • The massive cave church of Cairo's Zabbaleen community is carved into a mountain, seats 5,000 parishioners, is named for a 10th-century tanner, and is one of the largest Christian churches in the Middle East.

Umm Kulthum Museum

el-Manial • To call Umm Kulthum's following cultlike is an understatement. Perhaps the most famous Arabic singer of the 20th century, the museum filled with all things "Umm" creates a portrait both expansive (her vast recording career and collection of gowns) and intimate (rhinestone reading glasses and little black day book).

Coptic Museum

Misr al-Qadimah • In 1908, a rare collection of early Coptic art—paintings, stone reliefs, tapestries, and metalwork of the early Christian era—found a home at this singular museum where thousands of artifacts are surrounded by intricate and ornate wood carvings.

Babylon Fortress

Misr al-Qadimah • Built by Trajan, a soldier-emperor who expanded the reach of Rome as far as it would ever get, this first-century CE fortress is still striking, with its striped stone walls and two millennia of history. Recent digs revealed ancient river walls that have held back the Nile for more than 2,000 years.

Cairo Geniza of Ben Ezra Synagogue

Misr al-Qadimah • The synagogue, built in the year 882 CE, is believed to be located on the spot where little baby Moses was scooped out of the Nile. Almost 2,000 years later, more than a quarter million fragments of medieval Jewish texts were found in the basement.

Hanging Church

Misr al-Qadimah • In Arabic, this 7th-century Coptic church is known as al-Muallaqah, or "the suspended," as it literally hangs over an ancient Roman gate. Its roof mimics Noah's Ark and 29 steps lead to its intricately carved doors.

Darb 1718

el-Fustat • In 2008, Egyptian multihyphenate Moataz Nasr created this vibrant and eclectic art and culture space for young performers and artists, with galleries, an independent film series, and workshops.

The Umm Kulthum Museum celebrates the singer known as "the fourth pyramid."

The fossilized skeletons of enormous footed whales litter the Egyptian desert.

VALLEY OF THE WHALES

WADI AL-HITAN, AL FAYYUM GOVERNORATE

There was a time when whales walked the earth. During the Eocene epoch —56 to 33.9 million years ago—there lived a whale suborder known as the Archaeoceti. The five families within this subgroup all bore a characteristic that set them apart from modern-day whales: limbs equipped with feet and toes.

During the Eocene epoch, these footed whales lived underwater. Though they didn't use their feet to walk, they are a missing evolutionary link between contemporary whales and their terrestrial ancestors.

In 1902, the first fossilized Archaeoceti skeletons were discovered in Egypt's Western Desert southwest of Cairo. After decades of fieldwork, the bones of 1,000 animals have been identified. Today, hundreds of partial skeletons remain in the sand, on display to any visitor who is willing to make the long trek through the desert. Wadi Al-Hitan has been a protected area since 1989, and even though it is remotely located and under strict management, the fossils are still vulnerable to visitors. In 2007, Egyptian authorities accused a group of Belgian diplomats of ignoring signs and steering two four-wheel-drives onto one of the whale skeletons. Cars are now prohibited from entering the site.

The site is 93 miles (150 km) southwest of Cairo. There are no paved roads; 4-wheel-drive vehicles are your best option. Leave your car at the entrance to avoid running over any 40-million-year-old whales. Ⓝ 29.270833 Ⓔ 30.043889

COLOSSI OF MEMNON

AL BAIRAT, LUXOR

The twin colossi (which no longer resemble twins) have loomed over the Theban Necropolis since 1350 BCE, battered for millennia by scorching desert sun and sporadic Nile floods.

These ancient Egyptian statues each depict the pharaoh Amenhotep III, who ruled during the 18th dynasty. They once flanked the entrance to his lost mortuary temple, which at its height was the most lavish temple in all of Egypt. Their faded side panels depict Hapi, god of the nearby Nile.

Though floods reduced the temple to no more than looted ruins, these statues have withstood many natural disasters. In 27 BCE, an earthquake shattered the northern colossus, collapsing its top and cracking its lower half. The damaged statue did more than merely survive the catastrophe: After the earthquake, it found its voice.

At dawn, when the first ray of desert sun spilled over the baked horizon, the shattered statue would sing. Its tune was more powerful than pleasant, a fleeting, otherworldly song that evoked the divine. By 20 BCE, esteemed tourists from around the Greco-Roman world were trekking across the desert to partake in the sunrise acoustic spectacle. Some say the sound resembled striking brass, while others compared it to the snap of a breaking lyre string.

The unearthly song is how these ancient Egyptian statues wound up with a name borrowed from ancient Greece. According to Greek mythology, Memnon, a mortal son of Eos, the goddess of dawn, was slain by Achilles. Supposedly, the eerie wail echoing from the cracked colossus's chasm was Eos crying to his mother each morning. (Modern scientists believe early-morning heat caused dew trapped within the statue's crack to evaporate, creating a series of vibrations that echoed through the thin desert air.)

Well-intentioned Romans silenced the song sometime between 196 and 199 CE. After visiting the storied statues and failing to hear their ephemeral sounds, Emperor Septimius Severus, reportedly attempting to gain favor with the oracular monument, had the fractured statue repaired. His reconstructions, in addition to disfiguring the statue so the fixtures no longer looked like identical twins, robbed the colossus of its famous voice and rendered its song a lost acoustic wonder of the ancient world.

The colossi make for a good stop on the way to or from the Valley of the Kings, which is a 15-minute drive away. Ⓝ 25.720636 Ⓔ 32.610445

The twin colossi once emitted a mysterious, fleeting tune.

LIBYAN DESERT GLASS

Among the treasures buried in Tutankhamun's tomb was a jeweled, collar-style necklace featuring a scarab carved from pale yellow glass—a glass whose origin is still the subject of scientific debate.

Known as Libyan Desert glass or Great Sand Sea glass, the 98 percent silica substance is scattered in chunks all over the dunes of southwest Egypt. The glass formed

naturally under intense heat, but the exact manner of its formation is unclear. The prevailing belief is that a meteorite hit this part of the

desert approximately 29 million years ago, superheating the sand and causing it to form glass when it cooled. Another possibility is that the meteorite exploded in the atmosphere, radiating heat strong enough to create the glass.

The glass is scattered around the desert along the Libya-Egypt border. If you'd rather not forage in the sand, go to the Egyptian Museum in Cairo to see Tutankhamun's necklace.

Ⓝ 30.047778 Ⓔ 31.233333

BIR TAWIL

On the border of Egypt and Sudan is Bir Tawil, an 800-square-mile (2,072 km²) patch of land that neither country wants to claim.

A border dispute in which each nation wants to foist land onto the other is unusual, but Bir Tawil is unappealing for good reason. There are two versions of the Egypt-Sudan border: the political boundary, a straight line established in 1899, and the more wobbly administrative boundary, established in 1902. The 1899 boundary gives the Hala'ib Triangle, a prized coastal section of land, to Egypt. The 1902 boundary puts the Hala'ib Triangle in Sudan. If either claims Bir Tawil,

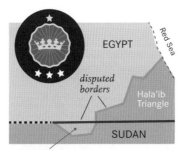

BIR TAWIL

it loses the much more valuable Hala'ib Triangle. And so explains the current stalemate.

Bir Tawil is one of the few bits of land on Earth to be regarded as *terra nullius*: unclaimed territory. There have, however, been attempts to establish sovereignty. In 2014, an American man named

Jeremiah Heaton flew to Egypt and journeyed 14 hours through the desert in order to plant a flag in the sand of Bir Tawil. His mission was to claim the region for himself so that his seven-year-old daughter's dream of being a princess could be realized.

Heaton, who received criticism in the British and American press for reviving white colonialism in Africa, has thus far been unable to gain international recognition for his "Kingdom of North Sudan."

Bir Tawil is 150 miles (241 km) south of Aswan, a city on the Nile that was founded in ancient Egypt as the frontier town of Swenett.

Ⓝ 21.881890 Ⓔ 33.705139 ➔➔

➔➔ Terra Nullius and the Discovery Doctrine

Terra nullius is a loaded phrase. Meaning "nobody's land" in Latin, it also refers to the belief, popular among European colonizers, that uncultivated land may be claimed in the name of the Crown despite the presence of indigenous inhabitants.

English settlers used the terra nullius justification to establish penal colonies in Australia during the 18th century, despite the presence of Aboriginal Australians. It wasn't until 1992 that the Australian High Court officially rejected the concept that the country

was terra nullius when the English arrived. Following this decision, Aboriginal Australians have been able to make claims on land for traditional use.

Closely related to the concept of terra nullius is the Discovery Doctrine, a set of principles

that guided Europe's colonization of the Americas and informed westward expansion in the United States. Its origins are in the papal bulls of the 15th century. Pope Alexander VI's 1493 papal bull, for example, declared that any land in the Americas not

inhabited by Christians was available to be "discovered." A Christian nation could claim sovereignty over such land, wrote Alexander VI, and explorers were to rid non-Christian inhabitants of their "barbarous" ways by instructing them in the Catholic faith.

LIBYA
GHADAMES

GHADAMES, TRIPOLITANIA

The old part of this ancient Roman oasis town, which is now uninhabited, is a maze of connected multistory mud-and-straw homes that are clustered together as though huddling against the swirling sands of the desert. Covered walkways between the buildings allowed people to socialize without having to face the heat of the Sahara. The passages linking the top floors of homes were used by women, while the ground-floor walkways were mostly used by men. Small ventilation holes in the walls let air flow through the alleys.

Some of the white walls of the homes are adorned with traditional designs of the Tuareg, the nomadic Berber people in the area. Red triangles, diamonds, moons, and suns are painted around windows and doors, above arches, and along stairs.

The newer part of Ghadames, which, unlike the old town, is equipped with electricity and running water, is still inhabited by around 11,000 people and welcomes overnight visitors.

There are flights from the Libyan capital of Tripoli to Ghadames, which is right near the spot where Libya meets the borders of Algeria and Tunisia.
Ⓝ 30.131764 Ⓔ 9.495050

The oasis town of Ghadames is known as the Pearl of the Desert.

The "Eye of the Sahara," a mysterious geological bull's-eye, is visible from space.

MAURITANIA

RICHAT STRUCTURE

OUADANE, ADRAR

The next time you're flying over Mauritania—or passing above Africa aboard the International Space Station—have a glance out the window and see if you can spot the Richat Structure. It shouldn't be too difficult: The circular feature is 30 miles (48.3 km) wide.

Also known as the Eye of the Sahara, the Richat Structure has somewhat mysterious origins. When the structure was first spotted from space in the mid-1960s, it was thought to be an impact crater from a meteorite. Geologists now believe that the massive bull's-eye is a heavily eroded mishmash of sedimentary, igneous, and metamorphic rock layers. After being pushed up into a dome formation—say, from a hot air balloon—these layers eroded at different rates, causing the striking pattern of concentric circles.

Though best viewed from above, the structure can be seen from the ground via a four-wheel-drive trip from the Mauritanian capital of Atar. Ⓝ 21.211111 Ⓦ 11.672220

LIBRARIES OF CHINGUETTI

CHINGUETTI, ADRAR

Soon after its founding around the 12th century, the desert mud-brick village of Chinguetti became a hub for trade, culture, and scholarship. Located on a trans-Saharan caravan route, it catered to the desert's nomadic population, receiving visitors with open arms—and open books.

The libraries of Chinguetti, owned and maintained by village families, contained a wealth of medieval Arabic manuscripts on science, mathematics, law, and Islam. Scholars, pilgrims, and the holy and venerated came to the village to pore over these handwritten leather-bound tomes and exchange ideas with one another.

Now desertification is causing the Sahara to encroach on Chinguetti. A few thousand people still live there, but sand is being pushed into the alleyways and swept against the walls. The libraries remain, but the dry air and swirling sand are a threat to the centuries-old manuscripts. Despite the risks, the families who own the texts prefer to keep them in place, and will display them for visitors using gloved hands.

Cars to Chinguetti leave from the nearby town of Atar. Chinguetti itself has few facilities, but some locals offer homestays, meals, and camel tours of the surrounding dunes. Ⓝ 20.243244 Ⓦ 8.836276

Chinguetti's holy manuscripts have been gathering dust since the Middle Ages.

MOROCCO
CHOUARA TANNERY

FEZ, FEZ MEKNES

Wedged among the ancient buildings and serpentine passageways of Fez's Old Medina is a grid of stone wells, each filled with colored liquid. This is Chouara, an 11th-century tannery that still operates as it did a thousand years ago.

Animal hides are brought here to be preserved, dyed, and turned into the handbags, jackets, and wallets sold in the surrounding souks.

The process begins with the raw skins being soaked in a mixture of cow urine, pigeon feces, quicklime, salt, and water. This loosens the hair from the hides and makes them softer. After a few days of steeping in this concoction, the skins are hauled out and hung from balconies to dry. Then comes the dyeing. Tannery workers plunge the skins into the colored wells, leaving them for a few more days to absorb the hue.

Visitors are welcome to observe the tannery in action and are even given a gift upon arrival: a small sprig of mint to hold under the nose when the smell becomes too much.

Fes El Bali, Fez. The tannery is in the old, walled part of the city El Medina, which also contains the University of al-Qarawiyyin. Established in the year 859, it is the oldest existing university in the world. Ⓝ 34.066361 Ⓦ 4.970973

The colorful wells of Morocco's leather tanning industry date back to the 11th century.

TREE GOATS OF MOROCCO

TAMRI, SOUS-MASSA

Morocco's argan trees are infested with hordes of fruit-hungry goats, who hop up into the branches to pick out the fruit. Grown almost exclusively in the Sous Valley in southwestern Morocco, the rare and protected argan trees (*Argania spinosa*) produce an annual fruit crop—these delicious morsels attract delightful tree-climbing goats.

Argan trees are not the most aesthetically pleasing plant in the world, with their rough, thorny bark and crooked branches. But their forests still tend to attract admirers, thanks to the odd sight of the hoofed animals perching on impossibly precarious limbs high in the treetops to enjoy their seasonal feast. The spectacle is far from just a single ambitious goat climbing a single tree—the goats tend to swarm into the trees. As many as a dozen goats can be seen munching away in the branches of a tree at any one time.

Local farmers condone and even cultivate this bizarre feeding practice, keeping the goats away from the trees while the fruit matures and releasing them at the right time. There is also a secondary benefit to the goats' habits: After the animals finish eating the fruit off the tree, they expel the valuable nuts found inside the fruit. The nuts are pressed to create highly sought-after argan oil, one of the most lucrative plant oils in the world.

This memorable rural scene mostly happens in June when the argan fruit ripen. Ⓝ 30.682889 Ⓦ 9.834806

The argan tree is a jungle gym for nimble, hungry goats.

World's Longest Conveyor Belt System

BOU CRAA, WESTERN SAHARA

The world's longest conveyor belt may not be as grand as the Great Wall of China, but it can be seen just as easily from outer space. The record-setting conveyance system is a winding chain of interlinked belts transporting phosphate from the mines in Bou Craa, Western Sahara, to the harbor town of El-Aaiún on the Atlantic Ocean, where it is shipped worldwide. The majority of the world's phosphate is mined in Bou Craa, the core of the so-called useful triangle in the Moroccan-controlled Western Sahara territory.

All told, the phosphate's leisurely journey covers a distance of 61 miles (98 km) from one end of the belt system to another. As the rocky ore makes its way across the landscape, strong desert winds blow the lighter particles of white powder off the belt, creating a bold ivory streak along the length of the transport system.

The start of the conveyor belt can be seen at the phosphate mines in Bou Craa. Ⓝ 26.188373 Ⓦ 12.696186

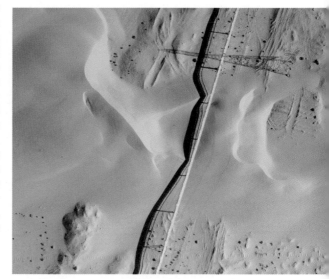

A conveyor belt so enormous it can be seen from space.

SUDAN

Pyramids of Meroë

MEROË, RIVER NILE

There are more pyramids in the northern region of the Sudanese desert than there are in all of Egypt. During Egypt's 25th dynasty—760 until 656 BCE—Meroë, now located in Sudan, was the capital of the Kingdom of Kush, ruled by Nubian kings who had conquered Egypt. The city, nestled against the Nile, contained a necropolis for royal burials.

As in Egypt, Nubian kings and queens were buried with gold, jewelry, pottery, and, occasionally, pets. Some royals were mummified, while others had their remains burned or buried whole. A sandstone pyramid, steeper and more narrow than the Egyptian variety, was built over each tomb.

In all, there were about 220 pyramids at Meroë. They remained relatively intact until the 1830s, when Italian treasure hunter Giuseppe Ferlini smashed the tops off 40 pyramids while searching for gold and jewels.

Meroë is a 3-hour drive north of Khartoum. A camel ride will get you to the pyramids. Bring water. Ⓝ 16.938333 Ⓔ 33.749167

Though less famous than their counterparts to the north, there are more pyramids in Meröe, Sudan, than in all of Egypt.

Explore the remains of Jacques Cousteau's underwater village.

Précontinent II

PORT SUDAN, RED SEA

Précontinent II is the last remnant of a series of three French underwater habitats built between 1962 and 1965. Developed by oceanography pioneer Jacques-Yves Cousteau, the underwater "village" tested the ability of humans to live underwater without interruption for extended periods of time, at increasing depths.

Précontinent I, a 16-foot (5 m) steel cylinder fixed 30 feet below the surface, was the first underwater habitat. It launched in the Balearic Sea off the coast of Marseille in September 1962. Two aquanauts, Albert Falco and Claude Wesly, lived among infrared lamps used as heaters, a record player, a radio, three telephones, a video surveillance system, a library, a TV, and a bed. In the bottom of the habitat was an airlock that allowed the two men to access the ocean, where they studied fish and took measurements for underwater topographical maps. A year later, two Précontinent II habitats launched about 22 miles (35.4 km) northeast, off the coast of Port Sudan. The first, named the Starfish House, lasted for four weeks and housed a group of oceanographers, as well as Simone Melchior Cousteau and the parrot Claude, who was supposed to warn the aquanauts of possible hazards in the air. The second habitat, Deep Cabin, was installed at a depth of 89 feet (27.1 m). Other structures included a tool shed and an air-filled hangar containing the Hydrojet Saucer DS-2, a two-person submarine equipped with three movable outside lamps, two cameras, a radio, a tape recorder, and a movable grappler. Précontinent III launched in September 1965 at 328 feet (100 m) below the surface, off the coast of Nice.

Of all the habitats, only part of Précontinent II remains underwater, and it has become the site of many diving tours from Sudan and Egypt. At the anchor place of the habitat you can find the remains of the toolshed, crusted with coral growth, and the fish cages, covered with sponges. A few meters deeper are the shark cages, covered with coral and crustaceans, and the hangar.

Shaab Rumi is a dive site 30 miles (48.3 km) from Port Sudan. Diving tours can be booked through various websites. Shaab Rumi is also a prime spot for shark sightings. Ⓝ 19.938736 Ⓔ 37.418697

TUNISIA
HOTEL SIDI DRISS

MATMATA, GABES

The small Berber village of Matmata is dotted with "troglodyte homes": traditional cave houses carved out of rock. Though the homes were created centuries ago, one of them, Sidi Driss, has a much more modern claim to fame: It was used as Luke Skywalker's childhood abode in *Star Wars: A New Hope* and *Attack of the Clones*.

The cave is now a hotel for *Star Wars* fans. For around $20 per night, you can live like a Jedi knight. It's not luxurious—the rooms are windowless, the beds are cots, and the occasional offensive odor travels on the wind—but it's certainly unique.

Shared taxis and buses leave from Gabes, 25 miles (40.2 km) away. ℕ 33.545687 Ⓔ 9.968319

Sleep like a Skywalker at Sidi Driss.

ALSO IN TUNISIA

Lac de Gafsa	Dougga
Gafsa · After appearing overnight in 2014, this mysterious desert lake has been dubbed both miraculous and possibly carcinogenic.	Twenty temples, an amphitheater, and a chariot-racing circle are among the highlights at this well-preserved ancient Roman town.

AGHLABID BASINS

KAIROUAN, KAIROUAN

Kairouan is in a semi-arid region prone to drought, without any nearby rivers or natural water sources. In the 9th century, a solution took the form of the majestic Aghlabid Basins, a huge and highly advanced work of engineering.

The Aghlabid Basins are composed of two connected cisterns which together form an open-air reservoir, fed by a 36-mile (60 km) aqueduct that sources water from the hills beyond town. Water flows into the smaller pool, which serves as a sort of filter, collecting stray sediments before the water is transferred to the larger basin, which is an impressive 16 feet (5 m) deep and 420 feet (128 m) in diameter.

The basins would fill up with rainwater, which would be used for washing or emergency hydration, though contamination always posed a major risk. Still, the system was a remarkably sophisticated engineering feat for its time and is considered the largest hydraulic installation of the period. Originally, there were at least 15; just two remain today. Though the pools appear circular, they are in fact 17-sided polygons.

Ave Ibn El Aghlab, Kairouan. You can visit the basins, but don't drink the water. While in Kairouan, swing by the Great Mosque. Established in the seventh century, it's one of the oldest places for Islamic worship in North Africa. ℕ 35.686541 Ⓔ 10.095583

Cisterns so well built they still stand 1,000 years later.

Built on stilts in the middle of a lake, the village of Ganvie is home to about 30,000 people.

West Africa

BENIN
GANVIE

GANVIE, ATLANTIQUE

In the 17th and 18th centuries, a portion of present-day Benin was known as the Kingdom of Dahomey. Established by the Fon people, a West African ethnic group, Dahomey became a major part of the Atlantic slave trade following the arrival of the Portuguese.

Fon hunters worked with Portuguese slave traders, traveling around the region hunting for people to sell. One of the ethnic groups they targeted was the Tofinu, who lived in what is now central Benin.

Knowing that the Fon's religious beliefs prevented them from venturing into bodies of water, the Tofinu fled their homes and established Ganvie, a community of bamboo huts built atop stilts on Lake Nakoué. Having provided protection for the Fon during the slave-trading days, Ganvie lived on, and has adapted to the demands of the 21st century. Motorized boats zigzag around its 3,000 buildings, which include a school, post office, church, bank, and mosque. About 30,000 people live in the village, traveling between huts by canoe and earning an income by fishing. **Ganvie is on the northern edge of Lake Nakoué, north of the coastal city of Cotonou, about 4 hours from Porto Novo. Ⓝ 6.466667 Ⓔ 2.416667**

BURKINA FASO
TIÉBÉLÉ

TIÉBÉLÉ, NAHOURI

The walls of the mud-brick homes at this village near the Ghanaian border are also canvases for cultural expression. Women of the Kassena ethnic group, who have lived in the region since the 15th century, work together to decorate the huts with geometric patterns, people, and animals. They use mud, chalk, and tar to paint, then cover the designs with a protective layer of varnish made from the boiled pods of a locust bean tree. **Tiébélé is 19 miles (30 km) east of the city of Pô, where you can hire a driver to take you to the village. Ⓝ 11.095982 Ⓦ 0.965493**

The women of Tiébélé turn every village wall into a geometric mural.

CAMEROON

LAKE NYOS

MENCHUM, NORTHWEST REGION

Lake Nyos killed over 1,700 people in a single night, but its victims did not drown. None were even in the lake—many died in their beds, in homes up to 15 miles (24 km) from shore.

The bizarre disaster began with the buildup of carbon dioxide in the lake, which sits in the crater of a dormant volcano. Gas rose from an underground magma chamber and dissolved into Lake Nyos, slowly creating a highly pressurized bottom layer saturated with carbon dioxide.

On the evening of August 21, 1986, just after 9 p.m., the lake erupted. A huge cloud of carbon dioxide burst from the water, smothering local villages and asphyxiating the people and animals within them. Those who survived spent hours unconscious

Seventeen hundred people died when these calm waters burped a bubble of carbon dioxide.

from oxygen deprivation. They awoke surrounded by bodies, with no indication of what had happened.

Since this catastrophic event, French scientists have implemented a degassing program at Lake Nyos. In 2001, they installed a pipe that runs to the bottom of the lake and allows the gas to

escape at a regular, safe rate. Two more pipes were added in 2011. A solar-powered alarm system monitors carbon dioxide levels—should the lake explode again, there will at least be some warning.

The lake, part of the Oku Volcanic Field, is about 200 miles (322 km) northwest of Yaoundé.
Ⓝ 6.438087 Ⓔ 10.297916

GABON

OKLO REACTOR

MOUNANA, HAUT-OGOOUÉ

At a University of Chicago athletic field on December 2, 1942, a crowd of excited physicists gathered to watch their nuclear reactor, CP-1, go critical. At the time, they believed they were witnessing the world's first self-sustaining fission chain reaction. In fact, CP-1 was the world's second uranium fission nuclear reactor—the first went critical approximately 1.7 billion years earlier, underneath the ground in the Oklo region of Gabon. This one was entirely natural.

Oklo's land is rich in uranium deposits, which France mined for decades beginning in the 1950s. In 1972, a routine analysis of samples from the Oklo mine showed an unusually low amount of uranium-235, one of the three isotopes found in naturally occurring uranium deposits. Ordinarily, the deposits consist of about 0.72 percent uranium-235. The Oklo sample contained only 0.717 percent uranium-235—not a huge difference, but enough to alert scientists to the fact that something unusual had taken place: a natural nuclear chain reaction.

The chain reaction began in the Precambrian era, when groundwater flowed through cracks in the ore and made contact with uranium-235. Generally, in a nuclear reactor, uranium-235 absorbs a stray neutron, causing its nucleus to split—fission—and releasing energy, radiation, and free neutrons. These neutrons then get absorbed into more uranium-235 atoms, causing more nuclei to split, which releases yet more neutrons in a chain reaction. Water acts as a neutron moderator, slowing down the fast-moving free neutrons that are released from split nuclei and giving them a better chance at further fission.

In all, 15 reactor zones have been discovered in the area surrounding Oklo's uranium mine. The waste products of one reactor remain, located on a slope of a mining pit and encased in a concrete block to prevent them from sliding into the trench.

The uranium mine, now closed, is on the N3 road in Mounana, a town of around 12,000 in the Oklo region.
Ⓢ 1.394444 Ⓔ 13.160833

GHANA
SACRED CROCODILE POND

PAGA, UPPER EAST REGION

The world's most docile crocodiles prowl the waters of this Paga pond. According to local tradition, each of the calm crocs represents the soul of a Paga villager. It is therefore forbidden to harm or disrespect the animals. But you're welcome to sit on their backs and pose for photos.

To see the crocs up close, you'll need to pay a guide, who will fetch a live chicken and whistle to summon the toothy beasts. Once your designated crocodile has sated itself with the flesh of the fowl and entered a state of post-gorging lethargy, you can pet its tail and sit astride its body. The crocodiles are not inclined to attack—probably because they are so well fed with fowl—but you are advised to steer clear of their snouts. Just in case.

The pond is on the Burkina Faso border, 25 miles (40.2 km) northwest of Bolgatanga. Ⓝ 10.98147 Ⓦ 1.115642

KANE KWEI CARPENTRY WORKSHOP

ACCRA, GREATER ACCRA REGION

A Ghanaian teacher was once buried in a ballpoint pen. A singer was laid to rest inside a microphone, while a laborer was interred in a hammer. These "fantasy coffins," built in the shape of items representing the deceased's occupation, passions, or aspirations, were made by craftsmen at Kane Kwei Carpentry Workshop.

The studio was established in the 1950s by Seth Kane Kwei, a member of the Ga ethnic group of coastal Ghana. The Ga believe that when someone dies, they move on to another life and continue to exert influence on their living descendants. Family members make sure to honor them and secure their from-the-grave goodwill by staging elaborate funerals involving hundreds of guests and a procession. The centerpiece is the casket, which is custom-designed to please the recently deceased.

Since Seth Kane Kwei's own death in 1992, the workshop has continued with a group of dedicated craftsmen who gladly sculpt coffins in the shape of lobsters, robots, sandals, high-top sneakers, bananas, and garbage trucks.

Should you be interested in a fantasy coffin, you can order one to be shipped anywhere in the world. You don't have to have your funeral in mind: In addition to their practical usage, fantasy caskets have acquired international value as works of art. A coffin in the shape of a Nike sneaker is on display at the Brooklyn Museum in New York, while an eagle-shaped casket holds court at the British Museum. Both are the work of Paa Joe, who was trained by Seth Kane Kwei.

Teshie First Junction, Accra. The open-air Kane Kwei workshop is on a dirt road, between a barbershop and a clothing store. Ⓝ 5.579425 Ⓦ 0.108690

With Kane Kwei coffins, death need not be a dull affair.

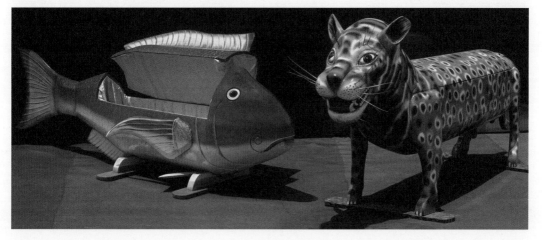

TENGZUG SHRINE

BOLGATANGA, UPPER EAST REGION

In order to visit the Tengzug Shrine, you must show respect by removing your shirt. Then you may walk the path toward the sacred site smeared with the blood of recently sacrificed animals.

The shrine is a place of worship for the Talensi, a northern Ghanaian ethnic group. Animal sacrifice is a significant part of the group's way of life, and as you wander through the village of Tengzug, you'll notice that the mud homes have adjoining shrines covered in chicken blood, feathers, and partial carcasses.

The main Tengzug Shrine at Tongo Hills is a cave atop a pile of boulders. Visitors—male and female alike—must enter topless. Inside are piles of feathers, sacrificial implements, and assorted remains of animals loved and lost. If the sights and smells of the cave are a bit too much to bear, turn your head to the hills—the vista is lovely.

Tengzug is 10 miles (16 km) southeast of Bolgatanga. Ⓝ 10.718635 Ⓦ 0.799999

MALI

ANTOGO FISHING FRENZY

BAMBA, GAO

Fishing is illegal at Lake Antogo, except for one day each year during the dry season. On that day, thousands of men—women are prohibited from participating—surround the small lake, wait for the gunshot that signals "go," and rush into the water, clamoring to seize catfish with their bare hands. After about 15 minutes of splashing and struggling, the fishermen emerge triumphant and mud-covered, carrying reed baskets full of gasping fish. The lake is all but empty and the ritual is over for another year.

The Antogo fishing frenzy is a tradition of the Dogon, a Malian ethnic group who inhabit the country's central Mopti region. Before desertification reduced the lake to its current small size, fishing happened year-round. Now that the fish are few, the annual ritual offers a fair chance for Dogon from all over Mopti to come together and capture food from the lake. Each year, men from multiple villages converge on the lake, located in a desert where temperatures often exceed 120°F (48.8°C).

The captured fish are presented to an elder from the nearby village of Bamba, who distributes them fairly among the gathered throng. The entire ritual, from catching the fish to sharing them, promotes unity among the disparate Dogon villages.

Lake Antogo is 120 miles (193 km) from Timbuktu. The date of the fishing frenzy is determined by village elders and changes every year, but generally occurs during May. Ⓝ 17.033644 Ⓦ 1.399999

Once a year, the world's wildest fishing trip takes place at Lake Antogo.

GREAT MOSQUE OF DJENNÉ

DJENNÉ, MOPTI

In 2014, the UNESCO Heritage–listed Great Mosque of Djenné sustained damage to its walls and had to be repaired by members of the community. But that wasn't cause for concern—it happens every year.

Like hundreds of other buildings in Djenné, the Great Mosque is made of mud. It was built in 1907, but the town's packed-mud architectural style dates back to at least the 14th century. To create the buildings, masons form mud and straw into bricks, allow them to dry in the sun, and stack them to form walls. A layer of mud plastered on top provides a smooth surface and better stability.

Though the buildings are sturdy and often sprawling—the Great Mosque can hold 3,000 worshippers—they are still vulnerable to the elements. Rain, humidity, and temperature changes cause cracks and erosion in the walls. Djenné's mud masons regularly band together and repair the mosque to keep it from falling apart.

Djenné is an 8-hour drive from Bamako, including a ferry ride across the Bani River.

Ⓝ 13.905278 Ⓦ 4.555556

Djenné's adobe architecture includes the largest mud-brick building in the world.

NIGER
LAST TREE OF TÉNÉRÉ

TÉNÉRÉ

For decades, a single, solitary acacia tree stood alone amid the vast desert of Ténéré. It was the only tree for over 250 miles in any direction, and became a landmark for travelers crossing northeast Niger.

In 1939, French military commander Michel Lesourd visited the tree to observe the construction of a well beside it. The acacia's roots were found to extend to a depth of 115 feet (35 m), where the water table began. "One must see the Tree to believe its existence," wrote Lesourd. He described it as a "living lighthouse."

roots, 10 stories deep

The last tree of Ténéré was destroyed in 1973 not by the harsh desert or the unforgiving weather, but by one human: a truck driver. The allegedly drunk Libyan man plowed into the acacia and snapped its trunk.

A simple sculpture of a tree, made from old pipes, fuel barrels, and auto parts, has since replaced the real one in the baked and barren Ténéré region of the Sahara. The fallen acacia still exists: It was taken to the National Museum of Niger in Niamey, where it stands in a fenced-in structure, safe from rogue drivers.

Around 150 miles (241 km) east of Agadez. Ⓝ 16.984709 Ⓔ 8.053214

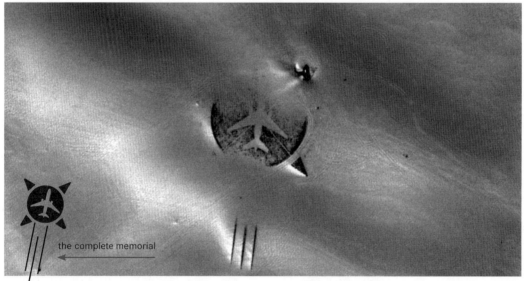

the complete memorial

Few people get to see this plane crash memorial in the Sahara, but those who do won't forget it.

UTA FLIGHT 772
MEMORIAL

TÉNÉRÉ

On September 19, 1989, UTA Flight 772 to Paris had been in the air for just over 45 minutes when a suitcase bomb placed in the hold by Libyan terrorists exploded, destroying the plane and killing all 170 people on board. Wreckage rained onto the Ténéré region of the Sahara desert in Niger, hundreds of miles from the nearest town.

Eighteen years after the crash, relatives of the victims journeyed to Ténéré to build a memorial. When they arrived, the parts of the plane not removed by crash investigators were still lying strewn in the sand.

Joined by 140 locals from Agadez, the nearest city, the group spent six weeks living in the desert and constructing a monument to the downed plane. Using dark stones trucked in from a site 44 miles (71 km) away, the workers built a 200-foot-wide (61 m) circle and filled it in to create a life-size silhouette of a DC-10 in the sand. A ring of 170 broken mirrors—each one representing someone aboard

the flight—lies at the perimeter of the circle. The crashed plane's starboard wing, brought in from its landing place 10 miles away, stands upright at the northern point of the circle. On the wing is a list of the 170 passengers' names.

The memorial is a tough, multiday drive from the nearest settlement, but it is visible to planes flying above it. Sand is gradually burying the rocks and mirrors.

Ténéré is a region in the south central Sahara, about 262 miles (421.6 km) east of Agadez. Ⓝ 16.864930 Ⓔ 11.953712

SENEGAL
GREAT GREEN WALL OF AFRICA

SENEGAL TO DJIBOUTI

It began as a wonderfully simple solution to the threat of the expanding Sahara desert: Plant a long green belt of trees across the entire width of the African continent to hold back the encroaching sands. Dubbed the "Great Green Wall," the plan was to grow a giant drought-resistant forest about 5,000 miles long and 10 miles wide across the southern edge of the desert, from Senegal in the east to Djibouti in the west.

The Sahara is currently the second-largest desert in size, smaller only than Antarctica. However, unlike its frozen relative, the Sahara is actually expanding at an alarming rate, threatening the farmlands in the Sahara and Sahel regions, where food security is an increasing problem.

The ambitious Great Green Wall initiative was started in 2007 by 11 African countries in order to fight drought, climate change, and creeping desertification. The name stuck, but the plan itself has evolved considerably over the last decade.

Rather than planting a narrow corridor of trees at the edge of the desert, the vision is now more of a mosaic of green landscapes across the entire arid region. The idea is to bring the land back to life by encouraging the natural regeneration of the drylands with a more grassroots approach that encourages green harvesting practices. The new goal is to regreen 100 million hectares of land by 2030. It's about 15 percent underway so far and still growing. The initiative now includes 21 African countries surrounding the Sahara on all sides.

Conservation and greening efforts in Senegal and Niger have seen the most success so far, restoring 9 million hectares of land.

Ⓝ 14.917014 Ⓦ 5.965215

AFRICAN RENAISSANCE MONUMENT

DAKAR

Atop one of the twin hills in the Mamelles district stands a mighty—and mightily confusing—monument. Sixteen stories tall, the bronze African Renaissance Monument is more than one and a half times the height of the Statue of Liberty. It depicts, in Soviet socialist realist style, a man with a bare, ripped torso holding an infant aloft in one arm and guiding a near-naked woman with the other.

In 2006, then-president of Senegal Abdoulaye Wade began planning a massive hilltop monument that would represent the country's emergence from centuries of slavery and colonialism. To build a budget-friendly monument, he turned to Mansudae Overseas Projects, a division of North Korea's government-run propaganda art factory. The company specializes in constructing huge, Soviet-style statues for cash-strapped nations.

The African Renaissance Monument was inaugurated in 2010 to mark the 50th anniversary of Senegal's independence from France. Unable to afford the $27 million price tag, Wade paid North Korea in the form of state-owned land in Senegal.

When the monument was unveiled, Wade was nearing the end of a 12-year presidency marred by alleged corruption, vote rigging, and self-serving changes to the constitution. His claim that intellectual property laws entitled him to 35 percent of revenue from tourism at the monument was met with understandable ire from fed-up Senegalese.

Despite this controversy, the monument still stands, surrounded by half-built houses and piles of litter.

Avenue Cheikh Anta Diop, Dakar.
Ⓝ 14.722094 Ⓦ 17.494981

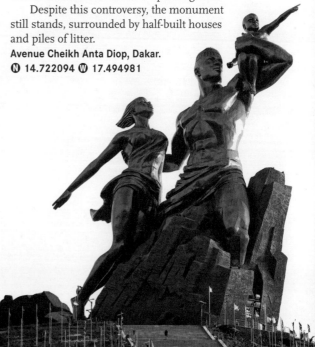

One and a half times taller than the Statue of Liberty, Senegal's much-derided sculpture was designed by a North Korean propaganda art factory.

LAKE RETBA
RUFISQUE

The pink waters and white shores of Lake Retba are deceptively inviting. Also known as Lac Rose, the lake has a salt content that rivals that of the Dead Sea, which makes for increased human buoyancy, as well as a busy salt industry. Salt collectors arrive daily, covered in shea butter to protect their skin from the harsh salinity, and spend up to seven hours a day collecting the precious mineral from the lake bed.

The lake's pink tint comes from the salt-loving microorganism *Dunaliella salina*, combined with a high mineral concentration. The water constantly changes hues, with the most stunning pink shade appearing during the dry season. In windy weather, and during the short wet season, the lake is less strikingly pink, due to the rain, which dilutes the salinity. With the salt levels reaching upward of 40 percent, Lake Retba can sometimes take a more sinister shade, appearing blood red, a much less comforting place for your imagination to go when gazing at the surreal view.

The lake is 25 miles (40.2 km) north of Senegal's capital, Dakar. In a car, the ride will take you less than one hour. Ⓝ 14.838894 Ⓦ 17.234137

ALSO IN SENEGAL

Fadiouth Shell Island

All the walls on this island are made with shells, as is the cemetery.

Salt collectors strike the riverbed to loosen the salt (above), which then dries in the baking sun (below).

The savvy voodoo shopper's source for chimp paws, desiccated cobras, and dog heads.

TOGO

AKODESSEWA FETISH MARKET

LOMÉ, MARITIME

When troubled by illness, relationship problems, or financial woes, voodoo practitioners in the West African nation of Togo go to the fetish market of Akodessewa. Located in the capital city of Lomé, the market has a row of tables piled high with dog heads, elephant feet, chimpanzee paws, desiccated cobras, and gorilla skulls. These are all fetishes, or talismans: objects infused with the power of the divine that are used to heal and protect.

Togo and neighboring Benin are where voodoo, known locally as vodun, began. Today, about half of Togo's population continues to hold indigenous animist beliefs. The fetish market, which is suffused with the smell of decaying flesh, is a sort of al fresco pharmacy, the perfect place to stock up on ingredients for rituals.

Tourists are welcome to peruse the offerings and visit one of the traditional healers in the huts behind the tables. During one of these consultations, the voodoo priest or priestess will ask you to describe your ailment, then consult with the gods to determine your prescription. Animal parts are ground up with herbs and held to a fire, which produces a black powder. Traditionally, a healer will make three cuts on your chest or back and rub the powder into the wounds. Tourists of a squeamish persuasion can opt to buy a wooden doll or just apply the powder to unbroken skin.

There are no set prices for the remedies; healers toss cowry shells to ask the gods what you ought to pay. If the price seems exorbitant, you are welcome to say so. The healer will keep consulting with the gods until you reach a mutually agreeable fee.

The market is located in the suburb of Akodessewa, just east of Lomé's airport. Ⓝ 6.137778 Ⓔ 1.212500

Central Africa

CENTRAL AFRICAN REPUBLIC
Dzanga Bai

BAYANGA, SANGHA-MBAÉRÉ

Ordinarily, forest elephants are an elusive bunch. Smaller than African bush elephants and now numbering under 100,000 due to poachers and deforestation, they travel the forests of the Congo Basin in small groups.

There is one place, however, where you can see 100 forest elephants at once: Dzanga Bai, a protected clearing surrounded by the dense forests of Dzanga-Ndoki National Park. Each day, the elephants stroll into the reserve along with forest buffalo, antelope, and wild boar. An elevated platform allows visitors to watch the wildlife on parade from a prime vantage point.

It's a peaceful scene, but not long ago, Dzanga Bai was a site of terrible violence. In May 2013, poachers stormed the clearing and killed 26 elephants for their ivory. The fight against poaching is ongoing and fraught with complications—forest elephant tusks are denser than the tusks of bush elephants, making them more valuable.

Following the 2013 poaching attack, Dzanga Bai reopened to visitors in July 2014. Researchers there are conducting an Elephant Listening Project, which studies how elephants use low-frequency sounds to communicate. They have been listening to the Dzanga Bai elephants since 1990.

The clearing is northwest of the village of Bayanga. It is accessible via a 40-minute walk through dense forest, on a path created by elephants. Ⓝ 2.950584 Ⓔ 16.367569

CHAD
Aloba Arch

ENNEDI

In the Ennedi Plateau of northeast Chad is a sight rarely seen outside China and the southwest United States: a natural arch of monumental proportions.

A natural arch is exposed stone in which a hole forms due to erosion or lava flow, leaving a frame shape in the rock. Aloba Arch spans about 250 feet (76 m), which is impressive in itself. But what really ups the drama factor is its height: The arch is located around 394 feet (120 m) above ground, which is about as high as the top floor on a 32-story building.

Natural arches spanning over 200 feet are rare. Of the 19 catalogued by the Natural Arch and Bridge Society, nine are in China and nine are in the Colorado Plateau in the southwest US, leaving Aloba as an awe-inspiring anomaly. (The Ennedi Plateau contains many other natural stone arches, but most of them have spans in the tens of feet, rather than the hundreds.)

The arches are several days' drive northeast from Chad's capital of N'Djamena. A 4-wheel drive is a must for navigating the sands. Ⓝ 16.742404 Ⓔ 22.239354

A towering arch in the middle of the desert.

DEMOCRATIC REPUBLIC OF THE CONGO

GBADOLITE

GBADOLITE, NORD-UBANGI

In the early 1960s, Gbadolite was a small village of mud huts. Then came Mobutu. When Mobutu Sese Seko seized control of the Democratic Republic of the Congo in 1965, it was the beginning of a 32-year reign characterized by tyranny against the people and extravagance for himself.

During his three decades of ruling the nation—which he renamed Zaire in 1971—Mobutu shut down trade unions, tortured dissidents, staged public executions, and embezzled billions of dollars. One of the self-serving ways in which he spent this money was to establish and maintain a luxury residence just outside of Gbadolite that became known as the "Versailles of the Jungle."

Powered by a hydroelectric dam Mobutu established in 1989, the newly lavish area featured well-appointed homes, schools, and hospitals, a five-star hotel, a Coca-Cola factory, and three large palaces, one of which was made up of Chinese pagodas. The Gbadolite airport had a VIP terminal accented with gold, and its runway could accommodate pricey supersonic Concordes. Foreign dignitaries would land here, then be whisked off in Mercedes-Benzes to Mobutu's private palace. There, they could take a dip in one of two swimming pools, lounge on Rococo furniture, and dine on sumptuous meals featuring gourmet ingredients flown in from France.

Following Mobutu's ousting in 1997, and his death from prostate cancer just a few months later, the shiniest parts of Gbadolite began to dull. Mobutu's hundreds of staff, including chauffeurs, chefs, and servants, stopped going to his palace. Weeds popped up among the marble, stained glass, and gold.

The gates to Mobutu's palace are still intact, but many of its roofs are gone. The steel beams of the ceiling form an eerie skeleton of the once-lavish residence. A makeshift school operates out of one of the Gbadolite buildings.

Some wall murals of Mobutu, which depict him in his signature leopard-skin hat, have survived the decay. His smiling face lives on in Gbadolite. **Gbadolite is about 8 miles (13 km) south of the Central African Republic border. Former workers at Mobutu's mansions, as well as their children, give tours of the ruins. Ⓝ 4.283333 Ⓔ 21.016667**

The grandeur of the "Versailles of the Jungle" has faded since the death of its despotic founder, Mobutu Sese Seko.

REPUBLIC OF THE CONGO

LAKE TELE

LIKOUALA

The Mokèlé-mbèmbé, Congo's version of the Loch Ness Monster, is said to live in this lake. Surrounded by tropical swampland, the circular body of water is difficult to access, which only fuels the stories about the apatosaurus-like creature supposedly lurking in its depths.

The cryptid has inspired many a proof-seeking pilgrimage to the lake, including a spate of trips during the 1980s led by American, British, Dutch, Japanese, and Congolese adventurers. In 1981, American engineer Herman Regusters claimed to have seen Mokèlé-mbèmbé during a two-week expedition, but none of the local men accompanying him claimed the same.

Monster-seeking trips like these have yielded little beyond muffled sound recordings and blurry photos of distant, indiscernible objects. But for cryptozoologists, the lack of resolution just fueled more imaginative speculation about what Mokèlé-mbèmbé gets up to over there. **Lake Tele is in the deepest jungle, surrounded by swamp forests teeming with gorillas, elephants, and swarms of bees. You'll need to fly into Impfondo (where you'll need to get a lake-visit permit from the ministry office), then drive to Matoko, get a riverboat to Mboua, and trek for 30 miles (48 km) through the wilderness. Ⓝ 1.346967 Ⓔ 17.154360**

East Africa

ETHIOPIA

ABUNA YEMATA GUH

EAST TIGRAY

If church can be an enlightening experience, imagine going to worship in a rough-hewn painted cave atop a towering sandstone pinnacle, only reachable via a dare-devil climb with 650-foot (198 m) drops on all sides.

At Abuna Yemata Guh, this risky and thrilling experience is common practice for a few dedicated priests. The monolithic place of worship is reachable only by a 45-minute ascent on foot. There are cliff faces to scale, rickety bridges to cross, and narrow ledges to traverse. After navigating the valley beneath the church, you must ascend the half-mile-high sandstone pinnacle, searching for rare footholds to avoid the long drop. Adding to the general sense of dread,

the route passes by an open-air tomb filled with the skeletal remains of deceased priests (although it's said that none of the priests died from falling off the cliff).

If the intense climb and the gorgeous view of the valley below aren't enough to take your breath away, the interior of the church surely will. The cave's ceiling is covered with two beautiful frescoes, featuring intricate patterns, religious imagery, and the faces of nine of the twelve apostles of Christ. The church also contains an Orthodox Bible with vibrant, colorful sheets made of goatskin. Abuna Yemata Guh is so sacred that some Ethiopian parents even risk bringing their babies all the way to the top of the cliff to have them baptized in the church.

The church is a 3.5-hour drive from Axum. The last portion of the climb, a vertical rock wall, must be done barefoot. Hire a guide to show you where to put your feet—and whatever you do, don't look down.
Ⓝ 13.915330 Ⓔ 39.345254

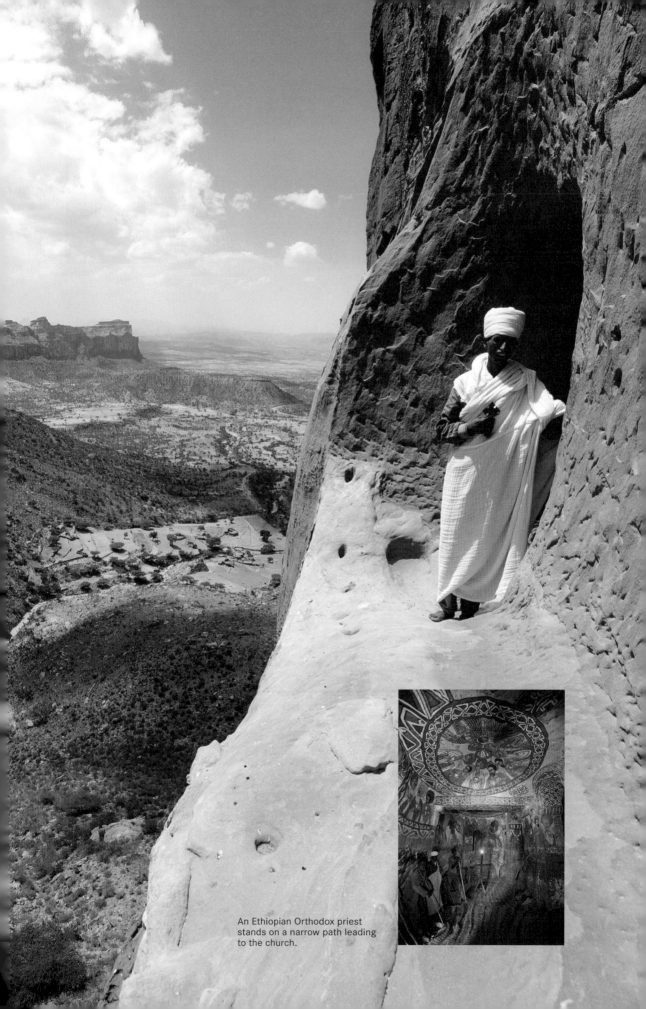

An Ethiopian Orthodox priest stands on a narrow path leading to the church.

The White Nile's vast swamps are the largest in the world.

SOUTH SUDAN
THE IMPENETRABLE SUDD

JONGLEI

The particularly squelchy chunk of land surrounding much of the White Nile in South Sudan constitutes the world's largest swamp. The Sudd, which means "barrier" in Arabic, is a vast wetland clogged with papyrus plants, water grasses, hyacinths, and other plants that have clumped together to create a giant impenetrable stew of greenery.

The size of the Sudd varies according to whether it's wet or dry season, but can expand to cover 50,000 square miles (130,000 km²)—roughly the size of the entire state of Louisiana. Swamp villages have been built on some of the floating islands of vegetation, which can measure up to 18 miles (29 km) across. Hippos and crocodiles hang out in the Sudd's shallower waters, while over 400 species of birds pay a visit during migration season.

The entire Sudd acts as a massive sponge, soaking up rainfall and the water that flows in from Lake Victoria in neighboring Uganda. This is bad news for boats, which carry saws to cut through the reeds and grasses. There have been proposals to establish channels that would cut a swath through the Sudd and allow for easier passage, but such an operation would disturb the ecosystem and displace its human inhabitants.

The Sudd spreads across the states of Unity and Jonglei. ⓔ 8.380439 ⓝ 31.712002

....

KENYA
KITUM CAVE

MOUNT ELGON NATIONAL PARK, WESTERN PROVINCE

Kitum Cave extends 600 feet (183 m) into an extinct volcano. Its salty walls are lined with scratches, troughs, and pits, which resemble the scars left by miners searching for diamonds or gold. But these carvings are not the work of humans—Kitum Cave's walls have been carved out by elephants.

The pachyderms that roam the park eat a diet of forest vegetation low in sodium. To get their fill of salt, elephants come to the cave and run their tusks along the walls, dislodging chunks of rock that they then crush and lick.

Elephants aren't the only animals that hang out in Kitum Cave. Buffaloes, antelope, leopards, and hyenas are known to prowl its depths. Beyond the inherent danger these animals pose, you'll need to be especially careful of the Egyptian fruit bats that swarm around the entrance. It is thought that the bats are vectors for Marburg hemorrhagic fever, an Ebola-like virus that two cave visitors contracted during the 1980s.

Salt-licking elephants are constantly renovating the interiors of Kitum Cave.

Both travelers—a 15-year-old boy and a 56-year-old man—died within days from the disease, for which there is still no vaccine.
The road to Mount Elgon leads from the town of Kitale, where you can get a minibus to the park. ⓝ 1.133333 ⓔ 34.583333

ALSO IN KENYA

Maasai Ostrich Farm

Kajiado · Take a ride on the world's largest bird—then eat its meat.

Gedi Ruins

Malindi · The remains of a mysterious town sit here surrounded by a tropical forest overlooking the Indian Ocean.

Marafa Depression

Malindi · The intricate folds and ridges of these sandstone gorges reveal whites, pinks, oranges, and reds in the rock.

TANZANIA

Ol Doinyo Lengai

NGOBRON, ARUSHA

Along the East African Ridge in Tanzania emerges a volcano known as Ol Doinyo Lengai, translating from Maasai to "Mountain of God." The name signifies a volcano of immense power, but the defining feature of Ol Doinyo Lengai is something else entirely.

This volcano, sprouting over 10,000 feet (3,000 m) tall in the middle of a plain, is the only active volcano on Earth that spews carbonatite lava instead of silica. This unusual composition makes the lava relatively cool: a mere 950°F (510°C), almost half the temperature of silicate magma. Carbonatite lava is black and gray in daylight, instead of the quintessential glowing red. When the lava solidifies, it turns white. And since the magma can cool and harden in seconds, it sometimes shatters in midair and sprinkles down the slopes.

Aside from the unusual temperature and color, the lava that pours from Ol Doinyo Lengai is also known to be the least viscous—or most "runny"—in the world. The lava doesn't just spout from the main crater either; little peaks on the volcano's surface called "hornitos" spew it too.

Ol Doinyo Lengai is a favorite among scientists, as it's easier to study than its dangerously hot counterparts—in fact, it's sometimes called a "toy volcano."

You can climb to the crater of the volcano with a guide. But it's a very taxing hike best reserved for the fit and well-equipped. Treks begin around midnight and return 9 to 10 hours later. ⑤ 2.763494 ⑥ 35.914419

A volcano frosted in white lava

Flamingos are among the few animals that can handle the hot, intensely salty waters of Lake Natron.

LAKE NATRON

MONDULI, ARUSHA

Visit Lake Natron during breeding season and you'll find it teeming with flamingos, their cotton-candy feathers contrasting beautifully with the mountainous backdrop. But this is no paradise: with a pH of 10.5—compared with ammonia's 11.6—the lake is caustic enough to burn your skin.

The shallow lake's high alkalinity comes from sodium compounds—primarily sodium carbonate—that flow in from the mountains. The water is hot—up to 140°F (60°C)—and often tinted a rusty red due to the presence of pigmented cyanobacteria.

The harsh conditions keep most animals away, but those that stay provide spectacular sights. A 2-million-strong flock of flamingos comes to Lake Natron every year to feed on algae and breed. The caustic conditions are perfect for warding off predators seeking to disturb the flamingo nests. On the downside, Lake Natron is the only regular breeding ground for East Africa's lesser flamingos, meaning that any environmental threats to the lake would have a severe impact on the species.

Proposed lakeside power plants and sodium carbonate processing facilities have thus far not materialized—a state of affairs that conservationists would like to preserve indefinitely.

Camp at the edge of the lake to see the flamingos at sunrise. ⑤ 2.416667 Ⓔ 36.045844

320-foot-long dune

moves 50 feet
per year

MAGNETIC SHIFTING SANDS

OLDUVAI GORGE, GREAT RIFT VALLEY

As the site of many early hominid fossil finds, Olduvai Gorge on the eastern Serengeti plains is widely regarded as the cradle of humanity. Right near it is a majestic pile of ash.

The ash—which originates from the Ol Doinyo Lengai volcano—is arranged in a crescent-shaped dune measuring roughly 320 feet (98 m) long. Wind is constantly reshaping the mound as its iron-rich magnetic grains fight back by clinging together. The result is a dune that is creeping across the desert at a rate of up to 50 feet (15 m) per year.

Ngorongoro Conservation Area. To appreciate the magnetic nature of the ash, grab a handful from the dune and throw it in the air—the grains find their way back to each other. ⑤ 2.920776 ⑥ 35.390521

RWANDA

KAKIRA IMIGONGO COOPERATIVE

NYAKARAMBI, EASTERN PROVINCE

In Rwanda, cattle are an important status symbol, and if you venture into the rural areas of the country you're almost guaranteed to cross paths with these gloriously long-horned denizens. You may even find yourself scraping their dung off your shoes. Or, if you're lucky, hanging it on your living room wall.

For generations, cow dung has been used in an art form found only in Rwanda: imigongo. Legend has it that in the 18th century, Prince Kakira was the first to use cow manure, mixed with ash and clay for color, to decorate the interior walls of his house. The practice took the name of the prince's domain, Gisaka-Imigongo.

Today's geometric imigongo artwork is generally painted on portable wooden panels, plates, or wall hangings. The vibrant paintings are composed of colors sourced from natural materials—rusty red from the natural soil, white from kaolin, or white clay, and black from the ashes of banana peels. There are several options for visiting an imigongo workshop, the most well-known being the Kakira Imigongo Cooperative. Here you can watch artisans making imigongo and even step inside a dizzying hut decorated in traditional imigongo style. Continue down the road between Nyakarambi and Rusumo and you'll see several other workshops along the way.

Nyakarambi is about 3.5 hours southeast of Kigali, the country's capital, by bus. ⑤ 2.271910 ⑥ 30.696677

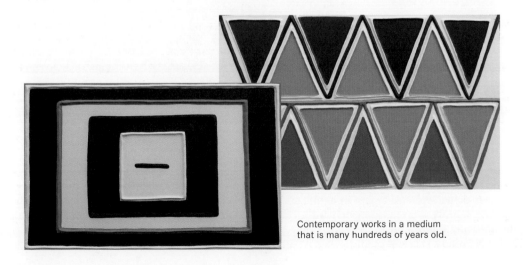

Contemporary works in a medium that is many hundreds of years old.

SOMALIA
THE MILKY SEAS

INDIAN OCEAN

Tales of a great glowing ocean had long been told within the sailing world, but the scientific community largely ignored them. Such bioluminescence, they reasoned, would require an impossible concentration of bacteria. Then a scientist named Steven Miller decided to do some further investigating.

In 2005, while searching for recorded accounts of the phenomenon, he came across the 1995 logs of the SS *Lima*, which recorded crossing milky seas 150 nautical miles east of Somalia. While it was presumed that no area would be large enough, or have a sustained enough glow, to be captured by satellite imagery, Miller, with the help of Steve Haddock, acquired archival data from the US Defense Meteorological Satellite Program for the night that the *Lima* recorded the phenomenon. When they overlaid it with the coordinates recorded by the *Lima*, they suddenly saw it shining up at them: a huge bright area off the horn of Africa.

Believed to be caused by the bioluminescent bacteria *Vibrio harveyi*, the glowing area is over 6,000 square miles (15,400 sq km) and is visible by satellite. It remains unclear how such a large congregation of bacteria can exist.

A few hundred milky seas have been documented around the world since 1915. The majority

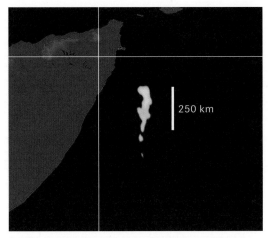
Satellite images show the bioluminescence at night.

show up in the northwest Indian Ocean, usually during summer monsoons. Their glow can last between several hours and several days at a time and is only visible at night.

If you have the time, budget, and inclination to venture 150 nautical miles from Somalia into the Indian Ocean, in the dark, you may encounter the milky seas. You'll just have to hope the stars—as well as enough bacteria—align. Ⓝ 11.350908 Ⓔ 51.240151

Southern Africa

BOTSWANA
AFRICAN QUADRIPOINT

CHOBE

There are several places where the borders of three nations touch, but the rare confluence of four nations in one spot exists only in Africa. Here, the corners of Zambia, Zimbabwe, Botswana, and Namibia meet.

The African quadripoint sits in the middle of the Zambezi River, which cuts between the countries. Quibblers point out that this is not a true quadripoint but instead a pair of tri-points separated by thin strips of real estate. Regardless, the jurisdictional headache of having four countries so close to one another has resulted in some conflict.

AFRICAN QUADRIPOINT
Zambia
Zimbabwe
Namibia
Botswana

At one point the ferry that carried people across the river from Namibia to Botswana became a point of contention, with both countries laying claim to the transport. A small fight broke out. Thank goodness it never escalated into a quadriputal war.

Zambezi River, an hour's drive west of Victoria Falls. The Kazungula Ferry travels across the river from Zambia to Botswana, via Zimbabwe. It's a 3-minute trip. Ⓢ 17.791100 Ⓔ 25.263334

MALAWI

LEPER TREE

LIWONDE, MACHINGA

A baobab tree in quiet, wildlife-filled Liwonde National Park bears a small, hand-painted sign that challenges the apparent tranquility of the scene. The sign reads: "The grave for people who suffered from leprosy in the past."

In Malawi, as in many places around the world, people with leprosy—also known as Hansen's disease—have often been ostracized. Though the bacteria that causes the disfiguring disease can be contagious, most of the world's population is naturally immune. Nevertheless, in accordance with traditional Malawian religious beliefs, those who died of leprosy could not be buried, as it was believed that they would contaminate the earth.

A look inside the Liwonde baobab, which is cut open on one side, shows the legacy of such beliefs. At the bottom of the hollow trunk lies a tangle of human skeletons. These were people with leprosy who got tied together and bundled into the baobab. It is unclear whether they were alive or dead at the time of their internment.

Liwonde National Park. The most prominent landmark in the park's southern area is Chinguni Hill, which is encircled by a dirt road. The tree is near the base of the hill. ⑤ 15.030231 ⑥ 35.247495

MOZAMBIQUE

THE LION HOUSE

GORONGOSA

The Gorongosa region, located in Great Rift Valley, is one of the most biodiverse places on the planet, and efforts have been made to preserve its unique ecosystems since the 1920s. By 1940, the wildlife reserve was such a popular attraction that a safari lodge was built to accommodate tourists. Unfortunately, it was built right on a floodplain.

Every year during the rainy season, the Mussicadzi River would flood the building, and the lodge was abandoned before it was even fully completed. Then the lions moved in. In 1960, Gorongosa became a national park, and today the magnificent animals and their unexpected residence are a famous landmark at the park.

For generations lions have been coming back to the house. Some of the estimated 50 to 70 living on the reserve use it as a safe haven for their cubs and a place to take shelter from the rain. The animals are known to ascend to the roof of the building for a better vantage point from which to watch their prey for hours, carefully choosing the best warthog or bushbuck to target for their next meal. And of course they use the house to do what cats do best: lie around and nap. Being at the top of the food chain has its advantages.

Fly from Maputo to Beira (a 3-hour drive from the park) or Johannesburg to Chimoio (a 2-hour drive). The park has well-appointed villas and bungalows for lodging, as well as a campsite for the more intrepid. ⑤ 18.690239 ⑥ 34.313589

It may look abandoned, but this shelter is a clubhouse of sorts for local lions.

A former diamond mining settlement is being claimed by the desert.

NAMIBIA

KOLMANSKOP GHOST TOWN

LÜDERITZ, KARAS

During the 1920s, the desert town of Kolmanskop was inhabited by hundreds of German diamond miners, and boasted a hospital, theater, casino, bowling alley, and gym. Now Kolmanskop is a ghost town, bleached by the sun and swallowed by sand.

The town was built in 1908 following the discovery of diamonds in the area. At the time, Kolmanskop lay in German South-West Africa, a colony that lasted from 1884 until 1915. Diamond mining operations were fast and furious until World War I caused a slump in sales. In 1926, a richer source of diamonds was discovered south of Kolmanskop. The town struggled on for a few more decades before being abandoned for good in 1954.

The homes of Kolmanskop still stand, but their floors are piled with sand, which has begun to reclaim the buildings. Some of the mini dunes are marked with wavy lines—the tracks of snakes that occasionally slither through the sandy halls.

Tours of Kolmanskop leave from the Insell Street boat yard in Luderitz, a harbor town 15 minutes away.
Ⓢ 26.705325 Ⓔ 15.229747

DEADVLEI

NAMIB-NAUKLUFT PARK

Rising from a parched white clay bed surrounded by soaring red sand dunes, the scorched branches of Deadvlei's trees twist toward a cloudless sky. Though long leafless and dead, the trees have yet to decompose—the climate is too dry to permit decay. Instead they stay stuck in the cracked and thirsty clay, skeletons of their former selves.

It's difficult to picture now, but a river once flowed into Deadvlei. Its trees bore flowers and provided canopies of shade. Then came the drought, around 1100 CE, which robbed the clay pan of its nourishing water. Sand dunes swept around the edges, blocking the flow of the river and leaving Deadvlei bare.

A few hardy plants have survived the stark terrain. Patches of salsola, a succulent saltbush, and nara, a bumpy-skinned melon, cling to the sand. Except for the camera-toting visitors, they're the only signs of life in a cinematic barren land.

Tours to Sossusvlei, the clay pan where Deadvlei lies, leave from Windhoek. It's a 6-hour drive and you can stay overnight. Ⓢ 24.760666 Ⓔ 15.293373

Seven-hundred-year-old scorched trees emerge from the salt pan, surrounded by the world's tallest sand dunes.

THE HOBA METEORITE

GROOTFONTEIN, OTJOZONDJUPA

The largest known meteorite on earth lies on a farm near the town of Grootfontein, on the very spot where it landed around 80,000 years ago. One of the reasons it remains in situ instead of sitting behind glass at a museum is its weight—at over 60 tons, it's roughly as heavy as a US Army tank.

Found in 1920, the Hoba meteorite measures 9.8 feet long by 9.8 feet (3 × 3 m) wide, and stands 3.3 feet high. Though a sizable crater must have been created at the moment of impact, 80,000 years' worth of erosion has erased the dent in the sand.

The meteorite's iron-and-nickel surfaces bear the marks of vandals—visitors to Hoba have been known to chisel off a piece of the space rock to keep as a souvenir. The addition of a surrounding amphitheater and anti-vandalism measures during the 1980s seem to have quelled attempts to take chips off the old block, but you can still touch the meteorite as much as you like.

The meteorite is about 16 miles (25.7 km) west of the town of Grootfontein, along the D2859 road. Ⓢ 19.588257 Ⓔ 17.933578

The largest meteorite ever found crashed to Earth around 80,000 years ago.

FAIRY CIRCLES OF SOUTHERN AFRICA

NAMIBIA DESERT

Small, circular patches of bare ground form like bald spots in the otherwise thick grass fields of Namibia and South Africa, in places where humans rarely set foot. The mysterious origin of these so-called fairy circles have bewildered scientists and spurred local legends about supernatural footprints and UFO landings.

Unlike their distant cousins, the crop circles of Britain, the fairy circles of southern Africa don't suddenly appear. In fact, they grow and shrink over time as though they were alive. Scientific research has established that the bald patches occur naturally; however, examination of the soil in and around the circles reveals no abnormal insects or parasites, no unusual fungi to speak of. In 2017 a study by a team of ecologists from Princeton University posited that the patterns are the result of termites establishing circular borders against competing colonies. Other experts have disputed this, however. All science has discovered conclusively thus far is that the fairy circles are not a hoax.

One spot to see the circles is NamibRand Nature Reserve, which is a 5-hour drive south of Windhoek, Namibia's capital.
Ⓢ 25.018789 Ⓔ 16.016973

Some call these mysterious circles the footprints of the gods.

caption tk

SOUTH AFRICA
ORLANDO TOWERS

JOHANNESBURG, GAUTENG

Orlando Towers, a self-professed "vertical adventure facility," caters to a niche crowd: those who have always wanted to bungee jump from a bridge suspended between the cooling towers of a decommissioned power plant, 33 stories from the ground.

From 1951 until 1998, the towers handled excess heat at Orlando Power Station. Following the closure of the plant, a rope access specialist named Bob Woods turned the towers into an extreme-sports venue. You can now rappel down the side of one of the towers, rock climb up the other, freefall off the rim into a giant net, or bungee off the bridge. Experienced BASE jumpers can even jump off one of the towers with no safety equipment, provided they bring their own parachute and sign a comprehensive legal waiver.

Since 2002 the once-drab towers have been covered in color. One is painted with murals representing South Africa, while the other is devoted to advertising space. The towers have become a landmark of Soweto, the ramshackle township that gained infamy as a ghetto for black residents of Johannesburg during apartheid.

Dynamo Street at Old Potch Road, Orlando, Soweto.
Ⓢ 26.253394 Ⓔ 27.927189

Bungee jumping from a brightly painted former cooling tower, anyone?

SEAL ISLAND

CAPE TOWN, WESTERN CAPE

In False Bay—named in the 17th century by disgruntled sailors who mistook it for the adjacent Table Bay—lies a rocky strip of land overrun with seals. Around 60,000 of the barking, flopping, waddling brown fur seals jostle for space on the half-mile-long, 164-foot-wide (50 m) Seal Island.

From a tour boat, the cacophonous jostling is a compelling sight, but it's the smell—a unique bouquet of rotting fish and excrement—that makes the boldest impression. This, however, is before you view the effects of the "ring of death," a circle of great white sharks that surrounds the island waiting for seals to enter the water. When they do, the sharks pursue them relentlessly.

It's not unusual to see a great white suddenly breach the surface and hurtle into the air with a seal struggling in its jaws. The sharks are fast, brutal, and capable of chomping seals to death in under a minute. It's a violent sight, and you can't help but root for the seal. Sometimes, after a thrilling battle, they get away.

To the sharks surrounding the island, the herds of noisy, smelly seals constitute a tasty buffet.

Seal Island cruises leave from Hout Bay. The trip takes about 45 minutes. Ⓢ 34.137241 Ⓔ 18.582491

VREDEFORT DOME

VREDEFORT, FREE STATE

When entering the small village of Vredefort, it may not immediately be apparent that you are at the center of one of the planet's most violent moments. Spread out from the town in a 185-mile (298 km) diameter are the rippling remnants of one of the oldest and largest known meteorite impact craters still visible on Earth. Though it can only be fully viewed from space, and 2 billion years of erosion have flattened the crater, the rippling rings around Vredefort speak to the sheer impact of the event when a 6-mile (9.7 km) wide mountain-size object slammed into the earth at over 25,000 miles per hour. **The crater is 75 miles (121 km) southwest of Johannesburg. Guided tours of the dome leave from Parys, a town north of the crater. ⑤ 26.997842 ⑥ 27.360668**

The oldest impact crater can be seen from space.

SWAZILAND

THE REED DANCE

LUDZIDZINI, HHOHHO

For a week every year, in late August or early September, tens of thousands of girls and young women storm Ludzidzini, the village of the royal family in Swaziland. Barefoot, bare-breasted, and adorned with brightly colored skirts, beaded necklaces, and pompoms, they parade in front of the king and his family, singing and dancing while holding machetes.

This annual ritual, known as the Umhlanga, or Reed Dance, is held primarily to celebrate the chastity of the girls and young women involved. Virginity is a prerequisite for participation, which reflects both a traditional social value in Swaziland and modern concerns about HIV transmission in a country where one in four people is living with the virus.

The ceremony begins with the girls being separated into groups according to their age. Each group then journeys to a patch of wetlands, where the girls cut and bundle reeds using their machetes. Over the next few days, the girls travel back and forth from the wetlands to the queen mother's palace, bringing back bundles of reeds intended to patch holes in the fence surrounding the palace.

After a day of rest and preparation, the girls return to the palace in bright sashes, skirts, and jewelry. The king and his family sit and watch as wave after wave of girls sing and dance before them. The public are also invited to attend these two days of celebrations, though photography is prohibited.

In addition to promoting the traditional social values of female virginity and cooperative labor, the ceremony has a practical purpose: The King of Swaziland, Mswati III, has often used the parade to scout for wives. His thirteenth wife, Inkhosikati LaNkambule, and his fourteenth wife, Sindiswa Dlamini, were both plucked from Reed Dances. **Ludzidzini Royal Village is between the capital city of Mbabane and Manzini. Exact dates of the Reed Dance differ each year, as they depend on astrology. ⑤ 26.460652 ⑥ 31.205313**

Young women prepare to dance for the Swazi king. One may become his next wife.

ZAMBIA
THE DEVIL'S SWIMMING POOL

LIVINGSTONE, SOUTHERN PROVINCE

The small pool with the terrifying view at the edge of Victoria Falls takes your average swimming experience and adds a hefty splash of anxiety. Situated just off tiny Livingstone Island on the Zambian side, the "Devil's Pool" invites you to sit at the top of the world's largest sheet of falling water in relative safety. A naturally formed rock barrier separates you from the roaring falls and keeps the pool's current weak, preventing you from getting swept over the edge and into the 355-foot-tall (108 m) waterfall.

Tour guides lead swims to the Devil's Pool from Livingstone Island when the water level is low enough—usually between August and January. ❷ 17.924353 ❸ 25.856810

Take a daring dip in the world's highest infinity pool, formed naturally by rocks.

The largest ancient structure south of the Sahara was part of a city that may have been home to 18,000 people.

ZIMBABWE
GREAT ZIMBABWE

MASVINGO, MASVINGO PROVINCE

The soaring stone walls that snake around the perimeter of what was once Great Zimbabwe provide an indication of the grandeur of the former city. Built by the Bantu people between the 11th and 15th centuries, Great Zimbabwe consisted of three parts: an ellipse-shaped Great Enclosure with 36-foot (11 m) walls, a citadel on a hill, and a scattering of stone dwellings in a valley.

Before it became overpopulated in the 15th century, leading to its abandonment, Great Zimbabwe was a thriving medieval trading center. Archaeological excavations, which began during the early 20th century, have unearthed glass and porcelain from China and Persia, as well as gold and coins from Kilwa, an island off Tanzania.

Excavations also uncovered eight carved soapstone birds, known as the Zimbabwe Birds. These are now Zimbabwe's national symbol, appearing on its flag, coat of arms, and banknotes.

Great Zimbabwe is about 17 miles (27 km) south of Masvingo, which itself is a 4-hour drive from Harare, the capital of Zimbabwe. ❷ 20.266667 ❸ 30.933333

At sunrise the dark baobabs provide contrast with the shifting pastel hues of the sky.

Islands of the Indian and South Atlantic Oceans

MADAGASCAR
AVENUE OF THE BAOBABS

MORONDAVA, MENABE

Along a stretch of dirt road that leads from Morondava to Belon'i Tsiribihina stand rows of baobab trees, their stout trunks glowing and fading as the sun passes overhead. This is the Avenue of the Baobabs, one of the more striking spots for appreciating the *Adansonia grandidieri*, one of seven baobab species endemic to Madagascar.

Hundreds of years old and standing up to 98 feet tall (30 m), the baobabs look like trees that have been uprooted and replanted upside down. Their branches, which only sprout from the very top of the trunk, are adorned with flat clusters of leaves that catch the light at sunset. Dusk and dawn are the best times to visit.

The baobabs are 45 minutes north of Morondava.
The roads are best navigated with 4-wheel drive.
Ⓢ 20.250763 Ⓔ 44.418343

- -

THE PIRATE CEMETERY

ÎLE SAINTE-MARIE, ANALANJIROFO

Here lies a dastardly fellow.

During the 17th and 18th centuries, the small island of Île Sainte-Marie near the East Indies trade route was the off-season home of an estimated 1,000 pirates. Buccaneers from all over the world lived in wooden huts adorned with flags that signified which captain's "crew" they belonged to.

When pirates died, they were buried in a scenic, palm-shaded hilltop cemetery overlooking the water. Legend has it that the notorious William Kidd is buried in a large black tomb in the cemetery, sitting upright as punishment for his dastardly deeds. He was actually buried in England, but his legendary ship, the *Adventure Galley* (rediscovered in 2000), was left docked near the island, and his booty is said to be buried somewhere in the surrounding sea. The crumbling cemetery, its graves half-covered by tall, swaying grass, is open to the public.

The cemetery is on the small island of Île Sainte-Marie, 4 miles (6.4 km) off the coast of eastern Madagascar. Hour-long flights to the island depart from the capital city of Antananarivo. Ⓢ 16.894317 Ⓔ 49.905893

TROMELIN ISLAND

Located almost 300 miles (483 km) east of Madagascar and measuring just 1.1 by 0.43 miles, Tromelin Island would be a mere splat of sand if not for its incredible, awful history.

In 1761, the French cargo ship *l'Utile* set sail from Madagascar bound for Mauritius—then known as Île de France. On board were approximately 160 slaves the crew had picked up in Madagascar, with the intent of selling them in Mauritius. But while en route, the ship ran into a reef. The stern shattered, sending the ship, 20 of its crew, and about 70 of the slaves to a watery grave. Many of the slaves who drowned were trapped belowdecks, with the hatches closed and, in some cases, nailed down.

The survivors struggled to Tromelin Island, a sandy, treeless, wind-battered speck equipped with nothing but turtles, seabirds, and coral. Some of the sailors managed to dig a well, but the lack of food and shelter made conditions intolerable. By salvaging wreckage from the ship, the survivors were able to build a seaworthy raft—one big enough to hold all the gentlemen and sailors, but not the slaves.

The white survivors climbed aboard the raft and set sail for Mauritius, promising to return for the remaining slaves. The rescue party never came—the governor of Mauritius balked at the idea of risking white lives to save what he considered human cargo.

Fifteen years after *l'Utile* was shipwrecked, a French warship captain named Bernard de Tromelin visited the island that now bears his name. There he discovered seven of the slaves from *l'Utile*—all women—and one baby boy who had been born on the island. The group had spent the previous decade and a half surviving on turtles and shellfish and sheltering in houses made from coral bricks. Little is known about the ultimate fates of these survivors, but it seems they were granted the right to live as free people on Mauritius.

A team of French archaeologists performed excavations on Tromelin Island in 2006 and unearthed cooking utensils made from copper salvaged from *l'Utile*, as well as remnants of the coral houses and evidence of a communal oven. The island is now home to a weather station that monitors winds and detects cyclones in the Indian Ocean.

There are no commercial flights to the island, but if you can find your own plane, you can land on the island's unpaved airstrip. Another option is to get there by boat, though there are no harbors—you'll need to anchor offshore. Accommodation is nonexistent. Bring a tent, a sleeping bag, and a lot of provisions. ⊗ 15.892222 ⊕ 54.524720

SEYCHELLES
VALLÉE DE MAI
PRASLIN

Praslin, the second largest of the Seychelles's 155 islands, is a paradise of secluded beaches, dense vegetation, and clear, tranquil waters. At the center of the island is Vallée de Mai, a forest home to a most unusual palm tree: the coco de mer. Endemic only to the Seychelles, the coco de mer produces the largest seeds of any plant in the world. Weighing in at up to 60 pounds (27 kg), the seeds are also remarkable for their distinctive shape. Simply put, they resemble a curvaceous woman's buttocks.

In 1881, devoutly Christian British general Charles Gordon visited Praslin and caught sight

The 60-pound fruit known as the "love nut."

of the scandalous seeds. So struck was he by their sensuous shape that he concluded the coco de mer was the tree of knowledge, and its seed the original forbidden fruit. That meant, of course, that Vallé de Mai was the Garden of Eden.

Though that geography may sound a bit wonky, at least according to the Book of Genesis, the coco de mer seeds are a suggestive sight worthy of the "forbidden fruit" label. A mythology has arisen around the coco de mer's supposedly aphrodisiac properties—the seed is regarded as a fertility symbol, which accounts for its popularity as a souvenir. In 2012, the Seychelles government imposed a ban on the export of coco de mer kernels in response to illegal poaching and trade. To take a seed home, you'll need to buy it from a licensed dealer and obtain an export permit. Expect to pay top dollar.

If you're content to just see the seeds, a hike through Vallée de Mai will expose you to plenty. You may also spot black parrots, a threatened species found only on the island of Praslin.

The park is open between 8 a.m. and 5:30 p.m. ⊗ 4.331692 ⊕ 55.740093

An Aldabra giant tortoise out for a stroll.

THE TORTOISES OF ALDABRA

ALDABRA ATOLL, OUTER ISLANDS

The Galápagos Islands may be the land most associated with giant tortoises, but there's another archipelago where these terrapins roam: Aldabra, a group of four islands located 435 miles (700 km) east of Tanzania.

Aldabra is the second-largest coral atoll on Earth. Over 100,000 giant tortoises live there—the largest population in the world. The tortoises, which can grow to 550 pounds (250 kg), share their remote home with green sea turtles, coconut crabs, hammerhead sharks, manta rays, and oceanic flamingos. A small research station houses a few scientists, but that's the extent of the human presence.

The Seychelles Islands Foundation oversees access to Aldabra. Trips are limited to those engaged in nature tourism and education, and some areas of the atoll are off-limits. To get there, you need to get a chartered plane to Assumption Island followed by a chartered boat or private yacht to Aldabra. ⓢ 9.416681 ⓔ 46.416650

....

SAINT HELENA, ASCENSION, AND TRISTAN DA CUNHA
TRISTAN DA CUNHA

An 8-mile-wide (13 km) part of a British Overseas Territory, Tristan da Cunha is the most remote populated island in the world. The nearest mainland city, located 1,743 miles (2,805 km) east, is Cape Town in South Africa. The journey from Cape Town takes seven days by boat—traveling by air is not an option, as there is no airport on the island.

Every inhabitant of Tristan da Cunha—269, at last count—lives in the island's only settlement, Edinburgh of the Seven Seas. Established in the early 19th century, the village is located on the north coast and is home to 70 families, all of whom are farmers. Electricity is supplied by diesel generators. The island's lone road, a narrow, winding path, is flanked by bungalow-style cottages, potato patches, and roaming cows. The looming volcanic cliffs and low-lying mist create a secluded, hazy setting.

It's a peaceful, pared-back existence with few anxieties—unless the volcano erupts. Such was the case in 1961, when earthquakes, landslides, and an eruption from one of the north vents sent the entire population fleeing to England via Cape Town. (Put off by England's busy streets and savage winters, most returned two years later after getting the all-clear from geologists.)

Now that the volcano has calmed down, life on Tristan da Cunha is an exercise in patience and planning. There is a grocery store, but orders must be placed months in advance so the goods can be loaded onto scheduled fishing vessels and delivered. A hospital equipped with X-ray machines, a labor and delivery room, operating room, emergency room, and dental facilities takes care of most health concerns, but patients requiring more specialized treatment must be transported to South Africa or the UK.

Boats leave from Cape Town. You'll need to get approval from island administrators before visiting the island. ⓢ 37.105249 ⓦ 12.277684

Oceania

Australia
New Zealand
Pacific Islands

**FIJI • GUAM • MARSHALL ISLANDS • MICRONESIA
NAURU • PALAU • PAPUA NEW GUINEA • SAMOA
VANUATU**

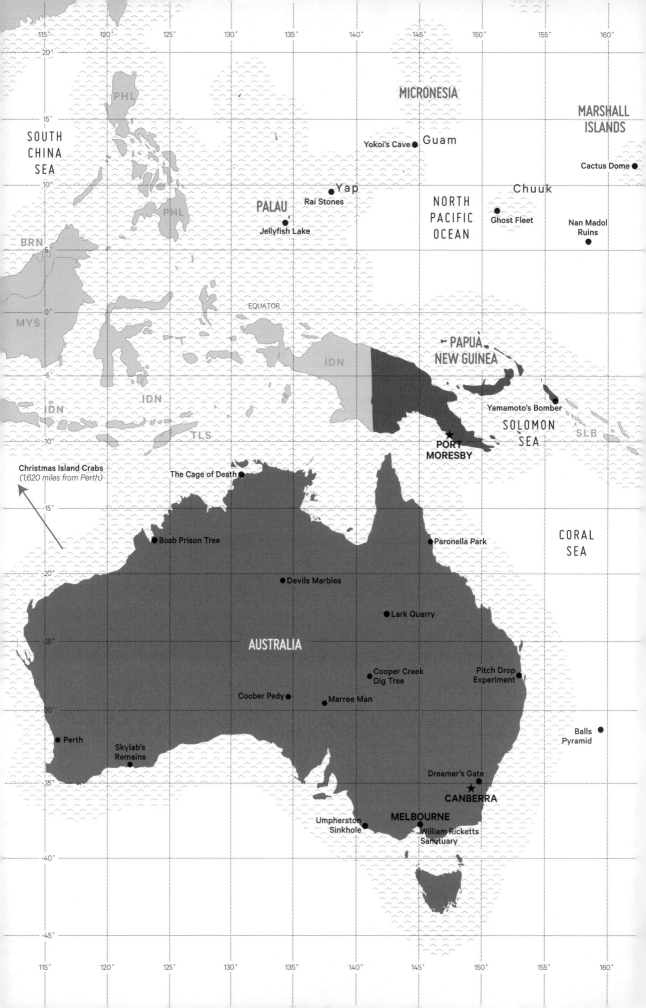

115°   120°   125°   130°   135°   140°   145°   150°   155°   160°

20°

MICRONESIA

MARSHALL
ISLANDS

15°

PHL

Yokoi's Cave ●   Guam

Cactus Dome ●

SOUTH
CHINA
SEA

10°

Yap

NORTH
PACIFIC
OCEAN

Chuuk

PALAU   Rai Stones

● Jellyfish Lake

Ghost Fleet ●

Nan Madol
Ruins ●

BRN

5°

MYS

EQUATOR

0°

IDN

IDN

PAPUA
NEW GUINEA

-5°

IDN

IDN

Yamamoto's Bomber ●

SOLOMON
SEA

SLB

TLS

PORT
MORESBY ★

-10°

Christmas Island Crabs
(1,620 miles from Perth)

The Cage of Death ●

CORAL
SEA

-15°

Boab Prison Tree ●

Paronella Park ●

-20°

Devils Marbles ●

Lark Quarry ●

AUSTRALIA

Cooper Creek
Dig Tree ●

Pitch Drop
Experiment ●

-25°

Coober Pedy ●

Marree Man ●

Balls
Pyramid ●

-30°

● Perth

Skylab's
Remains ●

Dreamer's Gate ★

CANBERRA ★

Umpherston
Sinkhole ●

MELBOURNE ●

William Ricketts
Sanctuary

-35°

-40°

-45°

115°   120°   125°   130°   135°   140°   145°   150°   155°   160°

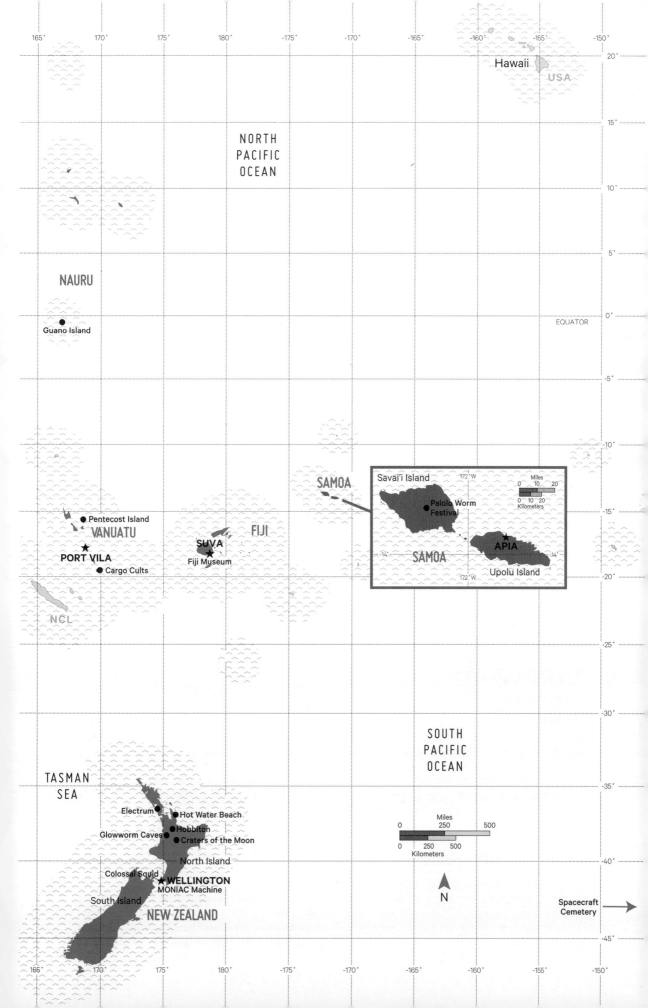

165°   170°   175°   180°   -175°   -170°   -165°   -160°   -155°   -150°

20°

Hawaii

USA

15°

NORTH
PACIFIC
OCEAN

10°

5°

NAURU

0°   EQUATOR

● Guano Island

-5°

-10°

SAMOA

Savai'i Island   172°W   Miles
                          0   10   20
                          Kilometers
                          0   10   20

● Palolo Worm
  Festival

● Pentecost Island   FIJI   -14°   SAMOA   -14°

VANUATU   ★ APIA

★ PORT VILA   ★ SUVA   Upolu Island

● Cargo Cults   Fiji Museum   172°W

-15°

-20°

NCL

-25°

-30°

SOUTH
PACIFIC
OCEAN

-35°

TASMAN
SEA

Electrum ● ● Hot Water Beach

Glowworm Caves ● ● Hobbiton

                  ● Craters of the Moon

North Island

-40°

Colossal Squid
          ★ WELLINGTON
          MONIAC Machine

Miles
0   250   500

Kilometers
0   250   500

N

South Island

NEW ZEALAND   Spacecraft
               Cemetery →

-45°

165°   170°   175°   180°   -175°   -170°   -165°   -160°   -155°   -150°

AUSTRALIA
DEVILS MARBLES

WAUCHOPE, NORTHERN TERRITORY

The Devils Marbles, known as Karlu Karlu ("big boulders") to local Aboriginal groups, consist of hundreds of rocks scattered across the landscape, varying in diameter from 1.5 feet to 20 feet (.45–6.1 m). Some boulders are stacked and appear to be balancing precariously atop one another.

According to Aboriginal mythology, the boulders are the work of Arrange, the Devil Man, who walked through the valley twisting a hair-string belt. As he twisted, clumps of hair fell to the ground, becoming rocks. On his walk back, Arrange spit on the ground, forming more boulders.

In 1953, a marble was transported to the town of Alice Springs and used in a memorial for John Flynn, the founder of a mobile medical service for the outback. The move was controversial—the site is sacred to local Aboriginal groups—and after more than 40 years, the rock was returned to its original location. In 2008, the government also gave back possession of the 7-square-mile (18 km²) Devils Marbles Conservation Area to its Aboriginal owners. Today, Aboriginal communities and local government work together to manage the site.

Wauchope, Northern Territory. The Devils Marbles are a long journey on the Stuart Highway from either Alice Springs (242 miles/389.5 km to the south) or Darwin (679 miles/1,092.7 km to the north). The nearest small town is Wauchope, a good place to stock up on supplies. Out of respect for indigenous residents, don't climb the boulders. ⓢ 20.566667 ⓔ 134.266667

Aboriginal myths attribute Wauchope's split, stacked, and balanced boulders to the Devil Man.

THE CAGE OF DEATH AT CROCOSAURUS COVE

DARWIN, NORTHERN TERRITORY

While you are being lowered into the first of Crocosaurus Cove's saltwater crocodile enclosures, you may notice claw marks on the walls of the acrylic cage in which you're standing. Try not to let that bother you—there are 1.5 inches (3.9 cm) of protective plastic between you and the 18-foot-long (5.5 m) lethal reptile.

Though this urban wildlife park houses other reptiles and fish, the main attraction is its collection of saltwater crocodiles. Compared with alligators, the saltwater species is larger, faster, and more inclined to attack humans. "Salties," as they're known locally, are abundant in the rivers and estuaries of northern Australia, where swimming is strongly discouraged.

Crocosaurus Cove offers a rare chance to splash alongside a saltie in the Cage of Death, a transparent cylinder that is lowered into the crocodile enclosures. Though no humans have ever been injured, the same can't be said for the crocodiles. In 2010, a crocodile named Burt—the 80-year-old star of *Crocodile Dundee*—lost a front tooth when he lunged at two football players who were taunting him from the cage.

In 2011, a cable holding the Cage of Death snapped and dropped a pair of tourists into the tank with an enormous crocodile named Choppa. Luckily for the couple, Choppa ignored them and they were quickly rescued.

58 Mitchell Street, Darwin. Thirteen bus routes stop along Mitchell Street. Unsurprisingly, you'll need to sign an indemnity release form before stepping into the Cage of Death. ⓢ 12.462333 ⓔ 130.839162 ▸▸

Despite the name, there's a good chance you'll survive the Cage of Death.

AUSTRALIA'S OTHER DEADLY CREATURES

Australia's reputation as a land of killer animals is a little unfair. Though the country is home to 21 of the world's most venomous snakes, marine creatures whose sting can kill within minutes, and five highly poisonous spiders, most of the continent's dangerous creatures do not seek out people to attack. A bite or sting usually happens in self-defense after a human unwittingly invades an animal's habitat. Here are some creatures—and one plant—to look out for during your travels.

1 BOX JELLYFISH
Named for the cubelike bell from which its lethal tentacles dangle, the box jellyfish is an almost-transparent creature that zooms silently through the water at up to 7 feet (2.1 m) per second. Its tentacles, the longest of which extend to 10 feet (3 m), have tiny harpoons that inject venom when touched. A kiss from a box jellyfish results in a temporary tattoo of its tentacles and up to 8 hours of agonizing pain. In rare cases, stings cause death by cardiac arrest.

TREATMENT: Pour vinegar over the tentacles to disable the stinging mechanism, then remove them from the skin using a towel or gloves.

2 STONEFISH
With their craggy, mottled complexion, stonefish camouflage themselves under mud or sand in the calm shallows of Australia's tropical waters. Accidentally step on one and up to 13 venom-filled dorsal spines will send neurotoxins coursing through your body, resulting in terrible pain, redness, swelling, muscle weakness, and short-term paralysis.

TREATMENT: Immerse limb in hot water to destroy the venom. In more serious cases, seek antivenom.

3 BLUE-RINGED OCTOPUS
This small, unassuming yellow cephalopod covered in neon-blue circles will not hesitate to bite when stepped on. The bite itself is painless, but the venom that spills forth from its salivary glands can cause muscular weakness, temporary paralysis, and respiratory failure. In many cases, the victim remains conscious and alert, but is unable to breathe or move.

TREATMENT: Utilize artificial respiration until the patient can breathe unassisted. There is no antivenom.

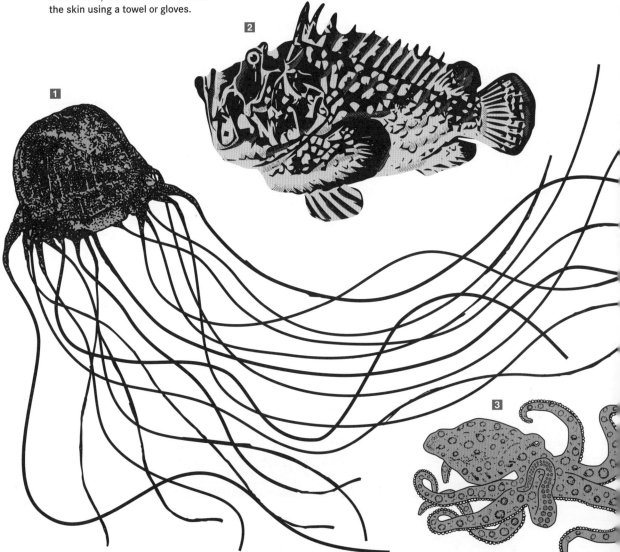

(AND ONE DEADLY PLANT)

4 COASTAL TAIPAN

Native to the seaside regions of northern and eastern Australia, the coastal taipan has a light brown, slim body, grows up to 6 feet (1.8 m) long, and has the largest fangs of any snake in the country at up to half an inch (1.3 cm) long. These sizable teeth can sink into your leg several times before you realize what's happened. When the taipan detects prey, it will freeze, raise its head off the ground, and then lunge and deliver multiple bites.

TREATMENT: The coastal taipan is the world's third-most-venomous snake, capable of disabling the human nervous system and issuing a one-two punch of neurotoxins that weaken the muscles, then prevent the blood from clotting. To avoid bleeding to death or suffering extensive muscle and kidney damage, bite victims should be administered antivenom as soon as possible.

5 SYDNEY FUNNEL-WEB SPIDER

Pervasive funnel-web phobia is an understandable phenomenon in Sydney. Unlike most other deadly animals, these 2-inch (5.1 cm), dark brown spiders have a habit of wandering into backyards, swimming pools, and homes. During summer, males leave their burrows and travel in search of a mate. A bite to an unsuspecting human causes symptoms within 30 minutes, including rapid heart rate, muscle spasms, sweating, tremors, and breathing difficulties. Though death is possible, there have been no recorded fatalities since the introduction of funnel-web antivenom in 1981.

TREATMENT: Get to a hospital for a dose of antivenom. In the meantime, apply pressure and a tight bandage, and immobilize the wound with a splint to prevent the poison from spreading.

6 GYMPIE GYMPIE

A 4-foot-tall (1.2 m) plant found in the forests of Queensland, the gympie gympie catches your eye with its large heart-shaped leaves, juicy pink berries, and dear little flowers. Then it stings you and all the prettiness is subsumed by a world of pain. Tiny hairs on the stalks and leaves dig into your flesh and break off, causing agony, swelling, and redness that can last for months.

TREATMENT: The strange but medically approved way to remove stinging hairs from the skin is to apply a hair-removal wax strip.

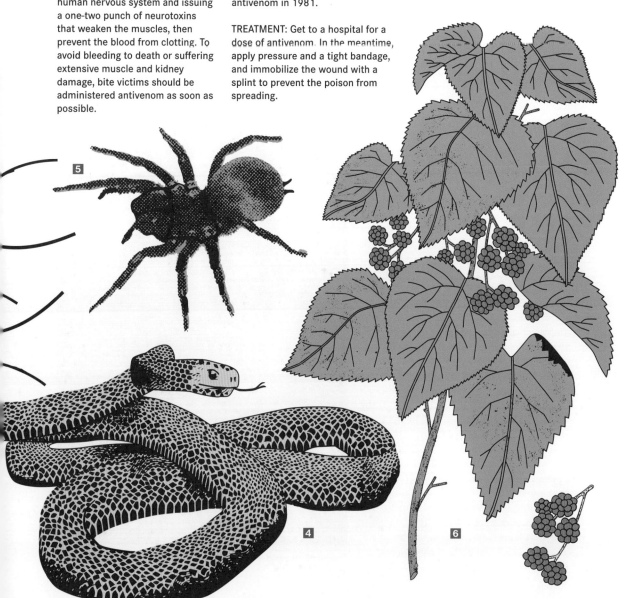

PITCH DROP EXPERIMENT

BRISBANE, QUEENSLAND

To view the experiment that the University of Queensland School of Mathematics and Physics boasts is "more exciting than watching grass grow," you'll need to go to the display cabinet in the school's foyer. There, beneath a glass dome, you will see a funnel filled with asphalt. It doesn't seem to be doing anything other than sitting there, but do not be deceived: You are looking at the world's longest running lab experiment in action.

The Pitch Drop Experiment began in 1927, the brainchild of UQ physics professor Thomas Parnell. His aim: to demonstrate that pitch—a term for thick, solid polymers such as asphalt—is not solid, but a very viscous liquid.

To prove this, Parnell poured a heated sample of pitch into a closed funnel and let it settle, a process that took three years. In 1930, he cut off the end of the funnel, allowing the pitch to flow freely. Which it did. Very, very slowly. The first drop fell into the beaker in 1938, with the second and third drops following in 1947 and 1954. With the installation of air-conditioning in the building came a reduction in the flow rate—the eighth drop, which hit the beaker in November 2000, took over 12 years to fall.

Just over 13 years later, in April 2014, the ninth drop fell. The next data point is expected to be collected in 2027.

Physics Annexe, University of Queensland, Brisbane. Get a bus from central Brisbane (Adelaide Street) to UQ (Chancellor's Place).
Ⓢ 27.497854 Ⓔ 153.013286

PARONELLA PARK

MENA CREEK, QUEENSLAND

Since childhood, baker José Paronella had dreamed of building a Moorish castle. In 1913, the adventurous 26-year-old left his village in Catalonia, Spain, and moved to tropical northern Australia. There, he eventually found wealth as a sugar cane farmer, and was finally able to pursue his dream.

In 1929, Paronella purchased a plot of rain forest in Queensland and began building his castle by hand, using sand, clay, old train tracks, gravel from the nearby creek, and wood taken from abandoned houses. By 1935, the structure had expanded to include a pool, café, cinema, and ballroom, as well as tennis courts and villa gardens with a grand staircase—all open to the public.

After Paronella's death in 1948, the building suffered decades of neglect, but thanks to conservation efforts, the castle is alive once again. Lush tropical plants have encroached upon and mingled with Paronella's hand-built stairs and fountains, making them look like they sprouted from their natural surroundings.

1671 Japoonvale Road, Mena Creek. Bus tours leave from Cairns, which is 75 miles (120.7 km) north of Mena Creek.
Ⓢ 17.671856 Ⓔ 145.917067

Fountains and lush gardens are all part of a Catalan baker's self-built fantasyland.

Site of an ill-fated decision that sent two explorers to their doom.

COOPER CREEK DIG TREE

COOPER CREEK, QUEENSLAND

An old eucalyptus tree on the banks of the Bullah Bullah water-hole marks the spot where a cruel twist of fate claimed the lives of two ambitious explorers.

In 1860, Robert Burke and William Wills led an expedition from Melbourne, aiming to travel to the northernmost part of Australia—a journey of around 2,000 miles (3,218.7 km). At the time, the desert terrain, where summer temperatures exceeded 122°F (50°C), had yet to be explored by non-indigenous people. Burke and Wills, neither of whom had any exploration experience, brought 19 men, 23 horses, 26 camels, and 6 wagons stuffed with far more supplies than was sensible. (A Chinese gong and a large oak table were among the more impractical baggage.)

After spending months journeying to Cooper Creek, Burke and Wills split from the rest of the group to make the trip to the northern coast. Those left at Cooper Creek were instructed to wait three months while the two men completed their journey to and from the coast. After holding out for more than four months, the Cooper Creek group buried food and supplies beneath a tree marked with the date and departed.

Nine hours later, Burke and Wills arrived back at Cooper Creek. They encountered the "Dig Tree," excavated the cache of supplies, and found a letter from the other group. Too exhausted to try to catch up with them, the men rested for two days. Before heading south, they buried a letter of their own in the cache, detailing their plans, in case a rescue party should arrive. But Burke and Wills made a crucial mistake: They did not change the date or message originally etched into the tree. When members of their original group returned to Cooper Creek carrying extra supplies, they saw no evidence that Burke and Wills had been there, and departed.

With their rations running low and all their animals dead, Burke and Wills stayed alongside the creek, too weak to carry water. Knowing the end was near, Wills returned to the Dig Tree and buried his diary. An entry on June 21, written a week before he and Burke died, reads thus:

"We have done all we could . . . our deaths will rather be the result of the mismanagement of others than of any rash acts of our own. Had we been come to grief elsewhere, we could only have blamed ourselves, but here we are returned to Cooper Creek, where we had every reason to look for provisions and clothing, and yet we have to die of starvation."

The tree is 23 miles (37 km) northeast of Innamincka, a tiny outback town in South Australia near the Queensland border. Markings on the Dig Tree are still visible. Ⓢ 27.617267 Ⓔ 141.078583

LARK QUARRY DINOSAUR STAMPEDE

WINTON, QUEENSLAND

Ninety-five million years ago, a herd of 150 dinosaurs—made up of chicken-size Skartopuses and ostrich-size Wintonopuses—ran for their lives when a predator (possibly a Tyrannosauropus) lurched onto the scene with teeth and talons bared. The chaotic exodus, which probably took just a few seconds, left a tangle of fossilized tracks on the ground—tracks which now form the world's only evidence of a dinosaur stampede. A conservation building constructed over the tracks protects them from erosion and damage.

Lark Quarry Conservation Park, Winton-Jundah Road, Winton. Ⓢ 23.016100 Ⓔ 142.411400

The world's only evidence of a dinosaur stampede.

SKYLAB'S REMAINS

ESPERANCE, WESTERN AUSTRALIA

On July 12, 1979, the United States' unmanned space station, Skylab, began its reentry into the Earth's atmosphere. Things got a little precarious when the space station missed its intended reentry target. The debris was supposed to fall 810 miles south-southeast of Cape Town, South Africa, but a 4 percent calculation error caused the debris to land about 300 miles east of Perth in Western Australia.

For the people of Esperance (current population 10,421), it was quite the event. Strange lights and sonic booms were just the start. NASA officials soon arrived, and locals were incentivized to hand over any debris they found. Local government offices handed out plaques to debris discoverers, and the *San Francisco Examiner* caused a frenzy by offering $10,000 to the first person to arrive at their office with an authentic piece of Skylab. The office, naturally, was in the US, and potential winners had just 72 hours to get there. Stan Thornton, a 17-year-old from Esperance, managed to claim the prize.

At the same time, the local Esperance Museum started to build its collection. Today, it contains all kinds of Skylab artifacts that fell to Earth, including large titanium nitrogen spheres and oxygen tanks, fragments of metal and insulation foam, ruined circuit boards, a portion of the main hatch, and a storage freezer.

Just outside the museum entrance stands a model of Skylab on a pedestal. A nearby billboard states:

IN 1979, A SPACESHIP CRASHED OVER ESPERANCE. WE FINED THEM $400 FOR LITTERING. PAID IN FULL.

While in the Esperance region, check to see if nearby Lake Hillier is pink. Sometimes it has a striking bubblegum hue. ⑤ 33.858962 ⑥ 121.893997

BOAB PRISON TREE

DERBY, WESTERN AUSTRALIA

During the 1890s, police used the bulbous, 15-foot-wide (4.6 m) hollow trunk of this 1,500-year-old boab tree as a temporary jail for Aboriginal prisoners en route to sentencing in the small town of Derby. Long before its use as a makeshift prison, the tree was part of an indigenous legend. The story goes that the boab, once tall and prideful, learned humility when the spirits turned it upside down, causing its roots to grow into the sky.

Broome Highway, Derby. Skywest flights from Perth to Derby (a 3-hour trip) depart every weekday. A fence around the tree prevents visitors from going inside it, partly out of respect for its connections to Aboriginal beliefs, but also because snakes like to sleep in the trunk. ⑤ 17.350738 ⑥ 123.669919

Rabble-rousers used to be flung into the belly of the Boab Prison Tree.

UMPHERSTON SINKHOLE

MOUNT GAMBIER, SOUTH AUSTRALIA

Mount Gambier is a city built on a porous foundation of eroding limestone caves and craters. In 1864, a gentleman named James Umpherston purchased a plot of land containing a large sinkhole. This was no oversight.

Far from being perturbed by the sinkhole's presence, Umpherston decided to transform the pit into a sunken recreational garden open to all. By 1886, he had filled the hole with a variety of ferns and flowers. Visitors flocked to the new garden, entering it via a set of wooden stairs.

After Umpherston's death in 1900, the garden began to deteriorate into an overgrown garbage dump. By 1976, however, plans were afoot to restore its former beauty. Department of Woods and Forest staff uncovered Umpherston's terraces, and planted new flowers and shrubs. Just like its original incarnation, the garden was an instant hit.

Umpherston Sinkhole continues to flourish, with its blooming pink and lilac hydrangeas and its edges dripping with hanging ivy that conceals the caverns below. Its popularity has extended to local possums, who scamper among the plants at night in search of food.

Jubilee Highway E, Mount Gambier. Mount Gambier is a 6-hour bus ride from Melbourne's Southern Cross station, or just over 6 hours from Adelaide's Central station. Ⓢ 37.835267 Ⓔ 140.802465

Ivy drapes over the edge of a 150-year-old sinkhole garden.

MARREE MAN

MARREE, SOUTH AUSTRALIA

Charter pilot Trec Smith was flying over the outback toward Coober Pedy in June 1998 when he saw it: a 2.6-mile-tall (4.2 km) drawing of a naked indigenous man, his left arm raised and ready to launch a hunting stick toward unseen prey.

The perfectly proportioned figure, formed by wide lines dug 10 inches (25.4 cm) into the ground, seemed to have been freshly carved. But despite the planning, precision, and sheer boldness required to create it, no one came forward to claim authorship—and apparently no one witnessed its creation.

The situation only got stranger. Anonymous press releases appeared, ostensibly written from an American perspective. They used US units of measurement, referred to local places with awkwardly formal names, and referred to the Native American Great Serpent Mound in Ohio. In June 1999, a fax from the UK revealed that a message had been buried beneath the Marree Man's nose. Authorities surrendered to curiosity and dug it up to discover a plaque that was decorated with an American flag, the Olympic rings, and a quote about Aboriginal hunting from a 1936 book on outback Australia.

The created-by-Americans angle seemed to be a red herring planted by an audacious eccentric. That's where Bardius Goldberg, now considered the most likely culprit, comes in. Goldberg, an artist prone to provocation, had been making Aboriginal-style dot paintings near the desert town of Alice Springs when he got into a dispute with the traditional landowner, Herman Malbunka. Goldberg then allegedly used a borrowed GPS and a tractor to send a spiteful message to Malbunka.

Unfortunately, Goldberg died in 2002 (he developed septicemia after losing a tooth in a bar fight), meaning the mystery of the Marree Man has never been officially solved. Goldberg's other schemes included planting eucalyptus trees in the shape of a giant kangaroo and installing a magically disappearing Virgin Mary in the wall of a house. To those who knew him, he was the only possible culprit.

The lines of the Marree Man have faded due to erosion, but the figure is still visible from the air. Tours to the Marree area, incorporating scenic flights over the Marree Man and nearby Lake Eyre, depart from Adelaide. Ⓢ 29.437780 Ⓔ 137.468077

The 2.6-mile-tall figure seems to have been created as a hoax by an eccentric artist.

ALSO IN AUSTRALIA

Litchfield Termite Mounds

Adelaide River · What look like craggy tombstones are actually houses built by ants.

Sun Pictures

Broome · The world's oldest outdoor cinema still screens multiple films per night.

Tessellated Pavement

Eaglehawk Neck · This plateau came into being when pressure at the Earth's crust caused cracks to appear in the rock at perpendicular angles, creating a tiled effect.

Eden Killer Whale Museum

Eden · See the full skeleton of Old Tom, a 22-foot-long (6.7 m) orca who once cooperated with hunters to herd fellow whales.

Hamelin Pool Stromatolites

Gascoyne · The rock-like formations in the shallow waters of Hamelin Pool Marine Nature Reserve are not rocks, but stromatolites: living, growing organisms that provide a rare glimpse of life on Earth as it was 3.5 billion years ago.

Wunderkammer

Melbourne · This downtown boutique sells artifacts and ephemera from the natural and scientific worlds.

Lake Hillier

Middle Island · The water in this lake is a startling bubblegum pink.

Undara Lava Tubes

Mount Surprise · White cockroaches, caramel-colored pseudoscorpions, and eyeless silverfish are among the rare insects and arachnids that lurk in these caves.

Twelve Apostles

Port Campbell · The "apostles"—which now number seven—are actually a line of limestone stacks off the coast of a national park.

Regent Street Station

Sydney · Groups of mourners with picnics in tow once assembled at this Gothic station to get the train to Rookwood Cemetery.

Museum of Human Disease

Sydney · Australia's only publicly accessible pathology museum offers a grim reminder of the consequences of an unhealthy lifestyle.

Fort Denison

Sydney Harbor · This tiny island, once home to the occasional banished starving prisoner, is also known as "Pinchgut."

Burning Mountain

Wingen · Mount Wingen has been smoldering for thousands of years due to a slow-moving, burning coal seam.

Newnes Glowworm Tunnel

Wolgan Valley · The path of a onetime railway tunnel is now home to thousands of glowing insects.

COOBER PEDY

COOBER PEDY, SOUTH AUSTRALIA

For most residents of Coober Pedy, opening a window to get some fresh air isn't an option. More than half of the desert town's 2,000 people live underground in houses excavated from rock, a lifestyle that protects them from the extreme dry heat.

Coober Pedy was established in 1915, after a 14-year-old named Willie Hutchison discovered opals in the ground while looking for water. The town has since become the world's largest producer of the white gemstones, which form when silica and water combine in

Living underground helps Coober Pedy residents stay cool during the brutal summers.

the cracks of sedimentary or igneous rock.

The cave-dwelling residents attend underground church services, browse underground art galleries, and manage underground hotels. For those recreational pursuits that simply aren't possible in a cave, there are creative modifications—at the town golf course, players begin games during the cool of night, using glowing golf balls and carrying a small piece of turf for teeing off. **The town of Coober Pedy is 526 miles (846.5 km) northwest of Adelaide. Two-hour flights to Coober Pedy on the Rex airline depart from Adelaide. Alternatively, an overnight Greyhound bus takes 11 hours. To avoid the hottest temperatures, visit between April and November. ❸ 29.013244 ❸ 134.754482**

DREAMER'S GATE

COLLECTOR, NEW SOUTH WALES

Once a five-inn town that attracted gangs of bushrangers—19th-century, forest-dwelling outlaws who robbed coaches—Collector has since quieted down to a 300-person village with few visitors. At its entrance is a striking sight: a 23-foot-tall, 112-foot-long (7 m, 34 m), sand-colored, Gothic-style gate that seems to have emerged organically from its sun-bleached surroundings.

The Dreamer's Gate is the work of local artist Tony Phantastes, who created it as a tribute to his deceased father. Phantastes began building it in 1993, using a skeleton of galvanized wire and piping, and adding burlap, plaster, chicken wire, and cement. The five-panel design incorporates twisting tree limbs, hands,

a sleeping man's face, and circular windows that show the landscape beyond.

In 1999, the local council issued a stop-work order, claiming the gate was structurally unsound. Phantastes fought back, but lost his case and, in an attempt at compromise, added steel support beams to the back of the gate.

Dreamer's Gate remains intact but unfinished. As the years pass, it becomes a little more bleached and rusted, its broken archway symbolizing Phantastes's incomplete dream. **Church Street, Collector. Collector is a 2.5-hour drive from Sydney. The gate is opposite the Bushranger Hotel, once frequented by Ben Hall's legendary bushranger gang. A monument at the hotel pays tribute to Constable Samuel Nelson, shot dead by an outlaw on that spot in 1865. ❸ 34.912724 ❸ 149.436323**

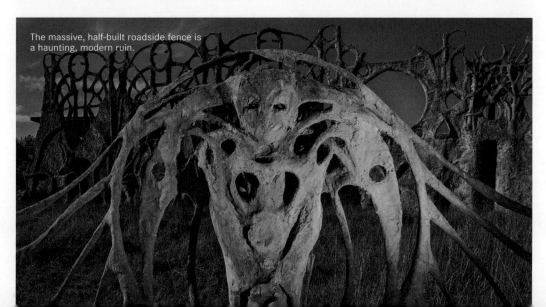

The massive, half-built roadside fence is a haunting, modern ruin.

AUSTRALIA'S BIG THINGS

In 1963, a 16-foot-tall (4.9 m) bagpipe-playing Scotsman appeared on the northeast corner of Scotty's Motel in Adelaide. The concrete structure, designed to attract travelers to the roadside lodge, sparked an Australian cultural phenomenon: the big thing.

Families road-tripping along the country's major highways during the 1980s and '90s encountered many an oversized object. Initially erected as promotional tools for stores, museums, and lodgings, the big things became attractions themselves. For many Australians, stopping for a photo in front of the Big Banana was a summer vacation ritual.

There are over a hundred big things in Australia, but most look a little run-down these days. Low-cost airline flights are gradually replacing the great Australian road trip. Low-tech big things now evoke feelings of nostalgia—and a bit of cultural cringe.

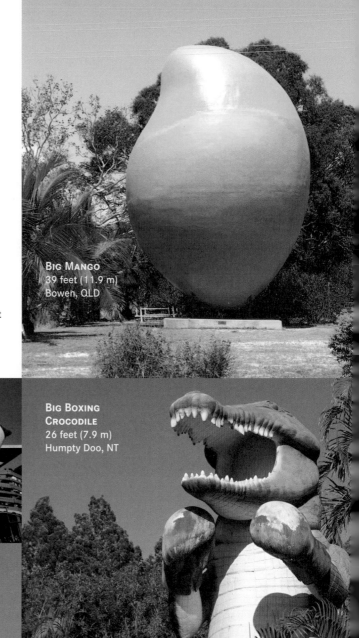

BIG MANGO
39 feet (11.9 m)
Bowen, QLD

BIG BOXING CROCODILE
26 feet (7.9 m)
Humpty Doo, NT

BIG BANANA (above)
16 feet (4.9 m)
Coffs Harbour, NSW

GOLDEN GUITAR
39 feet (11.9 m)
Tamworth, NSW

BIG MERINO
49 feet (15 m)
Goulburn, NSW

Giant Koala
46 feet (14 m)
Dadswells Bridge, VIC

Big Ned Kelly
20 feet (6.1 m)
Glenrowan, VIC

Big Prawn (above)
20 feet (6.1 m)
Ballina, NSW

Big Pineapple
53 feet (16.2 m)
Woombye, QLD

Big Galah
26 feet (7.9 m)
Kimba, SA

Long Beard and Earthly Mother.

WILLIAM RICKETTS SANCTUARY

MOUNT DANDENONG, VICTORIA

The winding mountain paths in the quiet forest of the William Ricketts Sanctuary are lined with 92 ceramic faces that seem to have grown straight out of the rocks and boulders. Each face depicts a real figure in the life of sculptor William Ricketts. Never trained in sculpture, Ricketts grew up surrounded by Aboriginal mythology, in which ancestral beings are believed to have created the land's natural features during what is called "the Dreamtime."

Ricketts began creating sculptures of indigenous elders, adults, and children in the 1930s—a time when Victorian government policy still removed Aboriginal children from their parents to be raised in white homes and institutions. In his depictions, Ricketts often sculpted white men wearing crowns made from bullets, with dead animals at their feet.

Ricketts continued sculpting until his death in 1993 at the age of 94. Opened to the public in the 1960s, his sanctuary offers a place for quiet reflection and the appreciation of nature.

1402-1404 Mt. Dandenong Tourist Rd., Mount Dandenong, Victoria. Get a train from Flinders Street Station in central Melbourne to the Croydon stop. From there, get a bus to the sanctuary. ⑤ 37.832715 ⑥ 145.355645

CHRISTMAS ISLAND CRABS

CHRISTMAS ISLAND

Christmas Island, an Australian territory in the Indian Ocean, is populated by 1,500 humans and 100 million crabs.

Each year at the start of the rainy season, the ground is transformed into a vast, churning red carpet as the island's crabs leave their forest burrows and scuttle to shore in order to spawn. During their perilous journey, which can take several weeks, the crabs must cross roads, withstand seaside winds, and steer clear of yellow crazy ants.

The ants, who, true to their name, move frantically and erratically when disturbed, were accidentally introduced to Christmas Island in the 1920s. Since then they have formed super-colonies, wreaking havoc on the island's ecosystem. Red crabs, despite their larger size and exoskeletons, are no match for the jets of lethal acid that swarms of ants spray into the crabs' eyes and mouths.

Concerned by the insects' destructive effect on red crabs and Christmas Island ecology as a

whole, the Australian government has established a seven-member Crazy Ant Scientific Advisory Panel. Tactics thus far include a four-year research study into the ants' reliance on honeydew, and the 2009 release of 13 tons of insecticide on super-colony areas. Though this last measure made a significant dent in the crazy ant population, their numbers are rapidly increasing once again.

Christmas Island is a 4-hour flight from Perth. Exact timing of the migration varies depending on the weather and the phases of the moon, but the crabs tend to start moving in November. ⑤ 10.447525 ⑥ 105.690449

BALLS PYRAMID

LORD HOWE ISLAND GROUP

Darkness had fallen. Two scientists were perched 330 feet (100.6 m) above the sea on a shard of an old volcano shaped like a giant jagged dagger. It was in this precarious position that they laid eyes on the best possible surprise: a nest of 24 giant stick insects, each the size of a human hand.

David Priddel and Nicholas Carlile embarked on their 2001 trip to Balls Pyramid, a 1,844-foot-tall (562 m) volcanic remnant off the east coast of Australia, motivated by a shaky belief: that the stick insect, long thought to be extinct, was still alive. The insect, also referred to as a "tree lobster" on account of its unusually large size, once roamed the forests of nearby Lord Howe Island. Following the 1918 introduction of black rats to the island—which escaped from a supply ship that ran aground—the insects disappeared, and by 1930 were considered extinct.

Balls Pyramid, located 12 miles (19.31 km) south-east of Lord Howe, is hardly lush with vegetation—it is almost entirely rock, its near-vertical cliff faces inhospitable to fauna and off-limits to mountain climbers without government permission. But beneath a spindly shrub growing from a crack, there they were: two dozen tree lobsters.

No one could figure out how they got there. Were they carried by birds? Did their eggs float across on the sea? At first, the Australian government couldn't decide whether they ought to be moved. But in 2003, a team from the National Parks and Wildlife Service scaled the pyramid and collected two pairs of stick insects for breeding in captivity. One pair died shortly after, but the pair dispatched to the Melbourne Zoo—"Adam and Eve"—met with success, producing eggs that became the foundation of the zoo's now-thousands-strong tree lobster population.

373 miles (600.3 km) northeast of Sydney. Flights link Sydney and Lord Howe Island, taking just under 2 hours. § 31.75416/ ☻ 159.25166/

Home of the tree lobster, long thought to be extinct.

NEW ZEALAND

ELECTRUM

MAKARAU

In addition to being one of New Zealand's wealthiest people, Alan Gibbs can control lightning. His farm is home to a sculpture called *Electrum*, the world's largest Tesla coil.

At night, from his balcony 50 feet (15.2 m) away, Gibbs can flip a switch that sends lightning streaming from the top of the 38-foot (11.6 m) structure, which consists of a simple sphere atop a column. When the coil discharges, it sends up to three million volts into the surrounding air. You can hear an earsplitting crackling sound and feel the hair on your head standing on end. That burning smell is ozone, the result of oxygen molecules breaking up and reforming in new combinations.

Electrum is the artistic realization of Gibbs's long-held fascination with lightning. To create the work, he commissioned late American artist Eric Orr, whose sculptures often combined fire, water, and a sense of high drama. With the help of electrical engineer Greg Leyh and teams in New Zealand and San Francisco, Orr designed and built a cylinder with a hollow sphere (known as a Faraday cage) on top. At its first test demonstration, during which a constant stream of lightning discharged amid a tremendous buzz, Leyh sat protected inside the sphere reading a book—an homage to the famous photograph of Tesla reading in a chair while a coil erupts into a lightning frenzy behind him.

At 38 feet tall, *Electrum* is the world's largest Tesla coil.

Since 1998, the sculpture has been part of Gibbs Farm—a large bayside property an hour north of Auckland with more than 20 large-scale, site-specific art installations. All have been commissioned by Gibbs, who collaborates with artists on the abstract-minimalist works. Adding to the unusual landscape are roaming zebras, giraffes, alpacas, emus, and goats. **Kaipara Coast Highway, Makarau. The farm is a private residence, but its art park is open to the public by appointment.** ⓢ 36.616196 ⓔ 174.491259

HOBBITON

MATAMATA, WAIKATO

In a hole in the ground there lived a hobbit—and that hole is located in Matamata, New Zealand. What remains of the Shire movie set for Peter Jackson's *Lord of the Rings* and *Hobbit* adaptations lies on Alexander Farm, a 2-square-mile (3.2 km²) family property with 13,000 sheep and 300 beef cattle.

Jackson selected the site after an aerial survey of the area revealed its hills were the perfect size and shape for the cozy hobbit houses described in J. R. R. Tolkien's books. To transform the farm into a Hollywood-approved

The little house where Frodo's perilous journey began.

Hobbiton, the film crew built a mill and bridge, brought in foliage, and wired individual fake leaves to a dead tree, all after enlisting the help of the New Zealand Army to pave an access road.

After taking a 1-hour guided tour of Hobbiton, visitors are welcome to bottle-feed a lamb or watch one being shorn. **501 Buckland Rd., Hinuera, Matamata. InterCity buses from Auckland take just over 3 hours to reach Matamata. A free shuttle runs from the bus stop to the farm.** ⓢ 37.879794 ⓔ 175.650222 ➤➤

➠ Epic Film Sets You Can Visit

BIG FISH
Private island in a river near Montgomery, Alabama, United States
The custom-built set of Spectre, the friendly, hidden town in this 2003 Tim Burton film, still sits on its little island. Years of weather have taken their toll, though—the buildings' rustic facades are wearing off to reveal the Styrofoam beneath.

The island is privately owned. Seek permission before visiting.

STAR WARS
Chott el Jerid, southwest of Nefta, Tunisia
The Lars Homestead, Luke Skywalker's Tatooine home, still stands in the Tunisian desert—thanks to some particularly dedicated fans. In 2010, *Star Wars* enthusiast Mark Dermul led a pilgrimage to the set location and was disheartened by the dilapidated state of the Skywalker igloo. After two years of fund-raising and negotiating with the Tunisian government,

Artists sculpt the face of Rameses II for Cecil B. DeMille's *Ten Commandments.*

Dermul and five friends returned to the desert and repaired the plaster set piece.

THE TEN COMMANDMENTS
Guadalupe, California, United States
For almost 90 years, the Guadalupe-Nipomo Dunes hid a massive bounty of Egyptian "relics." A 720-foot-long (219 m) Egyptian palace, 21 five-ton (4,535.9 kg) sphinx sculptures, and four 30-foot (9.1 m) pharaoh statues were among the set pieces for Cecil B. DeMille's *The Ten Commandments*, which was filmed in 1923. Despite building the largest set ever built at the time, DeMille ordered his workers to dismantle and bury the set after its month-long filming had been completed. The movie set lay hidden until 1983, when Peter Brosnan, a filmmaker and DeMille fan, set out to unearth the secret bounty. Brosnan and his crew found the "Lost City" after following clues featured in DeMille's autobiography, but lacked the funding for a proper excavation. It was not until October 2012 that digging finally commenced. Pieces of the set are still buried in the desert, but several unearthed objects are on display at the Dunes Center on Guadalupe Street.

Dig your own hot tub before the tide comes in.

HOT WATER BEACH

COROMANDEL PENINSULA, WAIKATO

Arrive on Hot Water Beach at the right time, and you'll be able to dig yourself a custom-size hot tub out of the sand, with adjustable water temperature. A small section of the beach sits on an underground geothermal water trough. A little digging between low and high tide releases the warm water, making it possible to create a personal spa.

Finding the temperature sweet spot can be tricky—on some patches of the beach, the underground water is hot enough to scald. The best approach is to fill a bucket with cold seawater and pour it into the hot tub if you start sizzling.

If diligently dammed, hot tubs will last for about four hours before being claimed by the sea as high tide approaches.

Check tide times before you go. Aim to arrive about 2 hours before low tide to claim your spot, start digging, and get the most time out of your hot tub before it washes away. Ⓢ 36.886044 Ⓔ 175.822721

CRATERS OF THE MOON

TAUPO, WAIKATO

Swirling wisps of steam billow from the basins and bubbling mud pools at Craters of the Moon, a geothermal field encircled by a raised wooden walkway.

The area was not always a hotbed of activity. The craters began to appear in the 1950s, when the installation of a nearby geothermal power station caused a reduction in underground water pressure, allowing hot water to come to the surface and escape as steam.

Since then, the land has been in a state of constant shift. New craters—up to 65 feet (19.8 m) deep—form during hydrothermal eruptions, which occur about once per year. Blowholes emitting steam and gas pop up more frequently—so much so that the walkway needs regular rerouting to bypass new vents and avoid scalding visitors.

Karapiti Road. Wairakei. Taupo is a 5-hour bus ride or 45-minute flight from Auckland. The Craters of the Moon site is 3 miles (4.8 km) north of the city center. Ⓢ 38.646667 Ⓔ 176.103753

A geothermal field dotted with steamy blowholes.

Bioluminescent larvae light the way through Waitomo's softly glowing caverns.

WAITOMO GLOWWORM CAVES

WAITOMO, WAIKATO

The tour of Waitomo's glowworm caves ends with a silent boat ride in the dark beneath a dense scattering of blue-tinged stars. Or at least that's what it looks like. The dots of light on the ceiling are actually bioluminescent fungus gnats.

This remarkable sight greeted local Maori chief Tane Tinorau and English surveyor Fred Mace when they explored the Waitomo caves for the first time in 1887. Entering through a stream and paddling on a raft by candlelight, the two men were astonished to discover the beauty of the caves, which formed approximately 30 million years ago. Return visits yielded greater rewards—the pair found an entry point on land and, by 1889, were guiding visitors through the caves for a small fee.

The Waitomo caves contain magnificent natural limestone formations that resemble cathedrals, pipe organs, and twisted columns. But the main attraction is, of course, the glowworms. Found only in New Zealand, *Arachnocampa luminosa* emit a blue-green light during their 6-to-12-month larval stage. The bioluminescence occurs due to chemical reactions in the gnat's excretory organs, and, along with dangling feeding lines, helps attract prey to the silk webs where the larvae live. The hungrier a larva is, the more brightly it glows. These are the gnat's glory days— after emerging from the pupal stage mouthless, they will die of starvation within 100 hours, devoting their short adult life to mating and, if female, laying about a hundred or so eggs.

39 Waitomo Caves Road, Waikato. The nearest major city is Hamilton, a 1-hour drive or bus ride away. Photography is forbidden in the caves and you are asked to remain silent when near the glowworms.
S 38.250961 E 175.170983

ALSO IN NEW ZEALAND

Baldwin Street

Dunedin ·
The steepest residential street in the world came about by accident: When drawing up road plans for Dunedin in the mid-1800s, London-based city planners used a standard grid system without regard for the local terrain.

Hundertwasser Public Toilets

Kawakawa ·
The crooked tiles, glass-bottle windows, and bursts of clashing color that make up the walls of this public restroom are the hallmarks of artist Friedensreich Hundertwasser.

Lake Tekapo

Mackenzie Basin ·
This turquoise lake gets its hue from "rock flour," a powder made when glaciers grind rocks as they go.

Te Wairoa Buried Village

Rotorua · In 1886 this settlement was buried beneath the ash of an erupting volcano.

Rere Rock Slide

Rere · The Wharekopae River cascades down this slanted 200-foot (61 m) rock formation, allowing daring visitors to slide down it on tires and boogie boards.

Mrs. Chippy Monument

Wellington ·
A bronze kitty adorns the grave of Harry McNeish, the polar explorer who brought the original feline to the Antarctic.

Bridge to Nowhere

Whanganui ·
A 130-foot-long (39.6 m) concrete bridge stretches across the untamed greenery of Mangapurua Gorge. Then it simply stops.

MONIAC MACHINE

WELLINGTON

The 1949 creation of crocodile-hunter-turned-economist Bill Phillips, the MONIAC (Monetary National Income Analogue Computer) demonstrates the workings of a national economy, using flowing water to represent the movement of money.

The 6-foot-7-inch (2 m) machine, which Phillips made from spare parts in his landlady's garage while studying at the London School of Economics, consists of transparent plastic tanks mounted on a wooden board, connected by plastic tubing. Each tank

How does a national economy work? Let the MONIAC explain with flowing water.

represents a part of the economy, such as imports, health, and education. Adjusting the flow rate of the water causes changes throughout the system, providing a clear simulation of the system-wide effects of spending, saving, investment, interest rates, and taxation.

Phillips created the MONIAC to demonstrate the ways in which small changes can have complex and far-reaching results within a national economy. Fourteen of the hulking, noisy machines were built following the initial prototype, but the advent of computers during the 1950s soon rendered them obsolete. One of the few surviving models is on display at the Reserve Bank Museum. Another can be found at the Science Museum in London. **Reserve Bank Museum, 2 The Terrace, Wellington. The museum is a 10-minute walk from the Wellington train station. ⊚ 41.278997 ⊕ 174.775217**

COLOSSAL SQUID AT TE PAPA MUSEUM

WELLINGTON

Like its cousin the giant squid, the colossal squid is an elusive beast. The cephalopod, which is shorter but heavier than the giant squid, lives 3,000 feet (914.4 m) deep in the pitch-black waters surrounding Antarctica. The first clues of its existence came in the form of two sucker-covered arms found in the belly of a sperm whale. Until 2007, only three complete colossal squid specimens had ever been captured and recorded.

In February of that year, the New Zealand fishing vessel *San Aspiring* was hunting near the Ross Ice Shelf when something tugged at the boat's fishing line with an unusually strong force. The crew pulled up the line to discover a 1,000-pound (453.6 kg) colossal squid attached to an Antarctic toothfish, refusing to let go. Knowing they'd happened upon something special, the fishermen hauled the squid on board, froze it, and plotted a swift course back to New Zealand.

Wellington's Te Papa Museum—a national institution focused on art, history, the natural world, and Maori culture—gratefully received the specimen, preserving it in formalin while staff pondered what to do with it. The squid remained in frozen storage for over a year until scientists thawed it in a specially built tank filled with ice and salt water. Webcams provided a live broadcast of the 60-hour thawing and examination process.

Though initially estimated at 30 feet (9.1 m) long, the squid measured 13 feet 9 inches (4.2 m)—a discrepancy attributed to postmortem tentacle

Dredged up from the Antarctic deep, Messie the squid has found a more cozy home.

shrinkage. Nicknamed "Messie," after its scientific name of *Mesonychoteuthis hamiltoni*, it is on display in a horizontal tank, forming the centerpiece of Te Papa's colossal squid exhibit. Here you will learn—or be reminded—that the squids have three hearts, rotating hooks on the ends of their tentacles, and an esophagus that passes through the center of a donut-shaped brain. **55 Cable Street, Wellington. Te Papa Museum is a 20-minute walk, or a 10-minute bus ride, from Wellington Station. ⊚ 41.290502 ⊕ 174.781737**

SPACECRAFT CEMETERY

PACIFIC OCEAN

As ships, stations, and other satellites come crashing down to Earth, many end up making planet-fall at the same patch in the Pacific Ocean, around 3,000 miles east of New Zealand and 2,000 miles north of Antarctica. For years, these downed science vessels have simply sunk down to the bottom of the sea in a place now known as the Spacecraft Cemetery.

While a great deal of debris and smaller satellites burn up on reentry, larger items—including entire space stations—need to be disposed of in a way that keeps the hazardous materials out of public circulation. So into the dark depths of the ocean they go. Among the more than 250 craft that have been scuttled at the spot since 1971 are unmanned satellites, waste freighters carrying astronaut poop, and, possibly most remarkably, the

Deep in the Pacific Ocean lies the technology of outer space.

entire decommissioned Russian space station, Mir.

Technically, the spacecraft cemetery surrounds the Oceanic Pole of Inaccessibility, which is the place on Earth farthest from any landmass. That makes it quite tricky to get to. (The ocean is also about 2.5 miles deep.) This is probably one place best appreciated from afar.

Ⓢ 43.579692 Ⓦ 142.720088

PACIFIC ISLANDS

FIJI

FIJI MUSEUM

SUVA, FIJI

Reverend Thomas Baker's grave mistake was allegedly attempting to remove a comb from the hair of a Fijian chief. For this breach of etiquette in 1867, the Methodist missionary became the last man to be killed, boiled, and eaten by villagers of Nabutautau. After that incident, Fiji abandoned cannibalism.

The sole of Baker's boiled shoe, as well as the specially designated "cannibal forks" used to eat him, are on display at the Fiji Museum. Other items in the collection, including a 44-foot-long (13.4 m), double-hulled war canoe and a copy of the 1874 deed of cession that granted the British ownership of the archipelago, piece together a portrait of Fiji's indigenous and colonial past.

At a tribal ceremony in 2003, Nabutautau villagers formally apologized to Reverend Baker's descendants for eating him, claiming the village had been experiencing "bad luck" since the event.

Thurston Gardens, Cakobau Road, Suva, Viti Levu.
Ⓢ 18.149635 Ⓔ 178.425746

A cannibal fork was used to keep human flesh from touching the lips of a chief.

GUAM
YOKOI'S CAVE

TALOFOFO

The accepted date for the end of World War II is August 14, 1945, even if Japan did not formally surrender until September 2. What some people don't know, however, is that for many Japanese soldiers the war ended much later.

An official count of 127 so-called holdouts or stragglers surrendered in various places in the Pacific Area between 1947 and 1974. This number does not include the many who died in their hiding places, only discovered decades later.

For these holdout soldiers, strong militaristic principles made surrender impossible: It was better to die or be captured than surrender. In some cases, they did not even know about the end of the war. Some of the holdouts continued fighting the American troops or, later, the police, while others just went into hiding. The stragglers believed it impossible to return to Japan, as they feared they would be treated as deserters and punished with the death penalty.

One of those stragglers was Shoichi Yokoi, a tailor by trade who was conscripted to the Japanese Army in 1941. Yokoi was part of the Japanese forces on Guam when the American troops under General Douglas MacArthur conquered the island in summer 1944. US forces advanced quickly, and while many Japanese soldiers were captured or killed, Yokoi and nine other men retreated deep into the jungle.

The men quickly realized that such a big group would be easily discovered. Seven of them left; what happened to them is unknown. The three remaining men, Yokoi included, split up to different hiding places in the area, but kept visiting each other. It took Yokoi three months to dig his "cave," not far from the Talofofo

A prisonlike underground cave served as a hiding place for Yokoi years after World War II.

Falls, about 7 feet (2.1 m) underground. Supported by large bamboo canes, the small underground room was about 3 feet high and 9 feet long, with a small hidden entrance and a second opening to provide an air supply. Inside, he hid all day and stored his few belongings. Yokoi only left his cave at night, lived on caught fish, frogs, snakes, or rats, and learned to use the unknown fruits and vegetables he found. Two of his biggest treasures were a self-made eel trap and a self-made loom, with which he made clothes from the fibers of hibiscus bark.

The three men heard around 1952 that the war was over. They were not sure if the information was true and feared for their lives if they were captured or surrendered, so they decided to stay in hiding. Around 1964, when Yokoi wanted to visit the other two men, he found them dead and buried them. He believed that they died of starvation. Other sources say they died in a flood.

Finally, in 1972, two local fishermen discovered Yokoi on the banks of the Talofofo River, and when, afraid for his life, he charged them, they captured him. He begged the two men to kill him. Instead they took him home, fed him his first real meal in 28 years, and brought him to the authorities. Two weeks later Yokoi returned to Japan and was welcomed as a hero. He felt differently. His famous words were: "It is with much embarrassment, but I have returned."

After Yokoi's death at age 82, the original cave was protected as a historical monument, but it collapsed. In its place, a replica of the cave was erected, along with a shrine and memorials for the last three Japanese stragglers. Some of Yokoi's belongings from his time in the cave can be seen in a museum at the entrance of the Talofofo Falls Resort Park. **From the entrance of the Talofofo Falls Resort Park, you can get a funicular to Talofofo Falls. From there it is about a quarter-mile walk to the cave. A monorail will also take you there. Ⓝ 13.322826 Ⓔ 144.736497**

MARSHALL ISLANDS
CACTUS DOME

ENEWETAK ATOLL

With its ring of verdant islands surrounding a deep sapphire lagoon, the Enewetak coral atoll was a beautiful place to launch the world's first hydrogen bomb. After capturing the atoll from Japan during World War II, the US evacuated the islands, exhumed their fallen soldiers to send home their remains for reburial, and conducted a series of nuclear tests.

Between 1948 and 1958, 43 weapons exploded over Enewetak. Among these was Ivy Mike, a hydrogen bomb 500 times bigger than Hiroshima's Little Boy. By the time testing ceased, the entire atoll was highly radioactive, its reefs and islands dotted with craters that each measured several hundred feet in diameter.

When evacuated residents began returning to Enewetak during the 1970s, the US government determined it ought to decontaminate the islands. In 1979, a military team arrived and gathered up contaminated soil and debris, mixing it with cement and piling the sludge into a 350-foot-wide (107 m) blast crater on Runit Island to the atoll's east. When the mound reached 25 feet (7.6 m) high, army engineers covered it with a saucer-shaped concrete cap. It was dubbed the Cactus Dome, after the Cactus bomb that caused the crater.

The US declared Enewetak safe for habitation in 1980. Currently, about 900 people live on the atoll, though none live on the Cactus Dome. A 2008 field survey of the dome noted that 219 of its 357 concrete panels contain defects such as cracks, chips, and vegetation taking root in joints.

You can charter a small plane from Majuro, the capital of the Marshall Islands, 90 minutes away. Prepare for a bumpy landing—the Enewetak airstrip is not well maintained. Ⓝ 11.552593 Ⓔ 162.333333

After decades of nuclear testing on the Marshall Islands, the US government covered its radioactive sins with a concrete dome.

FEDERATED STATES OF MICRONESIA
NAN MADOL RUINS

MICRONESIA

Off the coast of a remote Micronesian island lie the ruins of a once great city of man-made stone islands. These ruins represent the remains of megalithic

Man-made islets dot the coast of Pohnpei.

architecture on an unparalleled scale in Micronesia.

The construction of the nearly 100 artificial islets started around the 8th or 9th century, and the megalithic structures were built in the 13th to 17th century. This is about the same time as the stone construction of the Cathedral of Notre-Dame in Paris and Angkor Wat in Cambodia. The population of the city was probably more than 1,000. Most of the islets served as residential areas; however, some of them served a special purpose, such as food preparation, coconut oil production, or canoe construction.

There are no sources of fresh water or possibilities to grow food on Nan Madol, so all supplies had to be brought in from the mainland. According to local legend, the stones used in the construction of Nan Madol were flown to the location by means of black magic. Archaeologists have located several possible quarry sites on the main island, but the exact method of transportation of construction material has not been determined.

The complex of Nan Madol is constructed on a series of artificial islets in the shallow water next to the eastern shore of Pohnpei island. An island-hopper flight or sailboat will get you to Pohnpei. Ⓝ 6.840464 Ⓔ 158.331699

GHOST FLEET OF TRUK LAGOON

CHUUK

In February 1944, still reeling from the bombing of Pearl Harbor, the American military targeted a Japanese military base at what was then known as Truk Lagoon. Japan had converted the atoll into a major naval and logistical hub, building roads, trenches, and communications on its islands and stationing battleships, submarines, aircraft carriers, and other giant vessels in the waters.

The Project Hailstone mission began at sunrise on February 17. Five hundred aircraft departed from the nearby Marshall Islands, joining submarines and surface ships in the attack on Truk. Though the Japanese, fearing such a raid, had removed many of their larger ships from the area a week earlier, the damage was extensive.

Forty-seven ships and 270 aircraft were sent to the bottom of the lagoon. About 1,700 Japanese servicemen went down with them.

Truk's sunken vessels remain at the bottom of the lagoon, comprising the world's largest ship graveyard. Riddled with torpedo holes, the ships have released some of their contents. Gas masks, rotting shoes, unopened bottles of beer, and phonograph records drift silently along the coral-covered decks, a sobering reminder of the crew members' daily lives.

In addition to being the final resting place for warships, Truk Lagoon is a mass war grave for those who perished in the attack. In the 1980s, divers retrieved the remains of approximately 400 Japanese crew members. The bones were taken to a Japanese air

base and cremated, and the ashes interred at the National Cemetery for the War Dead in Tokyo. The remains of the other 1,300 servicemen are scattered in the lagoon.

Truk's ghost fleet attracts much marine wildlife, including sharks, manta rays, and turtles, as well as scuba divers. The ships continue to rust and deteriorate, causing ecological concerns—the three tankers on the lagoon floor contain about 32,000 tons (29 million kg) of oil, or about three-quarters of the amount spilled during the Exxon-Valdez disaster. **Truk Lagoon is also known as Chuuk Lagoon. Flights from Guam arrive at Chuuk airport, on Weno Island in the middle of the lagoon. The trip takes about 90 minutes. Ⓝ 7.416667 Ⓔ 151.783333**

The world's largest ship graveyard holds 47 vessels, 270 aircraft, and the remains of about 1,300 Japanese servicemen.

RAI STONES

YAP

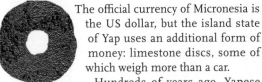

The official currency of Micronesia is the US dollar, but the island state of Yap uses an additional form of money: limestone discs, some of which weigh more than a car.

Hundreds of years ago, Yapese explorers journeyed 280 miles (450.6 km) west in bamboo canoes to the island of Palau, where they encountered limestone for the first time. After negotiations with the people of Palau, the Yapese established a quarry, using shell tools to carve disc-shaped stones they named *rai*.

The stones varied in diameter from a few inches to 12 feet (3.7 m) and weighed up to 8,000 pounds (3,628.7 kg). A hole punched into the center of each disc allowed the explorers to carry the larger stones on poles to their bamboo canoes. Keeping afloat during the long journey home was a more treacherous undertaking.

Back on Yap, rai became a sort of currency, customarily exchanged in marriages and as part of political deals and inheritances. The value of each rai depended on its size, but also on its provenance—if explorers died during the expedition to retrieve a stone, it acquired a higher value. A transaction did not require the physical exchange of a disc, merely the acknowledgment of a transfer of ownership. In fact, one of the rai stones in active circulation sits on the bottom of the Pacific Ocean, having tumbled from a canoe during a storm.

Rai stones were not immune to the vicissitudes of inflation. During the 1870s, an Irish American adventurer named David O'Keefe accompanied the Yapese to Palau, where he used imported tools to carve the limestone. His methods sped up the rai production process, with negative consequences: Yapese placed a lower value on O'Keefe's stones than on the discs carved with traditional shell tools, and the sudden abundance of rai brought down its overall worth.

The quarrying of rai stones ended at the beginning of the 19th century, but the Yapese still exchange discs to commemorate traditions. Many of the 6,500 remaining rai are displayed in rows at outdoor "banks"—jungle clearings and village centers. Theft is not a concern.

Sites include the villages of Maaq and Gachpar on Tomil Island. United Airlines flights to Yap depart from Guam twice a week. Ⓝ 9.533333 Ⓔ 138.116667

NAURU

GUANO ISLAND

YAREN DISTRICT

For a few decades after Nauru became an independent nation in 1968, its 6,000 citizens were among the richest, per capita, in the world. After being controlled since the 1840s by Germany, Britain, Australia, New Zealand, and Japan, Nauru's residents could finally call the 8-square-mile (20.7 km²) island their own—and they imported pricey sports cars to drive on its lone paved road.

Nauru's mighty wealth came from a single source: seabird droppings. Mining companies seized upon the phosphate from the fossilized guano—also known as bird (or bat) poop—in 1908, excavating and exporting it in abundance. The Nauru government, foreseeing the exhaustion of the phosphate supply, established a fund to channel mining money into investments that would secure the country's financial future. Unfortunately, much of the spending—such as the strange and disastrous investment in a four-hour-long 1993 West End musical about Leonardo da Vinci, which closed within five weeks of its premiere—yielded losses. When the phosphate ran out at the beginning of the 21st century, Nauru was left with no money, no natural resources, and no plan for recovery.

The plundered island's sudden poverty led to political instability, the 2005 grounding of its national airline, and unconventional approaches to generating income. Since 2001, Nauru has accepted financial aid from Australia in exchange for hosting a controversial refugee detention center. Asylum seekers hoping to gain entry to Australia by boat are diverted to Nauru and detained for months while the Australian government evaluates their requests for refuge.

Today, 9,500 Nauruans consume food and water imported from Australia—mining has left most of the land rocky, barren, and unsuitable for vegetation. Power shortages are common. Abandoned four-wheel drives and rusted equipment occupy the foreground of the island's coastal landscape, providing a constant reminder of its prosperous past and uncertain future.

The Republic of Nauru's Our Airline flies weekly to Nauru from Brisbane, Australia, and Nadi, Fiji. Ⓢ 0.530083 Ⓔ 166.931906

They don't sting.

PALAU
JELLYFISH LAKE

EIL MALK

A million golden jellyfish spend their days softly pulsating in a small saltwater lake in eastern Palau, their sting too soft to harm snorkelers. About 12,000 years ago, water from the Pacific Ocean flowed into the lake basin, bringing jellyfish with it—but not their predators. As a result, the golden jellyfish multiplied without restraint.

The jellyfish do have one nemesis—anemones that lurk in the shadows of the water, ready to eat them. The jellyfishes' consistent daily migration pattern helps keep them safe and well fed. They spend 14 hours bobbing up and down to gather plankton before chasing the sun from the east to the west, crisscrossing the lake each day.

Snorkeling is welcome in the lake, and the cnidarians will do you no harm as they waft past your body. The only danger is 50 feet (15.2 m) below the surface, where high levels of ammonia and phosphate may cause fatal skin poisoning. For this reason, scuba diving is prohibited.

East Eil Malk, also known as Mecherchar, is one of the southern islands in the Palau archipelago. United Airlines flies to Palau via Guam. Getting to the lake involves a boat trip and a steep 10-minute hike. Do not wear sunscreen, as it pollutes the lake. Ⓝ 7.161111 Ⓔ 134.376111

PAPUA NEW GUINEA
YAMAMOTO'S BOMBER

BUIN, BOUGAINVILLE

Deep in the jungle north of Buin lies the wreckage of a particularly significant Japanese World War II bomber. At dawn on April 18, 1943, this plane departed from Rabaul, Papua New Guinea. Onboard was Admiral Isoroku Yamamoto, commander in chief of the Japanese navy's Combined Fleet and mastermind of the attack on Pearl Harbor. Yamamoto was headed for a tour of Japanese front lines in the South Pacific, intending to boost morale following a series of setbacks in the area.

What the admiral and his officers didn't know was that US naval intelligence had intercepted and deciphered his travel plans. With Yamamoto's full itinerary in front of them, the US seized the opportunity to ambush his flight.

The mission—Operation Vengeance—was audacious. Eighteen American planes took off from Guadalcanal in the Solomon Islands, flying hundreds of miles north toward the Japanese bomber. The distance was so great that they had to carry extra fuel tanks. Flying over Bougainville, the Americans spotted Yamamoto's bomber and its escort planes. A dogfight ensued, and the admiral's bomber, spewing smoke, crash-landed in the jungle.

The Japanese rescue party who retrieved the admiral the next day said they found Yamamoto's body sitting upright under a tree, after he was thrown from the bomber. Rescue leader Lieutenant Hamasuna claimed that Yamamoto's white-gloved hand was still clutching the hilt of his sword—a detail that preserved the dignity of the admiral in the eyes of the dispirited Japanese.

To get to the wreckage, you'll need to take a 3-hour road trip from Arawa to Buin. Then it's an hour-long jungle trek to the crash site. Traveling with a local guide is recommended. Ⓢ 6.785649 Ⓔ 155.646687

ALSO IN THE PACIFIC ISLANDS

Great Pacific Garbage Patch

A Texas-size swirl of plastic fragments floats in the middle of the Pacific Ocean, made up of trash swept from the West Coast beaches of the US.

Alofaaga Blowholes

Savai'i, Samoa · Ocean water barrels through a series of coastal lava tubes, eventually blasting skyward through holes at the surface.

The wreckage of Admiral Yamamoto's World War II plane is still in the Bougainville jungle.

An Island to Oneself

New Zealander Tom Neale spent 16 years alone on Suwarrow, a tiny Cook Islands coral atoll 200 miles (321.9 km) from the nearest populated land. He rode out violent storms in a rickety shack, ate a diet heavy on fish and coconuts, and wore nothing but a loincloth on his sun-browned body. It is the remarkable tale of a shipwrecked survivor, but for one detail: Neale did not land on Suwarrow by accident. He traveled there willingly and enthusiastically, determined to live a simple, solitary existence on an island he could call his own.

Neale was 50 when he first set sail for Suwarrow in 1952. Formerly a shopkeeper in Tahiti, he became fixated on the atoll after meeting author Robert Frisbie and hearing him tell of its charms.

To prepare for his stay, which he planned to last for years, Neale stockpiled supplies—bewildering store owners in the small town of Rarotonga by buying their entire inventories of flour, sugar, kerosene, and coffee beans. As word spread about his grand plans, villagers offered gifts and even companionship—Neale politely refused the advances of several women who asked to accompany him, suspecting it would not be long before he came to resent their company. He did, however, choose two nonhuman companions: a cat named Mrs. Thievery (named for her favorite hobby) and her kitten, Mr. Tom-Tom.

Armed with tins of food, tools, seeds, and a motley collection of paperbacks, Neale arrived on Suwarrow following 6 days at sea.

Gradually, Neale adapted to island life. He spent the daylight hours building, cleaning, and tending to his garden, and ushered in nightfall sitting on a wooden box at the beach, watching the sun set while drinking a cup of tea. The necessary task of killing six pigs who threatened to destroy the garden brought Neale much anguish—after spearing the first one and hearing its screams, he wrote in his journal of feeling "melancholy," and decided to bury the animal rather than eat it.

Ten months after his arrival on Suwarrow, Neale received his first visitors: two couples on a yacht, who were astonished by the orderliness of his abode. (Not one to lower his living standards just because he lived in a shack, Neale boiled his sheets weekly, kept a tidy room, and ate using a tablecloth.) When the visitors departed a few days later, leaving well wishes and a half-drunk bottle of rum, Neale took up a new project: reconstructing a destroyed pier that had embarrassed him with its unsightliness.

For the next six months, he spent up to five hours every day dragging, rolling, and carrying large pieces of coral to the water's edge, setting them on the pier's fragmentary foundations. When the task was finally complete, Neale had single-handedly built a neat, structurally sound jetty using just rocks, patience, and hard work. The next day, a violent storm attacked

A latter-day Robinson Crusoe with his catch.

the island, completely destroying the newly finished pier.

Thus began a run of bad luck. Having exhausted his tobacco supply, Neale experienced torturous cravings. He dreamed nightly of soothing cigarettes, chocolate, beef, and fat, juicy duck. But the mental torture would soon pale in comparison to physical pain. Casting an anchor on the beach one day, Neale felt a searing stab along his spine and suddenly every movement was agony. Taking 4 hours to make the short journey back to his shack, Neale laid down in his bed and, between bouts of unconsciousness, hoped for a miracle.

Incredibly, a miracle indeed arrived—in the form of Peb and Bob, two American yachtsmen who stopped in at the atoll while en route to Samoa. (Peb, as it turned out, was more formally known as James Rockefeller Jr., a member of one of the US's wealthiest dynasties.) The duo, astonished to find Neale on the "uninhabited" island, fed him, massaged his back, and, having returned

him to good health, departed with a pledge that they would send a ship to fetch him. Two weeks later, the promised ship arrived, plucking Neale from his two-year life of island solitude and ferrying him back to Rarotonga.

Neale did not take kindly to being back among the comforts of civilization. Clocks were an intrusive nuisance, cars moved noisily and too fast, and trousers compared unfavorably with the comfort of a cotton loincloth. All Neale wanted was to return to Suwarrow, but the government forbade it. Disconsolate, he took a job in a warehouse. Six years passed before a friend with a 30-foot (9.1 m) boat offered to take Neale back to his beloved atoll.

Neale's second stay on Suwarrow lasted two and a half years, ending only when the increasing presence of pearl divers at the atoll began to wear on his patience. A 3-year break in Rarotonga allowed him to pen his island memoir, *An Island to Oneself*, before returning for his final, decade-long stay on Suwarrow. In 1977, stricken with stomach cancer, he was transported to Rarotonga, where he died at the age of 75.

Despite his long stretches of solitary living, Neale claimed he never felt lonely. The few times he wished someone was with him, he wrote in *An Island to Oneself*, were "not because I wanted company but just because all this beauty seemed too perfect to keep to myself."

SAMOA
PALOLO WORM FESTIVAL

SAVAI'I

For most of the year, Samoan palolo worms live in burrows in coral reefs, feeding on algae and slowly growing to their adult length of 12 inches (30.5 cm). But over one or two nights every October, they rise to the surface and engage in a swarming, floating, mucus-laden reproductive frenzy.

During the annual swarm, the worms release their tail segments (known as the epitoke), which contain sperm or eggs. The segments float up to the surface, where the casings dissolve, releasing their contents and triggering the reproduction process.

At that time, local families grab their nets and cheesecloth and wade into the water, hoping to scoop up a delicious serving of headless worms. Palolo, which has a salty, fishy flavor, is a delicacy in Samoa. Between filling buckets with the wriggling creatures, locals pop handfuls of the worm segments into their mouths completely raw. The next day, palolo on toast is the meal of choice.

Safotu, Fagasa, Asau, Papa, and Puleia reefs surrounding the island of Savai'i. The timing of the palolo swarm differs every year. Locals have developed a range of methods for predicting the date using the lunar calendar. Aim to be there 7 days after the full moon in October.
Ⓢ 13.613956 Ⓔ 172.420349

VANUATU
PENTECOST ISLAND LAND DIVING

PENTECOST ISLAND

There is a boy, perhaps 7 years old, standing on a platform that juts out from a tower made of tree trunks and vines. He is about 30 feet (9.1 m) above the ground. He is naked except for a traditional penis sheath attached to a vine belt. Tied around his ankles are the frayed ends of liana vines. Women in grass skirts cheer and dance. The boy closes his eyes, places his hands in the prayer position, and jumps. A loud snapping noise accompanies the moment when his body brushes the ground before bouncing back up and dangling from the vine. The boy is shaken, but smiles as two men help him stand. That was the warm-up. The really exciting stuff is yet to come.

The males of southern Pentecost Island have been land diving for centuries. The ritual, in which boys and men leap from increasingly higher levels of a 100-foot-tall (30.5 m) tower using vines as bungee cords, is performed to ensure a good yam harvest. Over the years, it has acquired additional meaning: Boys who make the leap following circumcision at age 7 or 8 gain acceptance into manhood.

Land diving takes place every year on Saturdays between April and June. At this time of year, the liana vines are at their most elastic. After spending up to 5 weeks building the tower, a team of men tills the soil at the landing patch to soften it. A village elder selects two vines for each jumper, taking height and weight into consideration. The margin for error is slim—too short and the jumper may swing back and hit the tower; too long and he may die or become paralyzed after hitting the ground hard.

The ritual begins with the youngest jumpers, who leap from the lowest platform. To ensure a plentiful yam harvest, the diver's shoulders must make contact with the ground. (As a safety precaution, the head is tucked against the chest during the dive.) The loud snap heard on impact is not—in most cases—a human spine breaking, but the snapping of the support beam.

As the age and experience of the divers increase, so does the level from which they leap. The ritual reaches a climax when a man dives from the very top. When he lands, villagers erupt into applause and cheers, surround him, and hoist him into the air.

Pentecost Island is a 50-minute flight from Port Vila. The land diving site is a 5-minute walk from the airport. Ⓢ 15.717317 Ⓔ 168.179243

Using vines as bungee cords, a man bravely leaps off a 100-foot tower to ensure a good yam harvest.

Tanna's true believers await an unconventional messiah.

CARGO CULTS OF TANNA

TANNA

On a small island in the southern part of the Vanuatu archipelago, devoted believers await the second coming of an American deity who will bring divine gifts in the form of TVs, refrigerators, and Coca-Cola. They are members of a cargo cult: an anthropological label for a tribal society that engages in religious practices designed to attract goods—or "cargo"—from more technologically advanced cultures.

Cargo cults rose to prominence during World War II, when hundreds of thousands of American and Japanese soldiers flooded into the islands of the Pacific region, bringing items that reflected material wealth and industrialization. Encountering mass-produced goods such as candy and radios—and having no concept of manufacturing processes—some island residents believed the goods were divinely created.

When the war ended and the soldiers went home, the cargo disappeared. Cult members believed that goods were dispatched to them by the gods, but intercepted by Westerners. They responded by setting up mock airstrips, airports, and offices, hoping to attract the cargo deliveries back to their rightful destination in Tanna.

Most of the cargo cults disappeared in the decades after the war, but the John Frum Movement lives on in Tanna. Cult members worship Frum, a messiah with mutable characteristics. To some, he is white. To others, black. For most, he is American, likely based on a soldier who brought cargo to Vanuatu during World War II: "John from America."

Though Frum's appearance varies, his mission is consistent: to shake off the restrictions of colonial rule and restore the independence and cultural freedom of the Tanna people. Cult followers believe Frum will return on February 15—an annual holiday known as John Frum Day—of an unspecified year, bearing food, household appliances, vehicles, and medicine.

Celebrations on John Frum Day have a distinctly American feel. Men in jeans with "USA" painted in red on their bare chests perform military drills, holding sticks of wood shaped like rifles. Above them, the American flag flies high from a bamboo pole.

The John Frum Movement coexists with other cargo cults in Tanna: The Tom Navy faction holds a US naval officer as its figurehead, and the Prince Philip Movement regards the Duke of Edinburgh as a pale-skinned mountain spirit and eagerly awaits his messianic arrival.

Sulphur Bay, Tanna. Flights to Tanna via Port Vila depart from Australia, New Zealand, Fiji, and New Caledonia. The center of the John Frum Movement is at Sulphur Bay. ⑤ 19.515486 ⑥ 169.456501

Canada

Western Canada

ALBERTA • BRITISH COLUMBIA • MANITOBA
NORTHWEST TERRITORIES • NUNAVUT
SASKATCHEWAN • YUKON

Eastern Canada

NEWFOUNDLAND AND LABRADOR • NOVA SCOTIA
ONTARIO • PRINCE EDWARD ISLAND • QUEBEC

WESTERN CANADA

ALBERTA
THE BANFF MERMAN

BANFF

In a glass case at the Banff Indian Trading Post is what looks like the back end of a snapper fish glued to the top half of a desiccated monkey. Tufts of white hair cling to the 3-foot-long creature's emaciated form. One webbed hand reaches out as if in the throes of death. A maniacal grin bares two rows of tiny, pointed teeth. This is the Banff Merman.

The legend of the merman began with Norman K. Luxton, founder of the Indian Trading Post and the Sign of the Goat Curio Shop. Accounts of its origin differ, but following a failed

Meet the mysterious 100-year-old man-beast of the Seven Seas.

around-the-world expedition, Luxton either caught, bought, or built the hokey-looking man-beast around 1915. The Banff Merman has been entertaining and provoking the imaginations of visitors ever since.

Indian Trading Post, 101 Cave Avenue Banff, 80 miles (129 km) west of Calgary. Next door is the Buffalo Nations Luxton Museum, also founded by Norman Luxton.
Ⓝ 51.171971 Ⓦ 115.571960

The Badlands Guardian

MEDICINE HAT

Gaze out of an airplane window above the Badlands east of Medicine Hat, and a Native American chief will stare back at you. Over millennia, erosion and weathering fashioned the rocky terrain into the shape of a human head, complete with feathered headdress. A gas well and road leading down from the chief's ear resemble earphones.

An Australian woman going by the name of "supergranny" discovered the head on Google Earth in 2006. Following a naming competition, the 820 × 740-foot (250 × 225.5 m) figure came to be known as the Badlands Guardian. (Rejected monikers include Space Face, Chief Bleeding Ear, The Listening Rock, Jolly Rocker, and Pod God.)

The Badlands Guardian is an example of pareidolia, the phenomenon of an overactive imagination perceiving recognizable shapes in ambiguous stimuli. Faces, particularly religious ones, are frequently found in inanimate objects—the Virgin Mary has appeared, among other places, in a grilled cheese sandwich, on an expressway underpass, and in a pile of chocolate drippings at a California candy factory.

The Badlands Guardian is east of Medicine Hat, a few miles south of Many Islands Lake. It is only visible by air—there is no public access to the site. Ⓝ 50.010600 Ⓦ 110.115900

Seen from the air, the folds of Medicine Hat's badlands resemble a man listening to music.

Also in Alberta

Sunnyslope Sandstone Shelter

Linden · Standing alone on a prairie, this shelter likely dates to the early 20th century, when homesteaders built it to protect themselves from the elements.

World's Largest Beaver Dam

IMPROVEMENT DISTRICT NO. 24

The beavers in Canada's Wood Buffalo National Park have been hard at work for decades, and their tree-chomping labor has paid off. The furry architects have created the largest beaver dam in the world.

The dam, which is about a half mile (.8 km) long, is so massive it even shows up on satellite images. It remained hidden within the Alberta wilderness until 2007, when a researcher spotted it while looking at Google Earth. The beavers are currently building new dams nearby which, when joined with the main structure, could add over 300 more feet (91.4 m) to its length.

Beavers are one of the few species capable of creating structures that are significant enough to be seen from space. The toothy critters are remarkable environmental engineers. Their dams reroute streams and even alter entire ecosystems. These creations, which are built to last, are barriers that form ponds, which act like defensive moats to protect the beavers from predators like wolves and bears.

It's likely the beavers began working on the Alberta dam sometime in the 1970s, making it a multi-generational architectural endeavor. The hodgepodge of mud, branches, stones, and twigs is cloaked in a layer of grass, meaning it's been there for a while. The dam stretches across a remote wetland area, which provides the creatures with both plenty of fresh water and bountiful building materials.

The isolated beaver dam is difficult to reach for any curious human. American researcher Rob Mark was the first to set foot on it, in 2014. His journey took nine days. Since the dam can be seen from space, you could always fly over it—in a standard plane or aboard a spacecraft. Ⓝ 58.271474 Ⓦ 112.252228

BRITISH COLUMBIA
SAM KEE BUILDING

VANCOUVER

In 1913, Chang Toy, owner of the Sam Kee import-export company, sold most of his corner property at Carrall and Pender Streets to the city of Vancouver for the construction and widening of West Pender Street. It was not the most amicable transaction—Toy was not adequately compensated, and the city's disrespect toward him was part of the anti-Chinese sentiment that prevailed at the time.

Left with only a strip of land to call his own, Toy recruited architects Bryan and Gillam to create a two-story building with attention-grabbing dimensions. The 6-foot-wide (1.8 m) structure is Guinness-certified as the narrowest commercial building in the world.

8 West Pender Street, Vancouver. The building is a 7-minute walk from the Stadium-Chinatown stop on the SkyTrain. Ⓝ 49.280416 Ⓦ 123.104715

The world's narrowest commercial building is 6 feet (1.8 m) wide.

FREE SPIRIT SPHERES

VANCOUVER ISLAND

Spending a night in a Free Spirit Sphere is a moving experience. The three spheres, named Eve, Eryn, and Melody, which are about 10 feet (3 m) in diameter, are suspended from trees in a forest just north of Qualicum Beach. When a breeze sweeps through the forest, the spheres sway gently.

Each 1,100-pound (500 kg) cedar-and-spruce orb is equipped with a bed, dining table, storage space, built-in speakers, and big circular windows for gazing at the forest. Spiral staircases and drawbridges provide access to the spheres, which hang about a story above the ground. Toilets and showers are located in separate buildings nearby—Eryn's outhouse is shaped like a mushroom.

The spheres are the work of Tom Chudleigh, who operates the property with his wife, Rosey. Chudleigh used shipbuilding techniques to handcraft them, aiming to create natural-looking, nutlike globes that blend in with the environment.

420 Horne Lake Road, Qualicum Beach. The ferry from Vancouver (Horseshoe Bay) to Nanaimo takes an hour and 40 minutes. Then it's an hour's drive north to the spheres. Ⓝ 49.378834 Ⓦ 124.616330

Sleep inside a softly bouncing wooden ball suspended from the trees.

THE TREE ON THE LAKE

PORT RENFREW

Living up to its name, Fairy Lake is in a remote and unspoiled landscape near the town of Port Renfrew. Sticking up out of the lake's stillness is a partially submerged log. Clinging to that log for dear life is a tiny, living Douglas fir tree. Tourists, boaters, and hikers come seeking it as a unique window into nature and rebirth.

The "bonsai" tree has attracted more than a few photographers to capture its struggle of endurance, including a winner of the National History Museum of London's Wildlife Photographer of the Year award. **Fairy Lake is on Vancouver Island, about 5 miles east of the town of Port Renfrew. Take Parkinson Road to the turnoff for Deering Road, follow that to the end, and turn right onto Pacific Marine Road. Follow that all the way to the lake. The little tree will be on your right, about a quarter mile past the turnoff for Fairy Lake Recreation Site. Ⓝ 48.589443 Ⓦ 124.349811**

Bonsai-like serenity and a symbol of survival.

VANCOUVER POLICE MUSEUM

VANCOUVER

Housed in a former coroner's court and morgue, this museum displays confiscated weapons, counterfeit currency, police uniforms, and other artifacts that chronicle Canadian crime-busting.

The best stories are found in the morgue, which retains its original autopsy bays, sinks, and drawers. It was here that a coroner conducted the autopsy of Errol Flynn after he died suddenly at the age of fifty in 1959. (The hard-living actor's recorded afflictions at the time of death included myocardial infarction, coronary thrombosis, coronary atherosclerosis, cirrhosis of the liver, and diverticulosis of the colon.)

A wry sense of humor pervades the museum's exhibits. A sign on one of the morgue drawers reads, PLEASE DO NOT OPEN MORGUE DRAWERS (DO YOU *KNOW* WHAT USED TO BE IN HERE??). The answer is not just "bodies"—one presiding coroner only used 17 of the 18 drawers, preferring to keep the last one as a beer fridge.

240 East Cordova Street. Get a bus along Hastings Street and walk a block north to Cordova. Ⓝ 49.282269 Ⓦ 123.099345

LARGE ZENITH TELESCOPE

MAPLE RIDGE

At the Liquid Mirror Observatory, scientists use a 20-foot-wide (6 m) spinning puddle of mercury to survey distant galaxies. While most reflecting telescopes incorporate solid mirrors made of glass and aluminum, the Large Zenith Telescope uses a pool of spinning mercury to reflect starlight. The centrifugal force of the rotating mercury forms a parabola, the shape required for the mirror to reflect light.

The main advantage of liquid metal telescopes is that they are significantly cheaper to build than their solid-mirror counterparts. The downside is that they can only point in a fixed direction—tilting the telescope would cause

mercury surface

rotating mirror platform

the reflective liquid to spill out. The Large Zenith Telescope is so named because it points toward the zenith—in other words, straight up.

Malcolm Knapp Research Forest, Maple Ridge. The observatory is 43 miles east of Vancouver. It's a 45-minute hike from the gate.
N 49.287579 **W** 122.572759

ALSO IN BRITISH COLUMBIA

Boswell Embalming Bottle House

Boswell · When he retired after 35 years in the funeral business, David H. Brown took half a million empty embalming fluid bottles and turned them into a two-story home.

Enchanted Forest

Revelstoke · In this old-world forest fairy-tale land, over 350 folk figurines are hidden among 800-year-old cedars.

Kitsault

Kitsault · The shiny new settlement that popped up in 1979 to cater to employees of a molybdenum mine lasted just 18 months before a molybdenum price crash rendered it a ghost town.

Hundreds of mineral-rich pools make up the giant painter's palette that is Spotted Lake.

SPOTTED LAKE

OSOYOOS

From fall to spring, there is nothing unusual about Spotted Lake. But come summer, the reason for its name becomes clear: Evaporation reveals hundreds of round pools on the bottom of the lake. Each spot is colored according to the type and concentration of its minerals.

Spotted Lake has long been a sacred site for the First Nations of the Okanagan Valley. Its minerals, which include magnesium sulfate, calcium, sodium sulphates, and traces of silver and titanium, are believed to have healing properties. During World War I, these therapeutic minerals were harvested and used to make ammunition.

Okanagan Highway 3, 6 miles (9.7 km) west of Osoyoos. The lake is on private land, but you can catch a glimpse from the highway.
N 49.078018 **W** 119.567502

MANITOBA

NARCISSE SNAKE ORGY

NARCISSE

For a few weeks every year, Interlake teems with piles of writhing serpents. In late April, tens of thousands of harmless red-sided garter snakes emerge from their winter dens, slithering over one another in search of a mate—the largest single concentration of garter snakes in the world. A multiweek reproductive frenzy follows, during which tangled balls of snakes constantly form and disperse. It's hypnotic and unexpectedly audible—on a dry day you'll hear the animals' scales rubbing together. **The dens are 4 miles north of Narcisse along Highway 17. To see the snakes mating, visit in late April or early May. Ⓝ 50.734526 Ⓦ 97.530355**

There's a whole lot of hissing going on.

NORTHWEST TERRITORIES

DIAVIK DIAMOND MINE

LAC DE GRAS

An open-pit spiral on an island in a lake, the Diavik Diamond Mine is spectacular when viewed from above. But the most remarkable thing about it is its remoteness. The mine is located 190 miles (306 km) north of the nearest town, Yellowknife in the Northwest Territories.

There is only one road to Diavik, and it can be used for just nine weeks each year. The reason? It's made of ice. At the end of every December, when the lakes and ponds have frozen, workers begin a six-week around-the-clock construction process to open the mine for resupply in late January. The route closes for the season by early April—the exact date depends on the thinness of the ice. Trucks bringing fuel, cement, explosives, and construction materials must stick to the road's 16-mph (25 kph) speed limit.

The mine began producing diamonds in 2003, and was soon yielding 3,500 pounds (1,588 kg) of the precious stones per year. In 2012, Diavik completed the transition from open-pit to underground mining in order to reach more diamonds. Its employees arrive and depart from a private airstrip. Heated access tunnels and readily available baked goods make the –20°F (–29°C) nights more bearable. **Lac de Gras, North Slave Region, Northwest Territories. Ⓝ 64.496100 Ⓦ 110.664280**

PINGO CANADIAN LANDMARK

TUKTOYAKTUK

The arctic region of Tuktoyaktuk is stippled with pingos, dome-shaped hills with a core of ice and a layer of soil on top. Just west of the Tuktoyaktuk, at Pingo Canadian Landmark, there are eight of these arctic landforms—including Ibyuk, the highest pingo in Canada at 160 feet tall and 984 feet wide (49 m by 300 m). The eight domes, which resemble baby volcanoes, are among the 1,350 pingos of the Tuktoyaktuk peninsula.

Three miles west of Tuktoyaktuk. Pingo Canadian Landmark is best accessed by boat from Tuktoyaktuk. Depending on the time of year, you may encounter caribou, grizzly bears, or snow geese among the pingos. Ⓝ 69.399722 Ⓦ 133.079722

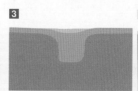
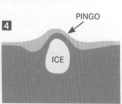

Pingos are hills made of earth-covered ice. Above, the formation of a pingo.

■ water-saturated sand ■ permafrost ■ soil ■ ice

NUNAVUT

HAUGHTON IMPACT CRATER

DEVON ISLAND

Twenty-three million years ago a meteorite slammed into Devon Island, the largest uninhabited island on the planet. The impact melted the surrounding rocks, leaving a 12-mile-wide (19 km) scar on the High Arctic landscape. Due to the cold, dry climate, which encases the ground in permafrost for most of the year, the island's geological conditions have remained stable ever since. They also bear a striking resemblance to a place humans have yet to visit: Mars.

The idea of using the Devon Island crater as a test lab for Mars exploration experiments originated with SETI Institute planetary scientist Dr. Pascal Lee in 1997. Working with NASA, Lee and a team of about 30 researchers make yearly summer visits to the spot, conducting field tests to help plan for Mars expeditions. Using a tent city as base camp, the scientists drive all-terrain vehicles to simulate rovers, operate automated drills to look for water, take

➤➤ Spaceship Architecture of the Arctic

In the Canadian Arctic, high winds, subfreezing temperatures, and the difficulty of transporting building materials create challenging design constraints for Nunavut's architects.

IQALUIT AIRPORT
Known locally as the Yellow Submarine, Iqaluit's airport terminal is built to withstand the elements. The airport's extra-long runway has been used by Airbus to cold-weather test new aircraft designs.

ST. JUDE'S CATHEDRAL
The "Igloo Cathedral" is the seat of the Anglican Diocese of the Arctic. It opened in 2012, replacing an earlier church that was destroyed by arson.

walks in spacesuit prototypes, and conduct mapping tests using robots.

Though human colonization of Mars is still but a distant dream, the Haughton crater experiments offer a practical look into how we might get there. New research projects take place every summer, and the eventual goal is for Red Planet–bound astronauts to use the crater as a training ground before blasting off to Mars for real.

Baffin Bay. Ⓝ 75.198235 Ⓦ 89.851182 ➡

The Mars-like landscape of Haughton crater is an ideal place to train astronauts for a Red Planet mission.

NAKASUK SCHOOL
The students who go to school in this two-story fiberglass structure don't much miss having windows during Iqaluit's dark winter months.

IGLOOLIK RESEARCH STATION
Built by the Canadian government in the 1970s, this UFO-shaped building holds research labs and offices for scientists from the Department of Environment.

NORTH WARNING SYSTEM SITE
The North Warning System is a 3,000-mile-long (4,828 km) string of early-warning radars in Cambridge Bay, built by the US and Canadian governments in the 1980s, to detect Soviet attacks across the North Pole.

GRAVES OF BEECHEY ISLAND

RESOLUTE

Standing eerily on Beechey Island, a peninsula off Devon Island in the Canadian Arctic, are four gravestones belonging to three members of an ill-fated expedition to the Northwest Passage and one of the men who went looking for them.

In 1845, Sir John Franklin led an expedition to find the Northwest Passage, a direct route from the Atlantic Ocean to the Pacific Ocean across the Arctic, on two ships that were called "unstoppable" at the time. They were stopped.

The expedition visited Beechey Island for a winter encampment. There, three members of the 129-person crew—John Torrington, William Braine, and John Hartnell—were buried near the shore on an otherwise desolate plain. The rest of the crew abandoned the ships later, when they got stuck in the ice near King William Island. Evidence has been found to suggest they resorted to cannibalism before perishing.

How the three young men died is still unknown despite the fact that their bodies stayed well preserved—essentially mummified—in the frozen arctic ground. Lead poisoning from their canned food was a leading theory, though it is disputed now. The men's remains were exhumed in the 1980s, examined, and reburied. In recent years, both of Franklin's ships have been discovered, and it is hoped that more mysteries can be solved.

The fourth grave marker at the site is that of Thomas Morgan. A member of one of the many expeditions launched to find out what had happened to Franklin and his crew, he died of scurvy in 1854. **Charter a plane from Edmonton to the very remote and very cold Arctic hamlet of Resolute. From there, climb aboard a well-stocked ship to journey to Beechey Island. And you come back now, you hear?** Ⓝ 74.714333 Ⓦ 91.825265

The markers stand out on the otherwise barren shoreline.

SASKATCHEWAN

TWISTED TREES

ALTICANE

Trembling aspen trees, so named for the way their leaves shiver in the wind, normally grow tall, straight, and thin. But a grove of aspens near Alticane, known as the "Twisted Trees," has somehow ended up as a crooked and mangled mess.

The oddest thing about the Twisted Trees is the fact that they are surrounded by perfectly normal trembling aspens. No one knows exactly when this patch of forest became so gnarled, but theories abound. One local legend tells of an alien who emerged from a UFO to urinate into the soil, causing it to become contaminated and warp the trees.

The scientific explanation is more mundane. Quaking aspen grow in vast groves consisting of what appear to be individual trees, but which are actually "clones" of an original source. The entire stand is a single giant organism.

At some point, a genetic mutation seems to have affected how these trees grow—and not just one tree, but the entire clonal forest. Though the mutation may have made some creepy, gnarly trees, it apparently wasn't devastating enough to impede their growth.

The Twisted Trees are about 3 miles southwest of Alticane.
Ⓝ 52.900372 Ⓦ 107.479533

The crooked aspens of Alticane twist their trunks for unknown reasons.

URANIUM CITY

URANIUM CITY

Candu High School, named after a type of nuclear reactor invented in Canada, is located on Uranium Road, not far from Fission Avenue in Uranium City.

As evidenced by its nomenclature, this northern Saskatchewan settlement is—was—a small town sustained by a single industry. Established in 1952 to house workers from the nearby Beaverlodge uranium mines, Uranium City flourished in the 1950s, '60s, and '70s thanks to British and American nuclear weapons programs.

Then, without warning, the town's reason for being vanished.

On December 3, 1981, Eldorado Nuclear Limited announced that the uranium mine would be shutting in six months. At the time, about 4,000 people lived in the city—almost all of them dependent on income from the mine. Candu High, freshly built, had just opened to students. But with jobs wiped out, a mass exodus soon took place by air and ice road—the only ways in and out of the city.

Today Uranium City is not quite a ghost town, though its abandoned, crumbling buildings make it look like one. Around 70 people still live in the settlement, enduring Januaries with an average daily low of –25.4°F (–31.9°C). There is no hospital, but among the ruins there is a school, a bar, a hotel, and a general store that receives grocery deliveries by air once a week.

Uranium City is a 4-hour flight from Saskatoon, departing twice weekly.
Ⓝ 59.569326 Ⓦ 108.610521

The closure of Beaverlodge Mine caused the collapse of Uranium City.

YUKON
WATSON LAKE SIGN POST FOREST
WATSON LAKE

The Sign Post Forest beside the Alaska Highway is a trail of wooden poles covered top to bottom with directional signs and license plates. Visitors are encouraged to show their hometown pride by adding a sign to the collection. (If you forget to bring one, the visitor's center provides the materials for you to make one.)

Sign Post Forest dates back to 1942, when an injured American soldier from Illinois was tasked with building signs in the area. Pining for home, he snuck in a sign that read "Danville, Illinois: 2,835 miles." The one-time lark soon became a popular tradition—there are now more than 72,000 signs in the forest. It is the pride of Watson Lake, which has a population of 800, or approximately 90 signs for each resident.

Mile 635, Alaska Highway, Watson Lake. The Sign Post Forest makes for a great pit stop during a road trip along the Alaska Highway—the 1,387-mile-long (2,232 km) road that links Alaska with the Yukon and British Columbia. Ⓝ 60.063716 Ⓦ 128.713954

Walk by 72,000 roadside signs—not on a highway, but in the woods.

SOURTOE COCKTAIL
DAWSON CITY

The story of the Sourtoe begins with Captain Dick. A former cowboy, truck driver, and professional wolf-poisoner, Dick Stevenson was poking around a cabin on the outskirts of town in 1973 when he found a jar. Inside, preserved in alcohol, was a human toe.

Known for his madcap schemes—he boasts of having organized "the first nude beauty contest north of the 60th parallel"—the captain wondered how he could best make use of the toe. Then, after several drinks, it hit him: *cocktail garnish.*

The Sourtoe, served every night at the Downtown Hotel since 1973, is Stevenson's enduring creation. Originally it adhered to a strict two-ingredient recipe: champagne plus pickled toe. Over the years, however, the Sourtoe rules have relaxed. Any liquid, alcoholic or otherwise, may now be used, but drinkers must abide by the official chant: "Drink it fast or drink it slow, but the lips have got to touch the toe." Those who accomplish the wince-inducing task receive a certificate of membership in the Sourtoe Cocktail Club.

The same toe is used for every drink—alcohol keeps it sterile—but incidents of accidental swallowing have resulted in a succession of donated toes. The first toe, amputated from a man's frostbitten foot in the 1920s, went down the throat of an intoxicated miner in 1980. Toe number two, donated when its owner developed an inoperable corn, went missing a short time later. A baseball player swallowed toe number three, another frostbite casualty, in 1983. Five toes have since been donated to the bar, the most recent arriving in a jar with a message: "Don't wear open-toed sandals while mowing the lawn."

Sourdough Saloon at the Downtown Hotel, 1026 Second Avenue, Dawson City. Ⓝ 64.062336 Ⓦ 139.433435

Does a square mile of sand just south of the Arctic Circle count as a desert?

CARCROSS DESERT

CARCROSS

A one-square-mile desert, surrounded by snow-covered mountains, in a Canadian territory just south of the Arctic Circle. How can this be?

The answer is that Carcross Desert, though certainly sandy and often referred to as the world's smallest desert, is actually the remains of a glacier. The Carcross area—"Carcross" is derived from "Caribou Crossing"—was once a glacial lake. Over thousands of years, as the glaciers retreated, the water level lowered, leaving behind the layer of silt that once formed the bottom of the lake. This silt, shaped by the wind into dunes, became the world's most adorable desert.

Summer activities at Carcross Desert include off-roading and sandboarding. In winter, when the sand is covered in snow, bring your skis and snowboards. **The teeny desert is an hour's drive south of Whitehorse. Ⓝ 60.187222 Ⓦ 134.694722**

LABRADOR SEA

NU

NU

HUDSON BAY

MB

NEWFOUNDLAND & LABRADOR

L'Anse aux Meadows

Newfoundland Island

QUEBEC

ONTARIO

PRINCE EDWARD ISLAND

Val-Jalbert

Cochrane Polar Bear Habitat

Canadian Potato Museum

Marconi National Historic Site

Sable Island

SNOLAB

MONTREAL

Diefenbunker

St. Joseph's Oratory

Oak Island Money Pit

NOVA SCOTIA

USA

Midlothian Castle

OTTAWA

NEW BRUNSWICK

Lower Bay Station

Sewers of Toronto

Bata Shoe Museum

USA

ATLANTIC OCEAN

N

Miles
0   200   400

Kilometers
0   200   400

NEWFOUNDLAND AND LABRADOR

L'ANSE AUX MEADOWS

ISLANDS BAY

The Vikings were here five hundred years before Columbus stumbled upon the Americas. Around 1000 CE, Vikings landed at the northernmost tip of Newfoundland and built a village. Known as L'Anse aux Meadows, it is the only recognized Viking settlement in North America.

The site was discovered in 1960 by Norwegian explorer Helge Ingstad. Excavations during the 1960s unearthed the remains of eight buildings as well as a stone oil lamp, a bone knitting needle, a sharpening stone, and traces of butternuts, a species of walnut that does not grow at the latitude of the settlement. This indicates that the Vikings must have traveled farther south to find sustenance.

The wood-and-sod buildings, which resemble Viking dwellings in Greenland, have been

The reconstructed lodgings of North America's first European visitors.

reconstructed to give visitors an idea of what L'Anse aux Meadows looked like. Site guides dressed as Vikings add to the immersive experience.

L'Anse aux Meadows is on the tip of the northern peninsula, 270 miles (434.5 km) north of Deer Lake. The site is open from June through September.
Ⓝ 51.598918 Ⓦ 55.530883

NOVA SCOTIA
OAK ISLAND MONEY PIT

OAK ISLAND

A deep, booby-trapped pit on uninhabited Oak Island may hold the Holy Grail. The Ark of the Covenant could also be down there, along with Marie Antoinette's jewels, Blackbeard's pirate treasure, and documents confirming that Francis Bacon was the actual author of Shakespeare's entire oeuvre.

Speculation over the contents of the pit began in 1795, when three men wandering on the eastern side of the island discovered a circular dent in the ground and a pulley attached to the branch of an adjacent tree. The men decided the scene was odd enough to grab shovels and start digging. After allegedly encountering layers of logs at 10 feet, 20 feet, and 30 feet down (3, 6, 9 m), the trio abandoned their burrowing.

This is where the story starts to get wilder and less plausible. Subsequent excavations by excited treasure hunters apparently uncovered pick marks, coconut fibers, and a stone inscribed with mysterious symbols. Once the dig reached below 90 feet (27.4 m), the pit began to flood. Attempts to bail out the water resulted in more water rushing in. "A trap," the diggers thought, "a clever trap to protect the treasure."

By 1861, people were literally dying to find the mythical riches that lay below. A boiler burst while workers were draining the hole with a steam-powered pump, mortally scalding one man and causing the pit to collapse again.

Despite over 200 years of treasure hunting—including corporate-funded remote-camera–enhanced

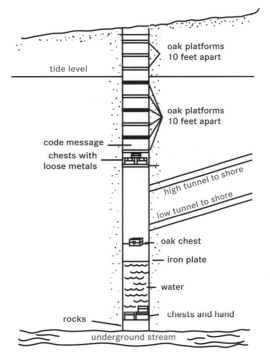

excavations during the 1960s—no one has solved the mystery of the Oak Island money pit. The likely story—that the pit is a naturally occurring sinkhole devoid of precious relics—goes ignored by the treasure hunters who still scour the island. A popular History Channel show features a new generation of hunters. So far, no treasure.

The island is privately owned and usually off-limits, but the Friends of Oak Island Society runs occasional tours. Ⓝ 44.512740 Ⓦ 64.288570

MARCONI NATIONAL HISTORIC SITE

GLACE BAY

On this spot in December 1902, Guglielmo Marconi ushered in the wireless age. Using a transmission station surrounded by four 200-foot (61 m) wooden aerials, Marconi sent and received Morse code signals to a station in Cornwall, England. It was the first official transatlantic use of electromagnetic waves for sending a message and the beginning of wireless global communication.

Marconi's station, constructed at Table Head in the small former coal mining town of Glace Bay, was relocated in 1905, but the tower foundations and a visitor's center remain. Now preserved as the Marconi National Historic Site, the center has a model of the original station as well as photos, artifacts, and information on the history of radio.

15 Timmerman Street, Table Head. The site is a half-hour drive from Sydney or a one-hour drive from Louisbourg. Ⓝ 46.210969 Ⓦ 59.952542

The age of radio began in Nova Scotia.

A place where wild horses roam free.

SABLE ISLAND

HALIFAX

Sable Island, which is made entirely of sand, is a low-lying stretch of land in the middle of the ocean. Due to its low profile and isolated location, the oversize sandbar has caused so many shipwrecks, it's earned the moniker "Graveyard of the Atlantic."

Sable Island is also known for its population of some 550 wild horses (descendants of the Shetland pony). A small number of scientists live on the island to study its flora and fauna, but it is otherwise empty of human activity. **Sable Island is 186 miles southeast of Halifax, Nova Scotia. Travelers to the island must register with Parks Canada. Ⓝ 43.934509 Ⓦ 59.914032**

ONTARIO

DIEFENBUNKER

OTTAWA

From 1962 to 1994, a small white shed in the middle of a field would have become national headquarters of the Canadian government in the event of a nuclear attack.

The "Diefenbunker," named after Prime Minister John Diefenbaker, is the largest of about 50 shelters built across Canada during the Cold War. Beneath the unassuming shed, a steel-lined blast tunnel leads to a four-story bunker with enough supplies to house over 500 government and military personnel for one month.

If a bomb were to hit, the prime minister and his staff would head directly to the bunker—alone, for there was no room to accommodate family members. Once there, they would strip and shower in the decontamination chamber, then make their way to the dormitory-style quarters. The spartan rooms contained bunk beds and little else—though the prime minister was granted the relative luxury of a single bed and a private shower.

Several of the bunker's design features aimed to lessen cabin fever and claustrophobia. In addition to the overall color scheme of serene blues and greens, the bunker's support columns were painted with vertical black stripes to make the ceiling appear higher. The floors of the narrow hallways have horizontal stripes, in an effort to make them look wider. Had these measures proved inadequate to keep someone calm and rational, a confinement cell was available.

As with other shelters built during the height of Cold War paranoia, the Diefenbunker was never used for its intended purpose. Decommissioned in 1994, the facility now operates as a Cold War museum. Stops on the tour include the situation room, a broadcast studio built to keep the surviving members of the nation informed, and a vault that would have kept the Bank of Canada's gold reserves safe from nuclear destruction. **3911 Carp Road, Carp. The bunker is 20 miles (32 km) west of Ottawa. Ⓝ 45.351819 Ⓦ 76.044741**

A nuclear shelter built for Canada's prime minister is now a Cold War museum.

Hundreds of screaming concrete heads adorn an eccentric teacher's 300-acre farm.

MIDLOTHIAN CASTLE

BURK'S FALLS

Peter Camani has a suggestion for where your earthly remains should go when you die. "Why settle for a small underground plot in the suburbs," he writes on his website, "when you have the option of joining a vibrant creation that fills the landscape?"

The "vibrant creation" to which he refers is a forest of 18-foot-tall (5.5 m) screaming heads made from cement and—if his idea catches on—the ashes of deceased humans.

The field of screams is just one component of Camani's ongoing art project on a 300-acre (1.2 km²) former farm just outside the village of Burk's Falls, Ontario. It all began in 1989, when the former high school art teacher began building a house on the property. Dubbed Midlothian Castle, the dwelling features a screaming head for a turret and a dragon for a

chimney that appears to breathe smoke whenever the fireplace is blazing.

In 1995, Camani began installing sculptures on the land surrounding the house. There are now over 100 scattered through the landscape—84 screaming heads, giant half-buried hands, trees with ghoulish faces, and the Four Horsemen of the Apocalypse.

Inspired by the Druids, Camani intends to continue sculpting screaming heads for as long as he's able. Though he has long envisioned a forest of sculptures made from cement and human ash—with the names and bios of the deceased written on them—he has only created one so far.

Midlothian Ridge, RR #1, Burk's Falls. The castle is around 150 miles (240 km) north of Toronto.
Ⓝ 45.595141 Ⓦ 79.537376

LOWER BAY STATION

TORONTO

Toronto's ghost subway platform has been empty since 1966.

Beneath Toronto's Bay subway station on the Bloor-Danforth line is Lower Bay, a platform that only operated for six months before it was boarded up.

The ghost platform opened in 1966 and was intended to ease commutes by joining the Bloor-Danforth and Yonge-University lines. In theory, passengers would benefit from being able to reach their destination without having to change trains. In practice, confusion reigned: Trains to the same destination arrived on different platforms, and travelers weren't sure whether to wait at the upper or lower location.

Since its closure in September 1966, Lower Bay has been used for film and television productions, often playing the part of a New York subway station. Although not usually viewable, the subterranean platform is occasionally open for special city events such as the annual Doors Open Toronto.

Bay Station, 64 Bloor Street West. The entrance to Bay Station is on Bloor Street West at Bellair Street. Ⓝ 43.669539 Ⓦ 79.392154

BATA SHOE MUSEUM

TORONTO

This museum tells the story of thousands of years of humanity, one pair of shoes at a time. The collection—which includes such historically resonant items as ancient Egyptian sandals, samurai shoes made of bear fur, and Queen Victoria's ballroom slippers—is drawn from the shoe stash of founder Sonja Bata, who began stocking up on fascinating footwear in the 1940s. The collection now numbers over 13,000 items, 1,000 of which are on display at any one time in the museum's permanent and rotating exhibits.

Around 13,000 shoes from all over history live in a shoebox-shaped building.

The shoes on show don't just illustrate fashion trends—they reflect their cultural contexts. A common theme is restriction and impediment, as seen in tiny lotus shoes once worn by Chinese women with bound feet as well as an impossibly tall velvet-covered platform shoe donned in the days of 16th-century Italy.

The museum has also managed to nab some cast-off footwear from 20th-century celebrities. See Robert Redford's cowboy boots, Elvis's blue patent-leather loafers, and an ankle boot that once cradled the foot of John Lennon.

327 Bloor Street West, Toronto. Ⓝ 43.667278 Ⓦ 79.400139

ALSO IN ONTARIO

Cheltenham Badlands

Caledon · These rolling red rock hills, striped with green from groundwater-induced oxidation, contrast impressively with the bright blue sky above.

Flowerpot Island

Ontario · On this delightful little island in Lake Huron, two rock pillars shaped like flowerpots guard the shore.

Ottawa Jail Hostel

Ottawa · Once a prison known for its inhumane practices, Ottawa Jail now welcomes backpackers for overnight stays in the cells.

Monkey's Paw

Toronto · This bookstore has the world's first "Biblio-Mat," a random-book vending machine.

SEWERS OF TORONTO

TORONTO

It takes a truly special set of circumstances to turn sewage into a landmark.

Toronto's subterranean waste management network is something to behold. The sewage tunnels in Toronto are wide and high-ceilinged, so large and well-built that they look more like soggy subway tunnels than rivers of waste water.

Daring adventurers and mischievous youths have long ventured into the city's underground passageways to map their trajectory and examine their current state. Each leg of the sewer system has its own story. The Garrison Creek Sewer running underneath the west end of the city, smoothly beveled and circular like a pneumatic tube, was once, as the name suggests, a creek. In the late 19th century, after that creek became full of human waste, the city wisely thought it best to just go ahead and bury the whole thing.

The tunnels are an unsung marvel of public engineering. That's to be expected from Toronto, a city that takes its sewage seriously, as evidenced by the ornate water treatment plant nicknamed the "Palace of Purification." That's where all the contents of these majestic tunnels end up—including explorers, if they follow the path long enough.

Entrances to the tunnels are exactly where you'd expect them to be—manholes, maintenance shafts, spillways, and water treatment offshoots—but entry is not technically allowed. Visiting is therefore difficult and granted only with permission and guidance by a public works employee.
Ⓝ 43.646747 Ⓦ 79.408311

Toronto's well-maintained sewer system is over 100 years old.

Take a relaxing dip with an 800-pound polar bear.

COCHRANE POLAR BEAR HABITAT

COCHRANE

A playful 800-pound (363 kg) bear named Ganuk is currently the sole ursine resident of Cochrane Polar Bear Habitat. The world's only facility dedicated solely to captive polar bears, Cochrane aims to care for rescued and zoo-raised bears while educating people on their conservation. Ganuk has free rein over the habitat's three expansive outdoor enclosures. His hobbies include digging, getting his head stuck in barrels, and eating bucket-size popsicles made with watermelon pieces, tuna, peanut butter, and marshmallows.

Ganuk can also literally paint you a picture of life in the habitat—zookeepers occasionally put nontoxic paint and canvases in front of him with the aim of encouraging his creative side. The resulting paw-printed abstract art is sold in the gift shop for up to $200 apiece.

Visit Ganuk between May and September and you'll be able to swim alongside him. There is a wading pool for humans right next to the bear pool, separated only by a 2-inch (5 cm) wall of glass.

1 Drury Park Road, Cochrane, a 7-hour drive from Toronto.
Ⓝ 49.057664 Ⓦ 81.023397

SNOLAB

LIVELY

A mile and a half underground, beneath the Creighton nickel mine, a team of astrophysicists is trying to solve the mysteries of the universe. They work at SNOLAB, a laboratory devoted to searching for neutrinos—neutral subatomic particles—and dark matter. The laboratory needs to be so far underground in order to shield the sensitive detection systems from interference caused by cosmic radiation.

The site is best known for its Sudbury Neutrino Observatory (SNO), an experiment that ran from 1999 to 2006, which used a 40-foot-wide (12 m) vessel filled with heavy water (water containing a large amount of the hydrogen isotope deuterium) to detect neutrinos produced by fusion reactions in the sun.

SNO's successor, SNO+, is currently being prepared. The new experiment will continue the search for neutrinos using a tweaked version of the existing equipment.

Creighton Mine, 1039 Regional Road 24, Lively, Greater Sudbury. Due to contamination concerns, anyone entering SNOLAB must shower and change on-site. ℕ 46.473285 ℕ 81.186683

Over a mile underground, a sphere studded with 9,600 photomultiplier tubes helps search for solar neutrinos.

PRINCE EDWARD ISLAND

CANADIAN POTATO MUSEUM

O'LEARY

The excitement starts building when you see the 14-foot (4.3 m) fiberglass potato mounted on a pole like a popsicle. The oversize tuber entices you

Get ready to have your potato-related assumptions challenged.

through the doors of a museum that is charmingly effusive about potatoes—particularly the Prince Edward Island potatoes harvested from the surrounding fields.

Journey through time and across continents at the Potato Interpretive Center, where you can trace the spud's origins in South America and follow it as it's introduced to Europe and North America. Take a moment to reflect solemnly on the diseased potato exhibit, where potatoes are displayed in miniature coffins beside signs detailing their causes of death. View a rust-encrusted 19th-century thresher in the Antique Farming Equipment room.

The museum experience ends, naturally, with a visit to the café, where french fries, potato cinnamon buns, and potato fudge compete for the chance to dazzle your taste buds.

For a potato-themed vacation, visit O'Leary in the last week of July for the annual Potato Blossom Festival, which celebrates the plants in full bloom. Events include a farmer's banquet, fireworks, and the Miss Potato Blossom pageant.

1 Dewar Lane, O'Leary. The museum is a 45-minute drive from Summerside northwest along Highway 2. It's open from mid-May to mid-October. ℕ 46.703346 ℕ 64.234841

QUEBEC
VAL-JALBERT GHOST TOWN

CHAMBORD

The village of Val-Jalbert, 150 miles (241 km) north of Quebec City, sprang up in 1901 when forestry entrepreneur Damase Jalbert built a pulp mill powered by Ouiatchouan River waterfalls. Though Jalbert died just three years later, the mill survived a resulting cash shortage and began to thrive under new owners. From 1909 until the early 1920s, Val-Jalbert was a prosperous community. Its 200 mill workers and their families had access to a school, a general store, a butcher's shop, and a post office, all enhanced with electricity.

In 1927, however, the reduced global demand for pulp forced the mill to close. At that time, Val-Jalbert had a population of 950. By the early '30s, it was a ghost town. Transformed into a tourist attraction in 1960, the village is now open for exploration from June to October. Many of the buildings have been restored while others sag inward, their wooden walls splintered and ridden with holes. Much of the mill's original machinery is intact, and the old butcher's shop now houses an old-timey photo booth.

Before you leave, head to the river's viewing platform for a close look at Ouiatchouan Falls, which, at 236 feet (72 m), is taller than Niagara Falls.
Highway 169, between Chambord and the city of Roberval. Ⓝ 48.444660 Ⓦ 72.164561

THE CRUTCHES OF ST. JOSEPH'S ORATORY

MONTREAL

Soaring 506 feet (154 m) above street level, the top of St. Joseph's dome is the highest point in Montreal. The hilltop basilica is the legacy of Brother André, a Quebecois man known for providing hope and reassurance to the sick. In 1904, he approached the city's archbishop for permission to build a shrine to St. Joseph, of whom he was a lifelong devotee. Afflicted by poor health since childhood, Brother André often prayed to St. Joseph and encouraged others to trust in his healing powers.

The archbishop couldn't fund Brother André's dream, but he did allow him to build a modest chapel. It wasn't until 1924 that construction on St. Joseph's Oratory basilica finally began. It was completed in 1967, 30 years after Brother André's death at the age of 91.

People who are unwell or chronically ill, or have limited mobility flock to St. Joseph's for comfort and the chance to be miraculously healed. The oratory's Chapel of Brother André is lined with rows of crutches left by those who claim to have been given the ability to walk again. (Brother André himself was canonized as a saint in 2010, so miracles are credited to his intercession as well as St. Joseph's.)

The heart of Brother André sits inside a glass box in the oratory's reliquary. In March 1973, a band of brazen thieves stole the organ. Over a year later, following an anonymous tip-off, the heart was recovered from a locker in the basement of an apartment building. It is now back on display.
3800 Chemin Queen Mary, Montreal. The oratory is near the Côte-des-Neiges metro station. There are 283 steps from the street to the basilica—pilgrims traditionally climb the middle set of 99 steps on their knees. Ⓝ 45.492171 Ⓦ 73.616943

Walking aids left by those who say Brother André restored their paralyzed legs.

NEW BRUNSWICK

World's Largest Axe

Nackawic · Built in 1991, this massive tool has a 50-foot (15.2 m) handle and a time capsule embedded in its axe head.

Old Sow Whirlpool

Deer Island Point · Legend says this tidal turbulence got its odd name because it sounds like a grunting pig.

USA

West Coast

CALIFORNIA • OREGON • WASHINGTON

Four Corners and the Southwest

ARIZONA • COLORADO • NEVADA • NEW MEXICO • TEXAS • UTAH

Great Plains

IDAHO • KANSAS • MONTANA • NEBRASKA • NORTH DAKOTA
OKLAHOMA • SOUTH DAKOTA • WYOMING

The Midwest

ILLINOIS • INDIANA • IOWA • MICHIGAN • MINNESOTA • MISSOURI
OHIO • WISCONSIN

The Southeast

ALABAMA • ARKANSAS • FLORIDA • GEORGIA • KENTUCKY
LOUISIANA • MISSISSIPPI • NORTH CAROLINA • SOUTH CAROLINA
TENNESSEE • VIRGINIA

The Mid-Atlantic

DELAWARE • MARYLAND • NEW JERSEY • NEW YORK
PENNSYLVANIA • WASHINGTON, DC • WEST VIRGINIA

New England

CONNECTICUT • MAINE • MASSACHUSETTS • NEW HAMPSHIRE
RHODE ISLAND • VERMONT

Alaska and Hawaii

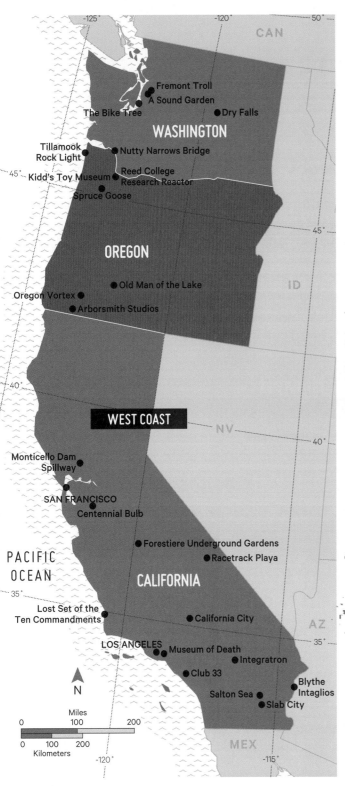

CALIFORNIA
BLYTHE INTAGLIOS

BLYTHE

Similar to the Nazca Lines of Peru, the Blythe Intaglios are huge designs scraped into the ground of the desert. There are six figures in three locations, the largest of which is a 171-foot-tall (52 m) human. The intaglios were likely carved by Mojave and Quechan Indians, but the date of their creation is unknown.

15 miles (24 km) north of Blythe on Route 95.

Ⓝ 33.800333 Ⓦ 114.531883

The Native Americans who scratched enormous human figures into the Colorado Desert could only have imagined what they'd look like from the air.

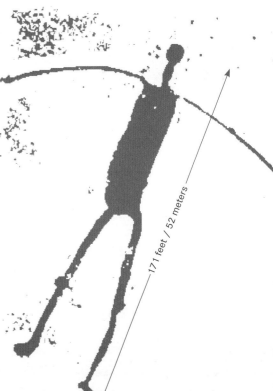

171 feet / 52 meters

SALTON SEA

BOMBAY BEACH

In the 1950s and '60s, Bombay Beach was a thriving seaside resort. Guests swam, water-skied, and golfed during the day, then headed to the North Shore Yacht Club to party into the night.

Now Bombay Beach is a bleached, rusted, abandoned wasteland. The water smells of salt, petrol, and rotting fish. The shores, once lined with sunbathers, are covered in green sludge and desiccated fish carcasses. It's an apocalyptic landscape.

To understand how this place turned from paradise to purgatory, you need to know the story of the Salton Sea. Bombay Beach lies not on the Pacific Coast, but in the middle of the Colorado Desert. In 1905, the Colorado River swelled, breached its levees, and flooded the desert valley known as the Salton Sink. The water flowed for two years, creating a 15 × 35-mile (24 × 56 km) lake dubbed the Salton Sea.

Though the creation of this inland sea—the largest lake in California—was an accident, it initially appeared to be a happy one. Birds flocked to the area, and fish thrived in the Salton Sea. Developers seized upon the rare setting and branded it the "Salton Riviera," a "miracle in the desert." Hotels, yacht clubs, homes, and schools sprang up along the shores as the Salton Sea became a resort destination. But disaster loomed.

By the late 1970s, the ecosystem was deteriorating rapidly. With no drainage outlet, almost zero yearly rainfall, and runoff flowing in from nearby farms, the sea was polluted with pesticides and turned saltier than the Pacific Ocean. Thousands of dead fish washed up on the beach and rotted. As they decomposed, the sand became coated in a layer of fragmented fish skeletons.

Hints of the Salton Sea's heyday still litter the shores. Boarded-up motels, rusting boat frames, and cracked concrete swimming pools covered in graffiti are a few of the sights that remain. People do live here—Bombay Beach is home to around 250 residents, who travel the barren landscape by golf cart and must drive 40 miles (65 km) to stock up on groceries.

There is one part of the Salton Sea that's shiny and new: The North Shore Beach and Yacht Club, long abandoned, was refurbished in 2010 and opened as a community center.

Start your visit at the Salton Sea History Museum, located at 72–120 South Lincoln Street, Mecca. Ⓝ 33.253533 Ⓦ 115.710179

Sun-bleached and over-salinated, Salton Sea turned from a resort paradise to a wasteland.

Sculptor Joe Holiday's woolly mammoth made of discarded truck tires.

SLAB CITY
NILAND

Known to its residents as "the last free place," Slab City is an isolated, off-the-grid desert community of squatters. Established in the early 1960s on a former United States Marine Corps training base, it is home to a motley mix of artists, travelers, retirees, and snowbirds. There is no local government, no running water, and no waste disposal system. Power comes from solar panels and generators; nightfall brings pitch darkness to the rattlesnake- and scorpion-infested sands.

Slab City's population varies from a few dozen in summer—when temperatures reach up to 120°F (49°C)—to a few thousand during the cooler months. Residents live in RVs, vans, tents, and converted school buses, and venture to a hot spring to bathe. Saturday is talent show night at The Range,

an outdoor concert venue with mismatched chairs and tattered couches for seating.

Within Slab City is a sub-community, East Jesus. The art collective grew from an old shipping container in 2006, and centers on an inhabitable, ever-growing artwork made entirely from salvaged materials. Among them are a giant mammoth made from blown-out car tires, a television graveyard, and a swing set made from the rusted skeletons of old car seats. According to its custodians, East Jesus is "populated by an ever-rotating cast of artists, builders, writers, musicians, freethinkers, merry pranksters, wandering messiahs, the dispossessed, the damned."

East Beal Road, Niland. Drive toward Niland on Highway 111, turn east on the street by United Grocery. Travel for 3.5 miles (5.6 km). Salvation Mountain marks the entrance. Ⓝ 33.258889 Ⓦ 115.466389

THE INTEGRATRON
LANDERS

Whisper while standing in the middle of the Integratron—an acoustically perfect dome in the desert—and you'll feel as though your brain is talking to you via vibrations. The sensation is odd and otherworldly, much like the Integratron itself.

In 1952, former flight mechanic George Van Tassel had a life-changing experience. As he described in his 1955 book, *I Rode a Flying Saucer*, Van Tassel was sleeping when a creature from the planet Venus woke him up, took him

aboard his spacecraft, and telepathically divulged the secret of eternal youth. Rejuvenation of the human body, according to the Venusian visitor, required the construction of a domed structure, built without metal and featuring time-travel and anti-gravity devices.

Armed with these instructions, Van Tassel set about building what he called the Integratron in the desert north of Joshua Tree National Park. The location was important—Van Tassel believed the spot contained powerful geomagnetic forces that, when harnessed by the Integratron, could recharge human cells.

Using wood, fiberglass, concrete, and glass—but no nails, screws, or any other metal—he constructed a two-story, 38-foot-high (12 m) domed building. The time-travel device and anti-gravity chamber, however, never came to be—Van Tassel died of a heart attack in 1978 with his creation incomplete.

These days the Integratron offers "sound baths," which involve up to 30 people lying in a circle on the floor, feet pointed outward, while a facilitator strikes a series of quartz bowls that resonate at different frequencies. (According to the owners, this experience provides relaxation and "sonic healing" by causing parts of the body to vibrate individually.)

The dome is so acoustically sensitive that soft sniffs and shuffles are clearly audible to people on the opposite side of the room. It is for this reason that sound baths begin with a stern warning: no snoring.

2477 Belfield Boulevard, Landers. The Integratron is a 2.5-hour drive east of Los Angeles. Public sound baths happen twice a month. You can also book a private bath. Ⓝ 34.293490 Ⓦ 116.403976

Experience a quartz-crystal sound bath inside a desert dome.

California Institute of Abnormalarts

North Hollywood • This venue for out-there music, B movies, and self-described freak shows, and home to a 100-year-old mummified clown is owned by an ex-mortician with a love for curios.

The Abandoned Old Zoo

Griffith Park • Built in 1912 and abandoned in the 1960s, the old Griffith Park Zoo is open to the public for hikes, picnics, or a climb inside an abandoned monkey cage.

Ennis House

Los Feliz • A monumental architectural wonder constructed mainly from concrete blocks, this Frank Lloyd Wright marvel has the cracks and pockmarks from nearly a century of seismic shifts, but its Mayan-inspired design hasn't suffered one bit.

Philosophical Research Society

Los Feliz • This library and bookstore has been at the center of altered consciousness, obscure religious philosophies, and study of the occult since its founding in 1934, but the library is a closed-stacks collection, so please don't try to take anything home. Karma (or maybe the librarian) will put a stop to that.

Snow White Cottages

Los Feliz • These eight storybook cottages, just a few blocks from Walt Disney's original studio, very likely inspired one of the most famous animated films of all time—and decades later ended up on the other side of the cinematic spectrum as a location in the David Lynch thriller *Mulholland Drive*.

Museum of Broken Relationships

Hollywood • The brainchild of two Croatian artists, this offshoot of the Zagreb original provides the brokenhearted with a place for their love affair leftovers, all donated anonymously, inviting the viewer to impose their own personal stories of heartache on the parade of seemingly mundane objects.

Holyland Exhibition

Los Feliz • The rumored real-life inspiration for Indiana Jones, Antonia Futterer was the last of a breed, an LA original. Tour his personal collection of Middle Eastern arts and artifacts, all packed into a hillside Los Feliz bungalow.

The Echo Park and Mar Vista Time Travel Marts

Venice • It can feel like an endless trek from Echo Park to Mar Vista, but these eccentric fronts for a nonprofit writing workshop have all the necessary supplies for your trips across town or to the fourth dimension, including dinosaur eggs, canned woolly mammoth chunks, Fresh-Start clones, and robot toupees.

Bob Baker Marionette Theater

Westlake • A Los Angeles Historic-Cultural Monument and the oldest children's theater in LA, with thousands of marionettes (not creepy ones!) and free cups of ice cream—who doesn't love a great puppet show?

Velveteria

Chinatown • With thousands of trippy, retro, black-lit beauties, the art of velvet painting is not only kept alive with this collection but elevated to a high (in more ways than one) art.

Skeletons in the Closet

LA County • This coroner's office gift shop will set you up with a supply of toe tags, body bags, and chalk-outline beach towels. The healthy mail-order business for their not-so-healthy-sounding catalog helps to raise money for safe teen driving programs.

The Bradbury Building

Downtown • Story goes that the architect of this deco downtown building—made famous in movies like *Blade Runner* and *The Artist*—wouldn't start building until he got an otherworldly OK from his dead brother.

Clifton's Cafeteria

Downtown • This psychedelic, kitschy, giant-redwood-themed cafeteria has been operating for 80 years under the gaze of stuffed bears and mounted moose heads, and is guided by its own golden rule: "Dine Free Unless Delighted."

Velaslavasay Panorama

University Park • This theater and exhibition hall—with a lush backyard garden—provides patrons with a 360-degree experience of wonder, a kind of early virtual reality from a time before the movies, when worlds on spinning painted backdrops could transport a crowd to dreamy and exotic landscapes.

Museum of Jurassic Technology

Culver City • For nearly 30 years, this stalwart curiosity cabinet has provided LA with hushed, soft-focus exhibits that are confounding, freakishly mind-bending, and challenge your sense of what is real.

The Wende Museum

Culver City • Housed in an inconspicuous business park is a stash of secret Eastern bloc spy equipment and Cold War–era paraphernalia—and a big stretch of the original Berlin Wall.

Saydel, Inc.

Huntington Park • Never pay retail for your religious effigies, magic soaps, and New Age candles—the folks at Saydel bring them to customers at low-low wholesale prices.

Old Town Music Hall

El Segundo • The Mighty Wurlitzer has been pumping out the tunes at downtown El Segundo's historic home for silent and classic movies since 1968 under the tickling fingers of in-house historian and organ master Bill Field.

The Bradbury Building's soaring interior.

CLUB 33

ANAHEIM

In Disneyland's New Orleans Square, near the exit to the Pirates of the Caribbean ride, is an unmarked gray-green door. The door itself is unmarked, but to its right is a sign bearing the number 33 and a brass speaker box with a panel that hides a buzzer. This is the entrance to Club 33, an ultra-exclusive, exorbitantly priced club that Walt Disney himself established so he would have a swanky place to entertain his VIP guests.

You must be a Club 33 member—or the guest of one—to dine at the secret restaurant. Membership requires an initiation fee of $25,000, followed by annual dues of $10,000. Membership is capped at 500 people, and it can take many years to be accepted.

Lunch or dinner at Club 33 is by reservation only. After being buzzed in through the secret door, you'll be ushered to the second-floor dining room, passing one of only two bars in Disneyland that serves alcohol. The restaurant is decked out in 19th-century New Orleans style, complete with a wooden elevator and wicker toilets. Food and drinks are served by doting staff wearing special Club 33 uniforms. They are only too happy to point out the original *Fantasia* animation cels on the walls and the table from the set of the first *Mary Poppins*.

Walt Disney never saw Club 33—he died in December 1966, five months before it opened. Evidence of his personal touch, however, remains. In one corner of the former trophy room is an animatronic California turkey vulture. Disney envisioned the bird surprising guests by talking to them via a voice actor hidden in a booth. Microphones were installed around the room for this purpose—but have since been disconnected.

33 Royal Street, Disneyland, Anaheim. To gain access, befriend a Club 33 member, book your meal months in advance, and prepare to spend a great deal of money on food, drinks, and exclusive souvenirs.
Ⓝ 33.810987 Ⓦ 117.921459

Jim Jones

Aileen Wuornos

John Wayne Gacy

MUSEUM OF DEATH

HOLLYWOOD

Your visit to the Museum of Death begins with a test: Look at the photo on the wall next to the front desk. It shows a man's freshly mutilated body, parts of it scattered across a road following a truck crash. If the picture makes you feel queasy, this place is not for you.

Established in 1995, the museum is a graphic, shocking ode to the myriad ways humans shuffle off this mortal coil. A 45-minute self-guided tour through the small building takes in capital punishment, cult suicides, traffic accidents, and serial murders. A display of body bags, coffins, and mortician instruments serves as a reminder that death is the great equalizer.

Standout exhibits include the Heaven's Gate room, a re-creation of the scene that greeted investigators when they entered a San Diego mansion in March 1997 to discover 39 cult members had committed suicide. Each person had swallowed a lethal dose of phenobarbital and—covered in a purple shroud and wearing brand-new Nikes—lay neatly on a bunk bed, believing their souls would be transported to a higher realm on an alien spacecraft. In the museum version, mannequins lie on a set of beds taken from the actual house. They wear shrouds and Nikes removed from two of the deceased followers.

High-profile cases such as the Black Dahlia, Charles Manson, and John Wayne Gacy receive name checks, but the more fascinating artifacts belong to lesser-known murderers. On one wall is a set of photos taken by a couple. The images depict the duo grinning at the camera as they hold up the shredded body parts of the man they have just killed. This being the days before digital cameras, the twosome were caught and charged with murder after they took the incriminating film to a lab to be developed.

6031 Hollywood Blvd., Hollywood. Take the metro to Hollywood and Vine and walk 2 blocks east.
Ⓝ 34.101943 Ⓦ 118.321201

LOST SET OF THE TEN COMMANDMENTS

GUADALUPE

In 1983, a trio of film buffs journeyed to the Colorado Desert in search of the lost Egyptian City of the Pharoah. Using clues gleaned from Cecil B. DeMille's posthumously published autobiography, they found sphinxes and pharaohs buried in dunes.

DeMille had the inside scoop because he built the City of the Pharaoh himself—it was the film set for his 1923 silent epic, *The Ten Commandments*. Built by a team of 1,500, the lavish set featured a 720-foot-long (220 m) palace decorated with hieroglyphs, four giant statues of Pharaoh Ramses II, and a grand path lined with 21 five-ton sphinxes.

When the shoot ended—behind schedule and over budget—DeMille was left with a massive array of plaster buildings and props. Transporting it all back to Hollywood would have been exorbitantly expensive, but the director didn't want to leave the set in the desert where low-budget filmmakers could use it to shoot their own epics. So DeMille dismantled the sets and buried the parts in the sand.

The City of the Pharaoh lay beneath the dunes for 60 years. When filmmaker Peter Brosnan read a cryptic joke in DeMille's autobiography about hapless archaeologists finding a lost Egyptian city in the dunes, he spearheaded the search for the Lost City of Cecil B. DeMille.

Brosnan and archaeologists surveyed the site using ground-penetrating radar. Lack of funds and permit issues with the county thwarted plans for a full-scale dig. The set pieces made of plaster crumbled into dust when unearthed.

Much of DeMille's city remains buried, but a few excavated artifacts—including a makeup compact, film reel tin, and re-created sphinx head—are on display at the nearby Dunes Center.
Guadalupe-Nipomo Dunes Center, 1065 Guadalupe Street, Guadalupe. ℕ 34.972501 Ⓦ 120.572081

CALIFORNIA CITY

CALIFORNIA CITY

From the air, this collection of streets resembles a printed circuit board. Its carefully planned cul-de-sacs and concentric curved roads are neat and densely packed. The layout of streets and services is logical, aesthetically pleasing, and well suited to a major city. There's just one thing missing: people.

In 1958, a former sociology professor named Nat Mendelsohn purchased 80,000 acres of land in the Mojave Desert. His grand plan was to create California's next great metropolis—a thriving, car-centric city to rival Los Angeles. Mendelsohn mapped out a network of roads, named them all, and oversaw their construction. The streets surrounded Central Park, an 80-acre green expanse incorporating an artificial lake. Model homes and architectural drawings showed an enticing, affordable version of the American Dream.

By January 1959, there were 65 homes in California City. But this influx of people did not herald a mass migration. As the years went by, a trickle of families established homes, but for the most part, the carefully laid out streets remained quiet and empty. Mendelsohn bailed on his planned city in 1969, selling it to a Denver-based sugar and mining company.

By 1990, the population was hovering at just over 6,000. In 2000, it was 8,388. As a major metropolis, California City was a total failure. But its cracked, sand-sloughed streets now attract off-road adventurers, who enjoy careening around the curves of the uninhabited roads on motorcycles and ATVs. The current population is around 14,000, but the houses are spaced oddly. Some blocks are crammed with homes, while others have just one dwelling. All are buffered by a swath of streets that carve up the vacant lots.
Located about 100 miles (160 km) north of Los Angeles, between State Route 14 and US Route 395. ℕ 35.125801 Ⓦ 117.985903

Miles of streets without houses are the only remains of a midcentury ghost city that was planned to rival Los Angeles.

RACETRACK PLAYA

DEATH VALLEY

When no one is looking, the rocks on the dry lake bed of Racetrack Playa move. Some have only traveled a few inches. Others have journeyed half a mile. All of them leave telltale trails—some straight; some curved; others erratic and jerky, as if the rock changed its mind along the way.

Until December 2013, no one had ever witnessed the rocks in motion, but plenty had offered theories to explain their movement. A 2010 NASA study concluded that melted snow had streamed from the surrounding mountains and flooded the playa. At night, according to NASA, the water froze around the bottom of the rocks, creating an "ice collar." Over the next month, more water from the mountains arrived, creating a slippery surface and allowing the ice-collared rocks to float on the playa. Fierce winds of up to 90 miles (145 km) per hour sent the stones skidding across the plain.

It was a sound enough theory, but actual evidence was hard to come by. No one is allowed on the playa when it is wet, as their footprints would scar the ground, and research must be noninvasive—meaning rocks can't be disturbed and cameras must be hidden in the landscape.

Then in 2013, paleobiologist Richard Norris and his cousin, research engineer James Norris,

The mysterious heavy stones of Death Valley can sail up to a half mile across the desert.

happened to be in the right place at the right time. In front of their eyes, wind pushed an ice floe across the playa, causing one of the rocks to slide along the slick surface of the lake bed. From their position on the mountainside next to the playa, the Norris cousins began taking photos. The evidence was in and the mystery solved.

Death Valley National Park. The 26-mile (42 km) road to Racetrack Valley begins near Ubehebe Crater. You'll need a 4-wheel drive vehicle. Once you reach the playa, cars are prohibited. Bring sturdy shoes.
Ⓝ 36.681069 Ⓦ 117.560258

FORESTIERE UNDERGROUND GARDENS

FRESNO

It took a few minutes of digging in the dirt before Baldassare Forestiere realized he'd made a terrible mistake. It was 1906, and the Sicilian had arrived in California to fulfill his dream of becoming a fruit merchant. But when he stuck a shovel into the 80 acres of Fresno land he'd just purchased, Forestiere was dismayed to discover hardpan, a layer of soil too dense for planting fruit trees.

The hard soil wasn't the only problem. Fresno sweltered in summer, regularly reaching 115°F (46°C). Determined to make the best of the situation, Forestiere came up with a new plan: He took the gardens underground, where the soil is softer and the air is cooler.

Fruit trees stay cool in a subterranean villa built over four decades.

It was a long-term project. Over 40 years, and without ever putting his design plans on paper, Forestiere hand-carved catacombs, arches, and alcoves beneath the hardpan surface. He planted oranges, lemons, grapefruit, mulberries, and grapevines. Skylights and open-air courtyards provided enough light to keep the fruits growing without overheating them.

Forestiere didn't just keep his gardens underground—he lived there himself. Taking advantage of the cooler subterranean temperatures (which range from 10 to 30 degrees lower than the surface), he installed a bedroom, bath, kitchen, and dining area.

The Forestiere Underground Gardens only stopped expanding when Forestiere died in 1946. Today the gardens are open to visitors. You can sample fruit from some of the trees Forestiere planted—it's for sale on site.

5021 West Shaw Avenue, Fresno. The gardens are a 10-minute drive north of downtown Fresno, right off Highway 99. Tours are available. They are closed during winter.
Ⓝ 36.807573 Ⓦ 119.881809

CITY GUIDE: More to Explore in San Francisco

Golden Fire Hydrant

The Castro • The gilded hydrant below Dolores Park earned its special status when it continued to function in the aftermath of the 1906 quake, saving much of the Mission District from burning down.

Head of the Goddess of Progress

Civic Center • The Goddess of Progress was a 20-foot-tall (6 m) bronze statue on top of San Francisco's original city hall. Her head, which weighs 700 pounds (317.5 kg), sits in the current city hall.

McElroy Octagon House

Cow Hollow • This eight-sided powder-blue home is a rare remnant of the octagon-shaped house-building craze of the second half of the 19th century.

Vaillancourt Fountain

Embarcadero • Despite drawing criticism since its installation in the early 1970s, this artistic jumble of angular cement pipes stands strong.

Westin St. Francis

Financial District • Since 1938, this hotel has provided a coin-washing service to prevent guests' hands being sullied by filthy cash.

Corporate Goddess Sculptures

Financial District • A dozen eerily faceless, draped figures loom over pedestrians from 23 floors up at 580 California Street.

Musée Mécanique

Fisherman's Wharf • Save up your quarters for the world's largest privately owned collection of coin-operated arcade machines.

California Academy of Sciences Herpetology Department

Golden Gate Park • The academy's 300,000-strong collection of jarred reptile specimens was amassed over 160 years. Viewing is by appointment only.

Drawn Stone

Golden Gate Park • A huge crack in the ground outside the de Young Museum was put there on purpose by the wry English artist Andy Goldsworthy.

Buena Vista Park Tombstones

Haight-Ashbury • Broken Gold Rush–era gravestones line the gutters of this park's paths.

Secret Tiled Staircase

Inner Sunset • The 163 colorful steps in this staircase form a vibrant mosaic that leads you to a smashing view of the city.

Sutro Egyptian Collection

Lakeshore • The antiquities housed here include two intact mummies, three mummified heads, and a mummified hand.

San Francisco Columbarium

Lone Mountain • This beautifully restored neoclassical atrium offers thousands of alcoves for burial urns. Reservations accepted.

Wave Organ

The Marina • Waves make music by crashing against the 20 pipes of this lovingly built organ, located on a jetty in the San Francisco Bay.

Palace of Fine Arts

Marina District • A piece of San Francisco's 1915 Panama-Pacific International Exposition survives in the form of this collection of classically inspired buildings, gardens, and fountains.

Institute of Illegal Images

Mission District • Mark McCloud's collection of acid blotters, amassed since the 1960s, makes for a uniquely hallucinogenic art gallery.

Good Vibrations Antique Vibrator Museum

Nob Hill • Shake things up with a visit to an institution that honors the Victorian cure for "female hysteria."

Seward Street Slides

Noe Valley • Two steep concrete slides provide thrills for the bold, provided you wear sturdy pants and bring your own cardboard sled. Adults must be accompanied by a child.

Cayuga Park

Outer Mission • Beside some elevated train tracks is a park filled with mystical wooden sculptures.

Yoda Fountain

The Presidio • A bronze version of the big-eared Jedi master stands atop a fountain at the Letterman Digital Arts Center.

Prelinger Library

SoMa • Organized in a unique way that encourages browsing, this privately funded library is open to all for "research, reading, inspiration, and reuse."

CENTENNIAL BULB

LIVERMORE

In June 2015, Fire Station 6 hosted a raging party in honor of a lightbulb. The occasion was a special one: It marked one million hours of service for the bulb, which hangs on a cable from the station's ceiling.

The Centennial Light Bulb, as it is affectionately known, was first screwed into a socket in 1901. Having shone ever since, with just a few minor interruptions, it has been Guinness-certified as the longest-lasting bulb in the world. Initially installed in the fire department's hose cart house, and moved to other fire stations over the years, it found a permanent home at Fire Station 6 in 1976.

There is no obvious reason why this light has lasted so long. Though its output has dimmed from 60 watts to four, the Centennial Bulb's glow has stayed steady for decades and shows no signs of weakening. There are no plans for what to do with it should the dark day of its demise arrive. **Fire Station 6, 4550 East Avenue, Livermore. You are welcome to visit the bulb if there are firefighters around to let you in. Ring the bell at the rear of the station and see if anyone answers. Ⓝ 37.680283 Ⓦ 121.739524**

MONTICELLO DAM SPILLWAY

LAKE BERRYESSA, NAPA COUNTY

Following heavy rain, a giant plughole funnels water from Lake Berryessa. The 72-foot-wide (22 m) Morning Glory spillway, known locally as the "glory hole," clears excess water to prevent spilling over the Monticello Dam.

While other drain-style spillways exist, the one at the Monticello Dam is the largest. Water rushes through the tapered pipe, under the dam wall, at up to 362,000 gallons (1,370,319 L) per second, traveling 700 feet (213 m) to exit at the south side of the canyon beneath the dam.

The deadly force of the flow means swimming near the dam is prohibited—in 1997, a UC Davis graduate student who defied the ban drowned after being pulled into the hole. During the dry season bikers and skateboarders have been known to circumvent the barbed-wire fences and use the exit section of the spillway as an unauthorized skate park.

The spillway is best seen during the rainy season when the lake is full. Ⓝ 38.512201 Ⓦ 122.104748

ALSO IN CALIFORNIA

Winchester Mystery House

San Jose · The former home of Sarah Winchester, heir to the Winchester gun fortune, contains doors to nowhere, stairs that stop suddenly, and secret passages.

Dymaxion Chronofile

Stanford · From journals to blueprints to dry-cleaning bills, Buckminster Fuller documented his life in staggering detail. The full archive is stored at Stanford University Library.

Lake Berryessa's massive overflow drain is known affectionately as the "glory hole."

OREGON

REED COLLEGE RESEARCH REACTOR

PORTLAND

Strictly speaking, a liberal arts college does not *need* a nuclear reactor. But there are myriad benefits of having one. Undergraduates at Reed College—an institution that does not offer a nuclear engineering program—have been using an on-campus reactor to conduct experiments for their theses since 1968.

Students using the reactor come from all majors, including English, philosophy, history, and art. Before being allowed to press any buttons, they must attend a year of seminars on nuclear safety and undergo a seven-hour exam administered by the Nuclear Regulatory Commission.

The water-cooled Reed reactor, which sits at the bottom of a 25-foot-deep (7.6 m) tank, generates neutrons that can be used to make materials radioactive. This allows students to determine the quantity of elements in a sample by measuring the amount of radiation they emit—a process known as neutron activation analysis. For instance, a history major might irradiate a pottery shard in order to find out where it came from by analyzing its trace elements.

Used only for university and community research, Reed's reactor is considered a "zero-risk facility" as far as public safety is concerned. That said, the student operators are still careful—following a federal inspection, they removed the family of rubber ducks from the surface of the tank water on the grounds that they violated safety protocols.

Reed College, 3203 SE Woodstock Boulevard, Portland. The reactor is on the east side of campus. Visits and tours must be arranged at least a week in advance. Ⓝ 45.480571 Ⓦ 122.630091

Undergraduate students operate this nuclear reactor—after going through stringent training, of course.

KIDD'S TOY MUSEUM

PORTLAND

It would be easy to miss the entrance to Kidd's Toy Museum but for the sign on the blue warehouse door. Beneath the official opening hours is a phrase hinting at the low-key nature of the place: "Other hours by appointment or chance."

Behind the blue door is a hoard of toy planes, trains, cars, mechanical banks, dolls, and collectible characters, dating mostly from 1869 to 1939. Every item is from the personal collection of Frank Kidd, who has spent a lifetime acquiring thousands of vintage toys.

Among the charming glimpses into childhoods past are some toys that evoke abhorrent beliefs of earlier eras—you'll see racist images and phrases on some of the mechanical banks, and the collection of golliwog dolls harks back to minstrelsy.

1301 SE Grand Avenue, Portland. The museum is in an unmarked building one block north of the Southeast Grand/Hawthorne light rail stop. Look for the blue door on the west side of the street, south of Southeast Main Street. Ⓝ 45.513518 Ⓦ 122.661068

THE SPRUCE GOOSE

MCMINNVILLE

"I put the sweat of my life into this thing. I have my reputation all rolled up in it and I have stated several times that if it's a failure I'll probably leave this country and never come back. And I mean it."

So said Howard Hughes in 1947 at a Senate War Investigating Committee hearing. "This thing" was the H-4 Hercules plane, also known as the Spruce Goose, the Flying Boat, and the Flying Lumberyard among Hughes's many detractors.

By the time he appeared before the Senate committee, Hughes had been working on the Spruce Goose for five agonizing years. In 1942, the US War Department needed to move troops and tanks across the ocean to the World War II front. German U-boats were attacking Allied ships in the Atlantic, so a plane big enough to house a tank was needed for the job. Hughes, the notoriously eccentric owner of the Hughes Aircraft Company, won the development contract.

There were several logistical issues right off the bat. Metals were needed for the war effort, so the plane was to be made of wood. It was to be the largest aircraft ever constructed—five stories tall, with a wingspan longer than a football field. The original contract called for three planes to be made within two years, but Hughes worked so slowly that the war was over well before he finished building one.

By 1947, Hughes had spent $23 million in government funds and the H-4 still hadn't flown. Skeptics questioned whether it was capable of flight at all. In August came the Senate hearings, during which Hughes curtly refuted allegations of misappropriating federal dollars. In November, determined to prove his critics wrong, Hughes invited members of the press aboard the flying boat for nonflight "taxi tests" in Long Beach harbor.

Howard Hughes's hefty wooden plane aimed high but flew for a total of one minute.

During the third test, however, the H-4 lifted off and flew 70 feet (21 m) for about a mile. That one-minute flight was the first and last time the Spruce Goose flew.

Ever the optimist, Hughes kept the H-4 in a climate-controlled hangar for the next 29 years, attended by a full-time crew. After Hughes died in 1976, the Spruce Goose eventually ended up at the Evergreen Aviation & Space Museum, where it remains to this day. You can walk through the massive fuselage and, for an extra fee, sit in the cockpit wearing a Hughesian fedora.

Evergreen Aviation & Space Museum, 500 NE Captain Michael King Smith Way, McMinnville. ⓝ 45.204228 ⓦ 123.145140

ALSO IN OREGON

Enchanted Forest

Turner · This charmingly homemade fairy tale park is still going strong despite being dubbed "Idiot's Hill" by its detractors.

Tree Climbing Planet

Oregon City · This farm just south of Portland is dedicated to teaching people the professional art of tree climbing.

OLD MAN OF THE LAKE

CRATER LAKE

A floating log may not seem note-worthy, but this one is special. The Old Man is a 30-foot (9 m) hemlock tree that has been bob-bing along vertically in Crater Lake since at least 1896. Bleached by the sun and blown across the water by wind currents, the tree protrudes about 4 feet (1.2 m) from the lake's surface.

The Old Man likely arrived in Crater Lake—a 6-mile-wide, 1,946-foot-deep (9.6 km, 593 m) blue pool that fills the crater of a dormant volcano—via landslide. Rocks were probably lodged in his roots, pulling his base down and allowing him to float vertically. The clear, cold water has kept the Old Man looking relatively youthful.

In the summer of 1938, two naturalists plotted the Old Man's

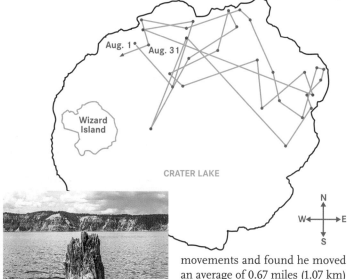

Tracking a month in the life of the floating log that has been drifting around Crater Lake since at least 1896.

movements and found he moved an average of 0.67 miles (1.07 km) per day. On one particularly windy August day he traveled 3.8 miles (6.11 km). When looking for him, keep his transient nature in mind. **Crater Lake National Park. The park is 80 miles (129 km) northwest of Medford. Ⓝ 42.868441 Ⓦ 122.168478**

A simple optical illusion explains the slanting Mystery House's weird physics-flouting properties.

OREGON VORTEX

GOLD HILL

At the slanted House of Mystery on Gold Hill, balls roll upward and brooms stand unsupported. Their apparent defiance of the laws of physics is just one of many strange phenomena one can observe at the Oregon Vortex.

The House of Mystery was once the office of a local mining company. Built in 1890, it was aban-doned within 20 years, after which it slid off its foun-dations and landed at an odd angle. Officially, the house fell because of a mudslide. But the owners of the site have another explanation: magnetic vortex.

In 1930, the house opened to the public as part of the Fabulous Oregon Vortex, an attraction

designed to demonstrate the land's alleged physics-flouting properties. In addition to seeing the mys-terious balls and brooms, you can participate in height experiments: When walking from one side of a plank to the other, you appear to change size.

Guides work the vortex angle during each dem-onstration, throwing in the odd ghost story and paranormal explanation. It's a fun premise—and watching someone change size before your eyes is certainly mind-bending—but the real cause of all the weirdness is simple optical illusion.

4303 Sardine Creek Left Fork Road, Gold Hill. The House of Mystery is open between March and October. Ⓝ 42.493002 Ⓦ 123.084985

TILLAMOOK ROCK LIGHT

CANNON BEACH

Things did not begin well for the lighthouse that came to be known as Terrible Tilly. In 1878, the government decided that ships sailing around Tillamook Head needed more light and better guidance. There was no suitable place to build a lighthouse on the headland, so attention turned to Tillamook Rock, a big chunk of basalt 1.2 miles (1.9 km) offshore.

In 1879, mason John Trewavas set off for the island to do some surveying. When he attempted to land on the rock, his body was swept into the tumultuous sea. This would be but one of many deaths and calamities caused by Tillamook's wild waves and unforgiving landscape.

A team of quarrymen eventually managed to build the lighthouse in 575 days, but the process was arduous: They had to rig a line between their ship and the top of the rock and use it to transport both their tools and themselves. Less than three weeks before the lighthouse opened, a ship called the *Lupatia* sailed close to the shore in thick fog. The next morning, the bodies of all 16 crew members washed ashore.

Lighthouse operators at Terrible Tilly had their own trials to contend with. Hunkered down with six months of supplies, the men lived a mentally and physically challenging existence, beset by frequent storms and blaring foghorns.

The Tillamook Rock Light operated for 77 years before being decommissioned in 1957. Then came a fittingly macabre twist. In 1980, real estate developer Mimi Morissette bought Terrible Tilly and turned it into a columbarium: a storage house for urns full of cremated human remains. Dubbed "Eternity at Sea," the postmortem museum amassed a collection of over 30 urns before the Oregon Mortuary and Cemetery Board took away its license in 1999. (Less-than-stringent record-keeping and improper urn storage were among the issues.)

There are still urns full of remains inside the Tillamook building—"honorary lighthouse keepers," Eternity at Sea called them—but the rock is primarily a seabird nesting spot and can only be safely accessed by helicopter. **The lighthouse rock is part of the Oregon Coast National Wildlife Refuge Complex and therefore off-limits during seabird nesting season. Ⓝ 45.937225 Ⓦ 124.019055**

Built to keep sailors safe from harm, Tillamook's lighthouse has instead attracted death.

ARBORSMITH STUDIOS

WILLIAMS

Arborsculpture is the craft of shaping living trees into works of art and architecture. The term was coined by Richard Reames, one of its pioneering practitioners and the owner of Arborsmith Studios—a combination nursery, design studio, and al fresco art gallery.

By grafting, bending, and pruning, Reames has shaped trees into helixes, peace signs, lattices, chairs, and gazebos. It's a process that requires a lot of patience—larger projects can take a decade or more to complete.

Reames decided to beome an arborsculptor after seeing the Tree Circus, a roadside display of sculpted trees in Scott's Valley, California. Axel Erlandson, who created the Tree Circus in 1947, never called what he did "arborsculpture"—he died in 1963, decades before the term arose—but his creations, which included a ladder tree, a phone booth tree, and trunks that split and spiraled, certainly fit the category.

Reames says that he would love to see arborsculpture revolutionize construction methods. In his ideal world, people would grow houses out of living trees instead of building them from dead ones.

1607 Caves Camp Road, Williams. Arborsmith Studios isn't open to the public, but Reames occasionally allows visitors to tour his studios by prior arrangement. Ⓝ 42.184718 Ⓦ 123.330013

Richard Reames bends and prunes living trees to sculpt them into artwork.

NUTTY NARROWS BRIDGE

WASHINGTON

NUTTY NARROWS BRIDGE

An aerial crossing above Olympia Way provides safe passage for squirrels.

LONGVIEW

Look to the trees above Olympia Way at 18th Avenue and you'll see something unusual: a miniature suspension bridge made of aluminum piping and an old fire hose.

In 1963, Amos Peters would look out the window of his Olympia Way office and see squirrels struggling to cross the busy road. After witnessing a string of hit-and-runs, Peters came up with an idea: a bridge that would allow the skittish animals to make a midair run across the street.

The 60-foot (18 m) Nutty Narrows Bridge opened to squirrel traffic later that year. In the decades since, three similar bridges have popped up around Longview. The city has taken the squirrel theme and run with it—since 2011 it has hosted an annual Squirrel Fest with live music, model railroads, and squirrel-themed face painting.

Olympia Way (between 18th and 19th Avenues), Longview. Squirrel Fest happens annually in mid-August. Ⓝ 46.141424 Ⓦ 122.940344

DRY FALLS

COULEE CITY

Dry Falls is the location of the world's most spectacular waterfall. Unfortunately, you're 12,000 years too late to see it.

As the ice dams of Lake Missoula gave way at the end of the last Ice Age, trapped water began flooding Idaho, Washington, and Oregon. The thundering torrents of water and ice flowed at 65 miles (105 km) per hour, carving trenches into the basalt bedrock.

The floods cascaded over the 3.5-mile-wide, 400-foot-tall (5.6 km, 122 m) cliffs in central Washington now known as Dry Falls, creating the largest waterfall ever known. (By comparison, Horseshoe Falls—the largest of the Niagara waterfalls—is only 167 feet tall and half a mile wide [51 m, 0.8 km].)

With the ice sheets thawed and the waters neatly contained in rivers, Dry Falls is now desiccated. But walk out onto the lookout platform, gaze at the sculpted basalt cliffs, and imagine a waterfall so powerful that it flowed ten times faster than all the world's rivers combined. That's what you would have seen at the end of the last Ice Age.

Dry Falls is 7 miles (11 km) southwest of Coulee City.
Ⓝ **47.607205** Ⓦ **119.364223**

At the end of the last Ice Age, the world's most incredible waterfall cascaded down these cliffsides.

From tiny seeds grow mighty trees—even if there's a bike in the way.

THE BIKE TREE

VASHON

In a forest on Vashon Island, there is a bike in a tree. Not in the branches of a tree—embedded in its trunk, 12 feet (3.7 m) above the ground.

The mystery of how this Douglas fir ate a child-size bicycle has perplexed visitors for decades. A heart-tugging story tells of a teenage boy who chained his childhood bike to a tree and went off to fight in World War I, never to return. It's a compelling tale, but it's not true.

According to Don Puz, who grew up in the area during the 1950s, the bike once belonged to him. In 1954, when Puz was nine, his family's house burned to the ground, killing his father. The community responded with donations for the bereft boy, including a shiny new bicycle. But it was a little small, and Puz soon outgrew it. One day, after playing in the forest, he left the bike behind.

There may have been some human intervention in the ensuing decades—it would be an amazing tree indeed that could envelop a bike so neatly—but the image of a rusted child's bike embedded in a mighty Douglas fir has sparked many an imagination. In 1994, local author Berkeley Breathed published a children's book, *Red Ranger Came Calling*, which weaves the bike tree into a Christmas story.

Off Vashon Highway, Vashon Island, just north of SW 204th Street. Ⓝ 47.422995 Ⓦ 122.460085

A SOUND GARDEN

SEATTLE

In a park beside Lake Washington, on the campus of the National Oceanic and Atmospheric Administration, what looks like a collection of TV antennae or weather vanes rises. But there's something strange about these metal towers: They emit a low, haunting hum when the wind blows through them.

The structures—12 in all—form a public artwork called *A Sound Garden*. Installed by sculptor Douglas Hollis in 1983, the piece consists of wind-actuated organ pipes suspended vertically from steel towers. Seattle grunge band Soundgarden was so inspired by the sculpture that they adopted its name.

Warren G. Magnuson Park, 7600 Sand Point Way NE. Stop in at the guard station at NE 80th Street. Photo ID is required. Ⓝ 47.651034 Ⓦ 122.347323

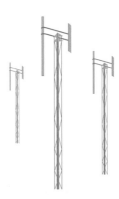

THE FREMONT TROLL

SEATTLE

In a freeway underpass beneath Aurora Bridge is a giant cement troll clutching a Volkswagen Beetle. Long, bedraggled hair obscures his right eye. His left eye is a silver hubcap.

The 18-foot-tall (5.5 m) concrete monster has lived under the bridge since 1990, when the Fremont Arts Council held a public art competition to enhance the underpass. Local artists Steve Badanes, Will Martin, Donna Walter, and Ross Whitehead sculpted the troll, adding a real VW Beetle to make it look like he'd just swiped a car from the road above.

Within months of the troll's unveiling, vandals broke into the car and stole a plaster bust of Elvis, which had been placed inside as part of a time capsule. The car has now been filled with concrete.

Visitors are encouraged to climb on the sculpture, but modifying the troll's looks is frowned upon. (This doesn't stop people from painting his lips pink, giving him tattoos, and tagging him with their names.)

Under the Aurora Bridge at North 36th Street and Troll Avenue North. Ⓝ 47.680257 Ⓦ 122.253201

ALSO IN WASHINGTON

Mystery Soda Machine

Seattle · Feeling lucky? Hit one of the "mystery" buttons on this battered old soda machine and see what pops out.

Hall of Mosses

Forks · Hike along a gothic, untamed trail of trees that drip with strands of moss.

The beloved cement curmudgeon beneath Aurora Bridge gets redecorated regularly.

Four Corners and the Southwest and Great Plains

Map labels:
- Oasis Bordello Museum
- Nekoma Pyramid
- MONTANA
- NORTH DAKOTA
- Air Mail Beacons
- Berkeley Pit
- Ringing Rocks
- Thunderhead Falls
- IDAHO
- SOUTH DAKOTA
- Museum of Clean
- WYOMING
- Carhenge
- Fly Geyser
- PhinDeli
- NEBRASKA
- SALT LAKE CITY
- Japanese Balloon Bomb Explosion
- NEVADA
- Toquima Cave
- UTAH
- Bristlecone Pines
- COLORADO
- Garden of Eden
- The Trembling Giant
- KANSAS
- Summum Pyramid
- Bishop Castle
- Strataca Salt Mine
- SALT LAKE CITY
- Ra Paulette's Caves
- Museum of Osteology
- Elmer McCurdy Grave
- Granite Mountain Records Vault
- Loretto Chapel Stairs
- OKLAHOMA
- Arcosanti
- Ozymandias on the Plains
- ARIZONA
- Lightning Field
- NEW MEXICO
- Wichita Mountains Buffalo Herd
- Titan Missile Museum
- TEXAS
- National Museum of Funeral History
- Prada Marfa
- Hamilton Pool
- Magic Lantern Castle Museum
- PACIFIC OCEAN
- GULF OF MEXICO

FOUR CORNERS AND THE SOUTHWEST AND GREAT PLAINS

N

Miles
0   150   300

0   150   300
Kilometers

Four Corners and the Southwest

ARIZONA

TITAN MISSILE MUSEUM

GREEN VALLEY

When you go underground at the Titan Missile Museum just south of Tucson, you travel back in time to the Soviet-fearing days of "duck and cover," big red buttons, and mutually assured destruction. The museum, formerly known as Complex 571-7, is one of 54 subterranean missile sites across the country that were active during the Cold War. Decommissioned in 1982, the silo still contains a 108-foot (33 m) missile—with the lethal bits removed.

The Titan II missile was capable of rapidly delivering a nine-megaton nuclear warhead to a target 6,300 miles (10,138 km) away. In other words, it could nuke Moscow within 30 minutes.

The launch process, simulated to exciting effect at the museum, began with a 35-character alphanumeric message from the president. The commander and officer at the launch center each copied down the message, then conferred with one another to make sure the codes they wrote were identical.

It was then time to open the Emergency War Order (EWO) safe, which contained authenticator

ARCOSANTI

MAYER

In 1970, Frank Lloyd Wright protégé Paolo Soleri took to the Arizona desert to break ground on an experimental community designed to forge a new way of urban living. Guided by principles of eco-friendliness, waste reduction, and what he called "elegant frugality," Soleri planned a hyper-dense city: Arcosanti. The name incorporates "arcology," his concept for architecture-plus-ecology.

Intended as a test site for Soleri's urban development theories, the self-contained Arcosanti was designed to house 5,000 people. Though almost five decades have passed since the laying of the foundation stone, the city is still in its early construction stages. Lack of funding has kept Arcosanti small—it is now home to between 50 and 150 inhabitants, depending on the season.

Over the years, thousands of volunteers have helped construct apartments, storefronts, an outdoor amphitheater, and a visitor's center, all rendered in concrete with lots of arcs and semicircles. Landscaping workshops and internships are still available for

Arcosanti's experimental community is run by eco-loving volunteers.

people who want to be part of the urban experiment. Work at Arcosanti is funded by sales of bronze and ceramic wind chimes.

The buildings are a little run-down and shabby; Soleri passed away in 2013, so they'll likely stay that way. But Arcosanti is a fascinating look at one man's ambitious alternative to urban sprawl. **13555 South Cross L Road, Mayer. Arcosanti is located between Sedona and Scottsdale. Ⓝ 34.345418 Ⓦ 112.116278**

ALSO IN ARIZONA

Santa Claus

Mohave County · At this abandoned Christmas-themed town in the middle of the desert, the faded festive decor is covered with graffiti.

Antelope Canyon

Page · Due to flash-flood risks, the Southwest's most beautiful slot canyon can only be visited with a guided tour.

Pumpkin Spring Pool

Littlefield · Don't swim in this naturally formed limestone bathtub—its waters are laced with arsenic.

cards used to confirm that the message did indeed come from the president. Also in the safe: two launch keys, which the commander and officer would insert simultaneously at separate control stations.

Once the keys had been turned, there was no going back: 58 seconds later, the missile would be on its way to the preprogrammed target. Launch crews never knew the targets—it's easier to launch a nuclear warhead when you don't know who it will kill—and the three preprogrammed targets at this Arizona site are still classified.

In addition to the rare up-close-and-personal look at an intercontinental ballistic missile, the museum occasionally offers overnight stays. You and three friends can snuggle up in the old crew quarters, mere feet from one of the most murderous devices ever created.

1580 West Duval Mine Road, Green Valley. The museum is 25 miles (40 km) south of Tucson. Thirty days' notice is required to book a cozy overnight stay. Ⓝ 31.902710 Ⓦ 110.999352

Step inside a decommisioned missile silo for a taste of Cold War tension.

Built without blueprints, Bishop Castle has a fire-breathing dragon and a bridge to nowhere.

COLORADO

Bishop Castle

RYE

In 1969, at the age of 25, newly married Jim Bishop started constructing a stone cottage for his family. Over the decades, as he kept building, that stone cottage became a castle. Today it is a multilevel marvel with three towers, a grand ballroom, and a fire-breathing metal dragon guarding the main eave. And Bishop still isn't done.

The castle doesn't adhere to any building codes. There have never been any blueprints, and Bishop is quick to point out that while his father helped a tiny bit with initial construction efforts, he has done the vast majority of the work himself. (Just to make sure this point is crystal clear, the small section that his dad worked on is painted with the words "Jim started the castle, not his father, Willard.")

Bishop sees his castle as a symbol of American freedom. Signs surrounding the building tell of the local government's unsuccessful attempts to regulate his work. "They tried but failed to oppress and control my God-given talent to hand-build this great monument to hard-working poor people," one reads (in part—it's a long sign).

Bishop plans to keep building until he is no longer physically able. When visiting, you may see him carrying stones or making an impromptu speech from one of the towers—he is known to unleash his political views on visitors at high volume.

12705 State Highway 165, Rye. Admission to the castle is free—funding for ongoing construction comes from gift shop sales and donations. The castle is open during daylight hours. From I-25, take exit 74 at Colorado City toward the mountains. It's 24 miles (39 km) farther along Highway 165.
Ⓝ 38.240728 Ⓦ 104.629102 ➸

Also in Colorado

Dinosaur Best Western

Lakewood · This franchise hotel got a multimillion-dollar, dinosaur-themed makeover in 2013, complete with a T. rex skull, dino murals, and a pterosaur-shaped weather vane.

Paint Mines Interpretive Park

Calhan · The sandstone spires of this geological park run wild along the color spectrum, from creamy white to orange, purple, gray, rust, and chocolate brown.

Blue Mustang

Denver Airport · This reviled red-eyed, blue-skinned 32-foot (9.7 m) sculpture of a rearing bronco caused the death of its creator when a section of the 9,000-pound horse fell on him. Some Denver residents believe that the horse is cursed.

Solomon's Castle

Cano's Castle

➡➡ Other American Castles

MYSTERY CASTLE
PHOENIX, AZ
In the 1930s, a man named Boyce Luther Gulley left his wife and daughter in Seattle and fled to the desert to build this castle. But this was not a case of abandonment. Gulley had just discovered that he had tuberculosis, and intended to build the castle for his daughter, Mary Lou.

The 18-room, three-story building, created using rocks, salvaged scrap, adobe, mortar, cement, and goat milk, was passed on to Gulley's abandoned family members when he died in 1945. The mother and daughter moved into the property and Mary Lou led public tours until her death in 2010.

CANO'S CASTLE
ANTONITO, CO
Vietnam vet Donald "Cano" Espinoza built this set of four gleaming towers single-handedly, using beer cans, hubcaps, and other discarded metal. He has cited as his main influences Jesus and "Vitamin Mary Jane."

SOLOMON'S CASTLE
ONA, FL
In 1974, sculptor and pun lover Howard Solomon began constructing a castle out of aluminum printing plates salvaged from a local newspaper plant. The building is now a gleaming, medieval-style castle standing three stories high and incorporating a sculpture garden and a 60-foot (18.3 m) replica of a 16th-century Portuguese battleship.

RUBEL CASTLE
GLENDORA, CA
Embedded in the external walls of Rubel Castle are glass bottles, forks, motorcycle parts, and other trash yard treasures collected by builder Michael Clarke Rubel. Beginning in 1959 at the age of eighteen, Rubel spent decades constructing the castle using stones and scrap donated by friends. A drawbridge, dungeons, and cars from the 1920s are among the surprises hidden behind the 20-foot-high (6 m) wall surrounding the compound.

CORAL CASTLE
HOMESTEAD, FL
When 26-year-old Latvian Ed Leedskalnin was jilted by his sweetheart the day before their intended wedding, he dealt with his distress by moving to the US and making a castle out of coral. The 5-foot-tall (1.5 m), 100-pound (45 kg) Leedskalnin somehow hauled 1,100 tons (997 MT) of coral blocks around to create a monument to lost love. A 500-pound (227 kg) heart-shaped stone table is among the hints of heartbreak incorporated into the architecture. A plaque laid into one of the walls reads, cryptically, YOU WILL BE SEEING UNUSUAL ACCOMPLISHMENT.

Human error and geothermal pressure combined to create this rainbow wonder.

NEVADA
FLY GEYSER

GERLACH

These multicolored, knobby cones of calcium carbonate that spew water from multiple spouts are not natural—humans had a hand in their creation. In 1964, a geothermal energy company drilled a test well in the Black Rock Desert. The water they encountered was not hot enough to use, so they plugged up the well. But the seal didn't hold, and water began erupting into the air.

Over the years, the geyser grew as minerals from the water settled on its surface. Fly Geyser and the terraced mound on which it sits now measure 12 feet (3.65 m) tall. Thermophilic algae have turned the cones various shades of green, yellow, orange, and red, giving the geyser a Martian look.

State Route 34, Gerlach. The geyser is on private property but visible with binoculars from State Route 34 near Gerlach. Property owners offer tours a few times a year. ⓝ 40.859318 ⓦ 119.331908

ALSO IN NEVADA

Clown Motel

Tonopah · Oh, just a motel on the edge of the desert, decorated with thousands of clowns, conveniently located next to an abandoned graveyard.

Neon Boneyard

Las Vegas · A 3-acre plot filled with disused neon signs charts Vegas's luminous history.

THE BRISTLECONE PINES OF THE GREAT BASIN

BAKER

At high elevations in a region of the western United States known as the Great Basin, a species of pine lives a quiet, secluded, and exceedingly long life.

Few other plants can grow in the hard rock where bristlecones thrive. The pines can live at least 5,000 years—longer than any other non-clonal organism. The trees are exceptionally hardy, surviving freezing cold temperatures, deep snow, and bracing winds. In many cases, portions of the bristlecone pine can die off and allow the tree to conserve its limited resources. Because of this, bristlecones aren't very tall and often appear dead or extremely weathered.

In eastern Nevada, a tree known as Prometheus was studied by a group of conservationists. Scientists drill cores out of trees in order to count and measure the rings that chronicle their growth. Unfortunately, when Prometheus was drilled for a core, the tool used for this process broke off inside. The researcher needed his tool back, and to get it, he had to cut the tree down. Once he'd retrieved his tool and the core from Prometheus, he was able to determine that the tree had lived 4,862 years.

An older tree hasn't been found since, though one known as Methuselah in California is believed to be over 4,800 years old. Most of the living groves of these trees are under better protection now and can be visited in several locations throughout the Great Basin and California.

Great Basin National Park. There are several bristlecone pine groves in the park—the most accessible is on the northeast side of Wheeler Peak. In summer, rangers lead walks through the grove. ⓝ 39.005833 ⓦ 114.218100

Some of the trees in this national park are among the oldest in the world.

310 / USA / FOUR CORNERS AND THE SOUTHWEST

Peer through protective fencing to see inside the shallow cave and take photos.

Toquima Cave

AUSTIN

In the center of Nevada is a cave lined with colorful pictographs painted by hand, thousands of years ago, using pigments of bleached white, bright red, and a yellowy turmeric orange. Unlike petroglyphs, the images are not carved into the rock but were added to the surface, most likely with fingers, in circular, crosshatched, beautiful snaking patterns.

The images, over 300 in all, date from around 1300 to 600 BCE. They were created by members of the Western Shoshone, a group of local Native American tribes. The cave depth is fairly shallow, so if it was used as a dwelling, it was probably short-term. Given the sweeping views from the cliff, the site may have been used as a place marker or geographical guidepost for finding food sources, tracking hunting grounds, or managing other tribal movements.

Archaeologists and anthropologists have found it a challenge to decipher the images. They may be keys to the land or, as some have posited, keys to other, less worldly, places. Cave shelters are seen as portals by some Native peoples, providing access to commune with the earth, experience visions, and seek understanding of what lies beyond. Whether used for the temporal or spiritual world, Toquima Cave and the pictographs hold great power for the Western Shoshone.

The cave is at Pete's Summit in the Toquima Range, about a 30-mile (48.3 km) drive southeast of Austin, Nevada. From Toquima Cave Campground, you'll need to hike half a mile or so. Remember that this is a sacred site—take nothing and leave nothing.
Ⓝ 39.187750 Ⓦ 116.790500 ➡

➡ Other Native American Sites

CAHOKIA MOUNDS
COLLINSVILLE, ILLINOIS
The largest pre-Columbian settlement in the Americas north of Mexico, Cahokia once had about 120 mounds, built beginning in the 9th century. One in particular, Mound 72, shows evidence of hundreds of sacrificial burials. Some of the skeletons were found with their fingers extended into the surrounding sand, suggesting to archaeologists that these people were alive when they were buried and tried to claw their way out.

At its height in roughly 1250, Cahokia was bigger than medieval London.

The settlement continued until perhaps the late 14th century, when it was abandoned for unknown reasons. Many theories have been proposed, including invasion and warfare, as well as lack of game animals and deforestation as a result of erosion.

Within the ceremonial complex there was a wooden monument built to mark the equinox and solstice.

Cahokia Mounds State Historic Site is just 8 miles from downtown St. Louis near Collinsville, Illinois.

Parowan Gap

LEO PETROGLYPH
RAY, OHIO
Nearly 40 images, collectively known as the Leo Petroglyph, are etched into a large slab of sandstone. It has familiar subjects like birds, fish, footprints, and stick-figure humans. Then there are the more abstract designs in the mix, including one that looks like a cartoon man with horns.

It's thought that people from the Native American Fort Ancient culture made the petroglyph around 1,000 years ago.

PAROWAN GAP
PETROGLYPHS
PAROWAN, UTAH
Just a few miles west of the small town of Parowan, and just at the edge of the dry "Little Salt Lake,"

lies a natural gap in the mountains, covered with hundreds of petroglyphs. They have been there for over 1,000 years.

Archaeologists have argued that the petroglyphs are a complex calendar system. Hopi and Paiute peoples have a variety of interpretations for the rock art as well, which includes representations of humans as well as depictions of animals and geometric shapes. Among the petroglyphs is a much more ancient reminder of the past: fossilized dinosaur footprints.

WASHINGTON HALEETS,
BAINBRIDGE ISLAND
Haleets, or Figurehead Rock, is about 100 feet (30.5 m) from the shore of Bainbridge

Island, and it disappears underwater during high tide. The sandstone rock is inscribed with several petroglyphs believed to have been carved by the native Suquamish tribe between 1,000 BCE and 500. The date has been narrowed down thanks to a facial piercing depicted on one of the characters on the stone: That specific type of piercing—a labret—was no longer used by the local indigenous people after about the year 500.

The purpose or meaning of the stone itself is a lot harder to discern. As it's located near a body of water, the rock may have marked a boundary of some sort. Or, as one local amateur astronomer has claimed, the rock may mark the lunar or solar calendar.

MAP ROCK
MELBA, IDAHO
This large basalt rock is believed to have been carved by the Shoshone-Bannock people to map the area of the upper Snake River, possibly as long as 12,000 years ago. It depicts the Snake and Salmon Rivers, as well as the animals and tribes that inhabited the territories in between. No one can decisively say what the carving's purpose was, which only contributes to its mysterious, ancient allure.

Map Rock is beside the Snake River, about 6 miles northwest of Walters Ferry along Map Rock Road.

NEW MEXICO
LIGHTNING FIELD

QUEMADO

A visit to the *Lightning Field* is not something you do on a whim. There are rules to be followed.

The field is a work of land art, installed in 1977 by sculptor Walter De Maria. It consists of 400 stainless steel, 2-inch-wide (5 cm) poles, each over 20 feet (6 m) high, arranged in a mile-wide grid.

To see it during the May to October visiting season, you must arrive in the small town of Quemado—a three-hour drive from Albuquerque—by 2:30 p.m. on your designated day. From there you'll be driven 45 minutes into the desert, where a rustic, six-person cabin sits beside the *Lightning Field*. The driver then departs, leaving you until 11 a.m. the next day to appreciate the art that surrounds you.

As the hours pass, the *Lightning Field* changes. The poles seem to shimmer. They turn gray and black, grow shadows, and reflect the brilliant orange of the setting sun. If you go in July or August, you

Walter De Maria's array of metal poles in the desert beckons fury from above.

may witness lightning—but despite the work's title, a storm isn't an essential part of the experience. **The Dia Art Foundation provides transportation to the *Lightning Field* from the tiny town of Quemado.** Ⓝ 34.343409 Ⓦ 108.497650 ➻

The artist Ra Paulette has carved over a dozen whimsical caves into the New Mexico sandstone.

RA PAULETTE'S CAVES

LA MADERA

"Manual labor is the foundation of my self-expression," says Ra Paulette, an artist who has spent decades carving intricately patterned caves into New Mexico's sandstone cliffs. Heading into the desert with a wheelbarrow strapped to his back, Paulette burrows into the rock to create chambers, arches, and columns, all of which he decorates with swirling flourishes.

Since 1990, Paulette has dug over a dozen caves, each one unique in design. Though some were created on commission, Paulette often veered away from the design requirements of his clients, instead carving out whatever designs his hands were instinctively drawn to. He is currently working on what he calls an "environmental and social art project": the Luminous Caves, a vast complex, lit via skylights, that will host gatherings and performances.

North of Santa Fe on US Route 285, at Ojo Caliente. The finished caves are not open to the public, but some of the interiors can be glimpsed through their skylights. Ⓝ 36.386554 Ⓦ 106.041037

LORETTO CHAPEL STAIRS

SANTA FE

Visit Loretto Chapel and you're guaranteed to witness a miracle. In the back right corner of the small church is a spiral staircase supposedly built by a saint.

Around 1878, the chapel nuns were in need of a way to access the newly built choir loft. A conventional staircase would have taken up too much space, but a ladder would have been inappropriate for the nuns to use when wearing their habits.

Perplexed by the problem, the nuns apparently prayed to St. Joseph, patron saint of carpenters. Lo, on the ninth day, a mysterious man appeared at the chapel door with a donkey in tow and vowed to build the stairs. Within a few months he had crafted an inspiring feat of engineering, a spiral staircase with no visible supports and no central column.

When the nuns went looking for the benevolent stranger to pay him and thank him, he had disappeared. They concluded that the miracle staircase was built by St. Joseph himself. The fact that there are 33 steps—equaling the number of years Jesus lived—only adds to the legend.

The spiral stairs are structurally sound but a little bouncy owing to their springlike double helix shape. They have been closed to public foot traffic since the 1970s, but if you book your wedding in the chapel you can stand on them to get your photo taken.

207 Old Santa Fe Trail, Santa Fe.
Ⓝ **35.685387** Ⓦ **105.937637**

ALSO IN NEW MEXICO

American International Rattlesnake Museum

Albuquerque · Glass cages of tail-shaking serpents line the walls of this museum, which is dedicated to showing the gentler, softer underbelly of the often-feared rattlesnake.

109 East Palace

Santa Fe · This innocuous-looking storefront was once the secret jump-off spot for Manhattan Project scientists working on the development of the atomic bomb.

The spiral staircase is said to have been constructed with the help of divine intervention.

LAND ART IN THE SOUTHWEST

Sun Tunnels, Lucin, UT

Four concrete cylinders big enough to walk in form *Sun Tunnels*, an outdoor artwork installed by Nancy Holt in 1976. Laid out in a cross configuration, the 18-foot-long, 9-foot-wide (5.5 m, 3 m) tunnels are positioned to frame the sunrise and sunset on the solstices. Each pipe has a cluster of holes drilled into its ceiling. They are not just random dots, but the patterns of constellations Draco, Perseus, Columba, and Capricorn. When the sun shines onto the tunnels, the constellations are projected on the interior walls.

Holt was part of the '70s land art movement along with her husband, Robert Smithson, whose 1970 work *Spiral Jetty* (shown below) is still in place at Great Salt Lake. The *Sun Tunnels* are a 4-hour drive west of Salt Lake City.

SPIRAL JETTY, GREAT SALT LAKE, UT

For over 30 years, *Spiral Jetty* (below) was hidden beneath the pink-tinged waters of Great Salt Lake. Artist Robert Smithson built the 1,500-foot-long (457 m) jetty in 1970, using mud, salt crystals, and basalt rocks. At the time, Salt Lake was experiencing a drought, and the water level was unusually low. When the rains returned, the lake swallowed the jetty.

It wasn't until 2002, during another drought, that the water lowered and *Spiral Jetty* reappeared. Unfortunately, Smithson wasn't around to see it return—he died in a plane crash three years after creating the work.

Encrusted with white salt and at the mercy of the elements—and the visitors who walk along it—*Spiral Jetty* looks a little worse for wear. It's a state of affairs Smithson would have appreciated. The artist, who coined the term "earthwork" for his brand of landscape-integrated art, had a fondness for entropy and the eroding power of nature. Rozel Point peninsula is on the northeastern shore of Great Salt Lake.

RODEN CRATER, FLAGSTAFF, AZ

In 1977, artist James Turrell purchased an extinct volcano northeast of Flagstaff in order to create a work of land art named *Roden Crater*. The centerpiece of this work, a naked-eye observatory housed in the 2-mile-wide (3.2 km) volcanic crater, is still under construction. Thus far, Turrell has installed a series of tunnels, viewing chambers, and a bronze staircase in the volcano. The projected completion date changes frequently, but something amazing is certainly in progress.

TEXAS

PRADA MARFA

VALENTINE

Along a silent stretch of Route 90, with only power lines and tumbleweeds for company, is a fully stocked Prada boutique.

Prada Marfa is a site-specific sculpture by Scandinavian artists Michael Elmgreen and Ingar Dragset. The shelves of the 15 × 25–foot (4.5 × 7.6 m) store are filled with Prada handbags and high heels, but none of the products are for sale, and the shop's door doesn't ever open.

The store was originally intended to be installed and left to the elements, so it would gradually deteriorate and be absorbed into the landscape. However, three days after the store's unveiling, vandals broke into Prada Marfa and stole every item on display. The products were replaced, the window glass thickened, and the concept tweaked: Representatives from the Art Production Fund and nonprofit cultural organization Ballroom Marfa now drop by periodically to pick up trash and paint over graffiti.

Route 90, 1.4 miles (2.25 km) northwest of Valentine. The Prada store is 37 miles (60 km) northwest of Marfa, a 2,000-resident town that has become a hub for contemporary art. Take a tour of the galleries and visit Donald Judd's installations at the Chinati Foundation. Ⓝ 30.603461 Ⓦ 104.518484

An artist's look-but-don't-touch homage to luxury consumerism in the middle of the desert.

NATIONAL MUSEUM OF FUNERAL HISTORY

HOUSTON

"Any day above ground is a good one." So reads the slogan of the National Museum of Funeral History, which celebrates life by showing how we honor its loss.

Founded in 1992 by undertaker Robert L. Waltrip and attached to an embalming school, the museum displays the country's largest collection of funeral artifacts. Items range from 19th-century horse-drawn hearses to memorabilia from Michael Jackson's memorial service.

The exhibit on 19th-century mourning customs provides a fascinating look at the Victorian response to death. Among the items are a wooden clock that reminded family members to mourn on the hour, a quilt made from ribbons that bound the flowers at a funeral service, and jewelry made from the hair of the deceased.

Other exhibits cover the history of embalming, papal and presidential funerals, and "fantasy coffins." Look out for the Snow White–inspired glass casket and the roomy coffin built for three.

415 Barren Springs Drive, Houston. Ⓝ 29.989561 Ⓦ 95.430324

See some of history's great hearses up close.

A roadside pair of legs puts a modern spin on the Romantic poem "Ozymandias."

OZYMANDIAS ON THE PLAINS

AMARILLO

You wouldn't know it, but these legs are the shattered likeness of an Egyptian king. Ozymandias is the Greek name for Rameses II and was the inspiration and name of the 1818 poem by Percy Bysshe Shelley.

A plaque near the gigantic legs reads:

In 1819, while on their horseback trek over the Great Plains of New Spain, Percy Bysshe Shelley and his wife, Mary Shelley (author of Frankenstein), came across these ruins. Here Shelley penned his immortal lines, among them:

I met a traveller from an antique land

Who said: Two vast and trunkless legs of stone

Stand in the desert . . .

And on the pedestal these words appear:

"My name is Ozymandias, King of Kings,

Look on my works, ye mighty, and despair!"

The pedestal near the monument also asserts that the visage of the king was destroyed by Lubbock football players after losing a game to Amarillo.

The hoax sculpture has been vandalized numerous times, most notably with the addition of socks to the legs. Occasionally the vandalism is sandblasted off the sculpture, but the socks always reappear. The locals seem to prefer the king's legs be kept warm.

The socks are on the east side of I-27. Ⓝ 35.101703 Ⓦ 101.909135

HAMILTON POOL

AUSTIN

There are swimming holes and then there's Hamilton Pool, a glorious fairy grotto where you can paddle in a natural spring protected by a canopy of limestone.

The grotto formed when the dome of an underground river collapsed due to erosion. Maidenhair ferns and moss-covered stalactites crept along the overhang, creating a verdant oasis in the Texas desert. A 50-foot (15 m) waterfall pours from the overhang into the turquoise pool.

The pool is 23 miles (37 km) west of Austin, off Highway 71. There's a quarter-mile hike down to the water—wear closed-toe shoes. Due to the small size of the beach (really just a patch of sand on the edge of the spring), capacity is limited to 75 vehicles and a one-in, one-out policy applies. Ⓝ 30.345135 Ⓦ 98.135221

This emerald-green grotto not far from Austin may be America's most beautiful swimming hole.

MAGIC LANTERN CASTLE MUSEUM

SAN ANTONIO

Prior to the invention of cinema, audiovisual entertainment came in the form of the magic lantern, a slide projector invented in the middle of the 17th century.

Early magic lanterns used candlelight and hand-painted glass slides to project dim images onto walls and cloth. Better and brighter light sources became available during the 19th century: limelight, arc lamps, and, eventually, incandescent bulbs.

As illumination improved, so did the special effects. By layering slides and moving them independently, magic lantern operators could make a dog appear to jump through a hoop or a skeleton seem to talk. Live narration and musical accompaniment added to the experience. A genre of scary supernatural shows known as phantasmagoria developed, featuring cackling demons, eerie ghosts, and unsettling melodies.

The Magic Lantern Castle Museum was founded by Jack Judson, who discovered a passion for collecting lanterns and slides when he retired in 1986. **1419 Austin Highway, San Antonio. Visits are by appointment only. Ⓝ 29.492141 Ⓦ 98.438667**

UTAH
THE TREMBLING GIANT

RICHFIELD

Though this golden grove of quaking aspens may look like a forest, the whole thing is actually a single organism. Every tree—or stem, technically—is genetically identical, and the whole forest is linked by a single root system. The Pando aspens reproduce asexually by sprouting new stems from the root structure.

With over 40,000 stems and a total weight of 13 million pounds (approx. 6,000 MT), the Pando clonal colony is the heaviest known organism in the world. It's also among the oldest living things on the planet—the root system is an estimated 80,000 years old.

One mile southwest of Fish Lake on Utah State Route 25. Ⓝ 38.524530 Ⓦ 111.750346

Though it may look like an ordinary forest, this grove of aspens is actually a single organism—the heaviest living thing in the world.

GRANITE MOUNTAIN RECORDS VAULT

SALT LAKE CITY

The history of your family is buried deep inside a mountain of solid rock just outside Salt Lake City. Granite Mountain Records Vault, or simply "The Vault," is a massive repository of genealogical records established in 1965.

The Church of Jesus Christ of Latter-day Saints built the vault to safeguard the genealogical information—such as records of births, deaths, and marriages—the church has been collecting on microfilm since 1938. The records collected are not just of church members, but everyone. This data is important to Mormons because they use it to trace their family trees in order to posthumously baptize their ancestors into the LDS faith.

Able to withstand natural disasters and nuclear blasts, the vault stores millions of microfilms in banks of 10-foot-high (3 m) steel cabinets, along with hard drives filled with digitized data. Heavy vault doors protect the six storage areas, which connect to one another via 25-foot-wide (7.6 m) tunnels. Natural conditions allow the temperature to stay at a steady 55°F (12.7°C) regardless of the season.

Due to the 200-year life span of microfilm, 60 full-time vault employees are currently converting the reels into digital images using microfilm scanners. This process was originally estimated to take 150 years, but technological advances and improved automation have reduced that to ten years. Much of the information stored in Granite Mountain is now remotely accessible via the Internet to anyone engaged in genealogical research.

The public may not visit the vault, purportedly due to concerns over contamination. The Church's history preservation department is particularly concerned about "blue jean dust"—the tiny fibers that fly into the air when pant legs brush against each other.

Little Cottonwood Canyon, Wasatch Range, Salt Lake City. The Vault is 20 miles (32 km) southeast of downtown Salt Lake City. Ⓝ 40.570561 Ⓦ 111.762052

ALSO IN UTAH

USPS Remote Encoding Facility

Salt Lake City · If your penmanship is poor, your hand-addressed letters will end up here to be decoded and redirected to the rightful recipient.

Inside this mountain are millions of family history records.

SUMMUM PYRAMID

SALT LAKE CITY

Inside an orange pyramid, right beside the Lincoln Highway, is a religious group willing to mummify your corpse. The religion, Summum, was founded in 1975 by Claude Nowell (aka Corky Ra), who claimed to have been visited by advanced beings who revealed to him the nature of creation.

According to Summum philosophy, death does not snuff out a person's awareness or ability to feel. Though bereft of a body, our spirit, or essence, sticks around—and gets thoroughly confused by the change in circumstances.

The solution: mummification. By preserving your body, Summum provides a "home base" for your posthumous essence. Secure in this wrapped-up, chemically preserved corpse, your essence can safely communicate and make plans to move on to its next destination.

The entire mummification process takes four to eight months and ends with your gauze-wrapped body being hermetically sealed in a sarcophagus, or "mummiform." Summum offers lots of customization options for your mummiform. You can go with a traditional golden Egyptian look featuring ankhs and scarabs, or you can choose a simple, streamlined capsule for the final send-off.

Corky Ra himself became the first Summum mummy following his death in 2008. His mummiform, and that of his cat, Oscar, is on prominent display at the pyramid.

707 Genesee Avenue, Salt Lake City. The Summum Pyramid hosts publicly accessible readings and discussions on Wednesday nights. Ⓝ 40.750707 Ⓦ 111.911651

Great Plains

IDAHO
OASIS BORDELLO MUSEUM

WALLACE

For decades, Oasis Bordello was a busy brothel—one of five that catered to the small silver-mining town of Wallace. Then, in January 1988, the working women caught wind of an imminent FBI raid. Late one night, they fled, leaving their rooms in a state that still exists today—with a few creative modifications.

Michelle Mayfield, a Wallace native, purchased the bordello building and opened it as a museum in 1993. Go on a guided tour of the rooms and you'll see mannequins dressed in the lingerie left behind by the women who worked there. Strewn around the former bordello are dog-eared magazines, flimsy nightgowns, toiletries, and an Atari 5200, as

Vacated in a rush just before a 1988 police raid, this brothel has been left untouched as a museum.

well as a bag of groceries—Minute Rice sits on the kitchen table, untouched since 1988.

Three stops on the tour leave no doubt as to the nature of the business: A peek inside a cupboard full of red lightbulbs is followed by the handwritten menu of services on the wall, complete with time limits and prices. In a drawer are battered kitchen timers used to enforce the prescribed duration of appointments.

605 Cedar Street, Wallace. Off Interstate 90, between Spokane and Missoula. Make sure to get a souvenir garter belt at the gift shop. Ⓝ 47.472574 Ⓦ 115.923529

MUSEUM OF CLEAN

POCATELLO

Don Aslett is the King of Clean. As the ruler of an empire of cleaning products and janitorial services, Aslett is a big advocate of cleanliness, not just

in terms of keeping your shower mildew-free but also for purifying your mind and spirit.

The Museum of Clean, which Aslett opened in 2011, is an institution dedicated to this clutter-cleaning philosophy. Its mission statement is to "sell the idea and value of clean"—Aslett's dream is to create "clean homes, clean minds, clean language, clean community, and a clean world."

The museum aims to sweep visitors into an unsullied state of mind via exhibits of brooms, tubs, toilets, and vintage vacuum cleaners dating from 1869 to 1969. An art gallery displays cleaning-themed paintings and spotless sculptures.

711 South 2nd Avenue, Pocatello. Ⓝ 42.859605 Ⓦ 112.441706

The Museum of Clean targets dirt in all its literal and metaphorical forms.

KANSAS
STRATACA SALT MINE

HUTCHISON

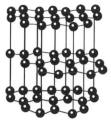

Six hundred and fifty feet (198 m) beneath the plains of Kansas lies a salt mine that's been operating since 1923. Some of the salt mined here ends up scattered on roads and highways in winter to prevent the buildup of ice. In an unused section of the mine you'll find a salt museum housing a crystal with a long and unlikely history.

In 1998, scientists discovered a strain of *Bacillus* bacterium lying dormant in a bubble within a 250-million-year-old salt crystal in New Mexico. At a lab in West Chester University, Pennsylvania, biologists were able to reanimate the bacterium by giving it fresh nutrients and putting it in a salt solution.

The discovery of this living bacterium from over 250 million years ago impacts our timeline of life on Earth—it is believed to be the world's oldest living organism.

3300 Carey Boulevard, Hutchinson (aka Salt City). Ⓝ 38.043184 Ⓦ 97.868482

Retired Civil War nurse Samuel Dinsmoor began sculpting his eccentric garden in 1905.

GARDEN OF EDEN

LUCAS

After serving in the Civil War as a Union nurse, Samuel P. Dinsmoor settled in Lucas, Kansas. It was there, in 1905, that he began building his own patriotic Garden of Eden.

The centerpiece of the garden was a "log" cabin that Dinsmoor sculpted out of limestone. Around the cabin he built tall, thin cement sculptures reflecting his Populist politics, Biblical interests, and distrust of authority. Adam and Eve, Cain and Abel, and the devil all make an appearance, as do snakes, angels, and a waving American flag. The most blatant political commentary is found in the "Crucifixion of Labor," a sculpture of a doctor, lawyer, banker, and preacher nailing a man labeled "Labor" to a cross.

In a corner of the garden is a pagoda-style mausoleum. Dinsmoor built it to house his own body and even posed for a double-exposed gag photograph depicting himself looking at his own corpse. When he died, Dinsmoor was embalmed and entombed behind glass, as per his plans. You can still see his smiling but slightly moldy face when you peer into the space.

305 East Second Street, Lucas. The tiny town is about 2 hours north of Wichita. Ⓝ 39.057802 Ⓦ 98.535061

MONTANA

TRANSCONTINENTAL AIR MAIL ROUTE BEACONS

WESTERN MONTANA

In the 1920s and '30s, prior to the development of radio navigation for powered flights, air mail pilots in the United States navigated their routes by following giant concrete arrows on the ground.

The 50- to 70-foot-long (15 to 21 m) arrows, painted yellow and installed alongside 50-foot-high (15 m) flashing beacons, lit up the national mail route, allowing pilots to take to the skies at night and greatly improving the delivery times for air mail. Hundreds of flashing beacons and concrete arrows were installed across the country. The system operated at full strength until radio-based navigation began to replace it in the mid-'30s.

During World War II, many of the navigational arrows and towers were destroyed out of fear that invading enemy bombers would use them to find their way to heavily populated areas. There are, however, some leftovers strewn across the States—most

Before radio navigation, huge concrete arrows guided pilots home.

of them sporting cracks in the concrete and faded paint jobs. Montana is the only state that continues to make use of its lighted towers. In the state's western mountain region, a series of 17 well-maintained beacons helps guide pilots home.

The beacons are spread along the mountainous ranges west of Helena. Ⓝ 46.229605 Ⓦ 112.781044

BERKELEY PIT

BUTTE

At the Berkeley Pit you can pay to stand on a viewing platform and gaze at a mile-long lake of toxic waste. The former open-pit copper mine operated from 1955 to 1982, after which groundwater began to fill the 1,780-foot-deep (542.5 m) hole. The lake is now poisoned with a toxic cocktail of heavy metals and chemicals, including copper, iron, arsenic, cadmium, zinc, and sulfuric acid. The reddish, iron-rich water at the surface shifts to a vibrant lime green below, where the copper concentrations are higher.

The water level in the pit is rising at the rate of roughly 0.7 feet (21.3 cm) per month. If it reached 5,410 feet (1.6 km) above sea level, pit water could contaminate the nearby groundwater of the Butte valley, home to more than 30,000 people. A water treatment plant was built in 2003 to prevent the Berkeley Pit water from ever reaching that critical level.

Though measures have been put in place to prevent the toxic pit from harming humans, other creatures have perished in its murky waters. In 1995 a flock of over 300 migrating snow geese landed at the pit and promptly dropped dead.

Exit 126 off I-90, Butte. The pit can be seen from a viewing platform on the Southwest rim, open from March to November. Ⓝ 46.017266 Ⓦ 112.512039

ALSO IN MONTANA

American Computer Museum

Bozeman · Founded in 1990 by husband-and-wife tech enthusiasts George and Barbara Kremedjiev, the American Computer Museum includes an original NASA moon mission navigation computer, ancient adding machines, and the room-size computers of yesteryear.

One of Butte's most striking sights is a pit full of toxic waste.

RINGING ROCKS

PIPESTONE

The most fun you can have 18 miles (29 km) east of Butte involves a pile of rocks and a BYO hammer. The Ringing Rocks, a half-mile-wide assemblage of angular stones, make pleasingly sonorous sounds when you strike them. The rocks sound different notes according to their size and shape. If removed from the pile, they no longer resonate with their bell-like ring.

The exact cause of the rock music is unknown, but it has something to do with the layout and density of the stone mass, which formed when magma cooled just below the Earth's surface around 78 million years ago. Uplift and erosion over the eons exposed the rocks and gave them their squared-off edges, which make it easy for visitors to tap out some tunes.

The rocks are off Interstate 90 in Deerlodge National Forest, on the southwest side of Dry Mountain. The roads aren't great, and you'll need to clamber up a few hills on foot. Watch out for bears along the way.
Ⓝ 45.943491 Ⓦ 112.237504

NEBRASKA
CARHENGE

ALLIANCE

England has Stonehenge. Nebraska has Carhenge. It's pretty much the same thing, give or take a few millennia of technological advancement.

After studying Stonehenge in England, Carhenge creator Jim Reinders returned to the family farm in Alliance with a plan: to create a replica of the prehistoric monument using junkyard automobiles. In the summer of 1987, with the help of family members, Reinders assembled 39 cars, all spray-painted gray, into a 96-foot-wide (29.2 m) circle—roughly the same dimensions as Stonehenge. The creation was inaugurated on the summer solstice with champagne, song, poetry, and a play written by members of the Reinders family.

In addition to providing an intriguing roadside stop for travelers, Carhenge is a memorial to Reinders's father, who once lived on the farm where the monument stands.

Three miles (4.8 km) north of Alliance, on Highway 87.
Ⓝ 42.142229 Ⓦ 102.857901

Built to the same dimensions as its Neolithic predecessor in England, only with cars.

SITE OF A JAPANESE BALLOON BOMB EXPLOSION

OMAHA

In the evening hours of April 18, 1945, a Japanese balloon bomb exploded in the evening sky above the Dundee district of Omaha.

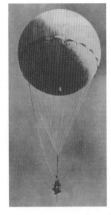

The bomb was one of more than 9,000 balloons the Japanese launched during a 6-month period at the end of World War II, and one of the nearly 300 that were found or observed in the United States. Also called "fire balloons," they were filled with hydrogen and carried bombs varying from 11 to 33 pounds.

Few people in Omaha knew a bomb had gone off at the corner of North 50th and Underwood. Some saw a flash of light, and others heard noises they thought were fireworks. One witness described "a ring of fire" in the sky. The plaque commemorating the incident notes: "The incendiary device flared brightly in the night, but caused no damage."

Japanese military leaders deployed these balloon bombs with the hopes of creating panic and widespread media attention, which would allow them to chart courses for future attacks. There were a few reports of explosions published in various outlets; however, the US Office of Censorship—a wartime agency set up during World War II to censor communications coming in or out of the US—sent messages to all media outlets asking them not to publish news of the balloon bombs, and the Dundee explosion, as well as several others, was not reported until after the war had ended.

The plaque commemorating the explosion is on the building at the southwest corner of 50th and Underwood Avenue. Look for the big green clock on the sidewalk. Ⓝ 41.266825 Ⓦ 95.987766

Not an Egyptian mausoleum, but a Cold War–era missile defense system.

NORTH DAKOTA
THE NEKOMA PYRAMID

NEKOMA

In a field behind a fence lies a 79-foot-tall (24 m), sinister-looking pyramidal frustum—a pyramid with the top cut off. This gray structure, and the clusters of exhaust towers beside it, look like an occult monument, or perhaps a bit of Egyptian architecture misplaced in the Great Plains. In fact, they are the remnants of an antimissile complex constructed during the Cold War.

The Stanley R. Mickelsen Safeguard Complex, as it was known, was built to house anti-ballistic missiles capable of intercepting incoming Soviet rockets. Radar inside the topless pyramid scanned the skies while 100 missiles underground sat ready to launch against a Russian attack.

Built at great expense, the Safeguard Complex was nonetheless short-lived. It became operational on October 1, 1975—one day before Congress voted to end the Safeguard program and decommission the Nekoma site.

North of Nekoma, where Highway 1 meets 81st Street. Ⓝ 48.589529 Ⓦ 98.356503

OKLAHOMA
MUSEUM OF OSTEOLOGY
OKLAHOMA CITY

In 1986, skull collector Jay Villemarette turned his hobby into a profession by establishing Skulls Unlimited, a business dedicated to cleaning, mounting, and selling animal skulls. (The cleaning process is fascinating: Flesh-eating dermestid beetles are let loose on the animal heads to chew away skin, muscle, and fat, leaving a dry and gleaming white skull.)

In order to showcase some of the more striking specimens from Skulls Unlimited, Villemarette opened the Museum of Osteology next door. Here you'll find over 300 carefully articulated specimens, including the skeletons of a Komodo dragon given by Indonesia to President George W. Bush, a rare Javan rhinoceros found in a shop in Paris, and a two-faced calf.

10301 South Sunnylane Road, Oklahoma City. Ⓝ 35.364772 Ⓦ 97.441840

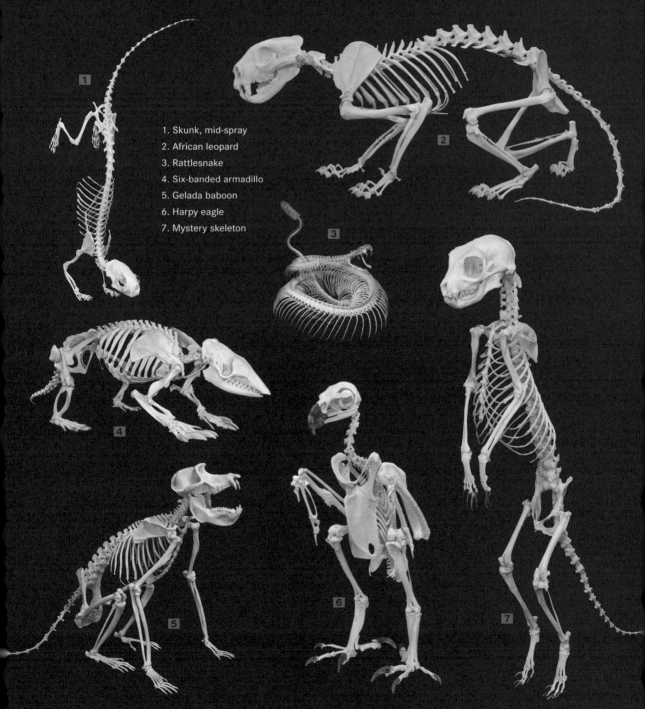

1. Skunk, mid-spray
2. African leopard
3. Rattlesnake
4. Six-banded armadillo
5. Gelada baboon
6. Harpy eagle
7. Mystery skeleton

WICHITA MOUNTAINS BUFFALO HERD

LAWTON

In 1907, 15 bison rode a train from New York to Oklahoma. Their 650 descendants now roam the plains of the Wichita Mountains Wildlife Refuge, a 92-square-mile (238 km²) area dedicated to protecting endangered animals.

The story of why six male and nine female buffaloes took a train trip across the country begins in 1905 with the formation of the American Bison Society. At the time, hunting and settlement had reduced the country's bison population to approximately 1,000—down from 60 million in 1830.

Spearheaded by William T. Hornaday and under the auspices of President Theodore Roosevelt, the society aimed to save the buffalo from extinction, increase the population, and provide a safe place for them to roam. Thankfully, the Wichita Mountains Wildlife Refuge had been established four years earlier—and the newly opened Bronx Zoological Park in New York was willing to spare a herd of bison.

The journey from New York to Oklahoma took six days by train and wagon. When they arrived at the preserve, the bison, who traveled in individual crates, received a rapturous welcome from curious crowds and members of the Native American Comanche tribe.

The animals have roamed free in the prairies ever since. The North American bison population is now around half a million, including the 650 of the Wichita Mountains Wildlife Refuge.

Visitors Center, Cache Meers Road, Lawton. The refuge is 59,000 acres. Your best bets for spotting buffalo are to bring binoculars and have a little patience. Organized nature tours, held throughout the year, get you closer to the action.
Ⓝ 35.750961 Ⓦ 98.682064

ALSO IN OKLAHOMA

Center of the Universe

Tulsa · Speak a few words inside this concrete circle, and your voice will become amplified for no discernible reason.

45th Infantry Museum

Oklahoma City · See the mirror from Hitler's Berlin bunker and a Mickey Mouse gas mask made for kids.

THE GRAVE OF ELMER MCCURDY

GUTHRIE

It was 1976. Crew members from the TV show *The Six Million Dollar Man* were preparing to shoot on location at the Pike Amusement Park in Long Beach, California. The plan was to capture Steve Austin, the titular pricey fellow, riding in one of the cars along the track of a spooky ride called the "Laff in the Dark." The ride featured a tunnel in which ghouls, demons, and skeletons would pop up and scare you as your car jolted from side to side in the dark.

While sprucing up the set, a stagehand spotted a mannequin hanging from a noose in the corner. He reached for the mannequin's arm and was surprised when it broke off in his hand. Looking at the dismembered limb, the worker was astonished to see what looked like bone beneath desiccated layers of skin. This was no mannequin. This was a man.

The hanging corpse in question belonged to Elmer McCurdy, an outlaw who died 65 years earlier. In 1911, the mischief-making vagabond robbed a train near Okesa, Oklahoma, then took his spoils—$46 and two jugs of whiskey—north, where he holed up in a barnyard on the Kansas border. Police pursued him and ended up killing him in a shootout.

McCurdy's body was taken to a funeral home in Pawhuska, but no one claimed it. Seeing a money-making opportunity, the undertaker embalmed him and allowed visitors to view the preserved corpse if they placed a nickel in its mouth.

Five years into this lucrative scheme, a carnival runner turned up at the funeral home claiming to be a long-lost relative of McCurdy and requested to take the body so it could be laid to rest properly. He was, of course, lying through his teeth. Within weeks, the McCurdy corpse was the star attraction of a traveling carnival.

For 60 years, McCurdy's mummy made the rounds of carnivals, wax museums, and haunted houses, until it turned up, inexplicably, at the Pike in Long Beach. By this time, the legend of Outlaw McCurdy was long forgotten, and the body assumed to be fake. After the *Six Million Dollar* discovery, police identified McCurdy and sent the body to Summit View Cemetery in Guthrie, Oklahoma, for long-delayed interment.

McCurdy's grave is marked by a stone that lists his death date as 1911 and burial date as 1977, with no elaboration on the matter.

Summit View Cemetery, North Pine Street, Guthrie. McCurdy's grave is in the Boot Hill section near Wild Bunch bandit Bill Doolin.
Ⓝ 35.878937 Ⓦ 97.425318

SOUTH DAKOTA
THUNDERHEAD FALLS

RAPID CITY

To see this 30-foot (9 m) waterfall, you will need to journey 600 feet (183 m) into a mountain. Thunderhead Falls is located in the tunnels of a disused gold mine established in the 1870s. To the miners tunneling for treasure, the gushing torrent that spewed forth was an inconvenient surprise amid more general disappointment— the mine never yielded any gold, and was abandoned by the time the 20th century rolled around.

With no gold in them hills, Thunderhead Falls was forgotten until 1949, when Vera Eklund boarded a sightseeing train from Rapid City to Mystic and noticed a stream of water flowing down the side of a mountain. Eklund and her husband, Albert, returned to the site to track down the source of the stream and found the underground waterfall. The Eklunds acquired the land and opened Thunderhead Falls to the public as a tourist attraction the following year. With a tromp through the musty tunnels, you too can experience the highs and lows of the gold-rush days.

10 miles (16 km) from Rapid City along Highway 44 West. Ⓝ 44.066968 Ⓦ 103.409214

Water rushes through an old gold mine deep inside a mountain.

ALSO IN SOUTH DAKOTA

Petrified Wood Park

Lemmon · A park the size of a city block is filled with 100 conical sculptures created out of petrified wood in the early 1930s.

Crazy Horse Memorial

Custer · Begun in 1948, this sculpture of the Oglala Lakota Chief, carved out of a mountain, is still in progress. Completion is a long way off, but the ultimate vision is to create the world's largest sculpture, at 641 feet (195 m) wide and 563 feet (172 m) high. For now, you can see the fully carved head, which is 87 feet (26 m) tall. (For comparison, the presidential heads at Mount Rushmore are 60 feet [18 m] tall.)

WYOMING
PHINDELI TOWN

BUFORD

Until 2013, PhinDeli was known as Buford. The town sign provided a unique photo opportunity: Planted beside the dusty main road, it read BUFORD; POP: 1; ELEV: 8000. That one crucial person tallied was Don Sammons, a Vietnam vet who moved to Buford in 1980.

Founded in 1866 during the construction of the First Transcontinental Railroad, Buford reached a peak population of around 2,000 people. As the rail line moved west, however, so did the workers. When Sammons, his wife, Terry, and son arrived in Buford in 1980 hoping for a quiet life, they got it: The trio comprised the entire population of Buford. In 1992, the family bought the town—consisting of a gas station, convenience store, modular home, garage, and surrounding land—for $155,000.

After Sammons's wife died and his son moved to Colorado, it was time for a change. In 2012, Buford went up for auction and was snatched up for $900,000 by mystery investors from Vietnam. The next year, the plan for the town was revealed: The PhinDeli Corporation, makers of Vietnamese coffee, intended to capture a share of the US market by establishing a branded town in the American heartland.

The town of PhinDeli now sells Vietnamese coffee in its convenience store. Though Sammons has moved to Colorado to be closer to his son, the population is still one: a caretaker who lives in the town's only house.

Interstate 80 between Laramie and Cheyenne. No visit to PhinDeli is complete without a trip to its only attraction: the Buford Trading Post. It has a restroom, gas, and, of course, coffee. Ⓝ 41.123688 Ⓦ 105.302292

Devil's Kettle

LAKE SUPERIOR

CAN

Hoegh Pet
Caskets

MINNESOTA

Marvin's Marvelous
Mechanical Museum

Kovac
Planetarium

DETROIT

Questionable Medical
Device Collection

LAKE
HURON

World's
Quietest
Room

WISCONSIN

Edison's
Last Breath

Dr. Evermor's
Forevertron

MICHIGAN

House on
the Rock

DETROIT

LAKE ERIE

CHICAGO

PA

Leather Archives

Crystal
Cave

Red Gate Woods

IOWA

INDIANA

OHIO

Villisca Ax Murder House

Rotary Jail
Museum

World's Largest
Ball of Paint

ILLINOIS

CINCINNATI

SubTropolis

Slocum Puzzle
Collection

Leila's Hair
Museum

American Sign
Museum   CINCINNATI

KS

MISSOURI

Cincinnati
Subway

OK

AR

TN

KY

ILLINOIS
LEATHER ARCHIVES & MUSEUM
CHICAGO

The sign above the door of this former church says LA&M in large white letters. A picture of a black boot to the left gives a tiny hint of what's inside, but no passerby would guess that this is a museum devoted to alternative sexual practices.

The Leather Archives & Museum documents the leather lifestyle, a subculture mostly associated with gay men, fetish, and BDSM—though the museum encompasses all sexualities and genders. The collection includes clothing, books, photos, and provocative paintings like *The Last Supper in a Gay Leather Bar with Judas Giving Christ the Finger*. The Dungeon displays fetish and BDSM items such as a stainless-steel male chastity device and a red leather spanking bench.

6418 North Greenview Avenue, Chicago. The museum is open from Thursday to Sunday. You must be 18 or older to visit the galleries. Ⓝ 41.998637 Ⓦ 87.668273

Galloping Ghost Arcade

Brookfield • Hundreds of arcade games await your coin-inserting, button-mashing presence in this suburban den.

Shit Fountain

East Village • This oversize bronze coil of feces is both a tribute to doggie defecation and a reminder to pick it up.

Lizzadro Museum of Lapidary Art

Elmhurst • Cut and polished stones, some carefully sculpted into mini boats and temples, are on display at this jade-lover's paradise.

U-505

Hyde Park • After sustaining much damage during World War II, the most unlucky U-boat in the German fleet is on display at the Museum of Science and Industry.

Oz Park

Lincoln Park • This *Wizard of Oz*–themed urban oasis features statues of the Tin Man, the Scarecrow, the Cowardly Lion, Dorothy, and Toto.

Busy Beaver Button Co.

Logan Square • Ever wanted to visit a museum dedicated solely to pinback buttons? Busy Beaver's got what you need.

Chicago Cultural Center's Tiffany Dome

The Loop • Completed in 1897, this 38-foot-wide, zodiac-themed Tiffany dome is made of about 30,000 pieces of glass.

Chicago Temple

The Loop • Those affected by vertigo may have trouble worshipping at the First United Methodist Church of Chicago, which is located on top of a 23-story skyscraper.

Money Museum

The Loop • See a money pit and stand in the shadow of a million bucks at this museum dedicated to the almighty dollar.

Pritzker Military Museum & Library

The Loop • The citizen soldier is the focus of this library, which opened in 2003. Along with more than 40,000 volumes on the subject, it offers military posters, recruitment art, soldiers' journals, and Civil War memorabilia.

SS *Eastland* Memorial

The Loop • Learn how a ship that sank in just 20 feet (6 m) of water, a mere 20 feet from shore, resulted in more than 800 deaths.

Bohemian National Cemetery

North Park • Established by members of the city's Czech community in 1877, this cemetery features a rare glass-fronted columbarium—a structure that stores the ashes of the deceased.

Pullman Historic District

Pullman • Take a stroll through the first planned industrial community in the United States, established in 1880.

Eternal Silence

Uptown • A shrouded statue in Graceland Cemetery imbued with creepy legends.

Garfield–Clarendon Model Railroad Club

Uptown • A small, long-running miniature train club has built one of the largest model rail lines in the United States.

Inez Clarke Monument

Uptown • Legend has it that this 19th-century statue of a wide-eyed young girl regularly comes to life and explores the surrounding Graceland Cemetery.

Fountain of Time

Washington Park • This concrete depiction of 100 humans at various stages of life is a solid reminder of the inescapable nature of time.

RED GATE WOODS

LEMONT

Standing on a grassy clearing in Red Gate Woods just outside Chicago is a gravestone with a most unusual inscription: CAUTION—DO NOT DIG.

The grave marker pays tribute not to a person, but a project: nuclear research. Buried beneath the stone is radioactive waste from Chicago Pile-1, the world's first artificial nuclear reactor.

Nicknamed CP-1, the reactor was built in 1942 as part of the Manhattan Project, the United States initiative to develop an atomic bomb during World War II. The reactor was a literal pile: In a squash court beneath the stands of Stagg Field, the University of Chicago's football field, Italian physicist Enrico Fermi and his team of scientists built a stack of uranium pellets and bricks of graphite, interspersed with cadmium control rods. On December 2, the control rods were removed and the reactor went critical.

Following the initial testing, CP-1 was disassembled in 1943, moved to Red Gate Woods, and rebuilt, with a radiation shield for safety, as a new reactor named CP-2. Another experimental reactor, CP-3, followed in 1944. When the Manhattan Project scientists were done with these reactors, they dismantled them and buried the remains in the woods, at spots marked Plot M and Site A. Both are now marked by granite monuments—Plot M has the headstone marked DO NOT DIG.

Though the buried waste is radioactive, the site poses no threat to public safety—Geiger counter readings in the area are consistent with standard background radiation levels.

Archer Avenue, Lemont. Ⓝ 41.699599 Ⓦ 87.921223

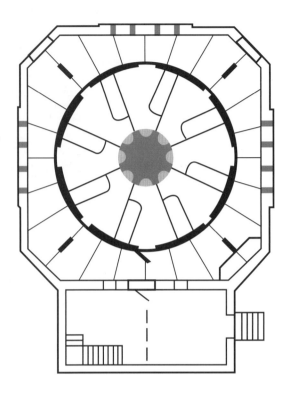

Spinning jails, built across the Midwest in the 1880s, rotated like carousels. Unfortunately, they also sometimes crushed prisoners' hands between the bars.

INDIANA
ROTARY JAIL MUSEUM

CRAWFORDSVILLE

In the spring of 1881, architect William H. Brown and iron foundry owner Benjamin F. Haugh, both of Indianapolis, filed a patent for a most ingenious innovation: a jail with revolving cells.

Their design consisted of a two-tier cylindrical cell block with a central column that served as both support and plumbing for the individual toilets in the cells. Each tier had eight wedge-shaped cells, but the surrounding structure had only one door. When a guard rotated a hand crank, the cell block spun, sending the prisoners on a disorienting carousel ride past the lone access point.

Brown and Haugh's invention quickly became a reality. In 1882, the first spinning jail, a two-tiered, 16-cell institution known as Montgomery County Rotary Jail, opened in Crawfordsville, Indiana. Other states in the Midwest soon got in on the idea—the three-tiered, rotating Pottawattamie County Jail, nicknamed the "Squirrel Cage Jail," opened in Iowa in 1885, followed by a single-story spinning jail in Gallatin, Missouri, in 1889. As many as 18 rotary jails were built in the United States, mostly in the Midwest.

Unfortunately, Brown and Haugh's novel, almost whimsical design had its flaws. Chief among them was the fact that a prisoner standing at the front of a cell with his hands resting on the bars had a decent chance of getting an arm crushed when the rotary mechanism was engaged. Natural light was scant, ventilation was poor, and mechanical problems could interfere with the operation of a jail. In the case of a fire, all the prisoners whose cells weren't aligned with the access door would likely be doomed.

In light of these problems, many rotary jails had their turntables immobilized during the 1930s. After operating in a modified state for decades, Montgomery County Jail closed for good in 1973. Pottawattamie County Jail sent its prisoners away in 1969, while the Gallatin jail shut up shop in 1975. All three now operate as museums. Montgomery County is the only one that still spins.

225 North Washington Street, Crawfordsville.
Ⓝ 40.043839 Ⓦ 86.901742

World's Largest Ball of Paint

ALEXANDRIA

Suspended from the rafters in a small shed behind the Carmichael family home is a 4,000-pound (1.8 MT) ball. Buried at its core is a baseball—the rest is paint.

When Michael Carmichael was a teenager in the 1960s, he and a friend were tossing a baseball in a paint shop and knocked over a gallon of paint. The ball was covered, and Michael's head was overtaken by an ambitious idea. Every day during his last two years of high school he applied a new coat of paint to the ball. He made it to 1,000 coats before losing interest. But a decade later, the idea resurfaced. In January 1, 1977, Michael rustled up a fresh baseball and presented it to his three-year-old son, who brushed on a coat of blue paint. Thus began the odyssey of the second, and current, Ball of Paint.

That ball has now been painted about 25,000 times. Michael, his wife Glenda, their children, their grandchildren, and a stream of visitors have all applied layers. Anyone is welcome to pick up a brush, and there is only one rule: Each new coat must be a different color than the last.

10696 North 200 West, Alexandria. The ball is located at the Carmichael family residence—call ahead to schedule a viewing or painting appointment. Ⓝ 40.258752 Ⓦ 85.709122

14-foot (4.3 m) circumference

What began as a painted baseball has turned into a spherical tribute to the power of persistence.

Slocum Mechanical Puzzle Collection

BLOOMINGTON

"Mechanical puzzles" are those brain-teasers that must be physically manipulated to achieve a specific outcome. Jerry Slocum began collecting mechanical puzzles as a child, eventually becoming the unofficial authority on the subject with the publication of his 1986 book, *Puzzles Old and New*. By 2006 he had accumulated over 40,000 mechanical puzzles, thanks in part to the International Puzzle Party, an annual private get-together for mechanical puzzle enthusiasts and traders, which Slocum inaugurated in 1978.

In 2006, he donated over 30,000 of the puzzles to the Lilly Library at Indiana University to create

Around 30,000 manually operated mind-benders make up the Slocum puzzle collection.

the Slocum Mechanical Puzzle Collection. In addition to the staggering number of puzzles, Slocum also donated thousands of books about puzzles. Among the pieces on display (only a few hundred out of the thousands in the collection) are an archaic Rubik's Cube with differing sizes of nails on each side, called a "texture cube"; a trick cup that seems normal until its drinker fills it too full and it drains away into the base; and more whimsical amusements like a Coke bottle with a wooden arrow through it. There are also countless intricate wooden geometrical curiosities that must be twisted and shifted together and apart.

Today, visitors to the library can actually try out a number of the puzzles and see countless others sitting in displays, just waiting to be solved.

1200 East Seventh Street, Bloomington. Ⓝ 39.167906 Ⓦ 86.518973

IOWA

VILLISCA AX MURDER HOUSE

VILLISCA

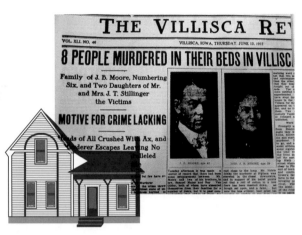

For a unique overnight stay, book a night in the home where eight people were once slaughtered in their beds as they slept.

In 1912, this house belonged to the Moore family: married couple Josiah and Sarah and their young children, Herman, Katherine, Boyd, and Paul. On the night of June 9, the family returned from Children's Day services at the local church, accompanied by two of the girls' friends: eight-year-old Ina Stillinger and her twelve-year-old sister, Lena.

Sometime between midnight and 5 a.m., an unknown person entered the house and murdered every person inside by striking their heads with an ax. From observations at the crime scene it appears that all were asleep at the time they were killed, apart from Lena, who exhibited a defensive wound on her arm and was positioned across her bed.

Over a century later, the case remains unsolved. The main suspect, traveling minister Reverend George Kelly, had taught at the church on June 9 and left town at approximately 5 a.m. the next day. He was tried twice but never convicted.

The Villisca Ax Murder House, as it is now bluntly known, was purchased in 1994 by Darwin and Martha Linn and restored to its 1912 state. You can tour the home by day, then spend the night in a room that was once a blood-soaked crime scene.

508 East 2nd Street, Villisca. All eight victims of the ax murders are at Villisca Cemetery, a 15-minute walk north of the house. Ⓝ 40.930704 Ⓦ 94.973316 ➡

➡ Other Murder Houses

LIZZIE BORDEN BED & BREAKFAST
FALL RIVER, MA

The tagline of this eight-room hotel is "Where everyone is treated like family!" Ordinarily that might sound like a good thing, but getting treated like Lizzie Borden's family means copping a hatchet to the head.

On the morning of August 4, 1892, the bodies of Lizzie's father, Andrew, and stepmother, Abby, were found in separate rooms of the family home. Both had been bludgeoned in the head with an ax. Lizzie, who had been in or near the house during the time of the murders, was arrested a week later and stood trial in June the following year.

Despite contradicting herself during her testimony and incurring

the ire of lead prosecutor Hosea Knowlton, Lizzie received an acquittal from the jury.

The house in which Abby and Andrew met their bloody ends is now a Borden-themed bed and breakfast. You can stay in the very rooms where Lizzie's parents took their last gasping breaths. Good night, sleep tight, don't let the ax murderer strike.

AMITYVILLE HORROR HOUSE
AMITYVILLE, NY

On the evening of November 13, 1974, 23-year-old Ronald "Butch" DeFeo Jr. murdered his parents and four younger siblings in their home at 112 Ocean Avenue. DeFeo then went to a bar down the road, where he ran in screaming for help, claiming his parents had been shot by a mob hit man.

When the deaths were confirmed and DeFeo was brought into the local police station for questioning, inconsistencies began to appear in his story. The following day, DeFeo confessed to the murders, telling police that once he started, he couldn't stop.

After DeFeo was given six consecutive sentences

Gruesome murders turned this family home into a morbid attraction.

of 25 years to life, the Lutz family, consisting of George and Kathy Lutz and their three children, moved into the house on Ocean Avenue. Less than a month later, they vacated the place permanently, claiming paranormal activity had made it impossible to live there.

The Lutzes' supernatural claims, which include descriptions of mysterious voices, slime oozing from the walls, and red glowing eyes appearing in the dark, were dramatized in the 1977 book *The Amityville Horror*, which has since been adapted into multiple films. The "based on a true story" tagline has never been corroborated with evidence.

The house at 112 Ocean Avenue (now 108 Ocean Avenue), an iconic part of American pop culture, is still private property—view it from afar if you like, but there's no need to warn the current inhabitants of the supposed supernatural peril. They've heard it all before.

MICHIGAN
HOEGH PET CASKETS

GLADSTONE

A tour of Hoegh Pet Caskets, established 1966, begins in the showroom. There, lined up on plinths against the walls, are blue, pink, white, and camouflage caskets ranging from 10 to 52 inches (25–132 cm) in length.

After seeing the finished products, it's time to see the factory, where 18 caskets are made every hour. The tour concludes at Hoegh's mock pet cemetery, where the recently bereaved can get ideas for conducting a final farewell to Spanky or Mittens.

The caskets, which are shipped all over the world, are not just for animals—they are also purchased by amputees who want to lay their severed limbs to rest.

311 Delta Avenue, Gladstone. Tours available daily.
Ⓝ 45.849229 Ⓦ 87.011343

Departed critters and amputated limbs are lovingly laid to rest in Hoegh's plush coffins.

MARVIN'S MARVELOUS MECHANICAL MUSEUM

FARMINGTON HILLS

At this overstimulating penny arcade you can play tic-tac-toe with a chicken, witness a mechanical depiction of the Spanish Inquisition, and marry a friend via the AutoWed machine.

The crowded lineup of vintage and new games, automata, and oddities belongs to Marvin Yagoda, who has been collecting coin-operated machines since 1960. The standard pinball, Skee-ball, and fortune-teller machines are interspersed with more atypical fare like Dr. Ralph Bingenpurge, a mechanical food inspector who vomits with violent and disturbing realism.

Marvin's is a good place to visit if you're unsure of what to do with your life—get a reading from a mechanical fortune-teller, then consult the career machine, which will tell you whether your ideal job is chorus girl, bootlegger, or soda jerk.

31005 Orchard Lake Road, Farmington Hills. Look for the big clock. Ⓝ 42.525442 Ⓦ 83.361727

Coin-operated oddities dance, dole out prizes, and, in one case, vomit continuously.

EDISON'S LAST BREATH

DEARBORN

In a display case at the Henry Ford Museum is a sealed test tube labeled "Edison's Last Breath?" The question mark is key: The great inventor didn't wheeze his final exhalation straight into the tube before falling back into the pillows and expiring. But the real story is just as compelling. And it begins with a long friendship between two prolific inventors.

In 1891, Henry Ford got a job as an engineer at the Edison Illuminating Company. The future car manufacturer regarded Edison as a personal hero, but the two men didn't meet until 1896. That year, Ford built his first vehicle: the four-wheeled, gas-powered Ford Quadricycle. Edison's positive response to the vehicle encouraged Ford to keep working on gas-powered cars. He left the Edison Illuminating Company and, in 1908, debuted the revolutionary Model T.

Edison and Ford's friendship remained strong well into the 20th century. In 1916, Ford purchased the property beside Edison's vacation home in Fort Myers, Florida. When Edison needed a wheelchair due to his failing health, Ford bought a matching one so they could race around the grounds.

In 1931, Edison died at his New Jersey home in the presence of his son, Charles. Beside the inventor's death bed was a rack of test tubes. Charles took one, had it sealed with paraffin, and sent it to Ford as a final memento of his dear friend.

20900 Oakwood Boulevard, Dearborn. The test tube is near the front door. Ⓝ 42.303109 Ⓦ 88.229686

MINNESOTA
WORLD'S QUIETEST ROOM

MINNEAPOLIS

You may think silence is peaceful until you visit Orfield Laboratories. The lab is home to an anechoic chamber: a room that has no echo. 99.99 percent of all sound made inside the chamber is absorbed by bouncy 3-foot-thick foam wedges that cover every surface.

Within seconds of entering, you will notice sounds you don't usually hear: The beat of your heart, the flow of your breath, and the gurgling of your digestive system start to become unnerving. Visitors often become disoriented, especially if lab founder Steven Orfield turns out the lights. Most don't last beyond a few minutes. Half an hour is unimaginable.

Manufacturers use the quiet room during product testing to gauge the volume of switches, displays, and other components.

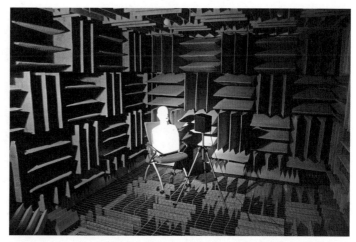

After just a few minutes in the noiseless room, aural hallucinations set in.

The chamber has been Guinness-certified as the quietest place in the world, with an ambient noise level of –9 decibels. (A quiet bedroom at night is around 30 decibels.) **2709 East 25th Street, Minneapolis. Ⓝ 44.957042 Ⓦ 93.232773**

ALSO IN MINNESOTA

House of Balls

Minneapolis · Local sculptor Allen Christian established this funhouse of found art as a physical incarnation of his idea that "we all possess the creative impulse and we owe ourselves the balls to express it."

QUESTIONABLE MEDICAL DEVICE COLLECTION

ST. PAUL

During the 1930s and '40s, American parents needing to take their kids shoe shopping could provide them with a fun incentive. Many stores at the time had shoe-fitting fluoroscopes, which used X-rays to show how a child's feet fit into their new shoes. The kid would insert his or her shoe-clad foot into the four-foot-high wooden box, and a salesperson would peer into a peephole to look at the position of the bones.

It wasn't until 1957—after the long-term effects of radiation exposure became better understood—that shoe-fitting fluoroscopes started getting banned in the US. (They made shopping for boots a real kick, but they also leaked radiation.)

The foot fluoroscope is one of hundreds of fraudulent and dangerous medical devices on show at the Science Museum of Minnesota. You'll also find a vibratory chair from 1900 (it shakes violently to stimulate digestion), a foot-operated breast enlarger pump from the mid-'70s, and the Relax-A-Cizor, a 1960s weight-loss device that delivered electric shocks to muscles.

Roger's Vitalator Violet Ray medical appliance was used in electrotherapy to cure a wide array of ailments.

Science Museum of Minnesota, 120 West Kellogg Boulevard, St. Paul. Ⓝ 44.953703 Ⓦ 93.089958

The right half of the waterfall goes into the river, while the left half just disappears.

THE DEVIL'S KETTLE

GRAND MARAIS

A large rock bisects the Brule River in Judge C.R. Magney State Park. The water that flows to the east tumbles 50 feet (15 m) down a cliff and continues toward Lake Superior. The water that flows to the west enters a hole and disappears.

Known as the Devil's Kettle, this water portal to nowhere has long puzzled Minnesotans. In attempts to trace the underground flow, researchers have dropped objects such as ping-pong balls and dye into the hole. So far, all efforts to map the water's path have proven fruitless.

Judge C. R. Magney State Park (Highway 61). Ⓝ 47.828945 Ⓦ 90.049609

MISSOURI

SubTropolis

KANSAS CITY

Beneath the limestone bluffs on the north side of the Missouri River lies a vast underground city. Known as SubTropolis, the 2-square-mile man-made cave is used for corporate workspaces and storage. According to its creators, it is the world's largest underground business complex.

Limestone mining began in the bluffs during the 1940s. Two decades later, the Hunt Midwest company began renting out office and storage space in the carved-out cliffs. Today, SubTropolis houses everything from the original *Gone With the Wind* and *Wizard of Oz* film reels to USPS commemorative stamps.

The unchanging ambient conditions—temperature of 65° to 70°F (18–21°C); humidity of 40 to 50 percent—assist with preservation and save energy by making it unnecessary to heat or cool the space.
8300 Northeast Underground Drive. See inside SubTropolis by participating in the annual Groundhog Run, a 5K foot race held in the complex each January. Ⓝ 39.157638 Ⓦ 94.478478

An eco-friendly mega warehouse hidden underground.

Leila's Hair Museum

KANSAS CITY

The wreaths, bouquets, and pieces of jewelry in Leila's Hair Museum are made from woven strands of human hair, shorn from Victorian heads.

Peaking in popularity in the mid-19th century, hair art and jewelry functioned as tokens of mourning, family heirlooms, and gifts between friends or lovers.

Locks of hair became personal mementos and served as "portraits" of an individual or family in an era when photography was not yet widely accessible. Some of the wreaths adorning the museum walls incorporate hair from multiple generations, twisted into flowers and vines that reflect the family tree. Friends and relatives of the recently departed wore bracelets made from the deceased's hair, or lockets with hair tucked inside.

Museum founder and cosmetology school owner Leila Cohoon began collecting hair art in 1949. The thousands of pieces on exhibit comprise the world's only museum dedicated to this near-extinct art form.
1333 South Noland Road, Independence. The museum is 1.5 miles (2.4 km) southeast of the Independence Amtrak station. Ⓝ 39.076007 Ⓦ 94.413452

ALSO IN MISSOURI

Glore Psychiatric Museum

St. Joseph · The Lunatic Box and the Tranquilizer Chair are among the exhibits that illustrate the starkly different way mental health was treated in the 18th and 19th centuries.

Leila Cohoon celebrates an extensive collection of Victorian jewelry made from human hair.

OHIO

CINCINNATI'S LOST SUBWAY

CINCINNATI

In the early years of the 20th century, Cincinnati's streets were clogged with slow-moving street-cars, crowds of pedestrians, horse carriages, and a few of those new-fangled contraptions known as automobiles.

At the time, the Boston, New York, and Philadelphia sub-ways had just started operating. Cincinnati needed a rapid transit system, and an underground rail-road seemed the obvious solution. The city raised money via bonds, and Cincinnati residents voted in favor of the subway in April 1917.

Unfortunately, this was pre-cisely the month that the US became involved in World War I. Suddenly, bonds stopped being issued and construction had to be halted. When the war ended 19 months later, building costs skyrocketed. The city resumed the subway project in 1920, but had to stop work in 1927 when the money ran out. More than 2 miles (3.2 km) of tunnels had been built, as well as seven sta-tions, but tracks were never laid.

Cincinnati still doesn't have a subway system. The stock mar-ket crash of 1929, the increasing popularity of the automobile, and the United States's involvement in another global war all contributed to the abandonment of the project.

The three above-ground sta-tions have been demolished, but the tunnels and four underground stations remain. Appearance-wise, little has changed since the '20s—parts of the Liberty Street station were converted into a nuclear fall-out shelter during the 1960s, and a water main was laid in the tunnel in 1957, but besides that it's just dusty platforms, musty smells, and stairs leading to nowhere. **The tunnel runs under Central Parkway for 2 miles (3.2 km), beginning at Walnut Street and ending just north of the Western Hills Viaduct. Tours of the tunnel are conducted once a year. Accessing the subway system at other times constitutes trespassing. Ⓝ 39.107302 Ⓦ 84.512853**

Despite decades of planning and construction, Cincinnati's underground train tunnels have never been used.

CRYSTAL CAVE

PUT-IN-BAY

Ohio's Crystal Cave is not a cave at all, but rather a single rock. It is the world's largest known geode, and its walls are lined with huge white-blue celestite crystals, some as much as 3 feet long.

This hidden gem was discovered about 40 feet (60.4 m) below the ground in 1897, by workers digging a well for the Heineman Winery. Upon exploring the cavern, winery owner Gustav Heineman found that his business was sitting on top of a vug, or large cavity within a rock. Emerging from the limestone walls of the cavity are countless crystals, composed of strontium sulfate, better known as the mineral celestite.

Heineman opened up the giant geode to visitors, and this unique attraction sustained the winery through the years of Prohibition. Today, Crystal Cave is even larger but perhaps less stunning than it once was, as many of the crystals were mined over the years to manufacture fireworks. Yet it remains a natural wonder unlike anything else.

The cave is best explored with a glass of wine or grape juice, as part of the overall Heineman Winery tour. ⓝ 41.646648 Ⓦ 82.826842

Come for the wine; stay for the world's largest geode.

AMERICAN SIGN MUSEUM

CINCINNATI

Some people rage against the indignities of middle age by buying a sports car. Tod Swormstedt founded a sign museum.

Swormstedt's self-proclaimed "midlife crisis project" began in 1999 as a real-world version of *Signs of the Times*, a trade magazine about sign making and outdoor advertising that he edited and published.

In 2005, his newly named American Sign Museum opened to the public. It is now crammed with fiberglass mascots, neon marquees, and hand-painted 19th-century signs advertising cobblers, druggists, and haberdashers. Tours

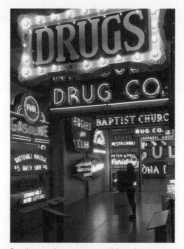

Get buzzed on neon at this ode to old-school Americana.

are accompanied by an ever-present buzz from all the neon. Visit on a weekday to get a glimpse of the neon shop, where employees from Neonworks of Cincinnati demonstrate how they make signs.

1330 Monmouth Avenue, Cincinnati. ⓝ 39.145530 Ⓦ 84.539904

Also in Ohio

Haserot Angel

Cleveland · Due to the effect of weathering and erosion, this bronze angel at Lakeview Cemetery appears to be weeping black tears.

WISCONSIN
HOUSE ON THE ROCK
SPRING GREEN

Opened to the public in 1960, this attraction is a window into the unusual mind of Alex Jordan, who built the home as a weekend retreat.

Jordan was a collector with eclectic tastes. Over decades, he filled the house with an astounding array of objects: pipe organs, dollhouses, antique weapons, coin-operated music machines, chandeliers, and miniature circuses, to name a few. Jordan died in 1989, but his house of treasures lives on.

The collection takes hours to walk through and can induce sensory overload. Two parts of the house really stand out: the Carousel Room and the Infinity Room. The Carousel Room contains the world's largest merry-go-round, featuring 269 animals—none of which are horses. The Infinity Room, built in 1985, is a cantilevered, glass-walled hallway that extends 218 feet (66.5 m) out over the valley. A walk through the house raises a lot of questions: Is this all real? Why is that massive sea monster battling a giant squid, and how does it relate to the robot orchestra? Don't look for answers. Just marvel.

5754 State Road 23, Spring Green. The town is about 2 hours from Milwaukee. Ⓝ 43.090644 Ⓦ 90.131808

By turns creepy, campy, and beautiful, House on the Rock features a carousel tricked out with angels, 20,000 string lights, and 182 chandeliers.

KOVAC PLANETARIUM

RHINELANDER

On an October afternoon in 1996, Frank Kovac and his fellow Boy Scouts ventured to Mud Creek Observatory and waited for the sun to set so they could gaze at the universe. But when it was finally dark, cloud cover made stargazing impossible.

Annoyed at the clouds for, in his words, "obscuring the universe," Kovac decided to create his own celestial sphere. He spent a decade building a 2-ton, 22-foot-wide (1.8 MT, 6.7 m) rotating globe and painting the interior with every northern hemisphere star visible to the naked eye.

The Kovac Planetarium is only the fourth mechanical globe ever created. Kovac treats visitors to a sky show that lives up to its motto: "Kovac Planetarium, Where the Universe Revolves Around You."

2392 Mud Creek Road, Rhinelander. Ⓝ 45.573826 Ⓦ 89.065458

DR. EVERMOR'S FOREVERTRON

NORTH FREEDOM

Nestled in the trees on a remote stretch of Highway 12 is the Forevertron, a 19th-century spacecraft built by an eccentric man named Dr. Evermor.

Dr. Evermor didn't exist until 1983. That's when former industrial wrecking and salvage expert Tom Every retired and assumed the alter ego of a Victorian professor and inventor. Having amassed a personal collection of beautiful old machinery components during his wreck-and-salvage days, Every set about sculpting a scrap-metal spacecraft with an 1890s aesthetic.

The Forevertron comes with a story: Its purpose is to launch Dr. Evermor into the heavens on a magnetic lightning beam. The big

glass egg at the top of the sculpture, latticed with copper, is the doctor's personal space capsule. An elevated gazebo beside the main sculpture allows royalty to watch the launch from a safe vantage point. The Celestial Listening Ears are designed to allow visitors to hear voices from space.

There is no set launch date for the Forevertron. Even if it never blasts into the heavens, it has already earned an impressive distinction: At 50 feet (15 m) high and 120 feet (36.5 m) wide, it's the largest scrap metal sculpture in the world.

US 12, North Freedom. The Forevertron is 5 miles (8 km) south of Baraboo, on a gravel road behind Delaney's Surplus Sales.
Ⓝ 43.375669 Ⓦ 89.768549

ALSO IN WISCONSIN

FAST Fiberglass Mold Graveyard

Sparta · The molds once used to make roadside sculptures, from menacing sharks to goofy giant mice to a towering Santa Claus, have been strewn across this grassy lot, making it look like the ruins of a particularly quirky civilization.

If all goes according to plan, this scrap metal sculpture will blast into space carrying its creator.

DELIGHTFULLY GOOFY DINOSAUR PARKS

Whether created for the purposes of entertainment, education, or some combination thereof, dino parks are a proud part of the great American road trip. Just don't rely on them for anatomical accuracy.

DINOSAUR PARK
RAPID CITY, SD

The half-dozen concrete dinosaurs perched on a hill overlooking Rapid City look pretty absurd. The round-jawed, smiling tyrannosaur appears to have double-jointed forelimbs. The duck-billed trachodon—now known as an anatotitan—stands upright and awkward, forced into a bipedal stance and looking resentful about it.

A stegosaurus, a triceratops, and a brontosaurus (since reclassified as an apatosaurus) stand nearby, looking as though they arrived from the same cartoonlike alternate dimension.

The dinosaurs were built in 1936 at the height of the Great Depression. Aside from an occasional fresh coat of bright green paint, they haven't changed

since. Though their design diverges wildly from the fossil record, the Rapid City dinos are imposing enough—until a car bound for Mount Rushmore stops by and kids clamber all over the stegosaurus spines.

CABAZON DINOSAURS
CABAZON, CA

Since the 1980s, travelers barreling down Southern California's Interstate 10 have been greeted by

a 150-foot-long (45.7 m) apatosaurus and a 65-foot-tall (20 m) T. rex.

Theme park artist and sand sculptor Claude K. Bell began building the steel-and-concrete dinosaurs, known as Dinny and Mr. Rex, in 1964. The main aim was to create hollow, climbable structures that would attract more customers to his Wheel Inn diner next door. But Bell also had a more

Argentinosaurus

personal motive: After spending years building sand sculptures and watching them disappear in the wind, he wanted to create something permanent.

Bell finished the apatosaurus in 1973 and began construction on the T. rex in 1981. He died in 1988, but not before seeing his dinosaurs achieve fame—they were featured in commercials, music videos, and the 1985 film *Pee-wee's Big Adventure*.

Since being sold in the mid-1990s, the Cabazon dinosaurs have changed dramatically, but not in a way that's visible from the outside. In short, they've found God. Dinny's belly now contains a gift shop and museum operated by creationists. Signs and displays espouse the view that dinosaurs were created along with humans 6,000 years ago.

Beside Dinny and Mr. Rex is an open-air robotic dinosaur museum. It features a medieval knight jousting with a velociraptor.

DINOSAUR LAND
WHITE POST, VA

Somehow, sculptures of King Kong, a giant cobra, and a monstrous praying mantis ended up here among the T. rexes and pterodactyls. And then there are the walk-through shark and octopus.

None of it makes much sense, but Dinosaur Land, built in the 1960s, still has enough dinosaurs to justify its name. Many have been sculpted in attack poses, making them particularly suitable for creative photo composition. Make sure you stop by the giganotosaurus that is casually chomping a pterodactyl out of the sky.

Pterodactyl

Tyrannosaurus rex

Triceratops

THE SOUTHEAST

CIA Museum
WASHINGTON, DC
The Great
Stalacpipe Organ
VIRGINIA
Vent Haven
Museum
Heigold House
KENTUCKY
NORTH CAROLINA
Devil's Tramping
Ground
Ozark Medieval
Fortress
The Body Farm
Fireflies of the
Great Smoky Mountains
Carnivorous
Plant Garden
TENNESSEE
Pearl Fryar's
Topiary Garden
Mars Bluff Crater
Georgia
Guidestones
ARKANSAS
SOUTH
CAROLINA
Unclaimed
Baggage Center
Crypt of
Civilization
ALABAMA
Oyotunji
Village
MISSISSIPPI
GEORGIA
ATLANTIC
OCEAN
LOUISIANA
Mississippi River
Basin Model
Angola Prison
Rodeo
Spear Hunting
Museum
University of
Florida Bat Houses
Historic Voodoo
Museum
St. Roch
Chapel
Lake
Peigneur
Weeki Wachee
Mermaids
N
FLORIDA
Miles
0   100   200
0   100   200
Kilometers
GULF
OF
MEXICO
Neptune
Memorial Reef
Skunk Ape Research
Headquarters
Stiltsville

ALABAMA

SPEAR HUNTING MUSEUM

SUMMERDALE

Eugene Morris was the greatest spear hunter in the world, according to Eugene Morris. From 2006 until his death at 78 in 2011, Morris maintained the Spear Hunting Museum, dedicated to celebrating his own accomplishments. Though the painted exterior—emblazoned with "Eugene Morris: The Greatest Living Spear Hunter in the World" next to a rendering of the man in action—has had to change, the museum lives on under the administration of his wife, Heather.

Inside the building are many of the 500 animals Morris has killed with spears, including buffalo, lions, zebras, bears, alligators, turkeys, and deer.

Photos of Morris on the prowl line the walls, as do the very spears he once launched into the abdomens of those he hunted down.

Formerly a gun hunter, Morris switched methods in 1968 because shooting animals had become too easy. He first tried bow hunting, then two-handed spears, and finally took to the wilderness with a spear in each hand, poised to strike whatever living creature crossed his path. Sometimes he threw both spears at once, killing two animals simultaneously.

Morris died sitting up, spear in hand. His will specified that the slogan on the museum wall be altered to read "Gene Morris: The Greatest Spear Hunter in Recorded History."

20216 Highway 59, Summerdale. The museum is between Robertsdale and Summerdale.

Ⓝ 30.519810 Ⓦ 87.707679

Passengers' lost property becomes shoppers' treasured bargains.

UNCLAIMED BAGGAGE CENTER

SCOTTSBORO

Every item being sold at this store was once lost in transit. The Unclaimed Baggage Center buys lost luggage from US-based airlines by the truckload and sells the contents to the public in a building the size of a city block.

The clothing, accessories, electronics, and luggage itself are the main offerings, but the staff has also unpacked 3,500-year-old Egyptian burial masks, a stuffed Canada goose, and Hoggle, the curmudgeonly dwarf puppet from the 1986 film *Labyrinth*. He and the salvaged ancient artifacts were never put on sale—they have a permanent home at the center's museum.

509 West Willow Street, Scottsboro, next to Cedar Hill Cemetery. Ⓝ 34.673176 Ⓦ 86.044589

ALSO IN ALABAMA

Monument to Hodges Meteorite

Sylacauga · This marble sculpture pays tribute to a meteorite that, in 1954, crashed into a local home.

ARKANSAS
OZARK MEDIEVAL FORTRESS

LEAD HILL

The plan was ambitious: A team of medieval enthusiasts would spend 20 years building a 13th-century castle using only tools and techniques from the Dark Ages.

The Ozark Medieval Fortress was intended to attract visitors who would pay for the privilege of observing a historic construction site. Opened to the public in 2010, the fortress lasted almost two years before lack of attendance forced its closure. Even the allure of falconry demonstrations and stone carving contests did not make up for the fact that it's pretty dull to stand around watching people build a fortress by hand.

The castle foundations have sat idle since 2012, awaiting a medieval-obsessed investor to get the project going again. There is a precedent for success: France's Guédelon Castle, which is based on the same concept as the Ozark fort, was founded by the same group in 1997. It is scheduled for completion in the 2020s and is flourishing as a tourist destination.

1671 Highway 14 West, Lead Hill. The fortress foundations and construction equipment are still in place, but walking among them requires trespassing beyond a fence. Ⓝ 36.438990 Ⓦ 93.036066

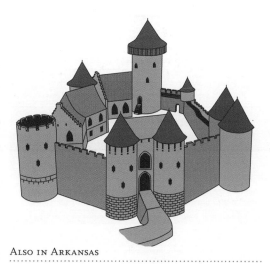

ALSO IN ARKANSAS

Gurdon Light

Gurdon · There's got to be a scientific explanation for this mysterious light that hovers above the railroad tracks, but inventing tall tales is more fun.

Billy Bass Adoption Center

Little Rock · Billy Bass was an animatronic singing fish that was a hugely popular gag gift in the early 2000s. The seafood diner Flying Fish has rows of Billies on its walls, each one given up for adoption by a customer in exchange for free food.

FLORIDA
UNIVERSITY OF FLORIDA BAT HOUSES

GAINESVILLE

When a fire destroyed the University of Florida's Johnson Hall in 1987, the bats living in the attic became homeless. In need of new eaves to inhabit, they nestled into the crannies of the running track bleachers and the tennis stadium. This was less than ideal for athletes and spectators.

In 1991, the university captured thousands of campus bats and relocated them to a giant, newly built, elevated bat house beside a lake. The bats escaped their new home within days. Four years later, they finally came around and moved in for good. Now around 300,000 bats live in the house and its neighboring barn, which was added in 2010.

With a combined capacity of 750,000, the house and barn are the world's largest occupied bat houses. At sunset, the bats emerge and stream across the sky in search of tasty bugs.

Museum Road between Village Drive and Radio Road, across from Lake Alice, University of Florida, Gainesville. The best time to see the bats is on dry, warm evenings in spring through early summer. Beware of falling guano. Ⓝ 29.644211 Ⓦ 82.362859

300,000 bats, cooped up in the world's largest bat houses, wait for sunset.

In shallow waters a mile off Miami stand the former party shacks of Stiltsville.

STILTSVILLE

MIAMI

In 1933, a Miami man known for his chowder—"Crawfish" Eddie—constructed a wooden shack on stilts a mile offshore. Built during the last gasp of Prohibition, the shack soon attracted drinkers and gamblers, who chased their beers and poker hands with a bowl of Eddie's famous chowder.

Crawfish Eddie's was the first shack in Stiltsville, a hodgepodge collection of offshore houses that became a playground for Miami's coolest sinners.

The Quarterdeck Club, an invite-only gentleman's establishment, appeared in 1941. Fishing buddies would anchor between buildings to drink, dine, and cast their lines into the shallow waters from the Quarterdeck's front dock.

The early 1960s was boom time for Stiltsville. Twenty-seven shacks crowded the sand flats, and the new Bikini Club offered free drinks for women in two-pieces and a secluded sundeck for naked lounging. The boom, however, was swiftly followed by busts both governmental and meteorological. The vice squad raided the Bikini Club and shuttered it for operating without a liquor license and possessing 40 unauthorized, undersize, out-of-season crawfish. Then came Hurricane Betsy in 1965, which swept away all but half a dozen shacks.

Many were rebuilt, but by this time the state's patience for Stiltsville shenanigans was wearing thin. Florida issued formal leases to the shack owners with an expiration date of 1999, declaring that any remaining houses would need to be removed. When the crucial date finally arrived—after Hurricane Andrew had destroyed all but seven of the stilt houses—community support helped Stiltsville owners negotiate a deal with the government. The shacks were saved and are now available to rent for parties.

The houses now lie within the boundaries of Biscayne National Park, and are co-managed by the National Parks Service and the Stiltsville Trust. Ⓝ 25.651305 Ⓦ 80.174227

The charmingly kitschy underwater mermaid ballet has been performed since the 1940s.

WEEKI WACHEE MERMAIDS

WEEKI WACHEE

Mermaids have lived in the waters of Weeki Wachee Springs since 1947. That's when swim coach Newt Perry developed an underwater mermaid show, performed at a depth of 20 feet (6 m) by glamorous women in bikini tops and fish tails.

To watch the mermaid show, spectators file into a 400-seat underwater theater built into one side of the spring. The lights dim, gentle music starts playing, and a faded blue curtain rises to reveal the water behind a 100-foot-wide (30.5 m) glass wall. As a voiceover describes the mermaids' world—"water as blue as the loveliest cornflower and as pure as the clearest glass"—one of the mythical creatures swims the length of the window, smiling and waving as the tendrils of her tail waft behind her.

The ensuing show is a lip-synced, music-enhanced retelling of *The Little Mermaid*, complete with handsome prince, evil sea witch, and a terrestrial wedding once the mermaid gets her legs. To breathe underwater, the scuba-certified performers inhale from free-flowing air hoses that snake around the spring. Fish and turtles are unwitting co-stars.

Since the arrival of Disney World in 1971, Weeki Wachee has struggled to attract visitors. During the 1960s there were nine shows a day. Now there are three.

Weeki Wachee Springs State Park, US 19 at State Road 50. Ⓝ 28.491034 Ⓦ 82.632138

ALSO IN FLORIDA

Pinecraft

Sarasota · Between December and April, busloads of Amish and Mennonite vacationers swap their frosty climes for the resort neighborhood of Pinecraft, where popular activities include shuffleboard and lounging—fully dressed—on the beach.

Robert the Doll

Key West · Held in a glass box at the Fort East Martello museum, this innocent-looking doll in a sailor uniform has a reputation for masterminding evil deeds.

Bok Tower Gardens

Lake Wales · A neo-Gothic 205-foot (62.5 m) tower on Iron Mountain houses 60 singing bells.

Cassadaga

Lake Helen · A community of spiritualists offers healing services, psychic readings, and nighttime spirit photography.

SKUNK APE RESEARCH HEADQUARTERS

OCHOPEE

Most Bigfoot sightings occur in the Pacific Northwest, but the Florida Everglades claim a local variant: the Skunk Ape. Bipedal, 6 to 7 feet (2 m) tall, and exuding an odor of rotten eggs mixed with moldy cheese, the Skunk Ape apparently stalks the grounds of the Big Cypress National Preserve.

No one claims to know more about Skunk Apes than Trail Lakes Campground owner and Skunk Ape Research Headquarters proprietor Dave Shealy. His obsessive quest to prove the ape's existence began at the age of ten when he spotted the Skunk Ape while on a hunting trip. Ever since, Shealy has scoured the park swamps looking for tracks, droppings, and the elusive creature itself. He claims a total of three Skunk Ape sightings.

Some of Shealy's findings are in his *Everglades Skunk Ape Research Field Guide*, which includes tips on planning an expedition and setting bait. ("If you

Dave Shealy's center is devoted to the search for the Everglades' most elusive primate.

plan to use deer liver, remember that it should be kept on ice until your site is chosen.") You can pick up a copy at the gift shop.

40904 Tamiami Trail East, Ochopee. Skunk Ape headquarters is on the Trail Lakes Campgrounds.
Ⓝ 25.892642 Ⓦ 81.279830

NEPTUNE MEMORIAL REEF

KEY BISCAYNE

A few miles east of Miami lies an underwater city. A pair of lions guard its entrance, which lead the way to stone roads, soaring gates, and crumbling ruins. Did an ancient civilization once live here? No. The "city" is a cemetery, and it was built in 2007.

Conceived as a living reef and modeled after the lost city of Atlantis, the site was created by cremation-services provider the Neptune Society. Anyone wishing to bury their loved one at the city can hand over the cremated remains—in person or by mail—to be mixed with cement and sand, poured into a shell- or starfish-shaped mold, and added to the reef. Family members are welcome to participate in the process, either by scuba diving or watching from a boat above. Postburial, they may visit the reef at any time for free.

If you want your remains to become part of the underwater city, you'll need to decide which part of the reef to join. There are 15 burial locations, ranging from standard placements (road railings; the "Fish Habitat Bench") to premium (gatekeeper columns) to exclusive (the Welcome Feature Centerpiece). Shipwreck diver Bert Kilbride, once listed as the oldest living scuba diver in the Guinness World Records, is interred in a place of honor at the top of one of the entry columns at the reef gate.

The Neptune Society has big plans for its undersea cemetery. Designed to attract fish and promote the growth of coral and marine organisms, the memorial reef will gradually take on a more authentic ancient-city look. The society's ultimate goal is a 16-acre metropolis containing the remains of 125,000 people. Currently, the reef is a quarter of an acre and is the final resting place of a few hundred. **The reef is just over 3 miles (5 km) east of Key Biscayne, 40 feet (12 m) under the sea. You are welcome to visit by boat and even dive at the site, but fishing is not permitted.**
Ⓝ 25.692940 Ⓦ 80.102861

At this underwater artificial reef, human remains are mixed into the architecture.

GEORGIA

CRYPT OF CIVILIZATION

ATLANTA

A pair of stockings, a bottle of beer, and a voice recording of Hitler: three of the artifacts by which future generations will judge 20th-century civilization. These three items sit alongside thousands of others in what is considered the world's first time capsule, sealed inside a former indoor swimming pool on May 28, 1940.

This "crypt of civilization" was the idea of Dr. Thornwell Jacobs, then president of Oglethorpe University. Frustrated by a dearth of primary sources during his research on ancient Egypt, Jacobs saw it as his "archaeological duty" to create an enduring, detailed record of life in the 20th century. When Jacobs made his plans known in 1936, the earliest date recorded in human history was equivalent to 4241 BCE. In accordance with this date from 6,177 years before, Jacobs decided his crypt should be opened in 8113—6,177 years into the future.

The question of what items would represent the sum of all human knowledge and experience was a tricky one to answer. After being inundated with unsolicited suggestions over three years, Jacobs and his crypt archivist, Thomas Peters, narrowed the options down to a few thousand essentials. A small sample of the inventory:

- *Gone With the Wind* script
- Microfilm reader and microfilms containing over 800 works, including fiction, the Bible, textbooks, news photographs, and drawings of human inventions
- Voice recordings of Hitler, Stalin, Mussolini, and Franklin D. Roosevelt
- Set of false eyelashes
- Potato masher
- Fishing rod
- Kodak camera
- Male and female mannequins
- Dental floss
- Toaster
- Donald Duck toy
- Steel plates used to print the *Atlanta Journal,* featuring articles on World War II

The time capsule, sealed behind a steel door in a 20-foot-long, 10-foot-wide (6 × 3 m) reinforced room, is scheduled to be opened on May 28, 8113. Jacobs and his staff took steps to ensure that 82nd-century individuals will be able to decipher the contents, regardless of societal changes—at the entrance of the crypt is a machine that teaches the English language.

Phoebe Hearst Hall, Oglethorpe University, 4484 Peachtree Road Northeast, Atlanta. You can't see inside the crypt until 8113, but you may visit its tightly sealed stainless-steel door. Ⓝ 33.874984 Ⓦ 84.333672

ALSO IN GEORGIA

Dotson Runway Graves

Savannah · When a new runway was laid at Savannah Airport in the 1980s, the preexisting graves of Richard and Catherine Dotson became part of the tarmac. Their two headstones, which lie side by side, flush with the runway, are clearly visible from departing and landing planes.

National Tick Collection

Statesboro · Scrutinize the differences among 850 species of tick at this overwhelming assemblage of specimens.

Sealed in 1940, Oglethorpe University's room-size time capsule is set to be cracked open in 8113.

GEORGIA GUIDESTONES

ELBERTON

When in need of life guidance, some turn to a higher power. Others look to four granite slabs in rural northeast Georgia.

In 1979 a man using the name R.C. Christian approached Georgia's Elberton Granite Finishing Company with plans to build a monument of four granite slabs, each almost 20 feet (6 m) tall, arranged in a cluster and topped with a smaller, horizontal slab. Each of the four vertical stones was to be inscribed with the same ten precepts for humanity, carved in eight languages.

These guidelines ranged from common-sense advice ("Balance personal rights with social duties") to New Age-y maxims ("Prize truth—beauty—love—seeking harmony with the infinite") to downright impractical instructions, served up with a hint of genocide ("Maintain humanity under 500,000,000"). The placement of the stones was carefully configured to align with solstices and equinoxes.

Armed with the detailed

No one knows who commissioned these mysterious megaliths, engraved in eight languages.

blueprints, the Elberton Granite Finishing Company duly created this mysterious monument and installed it in a field off Highway 77. A granite tablet was placed a few feet from the monument to provide some context for the Georgia Guidestones, as they have come to be known. It reads, in part, "Let these be guidestones to an Age of Reason."

The guidestones opened to the public in March 1980 and immediately became a magnet for conspiracy theorists. Over the years, visitors to the guidestones have left their marks by scrawling symbols and commentary on the monument, creating yet more intrigue.

There is still no definitive explanation for what the Georgia Guidestones mean, who actually commissioned them, or when the Age of Reason is due to be ushered in.

Guidestone Road Northwest. The stones are 7 miles (11 km) north of Elberton, just off Highway 77. Ⓝ 34.232056 Ⓦ 82.894389

KENTUCKY
VENT HAVEN MUSEUM

FORT MITCHELL

Vent Haven Museum is the only place in the world where you can walk into a room and see rows of ventriloquist figures sitting in chairs, all staring goggle-eyed in the same direction.

The museum's eerie displays grew out of the personal collection of William Shakespeare Berger (1878–1972), former president of the International Brotherhood of Ventriloquists. ("Vent" is slang for the profession.)

The most popular dummy at the museum is a replica of Charlie McCarthy, a figure in a top hat, tux, and monocle. Charlie and his human partner, ventriloquism pioneer Edgar Bergen, appeared on the *Chase and Sanborn Hour* radio show from 1937 to 1956. (The fact that a ventriloquist act achieved prolonged success in a nonvisual medium is one of the great mysteries of showbiz.)

Charlie's banter with Mae West on the December 12, 1937, show led to the actress being banned from NBC radio for 12 years. Her description of him being "all wood and a yard long" and teasing remarks about him giving her splinters the night before were deemed vulgar and obscene by the Federal Communications Commission.

33 West Maple Avenue, Fort Mitchell. The museum is open by appointment from May through September. Ⓝ 39.053008 Ⓦ 84.551937

ALSO IN KENTUCKY

Cumberland Falls

Corbin · On a clear night, with a full moon above, a moonbow, or lunar rainbow, appears in the mist above these waterfalls.

Heigold House

LOUISVILLE

Built in the 1850s, Heigold House still stands today as a testament to its owner's enduring belief in the American experiment. Well, at least its facade does.

Christian H. Heigold was a successful stonecutter who immigrated to Louisville from Germany in 1850, settling in a thriving neighborhood called The Point. There he quickly went about building a mansion, using his ample stonecutting skills to adorn the house with images of his family in scenes of Americana.

Louisville in the mid-19th century was a crucible of anti-immigrant sentiment, particularly targeting those of German Catholic and Irish descent. These tensions came to a head on August 8, 1855, when a Protestant mob attacked over 100 predominantly Irish and German businesses and homes, killing 22 people. No one was ever prosecuted for the violent riot, which came to be known as Bloody Monday.

The patriotic scenes Heigold cut into his home were a way of publicly proclaiming his American identity amid the rampant anti-immigrant sentiments. Even without the three-quarters of the original mansion, the facade abounds with details depicting Heigold's American idealism. A bust of James Buchanan is flanked on either side by the words HAIL TO BUCHANAN, NOW AND FOREVER and THE UNION FOREVER. HAIL TO THE UNION FOREVER; NEVER DISSOLVE IT. On the decorative lintel over the door, Heigold cut a scene depicting George Washington flanked by two figures, the Lady of Justice and the Lady of Culture, along with the words HAIL TO THE CITY OF LOUISVILLE.

After a laborious construction, Christian Heigold was not able to enjoy his home for long. He died in 1865, leaving the house to his son Charles. The passing of the elder Heigold marked the beginning of nearly a century and a half of unrest for the house and surrounding neighborhood.

By 1953, the city of Louisville began to buy and demolish properties in The Point to expand a dump site that had been encroaching on the neighborhood. The Point had virtually disappeared by then, having been flooded often by a diverted river. Buildings were demolished or covered in city waste, and the mayor had the facade of the Heigold House moved across River Road. After a developer bought the adjacent land to build luxury condominiums in 2007, the 70,000-pound facade was carefully moved again to its current location.

449–495 Frankfort Ave, Louisville. At night, spotlights illuminate the facade. It's a nice bit of drama.
Ⓝ 38.264259 Ⓦ 85.725211

A testament to one man's American identity in the face of anti-immigrant sentiment and unrest.

The inmates of Louisiana State Penitentiary put on a public rodeo and craft fair.

LOUISIANA

ANGOLA PRISON RODEO

ANGOLA

Every Sunday in October, inmates from the maximum-security Louisiana State Penitentiary host a publicly viewable rodeo. The prison—a former plantation nicknamed "Angola" after the original home of its slave workers—opens its doors to thousands of visitors who come to watch the bucking bulls, hear prison bands, and purchase crafts made by inmates.

The Angola rodeo tradition began in 1965 when a small group of prisoners and staff built an arena, intending to hold a rodeo purely for their own entertainment. What started as a way to pass the time turned into a huge public event. By 1969, visitors were cramming into a brand-new 4,500-seat stadium to watch inmates attempt their six-second bull rides. The current arena holds 10,000 people.

Inmates don't just participate in rodeo events—they are the ones selling hot dogs and candy apples, playing music for the crowds, and running market stalls featuring their own art, jewelry, leather goods, and woodwork. Easily distinguished by their black-and-white stripes, the prisoners chat freely with visitors but don't handle any money. The rodeo offers a rare chance to be among the public—three-quarters of Angola's 5,000-strong inmate population are serving life sentences.

End of Highway 66, approximately 22 miles (35 km) northwest of St. Francisville (Highway 61). Cameras are not permitted. Ⓝ 30.955436 Ⓦ 91.593903

HISTORIC VOODOO MUSEUM

NEW ORLEANS

Though all its offerings are crammed into just two dusty rooms and a hallway, the New Orleans Historic Voodoo Museum leaves a lasting impression. Founded in 1972 by local artist Charles Gandolfo, the museum focuses on Louisiana voodoo, which evolved from traditional West African vodun.

West Africans brought voodoo to Louisiana during the trans-Atlantic slave trade of the early 18th century. By the mid-19th century, the culture of New Orleans had begun to transform the spiritual practice. Voodoo spirits merged with Catholic saints, rituals gave way to processions, and Creole voodoo queens like Marie Laveau rose to prominence.

In 1932, a poorly acted, hastily shot horror movie—*White Zombie*—featured Bela Lugosi as an evil Haitian voodoo master with a crew of murderous zombies. The perverted pop-cultural portrayal of voodoo thrust it into the public eye. New Orleans stores capitalized on the trend by selling potions and voodoo dolls, while those who practiced genuine voodoo went underground.

Through its artifacts, the museum aims to convey the spiritual and historical context of Louisiana voodoo. Visitors can see traditional dolls and gris-gris pouches (amulets believed to provide luck or protection), and get a psychic reading from Dr. John, the resident voodoo priest. The gift shop sells love potions, snake skins, and chicken feet, which are used as protective charms.

724 Dumaine Street, New Orleans. Ⓝ 29.959903 Ⓦ 90.063851

ST. ROCH CHAPEL

NEW ORLEANS

There's a cemetery in the neighborhood of St. Roch (pronounced "rock"). At the center of that cemetery is a chapel. Inside that chapel, in a small room behind an iron gate, rows of prosthetic legs hang from the peeling walls. On shelves beneath sit plaster feet and false teeth, and a few pairs of artificial eyeballs.

Dedicated in 1867, the chapel honors St. Roch, who is associated with good health and healing. Born in the 14th century in Montpellier, Majorca—now part of France—St. Roch is said to have cared for and cured plague victims in Italy.

When a yellow fever epidemic hit 19th-century New Orleans, Reverend Peter Thevis, the pastor of Holy Trinity Catholic Church, prayed to St. Roch for relief and promised to build a shrine to him if the members of his parish were protected from the disease.

Though 40,000 New Orleanians succumbed to yellow fever, Father Thevis's community recorded no losses. The reverend held up his end of the bargain and built the St. Roch chapel and the surrounding cemetery. The gates opened to the public in 1876.

The room in the chapel has since become filled with offerings left by those in need of healing—as well as people who have prayed to St. Roch and recovered. Bricks on the ground are inscribed with the word "thanks" and littered with coins. Children's

The faithful leave tributes to St. Roch, including coins, flowers, and prosthetic limbs.

polio braces, crutches, and false limbs line the walls, interspersed with praying hands, rosaries, and figurines.

1725 St. Roch Avenue, New Orleans. ℕ 29.975445 Ⓦ 90.052018

LAKE PEIGNEUR

NEW IBERIA

Originally just 10 feet (3 m) deep, Lake Peigneur was once a popular but unremarkable fishing and recreation spot. However, on the morning of November 21, 1980, that all changed, when one of the largest man-made whirlpools in history flushed the lake and 65 acres of surrounding land—along with barges, big-rig trucks, and a Texaco drilling platform—down an enormous vortex.

Early that morning, the Wilson Brothers drilling crew knew something was amiss when their 14-inch drill bit became stuck and the entire platform shook. What they didn't know was that they had mistakenly drilled through the ceiling of the huge salt mine below. Wisely, they

abandoned the structure and, once safely on shore, watched in horror as their entire 150-foot rig sank like a magic trick into the shallow lake. Meanwhile, hundreds of feet below, 50 miners were scrambling to escape as water poured into the mine. Miraculously, there were no fatalities or serious injuries.

The damage from the all-consuming whirlpool was catastrophic and continues today. The freshwater lake became permanently salinated, forever altering the local ecosystem. Brackish water from Delcambre Canal and Vermilion Bay poured in through a newly formed 50-foot waterfall, while compressed air from the mine shafts created 400-foot geysers. The mine, which had been in operation for over 100 years, closed in 1986.

You can see views of Lake Peigneur and watch a short film about the drilling disaster at the Rip Van Winkle Gardens on Jefferson Island, located on the eastern shore of the lake. ℕ 29.978065 Ⓦ 91.984900

The remains of a flooded house.

The Army Corps of Engineers used Italian and German prisoners of war to build a scale model of 15,000 miles of waterway.

MISSISSIPPI

MISSISSIPPI RIVER BASIN MODEL

JACKSON

In the precomputer 1940s, when engineers needed to model a complex system, they would build an amazingly elaborate scale model.

The Army Corps of Engineers, the federal agency in charge of developing and maintaining the nation's water resources, built many such models, but none were on the scale of the Mississippi River Basin Model. Made in response to a series of catastrophic river floods, it simulated the effects of weather and flooding on the more than 15,000 miles (24,000 km) of waterways that make up the Mississippi River Basin. It was created at a scale of 1:100 vertical and 1:2,000 horizontal and covered over 200 acres of Buddy Butts Park.

Work on the model began in 1943 by Italian and German prisoners of war, who had been shipped over from North Africa. Though projected to be completed by 1948, the model took much longer than

expected to build. It wasn't truly finished until 1966, a full 23 years after it was started. Six years later, it was flooded for the last time.

By the early 1970s, the push toward computer modeling had begun, and by the 1980s, the model had become a burden for the Army Corps. In 1990, the site was transferred to the city of Jackson but was too expensive for them to maintain, so the city simply abandoned it.

The river basin model now sits surrounded and hidden by overgrown woods in Buddy Butts Park. It is open to the public to visit, but the tiny concrete banks of the rivers are now overgrown with comparatively giant foliage.

Buddy Butts Park, 6180 McRaven Road, Jackson.
Ⓝ 32.305984 Ⓦ 90.315903

Also in Mississippi

USS *Cairo*

Vicksburg · This iron-and-wood Civil War river gunboat was the first vessel to be sunk by a torpedo.

NORTH CAROLINA

STANLEY REHDER CARNIVOROUS PLANT GARDEN

WILMINGTON

Named in memory of Wilmington horticulturalist and carnivorous-plant lover Stanley Rehder, who died in 2012 at age 90, this garden is chock-full of meat-hungry flora. You'll see pitcher plants—which are known to swallow the odd frog or shrew—as well as Rehder's favorites: Venus flytraps.

In 2013, the garden took a major hit when thieves made away with approximately 1,000 flytraps—90 percent of the population. Fortunately, enhanced security and patient cultivation of replacement plants have helped the flesh-eating garden to flourish once more.

2025 Independence Boulevard, Wilmington. The garden is in the Piney Ridge Nature Preserve just behind Alderman Elementary School. Ⓝ 34.205827 Ⓦ 77.907280

Also in North Carolina

The Can Opener

Durham · The Gregson Street Railroad Trestle, or the Can Opener, is a truck driver's nightmare—the low-clearance rail bridge, built before the implementation of minimum height standards, regularly shaves the tops off trucks.

DEVIL'S TRAMPING GROUND

BENNETT

According to local legend, Satan likes to venture forth from the underworld and spend some quality time plotting the downfall of humanity at a camping spot in Chatham County.

A dusty circle of land in a forest northwest of Harpers Crossroads has come to be known as the Devil's Tramping Ground, based on stories of the Dark One that date back to the 1880s. Apparently, the devil regularly turns up at his favorite spot in the forest to pace in a circle, which accounts for the 20-foot-wide (6 m) patch of barren ground.

Beyond preventing the growth of vegetation, Beelzebub's cameos are said to have cursed the ground so that it causes objects placed there to move or disappear. There have also been reports of dogs whimpering and running when they encounter the cursed spot.

Signs bearing the name of the Devil's Tramping Ground Road are regularly stolen—presumably to serve as kitschy mementos. Unless, of course, it's a darker force that's "making" them disappear. **The ground is about 10 miles (16 km) south of Siler City on State Road 1100. ◎ 35.584783 ◎ 79.487017**

Where the devil comes to dance.

SOUTH CAROLINA
PEARL FRYAR'S TOPIARY GARDEN

BISHOPVILLE

When Pearl Fryar moved into a new house in 1981 he set himself a goal: to win the "Yard of the Month" award from the local gardener's club. Though he had no training in horticulture and no experience tending to plants, Fryar was determined to prove that he could grow a glorious garden. He visited local nurseries, took their discarded plants, and surrounded his house with them.

As the plants grew, Fryar began trimming them into diamonds, spirals, spheres, and cones. He won that coveted Yard of the Month award in 1985. By that time, he was well on his way to becoming the world's most celebrated topiary artist.

Fryar's garden now has 400 plants and trees, all pruned into fantastical shapes. **165 Broad Acres Road, Bishopville. ◎ 34.206793 ◎ 80.271868**

Originally motivated by a "Yard of the Month" award, Pearl Fryar has created a green wonderland with hundreds of ornamental shrubs.

OYOTUNJI AFRICAN VILLAGE

SHELDON

On the road into Oyotunji Village, a sign states, "You are leaving the United States. You are entering Yoruba Kingdom." Established in 1970, Oyotunji is an intentional community based on the culture of the Yoruba ethnic group of West Africa, particularly Nigeria. Its inhabitants live according to traditional Yoruba values and honor the Supreme Being Olodumare and the ancestral spirits through ritual dance, music, and ceremonies.

During its early days, Oyotunji was home to about 200 people. Now there are fewer than ten families living there, but the tight-knit community continues to host festivals—14 of which are open to the public—and a trading bazaar.

Oyotunji also offers Yoruba spiritual services, such as African naming ceremonies, divination readings, and communication with family members back home.

56 Bryant Lane, Sheldon. Oyotunji, just off Highway 17, is open for tours daily. Ⓝ 32.608852 Ⓦ 80.803306

ALSO IN SOUTH CAROLINA

Neverbust Chain

Columbia · This massive steel chain linking two office buildings was installed without permission but instantly beloved.

UFO Welcome Center

Bowman · Jody Pendarvis's homemade, rickety UFOs are intended to provide a rest stop for bewildered extraterrestrial visitors.

Oyotunji residents live according to the traditions of West African Yoruba and Fon cultures.

MARS BLUFF CRATER

MARS BLUFF

On March 11, 1958, an atomic bomb more powerful than the one dropped on Nagasaki fell out of a B-47 jet and onto Walter Gregg's back lawn.

The US Air Force plane had taken off from Savannah, Georgia, and was bound for England. There it would participate in Operation Snow Flurry, a series of mock bomb attacks. A real nuclear weapon was on board, just in case the war with the Soviet Union suddenly turned hot from cold.

Shortly after takeoff, a red warning light in the cockpit flashed to indicate that the bomb was not secured properly. Flight navigator Bruce Kulka went to inspect the situation and accidentally pressed the emergency release button, sending the 6-kiloton bomb plummeting toward Earth.

Mercifully, the bomb was not yet loaded with its uranium and plutonium core. But it did contain 7,600 pounds (3.4 MT) of payload-triggering explosives, resulting in significant damage to the rural ground on which it landed. When the dust cleared, a 50×70-foot wide (15×21 m), 30-foot-deep (9 m) crater scarred Gregg's yard. His house had been lifted off its foundation and was riddled with pockmarks and gaping holes. There were no human fatalities, but a few chickens perished in the accident.

The crater is still visible, but less dramatic—decades of forest growth have turned it into a peaceful little pond surrounded by trees.

Crater Road, Mars Bluff. The crater is on private property, but a historical marker sits by the access road. Ⓝ 34.200940 Ⓦ 79.657117

TENNESSEE

THE BODY FARM

KNOXVILLE

There is a 2.5-acre forest full of rotting human corpses at the University of Tennessee, but it's nothing to worry about—the bodies are meant to be there. The Knoxville institution is home to the country's first "body farm," a facility where forensic anthropologists and FBI agents get a close-up view of what happens when you die.

Anthropologist Dr. William M. Bass established the body farm in 1971 to advance the study of decomposition. Bodies are buried or left exposed within the wooded plot so they can be observed at various stages of the postmortem process.

By analyzing the effects of weather and insect activity on decomposition, students and researchers are better able to estimate the time of death. Law enforcement agencies also use the facility to sharpen criminal investigation skills—FBI agents, for example, practice exhuming and identifying human remains.

There are around 40 bodies in the farm at any one time, and donations are welcome (provided they're properly sourced). If you're interested in someday becoming part of the farm, make your intentions known to the university.

Don't mind the smell.

1924 Alcoa Highway, Knoxville. The body farm is not open to tours, but its staff gives talks, and the facilities are open to researchers. Ⓝ 35.940308 Ⓦ 83.942340

SYNCHRONIZED FIREFLIES OF THE GREAT SMOKY MOUNTAINS

ELKMONT

Like their bioluminescent counterparts in Malaysia, the little lightning bugs of the Great Smoky Mountains flash in sync to find a mate. After maturing from their larval stage, male fireflies stop eating and live for just three weeks. Given a mere 21 days to attract a partner, the fireflies flash en masse in order to help the females of the species find them.

Peak mating season lasts for about two weeks, between mid-May and mid-June. Visit the national park on a clear summer night and you'll find yourself in the middle of a romantic natural light show.

Elkmont, Great Smoky Mountains National Park. Firefly shuttles run from the Sugarlands Visitor Center to the Elkmont viewing area on evenings during mating season. Ⓝ 35.685606 Ⓦ 83.536598

ALSO IN TENNESSEE

Concrete Parthenon

Nashville · The trouble with the Parthenon in Athens is that it's falling apart. You could use your imagination to fill in the gaps, or you could head to Nashville's Centennial Park to see an intact, full-scale version.

Inside Luray Caverns, the cave itself becomes a musical instrument.

VIRGINIA
THE GREAT STALACPIPE ORGAN

LURAY, SHENANDOAH VALLEY

Deep underground in Luray Caverns is an unusual musical instrument designed by Leland W. Sprinkle. With its four-keyboard console, it looks like a standard variety church organ, with one crucial difference: There are no pipes. The "pipes" are stalactites and the instrument is a lithophone—a device that produces music by striking rocks of differing tones.

Sprinkle, a mathematician and electronics scientist at the Pentagon, came up with the idea for the "stalacpipe organ" after touring the caverns in 1954. He spent three years searching for stalactites that corresponded to the required musical notes, sanding them down to be pitch-perfect, and running 5 miles (8 km) of wires between the console and the rubber mallets that would strike each stalactite.

When the organ was first installed, Sprinkle himself took to the keys to entertain visitors. He even released a vinyl record of songs—it was promoted as "musical gems from solid rock" and sold in the Luray Caverns gift shop. These days the organ entertains cave visitors with automated renditions of such classics as "America the Beautiful," Moonlight Sonata, and, during the festive season, "Silent Night."

101 Cave Hill Road, Luray.
Ⓝ 38.664094 Ⓦ 78.483618

ALSO IN VIRGINIA

The Raven Room

Charlottesville · Edgar Allan Poe's old dorm room is now a shrine to the author's legacy.

CIA MUSEUM

LANGLEY

At the CIA's Virginia headquarters—a building formally known as the George Bush Center for Intelligence—there's a museum full of secret spy stuff. Its five galleries are hidden from public view, accessible only to CIA employees and special guests with security clearance.

In these rooms lie artifacts from decades of espionage dating back to World War II, when the CIA's predecessor, the Office of Special Services (OSS), was established. A German Enigma enciphering machine sits beside a letter written by an OSS officer on Hitler's personal stationery nine days after the dictator's suicide.

The Al Qaeda–focused gallery contains equipment and models used in SEAL training exercises in the lead-up to the 2011 raid on Osama bin Laden's Abbottabad compound. There's a scale model of bin Laden's hideout, as well as a wall from the full-size mock compound that was constructed for practice attacks. Bin Laden's AK-47, found beside his body, is on display, as is a brick from the real compound. And an Al Qaeda rocket-launching manual, scarred with burn marks.

Among the most fascinating exhibits are the unmanned vehicles and spy cams. Pigeon-mounted cameras, dragonfly drones, and robotic fish are a few of the devices that were trialed for stealthy surveillance. (The dragonfly drone, or insectothopter, was less than effective—developed during the 1970s, the remotely controlled insect had to be scrapped when it proved too susceptible to crosswinds.)

1000 Colonial Farm Road, McLean. The museum is not open to the public. Ⓝ 38.951791 Ⓦ 77.146607

MID-ATLANTIC AND NEW ENGLAND

The Mid-Atlantic

DELAWARE

JOHNSON VICTROLA MUSEUM

DOVER

The phrase "Put a sock in it!" originates from the days when people would stuff a sock into their Victrola horns to lower the volume. That's but one of the many fascinating facts you can learn when browsing this delightful collection of phonographs, also known as gramophones.

The museum is named after Eldridge R. Johnson, a Dover man who founded the Victor Talking Machine Company in 1901. Johnson's line of Victrola phonographs, which housed the device's horn inside a sleek wooden cabinet, became hugely popular when they were introduced in 1906.

In addition to the many phonographs on display, the museum has a "Nipper Corner"—Nipper being the terrier who served as the canine model for the legendary His Master's Voice logo.

375 S. New Street, Dover. Ⓝ 39.156455 Ⓦ 75.527210

The misfits and outsiders of the art world are celebrated at Baltimore's American Visionary Art Museum.

MARYLAND
AMERICAN VISIONARY ART MUSEUM
BALTIMORE

This museum honors the work of self-taught artists with an obsessive bent—those driven to paint and sculpt and create despite a lack of formal training.

Museum founder Rebecca Alban Hoffberger got the idea for the museum while working in a Baltimore hospital program aimed at reintroducing psychiatric inpatients to the community. Inspired by the intensity and imagination in the patients' artwork, Hoffberger created a home for visionary, outsider art.

Opened in 1995, the museum displays work that is playful, dark, funny, disturbing, and sometimes awe-inspiring, including a crocheted "horse dress" with giant equine eyes at the nipples and a 55-foot-tall (16.7 m) whirligig. The permanent collection is supplemented with temporary exhibits by guest curators. In these, too, the mood is varied: "The Art of Storytelling" featured Holocaust survivor Esther Krintz's tapestries of Nazi labor camps, while "What Makes Us Smile" featured a "Toot Suite" that honored the role of flatulence in the arts.

800 Key Highway, Baltimore. Each May the museum hosts the Kinetic Sculpture Race, in which human-powered vehicles traverse a 15-mile (24 km) course over land and water. Ⓝ 39.280035 Ⓦ 76.606742

ALSO IN MARYLAND

Urology Museum

Linthicum · See a collection of wince-inducing but beautiful bladder stones.

Inspiring figures immortalized in wax include Joe Lewis, Jackie Robinson, and Jesse Owens.

GREAT BLACKS IN WAX
BALTIMORE

The name of this museum may be light and quirky, but a visit to Great Blacks in Wax is a powerful, confrontational, and ultimately uplifting experience—even if the figures on display aren't quite up to the standard of Madame Tussaud's when it comes to verisimilitude.

Elmer and Joanne Martin founded the National Great Blacks in Wax Museum in 1983 to stimulate interest in black history and provide strong role models for African American youth. A tour of the exhibits, arranged in chronological order, begins with a walk through a replica slave ship where tightly packed rows of black slaves are chained by their necks. The Lynching Room, signposted with a graphic-content warning, contains life-size figures being hanged, beaten, and eviscerated.

Amid these vivid exhibits are over 100 wax figures of black civil rights leaders, entertainers, athletes, writers, and other luminaries—from Billie Holiday and Barack Obama to lesser-known figures such as Granville T. Woods, known as the "Black Edison." **1601 East North Avenue #3, Baltimore. Ⓝ 39.311749 Ⓦ 76.596842**

THE NUTSHELL STUDIES OF UNEXPLAINED DEATH

BALTIMORE

In 1943, Frances Glessner Lee began working on a series of detailed, dollhouse-style dioramas. Working at a scale of 1 inch to 1 foot, the 65-year-old forensics expert filled her minirooms with hand-sewn textiles, color-coordinated furniture, and bottles with hand-painted labels. Posed in each room was a minicorpse exhibiting just the right degree of decay.

Lee's dioramas were known as the Nutshell Studies. Created to assist forensic science students at Harvard, they depicted murder scenes, suicides, and lethal accidents. The clues in Lee's nutshells—such as blood spatter patterns, the position of the body, and the items found around it—allowed students to analyze and determine the nature of each grisly death.

To make each scene authentic, Lee read crime reports and police

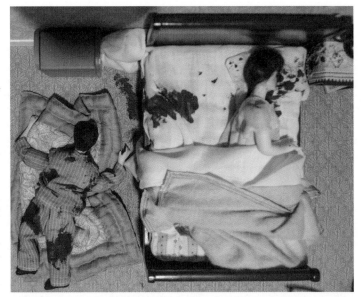

Tiny forensic dollhouses train detectives to solve crimes.

interviews to compile details. She was unflinching in her interior decoration: In one scene, "The Three-Room Dwelling," a husband and wife lie dead in their bedroom. Crimson footprints separate them from the corpse of their blood-spattered baby.

All 18 nutshell dioramas are displayed at the Maryland Medical Examiner's Office. The gory tableaus are still studied by detectives in training.
900 West Baltimore Street, Baltimore. Ⓝ 39.289109 Ⓦ 76.632637

NEW JERSEY
HOLMDEL HORN ANTENNA

HOLMDEL

In 1965, Arno Penzias and Robert Wilson accidentally discovered one of the greatest secrets of the universe.

The radio astronomers were using the Bell Labs horn antenna to scan for radio waves being bounced off NASA communications satellites. To Penzias's and Wilson's annoyance, an ever-present low hum interfered with their data collection. They checked their equipment, shooed away some pigeons that had been nesting in the antenna, and listened again. Still the hum persisted.

The noise was not coming from the antenna, or anywhere in New Jersey, or anywhere on Earth. It came from the universe itself. Penzias and Wilson had just stumbled upon cosmic microwave background.

Penzias's and Wilson's discovery provided the first observational evidence that the universe began with a Big Bang. The discovery earned them a

Once the pigeons were shooed away, scientists were able to detect the faint echoes of the Big Bang.

Nobel Prize in Physics. The decommissioned horn antenna they used for their explosive discovery is now a National Historic Landmark.
Holmdel Road and Longview Drive, Holmdel.
Ⓝ 40.390760 Ⓦ 74.184652

NORTHLANDZ

FLEMINGTON

Over 8 miles (13 km) of miniature train tracks run through this building, making it the largest model train layout in the world. Creator Bruce Zaccagnino began building the miniature railroads in his basement in 1972. After twice-annual open houses drew big crowds, Zaccagnino decided to open Northlandz to the public as a permanent attraction. It debuted in 1996 in a 52,000-square-foot (4,831 m²) building along Route 202.

The 135 trains of Northlandz cross over 400 bridges and pass by miniature cities, mountains, half a million trees, and crowds of teeny people. Then there are the odder sights, such as an outhouse factory and a crashed plane with survivors standing on its wings. There's a layer of dust on everything, and the lighting's a little dim, but the vastness and detail of the scenery transcend the moth-eaten vibe.

The world's largest model railroad began in a basement. It now incorporates a 30-foot mountain.

495 US Route 202, Flemington. About an hour north of Trenton. Ⓝ 40.517085 Ⓦ 74.819335

NEW YORK
DEAD HORSE BAY

BROOKLYN

Stroll along the beach at Dead Horse Bay and you'll be stepping on the faces of broken porcelain dolls, glass soda bottles from the 1950s, and fragments of 19th-century horse bones.

The debris strewn on the sand tells the story of the bay's past. Formerly part of Barren Island, Dead Horse Bay acquired its unsavory name in the 1850s, when it became the location for multiple horse-rendering plants. New York's former carriage-pulling equines arrived here to be transformed into glue and fertilizer. Having no use for their chopped, boiled bones, plant workers dumped them in the water. A horrid smell hung in the air.

The introduction of the automobile brought an end to carriage horses, and thus an end to horse-rendering plants. In the late 1920s the factories shut down and the city poured sand, silt, and garbage into the channel separating Barren Island from the mainland. The area functioned as a garbage dump until 1953, when the landfill was capped. Decades of erosion have uncovered the artifacts that dot the shore today.

Glass bottles make up most of the debris—hence the bay's nickname, Bottle Beach—but you

First a horse-rendering plant, then a landfill, Brooklyn's bottle-covered beach is now a scavenger heaven.

may also find saddle fragments, equine teeth, art-deco cosmetics cases, and broken toys. All are from 1953 or earlier, making the bay a garbage-strewn portal to the past.

Flatbush Avenue at Aviation Road, Brooklyn. Get a Brooklyn-bound 2 train to the last stop, Flatbush Avenue–Brooklyn College. From there, take the Q35 bus to Floyd Bennett Field. The bay is on the opposite side of Flatbush Ave. Ⓝ 40.581689 Ⓦ 73.898504

A little-remembered 1920 terrorist attack left holes along Wall Street.

SCARS OF THE WALL STREET BOMBING

MANHATTAN

The corner building at 23 Wall Street bears scars from a terrorist attack—one that occurred back in 1920. Just after noon on Thursday, September 16, a bomb placed on a parked horse-drawn wagon exploded, blasting 500 pounds (226 kg) of small iron weights into the air. Thirty-eight people died in the attack. One hundred and forty-three were seriously injured.

At the time, 23 Wall Street was the headquarters of J.P. Morgan & Co., the nation's most powerful bank. The perpetrators of the attack have never been officially identified, but anti-capitalist Italian anarchists were likely responsible.

The pockmarked limestone on the facade of 23 Wall Street was never repaired. These little marks are the only on-site hint of the attack—there are no signs or plaques to commemorate the bombing.

23 Wall Street, Manhattan. Ⓝ 40.706795 Ⓦ 74.010480

KEITH HARING'S *ONCE UPON A TIME* BATHROOM MURAL

NEW YORK

In May 1989, artist Keith Haring created the bathroom mural *Once Upon a Time*. He was 31, and it was his last major mural before his death in February 1990 of AIDS-related complications. The piece was created for The Center Show, a celebration of the 20th anniversary of the Stonewall riots, which are regarded as the start of the gay liberation and LGBT rights movement. The Center Show called upon LGBT artists to create site-specific works of art in the building of LGBT community hub The Center. Haring chose to create his provocative work in the second-floor men's bathroom.

The mural covers four interior walls with Haring's signature black-on-white line drawings. These are not the Haring images we are used to seeing on buttons, magnets, puzzles, and clothes; this is the private, sexual Haring come to life in a grandiose and unapologetic celebration of gay sexuality.

Unfortunately, time and the elements gradually took their toll on the mural. The bathroom was used as The Center's meeting room until 2012, when funds were raised for a major restoration of the work. The mural was restored and opened to the public in 2015.

Since Haring's works have sold at auction for up to $5.6 million, it is quite possible that this is the most valuable bathroom in America. Luckily, you can see it for free.

208 West 13th Street, Manhattan. The Keith Haring Bathroom and other Center Show works are open to the public during regular business hours at the Center. Ⓝ 40.738152 Ⓦ 74.001057

A one-of-a-kind mural that is as graphic as it is masterful.

CITY GUIDE: More to Explore in New York

Bronx Zoo Bug Carousel

The Bronx • Right next to the butterfly exhibit at the Bronx Zoo is the first—and likely only—carousel of hand-carved and elaborately painted insects.

High Bridge

Harlem River Drive • Connecting the boroughs of Manhattan and the Bronx, this 2,000-foot arched aqueduct soars above the Harlem River. The oldest bridge in the city, it reopened as a pedestrian walkway after four decades of neglect and abandonment.

Panorama of the City of New York

Queens • It took three years and more than a hundred model makers to build this panorama in time for the 1964 World's Fair. It knocked out the crowds with 10,000 square feet of every building in all five boroughs, each re-created in miniature.

Houdini's Grave

Queens • There's a Houdini museum in Manhattan, but in Queens you can visit the final resting place of the greatest illusionist of all time. Fans still gather to wait for his escape from the shackles of death, and they leave behind stacks of stones and packs of cards.

Castle William

Governors Island • In 1996 the Coast Guard—the last of the military tenants of Governors Island—finally folded up their charts, and the centuries-old military outpost opened to the public, including a historic fort that housed a hundred cannons.

Corpse Flower at the Brooklyn Botanic Garden

Brooklyn • Time it right, and lucky visitors may catch a whiff of one of the worst smells on the planet: the scent of the giant bloom of the Corpse Flower that the Brooklyn Botanic Garden calls Baby. Even when not in full bloom, the *Amorphophallus titanum*, or "titan arum," lives up to its name ("titan" that is, but Baby is awful cute).

Weeksville Heritage Center

Brooklyn • Brooklyn's largest African American cultural institution, this sparkling facility celebrates the little-known 19th-century community of Weeksville, intentionally created for free blacks and former slaves, with exhibitions, performances, and guided tours of the settlement's remains.

Fort Wadsworth

Staten Island • The traditional starting line of the New York Marathon, America's longest-manned military fort is now an abandoned hulk of ruins along the Verrazano Narrows, part of the Gateway National Recreation Area and perfect for melancholy picnics and beach bird-watching.

Floyd Bennett Field

Brooklyn • Part of the Gateway National Recreation Area of the National Park Service and named after the first person to fly over the North Pole, New York City's first local airport is now home to the Historic Aircraft Restoration Project.

Historic Richmond Town

Staten Island • A sizable piece of New York's late 17th- and early 18th-century past is preserved in a settlement of 30 structures in the city's farthest borough, including its oldest continuously operating farm, plus a 350-year-old home on its original site, one of the oldest in the country.

Roosevelt Island Smallpox Hospital Ruins

Roosevelt Island • These haunting ruins are a stone's throw from some of the most exclusive and expensive real estate on the planet. With a design by the architect of St. Patrick's Cathedral, this crumbling 19th-century relic maintains a sense of grandeur despite the suffering it once housed.

World's Largest Chess Board

Manhattan • Stuck to the side of an apartment building is the world's largest chess match. With pieces that measure more than two feet each, and with just one move a week (it takes a cherry picker to do it), it's also probably the world's slowest.

Holographic Studios

Manhattan • Bringing new life to a former blacksmith's forge, the world's oldest hologram gallery and laser laboratory has been creating, selling, displaying, and teaching the art and science of lasers since the 1960s.

Obscura Antiques and Oddities

Manhattan • In the back room of this charming store, with its astonishing variety of medical antiques, turn-of-the-20th-century taxidermy, and Victorian mourning jewelry, there is an exquisite 19th-century anatomical model (not for sale).

Angel Orensanz Foundation

Manhattan • The oldest surviving synagogue in the city is now a soaring art and concert space, where the music of Philip Glass has echoed through the pillars, and the designs of Alexander McQueen have shone under the filtered light of stained glass.

Dream House

Manhattan • Billed as a sound and light environment, the Dream House is a collaboration of a modern composer and a visual artist, harkening back to a time when Tribeca and Soho were neighborhoods with cheap rents and vibrant creative communities.

Mmuseumm

Manhattan • This tiny museum in a freight elevator specializes in the "overlooked, dismissed, or ignored," with unpredictable rotating exhibits that range from the shoe thrown at George W. Bush to the taxonomy of Corn Flakes.

City Hall Station

Manhattan • A lavish and abandoned subway station from 1904, complete with chandeliers and intricate skylights, greets the patient passengers who stay onboard the 6 train as it makes its downtown loop.

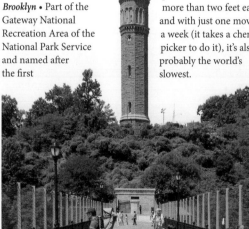

The High Bridge and its water tower date back to the 19th century.

THE SACRED GROVE

PALMYRA

In the Spring of 1820, a 14-year-old boy went to a quiet grove near his log cabin home to ask a big question. Confused over which religion he ought to join, the young man prayed to God for guidance. According to the boy, both God and Jesus then appeared, surrounded by white light and bearing a message: Do not join an existing religion, for their doctrines are incorrect.

Ten years later, that boy, Joseph Smith, published the Book of Mormon and formally established the Church of Jesus Christ of Latter-Day Saints. Smith's experience in the grove, referred to in LDS lore as the First Vision, was the moment he became a prophet.

The Sacred Grove, as it is known to Mormons, is now open to visitors year-round. The exact location of Smith's vision is unknown, but you can reenact his adolescent experience by walking from the replica log cabin to the forest and praying to the deity of your choice. A tour guide will gladly accompany you while telling tales from Smith's action-packed life.

843 Stafford Road, Palmyra. Start at the Hill Cumorah Visitors Center, located at 653 State Route 21. Ⓝ 43.040884 Ⓦ 77.239877

LILY DALE ASSEMBLY

LILY DALE

There's a saying in Lily Dale: "If you believe, you will receive." Small, peaceful, and remote, Lily Dale is a community of spiritual mediums who offer their psychic services. In order to move in, mediums must demonstrate their powers to the Lily Dale board of directors. If their messages from beyond the grave are of satisfactory accuracy, they are invited to join.

Visitors come to Lily Dale for readings, during which they hope to receive or convey messages to departed loved ones. The 40 or so resident mediums operate independently and set their own prices—visitors walk around the community, shopping for the spiritualist who suits them best.

Whether or not you believe in the residents' psychic abilities, Lily Dale is a tranquil place to spend a day. Besides the individual readings there are group

gatherings at the Inspiration Stump, during which a medium relays short messages to select people in the crowd. Stop by the pet cemetery, wishing tree, and healing temple to make the most of the entrance fee.

5 Melrose Park. Lily Dale is best visited in the summer months, when there are daily and weekly events for guests. Ⓝ 42.350730 Ⓦ 79.325898

SENECA WHITE DEER

SENECA COUNTY

For years, rumors circulated about the strange herd of white deer living in the former Seneca Army Depot. Some speculated that the "albino" breed was the result of an army experiment gone wrong, while others attributed the animals' appearance to an underground supply of radioactive military weapons.

The white deer were first spotted around 1941, when the US Army fenced off 24 square miles (62 km²) of land for a munitions storage site. Protected by the fencing, the deer population thrived, as did the recessive gene for all-white coloration.

As the white deer population proliferated through the 1950s, the US Army decided to protect the unique herd. Aiding the process of artificial selection, a depot commander hunted the brown deer population while forbidding GIs from shooting any white deer. Since then, the white deer population has grown to approximately 300, making it the largest herd of its kind in the world.

The Seneca Army Depot shut down in 2000 and has been closed to the public ever since. A nonprofit group has been fighting to turn the area into a conservation park and Cold War museum. Until then, dozens of deer remain visible from the highway, frolicking among the hundreds of abandoned bunkers.

A good vantage point for spotting deer is Route 96A, 6 miles south of Geneva. Ⓝ 42.747692 Ⓦ 76.858960

The largest Catholic relic collection outside the Vatican is located in Pittsburgh.

PENNSYLVANIA
St. Anthony's Chapel

PITTSBURGH

Pittsburgh may seem an unlikely pilgrimage destination, but the Catholic faithful flock to this chapel to see its collection of relics. St. Anthony's has thousands of saintly bone fragments and clothing remnants, held in jeweled reliquaries. Together they comprise the largest relic collection outside the hallowed halls of the Vatican.

The collection was established by Father Suitbert Mollinger, the Belgian-born priest who designed and built the chapel in 1880. Among the more notable relics are a sliver of wood from the Last Supper table, five fragments of the cross on which Jesus was crucified, and a particle from the Virgin Mary's veil. Mollinger, who died in 1892, used the relics during healing masses, which were aimed at restoring health and vitality to the infirm.

1704 Harpster Street, Pittsburgh. You can take a tour of the relic collection, but remember that the chapel is a place of worship. Photos are not permitted and silence is preferred. Ⓝ 40.464911 Ⓦ 79.983664

Center for PostNatural History

PITTSBURGH

A natural history museum tweaked for the 21st century, the Center for PostNatural History exhibits organisms that have been altered by humans via processes like selective breeding and genetic engineering.

The museum aims to examine the ways in which nature, culture, and biotechnology intersect. Its collection of living and preserved organisms includes genetically engineered glowing fish—which contain genes from bioluminescent jellyfish and coral—and a preserved "BioSteel" goat, which was genetically modified to produce spider silk proteins in its milk.

4913 Penn Avenue, Pittsburgh. The center is open on Sundays and the first Friday evening of every month. Ⓝ 40.465432 Ⓦ 79.944659

Mutant vegetables, transgenic mosquitoes, and a spider goat are exhibited at this unconventional natural history museum.

CENTRALIA

CENTRALIA

In October 2013, the eight remaining residents of the once 2,700-strong town of Centralia won a long court battle over the right to stay in their homes. The inhabitants of the former mining settlement are now free to keep living in an overgrown field crisscrossed by cracked roads that belch carbon monoxide from their crevices.

Located on a rich seam of anthracite coal, Centralia was settled as a mining town in the mid-1800s. In 1962, something happened that would transform Centralia from a quaint and lively small town into a bleak and hazardous wasteland: A fire in one of the underground mines began to burn out of control.

The exact cause of the fire is still disputed—some argue that it resulted from the volunteer fire department's annual burning of the landfill, while others claim that a coal fire from 1932 was never fully extinguished, and had been slowly spreading toward an abandoned strip-mine pit.

The scale of the problem did not become widely apparent until 1979. That year, mayor and gas-station owner John Coddington was checking the fuel levels of his underground tanks when he discovered that the gasoline had been heated to 172°F (77.7°C).

A real shocker came in 1981, when the ground tried to swallow Todd Domboski. The 12-year-old was walking in his backyard when the earth gave way and he fell 8 feet (2.4 m) into a smoking sinkhole. Domboski was able to hold on to tree roots at the sides of the hole until he was pulled to safety. The sinkhole was later found to be about 150 feet (46 m) deep and filled with lethal levels of carbon monoxide.

Following these troubling incidents, the government began claiming Centralia properties under eminent domain, condemning them, and relocating residents. The population fell from 1,017 in 1980 to 21 in 2000. Centralia lost its zip code in 2002.

Today, the remaining residents of Centralia have been granted the right to stay there for the rest of their lives, after which the government will take possession of their properties. Meanwhile, the fire rages on.

WARNING - DANGER

UNDERGROUND MINE FIRE

WALKING OR DRIVING IN THIS AREA COULD
RESULT IN SERIOUS INJURY OR DEATH

DANGEROUS GASES ARE PRESENT

GROUND IS PRONE TO SUDDEN COLLAPSE

Commonwealth of Pennsylvania
Department of Environmental Protection

Centralia is 2.5 hours northwest of Philadelphia.
Ⓝ 40.804254 Ⓦ 76.340503

GRIP THE RAVEN

PHILADELPHIA

The stuffed raven perched on a log in the display case of the Central Library's Rare Book Department is named Grip the First. Until his death and preservation in 1841—after which he was replaced by Grip the Second and Grip the Third—the raven was the beloved pet and sometime muse of Charles Dickens. So important was Grip, who had a habit of biting children's ankles, that the author paid tribute to him by including him as a character in his 1841 mystery novel, *Barnaby Rudge*.

Enter Edgar Allan Poe. In his review of *Barnaby Rudge*, Poe wrote that Dickens ought to have made Grip more ominous and

Barnaby Rudge with his raven.

symbolic. Four years later, clearly influenced by the novel, Poe published "The Raven," in which a "stately Raven of the saintly days of yore" induces grief and madness with its cry of "Nevermore." The raven's tapping in the poem echoes a line in *Barnaby Rudge*—when Grip first makes a sound, a character asks, "What was that—tapping at the door?"

Following Dickens's death, Grip ended up in the hands of Poe memorabilia collector Richard Gimbel. In 1971, Gimbel donated the bird, along with Poe's handwritten copy of "The Raven," to the library.

1901 Vine Street, third floor, Philadelphia. Get the subway (Broad Street line) to Race-Vine and walk 5 blocks west. Ⓝ 39.959605 Ⓦ 75.171023

EASTERN STATE PENITENTIARY

PHILADELPHIA

Prior to 1829, prisons were chaotic, unruly institutions where criminals of all ages and sexes lived in the same cells. Then came Eastern State Penitentiary. Influenced by Enlightenment thinking, the prison was the first to implement the "Pennsylvania System," a philosophy that kept prisoners isolated from each other and the outside world in the hope that their solitude would induce profound regret.

Eastern State's design was based on Jeremy Bentham's panopticon, with cell-block "spokes" radiating from a central observation post. Each cell was equipped with a bed, flushing toilet, skylight, and Bible. All other reading material, including letters from family members, was forbidden. A door on the back wall of each cell led to a small exercise yard, where inmates could spend up to one hour per day. During any activity requiring a prison guard escort, prisoners had to wear a hood to prevent eye contact with another human being.

After visiting the site in 1842, Charles Dickens wrote in *American Notes for General Circulation* that the solitary confinement system was "cruel and wrong." Decades of criticism—and a burgeoning prison population—led to the gradual relaxation of Eastern State's strict solitude policies.

Suffering from deteriorating mechanical and electrical systems, Eastern State Penitentiary closed in 1971. For the next 15 years it sat abandoned, an urban forest springing up among its stone walls. In 1994, the prison reopened for public tours. The cell blocks remain in a state of neglect—mint-green paint flakes from the walls and a shaft of light from each cell's skylight illuminates rubble, rusted bed frames, and stray old boots.

2027 Fairmount Avenue, Philadelphia. Look for Al Capone's cell, which he occupied for 8 months after being arrested for carrying a concealed weapon in 1929. Equipped with rugs, lamps, a writing desk, and radio, it re-creates the luxury to which he was accustomed. Ⓝ 39.968327 Ⓦ 75.172720

ALSO IN PHILADELPHIA

Camac Street

Take a stroll down the last of the city's woodblock-paved streets.

Mummers Museum

This museum displays extravagant costumes from the annual Mummers folk parade.

Al Capone's Eastern State cell was furnished with rugs and a radio—both luxuries, given the surroundings.

TOYNBEE TILES

MULTIPLE LOCATIONS (UNITED STATES, SOUTH AMERICA)

Mosaic rectangles with enigmatic messages, known as the Toynbee tiles, have been appearing on city streets for decades, and their origin and purpose are still a mystery. The tiles usually feature a cryptic message along the lines of: TOYNBEE IDEA—IN KUBRICK'S 2001—RESURRECT DEAD—ON PLANET JUPITER. Several hundred of these license plate–size plaques have been discovered since the 1980s, scattered randomly around major cities. They first appeared around Philadelphia and New York, and soon spread across the United States and into South America.

No one knows for sure why or how these tiles were laid.

The meaning of the "tiles," better described as adhesive patches that stick to concrete sidewalks and asphalt streets, has been interpreted as everything from a futurist utopian vision to a secret message from playwright David Mamet. (He denies this.) According to one popular theory, they were created by a Philadelphia carpenter who started a group that hoped to colonize Jupiter by resurrecting the dead there. Not surprisingly, his idea was not taken seriously by the media, and a few longer tiles have been found with side messages such as MURDER EVERY JOURNALIST I BEG OF YOU. Connecting the dots, it would appear that the tiler felt targeted for his beliefs of resurrection and chose to spread his message anonymously on the streets.

There are many theories on who the Toynbee tiler truly is and what their intent may be. But no concrete evidence has been found, and no one has ever laid eyes on the tiler. Some speculate that the typical tiles are laid simply by being tossed out of a hole in the floorboard of a car, which could explain the puzzling placement of many of the messages. **Many original tiles have been almost obliterated by constant foot and vehicle traffic, and some have been paved over in recent years. Others are well-preserved and easily read. There is an interactive online map of known tiles at toynbeeidea.com/portfolio/where. Ⓝ 39.951062 Ⓦ 75.165631**

MÜTTER MUSEUM

PHILADELPHIA

Named for Dr. Thomas Dent Mütter, who donated his collection of medical specimens in 1858, this museum is an enthralling mix of human skulls, diseased body parts, and anatomical models designed to educate aspiring doctors.

A highlight on the top floor is the Hyrtl Skull Collection: 139 19th-century crania arranged in eight rows. Each skull bears a description of the deceased's name, age, occupation, location, and cause of death. Though brief, the information is highly evocative—one 28-year-old Hungarian man died of "suicide by gunshot wound of the heart, because of weariness of life," while a Bosnian fellow was "killed in battle with Austrian sharpshooters."

Downstairs you'll find examples of exceedingly rare afflictions.

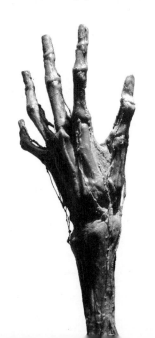

A skeleton in one of the display cases looks to be melting—the bones are the remains of Harry Eastlack, a man who suffered from a connective tissue disease known as fibrodysplasia ossificans progressiva. The condition gradually turns muscle and tendons into bone, immobilizing joints and imprisoning the sufferer in his own body.

A few steps away, in a glass display case, is what looks like a giant papier mâché snake. Brown, bulbous, and 9 feet (2.7 m) long, it represents the "mega colon" of a man whose large intestine accumulated 40 pounds (18 kg) of feces due to a nerve disorder. Turn around and you'll see a tiny skeleton curled into a sphere. This is a lithopedion, or "stone child," an extra-uterine fetus that died and calcified inside the mother, remaining undiscovered for 24 years.

19 South 22nd Street, Philadelphia. The museum is a short walk from 30th Street Station, Philadelphia's main train hub. Photography is not permitted. Ⓝ 39.953201 Ⓦ 75.176637

WASHINGTON, DC

GARGOYLES OF THE WASHINGTON NATIONAL CATHEDRAL

The sixth-largest cathedral in the world, this building is an elegant blend of flying buttresses, neo-Gothic spires, and a carefully sculpted Darth Vader.

The masked head of Anakin Skywalker sits between two arches high on the northwest tower. Unlike the dinosaur of Ta Prohm temple, there is no ambiguity about this bust—during the 1980s, while the church was still in its 83-year construction process, kids entered a competition to design a decorative sculpture for the cathedral. Twelve-year-old Christopher Rader submitted a crowd-pleasing drawing of Darth Vader.

The sci-fi villain is not the cathedral's only unconventional architecture. Other decorative sculptures

Grab binoculars to spot a Sith Lord on the northwest tower.

include a raccoon, a girl with braces, and a grinning man holding an umbrella. One of the stained glass windows honors the Apollo 11 moon landing and contains a fragment of lunar rock.

3101 Wisconsin Avenue, NW, Washington. You will need binoculars to see Darth Vader. From inside the cathedral, go through the wooden doors near the Abraham Lincoln statue. Stand on the grass to your right and turn around to look at the closest tower. You'll find him beneath the central point at the first peaked roof. Ⓝ 38.930655 Ⓦ 77.070747

FBI SPY HOUSE

WASHINGTON, DC

The three-story house at 2619 Wisconsin Avenue had a big front porch and was located in a residential neighborhood. Perfect for a family. Or the FBI.

In 1977, the Soviet Embassy moved into a new building complex across the road from the house. The FBI and the NSA soon snapped up 2619 Wisconsin Avenue to set up a secret spying station to keep tabs on Russian business.

This inocuous house hides a secret.

The house's cover was negligible. The curtains were always drawn and no mail was ever delivered, yet people were frequently seen coming and going. Cameras could be clearly spotted in the windows, filming all those who entered the Russian embassy.

The FBI's uses for the house may have gone beyond playing paparazzi. Operation Monopoly was a secret plan to dig a tunnel beneath the embassy to record conversations taking place within the

building in the hopes of gleaning secret information. The problem was that the FBI had little knowledge of the embassy's layout. The agency hoped the tunnel would run underneath a room where people congregated to spill secrets, but it was just as likely to end up beneath a storage closet.

Though the FBI acknowledges the existence of the tunnel, they have never revealed which house in the neighborhood they began digging it from. Speculators believe it was either this observation house on Wisconsin Avenue or an abandoned house around the side of the embassy on Fulton Street. The truth may never be known for sure, as the tunnel has been sealed.

2619 Wisconsin Avenue, Washington, DC. In February 2018, the street separating the house and the embassy was named Boris Nemtsov Plaza, after the Russian physicist and Putin critic who was assassinated in 2015. Ⓝ 38.924258 Ⓦ 77.072811

WASHINGTON MINI MONUMENT

WASHINGTON, DC

Near the Washington Monument is a manhole. And in that manhole is another Washington Monument.

The mini monument is a 12-foot-tall (3.7 m) replica of the 555-foot (169 m) original. It serves surveyors as a geodetic control point—a marker that provides a starting point for maps and measurements. It's part of the network of a million control points across the country that helps the National Geodetic Survey synchronize all the government's maps.

Geodetic control points are often metal caps or rods that are driven down into the ground, but this quirky control point mirrors the form of its next-door neighbor. It's been used for surveys since the early 1900s. Outside of surveying circles, it's largely forgotten.

The survey marker is underneath a manhole just south of the Washington Monument. Speak to a park ranger before trying to see it. Ⓝ 38.889150 Ⓦ 77.035211

Officially known as "Bench Mark A," this miniature is ¹⁄₄₆th the size of the original.

WEST VIRGINIA

CONGRESSIONAL FALLOUT SHELTER

WHITE SULPHUR SPRINGS

Guests staying at the luxurious Greenbrier resort during the 1960s often saw TV repairmen walking around the west wing of the hotel. What they didn't know was that these apparent maintenance workers were actually government employees tasked with tending to the secret on-site nuclear bunker.

As the Cold War heated up in the 1950s, it became clear to the Eisenhower administration that Congress needed a place to escape to in the event of nuclear war with the Soviet Union. The Greenbrier, long a favorite getaway of presidents and located just a couple of hours from Washington, was chosen to house the 1,100-person congressional fallout shelter. In 1958, under the cover of building a new wing of the resort, work began on a 112,000-square-foot (10,405 m²)

In case of nuclear attack, Congress would convene in a subterranean bunker beneath a swanky hotel.

bunker buried 720 feet (219 m) into the side of a hill.

Completed just in time for the 1962 Cuban missile crisis, the facility contained dormitories—with name-tagged bunk beds for Congress members—a clinic, a decontamination chamber, and a television broadcast center with a large, soothing backdrop of Capitol Hill. Some of the shelter's 53 rooms were hidden in plain sight. The Greenbrier's seemingly unremarkable Exhibition Hall was actually part of the bunker.

In the event of nuclear attack, concealed blast doors would seal off the rooms from the outside world, allowing the government to continue to function.

Like other Cold War bunkers, the Greenbrier's congressional fallout shelter was never used for its intended purpose. In 1992, journalist Ted Gup revealed the secret facility in an article for the *Washington Post*, resulting in its decommissioning.

Much of the bunker is now a private data storage facility, but a section is open to visitors by guided tour. The drab, utilitarian furnishings are quite the contrast to the five-star rooms located directly overhead.

The Greenbrier, 300 West Main Street, White Sulphur Springs. Amtrak's Cardinal train, running between Chicago and New York three days a week, stops at White Sulphur Springs. The resort is a 5-minute walk from the station. Ⓝ 37.785946 Ⓦ 80.308166

Green Bank's ban on radio waves has turned it into a haven for those who say they have electromagnetic hypersensitivity.

THE QUIET ZONE

GREEN BANK

Cell phones and wi-fi are not allowed in Green Bank. Since 1958, the small town has been part of the National Radio Quiet Zone, a 13,000-square-mile (33,670 km²) patch of land in which all electromagnetic radiation on the radio part of the spectrum is banned. This drastic measure is all in the name of science: Green Bank is home to an observatory with the world's largest fully steerable radio telescope. Radio waves in the vicinity would interfere with its operations.

The remote town with a population of around 150 offers a refuge for people who believe they are hypersensitive to electromagnetic transmissions. These "wi-fi refugees" report that their symptoms of aches, pains, and fatigue disappear in Green Bank. Despite these claims, the scientific community does not recognize electromagnetic hypersensitivity as a medical condition.

Whether its soothing effect on the electromagnetically overstimulated is scientifically verifiable or not, Green Bank offers something special for every visitor: the bizarre sight of cows, farmhouses, and vast green pastures dwarfed by a 485-foot (148 m) telescope.

National Radio Astronomy Observatory, West Virginia 28. The Green Bank observatory is open year-round for tours. Ⓝ 38.432896 Ⓦ 79.839717

New England

CONNECTICUT
HOLY LAND USA

WATERBURY

In the early 1950s devout Roman Catholic John Baptist Greco had a vision of a roadside theme park devoted to God. By the end of the decade, his vision had been realized. He called it Holy Land USA.

The theme park included a miniature Bethlehem, a re-creation of the Garden of Eden, biblical-themed dioramas, and various tributes to the life and work of Jesus Christ. But it was best known for its Hollywood-style sign reading HOLY LAND USA and its 56-foot (17 m) steel cross that could be seen for miles, especially when lit up at night. It is a town joke that Waterbury kids grow up thinking Jesus was electrocuted on the cross.

By the 1960s, Holy Land was attracting 50,000 visitors a year. But its popularity waned, and in 1984, the park—rundown, dated, and in need of a spruce-up—was closed for renovation. Greco had hopes of expanding the site to attract more tourists, but it never happened. He died in 1986.

Responsibility for the park passed to a group of nuns. For a while, they tried to keep the park clean and neat, but despite their efforts, Holy Land attracted vandals and graffiti artists. Statues were beheaded, dioramas destroyed, and tunnels blocked. Overgrown, dilapidated, and strewn with garbage, Holy Land has acquired an unholy reputation—a status sealed by the murder of a young woman there in 2010.

Slocum Street, Waterbury. Holy Land is down a dead-end road. It is up to you whether to believe the signs regarding surveillance cameras and prosecution of trespassers. Once inside, stick to the paths. Ⓝ 41.548636 Ⓦ 73.030328

CUSHING BRAIN COLLECTION

NEW HAVEN

Arrayed on shelves in a lush wood-paneled room at Yale's medical library are 550 jars filled with human brains. The collection once belonged to pioneering neurosurgeon Harvey Cushing, who preserved the brains from 1903 to 1932 as part of his tumor registry. When Cushing died in 1939, his undergraduate alma mater inherited the brains.

Cushing was among a handful of doctors operating on the brain during the early 20th century. At the time, about a third of patients who underwent brain tumor surgery did not survive the operation. Cushing introduced practices that dramatically lowered the mortality rate, such as monitoring blood pressure during surgery and operating with local anesthesia instead of ether. He was also the first to use X-rays to diagnose brain tumors.

Before they were restored and put on display in the medical library in 2010, the leaky jars holding Cushing's brain collection were locked in a basement under Yale's med student dorms. During the 1990s, students seeking a thrill would sneak into the dark, dusty storage room to view the fabled brains. Though these expeditions were unauthorized, students treated the specimens with care and apparently never swiped any. When moving the brains in 2010, Yale employees found a poster with names scrawled on it bearing the words "Leave Only Your Name. Take Only Your Memories."

Whitney Medical Library, Yale University, 333 Cedar Street, New Haven. Ⓝ 41.303218 Ⓦ 72.934003

ALSO IN CONNECTICUT

Crypt at Center Church on the Green

New Haven · When Center Church was built on a portion of New Haven's burial ground, 137 graves ended up in the basement.

A meeting of the minds—hundreds of them.

MAINE
WILHELM REICH MUSEUM
RANGELEY

A stone building with blue trim, once used as a laboratory, now holds much of the legacy of Wilhelm Reich, a psychoanalyst who believed that orgasmic energy could control the weather.

Reich began his career in 1919, working alongside Freud in Vienna. Influenced by Freud's theories on libido, Reich became fixated on what he called "orgastic potency": the complete release of energy and tension during orgasm. According to Reich, all neuroses—and even diseases like cancer—result from the inhibition of sexual energy.

Reich's work in the 1920s and '30s was unconventional—his "vegetotherapy" approach involved asking patients to strip to their underwear, after which he massaged them to loosen up their "body armor" until they screamed or vomited. During a series of bioelectricity experiments, Reich wired patients up to an oscillograph and observed changes in their bioelectricity as they engaged in sexual contact with each other.

Two weeks before the outbreak of the World War II, Reich moved to New York. It was here that he declared his discovery of "orgone," an omnipresent libidinal life force responsible for gravity, weather patterns, emotions, and health. Reich began building orgone accumulators: wooden booths lined with metal in which a subject could sit naked to absorb orgone energy.

Ten years later, in accordance with his new belief that the atmospheric accumulation of orgone radiation caused drought, Reich designed a cloudbuster. The machine consisted of a row of tubes aimed at

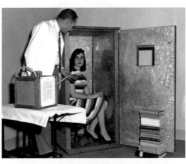

A woman sits in an orgone accumulator, designed by Wilhelm Reich to channel the omnipresent libidinal life force.

the sky, attached to hoses immersed in water. Reich believed that orgone energy would get sucked from the sky down through the tubes into the water, causing rain. In the mid-1950s, Reich switched his attention to UFOs, which he believed were spraying orgone radiation in an attempt to destroy Earth. He and his son traveled to Arizona, where they used cloudbusters as "spaceguns," aiming them at UFOs in an attempt to drain their energy.

By this time, Reich had attracted the attention of the FDA, which obtained an injunction to prevent him from shipping orgone accumulators out of Maine, where he then lived. When one of Reich's associates violated the injunction, the FDA ordered the destruction of Reich's accumulators, pamphlets, and books. Reich himself received a two-year prison sentence—the admitting psychiatrist at Danbury Federal Prison observed him to be experiencing delusions of grandeur. Eight months later Reich died in his cell bed after suffering a heart attack.

The museum at Orgonon, the idyllic site of Reich's Maine lab, contains equipment used in his eccentric experiments, as well as orgone accumulators, personal memorabilia, and original editions of publications burned by the FDA. Outside, a short walk into the woods, is a cloudbuster aimed directly at Reich's tomb.

19 Orgonon Circle, Rangeley. To really soak up the Orgonon energy, stay at Tamarack, one of the site's rental cottages, once the living quarters of the Reich family. Ⓝ 44.965682 Ⓦ 70.642710

INTERNATIONAL CRYPTOZOOLOGY MUSEUM
PORTLAND

An 8-foot-tall (2.4 m) Sasquatch guards the door of this museum, whose 10,000-item collection includes hair samples of the Abominable Snowman, fecal matter from a yeti, and a life-size mold of a coelacanth, a fish once thought to be extinct but rediscovered in 1938. Owner Loren Coleman, a lifelong cryptic enthusiast, is happy to talk to you about mothmen, chupacabras, tatzelwurms, and his own travels on the bigfoot-hunting trail. Pick up a yeti finger puppet or bigfoot-shaped air freshener in the gift shop.

11 Avon Street, Portland. Ⓝ 43.654222 Ⓦ 70.265869 ➤➤

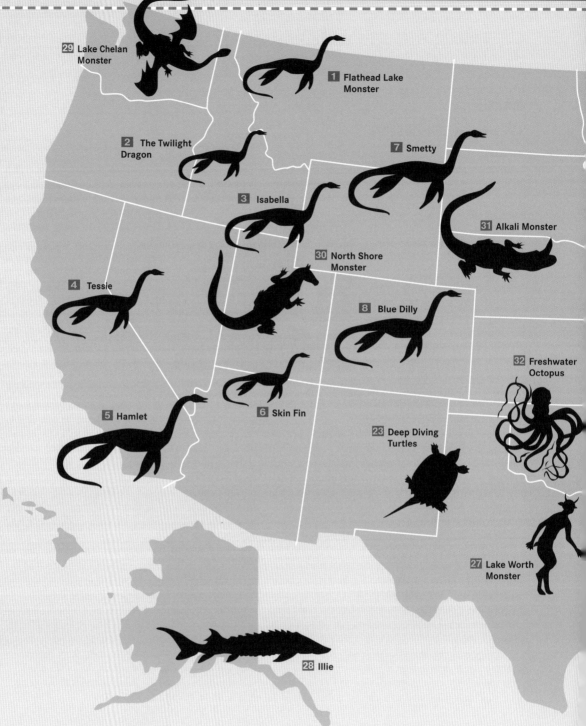

29 Lake Chelan Monster

1 Flathead Lake Monster

2 The Twilight Dragon

7 Smetty

3 Isabella

31 Alkali Monster

30 North Shore Monster

4 Tessie

8 Blue Dilly

32 Freshwater Octopus

5 Hamlet

6 Skin Fin

23 Deep Diving Turtles

27 Lake Worth Monster

28 Illie

LAKE MONSTERS OF THE USA

NESSIES

1. Flathead Lake Monster
Flathead Lake, MT

2. The Twilight Dragon
Payette Lake, ID

3. Isabella
Bear Lake, ID

4. Tessie
Lake Tahoe, CA

5. Hamlet
Lake Elsinore, CA

6. Skin Fin
Lake Powell, AZ

7. Smetty
Lake De Smet, WY

8. Blue Dilly
Lake Dillon, CO

9. Pepie
Lake Pepin, MN

10. Obojoki
Okoboji Lake, IA

11. Rocky
Rock Lake, WI

12. Lake Michigan Monster
Lake Michigan, MI

13. Bessie
Lake Erie, OH

14. Champ
Lake Champlain, VT

15. Poco
Pocomoonshine Lake, ME

16. Gloucester Sea Serpent
Gloucester Harbor, MA

17. Kipsy
Hudson River, NY

18. Chessie
Chesapeake Bay, MD

19. Normie
Lake Norman, NC

20. Altamaha-ha
Altamaha River, GA

21. Tarpie
Lake Tarpon, FL

22. Muck Monster
Lake Worth Lagoon, FL

9 Pepie

35 Mishebeshu

25 The White Monkey

15 Poco

14 Champ

11 Rocky

13 Bessie

16 Gloucester Sea Serpent

12 Lake Michigan Monster

10 Obojoki

24 Beast of Busco

17 Kipsy

18 Chessie

34 Herry

33 Whitey

19 Normie

20 Altamaha-ha

26 Tainted Keitre

21 Tarpie

22 Muck Monster

N

W

E

S

Whether scaly, slimy, or furry, America's mythical lake monsters have inspired a whole lot of small-town tales. Here are some of the fabled creatures that have made their mark on imaginations around the country.

GIANT TURTLES

23. Deep Diving Turtles
Bottomless Lakes, NM

24. Beast of Busco
Fulks Lake, IN

WEBBED HOMINIDS

25. The White Monkey
Saco River, ME

26. Tainted Keitre
Honey Island Swamp, LA

GOAT MAN

27. Lake Worth Monster
Lake Worth, TX

MONSTER FISH

28. Illie
Iliamna Lake, AK

WINGED ALLIGATOR-SNAKE

29. Lake Chelan Monster
Lake Chelan, WA

HORSE-HEADED ALLIGATOR

30. North Shore Monster
Great Salt Lake, UT

HORNED ALLIGATOR

31. Alkali Monster
Alkali Lake, NE

GIANT KILLER OCTOPUS

32. Freshwater Octopus
Lake Thunderbird, OK

HORNED BEAST

33. Whitey
White River, AR

GIANT EEL PIG

34. Herry
Herrington Lake, KY

AQUATIC LYNX MONSTER

35. Mishebeshu
Lake Huron, MI

MASSACHUSETTS

MAPPARIUM

BOSTON

In 1930, Boston architect Chester Lindsay Churchill was commissioned to design the new Christian Science Publishing Society headquarters. His orders: Build something that could compete with the other grand newspaper headquarters of the day. The *New York Daily News* building had its famous gigantic spinning globe. The *Christian Science Monitor* had to do one better.

Enter the Mapparium, a three-story-tall, inside-out stained-glass globe that is bisected by a glass walkway. Once illuminated with hundreds of lamps, it now glows with the light of LEDs.

The Mapparium is the only place in the world in which the surface of the earth can be seen without distortion. Even when looking at an accurate globe, the relative sizes of the continents are distorted by perspective, as the spherical shape causes different regions to appear at different distances from the eye. But with a view from the very center of a globe, the eye is the same distance from every point on the map.

It is fascinating to view Earth this way. Africa is huge. North America, Europe, and Asia are all jammed up against the North Pole. You have to look nearly straight up to see them. Sizes and locations of continents and countries you've always taken for granted are suddenly unfamiliar.

While the relative size and position of the continents are correct, the map's political boundaries are long out of date. The Mapparium hasn't changed since 1935. It's still possible to find Siam and French Indochina, but not Israel or Indonesia.

The Mary Baker Eddy Library, 200 Massachusetts Ave, Boston. While inside the Mapparium, stand in the middle and listen. You'll be able to hear the voices of anyone else inside with perfect clarity, regardless of where they're standing or how loudly they're talking. Ⓝ 42.345130 Ⓦ 71.086294

Test out the enhanced acoustics while standing at the center of the globe.

JAMES ALLEN'S BIOGRAPHY

BOSTON

Among the rare books, maps, and manuscripts of the Boston Athenæum, a private library established in 1807, is a small publication bound in a leathery light gray material. Titled *Narrative of the Life of James Allen*, it is a well-preserved example of autoanthropodermic bibliopegy: a book bound in the skin of its author.

James Allen was a New England bank robber and highwayman. His brazen ambushes during the 1830s landed him in Massachusetts State Prison, where he died of tuberculosis in 1837 at the age of 28. As ill health tightened its grip on the illiterate criminal, he began to dictate his memoirs to a warden, instructing him to deliver a skin-bound copy of the finished book to a man named John Fenno.

Though Allen had only met Fenno once, the circumstances of the encounter ensured he would never forget him. In 1834, Allen attacked Fenno on the Salem Turnpike. To the surprise of the highwayman, Fenno fought back, only fleeing after Allen scrambled for his gun and fired a shot, hitting the victim's torso. Miraculously, a buckle on Fenno's clothing deflected the bullet.

Arrested in 1835 based on a tip by Fenno, Allen nonetheless maintained an admiration for the target of his attempted robbery. As a token of respect, Allen bequeathed a unique gift: his life story, bound in his own tanned, dyed skin.

It is rare to see a book bound in the skin of its author.

10½ Beacon Street, Boston. Get the T (Red or Green line) to Park Street station. Guided tours for nonmembers are available on Tuesday and Thursday afternoons. Ⓝ 42.357945 Ⓦ 71.062029

MUSEUM OF BAD ART

BOSTON

Woman Riding Crustacean, one of the works in the Museum of Bad Art's 600-strong collection, is a portrait of a faceless, handless, footless naked woman astride a giant lobster. For reasons unknown, an amorphous black blob encases the woman and her animal. Like the other works in this museum's collection, there is a glaring gap between the artist's sincerity and skill level.

The museum began with a single painting found between two trash cans on a Boston street in 1993. Antiques dealer Scott Wilson spotted a portrait of an elderly woman dancing in a field of flowers under a yellow sky. In one hand she holds a freshly picked bouquet. In the other she holds a red armchair. Using this heartfelt but poorly rendered painting as a foundation piece, Wilson and his friend Jerry Reilly established a bad-art collection.

Since its inception, the museum has had rigorous standards. Nine out of every ten submissions are rejected

Ninety percent of submissions to the museum are rejected for being too good.

on the grounds that they display too much artistic competence. Those chosen—acquired via donations, thrift stores, yard sales, and trash heaps—exhibit wonky perspective, confusing symbolism, and lurid color combinations. Artwork depicting humans often omits hands and feet due to their being difficult to draw.

Around 30 items from the museum's collection are on show at each of its two Boston locations. Official museum commentary accompanies each artwork—*Juggling Dog in Hula Skirt* is described as "a fine example of labor-intensive pointlessism"—but guests are welcome to contribute their own interpretations in the visitor's book.

46 Tappan Street, top floor, Brookline. Get the T (Green line) to Brookline Hills station. There is another gallery at the Somerville Theatre, located at 55 Davis Square. Admission is free with every movie ticket. Ⓝ 42.331603 Ⓦ 71.127618

ETHER DOME

BOSTON

In the 1830s, surgery was a fast, brutal affair. Patients—plied with opium or whiskey, or punched unconscious if they were lucky—would be held down while doctors sawed off a leg or excised a tumor as quickly as possible. Top Scottish surgeon Robert Liston was famed for his ability to lop off a limb in under three minutes. (Once he cut off a leg in under three minutes, but was so caught up in the excitement of the feat that he accidentally removed the patient's testicles.) Diethyl ether, a volatile liquid narcotic, was used recreationally at the time—college students and bored socialites would take a big sniff and go on giggly "ether frolics"—but its pain-erasing properties had not yet been discovered.

The first public demonstration of ether as a surgical anesthetic occurred in 1846 at a Massachusetts General Hospital operating theater. A crowd of onlookers peered from the tiered seats as dentist William Morton administered ether vapors to Edward Gilbert Abbott. A few minutes later, with Abbott listless and unresponsive, surgeon John Warren sliced into a tumor on Abbott's neck. The absence of screams was encouraging.

When Abbott awoke and confirmed he had felt nothing, Warren turned triumphantly to the audience. "Gentlemen," he said, "this is no humbug!"

The Ether Dome, as the operating theater came to be known, was in use from 1821 to 1867.

Today the restored dome is open to the public when not being used for lectures and meetings. In addition to its ether-infused history, the room contains a collection of 19th-century surgical instruments, a skeleton, and Padihershef, an Egyptian mummy donated to the hospital in 1823.

55 Fruit Street, Bulfinch Building, 4th floor, Boston. While you're there, also take a look at the dome's architecture and the historic oil painting depicting the use of ether in an operating theater. Ⓝ 42.363154 Ⓦ 71.068833

CITY GUIDE: More to Explore in Boston

Dutch House

Brookline • Built for the 1893 Chicago World's Fair, this four-story Dutch Renaissance–style abode was dismantled and reassembled in Brookline.

Infinite Corridor (MIThenge)

Cambridge • The 825-foot (251.4 m) corridor that threads straight through multiple MIT buildings has garnered the nickname MIThenge—thanks to its east-west positioning, it aligns with the setting or rising sun twice a year.

Mark I at Harvard's Science Center

Cambridge • This 51-foot-long (15.5 m) World War II calculator harks back to the days when "computer" was a job title.

Metropolitan Waterworks Museum

Chestnut Hill • See the steam-powered pumping engines that supplied Boston's water back in the 1880s.

Madonna Queen National Shrine

East Boston • A 35-foot statue (11 m) of "Madonna, Queen of the Universe"—that's Mary, mother of Jesus, not the Material Girl—was built in 1954.

Granary Burying Ground

Historic Downtown • Wander among rows of 18th-century gravestones, many decorated with skulls and bones, at this burial ground founded in 1660.

Jamaica Pond Bench

Jamaica Plain • Installed in 2006 as guerrilla art, a U-shaped, seatless park bench has earned a permanent place in Parkman Memorial Park.

All Saints Way

North End • A wall in a narrow alleyway has become one man's shrine to Catholic saints.

Molasses Flood Plaque

North End • Pay your respects at the site of the Great Molasses Flood of 1919, during which the slow, sweet sludge killed 21 people and injured 150.

Venetian Palace Diorama

North End • In the main room of the Boston Public Library's North End branch is a miniature replica of the Doge's Palace, a grand bit of Venetian architecture first built in the 14th century.

Franklin Park Zoo Bear Dens

Roxbury • The bear dens of the first Franklin Park Zoo, built in 1912, have been left in their original wooded location for explorers to discover.

Museum of Modern Renaissance

Somerville • A former Masonic hall has been transformed into a mystical temple of art, complete with murals of flowers, mermaids, and druids.

Steinert Hall

Theater District • Since it closed in 1942, this ornate 19th-century concert hall, located four floors beneath a piano store, has sat waiting for the music to return.

Even the furniture is made of rolled-up newspapers.

PAPER HOUSE

ROCKPORT

The phrase "paper house" may invite images of something fragile, but the Paper House of Rockport has been standing strong since the 1920s. In 1922, mechanical engineer Elis F. Stenman started building a house with newspapers. Initially, it was a hobby. Stenman pressed the papers together to form the walls, and applied glue and varnish to make them sturdy.

When it came time to furnish the house, Stenman continued the newspaper theme, rolling papers into tiny logs, stacking them to form chairs, bookcases, and desks, and sloshing varnish on top for a lacquered wood effect.

Stenman spent summers in his newspaper house until 1930, after which the place opened to the public as a museum. Look through the layers of shellac and you'll see headlines and tales from the 1920s, including, on one desk, accounts of Charles Lindbergh's pioneering transatlantic flight.

52 Pigeon Hill Street, Rockport. The house is around 40 miles (64 km) northeast of Boston, in the coastal town of Rockport. It's open from spring through fall. Ⓝ 42.672947 Ⓦ 70.634617

....

NEW HAMPSHIRE

AMERICA'S STONEHENGE

SALEM

The name of this place sets you up for disappointment—it's nothing like the original. America's Stonehenge, formerly known as Mystery Hill, is a collection of small stone walls, modest rock arrangements, and underground chambers, all of which were constructed for undetermined reasons by persons unknown.

Radiocarbon dating of charcoal pits at America's Stonehenge reveals that people occupied the area during the second millennium BCE. Prevailing wisdom points toward a Native American presence at that time, but some people, including the site's current owners, suggest that the stone structures were the work of pre-Columbian Europeans. How such people might have ended up in New Hampshire millennia before the arrival of Columbus is anyone's guess.

A tour of America's Stonehenge incorporates "The Sacrificial Table," a hefty slab of granite with a groove around its perimeter—handy for draining the blood spilled during a ritual killing. This table looks very similar to the lye-leaching stones used during America's colonial era, which only confuses things further. The family of llamas that saunters around the site make for an adorable diversion when the muddled history becomes too frustrating.

105 Haverhill Road, Salem. Ⓝ 42.842852 Ⓦ 71.207217

BETTY AND BARNEY HILL ARCHIVE

DURHAM

Betty and Barney Hill were the first people to claim to have been abducted by aliens, back in 1961.

Late at night on September 19, 1961, married couple Betty and Barney Hill were driving home to Portsmouth, New Hampshire, from a vacation in Montreal when they spotted a moving light in the sky. Intrigued by the unusual sight, they pulled over. And that, according to the couple's later statements, is when things took a turn for the freaky-deaky.

The Hills said that as the light approached, they realized it was a spaceship. They could tell because they looked in the window of the craft and saw a dozen gray-skinned Reticulans staring back. During hypnosis sessions conducted after the incident, Betty and Barney spoke of being taken aboard the ship, subjected to invasive medical experiments, and returned to their car several hours later with scant recollection of the experience.

Abduction by gray-skinned aliens has become a sci-fi trope, but the now-clichéd imagery originated with the Hills' tale. The Betty and Barney Hill Archive at the University of New Hampshire contains correspondence, personal journals and essays, newspaper clippings, photos, slides, films, and audiotapes relating to the couple's alleged alien abduction. Standout items include transcripts of hypnosis sessions, the purple dress Betty was wearing on the night in question, and notebooks in which Betty documented all her UFO sightings from 1977 to 1991.

Dimond Library, University of New Hampshire, 18 Library Way, Durham. N 43.135515 W 70.933210

RHODE ISLAND
ROGER WILLIAMS ROOT

PROVIDENCE

Embedded behind glass in a wall at the John Brown House is the tree root that ate Roger Williams.

Williams, the founder of Rhode Island, died in 1683 and was buried in an unmarked grave on the family farm. There he remained for 177 years, until Providence community leader Zachariah Allen led an effort to locate and disinter Williams's remains in order to create a more fitting memorial to the esteemed man.

When the grave was dug up and the coffin opened, however, not a trace of Williams remained. In his place was the vaguely anthropomorphic root of an apple tree. Naturally, those who came upon the root assumed that it had grown into the coffin and eaten Williams, after which (having swallowed his essence) it assumed a stick-figure form.

This tree root, which may or may not have fed on the body of the state's founding father, is now on display at the John Brown House, Providence's oldest mansion.

52 Power Street, Providence. While in town, visit Roger Williams Park. N 41.822778 W 71.404444

ALSO IN RHODE ISLAND

John Hay Library

Providence · Books bound in human skin and H. P. Lovecraft's letters are among a few of the treasures this library has to offer.

Gun Totem

Providence · This 12-foot-high (3.6 m) pillar was made with 1,000 guns recovered during a 2001 firearms buyback program in Pittsburgh.

VERMONT
ROCK OF AGES GRANITE QUARRY

BARRE

The Rock of Ages is the world's largest deep-hole granite quarry. A minibus transports visitors up to the top of the quarry, where you can view this mammoth mine safely from behind a gate. Although much of its depths are under a well of milky-green water, the crater is astoundingly huge, plunging nearly 600 feet (183 m) deep.

Next to the quarry is an enormous cutting facility that has been in operation since 1885. In this 160,000-square-foot (14.865 m²) space, huge blocks of granite are moved around, cut, polished, and engraved for tombstones and monuments.

Before leaving, be sure to roll a few frames at the outdoor granite bowling alley. The Rock of Ages company experimented with granite bowling lanes in the 1950s, but the concept never caught on. A prototype from that trial period is on display at the quarry site and has been restored for family fun.

The bus ride to the quarry passes piles and piles of granite blocks, where quarry workers have simply dumped pieces of rock with fractures or cracks over the years. Called "grout piles" from the Scottish word for scrap (many Scots worked in the quarry in its early days), these piles can be seen all over the town. **N** 44.156731 **W** 72.491400

ALSO IN VERMONT

Dog Chapel

St. Johnsbury · This small village church celebrates the spiritual bond between canines and humans.

Most of America's granite headstones come from this massive crater.

Alaska and Hawaii

ALASKA
SPIRIT HOUSES

EKLUTNA

The cemetery behind St. Nicholas Orthodox Church in Eklutna has more than 100 tiny, colorful houses that look like chicken coops. Built to cover graves, the miniature buildings combine Russian Orthodox tradition and Native American practices.

Eklutna, located about 25 miles (40 km) outside of Anchorage, was the site of many Dena'ina Athabascan Indian villages about 800 years ago. Russian Orthodox missionaries arrived in the area around 1830 and the two communities slowly integrated.

Before the missionaries arrived, Athabascans cremated their dead. As the population became assimilated into Russian Orthodoxy, which forbids cremation, they began burying their deceased in the cemetery of St. Nicholas Church.

Spirit houses, an Athabascan tradition, provide a place for the deceased soul to dwell during the 40 days it is believed to linger in this world. When a body is buried, stones are piled on the grave and covered with a blanket to provide symbolic warmth and comfort to the person. Then the spirit house is placed over the blanket, and relatives paint it in colors that represent the family.

The final touch is an Orthodox symbol: a wooden three-bar cross. The bars represent, from the top, the sign placed on the cross during Christ's crucifixion, the bar to which his arms were nailed, and the footrest that supported his body.

Eklutna Historical Park, Eklutna Village Road, Anchorage. The cemetery is a 30-minute drive from downtown Anchorage and is open May through September.
Ⓝ 61.460946 Ⓦ 149.360985

A mix of Russian Orthodox and Native American traditions, small graveside houses keep the souls of the dead safe.

Skee-ball, igloos, a giant furry boot, Santa's "rocket ship"—all can be found at Mukluk Land.

MUKLUK LAND

TOK

Try as you might, it's difficult to determine the unifying theme of Mukluk Land. "Stuff from Alaska" is about as close as it gets.

Retired schoolteachers George and Beth Jacobs established Mukluk Land in 1985 as a way to share their Alaskan memorabilia with the public. The park, which touts itself as "Alaska's most unique destination," contains a junkyard, a room full of arcade games, an impressive collection of beer cans, a minigolf course, a giant cabbage, and a vintage red-and-white bus known as "Santa's Rocket Ship."

And then there are the dolls. A log cabin houses hundreds of them—in rows on the floor, seated on shelves, stuffed side-by-side into open suitcases, and crammed into a red plastic convertible. All face a window through which you can peer into the room. Entering the cabin is forbidden, a fact asserted by the open bear trap on the floor.

Once you've perused Engine Alley, Heater Heaven, and the rest of the rusting machinery on the grass, pose for a photo in front of the park's main attraction: the giant mukluk. The big red boot, festooned with white pompoms, is suspended at head level from the front gate.

Milepost 1317 Alaska Highway, Tok. The park is 3 miles (5 km) west of Tok (which rhymes with "smoke"). It's open June through August.
N 63.343807 W 143.098213

Also in Alaska

Mendenhall Ice Caves

Juneau · Take a walk inside a 12-mile-long (19 km), partially hollow glacier blessed with brilliant blue walls.

Lady of the Lake

North Pole · An abandoned WB-29 weather reconnaissance aircraft sits submerged in a lake in the Alaskan wilderness.

Musk Ox Farm

Palmer · This livestock farm harvests the strong, soft wool of the Alaskan musk ox, a horned, 600-pound (272 kg) species whose males emit a pungent musky odor during mating season.

Aurora Ice Museum

Fairbanks · Mind-blowing, neon-lit ice carvings and frozen fantasy scenes grace the largest year-round ice environment in the world.

City of Whittier

Whittier · Just one building houses the vast majority of this town's 217 residents.

ADAK NATIONAL FOREST

ADAK

There's no chance you'll get lost in the forest on Adak Island, a 275-square-mile (712 km²) splotch of tundra located toward the farthest end of the Aleutian Island chain that stretches west from the Alaskan peninsula. Adak National Forest—the smallest in the United States—consists of just 33 pines, all huddled together in the middle of a sprawling, treeless plain. A sign at the edge of the grove reads: "You are now entering and leaving the Adak National Forest."

The modest forest came about when members of the US military, stationed at Adak's air base during World War II, participated in a Christmas-tree-planting program to improve morale. In homage to the original purpose of the pines, the 300 residents of Adak decorate the forest with Christmas lights every December.

Off Hillside Boulevard, near Bayshore Highway, Adak. Flights to Adak from Anchorage take about 3 hours.
Ⓝ 51.906106 Ⓦ 176.658055

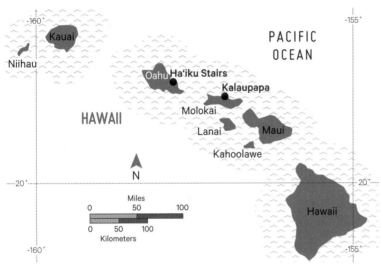

HAWAII
HAʻIKU STAIRS

KANEOHE, OAHU

To score a spectacular view of the sunrise—and avoid being chased away by a security guard—you'll need to start your hike up Haʻiku Stairs in the dead of night. The 3,922 steps, installed in 1942 in order to string antenna cables across the valley, became off-limits in 1987, when vandals destroyed three sections of the stairway. Undeterred, thrill-seeking hikers soon took to sneaking up the stairs, incurring the ire of local residents.

Though the city repaired the broken and rusted segments in 2002 with the intent of opening the Haʻiku Stairs to the public, community complaints and liability concerns have kept them closed. At just 18 inches (46 cm) wide, and more like a ladder in the steepest sections, the steps require climbers to travel single-file. A handrail on each side offers protection from tumbles down the mountain, but those rails—and the stairs—are often wet and slippery due to high humidity.

Each day at about 5 a.m., a security guard arrives at the foot of the stairs to enforce the no-trespassing rule. If you can find your way through the pitch-black jungle before the guard arrives, you'll be able to hike to the summit and back without getting into trouble. (As long as you are quiet and polite, the guard may even congratulate you or take a group photo when you arrive back at the bottom.) The reward for completing the adrenaline-fueled, mist-shrouded ascent is a glorious 360-degree view of Oahu.

Kuneki and Makena Streets, Kaneohe. Just a reminder: This climb is illegal. But if you're going to do it, bring a headlamp, water, a waterproof jacket, and gloves with grip. You'll see a gate—go past it on the right side and down the concrete road. Make a left at the first fork and a right at the second. You'll see an opening leading to a path on your left. Walk along it until you arrive at another paved road. Go left on the road and walk until you see the security guard's blue tent. Make a right into the jungle and go past the next gate on its left side. You've arrived.
Ⓝ 21.410265 Ⓦ 157.818364

Nicknamed the Stairway to Heaven, the Haʻiku Stairs ascend into the clouds above Kaneohe.

Isolated from the world by 1,600-foot cliffs, Kalaupapa was home to more than 8,000 exiled Hawaiian lepers.

KALAUPAPA

MOLOKAI

For over a century the island of Molokai served as a beautiful prison for people forcibly removed from society. In 1865, Hawaii's King Kamehameha V authorized the Act to Prevent the Spread of Leprosy. At the time, the condition, also known as Hansen's disease, was regarded as highly contagious and incurable. Those afflicted with the disfiguring disease faced exclusion from their communities, due to the belief that leprosy was a punishment.

The 1865 act allowed the Hawaiian government to arrest and exile anyone thought to be affected by leprosy. From 1866 until 1969, over 8,000 people were transported to the isolated colony of Kalaupapa on the north coast of Molokai. Most had leprosy. Some were mistakenly diagnosed. All spent their days surrounded by ocean on one side and 1,600-foot (487 m) sea cliffs on the other.

A lack of food and shelter made the colony's early years particularly miserable. In 1873 a Belgian Catholic priest named Father Damien de Veuster arrived at Kalaupapa. For the next 16 years, Father Damien improved conditions at the colony by arranging medical services, building homes, and attending to the sick. His close contact with patients proved fatal: He died from leprosy in 1889, at age forty-nine.

The introduction of sulfone drugs in the 1940s rendered leprosy noncontagious. Though compulsory isolation ended in 1969, many patients chose to stay at Kalaupapa. A few members of the colony still live among the historic community structures, which include a movie hall, a group home, and 14 cemeteries. These places are preserved so visitors can better understand the experiences of the people once confined to this prison in paradise.

Kalaupapa National Park, Molokai. Molokai is a 30-minute flight from Honolulu. Mule is the preferred mode of transport along the trail to Kalaupapa. All visitors must be over sixteen and join a tour offered by residents of Kalaupapa. Ⓝ 21.166395 Ⓦ 157.105464

ALSO IN HAWAII

Pineapple Maze at the Dole Plantation

Wahiawā · Race through the largest plant maze in the world.

Kamilo Beach

Naalehu · Formerly a stretch of pristine white sand, this beach has become a trash trap of the Great Pacific Garbage Patch.

Latin America and the Caribbean

South America
ARGENTINA • BOLIVIA • BRAZIL • CHILE • COLOMBIA
PERU • URUGUAY • VENEZUELA

Mexico

Central America
BELIZE • COSTA RICA • EL SALVADOR
GUATEMALA • HONDURAS • NICARAGUA • PANAMA

Caribbean Islands
BAHAMAS • BARBADOS • BERMUDA • CAYMAN ISLANDS
CUBA • CURAÇAO • DOMINICA • DOMINICAN REPUBLIC
GUADELOUPE • HAITI • MARTINIQUE • MONTSERRAT
PUERTO RICO • ST. KITTS AND NEVIS • TRINIDAD AND TOBAGO
ST. VINCENT AND THE GRENADINES

CARIBBEAN SEA

ATLANTIC OCEAN

Everlasting Lightning

CARACAS

VENEZUELA

Drowned Church

Pablo Escobar's Hippos

Armero
BOGOTÁ
Guayabetal Zip Lines
Caño Cristales

Sarisariñama

SUR GUY
GUY GUF

COLOMBIA

Amazon Stonehenge

ECU

EQUATOR

EQUATOR

Nazi Graveyard

Amazon River

Amazon Bore Surfing

Fordlândia

Lençóis Maranhenses

Sarcofagi of Carajía Gocta Falls

PERU

Boiling River of the Amazon

Chan Chan

Santo Daime

BRAZIL

LIMA
Ica Stones

Last Incan Grass Bridge

Uros

North Yungas Death Road
Witches' Market
LA PAZ

BRASÍLIA

BOLIVIA

Glowing Termite Mounds of Emas

Nitrate Towns

Salar de Uyuni

Mano del Desierto

PRY

Snake Island

SOUTH AMERICA

EQUATOR

The Unfinished Giants of Easter Island

SOUTH PACIFIC OCEAN

Miles
0   1,000
0   1,000
Kilometers

Ischigualasto Provincial Park

Robinson Crusoe Island

URUGUAY

CHILE

SANTIAGO

Laguna del Diamante

BUENOS AIRES

Laguna Garzón Bridge

MONTEVIDEO

PACIFIC OCEAN

ARGENTINA

ATLANTIC OCEAN

The Girl Who Died Twice

El Ateneo Grand Splendid

BUENOS AIRES

Marble Cathedral

SOUTH AMERICA

Miles
0   500   1,000
0   500   1,000
Kilometers

Falkland Islands

N

South Georgia

This historic, palatial theater is now one of the world's most beautiful bookstores.

ARGENTINA
EL ATENEO GRAND SPLENDID

BUENOS AIRES

With frescoed ceilings, ornate theater boxes, elegant rounded balconies, detailed trimmings, and plush red stage curtains, the El Ateneo Grand Splendid is hardly your average bookstore. Built in 1919, the majestic building began as a theater featuring tango legends, then became a cinema—the first in Buenos Aires to show films with sound. While the titles on offer tend to be more expensive than those of other city bookstores, the staggeringly opulent interior is reason enough to pay a visit.

Avenida Santa Fe 1860, Buenos Aires. Ride the subway to the Callao stop and walk three blocks north to Avenida Santa Fe. Ⓢ 34.595907 Ⓦ 58.394185

ALSO IN BUENOS AIRES

Castillo Naveira

Buenos Aires · This enormous neo-Gothic castle, hidden from the public, has a hall of armor and a stable of vintage cars.

Floralis Genérica

Buenos Aires · Every day this 105-foot-wide (32 m) giant metallic flower blooms anew.

Laguna Epecuén, Carhué

Buenos Aires Province · This Argentinean lake swallowed an entire village in 1985.

Museo del Mar

Buenos Aires Province · This museum holds a vast collection of seashells, fossils, and marine invertebrates.

Pedro Martín Ureta's Forest Guitar

Buenos Aires Province · A man's lost love inspired this giant guitar made entirely of living trees.

Xul Solar Museum

Buenos Aires · See the collected work of an artist of alternate worlds, inventor of languages, and dreamer of utopias.

TOMB OF THE GIRL WHO DIED TWICE

BUENOS AIRES

Most visitors to the beautiful baroque Recoleta Cemetery come to see the tomb of Eva Perón. But just a short walk south lies another curious sight: the crypt of Rufina Cambaceres, the girl who died twice.

In 1902, on her 19th birthday, Rufina was getting ready for a night out when she lost consciousness and collapsed. Three doctors declared her dead. The young socialite was placed in a coffin, given a funeral, and sealed in a Recoleta mausoleum.

A few days later, a cemetery worker, noticing signs of a break-in, entered the mausoleum. Suspecting a grave robber, he opened the casket to find Rufina's remains and scratch marks on the inside of the coffin. Rufina had been buried alive. Awakening in her coffin, she struggled to escape, clawing at the lid before she died of cardiac arrest.

Like many "buried alive" stories, it is difficult to separate truth from fiction, and Rufina's tale is told with varying layers of embellishment. In one version, her initial "death" is caused by the scandalous revelation that her boyfriend had been sleeping with his own mother.

Whether any of the stories are true or if they are the result of overactive imaginations, Rufina's tomb is worth visiting for its beauty alone. It features a full-size statue of the girl gazing out at the cemetery while holding shut the door to the very mausoleum that entrapped her.

Junín 1790, Buenos Aires. Pick up a free map at the entrance to Recoleta Cemetery. Rufina's grave is number 95, about three blocks south of Eva Perón's in the southwestern section. Ⓝ 34.588328 Ⓦ 58.392408 ➤

➤ Historical Methods of Preventing Premature Burial

During the 18th and 19th centuries, doctors understood that many people were accidentally being buried alive, but didn't yet know how to tell the difference between someone who was dead and someone who merely looked it. To solve this quandary, a variety of unusual methods were used to test for signs of life.

TOBACCO SMOKE ENEMAS were commonly used in 18th-century Europe to try to resuscitate the apparently dead. Smoke—blown through a pipe into the rectum using a bellows or from the mouth of an unflinching rescuer—was thought to bring people back from the brink of death. Drowning victims were often subjected to smoke enemas after being hauled from the water, with occasional (and probably only coincidental) success.

FOOT TORTURE was occasionally employed postmortem. Well-meaning physicians cut corpses' soles with razors, shoved needles under their toenails, and applied red-hot irons to their soles, all to ensure the person was really, truly, undeniably dead.

WAITING MORTUARIES, in which bodies were kept until they showed signs of putrefaction, were popular in Germany in the late 1800s. They were essentially hospitals for the dead, their

wards of corpses watched over by nurses. In order to mask the smell of rotting human flesh and organs, flower arrangements were placed beside each bed.

SAFETY COFFINS addressed the fear of premature burial by incorporating features such as air tubes, strings linking the body's hands and feet to an aboveground bell, flag, or lights, and for coffins installed in

vaults, spring-loaded lids. Despite the rash of safety coffin patents, there are no reported cases of the mistakenly dead being saved by such contraptions.

Safety coffins allowed the mistakenly buried to make their living status known.

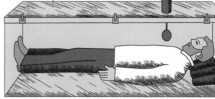

ESMA Museum

Núñez • A haunting and horrific museum of Argentina's "Dirty War," this former naval officers' school, one of 400 detention centers for political prisoners in the late 1970s and early '80s, opened its doors in 2008 to keep the memory of the military junta's "disappeared" from fading.

Remembrance Park

Belgrano • Along the Rio de la Plata, the Parque de la Memoria pays tribute to the tens of thousands lost to state-sponsored terrorism and violence in the late 1970s and early '80s—with emotionally expressive sculpture, sweeping lawns, wide ramps, and a wall of remembrance etched with the names of the victims.

Tierra Santa

Belgrano • Join the crowds flocking to catch the pop-up 40-foot Jesus, eat a "Last Supper" with some mannequin apostles, see a recreation of the Book of Genesis (did they have animatronic hippos back then?), and grab a selfie with Judas Iscariot.

Carlos Gardel Tomb

Chacarita • Like a tale from one of his own sad songs, tango composer and singer Gardel died in a plane crash at the height of his powers. His tomb at La Chacarita Cemetery features a life-size tuxedoed statue of the great entertainer, surrounded by dozens of bronze plaques from around the globe expressing undying love and gratitude.

The Weather Indicator at the Botanical Garden

Palermo • A marble obelisk topped with a bronze globe etched with zodiac symbols sits near a pond in the Carlos Thays Botanical Garden. A plaque tells you what it's called (a "Weather Indicator"), when it was made (1910), and who made it (Jose Markovich)— what it's supposed to do, or

Dance down the alley of El Caminito.

how it's connected to the weather, is a quiet mystery.

Castillo de Naveira

Lujan • Long kept hidden from public view, this sprawling neo-Gothic castle seems to rise out of the Argentine countryside and into a Grimm's fairy tale—it's a good hour outside the city, but worth the journey back to another time and place.

Recoleta Cemetery

Recoleta • A few of the mausoleums in this cemetery for Buenos Aires's upper crust have fallen on hard times, visited more often by the resident cats, but it's still one of the world's most beautiful resting places. The rows and rows of nearly 5,000 ornate vaults (including the tomb of Eva Perón) make for an extraordinary city of the dead.

The Golden Hall

San Nicolás • Teatro Colón is universally considered one of the three or four greatest opera houses in the world. There is more than a little touch of the Versailles in its Salón Dorado, a gallery positively dripping in gilt, and lined with mirrors of infinite reflection.

Barolo Palace

Monserrat • Until 1935, this 22-story office tower was the tallest building in South America. Its allegorical design—from Hell in the lobby, up through Purgatory, and finally to Heaven at the top—is modeled after Dante's *Divine Comedy*.

Block of Lights

Monserrat • Known as the Illuminated Block, or Manzana de las Luces, this 17th- and 18th-century complex of buildings, churches, and secret tunnels has played several crucial roles over the course of Buenos Aires history— educational, missionary, legislative, military—but the extent and original purpose of those tunnels remain a mystery.

Puente de la Mujer

Puerto Madero • An improbably cantilevered pedestrian crossing, the "Bridge of the Women" is, according to its architect, intended to evoke a pair of tango dancers, but its futuristic needle-nose design would be more at home on the set of *Star Trek* than in the dance hall—stick around to catch its 90-degree twirl as it opens for passing ships.

Urban Birding at Costanera Sur Ecological Reserve

Puerto Madero • Nature triumphs along the Rio la Plata at the huge Reserva Ecológica Costanera Sur, where a wide array of species have repopulated the reclaimed nature preserve, including roadside hawks, bar-winged cinclodes, vermilion flycatchers, scissor-tailed nightjars, and white-faced whistling ducks.

Russian Orthodox Cathedral

San Telmo • With its cobalt-blue onion domes, the Russian Orthodox Cathedral is very likely the only building in Buenos Aires that was designed in Saint Petersburg in the spirit of 17th-century Russia.

El Caminito

La Boca • This alley-long outdoor museum and permanent street fair is a riot of tango color and culture, lightheartedly carrying a solemn promise to keep the national dance a way of life.

Creole Museum of the Corrals

Mataderos • This small museum covering the history of the old meatpacking district is a little moth-eaten, but its charming, dusty quality is well suited to its focus on gaucho life—with cowboy artifacts, hundreds of antique lassos and knives, and some startling vintage slaughterhouse photography.

Hundreds of stone spheres dot the ball court.

ISCHIGUALASTO PROVINCIAL PARK

SAN JUAN, SAN JUAN

Nicknamed the Valley of the Moon on account of its odd geological formations, this park is home to giant petrified tree trunks and some of the world's oldest dinosaur remains. Among the odd stone formations is one called the "ball court," a field of hundreds of stone spheres formed over millions of years by wind and erosion.

The closest cities are San Juan (5 hours south) and La Rioja (3 hours northeast). Charter vans and buses depart from both locations.
Ⓢ 30.513765 Ⓦ 67.582397

ALSO IN ARGENTINA

Museo Rocsen	**House of Plastic Bottles**	**Perito Moreno Glacier**	**Petrified Forest**	**The Campo del Cielo Meteorite**
Nono · Photography, insects, toys, religious relics, fossils, and a Peruvian mummy are among the 25,000 objects in this eclectic 20-room museum.	*Puerto Iguazú* · One man built this one-bedroom cottage out of plastic drink bottles, CD cases, and milk cartons.	*Santa Cruz* · A growing glacier causes havoc when it dams Lago Argentino and then bursts—with spectacular results.	*Santa Cruz* · The two largest petrified trees on the planet are in this Patagonian park.	*Santiago del Estero* · The heaviest meteorite ever recovered on Earth landed at this site.

LAGUNA DEL DIAMANTE

SAN RAFAEL, MENDOZA

There are plenty of reasons why life should not exist at Laguna del Diamante. Located within one of the world's largest calderas—the bowl-shaped formations resulting from land collapsing after a volcanic eruption—the lagoon is surrounded by sulfur-spewing vents. The hyper-alkaline lagoon is five times saltier than seawater and has levels of arsenic that are 20,000 times higher than the amount deemed safe for drinking by the EPA.

Despite these inhospitable conditions, which mimic those of the early Earth, millions of bacteria known as "extremophiles" have managed to flourish. Scientists hope that the mysterious microorganisms can be used to discover new antioxidants or enzymes and may someday help to explain how life on Earth began.

The lake is 4 hours south of Mendoza, near the Chilean border. The road there is only passable from December to March. Four-wheel-drive tours depart from nearby San Rafael and Mendoza. Expect a bumpy ride. Ⓢ 34.149999 Ⓦ 69.683333

A toxic lake, on an active volcano, frequented by flamingos.

Stock up on llama fetuses at Bolivia's premier market for occult goods.

BOLIVIA
WITCHES' MARKET

LA PAZ

Dozens of vendors line this street, selling folk remedies, dried reptiles, and llama fetuses that are said to bring prosperity and good luck. "Witches" wander through the market offering fortune-telling services, spiritual advice, and traditional medicine cures. If you'd like a glimpse into your future, or help with a physical or spiritual ailment, look for the people wearing dark hats.

Calle Linares, La Paz. Taxis, micros (minivans), and *trufis* (cars with specific routes) are all cheap ways of getting to this cobblestone street between Sagarnaga and Santa Cruz. Ⓢ 16.496624 Ⓦ 68.138655

During the wet season, a thin layer of water transforms the salt plain's surface into a seemingly endless mirror.

SALAR DE UYUNI

UYUNI, POTOSÍ

Hotel Luna Salada is built almost entirely out of the most abundant local resource: salt.

The walls are salt bricks held together with salt mortar. You can eat at a salt table, sleep on a salt bed, and watch the sun set over the stark white of the Salar de Uyuni, the largest salt flat in the world.

Salar de Uyuni was created after a lake dried up thousands of years ago. It is a place where nothing seems to make sense. In the wet season, a thin layer of water turns the Salar de Uyuni into a mind-bending mirror, its 3,800 square miles (9,842 km²) of white desert reflecting the sky and creating the illusion of infinity.

Fierce sun during the day gives way to freezing temperatures at night. (This can be a nuisance at Hotel Luna Salada, due to limited hot water, so bring warm clothing and ask at the front desk about showering times.) Giant cacti are the only form of vegetation, but pink flamingos gather by the thousands at nearby Laguna Colorada.

NASA has used the Salar de Uyuni to calibrate its ICESat, a satellite that measures the elevation of ice sheets in Antarctica and Greenland. Because the surface of the salt flat is stable year-round, NASA scientists can calibrate their instruments by measuring the time it takes for the satellite's laser pulse to reflect off the ground.

The surreal landscape of Salar de Uyuni is complemented by a collection of rusted train cars in the desert. Uyuni was a transport hub for locomotives carrying minerals to the Pacific coast in the late 19th century. The decline of the mining industry in the 1940s resulted in many trains being abandoned in the desert. There has been talk of establishing a museum for the cars, but for now they sit in a line under an unrelenting sun.

Uyuni is a 10-hour overnight bus ride from La Paz. Buses also leave from Sucre in the morning. They stop in Potosí and then go on to Uyuni, where they arrive in the late afternoon. Ⓢ 20.280265 Ⓦ 66.982512

A hotel built entirely of salt.

North Yungas Death Road

LA PAZ

To one side is solid rock; to the other, a 2,000-foot (610 m) abyss. Between is a two-way, 12-foot-wide (3.65 m) highway known as Death Road.

One of the world's most dangerous routes, North Yungas Road was cut into the side of the Cordillera Oriental Mountain chain in the 1930s. Its steep descent, lack of guardrails, and tendency to be shrouded in fog and covered with falling rocks and mudslides explain why an estimated 200 to 300 people are killed there every year.

Though vehicles keep to the right side of the road elsewhere in Bolivia, North Yungas drivers keep their cars on the left so they can see the cliff's edge more clearly. The drop isn't the only thing to be concerned about—travelers must also watch out for the intrepid cyclists who arrive determined to barrel down North Yungas for thrills.

North Yungas Road is 43 miles (69.2 km) long, leading from La Paz, the capital, to the town of Coroico. Several companies in La Paz organize Death Road bike rides. Be prepared to sign multiple forms releasing them from responsibility for your demise.
⑤ 16.221092 ⑩ 67.754724

Bolivia's infamous Death Road has killed so many people, it's become a tourist attraction.

Also in Bolivia

Horca del Inca

La Paz · Above Lake Titicaca is a pre-Incan, 14th-century astronomical observatory.

Museo de la Coca

La Paz · A museum dedicated to the sacred leaf of the Andes.

Valle de las Ánimas

La Paz · Needlelike rock formations are densely packed into this "Valley of the Souls."

Great Train Graveyard

Potosí · On the outskirts of a desert trading village, high on the Andean plain, steel giants have been destroyed by salt winds.

Potosí Silver Mines

Potosí · A mountain of unimaginable riches bankrolled the Spanish Empire.

Fort Samaipata

Samaipata · Remnants of Inca and Mojocoyas culture can be seen in the rock carvings, plaza, and agricultural terraces of this hill.

Cal Orck'o

Sucre · Visit a limestone wall covered with 5,000 preserved dinosaur tracks from the Cretaceous period that was discovered in 1994 near a cement factory. It is the largest site of fossilized dinosaur tracks in the world.

Laguna Colorada

Sur Lípez · Explore a red lake 14,000 feet (4,267 m) above sea level that's home to extremophile bacteria and rare flamingos.

BRAZIL

AMAZON STONEHENGE

CALÇOENE, AMAPÁ

In 2006, archaeologists digging on the banks of the Rego Grande river in northern Brazil discovered a strange grouping of 127 giant stones. The megaliths, each standing over 10 feet (3 m) high, were arranged in circles in an open field. By analyzing ceramic shards found nearby, the archaeologists estimated the arrangement of stones is between 500 and 2,000 years old. The placement of the stones appears to be astronomically based—the shadow of one of the blocks disappears during the winter solstice—suggesting it might have been built as an observatory.

The vestiges of an ancient observatory, according to archaeologists.

Anthropologists have long argued that large, complex civilizations could not have existed in the Amazon, as the poor-quality soil could not have supported the agriculture necessary to establish large communities. But the Amazon Stonehenge and other recent findings have cast doubt on this assertion and opened up the possibility that thriving metropolises existed in the jungle thousands of years ago—it's just a matter of finding them.

The stones are in Calçoene, 240 miles (386 km) north of Macapá.
Ⓝ 2.497778 Ⓦ 50.948889 ➺

➺ Don't Follow That Man

The origin of the Amazon Stonehenge remains a mystery, but its discovery lends credence to the hypothesis that the South American rain forest may be teeming with the remains of lost cities. Such notions consumed the minds of explorers like Colonel Percy Fawcett, who ventured into the wilderness of Brazil's Mato Grosso region in 1925 in search of the city he dubbed "Z." Fawcett, his son, and his son's best friend all vanished without a trace.

In the decades following Fawcett's disappearance, over a dozen expeditions were launched in the hope of discovering his fate. None found conclusive evidence, and it is believed over 100 explorers have perished in the jungle looking for him. Here are a few who tried and failed:

Swiss trapper Stefan Rattin arrived at the British Embassy in São Paulo in 1932, claiming that he had encountered a long-haired, animal-skin–clad Fawcett five months earlier while hunting near the Tapajós River. According to Rattin, "Fawcett" told him he was being held captive and pleaded for help from the embassy.

With the blessing of Fawcett's wife, Rattin set off on a rescue mission with two men, walking through the jungle for weeks and building canoes out of bark. A later dispatch reported that the trio was about to enter hostile Indian territory. No one heard from them again.

Shortly afterward, English actor Albert de Winton, bored with Hollywood life, decided to become a genuine jungle explorer. Vowing to find Fawcett, he ventured into the wilderness, his publicist issuing a press release about his heroism. Nine months later, he emerged, thin and dressed in rags, and posed for photographs to send to the *Los Angeles Times*.

After replenishing himself in Cuiabá, de Winton headed back into the jungle. The only subsequent sign of him came a few months later, when an Indian messenger brought a crumpled note out of the forest declaring he had been captured. The unfortunate story of his demise followed years later: Members of the Kamayurá tribe had found him in a canoe, naked and deranged, and clubbed him to death.

In 1947, missionary Jonathan Wells warned New Zealand schoolteacher Hugh McCarthy against venturing into the Mato Grosso, but McCarthy was determined. The ever-cautious Wells gave him seven carrier pigeons for the journey. Over the next few months, three of the birds brought messages. The first reported a leg injury but remained optimistic. The second said McCarthy had abandoned his rifle and canoe and was living on berries and fruits, having exhausted his food supply. The third and final missive was simple and resolute: "My work is over and I die happily."

Percy Fawcett, doomed jungle explorer.

NAZI GRAVEYARD

AMAPÁ

On a small island on a tributary of the River Jary stands a 9-foot-high (2.7 m) wooden cross with an unusual decoration. Marked on the cross are the words "Joseph Greiner died here on 2.1.1936" and, above that, a swastika.

A Third Reich grave marker in the Amazon.

Greiner, a Nazi soldier, arrived in Brazil in 1935. He was accompanied by fellow scientist and SS officer Otto Schulz-Kampfhenkel. Their mission, known as the "Guayana Project," was to evaluate the area's suitability for colonization by the Third Reich.

Despite Schulz-Kampfhenkel's encouraging reports that the area offered "outstanding possibilities for exploitation" for "the more advanced white race," the Nazi colonization of Brazil obviously never took place. (Schulz-Kampfhenkel, however, was able to put aside his racial views long enough to father a child with an indigenous woman.)

Today, all that remains of this monomaniacal plan are the rotting grave of the Nazi soldier who perished in pursuit of it and a short film made while on the expedition, called *Rätsel der Urwaldhölle*, or "Riddles of the Jungle Hell."

Head southwest from Macapá on highway 156 until you hit the Amapá–Para border. The grave site is a little farther north. ⑤ 0.623461 Ⓦ 52.577819

AMAZON BORE SURFING

SÃO DOMINGOS DO CAPIM, PARÁ

Every year in February and March, during the spring tides of a new or full moon, the world's longest wave comes tumbling down the Amazon River at speeds of up to 20 miles (32.1 km) per hour. Referred to colloquially as *pororoca*, or "great destructive noise" in the Tupi language, its roar can be heard half an hour before it arrives.

Though the *pororoca* has the power to destroy trees, houses, and livestock, surfers from all over the world converge to compete in the annual Brazilian National Pororoca Surfing Championship. Braving wave heights of up to 12 feet (3.65 m), winners have experienced the ride of a lifetime, surfing the bore for more than 30 continuous minutes. However, Amazon bore surfing has its risks, including murky water, floating trees, poisonous snakes, and hungry alligators.

Surfers meet at São Domingos do Capim, a 2-hour drive east of Belém. The contest is usually held between February and April, but includes a lot of waiting, as the exact moment of the *pororoca* is always unknown. ⑤ 1.675948 Ⓦ 47.765834

SANTO DAIME AYAHUASCA CEREMONIES

BOCA DO ACRE, AMAZONAS

For followers of the Santo Daime religion, the violent expulsion of bodily fluids is both a regular and a desirable experience. Founded in the 1930s, Santo Daime mixes Christianity, shamanism, African animism, and the ceremonial ingestion of a psychoactive vine known as ayahuasca. Boca do Acre, Brazil, is the religion's psychedelic mecca, with people traveling from around the world to attend the ceremonies held here. Because ayahuasca is used for the purpose of healing, self-enlightenment, and spiritual communion, the Brazilian government has deemed it legal.

During ceremonies, which begin in the evening and last all night, participants are divided by sex, age, and—occasionally—virgin or non-virgin status, and given cups of brewed ayahuasca. As leaders sing and pray, the drug takes effect, causing out-of-body experiences, visions, loss of motor skills, and, most importantly, the "purge." Violent vomiting, diarrhea, and wailing are common and looked upon favorably; within Santo Daime, these expulsions signify evil spirits leaving the body.

Ayahuasca tourism brings visitors to Brazil, Peru, and Ecuador, where they are guided through a ceremony in groups under the instruction of local shamans. Experiences differ markedly, but many people report revisiting childhood traumas, letting go of their egos, and waking up the next morning with a sense of peace and clarity. Others just report vomiting.

Boca do Acre is a 5–10 hour drive from Rio Branco, depending on the state of the poorly maintained dirt roads. There is a local airport, but no commercial flights—you must charter a plane for the 25-minute trip from Rio Branco. ⑤ 8.740689 Ⓦ 67.384081 ➤➤

ENTHEOGENS

Entheogens, or psychotropic drugs used to enhance religious experience, have long been part of the spiritual practices of indigenous people, particularly in South America. Used in rituals to attain self-enlightenment, commune with nature, and enhance the senses, here are a few of the most fascinating:

1 **VIROLA TREES** contain a hallucinogenic resin in their bark. Colombian, Venezuelan, and Brazilian shamans prepare a snuff by collecting shavings from the inner layer of the bark and reducing them to a powder or paste. During Virola ceremonies, men and older boys use long tubes to blow the hallucinatory drug up each other's nostrils, then hop and crawl along the floor before losing consciousness.

2 **THE SAPO** is a large green tree frog whose skin secretions induce a racing heart, incontinence, and vomiting within minutes, before leveling off into a state of listlessness and, finally, euphoria. The Matsés Indian hunters traditionally apply the substance by burning their arms and rubbing the wounds with a stick dipped in the secretions. After the initial effects wear off, hunters are left with improved stamina and strength, a decreased appetite, and keener senses, all of which allow for stealthier stalking of animals.

3 **HUACHUMA**, or San Pedro cactus, is used in Peru for guidance, decision-making, and healing. It is ingested in the form of a bitter, dark-green liquid and begins to take effect within an hour or two. Drowsiness, a sense of detachment, and the feeling of being connected to all things throughout time may be felt for up to 15 hours. Sight and hearing may be enhanced for days afterward.

4 **AFRICAN DREAM ROOT**
is used by the Xhosa people of
South Africa to induce vivid and
supposedly prophetic lucid dreams.
The powdered root is mixed with
water and drunk in the morning,
allowing its effects to take hold at
bedtime. The Xhosa believe that
their deceased ancestors speak to
them during dreams, and regard
the dream root as a divination tool.

5 **SALVIA DIVINORUM**, a plant
native to Oaxaca, Mexico, has been
used in spiritual healing sessions
by Mazatec shamans for centuries.
According to Mazatec beliefs, salvia
is an incarnation of the Virgin Mary
who speaks to those who drink
the juice of her leaves. Due to the
mildness of salvia, which usually
produces only feelings of floating
and dizziness, light and noise are
said to chase the Virgin away.

6 **IBOGA** is the centerpiece of the
Bwiti religion, practiced in Gabon
and Cameroon. The root bark is
often ingested in large quantities
during initiation rituals in order to
bring about visions of the world
that lie beyond death. Iboga has
been found to reduce withdrawal
symptoms from other drugs, and
is used outside of Africa to treat
substance abuse.

SNAKE ISLAND

ILHA DE QUEIMADA GRANDE, SÃO PAULO

Off the shore of São Paulo lies an island forbidden to visitors by order of the Brazilian Navy. They have a good reason: Ilha de Queimada Grande, "Snake Island," is writhing with deadly golden lancehead vipers.

At its peak, the density of snakes on the island was believed to be about one per 11 square feet (1 m²), many of the reptiles being found overhead, hanging from the trees. In other words: death, every 3 feet, in all directions. Over the last decade, the golden lancehead population has declined—there are no mammals on Ilha de Queimada Grande, so the snakes must feed on visiting birds or resort to cannibalism. The serpents, found only on the 0.16-square-mile (.41 km²) island, are now classified as critically endangered. Estimates of the current count vary from 2,000 to 4,000—still one of the highest population densities of any snake.

Locals in the coastal towns near the Queimada Grande happily recount grisly tales about the island. In one, a fisherman unwittingly wanders onto the island to pick bananas and is bitten only moments after stepping ashore. The fisherman manages to stumble back to his boat before dying in a pool of his own blood. Unique to Snake Island, the golden lancehead is believed to have the fastest-acting venom of any lancehead viper. The effects of its bite include bleeding orifices, brain hemorrhaging, and kidney failure.

To visit Ilha de Queimada Grande you must get official permission from the Brazilian Navy. Ⓢ 24.487922 Ⓦ 46.674155

ALSO IN SÃO PAULO

Carandiru Penitentiary Museum

Now closed, this prison was famous for its terrible conditions and a prison break in which over 100 inmates escaped through a tunnel.

Instituto Butantan

A biomedical research center world-renowned for its collection of poisonous snakes, including 407 varieties of cobra.

LENÇÓIS MARANHENSES NATIONAL PARK

BARREIRINHAS, MARANHÃO

Known as "the bedsheets of Maranhão," Lençóis Maranhenses is an area packed with sand dunes, 15 miles (24.1 km) inland from the Atlantic in northeast Brazil. During the rainy season, the valleys between the dunes fill with water, resulting in an odd sight: a desert full of blue and green lagoons. Look closely and you'll see fish between the dunes, hatched from eggs transported from the sea by birds.

Entry to the park is via the town of Barreirinhas, about 4 hours east of São Luís. Tour buses depart daily from the São Luís Bus Terminal. Ⓢ 2.485938 Ⓦ 43.128407

In a park without greenery, lagoons and sand dunes sit side by side.

Henry Ford's $20-million jungle utopia didn't quite go according to plan.

FORDLÂNDIA

SANTARÉM, PARÁ

Traveling through thick Brazilian jungle up the Tapajós River, one arrives at a shockingly out-of-place tableau. Amid the monkeys and macaws stand the overgrown ruins of an abandoned American suburb, complete with houses surrounded by white picket fences, fire hydrants, and a golf course. It's Pleasantville, dropped in the middle of the rain forest.

Industrialist Henry Ford created his slice of Americana in the Amazon in the late 1920s. Troubled by the high price of rubber, Ford decided to build his own rubber plantation.

He bought over six million acres of Brazilian land and shipped in employees from Michigan to manage the model town. He named his settlement Fordlândia, and the workers—both American and Brazilian—were forced to live according to Ford's strict, teetotaling rules. This meant no smoking, no drinking, and attending wholesome poetry readings and sing-alongs.

Workers quickly became disgruntled. Local Brazilians didn't appreciate having to wear nametags, eat hamburgers, and learn square dancing, while the Midwestern managers of the plantation had trouble adjusting to the jungle climate and ever-present malaria. Strikes, knife fights, and mayhem became the rule. In 1930, the Brazilian workforce had had enough and rioted, chasing the American managers out of Fordlândia with machetes.

Worst of all, the rubber saplings planted by Ford—without the help of a trained botanist—were barely growing. Those that had taken root were soon hit by a catastrophic leaf blight. Fordlândia was officially a failure.

Henry Ford retired from the rubber industry in 1945, having spent $20 million—equivalent to over $200 million in today's dollars—without producing a single piece of rubber worthy of his cars. **Fordlândia receives few visitors but can be reached by a 10-hour river voyage via charter boat from Santarem.** 🌐 3.830107 🌐 55.497180

ALSO IN BRAZIL

Gruta do Lago Azul

Bahia · A brilliant blue lagoon hides in a limestone cave rich in fossils.

Curitiba Botanical Gardens

Curitiba, Paraná · Designed to resemble French royal gardens, Curitiba's lawn has one of the world's most incredible greenhouses.

Teatro Amazonas

Manaus · Brazil's 19th-century rubber barons built a grand opera house in the middle of the rain forest. Then the money ran out. The Teatro lay dormant for 90 years until an injection of government funds in 2001 brought the music back.

Victoria Amazonica

Manaus · The leaves of this gigantic plant, found in the shallow waters of the Amazon, grow up to eight feet (2.5 m) in diameter. Many are strong enough to support the weight of a child.

World's Longest Street

Pará · Lined with houses for its entire length, this street stretches for 311 miles (500 km).

New Jerusalem Theater

Pernambuco · The world's largest open-air theater spans 24 acres and hosts a massive re-creation of the Passion of Christ.

Escadaria Selarón

Rio de Janeiro · Jorge Selarón created these vibrant ceramic steps.

Largo do Boticário

Rio de Janeiro · Remnants of Rio's colonial past lie in this square tucked behind Corcovado ("Hunchback") Mountain, in Cosme Velho.

GLOWING TERMITE MOUNDS OF EMAS NATIONAL PARK

ALTO PARAÍSO DE GOIÁS

Termites thrive all over the world, building sprawling nests and wreaking occasional havoc on local lumber supplies. In Brazil, they build tall towers of cement-like Earth.

These termite mounds can grow quite large, with diameters

Beetle larvae give the mounds a bioluminescent quality.

nearing 100 feet (30.5 m) and towering heights of 16 feet (5 m) or more. Not only do they provide a home for up to several million termites; they're also nesting sites for many birds and home to hundreds of glowing *Pyrophorus* beetle larvae. At night, the termite mounds look like they're wrapped in Christmas lights.

While the adult beetles eat plants, the young are carnivorous, and their lights are a lure. Unsuspecting insects will make their way toward the pretty lights, only to be seized for a meal by the hungry larvae. And, yes, termites are a favorite food. In fact, the larval growth cycle is timed to take advantage of termite migrations, and many a termite will meet its end in the jaws of an inconsiderate houseguest.

The glowing mounds are best seen in the savannas during the summer, though they can be found in the jungles as well. The terrain can be quite rugged, but there are several private tour outfits who can guide you. ⊗ 14.005634 ⓦ 47.684606

CHILE

ROBINSON CRUSOE ISLAND

JUAN FERNÁNDEZ ISLANDS, VALPARAÍSO

In 1704, Scottish sailor Alexander Selkirk made a rash decision. Feuding with his cocaptain over their ship's seaworthiness as they sailed along the western coast of South America, Selkirk declared he would rather the vessel continue its journey without him. Taking him at his word, the crew dumped him on Más a Tierra, an island 419 miles (674 km) off the coast of Chile. (Selkirk's suspicions proved correct—the ship, *Cinque Ports*, sank shortly afterward, sending many of its sailors to the bottom of the sea.)

For the next four years and four months, Selkirk roamed the island alone, eating shellfish, chasing after goats with a knife, and digging up parsnips. To stave off boredom, he read his Bible and taught cats to dance. After hiding twice from Spanish privateers, he was finally rescued by English sea captain Woodes Rogers in 1709.

The most renowned castaway of all time, Selkirk is likely the inspiration for the title character in Daniel Defoe's novel *Robinson Crusoe*. In 1966, Más a Tierra was renamed Robinson Crusoe Island. Now home to a few hundred people, it is a place of extreme beauty, with coral reefs, white-sand beaches, blue lagoons, and abundant tropical fruits—not a bad place to be stranded.

Two-hour flights from Santiago depart several times per week. Hike to Selkirk's Lookout—a 3-hour trek that the marooned sailor made daily to watch for rescue ships. ⊗ 33.636666 ⓦ 78.849588

Only a third of Easter Island's *moai* were completed—hundreds of unfinished statues lie in the Rano Raraku quarry.

THE UNFINISHED GIANTS OF EASTER ISLAND

ISLA DE PASCUA, VALPARAÍSO

Between 1400 and 1600 CE, the Polynesian inhabitants of Easter Island carved 288 stone statues, or *moai*, and hauled them across the island, where they were installed on ceremonial pedestals. These representations were erected between the village and "chaos"—the ocean—as a wall of protection. Remarkably, the 288 figures represent less than a third of the statues that were created. The others lie either "in transit" at various places on the island or in the Rano Raraku quarry where they were carved. Most notable among the figures is "El Gigante,"

an unfinished 72-foot-tall (21.9 m) moai that surpasses the weight of two full 737 airplanes. It is questionable whether it could have even been moved using the wooden sleds, log rollers, and ropes that were presumably used to transport the island's other moai.

The mass of unfinished stone figures leaves many questions. What were the plans for El Gigante and the rest of the moai? Why carve so many and just leave them in a pile? It may have been a case of ambition eclipsing resources. Anthropologists have argued that the Easter Islanders used up all of their island's resources in the process of building their society. The two major tribes of Easter Island lived in a tropical rain forest, a

paradise of food and fishing, with plenty of time to put into the "great work" of statues.

According to Easter Island's resident archaeologist, Edmundo Edwards, the Polynesians used to sail back and forth across great distances among the Pacific islands, but eventually they used up all the large trees, thereby losing the ability to build large canoes. At this point, they became effectively trapped. The old middens (dumps for domestic waste) show that fish bones got progressively smaller, as the Polynesians could no longer sail out to deep fisheries.

Flights to Easter Island leave from Santiago. The trip takes about 5 hours. ⑨ 27.121191 ⓦ 109.366423

ALSO IN CHILE

El Tatio Geysers

Antofagasta · With over 80 active geysers, some of which you can bathe in, El Tatio is the third-largest geyser field in the world.

Sewell

Cachapoal · Founded in 1904 around a copper mine and once home to 15,000, this town was abandoned during the 1970s.

Villa Baviera

Linares · Formerly a cult known as Colonia Dignidad, Villa Baviera was a secretive German-Chilean community surrounded by barbed wire and led by ex-Nazi Paul Schäfer before his 2005 arrest.

Magic Mountain Hotel

Panguipulli · Located in a forest, this moss-covered nine-room hotel is shaped like a volcano and spews water from its roof. Entrance is via a cable bridge.

Villarrica Caves

Pucón · Travel hundreds of feet into this active volcano and see the hardened remains of a lava flow that once oozed out of the mountainside.

World's Largest Coca-Cola Logo

Arica · 60,000 empty bottles of Coke comprise a 30-year-old ad seen only from the air.

When "white gold" was no longer needed, Chile's mining towns fell apart.

NITRATE TOWNS

IQUIQUE, TARAPACÁ

Until 1909, Chile had something very rare and valuable: large deposits of sodium nitrate. Also known as "white gold" or "Chile saltpeter," sodium nitrate is used in the production of fertilizer and explosives. So valuable was this "white gold" that Chile went to war with Peru and Bolivia in 1879 over areas containing the chemical compound.

At the turn of the century, Chile's northern Tarapacá region was full of sodium nitrate mining towns. Workers from South America, Europe, and Asia formed communities around the mines. In the words of UNESCO, each town became a "distinct urban community with its own language, organization, customs, and creative expressions."

But something on the horizon would change all this. In 1909, German scientists Fritz Haber and Carl Bosch figured out how to chemically fix nitrogen—that is, how to make white gold on an industrial level. The discovery was disastrous for the Chilean saltpeter towns. By 1960, all lay abandoned. Today, their remains stand as rusting ruins in the inhospitable Atacama desert.
The Humberstone and Santa Laura Saltpeter Works are an hour east of Iquique on Route 16.
Ⓢ 20.205805 Ⓦ 69.794050

MANO DEL DESIERTO

ANTOFAGASTA, ANTOFAGASTA

The barren monotony of the Atacama desert is shattered by what looks like a buried giant reaching out for help. Mano del Desierto, a 36-foot-tall (10.9 m) hand protruding out of the sand, is the work of the Chilean sculptor Mario Irarrázabal, and was built in the early 1980s. Irarrázabal's work is known for its portrayal of human vulnerability and helplessness—two concepts that certainly come across when viewing the unnerving, half-submerged palm.
The hand is about an hour drive south of the town of Antofagasta, along the Pan-American Highway.
Ⓢ 24.158514 Ⓦ 70.156414

The Hand of the Desert has acquired graffiti on its palm.

Swirling arches of rock carved out over the millennia.

THE MARBLE CATHEDRAL AT LAKE GENERAL CARRERA

PUERTO RÍO TRANQUILO, GENERAL CARRERA

Within the banks of the deepest lake in South America is a marble "cathedral" formed by natural erosions. When sun shines onto the caves, the pale blue water reflects against the gray-and-white-striped marble, turning the whole scene aquamarine. Eaves and arches in the rock, created by water lapping at the marble, complete the cathedral effect.

Boat tours leave from the small town of Puerto Río Tranquilo, on the western shore of the lake. The nearest city is Coihaique, 5 hours north. ⑤ 46.475690 Ⓦ 71.291650

. . . .

COLOMBIA
BURIED CITY OF ARMERO

ARMERO, TOLIMA

Visit the eerily quiet former town of Armero and you'll see only a few buildings surrounded by weeds. Then you will realize that you are looking at the upper levels of those buildings. The ground floors are buried by mud that smothered the town more than 30 years ago.

Armero was home to almost 30,000 people on November 13, 1985. That was the day the nearby Nevado del Ruiz volcano erupted, sending torrents of mud and debris down its slopes at 40 miles per hour (64.3 km). Soon, a 15-foot (4.5 m) layer of the sludge had covered the town, trapping and killing 23,000 of its inhabitants.

Those who escaped instant death faced an agonizing 12-hour wait for relief workers to arrive. The mud, which pulled at their feet like quicksand, made rescue efforts frustratingly slow. People who had been buried up to their necks watched, helpless, as workers tried and failed to dig them out.

One such victim was 13-year-old Omayra Sánchez. Imprisoned in the mixture of water, mud, and the concrete remains of her own home, she smiled, sang, talked to rescue workers, and was interviewed. Volunteers made multiple attempts to dig Omayra out, but her legs were pinned by concrete. Sixty hours after becoming trapped, Omayra died. A photograph of her staring, helpless, into the camera while immersed in neck-high sludge was published around the world and became the symbol of the disaster.

Covered in mud and with more than two-thirds of its inhabitants wiped out, Armero became a ghost town. Survivors created a kind of cemetery, constructing tombs in place of the old houses and honoring their former residents with epitaphs. The Armando Armero foundation has established a Memory Interpretation Center on the site, where visitors can learn about the buried city and the volcano that destroyed it.

The ruins of Armero are a 5-hour drive west of Bogotá, Colombia's capital. Ⓝ 4.966666 Ⓦ 74.827318

CAÑO CRISTALES

LA MACARENA, META

From September to November, during the period between the wet and dry seasons, the Caño Cristales river, in Colombia's remote Meta province, becomes a liquid rainbow. The riverbed is carpeted with *Macarenia clavigera*, a species of river weed found nowhere else on earth, and the source of the Caño Cristales's notoriety. Pale green under the shade of riverbank foliage, the *Macarenia* turns a stunningly intense magenta under the full sun. Jet-black rocks, white water coursing over cascades, and the occasional crater of yellow sand complete the colorful tableau.

Until 2009, the river was off-limits to visitors due to the presence of FARC guerrillas in the region. Now the tourists are arriving again, brought to Caño Cristales by local guides who stick to authorized paths.

Vibrant river weeds give Colombia's "River of Five Colors" its rainbow effect.

Charter a flight from Villavicencio to the village of La Macarena, once a guerrilla stronghold. From town, it's a 15-minute ride in a motorized canoe up the Guayabero River, followed by a long hike down a FARC-built dirt road to the river. **Ⓝ 2.182991 Ⓦ 73.785850**

PABLO ESCOBAR'S HIPPOS

PUERTO TRIUNFO, ANTIOQUIA

Notorious Colombian cocaine baron Pablo Escobar once lived on this sprawling estate, spending his days riding his hovercraft over its many lakes, wandering among his collection of vintage cars, and strolling through his zoo filled with hippopotamuses and exotic birds.

Escobar was killed in a hail of gunfire by the Colombian police in 1993, and the hacienda became dilapidated. It has since been revived—this time as a theme park. There have been some problems, however. Locals are known to sneak in—on one occasion with a backhoe—and dig up the lawn and floors in search of treasure they believe Escobar buried.

Meanwhile, the four hippos Escobar imported from Africa have thrived and, in one case, escaped the confines of the estate. In 2009, a hippo named Pepe was found 62 miles (100 km) away and killed by the Colombian military. The group of wild hippos is now estimated at around 40. They are ruled by an alpha male named Pablo.

The hacienda is about 4 hours east of Medellin on Route 60. Visitors can feed baby hippos, tour the drug

The drug baron is long gone, but his hippos live on.

lord's personal effects, and even see the Cessna that carried Escobar's first load of cocaine to the US. **Ⓝ 5.886187 Ⓦ 74.642486**

GUAYABETAL ZIP LINES

GUAYABETAL, CUNDINAMARCA

If you want to cross the Rio Negro valley near Guayabetal, you have two options: Hike a steep forest path for four hours, or hitch yourself to a steel cable suspended 1,300 feet (396 m) above ground and hold on tight. Most locals opt for the latter.

The tools for crossing using the zip lines are simple: a length of rope used to form a seat, a steel roller with a hook to attach the rope, and a wooden yoke that straddles the cable and serves as a brake. The half-mile (0.8 km) trip takes less than 30 seconds.

The journey is not without its dangers. According to some reports, 22 people have plunged to their deaths. The most recent fatality occurred in 2004, when a 34-year-old man was decapitated while trying to cross with two other passengers lashed to him (they both survived). He'd already used the cable earlier that day to pass two beds, a doghouse, chickens, a television, a stereo, and three chairs across the valley without a hitch.

In the late 1990s, a Bogotá television news program aired an exposé on the cables, which included a clip of a six-year-old boy who lived on the far side of the valley zipping across the line to get to school. A public outcry ensued, provoking calls from Bogotá for the cables to be torn down. The lines were technically illegal, but because the Rio Negro Valley

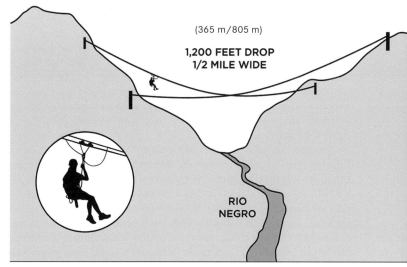

(365 m/805 m)

1,200 FEET DROP
1/2 MILE WIDE

RIO NEGRO

Proto zip lines once flew commuters across the Andes. Only a few remain.

spans two Colombian states—Meta and Cundinamarca—it had never been clear who held jurisdiction over them. In 2001, the government finally ordered 18 of the cables removed.

Locals saw the move not only as a threat to their livelihoods but as disrespectful of an old tradition that had served the community well for generations. The mayor of Guayabetal reportedly received death threats saying that if he complied with orders to remove the cables, he'd be "carried out in wooden pajamas"—a euphemism for a coffin. In an op-ed published in *El Tiempo*, a man who'd used one of the cables for 20 years without incident wrote, "If the authorities are so concerned with safety, they should take away airplanes, since not long ago one

crashed in the United States, killing all 260 passengers." To protest the impending removal, a local woman slid out to the middle of one of the lines and dangled there for hours.

In the end, all but four of the cables were removed. A school was built on the far side of the valley so that children no longer have to zip back and forth each day. Instead, a teacher from Guayabetal now crosses over at the beginning of the week and comes back to town for the weekend.

The zip lines are 2 hours south of Bogotá. If you can find the relatively well-hidden cables, you may be able to convince one of the locals to take you across, but you will be risking both their life and yours. Ⓝ 4.220892 Ⓦ 73.816551

ALSO IN COLOMBIA

Museo el Fósil	Malpelo Island	Peñól Stone	Las Lajas Sanctuary	Salt Cathedral
Boyacá · A bus-size crocodile-like fossil is the centerpiece of this roadside museum.	*Choco* · Dive for hammerheads and silky sharks in this biodiversity hotspot.	*Guatapé* · From afar, this 10-million-ton stone looks like two halves of a giant rock messily stitched together. Get closer and you will realize that the "stitching" is actually a spiral staircase.	*Nariño* · Built within a gorge, this Gothic Revival church is located at the site where the Virgin Mary supposedly appeared during the 18th century.	*Zipaquirá* · Explore a subterranean church in an old mine featuring floors that crunch underfoot, a large cross carved into the back wall, and blue and purple lighting.

PERU
SARCOFAGI OF CARAJÍA

CHACHAPOYAS, AMAZONAS

Staring down from a cliffside above a river gorge, the vertical Sarcofagi of Carajía (or Karijia) kept watch over the Utcubamba Valley for hundreds of years before researchers were able to climb up and investigate the mysterious mummies.

Created sometime in the 15th century by the Chachapoya civilization, the seven standing burial capsules—formerly eight; one collapsed during a 1928 earthquake—are located almost 700 feet (213 m) above the valley floor. While a great deal of the Chachapoya culture was lost after the Inca came to conquer, the sarcophagi survived largely intact due to their seemingly impossible location. Each of the figures stands a remarkable 8 feet tall (2.4 m) and change, constructed out of grass and clay. Some

of the graves even retain the human skulls that were installed atop the sarcophagi.

It was not until the mid-19th century that researchers were able to scale the cliff face and examine the mummies, dating them and speculating as to their construction. It is believed that the original architects of these graves worked from natural outcroppings that were later destroyed, either deliberately or naturally. While the sarcophagi are largely protected from the elements by the rock walls around them, birds and other small animals have done some damage. The researchers removed the contents of the sarcophagi to preserve the ancient innards from any further predation.

Hike or rent a horse from Cruz Pata, where you can also rent boots for navigating muddy trails.
🌐 6.163243 🌐 78.019354

Standing burial capsules topped with human skulls overlook the Utcubamba Valley.

THE BOILING RIVER OF THE AMAZON

PUCALLPA, UCAYALI

Hidden in the dense jungle of the Peruvian Amazon is a percolating, roiling river. The steaming turquoise waters, which can reach up to 200°F (93°C), are guided by ivory-colored stones and guarded by 60-foot (18 m) walls of lush forest and vegetation.

The headwaters of the Boiling River are marked with a boulder in the shape of a snake's head. According to legend, a giant serpent spirit called Yacumama, or "Mother of the Waters," gives birth to hot and cold waters and heats the river. The geothermal feature is unusual since it isn't located near a high-energy heat source such as an active volcano—usually a prerequisite for a boiling river.

Researchers led by geothermal scientist Andrés Ruzo believe that a fault led hydrothermal feature causes the river to reach such temperatures. The water seeps deep into the earth, heats up underground, and resurfaces through faults and cracks.

The 200°F river is believed to be sacred and have healing powers.

It may look like a natural hot tub, but don't jump in—you'll get third-degree burns within seconds. Ⓢ 8.820001 Ⓦ 74.730011

CHAN CHAN

TRUJILLO, LA LIBERTAD

Chan Chan is a giant, elaborate sand castle. Built by the Chimú people around 850 CE, the adobe city—the world's largest—is now an archaeological site. The 28-square-mile (72.5 km²) city, comprised of temples, houses, kitchens, gardens, and cemeteries, had a population of around 30,000 before falling to the Incan Empire in 1470.

The Chimú addressed the desert city's lack of water by building a complex irrigation system that included a 50-mile (80.4 km) canal to the Moche and Chicama rivers. Ironically, Chan Chan now faces the opposite problem: too much water. The city is slowly dissolving, as El Niño storms become fiercer and more frequent. Wind and torrential rains have substantially weakened the city, washing away the intricate animal friezes that decorate its walls. Peru's National Institute of Culture is supporting efforts to protect and preserve Chan Chan, but the city's substantial size makes it difficult to shelter from the elements. Time is running out, and the rains keep coming.

Off Avenida Mansiche, Trujillo. Only about 10 percent of the city is open to explore—a tour guide will be able to explain what lies beyond the publicly accessible portion. Ⓢ 8.105999 Ⓦ 79.074537

Conservationists struggle to maintain the art and architecture at Chan Chan, once the largest adobe city on Earth.

ICA STONES

ICA, ICA

For his 42nd birthday in 1966, Peruvian physician Javier Cabrera received an unusual present: a stone carved with what looked like an extinct fish. Over the next few years, Cabrera sought out more of the stones from a local farmer, who claimed to have found them in a cave. Eventually, the physician amassed a collection of more than 10,000. In addition to featuring animals, the carvings depicted strange scenes of ancient people battling Tyrannosaurs, conducting kidney transplants, and gazing through telescopes. Were these artifacts proof of a sophisticated ancient culture, or even evidence that humans and dinosaurs coexisted? Not quite.

Basilio Uschuya, the farmer who sold Cabrera the stones, confessed in 1973 that he had forged them. Then things got complicated: Uschuya retracted his admission soon afterward, claiming he lied to avoid being arrested for selling archaeological artifacts.

What ancient civilization—or modern charlatan—carved this stone?

Over 20 years later, when Cabrera opened a museum showcasing the stones, Uschuya changed his story yet again. This time he said he had carved most, but not all, of them. Cabrera was unfazed by the revelation, believing in the authenticity of the stones until his death in 2001.

Though the collection of carvings can't be dated due to its lack of organic material, archaeologists regard the stones as a hoax. This has not dissuaded many creationists and extraterrestrial enthusiasts from hailing the stones as the creations of "Gliptolithic Man"—an ancient, highly intelligent people who shared Earth with the dinosaurs before departing from the planet in spacecraft they built themselves. **Calle Bolivar 174, Ica. Ica is a 4-hour drive south of Lima, the capital. 11,000 of the stones are currently on display at Ica's Cabrera Museum, which is open to visitors by appointment. Ⓢ 13.450437 Ⓦ 76.150840**

FLOATING ISLANDS OF THE UROS

PUNO, PUNO

Though the origins of the Uros are shrouded in anthropological mystery, their basic story goes something like this: At some point in the distant, pre-Columbian past, a tribe of comparatively dark-skinned people migrated out of the Amazon and found themselves on the shores of Lake Titicaca. Oppressed by the local population and unable to find land of their own to tend, they ended up moving out into the middle of the lake on small floating islands they constructed from layers of cut totora, a thick reed that grows like kudzu in the lake.

In the middle of frigid Titicaca, the Uros found relative peace and scraped by for centuries as bird hunters and fishermen while living one of the most unique lifestyles on the planet. Today, some 1,200 Uros still live on an archipelago of around 60 artificial islands, strung out like a necklace near the city of Puno.

Stepping foot onto a floating island is a strange feeling, like walking on a giant sponge that squishes underfoot. Though the mats of reeds are up to 12 feet (3.6 m) thick, there is a persistent feeling that one could step right through to the cold lake below. **The Uros Islands are a half-hour boat trip from Puno. Disarmingly cute local children may sing for money during the ride. Ⓢ 15.818667 Ⓦ 69.968991**

In the middle of Lake Titicaca, a civilization that predates the Incas survives on floating islands of reeds.

Until 2005, the world's third-tallest waterfall was known only to those who lived beneath it.

GOCTA FALLS

COCACHIMBA, AMAZONAS

In May 2005, a German economist named Stefan Ziemendorff went for a hike in the remote Utcabamba valley of Peru. In the distance, he spied what looked to be an impossibly tall two-tiered waterfall that hadn't appeared before on any map. The following March, after returning with proper surveying equipment and measuring the falls at 2,531 feet (771 km), Ziemendorff held a press conference to announce that he had discovered the third tallest waterfall in the world. The rank of third-tallest has been hotly contested since then, but that's not the only debate.

Like many of geography's most heralded "discoveries," Ziemendorff's wasn't news to everyone. While the waterfall may have been a total secret to the outside world, there were 200 residents in an isolated village called Cocachimba who not only knew all about it, but lived almost directly underneath it. For 53 years, since the hamlet's founding, Cocachimbans had awakened each morning to one of the world's most picturesque views—and apparently never mentioned it to anyone. As it turned out, the locals had good reason not to bring it up—they were afraid of it.

A legend about the waterfall had been passed down for generations. According to locals, once upon a time, a man named Gregorio told his wife that he was taking off for a short trip. Not realizing that his suspicious wife had decided to trail him through the forest, he made his way toward the base of Gocta. There, the wife caught Gregorio cavorting with a beautiful blond mermaid at the foot of the falls and flew into a jealous rage. The frightened siren grabbed Gregorio and pulled him into the waterfall with her. He never reemerged, and locals came to believe that anyone brave enough to hike to the falls was chancing a run-in with dangerous, supernatural forces.

According to a town official, it took the safe return of dozens of tourists before the residents of Cocachimba shook their phobia of Gocta. The town has since come around to the benefits and beauty of the natural wonder that looms overhead.

Again, for waterfall enthusiasts, the question of whether Gocta even deserves its stature as the bronze medalist of waterfalls has been a subject of rancorous debate. It all comes down to your definition of what a waterfall is. If there's a break in the drop, as there is in Gocta, does that count as more than one waterfall? What if the water cascades over the side of an inclined cliff, rather than spilling off vertically, as is the case with several towering falls in Norway? And what if the water slows to only a trickle during the dry season? No matter which criteria you use, everyone agrees that Angel Falls in Venezuela tops the charts, particularly in terms of awe-inspiring spectacle.

Cocachimba is 5 hours east of Trujillo. Resident guides are happy to take you on a hike to the falls.
Ⓢ 6.028728 Ⓦ 77.888125

ALSO IN PERU

Toro Muerto

Arequipa · Multiple ancient cultures created this petroglyph field.

Sacred City of Caral-Supe

Barranca · "The oldest town in the new world" dates back to 3,000 BCE, the same era as the first dynasty of ancient Egypt.

Kuelap Fortress

Chachapoyas · The "Machu Picchu of the North," constructed around 500 CE by the Chachapoyas people, now consists of 400 ruined buildings enclosed by a huge, high-walled fortress.

Manú National Park

Cusco · One of the most biodiverse places in the world, this park is home to over 1,000 species of birds.

Qenqo Temple

Cusco · Death rituals and sacrifices were once commonplace inside this Peruvian megalith.

Band of Holes

Ica · This barren rock near Pisco Valley is dotted with neat rows of mysterious holes that stretch over mountain terrain.

Moche Pyramids

Lambayeque · At these pyramids, warrior-priests conducted rituals involving costumed battles and human sacrifice.

Huayllay National Sanctuary

Pasco · With its unusual formations in open fields, this rock forest is a dream destination for climbers.

The Inca town's distinctive layout includes quarries, terraces, and storehouses.

OLLANTAYTAMBO RUINS

OLLANTAYTAMBO

Dating back to the reign of 15th-century Emperor Pachacuti, who conquered the region, the town of Ollantaytambo contains some of Peru's best-preserved Inca ruins.

Ollantaytambo was home to the Inca elite. The town's primary attraction is the fortress on its outskirts, in a section known as the Temple Hill. Though originally built for worship, the fortress served as the last Inca stronghold against the Spanish conquistadors and is a site of one of the few battles in which the Inca successfully repelled Spanish forces. Other nearby attractions include the Temple of the Sun and the Princess Baths, both of which feature examples of Incan carvings.

Buses and combis run from Urubamba, about 30 minutes away. Ⓢ 13.258048 Ⓦ 72.263311 ➻

➤ Other Inca Ruins

Ingapirca

INGAPIRCA, GUAPÁN, ECUADOR

Ingapirca is Ecuador's largest site of Inca ruins. The city was home to the Inca and the indigenous Cañari, and after initial conflict, they merged to form a hybrid community.

The largest structure still standing on the site is the Temple of the Sun. It appears to have been built at such an angle that the sun would have shone directly into the doorway during the solstices. Advanced design is also on display in the startling underground aqueduct system that supplied the community with water.

A bus from Cuenca takes 2 hours to reach the ruins. While there, say hi to the llamas, who roam about freely.

CRADLE OF GOLD, CHOQUEQUIRAO, PERU

Known as the other Machu Picchu, Choquequirao ("Cradle of Gold") is filled with ruined buildings and terraces that sit below a flattened hilltop ringed with stones.

Only about one third of Choquequirao, a once vital link between the Amazon and Cusco, has been excavated. What has been uncovered to date follows traditional Inca construction: A temple and some administrative buildings are positioned directly around a central square, with living quarters farther out.

One of the most impressive features found in and around Choquequirao are two terraces that incorporate figures of llamas or alpacas. The shapes of the animals have been set into the large terraces using carefully carved white rock.

Choquequirao is a 2-day hike from Cusco. Experienced climbers only—this one's rough and tough.

HUÁNUCO PAMPA, PROVINCIA DE DOS DE MAYO, PERU

Though it was abandoned around 1539, Huánuco Pampa is remarkably well preserved. Apart from the strategic mountainous location, this site was probably quite unremarkable in its time. Its lack of grandeur may have been its saving grace. The conquistadores by and large neglected Huánuco Pampa, which helped it to survive and become the prime archaeological site it is today.

The site was an administrative center, built on a plateau conveniently defended by the steep slopes marking its perimeter. Huánuco Pampa was also a foodstuff storage hub. Its nearly 500 storehouses and numerous food processing centers show the massive planning and organizational skills the Inca needed to sustain their sprawling empire.

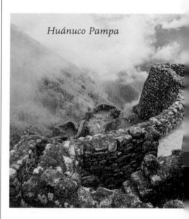

Huánuco Pampa

On a stroll through Huánuco Pampa today, you'll come across the remains of the baths, the main palace, and an enormous plaza with a pyramid.

Huánuco Pampa is a 5-hour drive from the city of Huánuco.

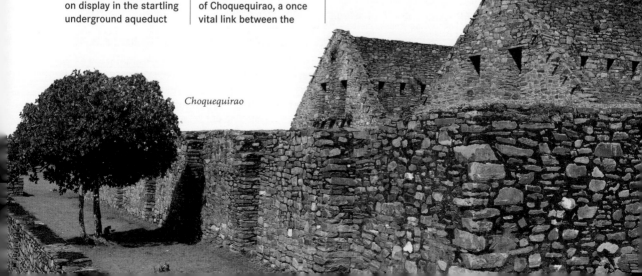

Choquequirao

The Keshwa Chaca has been rewoven from fresh grass every year since Incan times.

THE LAST INCAN GRASS BRIDGE

HUINCHIRI, CUSCO

The Incas never invented the wheel, never figured out the arch, and never discovered iron, but they were masters of fiber. They built ships out of fiber (you can still find reed boats sailing on Lake Titicaca). They made armor out of fiber (pound for pound, it was stronger than the armor worn by the conquistadors). And their greatest weapon, the sling, was woven from fibers and powerful enough to split a steel sword. They even communicated in fiber, developing a language of knotted strings known as *quipu*, which has yet to be decoded. So when it came to solving a problem like how to get people, animals, and goods across the steep gorges of the Andes, it was only natural that they would turn to fiber.

Five centuries ago, the Andes were strung with as many as 200 suspension bridges braided from nothing more than twisted mountain grass and other vegetation, with cables sometimes as thick as a human torso. Three hundred years before Europe saw its first suspension bridge, the Incas were spanning longer distances and deeper gorges than anything that the best European engineers, working with stone, were capable of.

Over the centuries, the empire's grass bridges gradually gave way and were replaced with more conventional works of modern engineering. The most famous Incan bridge—the 148-foot (45 m) bridge immortalized by Thornton Wilder in *The Bridge of San Luis Rey*—lasted until the 19th century, but it too eventually collapsed. Today, there is just one Incan grass bridge left, the Keshwa Chaca, a sagging 90-foot (27.4 m) span that stretches between two sides of a steep gorge, near Huinchiri. According to locals, it has been there for at least 500 years.

Despite its seemingly fragile materials, modern load testing has found that in peak condition, the Keshwa Chaca can support the weight of 56 people spread out evenly across its length.

In 1968, the government built a steel truss bridge just a few hundred yards upstream. Though most locals now use it instead of the grass bridge to cross the valley, the yearly tradition of rebuilding the Keshwa Chaca has not abated. Each June, it is renewed in an elaborate three-day ceremony. Each household from the four surrounding towns is responsible for bringing 90 feet (27.4 m) of braided grass cord. Construction takes place under the supervision of the all-important bridge keeper, or *chacacamayoc*. The old bridge is then cut down and thrown into the river. Because it has to be willfully, ritually regenerated each year, the Keshwa Chaca's ownership passes from generation to generation as a bridge across not only space, but also time.

The bridge crosses Apurimac Canyon, 5 hours south of Cusco. ⓢ 14.383056 ⓦ 71.493333

URUGUAY
Laguna Garzón Bridge

MALDONADO, MALDONADO

When Uruguay's Rocha and Maldonado counties sought to replace the tried-and-true way of crossing Laguna Garzón—via single-vehicle float rafts—they ended up with one of the most immediately recognizable bridges in the world today.

After six years of public hearings and negotiations with the local communities, Rafael Viñoly Architects found a way to meet the strict needs of the natural and cultural communities connected by the new bridge. The project's success hinged on its ability to incorporate the environmental laws of the area, which stipulate that just 35 percent of the stretch between the lagoons may be developed, while 50 percent must be devoted to green areas.

These prolonged negotiations resulted in the circular Laguna Garzón Bridge, which opened in 2015. Its design was partly motivated by safety concerns—the road's one-way half circles force motorists to slow down, thereby breaking up a mile-long stretch that otherwise might have been a tantalizing speedway.

The bridge is just under an hour's drive east of Maldonado. There is an observation deck and a fishing pier, so bring your rod if you fancy some roadside angling.
Ⓢ 34.802470 Ⓦ 54.572100

Also in Uruguay

Vizcaíno Creek Fossil Bed

Canelones · Thousands of fossils have been discovered at this site, including remains of the glyptodont, an extinct armadillo the size of a Volkswagen Beetle.

Valle del Hilo de la Vida

Lavalleja · Ninety cone-shaped mounds built from rock and believed to be over 1,000 years old dot this hill.

The Hand

Punta del Este · A giant hand emerging from the sands of Brava Beach is a monument to the drowned.

More than 1,000 vehicles cross this circular bridge daily.

Dense jungle gives way to cavernous sinkholes.

VENEZUELA

SARISARIÑAMA

SUCRE

One of the most remote locations in all of Venezuela, Sarisariñama is also one of the most bizarre landscapes in the world. High in the clouds on a *tepui*, or "tabletop mountain," are four giant sinkholes, each a near-perfect circle.

The largest of the sinkholes is 1,150 feet wide (350 m) and 1,000 feet deep (305 m). Adding to the mystery of the place is the local legend that gave the tepui its name. According to the Ye'kuana people, a flesh-eating evil spirit lived on the mountain, and it made the sound "sari sari" when consuming a meal of human meat.

Although you may not encounter actual person-eating spirits on the mountain, the desolation still adds a level of eeriness to the surroundings. Visitors to the area are often shocked at how the dense jungle pushes all the way to the sinkhole edges, making their presence more dramatic and even more unnerving.

The sinkholes are remote. Really remote. No roads go near Sarisariñama, and exploration of the tepui is best left to scientists. Ⓝ 5.008121 Ⓦ 64.147789

....

DROWNED CHURCH OF POTOSÍ

POTOSÍ, TÁCHIRA

In 1985, the residents of sleepy, bucolic Potosí received some unwelcome news: The government intended to flood their entire town in order to create the Uribante Caparo hydroelectric dam. The evacuation order came swiftly, and residents were relocated to nearby towns. The dam was completed and the town was submerged, but not all of Potosí disappeared quite so willingly. At low tide, the cross at the top of the 82-foot-tall (25 m) church spire would emerge from the water, a reminder of Potosí's former existence.

In early 2010, the El Niño weather phenomenon caused droughts across Venezuela and the water behind the Potosí dam gradually dried up, revealing the church in its entirety for the first time since flooding.

The site began to attract visitors and, with the area's water stores reaching critically low levels, locals gathered at the church to hold a mass and pray for rain. Their wish was granted—the skies opened and the Potosí church disappeared beneath the water once again.

Potosí is a 7-hour drive east of Caracas, the capital. The church steeple is now visible to varying degrees, according to rainfall and dam levels—check ahead. Ⓝ 7.948304 Ⓦ 71.653638

THE EVERLASTING LIGHTNING STORM

CONGO MIRADOR, ZULIA

There's something strange in the air where the Catatumbo River flows into Lake Maracaibo. For 260 nights out of the year, often for up to ten hours at a time, the sky above the river is pierced by almost constant lightning, producing as many as 280 strikes per hour. Known as the *relampago del Catatumbo* ("the Catatumbo lightning"), this everlasting lightning storm has been raging for as long as people can remember.

In 1595, Sir Francis Drake's attempt to take the city of Maracaibo by night was foiled when the lightning storm's flashes gave away his position to the city's defenders. This happened again during the Venezuelan War of Independence in 1823, when Spanish ships were revealed by the lightning and fell to Simón Bolívar's upstart navy.

In fact, the lightning, visible from 25 miles (40.2 km) away, is so regular that it's been used as a navigation aid by ships and is known among sailors as the Maracaibo Beacon. Interestingly, little to no sound accompanies this fantastic light show, as the lightning moves from cloud to cloud, far above the ground.

It's still unknown exactly why this area—and this area alone—should produce such regular lightning. One theory holds that ionized methane gas rising from the Catatumbo bogs meets cold air pouring down from the Andes, helping to create the perfect conditions for a lightning storm. **The best place to see the storm is from Congo Mirador, a village built on stilts on Lake Maracaibo. Head to Encontrados to make arrangements. Ⓝ 9.563214 Ⓦ 71.382437**

There is a dazzling lightning show over Lake Maracaibo almost every night of the year.

ALSO IN VENEZUELA

Colonia Tovar

Aragua · For over a century, residents of this German village in the cloud forest outside of Caracas spoke German and married only within their village.

Cerro Sarisarinama Tepui

Bolívar · Unique forests are found at the bottom of massive sinkholes on this tabletop mountain in one of the most remote places in the country.

Pedernales

Delta Amacuro · Explore mud volcanoes that are constantly bubbling up wet earth.

Médanos de Coro National Park

Falcón · A desert of massive sand dunes constantly shifts in the winds.

MEXICO

CENOTE ANGELITA

TULUM, QUINTANA ROO

It seems like a riddle: How can there be an underwater river?

In the thick jungle just outside the ruins of the Mayan city of Tulum, a series of sinkholes and caves lead to an amazing submerged world. One such opening is Cenote Angelita. The 200-foot-deep (60 m) pool cavern was created by the crumbling of porous limestone as water crept in and hollowed out the space. The gaping cavern was once even worshipped as a holy site by ancient Mayan cultures, hence its name; *cenote* is a derivation of a Mayan word meaning "sacred well," and *angelita* means "little angel."

The flooded Angelita cave has a unique quality: It seems that a separate river runs near the bottom of the water-filled pit. This illusion is a product of the water's chemistry. Different portions of the water in the caverns have different levels of salinity, causing the denser water to sink to the bottom, where it looks like a misty underwater river all its own.

The cenote is just southwest of the town of Tulum. Guides and transport may be arranged through tour agencies in Tulum. Ⓝ 20.137519 Ⓦ 87.577777

A flooded cave appears to hide an underwater river.

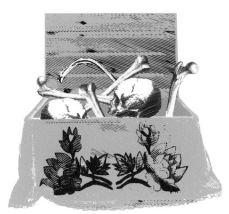

POMUCH CEMETERY

POMUCH, CAMPECHE

When a Pomuch resident dies, he or she is temporarily buried at the town graveyard. After three years, family members come to disinter the bones, clean them, and place them in a wooden box for permanent display. Each year after that, the families return on the Day of the Dead to participate in the ritual bone-cleaning.

In addition to reuniting families and allowing them to confront the pain of death, the tradition is tied to a belief that deceased relatives will become angry and wander the streets if their bones are not cared for properly.

Pomuch is a small town east of Campeche City. Ⓝ 20.137530 Ⓦ 90.174339

LAS POZAS

XILITLA, SAN LUIS POTOSÍ

Las Pozas is the creation of Edward James, an eccentric English poet, artist, and patron of the Surrealist movement. James sponsored Salvador Dalí, allowed René Magritte to use his London home as a studio, and was acquainted with such luminaries as Dylan Thomas, Sigmund Freud, D. H. Lawrence, and Aldous Huxley. Huxley introduced James to Hollywood types, who in turn introduced him to spiritualist Western visionaries, who then introduced him to the wilds of Mexico.

Won over by the country's lush vegetation and leisurely pace, James purchased a coffee plantation in 1947 and spent the next ten years cultivating orchids and tending to exotic animals. After an unprecedented frost in 1962 destroyed many of his plants, James started building the extraordinary sculpture garden that remains on the site today. The design of Las Pozas was inspired by both James's orchids and the vegetation of the jungle of La Huasteca, combined with architectural elements taken from the Surrealist movement.

Construction on Las Pozas began in 1962, and carried on for over 20 years. The gardens feature concrete structures with Surrealist names, like the "House on Three Floors Which Will in Fact Have Five or Four or Six," the "Temple of the Ducks," and the "House With a Roof Like a Whale." Stairs spiral up into the air, mismatched columns support uneven floors, and decorative arches range from ornately finished to seemingly incomplete.

In the 1960s and 1970s, James dedicated more and more of his resources to his "Surrealist Xanadu," as he referred to it, spending millions of dollars and employing hundreds of masons, artisans, and local

A Surrealist Mexican sculpture garden built by an eccentric English poet.

craftsmen. By the times James died in 1984, he had built 36 sculptures spread out over more than 20 acres of tropical jungle. Over the years, trunks and vines have snaked their way among the structures, adding to the surrealism of the scene.

20 de Noviembre, Xilitla. The closest international airport is in Tampico, a 3-hour drive from Xilitla. Ⓝ 21.396710 Ⓦ 98.996714

Minichelista

Hogar y Seguridad • In this café created by artists, you might find yourself sipping spicy coffee in a closet, eating off a typewriter, sharing fries on a glass-topped motorcycle, or hitting up a hookah alongside a robot.

Soumaya Museum

Granada • With a whopping 66,000 pieces of pre-Columbian, Mexican, and European art, this anvil-shaped museum was paid for, built by, and filled with the collection of Mexican magnate Carlos Slim Helú, one of the world's richest men.

Alameda Arts Lab

Centro • Art, science, and technology collide inside a bright-yellow 16th-century chapel, with futuristic electronic exhibits and artistic experiments.

Man, Controller of the Universe

Centro • Diego Rivera's original version of this controversial mural and its social-realist clash of capitalism and communism was done thousands of miles away in New York City's Rockefeller Center, but it so angered the Rockefeller family that it was completely painted over—only to be re-created here.

Palacio Postal

Centro • The city's main post office is everything a mail palace should be, a century-old gilded heaven for philatelists and architecture freaks alike.

Meteorites at the Palace of Mining

Centro • There are four meteorites on display at this early 19th-century school for mining engineers (there were five, but one went to live at the Institute of Astronomy), including the giant *El Morito*—at 14 tons, it's one of the largest chunks of space debris ever discovered on Earth, and the first one recorded in the Western Hemisphere.

Museum of Mexican Medicine

Centro • Not for the squeamish, this scientific repository houses wax figures sporting goiters, boils, and other ailments that are lit as if sculpted by Rodin, befitting the graceful 18th-century century palace they call home.

Caricature Museum

Centro • Housed in a Baroque building, this museum is dedicated to the promotion and preservation of Mexican cartooning, stretching back to the politics of the late 19th century and still happily thumbing noses and tweaking egos right up to today.

Room 2 at Templo Mayor

Centro • Most of the great temple of the Aztec city of Tenochtitlan was destroyed by the Spanish to make way for a cathedral, but along with the ruins many sacrificial artifacts have been found and are held in the museum's Room 2, including decorated skulls, pots of cremated bones, and altar vessels made to hold human hearts.

National Sanctuary of the Angel of the Holy Death

Centro • Three days a week, despite condemnation from the Vatican, believers gather in a modest storefront church to attend an untraditional mass, worshiping Nuestra Senora de la Santa Muerte—Our Lady of the Holy Death—Mexico's most cherished folk saint next to Santa Maria de Guadalupe.

Deportes Martinez

Doctores • In Mexico, freestyle wrestling, aka *lucha libre*, goes back more than 150 years, and the *luchadores'* go-to shop for spandex and iconic *máscaras* is Don Martinez's sports shop, just around the corner from Arena Mexico, the Friday-night fight venue.

MODO

Roma Nte • The space in this Art Nouveau mansion is tight so the 30,000 items in its collection are rotated in and out for an ever-changing display—some rare, some everyday, some edible, some wearable, all a feast for the eyes.

Old Toy Museum of Mexico

Doctores • This cacophony of a collection ranges from the 19th century through the 1980s, a vast jumble of miniatures and masks, vintage tin toys and action figures, plastic novelties and one-of-a-kinds: It's like wandering through the daydreams of a distracted schoolkid.

Museo Cabeza de Juárez

Cabeza de Juarez III • Built in 1972, the 100th anniversary of the death of president Benito Juárez, this giant head sculpture/museum is made from sheet metal and steel rods, and stares out gloomily from the middle of a traffic rotary.

La Casa Azul

Del Carmen • The deep azure-blue childhood home of Frida Kahlo, one she later shared with her husband, Diego Rivera, and, for a time, with Leon Trotsky, is now a museum of Kahlo's life and work.

Leon Trotsky Museum

Del Carmen • The Russian revolutionary lived in Mexico City for the last two years of his life. Visit the home he shared with his wife with its backyard tombs, bullet holes in the hallway, ominous brick guard towers, and Trotsky's nearly untouched study, the site of his 1940 assassination.

Admission is always free at the Soumaya Museum.

Dirt-smeared dolls hanging from trees form a creepy memorial for a drowned child.

THE ISLAND OF THE DOLLS

MEXICO CITY

As a gondolier steers you along Teshuilo Lake to La Isla de las Muñecas, you'll see two giant teddy bears sitting sentry on the shore. Beyond them are the main attraction—hundreds of dirt-encrusted dolls nailed to trees, strung along wires, and pinned to a dilapidated wooden shack.

Some dolls are missing limbs. Others have spider webs forming in their eye sockets. Their faces have been bleached and discolored by the sun, and their hair is stringy and matted. Their clothes are gradually rotting away. Most are attached by their necks, their heads sagging forward, giving them the appearance of having been hanged.

Dolls began appearing on the island in the 1950s, when a man named Don Julian Santana Barrera, ostracized from his hometown for his religious preaching, left his wife and children and moved there to live in isolation. A local legend told

of a girl who had drowned in the surrounding lake. Santana Barrera became fixated on her and was convinced that her spirit lingered on the island. In order to appease her, and to protect himself from any evil spirits lurking in the lake, he began collecting dolls from the trash and arranging them into makeshift memorials.

Over the next five decades, Santana Barrera collected hundreds of plastic children. An avid gardener, he traded produce for dolls and suspended them carefully from trees, wires, and the walls of his wooden hut. He continued to be haunted by the spirit of the drowned girl—though there is no evidence that the girl ever existed.

In 2001, Santana Barrera's nephew, Anastasio Velazquez, came to the island to help his uncle plant pumpkins. As they fished in the canal, Santana Barrera, then 80, sang passionately, claiming that

mermaids in the canal were beckoning to him. Velazquez left briefly to work on the garden. When he returned, he found Santana Barrera lifeless, lying facedown in the canal in the spot where the girl is said to have drowned.

Though the troubled man behind the dolls is gone, his unsettling creations live on. Velazquez keeps the private island open to visitors, many of whom bring dolls of their own as tributes for the "girl of the lake."

Teshuilo Lake, Xochimilco, Mexico City. Get the metro line to Tasqueña station, then the light rail to Xochimilco, a district of canals and artificial islands. From there, walk to Cuemanco landing, where you can hire a gondola. Make sure the gondolier is willing to ferry you to the island, as it's not part of the standard route. The trip takes about 2 hours. Ⓝ 19.272847 Ⓦ 99.096510

GREAT PYRAMID OF CHOLULA

SAN PEDRO CHOLULA, PUEBLA

When the Spanish arrived at the city of Cholula in 1519, they were pleased to find a large hill just itching to have a Catholic church built on top. What they didn't realize was that it was no mere hill—beneath the overgrown grasses was a pyramid with a volume larger than that of the Great Pyramid of Giza.

Construction on Cholula's great pyramid began around the first century BCE. During the many pre-Columbian power shifts in Mexico, each conquering culture—the Olmecs, the Toltecs, and the Aztecs—built its own additions to the structure, creating a stack of pyramids in different architectural styles.

At some point before Hernán Cortés and his army arrived in Cholula, the pyramid fell out of favor as a place for religious ritual. It became overgrown, slowly transforming into what looked like a big hill. Veiled by nature, the pyramid avoided the fate of surrounding temples and sacred sites, which Cortés destroyed and replaced with churches per colonial policy. The Church of Our Lady of the Remedies, built on top of the "hill" in 1594, is still there.

The pyramid was not revealed again until 1910, when diggers preparing the construction of an asylum at its base uncovered the foundations. Archaeologists have since excavated the pyramid's stairways, platforms, altars, and over 5 miles (8 km) of tunnels snaking through the structure's innards. **Av 8 Norte #2, Centro, Puebla. Hike to the hilltop church for a great view of Puebla. Ⓝ 19.105270 Ⓦ 98.225566**

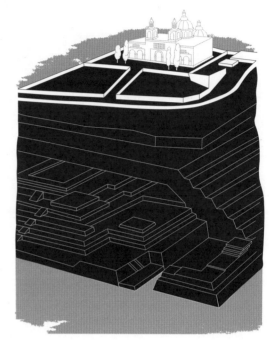

Cholula's ancient pyramid hides under a grassy hill.

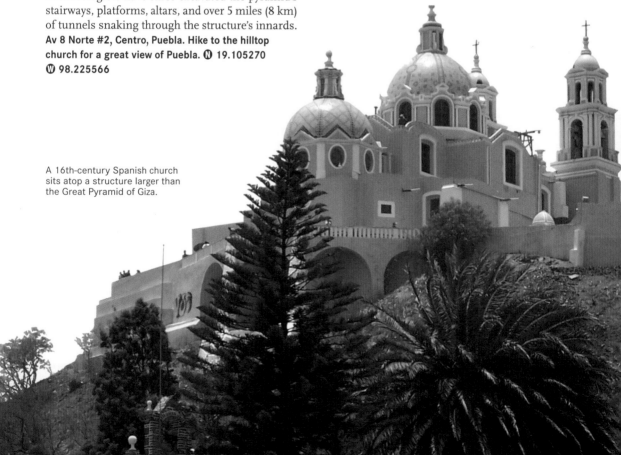

A 16th-century Spanish church sits atop a structure larger than the Great Pyramid of Giza.

Mapimí Silent Zone

MAPIMÍ, DURANGO

According to legend, there is a patch of desert 2.5 miles (4 km) from San Ignacio where cell phones don't work, the animals are mutants, and aliens do flybys in UFOs. Mapimí Silent Zone, so called due to a belief that radio waves can't be transmitted within the area, is Mexico's answer to the Bermuda Triangle. The fact that both zones—as well as the Egyptian pyramids—are located between the 26th and 28th parallels only fuels the fire of conspiracy theorists' imaginations.

Mapimí's supposed magnetism can be traced back to July 11, 1970, when a US Air Force Athena test rocket lost control, accidentally invaded Mexican airspace, and landed in the desert region of Durango, hundreds of miles from its planned New Mexico destination. The rocket was carrying two small containers of cobalt-57, a radioactive element.

A team of covert specialists brought in to find the fallen rocket conducted aerial searches lasting three weeks. When they finally recovered the rocket, a road was built to transport the wreckage, as well as a small amount of contaminated topsoil. All these operations were carried out under tight security, spurring rumors among the locals.

Rumors became legends: People claimed that radios didn't work, reported sightings of very tall people in "tight silver suits" (which may have held some truth, as during the missile cleanup people might have seen men in silver bio-suits), and spoke of concentrated "Earth energy," "light spheres," and UFOs. A seemingly malformed species of desert tortoise with triangles on its shell sparked cries of mutation. (In fact, the patterns are a normal variation among the Bolson tortoise population of Mexico.)

People now come from all over to explore the area, look for the elusive "silent zones," and sometimes attempt communication with otherworldly beings. Though visitors may be surprised to find their compasses and radios working just fine, an experienced guide will remind them that since the zones move, it can be hard to locate them.

Unfortunately, these new age and paranormal enthusiasts, known locally as *zoneros* or *silenciosos*, are now having an adverse effect on the desert area that contains the Silent Zone. By collecting and keeping both natural and historical artifacts they find in the desert, they are depleting the area of its finite resources.

The zone is east of Federal Highway 49, in the Chihuahuan Desert. Part of the Silent Zone is located in the Mapimí Biosphere Reserve; please respect the reserve and keep any supernatural activities subtle.
Ⓝ 26.738181 Ⓦ 103.722721

La Mona

TIJUANA, BAJA CALIFORNIA

In 1987, a scruffy part-time art student named Armando Garcia approached Tijuana city officials with a simple plan: to build a humongous naked woman in the middle of the city to mark the 1989 Tijuana centennial. Unsurprisingly, they declined the offer.

Garcia was undeterred, simply relocating the work to his neighborhood, an overlooked ghetto of Tijuana. Two years later, despite the doubts of his professors and classmates, he had built it: a 5-story, 18-ton nude woman rising from hovels and a trash dump. Her right arm, pinky finger extended, points toward the sky. It is a sly gesture that mimics the location of Tijuana on a map of Mexico.

The huge woman, officially named *Tijuana III Millennium* by Garcia but known locally as *La Mona*, or "the doll," was modeled after one of Garcia's ex-girlfriends. For several years, Garcia lived inside the hollow woman with his wife. Their bedroom was located in the woman's breasts, the study in her head, the kitchen in her stomach, and the bathrooms, appropriately, in her behind.

Garcia has since moved to another house in Puerto Nuevo called *La Sirena*. It, too, is in the shape of a giant nude woman.

Ensenada Street, Aeropuerto, Tijuana. The Aeropuerto neighborhood is just southwest of Tijuana International Airport. Local taxi drivers will know how to find La Mona. Ⓝ 32.539038 Ⓦ 116.993191

Armando Garcia's woman-shaped home is hard to miss.

Hierve El Agua

San Pablo Villa de Mitla

Sometimes nature creates counterfeits: a fish that looks like a plant, a fruit that looks like a vegetable, or, in the case of Mexico's Hierve El Agua, a rock formation that looks like a waterfall.

At a distance, this enormous structure looks exactly like a frozen waterfall, a seeming impossibility in the hot temperatures of San Pablo Villa de Mitla, the town closest to the rock. The rocks are, in fact, mineral deposits on top of a limestone mountain. On the mountain's ledges sit two freshwater pools noted for their medicinal properties and having springs that are saturated with calcium carbonate and magnesium. Water from the pools drips through the cliffs, depositing the minerals onto the side of the mountain. Over time, these deposits have accumulated in staggered columns.

The name of the place, which means "the water boils" in Spanish, comes from the way the water bubbles as it travels through the spring. The Zapotec people, who lived in the area more than 2,000 years ago, revered these pools and directed the spring waters to irrigate their plants. Over thousands

A freshwater pool tops off what appears to be a frozen waterfall.

of years, their canals have petrified into this unusual rock sight.

Take a bus from Oaxaca or Mitla. The park's hours aren't consistent, so make sure to call ahead before setting out. Ⓝ 16.865684 Ⓦ 96.276006

Also in Mexico

San Juan Parangaricutiro

Angahuan · The towers and top floor of this church are all that protrude from a layer of lava that smothered the town in 1944.

The Mummies Museum

Guanajuato · With their mouths gaping open, their arms clutching at themselves, and their tissue-thin skin ripped to reveal bone, these 118 mummies do not appear to be resting in peace.

Statue of José Maria Morelos

Janitzio · A staircase spirals up inside this 131-foot (40 m) statue of a Mexican independence hero. Above the stairs are murals depicting the life of Morelos and his role in the country's history.

Little Boy Zero

La Gloria · Edgar Hernandez, the five-year-old patient zero of 2009's global swine flu pandemic, is immortalized in this bronze statue.

Museum of Perversity

Manzanillo · The graphic dioramas here that depict torture, violence, and cruelty are intended to turn visitors into human-rights activists.

Mercado de Sonora

Mexico City · This market is a one-stop shop for herbal medicine and occult supplies. Stock up on dried skunk, amulets, and ingredients for love spells.

City of Books at Biblioteca Vasconcelos

Mexico City · A jaw-dropping megalibrary contains the complete, perusable personal book collections of five of Mexico's greatest thinkers.

Quetzalcoatl's Nest

Naucalpan · Visit condos designed in the shape of a feathered Aztec snake god, complete with gaping maw.

Cosmovitral Botanic Garden

Toluca · Stained-glass windows bathe this artful garden in cosmic light.

Tree of Tule

Tule · The Montezuma cypress's spectacular girth earns it a place in the record books, while its gnarled bark inspires the imagination. Visitors have found likenesses of human faces, lions, jaguars, and elephants.

Festival of the Exploding Hammers

San Juan de la Vega · Each February, brave and/or reckless locals strap explosives to sledgehammers and throw them down with all their might.

CAVE OF THE CRYSTALS

NAICA, CHIHUAHUA

In 2000, workers at Naica, Mexico's largest mine, were excavating a new tunnel 1,000 feet (305 m) underground when they broke into an extraordinary cave. This chamber, now known as the Cave of the Crystals, contains some of the largest crystals ever found. Its crisscrossing shards of selenite measure up to 39 feet (12 m) long.

The unusually immense crystals formed over half a million years in water that was a steamy and stable 136°F (57.7°C). These conditions allowed a particular mineral in the cave, anhydrite, to absorb water and transform into gypsum, its lower-temperature, stable form. Gypsum deposits gradually built up, forming the giant selenite crystals. When mining operations began in the area, workers pumped water from the surrounding caves, inadvertently draining the crystal cave and exposing its treasures.

Conditions in the Cave of the Crystals are very hazardous to humans. Ambient temperature is around 125°F (51.6°C), and the 90 to 99 percent humidity creates a stifling environment in which higher brain functions quickly deteriorate and breathing becomes difficult. The terrain is uneven and the smaller crystals have sharp edges, making walking tough.

Scientists and researchers have been exploring the cave since 2006. They do so wearing cold-water respirators and suits lined with ice. Even with this special equipment, the explorers can only stay in the cave for 45 minutes at a time.

Naica's gigantic crystals were discovered in 2000.

Unfortunately, the water-draining process that revealed the Cave of the Crystals is also destroying it. Selenite deteriorates when exposed to air. Currently, the mine's water-pumping operations keep the cave dry. To preserve the crystals and allow them to grow larger, the cave must be flooded again, which would cut off human access. The dilemma is whether "saving the cave" means maintaining scientific access to it or allowing its crystals to grow unobserved.

The mine and cave are located in the southwest part of Naica, a town with around 5,000 residents. Due to its fragility and oppressive conditions, the cave is only accessible to researchers.

Terreros 7, Naica. Naica is a 2-hour drive south of Chihuahua City. Ⓝ 27.850833 Ⓦ 105.496389

THE CAVE OF SWALLOWS

AQUISMÓN, SAN LUIS POTOSÍ

If you fell into the Cave of Swallows, it would be at least 10 seconds before you hit the floor. The limestone sinkhole is 1,093 feet (333 m) deep. That's deep enough to fit the Chrysler Building with the Statue of Liberty balancing on top.

BASE jumpers used to fling themselves into the abyss regularly, using a mechanical winch to make the long journey back up. Now, however, BASE jumping and motorized winches are no longer allowed. The noise and constant high-speed descents were disrupting the resident birds as well as the nearby humans.

To see down to the the the bottom of the cave—which, incidentally, is covered with guano and crawling

Rapelling into the unknown.

with insects, snakes, and scorpions—you'll need to throw a rope into the abyss and rappel down. The hard part is climbing back up, which takes 40 minutes if you're super humanly fit, and 2 hours if you've been known to skip a few sessions at the gym. If you'd rather not descend into the fathomless chasm, you can tie a safety rope around your waist and peer over the edge.

The Cave of the Swallows is named after the thousands of birds who nest in the cave walls, spiral out of the sinkhole every morning, and return every night. They are not actually swallows—they're a combination of white-collared swifts and green parakeets.

The cave is a 30-minute drive west of the small town of Aquismón. Ⓝ 21.599836 Ⓦ 99.098964

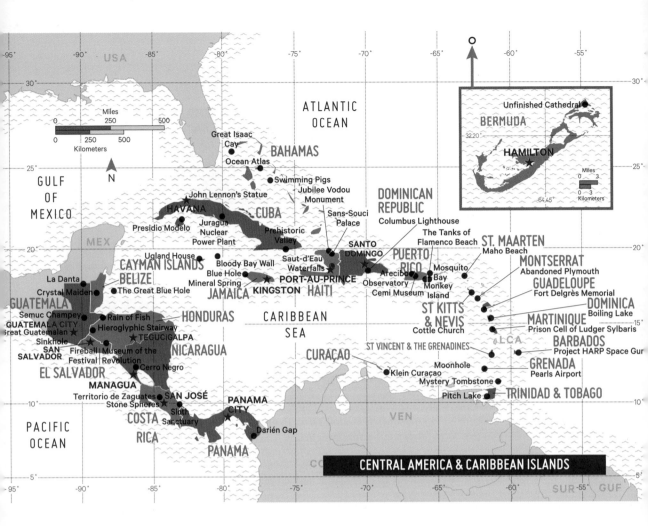

CENTRAL AMERICA & CARIBBEAN ISLANDS

Central America

BELIZE

THE CRYSTAL MAIDEN

SAN IGNACIO, CAYO

To reach the caverns of Actun Tunichil Muknal, you'll need to endure a bumpy 45-minute drive, a 45-minute hike through the jungle, three river crossings on foot, and a claustrophobia-inducing swim into the narrow mouth of the waterlogged cave. But at least you'll make it out alive.

During the late Classic period of their civilization (700 to 900 CE), the Maya came to the cave to perform sacrificial rituals, believing it to be a gateway to Xibalba, the underworld. Carrying flaming torches, burning incense, and holding ceramic pots containing edible offerings, they led people inside to be killed and offered to the gods.

Archaeologist Thomas Miller discovered Actun Tunichil Muknal, also known as ATM, in 1986. Later excavations uncovered the bones of 14 people, including six children under the age of three, in a large chamber called the Cathedral. Cranial trauma and the positioning of the remains indicated they were fatally struck on the head and thrown to the ground. Left undisturbed in the dripping cave for approximately 1,200 years, the bones are coated in calcite crystals, giving them a sparkling, puffy appearance. Hundreds of pieces of broken pottery surround the human remains—following sacrificial ceremonies, the Maya would smash the ceramic pots to release the energy contained within.

A full skeleton, lying on its back with its head raised as if to look at you, stands out among the scattered bones. Calcification has softened its harsh contours, and the crystals dusting the bones glitter in the light of your headlamp. This is the "Crystal Maiden." She died probably at 18—in a particularly violent way, judging by her two crushed vertebrae.

Due to site preservation requirements you must go with a guide—you can find several in San Ignacio. Cameras are no longer allowed, after a tourist dropped one on a skull estimated to be a thousand years old in 2012. Bring dry socks to wear in the Cathedral, where shoes are not permitted. Wear shoes you can swim and hike in. You'll be given a helmet with a headlamp.

The caverns are a 2-hour drive southwest of Belize City.
Ⓝ 17.117496 Ⓦ 88.890467

COSTA RICA
TERRITORIO DE ZAGUATES (LAND OF STRAYS)

CARRIZAL ALAJUELA

Over one million stray dogs roam Costa Rica, and the numbers tick higher every day. Many street dogs are taken into shelters, but purebreds are more likely to be adopted than mutts. One rescue organization is different: Up in the mountains, *Territorio de Zaguates*, or the Land of Strays, celebrates the unique mix of each dog it cares for.

Veterinarians at Territorio de Zaguates do their best to analyze the physical traits of each of the hundreds of rescue dogs that live at the free-range shelter and make guesses at their breeds' lineage. They then give every mutt its own unique pedigree, with names like the Long-Legged Irish Schnaufox or the Fire-Tailed Border Cocker.

When the shelter's head vet appeared on television to talk about the special breeds bestowed upon the canines, he emphasized their uniqueness, boasting that "these dogs exist only in our country." Dog lovers went wild, calling in to reserve the Bunny-Tailed Scottish Shepterrier or the Furry Pinscher Spaniel for themselves. The shelter grew in popularity, leading to more adoptions of these one-of-a-kind pups.

Territorio de Zaguates formerly sponsored public hiking events where visitors could frolic in the mountains with hundreds of pups. The park is currently closed to the public but there are plans to reopen the sanctuary for tours and visits with the pack. Ⓝ 10.096143 Ⓦ 84.156100

Also in Central America

Costa Rica

727 Fuselage Home

Quepos · Stay in a beachfront hotel repurposed from an old Boeing 727 fuselage.

Guatemala

Mapa en Relieve

Guatemala City · For a smaller, steeper, more-turquoise version of Guatemala, head to the open-air relief map at Minerva Park.

Nicaragua

Footprints of Acahualinca

Managua · Over two thousand years ago, a dozen or so people went for a stroll through Managua. Their footprints, embedded in volcanic ash which then solidified, are still visible today.

Panama

Ancón Hill

Panama City · Surrounded on all sides by Panama City, a tiny patch of jungle wilderness remains protected amid a rapidly industrializing and burgeoning urban center.

A young woman sacrificed around 1,200 years ago has transformed into a glittering skeleton.

STONE SPHERES

SAN JOSÉ

Clearing land along the Diquis Delta for future banana plantations in 1939, the United Fruit Company uncovered something unexpected: hundreds of spherical stones, measuring up to eight feet (2.4 m) across.

To this day, it is unclear who shaped the stones, when they did it, and for what purpose, but their perfect roundness and smooth surfaces indicate they are man-made, rather than naturally formed. They were likely shaped into balls from larger boulders, using a combination of fracturing, chiseling, and grinding.

Almost all of the stone spheres have been moved from their original locations, making it even more difficult to determine their

Formed by an ancient civilization, Costa Rica's mysterious stone balls have become prized lawn ornaments.

archaeological context. Treasure seekers have blown up some of the balls, acting on the belief that there is gold hidden inside. There is not.

Six of the spheres are in the courtyard of Costa Rica's national museum in San José, Calle 17, Cuesta de Moras. Ⓝ 9.932609 Ⓦ 85.071967

EL SALVADOR

FIREBALL FESTIVAL

NEJAPA, SAN SALVADOR

Every August 31, once the sun goes down, young men with painted faces crowd the streets of Nejapa to hurl flaming fuel-soaked rags at one another. Hundreds of onlookers cheer as the *bolas de fuego*, or "fireballs," fly through the air.

For over 30 years, the annual fireball festival has commemorated the 1658 eruption of the El Playon volcano, which buried the town of Nexapa and forced its residents to build a new settlement: Nejapa. The

fireballs, which are made from rolled-up rags soaked in barrels full of kerosene, represent the flaming rocks spewed from the volcano. The festival also honors San Jerónimo, the town's patron saint, who is said to have fought the devil in a fiery struggle.

To protect themselves from burns, fireball festival combatants wear gloves and waterlogged clothes. Even with these precautions in place, dozens of people each year have to be treated for burns.

Nejapa is a small town 30 minutes north of San Salvador, the capital. Ⓝ 13.819263 Ⓦ 89.233773

Once a year, flaming rags are flung in the air to commemorate a volcanic eruption.

Hidden in the dense Guatemalan jungle is one of the world's largest pyramids.

GUATEMALA
LA DANTA

CARMELITA, PETÉN

An enormous stone structure pokes above the trees in the northern Guatemalan jungle. It looks like a strange, lonely volcano randomly plopped in the vegetation. But the structure is actually one of the largest pyramids on the planet, which stands within the ruins of El Mirador, the "lost city of the Maya."

The ancient city of El Mirador thrived between the 6th and 3rd centuries BCE, before being abandoned and swallowed up by the jungle. The site laid dormant for hundreds of years, until archaeologists began excavating. Thousands of structures were unearthed within the pre-Columbian city, but perhaps none are as impressive as the La Danta temple.

La Danta stands a staggering 230 feet tall (70 m). It has a total volume of nearly 99 million cubic feet, making it one of the world's largest pyramids and among the most enormous ancient structures on Earth. It's been calculated that 15 million days of labor were needed to construct the gigantic monument. A staircase leads up the temple's eastern face, rewarding those who climb it with views of a vibrant canopy of trees stretching as far as the eye can see.

You can reach El Mirador from Flores via helicopter. It's also possible to hire a guide and hike from the village of Carmelita. Hiking to the lost city takes several days, and you'll walk through jungle inhabited by the venomous fer-de-lance snake. Ⓝ 17.756152 Ⓦ 89.919017

The arduous journey to Semuc Champey ends in a natural paradise of turquoise pools and limestone caves.

SEMUC CHAMPEY

LANQUIN, ALTA VERAPAZ

Tucked away in the densely forested mountains of Alta Verapaz lies an idyllic limestone paradise. Virtually inaccessible to all but the heartiest four-wheel drive vehicles, the Semuc Champey natural monument boasts six stunning tiered turquoise pools and an extensive cave network, complete with underground waterfalls. The shockingly blue pools rest on top of a natural limestone bridge covering a portion of the Cahabón River.

The site is located far from any large settlement down rough, rock-strewn roads. However, the difficulty of getting to this unique natural landscape is rewarded many times over by the sights and experiences awaiting guests upon arrival. If you choose to take a guided tour, you'll start with an optional rope swing leap into the river before grabbing a candle and wading through a series of watery caves. The above-ground portion of the tour meanders through the forest before dropping guests at their final activity: a relaxing swim in the limestone pools. **While it is possible to rent a car and drive on your own, the easiest and safest way to get to Semuc Champey is by booking a minibus through a travel agency in one of Guatemala's larger cities. Minibuses will drop you off at Lanquín, the town closest to Semuc Champey, and from there you can either walk for about 2.5 hours or take a 4x4 pickup truck taxi to the entrance of the falls. Ⓝ 15.533352 Ⓦ 89.961379**

HONDURAS
RAIN OF FISH

YORO, YORO

The *Lluvia de Peces*, or "Rain of Fish," is said to occur at least once and sometimes twice a year in the small town of Yoro: During massive rainstorms, hundreds of small silver fish supposedly cascade from the heavens.

The fantastical story says that from the 19th century onward, every May or June, a large storm has rolled through the town bringing heavy rain. When the maelstrom passes, the streets are alive with gasping fish.

In the 1970s, a team from the National Geographic Society actually witnessed the flapping fish—one of the few credible sightings of the phenomenon. They did not, however, find proof that the fish came from the sky.

The "animal rain" weather phenomenon has been reported around the world for centuries, though the scientific understanding of it remains sketchy. The simplest explanation for these falling fauna is that large rainstorms flood rivers and force certain animals out of their homes, causing them to fill the streets. Another simple explanation is that a flash flood can deposit fish far from their waters before quickly receding, leading bystanders to believe that the animals must have come down with the rains.

While it's extremely rare, animals do occasionally fall from the sky when they get picked up by waterspouts. Waterspouts are small tornadoes that form over a body of water. Though they do not suck up water into the air (the "spout" is actually condensation), the whirlwind has the power to lift small animals from the water and release them over land.

Among the most mysterious elements of Yoro's "Rain of Fish" is that the fish themselves are not local to the area and may come from as far away as the Atlantic Ocean, some 140 miles (200 km) to the north. A less exciting theory postulates that the fish live in underground rivers and are forced up onto the streets rather than falling down onto them. This hypothesis is supported by the 1970s National Geographic team's discovery that the silver fish are completely blind.

In Yoro, the explanation is often religious rather than scientific. In the 1860s, Father José Manuel Subirana, a Catholic priest living in the area, prayed for sustenance for the hungry. At the end of his marathon prayer session, it is said to have rained small fish. Since 1998, an annual festival has been held in honor of the Lluvia de Peces miracle. It includes a parade, during which revelers carry effigies of Father José Manuel Subirana through the streets. **Buses run between the Honduran capital of Tegucigalpa and Yoro—a 125-mile (201 km) journey. The festival is usually held in June, coinciding with the first major rainfall of the season. Ⓝ 15.133333 Ⓦ 87.142289**

HIEROGLYPHIC STAIRWAY OF COPÁN

COPÁN

The city of Copán in what is now western Honduras served as a political, civil, and religious center of the Mayan civilization for over 400 years. The site is host to a number of marvelous ruins, the most striking of which must be the epic stairway in the temple-pyramid of Structure 26.

This construction, which forms the longest discovered Mayan text, was originally commissioned by the 14th governor of Copán, K'ak Joplaj Chan K'awiil, and completed about six years after his death in the year 755. The pyramid is nearly 100 feet (30.5 m) high and etched with around 2,000 glyphs. This collection of symbols offers a rare window into the rich history of the Copán Valley and the culture that ruled it for so many years.

Researchers, first stumped by the hieroglyphs, came to realize that the staircase is a record of the royal history of Copán, listing the names of kings, their births, their deaths, and the defining events of their rule. The happy realization that the stones were arranged chronologically was somewhat tempered by the fact that archaeologists in the 1930s—not 100 percent clear on Mayan syntax—had liberally rearranged the stone blocks in an attempt at reconstruction. Only the bottom 15 stairs remain in their original positions.

Despite the jumble, modern archaeologists have figured out that the stairs document the rule of 16 kings, beginning with Yax K'uk Moh at the bottom step and ending with the death of a ruler known as "18-Rabbit" at the top. It is also believed that there is special emphasis on the story of the 12th king, K'ak Uti Ha K'awiil, whose burial plot was discovered inside the pyramid that supports the staircase.

The ruins are a 3-hour bus ride from San Pedro Sula. Ⓝ 14.837331 Ⓦ 89.141511

A statue of a Mayan ruler dressed as a Teotihuacan warrior sits at the base of the stairs.

NICARAGUA
CERRO NEGRO
LEÓN, LEÓN

Cerro Negro, South America's youngest volcano, is the world's first location to offer ash boarding. Also known as volcano surfing or volcano boarding, the sport involves strapping a wooden plank to your feet and coasting down the 1,600-foot (488 m) ash-and-pebble slope of Cerro Negro. Boarders wearing gloves, goggles, and jumpsuits reach speeds of up to 50 miles (80.5 km) an hour, kicking up clouds of dust on the way down. Those of a more timid disposition can opt to sit on the board or simply run down the steep slope.

The ascent is less thrilling—it's an hour-long hike—but the summit brings its own rewards. A stunning

Surf down the slopes of an active volcano.

360-degree panoramic view reveals the chain of active and dormant volcanoes, lined up one after the other, surrounded by blue skies and lush green foliage. Cerro Negro itself, which first appeared in 1850, is an active volcano whose crater often emits smoke. It has erupted 23 times, most recently in 1999.
Boarding tours leave from León, an hour southwest of the volcano.
Ⓝ 12.506864 Ⓦ 86.703906

PANAMA
DARIÉN GAP
DARIÉN PROVINCE

The Pan-American Highway stretches all the way from the northern shore of Alaska to the southern tip of South America with just one break: a 54-mile (87 km) missing piece on the Panama–Colombia border known as the Darién Gap. Visit and you will encounter a wild jungle oasis that is home to many rare plants and wildlife. You also may not make it out alive.

The Darién region is home to members of the Revolutionary Armed Forces of Colombia (FARC), a Marxist–Leninist guerrilla group engaged in a decades-long armed conflict with the Colombian government. The overgrown jungle provides plenty of hiding places for the storage and trafficking of drugs—activities that earn FARC hundreds of millions of dollars each year. Many travelers attempting to cross the Darién Gap have gone missing, been kidnapped, and been held hostage by rebels on both sides of the border.

The current Colombian and Panamanian governments have no desire to build a road that would complete the Pan-American Highway. It's too expensive and too dangerous, and development would damage the jungle's fragile ecosystem. In the words of explorer Robert Young Pelton, who was kidnapped and held hostage in the Darién Gap in 2003, "It's probably the most dangerous place in the Western Hemisphere . . . Everything that's bad for you is in there."
The thick jungle and militia presence make the Darién Gap a destination for only the most foolhardy. To travel between Central and South America more safely, buy a plane ticket or hop aboard one of the many yachts that make the trip from Panama to Colombia. Ⓝ 7.868171 Ⓦ 77.836728

The only gap in 30,000 miles of Pan-American Highway is a very dangerous place.

Caribbean Islands

BAHAMAS
SWIMMING PIGS

BIG MAJOR CAY

"Uninhabited island full of feral pigs" may not sound like a delightful vacation destination. But consider this: These pigs are friendly, and they want nothing more than to frolic with you in the clear, refreshing waters of Big Major Cay, also known as Pig Beach.

The swimming pigs hang out during the day on the beach and in the waters of the appropriately named Pig Beach. When a boat approaches from the adjacent resort island of Fowl Cay, the eager swine throw themselves into the water and paddle up to greet their guests. A steady stream of visitors ensures they are well fed and well loved.

It is unclear how pigs got to Big Major Cay in the first place, but they were likely left there by sailors

Friendly wild pigs float in the warm Bahamian waters.

stopping off on the way to bigger bits of land.

To get to Big Major Cay from Nassau, take a plane to Staniel Cay, then a boat north. The pigs like it when you bring potatoes. ℕ 24.183874 Ⓦ 76.456411

OCEAN ATLAS

NASSAU, NEW PROVIDENCE

The world's largest underwater sculpture is submerged beneath the sea in the crystal Bahamian waters off the coast of Nassau. Entitled *Ocean Atlas*, the giant sculpture is a contemporary take on the ancient Greek myth of Atlas. But rather than a Titan condemned to carry the heavens on his back for eternity, it depicts a young Bahamian girl supporting the ceiling of the ocean on her shoulders.

Created by artist, naturalist, and diver Jason deCaires Taylor in 2014, *Ocean Atlas* is over 16 feet tall and weighs 60 tons. Located just off the coast of New Providence, the most populous island in the Bahamas, the watery wonder is meant to deter tourists from endangered reefs and encourage coral colonization. The artwork is forged from sustainable, pH-neutral materials designed to kick-start the growth of local coral. It's an environmental gesture intended to portray the positive potential of human interaction with the natural world, even as the Earth's oceans face numerous threats from climate change and human activity.

The artist has designed three other submerged museums and installations around the world: Vicissitudes, the world's first underwater sculpture park, located in Grenada's Molinere Bay; MUSA (Museo Subacuático de Arte), an underwater sculpture park in Cancún; and Museo Atlántico, the first submerged contemporary art museum in the Atlantic Ocean, off the coast of Lanzarote, Spain.

Ocean Atlas is submerged just off the coast of Nassau within Clifton Heritage National Park. You can book a snorkeling tour of the sculpture online. ℕ 25.013896 Ⓦ 77.551996

A modern Atlas sits beneath the sea.

BARBADOS
PROJECT HARP SPACE GUN

SEAWELL, CHRIST CHURCH

Put simply, Project HARP was established to create a cartoonishly large gun to shoot satellites into space. Short for High Altitude Research Project, the 1960s experiment was a joint initiative between the United States and Canada to study the use of ballistics to deliver objects into the upper atmosphere and beyond. Numerous space guns were built, but the most impressive surviving relic of the program is the gigantic, abandoned gun barrel in Barbados.

Engineer Gerald Bull

The gun was designed by the brilliant and controversial ballistics engineer Gerald Bull, who spent his life in passionate pursuit of his dream to build a long-range super-gun (an obsession that would later, after Project HARP was shut down, lead him to design weapons for the Iraqi government). Bull was assassinated in 1990 inside his apartment. His killing remains unsolved.

The Barbados gun was built from a 65-foot-long (20 m) naval cannon, the kind that might be seen on a battleship. That cannon was later joined to another barrel, extending the length to 118 feet (36 m) and making the gun too big for effective military application but seemingly perfect for satellite delivery. At its peak in 1963, this giant piece of artillery was able to fire an object a staggering 111 miles (178 km) into the sky, setting the world record.

The Barbados gun was abandoned by 1967 and left to rust on its original launch site on a small cliff overlooking the Atlantic Ocean. After years of neglect, it looks more like a painted sewer pipe than a mammoth space cannon.

The abandoned space gun is located on an active military base and is only accessible with permission. Ⓝ 13.077242 Ⓦ 59.475511

BERMUDA
THE UNFINISHED CATHEDRAL

ST. GEORGE'S, ST. GEORGE'S

St. Peter's will never be completed, but the open-air ruin now has its own appeal.

Grass grows where the pews ought to be, half the support pillars have crumbled, and the roof is long gone. The unfinished church at Somers Garden is the result of conflicts in the congregation, money troubles, and one almighty hurricane.

Construction on the Protestant cathedral began in 1874. The building, designed to seat 650, was intended to replace St. Peter's Church, an Anglican place of worship established shortly after the 1612 English settlement of St. George's.

St. Peter's Church still stands, but the new cathedral remains unfinished. The first hurdle came when the congregation split and a group of former parishioners left to build their own Reformed Episcopal Church. In 1884, a cathedral in nearby Hamilton burned down, requiring funds to be diverted from the construction project. By 1894, with the unfinished cathedral having suffered from financial setbacks, storm damage, and squabbles within the Anglican community over its legitimacy, the congregation decided they would rather renovate St. Peter's than complete the new cathedral.

Thirty years later, a hurricane caused substantial damage to the western end of the unfinished cathedral, sealing its fate as a modern ruin. Though the building has no ceiling, no floor, and no windows, it is a popular site for wedding ceremonies.

Blockade Alley, St. George's. Public buses run to nearby Somers Garden. Ⓝ 32.382350 Ⓦ 64.676251

ALSO IN BERMUDA

Somerset Bridge

Somerset Island · The world's smallest drawbridge is just wide enough for a sailboat mast.

CAYMAN ISLANDS

UGLAND HOUSE

GEORGE TOWN, GRAND CAYMAN

There are nearly 100,000 corporate entities worldwide that use the Cayman Islands' zero percent tax rate to dodge corporate taxes, a number higher than the territory's population itself. These corporations could together form a miniature city or a major financial district, but thousands of their offices have the exact same address.

The five-story Ugland House in George Town covers a mere 10,000 square feet of land but is the official home of a whopping 18,857 corporate entities. That equals one corporation registered for every three square feet of space in the building.

The Cayman Islands' image as a tax-free paradise has its own mythological origins. In 1794, a convoy of 10 British ships en route from Jamaica met disaster on the treacherous reefs of Grand Cayman. As the passengers and crew struggled to survive amid the breaking waves, island residents from the East End and Bodden Town, having heard the ships' distress signals, paddled out to the reefs in canoes to attempt a rescue. In the darkness and pounding surf, the Caymanians saved 450 of the stranded souls. Amazingly, only 6 people lost their lives in the disaster.

The heroism of the Caymanians in rescuing the English sailors and passengers fueled a legend that lingers to this day. The story goes that one of the passengers rescued from the wrecked ships was a son of King George III. When the king learned of the islanders' bravery, he rewarded them by decreeing that the Cayman Islands would forever be free of taxation and war conscription. However, there is no record that any member of the royal family was on one of the ships or that the king ever issued such a decree.

121 S Church Street, George Town. When you're done scoping out Ugland House (you can't go inside), head to the East End, where you'll find a simple memorial commemorating the maritime disaster. Ⓝ 19.292199 Ⓦ 81.385544

CUBA

PRESIDIO MODELO

NUEVA GERONA, ISLA DE LA JUVENTUD

During their four decades of operation, the circular cell blocks of Presidio Modelo housed political dissidents, counterrevolutionaries, and even Fidel Castro. Cuban president-turned-dictator Gerardo Machado oversaw the prison's construction in 1926. Modeled after Jeremy Bentham's Panopticon design, with tiered cells surrounding a central observation post, the prison provided constant surveillance of its inmates.

Fidel Castro spent two years at Presidio Modelo after leading a 1953 attack on Moncada Barracks that killed dozens and ignited the Cuban Revolution. The future Communist leader and icon spent his sentence penning "History Will Absolve Me," a revolutionary manifesto that formed the basis for his junta.

When Castro seized power in 1959, the prison soon became overcrowded with enemies of the socialist state. Designed to hold 2,500 inmates, Presidio Modelo housed over 6,000 inmates by 1961. Riots and hunger strikes broke out regularly, leading to the prison being closed for good in 1966.

Today, the buildings are open as a museum and national monument. **Isla de la Juventud is south of the main island of Cuba. A boat from the port in Batabanó takes around 2 hours, or you can get a half-hour flight from Havana. The prison is just east of Nueva Gerona. Ⓝ 21.877609 Ⓦ 82.766451**

Presidio Modelo's circular cell blocks made prisoner surveillance easy.

JURAGUA NUCLEAR POWER PLANT

JURAGUA, CIENFUEGOS

In 1976, Communist companions Cuba and the Soviet Union signed a deal to build the Juragua nuclear power plant. Construction on the first of two nuclear reactors began in 1983 with a target operational date of 1993. But a few years before the reactor's scheduled completion, the USSR collapsed. The flow of crucial Soviet funds ceased, 300 Russian technicians went home, and Cuba was forced to suspend construction on its badly needed power plant.

Lacking nuclear fuel and without the primary components installed, the plant sat in limbo until December 2000, when Russian president Vladimir Putin paid a visit to Cuba. Putin offered Fidel Castro a belated $800 million to finish the first reactor. Despite Cuba's reliance on imported oil for power, Castro declined. Project status: officially abandoned.

The unfinished plant, a huge, domed concrete structure, sits on the Caribbean coast, across the bay from the city of Cienfuegos. You can get a closer look by going to Castillo de Jagua, an 18th-century Spanish fortress two miles from the plant. Access to the plant itself is prohibited.

The plant is a few minutes away from the town of Jagua.
Ⓝ 22.066660 Ⓦ 80.513275 ➤➤

➤➤ Abandoned Nuclear Power Plants

HANFORD SITE
WASHINGTON
Located on Washington State's Columbia River and surrounded by a wildlife refuge, the 560-square-mile (1,450 km²) Hanford site is the largest radioactive waste dump in the US.

Selected as the location for a plutonium production complex in 1943, the first nuclear reactor at the site served up its initial batch of plutonium in November 1944. By February 1945, Hanford had a trio of identical reactors producing plutonium.

Plutonium produced at Hanford ended up in Fat Man, the bomb that killed approximately 80,000 people in Nagasaki. Almost all of the 50,000 construction workers who built the plant had no idea they had contributed to the creation of a nuclear weapon until news of the Hiroshima bomb reached them.

Decommissioned after the Cold War, the Hanford complex left 53 million gallons of radioactive waste stored in leaking underground tanks. A multidecade cleanup is currently underway, with a projected completion date of 2040.

EXPERIMENTAL BREEDER REACTOR I (EBR-I)
IDAHO
Built as a research facility in 1951, this plant in Idaho's Arco desert became the first nuclear reactor to generate electricity. Deactivated in 1964, the site is now a museum. Visit to see two nuclear reactors, press buttons and flip switches in the control room, and use mechanical manipulator claws that once handled radioactive waste.

In the parking lot are two prototype reactors designed to power nuclear bomber aircraft. Both the United States and the Soviet Union researched nuclear-powered planes during the Cold War, but neither country produced a working model.

WUNDERLAND KALKAR
GERMANY
The swing ride at the Wunderland Kalkar amusement park north of Düsseldorf is in the cooling tower of a former nuclear power plant.

Wunderland Kalkar offers amusement park thrills in the shadow of a nuclear cooling tower.

Construction on the plant and reactor SNR-300 began in 1973 and took 12 years to complete. During its construction, the community was vocal about its concerns over nuclear power. In 1985, the reactor began partial operation. Then came the Chernobyl disaster of April 26, 1986. Concerned about safety and wanting to avoid high operating costs, the state government halted the opening of the plant.

Five years later, with SNR-300 officially canceled and its valuable parts sold and shipped away, Dutchman Hennie van der Most purchased the land. He then took the obvious next step: turning a nuclear power plant into a family amusement park.

Kernwasser Wunderland ("Corewater Wonderland") opened in 2001 with over 40 rides, a 437-room hotel, bars, restaurants, and a bowling alley. The star attraction is the cooling tower, now painted to resemble a snowy mountain landscape. A rock-climbing trail snakes up its outer wall, while the inside is home to a swing ride and "Echoland"— just shout and you'll understand why.

CURAÇAO
KLEIN CURAÇAO

WILLEMSTAD

Measuring just 1.2 square miles in size, the flat, abandoned coral atoll of Klein Curaçao is home to a deserted lighthouse, the shipwrecks of vessels it failed to save, several collapsed ancient stone buildings, and a burial site.

The northern side is a tropical paradise of palm trees, white beaches, and crystal waters. The southern, windward side, more exposed to the elements, is an unforgiving shoreline of pounding surf and ragged coral reefs. Here lie the shipwrecks of Klein Curaçao. There's about half left of the oil tanker *Maria Bianca Guidesman*, which ran aground in the 1960s. Next to the *Maria Bianca* are the remnants of a once glorious 30-foot (9 m) luxury boat that smashed against the sharp coral reefs.

Crumbling stone structures, perhaps former homes to passing fishermen, dot the island. On

A long-abandoned lighthouse sits on the southside of paradise.

the northeastern end there is also a simple burial site, marked by a bleached, plain wooden cross without a name.

Standing alone at the center of the island is the lighthouse. Once painted a vibrant coral pink, it was built in 1850. Its wooden stairs are still intact, as are the two stories of rooms where the lightkeepers lived.

In 1888, the German navy attempted to build a base at Klein Curaçao as part of a hoped-for colonization of the Caribbean, but they were driven off by the windswept conditions of the remote outpost when a tropical storm swept away the first foundations of a wharf.

Klein Curaçao is a 2-hour sail southeast from neighboring Curaçao. Several companies offer day trips by catamaran.
Ⓝ 11.984563 Ⓦ 68.644221

DOMINICA
BOILING LAKE

ROSEAU

The lake on Watt Mountain is not a good place for a refreshing dip: Drinking or bathing in the water will result in death, or at least severe burns.

Morne Watt (Watt Mountain) is a stratovolcano, its boiling lake a flooded fumarole—a direct line to the molten subsurface of Earth, with vents pumping scalding steam and gases into the water. A thick cloud of vapor rises from the bubbling blue-gray lake. Water temperature is around 194°F (90°C).

You need to be fit to visit the lake—it's a 3-hour hike from the nearest road, over difficult terrain. En route, you'll pass through the Valley of Desolation, a sulfurous expanse of volcanic vents, hot springs, and bubbling mud. Ⓝ 15.333608 Ⓦ 61.324139

This mountaintop lake churns, bubbles, and steams in a perpetual boil.

The cruciform building that may (or may not) hold Christopher Columbus's remains.

DOMINICAN REPUBLIC
THE COLUMBUS LIGHTHOUSE

SANTO DOMINGO ESTE, SANTO DOMINGO

In 1506, Christopher Columbus died in his mid-fifties in Spain. But death was not the end of his adventures—his body continued to travel in a centuries-long shell game.

Immediately after his death, Columbus was buried in Valladolid, the town in which he spent his last days. Then, on the wishes of his son Diego, the body was moved to Seville. But that wasn't Columbus's final destination—Diego wanted a grander tribute for his father. He headed back to the Dominican Republic, where in 1514 he laid the cornerstone for the Cathedral of Santa María la Menor that would hold Columbus's remains. Unfortunately, frequent traveler Diego died in 1526 in Montalbán, Spain, before the cathedral was finished. His body was transported to Seville and interred next to his father.

The bodies of father and son stayed in Seville for the next 16 years, but when the Cathedral of Santa María la Menor was completed in the Dominican Republic, Diego's widow put the wheels in motion to have both bodies moved there. In 1542, the remains sailed the ocean blue again, joining the body of Christopher's brother, Bartholomew, who had died in Santo Domingo the year before.

There they remained, for more than 200 years, until the Spanish were ousted from the Dominican Republic in 1795. On their way out, Spaniards took the explorer's body with them to the other Spanish stronghold in the Caribbean: Havana, Cuba.

Back in the Dominican Republic, nearly a century later, a construction worker working on the cathedral renovation uncovered a lead box—unimpressive, save for the inscription on the inside of the lid: "The illustrious and excellent man, Don Colón, Admiral of the Ocean Sea."

At first pass, it seemed obvious that the Spanish must have, in their haste, taken the wrong box. But there's a catch—both father, Christopher, and son, Diego, were known as Don Colón in their lifetimes, and both held the title Admiral of the Ocean Sea.

In 1898, the Spanish left newly independent Cuba. They took the (assumed) remains of Columbus back to Seville and placed them in an elaborate cathedral tomb. Back in the Dominican Republic, a 1931 design competition resulted in the 688-foot-long (210 m) cruciform memorial complex that allegedly now holds the boxed remains of the explorer.

Thus far, science has not solved the mystery of the mixed-up remains. DNA analysis of the Seville remains in 2003 was inconclusive, and Santo Domingo authorities will not permit any exhumations.

Though it's referred to as a lighthouse, the building that (maybe) houses Columbus's remains is actually a blocky, gray, seven-story museum. It is also home to Pope John Paul II's robes and a popemobile.

Avenida Faro a Colón, L2 13, Santo Domingo Este. The lighthouse is in the Sans Souci part of Santo Domingo, near the cruise terminal. Buses marked "Corredor Independencia" and "Ave Las Americas" will get you within a 20-minute walk.
Ⓝ 18.478714 Ⓦ 69.866531

A stone circle on the slope of a volcano commemorates the leader of an anti-slavery uprising.

GUADELOUPE
FORT DELGRÈS MEMORIAL

BASSE-TERRE

In 1802, Louis Delgrès, a free man of color born in Guadeloupe, led a doomed rebellion against Napoleon's General Antoine Richepanse to prevent the return of slavery in the French Caribbean. Now the fort where he made his last stand bears his name.

Delgrès was an idealist and a distinguished soldier in many battles for the French Republic. He was even captured and sent to England as a prisoner once or twice. When, in 1802, Napoleon Bonaparte sent General Richepanse to Guadeloupe to restore it to its "pre-1789" state

(i.e., to reinstate slavery), Delgrès led an armed rebellion of civilians and soldiers of color.

Unfortunately, the rebels were no match for the French army. They retreated into this fort, where Delgrès issued a proclamation "to the entire Universe" explaining what he was fighting for. Then, when it became clear there was no hope of victory, Delgrès and 400 of his followers holed up in a plantation on the volcano's slope and blew themselves up, along with as many French soldiers as they could.

Slavery was reinstated— though some say the rebellion's failure motivated the successful

liberation struggle in Haiti. As for General Richepanse, he got yellow fever and died a few weeks later and is now buried in the military cemetery at the very top of the fort complex.

The fort's memorial to Louis Delgrès is a sort of cross between a meditation maze and Stonehenge, with Delgrès's head in the center. If you venture into the stone spiral, you'll be able to pick out some carvings on one of the rocks that read LIBERTÉ and JUSTICE.

Basse-Terre's southwest coast is where you will find the fort. Informational signs are in French.
Ⓝ 15.988921 Ⓦ 61.722995

ALSO IN THE CARIBBEAN

ANTIGUA AND BARBUDA

Kingdom of Redonda

Redonda · Multiple kings claim to rule this hotly contested island micronation that was founded on an uninhabited island in 1865.

BAHAMAS

Bimini Road

Bimini Islands · These evenly spaced underwater stones raised hopes that Atlantis had finally been found. Further examination showed that the "road" was a naturally occurring rock formation.

CAYMAN ISLANDS

Hell

Grand Cayman · A patch of jagged limestone formations has come to be known as Hell. Hell postcards with Hell postmarks are available from the local post office.

GRENADA

Mopion

Resembling the prototypical cartoon desert island, this tiny sandbar, supposedly the Caribbean's smallest island, is home only to a single umbrella.

HAITI

SAUT-D'EAU WATERFALLS

HAUT SAUT D'EAU, CENTRE

According to Haitian Catholics, the Virgin Mary once appeared in a palm tree next to the Saut-d'Eau waterfalls. According to Vodou practitioners, the apparition was the *Iwa,* or spirit, Erzulie Dantor. Though the tree was chopped down, members of both faiths have trekked to the waterfalls every July for over a century in search of spiritual and physical healing.

An annual pilgrimage takes place during the festival of Our Lady of Mount Carmel, from July 14 to the 16th. (July 16, 1843, is when the Virgin is said to have appeared in the tree.) The sick and needy come to the 100-foot-tall (30 m) waterfall to pray, bathe, and cleanse themselves with medicinal herbs, hoping to feel the presence of the Virgin Mary—or be possessed by the spirit of Erzulie Dantor. Hundreds of pilgrims crowd the base of the falls, arms raised in reverence toward the torrent of water. Some fall into a trance and must be supported by others so they don't drown.

Pilgrimages to Saut-d'Eau increased following the catastrophic Haitian earthquake of 2010. **The waterfalls are near Mirebalais, an hour drive north of Port-au-Prince. Ⓝ 18.816902 Ⓦ 72.201512**

Thousands of Haitians travel to the falls each year to seek the healing powers of the Virgin Mary of Mount Carmel and her Vodou counterpart, Erzulie.

MARTINIQUE
Prison Cell of Ludger Sylbaris

ST. PIERRE, ST. PIERRE

A glance at the windowless stone cell that Ludger Sylbaris once occupied may elicit pity for the man—until you learn that this building saved his life.

On May 7, 1902, the town troublemaker ended up in solitary confinement after being arrested for drunk and disorderly conduct. The next day, Mount Pelée, a volcano just north of St. Pierre, erupted, sending a cloud of superheated gas and dust racing toward the city. Within a minute, St. Pierre was leveled. Thirty thousand people burned to death instantly. There were just three survivors: a shoemaker who lived at the edge of town, a girl who escaped on a boat, and Ludger Sylbaris.

Trapped in his cell, Sylbaris couldn't fully escape the intense heat as the ash came flying in through the tiny slot in the door. Suffering from burns and desperate to cool down, Sylbaris urinated on his clothes and stuffed them into the slot. Four days later, rescuers freed him from his prison.

Having survived the worst volcanic disaster of the 20th century, Sylbaris became a celebrity, even touring the world with Barnum & Bailey's circus. Posters billed him as "the only living object that survived in the 'Silent City of Death.'" St. Pierre, once the cultural capital of Martinique, is now a modest town, home to less than 5,000 people.

The stone prison cell that saved a man from the deadliest volcanic eruption of the 20th century.

Rue Bouille, St. Pierre. The closest international airport to St. Pierre is at Le Lamentin, a 45-minute drive away. ⓝ 14.742798 ⓦ 61.174719 ➺

➺ Other Sole Survivors

JULIANE KOEPCKE
It was noon on Christmas Eve of 1971, and Juliane Koepcke had just attended her high school graduation ceremony in Lima, Peru. Accompanied by her mother, a German ornithologist, Koepcke boarded LANSA Flight 508, bound for Pucallpa, a city in eastern Peru.

The standard flight time was 50 to 60 minutes. Forty minutes into the journey, a bolt of lightning struck the plane. The fuel tank on the right wing ignited, causing the plane to burst apart.

Juliane Koepcke woke up under her seat on the floor of the Amazon rain forest approximately 20 hours later. Concussed, suffering from a broken right collarbone, and squinting through blood-red eyes due to ruptured capillaries, Koepcke spent half a day fading in and out of consciousness until she managed to stagger to her feet. Her first concern was finding her mother. Despite a full day of searching, she never found her. But Koepcke did encounter some of the 92 passengers who died in the crash.

Though Koepcke could hear rescue planes in the sky, she had no way of signaling to them through the dense foliage. Realizing she would have to rely only on herself to survive, she found a stream and followed it. After nine days of floating and wading, she finally found a motor boat moored on the water and a path leading to an empty shack.

Koepcke was lying in the shack, too exhausted to move, when she heard voices. A trio of locals appeared, utterly shocked to see her after hearing of the crash on the radio. They gave Koepcke food, tended to her wounds, and took her to the hospital at the nearest small town.

It was several more days before rescuers located the wreckage and confirmed Koepcke was the only survivor.

RANDAL McCLOY

Early in the morning on January 2, 2006, the first day back at work after the New Year's break, 26-year-old Randal McCloy began his shift at the Sago coal mine in West Virginia.

At 6:30 a.m., 2 miles (3 km) inside the mine, a huge explosion rumbled the earth. A sealed passage, blocked due to its high methane levels, had blown open, sending clouds of toxic methane and carbon monoxide rushing through the mine tunnels.

McCloy and his 12 coworkers attempted to drive to the surface, but fallen debris from the explosion made the journey impossible. Each miner carried an emergency "self-contained, self-rescuer" pack, which provided an hour of breathable air, but 4 out of the 13 packs weren't working. Out of options, the men hunkered down in a tunnel section, creating a makeshift tent by nailing plastic sheeting to the ceiling and weighing it down with coal.

The miners took turns ramming an 8-pound (3.6 kg) sledgehammer into a wall bolt to signal their location to rescuers. They listened for blasts above ground—signals that would indicate they had been found. None came. It would be 12 hours before surface crews could even begin the rescue mission, due to the high levels of carbon monoxide and methane.

Four and a half hours after the explosion, the miners were weak and disoriented from carbon monoxide poisoning. They recited prayers together and borrowed one another's pens to scrawl notes to their families. Junior Toler, a 51-year-old section foreman who had spent 32 years in coal mines, wrote, "Tell all I see them on the other side. I love you. It wasn't bad. I just went to sleep."

One by one, the men lost consciousness and collapsed. Forty-one hours after the explosion, a rescue crew finally reached the tunnel, where they found McCloy barely alive beneath the body of a coworker. One of the rescuers relayed the news of the other miners' deaths to the surface via walkie-talkies, but the distance garbled the signal, resulting in an awful miscommunication: The media and miners' families, gathered at a nearby church, were told that all of the trapped miners had survived. Three hours of singing and rejoicing followed before they finally learned the horrific truth.

McCloy spent weeks in a medically induced coma while receiving hyperbaric oxygen therapy. With damage to his brain, heart, kidneys, and liver, as well as a collapsed lung, the prognosis was poor. But following months of inpatient rehabilitation, McCloy was walking, speaking, and able to return home.

VESNA VULOVIĆ

Vesna Vulović has no memory of what occurred on January 26, 1972. That afternoon, the 22-year-old Serbian flight attendant boarded JAT Yugoslav Airways Flight 367 in Stockholm, bound for Belgrade with a stopover in Copenhagen. She wasn't scheduled to work—she had been mixed up with a different Vesna— but took the opportunity to visit Denmark and add some miles to her tally.

The Stockholm-to-Copenhagen leg of the journey was unremarkable. Then came the two-hour flight to Belgrade. About 40 minutes after takeoff, the plane exploded. Twenty-seven people died. One survived: Vesna Vulović.

Vulović fell 33,330 feet (10,159 m), earning her a place in the Guinness Book of Records for surviving the highest fall without a parachute. The wrecked fuselage landed in Srbská Kamenice, in what is now the Czech Republic. A former World War II medic found Vulović pinned under a food cart in the middle section of the plane. She had sustained a fractured skull, three broken vertebrae, and two broken legs, and was temporarily paralyzed from the waist down.

Three days later, Vulović awoke from a coma. With no recollection of the flight or the crash, she was astonished to read the details in the newspaper. It would be 10 months before she could walk again.

The official cause of the explosion on Flight 367 was a suitcase bomb in the front luggage compartment, planted by the Croatian terrorist group Ustaša. In 2009, however, a Czech journalist and two German journalists challenged this explanation based on newly acquired documents. Their assertion—that Czechoslovakia's air force shot down the plane at low altitude after mistaking it for an enemy aircraft—has been refuted by Vulović herself.

The city of Plymouth was buried in ash when Montserrat's volcano erupted.

MONTSERRAT
ABANDONED PLYMOUTH

PLYMOUTH

On February 11, 2010, vacationers flying from Toronto to St. Lucia on a Boeing 737 heard the pilot make an unexpected announcement: "Ladies and gentlemen, if you look to the left of the plane, you'll see a volcano erupting."

The volcano that was indeed hurling a plume of ash into the sky was the Soufrière Hills volcano on the Caribbean island of Montserrat. It was a fantastic sight, but not an uncommon one. Soufrière Hills began to erupt in 1995—for the first time since the 17th century—sending lava flows and ash falls over the 10-mile-long (16 km) island. The affected areas were evacuated and no one was killed. However, just two years later, the volcano went off again, this time killing 19 people. Continuing eruptions destroyed the capital city of Plymouth and covered the entire southern half of the island in a thick layer of ash.

The south side of the island was declared uninhabitable and remains an exclusion zone. Over half of Montserrat's 12,000 residents never returned after being evacuated. Those who stayed live on the north side of the island and have grown accustomed to the ongoing eruptions at Soufrière Hills. The island's economy is even benefiting from volcano-focused tourism, such as helicopter flights over devastated Plymouth and boat rides offering views of the smoking mound.

Montserrat is a 15-minute plane ride or 2-hour ferry ride from Antigua. The southern part of the island is off-limits, but you can see the volcano by boat. Ⓝ 16.707232 Ⓦ 62.215755

....

PUERTO RICO
MONKEY ISLAND

CAYO SANTIAGO

Half a mile off the eastern coast of Puerto Rico is Cayo Santiago, an island teeming with free-ranging Rhesus monkeys. Researchers from Harvard, Yale, and the University of Puerto Rico's Caribbean Primate Research Center visit the island to study the monkeys' behavior, development, communication, and physiology.

The simian population numbers around 800. All monkeys on the island are descendants of the 409 monkeys imported from India in 1938 to establish the facility. Cayo Santiago has no human inhabitants. Visitors are not permitted, and with good reason: Rhesus monkeys may carry Herpes B, a virus that can be fatal to humans.

Kayak trips to Monkey Island leave from Punta Santiago. You'll be required to stay 30 feet (9 m) from the island, which is still close enough to spot some monkeys running wild. Ⓝ 18.156404 Ⓦ 65.733832

THE TANKS OF FLAMENCO BEACH

CULEBRA

With its soft white sand, turquoise-tinted water, and proximate empanadas, Flamenco Beach is considered one of the best beaches in the world. But there is one incongruous sight in this paradise: a pair of rusting battle tanks, left on the sand as a souvenir from the US Navy.

In 1901, following Spain's ceding of Puerto Rico to the US, President Theodore Roosevelt allocated all of Culebra's public land to the Navy. Soon, troops were conducting test landings and ground maneuvers on the island. In 1939, the Navy began using Culebra for bombing practice. Bombardment reached its peak during 1969, when pilots trained for the war in Vietnam. Missiles hit the island on 228 days of that year.

By 1970, the 700 residents of Culebra were well and truly fed up with the Navy using their home as a bombing ground. Unexploded ordnance littered the island, and the ground bore craters and pockmarks from the shelling. A naval attempt to evict the entire population of Culebra was the last straw. In the summer of 1970, residents began a series of nonviolent protests, aiming to rid the island of naval occupation.

Locals continue to add new art to these abandoned tanks.

After seven months of marches, sit-ins, and human blockades of naval sites, the Culebra activists succeeded. In January 1971, the Navy agreed to stop using the island as a test location by 1975.

Though it's been decades since the Navy left, the tanks on the beach, painted over and over by locals, remain.

Tanks are back in the brush and on the shoreline on the far west side of the beach. Ⓝ 18.316951 Ⓦ 65.290032

ARECIBO OBSERVATORY

ARECIBO

Few telescopes are as awe-inspiring as the one at Arecibo Observatory. At 1,000 feet (304 m) across and 167 feet (51 m) deep, the Arecibo dish is the largest and most sensitive radio telescope in the world. Built into a natural limestone sinkhole, it is made of nearly 40,000 perforated aluminum panels.

Cornell University professor William E. Gordon opened the observatory in 1963, aiming to study the scattering of radio waves off molecules in the Earth's upper atmosphere. Since then, significant astronomical discoveries have been made at Arecibo, including the detection of the first planets outside our solar system. The telescope has also been at the center of several projects in the search for extraterrestrial intelligence.

In 1974, astronomers Frank Drake and Carl Sagan wrote the Arecibo message, a binary string that was beamed from the telescope toward the star cluster M13 some 25,000 light-years away. If the message is eventually decoded by an intelligent race, the extraterrestrial recipients will be greeted with a 23-by-73-pixel bitmap image depicting a human being, chemical formulas, the solar system, and even the telescope itself.

PR-625, Arecibo. While you can't walk on the telescope, you can look at it from a viewing platform and see space-related exhibits at the visitor center. Ⓝ 18.346318 Ⓦ 66.752819

Arecibo's 1,000-foot-wide dish scans the skies for signs of extraterrestrial life.

The museum is named for (and shaped like) its subject.

CEMI MUSEUM

JAYUYA

To the indigenous Taíno people of the Caribbean, the *cemi* is an ancestral spirit as well as a small, usually three-pointed object that holds that spirit. Fashioned from stone and other materials, cemis have a central point representing a mountain peak on which sits Yaya, the Creator. The mouth-like point represents Coabey, the land of the dead. Finally, the third point represents the land of the living.

The Cemi Museum building takes the shape of one of these sacred symbols, and when viewing the structure against the backdrop of the surrounding mountains, it is easy to see how this symbol evolved as a stylized mirror of the topography.

Inside the small museum there is a display of Taíno cemis and artifacts, including a carved, pointed wooden tongue depressor used in ritual vomiting ceremonies. There is also a mural showing a series of petroglyphs that are also believed to have been created by the Taíno.

The museum is a 10-minute drive southeast of Jayuya. To see the Taíno petroglyphs in situ, go to La Piedra Escrita, a boulder in the Rio Saliente that is accesible from the shore. Ⓝ 18.209674 Ⓦ 66.561614

ST. KITTS AND NEVIS

COTTLE CHURCH

CHARLESTOWN, NEVIS

In 1824, Cottle Church became the first racially integrated place of worship in the Caribbean. John Cottle, a plantation owner and the former president of Nevis, established the church so that his family and slaves could worship together. At the time, black people were banned from attending Anglican services.

For his defiance of the law, Cottle is generally regarded as a kind and lenient figure. His lenience, however, did not extend to his construction methods: Black slaves built the church.

The Cottle Church ruins are hidden in the woods north of Charlestown. Look for the small sign on the main road just south of the Newcastle Airport and follow the dirt track. Ⓝ 17.196473 Ⓦ 62.596157

A house of worship for both slaves and their owners, Cottle Church was completed in 1824.

TRINIDAD AND TOBAGO
MYSTERY TOMBSTONE

PLYMOUTH, TOBAGO

The grave of Betty Stiven, who died in childbirth in 1783, aged 23, presents a riddle on its tombstone. "What was remarkable of her," the inscription reads, "she was a mother without knowing it and a wife without letting her husband know it, except by her kind indulgences to him."

Some local theories on this mystery point to a passionate and taboo interracial romance that would have required secrecy and the denial of matrimony. But what of the child who somehow came into the world without Stiven realizing? There's a theory for that, too—and it actually makes sense.

According to this version of events, Betty met Alex Stiven and they fell in love. He wouldn't marry her, so she got him drunk, then had a priest perform a sneaky marriage. This takes care of the "wife without letting her husband know" part.

As for the "mother without knowing it" detail, Betty allegedly got pregnant and then, before realizing she was with child, came down with meningitis. She spent the rest of her life in a coma, but not before delivering the baby, who died in the process

Within thefe Walls are Depofited the Bodies of M.RS BETTY STIVEN and her Child She was the beloved *Wife of ALEX.B STIVEN* to the end of his days will deplore her Death which happened upon the 25.th day of Nov. 1783 in the 23.rd Year of her Age what was remarkable of her *She was a Mother without knowing it and a Wife without letting her Hufband know it except by her kind indulgences to him*

Betty Stiven's epitaph contains a puzzle.

and was buried beside her. (It is medically possible to give birth while comatose, so that part of the story, at least, could check out.)

The tombstone is enclosed by an orange fence and is well marked. Flights from Port of Spain in Trinidad arrive at A.N.R. Robinson International Airport near Canaan. From there, take the Claude Noel Highway toward Plymouth. Ⓝ 11.221079 Ⓦ 60.778723

PITCH LAKE

LA BREA, TRINIDAD

With the fragrance of a freshly paved road and a viscosity that varies with every step, Pitch Lake is not your average watering hole. The 250-foot-deep (76 m) asphalt lake is the size of around 75 football fields, making it the largest of the world's three naturally occurring pitch lakes—the others are located in Los Angeles and Venezuela.

In some spots, the surface of Pitch Lake is solid enough to walk on. In others, it is more like quicksand. To make matters more confusing, water collects in patches in the basin, resulting in a mix that is sometimes as thin as regular lake water, and other times as hard as rock.

English writer and explorer Sir Walter Raleigh encountered the lake in 1595 and used its pitch

The world's largest asphalt lake is thick enough to walk on.

to caulk his ship. More formalized mining began in 1867 and continues to this day. Asphalt from Pitch Lake has been used to pave roads in over 50 countries, including the runways at New York's JFK airport and the streets of Westminster Bridge in London.

Southern Main Road, La Brea. Pitch Lake is about a 90-minute drive from Trinidad's capital, Port of Spain. Ⓝ 10.232618 Ⓦ 61.628047

ST. VINCENT AND THE GRENADINES
MOONHOLE

BEQUIA, GRENADINES

Named for the stone arch through which you can see the moon set twice a year, Moonhole is a community of 19 homes made from stones and scavenged materials. The beachfront houses, built on the small island of Bequia during the 1960s, are open to the elements: There are no doors to lock and many of the walls have windowless archways.

Some of the homes are now available to rent and come complete with solar-powered refrigerators, hot water, and bars made from whale ribs.

Bequia is a 25-minute ferry ride from Kingstown, the capital of St. Vincent. Moonhole is a 20-minute taxi ride. Ⓝ 12.992146 Ⓦ 61.276701

Moonhole's residents live beneath a stone arch in homes made from salvaged materials.

Antarctica

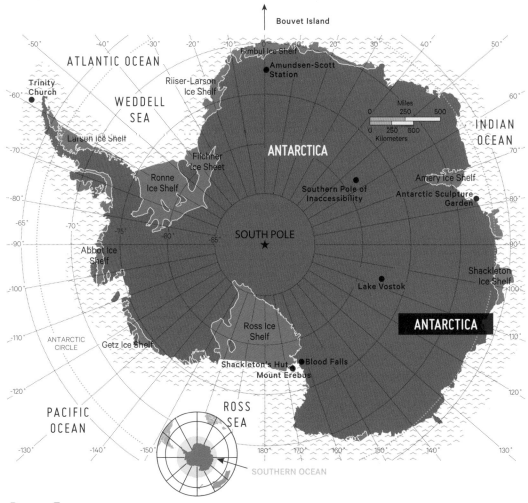

Blood Falls

MCMURDO DRY VALLEYS, VICTORIA LAND

Taylor Glacier is hemorrhaging blood—at least that's what it looks like. On the east end of the frozen mass, a five-story stream of rust-colored water flows into Lake Bonney, staining the ice.

This crimson water has been trapped beneath a glacier for 2 million years. Ocean water flooded East Antarctica 5 million years ago, creating a salty lake on the iron-rich bedrock. Taylor Glacier formed atop the lake, sealing it off from sunlight and oxygen and gradually burying it beneath 1,300 feet (396 m) of ice. Despite the absence of oxygen, the hidden reservoir of groundwater is rich with microbial life. At least 17 different microorganisms have been identified in Blood Falls's high-salt, high-iron water, which is now rising through fissures in the glacier. When it meets the air, the water oxidizes, resulting in the bloodlike hue.

Beyond its striking appearance, Blood Falls is interesting to scientists because the glacier's surviving microbes hint at the ecosystems that might be found on Mars and in other harsh, low-oxygen habitats.

The Dry Valleys are accessible only by helicopter from McMurdo Station, Scott Base, or via a cruise ship in the Ross Sea. Cruises depart from New Zealand.
Ⓢ 77.716686 Ⓔ 162.266765

Red water, trapped for 2 million years beneath a glacier.

✵ Antarctica: A note on how to get there

Though seven nations have claimed land in Antarctica, no country owns it. The continent operates according to the Antarctic Treaty of 1959, which defines the continent as a scientific preserve, regulates the research activities of each nation, and prohibits new territorial sovereignty claims.

Travel to Antarctica requires an abundance of two things: time and money. Many visitors arrive on a cruise ship from the Argentinian port of Ushuaia, located on the southern tip of South America. A few tourist ships also launch from Australia, New Zealand, Chile, and Uruguay. Trips take place during the austral summer (from November to March), and cost several thousand dollars depending on length and itinerary.

Commercial flights to the continent—most of which depart from Australia—do not land, but offer sightseeing from above. To fly into Antarctica, you generally need to nab a space on one of the military flights that shuttle in staff and supplies to the research stations. Supply flights also take place between November and March.

Regardless of how you get there, make sure you are healthy when venturing to Antarctica. There are no hospitals, and medical evacuation, when possible, is arduous and expensive.

In 1958, Soviet explorers staked their claim on the South Pole with a Lenin bust.

SOUTHERN POLE OF INACCESSIBILITY

The Southern Pole of Inaccessibility—as distinguished from the geographic South Pole, 550 miles (885 km) away—is the point in Antarctica farthest from the ocean. This inhospitable spot, on which few humans have trod, has an average yearly temperature of –72.8°F (–58.2°C). It is marked by a bust of Vladimir Lenin.

In 1958, a team of 18 determined Soviet explorers reached the Southern Pole of Inaccessibility for the first time. The team journeyed there from Mirny, a Soviet station established on the coast of the Davis Sea two years earlier. Aboard their tractors were components for the prefabricated wooden huts that would form a new four-person research station.

When they arrived, the team assembled the huts, raised the Soviet flag, and added one final touch to the top of the chimney on one of the buildings: a Lenin bust, positioned to face Moscow. The base station was used only for a few weeks to monitor weather before being abandoned to the elements. The communist revolutionary's sculpted head is often half-submerged in snow.

The exact point of the Southern Pole of Inaccessibility is the subject of debate—the movement and melting of ice sheets alter the coastline, affecting measurements. The bust is located at ⓢ 82.099907 ⓔ 54.967117

LAKE VOSTOK

VOSTOK STATION, PRINCESS ELIZABETH LAND

Buried in ice 2 miles (3.2 km) beneath Russia's Vostok research station lies a lake that's been sealed away from the world for an estimated 15 million years.

Measuring 160 miles long by 30 miles wide (258 km × 48 km), Lake Vostok is the largest of Antarctica's subglacial "ghost lakes." Its existence was confirmed in 1993, via radar altimeter data from a remote-sensing satellite.

The air temperature at Lake Vostok has plummeted as low as –128°F (–88.8°C), the lowest temperature ever recorded on Earth. The underground lake's average water temperature is comparatively balmy at 27°F (–2.7°C). Though that's below the usual freezing point, the lake stays in a liquid state due to the pressure exerted by the ice above, which also provides insulation. Geothermal heat from beneath the lake may also play a role.

The search for signs of life in the lake began during the late 1990s, when scientists began drilling into the ice core to retrieve samples for analysis. As their probes approached the water, concerns arose that the drilling fluids used, Freon and kerosene, might contaminate any samples they collected. With

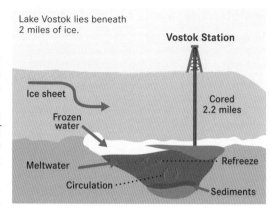

Lake Vostok lies beneath 2 miles of ice.

over 300 feet to go before they reached the lake, the team chose to stop drilling.

In 2012, using silicone oil as a drilling fluid, Russian scientists reached the surface of the lake. Analysis of the samples showed DNA from over 3,500 organisms. That so much life could exist in such an inhospitable environment gives hope to scientists that life may someday be found outside planet Earth.

Vostok Station, home of the big drill, is at the southern Pole of Cold, around 800 miles (1,287 km) southeast of the South Pole. Ⓢ 77.499996 Ⓔ 106.000028

ANTARCTIC SCULPTURE GARDEN

DAVIS STATION, PRINCESS ELIZABETH LAND

His proper name is *Man Sculpted by Antarctica*, but he's better known as "Fred the Head." He stands outside the meteorology building of Australia's Davis Station, and resembles Easter Island moai. Fred is the creation of a plumber named Hans, who carved the sculpture out of an old wooden pole during his winter stay in 1977.

Exposed to the winds and snow for decades, Fred has acquired a weathered complexion and become a totem for those enduring the long, dark Antarctic winters. In 2003, Davis artist-in-residence Stephen Eastaugh was so inspired by Fred that he created a sculpture garden using the wooden head as a centerpiece. Visitors are invited to add their own creations to Eastaugh's wood and metal sculptures, but they must first get permission from Davis's station leader and environmental adviser.

Flights to Davis via Casey, another Australian Antarctic station, leave from Hobart, Tasmania. Ⓢ 68.576206 Ⓔ 77.969449

There may not be any plants in this garden, but creativity flourishes.

SHRINES OF THE AMUNDSEN–SCOTT STATION ICE TUNNELS

SOUTH POLE

The web of ice tunnels beneath Amundsen-Scott Station serve as conduits for the research base's power lines, supply pipes, and sewage removal. But the tunnels aren't just utilitarian. Recesses carved into the frozen walls contain shrines to completed projects, departed scientists, and Antarctic in-jokes that defy explanation.

The tunnels were constructed over three summers as part of a station that replaced the original Amundsen-Scott base established in 1956. Completed by excavator, chainsaw, and pickax in 2002, the halls are a constant –60°F (–51.1°C) and measure 10 feet high by 6 feet (3 m × 1.8 m) wide. Or, at least they used to—much like a household

FIRST ELEVATED STATION CREW · WINTER 2003 ·

South Pole Station's winter 2003 crew left behind a pig's head shrine.

freezer, ice has been building up on the walls, reducing the size of the tunnels by several inches.

The extreme cold keeps each shrine beautifully preserved. Flowers, strings of popcorn, prayer candles, tinned caviar, and a hard hat are among the eclectic items on display.

Then there is the sturgeon, set in an alcove beside a document detailing its backstory. Back in the 1990s, Russian researchers staying in Antarctica gifted the fish to American scientists at McMurdo Station, located 850 miles (1,368 km) from the South Pole. The sturgeon sat unappreciated in a freezer for months, and was on its way to being thrown out when a researcher headed from McMurdo to Amundsen-Scott Station decided to bring it along as a gift.

The frozen fish, enshrined in the tunnels, is now the research base's only permanent resident. **Once you've checked out the tunnels, make sure to pose for a photo beside the ceremonial South Pole, marked by a red-and-white post surrounded by the flags of nations that have signed the Antarctic Treaty. ❺ 72.294154 ❻ 0.696294**

BOUVET ISLAND

BOUVET ISLAND

Located between Antarctica and South Africa, 1,404 miles (2,260 km) from the nearest human settlement, Bouvet is, by definition, the most remote island on Earth. Should you reach its shores, you will find it unwelcoming in the extreme. An ice-covered volcano lies at its core, and storms rage around the island for over 300 days per year.

Discovered in 1739, the island is so isolated that it was accidentally "lost" for nearly 70 years. No one actually set foot on Bouvet until 1927, when a group of Norwegians scrambled up its glacial cliffs. In 1964, an abandoned lifeboat with no national markings was discovered on the island. From the supplies spread about, it was clear someone had been there, yet ships did not normally come within 1,000 miles (1,609 km) of Bouvet, and the lifeboat was equipped only with oars and no mast. Despite a search, no bodies or tracks were found. As of today, fewer than a hundred people have ever set foot on the island—not counting whoever was in that lifeboat. **Assuming no budgetary restrictions, the best way to get on the island is to fly a helicopter from the deck of a ship and land delicately on Bouvet's icy surface. Bouvet is a dependent territory of Norway, so Norwegian laws apply. ❺ 54.432711 ❻ 3.407822**

ALSO IN ANTARCTICA

Wilson's Stone Igloo

Cape Crozier · See the remains of a shelter built during what Scott expedition survivor Apsley Cherry-Garrard described as "the worst journey in the world."

Discovery Hut

Hut Point · Built by the British in 1902, this wooden hut was used to store tinned meats, flour, and coffee for expeditions.

McMurdo Dry Valleys

McMurdo Sound · The snow-free peaks and troughs of this region comprise one of the world's most extreme deserts.

Chapel of the Snows

McMurdo · This is the third incarnation of the world's second-southernmost place of worship—the previous two burned down.

IceCube Research Station

South Pole · This particle detector uses a telescope buried a mile under the ice to look for neutrinos.

Buckminster Fuller's Dymaxion Map

All maps are, in one way or another, a lie. The problem isn't with the cartographer but with geography. When we flatten our globe to make a two-dimensional map, pulling and stretching it like taffy to make a rectangle, we distort the world and suddenly Greenland looks like it's the size of Africa. Greenland is not the size of Africa.

Inventor, architect, and designer Buckminster Fuller was aware of this map problem. "All flat surface maps are compromises with truth," he said. His solution, which premiered in *Life* magazine in 1943, was both beautiful and simple. Fuller turned the earth into an icosahedron, a three-dimensional shape made up of twenty equilateral triangles. These smaller triangular surfaces minimized the distortion problem. While it makes for a strange and jagged map, it creates a much truer picture of the world.

Unfolding the world this way did more than just fix the size of Greenland. It also created a new way to visualize the arrangement of Earth on a map. In this particular layout of Buckminster Fuller's map, the continents appear as one great land mass stretching from Australia to Antarctica.

It's for that reason that we chose the Dymaxion map for our world trip map. The exact trip you see may not be practical, or even entirely possible, but this map is a beautiful way to visualize an epic journey.

One great loop around the island of Earth.

We'll start in a cold place, the Davis Station Sculpture Garden in Antarctica, move through to the warmer climes of Australia, and then circle back again. It's everything you need to take the most incredible Atlas Obscura trip around the world possible . . . plane, boat, car, train, bicycle, horse, and camel not included.

R. Buckminster Fuller holding his folded Dymaxion map. Photographed by Andreas Feininger for Life *magazine, 1943.*

Atlas Obscura's Trip Around the World

Buckminster Fuller's Dymaxion map represents his belief in equality. When folded, it becomes a round Earth with one continuous landmass, its face made up of 20 triangles all equal in size, with no definitive center and no north/south or east/west.

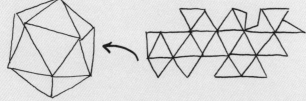

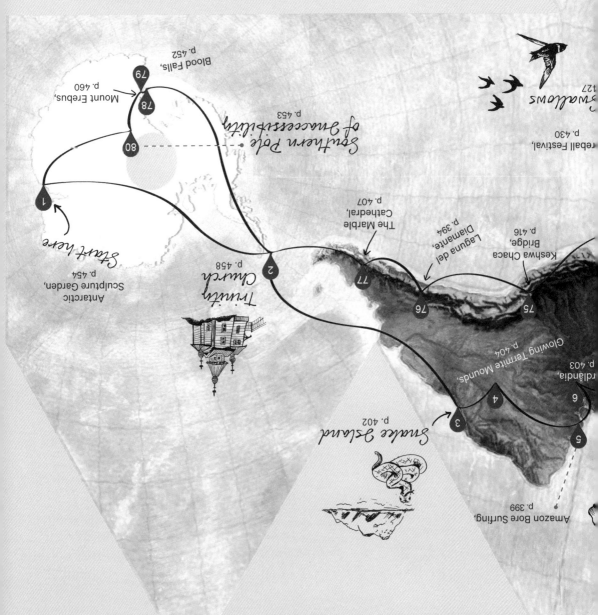

Blood Falls, p. 452

Mount Erebus, p. 460

79

78

80

Southern Pole of Inaccessibility p. 453

1

Start here

Antarctic Sculpture Garden, p. 454

Trinity Church p. 458

2

The Marble Cathedral, p. 407

Laguna del Diamante, p. 394

Keshwa Chaca Bridge, p. 416

77

76

75

Swallows p. 427

...reball Festival, p. 430

Glowing Termite Mounds, p. 404

...rdlândia, p. 403

3

4

6

5

Snake Island p. 402

Amazon Bore Surfing, p. 399

Annual Festivals Around the World

JANUARY

Harbin International Ice and Snow Sculpture Festival
Harbin, China
For the world's competitive ice and snow sculptors, there is no bigger stage or more serious contest. The scale of these frozen structures is staggering: The festival grounds are split into an exhibition area for massive snow sculptures and an entire city constructed of ice blocks.
JANUARY 5

The Burning of the Clavie
Burghead, Scotland
In a ritual dating back to Roman times, villagers parade a "clavie"—a blazing wooden cask mounted on a pole—to the ruins of an ancient altar where it is built up into a great bonfire.
JANUARY 11
(New Year's Eve by the Julian Calendar)

FEBRUARY

Busójárás Monster Parade
Mohács, Hungary
Goat-horned monsters and mysterious women in lace masks parade through town, jangling bells and twirling noisemakers during this Carnival celebration.
SHROVE TUESDAY

Sa Sartiglia Festival
Oristano, Italy
Equestrian performers and competitors don blank-faced porcelain-doll masks and race elaborately decked-out horses through the streets. The riders attempt to spear star-shaped rings hung in front of the local chapel, which sometimes requires standing on top of their galloping horses.
LAST SUNDAY AND TUESDAY BEFORE LENT

Da Shuhua Molten Iron Throwing
Nuanquan, China
This annual tradition was dreamed up approximately 500 years ago by blacksmiths who wanted to participate in the annual Lunar New Year festivities but couldn't afford

Festival of the Exploding Hammers
San Juan de la Vega, Mexico
Commemorating Juan de la Vega's triumph, aided by San Juan Bautista, over local outlaws, the braver locals strap homemade firecrackers to the end of sledgehammers and slam them onto a sheet of metal, detonating the package to the delight of the crowd.
SHROVE TUESDAY
(Feast of San Juan Bautista)

the luxury of traditional fireworks. Instead, the blacksmiths tossed cupfuls of molten iron against the city gate. The result was a spectacular shower of pyrotechnic beauty.

LUNAR NEW YEAR

MARCH

Frozen Dead Guy Days

Nederland, Colorado, USA
A rollicking festival honoring the town's one and only cryogenically frozen resident, Bredo Morstoel. Popular events include Ice Turkey Bowling, the Parade of Hearses, Tuff Shed Coffin Races, and the Salmon Toss.

SECOND WEEKEND IN MARCH

APRIL

The Chios Rocket War

Vrontados, Greece
Two churches shoot tens of thousands of small homemade rockets at one another. The goal, as much as there is one, is to hit the opposing church's bell tower.

ORTHODOX EASTER DAY

MAY

Festival of the Snake Catchers

Cocullo, Italy
The Snake Catchers procession, held in this small village in central Italy, honors St. Dominic, who cleared the area of snakes, and the pagan snake goddess, Agnizia. A statue of St. Dominic,

completely covered in snakes, is paraded away from the church, along with musicians and a coterie of snake catchers.

MAY 1

Rock-Throwing Battle

Santiago de Macha, Bolivia
Tinku, a Bolivian Aymara and Quechua tradition of ritualistic combat, represents the fight of indigenous peoples against colonial oppression. Tinku events take place all over the country in May, but the Macha festival is the most notoriously bloody. The festival begins with men and women dancing together, only for the women to back away from the men as things escalate into an all-out brawl.

EARLY MAY

JUNE

Kirkpinar Oil Wrestling Festival

Avarız Köyü, near Edirne, Turkey
In the world's oldest regular sporting event (besides the Olympics, that is), brawny wrestlers—naked but for their prized leather trousers—are doused in olive oil to grapple until one wrestler pins the other or lifts him above his head. The original wrestlers were said to have fought to the death. These days, competitors fight for the $100,000 cash prize.

LATE JUNE

JULY

L'Ardia di San Costantino Festival

Sedilo, Italy
One part horse race, one part religious pilgrimage, this yearly race is run by brave horsemen atop their faithful steeds, reenacting the victory at Rome of the emperor Constantine over his rival Maxentius in the year 312.

JULY 6–7

The Festival of Paucartambo

Paucartambo, Peru
Every year, *campesinos* from the Sacred Valley trek to a remote town to dance in the festival of the Virgen del Carmen. Each regional group performs in full regalia to reenact their village's origin story. They represent everything from wealthy Spanish-blooded landowners to tempting devils in Chinese dragon–style headdresses.

THIRD WEEK IN JULY

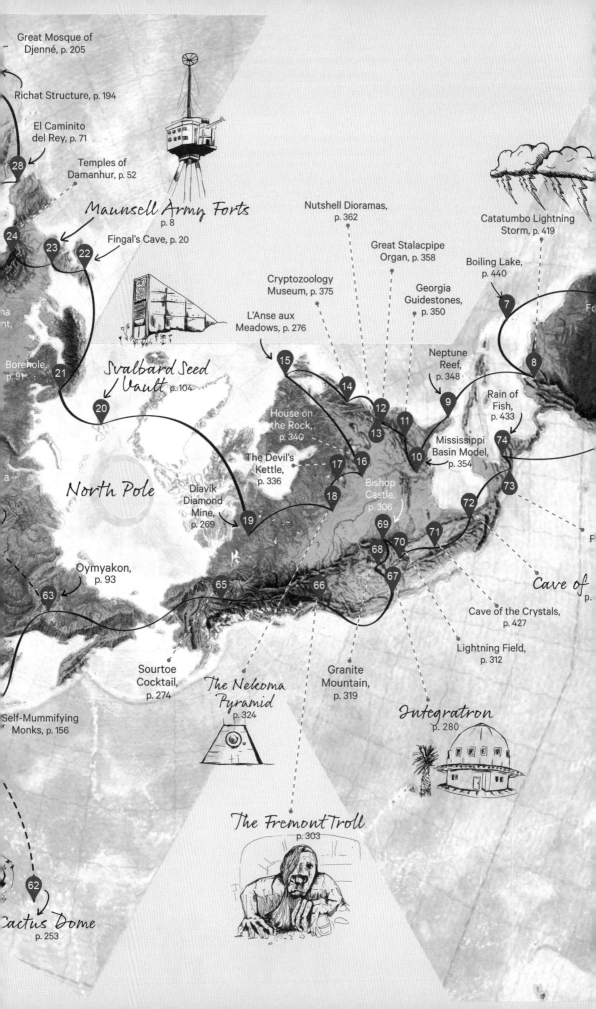

Great Mosque of
Djenné, p. 205

Richat Structure, p. 194

El Caminito
del Rey, p. 71

28

Temples of
Damanhur, p. 52

24

23

22

Maunsell Army Forts
p. 8

Fingal's Cave, p. 20

Nutshell Dioramas,
p. 362

Catatumbo Lightning
Storm, p. 419

Great Stalacpipe
Organ, p. 358

Boiling Lake,
p. 440

Cryptozoology
Museum, p. 375

Georgia
Guidestones,
p. 350

7

L'Anse aux
Meadows, p. 276

Borehole,
p. 91

21

*Svalbard Seed
Vault* p. 104

20

15

14

12

13

11

Neptune
Reef,
p. 348

8

9

Rain of
Fish,
p. 433

74

House on
the Rock,
p. 340

The Devil's
Kettle,
p. 336

17

16

10

Mississippi
Basin Model,
p. 354

73

North Pole

Diavik
Diamond
Mine,
p. 269

19

18

Bishop
Castle,
p. 306

69

72

71

68

70

Oymyakon,
p. 93

63

65

66

67

Cave of
p.

Cave of the Crystals,
p. 427

Sourtoe
Cocktail,
p. 274

*The Nekoma
Pyramid*
p. 324

Granite
Mountain,
p. 319

Lightning Field,
p. 312

Integratron
p. 280

Self-Mummifying
Monks, p. 156

The Fremont Troll
p. 303

62

Cactus Dome
p. 253

33 Deadvlei, p. 221

Kolmanskop —
Ghost Town, p. 220

34

31

30

29

32 Oklo Reactor,
p. 202

Kane Kwei,
p. 203

Avenue of the
Baobabs
p. 226

Capuchin
Catacombs, p. 60

35

27

Abuna
Yemata Guh,
p. 212

Valley
of Whales,
p. 190

Easter Rocket
War, p. 49

26

25

37 **38** **39**

40

Buzludzha
Monume
p. 76

Socotra
Island
p. 122

36

Précontinent II,
p. 199

Baalbek
Trilithon,
p. 118

Kola

41

Door to Hell,
p. 139

Nek Chand's
Garden, p. 127

Kyaiktiyo Pagoda
p. 175

Chand Baori
Stepwell, p. 130

43 **42**
44

Skeleton Lake,
p. 127

45

Tungus
Event
p. 90

Root Bridges of
Cherrapunji, p. 132

46

Dochula Pass
Caves, p. 126

64

47

Hengshan
Hanging Temple,
p. 142

Synchronized
Fireflies
p. 172

48

Guoliang
Tunnel,
p. 144

56 **57**

58

49

Third Tunnel
of Aggression,
p. 162

61

50 Skylab Remains,
p. 238

Marree Man
p. 240

Tana Toraja
Funeral Rights,
p. 166

59

60

Battleship Island,
p. 160

55

G-Cans, p. 154

51

Jellyfish Lake
p. 257

Waitomo
Glowworm
Caves,
p. 249

54

Ball's
Pyramid
p. 245

52

Electrum, p. 246

53

AUGUST

Dragon-Slaying Festival

Furth im Wald, Germany
The *Drachenstich*—one of the oldest folk plays in Germany—has been performed in this medieval "City of Dragons" since 1590. The festivities include 1,000 locals dressed in historical costume, at least 250 horses, a hero knight, and his wife who needs to be rescued from a 50-foot-long (15 m) fire-breathing dragon-robot.

SECOND WEEK IN AUGUST

Roggenburg Leiberfest

Roggenburg, Germany
On Assumption Day, this Bavarian village brings out their dead. Led by a large brass brand, the exquisitely adorned and bejeweled mummified bodies of four local saints are disinterred from their place of rest at the abbey and paraded through the village.

AUGUST 15

Drunken Dance Festival

Tokushima, Japan
Some 80,000 participants and 1.3 million spectators descend upon the city of Tokushima for Awa Odori, a three-day dance festival where colorfully dressed dance teams chant, sing, and perform different versions of a signature dance step. As the most famous Awa Odori song puts it, "The dancers are fools / the watchers are fools / both are fools / so why not dance?"

AUGUST 12–15

SEPTEMBER

Exeter UFO Festival

Exeter, New Hampshire, USA
UFO enthusiasts from around the country gather in this small town, the location of a 1965 UFO sighting, to listen to lectures and participate in alien fun for believers and skeptics alike.

LABOR DAY WEEKEND

OCTOBER

El Campello Moors and Christians Festival

El Campello, Spain
To commemorate the 13th-century struggle between the Christian kingdoms to the north of the Iberian Peninsula and the Moorish (Muslim) occupiers in the south for control of the country, the coastal town of El Campello puts on an intricately choreographed reenactment of the arrival of the Moorish fleet.

SECOND WEEK IN OCTOBER

Feast of St. Jude

San Hipólito Church, Mexico City
In honor of St. Jude, the patron saint of lost causes and desperate situations, nearly 100,000 of Mexico's working class, poor, and marginalized come to San Hipólito carrying red and white roses and hauling full-size wooden statues to sing, pray, and find strength.

OCTOBER 28

NOVEMBER

Bonfire Night

Ottery St. Mary, England
Each Guy Fawkes Day, Ottery's residents hoist burning barrels on their shoulders or heads and run through teeming crowds. Only established locals are allowed to carry the flaming barrels. And while the fire department is on hand, other health and safety regulations are encouraged to take the night off.

NOVEMBER 5

DECEMBER

Gävle Goat

Gävle, Sweden
Every year, the good people of Gävle build a huge straw Yule goat—an ancient Nordic Christmas (and probably pagan) celebration of the solstice—and display it in the town square. And every year (starting in 1966), vandals attempt to destroy the goat. It's been torched, stolen, smashed, run over by a car, and once nearly thrown in the river.

DECEMBER 1

Bonfires on the Levee for Papa Noël

St. James Parish, Louisiana, USA
Through the month of December, families of St. James Parish build pyres along the levee, some using fireworks as kindling. Each night the community lights one bonfire. On Christmas Eve, all the remaining pyres are lit, and the town comes out to walk around, taking in the displays.

DECEMBER 24

Harbin Ice Festival in the daytime, and at night, right.

SHACKLETON'S HUT

CAPE ROYDS

The shelves are lined with tins of curried rabbit, stewed kidneys, ox cheeks, and sheep tongues. Long johns hang off washing lines slung from the walls, and boots sit in rows underneath the makeshift beds built from wooden crates. Ernest Shackleton's hut looks just as it did when the explorer abandoned it in 1909.

Shackleton and his team of 14 men assembled the prefabricated timber hut in February 1908, having lugged it from London via New Zealand. The building was to serve as a base during the Nimrod Expedition, Shackleton's quest to be the first to reach the South Pole.

The four-man trip toward the pole had a bittersweet outcome: With their ponies dead and their food supply dwindling, the quartet turned back 112 miles (180 km) from the South Pole—the closest anyone had gotten at the time.

The contents of Shackleton's hut, naturally preserved in the frozen climate, offer a fascinating insight into the Heroic Age of Antarctic Exploration, the era beginning in the late 19th century in which pioneering explorers like Shackleton, Scott, and Amundsen led perilous, often fatal expeditions. Among the items on his packing list, intended to sustain 15 men for up to two years, were 1,600 pounds of the "finest York hams," 1,260 pounds of sardines, 1,470 pounds of tinned bacon, and 25 cases of whisky (that's 726 kg, 572 kg, and 667 kg, respectively).

Century-old curried rabbit and tins of ox cheek remain just as Shackleton left them in 1909.

The discovery of this last item was the cause of much excitement when, in 2010, conservators retrieved a crate of Mackinlay whisky from a stash of booze hidden beneath the hut. Three of the bottles underwent chemical analysis in Scotland, after which Mackinlay used the flavor profile to create a replica whisky. The original bottles were returned to the hut, where they sit in tribute to a long-departed gentleman explorer.

Visitors to the hut must be accompanied by a guide. A maximum of 8 people are allowed inside at one time, and all are required to sign the logbook. ⓢ **77.552922** ⓑ **166.168368**

✎ Self-Surgery in the Antarctic

On April 29, 1961, 27-year-old Russian physician Dr. Leonid Rogozov experienced pain in his side and began to feel very unwell. Rogozov was one of a dozen men stationed at the Soviet Novolazarevskaya research base, and the only physician on staff. As the pain grew more intense, and a violent snowstorm made evacuation by plane impossible, Rogozov confronted a terrifying truth: He would have to perform his own appendectomy.

Lying on his back and using a mirror for guidance, Rogozov spent 2 hours digging around in his anesthetized abdomen as his colleagues looked on. Weakened and suffering from headspins, the determined doctor took 20-second rests every 5 minutes to gather his strength. Rogozov's journal entry on the operation recounts a close call: "At the worst moment of removing the appendix I flagged: My heart seized up and noticeably slowed; my hands felt like rubber. Well, I thought, it's going to end badly."

Despite the physical strain, Rogozov completed the operation and made a full recovery, going on to live for another 29 years. Some of the surgical instruments used during the operation are on display at the Museum of the Arctic and Antarctic in St. Petersburg.

Rogozov is not the only Antarctic patient who has resorted to self-administered surgery. In March 1999, Dr. Jerri Nielsen was stationed at the US Amundsen-Scott station at the South Pole when she found a lump in her breast. With transport off the continent impossible until October, Nielsen performed her own biopsy and sent images to oncologists in the United States for diagnosis.

When it was confirmed that she had breast cancer, Nielsen self-administered hormones and chemotherapy drugs using supplies air-dropped from military planes.

When the air temperature warmed to about –60°F (–51.1°C), Nielsen was flown to the US for treatment. She went into remission following a mastectomy, but the cancer returned and she died from the disease in 2009.

TRINITY CHURCH

BELLINGSHAUSEN STATION, KING GEORGE ISLAND

When it comes to unique weddings, it's hard to beat the union of Chilean Antarctic researcher Eduardo Aliaga Ilabaca and Russian scientist Angelina Zhuldybina. In January 2007, the couple donned their formal wear, walked through the snow, and tied the knot at Trinity Church, the southernmost Orthodox church in the world.

Standing 50 feet (15.2 m) tall and constructed from Siberian pine, Trinity was built in 2002 in Altai, a federal subject of Russia that borders Kazakhstan and Mongolia. From there, the church was transported 2,500 miles (4,023 km) to Kaliningrad (a Russian exclave on the Baltic Sea between Poland and Lithuania), dismantled, and brought to King George Island. A delegation of 20 religious leaders attended the official consecration, which took place in February 2004. Two priests now conduct services at the church, staying for a year before being swapped for new staff.

Trinity Church is within walking distance of Russia's Bellingshausen research station, making it a convenient Sunday morning trip for Russian Orthodox scientists. Weekly services, weddings, and baptisms are all on offer—with the Southern Ocean providing a natural, albeit alarmingly cold, source of water for the baptism ritual.

The church is on a hill near Bellingshausen Station, a Russian research base at Collins Harbor.

Ⓢ 62.196405 Ⓦ 58.972042

With its golden wall of saints, the southernmost Orthodox church in the world is the perfect spot for an adventurous elopement.

Sunlight illuminates the ceiling of an ice cave on the southernmost active volcano on Earth.

MOUNT EREBUS

ROSS ISLAND

When British polar explorer James Clark Ross came across this volcano in 1841, he named it after his ship. But Mount Erebus has since proven itself more like the original Erebus of Greek mythology, son of Chaos and god of darkness.

The mountain that bears Erebus's name is a 12,448-foot (3,974 m) active volcano brimming with boiling lava. It is an odd conflation of fire and ice: Heat and gas from the 1,700°F (926.6°C) lava lake filter up to the slopes, melting the packed snow and carving out ice caves.

Since 1979, an area on Mount Erebus's lower slopes has been regarded as a tomb. That year, an Air New Zealand sightseeing flight crashed into the mountain, killing all 257 passengers on board. The plane had been flying in a whiteout, using coordinates that differed from the approved route. Though an extensive recovery effort took place, wreckage from the crash is still on the mountain. A memorial cross stands nearby, along with a capsule containing messages from relatives of the victims.

Although the volcano is always active (sometimes hunks of molten rock shoot through the air), Mount Erebus is open to climbers in the Antarctic summer. Entry into the crash site area is prohibited unless you have a permit issued by the relevant New Zealand authorities. ⓢ 77.527423 ⓔ 167.156711

ACKNOWLEDGMENTS

In accordance with ancient Bolivian custom (see La Paz Witches' Market, page 395), our relationship with Workman Publishing began with the gift of a mummified llama fetus. When presented with the rank carcass, which is traditionally buried under the foundation of a new building as an offering to the fertility goddess Pachamama, Suzie Bolotin did not vomit. Instead she had it framed and mounted on her wall. We knew we had found the right publisher.

Indeed, we could not ask for better partners than the imaginative, exacting, and ever-patient team at Workman. Thank you, Suzie Bolotin, Maisie Tivnan, and Janet Vicario for making a bet on *Atlas Obscura*, and then for hanging with us through all the ups and downs of producing this insane book. We've had a great crew supporting us: Sun Robinson-Smith, Danny Cooper; Justin Krasner; our production editor Amanda Hong; our typesetters Barbara Peragine and Jaclyn Atkinson; Monica McCready; Doug Wolff; Carol White; Orlando Adiao; and our photo researchers Bobby Walsh, Melissa Lucier, Aaron Clendening, Sophia Rieth, and Angela Cherry. And, of course, Workman's wonderful publishing and marketing team: Selina Meere, Jessica Wiener, Rebecca Carlisle, and Thea James.

We're grateful to the incomparable Elyse Cheney and Alex Jacobs for shepherding this book through all its stages. To project manager Marc Haeringer for keeping us on track even when the train got really wobbly. To Meg Neal for her contributions to the revised edition. And to our entire team at AO HQ who have put so much of themselves into building *Atlas Obscura*. Thank you, David, David, Dan, Tyler, Megan, Sommer, Jordan, Alexa, Michael, Mike, Reyhan, Eric, Lex, Luke, Rachel, Sarah, Cara, Blake, Hana, Anika, Erik, Rose, Matt, Erin, Michelle, Rebecca, Ryan, Tao Tao, and Urvija. To the folks who were there with us in the early days, this book is yours too. Annetta, Seth, Allison, Nick, Adam, Aaron, and Rachel: Thank you.

JOSH:

It has been a tremendous pleasure working on this project with such extraordinary people. Ella, you are simply a wonder. I admire your diligence, good humor, and grace so much. Marc, my brain hurts imagining how we could have ever pulled this off without your organizational wizardry. Dylan, thank you for always being a wonderful partner, friend, and human being. How much longer can we keep Derweze waiting?

DYLAN:

Ella and Marc, that this book exists is the eighth wonder of the world. Thank you for five years of dedication and creativity. Maisie. Suzie. Janet. Dan. Megan. Allison. Nick. Annetta. Seth. Rachel. Eric. You all had a hand in *Atlas Obscura* becoming real. Thank you. Mom and Dad, as you know, you made me this way. Michelle Enemark for being there in every way for nearly half my life and to Phineas for coming into existence. Josh, thank you for everything. For trusting me, for guiding me. You are my friend and an inspiration. Derweze can't wait. I booked tickets.

ELLA:

Dylan and Josh, your philosophies on exploration and discovery have changed how I see the world. Thank you for trusting me with your most treasured wonders. Thank you, Marc Francois Haeringer, for your unwavering support, diplomacy, and artisanal charcuterie plates. Thank you, Opus and Jez, for making soothing noises as I lay on various floors and couches and moaned that this would never, ever be finished. Eric, thank you for all the Grund mornings. And thank you to Mum and Eclair for the many ways in which you tether my flailing self to the earth.

PHOTO CREDITS

INTRODUCTION, P. 6
Daniel Mihailescu/AFP/Getty Images.

GATEFOLD
Alamy Stock Photo: Tibor Bognar p. 2 (left); dpa picture alliance p. 2 (middle); Robert Harding p. 1 (middle); JASPERIMAGE p. 1 (left); Guido Paradisi p. 1 (right); Chris Willson p. 2 (right). **Shutterstock.com:** aphotostory pp. 1–2 (background), 2 (btm).

AFRICA
Adobe Stock: 3drenderings p. 227 (top); Marina Gorskaya p. 204 (top); Morphart p. 210 (top); Piccaya p. 205; R. Gino Santa Maria p. 186 (top); Siloto p. 219 (top). **Camille Moirenc/AGE Fotostock** p. 194 (btm). **Alamy Stock Photo:** age fotostock pp. 195 (btm), 201, 226 (btm); blickwinkel p. 228 (btm); brianafrica p. 225 (btm); Rungtip Chatadee p. 188; Gilles Comlanvi p. 200 (top); Michael Runkel Egypt p. 186 (btm); Eddie Gerald p. 227 (btm); Oliver Gerhard p. 219 (btm right); Mike Goldwater p. 214 (top); Robert Harding p. 222 (btm); Blaine Harrington III p. 223 (top); Kim Haughton p. 199 (top); Hemis p. 197 (btm); Historic Collection p. 189; Seth Lazar p. 202 (top); Sulo Letta p. 196; Look Die Bildagentur der Fotografen GmbH p. 213 (inset); Henri Martin p. 208 (inset); Andrew Michael p. 223 (btm); National Geographic Image Collection p. 198 (top); B. O'Kane p. 185; Pictures Colour Library p. 187; Robert Estall photo agency p. 224 (btm); p. 203 (composite); Neil Setchfield p. 221 (btm); Mike P. Shepherd p. 192 (top); Kumar Sriskandan p. 225 (top); Fredrik Stenström p. 226 (top); Universal Images Group p. 194 (top); p. 224 (top); Universal Images Group/DeAgostini p. 210 (btm); John Warburton-Lee Photography p. 228 (btm); Tim E White p. 207 (btm). **Matteo Bertolino/matteobertolino.com** p. 204 (btm). **© William Clowes** p. 211. **Getty Images:** Nigel Pavitt/AWL Images p. 215 (btm); Pascal Deloche/Corbis Documentary p. 209 (top); Anup Shah/Corbis Documentary p. 216 (top); Nik Wheeler/Corbis NX p. 208 (background); De Agostini/G. Dagli Orti p. 191; Marc Guitard/Editorial RF p. 213 (background); Leonid Andronov/iStock p. 199 (btm); pascalou95/iStock p. 193 (btm); DigitalGlobe/ScapeWare3d p. 206 (middle); Reinhard Dirscherl/WaterFrame p. 197 (top). **Ian Redmond/Nature Picture Library** p. 214 (btm).

Courtesy Photos: The following images are used under a Creative Commons Attribution 3.0 United States License (https://creativecommons.org/licenses/by/3.0/us) and belongs to the following Wikimedia Commons user: Ji-Elle p. 217 (btm left, middle & btm right). **Public Domain:** Dr. Steve Miller, from the Naval Research Laboratory/U.S. Navy p. 218 (top).

Atlas Obscura **Contributor:** Courtesy Megan E. O'Donnell p. 219 (btm).

ANTARCTICA
Aha-Soft/Adobe Stock p. 457 (btm). **Alamy Stock Photo:** B. O'Kane p. 458 (btm); Cavan Images p. 452 (btm); Robert Harding p. 458 (top); Colin Harris/era-images p. 457 (btm). **Courtesy of Stephen Eastnaugh/Australian Antarctic Division** p. 454 (btm). **Andreas Feininger/The LIFE Picture Collection/Getty Images**

p. 456. **Kristina Gusselin** p. 455 (top). **Carsten Peter/National Geographic Stock** p. 459. **Stein Tronstad** p. 453.

ASIA
Adobe Stock: Anthonycz p. 133 (top); bluebright p. 142 (btm); Rada Covalenco p. 144 (top right); evegenesis p. 145 (btm); forcdan p. 119 (top); frog p. 136 (top); kim1970 p. 144 (top left); R.M. Nunes p. 165 (top); SoulAD p.159 (top); Telly p. 145 (middle right). **AGE Fotostock:** Angelo Cavalli p. 175 (btm); Deddeda p. 177(top); Ivonne Peupelmann p. 166; Topic Photo Agency IN p. 164 (btm). **Alamy Stock Photo:** Aflo Co. Ltd p. 160; afrisson p. 133 (btm); age fotostock p. 134 (inset background); age fotostock p. 163; Agencja Fotograficzna Caro p. 146; Mark Andrews p. 150 (top right); Vladislav Ashikhmin p. 164 (btm); Asia Images Group Pte Ltd p. 137; Don Bartell p. 150 (top left); Curtseyes p. 138 (top); Luis Dafos p. 136 (btm); DestinationImages p. 127 (btm); Paul Doyle p. 117 (btm); dpa picture alliance p. 141 (inset background); Kristaps Eberlins p. 118 (btm); Dominic Dudley p. 138 (btm); Michelle Gilders p. 162 (btm); Manfred Gottschalk p. 167; Simon Grosset p. 149 (btm); hanohikirf p. 119 (btm); Marc F. Henning p. 145 (middle left); Imagebroker p. 122 (top) and p. 165 (btm); Ellen Isaacs p. 132 (btm left); LOOK Die Bildagentur der Fotografen GmbH p. 143; Don Mammoser p. 131; MJ Photography p. 130 (top); Will Moody p. 123; Nokuro p. 174; Novarc Images p. 132 (btm right); NPC Collection p. 157; NurPhoto.com p. 176; PhotoStock-Israel p. 117 (top); Paul Rushton p. 147; Olena Siedykh p. 126 (top); Jack Sullivan p. 118 (top); Keren Su/China Span p. 148 (btm); SuperStock p. 134 (inset); Jeremy Sutton-Hibbert p. 161; tonyoquias p. 178; Travel Asia p. 128 (btm); John Warburton-Lee Photography p. 121; Henry Westheim Photography p. 142 (top); Tim Whitby p. 139 (btm); Xinhua p. 152. **AP Photo:** David Guttenfelder p. 162 (top); Shizuo Kambayashi/STF p. 158. **Christian Caron** p. 130 (btm). **Getty Images:** AFP p. 124; Patrick AVENTURIER/Gamma-Rapho p. 180; Bloomberg p. 154 (btm); Amos Chapple/Lonely Planet Images p. 132 (top); Alireza Firouzi p. 113; gaiamoments p. 172 (top); Christian Kober/AWL Images p. 141 (inset); Eric Lafforgue/Art in All of Us/Corbis News p. 120; Lugaaa p. 175 (top); Quynh Anh Nguyen p. 129; Olive/Photodisc p. 128 (top); Brian J. Skerry/National Geographic Image Collection p. 155; George Steinmetz p. 168; Andrew Taylor/robertharding p. 173 (inset); YOSHIKAZU TSUNO/AFP p. 154 (top); VCG/Visual China Group p. 145 (top); Nik Wheeler p. 114 (btm); Fei Yang p. 144 (btm). **Chris Backe/worthygo.com** p. 179 (top). **Reuters:** Andrew Biraj p. 125; Amir Cohen p. 116 (btm); Thomas Peter p. 159 (btm). **Rehan Khan/Rex USA** p. 135 (btm). **Abedin Taherkenareh/EPA/Shutterstock** p. 112 (top). **UncorneredMarket.com** p. 135 (top).

Courtesy Photos Ehsan Abbasi p. 112 (btm); Ken Jeremiah p. 156.

Atlas Obscura **Contributors:** Chris Backe in South Korea p. 181 (top); Rachel Hallman p. 153; Nienna Mees p. 115; Sam Poucher p. 181 (btm); Jordan Samaniego p. 177 (btm); Anna Siri p. 169, 173 (inset background).

CANADA
Adobe Stock: PremiumGraphicDesign p. 269 (middle); Nadezda Razvodovska p. 276 (left). **Alamy Stock Photo:** 914

Collection p. 266 (top); All Canada Photos p. 268 (btm), p. 269 (top), p. 271 (middle right), p. 275, p. 276 (right); Alt-6 p. 284 (top); blickwinkel p. 274; Yvette Cardozo p. 270 (btm), p. 282; Chronicle p. 277 (btm); Cosmo Condina p. 278 (btm); dpa picture alliance archive p. 272; iconim p. 265 (btm); INTERFOTO p. 273 (btm); Andre Jenny p. 267 (btm), p. 283 (btm); Lannen/Kelly Photo p. 284 (btm); Susan Montgomery p. 280 (btm); Radharc Images p. 273 (top). **Getty Images:** Bloomberg p. 281 (inset); DigitalGlobe/ScapeWare3d p. 265 (top); Finn O'Hara/Photodisc p. 270 (middle); Carlos Osorio/Toronto Star p. 280(top); Chris Sheppard/500px p. 267 (top); Brian Summers/First Light p. 271(btm); xPACIFICA/National Geographic Image Collection p. 278 (top). **Rex USA:** Jon Freeman/Shutterstock p. 271 (top); REX Shutterstock p. 266 (btm). **LBNL/Science Source** p. 283 (top).

Courtesy Photos: Banff Indian Trading Post p. 264 (btm); Joshua Foer p. 271 (middle left); Keith Watson p. 279.

EUROPE
Adobe Stock: annexs2 p. 72 (top); Martina Berg p. 43 (btm); chicha1mk p. 84 (top); Rimas Jas p. 83; Igor Kisselev p. 101 (top); Jules Kitano p. 102 (btm); lenka p. 2; martialred p. 90 (btm); mino21 p. 95 (top); Nikokvfrmoto p. 51 (btm); Sved Oliver p. 97; Alexander Potapov 30 (top); sdp_creations p. 35 (top); skvoor p. 79 (top). **AGE Fotostock:** BEW Authors p. 85 (top); DEA/A DAGLI ORTI p. 32; DOMELOUNKSEN p. 28 (btm); Patrick Forget p. 38 (top); Paula Mozdrzewska p. 85 (btm); Christine Noh p. 105; Werner Otto p. 44 (btm); Marco Scataglini p. 66 (btm). **Alamy Stock Photo:** Jon Arnold Images Ltd p. 50; ASK Images p. 41 (btm); Hans-Joachim Aubert p. 84 (btm); bilwissedition Ltd. & Co. KG p. 7 (top); Michal Boubin p. 78; James Byard p. 17 (inset background); Christ Cathedral p. 17 (inset); Chronicle pp. 3, 15 (btm); Cuboimages srl p. 57; deadlyphoto.com p. 104 (btm); Vincent Drago p. 86 (top); EmmePi Travel p. 96 (top); Julio Etchart p. 51 (top); Mark Eveleigh p. 69 (btm); Everett Collection Historical p. 14 (top); Everett Collection Inc p. 41 (top); Jerome Flynn p. 11; Peter Erik Forsberg p. 79 (btm); Leslie Garland Pictures p. 98 (btm); David Crossland/Germany Images p. 45; Michele and Tom Grimm p. 74 (btm); GL Archive p. 35 (btm); Robert Harding Picture Library Ltd pp. 16, 100 (top); HelloWorld Images p. 81; Hemis p. 63; Peter Horree p. 62; imageBROKER p. 33; ITAR-TASS News Agency p. 92; ITAR-TASS Photo Agency p. 90 (top); Ton Koene p. 65; Douglas Lander p. 107 (inset); Yannick Luthy p. 80; David Lyon p. 18; Paul Mayall Germany p. 43 (top); Jeff Morgan 05 p. 48 (btm); Eric Nathan p. 99; David Noton Photography p. 31 (top); OK-SANA p. 100 (btm); Pandarius p. 37; Sean Pavone p. 70 (top); Alan Payton pp. 9, 20 (left); Prisma by Dukas Presseagentur GmbH p. 72 (btm); Profimedia.CZ a.s. p. 28 (top); QEDimages p. 5 (btm); Reciprocity Images Editorial p. 46 (btm); Bjarki Reyr MR p. 86 (btm); Peter Robinson p. 20 (right); Mauro Rodrigues p. 67; Denny Rowland p. 7 (btm); Adam Radosavljevic/Serbia Pictures p. 94 (btm); SPUTNIK p. 91 (top); Gerner Thomsen p. 93 (top); Urbanmyth p. 47; Ivan Vdovin p. 39; Guido Vermeulen-Perdaen p. 56 (btm); VPC Photo p. 58 (btm); Jasmine Wang p. 6; Sebastian Wasek p. 71; Rob Whitworth p. 69 (top); YAY Media AS p. 94 (top); Shau Hua Yi p. 82 (btm). **Scala/Art Resource, NY** p. 56

(top). **Natika/Can Stock Photo** p. 5 (top). **Christian Payne/Documentally** p. 10. **Getty Images:** William A. Allard/National Geographic pp. 60–61; Arctic-Images/Iconica p. 103; DEA/PUBBLI AER FOTO/DeAgostini p. 91 (btm); DEA/S. VANNINI p. 68; Geography Photos/Universal Images Group p. 76; Ton Honan/PA Images p. 17 (btm); Hulton Archive p. 12; ARIS MESSINIS/AFP p. 49 (btm); Daniel Mihailescu/AFP pp. viii, 88 (btm); nimu1956/E+ p. 59; Maryam Schindler/Picture Press p. 101 (btm); Science & Society Picture Library/SSPL p. 54 (top); Yulia-B/iStock p. 93 (btm). **Paul Léger:** p. 36. **Ricardo Ordonez/Reuters** p. 70 (btm). **ITV/Shutterstock/Rex USA** p. 21. **Science Source:** p. 108 (middle & btm). **Shutterstock.com:** Alexandr Makedonskiy p. 96 (btm); Gigi Peis p. 15 (top). **Temple dell'Umanita Association:** p. 52 (top). **Guido Alberto Rossi/Water Rights Images:** p. 53 (top).

Courtesy Photos: Stephen Birch p. 8; Jennifer Boyer p. 102 (top); © Hellbrunn Palace Administration p. 27; Paul Hyland p. 14 (btm); Collections Mundaneum p. 29; Jan Kempenaers/Courtesy of Little Breeze London p. 77 (all); Dawn Mueller p. 42; © Nick Palalino, 1999 p. 64 (btm); Kjartan Hauglid. © Emanuel Vigeland Museum/Bono p. 106. **Creative Commons:** The following image is used under a Creative Commons Attribution 3.0 United States License (https://creativecommons.org/licenses/by/3.0/us) and belongs to the following Wikimedia Commons user: Msemmett p. 7 (middle). The following image is used under a Creative Commons Attribution-ShareAlike 4.0 International License (https://creativecommons.org/licenses/by-sa/4.0) and belongs to the following Wikimedia Commons user: Romain Bréget p. 30 (btm). **Public Domain:** World Esperanto Association {{PD-old-70}} p. 26 (top).

Atlas Obscura **Contributors:** Scisetti Alfio p. 44 (top); Atlas Obscura p. 73; Michael Bukowski & Jeanne D'Angelo p. 87 (all); Christine Colby p. 13 (top); Peter Dispensa p. 40; Michelle Enemark p. 88 (top); Ophelia Holt p. 34; Courtesy of Nikolaus Lipburger, Kugelmugel p. 23; Michael Magdalena pp. 19, 49 (btm); Roger Noguera p. 82 (top).

LATIN AMERICA
Adobe Stock: BuckeyeSailboat p. 436 (top); lacotearts p. 399 (middle); luciezr p. 412 (btm); martialred p. 439 (top); ocphoto p. 412 (top); Viktoria p. 446 (btm); VKA p. 433. **AGE Fotostock:** CSP_marconicouto p. 394 (btm); GUIZIOU Franck p. 430 (top). **Alamy Stock Photo:** age fotostock p. 431; Aurora Photos p. 423; Michele Burgess p. 405; Maria Grazia Casella p. 402 (btm); Cavan Images p. 443; dpa picture alliance archive p. 439 (btm); Exclusivepix Media p. 417 (inset); Julio Etchart p. 406 (top); Mark Eveleigh p. 435 (btm); Robert Fried p. 444 (top); Bernardo Galmarini p. 393; Mark Green p. 413; Robert Harding p. 418 (top); Hemis p. 442; Robert Adrian Hillman p. 429 (btm); George H.H. Huey p. 440 (btm); imageBROKER pp. 394 (top), 396 (btm & top), 406 (btm), 407, 416; LatitudeStock p. 449 (btm); Eric Laudonien p. 438 (top); LOOK Die Bildagentur der Fotografen GmbH p. 447 (btm); Martin Norris Travel Photography p. 429 (btm); John Mitchell p. 441; Efrain Padro p. 448 (top); Dipak Pankhania p. 411 (btm); Wolfi Poelzer p. 438 (btm); MARIUSZ PRUSACZYK p. 432; Carrie Thompson p. 422; Tom Till p. 408 (top); travelstock44 p. 392

(top); Michael Ventura p. 448 (btm); Fabrice VEYRIER p. 420; Westend61 GmbH p. 446 (top); Xinhua p. 419 Zoonar GmbH p. 426. **Dave Bunnell/Caters News** p. 427 (btm). **Kiki Deere/kikideere.com** p. 403. **Getty Images:** AFP p. 430 (btm); cdwheatley/iStock p. 447 (top); DEA/G.SOSIO/De Agostini p. 437 (btm); diegograndi/iStock p. 434; Dan Herrick/Lonely Planet Images p. 436 (top); Richard Maschmeyer/robertharding p. 414 (inset background); MSeis/iStock p. 410; Carsten Peter/Speleoresearch & Films/National Geographic p. 427 (top); rchphoto/iStock p. 415 (btm); Henryk Sadura p. 414 (inset); Frans Sellies p. 440 (top); Topical Press Agency/Hulton Archive p. 398 (btm); Rosanna U/Image Source p. 415 (top right); ullstein bild p. 399 (top); Uwe-Bergwitz/iStock p. 415 (top left); Edson Vandeira p. 404 (top); xeni4ka/iStockEditorial p. 417 (inset background). **Edgard Garrido/Reuters** p. 425 (btm). **Sofia Ruzo** p. 411 (top).

Creative Commons: The following images are used under a Creative Commons Attribution 3.0 United States License (https://creativecommons.org/licenses/by/3.0/us) and belong to the following Wikimedia Commons users: Shaddim p. 437 (top); Yurileveratto p. 398 (top).

Atlas Obscura **Contributors:** John Allen p. 421 (btm); cgracemo p. 397; Each Day I Dye p. 424 (btm); Mark Harrison p. 408 (btm); Allan Haverman pp. 391, 395; Courtesy of Kirk Horsted p. 450; Jason Decaires Taylor p. 436 (btm).

OCEANIA
Adobe Stock: Wolfgang Berroth p. 232; Tommaso Lizzul p. 236 (btm). **AGE Fotostock:** Jean-Marc La-Roque p. 243 (pineapple); Keven O'Hara p. 247 (btm); Joe Dovala/WaterFra p. 255. **Alamy Stock Photo:** Bill Bachman p. 244 (top); Robert Bird p. 248 (top); chris24 p. 242 (guitar); Steve Davey Photography p. 261; Philip Game p. 254; Iconsinternational.com p. 243 (Big Ned); National Geographic Image Collection p. 243 (koala); Martin Norris Travel Photography p. 238 (btm); Christine Osborne Pictures p. 242 (banana); Aloysius Patrimonio p. 238 (top); Stefano Ravera p. 242 (mango); Andrew Sole p. 248 (btm); Jack Sullivan p. 243 (prawn); John White Photos p. 243; Big Galah; Wiskerke p. 242 (merino); Ian Woolcock p. 239; Zoonar GmbH p. 242 (crocodile). **Getty Images:** The Asahi Shimbun p. 253; Ben Bohane/AFP p. 262; Don Kelsen/Los Angeles Times p. 247 (btm); Desmond Morris Collection/UIG p. 251 (btm); Mitch Reardon/Lonely Planet Images p. 237 (top); Oliver Strewe/Lonely Planet Images p. 258; Michele Westmorland/The Image Bank p. 257; Whitworth Images p. 245 (background).

Steven David Miller/Nature Picture Library p. 237 (btm). **Clive Hyde/Newspix** p. 233. **Martin Rietze/MRIETZE.COM** p. 249; **Patrick Horton/Shutterstock.com** p. 252.

Courtesy Photos: Patrick J. Gallagher p. 241 (btm); David Hartley-Mitchell p. 246 (top); Malcolm Rees p. 250 (btm); **Creative Commons:** The following image is used under a Creative Commons Attribution 3.0 United States License (https://creativecommons.org/licenses/by/3.0/us) and belongs to the following Wikimedia Commons user: Peter Campbell p. 240. The

following image is used under a Creative Commons Attribution-ShareAlike 2.5 Generic License (https://creativecommons.org/licenses/by-sa/2.5) and belongs to the following Wikimedia Commons user: Peter Halasz p. 245 (inset). **Public Domain:** NASA p. 251.

Atlas Obscura **Contributors:** Céline Meyer p. 246 (btm); Amanda Ulliek p. 241 (top).

USA
Adobe Stock: airindizain p. 381 (btm); davidevison p. 369; Diverser p. 359 (btm); Dominic p. 310 (top); Imagewriter p. 326 (top); kovalto1 p. 340 (btm); opin47 p. 300 (top); Sean Pavone Photo p. 350 (top); Alexander Potapov p. 321 (top); sljubisa p. 323 (top); tanais p. 354 (btm); valdezrl p. 312 (top); Vector Tradition p. 334 (btm). **Alamy Stock Photo:** Irene Abdou p. 371 (top); Nathan Allred pp. 314–315 (background); Alan Bozac p. 329 (btm); Pat Canova p. 346 (top); Chronicle p. 382 (top); Cultura RM p. 372 (inset background); D Guest Smith p. 329 (top); Danita Delimont p. 322 (btm), p. 367 (top); Design Pics Inc p. 388; Don Despain p. 317 (btm); dpa picture alliance p. 315 (inset); Randy Duchaine p. 375 (top); Education & Exploration 3 p. 348 (top); Richard Ellis p. 355 (btm); Everett Collection Historical p. 364 (top); Franck Fotos p. 332 (btm); Zachary Frank p. 301; Oliver Gerhard p. 373; Joseph S. Giacalone p. 298 (inset); Michelle Gilders p. 320 (top); Jay Goebel p. 317 (top); Robert Harding p. 311; Blaine Harrington III p. 307 (top right); Clarence Holmes Photography p. 365; Janet Horton p. 302 (top); Independent Picture Service p. 340 (top); Inge Johnsson p. 308; Richard Levine p. 370 (top); Ilene MacDonald p. 307 (top left); Mary Evans Picture Library p. 350 (btm); National Geographic Image Collection p. 310 (btm); Luc Novovitch p. 305 (top); B. O'Kane p. 290 (btm); Edwin Remsberg p. 362 (top); RMF stock p. 287 (background); RosaIreneBetancourt 7 p. 339 (top); Philip Scalia p. 360; SCPhotos p. 387; Jim West p. 323 (btm); Zanna Pesnina p. 294; ZUMA Press, Inc. pp. 287 (inset), 288, p. 316 (top), 347, 361, 379 (btm); **Brad Andersohn** p. 295 (inset). **AP Photo:** Wilfredo Lee 348 (btm); Douglas C. Pizac p. 319 (top). **Boston Athenæum** p. 379 (top). **Brendan Donnelly** p. 291 (middle left, center & right). **Zach Fein** p. 338. **Getty Images:** Allentown Morning Call/MCT p. 370 (btm); John Ashmore p. 336; Raymond Boyd p. 351; John B. Carnett/Bonnier Corporation p. 357 (middle); Bryan Chan/Los Angeles Times p. 293 (btm); Scott Gries p. 364 (btm); Paul Hawthorne p. 333 (top); Kevin Horan/The LIFE Images Collection p. 333 (btm); Karen Kasmauski p. 378; MagicDreamer/iStock p. 318 (btm); Keith Philpott/The LIFE Images Collection p. 337 (btm); Rischgitz/Stringer p. 368; Joel Sartore/National Geographic p. 358 (top); Dieter Schaefer p. 309; Scott T. Smith/Corbis Documentary p. 314 (inset); Universal History Archive p. 299.

Ahenredon/Shutterstock.com p. 383. **Skeletons: A Museum of Osteology/Skulls Unlimited International, Inc.** p. 325 (all).

Courtesy Photos: Richard Reames-Arborsmith Studios p. 300 (btm); Clark R. Arrington p. 356; Allison Meier/flickr.com p. 326 (btm); Ryan Cheung/flickr.com p. 353 (btm); © 2016 Google, Imagery © 2016 DigitalGlobe, Landsat, U.S. Geological Survey p. 292 (btm); Paul Hall p. 327 (top); Megan

Mahlberg p. 332 (top right); Mukluk Land p. 385(all); Leather Archives & Museum p. 328 (btm); Brad Kisling/Museum of Clean p. 320 (btm left & right); Steven Orfield of Orfield Laboratories, Inc. p. 335 (top); Paper House p. 381 (top); Nicholas Pena p. 312 (btm); Steven Pierson p. 331 (top); The Archives, Philip Weltner Library, Oglethorpe University p. 349; Center for PostNatural History p. 367 (btm); Science Museum of Minnesota p. 335 (btm); Unclaimed Baggage Center p. 345 (top); Bruce Wicks p. 330 (top & btm right); Cushing Center, Harvey Cushing/John Hay Whitney Medical Center Library, Yale University p. 374. **Creative Commons:** The following image is used under a Creative Commons Attribution-ShareAlike 4.0 International License (https://creativecommons.org/licenses/by-sa/4.0) and belongs to the following Wikimedia Commons user: Dppowell p. 322 (top). **Public Domain:** Federal Aviation Administration p. 297 (top); Library of Congress/National Park Service/Benjamin Halpern p. 324 (btm); U.S. Army p. 324 (top); U.S. Army Corps of Engineers p. 354 (top); The U.S. Food and Drug Administration p. 375 (top).

***Atlas Obscura* Contributors:** Ashley Avey p. 306 (inset); Atlas Obscura p. 371 (btm); The Beautiful Lashes p. 293 (top); Dave Bell/davebellphotography.com p. 295 (inset background); Kyle Bennett 69 p. 321 (btm); Steve Doerk p. 296 (top); Jesse Doyle p. 306 (background); Jerome Glass p. 304 (btm); Jessica Leigh Gonzales p. 289; Brett Klynn p. 297 (btm); Eric S. Kienzle p. 305 (btm); Allison M. p. 363 (top); Moonspenders p. 303; Jared Nagel p. 334 (top); Noaa's National Geodetic Survey p. 372 (inset); April Packwood p. 339 (btm); Traci Paris p. 363 (btm); Amanda Petrozzini p. 341 (all); Brian Pozun p. 384 (btm); M Reniche p. 286 (desert); Space age Juliet p. 362 (btm); Tammy p. 352 (top left); Tammy 352 (top right); Trey Tatum p. 353 (top); Tremperj p. 346 (btm); Jane Weinhardt p. 313 (top).

INDEX

Atlas Obscura, publisher of the definitive guide to the world's hidden wonders, is a travel company defined by storytelling. It was founded in 2009 by Dylan Thuras and Joshua Foer with a mission to inspire wonder and curiosity about the world. Our editorial team reports on hidden places, incredible histories, scientific marvels, and gastronomic wonders. Atlas Obscura creates hundreds of unique global trips and local experiences every year, bringing our community with us to visit the world's most unusual places and try the world's most extraordinary foods.

Gastro Obscura

A FOOD ADVENTURER'S GUIDE

★ ★ ★ ★

CECILY WONG • DYLAN THURAS

with additional writing by Rachel Rummel, Anne Ewbank, and Sam O'Brien

WORKMAN PUBLISHING • NEW YORK

An Important Note to Readers

Not everything in *Gastro Obscura* should be eaten. Some of the foods in this book are a wonder to learn about, but do harm to partake in. As for the rest, we encourage you to try them.

....

Library of Congress Cataloging-in-Publication Data
Names: Wong, Cecily, author. | Thuras, Dylan, author.
Title: Gasto obscura : a food adventurer's guide / Cecily Wong, Dylan Thuras
with additional writing by Rachel Rummel, Anne Ewbank, and Sam O'Brien.
Description: First edition. | New York : Workman Publishing, 2021. |
Series: An Atlas Obscura book. | Includes index. |
Identifiers: LCCN 2021025589 | ISBN 9781523502196 (hardcover) |
ISBN 9781523502196 (kindle edition)
Subjects: LCSH: Dinners and dining—Anecdotes. |
Food—Anecdotes. | Voyages and travels--Anecdotes.
Classification: LCC TX737 .W66 2021 | DDC 641.3—dc23
LC record available at https://lccn.loc.gov/2021025589

Art direction and design by Janet Vicario
Illustrations by Alan Berry Rhys
Photo research by Sophia Rieth and Aaron Clendening
Photo credits listed on page 414

Workman books are available at special discounts when purchased in bulk for premiums and sales promotions as well as for fundraising or educational use. Special editions or book excerpts also can be created to specification. For details, contact the Special Sales Director at specialmarkets@workman.com.

Workman Publishing Co., Inc.
225 Varick Street
New York, NY 10014-4381
workman.com

WORKMAN is a registered trademark of Workman Publishing Co., Inc.

Printed in South Korea on responsibly sourced paper.
First printing September 2021

10 9 8 7 6 5 4 3

CONTENTS

INTRODUCTION

Eating may be the most immersive, visceral travel experience. It requires an engagement of every sense, from the sound of dishes clattering in an alleyway kitchen, to the smell of garlic hitting hot oil, to the joy of seeing a plate of food before you as you sit, utensil in hand, about to taste. Humans around the world are bound by the necessity and pleasure of eating, and there is no faster way to glimpse the heart of a place than by experiencing its food.

A guiding mantra at Atlas Obscura is that wonder can be found around every corner—not just in uncharted and far-flung locales but down the street, down some stairs, into the Victorian-era public toilet that now houses a London coffee bar. While travel is a beautiful way of seeking wonder, you'll find within these pages that adventures don't always require a plane ticket. From the award-winning smokehouse in an Arkansas living room, to the Thai food stalls in a California parking lot, to the Mexican auto body shop that transforms into a taqueria every night—wondrous food is everywhere.

Gastro Obscura is a book that scratches the surface of a mind-bending world of eating. We love tasty food, but we aim to be explorers rather than gourmands. Seekers rather than epicureans. This book is more than a menu of foods worth tasting—it's a collection of forgotten histories and endangered traditions, obscure experiences, culinary ingenuity, and edible wonders. It's a noisy, delicious, action-packed feast that spans seven continents, and over 120 countries and, as often as possible, tells you exactly where and how to experience things for yourself.

Most of the entries in this book came from the Atlas Obscura community—over half a million incredible users who share tips with us every day—and our remarkable team of editors who scour the earth to find even more wonders. What you hold in your hands is a massive, collaborative effort made possible by every person who pointed us to a surprising restaurant, a charming fruit, or a Canadian hockey arena above the Arctic Circle that locals have turned into a thriving greenhouse.

We have always believed that wonder can be found wherever you are open to searching for it. Well, here it is, sitting right in front of you, waiting to be eaten. Dig in.

Cecily Wong and Dylan Thuras

Every morning, dabbawalas throughout Mumbai transport homemade lunches to office workers, using codes on the packages to indicate their destination.

Europe

GREAT BRITAIN AND IRELAND

WESTERN EUROPE ∘ EASTERN EUROPE

SCANDINAVIA

GREAT BRITAIN AND IRELAND

FRIDAY NIGHT PUDDING FEAST

THE PUDDING CLUB AT THE THREE WAYS HOUSE HOTEL • ENGLAND

How to try it
Interested parties must call the hotel and book in advance. After gorging on pudding, you can sleep in one of the hotel's seven dessert-themed rooms.

From the outside, the Three Ways House Hotel is a typical 19th-century British bed-and-breakfast, made out of golden stone and engulfed in ivy. On Friday nights, however, the hotel plays host to the Pudding Club—an institution with a self-proclaimed mission of preserving the "great British pudding."

Since 1985, dozens of dessert-lovers from around the world have gathered weekly to gorge on a banquet of British puddings, presented with pomp by the hotel's resident Pudding Master—the mastermind who curates the menu. Traditionally, British pudding is a cake-like dish made with suet, or hardened animal fat, that's steamed for hours and can be sweet or savory. But the word can also apply to desserts in general, and at the Pudding Club, the Friday feast includes traditional puddings like jam roly-poly, spotted dick, and sticky toffee pudding, as well as non-steamed puddings like rice pudding, sliced-bread-and-fruit summer pudding, apple crumble, passion fruit roulade, and syrup sponge cake.

The seven-course pudding extravaganza is a feat of endurance, and those who make it through the evening are awarded a certificate. According to Pudding Master Lucy Williams, the club is not just about indulgence, but celebrating dishes that have fallen out of modern favor.

The Three Ways House Hotel was originally a doctor's house.

BRAWNY LIQUID BEEF

BOVRIL • ENGLAND

How to try it
Beloved Bovril is widely available in British supermarkets. If you're interested in how the beef extract has been marketed over the decades, visit the Museum of Brands in Notting Hill, London. It has a bunch of old Bovril posters and vintage-style merchandise.

In 1870, as Napoleon III led his troops into the Franco-Prussian War, he ordered one million cans of beef to feed his men. The request went to a Scottish butcher living in Canada named John Lawson Johnston, who tweaked a recipe for meat glaze to make "beef fluid," a thick, glossy paste that tastes exactly as you might guess: very salty and very beefy. The result was Bovril, England's iconic concentrated beef paste.

Bovril was touted as a constitution-boosting, meaty superfood that could be spread on buttered toast or diluted and drunk as a restorative tea. Marketing claims (some endorsed by real scientists) declared the paste could make the infirm well, the elderly strong, and the young healthy. One advertisement even claimed that "Bovril fortifies the system against influenza."

Victorians loved the beef-in-a-jar. From breakfast tables to hospitals to football stadiums, a hot thermos of Bovril tea became the preferred way to warm up and gain strength. The foodstuff was considered patriotic—it fed British soldiers during the Boer War—and it was celebrity approved.

Ernest Shackleton ate Bovril during his 1902 Antarctic expedition. Famous Victorian strongman Eugen Sandow claimed Bovril gave him strength. Even Pope Leo XIII was depicted in a Bovril ad (albeit without his permission) drinking a mug of beef broth above the slogan: "Two Infallible Powers: The Pope and Bovril."

Fluid beef made Johnston a very wealthy man. In 1896, he sold Bovril for £2 million and died four years later, in Cannes, on a yacht.

Early 20th-century ads for England's favorite liquid-beef-in-a-can.

A KINGLY LIQUOR TO DRINK WHILE DRIVING

THE KING'S GINGER • ENGLAND

King Edward VII was 62 when he took the throne from his mother, Queen Victoria, in 1901. Elderly and overweight, he still partied hard. His joyrides around the English countryside in his topless Daimler exposed him to the very British elements (chilly and damp) and concerned the royal physician.

In 1903, the doctor commissioned an established London merchant, Berry Bros., to formulate a warming, fortifying beverage to put in the aging monarch's driving flask. The result was The King's Ginger, a brandy-based elixir with ginger, honey, and lemon, designed specifically "to stimulate and revivify His Majesty during morning rides."

The king loved his new zesty liqueur. Not only did he drink it in his "horseless carriage," he brought it along while hunting and generously passed around the bottle. By the time Edward died in 1910, the royal family was hooked. Berry Bros. continued to make and sell The King's Ginger exclusively to nobility, who purchased hundreds of cases of it every year in unlabeled bottles.

In recent years, a bartender asked the maker, now Berry Bros. & Rudd, for a standardized version of the elusive drink, and the company enlisted a Dutch distiller to make the beverage for the masses. A modern version debuted in 2011, using a base of neutral grain spirits instead of brandy, along with ginger, lemon oil, Glenrothes single malt scotch, and sugar. At 82 proof, it takes just a few sips to get your engine revving.

How to try it
Find The King's Ginger (for the masses) online and at retailers across the UK, USA, Australia, and New Zealand.

NOTTINGHAM'S SUBTERRANEAN DRINKING DEN

THE LOST CAVES • ENGLAND

How to try it
The access to the Lost Caves is somewhere in the vicinity of the Mecure Hotel and the Lost Property Bar. Dress warmly. Any more information would spoil the fun.

Damp, dimly lit, and decorated with skulls, chandeliers, and stuffed animals, this secret drinking establishment is part of the extensive cave system that's cut into the soft sandstone below the city of Nottingham.

Accessed via a dark and uninviting alley, through a heavily disguised door with a brass skull handle, you'll find a staircase to the basement beneath a 200-year-old building. In this basement, a further series of rock-cut steps leads into the cavernous void beneath the city. The final descent into the Lost Caves is by escort, as there is a strict maximum occupancy. Inside, 26 feet (8 m) below the venerable George Hotel (now the Mecure), which has accommodated guests as diverse as Charles Dickens and Elizabeth Taylor, is a most unlikely cocktail palace.

When, why, and by whom these deep grottoes were excavated is unknown; however, they appear to have been adapted for the purpose of storing and brewing ale on rock-cut ledges. Today, instead of barrels of beer, the cushion-padded rock ledges are used as seating for the bar's subterranean drinkers.

Beneath the streets of Hockley is one of Nottingham's best-kept secrets.

OUTLAWED ICE-CREAM WARE

PENNY LICK • ENGLAND

How to try it
Penny licks are a rare collectible these days. Wash well before using.

Penny licks were England's most nefarious ice-cream paraphernalia. As the name suggests, a few licks of ice cream cost just a penny. Included in that price was the sizable risk of contracting tuberculosis.

In the mid-1800s, ice cream had become a beloved and affordable treat, sold all over the streets of England. Ice-cream vendors called Jacks served tiny scoops in glass cups called penny licks, which came in three sizes: the standard and most popular penny lick, the wee ha'penny (halfpenny) lick, and the larger tu'penny (two penny) lick.

These small glasses were designed especially for ice cream—or more specifically, for an ice-cream optical illusion. As Jacks paddled the dessert into the cup, the conical shape and thick glass magnified its contents so that even the tiniest serving appeared bountiful.

After finishing their ice cream, customers licked their glasses clean and handed them back to the Jack, who would serve the next customers from the unwashed cups.

When tuberculosis swept the nation, the medical establishment pointed to the penny licks. An 1879 English medical report blamed a cholera outbreak on the reuse of glassware, and fear of tuberculosis led the city of London to ban penny licks in 1899. Some vendors continued to use the illicit ice-cream cups through the 1920s and 1930s, until a breakthrough in ice-cream technology eradicated the need for their glassware for good. The mighty waffle cone emerged as the new single-use vessel of choice, knocking out the penny lick with its portability, edibility, and complete absence of infectious disease.

"THE NOTED EEL-AND-PIE HOUSES"

M. MANZE • ENGLAND

The M. Manze Eel and Pie House at 87 Tower Bridge Road is the oldest eel-and-pie shop still standing in London. Open three or four hours a day, Manze's serves only lunch, and their lunch menu consists of just two things: eels and pies.

Throughout the 1700s, eels were so plentiful in the River Thames that a net cast at any spot would pull up a hearty catch of cheap protein. Working-class East Londoners, or Cockneys, grew to love them, and eels became the go-to meal for the city's workhands. Capitalizing on the eel craze, pie shops (which generally trafficked in mutton and potatoes) started serving them up how their clients liked them: naturally jellied.

How to try it

M. Manze has three locations in London— the Tower Bridge location is the oldest. The second oldest, on Peckman High Street, was built in 1927.

Thanks to a huge amount of collagen, eels are gelatinous by nature. With skin and bones intact, round chunks of eel are boiled in water flavored with vinegar, bay leaves, peppercorns, and onion, then left to cool in the liquid, which gently congeals into a translucent jelly. These quivering hunks of cold, tender meat are considered Britain's first fast-food takeaway, commonly scooped into cups, doused with hot chili vinegar, and eaten on the go.

By the end of World War II, London boasted more than 100 eel-and-pie shops—but as the Thames grew polluted, supply decreased and the city's interest in eel eating waned.

At Manze's, eels are still king. They can be ordered cold and jellied or hot and stewed, or served with mash and slathered in "liquor"—an alcohol-free parsley sauce that also goes on pies. The small, no-frills shop is operated by the grandson of the original owner, Michele Manze, who came to London in 1878 from the Italian village of Ravello. The decor, with its green-and-white tiles and long communal tables, hearkens back to Victorian days, when eels reigned supreme.

A server at Manze's adds parsley sauce to a plate of mash and pie.

TABLE ETIQUETTE IN THE *Victorian Age*

Nineteenth-century England was rife with highly specialized eating utensils, serving devices, and table decor—especially extravagant in well-to-do homes. Designed in the spirit of gentility over essential function, Victorian kitchen gadgetry served a higher purpose, which was impressing dinner guests, brandishing status, and proving just how fabulous a fussy table could be.

ICE-CREAM FORKS

The first recorded owner of a table fork was an 11th-century Byzantine princess who died of plague. Some said this was an apt punishment for using a fork, which looked suspiciously like the devil's pitchfork. The Victorians had no such concerns, and forks were used with abandon. A spoon could be used when eating a bowl of ice cream but the ice-cream fork—a shallow, three-tined protospork—was used exclusively for eating ice cream served on a plate.

MUSTACHE CUPS

Impressively shaped mustaches of the era looked stately and dignified until confronted with a hot cup of tea. The heat melted the mustache wax, causing the corners to droop.

In the 1870s, British potter Harvey Adams invented the mustache cup, featuring a patented, wing-shaped ledge that created a handy barrier between facial hair and tea.

The cups came in many shapes and sizes, from the large pint-size "farmers' cups" to small porcelain pieces sculpted like conch shells or embossed with the name of the owner.

CELERY VASES

Wild celery, native to the Mediterranean, wasn't cultivated in England until the early 1800s, and it didn't grow easily. Those who succeeded in obtaining some celery needed a way to flaunt it. Glass-blown celery vases—featuring embellishments like fluted edges and the owners' name engraved on the bottom—were used as centerpieces on fashionable tables.

PICKLE CASTORS

These jewel-toned, pressed-glass jars were a mainstay on posh Victorian tables. The castors were fitted in a silver holder, accompanied by small silver tongs, and were embellished with anything from personal messages to gargoyles.

Beyond their role as ritzy table decor, pickle castors signaled that a home employed enough servants to prepare pickles, and display the produce.

PIE BIRDS

Placed in the middle of a pie, the small, hollow ceramic birds released steam from the hot filling, while appearing to blow huge gusts of air through their upturned mouths.

The idea was that this bird chimney would vent the pie and keep any juices from bubbling over, but as any baker knows, a few cuts with a knife would perform the same trick, albeit without the avian whimsy.

MEAD-MAKING PARADISE

THE HOLY ISLAND OF LINDISFARNE

In the 7th century, at the request of King Oswald of Northumbria, Irish monk Saint Aidan established a monastery on the isolated tidal island of Lindisfarne. The monastery, which survives in ruins, would become the base for spreading Christianity throughout Anglo-Saxon England. Many also believe that the Lindisfarne monks were excellent mead-makers, who crafted the golden liquid in the name of spirituality. Mead is one of the oldest tipples in the world, appearing in ancient Greek texts, Hindu scriptures, and Norse mythology, in which drinking certain meads was a pathway to scholarly intelligence.

Often called the elixir of the gods, it's fitting that some of the finest mead is produced on "Holy Island." While monks no longer helm the operation, mead-maker J. Michael Hackett was drawn to the history of Lindisfarne. In the early 1960s, he opened St. Aidan's Winery on the island and set about making a modern version of the ancient brew, which he called Lindisfarne Mead. Drawing cues from the ancient Romans, who included grape juice in their meads, the team at St. Aidan's starts with a base of fermented honey, adding aromatic herbs, fermented wine grapes, and water drawn from a local well. A neutral spirit fortifies the holy mixture, which tasters describe as light, silky, and dry. The medieval mead from the tiny island (population 180) is now distributed internationally.

How to try it

St. Aidan's Winery is open to the public during Lindisfarne Island's "open tide" times, when the island is safely reachable by causeway. About twice a day, during high tide, the island becomes inaccessible.

Indian Curry IN BRITAIN

During their 200-year occupation of India, the British developed a fondness for the country's complex, pungently spiced cuisine. Curry, especially, made a big splash in the 19th-century English diet: Housewives worked hard to re-create Indian flavors with domestic ingredients while Queen Victoria, credited with making curry fashionable in England, employed an Indian staff who prepared food for the royal family.

To make the dish more accessible, Brits invented curry powder in the 18th century. The spice blend, with its base of turmeric, garlic, cumin, and fenugreek, was a far cry from Indian cooking, where different dishes were spiced uniquely and the catch-all word *curry* did not exist. (The word *curry* is likely a bastardization of the Tamil word *kari*, which, depending on how it's pronounced, can mean "to blacken" or "to bite." Fifteenth-century Portuguese colonists took it as an all-purpose word for Indian food: curry.) As British influence spread around the globe, so did curry powder, which was introduced as a British food to countless cuisines in places like Japan, Thailand, and the Caribbean. Even Indians, working abroad as indentured laborers, were given rations of curry powder with their pay.

In the mid-20th century, Bangladeshi immigrants arrived in London, mostly jumping ship at the port after toiling in the engine room on long steamship voyages from India. The new arrivals bought up small cafés and "chippies" (fish and chips shops) that had been damaged by the bombings in World

A chef tends to trays of yellow curry in a stall at the Southbank Centre food market in London.

War II and could be had for a bargain. Alongside the English standards, these new shops sold curry and rice for the growing South Asian community. They also stayed open late— a strategic move to attract the English drinking crowd, who began to order curry as their post-pub meal, sometimes with rice, sometimes with chips.

The influx of Indian immigrants throughout the 20th century kept curry pumping through the country. Chicken tikka masala, the creamy tomato curry found on every Indian restaurant menu, is perhaps the dish that best represents the

British Indian palate. Most food historians believe the dish was created in the UK by an accommodating Indian chef. When his Indian chicken preparation was too dry for gravy-loving English tastes, the chef drowned the tandoori meat in sauce, creating a curry that sells tens of millions of servings every year. As of 2015, one of every five restaurants in the UK serves curry, and the most popular among them is chicken tikka masala.

What was once a cheap option for takeout has become a point of pride for Britain. Michelin stars and international honors now decorate the walls of

many Indian restaurants in the UK. The British Curry Awards, modeled after the American Academy Awards, is a televised black-tie affair that holds a distinguished place on the British social calendar (former prime minister David Cameron called them the "Curry Oscars"). Culinary luminaries, along with celebrities, come together to honor the best Indian restaurants in the UK. The neon-lit venue holds 2,000 esteemed guests, and the ceremony is syndicated around the world, from Europe to Australia, the Middle East to South Africa, where it's enjoyed by millions of curry fans.

A FABLED FISH HEAD PIE

STARGAZY PIE

Tom Bawcock's Eve, a Christmastime festival held in the Cornish seaside village of Mousehole, celebrates the night that Tom Bawcock, a 16th-century Mousehole folk hero, sailed out to fish despite dangerous storms. As the story goes, he returned with enough catch to end a local famine. In some versions of the tale, Bawcock brought along his cat, who helped calm the storm.

To honor the brave fisherman, revelers tuck into stargazy pie, a classic savory fish pie of potatoes, eggs, and white sauce, with the added flourish of intact fish heads (and sometimes tails) craning their necks through the crust, as though looking up at the stars. An anchovy-like fish called a pilchard is typically used, but really any small fish will do—so long as it has a head.

How to try it

Tom Bawcock's Eve is held annually on December 23. The Ship Inn, a historic pub perched on the edge of the harbor's wall, gives out free stargazy pie to celebrate the holiday, often doled out by a local fisherman dressed as Tom Bawcock.

A COFFEE BAR IN A VICTORIAN-ERA URINAL

THE ATTENDANT, FITZROVIA • ENGLAND

How to try it

The Attendant has other shops in London, but only the Fitzrovia location (27A Foley Street, London) has the urinals.

These ornate, underground urinals once served the Victorian gentlemen of London. Now they serve diners espresso, flat whites, and avocado toast. Walk down the stairs to take your seat at one of the full-size, porcelain urinals and sip your coffee among the most elite, historical toilets in Fitzrovia.

Originally built in the 1890s, these public toilets were closed in the 1960s. They sat boarded up for more than 50 years before being reimagined as an upscale coffee bar.

HEALTH MILK ON A BUDGET

ARTIFICIAL ASSES' MILK • ENGLAND

How to try it

Making artificial asses' milk has fallen out of fashion, but if you must, snail season starts in the summer.

Since antiquity, donkey milk has been used as a cure-all and cosmetic—by those who could afford it. Cleopatra was said to bathe in tubs full of asses' milk to preserve her skin. Hippocrates recommended donkey milk for a range of conditions, including liver problems and fever, and from the 1700s to the early 1900s, Europeans considered donkey milk a superfood that cured lung problems, blood problems, and even hysteria. Poet Alexander Pope drank donkey milk for his many health issues, writing in a 1717 letter, "I also drink asses' milk, upon which I will make no jokes tho' it be a fertile subject." The composition of asses' milk closely resembles human breast milk, and so orphanages and new parents found it a helpful supplement.

But asses' milk was not cheap, and those looking for an affordable alternative attempted to replicate the natural product. An 18th-century recipe for "Mock Asses Milk" begins with boiling barley in water, adding hartshorn (ground-up deer antlers), enrigo root (a thistle-like plant believed to soothe coughs), and a handful of snail shells, and then diluting the brew with cow's milk.

Snails show up in almost all the renditions of ersatz donkey milk—often tossed in whole. The "Mock Asses Milk" author included a finger-wagging note at the end of his recipe, saying, "You may leave out the snails if you don't like them, but it is best to use them."

The Knights Templar Longevity Diet

Graybeards were a rare sight in the 13th century. Male life expectancy—even for the wealthy—was just 31 years. For those who made it to their twenties, that number jumped to 48 years. The Knights Templar, then, were an extraordinary exception: Many members of the Catholic military order lived long past 60, and even then, they usually died at the hands of their enemies rather than from illness. While many believed the knights' longevity was bestowed upon them from above, modern research suggests the order's strict dietary rules could have been the vital force behind their health.

The knights, an order of renowned fighters, warriors, and jousters, are believed to have lived genuinely humble lives. Early in the 12th century, a long and complex rulebook called the Primitive Rule of the Templars established the knights' vows of poverty, chastity, and obedience. Knights were ordered to eat together silently, and table items were to be passed "quietly and privately . . . with all humility and submission." The men also ate in a kind of buddy system. Due to an alleged "shortage of bowls," two knights shared one eating vessel, and each man was ordered to monitor his eating partner, making sure he wasn't taking more than his share or eating too little. (As the order was notoriously rich, this bowl sharing was likely a demonstration of abstinence.)

Balancing the fasting demands of the devout and the nutritional requirements of active, military lives, the knights alternated days of meat eating and vegetarianism. Three days a week, the knights ate meat—usually beef, ham, or bacon— which was especially abundant on Sundays. Meatless days brought bread, milk, eggs, cheese, grains, and vegetable stews to the table. On Fridays the knights fasted, which meant land animals were replaced by fish. Their varied diet was supplemented with wine, served in moderate and diluted rations. By medieval standards, these practices put the knights at the apex of clean and sensible living, which extended their lifetimes well beyond what was considered, at the time, possible without divine intervention.

Jacques de Molay (ca. 1243–1314), last Grand Master of the Knights Templar.

DORMANT UNDERGROUND DAIRY

BOG BUTTER • IRELAND

How to try it

If you have a bog nearby, wrap some butter in a cheesecloth and towel, bury it, and leave it there for at least a few months. Remember to make a note of your burial site.

When digging up peat in rural Ireland, it's not uncommon to bump into a huge block of butter. Wrapped in animal skins or packed into a wooden or earthenware container, chances are the butter has been buried for hundreds of years, and while it might be too funky to actually be tasty, it's likely still safe to eat.

Bog butter is exactly what it sounds like: cow's milk butter buried in peat bogs. (It can also refer to underground beef tallow, but that's less common.) Bog butters are typically several hundred years old, but some have been around for multiple millennia: A 3,000-year-old bog butter was recently taste-tested and described as having an extremely moldy aftertaste.

The butter, of course, was not intended to be eaten centuries later. Bogs are cool, low in oxygen, and high in acidity, and therefore excellent places for preserving perishable items (also evidenced by the remarkably well-preserved human remains extracted from bogs). The bog was likely used as a refrigerator, and the owners of the butter never came to get it—or simply forgot where they left it. Other theories suggest that the butter was an offering to the gods or was being hidden from thieves and invaders. Whatever the reason, a lot of butter was abandoned in the bogs around Ireland and the UK and is still being found today. The older the butter, the funkier the flavor. Recently, there have been experiments that intentionally age butter in bogs. They found that if you let the butter bog age for just a few months, the taste can be pleasantly earthy, like good Parmesan cheese.

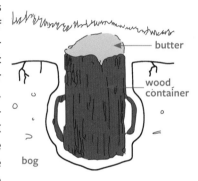

HONEYCOMB TOFFEE AND PURPLE SEAWEED

DULSE AND YELLOWMAN • NORTHERN IRELAND

How to try it

The Ould Lammas Fair typically occurs on the last Monday and Tuesday of August. The dulse and yellowman are sold separately and can be combined.

Before there was salted caramel popcorn or chocolate-covered pretzels, there was dulse and yellowman, an old-school sweet-and-salty treat sold at the Ould Lammas Fair in Ballycastle, the oldest fair in Northern Ireland, with roots in the 17th century.

Yellowman, the sweet half, is a golden, toffee-like honeycomb made from brown sugar, golden syrup, butter, vinegar, and baking soda. The last two ingredients create a carbon dioxide reaction, which gives the candy a unique crunchy and bubbly consistency. Smashed with a hammer, yellowman is usually sold in uneven shards.

Dulse, the salty counterpart, is a type of seaweed harvested at low tide along the coasts of Northern Ireland. Irish monks began harvesting this seaweed (an activity known as "dulsing") some 1,400 years ago. It can be eaten raw or tossed into soups, but most often dulse is dried in the sun and turned into chewy, reddish-purple seaweed chips.

Why these two became a classic combination is open to debate, but dulse and yellowman have been sold alongside each other for hundreds of years. A local shopkeeper and bog-oak carver named John Henry MacAuley memorialized their partnership in a ballad about the fair, which included the lines, "Did you treat your Mary Ann to some dulse and yellowman / At the Ould Lammas Fair in Ballycastle-O?"

A vendor sells yellowman at Lammas Fair.

AN EDIFICE TO AN ELITE FRUIT

DUNMORE PINEAPPLE HOUSE • SCOTLAND

On Christopher Columbus's second voyage to the Caribbean, in 1493, he and his men stumbled upon a deserted village on the island now known as Guadaloupe. They found a pile of fresh produce, among them the strange, impossibly sweet fruit that Columbus described as resembling a pinecone, with the sweet interior of an apple. Smitten, he brought the pineapple back to Spain, where Europeans quickly developed a passion for the tropical fruit.

Sugary foods and fresh fruits were a rarity in 16th-century England, and the pineapple became a highly sought-after item, not just for eating but for showing off. Only the richest and best connected had access to the exotic fruit, which had to be transported on long, blistering journeys across the ocean, and often spoiled before reaching port. By the 17th century, pineapples were in such demand that a thriving rental market emerged: A pineapple could be hired for a party, used as a centerpiece, then returned so it could be bought and eaten by someone wealthier. (An 18th-century pineapple cost about $8,000 in today's currency.) Ship captains also used the fruit as status symbols, displaying them outside their homes as a way to announce their return from exotic travels abroad.

The Pineapple House in Airth, Scotland, is perhaps the world's most extravagant proclamation of wealth and homecoming. John Murray, the fourth Earl of Dunmore, left his ancestral home in Scotland for the wilds of the colony of Virginia, where he became the last English governor of the region. When he returned to Scotland in 1776 (with a reputation for terrible diplomacy), he constructed a behemoth 45-foot (13.7 m) pineapple atop his mansion, announcing to his neighbors that he was home, and he was wealthy. The house may be a symbol of colonial excess but the masonry work is exceptional, full of artistic detail and technical merits, and in 1973 the house was restored by the National Trust for Scotland.

How to try it
The Dunmore Pineapple House is open to the public and available to rent for holidays. It sleeps four.

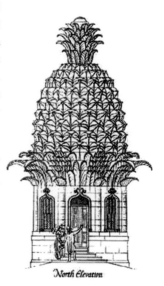

North Elevation

THE LEADING IRON SOFT DRINK

IRN-BRU • SCOTLAND

Originally called Iron Brew, the bright orange soda of Scotland was forced to change its name after World War II, when British legislation cracked down on food labeling. Suddenly, the words on packaging had to reflect what was actually inside, and the problem wasn't iron: The soda, which has a light but discernible taste of rust, contains .002% ammonium ferric citrate. The issue was that Iron Brew wasn't actually brewed, and so it became Irn-Bru. The sweet, creamy soda remains the most popular soft drink in Scotland, outselling even Coca-Cola.

That Irn-Bru contains iron is a point of pride for the drink. Advertisements, which have attracted controversy over the years, feature drinkers gaining muscleman strength and women shaving their newly grown beards. The blatantly false phrase "Made in Scotland from Girders" was used for years (the iron in Irn-Bru is a food additive). The drink has been compared to liquid bubble gum with a spicy aftertaste similar to ginger, although many devotees contend the flavor is impossible to describe faithfully. It's often called Scotland's other national drink because the beloved soda falls second only to whisky.

The equivalent of 20 cans of Irn-Bru is sold every second.

HAGGIS HURLING

THE WORLD HAGGIS HURLING CHAMPIONSHIP • SCOTLAND

A stuffed sheep's stomach soars through the air, spinning rapidly before thudding to the ground. The boiled exterior, free from any tears, still holds the contents crammed inside. It is a well-thrown haggis.

Haggis hurling is one of Scotland's stranger sports. Contestants climb atop a platform, usually an overturned whisky barrel, and lob a boiled sheep's stomach stuffed with sheep pluck (a sheep's heart, liver, and lungs), onion, oatmeal, suet, and spices. The goal is to throw the haggis, Scotland's national dish, as far as possible. Each haggis is inspected prior to hurling to ensure the food hasn't been enhanced with firming agents.

Haggis hurling as we know it today began when Robin Dunseath, an Irishman, placed a newspaper ad about reviving the "ancient sport" at the 1977 Gathering of the Clans (a two-week gathering of descendants from Scotland's various clans).

Dunseath alleged that the game arose from a 17th-century custom where women tossed haggis to their husbands while they worked in the bogs and the men caught the airborne puddings in their kilts.

Dunseath eventually became the president of the World Haggis Hurling Association and wrote an entire book, *The Complete Haggis Hurler*, about the sport's history. Decades later, he revealed the whole thing was a hoax—he originally placed the advertisement to gauge the gullibility of the Scots.

But his revelation didn't end the fun. Haggis hurling is still popular at Highland games and festivals throughout Scotland and countries with suitable numbers of Scots. The World Haggis Hurling Championship is held annually. The current world record belongs to Lorne Coltart, who managed a 217-foot (66 m) throw at the Milngavie Highland Games in 2011. Dunseath, meanwhile, has distanced himself from the sport he invented and has said that he finds it surreal that people—gullible or not—still hurl haggis.

A competitor at the 2015 World Haggis Hurling Championship.

The Village Sin Eater: The Worst Freelance Gig in History

When a loved one died in parts of England, Scotland, or Wales in the 18th and 19th centuries, decorum required that the family place bread on the chest of the deceased, then call upon a paid professional to absolve the departed of all worldly transgressions. This professional was not a priest, but the local sin eater, whose job it was to eat the chest bread and, with it, all the misdeeds of the deceased.

This was not a metaphorical service. The family who hired the sin eater believed that the bread literally soaked up their loved one's sins, and once it had been eaten, all the misdeeds were passed to the hired hand. The sin eater's soul was considered sullied with the depravities of countless men and women, and although the service was distasteful, it was also an essential step in getting loved ones to heaven.

The literal price of absorbing a lifetime of sin wasn't much better. For each service, the sin eater made a mere four English pence, the equivalent of a few US dollars today. Those who were willing to risk their souls were very poor, but perhaps they were on to something else: The bread and ale they were required to consume, while technically representative of sin, was still a free meal of bread and ale.

The origins of sin eating are murky, but the practice likely grew from older religious traditions. Historically, scholars believed it came from pagan rituals, but some academics now think it developed from a medieval custom: Before a funeral, nobles once gave food to the poor in exchange for prayers on behalf of the deceased. Symbolic breads like the ones eaten on All Souls' Day, which represent the dead and are eaten by the living, may also connect to sin eating.

The last known sin eater in the United Kingdom was Richard Munslow, who took on the role after losing his three children to whooping cough. He died in 1906. Nearly 100 years later, he was commemorated with a churchyard ceremony and a proper funeral of his own.

WELSHMAN'S CAVIAR

BARA LAWR • WALES

How to try it

Try laverbread toast as part of a Full Welsh breakfast at the Pettigrew Tea Rooms in Cardiff. (The rest of the Full Welsh: sausage, bacon, egg, mushrooms, tomatoes, baked beans, and black pudding.)

Laverbread, or bara lawr in Welsh, might be the only "bread" you can spread on toast.

The thick, sticky, and nutritious goop is made by boiling laver, a green-black seaweed that grows along the Welsh coastline. Packed with protein and minerals, especially iron and iodine, the seaweed has a briny flavor akin to oysters or olives. You can eat the seaweed raw, but most prefer the taste after it's been boiled for about six hours and then kneaded into a paste (the kneading may be the reason it's called laverbread). The resulting spread tastes of the sea, salty and crisp.

Whether fried in bacon fat, mixed with oatmeal into laverbread cakes, or simply spread on a slice of toast, bara lawr is an essential part of a full Welsh breakfast.

This former food of last resort for early Welshmen is now a point of pride. Welsh actor Richard Burton called this local delicacy "Welshman's caviar." In 2017, the European Commission bestowed the humble laverbread with a protected-food designation, which it shares with iconic food and drink like Parma ham and champagne.

Wild laver growing at Freshwater West, a beach in Pembrokeshire, Wales.

WESTERN EUROPE

THE CASTLE BEER SPA

STARKENBERGER BEER POOLS • AUSTRIA

Inside the 700-year-old castle owned by Austrian brewer Starkenberger, you can enjoy a complete beer-centric experience with beer trivia, beer history, beer drinking, and the natural extension of these activities: bathing in beer.

The seven 13-foot-deep pools each contain some 42,000 pints of warm beer (and some water). Bathers can sit and relax, fully immersed in ale, which is rich in vitamins and calcium—said to soothe the skin and help cure open wounds and psoriasis.

The pools opened in 2005 when the old fermentation cellar of the 700-year-old castle became obsolete. The beer pool is kept quite hot, so order a cold one while you soak. Drinking from the pool is ill-advised.

How to try it

Starkenberger Castle is located in Tarrenz, in western Austria, perched at the top of a hill. At about $300 for a two-hour session, bathing in beer isn't exactly affordable, but it's considerably cheaper than the 42,000-pint DIY option.

The walls of the spa feature painted murals.

INTERNATIONAL COLLECTION OF SOURDOUGH STARTERS

SOURDOUGH LIBRARY • BELGIUM

Hidden inside a Belgian baking corporation's research center is a sourdough library: 107 sourdough starters kept alive and fed to preserve the biodiversity of bread. Glass-door fridges line the walls, the Mason jar samples displayed almost jewel-like, two to a shelf. Karl De Smedt, who has run the library since 2013, knows the story behind each starter. His quest is to find and identify as many sourdough starters as possible. And according to Mr. De Smedt, he is the world's only sourdough librarian.

The starters on the shelves are leavened naturally, with living yeasts and bacteria from their home environments. When part of the starter is added to flour and water and baked, it results in a loaf of sourdough bread. Before the rise of commercial yeasts some 160 years ago, most of the world's bread was made with starters. Depending on the microbes in the ingredients, the air, and even on the baker's hands, each starter has the potential to produce a uniquely flavored loaf.

De Smedt regularly travels to add starters to the collection, which currently contains samples from approximately 20 countries including Japan, Hungary, China, and Italy. Each was made by different people and with different ingredients, from juice to holy water. Every few months, the starters are fed with flour from their home bakeries so that their microbial makeups don't change too much. Regular feedings can keep bacteria colonies alive indefinitely, so some starters have illustrious histories that can be traced back decades. In De Smedt's library, for example, there are starters sourced from the descendants of Yukon gold miners, who used the bubbling mix to make bread and flapjacks for hungry miners.

How to try it

The Sourdough Library, located in St. Vith, Belgium, is not open to the public. However, if you reach out to Karl De Smedt on social media (his Instagram is @the_sourdough_librarian), he's known to give tours.

A HEDONISTIC GAUNTLET

MARATHON DU MÉDOC • FRANCE

Runners competing in the annual Marathon du Médoc must complete a 26.2-mile (42.2 km) run in the September heat, while wearing a costume not intended for racing, and stopping along the way to drink 23 glasses of wine and nibble on local specialties like foie gras, oysters, steak, and ice cream. Many of the runners even begin the race hungover: The night before, it's tradition to partake in a "pasta party" that features copious amounts of local wine.

The 10,000 or so participants dressed as Smurfs, adult babies, grapes, and hula dancers traverse a stunning landscape of vineyards, stopping at designated chateaus to eat and imbibe. Along the route there are bands and orchestras playing music where runners can pause for a dance break and lakes to jump in for cooling off. During breaks, racers drink water and pop Imodium to stabilize their weakening constitutions, which doesn't always do the trick. All that bouncing shellfish and bordeaux leads to frequent sightings of cartoon characters vomiting along the side of the road, then starting up again.

The idea is to finish, not to win. The race lasts for six and a half hours and a common technique is to use the full amount of time to enjoy the journey as much as possible. Still, running 26 miles is never an easy feat. Even when emboldened by liquid courage, it's best to channel the wisdom found on a sign once seen along the course: "Pain is just the French word for bread."

The costumed, culinary marathon runs through the Médoc wine region before the grape harvest.

THE INSCRUTABLE LIQUEUR OF LIFE

GREEN CHARTREUSE • FRANCE

In 1084 CE, St. Bruno of Cologne formed an order of silent monks called the Carthusians. They resided in a valley of the Chartreuse Mountains, a region of the French Alps near Voiron. By 1605, they were a large, well-respected order, and King Henri IV's Marshal of Artillery presented the Carthusians with an ancient alchemical manuscript for an elixir that would prolong life.

After looking over the document, even the most learned of monks were at a loss. The concoction called for 130 different plants. It required advanced distillation, infusion, and maceration techniques. No one attempted the recipe until 1737, and even then, it's assumed the monastery's apothecary took creative liberties.

A lone monk delivered the first bottles of the potent herbal tonic (which was 69 percent alcohol) to surrounding villages by mule. In 1764, the Carthusians adapted the recipe into a milder liqueur called Green Chartreuse. The update, which was still potent at 55 percent alcohol, is the version we consume today: herbaceous and sweet with sinus-clearing heat. The monks themselves recommend serving it cold, either chilled or on the rocks.

Despite increasing demand, the order has continued the tradition of having just two monks handle the entire process, passing down the recipe through the generations. Today, only Dom Benoît and Brother Jean-Jacques know all the ingredients and how to turn them into the beloved vegetal liqueur. Once they've readied a batch, they age it in huge oak casks inside the world's longest liqueur cellar. Several years later, the same men test the product and decide if it's ready for bottling.

Champagne Was Once an Energy Drink

On July 24, 1908, the London Olympic marathon went down in history as one hell of a race: Fifty-five runners started off from Windsor Castle, but only 27 made it to the finish line. The majority of runners quit before the halfway mark, and a number of them were drunk.

Before the mid-20th century, brandy, champagne, and strychnine (best known now as rat poison) were thought to be performance enhancers, a tradition with roots in ancient Greece and imperial China. The drinks were doled out to endurance athletes by trainers, who often followed behind in cars or on bicycles, as a midrace boost. Alcohol was commonly accompanied by drugs, such as heroin and cocaine, to dull pain and increase aggressiveness. Stimulant drugs ran unchecked until the 1920s, while alcohol was used all the way into the '80s. (Champagne was especially revered for its rejuvenating effervescence.)

Irish-American Olympian Johnny Hayes crossing the finish line to de facto victory.

At the 1908 Olympic marathon, however, the potent draughts proved unreliable. Twenty-year-old Canadian runner Tom Longboat, the favorite to win, fell victim to the brutal summer heat and, at mile 17, turned to champagne. Two miles later, he collapsed and was out of the race. Meanwhile South African Charles Hefferon took a massive four-minute lead, but two miles from the finish line he also accepted champagne, which caused such intense stomach pain he let two runners pass and finished third.

At the finish line, 80,000 spectators watched as the front-runner, Italian pastry chef Dorando Pietri, reeled toward the end. In the last quarter mile alone, an exhausted and dazed Pietri had collapsed five times, had run in the wrong direction, and had his heart massaged by concerned medics. Worry for Pietri's life resulted in a doctor supporting him across the finish line, causing his eventual disqualification and a redistribution of the race's medals. Some say Pietri was simply drunk, while others believe both he and Longboat were suffering from strychnine poisoning.

But not all the boozed runners fared poorly. De facto gold medalist Johnny Hayes admitted to an energizing gargle of brandy during the race, and bronze medalist Joseph Forshaw also turned to brandy in order to treat a stubborn side stitch. At the time, trainers believed that dehydration was better treated with wine than water (the 1924 Paris Games stocked its rehydration stations with glasses of wine), which is a theory that has since been dismantled by science, along with a mess of soused runners.

24-HOUR MOLLUSKS

OYSTER VENDING MACHINE • FRANCE

How to try it

The oyster vending machine is located at La Maison Neuve on Ars-en-Ré. It accepts credit cards.

There are a wide variety of oyster shops on France's Île de Ré, but none stay open throughout the night. Oyster farmers Brigitte and Tony Berthelot, whose shop L'Huîtrière de Ré is open six days a week, make their mollusks available at all hours with a vending machine that dispenses fresh oysters 24/7 next to their shop.

The vending machine was specially fitted for oysters, which are available in packages of two to five dozen. A dozen oysters runs about $8, which is the same price as next door at their store. (For safety and health reasons, all oysters are sold closed.) Customers who order ahead of time can text their request to the store and have their order placed in the vending machine, where it can be retrieved with a personalized code. With this option, they can add on other grocery items like pâté and sea asparagus, which will be waiting beside their oysters.

COCAINE-LACED WINE

VIN MARIANI • FRANCE

How to try it

The days of cocaine-laced bordeaux are over, but try regular bordeaux—it's very good.

In 1859, Italian scientist Paolo Mantegazza published a paper on the potential benefits of a little-studied South American plant called coca. Inspired by the findings, a French chemist named Angelo Mariani invented a potent tonic—bordeaux wine spiked with 6 milligrams of coca leaf per ounce.

Vin Mariani became a smash hit in Paris, then spread throughout Europe and the United States. This was due in part to Mariani's aggressive marketing campaign, which involved commissioning famous artists to design advertisements. An endorsement from the pope didn't hurt, either. The pontiff praised the fortifying effects of the tonic wine "when prayer was insufficient." Throngs of celebrities—from Ulysses S. Grant and Thomas Edison to Queen Victoria, Henrik Ibsen, and Jules Verne, sang the praises of Vin Mariani. And a volume of *Medical News* from 1890 confirms that "no recognized medical preparation has received stronger endorsement at the hands of the medical profession."

Vin Mariani was potent stuff. When cocaine and alcohol are imbibed together, a third chemical compound, called cocaethylene, forms as the intoxicants are metabolized in the liver. This intense psychoactive is more euphoric, powerful, and toxic than cocaine or alcohol alone.

In this 1899 advertisement, Pope Leo XIII endorsed the popular cocaine wine.

Mariani, hailed as the world's first cocaine millionaire, didn't stop with wine. He made coke-laced teas, throat lozenges, cigarettes, and even a signature spread called Mariani margarine.

But all parties must come to an end. In 1906, the United States began enforcing labeling regulations, and the dangers of cocaine became more widely known. A coca-less version of Vin Mariani was produced in the United States, but it lost sales to a competing beverage that was also originally based on coca: Coca-Cola.

THE WORLD'S LARGEST FRESH FOOD MARKET

RUNGIS MARKET• FRANCE

Five miles south of Paris, in a suburb called Rungis, lies a little-known epicenter of international gastronomy. Occupying about 578 acres, Rungis Market has a seafood section the size of a soccer field, a fromage pavilion with hundreds of different cheeses, ceiling-high towers of lettuce and oranges, and a department specifically for game meat. Beyond the onslaught of groceries, there are also 19 restaurants, a bank, a post office, a hotel, gas stations, and the market's own police force.

It takes about 13,000 workers to run Rungis Market, many of whom are second- or third-generation vendors. Work begins around midnight, with the various departments opening their doors beginning at 2 a.m. (Seafood opens first, fruits and vegetables last at 5 a.m.)

A version of this market has existed since the 5th century, but the location has changed throughout time. In 1135, Louis VI moved it from the banks of the Seine to Paris's city center, where it became the famed Les Halles. It remained in Les Halles until 1969, when it moved to its current location in Rungis.

How to try it
To visit the market you'll need to book a tour, which often includes breakfast at Rungis. Shopping requires a buyer's card, which costs an annual fee.

More than one million tons of fruits and vegetables pass through the Rungis Market each year.

HAND CHEESE WITH MUSIC

HANDKÄSE MIT MUSIK • GERMANY

How to try it
Try the Frankfurt restaurant Lohrberg-Schänke, which serves hand cheese along with other Hessian specialties.

Handkäse mit Musik is a specialty of the southern Hesse region, where slices of the handmade rounds (hence the name "hand cheese") are paired with tart Apfelwein, or apple cider. Buttered bread is a popular vehicle for the translucent, smelly cheese, along with a smear of onion and a sprinkle of caraway seeds.

Locals say that after eating this cheese, the music comes later—a nod to the flatulence that accompanies eating raw onions.

Beyond stinky-cheese lovers and fart-joke enthusiasts, Handkäse mit Musik has gained a strong following of dieters, bodybuilders, and runners. The cheese is high in protein, low in fat, and really gets digestion moving.

SPAGHETTI ICE-CREAM SUNDAE

SPAGHETTIEIS • GERMANY

How to try it
Dario Fontanella's family ice-cream parlor is still going strong. You can eat the original Spaghettieis at Eis Fontanella in Mannheim.

Telling a kid they're getting ice cream and giving them a plate of dinner food instead will likely result in outrage and despair. Unless the plate is Spaghettieis—an ice-cream replica of Italy's national dish and a ubiquitous German treat.

Dario Fontanella, the man responsible for this ice-cream artifice, was the son of a northern Italian immigrant who arrived in Mannheim, Germany, in the 1930s and eventually opened an ice-cream parlor. In 1969, Fontanella decided to honor his family's homeland with dessert.

Fontanella re-created an iconic bowl of spaghetti, tomato sauce, and parmesan cheese by feeding vanilla gelato through a chilled spaetzle press. This device extruded thin strands of ice cream shaped just like the egg noodles it was designed to produce. Fontanella placed his ice-cream "spaetzle" on a bed of whipped cream and topped it with strawberry "tomato" sauce and white chocolate "parmesan" shavings. A wafer or cookie on the side mimicked a piece of Italian bread.

Today, the dessert is so well-known that no German child would think twice before diving into a bowl of the faux-spaghetti. And even though Fontanella was awarded the Bloomaulorden—the highest citizen's award in Mannheim—he never patented the creation. As a result, just about every German ice-cream parlor makes some version of the frozen delight. Outside the country, the sundae that masquerades as dinner remains relatively unknown and can still trick children.

A SHRINE TO VOLCANIC TOMATO PASTE

TOMATO INDUSTRIAL MUSEUM • GREECE

When the Vlychada tomato-paste factory opened in 1945, Santorini was still a sleepy island. There was no electricity; coal powered the machinery, and seawater was pumped in to wash and steam the tomatoes. Farmers reached the factory on foot, leading mules carrying woven baskets full of tomatoes. The factory was a gathering place for islanders, who took immense pride in the singular tomatoes produced from their soil.

Domati Santorini may look like standard cherry tomatoes, but they are uniquely marked by the island's climate and geology. Santorini sits on an active volcano, which erupted in 1646 BCE and covered the island in rich volcanic ash. The local tomato's sweet flavor, intense aroma, and thin skin come from these ancient nutrients, along with its ability to thrive with minimal water. (Like many crops on the dry island, they pull the moisture they need from the morning mist and require no irrigation.) The already concentrated flavor makes exceptional paste, or pelte, and tomato factories flourished from the 1920s to 1970s. The tomato business has since declined, but the iconic crop is still a pillar of Santorini cuisine and its heyday has been memorialized at the Tomato Industrial Museum.

Despite the dreary name, the museum's exhibits give insight into a lost side of the island, before tourism became the main industry. Beyond processing equipment and historical materials, the museum shows interviews of elderly former factory workers telling stories about a bygone era, which you can watch while eating bruschetta and sipping a glass of local wine.

How to try it
Guided tours run every 30 minutes and are included with the €5 admission. Also included is entrance to the contemporary art gallery next door.

A RARE AND NAMELESS SEAFOOD

FRIED OCTOPUS INK SACS • GREECE

The small, mountainous island of Kalymnos has some of the best, most obscure seafood in all of Greece, and fried octopus ink sacs might be the most unknowable of them all. Not only is this dish difficult to find, it has no official name.

The key to a good fried ink sac is to avoid puncturing it so that it holds its delicate shape and retains most of the ink inside. After briefly boiling it to harden the skin, chefs carefully cover the nugget in flour and lightly fry it in olive oil. Typically seasoned with just salt and pepper, the texture is like thick oatmeal, while the flavor has the rich gaminess of chicken liver.

The ink sacs are a part of Kalymnos's long history of embracing offal. When sea-sponge harvesting was the island's main industry, divers would be at sea for months and subsisted on every part of the fish they captured. Although the industry has been greatly diminished by sponge disease outbreaks, the divers' food philosophy has left its mark on local cuisine. A search through the island's fish markets and tavernas will reveal the likes of two-pound octopus roe, parrotfish intestines, and sea squirts preserved in saltwater.

How to try it
Sink your teeth into some ink sacs at O Sfouggaras, a beachfront restaurant in the southern Kalymnos village of Vlichadia.

TOM CARVEL

(1906–1990)

When listing the innovations of the Greeks—among them philosophy, geometry, alarm clocks, and the Olympics—soft-serve ice cream doesn't come readily to mind. But Tom Carvel, born in Athens as Thomas Karvelas, is the man behind this iconic invention.

An immigrant, Carvel lived on New York City's Lower East Side and scraped together a frugal living shining shoes, fixing cars, and drumming in a Dixieland band. At the age of 26, a doctor found a tubercular spot on his lung and gave him three months to live. In search of fresh air, Carvel borrowed $15 from his future wife, Agnes, and fled to upstate New York to live out his few remaining days selling ice cream from the back of a truck.

On Memorial Day weekend in 1934, two years after his diagnosis, a flat tire forced Carvel to pull off to the side of the road, derailing his plans to sell cold treats on one of the busiest ice-cream days of the season. But passing cars mistook him for a roadside stand and stopped for ice cream, delighted by the unique texture of his melting desserts. Business was better than usual, and so Carvel decided to stay put, striking an agreement with the pottery store next door for use of their electricity. In 1936, Carvel was still alive and still selling his (slightly melted) ice cream, so he expanded into the pottery store, which remained a Carvel shop for 72 years.

Taking hold of his second chance at life, Carvel went to work. Distilling knowledge he gained while working in Army post exchanges during World War II, Carvel built his own machinery. He engineered a system that used a short icy barrel, where cream would freeze instantly along the wall, with sharp blades that would scrape the cold cream into soft ribbons. And although ice cream was his medium, he is perhaps best known as the "father of franchising." He began peddling fully built stores, which included training, equipment, recipes, and his trademark.

Carvel became the unlikely mascot of his growing ice-cream empire. He was known for a deep, gravelly, attention-grabbing voice, described as "terrible, but mouthwatering," which he broadcast widely through the radio commercials he famously performed live and unscripted. For decades, Carvel was one of the best-known voices in advertising, doling out ad-libbed commentary on achieving the American Dream. He is credited with the invention of not just soft-serve, but also the ice-cream cake, the "buy one get one" coupon, and a College of Ice Cream Knowledge. He held more than 300 patents, copyrights, and trademarks.

When Carvel died in 1990, there were approximately 800 ice-cream stores operating under his name, and by most accounts, he'd made a triumphant exit (he'd recently sold his business for $80 million). But scandal surrounds the octogenarian's passing. Carvel's niece, Pamela, and his widow, Agnes, spent two decades in court battles against the president and vice president of Carvel's foundation and trust—whom Pamela accused of murdering her uncle with poison. Although much of the proceedings ended inconclusively (Pamela's request for the body to be exhumed was denied), Carvel's legacy remains formidable—his ice-cream powerhouse is still thriving in his adopted country.

LSD NIGHTMARE FISH

n Arabic, it is known as "the fish that makes dreams," which is a mild way of describing the visions the salema porgy is capable of inducing. Certain porgies contain a toxin known to trigger several days of vivid, sometimes frightening hallucinations, which scientists equate with the effects of taking LSD.

The potent silvery sea bream lives off Africa's east coast and throughout the Mediterranean. Ancient Romans supposedly used the fish as a recreational drug, while Polynesians employed its psychedelic powers during ceremonies. The effects can last for days and can include dark, demonic hallucinations. A 2006 study published in *Clinical Toxology* examined two cases of men who ate salema porgy on the French Riviera. One man had auditory hallucinations of "human screams and bird squealing." The other "was not able to drive anymore as he was seeing giant arthropods around his car."

Scientists understand very little about the forces at work behind the fish's hallucinogenic side effect, which is officially known as ichthyoallyeinotoxism. One theory is that it's the result of something in the phytoplankton they eat. There might also be seasonal influences at play: The 2006 study reports that levels of the trip-inducing toxin are highest during autumn, but most poisonings happen in late spring and summer. Further complicating things is that most salema porgy aren't hallucinogenic at all, and those that are lack uniform poison distribution. The head is a common psychedelic source, but some sections are toxin-free, and unfortunately you won't know for sure until you're chasing enormous spiders from your car.

How to try it

Salema porgy is available throughout the Mediterranean, particularly around the French Riviera.

From the outside, you can't tell which of these porgies will give you nightmares.

||||||||||||||||||||||||||||||||||||||||||||||||||||||||||||||||||||||||||||||||||||||||||||||||||||||||||||||||||||||||||||||

Unicorn Horns

···

The Whimsical Way to Test for Poison

For centuries the great minds of Europe, from Aristotle to Leonardo da Vinci, believed unicorns were real. So did physicians, who claimed the pure white horn of the unicorn could detect poison—a valuable tool at a time when illnesses and ailments were often chalked up to poisoning. The theory went that the horn, when dipped in food or wine, would smoke or sweat if it came in contact with poison.

By the Middle Ages, the unicorn horn was the must-have item among the royal and the royally rich (especially those with enemies). But how did they get a unicorn horn in a world without unicorns?

For years, the Vikings held the secret: Out sailing in Arctic waters, they hunted narwhal whales for their single ivory tooth, which grew up to nine feet in length and swirled, tapering to a point. Back ashore, the Vikings sold the tusks as unicorn horns, and by the 12th century, the twisted shape of the narwhal tusk was the accepted image of a unicorn's magical extremity.

Rare and irrationally expensive, "unicorn horns" became both status symbol and mystical tool. Lorenzo de Medici owned a narwhal tusk that was worth 6,000 gold coins, while Queen Elizabeth I reportedly received one worth £10,000 (the price of an entire castle). Danish rulers were once crowned on a "unicorn horn" throne, which is still on display at Copenhagen's Rosenborg Castle. Remarkably, there was not a single case of a horn smoking, sweating, or detecting poison, which did not deter the booming, centuries-long unicorn horn trade.

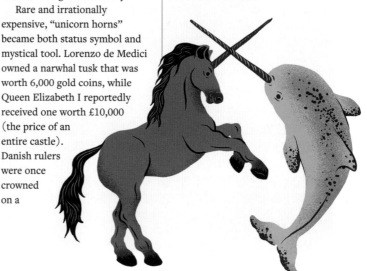

RENAISSANCE WINE WINDOWS

BUCHETTE DEL VINO • ITALY

How to try it

According to Florence's Wine Windows Association, there are 152 visible wine windows in the center of the city, which can be found by using the association's interactive map. To make use of a functioning wine window, visit Babae, located at Via Santo Spirito 21/R.

Around the city of Florence, be on the lookout for small windows along the street level, most of them plastered over and painted. Called "buchette del vino" in Italian, these sealed-up portals were once used for the easy distribution of Italy's favorite beverage, and hence their name: wine windows.

In 1559, Cosimo de' Medici decreed that noble families could sell wine from their vineyards directly from their palaces. Anyone on the street could knock on the windows built into the facades of the Renaissance palaces, asking for wine service. A servant would take the customer's empty bottle and their payment, refill the bottle in the cellar, and pass it back to the street.

When bubonic plague swept through the city in the 17th century, the system became even more valuable. The windows allowed vendors to sell wine without hazardous hand-to-hand or face-to-face contact. At a time when drinking water was often contaminated with disease, wine was prized for being both sanitary and medicinal.

By the 20th century, the buchette del vino had fallen from favor, but several windows have recently reopened in a new era of social distancing. Babae, for example, a restaurant in Florence's Santo Spirito neighborhood, revived its centuries-old wine window and safely dispenses glasses of red.

The Wine Window Association has placed plaques beneath some of Florence's prominent buchette del vino.

MAGGOT PECORINO

CASU MARZU • ITALY

You slice into a wheel of perfectly aged pecorino, peel back the top, and find a wriggling mass of maggots. If it's casu marzu, all is going according to plan.

"Rotting cheese" in Sardinian, casu marzu is the product of larvae-driven fermentation. Cheese makers initiate the process by cutting a small hole in a wheel of sheep's milk cheese and leaving it outside. Flies—*Piophila casei*, to be exact—slip in through the opening and lay eggs. After the larvae hatch, their excretions break down the cheese's fats and proteins, creating a soft, creamy texture.

When the gooey liquid known as lagrimas ("tears") leaks through the rind, the cheese is ready to eat. It is pungent and sharp, a bit like ripe gorgonzola, with a mild acidity left in the larvae's wake.

Even though the creamy hunk of cheese might look harmless, approach with caution. As *The Science of Cheese* points out, "Cheese skippers [maggots] are able to jump a few inches, so consumers are advised to protect their eyes" when unsealing the wheel.

Sure, a maggot to the eye would be unfortunate, but the larvae can do far more damage to your insides if they're alive when eaten— including pain, nausea, and vomiting. But you can't just buy cheese with the maggots already dead; that's a sign it's gone bad. The solution? Plenty of people take the risk and eat the live maggots. Alternatively, they mash them to death and smear the cheese on pane carasau, a type of flatbread. Or they seal a piece of cheese in a zipped plastic bag. When the sound of pattering maggots stops, it's snack time.

Although casu marzu is the most famous maggot-infused cheese, it's not the only one. Elsewhere in Italy, there's marcetto in Abruzzo, casu du quagghiu in Calabria, saltarello friulano in Friuli, and cacie' punt in Molise.

How to try it

Due to health risks, casu marzu's legal status is murky (it's banned in the EU), so you've got to do some sleuthing to find it. A simple inquiry at a Sardinian cheese shop will usually point you in the right direction.

|||||||||||||||||||||||||||||||||||||||||||||||||||||||||||||||||||||||||||||||||||||||||||||||||||||||||||||||||||||||||||||||||||||||||

The Gladiator Diet

What epitomizes the Western ideal male physique more than the Roman gladiator? Lean and rippling with muscle, gladiators are portrayed in classical art and contemporary pop culture as specimens of corporeal perfection—when in reality their abdominals and pectorals were likely covered in a quivering layer of subcutaneous fat.

The excavation of a 2,000-year-old gladiator grave, which housed the bones of 67 fighters, showed that gladiators carb-loaded. Using a technique called isotopic analysis, Viennese researchers tested the gladiators' skeletal remains for elements such as calcium and zinc and found the fighters ate little meat, but plenty of carbohydrates and calcium. Their findings were confirmed by Pliny's *Natural History*, where gladiators are referred to by the nickname *hordearii* ("barley eaters").

According to the researchers, the largely vegetarian diet was not the result of poverty, but a way to improve gladiators' performance on the battlefield. Weight-adding foods such as carbohydrates provided a layer of bodily protection, which meant nerve endings would be less exposed and bleeding cuts less perilous. As an added benefit, the extra protective layer of fat created a more satisfying spectacle: Flesh wounds would gush blood, but the gladiator could keep on fighting.

Like modern athletes, gladiators also took calcium supplements. They drank potent brews made of charred plant or bone ash; the calcium level in their bones was exorbitant compared with the bones of average citizens.

Before a big gladiator game, fighters were sometimes invited to a celebratory banquet, where they had the rare opportunity to eat more decadent foods, such as meat. But attending these banquets was also a risk, as drunk and disorderly hosts and guests were liable to start the bloodshed early, and in the pursuit of entertainment, some gladiators lost their lives before the competition officially began.

THREADS OF GOD

SU FILINDEU • ITALY

How to try it

Book a trip to Sardinia during the Feast of San Francisco in May and October. Don't forget your walking shoes.

Twice a year, pilgrims in Sardinia trek from the city of Nuoro to the village of Lula under cover of night. They walk in solidarity, forgoing sleep and shelter—sometimes by the hundreds, sometimes by the thousands. Twenty miles later, at the entrance of Santuario di San Francisco, they reach their destination.

These seekers persist not to find the sanctuary itself, but to eat what may be the rarest pasta in the world. Su filindeu—literally "threads of God" in Sardinian—is unfathomably intricate. It's made by only three women on Earth, all from the same Sardinian family, who work every day to produce and stock enough pasta to feed the pilgrims who arrive, just twice a year, for the Feast of San Francesco. In Nuoro, this tradition has been passed down through the women of the Abraini family for nearly 300 years.

The ingredients are simple: semolina wheat, water, and salt. The serving preparation is similarly uncomplicated: gamy mutton broth and a helping of tangy pecorino cheese. Making the pasta, however, is nearly impossible. Engineers from the Barilla pasta company attempted, unsuccessfully, to build a machine that could reproduce the technique. Celebrity chef Jamie Oliver also visited Sardinia in hopes of mastering the elusive noodle. After two hours, he gave up.

Paola Abraini, the current matriarch of the su filindeu tradition, says the hardest

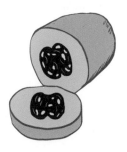

part is "understanding the dough with your hands." She kneads the mixture until it feels like modeling clay, then separates it into smaller pieces and works them into cylinders. If the semolina lacks elasticity, she dips her fingers in a bowl of salt water. If it feels dry, unsalted water does the trick. The balance, says Abraini, can take years to understand. She should know, because she's been at it for more than 40.

When the consistency reaches perfection, Abraini stretches the dough in the air like an accordion, then doubles it and pulls again. With each pull the strands multiply, growing increasingly thin. After eight pulls, she's left with 256 wispy threads. She gingerly stretches the fine pasta across a circular wooden frame, crisscrossing three layers of noodles to form an intricate "woven" pattern. After the su filindeu dries in the sun, it's broken into square pieces and put aside for the pilgrims.

Paola Abraini, matriarch of the only family that can make su filindeu, displays her mastery.

SMUGGLER'S SALAMI

CACIOCAVALLO DELL'EMIGRANTE • ITALY

Imagine it's the early 20th century. You're leaving your hometown in southern Italy, about to board a ship that will take you thousands of miles across the Atlantic to build a new life in the United States. Naturally, you begin to think about comfort foods. In the New Country, you'll want your beloved cheese and cured pork. The cheese is easy, permitted to freely cross into America. But how will you bring the soppressata, when meat is banned from entering the country? A group of migrants from Vallo di Diano in Salerno managed to solve the riddle: You hide the pork inside the cheese.

Caciocavallo dell'emigrante, literally the "caciocavallo of the migrant," is the ingenious method of concealing one illegal delicious thing (spicy pork soppressata) inside a second—legal—delicious thing (a ball of caciocavallo cheese). The name of the cheese, which refers to a cavallo ("horse"), derives from the traditional cheese-making technique of hanging it in pairs, linked by a rope that resembles reins.

Today, there are only a handful of cheese makers who still create this contraband cheese-salami ball, following a recipe that has been handed down, mostly orally, across generations.

How to try it
Depending on your country's meat-import regulations, you might be able to order caciocavallo of the migrant from Italian retailers online. But for the real thing, you'll need to go to Salerno.

SICILY'S MANNA BAKERY

FIASCONARO • ITALY

How to try it
Fiasconaro is located in Castelbuono's Piazza Margherita. It ships its panettone all over the world, but those able to visit the bakery are rewarded generously with samples.

For centuries, scholars have debated the origins of manna, the mysterious substance that, according to the Bible, God provided as food for the Israelites while they traveled through the desert. But in Pollina, a region in the Madonie mountains of Sicily, there's no debate: Manna is the dried sap of *Fraxinus angustifolia*, the narrow-leaf ash tree. A substance with ancient roots, manna has been cultivated in Sicily since around the ninth century, when Arabs introduced the practice of collecting the ash tree's resin. Today, manna is collected by a small handful of producers, many of them over the age of 70, during a fleeting harvest window at the end of summer. With the advent of cheap sugar and modernization, it's a tradition in decline, but a local sweet shop is working to put manna back on the map.

Fiasconaro is an artisan bakery in the town of Castelbuono. Among its specialties is a panettone—Italy's traditional Christmas bread—drenched in manna icing. Sicilian manna has a delicate, natural sweetness some describe as a cross between honey and maple syrup. The biblical substance, all sourced by hand from the region's harvest, also flavors the bakery's gelato and a thick, spreadable cream that's well worth a culinary pilgrimage.

Manna drips from incisions on a narrow-leaf ash tree.

A VERY DISTRACTING EASTER CAKE

CASSATA SICILIANA • ITALY

How to try it
Pasticceria Oscar in Palermo makes an excellent traditional Cassata Siciliana.

Sicilians have a proverb: *Tintu è cu nun mancia a cassata a matina ri Pasqua*, or "Sad is the one who does not eat cassata on Easter morning." Cassata Siciliana is the superstar of Sicilian Easter, an elegant, baroque-style confection with a liqueur-soaked sponge cake, layers of sweetened ricotta, pistachio-tinted marzipan, white glaze, and colorful candied fruit. Traditionally served at Easter, the cake is a decadent way to break the Lenten fast.

Nuns, who began the tradition of making cassata for Easter, were the first to experience the beguiling power of the delicious cake. In 1574, nuns at a convent in the Sicilian village of Mazara del Vallo liked making and eating the cake so much that they neglected their prayers, and the local diocese banned cassata making during Holy Week.

The version enjoyed today was invented by Salvatore Guli, a 19th-century Palermo baker who added marzipan and colorful decorative swirls to the cake's exterior—taking inspiration from the nuns of Palermo's Martorana convent, who famously made marzipan that resembled fruits. The flavors that make cassata Siciliana so uniquely delicious show-case the island's multicultural history. Sugar, almonds, lemons, and oranges came from ancient Arab influence. The sponge cake came from Spanish rule and the white fondant icing from the French conquest.

CURED TUNA HEART

CUORE DI TONNO • ITALY

Every year between May and June, bluefin tuna migrate through the Mediterranean Sea. They travel through Gibraltar, up to Corsica, and down to Sardinia, where fishermen set up nets during the fleeting season. The short window of time, coupled with increased regulation around this prized and increasingly rare fish, means that Sardinian chefs make use of every possible part of the bluefin, including the heart.

To prepare cuore di tonno, a fresh tuna heart is salted and pressed under weights for about three weeks. After the organ has been drained of its moisture, it's left to dry in the open air until the black, briny mass is rock hard. The ocean-heavy odor might recall the bilge of a ship, or another Sardinian specialty, bottarga (cured tuna roe). The practice harks back to a time before refrigeration, when the abundant summer catch had to be cleverly preserved and rationed throughout winter.

Like bottarga, cuore di tonno is a powerhouse of flavor, and a few shavings off the block will impart a salty, savory, metallic tang to a dish. A shower of grated tuna heart over fresh ribbons of pasta topped with an egg yolk is a classic application, but the delicacy can also be added to soups and sauces or sliced thinly, doused with olive oil, and eaten as an antipasto.

The tuna hearts are left out to air-dry until they are rock hard.

How to try it
The menu at Al Tonno di Corsa in Carloforte, Sardinia, revolves around tuna and includes both tuna heart salad and bottarga.

Fish Sauce Factories

Fish sauce was a wildly popular Roman condiment. Called garum, it was made by salting fish entrails and allowing them to ferment into golden, pungent, umami-laden liquid.

Archaeologists have excavated an immense, sprawling trail of fish sauce factories across the ancient Roman Empire, dotting the coastlines from the western Mediterranean to the northern reaches of the Black Sea.

The factories, which date between the 2nd century BCE and the 6th century CE, featured a central patio, rooms to clean the fish and store the product, and an array of sunken rectangular basins for fermenting the garum, typically built from cement and lined with a paving material called opus signinum that kept precious liquid from seeping out. Finished fish sauce was poured into amphorae (slim ceramic jars) and distributed throughout the empire in what was a booming, sophisticated network of production and transport.

Garum factories made use of every fishy morsel: The flesh of large fish was salted and dried, while the entrails, along with less desirable small fish, were used to make garum. Like other fermented products (think wine), garum varied hugely in quality. The purest sauce, distilled from tuna parts, could fetch $500 a bottle in today's currency, while cheap baitfish-and-viscera varieties were the fish sauce of commoners and enslaved people. For everything in between, mackerel was the fish of choice.

The densest concentration of factories was found along

OF THE ROMAN EMPIRE

fish migration routes, enabling fishermen to bring their catch ashore and directly to the processing sites. The Strait of Gibraltar, which every spring still plays host to schools of traveling bluefin tuna, was surrounded by factories that would process the massive annual catch. Shoals of sardines around the western tip of France made the region of Brittany another fish factory hot spot, home to an enormous site called Les Plomarc'h, which cranked out cheap garum for the Roman army. Away from the migratory fairways, the salting sites were modest; this is especially true closer to Rome, where there was a demand for fresh fish at market.

Garum was used as something of a mother sauce: By adding honey, vinegar, herbs, or oil, Romans created dozens of derivative condiments. In the famed first-century Roman cookbook *Apicius*, more than 75 percent of the 465 recipes call for garum. Excavations of Pompeii revealed that Romans of all social classes had easy access to fish sauce and used it daily: The city's signature garum container, the urceus, was found everywhere throughout Pompeii's ruins, in shabby shops and wealthy homes, even kosher versions in Jewish kitchens. Across the empire, garum amphorae have been recovered underwater, lost in ancient shipwrecks, and on land from Britain to Africa, showcasing the expansive, formidable reach of Rome's fallen condiment.

Delicious Diaspora

DUTCH INDONESIANS IN THE NETHERLANDS

Until the very end of the 16th century, the Portuguese ruled the spice trade world, sailing between Indonesia and Portugal on a nautical route they fiercely guarded. That all changed in 1592, when a Dutch cartographer published a chart with detailed instructions on how to sail to Indonesia, known then as the East Indies.

Shortly after, three Amsterdam merchants began plotting an expedition in secret: A spy was sent to Lisbon, posing as a merchant, to confirm the cartographer's charts, which were also cross-referenced with intelligence from other knowledgeable Dutch travelers. With this information, the men raised enough capital to build four ships, hire 248 crew members, and set sail in 1592.

By most accounts, the voyage was a catastrophe. The roundtrip journey took more than two years, during which they lost 154 men, killed one Javanese prince, were stranded six months on Madagascar, and held for ransom, raided, and generally disgraced. But they did return with pepper, nutmeg, and mace, all of which were so valuable at the time that the expedition was still deemed a profitable success. In 1602, the Dutch set up a trading post in Java, eventually taking forcible control of the entire country and remaining there until Indonesia gained independence in 1949.

Three hundred years of colonial rule and intermarriage led to a braiding of cultures and a mixed-race community known as "Indos." Today, roughly 10 percent of the Dutch population has some Indonesian blood. And Indonesian cuisine—spice-heavy, sweet, sour, and spicy—has found its place among traditional Dutch fare, sometimes evolving into new Indo dishes unique to the Netherlands.

Rijsttafel is the ultimate example of Netherlands-specific Indonesian cuisine. Dutch for "rice table," rijsttafel was created in Indonesia for the Dutch colonists as a way to indulge in a large assortment of dishes from the numerous islands. Rijsttafel consists of many small plates, typically a dozen or more curries, stir-fried vegetables, satays, fritters, and stews, served with rice in various preparations, together on the same table. Not only was this meal indulgent for the colonists, it was also meant to impress visiting dignitaries with its breadth and magnitude. Since Indonesia's independence, rijsttafel is not easily found on the islands—Indonesians are less interested in excess and find that mild Javanese dishes, for example, don't necessarily go well with the heavily spiced food of Sumatra. But the rice table is alive and well in the Netherlands, where the meal is loved on land and—even today—by seafaring Dutch: A Dutch naval tradition is to eat rijsttafel every Wednesday afternoon.

Spekkoek (or "lapis legit" in Indonesian) is a riff on a German multilayered spit cake, called Baumkuchen, where batter is brushed onto a rotating spit, layer by layer. When Dutch traders arrived with this recipe, Indonesians added spices (cinnamon, clove, nutmeg, mace) to the batter and built the layers in a pan, using a broiler to cook each delicate stratum before carefully adding a dozen more. This labor-intensive preparation required butter from the Netherlands and spices from Indonesia, resulting in a special-occasion cake that's still expensive today (in Amsterdam, spekkoek goes for about €20 a kilo, about 2.2 lb).

Friet saté pairs the ubiquitous Dutch french fry with a generous topping of peanut sauce (called saté sauce because it's typically used for meat skewers).

Split pea soup with rice and sambal (spicy chili sauce), **macaroni and cheese packed with lunch meat** (hot dogs, Spam, or corned beef), and **steamed meatloaf with sweet soy sauce** are all classic Indo comfort foods.

THE WORLD'S FIRST FLOATING FARM

FLOATING FARM • NETHERLANDS

How to try it

Floating Farm is located in the Merwehaven, a harbor within Rotterdam's port. It's currently open to the public on Fridays and Saturdays from 11 a.m.–4 p.m.

In 2019, a new farm opened in one of Europe's largest and busiest ports—not in the area, but literally floating in the port of Rotterdam. Called Floating Farm, it's the first of its kind, though hopefully not the last.

The idea came to CEO and founder Peter van Wingerden while in New York City during Hurricane Sandy. In the wake of the flooding, he watched the largely imported produce disappear from city markets and realized the world of tomorrow would need to produce food closer to consumers—and it might need to float. His solution for the future is now realized in the three-story concrete platform that's home to 35 cows producing 700 liters of milk every day.

The farm is unparalleled in its sustainability. Half the farm's energy comes from 50 solar panels floating beside it in the shape of a milk bottle. On the farm's top level, cows graze from a mixture of hay and grass clippings from local parks and golf courses, and drink purified rainwater collected from the roof. Their manure is converted into fertilizer, which is used to regrow the very fields from which they'll later eat.

Only two humans are needed to operate the farm. Most of the work is performed by robots, using AI to milk, feed, and clean up after the cows. The milk itself is processed on the farm's second floor, and the pasteurized milk and yogurt are sold on-site and in grocery stores throughout the city.

This three-story floating farm is home to 35 lactating cows.

BLOOD-SUCKING SEA MONSTER

LAMPREY • PORTUGAL

If you're a species that has spent millions of years sucking blood, getting cooked in a vat of your own is due punishment. Such is the plight of the parasitic sea lamprey, which gets boiled in a bloodbath as part of traditional Portuguese cuisine.

At first glance, lampreys might seem more like monsters than meals. These parasites resemble wormy eels with sharp, winding rows of teeth. In the North American Great Lakes, they're not seen as dinner, but as parasites that kill other species and accumulate mercury.

But one man's horrific, prehistoric pest has been another man's delicacy for thousands of years. Roman servants prepared lamprey at Julius Caesar's banquets. During the Middle Ages, only members of the upper class had access to its hearty, prized meat. Across southwestern Europe, Christians were drawn to lamprey's texture, akin to slow-cooked steak, and its lack of fishy aftertaste. Demand was especially high during Lent, when eating land animals was forbidden.

In Portugal, stewed lamprey is still a suitable beef replacement. From January through April, you'll find this creature marinated in its own blood and served with rice all over the country. Every March, 30,000 gourmets flood the small village of Montemor-o-Velho for the annual Lamprey and Rice Festival. During the Christmas season, nuns, bakers, and families celebrate by fashioning sea monsters out of sweet egg yolk. This treat, known as lampreia de ovos, features a lamprey replica covered in icing—a more kid-friendly version than the blood-coated dish.

How to try it

Fresh lamprey is seasonally available in restaurants across Portugal, as well as in Spain and France. In Finland, lamprey is served pickled year-round.

DECOY SAUSAGE

ALHEIRA • PORTUGAL

After the Spanish Inquisition spread to Portugal in the 16th century, Jews had to tread very carefully. The ruthlessly pro-Christian era was deeply anti-Semitic, and those practicing Judaism were persecuted, exiled from the country, or burned at the stake in Lisbon's Rossio Square.

Even practicing Judaism in secret was a dangerous game. Informants were everywhere, pouncing at the opportunity to report an overheard Hebrew prayer or, equally incriminating, a lack of hanging sausages. To protect themselves, the Jews of Mirandela created alheira, a decoy sausage that looked just like the porcine variety but was made with kosher-friendly poultry and bread. Hanging in their homes and gracing their dinner tables, the sneaky sausage likely saved hundreds of lives.

Today, not all alheira is kosher, and pork fat is often mixed into the filling, which can contain anything from veal to duck to salt cod. The garlicky smoked tube meat (alheira gets its name from the Portuguese word for garlic, *alho*), typically served with fries and a runny egg, has earned a near universal place on Portuguese menus, beloved now for its taste rather than its life-saving abilities.

How to try it

Head to the northeastern city of Mirandela, where the alheira is protected by a PGI (Protected Geographic Indication) certification. All sausages are produced according to strict regulation and are considered the best in Portugal.

BACON FAT PUDDING

PUDIM ABADE DE PRISCOS • PORTUGAL

How to try it
Casa dos Ovos Moles in Lisbon makes traditional, Braga-style bacon pudding they sell by the kilo (the equivalent of 2.2 lb), the half kilo, or in individual servings.

In the northern Portuguese city of Braga, in the parish of Priscos, there once lived a man named Manuel Joaquim Machado Rebelo. Known as the Abbot of Priscos, Rebelo became one of the country's most lauded chefs during the 19th century, preparing elaborate banquets for the royal family and Portugal's elite. The abbot was notoriously close-lipped about his recipes, but he did let one slip, and his formula for pork fat and wine pudding became his legacy.

Pudim Abade de Priscos begins with a golden liquid caramel slathered around a pudding mold. Poured into the caramel skin is a classic custard of sugar, egg yolks, and cinnamon, amped up by two regional ingredients: port wine and pork fat. The effect is a smooth, velvety bite with the subtle unctuousness of lard, cut by the wine's sweet acidity. Two hundred years later, the Abbot's bacon fat pudding is still considered a first-class recipe and a Portuguese classic. It's often described as a magic trick of gastronomy because the custard is so ethereal it vanishes in your mouth.

THE SAUCIEST SANDWICH IN PORTO

FRANCESINHA • PORTUGAL

How to try it
Porto is the hotbed of francesinhas; try Lado B Café for a saucy version, or Café Santiago F for a cheese-centric rendering surrounded by fries.

Your typical francesinha, or "little French woman," is a sandwich only by definition. Indeed there is bread, and between that bread is meat, but the word *sandwich* does not do justice to the magnitude of the meat, which is a trio of cured ham, steak, and linguiça sausage. Nor does it suggest that the meat and bread are covered in gooey melted cheese, then slathered in a secret sauce that contains beer, tomato, chilies, and, allegedly, even more meat. A runny egg adds surplus lubrication, which means there is typically a side of french fries for dipping in the "sandwich."

Residents of Porto, where the behemoth was born, suggest limiting yourself to two francesinhas a month, both for general health and safety as well as to ration your delight throughout the year. Delight rationing has been an ongoing issue for this dish: Originally a popular food for bachelors, the sandwich was once considered so decadent, it was inappropriate for a woman to order one.

A HOME FOR MACANESE CUISINE

CASA DE MACAU • PORTUGAL

For more than four centuries, Portugal controlled the small island of Macau, just off the coast of southern China. When Portuguese traders first landed in the 16th century, Macau was under the control of the Ming dynasty, who used it as a commercial port until around 1550. After a rocky start, relations improved when the Portuguese helped rid the coastline of pirates, and the Chinese allowed the Portuguese to settle. By the mid-19th century, the Portuguese had colonized the island. They erected Portuguese-style buildings, controlled the port, and enslaved Macanese women—and women from other Portuguese colonies—as wives.

Tasked with cooking for their European husbands, the wives from Macau, Goa, and Malacca (all former Portuguese colonies) improvised the dishes they'd never tasted. Bacalhau, the Portuguese dried codfish, was braised in soy sauce and tamarind. Coconut milk replaced cow's milk and sweet-and-savory Chinese sausage, called lap cheong, was used in place of chouriço. Wives learned to bake pastéis de nata, the predecessors to the Chinese egg tarts known as dan tat. They made samosas that tasted more like egg rolls and Portuguese-style fried rice.

In Lisbon, the Casa de Macau helps preserve this historic gastronomy. The private association, according to its president, was founded to unite the Macanese diaspora: Portuguese raised in Macau who have returned to Europe and those with mixed Portuguese and Macanese blood. (The term *Macanese* is still complicated because it describes natives of Macau, both with and without Portuguese heritage.) At special events throughout the year, the Casa de Macau serves a Macanese meal in a Macanese-style dining room, decorated with East Asian art and pictures of the founders on the wall.

How to try it

Casa de Macau is located outside Lisbon's city center, at Avenida Almirante Gago Coutinho, 142.

Pastéis de nata.

Macau's inner harbor, ca. 1880.

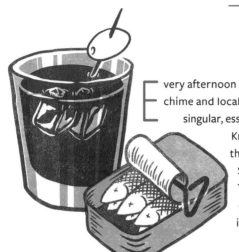

VERMOUTH HOUR

LA HORA DEL VERMUT • SPAIN

Every afternoon in Madrid, when the sun is at its highest, internal clocks chime and locals begin to fill the neighborhood bars, gathering for the singular, essential purpose of preparing their appetites for lunch. Known as vermouth hour ("la hora del vermut" in Spanish), this daily ritual is fundamental to the routines of many Spaniards, occurring just before the big daytime meal. The objective is to tease open your hunger with an aperitif (an alcoholic drink meant to stimulate the appetite), and in Spain, the daytime standard is vermouth—so popular

A Sip Before Dinner

Aperitifs are a glorious facet of the European lifestyle. Like a slow seduction before a meal, aperitifs open the palate and arouse the appetite before you settle into the main event. A pre-meal glass of liqueur or fortified wine—enlivened with a mix of fruits, roots, and spices—is a tradition that extends across the continent, because when it comes to extracting maximum pleasure from everyday eating, no one does it like the Europeans.

LILLET
A key ingredient in James Bond's favorite martini, Lillet is 85 percent white bordeaux wine, 15 percent macerated-citrus liquor. (France, 17% ABV*)

OUZO 12
Fiery and sweet, anise-flavored ouzo turns from clear to cloudy when poured on ice. (Greece, 38% ABV)

GINJA SEM RIVAL
Ginja, the local sour cherry, steeped in aguardente ("fire water") is the most traditional drink of Lisbon, served as a thick, sweet shot—with or without the cherries. (Portugal, 23.5% ABV)

*alcohol by volume

it's usually available on tap, in at least a few varieties. The classic Spanish vermouth is red, sweet, and herbaceous, made from a white wine that's been fortified with brandy and left to steep with a combination of warm spices, bitter herbs, and fruits such as orange, cherry, or grapefruit. Straight from the tap, served over ice or straight up, Spanish vermouth is notoriously smooth and easy to drink—much less sweet than the traditional Italian variety. Snacks are also a major component of la hora del vermut. Mussels, anchovies, and the ubiquitous jamón (ham) all make for excellent accompaniments; olives are pretty much obligatory. Spaniards are known for their late schedules—lunches in the early evening and dinners at 11 p.m. are commonplace here—and so a glass of vermouth and a hearty snack is a welcome early-afternoon repast.

How to try it

Every bar in Spain will have a selection of vermouths, often on tap, most of which are produced within the country. In Barcelona, Quimet & Quimet has been pouring vermouth for more than a century in a quintessentially old-school joint. At Bar Electricitat, they leave a bottle of vermouth on your table and you tell them how many glasses you've had.

Becherovka kiosk in Karlovy Vary, the liqueur's hometown.

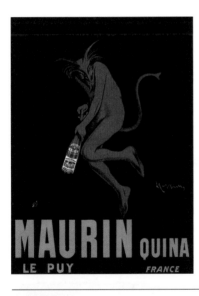

RABARBARO ZUCCA
Chinese rhubarb, bitter orange peel, and cardamom make a sweet, botanical tipple. (Italy, 16% ABV)

BECHEROVKA
A closely guarded, medicinal synthesis of cinnamon, clove, chamomile, and ginger. Technically a digestif meant for after-dinner sipping. (Czech Republic, 38% ABV)

MAURIN QUINA
A fortified wine laced with cherries, quinine (bark extract), and bitter almonds. (France, 16% ABV)

YANHELIVKA
With hints of dill, ginger, mesquite, and lemon, this Ukrainian blend is also touted as an aphrodisiac. (Ukraine, 33% ABV)

MANDARINE NAPOLÉON
The recipe for this cognac flavored with mandarin peel was inspired by Napoleon, who liked his cognac with a touch of orange. (Belgium, 38.5% ABV)

FRIED LEMON LEAF CHALLENGE

PAPARAJOTES • SPAIN

How to try it

Paparajotes are available only within Murcia, typically during the spring, when you can find them at festivals such as Bando de la Huerta. During the off-season, the paparajotes at Rincón de Pepe and La Parranda Taberna are very tasty.

No matter how well you speak castellano or tolerate the blazing summer sun, Murcianos of southeastern Spain can always tell whether you're a local by how you eat a paparajote—the traditional treat of the citrus town—made by battering a lemon leaf, deep-frying it, and dusting it with cinnamon and sugar. Take a bite of the paparajote and your cover is blown. The lemon leaf, which is unpalatably bitter, is not for eating. Its purpose is to give the paparajote shape and a slight citrus tang. To pass the test, pick up the leaf by its stem, pull the batter off, and eat the crispy, sugary, donut-like shell. Discard the lemon leaf, and you've passed a cultural test as well as enjoyed the delightful, hyper-regional sweet that leaves most tourists cringing from lemon peel mouth.

MONASTERY FOOD CAFÉ

CAELUM • SPAIN

How to try it

Caelum is open from 10 a.m. to 8:30 p.m. every day, including Sundays.

Within Barcelona's medieval Jewish quarter, Caelum ("heaven" in Latin) provides a treasure trove of delicacies made in monasteries all around Spain. The café specializes in sweets, such as the nun-made egg yolk candy Yemas de San Leandro from Seville, and Tocinillo de Cielo, a custard invented by 14th-century nuns in Jerez de la Frontera.

The ground floor holds the cozy café, complete with an elaborate window display of heavenly cakes and pastries, where visitors can enjoy their chosen treat along with coffee and tea. Afterward, a trip to the building's basement offers a surprising piece of medieval history. Below the café are the remains of the quarter's public baths, whose stone walls and vaulted ceilings are right at home among the centuries-old monastic delights.

AN ENCHANTING PARTY PUNCH

QUEIMADA • SPAIN

At every good Galician punch party, the host recites an incantation, then sets the bowl of punch on fire. Like any proper host, she wants to ward off the evil spirits and invite good fortune for her guests. After the alcohol burns in a brilliant blue flame, she ladles the queimada into cordial glasses.

The taste of the caramelized sugar and lemon peel, the earthy coffee beans, and the heat of orujo brandy swirl magically together in the glass. The first sip banishes evil spirits, the second clears your mind of hate, and the third fills your soul with passion.

Queimada is a traditional punch of Galicia, and the ritual surrounding its consumption is known as conxuro da queimada ("the spell of queimada"). Although the drink's origin is unknown, it draws from the cultures of Celtic Druids, the Moors, and Spanish colonies in South America. Galicians perform the ritual at events such as weddings or dinner parties. If you can't get an invite to either, visit Galicia in June or October: There are queimada performances on Halloween, which is derived from the Celtic holiday of Samhain, and St. John's Night (also known as Witches' Night) on June 23.

How to try it

Instructions on how to conduct your own conxuro da queimada can be found online, but if you try this at home, make sure to use a clay pot or earthenware bowl, which best contains the fire.

WAFFLE ROULETTE VENDORS

BARQUILLEROS DE MADRID • SPAIN

Barquillos are simple treats: waffle dough pressed into a checkered pattern, then rolled into tubes, cones, or other shapes. But to get one (or ten), you'll have to play for it. Waffle vendors, called barquilleros, will remove the outer metal canister and begin a game of roulette using a wheel on its top. You can pay once to spin for either one or two barquillos, or pay more and spin as many times as you want, racking up waffles until you stop or the ticker lands on one of the four golden markers, at which point you lose everything.

How to try it

Barquilleros de Madrid, the shop run by the Cañas family, is located at Calle de Amparo 25.

The traditional barquillo nearly vanished during the food shortages under Francisco Franco's dictatorship. Luckily, the Cañas family of Madrid persisted in carrying on the barquilleros' legacy, and today Julián Cañas, a third-generation barquillero, maintains a shop in the city's Embajadores neighborhood. On weekends, Cañas and his sons also roam Madrid's plazas and parks with baskets of waffles under their arms and roulette tins on their backs.

Barquillos can also be found in pastry shops, but for the most authentic experience, look for a barquillero in public spaces such as the Plaza Mayor, El Rastro market, or El Retiro park. The roaming, gambling members of the Cañas family also make appearances at fiestas such as the San Isidro Festival.

Barquilleros at Madrid's Las Fiestas de la Paloma in 2015.

THE ART OF TABLE-SIDE FROTHING

ASTURIAN CIDER POURING • SPAIN

How to try it
In Asturias, you don't order a glass of cider. The drink comes by the bottle, which includes the tableside pouring and frothing service.

In Spain's northern region of Asturias, cider pouring is more performance art than table service. At local cider bars, known as sidrerías, servers pop the cork and hoist the open bottle high into the air. From this altitude, the elevated hand tips the bottle while a lowered hand catches the cloudy liquid in a glass until it's roughly a quarter full.

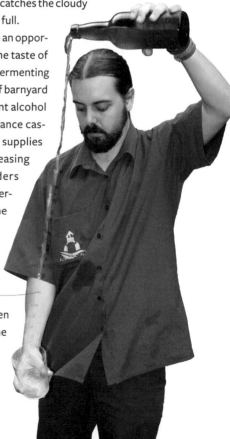

The servers aren't just capitalizing on an opportunity for theatrics, they're enhancing the taste of the beverage. Asturian cider, made from fermenting five kinds of apples into a funky medley of barnyard flavors, contains approximately 6 percent alcohol and is almost entirely flat. The long-distance cascade into the glass creates a splash that supplies effervescence and foam while also releasing the cider's aromas. Because bartenders might spill a few drops in the process (perhaps due to all their no-look pours), some establishments litter the floor with sawdust to absorb the constant splashing and spills.

A long-distance pour at a sidería in the Spanish town of Ribodesella.

Rather than sipping and savoring the tart drink, patrons shoot their small pour back in one swift go. The drinker then shakes out any last dregs of cider onto the floor to freshen the cup for the next drinker, and the entire pouring ritual begins again.

EASTERN EUROPE

PICKLED BAR CHEESE

NAKLÁDANÝ HERMELÍN • CZECH REPUBLIC

U Fleků, the oldest barhouse in Prague, serves the quintessential Czech bar snack: a soft, round cheese called hermelín, with a creamy white interior. Sliced in half lengthwise, the cheese is layered in a jar with spice-and-herb-infused oil that typically includes onion, garlic, bay leaves, black peppercorn, and, for a spicy variety, red pepper. Left to marinate for about ten days, the cheese picks up all the pungent flavors of the oil, which mingles with the mushroom notes of the cheese, growing increasingly powerful as the mixture ages. The cheese retains its gooey texture, which is why a few slices of deep-fried brown Czech bread, called topinki, are always within reach.

Despite it's name, the cheese isn't actually pickled—it's marinated. But less ambiguous is the proper way to eat this herbaceous delicacy: with a fork in one hand and a cold Czech beer in the other.

How to try it
At U Fleků, you can eat pickled hermelín at communal tables while waiters roam for business, carrying big trays of housemade dark lager, which is the only beer served here.

HOW TO ENJOY A FLUFFY BEER

MLÍKO • CZECH REPUBLIC

The Czechs, inventors of the pilsner, drink the most beer per capita of any nation on Earth. With a beer culture this pervasive, it's only natural that they'd create a philosophy around how to pour and enjoy their favorite drink. At a bar in Prague, beer drinkers not only choose their favorite brew—they also select their preferred pouring method. Mlíko, or milk beer, which renders a whole beer white and foamy, resembling a tall glass of milk, might be the most misunderstood style.

How to try it
The traditional pilsner pub Lokál Hamburk in Prague is especially adept at transforming beer into beer fluff. Mlíko should cost half the price of a standard pour.

Outside the Czech Republic, too much foamy head on a beer is considered an amateur move, a watery nuisance that takes up valuable space in the glass. But the foam in mlíko is a different substance entirely, made by opening the tap just slightly and finessing a thick, creamy lather into the mug. The mlíko foam has a cloudy, velvety body and sweet taste—nothing like the sensation of gulping air that comes

A bartender pours a milk beer in Pilsen, home of Pilsner Urquell.

from a poorly pulled draft. Because the foamy milk beer is less alcoholic than a regular pour, mlíko makes a great nightcap, an easy lunchtime beer, or the beverage of choice when in a rush because the foamy drink is easy to down quickly.

Mlíko is the lightest of the Czech pouring styles, with just a sliver of amber liquid on the bottom. The standard pour, called hladinka, is three parts beer to one part foam. Another pour, called a šnyt, contains about two parts of beer, three parts of foam, and a couple of inches of empty glass—a style that comes to the rescue when drinkers need to start slowing down but can't bear the embarrassment of ordering a small beer.

TINY-HOUSE WINE STORAGE

VRBICE WINE CELLARS • CZECH REPUBLIC

Vrbice is a town of about 1,000 people, located in the winemaking district of Břeclav. The village stands like an island surrounded by a sea of vineyards, which produce some of the best wine in eastern Europe. The village is known for its picturesque wine cellars.

The most famous of the cellars, the Stráž cellars, were built in the 18th and 19th centuries. Cut into the village's sandstone hillside and adorned with elegant Gothic arches, the cellars look like tiny houses from a fairy tale. Inside, the long corridors are stocked with wine. The interior walls are dusted with mold that, together with the stable temperature and humidity belowground, help to create an ideal environment for maturing wine. In certain cases, the original builders kept digging, stacking multiple layers of cellars, one above the other: The largest of Vrbice's cellars, called U Jezírka, goes seven stories deep.

How to try it

Vrbice is located in the southeast Czech Republic. Many of the cellars are available for visits and will offer tastings of the region's wine.

FERMENTED-BREAD SODA

KALI • ESTONIA

Dense, sweet Estonian black rye—so sacred that old folklore demands that a loaf fallen to the ground should be picked up immediately and kissed before returning it to its proper place—is a mainstay on every Estonian table. Locals have also found a way to drink their favorite carbohydrate, parlaying their rye into a fizzy drink that's become the country's most popular soda.

The rye bread, already made from a fermented batter, is fermented again to make kali. Rye slices are boiled until soft, then mixed with yeast, sugar, and maltose. After the mixture has fermented for a day, it's sieved through a cheesecloth, sweetened with additions such as lemon and raisins, and ready to drink. The slightly alcoholic drink tastes like a cross between dark beer and kombucha—malted, sour, and effervescent. It's an easy-drinking refreshment that's far more nutritious than the average cola: Rye bread provides vitamin B and magnesium, and the lactic acid from the fermentation can aid digestion.

Street vendors once pushed carts around Tallinn's cobbled streets selling kali by the glass, but today you can find bottled versions of what many call "Estonian Coca-Cola" on supermarket shelves. But Estonians swear the supermarket brands are just not the same as traditional kali, and they'd be correct: Many commercial brands of kali are not fermented, which makes the taste more soda than soda beer.

How to try it

Ochakovsky is a Russian commercial brand of kvass (their equivalent of kali) available in Eastern European grocery stores and online. In Estonia, you'll find home-brewed kali everywhere.

Other Fortified Sodas

These are sodas made with ingredients that claim to aid everything from digestion to arthritis to diabetes.

CARIBBEAN	VIETNAM	SWITZERLAND	SOUTH KOREA	USA
Mauby Fizz	Tribeco	Rivella	Tamla Village Co.	Dr. Brown's Cel-Ray
made with tree bark, anise, vanilla	made with white fungus, swiftlet bird's nests	made with milk whey, minerals	made with Jeju onions	made with celery seed

When the Soviet Union Paid Pepsi in Warships

In the summer of 1959, many Russians got their first taste of Pepsi. Accustomed to carbonated mineral water and bread-based sodas, many Russians' first impression of Pepsi was that it smelled like shoe wax and tasted too sweet. But the American brand was determined to enter the untapped market—even if the communist government couldn't compensate them in the traditional manner.

It all began with a rare exchange of culture at the American National Exhibition in Moscow, which was meant to showcase Americana through exhibits sponsored by US brands. Pepsi executive Donald M. Kendall went to Moscow with the mission of getting a Pepsi in the hands of Soviet leader Nikita Khrushchev. The night before the exhibition, Kendall

Vice President Richard Nixon watches Kliment Voroshilov and Nikita Khrushchev sample Pepsi for the first time.

approached then Vice President Richard Nixon at the American embassy, and he agreed to lead Khrushchev to the Pepsi booth. The next day, Nixon delivered as promised, and a photographer snapped a picture of the two world leaders sipping cups of Pepsi.

For Kendall—who catapulted up the ranks of Pepsi, eventually becoming CEO—the USSR was the land of opportunity. In 1972, he negotiated a cola monopoly that locked out Coca-Cola until 1985. Cola syrup began flowing through the Soviet Union, becoming what the *New York Times* named "the first capitalistic product" available in the USSR. But it wasn't business as usual.

Soviet rubles were worthless internationally and prohibited from being taken abroad, so the USSR and Pepsi had to barter. Cola was traded for Stolichnaya vodka, which Pepsi sold in the US. But when an American boycott banned Stolichnaya, they had to trade for something else: In the spring of 1989, Pepsi became the middleman for 17 used submarines, a frigate, cruiser, and destroyer, which a Norwegian company bought for scrap. In return, Pepsi was allowed to double the number of soda plants in the USSR.

In 1990, a new $3 billion deal was signed. Pepsi agreed to sell Soviet-built ships abroad in order to finance their expanding Russian enterprises, which now included another American institution: Pizza Hut.

But a year later, the Soviet Union fell, taking with it Pepsi's monopoly and business deals. Suddenly, their long balancing act turned into a scramble to protect their assets in a free-for-all made more complex by redrawn borders, inflation, and privatization. The new Pizza Huts were hobbled—their mozzarella was sourced from Lithuania. Plastic soda bottles were located in Belarus and Pepsi's new ship business was stranded in now-independent Ukraine.

Kendall, who had since retired, lamented that the Soviet Union had essentially gone out of business. Over several months, Pepsi pieced parts of the deal back together as Coca-Cola aggressively entered the former Soviet Union. Despite a huge marketing push from Pepsi (they launched a giant replica Pepsi can to the Mir space station and erected two billboards over Pushkin Square), Coke beat out Pepsi as Russia's most popular cola in 2013, ushering in a new era where soft drinks, vodka, and destroyers had to be bought with legal currency.

Pepsi advertisement above Pushkin Square in 1998.

ANCIENT GEORGIAN WINE VESSELS

QVEVRI • GEORGIA

n 2017, archaeological excavations in southern Georgia unearthed terra-cotta jars from the 6th century BCE, which meant Georgians have been making wine for 8,000 years, predating even the Greeks and the Romans. Called qvevri, the oversize, lemon-shaped jars are used for fermentation and storage and belong exclusively to the Georgian winemaking tradition.

Producing a qvevri, which is always made by hand, requires considerable craftsmanship. A slight imbalance of weight or thickness can make a qvevri crack or wobble. Selecting the right clay, which imparts essential minerals to the wine, is also critical. There are only a small number of remaining craftsmen, who likely learned the trade from their parents. It can take months to make a single qvevri—but once it's done, it can last for centuries.

To make traditional Georgian wine, pressed grapes, along with their skins, stalks, and pips, are loaded into a beeswax-coated qvevri that's buried beneath the ground. The qvevri is sealed shut, and the mixture is left to ferment for about half a year. The distinctive shape of the qvevri allows the grape seeds and skins to sink to the bottom, while the juice stays on top to mature. Winemakers say using the qvevri makes their wine naturally stable, eliminating the need for chemical preservatives.

Between vintages, qvevris are rigorously cleaned with lime, water, and a special brush made from cherry bark, then relined with beeswax. Cleaning a qvevri can be almost as taxing as making one, especially when it's already set in the ground. Although qvevri vary greatly in size, the largest can hold approximately 2,600 gallons (10,000 liters) and are big enough for a person to roam around inside.

How to try it
Visit the cellar and taste the wine at the Alaverdi Monastery in eastern Georgia, where they've been following tradition for more than a thousand years.

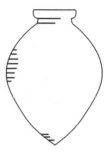

An ancient monastery's winemaking room, containing rows of subterranean qvevri.

THE ELOQUENT, EXISTENTIAL TOASTMASTER

TAMADA • GEORGIA

How to try it
Supras are generally invite-only affairs.

A Georgian feast is called a supra, and presiding over every supra is a tamada, or toastmaster, who leads the diners on a long and winding existential journey throughout the meal. A few times an hour, the tamada will rise and speak to the guests, who may consist of a casual gathering of friends or an elaborate wedding celebration. He doesn't shy away from the difficult topics: A good toastmaster will address matters of the mind and soul, themes of life, death, God, and humanity, and will speak of them with honed finesse. There will be metaphors and historical references, all bound by a rhythm that's nearly poetic. He will raise his glass to his fellow diners and sit until it's time to toast again.

Hospitality is deeply rooted in Georgian culture and to be a tamada is a significant honor, typically bestowed upon the eldest and most well-spoken man at the table. (Women tamadas are a recent development and still rare.) If a tamada is especially skilled, he'll be asked to officiate the ceremonies and meals of those beyond his circle, often becoming locally famous. Respected as men of stature and ideas, tamadas are almost never paid. They provide a service to the community, and their community venerates them with deep gratitude.

A traditional Georgian feast in the town of Mestia.

The younger generation has openly embraced the tradition, and though they may conduct their supras a little differently (less food, more women as tamadas), they still prize the discourse around the big questions of existence and the fellowship that happens around a table.

CAMPFIRE BACON FAT

SÜLT SZALONNA • HUNGARY

How to try it
A slab of smoked fatback from your butcher, cut into chunks and skewered, will work perfectly. Rye bread is the preferred accompaniment.

Imagine a block of pure pork fat—no muscle, no skin—lightly smoked and cut into cubes. When slid onto a wooden skewer (preferably cut fresh from a fruit tree) and melted over an open fire, this becomes the beloved Hungarian campfire treat known as sült szalonna. As the cube sizzles and begins to drip salty, liquid pork, a thick slice of bread catches the fat and soaks up the flavor. After a few cycles of plunging the skewer into the flames and dangling it over the bread, the slice should be entirely saturated in fat and ready to be decorated with bits of red onion, tomato, cucumber, or—in classic Hungarian style—with paprika.

SPIT-ROASTED CAKE

SAKOTIS • LITHUANIA

Most cakes are created in about the same way: You mix a batter, pour it into a pan, and bake it in an oven. Spit cakes, in dramatic contrast, are cooked by flinging batter onto a rotating dowel over an open flame.

Variations of spit cakes are popular across Europe. In Hungary, Slovakia, and the Czech Republic, spit cakes tend to be tubular; in Germany, Baumkuchen looks like donuts stacked one on top of the other.

One of the most dramatic spit cakes, though, is the Lithuanian version, sakotis. In the final stages of the cooking process, bakers increase the speed at which the spit rotates, which causes spikes to form as batter is flung toward the fire. The result is a cake that resembles a Christmas tree. Sakotis, after all, means "branchy tree."

Making sakotis can easily take five hours. Bakers ladle batter along the spit in regular stages, and the skill comes from knowing just how much batter to add—and just how long to wait—so all the batter stays on the cake. By piling more batter in the middle, and then cutting the final product in two, bakers can achieve a treelike appearance. For fancy affairs, like weddings, they may decorate enormous sakotis that stand taller than some guests, with sugary flowers, nuts, and drizzles of chocolate. The cake itself is spongy and moist yet firm with a slight chew. It smells pleasantly of vanilla but tastes like a classic, eggy yellow cake.

In 2015, to inaugurate a tree cake museum, the company Romnesa organized the baking of a record-holding, 12-foot-long (3.7m) spit cake.

How to try it

You can buy sakotis all over Lithuania. In Vilnius, Lithuania's capital, you'll find towers in the windows of bakeries, slices served in cafés, and packaged trees on supermarket shelves.

A slotted spoon helps with even batter distribution.

ORNAMENTAL SMOKED CHEESE

OSCYPEK • POLAND

How to try it

Counterfeit oscypek is a problem in Poland, with many forgers swapping in cow's milk and using dyes to mimic the smoked color. Ensure it's the real deal by going straight to the source: U Jancoka, a highland guesthouse, is operated by cheese-making shepherds.

Fewer than 150 people are qualified to produce the Polish highland cheese oscypek. Shepherds, known as bacas, are typically at the helm of this traditional operation. They care for the sheep that graze in the Tatra mountain range of southern Poland and use their milk to create beautiful spindles of golden, smoked cheese.

A Balkan tribe called the Vlachs introduced shepherding and cheese making to the mountain's meadows nearly 1,000 years ago, and modern bacas continue to operate in ancient fashion. They work in small huts, using only wooden tools, often retaining their traditional dialect and dress. Fresh batches of cheese are cast in sycamore molds, which are carved with intricate decorations. Historically, the molds depicted imagery related to the cheese's function (often as currency or gifts), but today the designs are purely ornamental. The molds can be ovals, barrels, hearts, or animals, but only the spindle-shaped variety has earned protected status from the European Union, and those spindles must weigh between 21 and 28 ounces (600 and 800 grams), measure between 7 and 9 inches (17 and 23 centimeters) in length, and be produced between April and October, during the sheep's grazing season.

When the cheese has taken on its form, bacas soak it in saltwater, hang it from a beam, and smoke it using pine or spruce wood. This gives the exterior a slick golden hue while preserving the creamy white interior. The finished product has the texture of firm mozzarella, but the flavor is briny, smoky, and sharp, with notes of toasted chestnut. Grilled until soft and stretchy and topped with fruit preserves, oscypek might taste even better than it looks.

Transylvania

Transylvania is home to a slow-paced pastoral lifestyle. Villages have been slow to modernize: Especially in the 12th-century Saxon villages, many people don't have cell phones and still prefer horse-drawn carriages to cars. Locals often live off their land and their animals, producing small batches of old-world, artisanal food. The farm-to-table lifestyle means things taste better, but little travels beyond the region's borders—so to taste their land, you'll have to go. Here's the best of Transylvania:

Magiun of Topoloveni is a fruit spread made from four (or more) Romanian plum varieties, cooked for ten hours until it becomes a sticky, dark brown paste. The plums here are so sweet that the recipe never uses sugar.

Inima de Bou ("heart of ox") tomatoes were the favored variety of the Saxons—intensely sweet, pulpy, and thin-skinned. They are disappearing in most of Romania, but still grow in their native Transylvania, albeit in much smaller quantities.

A shepherd in the Hășmaș Mountains making cheese in a hut.

Șuncă (ham) is a point of pride in Transylvania, where pigs are raised and processed without machinery—just as they were centuries ago—and have a naturally complex and meaty flavor lost in commercial operations.

Brânză de burduf is a soft sheep's milk cheese produced on the slopes of the Bucegi Mountains and aged in the bark of a fir tree, which produces a uniquely spicy and verdant taste.

Kürtöskalács (chimney cake) is made by wrapping dough around a wooden spit that rotates over hot cinders. As it barbecues, the dough turns into a chewy, peelable cake while a coating of sugar becomes a sticky caramel coating.

MAGICAL CHEESE-RIPENING CAVE

GROTTO OF TAGA · ROMANIA

How to try it

Due to the very limited production of the cave, Năsal cheese is difficult to find outside of Transylvania.

According to Transylvanian legend, the commune of Taga was once controlled by a cruel and wealthy count. The people were starving and, to feed themselves, were forced to steal the count's cheese, which they hid in the town cave. When they came to retrieve the contraband cheese, they discovered it had changed color, from white to reddish-yellow, and had acquired a funky smell. To their surprise, the transformed cheese was delicious. When the count discovered what they'd done, he took the cheese—and the cave—for himself.

Although the story is legend, the cave is very real, and it remains the only place in the world that can produce this hyper-regional, soft cow's milk cheese called Năsal, after the small village where the cave is located. Năsal is a smear-ripened cheese, which means bacteria or fungi grow on the rind. The cave in Năsal contains naturally occurring *Brevibacterium linens*, a bacteria present on the human skin that causes foot odor, which—in tandem with a stable temperature and humidity—gives the

Wheels of Năsal cheese age in the grotto.

cheese a deep and earthy flavor impossible to re-create elsewhere.

Since the 19th century, when a Romanian architect and his son began producing the cave cheese, Năsal has been steadily gaining a devout following, even winning a gold medal at the Paris World Expo. A commercial operation began in 1954, which tried to expand the facility beyond the cave, but the cheese suffered, the price increased, consumption waned, and so the cave was closed in 2013. After enormous public outcry, the cave reopened less than a year later. Today, the cheese of Năsal lives on, feeding off that dank, delicious foot bacteria that makes it uniquely Transylvanian.

BLOOD CANDY NUTRITIONAL SUPPLEMENT

GEMATOGEN · RUSSIA

How to try it

Gematogen is widely available in Russia, typically at the pharmacy, and in Russian grocery stores worldwide.

Gematogen has all the hallmarks of candy: the dark appearance of chocolate, the sticky chewiness of caramel, and plenty of sweetness. These features do an impressive job of masking all the cow's blood, which is the main ingredient in this Soviet-era treat.

The packaging, which features smiling cartoon children and animals, also does wonders for marketing the bloody contents. In fact, many young Russians grew up eating the treat without realizing what it contained. Sold at pharmacies and drugstores, gematogen was dispensed more like medicine than candy. Adults were prescribed daily doses of about 1.75 ounces (50 g), children under the age of 13 needed an adult's consent, and pregnant women and breastfeeding mothers required a consultation before eating it. These days fresh cow's blood is often swapped out for powdered stuff, but it remains the leading candy bar for anemia, malnutrition, and fatigue.

THE HIGH-TECH WAY TO FEED COSMONAUTS

MIR SPACE STATION DINING TABLE ∘ RUSSIA

The Mir station was the world's first experiment with long-term space habitation, orbiting Earth from 1986 to 2001, with the capacity to support three crew members (among them cosmonaut Valeri Polyakov, who still holds the record for longest continuous space sojourn at 437 days). To feed these space workers in the compact microgravity station, the Russians designed a high-tech table for communal dining.

Located in the station's core module, the multicolored space table had slots where cosmonauts could heat up tins and tubes of food such as liver stroganoff and chicken in white sauce. Other cans, such as caviar and cheese, were eaten at space temperature. About 65 percent of each meal was composed of freeze-dried food, which could be reconstituted from a spigot in the table that dispensed hot and cold water. A built-in vacuum system sucked up any stray crumbs, but the meals were designed with easy cleanup in mind: Crumbly things were prebroken into bite-size pieces and flaky items were coated with an edible film that kept everything together. (According to American astronaut Andy Thomas, the space food in general was surprisingly delicious, especially the soups and fruit juices.) The table itself could be folded against the wall to create room when not in use, but that rarely happened because the cosmonauts found they could simply float over it.

The Mir station was in service for 15 years, three times longer than expected, and it had the battle scars to prove it: There were mold breakouts, a fire, and a collision with a cargo spacecraft. After being decommissioned, the body of the space station was mostly broken up, but the table was brought back to Earth and currently resides at the Memorial Museum of Cosmonautics in Moscow.

How to try it

The Memorial Museum of Cosmonautics is open seven days a week and costs 250 rubles, or about $4.

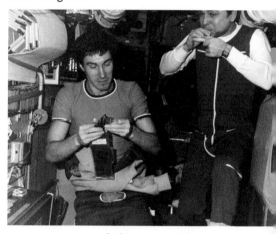

Soviet cosmonauts Sergei Krikalev and Aleksandr Volkov eating lunch aboard the Mir station in 1988.

The dining room and kitchen were centrally located in the station's core module.

THE BRIEF, HIGH-FLYING ERA OF

From 1928 to 1937, when the *Hindenburg* disaster incinerated the future of zeppelin travel, the German-owned airships offered a dining experience to rival a modern luxury cruise ship. The menus leaned heavily toward the German palate, with an emphasis on cream and meat, modeled after the cuisine of traditional, high-end European hotels.

Zeppelins, which were the size of buildings, flew significantly lower than modern planes do and therefore avoided the dry, pressurized air that dulls taste and smell on today's commercial flights. Food tasted like itself, which helped passengers enjoy the 7.5 pounds (3.5 kg) of lavish victuals they were allotted each day, including fattened duckling, champagne braised cabbage, lobster, and caviar.

The emphasis on German cuisine was a strategic choice. Although there was hope that these commercial zeppelin flights would one day be profitable, they were primarily a way to demonstrate a kind of German cultural strength. After being trounced in World War I, the Germans used zeppelins to show the world they were at the cutting edge of luxury and transport, sparing no expense to make their point. Tables were laid with vases of fresh flowers and blue-and-white china. Plates and teapots were inlaid with real gold. The dining room of the *Hindenburg* was furnished with lightweight, state-of-the-art aluminum Bauhaus furniture. (Napkins, oddly, were seriously regulated: Passengers were given a single white cloth napkin, in a personalized envelope which they had to keep and reuse for the entire journey.)

Drinking was perhaps the most popular activity aboard a zeppelin. The well-stocked bar had as many as 15 varieties of wine, as well as mixed drinks divided into "Sours," "Flips," "Fizzes," "Cobblers," and "Cocktails." Prairie oysters, a hangover cure made with hot sauce and a whole raw egg, were listed on the bar menu below the libations.

Zeppelin Dining

Europe's largest market is housed in giant zeppelin hangars.

At the turn of the 20th century, five giant neoclassical and art deco style hangars were built in the center of Riga, Latvia, to house zeppelins. When the German-made airships fell from favor, the hangars were turned into Riga's Central Market, the largest market bazaar in Europe. The market spans 778,000 square feet and houses 3,000 trade stands. During the Nazi occupation, the space was used to house troops and army supplies, but the market was reinvigorated under the Soviets.

Each of the five hangars in Riga's Central Market has a theme: meat, fish, dairy, produce, and general gastronomy.

Russians Once Preserved Their Milk with Frogs

Before the boon of refrigeration, Russian tradition held that a live frog dropped in a pitcher of milk would prolong its freshness.

There are Russian fables about frogs in milk. One proverb tells of two frogs who have fallen into a jug of milk, one who gives in to despair and drowns, and the other who stays afloat by swimming furiously. By morning, the sprightly frog has churned the milk into solid butter and escapes. Another story describes Babushka-Lyagushka-Shakusha, the magical, sentient "Grandmother Hopping Frog," swimming around in a bath of milk.

So was the preservation trick simply based on an old wives' tale? In 2012, these wives of yore were vindicated: A team of Moscow scientists proved that the secretions from certain frogs have antibacterial and antifungal properties, which may have helped in the preservation of milk. Inspired by a childhood of drinking frog milk, lead scientist Dr. Albert Lebedev discovered 76 antimicrobial peptides in the Russian brown frog, many of which had antibiotic compounds that protect against bacteria in their wet habitats. Some of these compounds were as effective at killing salmonella and staph bacteria as modern prescription antibiotics.

Still, it's not recommended to drop any random frog into your milk because they can also spread harmful pathogens. The scientific pursuit of amphibian-inspired medicine is an ever-expanding and exciting world (a different frog, the North American mink frog, secretes a chemical effective against the drug-resistant bacterium *Acinetobacter baumannii*), but when it comes to milk, the refrigerator—along with the expiration date—is undeniably the best line of defense.

MILK VODKA

ARAGA • RUSSIA

How to try it

Araga is primarily made at home in the countryside, so you likely won't find it in stores. In Tuva, your best shot at tasting it is to get an invitation to a local family's yurt.

For centuries the nomadic people of Tuva, a remote region of Russia just north of the Mongolian border, have turned the milk from their yaks, cows, and goats into a bevy of useful food products stable enough to withstand long journeys. Among them is araga, the Tuvan moonshine distilled from fermented sour milk.

Araga is produced in a homemade still called a shuuruun, crafted from the hollowed-out trunk of a poplar tree. The wooden cylinder is set inside a large pot over the stove and sealed off at the top with a container of cold water. As the fermented milk, or khoitpak, heats up at the bottom of the pot, the steam trapped inside produces condensation, which slowly trickles out of the shuuruun's long spout. The result is a clear, sour liquor of 5 to 20 percent alcohol that tastes milder when warm. Considered a special drink, araga is reserved for celebrations and rituals and is mostly served to the community elders: An old Tuvan custom states that a man must be married before his first taste.

STURGEON SPINAL CORD

VYAZIGA • RUSSIA

Sturgeon—famous producers of the ultimate luxury food, caviar—are prized in Russia for another delicacy: vyaziga. Made from the fish's spinal cord, vyaziga is used in Russian cooking to impart a rich, intense flavor that comes from the sturgeon's marrow. The decadent ingredient was famously served in a second-course consommé in the last, fateful meal for first-class passengers aboard the *Titanic*.

Because sturgeon lack vertebrae, the spinal cord can be pulled from the body in one very long piece (the stretchy, gelatinous cord can be multiple feet long). Once harvested, the cord is dried and then crushed into powder, which is typically reconstituted in water to make to make a thick, sticky paste.

In Russia, the dish most often associated with vyaziga is the kulebyaka: a pie so complicated, time-consuming, and expensive to make that most Russians have only read about it in stories by Nikolai Gogol and Anton Chekhov (who referred to it as a "temptation to sin"). The intricate kulebyaka is an oblong construction of many layers, each layer separated from the next by a "pancake" made from dough rolled out very thin. Fish, such as salmon or sturgeon, makes up the base layer, which supports a balancing act of rice, creamed mushrooms, onions, eggs, and boiled cabbage, all held together by a paste of vyaziga. Wrapped in pastry, the pie is often decorated with little fish, leaves, or flowers made of dough.

How to try it

Vyaziga is still available in Russian grocery stores and is considered essential to making a true kulebyaka.

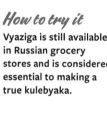

Although still used, vyaziga is less common in Russian cooking today. This decline in popularity is mostly due to the overfishing of sturgeon, but the ingredient has also suffered from its association with the downfall of some of history's most opulent eaters.

SIBERIAN SASHIMI COMPETITION

FESTIVAL STROGANINA • RUSSIA

How to try it

Festival Stroganina takes place in early December. Although there's no easy way to get to Yakutsk, the most reliable method is to fly: It has a small airport with a single runway.

The Russian city of Yakutsk is located fewer than 300 miles (483 km) from the Arctic Circle. Many of Yakutsk's residents are descended from the Yakut people, who have lived in the region since the 7th century and are famous across Russia for their hunting and fishing prowess. Despite experiencing the coldest temperatures of any major city on Earth, Yakutsk's locals like to be outdoors hunting, ice fishing, and in December (when lows average about –40°F) throwing an open-air celebration for their culinary specialty, stroganina—thin slices of sashimi stripped from the flank of a frozen whitefish.

The festival's opening ceremony is a judged presentation of these curls in elaborate stroganina sculptures, ranging from friendly snowmen to towering mammoths. The main event is a partnered trial: Men hold the frozen fish vertically by its tail and slide a sharp Yakutian knife (a 4-to-7-inch asymmetrical blade specially designed for long slices) along the fish's abdomen, producing elegant, diaphanous curls of sashimi. Their female partners dash back and forth between fish and plate, collecting stroganina and arranging it as artfully as possible. During judging, time is weighed against beauty, and a winner is chosen by a panel of fishermen, government officials, and sashimi enthusiasts. Knife vendors, fish salesmen, and merchants of fish-skin clothing and gloves round out the stroganina-themed celebration.

The Siberian sashimi is served simply, with salt and pepper, and should melt with the heat of your mouth. The bite-size blast of protein also makes an ideal chaser. As one saying goes, only sled dogs eat stroganina without vodka, and at the Festival Stroganina, there is plenty of vodka and champagne flowing into glasses carved from ice.

A Yakut woman in national clothing holding frozen ribbons of stroganina.

CHERNOBYL'S EXCLUSION ZONE CAFETERIA

CANTEEN 19 • UKRAINE

On April 26, 1986, a reactor at the Chernobyl nuclear power plant exploded, causing the world's biggest nuclear power disaster. The explosion killed dozens of workers and first responders, and scientists still dispute how many people have since died from radiation-related cancers. Today, forestry workers, biologists, and construction crews continue efforts to dismantle the reactor and remove waste in the 1,000-square-mile (2,600 km²) Exclusion Zone. When they're ready to take a break and eat, many of them head to Canteen 19.

Canteen 19, the Exclusion Zone's most popular dining hall, serves hearty Eastern European fare, including borscht, schnitzel, kompot, and sweet, cream-filled crepes. In addition to Chernobyl workers, the canteen feeds tour groups on Ukrainian government–sanctioned trips. (To enter the Exclusion Zone, guests must sign up for a tour or hire a private licensed guide, have their passports checked by the Ukrainian government, and pass through a military checkpoint.)

Diners must pass through a radiation detector before entering the austere canteen, which looks like an institutional lunch line, with white-uniformed workers scooping up meals from a line of prepared foods. The cafeteria offers a glimpse into contemporary Chernobyl life, as well as the opportunity to eat alongside the people still cleaning up after the disaster.

How to try it

Canteen 19 is open from 9 a.m. to 6 p.m. Many tour operators will make a stop here for lunch, which, if not included in the tour, costs about $10.

PORK LARD PLAYGROUND

SALO ART MUSEUM • UKRAINE

No trip to the city of Lviv is complete without a little pork fat art. Called salo in Ukraine, the salt-cured fat is usually eaten raw, often on bread, with just black pepper and paprika to counter its rich fattiness. The shelf-stable fat (which, thanks to salt-curing, is safe to eat for up to two years) also makes a great medium for sculpture, as evidenced by the Salo Art Museum.

Although a museum in name, the space is more like a contemporary art gallery housed in a restaurant that becomes a nightclub on the weekends. Human busts,

How to try it

The Salo Art Museum is open 7 days a week.

body parts, aliens, and animals are all whittled from the creamy, butter-textured fat, and line the walls of the industrial space. A giant replica of a human heart—which set the record for largest heart made out of lard—is proudly preserved behind glass. Rounding out the lard experience is the museum restaurant, which doubles down on the art theme. Most meals are served with small salo statues carved into strikingly realistic lions, pigs, soldier heads, and Elvis Presleys. There's also salo sushi, salo chocolate, and a vast supply of booze to cut through any lingering feelings about having eaten a pig constructed of pig fat.

After hours, the white couches and neon lighting transform the space to a nightclub with a live DJ, because when it comes to salo, it's never too far.

The works on display are among the world's most caloric figurines.

BUTTER WEEK

MASLENITSA • UKRAINE

How to try it

Maslenitsa is celebrated all over Ukraine the week before Lent, with particularly large parties (and publicly burning effigies) in Kyiv.

Before it was named Maslenitsa (literally "of butter"), this week-long celebration was a pagan festival to cast off winter and welcome spring. But when Christians joined the festivities, the party gradually evolved into a pre-Lenten feast that heavily featured the most decadent food permitted during fast days: dairy.

Also known as "Pancake Week," Ukrainian Maslenitsa is now a jubilant time for reconnecting with family and loved ones, particularly over pancakes. Each day brings a different theme, and a different person with whom to eat pancakes. Monday is for women, with men making the pancakes. On Wednesday, mothers-in-law traditionally invite sons-in-law for pancakes. Friday, the roles reverse and the son-in-law plays host. Saturday is for sisters-in-law. On Sunday, everyone eats pancakes together. Called mlyntsi, the pancakes are typically crepe-thin, made from a loose, dairy-heavy batter. As they're served all day long, mlyntsi can be sweet or savory, eaten with cottage cheese, fruit preserves, mushrooms, or caviar.

Revelers burn an effigy of "Lady Maslenitsa."

To accompany the pancake binge, Maslenitsa brings a revival of folk customs: Dancing and singing in traditional dress, ice skating, competitions, and snowball fights are loud and vivacious, meant to break the stillness of the cold months. On the final day, an effigy is burned that symbolizes death and resurrection—a ritual surviving from pagan times. The pancakes, too, are often considered a nod to the old tradition. Pagans worshipped the returning sun, and pancakes, being round and hot and yellow-hued, are their culinary representation.

WEDDING BREAD

KOROVAI • UKRAINE

On the Saturday preceding a Ukrainian wedding, seven married women gather to make korovai, a wedding bread that symbolizes the community's blessing of a new union. These women, who knead the dough and sing folk songs, must be happily in their first marriage, infusing the bread with their good fortune. When it's time to bake the dough, a happily married man must place the bread in the oven. Then everyone prays for the best. A cracked or malformed korovai is a bad sign for the marriage, but the higher it rises and the more decorations or layers it contains, the better the marriage will be.

Though wedding breads are a part of ceremonies across much of eastern Europe, Ukrainian korovai tends to be the most ornate. Each flourish crafted from dough has a specific meaning: Roses symbolize beauty, ears of wheat mean future prosperity, and a wreath of periwinkle represents the strong connection that binds the couple. Two birds often grace the top of the bread, one baked with its wings outstretched to represent the groom, the other with wings furled to symbolize the bride.

During the wedding, the korovai is displayed prominently beside the altar. Afterward, every guest must eat a piece. In some versions of the tradition, the bride and groom both break off a bit of bread, and whoever comes away with the bigger slice will be the head of the household.

How to try it
A few Ukrainian bakeries online will ship their korovai internationally. Prices start at about $100 and increase as the bread becomes more elaborate. It all depends on how happy you'd like your marriage to be.

SCANDINAVIA

SPICY BIRTHDAY RITUAL

PEBERSVEND • DENMARK

How to try it
Every day, unmarried people turn 25 and 30 in Denmark; keep an eye out for celebratory spice attacks.

Hundreds of years ago, traveling spice salesmen were notorious bachelors. They never stayed in one place for long enough to settle down, and a man who remained single was called a pebersvend—literally, a "pepper companion." Today, Danes still refer to unmarried adults as spice salesmen. (A single woman is a pebermø, or "pepper maiden.") To celebrate an unwed person's birthday, Danes like to douse them in spices.

A 25th birthday calls for getting "cinnamon-ed." Often, friends attack the birthday pebersvend or pebermø by tying them to a post, making them don goggles, and then pelting them with handfuls of ground spice. At age 30, the cinnamon attack is upgraded to pepper, and the birthday victim is likely to receive at least one pepper grinder as a gift.

SAUNA SAUSAGE

SAUNA MAKKARA • FINLAND

How to try it
Some Helsinki markets will sell meat specifically labeled "sausage for sauna." But if you can't find sauna sausage, Polish kielbasa will do.

In Finland, the sauna is a cultural institution. Finns once gave birth and washed their dead in the heated rooms because they were the cleanest spaces in the home. Now there are 3.3 million saunas for a population of 5.5 million, meaning just about every household has one.

As with any treasured national pastime, there are rules. First, you must strip and shower. When you enter, lay a towel on your seat and prepare to get hot: The temperature should be 158–212°F (70–100°C). It's good to work up a healthy sweat, but if you start to feel dry, simply ladle some water onto the hot stones to create steam, known as löyly. When you've had enough, go outside and cool off by jumping in a lake or rolling in snow.

With all that sweating and jumping, you're probably hungry, which means it's time for sauna sausage. While you were sizzling inside the steam room, so was your meal. Makkara, a traditional Finnish sausage, is often heated over the hot stones of a sauna stove, known as a kiuas. For a crispy exterior, the bare sausage goes directly on the kiuas. For tender sausage and easy cleanup, wrap them in foil or get yourself a special holder made of Finnish soapstone and used exclusively for the cooking of sausage in saunas.

The sausages, which typically come plain or with cheese inside, pair perfectly with the sweet-hot zing of mustard. Called sinnapi, Finnish mustard is often made on the stovetop at home, using mustard powder, sugar, lemon juice, vinegar, and the special ingredient: a big glug of cream. Cooked down to a thick, amber spread, sinnapi is a crucial sausage condiment that cannot be swapped out for any old supermarket mustard.

Sausages cooked in special holders are extra tender.

Finnish Mustard

5 tablespoons hot dry mustard
   (such as Colman's)

½ cup sugar

1 teaspoon salt

1 cup cream

1 tablespoon olive oil

2 tablespoons apple cider vinegar

1 tablespoon lemon juice

1. Mix together the mustard, sugar, and salt, making sure to remove all lumps. (Use a sieve if necessary.)

2. Transfer the dry mixture to a small saucepan and add the cream one tablespoon at a time, incorporating each spoonful before adding another.

3. Add the olive oil, vinegar, and lemon juice and stir.

4. Bring the mustard to a boil over medium heat, then lower the heat and simmer for 7 to 8 minutes, stirring constantly.

5. Let cool, transfer to a sealable jar, and keep in the refrigerator.

MUSTARD

Before mustard was a condiment, it was a poultice for bronchitis and toothaches, an ointment for skin inflammation, and a powdered additive to a soothing, sleep-inducing bath. As early as the 5th century BCE, the Greeks prized the easy-to-grow plant for its antiseptic properties and ability to stimulate blood circulation. Scientist Pythagoras found that the essential oils, when applied to a wound, pulled toxins from the body, which led him to use mustard as a treatment for scorpion stings. Physician Hippocrates applied mustard plasters to chests and let the heat from the dressing loosen phlegm and ease breathing.

Around the 4th century CE, the Romans had a new idea. They mixed young wine with the crushed seeds of the medicinal plant, tasted the paste, and named the new flavor sensation "flaming hot must." Long before the Silk Road opened to Europe, mustard (mustum being the Romans' unfermented grape juice, and ardens the Latin for "fiery") was one of the continent's first breakout spices, and it soon spread to the rest of the world.

Because of its antibiotic properties, an unopened jar of mustard will rarely spoil. It doesn't require refrigeration, will not develop mold or bacteria, and will never become unsafe to eat. Coupled with the distinctive zing that flatters everything from Indian curries to American hot dogs, dim sum to barbecue sauce, nearly every region in the world has developed their own application for the spicy, versatile, and medicinal plant.

Dijon

In the French city now synonymous with the condiment, they made their mustard with verjus, the tart juice of unripe grapes, which made a sharper, more sophisticated variety soon coveted around the country. The Duke of Burgundy, an avid 14th-century mustard lover, held a gala where guests reportedly consumed 85 gallons of Dijon in a single sitting. Pope John XII of Avignon declared a new Vatican position called Grand Moutardier du Pape, or Grand Mustard Maker to the Pope, and appointed his nephew, believed

to be a dilettante living near Dijon, to mix all his mustards. (The idiom "the pope's mustard maker," which refers to a pompous person in an insignificant role, came from this appointment.) By 1855, a man named Maurice Grey was winning awards for his Dijon-mustard-making machine, the first of its kind to automate the process. He sought out a financial backer and found Auguste Poupon. Together, combining their last names to form the Grey Poupon brand, they rolled out their signature Dijon, prepared with white wine and manufactured at high speed.

Colman's

Jeremiah Colman, an English miller, pioneered the technique of grinding mustard seeds into a fine powder without allowing the oils to evaporate, which preserved the spicy, intense flavor. In 1866, Colman became the official mustard maker to Queen Victoria and later, during World War II, his mustard was one of the few foods that wasn't rationed because it was essential to flavoring bland wartime food.

Kasundi

Traditionally, Bengalis had elaborate rituals surrounding the harvest and washing of mustard seeds to make the traditional mustard relish, kasundi. On a spring day called Akshaya Tritiya, groups of married women bathed in odd numbers, then washed the mustard seeds facing east, chanting in wet saris. Over the next week, the seeds were ground into a pulp, spiced, and mixed with water, salt, and green mango, before fermenting in a clay pot. Originally, only Brahmins (the highest Indian caste) were allowed to make the mustard sauce, but it's now open season for kasundi making. The spicy chutney is the preferred dipping sauce for fried foods, especially the beloved Bengali vegetable fritter, called a chop.

Mostarda di Frutta

The 14th-century dukes of Milan were trendsetters in mixing sweet and spicy. Chunks of fruit such as apples, quince, or cherries were preserved in sweet and hot mustard syrup, then served atop their ducal roasts. In Italy today, the term *mostarda* refers to the hot and fruity condiment.

Chinese Mustard

This thick, pungent paste inflames the nasal passages like horseradish or wasabi. There is no special ingredient to the mixture, just ground brown mustard seeds (*Brassica juncea*, or Chinese mustard) mixed with water. After about 15 minutes, the paste reaches peak potency, then slowly declines. A good swap for Chinese mustard powder is Colman's, which is a blend of *Brassica juncea* and the slightly milder white mustard, *Sinapis alba*.

HELSINKI'S POP-UP RESTAURANT PARTY

RESTAURANT DAY • FINLAND

On Restaurant Day in Helsinki—which occurs on the third Saturday of February, May, August, and November—anyone can open a restaurant, anywhere. All around the Finnish capital, citizens sell ceviche from pop-up stands, muffins from jewelry stores, and homemade food from old train depots, borrowed kitchens, bus stops, stairwells, and the occasional boat. Anything goes: Restaurants are erected for babies, currywursts are slung from dark basements. In a city where residents don't engage in much small talk, Restaurant Day has altered Helsinki's social fabric. It's a day for people to talk to one another, to approach strangers and chat about what they're cooking.

Restaurant Day got its start in 2011, when Helsinki resident Timo Santala wanted to start a mobile bicycle bar, selling drinks and tapas, and was frustrated by the city's red tape. Santala imagined a day where a restaurant could open with no licenses and no limitations, and inaugurated Restaurant Day in May 2011. Since then, the free-for-all food carnival has become so beloved that the city government decided to support the festivities. (It helps that there have been no known cases of Restaurant Day food poisoning.)

The rogue entrepreneurial holiday has spread to other countries, too, from Iceland to islands in the South Pacific—where communities are connecting over shared food and conversation. In Russia, a Restaurant Day chef cooked chicken in the seam of an old Soviet car motor. In Nicaragua, one restaurant owner took payment in the form of a poem or a song.

SNOWMOBILE COFFEE IN THE HUGGING TREE FOREST

HALIPUU'S CAMPFIRE BARISTA • FINLAND

The Campfire Barista, Steffan Wunderink's one-of-a-kind café, offers up exceptional drinks prepared over an open fire that he drags behind a snowmobile through a forest in the far northern reaches of Finland.

The forest, which belongs to his wife's grandfather, was a gift from the Finnish state after the family lost their home during World War II. Instead of using the forest as timber, the family decided to put the trees up for adoption and invite tourists to come spend time with them. It was while working as a guide on this land—now known as HaliPuu (Hugging Tree) Forest—that Wunderink became the Campfire Barista.

Using an open fire as his stove, Wunderink gained a reputation for his wondrously smoky, espresso-based drinks, as well as a chai latte made from an antioxidant-rich native mushroom called chaga. When a local complained about having to trek into the forest for her daily caffeine fix, the C.F.B. went mobile.

Wunderink bought a snowmobile and built a sled that could safely hold a wood-fired grill. Then, in a windfall of upgrades, he partnered with a friend with ties to a single-estate, biodynamic coffee farm in India, who also happened to operate a solar-powered coffee roaster out of a converted sea container in town.

During winter months, you can catch Wunderink's café in front of the tourism office in the center of town, in his family's forest, or at a number of public events. In the warmer months, without a snowpack to ride on, he's restricted to stationary events and festivals. His menu has expanded beyond espresso-based drinks and chaga chai to organic teas, warm black currant juice, and lingonberry marshmallows you can roast over his fire.

FERMENTED BIRDS IN A SEAL SKIN

KIVIAK · GREENLAND

This Inuit tradition begins with a hunt: Using just sight and feel, a skilled hunter casts a long-handled net high into the air to catch small auks mid-flight, netting hundreds of birds over the course of a single day. The summer months, when the weather is moderate and the birds plentiful, are the time to make kiviak so it will be ready by winter, when hunting sites are perilously icy and sustenance scarce.

Auks are small Arctic birds, about half the size of puffins, little enough to be held in a palm. Up to 500 auks are needed for a kiviak, which takes the birds—left whole with feathers intact—and stuffs them into the cleaned skin of a seal. Once packed with auks, any excess air is removed from the seal sack, often by jumping on it, then the opening is sewn shut and the seam is rubbed with seal fat, which repels flies. The massive bird-and-seal package is buried under a heap of stones and left to ferment for a minimum of three months (but will keep for up to 18). The seal skin retains a thick layer of blubber, and the fat allows the tiny birds to slowly soften as they age, bones included. Save for the feathers, every part of the bird will be eaten.

Come winter, when the Greenland days are long and dark, kiviak provides a celebration. The fermented auks are considered special-occasion food, saved for birthdays and weddings, and unearthing the bundle means a long-awaited feast. The birds remain mostly intact, but the meat and innards are almost creamy, with a taste often compared to the ripest of gorgonzola cheese crossed with the anise flavor of licorice. Kiviak is always eaten outdoors because the smell is as pungent as the taste. It is also imperative that the birds be auks: In 2013, several people in the town of Siorapaluk died from eating kiviak made from eider birds, which don't ferment as well as auks.

How to try it

Kiviak is hard-won food, but if you're willing to trek to eastern, western, or polar Greenland, you can try to wrangle an invitation to a local birthday party.

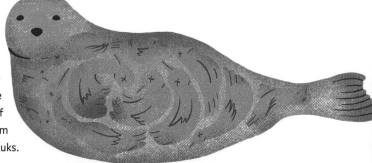

Engastration

The centuries-old culinary technique of stuffing one animal inside another animal, sometimes beyond sense or recognition.

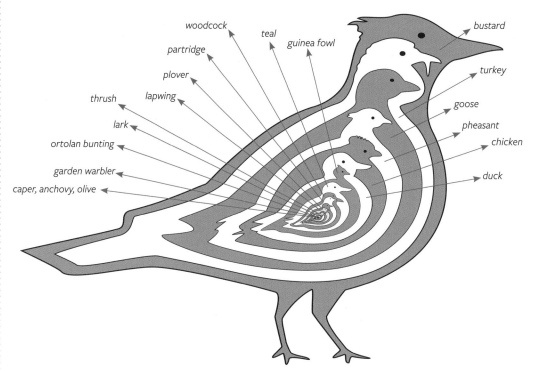

woodcock
teal
guinea fowl
bustard
partridge
turkey
plover
goose
thrush
lapwing
pheasant
lark
chicken
ortolan bunting
garden warbler
duck
caper, anchovy, olive

RÔTI SANS PAREIL ("UNPARALLELED ROAST")

A French recipe from 1807 instructs the cook to stuff a caper into an anchovy, which is then placed into the cavity of an olive, which can be stuffed easily into a garden warbler, which fits nicely into an ortolan bunting, and then, with some finesse, into a lark, which is fitted inside a thrush, then pushed into a lapwing and shoved into a plover, which slides into a partridge just before being rammed into a woodcock, muscled into a teal, shunted into a guinea fowl and crammed into a duck, then a chicken, then a pheasant, before the final, large-bird sprint, which shoves the menagerie into a goose, which should fit into a turkey and, if all goes well, slides snugly into a bustard. Slow-cooked in a hermetically sealed pot of broth, your 17 birds will be ready to eat in 24 hours.

TROJAN BOAR

This ancient Roman recipe begins with a gutted 1,000-pound (454 kg) hog, washed twice in wine and rolled in musk and pepper. Half the enormous cavity was filled with a collection of thrushes, sow's udders, gnat snappers, and eggs, while the other half was plugged up with polenta. Oysters and scallops were inserted in the mouth and pushed down into the belly, then the whole hog was sewn up, washed in liquor, and roasted. Aptly nicknamed after the Trojan horse, this engorged boar was served up at brawny events like gladiatorial contests, chariot races, and the inaugurations of emperors.

BEDOUIN STUFFED CAMEL

The whole stuffed camel is a gastronomic legend—or is it? Fish, stuffed with hardboiled eggs and rice, are packed into chickens that are stitched into a couple of lambs, maybe a goat, and loaded into the body of a camel, which is boiled then roasted on a spit. This camel, allegedly prepared at prominent wedding feasts in Saudi Arabia and the United Arab Emirates, appears in culinary memoirs and many cookbooks, but firsthand accounts are still rare. *Guinness World Records* claims the camel is "the largest item on any menu in the world," and pictures of the desert delicacy do exist; still, the skeptics remain convinced that the Saudis are pulling off an elaborate, impressively executed camel joke.

FERMENTED SHARK

HÁKARL • ICELAND

When trying hákarl—the dried and fermented shark of Iceland—it's common to gag. Even a bite-size cube has an extraordinarily high ammonia content, which smells (and some say tastes) like urine. But Vikings would advise you to pinch your nose and be thankful for their innovation. Had the shark not been fermented per their specifications, you might not even live to be repulsed because the meat would have been chock-full of poison.

When fresh, Greenland sharks contain large amounts of trimethylamine oxide, which can cause powerful, uncontrollable intoxication when eaten. The Vikings, when confronted with a meaty creature that grew up to 24 feet long, devised a method for draining the poison from its flesh. They buried a cleaned shark in a shallow pit of gravelly sand, placed rocks on top of the sand to weigh the shark down and press the liquid from its body, and left it to seep and ferment for 6 to 12 weeks. After digging the shark up, they cut it into strips and hung the pieces to dry for several months. The finished product lasted practically forever, making for perfect Viking food.

But what's great for a Viking is not always great for a modern palate. Putrid pee aroma aside, hákarl is a hardcore piece of meat. Soft, white bits from the body are often described as a gruesome cross between fish and blue cheese, and the reddish belly meat is unapologetically chewy. Even Icelanders are polarized by this food; many, in fact, have never tried it themselves.

In recent years, hákarl has become popular with tourists, who keep the traditional industry alive and don't mind that modern curing methods involve more plastic containers than dirt and rocks.

Pieces of fermented shark hang in an open warehouse.

How to try it

Most of the country's hákarl is produced at the Bjarnarhöfn Shark Museum, where you can sample a piece. The midwinter Þorrablót festival, which celebrates Icelandic heritage, is another place you'll be sure to find it.

VOLCANIC SPRINGS BANANA PLANTATION

GARÐYRKJUSKÓLI RÍKISINS • ICELAND

How to try it

The plantation is not a traditional tourist site, but visitors can call ahead to see the fruit. The school is located at Reykjumörk Street, whose name translates to smokefield, with several fumaroles along the way making the air hazy and warm.

Less than 200 miles (322 km) from the Arctic Circle, the plantation at the Icelandic National Gardening School is a tropical oasis. Surrounded by volcanic hot springs, the plantation's easy access to geothermal energy and an unusually warm climate allow them to grow warm-weather crops like bananas as well as avocados, cocoa, and coffee. Many Icelanders will tell you it's the largest banana plantation in all of Europe—and it might be, depending on who's measuring.

The Icelandic banana-growing experiment began in the 1940s, when import taxes on produce were high and geothermal energy was cheap. For nearly a decade, Icelanders ate local bananas grown in geothermal-heated greenhouses that held at a steady 70°F (21°C). But in 1960, the government removed the import duties on fruit, and Iceland's greenhouse bananas could no longer compete against the international market. Today, most bananas sold in Iceland are shipped into the country from tropical climates, but the plantation in Reykir still manages several hundred trees that produce 1,000 to 4,400 pounds (500 to 2,000 kg) of bananas annually.

Whether the plantation can be called the largest in Europe is up for debate. Technically, Spain and France control larger plantations, but they're located in their respective warm-weather colonies on the Canary Islands, Martinique, and Guadeloupe. The plantation in Iceland, which is completely isolated from the outside banana world, may end up serving a different purpose: A fungal pathogen called Panama disease has been wreaking havoc on banana plantations and many fear it could wipe out the world's most widely consumed banana, the Cavendish. (This has happened before: The Cavendish's predecessor, the Big Mike, was lost in the 1950s.) Quarantined in the far north, the Icelandic bananas might end up being the last bananas standing.

Bananas thrive in a steamy greenhouse—even in chilly Iceland.

Showboating Royals

During the Middle Ages, showing off often went too far—especially at banquets, where royals loved to flaunt how rich, creative, and hilarious they were. Among nobility, throwing the most elaborate feast became such competitive sport that a new term was coined for their preferred method of showboating. Sotelties, or entremets in French (literally "between courses"), were dishes meant not to eat, but to entertain: Fish suspended in jelly appeared to be swimming, dough castles were plastered in gold leaf, slivers of almonds mimicked the spikes of a hedgehog, and meatballs were made to look like oranges. Cute at first, by the 14th century the practice was getting out of hand. Frantic for ways to remain on top, royal kitchens in England and France began reaching for more ostentatious farces. Animals became the medium of choice (another flashy move, as vegetables were considered food for the poor), and although some did laugh, chances are those people were megalomaniacs.

Redressed birds were a classic banquet centerpiece. Swans and peacocks, with their elegant plumage, were meticulously skinned to get their feathers off in one neat piece. After the birds were roasted, cooks redressed them in their skins. To keep things interesting, sometimes a bird was sewn inside the feathers of a different bird because the only thing droller than a roasted peacock sewn back into its skin was a goose replacing that peacock.

The **cockentrice** was allegedly created for King Henry VIII to impress the visiting king of France. The recipe, written like a surgical guide, instructs the chef to procure a capon and a pig, then to scald and clean them both before cutting each animal in half at the waist. Using a needle and thread, the front half of the pig is stitched to the back half of the capon, creating a new hybrid animal guaranteed to dazzle. (The order could also be reversed: chicken top, pig bottom.)

Singing chickens were made by sewing shut the bottom of a bird's neck, filling the cavity with mercury and ground sulfur, and sewing the neck again at the top. When reheated, the chemicals pushed air through the restricted passage of the neck and produced a sound akin to singing. This technique was used to prank chefs, too: Chickens were known to wail and jump from pots in what may have been the creepiest kitchen of all time.

Regular pigs became **fire-breathing pigs** when their mouths were stuffed with alcohol-soaked cotton, then lit on fire to create the optical illusion. For extra-special occasions, many animals were assembled and made to sing and breathe fire in religious and allegorical spectacles.

Chickens were the primary victims in the gruesome movement to make living food that looked dead. Submerged in hot water, they were plucked alive and glazed, then put to sleep by tucking the bird's head beneath its wing. When awakened at the table, the chicken would flee down the table, knocking over glasses and jugs and making women shriek in what royals considered a top-notch joke. Lobsters also made good fodder: After being doused in extra-strong brandy, live lobsters turned red and could be easily mixed in with the platter of cooked lobsters.

The top half of a pig sewn into the bottom half of a capon was a dish meant to impress the king of France.

How to try it
Laugarvatn Fontana is
a hot spring spa that
leads tours of its on-
site geothermal bakery
twice daily. A tour
includes a tasting of
the bread hot from
the ground, served
with butter.

HOT SPRING RYE BREAD

HVERABRAUÐ • ICELAND

Every day, a small but devoted group of Icelandic bakers trudges out to the near-est geothermal spring, digs a hole in the hot black sand, and deposits a box full of just-mixed bread dough. About a day later, they go back out and dig up the box. Inside they find a hot loaf of rye bread, gently steamed by the heat of the spring, that's dense, chewy, nutty, and just a little bit sweet.

Iceland comprises a labyrinthine network of under-ground volcanic hot springs, and more than 50 percent of the country's energy comes from geothermal sources. The bread must also absorb some of this power, because after a few bites of this hearty loaf, you might feel ready to climb a mountain or ford an icy river. Hverabrauð means, literally, "hot spring bread," but one of the food's nicknames—þrumari, or thunder bread—hints at another powerful side effect. All that fiber, after all, can wreak havoc at the other end of your digestive system.

Of course most Icelanders bake their rye bread (rúgbrauð) in modern ovens, but those who opt for geo-thermal heat swear the taste and texture is vastly superior.

A baker digs up geothermal bread on the shore of Lake Laugarvatn.

BEER ON HORSEBACK COMPETITION

BEER TÖLT • ICELAND

Icelandic horses are famous for their tölt—a smooth, lateral gait unique to the northern breed. The steady, four-beat stride can pick up velocity while remaining comfortable for riders, letting them remain fairly still in the saddle while their steeds zip around the track. To prove just how steady their horse can be, there is the beer tölt, a game in which the rider holds a full mug of beer while putting his mount through its paces. The objective is to spill as little beer as possible because the rider who loses the least gets to drink the most.

The beer tölt is a reliable feature at Icelandic horse shows. Competitors ride at various speeds, in forward and lateral directions, holding the mug with a single hand. Sometimes there is music. The sight of a dozen eques-trians, each holding a beer with intense concentration as their horses bounce jauntily beneath them, is as impressive as it is ridiculous—and is an ideal way to show off your steady horse, your quirky personality, and your respect for beer.

How to try it
Friðheimar Farm in
Selfoss, southern
Iceland, features
various horse shows
including the beer tölt.

ICELANDIC HOT DOGS

PYLSUR • ICELAND

Compared with more intimidating Icelandic specialties like sour rams' testicles and fermented shark, the Icelandic hot dog known as pylsa is a comparatively accessible, and notoriously delicious, national dish.

Pylsur (just one hot dog is a pylsa) are built from a triumvirate of meats: lamb, pork, and beef. They also feature two kinds of onions, crispy-fried and raw, and a selection of condiments including ketchup sweetened with apples and a special sauce known as remolaði. The latter condiment is the Icelandic cousin to France's remoulade, a mayonnaise-based sauce spiked with pickles, vinegar, and onions.

The subtle blend of meats is the key to the pylsa's complex flavor. Beef provides the fat, pork the texture, and lamb a subtle gaminess. Icelandic lambs have a very nice life—they roam freely around the island, feasting on berries and vegetation, which make their meat abundantly flavorful. Icelanders also cook their hot dogs in a mixture of water and beer. The country's most famous supplier, Bæjarins Beztu Pylsur (literally "The Best Hot Dogs in Town"), is a contender for the title of world's greatest hot dog stand. The historic chain, which has been serving hot dogs since 1937, is a national institution with a perpetual line that's included celebrity chefs from around the world and former US president Bill Clinton.

How to try it
Bæjarins Beztu Pylsur has five locations in Reykjavík, the oldest being in Tryggvagata, near the harbor. Try ordering "one with everything" (eina með öllu).

Other Famous Hot Dogs

NEW JERSEY, USA
Italian

Fried hot dog, fried potatoes, bell peppers, onions in pizza bread

MEXICO
Sonora

Bacon-wrapped hot dog with beans, onions, tomato, chilies

SWEDEN
Tunnbrödsrulle

Hot dog with fresh onions, mashed potatoes, lettuce, shrimp salad, in a flatbread

KOREA
Potato Dog

Hot dog on a stick dipped in batter with crinkle-cut french fries, deep fried, drizzled with ketchup

COLOMBIA
Perro Caliente

Boiled hot dog with pineapple salsa, coleslaw, potato chips, Costeño cheese, salsa rosada (ketchup and mayo), quail egg

A NORWEGIAN LOVE STORY

FROZEN PIZZA • NORWAY

How to try it

A classic Norwegian
way to eat frozen pizza
is adding extra cheese
before baking, then
drizzling it with
ketchup.

*The average grocery store
needs two aisles to house
their frozen pies.*

Norwegians eat more pizza (per capita) than any nation on Earth. And of the 50 million pizzas consumed each year, 47 million of them are pulled from the freezer and baked at home.

Pizza arrived in Norway in the 1970s and was the first foreign food to burst onto the local scene. An American named Louis Jordan, who learned to make pizza from a Neapolitan living in New Haven, Connecticut, opened a small pizzeria in Oslo called Peppes with the help of his Norwegian wife, Anne. Peppes boasted nine varieties of American- and Italian-style pies, which were a thrilling culinary departure from the traditional meat-and-potatoes fare of the time. Peppes, which remains one of the most popular pizza chains in Norway, quickly expanded.

The frozen pizza movement came a decade later, when the brand Grandiosa set out to make a pie large enough for a family to share. The cheesy baked good was still new to the general population, and according to Norwegian pizza lore, the factory manager who agreed to produce the frozen pies did so without actually knowing what a pizza was. The company placed their bets on tomato sauce, Jarlsberg cheese, and paprika, and never looked back: This signature recipe still sells nine million pies every year.

THE GREAT CARAMEL CHEESE ACCIDENT

BRUNOST TRUCK FIRE • NORWAY

How to try it

Stock up on varieties of
brunost at Fenaknoken,
an Oslo delicatessen.
While there, you can
also pick up some
reindeer sausage and
cloudberry jam.

In 2013, a truck carrying 60,000 pounds (about 27,000 kg) of brunost—Norway's favorite caramelized cheese—was barreling through a tunnel in Tysfjord when it caught fire. The blaze spread to the truck's cargo, whose fats and sugars fueled the flames and kept the fire raging for five days, emitting so much toxic gas that firefighters could not approach until the cheese had burned through. The tunnel was ravaged and closed for weeks, but the biggest national tragedy was the loss of all that good brunost—the decadent "brown cheese" loved by Norwegians. One member of the Norwegian Roads Administrations lamented, "I didn't know that brown cheese burns so well."

Brunost is not technically a cheese, but a by-product of cheese making. Leftover whey is simmered with milk or cream into a sweet, caramelized paste with a fudge-like texture and salty-sweet, almost tangy flavor. The only acceptable tool for cutting a brown cheese is an ostehøvel—the great Norwegian invention that we know simply as a cheese slicer. Eating brunost has fewer rules and the sweet cheese can find its way into almost any meal. Rye toast, waffles, and sandwiches (strawberry jam plus brunost makes a Norwegian version of a peanut butter and jelly) are all perfect vessels for brown cheese. Brunost, in all its beautiful versatility, can also be melted into stews, mixed into meatballs, and used to sustain weeklong fires that ruin tunnels and make international news.

Weaponized Food

Food has long been a dependable vessel for murder. Typically paired with poison, edibles are widely regarded as a neat, quick, and (relatively) civilized way to slay an enemy. During the Joseon dynasty in Korea, a ceremonial cocktail called sayak was used exclusively to execute the very elite (regular people were decapitated or hanged). Mathematician Alan Turing died from a bite of a cyanide-laced apple (whether it was intentional or an accident is still a matter of debate). Although poison is the obvious choice, history proves there are many ways to off a person with groceries.

CHOCOLATE BOMBS: The Nazis were known to put bombs in so many things—thermos flasks, mess tins, motor oil cans, watches—that the British intelligence service hired an artist to draw 25 detailed mock-ups of Nazi booby-trap bombs as a manual for agents who might need to defuse them. Among these drawings was one of an exploding chocolate bar intended to kill Winston Churchill, along with anyone within several yards. Dark chocolate (nearly impossible to find at the time) concealed the explosive steel-and-canvas device, which was wrapped in black-and-gold paper and earmarked for Churchill's living room. Fortunately for the prime minister, the Nazis' plan was intercepted before he could be tempted by the candy.

CHEESE CANNONBALLS: In 1841, Uruguayan Navy Commodore John H. Coe ran out of cannonballs in the middle of battle. He and his opponent, Admiral William Brown of Argentina, had been engaged in close combat, their iron cannonballs shot from the decks of their ships, about 33 yards (30 m) across the water. Cannonballs gone, Commodore Coe remembered a stock of cheese that hadn't aged well—it was so hard, a lieutenant had broken a knife trying to cut it. Coe loaded the cannon with the compacted Edam and fired away. Cheese cannonballs struck the main mast, tore holes through the sails, and flew through a porthole, killing two men. The Argentinians retreated, unwilling to lose more men to defective dairy, and the battle was won.

MAD HONEY: Made from a rare species of rhododendron that contains a natural neurotoxin called grayanotoxin, mad honey is produced around the Black Sea region of eastern Turkey, where the locals call it deli bal. Overconsumption can lead to nausea, numbness, and hallucinations, which is exactly what happened in 67 BCE, when the army of King Mithridates left chunks of mad honeycomb along the road used by the invading Romans. Unable to resist, the Romans gorged themselves on the sweet snack, and when they began to lose physical and mental capacity, the Persian army came back and finished the job.

POISON MILKSHAKE: Fidel Castro is said to have survived some 600 assassination attempts during his rule as prime minister and president of Cuba. Playing into his weakness for ice cream (he famously concluded a large lunch with Gabriel García Márquez by eating 18 scoops), the CIA planned to slip a capsule of poison into his chocolate milkshake. But when the assassin went to retrieve the pill from the freezer it was stuck, and it tore open when he tried to get it out. "This moment was the closest the CIA got to assassinating Fidel," said Fabian Escalante, former head of the Cuban secret service, which makes sense if you consider the other attempts: a bacteria-filled wetsuit, LSD cigars, an exploding conch shell, and thallium salt intended to make his beard fall out and thus cause him to lose the respect of his people.

*The subaquatic dining
room can seat up to
40 guests.*

THE WORLD'S LARGEST UNDERWATER RESTAURANT

UNDER • NORWAY

Under, submerged off the coast of Lindesnes on the southern tip of Norway, is the first underwater restaurant in Europe and the biggest in the world. Sixteen feet below sea level, visitors dine on local delicacies while watching fish glide across the submerged panoramic window. In Norwegian, the word *under* means both "below" and "wonder."

The architecture firm behind Under, Snøhetta, has designed other wondrous structures (including the iconic Oslo Opera House) but constructing a subaquatic restaurant posed unique challenges. They needed to ensure the building could withstand a harsh ocean environment of waves, storms, and constant water pressure. Beyond sound construction, the architects designed the restaurant to slowly integrate into its surroundings, eventually functioning as an artificial reef where underwater life can grow.

From the outside, Under looks like a container that fell off a truck and slid into the water. But after walking inside and descending the stairs, visitors enter a whole new world. The minimalist dining room, with dark silhouetted tables and chairs, is bathed in the soft aquamarine glow of the sea. In addition to the underwater entertainment, the fixed seasonal tasting menu features hyperlocal foods intended to take diners outside their comfort zone, including shellfish, seabirds, wild sheep, sea kale, and arrowgrass.

How to try it
There is a long waiting list to dine at Under, and the tasting menu isn't cheap. You can check availability and make reservations on the restaurant's website.

THE VIKINGS' SOLUTION FOR SCURVY

SPRUCE BEER • SWEDEN

Sailors and scurvy once went hand in hand. Long sea voyages required foods that could keep for long periods of time, which meant fresh produce, along with the vitamin C it contained, was an impractical luxury. Especially in

Scandinavia and the Great White North, the Vikings endured some bleak, barren winters—but what they lacked in produce, they made up for in pine trees.

For several centuries, maritime explorers boiled the tips of evergreens into a drink called spruce beer, which contained enough vitamin C to keep them relatively scurvy-free. Before the disease had a medical name, the Vikings believed the liquid spruce kept them healthy, boosted strength in battle, and enhanced fertility.

By the 16th century, European explorers in North America were recording the use of spruce to fight scurvy. In Newfoundland, it became one of the most popular, readily available drinks around. Even Captain James Cook, in his 1784 book *Voyage to the Pacific Ocean*, describes two of his men brewing the fragrant beer for the crew's daily consumption. The elixir was carried on British navy ships and drunk by British and colonial American armies, until the end of the 1800s, when the practice died out in favor of other vitamin sources.

Spruce beer tastes a lot like drinking a Christmas tree. Fans describe it as crisp and refreshing, while detractors equate the strong flavor to pine-based cleaning products.

How to try it

Today, Canada is the leading market for spruce beer, which can be shipped globally, but anyone can make a home brew following 18th-century recipes available online.

THE NOBEL PRIZE BANQUET HALL

STADSHUSKÄLLAREN • SWEDEN

The Stadshuskällaren, or the City Hall Cellars, is the venue for the Nobel banquet, which takes place each December 10 and is attended by geniuses, humanitarians, and Swedish nobility. On all other days of the year, however, you can visit the restaurant as a regular person and eat a banquet from ceremonies past.

Every banquet, from every year, is available to order. The 2017 Nobel banquet, for example, with its crispy saddle of lamb and frosty bilberry bavarois, is available to order, plated on the bespoke green-and-gold Nobel china used at the actual banquets each year. For a unique historical experience, visitors can have a banquet from a Nobel year that fêted one of their cultural heroes. Fans of Gabriel García Márquez can have the banquet from 1982 (with Arctic char in dill cream sauce and Nobel ice cream), and Marie Curie devotees can toast her 1911 chemistry prize by dining on fonds d´artichauts duchesse and poularde fermière (artichoke bottoms "duchess style" and farm chicken).

Unfortunately, Nobel banquets don't come cheap. The price of the previous year's banquet is currently 1,865 SEK ($200) per person. Vintage menus (anything earlier than the previous year) have varying prices, require a party of 10 or more, and need to be booked at least a week in advance. If that sounds too lavish, you can always stop into the restaurant for lunch and gawk at the Stadshuskällaren's vaulted ceilings and lush decor.

How to try it

The Stadshuskällaren is located at Hantverkargatan 1 in Stockholm, and is open for lunch Monday to Friday (11:30 a.m. to 2:30 p.m.) and for dinner Wednesday to Saturday (5 p.m. to 11 p.m.).

The restaurant, open since 1922, still retains some original furnishings.

EUROPE'S DELIGHTFUL
Food Museums

THE HERRING ERA MUSEUM

Siglufjörður, Iceland

Iceland's largest maritime museum re-creates the boom days of the herring rush in the country's northernmost town. From the early 1900s to 1969, the tiny village exploded with thousands of herring workers who came to salt and process the summer catch. The museum is housed in an old salting station and brings to life the work and living quarters of the period and place, which Icelanders call "the Atlantic Klondike."

THE FOOD ADDITIVES MUSEUM

Hamburg, Germany

Tucked away in a wholesale market, this museum shines a light on the mysterious world of emulsifiers, stabilizers, dyes, thickeners, sweeteners, preservatives, and flavorings. Learn why we eat so much sawdust and how the world slowly legislated against the use of poisonous additives, such as arsenic.

THE DISGUSTING FOOD MUSEUM

Malmö, Sweden

A collection of 80 polarizing foods from around the world, including guinea pig, durian, and maggot-infested cheese, the museum highlights the subjectivity of disgust. Showcasing foods beloved in one country and loathed in another, there are plenty of opportunities for smelling and tasting, encouraging visitors to challenge their notions of disgust.

Above: Goat's rennet cheese (sallu sardu); Left: Fresh durian fruit

THE BAKED BEAN MUSEUM OF EXCELLENCE

Port Talbot, Wales

Previously an IT worker for British Petroleum, in 1986 the man once known as Barry Kirk sat naked in a bathtub of baked beans for 100 hours, setting a world record. The event led him to change his name to Captain Beany and open a bean-centric museum in his two-bedroom apartment. The tiny museum is packed with baked-bean tins and memorabilia from around the world, a "Branston Bathroom," and a "Heinz Kitchen."

Asia

THE MIDDLE EAST • SOUTH AND CENTRAL ASIA

EAST ASIA • SOUTHEAST ASIA

THE MIDDLE EAST

THE ORIGINAL FRUIT LEATHER

T'TU LAVASH • ARMENIA

Sun-dried fruit leather has added color to Armenian markets for centuries.

How to try it
Vendors sell t'tu lavash along the path to Geghard Monastery, a medieval site named after the spear that stabbed Christ at the crucifixion.

Armenia is a country blessed with fruit. Each year, the small landlocked nation is blanketed in grapes, pomegranates, figs, apples, and apricots. With such incredible seasonal bounty, Armenians make t'tu lavash, a dried, rolled fruit leather that, when unwound, can be as large as a tablecloth. The technique hails from ancient times, when the dried fruit sheets made for practical food storage. The sweet, tart snacks are still popular today. T'tu lavash means "sour lavash," and lavash refers to the ubiquitous flatbread served around the country. The fruit leather is eaten plain, wrapped around nuts, or melted into a soup with fried onions called t'ghit, which is served with a side of regular lavash.

HAND-PULLED COTTON CANDY

PASHMAK • IRAN

How to try it
Haj Khalifeh Ali Rahbar is a sweetshop in the city of Yazd that sells pashmak, along with nearly every kind of Persian sweet imaginable.

Iran's cotton candy, called pashmak, requires both man and machine to achieve its soft and fuzzy, melt-in-your-mouth strands. (In Persian, pashmak means "like wool.") Compared to Western cotton candy, where hot sugar syrup is pushed through the tiny holes of a spinning drum before quickly solidifying into wispy candy, pashmak is old school. It's made by caramelizing water and sugar in a massive vat, then stretching and kneading the mixture on a large work surface as it cools, until it acquires the texture of taffy. Rolled by hand into a dense, sticky ring, the caramel is then placed atop a mass of flattened dough made from toasting flour in butter. The two substances slowly combine with the help of skilled hands and a special machine with octopus-like appendages. The mechanized arms start in a tight cluster, then expand, stretching the candy and dough outward.

The human hands push the mixture back to the center, then the pashmak octopus expands and stretches the candy again. This slow, laborious process happens over and over, until the delicate strands begin to emerge and the mixture takes on the fluffy, frayed appearance of wool.

The finished product—which comes in flavors from sesame to cardamom—is cut up, boxed, and sold in the country's sweetshops. In Iran, pashmak is often a topping for ice cream or a garnish for cake. Its light, ethereal texture gives away none of the candy's dense beginnings, but the flavor is notably complex. While pashmak is sweet, it's also nutty and buttery from the toasted flour, making it a sophisticated version of the colorful fairground variety.

What Iranian cotton candy lacks in color and fluff, it makes up for in buttery, toasted flavor.

Other Sweets from Iran

Frozen Treats

FALOODEH

One of the world's oldest frozen desserts, dating back to the days of yakhchals. The 2,500-year-old treat is a kind of sweet noodle slush, made by combining cooked vermicelli with crushed, rose water–flavored ice. The crushed ice is soft, refreshing, and lightly floral, while the noodles give a chewy texture. Topped with a squeeze of lime, faloodeh is still one of Iran's most popular treats.

BASTANI-E NOONI

Flavored with the traditional blend of saffron and rose water, this Persian ice-cream sandwich is encased between two thin crispy wafers and rolled in pistachios. Although bastani-e nooni are available year-round, they become especially popular during Nowruz, the Persian New Year.

The Single Iranian Seed
That Launched America's Pistachio Industry

In 1979, a group of Iranian college students stormed the American Embassy in Tehran, taking dozens of hostages. The crisis dominated relations between the two countries, influencing politics for generations—and proved beneficial for American pistachio production. When the American government slapped a retaliatory embargo on Iranian pistachios, California's nascent pistachio industry exploded. Today, Iran and the United States are neck and neck for the accolade of the world's top producer.

From a botanical perspective, this was a remarkable turnaround. Pistachios are notoriously difficult to cultivate. They like hot, dry climates, but they also need cold winters to fruit. Pistachio trees also take about a decade to mature, and even then many trees produce nuts only in alternate years.

Iran's climate, especially the high-altitude desert town of Rafsanjan, is uniquely suited to the finicky crop. The nut was brought to the United States in the late 19th century by Middle Eastern immigrants, hungry for a taste of home. These pistachios were "non-fertile," good for snacking but not for planting.

In 1929, California's Chico New Plant Introduction Station sent William E. Whitehouse, a deciduous tree researcher and "plant explorer," to Iran with a singular mission: to collect pistachio seeds for planting. For six months, he searched for pistachios and returned to Chico with 20 pounds of different varieties. The station planted and evaluated 3,000 trees, and one pistachio rose above the others—the round, unblemished, crisp-tasting Kerman, from a prominent orchard in Rafsanjan. A female mother tree planted around 1931 at the Chico research station is the source of all pistachios commercially grown in California.

For decades, pistachio planting stayed small-scale and demand was still fulfilled by Iranian imports. The fledgling American industry didn't have its first commercial harvest until 1976.

Then came the 1979 hostage crisis and the sanctions that followed. The American pistachio industry took the opportunity to organize; even after the sanctions were lifted, there was still a 300 percent tariff on importing the Iranian nuts.

The pistachio is heralded as "the single most successful plant introduction to the United States in the 20th century." The hard-to-grow plant is now a $1.6 billion industry in California alone, where Whitehouse's single, all-important seed has family members spread across 200,000 acres.

In Zarandieh, Iran, a man hauls fresh pistachios to be dried in the sun.

ANCIENT PERSIAN ICE HOUSES

YAKHCHALS • IRAN

Standing tall and majestic like giant clay beehives, yakhchals are a feat of ancient Persian ingenuity. Long before electricity or refrigeration, these conical structures made eating ice cream in the desert possible as early as 400 BCE. Constructed from a special mixture of sand, clay, egg whites, lime, goat hair, and ash called sarooj, the visible portion of the yakhchal sits atop a vast underground chamber where ice was made and stored. In an incredible act of engineering, the chamber was fed by a series of underground channels called qanats, which flowed from an aqueduct. Using a combination of wind towers, strategic venting, and shade from the outer walls, water typically froze overnight. Additional ice was often brought from the mountains and stored in the yakhchals to facilitate the cooling process. The ice was then cut into blocks that could be transformed into frozen treats. With all that pent-up cold air, yakhchals also functioned as early refrigerators, storing perishables such as meat and dairy that would otherwise spoil in the heat of the desert.

How to try it

Many yakhchals still stand in Iran today. One of the easiest to find is near the Narin Castle in Meybod, but there are also some in Yazd and Kerman.

The advanced technology of this majestic ice house, one of four in the city of Abarkuh, dates back more than 2,000 years.

How Bootleg Fast Food Conquered Iran

Before the 1979 revolution, when religious clerics took control of the country, Iran's capital, Tehran, was a cosmopolitan city full of Western influences: secularism, miniskirts, and fast-food chains such as McDonald's and Kentucky Fried Chicken. But when Ayatollah Ruhollah Khomeini came to power, he pushed a return to traditional Islamic values. Everything Western became contraband, including American-style fast food.

When Khomeini died in 1989, citizens grew gutsier about flouting the ban on Western culture. Many Iranians maintained contact with the West through satellite television and relatives abroad. Others traveled to places such as Dubai, where they saw the far-reaching success of fast food. Iranian entrepreneurs wanted to bring these food options to Iran, but sanctions, tariffs, and a fraught relationship between Iran and the United States made it impossible to get the real thing. Instead, they opened imitations: Mash Donald's, Subways, Sheak Shack, and Pizza Hot.

Menu item names, such as Dahbel Dahn (KFC Double Down) and Wooper, were adjusted to fit the Persian vernacular's rich vowels. In other cases, traditional ingredients met Western formats to create one-of-a-kind dishes, such as

Tehran's ZFC (above) and Pizza Hot (below)

lavash-wrapped burritos stuffed with jujeh (chicken) kebab, grilled vegetables, saffron rice, and yellow raisins.

In most countries, these eateries would have to worry about lawsuits from Pizza Hut, Shake Shack, and KFC. But Iran's murky relationship with the United States gives these entrepreneurs some leverage. Although legal institutions in Iran exist for McDonald's lawyers to shut down Mash Donalds (in 2010, Baskin-Robbins managed to close five bootleg ice-cream shops), the dysfunctional political relationship between the two countries makes enforcing intellectual property rights frustrating at best. Most companies with little or no legitimate presence in Iran are inclined to devote their resources to enforcing trademarks in bigger markets.

The larger concern for the enterpreneurs behind Sheak Shack and Subways is the Iranian government. Even imitations are considered symbols of American imperialism, and authorities can—and will—shut them down for promoting gharbzadeghi, a Persian term for "westoxification." The restaurant owners must strike a balance: imitating Western chains enough to draw Iranians who want to try those brands, but not so closely that the government accuses them of corrupting and Westernizing the country.

DESERT IN BLOOM

KASHAN ROSE WATER FESTIVAL • IRAN

How to try it

The city of Qamsar, located 134 miles south of Tehran, becomes a rose-scented festival hub every May.

Most of the year, Kashan County is a monochromatic landscape of arched, khaki-colored buildings spread on dusty, windswept hills. But each spring, this desert region bursts into bloom and the land fills with roses, in soft pastels and electric pink, scattered across a bed of green. From May to June, local workers carefully wade through the thorny bushes of the region's gol Mohammadi, or Mohammadi rose, picking thousands of pounds of the flower to distill into rose water.

Visitors from across Iran and the world pour into the otherwise sleepy city of Qamsar to celebrate the fragrant harvest. Modern rose water production is often industrial, but some Kashan County producers still distill the liquid using a centuries-old process called golab-giri. This technique involves slowly boiling the petals in sealed copper pots and letting the steam rise and slowly collect in tubes—much like distilling hard liquor. The tubes lead outside of the pot and into

Roses in Kashan are gathered into large vats before being distilled into rose water.

a pitcher where, over the course of a few hours, the condensed liquid is collected. This potent distillate yields both rose oil, a highly concentrated liquid prized for its fragrance, and rose water, which is less expensive and used in traditional medicine and Persian cooking.

During festival time, rose water is available everywhere, fresh from the manufacturer or bottled at the central bazaar. Iranian rose water is widely considered the best in the world because the country's producers take great pride in getting the petals swiftly from the fields to the copper pots to preserve the roses' natural aroma and flavor.

MARSH TAFFY

KHIRRET • IRAQ

In midsummer every year, the souks of southern Iraq are tinged with the gold dust of khirret (pronounced "khar-ee-at"), a crunchy candy made from the pollen of an aquatic plant that grows in the region's marshes. The delicately sweetened confection is bright yellow and tightly compressed, like a chunk of chalk or a solid clump of mustard powder.

The Ma'dan people who live in the marshes of al-Ahwar, a UNESCO World Heritage Site, eat every part of the bardi plant (*Typha domingensis pers*), which also goes by the name "cattail." During the springtime, the male flowers release pollen, which is stripped off the plant to make khirret (khirret means "the stripped"). The canary-colored pollen is set out to dry in the sun, filtered to remove impurities, then mixed with sugar, wrapped in cheesecloth or a bag, and steamed. The steam binds everything together, and the solidified khirret is ready to be sold at market.

Khirret is considered a festival food for Iraqi Jews. One theory is that the marsh reeds became sacred for the Jewish community because baby Moses was kept hidden and safe among the Egyptian papyrus reeds, which resembled the ones found in Iraq. Baghdadi Jews traditionally served khirret during Purim until around the mid-20th century, when the group started a mass migration to Israel. Although khirret didn't make the trip with them, it remains a seasonal delicacy in southern Iraq.

How to try it
During the summer, check markets in Basra and Nasiriyah for the compressed pollen candy.

A THORNY FRUIT RIPE WITH SYMBOLISM

SABRA/SABR • ISRAEL

How to try it

The prickly fruits are available during the summer and are sold in Israeli and Palestinian markets, often peeled or with their thorns removed. The cactus makes excellent jam, juice, and syrup, but is commonly eaten ripe and raw, regardless of who is doing the eating.

For Israelis and Palestinians living in one of the most disputed regions in modern history, the prickly pear cactus is political. The small oblong fruit with thick, spiny skin and sweet, acidic flesh grows abundantly in the area and is eaten in both countries. Called sabra in Hebrew and sabr in Arabic, the fruit has become a core but conflicting symbol of Israeli and Palestinian national identities.

On one side, the sabra is the symbol of an Israeli ideal: tough on the outside, yet soft and sweet on the inside. It also connotes a person with roots in the soil, namely a Jew born and raised in Israel. The tall prickly pear bushes, which grow in flat paddle shapes and yield both fruits and flowers during the summer months, are often planted around Israeli homes and buildings.

Among Palestinians, the symbolism of the fruit is more of perseverance than of strength. Sabr, which is also the Arabic word for "patience," grows in the most inhospitable of environments. It takes root in sand and rocks, resists droughts, and still manages to produce a sweet, delicate fruit. In many of the Palestinian communities now occupied by Israel, the cactus has become an emblem of Palestinian dispossession. Although eating is the main use of sabr, one West Bank artist, Ahmed Yasin, uses the cactus as a canvas, transforming the plants in his backyard into a gallery of political scenes he uses as a form of cultural resistance.

BEN-GURION'S LITTLE CRUMBLES

PTITIM • ISRAEL

How to try it

Osem, the original creators of ptitim, are still making their little crumbles, which can be bought everywhere in Israel or ordered online.

In 1953, the newly formed state of Israel was short on rice. Hundreds of thousands of Jewish immigrants had been expelled from Arab countries across the Middle East, and the state struggled to feed its new inhabitants. Into this grain-shaped void stepped David Ben-Gurion, founder of Israel and the country's first prime minister.

At the request of Ben-Gurion, local food company Osem began producing ptitim, or "little crumbles," a rice-like pasta made from wheat flour. These "grains" were extruded, cut, dried, and then toasted, which made them shelf-stable while imparting a nutty flavor. Hearty, with a uniquely chewy texture, ptitim was a great success and remained popular long after the end of Israel's early austerity measures.

While originally shaped to mimic rice, ptitim eventually morphed into the orb shape much of the world recognizes today as Israeli couscous (not to be confused with traditional North African couscous). According to kitchen lore, this misnomer was coined in the 1990s by New York chef Don Pintabona, who sampled ptitim at the home of Israeli chef Mika Sharon.

DESERT TRUFFLE MARKET

FAGGA SOUK · KUWAIT

I n the early spring, the truffle souk in Al Rai, just northwest of Kuwait City, bustles with connoisseurs sniffing for white-and-beige culinary gold. The demand for desert truffles, called fagga in Kuwait, is so high that more than 500 vendors apply each year for the 120-odd available stalls.

The deserts of the Middle East and North Africa are prime ground for desert truffles, which are lighter in color, less pungent, and cheaper than their European counterparts. Though they hail from the fungi kingdom, desert truffles look more like potatoes. Spongy with an earthy taste, the mushrooms act as a flavor enhancer for meats, stews, and sauces. They can also be eaten on their own, with a little olive oil and cilantro, or added to kabsa, a spiced meat-and-rice one-pot dish popular in the Gulf countries.

Since the Iraqi invasion in 1990, nearly all the truffles that make it to the souk come from neighboring countries such as Iran, Saudi Arabia, Libya, Morocco, and Tunisia. Kuwaiti foragers who once roamed the desert for the fancy fungus are now rightfully afraid of unexploded landmines left behind by the Iraqi army. Kuwait's changing landscape and climate are also to blame. Growing truffles requires rain, which can be irregular, and space, which is being diminished by urban encroachment. Foraging in other countries, especially war-torn regions such as Syria and Iraq, can be just as dangerous, with reports of truffle hunters captured and killed by suspected Islamic State militants.

When rain and lightning fall on the desert midwinter, Bedouins rejoice. Although not fully understood, lightning seems to encourage truffle growth underground. Once the fungi mature, they begin to crack the soil, which shows harvesters where to dig for the desert delicacy. At market, a kilo fetches about $25–$65.

How to try it
The truffle souk is located in Al Rai, where truffles are flown in daily during the season.

Competition is fierce to become one of the lucky hundred-plus vendors of desert truffles in Kuwait.

LAMB TAIL CONFIT

AWARMA · LEBANON

I n Lebanon, awarma is a dish with roots invented before the advent of refrigeration. After butchering sheep during the warmer months, villagers would cook the meat slowly in its own fat—a technique called confit, which was traditionally a method of preservation. Sealed tightly, awarma could last for several months in the pantry and provide meat throughout the winter.

Awarma is made by rendering cubes of fat from the tail of a sheep (fat-tailed sheep, whose fat accumulates in massive baggy deposits, are common in the Middle East), then adding minced sheep's meat, salt, and cooking it until softened and brown. The versatile, unctuous dish is commonly cooked with eggs and eaten for breakfast, but it can also be added to kibbeh (a spiced meat and grain mixture), sprinkled atop hummus, or used to add meaty oomph in soups, stews, and pilafs.

How to try it
Al Soussi restaurant in Beirut is beloved for their traditional breakfasts, including a fluffy plate of eggs and awarma.

Fat-Tailed Sheep
ARE BOTH REAL AND DELICIOUS

According to Herodotus, the 5th-century Greek "father of history," travelers passing through Arabia would encounter flying snakes, birds building nests out of cinnamon, and sheep with tails so massive they dragged on the ground or were supported by custom-made wheeled carts. While Herodotus was notorious for peppering his histories with fantasy, the fat-tailed sheep are very much real.

For millennia, people have bred sheep with huge, fat-heavy tails. (About 25 percent of the world's sheep are still fat-tailed varieties, mainly found in the Middle East, Central Asia, and Africa.) Some breeds have bulbous, curled tails, while others have flat, wide tails like paddles. The broad tails of the Awassi sheep, a nomadic breed prized for milk production, can weigh about 26 pounds (12 kg)—which is modest compared to an 80-pound (36 kg) tail described by 16th-century chronicler Leo Africanus.

For sheep, extra tail fat provides energy reserves in harsh climates. In the desert, sheep must traverse extreme distances for grassland and water and so, like camels' humps, they store calorie reserves in their tails. For humans, the tail fat makes an excellent preservative and cooking grease. Located near the surface of the animal's skin, rather than close to the heat of the body, the tail fat is exposed to colder temperatures. Because of this, it has a lower melting point and a texture that's buttery and soft, rather than waxy, with a subtle lamb flavor.

Butchers often sell the sheep's tail separately. Bits of tail fat are commonly mixed into meats for kebabs, to give it extra juiciness and meaty flavor. The crackling rendered from pieces of tail fat can be served as an appetizer, while the liquefied fat might be brushed on baklava.

Artists from Israel to India immortalized fat-tailed sheep with rock paintings, mosaics, and glorious golden canvases. (There's even a mention of fat-tailed sheep in the Bible.) For Europeans and Americans, however, who were used to thin-tailed sheep, the creatures were a jaw-dropping concept. Up until the 20th century, travel accounts and farmer's almanacs described fat-tailed sheep with the whimsical wonder of Herodotus, complete with the attached cart. The fanciful nature of these depictions led skeptics to question whether sheep with tail carts were mythical (photographic evidence remains scarce), but scholars still argue the carts are real, citing 19th- and 20th-century references to sheep-tail carts in Afghanistan.

Many a traveler has written of woolly mythology that just might be true: sheep with tails so fat, they pulled them on carts.

Black nigella seed paste, when sweetened, makes for a striking pie that can only be found in Palestine.

BLACK TAHINI

QIZHA • PALESTINE

To love qizha, first you must know about it. The region's ongoing border dispute, which keeps many Palestinian products from leaving their home, means that few outside of Palestine know about the dark, tahini-adjacent paste. Made by roasting and grinding black nigella seeds, along with black sesame seeds for fat, qizha is shiny and viscous, the color of tar. It's bitter yet sweet, with an herbal undertone of mint. When visitors do discover qizha, many develop an addiction, and when they leave the country, they can't find it again.

The Palestinian city of Nablus is known as the culinary capital of the West Bank, and qizha is among their specialties. Qizha is typically sweetened and made into dessert. Qizha halwa and qizha semolina pie are customary, as is taking doses of the paste like medicine. In Arabic, nigella seeds are called hubbat al-baraka, or "seeds of blessing," for their range of purported health benefits. Especially among the older generation, Palestinians are known to eat it daily for its anti-inflammatory and antibacterial properties.

How to try it
In Nablus you can find top-notch qizha at Breik Roasting, which also sells local spices, coffee, and soap.

SWEET NOODLE OMELET

BALALEET • QATAR

How to try it

Balaleet is an affordable, often homemade dish. Shay Al Shoomoos is a restaurant owned and operated by a Qatari mother of five, Shams Al Qassabi, who is a rarity in the male-dominated business scene of Qatar. Located in the Souk Waqif, she makes an excellent sweet noodle omelet.

Eid al-Fitr marks the end of the monthlong Ramadan fast with a feast of special foods. For Qataris and their Gulf neighbors, that means food like balaleet. It's a noodle dish, but it's also an omelet. It's sweet but also savory. Soft but crispy. Almost always breakfast, but sometimes lunch or dinner.

Balaleet begins with rice noodles, which are parboiled, then fried in a pan with butter, sugar, cardamom, and saffron. (To get fancier, add curry, turmeric, or ginger.) The noodles should brown a bit, making some parts soft and others crunchy, before being finished with a sprinkling of rose water. Next, there's the omelet, which should be cooked in hot oil very quickly so it forms a nice crust. With the omelet draped over the noodles, and then a handful of pistachios sprinkled over the top, each bite should be aromatic, salty, sweet, crunchy, and extremely delicious.

SILK ROAD CHILI POWDER

ALEPPO PEPPER • SYRIA

How to try it

The Syrian war has all but ended Aleppo pepper exports from the country. Turkish growers have picked up the production, using Syrian seeds to grow the plants.

Spices have flowed in and out of Aleppo for millennia. The city was a central trading point along the Silk Road, and its souks were collectively one of the great wonders of the ancient world. Heaped into great piles alongside goods from across the world, these spices were mixed with ingredients and recipes brought from Asia, Anatolia, and beyond, making for new dishes found nowhere else. (Supposedly, the sultans of the Ottoman Empire sent their chefs to Aleppo to spy.) Today, the world still covets Syria's spices, especially the Aleppo pepper.

A variety of *Capsicum annuum*, the Aleppo pepper was brought back from South America and introduced to Europe in the 1400s. Soon the peppers were growing across the Middle East, including the fertile ground of Syria, where the chilies took on a new flavor. The peppers became so connected to Syria that their name in Arabic, baladi, means "my country."

Traditionally, the spice was made by local families who processed the fresh peppers by hand—cleaning them with a dry cloth, gutting them, and drying them on rooftops around the country. Once dried, the peppers were ground with salt and olive oil and dried again to produce bright red, salty flakes with a sweetness like raisins or sundried tomatoes and a mildly spicy, earthy flavor.

In the late 20th century, chefs around the world began falling for the Aleppo pepper. Their discovery coincided with the loosening of Syrian state rules and international interest in the country's culinary scene. But when the Syrian Civil War broke out in 2012, the authentic Aleppo pepper became nearly impossible to get, which created a market for fake Aleppo pepper. Seeds were carried out by refugees and planted in Turkey, which now grows most of the "Aleppo pepper."

Aleppo is now in the difficult process of restoring life as it was before the conflict. Aleppo is considered by many to be the culinary capital of the region, and there is hope that the centuries-old, now world-famous, pepper will flourish in the city again.

In the covered souks of the ancient city of Aleppo, shoppers can get everything they need, from peppers to soap to rugs.

Dallah
THE WORLD'S MOST WELCOMING COFFEEPOT

The Arabic coffeepot, called a dallah, is the region's universal symbol of hospitality. Tall and elegant with a dramatic, arched spout and a slim, tapered waist, the dallah is the first thing used to welcome friends, visitors, and business associates. Upon entering a home or celebration, coffee preparation begins. In the United Arab Emirates, this involves a ceremony called gahwa, in which coffee beans are freshly roasted in a skillet, ground with cardamom using a pestle, brewed in a dallah, often filtered into a succession of smaller dallahs, then served to guests little by little, filling their cup just part of the way. The pouring process repeats for each guest until they shake their cup, indicating they've had enough.

The gahwa speaks to the core significance of coffee in the UAE, and the Arabian Peninsula in general—its power to gather people together and facilitate relationships, conversation, and ideas. The ritual of drinking together creates regular opportunities to exchange hospitality and sustain the region's oral traditions. Coffee is also a sign of wealth and generosity, which is why the dallah is featured on the one dirham coin in the UAE and has been used as a watermark on the country's banknotes. The dallah has become an emblem of warmth, strength, and welcome—and the coffeepot now stands all over Arabia in the form of statues, fountains, and entryways.

Dallah Fountain in Fujairah, United Arab Emirates

Dallah Fountain in Jeddah, Saudi Arabia

Dallah roundabout in Al Khor, Qatar

Dallah Sculpture in Abu Dhabi, United Arab Emirates

Dallah Sculpture in Doha, Qatar

Entrance to Capital Park in Abu Dhabi, United Arab Emirates

SOUTH AND CENTRAL ASIA

MENDED TEAPOT SOUP

CHAINAKI • AFGHANISTAN

How to try it

Bacha Broot, in the Old City near the bird market, is Kabul's oldest restaurant. Per tradition, men and women sit in separate rooms to eat their chainaki.

The tea shops of Afghanistan, called chaikhanas, have long been a refuge for locals in need of a break. Ranging from small rooms with mud floors to more luxurious guest houses, chaikhanas dot any well-traveled road, offering liquid Afghan hospitality: black or green tea, often sweetened and spiced with cardamom. In some shops, tea is dispensed into short glasses from a samovar. In others, the whole teapot is given to the guest to pour themselves.

With limited space and specialized equipment, chaikhana owners came to the handy realization that teapots could be used for more than just tea. Chainaki is a lamb or goat soup cooked slowly in a teapot. In the morning, a collection of teapots is filled with simple ingredients: a few pieces of meat, some chopped onion, a spoonful of split peas, salt, and a glug of water. Topped with the lid, the ceramic vessels are placed on a stove or tucked into hot embers where the meat slowly softens and the water transforms into a deeply savory broth. When a chainaki is ordered, a teapot is removed and served. The traditional way to enjoy teapot soup is by tearing naan into a bowl, pouring the hot soup over it, then eating it with your hand—always just one hand, always the right.

The teapots used for soup are often salvaged, which gives the dish a well-loved, eclectic presentation. In Afghanistan, broken teapots are taken to a professional mender called a patragar, who repairs them by drilling tiny holes in the pieces, stitching them together with thin metal wire, then closing up the gaps with a paste of egg whites and gypsum.

Broken teapots are given new life at chainakis, where they are used to pour soup over torn pieces of bread.

THE ALL-IMPORTANT MULBERRY

TOOT • AFGHANISTAN

Tall, bushy mulberry trees, many with centuries-old root systems, grow all across Afghanistan. In the summer, when they bear fruit, farmers spread out sheets beneath the branches and shake the trees, letting the ripe berries fall. In a country teeming with fruit, mulberries are among the most abundant and play a central role in the Afghan diet.

During the summer, fruit stands line the roads, selling mounds of fleshy mulberries. Although locals do eat them fresh, most mulberries are bought for drying, which also happens during the hot season. Roofs and yards are filled with berries shriveling in the sun. Dried mulberries are an Afghani pantry staple, stashed away for the winter when fresh produce becomes scarce. They're used as a condiment for bread, or as a self-contained tea bag when dropped in hot water. In a practice that originated with caravanning nomads, the dried berries were mixed with nuts and pressed into nutrient-packed blocks called chakidar, which were tied into the end of a traveler's turban and eaten as a snack. In the north of the country, where mulberries are especially plentiful, ground berries stand in for flour in a mulberry bread called talkhun.

How to try it

From June to September, mulberries blanket Afghanistan. The best berries are said to grow in the north, along the route from Kabul to Balkh.

Mulberry Bread

Makes 16 bars

½ pound dried mulberries

½ pound shelled walnuts

¼ teaspoon kosher salt

2 tablespoons water

16 walnut halves for topping

Fresh mulberries

Dried mulberries

1. Put all of the ingredients except the walnut halves in a food processor fitted with a metal blade and puree for 1 to 2 minutes until they form a thick, smooth, sticky paste.

2. Line an 8 x 8-inch baking pan with parchment or wax paper with the paper draping over two sides of the pan, to make removing the bars easier.

3. Press the mulberry–walnut mixture into the pan, making an even layer all over the bottom of the pan. Distribute the walnut halves evenly, making 4 rows of 4 walnuts, then gently press them halfway into the mixture.

4. Refrigerate for an hour to firm up the bars. Using the edges of the wax paper, lift the mixture out of the pan and set it on a cutting surface. With a sharp knife, cut it into 16 squares with a walnut in the center of each square. Store in a sealed container at room temperature, or the refrigerator if you prefer them cold.

A VERDANT 19TH-CENTURY TEA GARDEN

LAKKATURA • BANGLADESH

How to try it
The easiest way to
get to the estate is
by CNG (a kind of
auto-rickshaw used
all over Bangladesh)
from Sylhet city center.
Upon arrival, you can
report to the main office
and hire a guide or
simply wander around
the garden by yourself.
For seven color tea,
head to Nilkantha Tea
Cabin, about two hours
south of Lakkatura.

n the northeastern city of Sylhet, an area renowned for the beauty of its tea gardens, Lakkatura is often considered the most picturesque. It is also one of the largest tea gardens in the country, covering a total of 3,200 acres. Officially established in 1875, the estate now produces an astounding 550 tons of tea each year. Tea has a long history here. Long before the region started producing it, Bengal was the terminus for the Tea Horse Road, the ancient caravan path that brought Chinese goods, most important, tea, to South Asian buyers.

The Lakkatura estate is a lush, quiet expanse intersected by a number of dirt roads. Some roads are used to transport tea and take visitors on rides through the carpeted hills of neatly manicured tea plants. Others are thoroughfares, part of a larger network that connects the garden to rural villages around the estate. During the harvest, makeshift villages pop up around the plantation to house the workers who come to pick and process the tea.

The British East India Company first introduced tea cultivation to Bengal in 1840, but it wasn't until 1857 that tea became a commercial occupation. In 2018, Bangladesh produced more than 80,000 tons of tea, making it the tenth-largest tea producer in the world. In Sylhet, tea is so plentiful a local teashop owner invented "seven color tea," or saat rong in Bengali. Using a secret recipe, he makes seven distinct tea mixes with spices and milk and layers them based on their densities to create a striking, stratified glass that has attracted the prime minister of Bangladesh, as well as a Qatari ambassador who reportedly enjoyed it so much, he paid 7,000 taka, or about $83, for his glass.

THE KNIFE THAT REQUIRES FEET

BOTI • BANGLADESH

Peer into most Bengali kitchens and you'll find women sitting on the floor, cutting up fish and vegetables in a swift rhythmic motion that requires both hands and feet. Unlike most knives, which are wielded over the food, the boti flips the script. Women maneuver an ingredient around the boti's blade, which stays completely stationary, and use its sharp edge to whittle the skin off potatoes or slice cucumbers.

A boti has two main features: a long, flat wooden board and a curved, upright blade. One foot is used to weigh down the board, either by squatting on it or sitting with a leg folded on top. The blade—which rises from the board, sharp side facing the cook—can shave a piece of garlic as well as it can dismember an entire pumpkin.

Watching a woman skillfully work a boti is mesmerizing. Her fingers boldly evade the blade, busting open heads of cabbages and broccoli with force, then carving out uniform, practiced shapes with the velocity and precision of machinery. For the biggest celebrations, Bengali women gather with their botis and sit together on the floor, in a colorful mess of peels and produce. For many Bengalis, the boti makes handheld knives irrelevant. Perhaps the only disadvantage, as women get older, is sitting on the floor—but there is a boti for that: Newer models are made to be screwed into a table, so cooks can sit in a chair while whittling.

THE LOST SUPERIOR PEPPER

LONG PEPPER • INDIA

India is the birthplace of two important peppercorns: one black, one long. Black pepper, now ubiquitous on tables around the world, is native to Kerala, on the southeastern coast, while long pepper grows in the north of India. Long pepper, with its tight and conical shape, was the first pepper to make its way from India to the Mediterranean and into the kitchens of ancient Greece and Rome. At the time, around the 6th century BCE, the piquant flavor was unlike anything Westerners had tasted before. Mustard and horseradish grew natively, but they'd never tried a spice that attacked their mouth like the blunt, earthy long pepper.

By the 4th century CE, black pepper entered the market. Unlike long pepper, the new pepper could grow outside its native home and as a result was significantly cheaper. Black pepper rose to prominence, usurping what many believe to be the superior-tasting long pepper.

Black and long pepper are closely related. They share an active compound called piperine, which activates the human body's heat-sensing pathways. But while black pepper delivers its flavor boldly and at once, long pepper is more complex. At first, long pepper's spice is more subtle, lingering, then growing in power and eventually tingling the way black pepper does. Long pepper also has a fruity mellowness, a citrusy bite similar to Sichuan peppercorns.

Today, as the Western world eats black pepper, long pepper is still popular in its native India. The floral, more understated pepper is used in the spicy soup rasam, lentil curries, and Indian pickle and is an essential ingredient in the mutton stew nihari.

ROCK STAR FRUIT

BASTARD OLEASTER · INDIA

Bastard oleaster doesn't just sound like a rock star, it looks like one, too. The small red fruit, which resembles a cherry tomato, appears to be dusted in silver glitter. Cut one open and you'll find an equally dramatic interior: an elongated seed with a striped pattern, kind of like a lightning bolt.

This fruity bastard tastes sour and a bit astringent. It has a slight tomato taste, which isn't surprising given that these fruits are packed with lycopene, a compound found in tomatoes. In northeast India, where they grow, bastard oleasters are a popular street snack. Vendors sell small bags of whole, sparkling fruits along with salt, which helps cut the astringency and sourness. The seeds are edible, but they have a fibrous hull that's difficult to chew. Those willing to work can split open the seeds to eat the kernel inside, but more often they're discarded.

How to try it

You're unlikely to find bastard oleasters outside of northern India. They occasionally show up at street markets in the city of Guwahati, but a better bet is to travel to the city of Shillong, where the fruits are sold as a snack outside bus stations.

Women from all walks of life gather at the annual Pongala Festival, huddling around brick stoves to create rice pudding worthy of a goddess.

FOUR MILLION WOMEN MAKING RICE PUDDING

PONGALA • INDIA

On the ninth day of Attukal Pongala, a festival dedicated to the Hindu goddess Bhadrakali, Indian women find refuge in numbers. Considered the largest spiritual gathering of females in the world, four million women from all over India descend upon the city of Thiruvananthapuram in Kerala each year. They spread out over 15 miles (24 km), washing rice, grating coconuts, and gathering bricks for small makeshift fires. The sari-clad pilgrims have come to make an offering to the goddess. To do this, they cook a staggering amount of rice pudding called pongala.

The basic ingredients of pongala—clarified butter, coconut, rice, and cane sugar—are simple and affordable, which makes the ceremony accessible to any woman who wants to participate. (In fact, it was women from the "untouchable" Dalit caste who pioneered the event.) For each new ceremony, the women use a new cooking vessel, which they carefully select from the mountains of pots on offer throughout the city. For 24 hours, Thiruvananthapuram transforms into a sacred kitchen. The millions of women place their brick stoves side by side, forming a concentric circle around the Attukal Bhagavathy Temple. Devotees claim all available public space, setting up temporary hearths on streets, sidewalks, courtyards, bus stations, and railway platforms. At the sounding cue of a loudspeaker, the women strike matches, light their fires, and prepare their pongala offerings.

The goddess Bhadrakali is a fierce incarnation of Devi, who annihilates evil and brings prosperity to her followers. In this form, she is black or blue, wields a sword and sickle, and wears a necklace of skulls and a belt of severed heads. The ferocious deity is believed to embody fury as well as benevolent protection and is often worshipped as a universal mother figure. She is perhaps best known by her more affectionate name: Attukal Amma, or Mother.

When the pongala pot overflows, erupting in white foam, the goddess has accepted the offering. The atmosphere is highly emotional, with celebrants crying and chanting, sharing rice pudding, and basking in the strength of female solidarity.

How to try it

The pongala offering takes place as part of a ten-day festival that typically falls in February or March. Contact the Attukal Bhagavathy Temple for exact dates.

How to try it

The Golden Temple is in Atta Mandi in Amritsar's south. Shuttle buses run from the city's bus terminal.

A HOLY KITCHEN FEEDING THOUSANDS FOR FREE

LANGAR AT THE GOLDEN TEMPLE • INDIA

Everyone who arrives at Shri Harmandir Sahib, also known as the Golden Temple, eats for free. The gilded Sikh structure is the main attraction in the city of Amritsar, which means the temple's kitchen serves about 75,000 free meals every day. On special occasions, the number can reach 100,000 or more.

This ritual, which is run almost entirely by volunteers, is part of a centuries-old practice known as langar, started by the first Sikh Guru, Guru Nanak. Langar is a display of humility and equality. Regardless of class, caste, or gender, everyone must

Volunteers prep thousands of vegetables for the temple's 24-hour kitchen.

sit on the floor of a Sikh temple, side by side, and eat the same simple vegetarian meal, without the exchange of money.

Serving the thousands of visitors and pilgrims who come to the Golden Temple is a monumental task. The kitchen comprises multiple buildings, filled with rooms dedicated to specific preparations. In one room, volunteers sit in circles and chop vegetables for the sabzi, a vegetarian stew. In another room, a team cooks the sabzi, stirring giant wood-fired vats with wooden spoons the size of oars. The making of dal, the all-important lentil curry, requires its own building, a water hose, and about 28,660 pounds (13,000 kg) of lentils every day.

In recent years, rising demand has led the temple to supplement volunteers with machinery, including a device that can churn out 25,000 rotis in an hour. Each piece of bread, hot from the oven, is hand painted with ghee (clarified butter), before being sent out to the dining room.

At mealtime, thousands of people file into two large dining halls. They pick up a metal cafeteria tray, a cup for water, and cutlery, then take their place on the floor in rows. The volunteers walk down the row, holding steaming buckets of dal, sabzi, and rice pudding that they ladle into the compartments of the tray. When the rotis come, diners hold out their hands in a sign of respect, and the bread is placed in their open palms.

Early 19th-century Sikh leader Ranjit Singh donated the gold for the temple's exterior.

The meals are filling, nutritious, and simple. And although the food is indeed tasty, many visitors come as much for the ritual, for the exercise of eating together in equality and harmony, as they do for the meal.

FEEDING ANCESTORS BY FEEDING CROWS

SHRADH • INDIA

In the Hindu faith, it is said the dead visit the living on Earth every year on the anniversary of their passing. They come as crows, and it is the responsibility of the living to feed their ancestors their favorite foods, as part of a ritual known as shradh.

On these death anniversaries, called the tithi, relatives cook a feast that might contain half a dozen dishes of rice and dal, savory vadai fritters, and sweet vermicelli pudding—all tailored to the tastes of the deceased. The relatives spread out a banana leaf and take turns ladling the dishes onto it, which they will then carefully wrap and take outside to present to a crow. Sometimes, finding the crow can be the hardest part. If there is no crow outside, a relative might caw, trying to call a bird to where they are. If that doesn't work, the family will pack up the banana leaf and go roving for crows, getting into the car and driving slowly, scanning trees and rooftops. When they find the crow, they spread out the banana leaf and invite it to feast. The bird must eat the food in order to conclude the shradh, which signifies to the living that the soul of the loved one is sated and at peace.

How to try it

Shradh is especially important when honoring dead parents. It is typically performed by the eldest son, but daughters perform the ritual in the absence of sons.

SPICED CANNABIS MILK

BHANG • INDIA

Nicknamed the "Festival of Love and Colors," Holi is a joyous spring festival when revelers run through the streets, dousing one another in bright pigments and colored water. It's also the one time of the year when more conservative members of the family, such as grandmothers or uncles, might cut a little loose by getting loopy on bhang.

Bhang is an edible preparation of cannabis, most popularly incorporated into spiced, milk-based drinks. There's bhang thandai, flavored with almonds, fennel, rose water, saffron, and more, and bhang laasi, which brings yogurt to the party. Like other types of ingested cannabis, the effects of bhang are often hallucinogenic, leading to heightened physical and mental sensations that can be mild or severe, depending on the dosage, and can last an entire day.

MUMBAI'S EXTRAORDINARY

Dabbawala is a term for a "lunch box person," one of the 5,000 deliverymen (and a small handful of deliverywomen) who transport 200,000 homemade, multicourse meals to office workers, students, and other hungry people across Mumbai each day.

Starting at about 8 a.m., dabbas (lunch boxes) are picked up from apartment buildings across the city. A dabba contains three or four stackable cylindrical compartments. One compartment will typically contain rice or rotis. Another might hold dal or a curry, then vegetables, yogurt, or dessert. Although these meals are typically cooked at the recipient's home (generally by family members or domestic help), most workers commute during the morning rush hour, when there's no space on the train to carry their lunches. Instead of bringing the food themselves, dabbawalas—who are all

employed by the Nutan Mumbai Tiffin Box Suppliers Trust—trail behind them.

The dabba system, as we know it today, started in the late 19th century, when Mumbai was still known as Bombay and India was under rule of the British Raj. Indians from all over the country flocked to work in the city, and by 1891, Bombay's population had reached nearly 820,000. Parsis, Hindus, Muslims, Christians, Jews, and Jains worked side by side, bringing food from their homes to their new city.

Legend has it that the system arose when a Parsi banker hired a Maratha worker to pick up a homemade lunch from the banker's house, then deliver it to his office four miles away. Mahadeo Havaji Bacche, the deliveryman, was one of the many men parked at a nearby intersection, waiting for odd jobs. Bacche saw an untapped opportunity to deliver home-cooked meals

Indian law forbids the possession of hashish (resin) and ganja (buds)—but not industrial hemp, and not bhang. Regulation is up to each of the country's states, many of which explicitly allow its consumption. In Rajasthan, for instance, there are government-authorized bhang shops selling cookies and chocolates alongside drinks.

Bhang's roots go back some 3,000 years, to the Vedic period, and the substance (and cannabis in general) plays a prominent role in the mythology of the powerful ascetic-monk god Shiva. Holi is perhaps the best time to drink the ancient elixir, when there are enough sounds and sights to match the happy-go-lucky sensation of bhang.

Lunch Box Delivery System

to office workers, and in 1890, he hired a hundred Maratha workers to make it happen.

In the early days, dabbas were made at home by either a wife or a housekeeper, but today dabbas are sourced from many places. In addition to foods cooked at home, dabbawalas also have connections with kitchens that specialize in home cooking, many of which employ women-driven workforces as a way to encourage financial independence.

The modern dabbawala system is a relay between workers on bicycles, workers riding trains, and workers pushing carts and carrying crates. The lunch boxes change hands multiple times before reaching their destination, and each leg is guided by the series of numbers and letters on the label. Take B 5 W 6N2, for example. The B and the W stand for the lunch box's origin, Borivali West. The 6N2 denotes the

delivery destination: The 6 is the locality, the N is the building, and the 2 is the floor. The 5 refers to the destination train station. (In congested Mumbai, the dabbawallas rely on the rails.) This coded system yields a startlingly consistent and on-time delivery rate. It is so reliable: it bears a 99.9999 percent accuracy rate, or about one mistake for every 16 million deliveries.

Once lunch is over, the same relay is carried out in reverse. The empty dabbas are picked up, sorted, transported, and dropped back home. This round trip service costs 1,200 rupees (about $15) per month. The dabbawalas make about 15,000 rupees a month, or about $200.

Each day, thousands of deliverymen perform a complex relay across Mumbai with 200,000 lunch boxes.

THE LAST WILD APPLE FORESTS

ILE-ALATAU NATIONAL PARK • KAZAKHSTAN

How to try it

The apple forests now exist only in patches. There are various protected sections in the Ile-Alatau National Park, but hiring a guide to take you there is recommended as they are difficult to find.

n the early 20th century, biologist Nikolai Vavilov first traced the apple genome to a small Kazakh town called Almaty. The apples he found there were strikingly similar to the American classic Golden Delicious. Even more incredible, the apples in Almaty were growing wild, dangling from a thicket of unevenly spaced trees, a phenomenon that existed nowhere else in the world.

Long before human cultivation, scientists believe birds, bears, and horses transported apple seeds from their native Kazakhstan into places like Syria, where the Romans found the fruit and carried it farther around the world. As the apple spread, it became increasingly difficult to pin down its true birthplace, until modern gene sequencing proved that the wild Kazak apple, known as *Malus sieversii*, was indeed the progenitor of the domestic apple. Almaty and its surrounding land was recognized as the origin of almost all apples. (Almaty means "father of apples.")

What remains of Kazakhstan's wild apple forests can be found along the Tian Shan mountain range, where the trees are protected and growing safely. Pomologists report that the wild apples have a variety of flavors depending on how the bees pollinate the blossoms. There are honey- and berry-flavored apples, sour crabapples, apples that taste like licorice, and a few strains that would be sweet enough for the modern supermarket.

The Zailiyskiy Alatau mountain range surrounds Almaty, Kazakhstan.

FERMENTED POCKET CHEESE

KURT • KYRGYZSTAN

Kurt is the invention of nomadic herders. Around Central Asia, where shepherds have roved with their animals for millennia, the dried cheese ball is a dietary staple, made slightly differently depending on where you are and what's available. In Kyrgyzstan, kurt is made by fermenting milk—which can come from a cow, sheep, goat, camel, or mare—then draining the whey from the curds. The soft, soured curds are rolled into balls (some traditions prefer discs, strips, or chunks) and dried in the sun until they are so hard, they must be gnawed. A well-made ball of kurt will keep for years.

These caloric dairy bombs are put to endless use. Kurt makes a ready-to-eat snack, but it's also a kind of creamy bouillon, dissolved into soups and stews, or melted into water for a hot drink. Kurt is also crumbled and used as salt, or dissolved into soda, or tossed into salad.

Sundried, fermented cheese has been around for thousands of years. In 2006, archaeologists in Xinjiang, China, unearthed a coffin containing a woman with chunks of kurt around her neck and chest. The archaeologists determined that the woman (nicknamed the "Beauty of Xiaohe") was buried around 2000 BCE, making the kurt approximately 4,000 years old. In 2017, this preserved kurt was considered the second oldest piece of cheese in the world, trailing behind a 7,000-year-old remnant found in Croatia. The nomadic people who occupy the Tian Shan Mountain area, where the Beauty of Xiaohe was found, still make cheese almost exactly the same way.

How to try it
Kurt balls are sold in markets around Kyrgyzstan, and its many derivatives can be found around the larger Central Asia region.

BOTTOMLESS MILLET BEER

TONGBA • NEPAL

On the narrow trails of the Himalayas, where travelers must carry their meals on their backs, multiuse ingredients are essential. Tongba, a brew-it-yourself millet libation, is one such staple. As long as there's a steady supply of hot water, one cup of the cooked, fermented millet can be easily stretched into several rounds of warming, yeasty beer.

Tongba provides near-instant gratification. Simply pour hot water over the millet, let the grains steep until the liquid turns cloudy, then stick in a straw and enjoy. A tongba straw is closed at the submerged end but perforated on the sides, which lets in liquid while filtering out the grains. When the mug runs dry, the process can be repeated four or five times without losing much flavor or potency. Depending on the millet, the alcohol content will vary, but it's usually lower than regular beer and provides a slow, mellow buzz. The taste is yeasty and earthy, with hints of bread and mushrooms.

The incredible refillable brew is especially important to the Limbu people of eastern Nepal, who use the drink for ceremonies, celebrations, and religious offerings. Today, the practice has caught on in the surrounding mountainous regions of Tibet, Bhutan, and India, as well as in restaurants across Nepal, where pitchers of hot water are placed on the table. The traditional drinking vessel is a cask-like mug, which is also called a tongba.

How to try it
Small Star in Kathmandu is a loud (and relatively expensive) local eatery known for traditional meals and exceptional tongba.

Several salt replicas of monuments have been built inside the Khewra mines, like this rendering of Minar-e-Pakistan, a national landmark in Lahore.

SALT MINE METROPOLIS

KHEWRA SALT MINES • PAKISTAN

The Khewra salt mines are the second largest in the world—behind the Sifto Canada, Inc., salt mine in Goderich, Ontario—turning out 325,000 tons of salt per year, and an estimated 220 million tons over its lifetime.

The massive mine, which covers an area of 1,184 square feet (110 square m) and runs 11 stories (748 feet, or 228 m) deep, has a tunnel system of 25 miles (40 km). To keep the huge space from collapsing in on itself, only 50 percent of the salt is mined, while the other half serves as structural support. Over the years, workers have constructed some incredible structures within the mine, including a miniature Badshahi Mosque—the famous Mughal-era masjid in Lahore—complete with a small salt minaret, as well as small salt versions of the Great Wall of China, the Mall Road of Murree, and Pakistan's national poet Allama Iqbal. All the miniatures are built from salt bricks, which vary from red to pink to white. Beyond the sculptures, there is a 20-bed clinic that treats asthmatic patents with salt therapy, and its own fully functioning post office, for use by the workers, which is the world's only post office built from salt.

Although a popular tourist destination today, the salt mines were the scene of brutal oppression and forced work by the British in the 1800s. Miners were locked in and not allowed to leave until they fulfilled their quotas. This policy included pregnant women, and a number of children were born within the mine. Strikes were met with violence, which is on display in the mines: The graves of 12 miners shot and killed in 1876 can be seen at the middle gate.

How to try it

An electric railway, in place since the 1930s, now brings tourists into the mine, but you can choose to walk the tunnels. It's easy to taste the output of Khewra, which is known as Himalayan salt and sold in many grocery stores.

Other Salty Wonders

DANIEL CAMPOS, BOLIVIA

Salar de Uyuni

The largest salt flat in the world is spread over 4,247 square miles (11,000 square km) in an endless sheet of hexagonal tiles. Generations of saleros historically harvested the flats, but their way of life is disappearing in a modernizing Bolivia. Today, the flats are mostly scenic. During the wet season, the expanse transforms into an enormous salt lake that perfectly mirrors the sky.

MOUNT ELGON, KENYA

Kitum Cave

This salt-rich cavity extends some 600 feet (183 m) into an extinct shield volcano and functions as a salt lick for animals in the Kenyan wild. When the cave was first discovered, the marks and scratches on its walls were assumed to be the work of ancient people, but they were actually left by elephants, who used their tusks to pull chunks off the wall and eat the salt, slowly excavating the cave over hundreds of years.

GRAND SALINE, TEXAS

The Salt Palace

This town's salt-mining history dates back to 1845. The Salt Palace is constructed entirely of salt, erected next to a salt deposit that's an estimated 16,000 feet (4,877 m) deep and contains a supply to last about 20,000 years. In Grand Saline, salt is everything. A museum for Morton Salt, North America's largest producer, the palace boasts a wall that visitors like to lick.

Salar de Uyuni in Bolivia stretches over 4,000 miles.

MAD HONEY

DELI BAL • TURKEY

When bees feed on the pollen of rhododendron flowers, their honey can pack a psychotropic punch. Depending on how much a person consumes, reactions can range from hallucinations and a slower heartbeat to temporary paralysis and unconsciousness. There are hundreds of types of rhododendrons, but only a few contain grayanotoxin, the compound that makes honey psychedelic. These special rhododendrons grow in the high Turkish mountains that line the Black Sea, where locals have been cultivating deli bal, or mad honey, for millennia and using it with strategic aplomb.

Mad honey was deployed in 67 BCE as a trap for invading Roman soldiers. Loyalists to King Mithridates placed honey along their path, which the Romans were unable to resist. When paralysis settled in, Mithridates's men came back to kill them.

By the 18th century, Europeans had developed a taste for the honey, which they imported by the ton and mixed into their drinks for a psychedelic tipple.

In smaller doses, mad honey is used in Turkey as folk medicine. About a teaspoon of the potent, red-hued nectar is believed to relieve hypertension, diabetes, and gastric pain among other things. More than a tablespoon is when poisoning symptoms generally kick in, but the potency can vary greatly from batch to batch.

How to try it

The mountain towns along the Black Sea are where to find the purest mad honey, but shopkeepers may be reluctant to sell it to outsiders.

Sea bass biryan

SULTAN CUISINE FROM THE OTTOMAN EMPIRE

ASITANE RESTAURANT • TURKEY

On a quiet side street in Istanbul, Asitane Restaurant prides on itself re-creating Ottoman cuisine. It's harder than it sounds. During the Ottoman period (1299–1922), secretive guilds prohibited chefs from writing down recipes. Complicating things further, any records of classical Ottoman preparations are in Ottoman Turkish, written in Arabic script, instead of modern-day Turkish, which

How to try it

Asitane is located at 6 Kariye Cami Sokake, in the Fatih district west of Istanbul's city center. They are open every day, 12 p.m.–11:30 p.m.

is written in the Latin alphabet. Undaunted, Asitane hired a team of academics and researchers to search for menus detailing historic feasts held by sultans, records of foods purchased for palace kitchens, and written accounts by foreign travelers. Slowly, the culinary detectives built a repertoire of hundreds of recipes, including many that are tied to specific dates. Historical specialties at Asitane include almond soup from 1539 served with pomegranate and nutmeg, 17th-century fried liver rissoles dunked in sweet-and-sour molasses, and slow-cooked goose atop almond pilaf. A perennial favorite is baked fruit (quince in the winter, melon in the summer) stuffed with lamb and beef. The hard-won, centuries-old dishes painstakingly re-created in the Asitane kitchen are perfect for anyone hungry for a literal taste of history.

MAGIC ORCHID THICKENER

SALEP • TURKEY

Consider the glamorous orchid: Most know the plant for its long stems, elegant blossoms, and hard-to-grow reputation. But in Turkey, the orchid is best loved for a hidden talent. Dried up and ground, the tubers of wild orchids make a flour called salep, which locals use as a special thickener in two essential Turkish foods.

When combined with hot milk, sugar, and spices, salep becomes a drink, also called salep, that dates back to the Ottoman Empire. The texture is viscous and smooth, coating the throat and mouth in a soothing way that's especially desirable during cold winter days. Salep is also traditionally considered a medicinal drink, with the power to heal respiratory and gastrointestinal problems.

A dondurma vendor pulls the ice cream high in the air.

The incredible flower is also what gives Turkish ice cream its signature texture. Called dondurma, Turkish ice cream is equal parts dessert and performance art. Vendors use a long metal rod to beat and knead the ice cream in a metal drum, which they then pull high into the air, creating a vertical trail of thick, elastic ice cream. Twirled onto the rod, vendors deposit a blob of ice cream onto a cone and hand it to a customer. Salep powder makes the ice cream thick and stable (dondurma is sometimes served like shawarma, sliced from a large mass with a knife), while also making it less prone to melting. As for the sticky elasticity, that comes from a pine resin called mastic sap, which also makes it chewy.

Salep has become such a popular product that Turkey's wild orchid population is being destroyed. It is now illegal to export real salep, and more and more shops are substituting rice flour or guar gum. Although the ancient flour performs some excellent tricks, as with everything, it's best in moderation.

How to try it

In Turkey, it's getting increasingly hard to find the real thing. Ali Usta in Istanbul serves both the hot drink and the ice cream.

SOVIET-ERA CARROT KIMCHI

MORKOVCHA • UZBEKISTAN

How To Try It

Look for morkovcha in big, bustling Uzbek bazaars, such as Chorsu Bazaar in Tashkent and Central Bazaar in Samarkand.

To those who don't know its history, morkovcha is a simple carrot salad. Julienned carrots are pickled in white vinegar and oil and seasoned with coriander, red pepper, and fresh garlic. Its name, which means "Korean carrots," hints at a deeper significance.

In the 1860s, faced with drought and famine, thousands of Koreans from the province of Hamgyong crossed the border into Russia. At first their new country embraced them, but there was soon pressure to assimilate to Russian culture and the Orthodox Christian faith. As the Russian czars tried to convert the first wave of immigrants, more arrived, many escaping the Japanese occupation. By the 1930s, nearly 200,000 Koreans, known as Koryo-saram, had settled in what was then the Soviet Union. Many Koreans assimilated, accepting Russian values, eating European food, and enlisting in the imperial army. But some Koreans remained in enclaves, preserving their culture and traditional cuisine.

In 1937, as tensions rose between the USSR and Japan, Joseph Stalin decided the Koryo-saram were an "unreliable people" and forcibly and violently relocated the population to remote parts of Uzbekistan and Kazakhstan. Many Koryo-saram died on the monthlong journey. Those who survived were forced to start over with nothing in an unknown land.

Morkovcha is an example of the cuisine that emerged from this brutal diaspora. Koryo-saram food is shaped both by early Russian influence and by the crops they found in Central Asia. When common Korean ingredients such as napa cabbage weren't available for kimchi, carrots were a handy substitute. Coriander seeds and fresh cilantro, both staples of Uzbek cuisine, made their way in, too.

As Soviet Koreans moved around the USSR to study and work in the 1960s, their cuisine spread and morkovcha became a staple outside the diaspora. The crunchy, garlicky, sweet-and-sour salad is so well loved that many Uzbek grocery stores sell packaged spice mixes so customers can make it at home.

BREAD STAMPS

CHEKICH • UZBEKISTAN

Uzbekistan's non is a round, flat bread that's light, chewy, and treated with such respect that every loaf is decorated with a stamp especially made for bread beautification. Called chekich, these stamps have fine, needle-like points that make tiny perforations into the dough. After they've been poked, the non is slapped against the blistering walls of a tandyr, or tandoor oven, where the bread will rise around the tiny holes, leaving an elegant, intricate design.

Besides being attractive, the designs affect the bread's texture, giving a unique blend of chewy, crunchy, and soft, depending on how much of the dough has been stamped. In Uzbekistan, the care given to bread borders on worship. Their non is ancient (the *Epic of Gilgamesh*, one of the earliest surviving works of literature, references Uzbek-style non), and there is a bread tradition for every occasion. Engaged couples are given pink and yellow non. Those leaving on a trip take a bite from a piece of non, then leave the rest behind for their safe return. If non is dropped on the ground, it is picked up and placed on a ledge or tree branch for birds to eat, while saying "*aysh Allah*" or "God's bread."

Though the bread is eaten every day, at nearly every meal, bakers take the time to lovingly stamp each loaf. As a common Uzbek proverb goes: "Respect for non is respect for country."

How to try it

Conveniently, chekich can be found at the same bazaars that have morkovcha (p. 114). Make a day of it!

Though the intricate designs may suggest otherwise, loaves of non are an everyday food in Uzbekistan.

EAST ASIA

FERMENTED TEA GOLD RUSH

PU'ER TEA • CHINA

How to try it
For full immersion, taste tea varieties at the Pu'er Tea Institute, south of Pu'er City in the autonomous Xishuangbanna prefecture.

W inding through the southwestern mountains of China, east of Tibet, is an ancient caravan trail once used by traders to transport tea. The Tea Horse Road begins in Yunnan Province, which many believe to be the birthplace of tea. Around the 8th century, to make transportation easier, sellers compressed their tea into discs and wrapped them in bamboo leaves, which could be bundled and strapped to their animals. On the journey, the goods were exposed to sunshine, heat, and rain, causing the tea cakes to ferment. The region's famous specialty tea, pu'er, was born.

Like wine grapes, tea leaves are affected by terroir, cultivation, processing, aging, and storage. The very best pu'er grows wild in the rain forests of Yunnan Province, where hundred-year-old trees with deep root systems produce rich, complexly flavored leaves. (Bordered by Vietnam, Myanmar, and Laos, these forests look more like Southeast Asia than mainland China.) The picked leaves are fired in a wok, a process that removes moisture and breaks them down slightly, and then kneaded by hand and left to dry in the sun. After extensive tasting, the tea is blended with other tea leaves, pressed into discs, and left to ferment.

In the late 1990s, wealthy tea drinkers from Hong Kong to Taiwan became fascinated with pu'er, then fixated, then absolutely loony for it. The pu'er market exploded. The Chinese middle class invested like it was gold. Speculators bought all the tea they could, with little regard for quality. There were forgeries. Tea was shipped into Yunnan, stamped as pu'er, and sold as if it had come from the province. Labels were intentionally made to mirror the packaging of popular luxury brands. A decade before the boom, a kilo of pu'er sold for pennies. In 2006, right before the bubble burst, the same kilo went for hundreds of dollars.

The mountainous region of Yunnan, China, is an ideal place to grow pu'er tea, as its rolling slopes allow even rainfall distribution to plants at every level.

Among aficionados, pu'er is treated like wine or cheese—as a living product that will change and develop for the duration of its life. Microbes are important—the Yunnan forests are rich with unique bacteria—as is the location where the tea was aged, how long it was aged, and by whom. In 2005, 500 grams of a 64-year-old "vintage" sold for $150,000.

While the pu'er frenzy has quieted, pu'er drinkers still make up a robust, devoted community. In China, pu'er is a popular gift, and the most sought-after tea (grown in places such as Lao Banzhang) gets bought before it can leave the country. Those who source for foreign demand have to make strategic partnerships with farmers, who keep their harvesting sites secret.

To drink pu'er, a small chunk of tea is broken from the cake and "rinsed" with an application of hot water, which is discarded. The second brew is good to drink, and many people brew their pu'er many times after that, enjoying the way the flavor changes. The finest pu'er is measured in both flavor and how it feels in the body. Many describe drug-like highs, both the calm, muscle-relaxing variety and the sweaty, panicked kind. The taste is almost impossible to describe—some dark, some earthy, some sweet, some harsh—as every brick tastes different.

Pu'er tea is one of the few teas protected by the Chinese government and must come from the Yunnan Province.

BOUNCY MEATBALL SHOP

FEI XIA LAO ER • CHINA

Every day at 3:30 p.m., the staff at Fei Xia Lao Er start breaking down fresh, still-warm slabs of beef and transforming them into meatballs that, when thrown against a table, will bounce a foot in the air. Along the windows of the small shop, a row of young workers sit on stools, ready to perform the 4 p.m. show that's taken place every day for 30 years. In each hand, they hold a metal baton. Before them is a solid hunk of beef. In 25 minutes, it will be paste.

If you didn't see the beef, you might think the employees were beating a drum. But with each rhythmic rise and fall of the metal batons, the quivering block of meat slowly loosens. The workers strike the meat, fold it, then strike again. According to owner Liping Hong, the pounding motion is not about strength, but posture. With the correct form—picked up from the elders in Hong's hometown—the pounding should be "easy."

The beef paste is ready when it's a light pink color, jiggly, and almost fluffy. Seasoning and starch are added, then the mixture is squeezed between the thumb and forefinger into little balls that are plopped directly into a vat of boiling water. The staff at Fei Xia Lao Er make 3,200 meatballs every day, which are usually gone within 24 hours.

The texture of the meatballs is light, refreshing, and springy. This is all thanks to the hand-pounding. Machinery destroys the muscle fiber in beef, whereas the slow beating keeps the fiber intact and gives the meatball its signature bounce.

How to try it

Fei Xia Lao Er is located on Feixia N Road in Shantou, but bouncy meatballs are a traditional specialty all over the Chaoshan region.

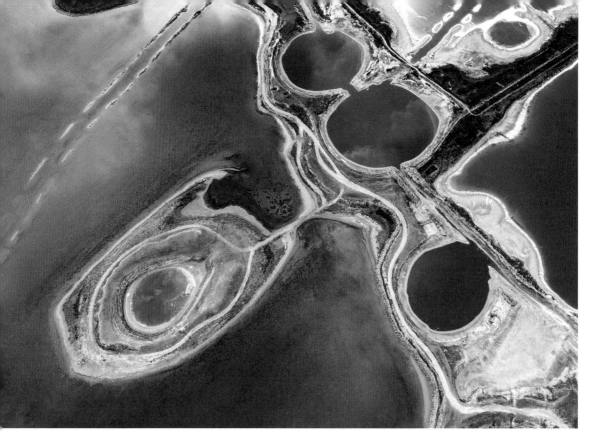

CHINA'S DEAD SEA

YUNCHENG SALT LAKE • CHINA

How to try it

There are several buses that run from downtown Yuncheng to the lake. Other salt lakes in China have suffered extreme pollution due to tourist attention. Help keep Yuncheng from the same fate by carrying your trash out with you.

When summer comes, the glassy water of Yuncheng Salt Lake in China's Shanxi Province turns a shocking rainbow. From above, the lake looks like a painter's palette, with dabbles of magenta, green, and aquamarine across the landscape.

Known as "China's Dead Sea" for its salinity, the vast lake has long been the focal point of Yuncheng's culture and economy. Chinese historians estimate that locals have harvested salt from the lake for more than 4,000 years. By the sixth century, Yuncheng Lake was responsible for a quarter of China's overall salt production. Local lore reports wars fought over possession of the lake, and nearby temples are dedicated to salt gods.

Today, most travelers come to the lake not to worship the salt gods, but to marvel at the landscape's surreal charm. As opposed to the Dead Sea, which is filled with chloride and is hostile to life, Yuncheng Lake is filled with sulfate, which supports a lush ecosystem. In the summer, algal blooms turn the water technicolor thanks to *Dunaliella salina*, an algae species that changes color when it reacts with salt. In winter, when the temperature dips below 23°Fahrenheit (-5°C), the salt forms crystals of mirabilite, also known as Glauber's Salt, transforming the landscape into a twinkling winter fantasy.

Yuncheng salt was traditionally harvested for culinary use through a five-step process that the Shanxi Province has officially recognized as a piece of the region's intangible heritage. Since the 1980s, however, producers have abandoned this process and pivoted toward industrial harvesting. Locals hope that the influx of visitors interested in marveling at the lake can also help inspire the preservation of local salt-harvesting traditions and the rich ecosystem that has given rise to an extraordinary natural beauty.

NAKED BOY TEA PET

PEE-PEE BOY • CHINA

How to try it
Pee-pee boys can be
purchased online.

In recent years, "tea pets" have made their way into the contemporary Chinese tea ceremony. The small figurines, shaped like animals, plants, or mythical creatures, are meant to be cared for by their owners, who "bathe" their little companions by pouring hot water over their bodies. Among China's favorite pets is "pee-pee boy," a hollowed-out child with a large head and a small penis.

Pee-pee boy is more useful than he first appears because his body functions—via bodily function—as a thermometer. When preparing tea, pee-pee boy takes a dip in room-temperature water, which he draws in through the hole in his member until he is half full. To check the temperature of your tea water, simply pour it over pee-pee boy's head, and if the water is hot enough, your tea pet will emit a long, arching liquid stream. If the water's too cold, pee-pee boy will lose his nerve.

Although the origins of pee-pee boy are unclear, the physics behind his steady stream are scientifically sound. A 2016 study exploring the thermodynamics of several pee-pee boys found that hot water poured over the noggin makes the air within the body expand, causing pressure to build and release a jet of "pee" seconds later. The correlation was simple: the hotter the water, the farther the stream. Additional factors affecting whizzing distance included head size (pee-pee boy's cranium is disproportionately large), ceramic thickness, penis size, and hole diameter.

Hollow ceramic figurines date back to the Tang dynasty (618–906 CE). If they were used like tea pets, researchers speculate that they could be the world's first thermometers, preceding Galileo Galilei's late-16th-century invention of the thermoscope.

This small urinating boy may look like trouble, but he is one of China's favorite "tea pets."

A WORKING REPLICA OF THE *FRIENDS* COFFEE SHOP

CENTRAL PERK BEIJING • CHINA

How to try it
Central Perk Beijing
is located at 0616
Chaowai SOHO Building.
According to visitors,
the sixth floor of the
building is vast, with
many vacancies, so you
may not find it right
away.

Tucked away on the sixth floor of Beijing's Chaowai, SOHO Building A, is a shockingly good replica of Central Perk, the coffee shop hangout on the American sitcom *Friends*. Not only is it fitted with identical brick walls, tables, and the ever-present orange couch, it's also a fully functional coffee shop where customers can sip java, relax, and pretend they're in the show. There is even a resident Smelly Cat.

Created by owner Du Xin, who describes the show as his religion, Beijing's Central Perk is a mecca for Chinese fans of *Friends*, as well as those who simply want to practice their English. A TV plays episodes of *Friends* on loop with Chinese subtitles, which students say is a great way to pick up colloquialisms and mannerisms that aren't taught in the classroom. In the space next door, Du has also constructed a replica of the character Joey Tribbiani's apartment, complete with foosball table, dartboard, Etch A Sketch, and oversize TV console.

DOUBLE-YOLK EGG CITY

GAOYOU • CHINA

How to try it

Gaoyou holds an annual China Double-Yolk Duck Egg Festival, typically in April. Year round, salted double-yolked eggs are served in the region's teahouses, generally as a component of zaocha, or morning tea.

Two-yolked eggs are usually a rare, statistically random occurrence. But in the eastern Chinese city of Gaoyou—a place synonymous with double-yolked duck eggs—farmers found a way to engineer a vast supply of this local specialty.

Gaoyou, a city with a population of nearly one million, has a long and close relationship with ducks. The duck industry dates back to the 6th century, and locals still gift ducks on occasions ranging from marriages to a child's first day at school. Double-yolked eggs—believed to be more nutritious than regular eggs, as well as a sign of good luck—are held in especially high regard. For generations, locals bred Gaoyou's local duck variety to produce double-yolked eggs, which occur when a fowl ovulates twice in the process of formulating an egg. The resulting duck lays anywhere between 2 to 10 percent double-yolkers.

To check an egg for double yolks, farmers shine a bright light on the shell, which reveals either one gray yolk shadow or two. This process, known as candling, is done on a commercial scale in Gaoyou, where workers pick eggs off a backlit conveyor belt. Once removed from the pack, the special eggs are brined in vats of salt water before gracing lucky tables across the region.

A backlit conveyor belt helps workers identify the duck eggs with two yolks.

NOCTURNAL CRAB CONDIMENT

GHOST CRAB SAUCE • CHINA

On early autumn nights when the tide is low, the beaches off the southern coastal city of Beihai come alive with tiny skittering ghost crabs, darting beneath the moonlight. The miniature crabs, just two centimeters long, have spectral white legs and transparent, ghoulish blue bodies. Also known as sand crabs for their ability to camouflage themselves on the beach, the tiny crustaceans are a species that has remained nearly unchanged for millennia.

During ghost crab swells, Beihai locals put on rubber boots and come out to chase them. Carrying long sticks attached to nets, they scoop the critters however they can, bending to gather them in their hands or swooping them up in their nets. Ghost crabs are incredibly fast, able to sprint about five feet (1.5 m) in a second, so the nocturnal hunt is frenetic, with humans dashing after masses of micro crabs as they try to burrow into the sand.

Ghost crabs, which are sensitive to pollutants, are often a sign of a healthy beach. The people of Beihai like them for their nutrient-rich taste, which they absorb from seawater and algae. Ghost crab sauce is an essential condiment in the southern Chinese city, made from pounding the cleaned and gutted crabs, adding salt and liquor, then letting it ferment for about a month. The pungent, fishy sauce, with its shell-and-meat-studded texture, is used as something of an all-purpose seasoning. The most popular preparation is steamed with cowpeas (a green bean), but the complex, raw, and richly flavored liquid is happily poured over pretty much anything.

How to try it
Ghost crab sauce is highly regional and almost always homemade. The crabs themselves are found on coasts from North America to South Africa.

← 2 cm →

THE WORLD'S OLDEST SANDWICH

ROU JIA MO • CHINA

Rou jia mo, one of China's most popular street foods, has been around since the Qin dynasty (221–207 BCE). Translated as "meat in bread," rou jia mo is widely considered the world's first sandwich, the progenitor of the burger, and one of the tastiest, most interesting foods in the country.

The Han Chinese were the original sandwich makers. Although rice is the starch Westerners most associate with Chinese food, the northern provinces have a distinct cuisine that revolves around mo, or bread. Few details exist about the first rou jia mo, but historical records show the ancient Chinese were combining bread and meat 2,000 years before the Earl of Sandwich. During the Tang dynasty (618–907), the Silk Road originated in the city of Xi'an, now the capital of Shaanxi Province. Traders and merchants from the Middle East and India arrived in the ancient Chinese capital, bringing knowledge and spices, which went into flavoring the world's first sandwich.

How to try it
Anywhere in China, rou jia mo is hard to miss, but around Shaanxi Province, shops sell every imaginable variation. In Xi'an, try Cheng's for "juicy" filling, Ziwu Road Zhang for "chewy" filling, Dongguan Li's for "dry" filling, or Qinyu for just lots of filling.

A Xi'an street vendor prepares lamb rou jia mo.

Traditional, street-style rou jia mo is made with 20 spices, including ginger, star anise, cardamom, galangal, bay leaves, Sichuan peppercorn, cinnamon, and cumin. Swirled into a stock of sweetened soy sauce and Shaoxing wine, the broth is used to slowly braise chunks of pork belly. The stock is the most important part of the dish, used over and over again. Called Thousand Year Old Sauce, the liquid takes on the rich oil of the meat, reducing and growing more profound in flavor with each batch. (This is a technique used in other Chinese dishes such as Chairman Mao's favorite red-braised pork belly, which makes an excellent rou jia mo filling.) The bun, or mo, is a simple wheat flour dough that's formed into hand-size discs, then baked in a traditional clay oven or fried in a pan. Split open and stuffed with meat, cilantro, and vendor-specific toppings, a rou jia mo on the street in China will cost about 5–10 yuan ($0.75–$1.50 USD).

Thanks in part to the Silk Road, modern-day Xi'an is now home to about 70,000 Muslims and a lively Chinese Muslim food scene, awash in hand-pulled noodles and mutton stews. Adapting the regional sandwich recipe to suit their tastes and religious dietary restrictions, they introduced lamb and beef rou jia mo, which are now as ubiquitous in Xi'an as the Han pork belly classic.

Chairman Mao's Red-Braised Pork Belly (Hong Shao Rou)
4-6 servings

2 pounds pork belly, cut into ¾-inch pieces

6 slices ginger (divided)

2 tablespoons oil

3 tablespoons granulated sugar or 40 grams rock sugar, plus ½ teaspoon to finish

3 scallions, diced, with the white and green parts separated

½ cup Shaoxing wine

3 tablespoons light soy sauce

1½ tablespoons dark soy sauce

1 piece of cinnamon

2 star anise

4 bay leaves

1–2 dried chili peppers (optional)

4 cups water

1. Put the pork belly and 3 slices of ginger in a pot, cover with cold water, and bring to a boil with the lid on. Once the pot boils, turn down the heat and simmer for 1 more minute. Drain, rinse the pork belly clean, and set aside.

2. With the wok set over low heat, add the oil and sugar. Slowly melt the sugar, then add the pork belly, the remaining 3 slices of ginger, and the white parts of the scallions. Turn up the heat to medium and stir, coating the pork in the melted sugar.

3. Add the Shaoxing wine, light soy sauce, dark soy sauce, cinnamon, star anise, bay leaves, dried chili pepper, and water. Stir. Simmer over medium low heat for 1 hour.

4. Add the remaining ½ teaspoon of sugar and green parts of the scallions.

It's said that Chairman Mao (above) ate this dish every day.

The Mandatory Canteens
OF COMMUNIST CHINA

In 1958, Chinese communist cadres descended upon the homes of farmers with an official government mission: to confiscate food supplies and cooking equipment, and to destroy private kitchens. Effective immediately, cooking and eating meals at home became illegal.

The measure stemmed from Chairman Mao Zedong's Great Leap Forward, a series of communist government initiatives intended to revolutionize the Chinese countryside. In order to build a new socialist consciousness in China, Mao pushed agricultural collectivization. He abolished private property, divided all work among households, and grouped farmers into cooperatives of about 23,000 members. The system was called the People's Commune, and it centered around a free canteen system designed to feed commune members.

The People's Commune contained 2.65 million canteens, constructed from confiscated tables, utensils, and kitchen equipment. A ringing bell signified the start of mealtimes, when farmers would line up single file to be served cafeteria-style before sitting down in a central dining area. The meals were free, but there was no other choice.

At first, the canteens were treated like a miracle. A popular slogan invited diners to "open your stomach, eat as much as you wish, and work hard for socialism." Farmers reveled in the new system and gorged themselves on pork and vegetables, sometimes eating when they weren't hungry. Government propaganda led citizens to believe that more grain was being produced than actually was, and that food was plentiful. Leftovers were thrown away and massive amounts of food were squandered.

Problems arose almost immediately, and signs of famine appeared as early as the winter of 1958. Historically, Chinese farmers maintained food stockpiles to prepare for shortages or slow harvest years. Without them, they were hostage to the dwindling food supply of the canteens.

By spring of 1959, the famine had metastasized beyond control. The carefree days of feasting quickly morphed into hunger. Survivors remember the canteen meals grimly: buns made from corn and bark, served with water. It was not uncommon for laborers, still toiling in the fields to hit massive quotas, to receive as little as 150–200 grams of food for a meal. Rice was unavailable and was substituted with watery wheat porridge, sweet potatoes and their leaves, and hemp "noodles," made by cutting roots into strands. Farmers also ate the bark from parasol and loquat trees.

Massive exploitation further exacerbated the problem. Corrupt leaders ate as much as they wanted from the canteens. Meanwhile, farmers had little incentive to work because everyone received the same food. By the end of 1960, the rising death toll and drastic food shortages forced the government to acknowledge that the canteen system had failed. After a series of debates with high-ranking officials, Mao finally relented. By 1962, all communal canteens were eliminated. The famine killed an estimated 30 million people, making it one of the worst in human history.

Despite the canteen system's devastating consequences, restaurants that hearken back to Mao's China have opened in cities such as Beijing and Chongqing. Staff don the traditional communist suits and use gimmicks to project nostalgia about a "simpler" time and a China that no longer exists. In an ironic twist, these ultra-capitalist modern restaurants, with their abundance of food, may have been closer to what Mao originally imagined for his communal canteens.

Chinese citizens eat as much as they can at a People's Commune canteen in 1958.

How to try it

The addition of gondolas has greatly increased the traffic to Mount Hua, and there is often a wait to make the climb from the northern peak.

A PERILOUS CUP OF ELEVATED TEA

HUASHAN TEAHOUSE • CHINA

Nestled atop the highest peak of China's holy Mount Hua is a temple that offers a cup of tea—a drink central to Daoist philosophy—more than 7,000 feet (2133 m) in the air. The trek, which has been called one of the most dangerous hiking paths in the world, has attracted pilgrims for centuries. Mount Hua is one of China's five sacred mountains and has been a religious site since the 2nd century BCE, when a Daoist temple was built at its base.

To reach the temple, hikers must first reach the northern peak by climbing a series of steps carved into the mountain known as the Heavenly Stairs, which takes about 4–5 hours. (This is the only leg of the ascent you can take via gondola.) Once at the northern peak, the real work begins. Getting to the southern peak requires another 2–3 hours of climbing, but instead of traditional trails, hikers must sidle along the sheer mountainside, balancing across a thin ledge made of what looks like scrap wood suspended hundreds of feet in the air. (This is called the "plank walk.") At certain points, the planks fall away, leaving nothing but a horizontal chain to hold and some pegs to stand on. Regulations now require hikers to use safety harnesses and carabiners, but the paths are so narrow that climbers often unhook their carabiners to pass each other. Finally, a set of worn stairs leads to the temple, and their sharp grade offers no respite.

Inside the temple, while the monks go about their daily rituals, visitors can sit down for a well-earned cup of tea. In Daoist philosophy, drinking tea facilitates meditation and creates a connection to nature. The tea served at the temple teahouse is made with natural water—collected from rain, melting snow, and mountain springs—or bottled water ferried to the top. Those who have completed the climb say the elevation, view, and temple setting make for one of the most satisfying cups of tea you'll ever experience.

THE WORLD'S LARGEST FLOATING RESTAURANT

JUMBO KINGDOM • HONG KONG

How to try it
Jumbo Kingdom
provides free boat
shuttles to and from the
Aberdeen waterfront.
(Don't be fooled by a
sampan taxi offering a
cheap ride.) Dim sum,
served during lunch,
is regarded by many
as the most lively and
affordable meal on offer.

Glistening in Hong Kong's Aberdeen Harbor is Jumbo Kingdom, a floating behemoth of a restaurant that functions more like a city. The kingdom contains a collection of restaurants serving different styles of Cantonese fare, with grand staircases and skinny walkways crisscrossing between the various establishments. Built by Dr. Stanley Ho, known as Macau's "King of Gambling," the complex was completed in 1976 after four years of work and was modeled on an ancient Chinese imperial palace.

The exterior is decked out in neon lights and upturned eaves with yellow flourishes, a color once reserved for imperial buildings. Inside, there is no shortage of dragons, pagodas, and Ming dynasty–era details: In one banquet hall, there is a gold and red "dragon throne" that took sculptors two years to carve. Beyond the dining areas, which can seat more than 2,000 people, there's a seafood tank barge that guests can visit (the daily catch arrives each morning by fishing boat), a 130-foot (40 m) kitchen boat, a cooking school, a Chinese tea garden, and a theme park.

THE COGNAC OF CONDIMENTS

XO SAUCE • HONG KONG

How to try it
Bottled XO sauce is
available in Chinese
grocery stores, but the
best versions are
homemade.

The term XO, when applied to cognac, means "extra old." But in Hong Kong, it simply means luxury. The island's elite have long nursed an obsession with the super-aged French liquor, so when a chef created "XO sauce" in the 1980s, Hong Kongers knew it had to be fancy.

The cognac-inspired condiment is a sweet and spicy, unctuous medley of minced seafood that requires lots of patience and a hefty amount of cash to create. It begins with a wok of hot oil, which must be carefully monitored throughout the lengthy, multi-step frying process. Each ingredient in the sauce goes in separately, is fried until golden, then removed and reserved until the very end. Garlic and shallots get the oil bath first, then the mélange of dried seafood, all of which must be rehydrated and chopped prior to frying. Diver scallops and shrimp are mandatory (cod roe and baby anchovies are happy additions). Jinhua ham, China's version of prosciutto, is the last item to take a dip in the pool. If along the way something gets burned, the sauce is in trouble. Not only are the items pricey (dried diver scallops can go for $300 a kilo), but the fragrant oil is a key ingredient, swirled with the fried bits, sugar, and chili peppers at the end to create the sumptuous alchemy of XO sauce.

Like cognac, a little XO sauce goes a long way. A spoonful atop a steamed fish or a bowl of greens draws out sweet, salty, and savory elements in dishes that would otherwise lack a dynamic range.

Farthest Flung
CHINESE RESTAURANTS

There are more Chinese food joints in the United States than McDonald's, KFC, Wendy's, and Burger King combined. No food has more completely mapped every small town, hamlet, and neighborhood than Chinese cuisine, and it's not just in the United States. Thanks to an expansive diaspora, Chinese restaurants have spread out across the world, and you can find Chinese food from Ecuador to Ethiopia. Here are a few of the farther-flung locations:

1 In Ushuaia, Argentina, at the southern tip of the world, you can get a Chinese buffet at **BAMBOO.** Because it is often the launching point for visiting Antarctica, it isn't uncommon to find large groups of Chinese tourists eating there on their way to the frozen continent.

2 On the island of Tromsøya, above the Arctic Circle, on the fjord-filled northern edge of Norway, you can find **TANG'S**, a traditional Chinese restaurant.

3 Easter Island, with a population of 5,700, has **KAI SUSHI RAPANUI,** a mixed Japanese and Chinese spot.

4 In Lisbon, Portugal, people's apartments form a network of Chinês clandestinos, nonofficial Chinese restaurants.

5 Going to Greenland? Stop at the **HONG KONG CAFE** in Ilulissat, population 4,541, and get some fried spare ribs with your fried rice.

6 **SAM AND LEE'S RESTAURANT** in Utqiaġvik, Alaska, the northernmost city in the United States, may well be the northernmost Chinese restaurant in the world. The restaurant is run by Ms. Kim, who also makes a mean stack of pancakes, reindeer-and-cheese omelets, and the restaurant's own creation, the "Kung Pao" pizza.

7 In Antarctica, although there technically isn't a Chinese "restaurant," the **CHINESE GREAT WALL STATION** does have a team of Chinese chefs, and researchers from other stations go out of their way for a taste of the roasted mutton and peppery chicken spiced with fresh herbs grown in a soilless base.

8 Montana might not be your first thought when it comes to great Chinese food, but the **PEKIN NOODLE PARLOR** in Butte is a classic. Immediately identifiable by its iconic glowing neon "Chop Suey" sign, Pekin Noodle Parlor is the nation's oldest continually operating Chinese restaurant. It started serving chow mein back in 1911. On the restaurant's one hundredth birthday, the owner cooked dinner for the whole town.

9 In the city of Mamoudzou, on the island of Mayotte, floating in the channel between Madagascar and the east coast of Mozambique, you can find dozens of Chinese restaurants, including the high-end French-Chinese fusion **L'ORIENT EXPRESS**. Madagascar was a French colony and also has one of Africa's largest Chinese populations.

10 Visiting Nauru—a tiny island country of 11,347, the second smallest country population in the world behind Vatican City—and worried about getting good Chinese? Don't be—you can choose from one of the more than 138 Chinese restaurants, mostly operated by the 8 percent of the island that are Han Chinese.

11 In the city of Cerro de Pasco, a Peruvian mining town at an elevation of 14,232 ft (about 4,338 m), one of the highest cities in the world, you can still get an egg roll at **CHIFA YING FU.**

12 In Oklahoma City, beneath the streets is a system of tunnels built in the 1970s known as "the Underground." What's down there? Why, **CHINA CHEF,** of course, open for more than two decades, despite being notoriously hard to find in the maze of tunnels.

A TRADITIONAL AMIS EATERY

BANAI'S SHOP • TAIWAN

How to try it
Taiwan has three
outposts, two in Taipei
(Ximen and Shilin) and
one in Taichung.

Tucked on a side street off the main drag of Dulan, a small village along Taiwan's eastern coast, is Banai's Shop, a cozy "quick fry" restaurant specializing in traditional Amis dishes. While the Amis people are Indigenous to this part of Taiwan, a visitor to this popular backpacker town might not immediately guess it from the cute hostels and international eateries that dot its main thoroughfare. Banai's Shop, opened eight years ago by Ms. Ye Shuyuan (Banai is her Amis name), stands out for its tasty, traditional flavors, community-sourced ingredients, and welcoming atmosphere. In addition to Ms. Ye's warm presence, the restaurant's long wooden tables are also often filled with locals who are happy to give tourists recommendations on what to order and aren't shy to share a helping from their plates or a pour of liquor.

Some of the restaurant's more unique offerings include mountain boar stir-fried with bell peppers, cold mountain boar skin marinated in vinegar and topped with fresh cilantro, flying fish fried rice and honey-glazed flying fish (available only during April and May), brook shrimp stir-fried with scallions and chilies, and "Lover's Tears," a green fungus found in the mountains after rainfall, stir-fried with eggs and Thai basil. Traditional millet wine is also available, homemade by local women and sold in tall, unmarked glass bottles. The unfiltered liquor is clean and sweet, making it a great accompaniment to the hearty, bold fare.

TRADITIONAL PYROTECHNIC FISHING

JINSHAN FIRE FISHING FESTIVAL • TAIWAN

How to try it
Tours are about four
hours long and offered
only in Mandarin. They
include an introduction
to the history of Jinshan
fire fishing, a dinner
of noodle soup, and
a dazzling view of the
fishermen at work.

It's pitch-black on Taiwan's northern waters, when suddenly a boom and blaze of fire explode into the night sky, releasing the sour stench of sulfur. All at once, thousands of tiny sardines leap from the Pacific Ocean, hurling themselves toward the scorching flames. As the fire rages on the boat, several aging fishermen work feverishly to catch the fish before they plunge back into the sea.

Traditional sulfuric fire fishing is a century-plus-old practice found only in Jinshan, a sleepy port city near the northern tip of Taiwan. Fishermen use a bamboo torch and the flammable gas produced by sulfuric rocks (abundant in Taiwan) to ignite a fire fierce enough to drive hordes of sardines to the water's surface. Always timed with a moonless night, when the fish are hungry for light, the fishermen ignite their fire and cast their nets. They work through the night—each playing an essential role such as steering the boat or controlling the flames—for up to 12 hours. The practice is backbreaking, treacherous, and in danger of disappearing.

In its glory days, fire fishing was used by thousands. The technique was first developed by the Pingpu aboriginal tribe and honed during Japanese colonial rule in Taiwan. As of 2019, there are a mere four fire-fishing boats remaining and a dwindling number of fire fishermen, many of them well into their 60s and 70s. The

island's youth have not shown interest in carrying on the fickle, punishing work, which led the government to set up the Jinshan Fire Fishing Festival, where outsiders can witness the nocturnal spectacle.

Like fireworks on the sea, sulfuric flames ignited by Jinshan fishermen attract sardines to the surface.

From May to July, sightseeing tours bring boats of onlookers alongside the fire-fishing boats. The idea is to raise awareness and appreciation for the practice and hopefully save it from extinction. Many fishermen perform the work with a sense of resigned pride, knowing their tradition will inevitably be surrendered to history. For them, fire fishing is both art form and vocation. They feel the cultural significance in what they do, and the strong connection to their island and their ancestors. Yet at its core, fire fishing was a way to make a living, and that way of life is slowly vanishing in a modern world.

PIG'S BLOOD CAKE

ZHU XIE GAO • TAIWAN

In the frenetic, glowing chaos of a Taiwanese night market, all is not what it seems. Propped up on a stick is what looks like a frozen treat, rolled in peanuts and sprinkled with green flecks that, at first glance, you might not recognize as cilantro. Inside is another surprise. The handheld blocks are made of pig's blood and sticky rice, which combine to make a semi-gelatinous, cohesive texture that maintains the integrity of each grain. (The chewiness is reminiscent of Korean rice cakes or Japanese mochi.) Vendors bathe the cake in a pork-soy broth that adds a sweet, umami flavor, then roll it in peanut flour and cilantro. The final product is savory, meaty, herbal, and complexly delicious.

How to try it
Find pig's blood cakes at the Rahoe Night Market, one of the oldest markets in Taipei.

BLOOD

Rich in protein and iron, blood is a versatile, shape-shifting ingredient that can thicken or emulsify, congeal into solids, or melt into soup. But when blood goes bad, things get dangerous, which makes for a thin line between healthy and hepatitis.

Gematogen Blood Candy

This soft, chewy stick of molasses-sweet candy wasn't made for pleasure, but for treating low levels of iron and vitamins in Soviet-era Russia, thanks to the primary ingredient: cow's blood. Sold at pharmacies and drugstores, gematogen was dispensed more like medicine than candy. Adults were prescribed daily doses of 50 grams, children under the age of 13 needed an adult's consent, and pregnant women and breastfeeding mothers required a consultation before eating it. These days fresh cow's blood is often swapped out for powdered blood product, but it remains the leading candy bar for anemia, malnutrition, and fatigue.

Blood Tofu

When left out in a clean environment, fresh blood congeals into a jelly-like solid. All it takes is about ten minutes, then the soft block of blood can be cut into pieces and gently boiled to firm up the texture ever so slightly. The result is a silky, ephemeral cube that bursts and melts in the mouth, similar to soft tofu, but with the rich, acerbic flavor of blood. Likely a Chinese invention, blood tofu is eaten across Asian cultures. Duck blood tofu is a staple in hot pot; pig blood tofu tops Thailand's pork blood soup. In the Philippines, chicken blood tofu is cut into rectangular slabs, skewered, and grilled to make a popular street food called Betamax, named after its resemblance to the old-school video cassettes.

Yak Blood

Twice a year, thousands of Nepalese gather in the high Himalayas to drink fresh yak's blood, straight from the animal. At the Yak Blood Drinking Festival, which occurs in the districts of Mustang and Myagdi, local yak owners sell blood by the glass, dispensed from a slit in the animal's neck. The yak is bled alive, without the intention of killing it, and a single animal can provide blood for about 20–50 customers. (In 2019, a glass cost a hundred rupees, or about $1.)

The Nepalese who attend the festival are usually seeking cures for medical ailments. The yaks are known to graze on rare herbs that only grow at staggering altitude, like the wildly expensive caterpillar fungus, and drinking the yak's blood is meant to pass on these medicinal properties. People from around the country arrive with gastric problems, allergies, high blood pressure, asthma, and kidney dysfunction to drink a glass from the source—and many return year after year, citing relief from symptoms.

131

Blood Clams

When you open a blood clam, you know it immediately. The bite-size cockles are filled with hemoglobin, the dark red protein found in human blood. (Most clams have clear blood.) In places like Asia and Central America, blood clams are a delicacy, generally eaten raw or briefly cooked. But clam blood, like human blood, can carry disease. Hemoglobin allows the mollusks to live in places without much oxygen, but they also must filter a lot of water, making them more susceptible to bacteria and viruses. (In China, a 1988 outbreak of hepatitis A killed 31 people and was linked to contaminated blood clams.) But the ghoulish clams still have a big following and are said to have a cleaner flavor and crisper texture than clear-blooded clams.

Blood Pancakes

Throughout Scandinavia, blood is a common ingredient in breakfast pancakes. The blood—which can be cow, pig, or, in the case of the Sami people of northern Norway, reindeer—whips up nicely into a foam, is packed with protein, and binds the batter almost like an egg. Blood pancakes are nearly black in color, dense, and more nutritious than bloodless pancakes. They're so popular in Europe's northern reaches that the Finnish company Atria makes frozen pig-blood pancakes, available at grocery stores.

Maasai Blood Drinking

Traditionally, the Maasai of southern Kenya and northern Tanzania consume a diet of primarily cow's milk and blood, which is carefully retrieved from the living cow's jugular artery, then quickly resealed. Blood and milk are regarded as "both ordinary and sacred food," used as a regular source of calories and in ritual and ceremony. Cattle blood is considered beneficial for people with weakened immune systems, as well as for hangovers, or simply for breakfast. In a study conducted in 1935, a Canadian dentist found the tribesmen were unusually healthy—entirely free of disease, including cardiovascular problems, and with almost no cavities. (Subsequent studies showed they had half the cholesterol of the average American.) More recently, pasture land has dwindled and many Maasai have been forced to eat more grain and drink less milk and blood, which has shown negative consequences for their health.

A Maasai man dressed in a traditional red shuka holds a gourd full of fresh blood.

CATERPILLAR FUNGUS

YARTSA GUNBU • TIBET

The Talon Club inside The Cosmopolitan of Las Vegas serves a bowl of "Cordyceps Soup" for $688. It's the most expensive soup in the world, made with chicken, red dates, longan berries, and a quarter ounce of caterpillar fungus. By weight, this tasteless parasitic fungus is one of the priciest substances on earth—more than truffles, more than gold—sourced on the grassy plains of the Tibetan Plateau.

Every May and June, Tibetans spread across the high, grassy plains of the Tibetan Plateau and search for slender brown protrusions that jut from the soil. At first glance, they look like sticks, but they're actually the fruiting bodies of *Ophiocordyceps sinensis*, a fungus that attacks living caterpillars, then consumes them from the inside out. While the ghost moth caterpillar feeds underground, the fungus Tibetans call yartsa gunbu infects it. Once it has consumed most of the body, the fungus takes control of the caterpillar and sends it toward the surface, where the fungus erupts from its head, sending up its "stick." Aboveground, the fruiting body will release spores that go on to infect other caterpillars.

Yartsa gunbu has been a part of Tibetan food and medicine since at least the 1400s, used to treat everything from heart arrhythmias to impotence to cancers. Though little research exists, the fungus is believed to have extensive medicinal properties. Wealthy Chinese buyers have long prized the fungus, but in recent years, the craze has become mainstream.

In the 1990s, stories began circulating about how the fungus helped Chinese athletes break world records. Since then, the value of the parasitic fungus, once traded by locals for food, has increased more than ten times. (A single pound can sell for $50,000.)

The fungal gold rush on the Tibetan Plateau has made a huge impact on the rural region. Some of the change has been positive: Villages have installed solar panels and many households have more money for basics. But the race to find this limited resource has resulted in violent competition, including numerous murders. Many Tibetans have abandoned traditional herding in favor of the fungus hunt, leaving them vulnerable in low-crop years, which are growing more frequent due to overharvesting and global warming.

A Tibetan family digs for valuable caterpillars in the hills of Serxu.

BAMBOO WATERSLIDE NOODLES

NAGASHI SOMEN • JAPAN

n Japanese, nagashi means "flowing." When paired with somen, a cold, white wheat noodle popular during the summer, you get an action-packed meal that requires catching noodles with chopsticks as they float down a bamboo waterslide.

Popularized in the southern town of Takachiho in 1959, the House of Chiho restaurant dreamed up nagashi somen as a way to capitalize on the pure, local spring water. In a tradition that continues today, staff fill long chutes of halved bamboo trunks with cold running water. Once they yell, "Ikuyo!" or "It's coming!" they deposit cooked noodles into the chute for diners downstream to snatch from the current. At most establishments, a basket at the end of the waterworks collects uncaught noodles, and the staff retrieves them for customers. But at the well-known Hirobun restaurant in Kyoto, what you catch is what you get, until red-dyed somen floats through and signals the end of the meal.

Noodle waterslides are not just for restaurants. Home cooks can buy bamboo half pipes to set up nagashi somen in the house. Alternatively, there are special machines that spin noodles around circular basins or send them down miniature waterslides that look like toys. In 2016, the citizens of Gose, in Nara Prefecture, set the Guinness World Record for "longest distance to flow noodles down a line of bamboo gutters." Their nagashi somen chute was 10,871 feet (3,317 m) long.

How to try it

House of Chiho, located beside a picturesque gorge in Takachiho, still sends noodles flowing through local spring water. It's a 3-hour, 30-minute bus ride from Fukuoka City.

A woman slurps noodles she successfully snatched out of a bamboo waterslide in Takamatsu, Japan.

RAILWAY STATION DELICACIES

EKIBENYA MATSURI • JAPAN

t's always a festival (in Japanese, a matsuri) of feasts between tracks 6 and 7 at Tokyo Station. Here, at Ekibenya Matsuri, travelers bustle around choosing from nearly 200 different kinds of ekiben, portable meals meant to be eaten on the Shinkansen bullet train and other local trains that set off from the cosmopolitan city's central train station.

At each train stop in Japan Railways' vast network, vendors sell ekiben containing the specialties of that particular region. In Hyogo Prefecture, this might mean the hipparidako meshi ekiben: a rice, octopus, eel, and vegetables dish served in a miniature takotsubo, modeled on the traditional earthen pot designed to catch octopus in the area. At Shizuoka Station, travelers might line up for the tai meshi, a locally popular dish of sea bream and rice. But circling the displays at Ekibenya

How to try it

The average price of a box at Ekibenya Matsuri is about $10. Ask for a warmed bottle of miso soup when you pay, or grab a bottled matcha, or even single-serve bottles of wine, which they also sell.

Matsuri, you can find most of these region-specific novelties stacked against one another in a single frenetic train station shop.

You can indulge your inner child with an ekiben shaped like a train. Or take advantage of seasonal ekiben, made only with location-specific seasonal produce. Then there's the high-tech self-heating ekiben, packaged in a box that heats up when a string is pulled. Or you might keep it traditional with the Daruma bento, packaged in a box that looks like Daruma, a doll meant to represent Bodhidharma, the founder of Zen Buddhism. The box has a slit at the mouth and can be used as a coin bank, making it a lucky keepsake.

THE ANCIENT ART OF LIFELIKE LOLLIPOPS

AMEZAIKU • JAPAN

How to try it

The Amezaiku Ameshin confectionery is located in the Tokyo Skytree Town mall in Asakusa. For 3,000 yen (about $28), you can also take a two-hour workshop, where a candy artist will teach you to make a rabbit. Instruction is offered only in Japanese.

Within three minutes, the window to make amezaiku is over. Molten sugar is pulled from the pot at nearly 200°F (93°C), just soft enough to manipulate the formless glob into a stunningly lifelike creature. Using just their hands and a pair of tiny scissors, amezaiku masters mold and snip the candy, forming the delicate gills of a goldfish or the three-pronged feet of a frog. The procedure is creative, and it's also precise. Artists can create the same animal over and over again, nearly identical each time. After the candy has cooled, the figurines are painted with food coloring, bringing them further to life with a transparent glaze.

According to candy artist Shinri Tezuka, making the candy is all about thinking ahead, anticipating the next snip and tuck before the candy cools. Tezuka is one of Japan's most prominent and last remaining amezaiku artists. He is also entirely self-taught because there is no longer a school teaching the craft. His Tokyo shop, a neat stall in a high-rise mall, is stocked with classical offerings such as animals and flowers, but in accordance with tradition, Tezuka also makes special orders.

Amezaiku is an ancient practice, brought to Japan from China during the Heian period (794–1185). The ornate sugar sculptures were first used as offerings to the spirits, but during the Edo period (1603–1868), artists took to the streets, snipping and molding their confections as entertainment, often to the specifications of their customer. Tezuka takes pride in the old-school craftsmanship, in knowing the sugar well enough to produce whatever a customer can imagine. As one of the last artisans practicing the art, his shop is one of the few places in Japan preserving the ancient disappearing tradition.

Candy artist Shinri Tezuka's creations—like this pair of koi—are almost too beautiful to eat.

THE ORIGINAL SUSHI

FUNAZUSHI • JAPAN

Sushi has come a long way since the 8th century, when making sushi meant salting a fish and letting it ferment for years. Called narezushi, the earliest sushi was primarily a preservation method: A gutted fish was fermented with salt and uncooked rice, which slowly transformed into a soft and pungent food.

In Shiga Prefecture, traditional narezushi is still the specialty. For centuries, locals have carried on the dying art of making a type of narezushi known as funazushi, made exclusively with the local carp found in nearby Lake Biwa. The fish is gutted, salted, and packed into wooden barrels. After a year, the carp is mixed with rice and packed away again for another two to three years. The result is a cured, prosciutto-like fish with a ripe smell and cheesy flavor.

In Takashima City, a family-run shop has been making funazushi since 1619, and is currently being operated by the 18th generation of the family. Called Kitashina, the shop is one of the few left in Japan preserving the country's ancient sushi.

In 8th-century Japan, an order of sushi looked more like this.

How to try it
Kitashina is located at 1287 Katsuno, Takashima, Shiga. Like most aged products, funazushi can be very expensive.

Themed Dining

Tokyo is home to some 160,000 restaurants, the most Michelin-starred restaurants in the world, and these four fantastical haunts where the cuisine is really not the point.

KAWAII MONSTER CAFE feels like a party thrown by the monsters in your closet. Located in Harajuku, Tokyo's fantasy playground, visitors enter through the mouth of a googly-eyed monster and are greeted by a merry-go-round of life-size desserts. The compact space contains a psychedelic "Mushroom Disco" as well as a "Milk Stand," where bunny and unicorn heads drink from baby bottle chandeliers. Monster girls roam, serving food and dancing. (In Japanese, kawaii means "cute.")

ROKUNEN YONKUMI offers a dose of nostalgia by re-creating the Japanese elementary school experience. Upon entry, diners become "students" by putting on a school bag and hat. Seated at wooden desks inside the classroom, "teachers" serve classic elementary school fare like sugary fried bread (agepan) on traditional aluminum dishware. At the end of your meal, you have the option of taking a test.

NINJA AKASAKA is modeled after feudal Japan, where diners step four centuries into the past as silent, black-clad mercenaries guide them across a drawbridge, through winding corridors, past secret doorways, and into the hidden dining room. Patrons order from scrolls, then the ninja-trained waitstaff disappears. But not for long. They regularly reappear, out of thin air, to perform sword tricks and martial arts.

DETECTIVE BAR PROGRESS straddles the line between fantasy and reality. With its yellow "Keep Out" tape across the door and outline of a splayed body on the floor, this bar feels like detective cosplay. But the bartenders here are real detectives. By day, they track down missing people or sleuth around crime scenes, and at night, they'll pour you a drink and tell you about their jobs.

JAPANESE NAVAL CURRY

KAREE • JAPAN

How to try it

Submarine curry is served at the café inside the Japan Maritime Self-Defense Force Museum in Kure. It's a 40-minute drive south of Hiroshima. You can't miss the building—there's a giant black-and-red submarine out front.

The Meiji era, which began in 1868, was a time of increasing foreign influence and domestic militarization. Japan needed to feed its troops, and their current system wasn't working. At the time, eating polished white rice was a sign of refinement and wealth. To attract recruits, the Imperial Navy and Army offered unlimited white rice and many soldiers ate little else, which led to a vitamin deficiency called beriberi. Caused by a lack of thiamine, an essential nutrient absent in white rice, beriberi killed Japanese royals and commoners alike. The deficiency soon became a drastic problem, laying low thousands of soldiers during the 1904–1905 Russo-Japanese War.

To save their sailors, Japanese officials examined the food provided in other navies, particularly Britain's. Many British ships served "curry": a mix of tinned curry powder, butter, meat (typically beef), root vegetables, and a sauce thickened with flour. Because both meat and flour contain thiamine, curry was a silver bullet against beriberi. Served over a heaping portion of rice, it could also feed an entire mess hall.

Soon, Anglo-Indian curry became a standard meal in the Japanese navy. (Navy officials were more inclined to accept dietary innovation than the army, which suffered beriberi long into the 20th century.) In 1908, the official *Navy Cooking Reference Book* was issued with a recipe for curry that has been enshrined as the traditional gold standard.

The naval curry tradition continues in the Japan Maritime Self-Defense Force, where sailors are served curry every Friday. Each ship takes pride in having a unique curry recipe, many of which have made it ashore. In Kure, Hiroshima, dozens of restaurants serve curry recipes eaten aboard active ships, from the JS *Samidare* to the JS *Umikiri*.

Japanese naval uniforms, ca. 1908.

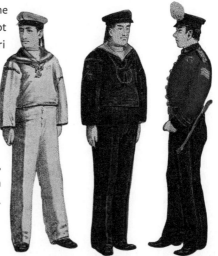

Delicious Diaspora

"YOSHOKU" JAPANESE WESTERN FOOD

In the 19th century, when Emperor Meiji opened his island nation to the Western world, his citizens were shocked to discover how large Europeans and Americans were. Japanese sent to study the West returned with tales of tall, brawny white men who ate not only meat (illegal in Japan until 1872), but a bevy of foods they'd never seen before. The new, modernizing Japan decided to embrace Western-style eating as a means of growing physically strong and internationally competitive.

Yoshoku cuisine, or "Western food," developed from this early contact with the West. Pasta, hamburgers, sandwiches, and deep-fried cutlets are at the foundation of this fare, but tailored to Japanese tastes, these dishes are often unrecognizable to Westerners. Yoshoku defies conventional categorization. It's a nostalgic food, served in family-run restaurants, but it can also be trendy date-night food or high-end restaurant fare. Within Japan, these Western-hybrid dishes are universally known and loved, creating a traditional comfort cuisine inspired by the diets of large foreigners.

Hambagu takes the hamburger and makes it a fork-and-knife (or chopsticks) affair. The beef patty, which is mixed with breadcrumbs and egg, is cooked in a pan and coated in demi-glace, then served with rice and vegetables.

Omurice combines the words *omelet* and *rice*, telling you exactly what to expect. The original combination was simply a mound of rice draped in a sheet of egg, but in recent years the rice is often mixed with ketchup or stir-fried with meat and vegetables, and then the omelet is drizzled with ketchup. Omurice is a classic accompaniment to naval curry (kare). Another variation is omusoba, where soba noodles are covered in an omelet blanket.

Portrait of Emperor Meiji and the Japanese imperial family during the Meiji period, ca. 1900.

Napolitan, named after the Italian city, was one of Japan's earliest pasta dishes and is now a classic. The country is dotted with coffee shops that specialize in the dish, which is made by cooking spaghetti until soft, then pan-frying the noodles with lunch meat, onion, bell pepper, and a ketchup-based sauce. Napolitan is often served with hambagu.

Napolitan

Sando is a Japanese sandwich, an unlikely star on the country's culinary scene. Sando bread is soft, white, and crustless, which hearkens back to the factory-made loaves that substituted for rice during the lean years after World War II. Today, sandos can still be bought for cheap in convenience stores across the country (a classic Japanese sando set is a trio of egg salad, ham and cheese, and tuna fish). Or you could go high-end: Grilled Wagyu beef sandos and fried Wagyu katsu sandos, running about $200 each.

Tacoraisu, or taco rice, hails from the southern island of Okinawa. Relatively new to the Yoshoku canon, the dish was developed by a 20th-century Okinawan cook who began selling tacos to the hundreds of American GIs stationed there. One day, he swapped out the tortilla for rice and piled on the seasoned ground beef, shredded cheese, lettuce, and chopped tomatoes.

Taco rice was a massive hit with both Okinawans and Americans, before spreading to the rest of the country. At the Taco Bell in Tokyo, taco rice is on the menu and comes with French fries.

Tacoraisu

Katsu sando

Hambagu

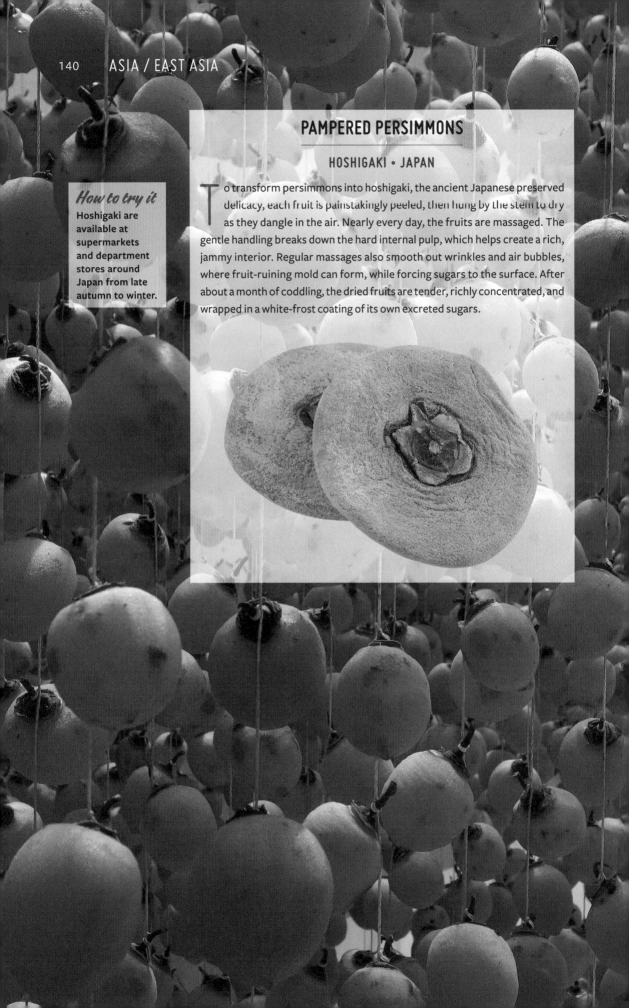

PAMPERED PERSIMMONS

HOSHIGAKI • JAPAN

How to try it

Hoshigaki are available at supermarkets and department stores around Japan from late autumn to winter.

To transform persimmons into hoshigaki, the ancient Japanese preserved delicacy, each fruit is painstakingly peeled, then hung by the stem to dry as they dangle in the air. Nearly every day, the fruits are massaged. The gentle handling breaks down the hard internal pulp, which helps create a rich, jammy interior. Regular massages also smooth out wrinkles and air bubbles, where fruit-ruining mold can form, while forcing sugars to the surface. After about a month of coddling, the dried fruits are tender, richly concentrated, and wrapped in a white-frost coating of its own excreted sugars.

Luxury Fruit of Japan

The tradition of Japanese gift giving, especially in business, can be something of a competitive sport. Companies vie to procure thoughtful, impressive gifts for their partners and clients, often spending vast sums of money to source something delightfully obscure. Japan has two traditional gift-giving seasons, Ochugen in summer and Oseibo in winter. Given such demand for specialty products, a world of luxury fruit has flourished. Bred and cultivated to be superior in taste and striking in appearance, these wildly priced, edible gems are now power players in the high-end gift-giving game.

DENSUKE WATERMELON

Prized for its black exterior and sweet and crunchy pink flesh, this pricey melon is limitedly grown in Hokkaido.

Average Price: 2,000 yen (about $20)

Sold at Auction in 2008: 650,000 yen ($5,927)

TAIYO NO TAMAGO ("EGG OF THE SUN") MANGO

Allowed to fall naturally from the tree when ripe into a net, they must be 350+ grams and have a high sugar content of 15+ percent.

Average Price: 5,000 yen ($45)

Sold at Auction in 2019: 500,000 yen for two ($4,659)

BIJIN-HIME ("BEAUTIFUL PRINCESS") STRAWBERRIES

The size of a tennis ball, these "scoop-shaped" berries took 15 years to perfect, and about 500 are grown each year

Average Price: 500,000 yen for one ($4,395)

RUBY ROMAN GRAPES

The size of a ping pong ball, each grape must weigh 30+ grams.

Average Price: 100,000 yen per bunch ($880)

Sold at Auction in 2017: 1.1 million yen for a bunch of approximately 30 grapes ($9,745)

YUBARI KING MELONS

Exclusively from Yubari, only one melon is grown per plant, allowing the single fruit to receive all the plant's nutrients. The melons also wear hats to protect from the sun.

Average Price: 10,000 yen ($91)

Sold at Auction in 2018: 3.2 million yen for two ($29,251)

A seller auctions off Egg of the Sun mangoes in the wholesale market in Miyazaki.

SUMO WRESTLER STEW

CHANKO NABE • JAPAN

Sumo wrestling has no separate weight classes, which means the heavier competitor has the advantage. In recent years, largely due to an influx of Hawaiian and Mongolian wrestlers, the average weight of champions has soared from just under 300 pounds (136 kg) in the 1930s to well over 400 (181 kg) today. To keep up, Japanese wresters eat chanko-nabe—a stew they consume, with ritualistic regularity, at nearly every meal for the duration of their career.

Chanko-nabe is a big communal pot of bubbling broth, to which ingredients are continually added and removed in a process similar to shabu shabu, or hot pot. Each training house typically has a signature broth recipe, which may be chicken, soy, or salt-based. Into the broth goes fish or meat, tofu and vegetables, and chunks of calorie-dense mochi (a starchy cake made from pounded glutinous rice). The sumo stew is cheap, hearty fare and, in ordinary quantities, not intrinsically fattening. But sumo wrestlers skip breakfast to work up an appetite, then eat as many as ten bowls for lunch, washed down with copious amounts of beer. After lunch, the wrestlers nap.

Despite the gluttonous mealtimes, structure and rigor dominate the sumo heya, or "clubhouse." Each wrestler has chores to perform, a surprising number of which revolve around chanko. Junior wrestlers are tasked with setting up the eating area, cycling to buy groceries, or chopping vegetables. (The highest-ranked wrestlers are usually tasked only with making public appearances or entertaining patrons.) While their superiors snooze, junior wrestlers rise early to train and prepare the meal. At lunchtime, the heavyweights sit around the pot first, reaching for soupy morsels they eat with rice. When their rice bowl is empty, they raise their hand and the junior wrestlers, who are expected to watch and anticipate their needs, refill their bowls. Only when a senior wrestler has finished can someone lower in rank sit down and take his place. As a result, junior wrestlers are often left with the dregs of the stew, which they must bulk up with things like instant noodles.

While chanko chores are considered entry-level, being in charge of the kitchen—chankocho—is a position of respect because it gives the wrestler a valuable skillset for his future. Not every wrestler can be a champion, and chanko can be the route into a new profession. Many retired wrestlers work at sumo-themed restaurants called chankoya, where high-end seafood chanko is the main attraction. The most famous wrestlers might even open their own eponymous chankoya, where their stardust is as much of a draw as their stew.

How to try it

The Ryogoku district in Tokyo is where you'll find the sumo stadiums and clubhouses, as well as chankoya. Hananomai Ryogoku Kokugikanmae, located right outside Ryogoku's train station, is shaped and decorated like a sumo dojo.

Sumo wrestlers serve chanko-nabe before a tournament at Osaka's Musashigawa Sumo Stadium in 2007.

GIANT RICE STRAW SCULPTURES

WARA ART • JAPAN

The rural, coastal Niigata Prefecture is the second largest producer of rice in Japan, known for its scenic expanse of rice paddies. Each fall, the rice is harvested and the grain extracted, which leaves a huge amount of leftover rice straw, called wara.

How to try it

The sculptures go on display in late August at the Wara Art Festival in Niigata's Uwasekigata Park. The sculptures remain up until the end of October.

Wara doesn't go to waste. The heaps of straw get repurposed as fertilizer, roofing, livestock feed, and most memorably as enormous wara sculptures that transform the rice fields into outdoor art installations. Since 2008, students from Tokyo's Musashino Art University have arrived in Niigata each fall to erect giant fantastical animals from the rice by-product. Made by braiding the straw, then attaching pieces to a wooden frame, the shaggy, golden building material makes strikingly realistic lion manes, gorilla fur, and tarantula fuzz. In 2017, to celebrate ten years of wara animals, the students were challenged to build sculptures twice the size of years past, and so they constructed 20-foot (6 m) dinosaurs and hippos, large enough for visitors to pose in their mouths.

*Students constructed
a giant gorilla for the
2017 festival's supersize
challenge.*

THE REAL MONGOLIAN BARBECUE

BOODOG • MONGOLIA

How to try it
Winter is the traditional season for boodog in Mongolia.

Mongolian warriors carried what little they owned on horseback, which meant they couldn't be weighed down by heavy cookware. To fit food preparation into their nomadic lifestyle, they used an animal's carcass as crockery. The unlucky marmot or goat that got stuffed with its own meat and cooked over an open

Two men drop hot stones into a goat carcass for boodog-style barbecue.

flame came to be known as boodog—the real Mongolian barbecue.

To prepare boodog (pronounced "baw-dug"), a butcher slices the animal, neck to groin, and carefully removes the meat and bones while keeping the rest of the skin intact. After seasoning the meat (including the liver and kidneys), the butcher stuffs it back inside with hot stones and vegetables and reseals the neck.

While ancient Mongolians roasted boodog over a fire, modern cooks use a blowtorch. The flame burns off most of the animal's fur, and what remains is scraped away with a knife. After a couple hours under the blowtorch, when the seal around the neck starts to drip with fat, the animal is ready to eat. But before digging in, diners must first pass around the hot stones; it is believed that holding the warm, smooth rocks reduces stress and fatigue.

A succulent stuffed goat is enough to feed an army of hungry Mongolians—and it did. According to the president of the Mongolian Chefs Association, Genghis Khan threw boodog banquets when his warriors were victorious.

With boodog, the animal torso doubles as a serving bowl.

SHOE SOLE CAKE

UL BOOV • MONGOLIA

When Mongolians celebrate the Lunar New Year with a days-long holiday called Tsagaan Sar, the centerpiece is usually a fabulous ul boov. Ul boov means "shoe sole cake"—a humble name for a towering dessert that's steeped in tradition.

Ul boov is built from layers of fried cakes, each embossed by a wooden stamp that leaves a design like the tread of a shoe. These stamps are passed down through generations and every stamp is unique, which means ul boov designs can identify families like a fingerprint. The height of an ul boov corresponds with age and social status: Young couples make three-layered cakes, elders make seven layers, and most everyone else makes five. (The layers always occur in odd numbers because they symbolize happiness.) The stacking of the cakes is a ritual in itself, performed with the precision and care of lighting a menorah.

To decorate an ul boov, wrapped candies, sugar cubes, and dried milk curds called aarul are placed on top. Fully adorned, the cake is meant to symbolize the sacred Buddhist site, Mount Sumeru.

How to try it

Ul boov is typically a homemade holiday treat. You can find recipes online, but you'll have to borrow a stamp.

NORTH KOREAN DIPLOMACY NOODLES

PYONGYANG NAENGMYEON • NORTH KOREA

How to try it

Pyung Hwa Ok, or "House of Peace," is a restaurant specializing in Pyongyang naengmyeon, located in South Korea's Incheon International Airport.

In many ways, naengmyeon is a simple dish. Typically made from buckwheat flour, the slim, exceptionally chewy noodles are served in an iced beef broth, topped with meat slices, boiled egg, slivers of cucumbers or radish, and seasoned with spicy mustard and vinegar. Created during the Joseon Dynasty, which spanned 1392 to 1910, naengmyeon has been around for centuries. But in April 2018, when the leaders of North Korea and South Korea met for an unprecedented diplomatic summit, the cold noodles were thrust onto the world stage.

For the first time in 11 years, both Korean leaders, North Korea's Kim Jong-un and South Korean president Moon Jae-in, agreed to meet in the DMZ (the demilitarized zone between their two countries). Surprising everyone, Kim Jong-un showed up with a batch of naengmyeon, a noodle maker, and jokes about noodles from a "faraway" land, before conceding that it wasn't that far.

After a 2018 summit, the cold noodles loved on both the north and south sides of the Korean border became a symbol for thawing relations between the countries.

With this simple gesture, the popularity of the humble dish exploded in South Korea. On the day of the summit, the noodles were more talked about than the summit itself, and restaurants that served naengmyeon had lines out the door. Many of the diners expressed that they were eating them in honor of the peace talks. Naengmyeon, after all, was a reminder of their shared heritage.

In North Korea, where the noodles originated, naengmyeon holds special patriotic pride. It's the signature dish at Okryu-gwan, the country's most important restaurant and perhaps the most significant source of North Korea's culinary heritage. During the Korean War, when people fled from the north to the south, they popularized the cold beef broth noodles from their side of the border. (When served with broth made from beef and radish water kimchi, the noodles are considered the North Korean style, "Pyongyang naengmyeon.")

The noodles have long been a refreshing meal in the humid Korean summer, but since the 2018 summit, they have also become an edible symbol of peace, with one restaurant serving the dish as "reunification naengmyeon."

AN ENTIRE UK BREWERY TRANSPORTED TO NORTH KOREA

TAEDONGGANG BREWING COMPANY • NORTH KOREA

The team first arrived in the rural English town of Trowbridge in the summer of 2000. There were two brewers, two engineers, and eight government officials. They were all from North Korea, and they had come to take the brewery.

Their leader, Kim Jong-il (nicknamed "Kim Jong-ale" by the residents of Trowbridge) had recently decided that North Korea needed a proper state-run brewery. But instead of building a brewery from scratch, the North Korean leader decided to go shopping for one.

How to try it

Taedonggang is very difficult to get outside of North Korea. To try it, you'll have to visit, which makes it an elusive task for many.

For £1.5 million, the North Korean bought the 175-year-old Ushers of Trowbridge Brewery. A team of Russians came in to entirely dismantle the brick-walled factory, then the North Koreans shipped all four million pounds of it back to Pyongyang. The crew left nothing, taking every vat, keg, pipe, nut, bolt, tile, and toilet seat in the brewery. They wanted to take the brewmaster himself but had to settle for just his knowledge. Korean translators spent weeks with him poring over beer-making schematics.

A mere 18 months later, in 2002, the Russian team had reassembled the factory on a cabbage field in East Pyongyang. Since named the Taedonggang Brewing

A mural of the late North Korean leader Kim Jong-il holding a beer hangs near the entrance of the brewery.

Company, the brewery produces seven styles of beer, named pragmatically from light pilsner "Beer Number One" ("Taedonggang 1") to dark, chocolatey dunkel "Beer Number Seven." Taedonggang is considered some of the best beer available on the Korean Peninsula, and even within Asia.

Despite the improved state-run brewing game, most North Koreans still prefer cheaper, harder stuff such as the local liquor, soju. Rural North Koreans must use food rations to buy beer, which makes it a luxury item few can afford. In the country's capital, men receive beer vouchers (usually 1–2 liters a month) that can be redeemed in a Pyongyang bar. But for the most part, beer is still an urban, middle-class affair, more akin to a nice glass of wine than a party beverage.

Although North Korea and the Taedonggang Brewing Company would like the world to focus on their surprisingly good beer, the brewery still remains the property of a mysterious and harsh dictatorship. In 2016, Pyongyang held its first-ever beer festival, which attracted 45,000 visitors. In 2017, however, the festival was canceled by the government without explanation.

KOREAN NUN CUISINE

JINGWANSA TEMPLE FOOD • SOUTH KOREA

How to try it
Jingwansa is located in Bukhansan National Park, about an hour north of Seoul's urban center. Buses run from Gupabal subway station. Anyone can reserve a stay at the temple, take a cooking class, or tour the property.

Jingwansa, a 12th-century Buddhist temple, sits atop a mountain in Seoul's Bukhansan National Park. Women with shaved heads and gray robes run the entire operation. These Buddhist devotees are renowned for their cuisine, which epitomizes the ancient art of Korean temple fare. It's vegan and free of MSG, garlic, onion, and leeks. Temple food is meant to facilitate meditation, and Buddhist teaching advises eschewing these ingredients because they are believed to incite lust, among other things. Although the kitchens of many monasteries follow similar principles, high-profile visitors from around the world flock to Jingwansa in search of culinary enlightenment.

Korean temple cuisine is far from bland. At Jingwansa, they ferment, spice, dry, marinate, and pickle ingredients to create a wide array of pungent, spicy, and tangy dishes. They also ferment up to 30 different soybean pastes at a time, some of which have been aging beneath the sun for 50 years. Visitors have reported eating more than 25 dishes in one meal, sampling fermented radishes, chestnut stew, crispy greens, marinated tofu, mushroom fritters, and sweet sticky rice squares sprinkled with fruit and nuts—a treat traditionally eaten on the nuns' head-shaving day.

The female order has maintained its status as the preeminent location for temple cuisine for centuries. In Korean Buddhism, monastic mealtime is a practice referred to as baru gongyang, or "offering." Diners eat in silence from a wooden bowl using wooden chopsticks. Historically, Jingwansa hosted suryukje, an annual ritual in which the dead are led to heaven through chanting and food ceremonies. The establishment has become increasingly popular as a culinary pilgrimage site, but the nuns continue to cook with old-school standards and still use vegetables grown on temple grounds.

A quiet sunrise over Seoul's Bukhansan mountains echoes the silent mealtimes at the Jingwansa temple.

Buddhist TEMPLE CUISINE

Respect for animal life and devotion to vegetables is the backbone of Buddhist temple cuisine. Local, seasonal produce, simple hand tools, and zero waste are tenets of religious gastronomy, which seeks to prepare the body for spiritual work. These vegetarian restaurants, all housed within active temples, specialize in nourishment for meditation.

Daitoku-ji Temple • Kyoto, Japan

Izusen Restaurant cooks shojin ryori, or "devotion cuisine," which developed alongside Japanese Zen Buddhism. Elegant, visually striking, and painstakingly prepared, the process of making devotional food is considered a meditative experience in itself. At Izusen, Buddhist cuisine is at its most refined. Surrounded by a tranquil garden on the temple grounds, diners enjoy dainty, impressive courses of wild plants, tofu, seaweed, and vegetables, served in the round lacquered bowls used by monks to collect alms.

Po Lin Monastery • Hong Kong

Located at the bottom of the Big Buddha statue on Lantau Island, the café at Po Lin Monastery is a plant-based paradise in meat-centric Hong Kong. The menu has three options: a general meal, a deluxe meal, or a snack, all comprised of whatever the kitchen has prepared that day. To prevent waste, the quantity of dishes served depends on how many people are eating together. The bean curd, which is made daily, is the monastery's specialty.

Wat Suan Dok Temple • Chiang Mai, Thailand

Just behind the 700-year-old golden-domed Wat Suan Dok is Pun Pun, an organic café serving Thai food made with produce from the restaurant's garden. Beneath the shade of Pun Pun's giant Bodhi tree, watch orange-clad monks pace the temple grounds as you eat coconut milk curry, banana flower salad, and fermented mushroom sausage.

Jiming Temple • Nanjing, China

Perched high on a hill, atop a long staircase fluttering with prayer flags, Jiming Temple is home to a small, cloistered vegetarian restaurant. The simple café surprises with views of Nanjing's ancient walls and Xuanwu Lake, and is especially good at mock meats. While you won't find seitan or tofu "meats" in other Buddhist cuisines (like Japan, where meat eating was taboo until the 19th century), the Chinese have long had a taste for meat and have been making plant-based substitutes for centuries.

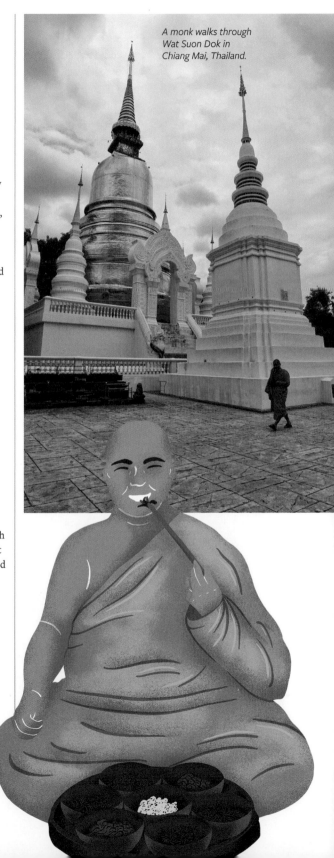

A monk walks through Wat Suon Dok in Chiang Mai, Thailand.

URINE-FERMENTED SKATE FISH

HONGEO • SOUTH KOREA

How to try it

Indongju Maul,
a restaurant in
Mokpo's east,
is a popular place
to try fermented
skate. It's served
with sliced pork,
soy-marinated
crab, and kimchi.

Back in the 14th century, South Korean fishermen realized the skate they caught could travel long distances without spoiling. While other fish would rot by the time it reached inland, the flat-bodied, bottom-dwelling skate was somehow spared. The side effect to this miraculous preservation, however, was hard to miss. The fish smelled overpoweringly of ammonia, as if it had urinated through its skin—because it had.

Instead of urinating like other animals, skate expels waste by secreting uric acid through its skin, which in turn ferments the flesh. Koreans began eating the caustic-smelling fish as aged sashimi, alongside boiled pork belly and kimchi in a combination known as samhap ("harmonious trinity").

Today, hongeo is polarizing even within Korea. In hongeo's birthplace of Jeolla Province, the dish is considered a luxury item with almost mythical status for its ability to preserve itself. Especially in the port city of Mokpo, where skate fishing is a lucrative business, hongeo is an expensive dish reserved for special occasions, wealthy people, and men in search of libido enhancement. Outside these southwest regions, however, many Koreans find the fish deeply unappealing. The texture, which is chewy with lots of cartilage and mushy bone, is almost as challenging as the smell, which is often compared to an outhouse. Even those who love it recommend breathing in through your mouth and out through your nose when trying to get a piece of hongeo down.

IMPOSSIBLE SLIME FISH

HAGFISH • SOUTH KOREA

Hagfish, with their bald, loose-fitting skin (think naked mole rat), are scavengers who search the ocean floor for dead or dying creatures, burrow inside, and eat their way out. Commonly referred to as both "slime eels" and "snot snakes," hagfish are actually neither snakes nor eels, but rather jawless fish. The misnomers come from their eel-like appearance and their notable ability to excrete up to 20 liters (about 5 gallons) of milky mucus when under stress.

The mucus is a unique defense mechanism that has allowed hagfish to roam the oceans for 300 million years. When a predator attacks, the hagfish's slime coats its gills, suffocating the predator. The slime deters human predators too, but in Korea it's a part of the gastronomic appeal. Hagfish slime, which is fibrous and full of protein, can be used as a substitute for egg whites. To "harvest" the slime, hagfish are sometimes kept in cages, which are rattled to agitate the fish.

In Korean fish markets, it's common to see hagfish skinned alive and grilled with onion and garlic. In a punishing spectacle, hagfish writhe in circles, discharging snot until the hot barbecue kills them. They can also be broiled in sesame oil, salted, and served with a shot of liquor. Like many phallic-looking animals, the hagfish is valued as an aphrodisiac.

But edibility isn't the slime's only virtue. The fibrous thread is an incredibly strong and versatile material, a hundred times thinner than human hair yet ten times stronger than nylon. Researchers are working on ways to use hagfish slime in everything from airbags to bandages to bungee cords. Engineers in the US Navy even hope to create an artificial version of the slime for missile defense systems.

How to try it

Hagfish are available in fish markets around Korea, but Jalgachi Market in Busan is a good place to start.

Hagfish slime is stronger and more useful than it appears.

ARMY BASE STEW

BUDAE JJIGAE • SOUTH KOREA

One of South Korea's most beloved fusion dishes, budae jjigae, began with desperate wartime dumpster diving. Translated as "army base stew," budae jjigae was once made with American throwaways saved by resourceful South Koreans, who transformed the scraps into a one-pot meal that's become a complicated vestige of US imperialism.

During the Korean War, while citizens struggled with food scarcity, a US army base an hour north of Seoul was stocked with ample quantities of American food. Most notably, the Americans had plenty of meat, which most Korean stores no longer carried. Koreans began lining up outside the mess halls, trying to purchase the soldiers' leftovers. Whatever wasn't eaten or bought was thrown away, so many

How to try it

Bada Sikdang near the American army base in Itaewon is a well-known hole-in-the-wall. Their budae jjigae comes draped in a bright-yellow slice of American cheese.

people resorted to scavenging through the dumpsters, picking through cigarette butts and inedible waste to piece together a meal.

What the Koreans found was processed Americana—canned beans, cheese products, Spam, hot dogs, and ham—which they tossed into a pot with kimchi, vegetables, chili paste, and instant noodles. The result was budae jjigae, a surprisingly cohesive stew that was spicy, filling, and sustaining.

After the war, the meat shortage continued. Among the South Koreans who survived, many had developed a taste for budae jjigae, which became even harder to source after the government passed import laws preventing Koreans from buying American products. In response, a black market for army-base stew ingredients flourished. Retail stores for American soldiers stationed in Korea (known as "post exchanges") became sites for illegal trading, facilitated by Korean women involved with American soldiers. American processed meat was the only meat many people had access to, so demand remained high. (Spam was illegal until the 1980s, when a Korean company began producing it.)

The American product ban was eventually lifted, and budae jjigae evolved into a popular comfort food. It's now common on South Korean menus, particularly in college neighborhoods, although even posh neighborhoods such as Gangnam have restaurants specializing in the wartime stew.

Budae Jjigae   *4 servings*

Seasoning Paste

½ packet Korean ramyeon noodle seasoning

3 tablespoons Korean chili flakes

1 tablespoon gochujang

1 tablespoon minced garlic

2 tablespoons soy sauce

½ teaspoon black pepper

Stew

1 can (12 ounces) Spam, sliced

1 can (8 ounces) pork and beans

7 ounces hot dogs or Vienna sausage, sliced

1 package firm tofu, sliced

1 cup sour kimchi, sliced

½ onion, sliced

8 ounces mushrooms, sliced

1 packet Korean ramen noodles

32 ounces low-sodium chicken stock

1 or 2 slices American cheese

white rice (optional)

1. In a small mixing bowl, combine all ingredients for the seasoning paste. Set aside.

2. In a large shallow pot, arrange all the stew ingredients as you please, up to the ramen noodles, which should be set on top.

3. Add the seasoning paste to the pot and pour the broth over.

4. Bring to a boil over medium high heat. When it starts to boil, spread the seasoning paste around the pan, untangle the ramen in the broth, and cook until the noodles are tender yet firm.

5. Drape the cheese over the top. Serve immediately. (Combine with rice for a more filling stew.)

Desperate resourcefulness was the origin of this scrappy, surprisingly delicious wartime stew.

A diver flashes a smile while emptying her net of shellfish.

JEJU ISLAND'S FREE-DIVING SEA WOMEN

HAENYEO • SOUTH KOREA

Jeju Island, the largest island in South Korea, is home to a centuries-old tradition of divers who can plunge 30 feet on a single breath to collect shellfish on the ocean floor. They wear wet suits and goggles but do not use oxygen masks. Called haenyeo, all of these free divers are women, and many of them are in their 80s.

In historically patriarchal South Korea, these deep-diving fisherwomen have become the heads of their households. Their dives yield sea life like sea urchins, abalone, conches, seaweed, and sea snails, which the divers clean and sell to support their families. It's difficult work; the women dive for six to seven hours a day in ice cold water and earn only modest wages. But the practice is also deeply rooted in community and tradition. Many haenyeo carry on in the profession for the intimacy it fosters with fellow divers, as well as with nature.

The haenyeo's numbers are dwindling in modern South Korea, with fewer than 4,000 skilled divers still practicing. (In the 1960s, there were over 20,000.) But in recent years there's been a concerted effort to preserve the women's legacy, and Jeju Island now boasts a haenyeo museum and haenyeo schools.

How to try it

The sea women's home base is next to the volcanic crater of Seongsan Ilchulbong (also called Sunrise Peak). Depending on weather conditions, Beophwan Jomnyeo Village Haenyeo School provides haenyeo experience activities from June to mid-October, offered in Korean/Jeju dialect. The Jeju Haenyeo Museum is open year-round.

KIMCHI-MAKING SEASON

GIMJANG • SOUTH KOREA

How to try it

Gimjang is not a specific day, but a season that occurs between October and November. (The Kimchi Festival takes place during this time.) Seoul's Museum Kimchikan is a great place to dive into kimchi's 1,500-year-old history.

More than a million tons of kimchi is eaten across South Korea each year. Of that, a mere 7 percent is commercially produced. When it comes to kimchi, South Koreans don't mess around. The good stuff is made at home, in staggering quantities, during the annual pickling season known as gimjang.

Every fall around late October, South Koreans begin watching the price of cabbage. National news programs dedicate segments to price spikes and dips, letting their viewers know how much this year's kimchi making will cost. During gimjang, families gather to make pogi kimchi, the most recognizable variety, made by coating heads of napa cabbage with a complex, pungent red pepper paste and aging it, sometimes underground in earthenware pots, sometimes in high-tech kimchi fridges. Farmers' markets pop up around the country, and everyone pitches in, donning rubber gloves to rub the bright red paste into dozens of heads of cabbage. (A typical family might prepare anywhere between 50 and 150 cabbages.)

In 2013, gimjang was recognized by UNESCO and added to their list of Intangible Cultural Heritage. The annual pickling affair draws the nation close. Women across South Korea watch the weather, settling on the right day to set up their production, often banding together with other families to make tremendous batches they can divvy up. Another tradition is for new wives to learn their mother-in-law's recipe because many husbands prefer the kimchi of their childhood.

Access to kimchi, which is eaten with nearly every meal, is considered something of a South

Volunteers at the 2014 Kimchi Festival slather napa cabbage in bright red paste.

Korean civil right. The spoils of gimjang are distributed to those who need it, which can be anyone from bachelors to women who are bad at making kimchi but will not suffer the indignity of buying it at the store. At the Seoul Kimchi Festival, which has taken place during every gimjang since 2014, thousands of apron-clad volunteers line up along a sea of tables to make more than a hundred tons of kimchi. The community bounty is presented to those who cannot afford to make it themselves, ensuring that when winter strikes, there will be enough crunchy, sour, slightly fizzy cabbage to sustain many South Koreans through the long cold season.

SOUTHEAST ASIA

STICKY DIPPING PASTE

AMBUYAT • BRUNEI

Eating ambuyat requires a sticky, multistep dance: Using a pair of bamboo tongs called chandas (think cheater chopsticks), diners dip into the starchy goo so that it adheres to the utensil and can make its way from bowl to dipping sauce to mouth, where it's slurped down, no chewing required.

How to try it

Aminah Arif Restaurant in Brunei's capital, Begawan, is the place to twirl and dip to your heart's content.

Made by slowly mixing the interior pulp of the rumbia tree with water, the gelatinous starch has little flavor of its own, which makes it an ideal vehicle for dipping sauce, or cacah. Most typical is binjai cacah, a sour and spicy combination of lime, onions, garlic, and binjai, a local fruit with a sweet-and-sour flavor. Ambuyat is a communal meal, served in a large bowl with several chandas, at least one sauce, and dishes of fresh, raw vegetables for a crunchy interlude between each sweet-and-sour swallow.

CUSTARD-FILLED PUMPKIN

SANG KAYA LAPOV • CAMBODIA

On the outside, it's a pumpkin. On the inside, it's creamy, quivering custard. Known in Cambodia as sang kaya lapov, this is the most elegant dessert you'll ever find hidden inside a squash. The pumpkin, which is hollowed out like a Halloween jack-o'-lantern, makes a perfect, edible vessel for coconut milk custard, which is poured into the cavity. Topped with the pumpkin lid and steamed until

How to try it

Sang kaya lapov is sold in Cambodian markets and sweet shops, generally by the slice. It can also be found in Thailand by the name sangkhaya fak thong.

the custard is set and the pumpkin flesh is soft (between 40 minutes and 3 hours, depending on your pumpkin), this dessert in disguise is a customary centerpiece on Cambodian New Year tables. The recipe likely hearkens back centuries, when Portuguese conquistadores arrived in Cambodia and passed on their affinity for eggy sweets.

The perfect sang kaya lapov will cut into neat, silky slices that hold together like a custard pie. While the preparation may seem straightforward, this is a difficult recipe to master. Custards curdle, pumpkins fall limp, and you won't know until you cut it open.

WORM COURTSHIP FESTIVAL

BAU NYALE• INDONESIA

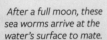

How to try it
Seger Beach, in the
south of Lombok,
is the center of the
celebration. It can be
hard to predict exactly
when the worms will
emerge, but it always
follows February's full
moon.

According to legend, there once was on the island Lombok a princess so beautiful that suitors flocked from across the land, igniting a fierce competition to win her hand in marriage. The princess, distraught by seeing her people fight, threw herself into the sea. The villagers waded into the water to search for her, but all they found were thousands of green and purple sea worms. The princess herself was never found, but the discovery of worms brought the village peace because they came together to partake in the bounty.

Inspired by this legend, every year thousands of Sasak people, an ethnic group that lives on Lombok, make the journey to the southern and eastern beaches of their island to catch nyale, or sea worms, and participate in the courting festival known as Bau Nyale (literally translated as "Catch Sea Worm"). Leading up to the event, men engage in ritualistic combat using shields and rattan (a vine-like palm) sticks, athletes race horses on long stretches of beach, and vibrantly dressed women parade through the streets in glittering Sasak regalia. Nearing nightfall, groups of men and women head toward the sea where a game of poetic flirtation called pantun takes place. Using couplets to express their interest in each other, young people call back and forth in a traditional style, their words cheeky and heavy with innuendo.

After a full moon, these sea worms arrive at the water's surface to mate.

As for the nyale, they're also engaged in a courtship ritual. Sometime after February's full moon, the worms are triggered by the lunar cycle. They emerge from their coral homes to release their tails, filled with eggs or sperm, to the water's surface where the mating can occur. (Their bodies stay alive and well.) Equipped with nets and buckets, locals wade into the tides to collect the mass exodus of sea creatures. Eating nyale is said to bring beauty, prosperity, and fertility. The worms can be prepared in a variety of ways, like roasted in banana leaves, fermented with shrimp paste, or cooked in a soup called kalek moren with fresh-grated coconut.

Courtship Foods

Much like humans take dates to dinner, many animals practice a ritual called "courtship feeding," in which the suitor brings an offering of food to a desired mate, who eats it before, during, or after intercourse. Male nursery web spiders, for example, catch an insect (generally a fly) in their web, wrap it in silk, and present it to their chosen female. While she's busy consuming what he's brought, the male begins copulation.

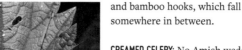

But things don't always go smoothly. Female nursery web spiders are sexual cannibals, which means the male is always at risk of being eaten. Studies have found that the bigger the gift, the lower the risk of being cannibalized. Yet some males are still prone to ungentlemanly behavior: They choose to eat the insect, present the female with a gift-wrapped, nutritionless exoskeleton, and try to get the job done before she figures it out and murders him. (Females are also known to take the meal and run away.)

In the human world, using food as a way to win a mate is generally less cutthroat. Still, there's plenty of innuendo in the type of food, how it's presented, and what's inside.

ARMPIT APPLE: In the 19th century, rural Austrian women attended dances where they would prance with the eligible bachelors, all while keeping a slice of apple tucked into their armpit. When the music stopped, the women would remove the pheromone-soaked fruit and offer it to the man of their choice. To return the compliment, the man had to eat the apple, signaling that he enjoyed the woman's personal fragrance.

SISTERS' MEAL FESTIVAL: Amid the bullfighting, dragon dancing, and horse racing that takes place at the annual celebration in China's Guizhou Province, there is a courting ritual that centers on glutinous rice. Unmarried women from the Miao minority group climb the mountains to pick wildflowers that they use to dye the rice bright colors. They then roll the rice into balls, hiding different symbols inside, and give out their "sister rice" to the Miao men who come to sing to them. Each symbol bears a message for their potential suitors: two chopsticks means love, one chopstick refusal, and then there's cotton, parsley, pine needles, and bamboo hooks, which fall somewhere in between.

CREAMED CELERY: No Amish wedding is complete without creamed celery, the traditional stove-top dish of chopped celery in a white, slightly sweetened sauce. Amish weddings are big affairs with hundreds of guests, so those preparing to marry need a lot of celery (even more if they're making Amish casserole, which they probably are). As Amish weddings are often kept secret until the last minute, the most surefire way to uncover impending nuptials is to check the garden: If it's full of celery, someone's getting married.

BRIK: The North African savory pastry, called brik, is made by wrapping a phyllo-like dough around a filling of tuna, capers, chilies, and a raw egg. The filled pastry is fried just long enough for the egg white to set but the yolk to remain runny. When men in Algeria and Tunisia are ready to wed, they must prove their aptitude for marriage by eating a brik. If they can finish the pastry without spilling a drop of oozing yolk, they are considered husband material.

CZERNINA: If you were a suitor in 19th-century Poland, receiving a bowl of duck blood was a sign that your marriage proposal had been denied. Serving czernina, a thick, black, fruit-and-vinegar-laced blood soup, was a way for peasant families to deliver bad news. The shaming sometimes happened publicly, delivered to the table with other diners who, while enjoying their bloodless soups, understood that the man had been officially rejected.

The Hidden History of the Nutmeg Island Traded for Manhattan

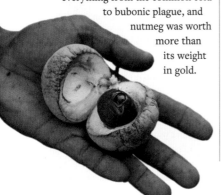

In 1677, the Dutch traded Manhattan to the British for their claim on a tiny island named Run. Less than one square mile, Run is one of Indonesia's Banda Islands—once believed to be the world's only source of nutmeg. At the time, Europeans were crazy for nutmeg. They believed the mysterious brown spice cured everything from the common cold to bubonic plague, and nutmeg was worth more than its weight in gold.

The Bandanese began cultivating the spice early in the second millennium, and the Banda Islands quickly became the key port for the nutmeg trade, frequented by Chinese, Malay, and Javanese. By the 15th century, Arabo-Persian merchants arrived, who sold the spice to Europeans and incited their lust. Eager to cut out the middlemen, Europeans began sailing to the Banda Islands, hoping to take control of the trade.

In the 1510s, the Portuguese were the first to invade but were handily defeated by the Bandanese. Next came the Dutch in 1599, then the British in 1603. The Dutch led a violent, genocidal crusade against the Bandanese, while also warring with the British for claim on the string of islands. In 1677, the British lost the Second Anglo-Dutch War, which ended in the Treaty of Breda. This treaty granted the British the island of Manhattan—then a swampy parcel of land known as New Amsterdam—while giving the Dutch victors what they wanted most: the tiny island of Run, which completed their monopoly of the Banda Islands.

Today, Run is part of Indonesia, which declared independence in 1945. The remote, tranquil island still cultivates what many believe to be the world's finest nutmeg—sweet, warm, and aromatic—while the Dutch go down in history as brokering one of the worst land deals of all time.

CHILI WOOD

MAI SAKAHN • LAOS

How to try it

Mai sakahn is available at morning markets across Laos and easily found in Luang Prabang and Vientiane. Keep in mind that the bark must be used immediately, or else tightly wrapped and kept in the freezer.

Among the lush, wild foliage of northern Laos, the plant known as mai sakahn doesn't stand out—but looking good isn't the main attraction. Also known as chili wood, the bark of the plant contains supercharged, peppery powers. A single sliver of the stuff laces soups and stews with a hot, tingly flavor, similar to Sichuan peppercorns but with even more of a kick.

Mai sakahn is a species of black pepper plant that grows across Southeast Asia. The taste is between pepper and chili, with a hint of herbal bitterness. In Laotian markets, the plant is sold as a woody stem or stump, and cooks splinter the bark themselves just before adding it to the pot. It's the most important ingredient in Laos's famous mor lam, a buffalo stew made with lemongrass, eggplant, and other riverside ingredients.

ONION SOUP MANGO

BAMBANGAN • MALAYSIA

Most fruit enthusiasts have tried only the sweet and tropical common mango, also known as *Mangifera indica*. The bambangan, however, is *Mangifera pajang*. The rare—and endangered—mango variety is found only on the island of Borneo, particularly in the state of Sabah. With their rough brown skin and hefty size (a single fruit can reach more than 5 pounds, or 2.3 kg), bambangans don't look much like the average mango. With their funky, durian-like smell and savory onion-soup flavor, they don't taste like them either.

While some do enjoy the sulfuric fruit on its own, it's most commonly used in dishes such as salads and chutneys. To make bambangan pickles, the fruit is sliced and mixed with chilies, salt, and shavings of the fruit's large white seed. After a week in an airtight container, the pickles are used as an accompaniment to fish dishes.

How to try it

Bambangans make appearances at markets throughout the island of Borneo, but are easiest to find in the East Malaysian state of Sabah. Due to their smell, they are often found alongside durians on the periphery of local markets rather than inside.

MATCHMAKING ORANGE FESTIVAL

CHAP GOH MEI • MALAYSIA

On Chap Goh Mei, the 15th night of Lunar New Year, groups of Malaysian revelers congregate at the edges of lakes and straits, their hands cupping vibrant oranges covered by words written in permanent marker.

At the onset of the New Year, celebrants often give oranges (which represent wealth in the coming year) to their friends and families. But on the last day of celebration, single women in Malaysia co-opt the symbolic orange to help them find love. Starting in the late 19th century, eligible women on Penang Island wrote on the rinds and tossed oranges into the water. Male suitors were meant to pluck a floating orb, then find the affiliated lady. Singles initially performed this ritual so that fate

How to try it

Merrymaking and orange tossing ensues along the waterfront strip of Esplanade on Penang Island. For those not able to attend, a virtual Chap Goh Mei river filled with floating oranges can be accessed from an app called Wowwwz.

might bring them a spouse, but today, women add their phone number or social media handle and try to land a date. Although the tradition started in Penang, groups now gather at bodies of water throughout Malaysia for the annual rite.

Though love is in the air, some participants are guided by entrepreneurial spirit rather than romance. Vendors scoop up oranges from the water, then resell them in the street—contact details and all—to interested bachelors.

EDIBLE BIRD'S NEST FARMING

SWIFTLET HOTELS • MYANMAR

How to try it
Farmed swiftlet nests are a good deal more sustainable than wild ones—but before you stock up, remember it's still a tasteless food with no proven medicinal or nutritional value.

Nestled throughout the southern city of Myeik are boarded-up houses and a few windowless concrete structures. From the outside, they look abandoned, but inside they are fully occupied. Loudspeakers inside the buildings blast a high staccato chirping sound, the mating call of the white-nest swiftlet, and hundreds of the small birds pour out of the sky and in through open windows at the top of the building. They are the swiftlet hotels of Myeik.

Swiftlet nests, which are clear, gelatinous, and made almost entirely of bird saliva, have been prized in Chinese medicine and cooking for hundreds of years. They are the main ingredient in the infamous bird's nest soup and are believed to slow aging, provide disease immunity, and increase sexual vigor. The edible bird's nest industry is massive—estimated to be worth at least five billion dollars annually, with two billion of it generated in Hong Kong alone.

Historically, the nests were gathered in caves in Borneo. Using ropes, bamboo poles, and handmade rattan ladders dangling from the cave's ceiling, the local Ida'an people climbed hundreds of feet in the air to scrape the nests from the cave walls. The work was incredibly dangerous. The pitch-black cave was lit only by torchlight, and people fell regularly to their deaths. Demand quickly outpaced natural resources, and the wild swiftlet population was under severe threat.

In the 1980s, a solution arrived in the form of swiftlet hotels. Typically converted from old houses and abandoned factories, then eventually built to order, these hulking windowless buildings now stretch across Thailand, Vietnam, Myanmar, Malaysia, and Indonesia. There is a get-rich-quick quality to the business model that has helped swiftlet farming grow rapidly. The initial costs are low (an old building, a stereo system), and if the farmer succeeds in establishing a population, it can be quite lucrative. Depending on the source, a kilo of birds' nests can go for more than $2,500.

The rise of swiftlet farming is perhaps the largest avian domestication project in modern history. The empty buildings act like massive artificial beehives, and the swiftlet farmers their keepers. Although the overall result has been an increase in swiftlets, there have been mixed results for wild populations. Wild nests are now even more valued, fetching as much as $10,000 a kilo, and the behavior of swiftlets has changed, with generations of birds learning to seek houses rather than caves.

FLOATING GARDENS

INLE LAKE • MYANMAR

Around a quarter of Myanmar's Inle Lake, the country's second largest body of water, is topped with man-made gardens. Farmers atop boats glide between their plots, plucking produce from patches of "land" that rise and fall with the currents. To create these tiny garden islands, farmers gather clumps of water hyacinth and seagrass from around the lake, which they weave and compress into a flat, raft-like structure. On top, they add a thick layer of silt, then the floating parcel is secured with long bamboo poles that are staked into the lake's muddy bottom. With direct access to the water's vast nutrients, the miniature islands are prime, fertile bits of land.

More than 90 percent of the gardens' yields are tomatoes, which are sold at market hundreds of miles away in Yangon and Mandalay and make up roughly half of the tomatoes eaten in Myanmar. Depending on the season, farmers can also harvest beans, cucumbers, flowers, and gourds, but tomatoes, their most lucrative crop, are given top priority.

The practice of farming atop the lake, rather than around it, is thought to have started in the 19th century before intensifying in the 1960s. The unusual agriculture has boosted the region's economy, but there is increasing concern that chemical fertilizers, pesticides, and runoff are destroying the lake's natural ecosystem, and new measures have been taken to preserve the floating aquaculture.

How to try it

Inle Lake is located in Taunggyi, about 150 miles (241 km) southeast of Mandalay. Many companies offer boat tours of the gardens and the surrounding homes on stilts.

The man-made Kela Floating Gardens on Inle Lake yield produce sold throughout Myanmar.

HERITAGE FILIPINO RECIPES IN AN ANCESTRAL HOME

ATCHING LILLIAN RESTAURANT • PHILIPPINES

The province of Pampanga is often seen as the culinary heart of the Philippines, and Kapampangans are rightly proud of their cuisine. Local chef and historian Atching Lillian is a champion of what she calls "Heirloom Recipes," which focus on the rich heritage and stories behind her province's foods. From her ancestral home, where her family has lived for more than a century, Lillian runs a restaurant where she teaches visitors this inherited history.

Lillian prepares adobo, for example, without the customary soy sauce—in accordance to traditional recipes she's discovered. Her signature creations, called San Nicholas cookies, are a religious treat from the Spanish colonial era, made with 100-year-old molds, from a 300-year-old recipe. Many of her recipes were found in archives, and Lillian takes pride in preparing these dishes in the most traditional manner possible. (Just like her ancestors, Lillian doesn't weigh or measure ingredients.) With Lilian as guide, visitors are taken on a rare culinary journey that spans centuries of Pampanga's history, and lets them eat like it's 1699.

How to try it

For a culinary demonstration at Atching Lillian's, you'll need a party of ten or more. Reservations can be made through Facebook or by calling 09157730788. In the Kapampangan language, the restaurant is called Kusinang Matua ng Atching Lillian, or the "Old Kitchen of Atching Lillian."

BOODLE FIGHT

KAMAYAN • PHILIPPINES

Kamayan is a Tagalog word that translates to "by hand" and refers to the traditional Filipino style of eating—communally, and without plates or utensils. Though the practice faded under pressure from colonial rule, kamayan-style banquets are enjoying a resurgence, both within the Philippines and abroad, wherever the Filipino population can sustain a massive free-for-all feast.

A typical kamayan meal features a long table covered in smooth, waxy banana leaves, which all function together as an enormous plant-based plate. Down the middle is usually a foundation of rice, upon which traditional Filipino fare is piled: grilled chicken and pork, fried fish, shrimp, lumpia (a Filipino-style egg roll), pancit (stir-fried noodles), longganisa (sweet sausage), and whatever else will fit. Chunks of fresh fruit are fit into crevices, mango-tomato salsa is

How to try it

Whether called kamayan or boodle fight, the traditional feast is now being served from Manila to the United Arab Emirates to Los Angeles. In the Philippines, Villa Escudero Waterfalls Restaurant in San Pablo City lets diners go barefoot while they eat in the middle of a small river with a waterfall.

piled on top. Standing, diners scoop their hands into the piles, lifting bites to their mouth that they deposit with their thumb.

Kamayan meals are often referred to as a "boodle fight." The term hearkens back to an American military practice, brought to the Philippines during the US occupation of the country. During a boodle fight, officers of different ranks would engage in ritual eating contests while standing shoulder to shoulder around a table. There is controversy around the term because it turns the traditional style of Filipino eating, without utensils, into a colonial game. But many Filipinos have claimed the word as their own, evidenced by the many boodle fight restaurants and catering services available throughout the country.

MAY MANGO MADNESS

GUIMARAS MANGO FESTIVAL • PHILIPPINES

The province of Guimaras, a small island nestled between Panay and Negros, is the Filipino mango hub. Orchards blanket the island, bearing an abundance of stunningly sweet manga, or mangoes. While a large percentage of these bodacious fruits leave the country, each May Guimaras puts on a two week celebration for the locals, where the majesty of their mangoes is celebrated in almost every imaginable way.

During the Manggahan Festival, the island comes out to paint the streets yellow. In a mango-themed parade, performers wielding mango props dance in mango skirts. Competitive athletes register for sporting events such as the Amazing Guimarace, the Tour de Guimaras, and a Motocross Challenge. For the true fruit lover, there's the "Mango Eat All You Can," where for a hundred Filipino pesos (about $2), participants are set loose in a space filled with mango treats for 30 minutes.

In 1992, Guimaras was formally recognized as its own province. Locals celebrated the first Manggahan Festival in 1993, in honor of their provincial founding. Two decades later, the festival is bigger and longer than ever. All five municipalities of Guimaras use the event as an opportunity to showcase the island's culture, celebrate their community, and give thanks for the island's natural bounty.

How to try it

The Manggahan Festival takes place each May for two weeks. Outside the festival, you can visit the Trappist Monastery on Guimaras, Our Lady of the Philippines, where the order of monks make mango products that you can buy in the gift shop.

A Filipina dancer at the 2017 Manggahan Festival carries dozens of mangoes on her head.

MARIA YLAGAN OROSA

(1893–1945)

Ketchup, originally a Southeast Asian sauce, has been made over the centuries with everything from fish to walnuts to tomatoes. In the Philippines, pulped bananas are turned into ketchup, sweetened with sugar, soured with vinegar, and reddened with food coloring. One innovative food scientist is credited with creating a readily available domestic version of the condiment: Maria Ylagan Orosa.

As a young woman, Maria Ylagan Orosa was uncommonly courageous. Boarding a ship to the United States in 1916, she exchanged the warm Philippines and her family for chilly Seattle and her classmates at the University of Washington, where she pursued a degree in chemistry. After graduating, she became an assistant state chemist for Washington.

But in a few years, she went back home to the Philippines, taking up a role in Manila's Bureau of Science. (At the time, the US occupation of the Philippines was at its midpoint.) There, she experimented with Filipino produce, developed recipes, and sent economists (often dubbed "Orosa girls") to the countryside to showcase food-preservation methods and ingenious cooking techniques for those with little access to electricity or resources. Meanwhile, she developed hundreds of inventive recipes. In place of imported goods, she made soft drinks from local calamansi limes,

A bust of Orosa in her hometown of Batangas.

cookies from cassava, and a multitude of ingredients to make ketchup, including the banana. American newspapers reported on her experiments as well, especially about her attempts to ship frozen mangoes to the United States in a time when neither mangoes nor frozen food were especially common there.

All these achievements made her the Philippines' "foremost food specialist and food chemist," as a resolution naming a street in her honor proclaimed. But her life was to be cut unfortunately short. In the midst of World War II, she refused to leave Manila. When the Japanese invaded, Orosa secretly fed guerilla fighters and prison camp internees. But during the 1945 Battle of Manila, the city itself became a war zone. As American and Filipino troops fought to liberate the city, a piece of shrapnel struck Orosa, injuring her and sending her to a hospital. During a fierce artillery battle that pelted the hospital on February 13, Maria Orosa died, along with hundreds of others.

Orosa never commercialized her creations, and banana ketchup became popular only after her death. But she is survived by a large family living around the world, and tributes to her accomplishments have slowly trickled in over the decades. Today, her name adorns a street in Manila, and the nation's Rural Improvement Club considers her their founder. And, of course, there's the ketchup.

How to try it

Jumbo Seafood in Singapore's East Coast Seafood Centre offers yusheng, among other Lunar New Year specialties. Their version is quite large and designed to share with a group.

LUCKY SALAD TOSS

YUSHENG • SINGAPORE

To welcome the Lunar New Year, Singaporeans toss a raw fish and shredded vegetable salad called yusheng, which happens to be a very auspicious homophone. In Mandarin, yu is the word for fish, but it also sounds like the word for abundance. Yu sheng, which literally translates to "raw fish," also sounds like the Mandarin phrase for an "increase in abundance." Playing up the double meanings, many ingredients in the dish also have significance rooted in popular Chinese sayings: lime for luck, peanut crumbs to symbolize gold and silver, green radishes for eternal youth, and shredded white radish for prosperity in the workplace.

The ingredients are added one by one, and with each addition, the salad-maker says a well-wishing phrase. Once all the ingredients have been placed in the dish, all diners stand up and toss the ingredients into the air with their chopsticks while saying "lo hei," a Cantonese phrase that conveys well wishes for the new year. The higher you toss, according to tradition, the higher your fortune will be. Finished with a sweet plum and Chinese five-spice dressing, tossing yusheng might be auspicious for the future, but eating it gives instant returns in the present.

GILDED TOWER OF GIN

ATLAS BAR • SINGAPORE

With its majestic art deco exterior, Singapore's Parkview Square office building has earned the nicknames "Gotham" and "Batman building" among locals. Step inside its lobby and you'll find a warm, ornate space filled with red carpets, leather booths, and a giant golden tower that contains 1,300 bottles of gin from around the world.

This 26-foot (8 m) tall tower is part of Atlas Bar, which opened in 2017. Visitors and workers (the building houses various organizations, including the embassies for Mongolia, Austria, and the United Arab Emirates) can sip gins from regions as far-ranging as Bolivia, Belgium, and Japan, and dating back as far as 1910. Doubling down on its Gilded Age vibe, the bar's cocktail menu revolves heavily around gin and champagne.

How to try it
Atlas Bar is open from 12 p.m. to 2 a.m. daily.

The interior of Atlas Bar allows customers to feel like they are traveling through time and around the world with 1,300 types of gin.

A 45-YEAR-OLD SIMMERING STEW

NEUA TUNE AT WATTANA PANICH • THAILAND

How to try it
Wattana Panich is located at 336 338 Ekkamai Road.

The giant pot of neua tune, a beef stew popular in Bangkok, the Thai capital, has been simmering since owner Nattapong Kaweenuntawong was a child, more than 45 years ago. Growing up, Kaweenuntawong studied the stew's flavor profile and learned its nuances from his father. Today, he balances the flavor himself daily. Employing a centuries-old practice called Hunter's Stew or Perpetual Stew, Kaweenuntawong uses some of the previous day's leftover broth to start the base of the following day's soup. There is no recipe for the dish; he simply tastes until it's right.

A secret blend of spices and herbs, stewed beef, raw beef slices, meatballs, tripe, and other organs swim about the deeply savory, bubbling vat. While new restaurants and high-end condominiums now dwarf the humble one-story bistro in Bangkok's busy Ekkamai neighborhood, the complex, time-enriched flavor of their signature dish keeps Wattana Panich in brisk business.

Kaweenuntawong's mother tends the bubbling vat of stew.

AN ENCHANTING, COLOR-CHANGING EXTRACT

BUTTERFLY PEA FLOWER • THAILAND

How to try it
Butterfly pea flower is ubiquitous across Southeast Asia wherever there are hotels, spas, or markets selling blue dumplings and purple rice. It's also sold online in tea blends, powder form, and as a "cocktail colorant."

The secret to unlocking the transformative powers of butterfly pea flower, or *Clitoria ternatea*, is acid. When dropped into pure water with a neutral pH of 7, the liquid turns a cosmic blue. Add a squirt of lemon, dropping the pH, and the color turns to purple. One more squirt and it changes again, this time into a vibrant magenta. The indigo-colored plant is found across Southeast Asia and has been used for centuries to dye foods and create lava lamp–looking drinks. In Thailand, a blue tea called dok anchan, spiked with lemon and honey, is the traditional welcome drink at hotels and spas.

With a mild herbal taste that's likened to black tea, butterfly pea is gentle in flavor. As with other foods with deep blue hues, the plant is considered extremely healthy thanks to antioxidants called anthocyanins, which combat inflammation and a host of other ailments, including high blood pressure, immune-system issues, and even certain types of cancer. None of this is new to Southeast Asians, especially practitioners of Ayurveda, who have used the blossom medicinally for hundreds of years.

Recently, butterfly pea flower has entered the modern craft-cocktail scene. Using either whole petals or dried flower powder, bartenders have invented drinks

that show off the plant's dynamic range of colors. A squirt of citrus might be added before the customer's eyes to make the drink flare lavender, then, as the ice melts and the liquid dilutes, the drink will gradually descend into sapphire.

DICTATOR'S DELIGHT

PAD THAI • THAILAND

How to try it
Pad thai is available in nearly every home-style restaurant in Thailand, as well as at night markets, from street carts, and in food courts across the country.

Dictators often make unreasonable demands. Plaek Phibunsongkhram, prime minister and military dictator of Thailand, began his reign with a dozen edicts called the 12 Cultural Mandates, meant to build a unified national identity. Beginning in 1939, a year after Phibunsongkhram helped overthrow the Thai monarchy, his countrymen were ordered to start calling the country Thailand instead of Siam, to "eat meals at set times, no more than four daily," to "sleep approximately 6–8 hours," to dress appropriately, to honor the flag, and very specifically, to wear hats. Languages of ethnic minorities were banned, the traditional garments of local tribes were made illegal, and in what might have been his strangest dictate, Phibunsongkhram invented a new national dish called pad thai.

Meant to reduce rice consumption and encourage noodles, which could be made using a fraction of the grain, Phibunsongkhram stated in a speech: "I want everyone to eat noodles. Noodles are healthy, and have a variety of tastes, from sour to salty to sweet. Noodles can be made in Thailand, are convenient to make, and have excellent taste." Before Phibunsongkhram willed it into the world, pad thai was essentially nonexistent.

Rice noodles were most likely brought to the country by the Chinese—ironic for a campaign built on creating a strong Thai identity—but the dish features Thai flavors of tamarind, palm sugar, and chilies. And the name made Phibunsongkhram's intent clear: It was pad THAI.

With the full power of the Thai government and military behind the newfangled noodle dish, the Public Welfare Department began distributing recipes and food carts, from which pad thai was to be sold. (Other foreign food vendors were banned.) Incredibly, his plan worked. Pad thai remains the national dish of Thailand. It's eaten widely across the country and considered the poster child for Thai food abroad. The dictator's noodles were an undisputed success, but not all of Phibunsongkhram's mandates worked so well: Hat-wearing in Thailand is now optional.

ALL THEY CAN EAT

MONKEY BUFFET FESTIVAL • THAILAND

How to try it

The Monkey Buffet Festival takes place on the last Sunday of every November, at Phra Prang Sam Yot temple. Be warned: Once the monkeys have had their fill, they're known to get rowdy with the leftovers.

On the last Sunday of November, among the ruins of Thailand's 13th-century temple Phra Prang Sam Yot, an exquisite banquet awaits the guests of honor, all of which are monkeys. The province of Lopburi is home to thousands of macaques, and feting them each year is believed to bring good luck to the area and its people.

Known as the Monkey Buffet Festival, the party kicks off with an opening ceremony that features performances by human dancers in monkey costumes. When the real monkeys arrive, hosts remove sheets from the banquet tables, revealing decorative spreads of beautifully ripe watermelons, durians, pine-apples, and anything else a monkey could ask for. The macaques jump freely across tables, climbing and feasting on towering pyramids that contain nearly two tons of edible offerings.

Monkeys jump from table to table and feast on beautiful produce arrangements at the 2010 Monkey Buffet Festival.

Respect for monkeys traces back at least 2,000 years to the epic tale of Rama, the divine Hindu prince, and his struggle to rescue his wife, Sita, from the clutches of a demon lord. According to the tale, the monkey king Hanuman, along with his army, stepped in to help rescue Sita. Since then, monkeys have been revered as a sign of fortune and prosperity, and the annual buffet in Lopburi is a way for Thais to mark their appre-ciation and to keep the good luck coming.

EGG COFFEE

CÀ PHÊ TRÚ'NG • VIETNAM

In modern-day Hanoi, coffee drinkers rely on a steady stream of condensed milk to smooth out the heavy-duty Robusta brew served in most Vietnamese coffee shops. In fact, ordering a cà phê sũ'a ("milk coffee") will automatically get you a hot Robusta with sticky-sweet condensed milk. When French colonists introduced coffee to Vietnam in the 1800s, fresh milk was hard to come by. Dairy wasn't part of the local diet, and whatever milk could be found spoiled easily in the tropical heat. Luckily, a New Yorker named Gail Borden invented commercial condensed milk in the 1850s, which the French brought over to Vietnam. The thick, shelf-stable milk became standard in the country's coffee—but in 1946, Nguyen Van Giang didn't have either kind of milk, and so he turned to eggs.

The onset of the French War (also known as the First Indochina War) had caused a milk shortage in Vietnam, and Giang, a bartender working at Hanoi's Sofitel Legend Metropole Hotel, needed something to make a creamy coffee. He whipped in an egg, which foamed almost like milk, and invented cà phê trú'ng, or egg coffee. Today, the rich, fluffy combination is as much a dessert as it is a drink, now made using just the yolks, which are whipped with milk and sugar and heated into an unctuous topping for Robusta coffee. Egg coffee is always served in a small glass, often cradled by a bowl of hot water to keep the treat warm. Otherwise it's cold and strong, like a refreshing glass of liquid tiramisu.

How to try it

Nguyen Van Giang's son, Van Dao, serves the most popular egg coffee in Hanoi at the shop his father opened, called Café Giang. His sister also owns an egg coffee shop called Dinh Café.

Egg coffee can be drunk at any temperature, but it is usually kept warm in a bowl of hot water.

NOODLES DRAWN FROM A SINGLE WELL

CAO LẦU • VIETNAM

Cao lầu, in its traditional form, can never be globalized. While everything in the dish is ostensibly replicable—a bed of greens and herbs, topped with noodles, barbecue pork, crispy rice crackers, pork crackling, and a ladle of pork broth—the traditional rice noodles cannot be made anywhere else but the city of Hội An because they rely on the water from a single well.

All the cao lầu noodles in Hội An, a city of 150,000, are made by a secretive handful of people. The most important cao lầu family has an empire that extends back four generations, when a chef from China taught the current noodle-maker's great-grandfather the recipe. For the first two generations, the water that went into the noodles was drawn from a famous 10th-century well in Ba Le, which has been ascribed mystical and medicinal properties by the locals, thanks to its alum- and calcium-rich composition. In recent years, the family decided to dig their own well to supply their noodle making. (The water, they assure, is just as good.) The second ingredient that makes the noodles hyper-regional is the wood ash they add to the water, made from burning local trees such as the cajuput. Together, the ash-and-water mixture gives the noodles their dense, chewy texture and flaxen color.

How to try it

Cao Lầu Không Gian Xanh is a casual café with an exceptional cao lầu. A bowl is 30,000 dong, or about $1.25.

Every morning, save for one day during the Vietnamese Lunar New Year, called Tet, the family makes cao lầu noodles by hand: boiling and pounding rice, working it into a dough, steaming, kneading, rolling, and cutting. The dough is steamed twice, there's no electric machinery, and few know how to do it outside of a man named Ta Ngoc Em and his family. Fearing that the culinary heritage might be lost if anything were to happen to them, a government official arrived at their home and implored them to share the recipe with others, just in case. The family has since loosened their vow of secrecy and has allowed outsiders to witness their process.

A bowl of cao lầu is always eaten with chopsticks, never with a spoon, because the five spice seasoned broth is meant more as a sauce than a soup. The city's famous noodles, all delivered fresh from the same kitchen, are available at restaurants and stalls all over Hội An—and nowhere else.

Cao lầu noodles are the hyper-regional specialty of Hội An.

Also from a Single Well

BAN SOY SAUCE

The water from the only well in Ban Village is not used for bathing or cooking, but for making a soy sauce many consider the best in Vietnam. Ban soy sauce, a staple of North Vietnamese cooking, is a light, caramel-colored condiment made by fermenting large-grain sticky rice and small-grain soybeans in large ceramic jars. Fermentation takes place during the warmest months, between March and August, when the village yards are packed with hundreds of ceramic jars.

Most people have never tasted traditional fermented soy sauce. Commercial soy sauce is not fermented; rather, it uses hydrochloric acid to break soybean protein into amino acids. While the commercial process takes mere days, fermenting soy sauce takes months, if not years. It allows time to transform the water, grain, soybeans, and mold into a complex and salty, umami-rich liquid.

Compared to other naturally brewed soy sauces, ban soy sauce is milder and sweeter, thanks to the village's pure water and natural resources. The coveted condiment is used as a dipping sauce, a grilling marinade, and a gift for homesick Northerners who now live far from the well.

Africa

NORTH AFRICA · WEST AFRICA

EAST AFRICA · SOUTHERN AFRICA

NORTH AFRICA

WILD PIGEON TOWERS

DOVECOTES • EGYPT

How to try it
You can see clusters of mud-brick pigeon towers in Mit Ghamr, a two-hour drive north of Cairo. Back in Cairo, Kababgy El Azhar Farahat is a classic alleyway restaurant that serves some of the city's best pigeon, including hamam mahshi and pigeon soup.

Dovecotes on the road between Alexandria and Cairo.

Dovecotes rise from Egyptian cities like earthen chimneys, each home to mother pigeons and their young squabs. Pigeons are prized in Egypt for their meat and their excrement, called guano, which makes an excellent fertilizer. The hollow, conical birdhouses have been used in Egypt since ancient times. Dovecotes come in all sizes; some are attached to buildings, others freestanding. Their small alcoves provide a welcoming nest for the flocks of wild pigeons who spend the day flying around looking for food, then return to the dovecote at night to roost.

The dovecotes also provide the country with a steady supply of pigeon meat—a staple of the local diet. Young pigeons, or squabs, are considered the most succulent and are used for the stuffed pigeon dish hamam mahshi. Plucked from their dovecote at around six weeks, often before they learn to fly, the small birds are stuffed with rice or freekeh (a toasted, cracked young green wheat) mixed with onions, chopped giblets, cinnamon, cumin, and nuts. Trussed up tightly, the squab is roasted or grilled until the skin is crispy and the stuffing has soaked up the bird's flavorful juices.

The 2,000-Year-Old Magic of Egyptian Egg Ovens

In 1750, French entomologist René-Antoine Ferchault de Réaumur visited an Egyptian egg incubator and declared, "Egypt ought to be prouder of them than her pyramids." An ingenious—and ancient—system of mud ovens designed to replicate the conditions under a broody hen, these egg ovens could hatch thousands of fertilized eggs in two to three weeks.

From the outside, many incubators looked like smaller, rounder versions of the pyramids. Réaumur wrote a detailed description of what he saw: two symmetrical wings separated by a central corridor, with each wing containing up to five sets of two-tiered chambers. Fertilized eggs were placed in the lower tier and kept warm by a smoldering, dung-fueled fire in the upper tier. Réaumur observed the hatchery workers, who stayed on the premises to monitor the fire and turn the eggs regularly, which kept the embryo membrane from attaching to the shell and creating deformities in the chick. In the final days of incubation, the workers monitored the eggs with additional attention because too much external heat risked causing early hatching. Hens instinctively regulate their eggs' temperature with their bodies. The Egyptian egg hatchers mimicked this process by gently pressing the eggs to their eyelids—one of the most sensitive parts of the human body.

Back in France, Réaumur tried to replicate the Egyptian method, but the cold European climate meant that the hatchers required stronger heat and more fuel than was cost-effective. In 1879, a Canadian farmer named Lyman Byce invented the coal lamp incubator with an electric temperature regulator, which was widely commercialized and used internationally—including in Egypt.

Over the 20th century, most traditional Egyptian egg ovens were replaced with electric incubators, but approximately 200 ovens are still in operation. Although modern advances are slowly creeping in—some hatchery workers now incorporate metal trollies, automatic egg turners, and thermostats—the 2,000-year-old technology is as effective as ever.

A diagram of the inside of the fire-fueled egg incubator.

Edible Beauty Products

The ancient Egyptians have a reputation for beauty, vanity, and making use of the natural—often edible—world to supply their extensive beautification routines. Cleopatra was rumored to have had hundreds of lactating donkeys to provide milk for her regular anti-wrinkle baths. Egyptians used burnt almonds to fill in their eyebrows and animal-fat creams to moisturize their faces. Cosmetics were so important to Egyptians that many chose to be buried with them.

Body hair, considered a sign of poor hygiene and low class, was deeply undesirable. (An exception was made for eyebrows.) The earliest Egyptians fashioned tweezers from shells and razors from bronze. Around 1900 BCE they came up with a more effective, less painful method for hair removal: caramel wax. Egyptians boiled a mixture of oil and honey until it formed a thick syrup. The cooled caramel was then applied to fuzzy patches of skin, covered with a piece of muslin cloth, and ripped off. The technique (recently rediscovered by the modern hair-removal world and rebranded as "sugaring") soon spread across the Middle East to places like Iran and Turkey. Egyptians may be the most famous ancient beauticians, but they weren't the only ones using edible cosmetics.

MAYA AVOCADO-BANANA HAIR PASTE: During the Maya classical period, which lasted from 250 to 900 CE, head shape was the all-important marker of status and beauty. A high, elongated forehead that sloped

Ancient Egyptian princess Nefertiabet, whose name means "Beautiful One of the East."

SAND-BAKED BREAD

TAGUELLA • LIBYA

How to try it

Due to major unrest in Libya, it's safer to try taguella in neighboring Niger. The desert trade town of Agadez would be a prime place, but violent crime is also common there. Please check travel advisories before making any plans.

For the nomadic Tuareg people of North Africa, the desert is their oven. When they want to bake bread, they spread hot coals over the sand and dig a round, shallow divot in the center. They place their dough—a wet, unleavened mixture of semolina or millet that's been kneaded and shaped into a flat, round disk—into the blazing hollow and cover it quickly with hot sand and stones. A crust will form on the dough before the sand has time to seep into it. After about 20 minutes, the baker will uncover the bread, flip it, and re-cover it to ensure even heat distribution. Called taguella, the chewy, charred bread is a staple of the Tuareg diet. It's typically torn into bite-size pieces, placed in a bowl, and used as a base for stew.

Two Tuareg men baking bread in the Libyan desert.

backward to a point was so desirable that Maya parents would mold the soft skulls of their newborn babies, often strapping two boards to an infant's head to press it into the desired shape. To accentuate a good pointy head, well-to-do women wore high ponytails that they decorated with braids, ribbons, and headpieces, which in turn strained their scalps and damaged their hair. Thankfully, they had avocados packed with vitamins B and E, which facilitate hair growth and repair scalp damage. They also had bananas, with folic acid, to keep their hair shiny and strong. Whipping the two together with a protein-packed egg and moisturizing oil, the Maya made a hair and skull cream that still works today.

ANCIENT GREEK COLD CREAM: Second-century Greek physician Galen is considered the inventor of cold cream, which he made by vigorously blending olive oil, beeswax, and rose water. Called cold cream for its cooling effect on the skin, Galen's invention was a moisturizing marvel for the ancient Greeks. Today, commercial cold cream is made with shelf-stable mineral oils and borax, which keeps the mixture from spoiling and separating, but Galen's original formula can still easily be made in the kitchen. No time for scratch-made

A 19th-century geisha.

cold cream? Modern Greeks are known to use yogurt instead.

CHINESE AND JAPANESE RICE POWDER: Ancient Romans and Greeks used white lead to lighten their skin, which slowly poisoned them, until they made the switch to chalk. The ancient Chinese and Japanese, who also dabbled in lead, eventually settled on rice powder.

Chinese women dusted their faces with the finely ground rice, and geishas mixed the powder with water to paint their faces. (Some geishas would also bathe in rice water.) In modern Asia, rice is still a key cosmetic ingredient. The milky liquid drained from soaked rice, which many believe tones the skin and lessens the effects of sun damage, can be applied to the face with a cotton ball.

VICTORIAN LEMON EYE DROPS: Nineteenth-century England was a time of many treacherous beauty practices. Women bathed in arsenic to keep their skin white, numbed their eyelids with cocaine, and filled out their eyelashes by sewing in hair from their head. They also squeezed lemon juice into their eyes, which dilated their pupils and gave them the desirable big, glassy appearance—and also caused the inevitable corneal abrasions and, with excessive use, blindness.

GRANARY FORTRESS

QASR AL-HAJ • LIBYA

How to try it

Qasr al-Haj is located in a remote area southwest of Tripoli. The granary can be visited, but because it is a functional storage facility, the storage rooms should not be entered without the guidance of the caretaker or permission of the owners.

The Qasr al-Haj is one of the most stunning pieces of Berber architecture in Libya. Even though the name means "Fortress of Haj," the structure is neither a fortress nor a fortified city. It's a 12th-century storage facility—built to warehouse the harvests of the seminomadic people of the region, as well as travelers on the Haj pilgrimage to Mecca—that's still in use today.

From the outside, the circular building is nearly featureless. A single door opens to a vast expanse of courtyard surrounded by 114 cavelike storage rooms. The rooms are arranged on several different levels. The lowest, which lie partially underground, are used to store olive oil, while the upper levels are dedicated mainly to barley and wheat. A staircase leads to the top, where a walkway makes a full circle around the structure. Each room serves as a vault of sorts, much like in a bank, where a family or individual can securely store their foodstuffs. Historically, the granary was also used as a grain "stock exchange," its courtyard a marketplace for buying and trading goods.

Sheikh Abu Jatla, the 12th-century ruler who built the granary, rented the storage rooms in exchange for a small amount of grain, which he is said to have distributed among the poor.

Other Granary Fortresses

For at least 11,000 years, humans have stored grain in bulk. In many societies, a granary was the equivalent of a bank, protecting from local "economic" factors like animals, thieves, and weather extremes. Before formalized currency, grain was one of the earliest forms of money. Ancient Egyptians deposited and withdrew their grain from a centralized collection site, while Babylonians, who used silver as currency, determined its value in relation to barley.

① KSAR OULED SOLTANE (TATOUINE, TUNISIA) is a 15th-century Berber granary built on a hill, which protected it from raiders. Divided into two courtyards, the original structure was built entirely of mud (in 1997, the granary was restored using cement) and contains hundreds of storage vaults. Ksar Ouled Soltane rose to international fame when it was used as the slave quarters in the movie *Star Wars: The Phantom Menace.*

② AGADIR ID AISSA (AMTOUDI, MOROCCO) is one of Morocco's many spectacular igoudar (the plural form of agadir, which means "granary"), and among the oldest and best preserved. Built some 900 years ago by the Berbers, who are Indigenous to Morocco, Agadir Id Aissa stored not only grain but valuable documents, precious metals, and anything else in need of fortification, including animals, medicines, beehives, and civilians.

Perched high above the small oasis town of Amtoudi, Agadir Id Aissa can be reached only by foot, mule, or donkey. As with all igoudar, the local guardian of the key—which is generally the size of a forearm—grants entrance into the labyrinthine storage facility.

③ THE HECANG GRANARY (GOBI DESERT, CHINA) is contained within the massive fortress built during the Han dynasty (206 BCE–220 CE) and supported soldiers building the Great Wall. The fortress was designed to disguise itself from enemies in the desert, shielded to the north and south by tall sand dunes. It was also strategically located along a remote part of the Silk Road, and its granary stores helped feed traveling merchants. While the site is now mostly in ruins, it's a rare surviving example of a Han dynasty earthen structure.

PUBLIC OVEN IN A PORTUGUESE FORTRESS

EL JADIDA COMMUNITY OVEN • MOROCCO

How to try it

El Jadida, a recent addition to UNESCO's World Heritage Sites, is a 90-minute drive from Casablanca. The fortress also features a cistern where a scene in Orson Welles's *Othello* was filmed.

Most Moroccans have an oven in their home, yet they leave the baking to the local oven attendant, who makes a living tending to the neighborhood's communal oven.

In El Jadida, a quiet port city on the Atlantic coast, the oven is located in a 16th-century Portuguese fortress. The city, orginally known as Mazagan, was once a colony of Portugal and a stopping point for spice traders on their way to India. Abandoned in 1769, the city stood vacant for half a century. In the mid-19th century, a multicultural mix of Muslims, Jews, and Christians repopulated the town and turned the fortress into a commercial center. They renamed the city El Jadida, or "The New." The wood-burning oven inside the fortress is used for far more than baking bread. Along with their dough, El Jadida's fishermen and homemakers bring in meats, fish, and pizzas to be deftly baked by the oven operator.

El Jadida residents bring their bread dough to the oven attendant, who bakes it in the communal oven.

STUFFED CAMEL SPLEEN

TEHAL • MOROCCO

How to try it

A camel spleen sandwich should cost about 12 dirham, or a little more than $1.

Among the chaos of the Fez medina market, you'll find giant bulging loaves of meat, easily more than a foot in length, hanging out in metal trays. When a customer orders, vendors will slice off a slab and sear it on a griddle. They take requests: Herbs, vegetables, and even an egg can be added to the mix before it is scooped into batbout, a type of Moroccan pita bread.

Holding the meat mass together is a camel's spleen, stuffed taut with ground meat—generally a medley of camel, cow, and lamb—seasoned with spices, olives, and preserved lemon. Called tehal, it has a dark, compacted appearance akin to Scottish haggis. Traditionally, tehal is prebaked in one of Morocco's many communal bread ovens and then sliced and cooked to order in the marketplace. It's a popular lunch for working locals, who line up to grab a quick and portable camel-cinched meal.

A jam-packed camel loaf at the Fez medina.

BATHHOUSE TAJINE

TANJIA • MOROCCO

Tanjia, which is a name for both the cooking vessel and the dish inside it, practically cooks itself. The glazed terra-cotta jug, which resembles the amphorae used to store liquids in ancient Greece and Rome, acts like a single-serving slow cooker. To prepare a tanjia, you will have to make two stops. The first is to the butcher, who will fill your jug with meat, typically beef or lamb. Cuts like collar, neck, and tail work well for this dish because they release fats and gelatins that help braise the meat and create a rich, silky sauce. The butcher also takes care of the seasoning—saffron, cumin, preserved lemon, garlic, a dollop of fermented butter, and a drizzle of olive oil. After sealing the tanjia with a piece of parchment, you'll take it to stop number two: the local hammam, or bathhouse. Give your tanjia to the attendant, who will nestle the jug of meat into the hot ash of the coal-burning oven used to heat the bathwater, and leave it to slowly cook for at least half a day. (Some will drop off their tanjia in the evening and pick it up the next morning.) The long, gentle simmer renders the meat so tender it practically melts and yields a sauce that's bright, fragrant, and unctuous.

Because tanjia requires no cooking skills, it has a reputation for being a bachelor's meal. Traditionally, men who worked at the souk had Friday off and would eat tanjia together after a relaxing morning in the park.

A tanjia filled with lamb and olives, closed at the top with parchment.

How to try it

Marrakech is the city most famous for tanjia. Many butchers will rent you a tanjia to take to the bathhouse, which also charges a small fee for cooking and tending to your meal.

ARGAN OIL ALMOND BUTTER

AMLOU • MOROCCO

How to try it
Amlou is among the
many argan-centric
products available
at APIA, a store in
Marrakech's upscale
Gueliz district.

Argan oil, the Moroccan cooking staple and internationally prized age-defying cosmetic, is no picnic to produce. The argan tree, which is notoriously thorny, grows exclusively in southwestern Morocco and produces fruit just once a year. The fruit itself is something of a puzzle. Peel the outside flesh to reach the nut. Open the nut, which is extremely hard, to reach the oily kernel (there is often just one, but never more than three). To extract the oil, the kernels must be toasted, ground, and pressed by hand. It can take 20 hours to produce a single liter, which explains the $130 price tag—and the "liquid gold" nickname. Most of the world dispenses argan oil judiciously, or drop by drop as a beauty serum, but southern Moroccans use it to make a sweet nut butter called amlou.

To make amlou the traditional way, toasted almonds and argan oil are ground on a millstone—another laborious process that often requires shifts from the whole family. The pulverized almonds, which release their own fats, thicken the argan oil and create a viscous, nutty liquid that's lightly salted and sweetened with honey. Sticky, silky, and glistening with oil, amlou is used as a dip or spread for whatever needs a little liquid gold.

Amlou

(about 1 cup)

¾ cup (104 grams) raw almonds

4–6 tablespoons (32–48 grams)
    pure argan oil

2 tablespoons (42 grams) honey

Sea salt, to taste

1. Preheat the oven to 350°F (177°C). Spread the almonds on a sheet pan and toast in the oven for about 15 minutes, until they are dark brown and very fragrant. Set them aside to fully cool.

2. Once the nuts have cooled, transfer them to a food processor and pulse until they are very finely ground and oily.

3. Transfer the nut paste to a mixing bowl. Add the argan oil, honey, and salt. Stir well. Store in a tightly sealed container at room temperature. The amlou will keep for up to one month.

The traditional way to
make amlou is by hand,
using a millstone.

French Doctors Once Feared Tea-Drinking Would Destroy Tunisian Society

TUNISIA

In 1927, at a meeting of the Academy of Medicine in Paris, a French-trained Tunisian doctor, Béchir Dinguizli, announced a "new social scourge" spreading like an "oil stain" across Tunisia. If not stopped by French authorities, the doctor warned, it had the power to corrupt morals and paralyze Tunisian society. Soon after, the French paper *Le Matin* ran a front-page article about the "new intoxication." The alarming threat? Tea.

Tunisia, a French colony from 1881–1956, was only introduced to tea after the Italo-Turkish War of 1911–1912, which sent an influx of tea-drinking refugees from Tripolitania (modern-day Libya) into Tunisia. When locals began to drink tea, too, French colonists—accustomed to coffee, which they believed was the drink of the Enlightenment—accused them of teaism.

According to Dinguizli, teaism was an addiction comparable to alcoholism, a form of chronic poisoning with nervous tremors, amnesia, palpitations, blurred vision, serious disturbances of the nervous and circulatory systems, a general weakening of the body, and even a marked decrease in birth rates. Later authors delineated additional mental consequences, such as hallucinations, delusions, and even psychoses.

Beyond the medical concern, French colonists believed that tea addicts would do almost anything to satisfy their habit, and those succumbing to the "vice of tea" were potential criminals. They tried banning illegal coffeehouses, which served tea, and increasing custom duties. There were calls for educational posters and films on the dangers of tea, for creating a state monopoly on tea, and for a law making tea a prescription drug available only at pharmacies.

Alas, Tunisians did not respond to the French scare tactics of teaism, and locals continued to drink tea. In 1956, Tunisia gained independence, and today tea is practically the country's national drink.

WEST AFRICA

TASTE TRIPPING FRUIT

MIRACLE BERRY • BURKINA FASO

How to try it

Fresh miracle berries and whole plants can be ordered online. Across West Africa, the fruit is known by a dizzying number of local names.

At first, miracle berries (*Synsepalum dulcificum*) taste like bland cranberries, but eating just one can alter the taste of sour foods for up to an hour, turning them impossibly sweet.

In 1968, scientists isolated the berry's unique protein that turns sour flavors sweet. Named miraculin for its "miraculous" effects, the protein binds to taste buds and lingers on sweet receptors, activating them only in sour environments. The berry must be fresh; heat or refrigeration renders the fruit ineffective.

In recent years, miracle berries have become the stars of "flavor-tripping" parties. Participants (mostly in the United States) kick off the night by scraping the flesh from the fruit with their teeth, letting the juice coat their mouth, and spitting out the seed. Soon a smorgasbord of foods that shouldn't taste sweet do: Lemons become lemonade, and goat cheese morphs into cheesecake.

Though little studied, there are also medical uses for miracle berries. For example, miraculin allows diabetics to enjoy sweetness without ingesting sugar, and it helps chemotherapy patients experience a fuller spectrum of taste.

In Burkina Faso and throughout West Africa, where the berry plant is native, some families and farmers still grow the fruit, but its use has declined. Cheap, plentiful sugar has robbed the miracle berry of its magic.

Another Miraculous Berry

Serendipity

The serendipity berry (*Dioscoreophyllum cumminsii*) is a West African fruit that grows in the rain forests of southern Nigeria and in the tropical regions between Sierra Leone and Eritrea. It contains monellin, a potently sweet protein that's approximately 1,500 to 3,000 times sweeter than sucrose (table sugar), which makes it an exciting natural sugar alternative. Alas, like the miracle berry, the serendipity berry loses its powers when heated above 122°F (50°C), the temperature at which monellin breaks down and the sweetness disappears. For now, extracting the protein is expensive, and commercial viability remains to be seen.

Coating your mouth with the flesh of the miracle berry will temporarily make sour foods taste sweet.

PSYCHEDELIC ROOT

IBOGA • GABON

Iboga (*Tabernanthe iboga*) sprouts green leaves, bears small fruit, and carries within its roots an important part of Gabon's Bwiti culture: one of the strongest psychedelic compounds in the world.

In powdered form, the dried peelings of the iboga root resemble instant coffee. A small dose works like coffee, too, and Bwiti hunters sometimes use it as a stimulant. In moderate doses, the root is employed to treat a host of physical maladies. In large doses, it becomes a ritualistic substance for initiating a newcomer into the Bwiti religion—a spiritual discipline that incorporates animism, ancestor worship, and Christianity.

When people undergoing initiation enter a Bwiti temple, they're first covered in powdered clay, and then they consume iboga, as dried chips, spoonfuls of powder, or (less commonly) mixed with tea. For the rest of the night—and sometimes for several days—initiates remain under the care of other Bwiti as they experience out-of-body, hallucinatory experiences caused by the plant's active alkaloid, ibogaine. The root-inspired visions help the Bwiti connect with ancestors, which is a central aspect of their religion.

In recent decades, foreigners have developed a reputation for abusing the plant and using it for wild drug trips instead of spiritual journeys. But in 1962, a heroin addict in New York City found a use for the plant that changed his life and many others: After trying ibogaine, he was rid of his desire for heroin, and he spent the rest of his life advocating for the natural medicine. Many addicts now swear by iboga's ability to prevent opiate withdrawal, and while more research is necessary, ibogaine is available at rehab clinics wherever it's legal, from Canada to Mexico to Europe.

How to try it

Iboga is a powerful psychotropic and for practitioners of Bwiti, a powerful spritiural conduit. It is not something to ingest casually.

The hallucinogenic root bark of the iboga plant.

WORLD'S LARGEST LAND SNAIL

GIANT GHANA SNAIL • GHANA

Giant Ghana snails (*Archachatina marginata*) can live for up to a decade, during which time they can grow up to 8 bulky inches (20 cm) long, making them the largest land snails in the world. To maintain their size, these gastropods will eat practically anything, including house paint, stucco, and 500 types of plants. The snails are hermaphrodites, and each lays hundreds of eggs each year, which means that a small group of ravenous giant snails can swiftly turn into a horde of ravenous giant snails. Some countries fear that the snails will destroy their ecosystems (in 2014, 67 snails intended for human consumption were seized at Los Angeles International Airport and promptly incinerated). But in Ghana—where snails are harvested from safe, known locations—the bigger the better because these hefty critters make for delicious meat.

How to try it

Giant snails are easily found in West Africa. They are a popular street food and are generally sold as kebabs or in a spicy pepper sauce.

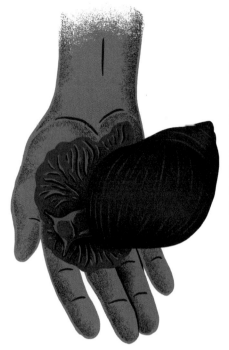

Chili-spiced snails, snail soup, peppered snails, snail kebabs, fried snails, marinated minced snails—all are considered delicacies. In the marketplace, vendors carry metal trays on their heads, hawking snails, while street stalls serve the chewy, briny meat on toothpicks as a quick snack. The snail can be harvested in the wild, but sustainable snailery farms are becoming increasingly common in West Africa.

To shuck the snails, a thin metal stick is inserted into the shell and used to pull out the meat, which is then trimmed and washed in lime juice to remove the slime. The meat is then ready for the pot. The snails are a near-perfect protein—low in fat and rich in iron, potassium, and phosphorus.

PASSENGER JET RESTAURANT

LA TANTE DC 10 • GHANA

Anyone can board the McDonnell Douglas DC-10 jet parked on Airport Road, just outside Accra's international airport—but it won't take you anywhere. Once operated by Ghana Airways and flown to Europe and the United States, the aircraft was impounded in 2005 at London's Heathrow Airport as a result of unpaid company debts. (Ghana Airways is now defunct.) Brought back to Ghana, the jet now serves as a restaurant called La Tante DC 10, known locally as the Green Plane.

How to try it
La Tante DC 10 is located a few minutes away from the terminals at Kotoka International Airport. It's open from noon to 10 p.m.

Customers board just as they would on an operational vessel, by climbing up a covered stairway. At the top, they are greeted by waitstaff dressed as flight attendants. The first-class seats serve as a waiting area and bar, and the economy section houses the dining room, composed of tables with rows of airplane seats facing each other. (To make room, the plane's capacity was reduced from 380 seats to 118.) While spaghetti and sandwiches are on the menu, the offerings skew largely toward local fare. Under the heading "Proud to Be Ghanaian," the fuselage restaurant offers West African favorites like palm nut soup, jollof rice, guinea fowl, and tilapia. To keep everything as authentic as possible, the restaurant's bathroom is the same tiny one you'd use if the jet was in the air.

Before being converted into a restaurant, this plane flew internationally.

SACRED FISHING FRENZY

LAKE ANTOGO · MALI

Once a year, men run into Lake Antogo to catch catfish by hand.

Fishing is illegal at Lake Antogo except for one day a year, when thousands of men gather at the shore waiting for the gunshot that signals "go." Carrying baskets, the men rush the shallow, muddy lake and capture as many catfish as they can, using just their hands. The scene is dense and chaotic, but it doesn't last long: After about 15 minutes, all the fish in the lake have been scooped up, and the ritual is over for another year.

The Antogo fishing frenzy is a tradition of the Dogon, a Malian ethnic group who inhabit the country's central Mopti region. The Dogon consider the lake sacred because it's a rare oasis in the Sahara, and for a time it provided year-round fishing. Since desertification reduced the lake to its current small size, the annual ritual offers a fair chance for Dogon from all over Mali to come together and capture food from the lake. (Women are prohibited from participating.) The frenzy takes place during the dry season, when the water is low and the fish are easy to capture. After the lake has been emptied, all the fish are presented to an elder from the nearby village of Bamba, who distributes them fairly among the participants.

How to try it
The date of the fishing frenzy is determined by the village elders and changes every year, but it generally occurs during May.

GROUNDNUT SNACKS

KULI KULI • NIGERIA

How to try it

You'll most likely find fresh kuli-kuli sold at roadside stands or markets, but you might also find a few packaged brands, such as Kozee, sold in Nigerian grocery stores or online.

In Nigeria, peanuts, colloquially known as groundnuts, form the base for an array of crunchy snacks called kuli-kuli. Every shape of kuli-kuli is made from the same labor-intensive mixture: Peanuts are dry-roasted, stone-ground into a paste, and then mixed with ginger, chicken bouillon, chilies, and other spices. To give the deeply savory snack its iconic crunch, the paste is pressed to remove any excess oil before being formed into its many iterations—skinny sticks, nugget morsels, flat cakes, rings, spirals, noodles—and deep-fried. Kuli-kuli is generally eaten plain or with a sprinkle of sugar. Broken up, it makes a topping for salad or yogurt. Because the peanut-rich fritter is high in protein and fat, it can also be dropped into a blender to pump up a protein shake.

AN ISLAND MADE OF CLAMSHELLS

FADIOUTH • SENEGAL

How to try it

From Joal, the lively fishing village packed with brightly painted pirogues (traditional wooden boats), Fadiouth can be reached by a 1,312-foot (400 m) wooden bridge or by boat. On Sundays, there is a Catholic mass.

Fadiouth, attached by bridge to the mainland fishing village of Joal, is considered a man-made island because it's formed primarily from clamshells. For hundreds of years, the inhabitants of Joal-Fadiouth, as the area is known, dined on clams and threw their shells into the water just off the busy fishing port. The shells' slow accumulation, held together by the roots of baobab and mangrove trees—along with subsequent intentional shell construction—has created an awe-inspiring land mass built from millions of tiny natural pieces that glint white and pearly in the sun.

Apart from being a literal island of shells, Fadiouth has another special claim: In a country that is 90 percent Muslim, the shell island's residents are 90 percent Christian and 10 percent Muslim, and the two live together in harmony. One of the main draws of Fadiouth is the cemetery where people of both faiths are buried side by side, set against a panoramic view of the water. Today, the penchant for natural construction has not been lost: In the afternoons, when the tide is low, women can be seen collecting the shells of mussels, oysters, and clams, which will eventually become building material on the islands.

Fadiouth's cemetery, built from shells.

SENEGALESE EGGROLLS

NEM • SENEGAL

During the French Indochina War (1946–1954), France sent more than 50,000 West African soldiers—recruited from various colonies—to what is now Vietnam, Cambodia, and Laos. Many of these soldiers were Senegalese, and the corps became known as tirailleurs sénégalais ("Senegalese riflemen").

While stationed in Vietnam, some Senegalese soldiers married local women, about a hundred of whom accompanied their husbands back to Senegal after the French were defeated. The tight-knit community of women set up stalls in Dakar's downtown food market, where, among other dishes, they fried nem—small Vietnamese spring rolls filled with glass noodles and ground meat or shrimp.

Today, nem are everywhere in Senegal, sold streetside throughout the city and at countless restaurants. But despite the ubiquity of the spring rolls, Dakar's old-timers say the quality has declined in recent years because most of the community linked directly to Vietnam has passed away. But those who remember the original rolls say that Saveurs d'Asie, a local chain owned by the son of a Vietnamese immigrant, is one of the few remaining outposts still frying up the real deal.

How to try it
Saveurs d'Asie is a small chain with four outposts across Dakar. Le Dragon, one of Senegal's oldest Vietnamese restaurants, has a section on its menu especially for nem.

◆◆◆◆◆◆◆◆◆◆◆◆◆◆◆◆◆◆◆◆ **REGION OF WONDER** ◆◆◆◆◆◆◆◆◆◆◆◆◆◆◆◆◆◆◆

Asmara, Eritrea

In 1939, more than half the population of Asmara, the Eritrean capital, was Italian. The African city was the seat of Mussolini's colonialist expansion into Africa, and he encouraged Italians to move to what he called La Piccola Roma, or "Little Rome." Mussolini brought in top Italian architects who erected art deco- and Futurist-style cinemas, cafés, and villas—hundreds of which still stand today. When the Italians left in the 1940s, control shifted to the British and then the Ethiopians, until finally Eritrea gained its independence in 1991. There is little tourism and no free press, which means the capital's wide, bicycle-filled boulevards and modernist buildings, in varying states of beauty and disrepair, are rarely seen by outsiders. (In 2017, Asmara became a UNESCO World Heritage Site, making it the first modernist city to receive the accolade and the preservation assistance that comes with it.) Beyond the architecture, the cuisine of this time-capsule city—which traditionally features boldly spiced, aromatic stews and curries—was also marked by Italian influence. Many Italian staples have

The local spice blend berbere gives Eritrean spaghetti sauce a fiery kick.

been folded into Eritrean cuisine— some of them remaining faithful to the traditions of the European colonizers, some of them taking on an Eritrean twist.

Spaghetti al sugo e berbere is the Eritrean take on the Italian classic. Tomato sauce is laced with the local spice mixture berbere, which includes chili peppers, ginger, nigella, and fenugreek. The fiery powder, which makes an appearance in many Eritrean dishes, is also

commonly melted into butter for a simple, spicy spaghetti sauce. In Asmara, berbere-spiced spaghetti can be eaten with your fingers using a piece of injera, the local crepe-like bread and universal carb.

Lasagna is a ubiquitous Asmara party food, especially prevalent during the holidays. (The sweet Italian Christmas bread panettone is also traditional.) Recipes hail from an older generation who worked in the homes and business of Italians,

A man buying breakfast pastries for sale at a café in Asmara.

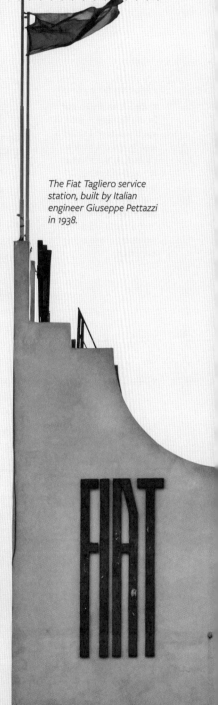

The Fiat Tagliero service station, built by Italian engineer Giuseppe Pettazzi in 1938.

picking up culinary knowledge along the way. Over the years, Eritrean lasagna has morphed into a dish that accommodates local ingredients: less cheese, more berbere-spiced beef (never pork). The cheese is generally mozzarella or cheddar, rarely ricotta, and the final casserole has a spicy, meaty density unique to the Eritrean lasagna-making tradition.

Coffee is served ceremonially in most of Eritrea: Hosts roast the beans by hand, grind them with a mortar and pestle, brew the coffee in a special clay pot, and then serve it in three leisurely rounds. In Asmara, coffee culture skews more Italian, and java is enjoyed quick and small as espresso-based drinks at any of the numerous bars around the city. The machines are old, with the same Eritrean baristas manning the machines for years. Along with coffee, the clientele enjoys the pastries they inherited from the Italians, like cream-filled, flaky sfogliatella.

A Gaggia espresso machine at Asmara's Bar Impero.

FALSE BANANA

ENSETE • ETHIOPIA

How to try it

Kocho is easily found in the Gurage region in southwestern Ethiopia and in the country's capital, Addis Ababa. If you find kocho outside Ethiopia, it will generally have been pit-fermented in the traditional manner before being exported.

The ensete looks like a banana plant, is harvested like a root vegetable, and tastes like flatbread. It's a cousin of the banana, but this plant's inedible fruit is nothing like that sweet yellow berry (banana is indeed a berry). Betrayed by the ensete's misleading appearance, English speakers named it the "false banana." But the fruit is not what makes the ensete worth planting.

The most prized part of the ensete is the starchy pith inside the plant's pseudo-stem and corm—the bulbous organ that grows underground, at the stem's base. In order to harvest the pith, the entire plant must be pried from the dirt and dismantled by hand. The corm and stem are scraped with a bamboo hand tool to collect the white fleshy pith, which is then combined with yeast, buried in a pit lined with ensete leaves, covered with more leaves and rocks, and left to ferment for at least three months and up to two years (it gets better with age). The subterranean fermentation yields a doughy paste, called kocho, that is made into porridge, drinks, and most commonly a flat, bread-like disk that's also called kocho. Kocho bread can be eaten in its pure, sticky form, or it can be toasted to a crispy, cracker-like texture.

Although almost unknown outside Ethiopia, ensetes are a staple crop for roughly 20 million people in the country's southwestern region. The plant's ubiquity, utility, and nutritional value make it a critical commodity. The plants can be harvested throughout the year, which provides a buffer against famine when seasonal crops fail. Fermented ensete paste is sold and traded at market, and ensete pits are regarded as commercial assets. After the dismantling and pulping process, the tough leftover fiber is turned into ropes, mats, and sacks—making ensete a plant that provides just about everything but bananas.

A Dorze woman preparing traditional bread, called kocho, from the ensete plant.

BEER, WINE, AND SODA MIX

TURBO • ETHIOPIA

Walk into any dive bar in the Ethiopian capital, Addis Ababa, and you're likely to see a group of jubilant souls sitting around a jug of turbo, a perennial favorite among locals who want their booze cheap and potent.

Turbo is simple to prepare: Take a plastic jug and pour in a bottle of local white wine (typically the Awash brand), a large bottle of local Bedele Special beer (look for the spider monkey on the front), and a bottle of Sprite. The large-format cocktail is part of the Ethiopian culinary tradition of spris, the Amharic word for "mix." Spris applies to cocktails (red wine and Coca-Cola is another favorite), but the concept extends far beyond the bar. Order a spris in an Ethiopian café and you'll get a cup that is half tea and half coffee. A spris in a juice shop will be a seasonal mix of three freshly squeezed fruits. But none of these spris will get you dancing as fast as turbo, which is light, sweet, and notoriously drinkable.

How to try it

Jambo House in Addis Ababa is a sweaty and riotous underground bar known for its dance scene and free-flowing jugs of turbo.

ETHIOPIAN BEEF TARTARE

KITFO • ETHIOPIA

If you visit one of Ethiopia's kitfo houses, you will notice that the menu offers just one dish: kitfo, finely ground, lean raw beef mixed with a clarified herb butter called kibbeh and a spicy chili blend called mitmita. The beef is almost always grassfed, which provides maximum herbal, meaty flavor and a smooth, unctuous texture that requires almost no chewing. The glistening beef is typically served with gomen (collard greens), ayib (Ethiopian cheese), and a piece of injera (spongy sourdough flatbread) that is meant to be used as a delivery vessel.

There are risks associated with eating kitfo, including worms, so butchers often take the meat from between the shoulders of an ox because it's traditionally thought to be a worm-free part of the body. In Ethiopia, raw meat is an important, often celebratory food. Another dish, tere siga, translates as "raw meat," and it is exactly that: a slab of uncooked meat, generally beef, cut into pieces and dipped in mitmita.

Ethiopian children are generally allowed to eat raw meat at around the age of five or six, when their systems are deemed strong enough to defend against foodborne illness. But old or young, some never develop a taste for it, which is why kitfo can also be slightly cooked, in a preparation known as lebleb.

How to try it

Yohannes Kitfo, a restaurant in Addis Ababa, is famous for the dish. A serving costs about $6 and serves two or three people.

A plate of kitfo with typical side dishes, collard greens and cheese.

LAST OF THE WILD ARABICA PLANTS

MANYATE COFFEE VILLAGE • ETHIOPIA

How to try it

Bale Mountains National Park is located 250 miles (402 km) southeast of Addis Ababa. Directions are available on the park website.

Protected within Bale Mountains National Park is Harenna Forest, a tangle of dense greenery hidden beneath the shroud of often-present, low-lying clouds. Ethiopia is the birthplace of coffee, and within this forest are some of the world's last wild coffee plants.

Most people have never tasted wild coffee, and they probably never will: According to a 2017 study, the wild plants are at a "high risk of extinction" in the next few decades, largely due to climate change's negative effects on coffee-growing land. For now, arabica flourishes in the high-elevation, mountainous reaches of the Harenna Forest, where massive, mossy trees provide the shade that the wild plants need. About 3,000 farmers living in the area depend on the crop, known as "forest coffee," for income. The plants produce bright-red fruit, called cherries, which harvesters collect and then spread out on frames to dry naturally beneath the sun. The wild coffee they gather has not been well studied, and its wildness has been a subject of beguiling speculation among many coffee professionals, who believe the forest holds more than a hundred untapped varieties of arabica.

At Manyate Coffee Village, situated on Harenna's southern edge, you can sample a cup of wild coffee. Residents of Manyate have established a community group, known as the Sankate Association, to better develop the forest's small-scale industries. Sankate's coffeehouse offers traditional Ethiopian coffee ceremonies, and during harvest season, guests can pluck their own ripened coffee cherries.

Gushuralle Peak in Ethiopia's Harenna Forest.

The Controversy of Caffeine

Caffeine is the most commonly consumed psychoactive drug in the world. Despite scientific evidence that caffeine is habit-forming, performance-enhancing, harmful in large doses, and difficult to quit, it goes unregulated around the world. But caffeine wasn't always universally accepted. Catholics once deemed the drink "satanic" because of its association with Islam and Mecca, and 17th-century sultan Murad IV was known to dress as a commoner and walk the streets of Constantinople decapitating subjects he found drinking coffee. Since then punishment has eased, but caffeine still has its detractors.

MORMONS: The Doctrine and Covenants, one of the scriptures of Mormonism, contains a section called the "Word of Wisdom" in which God delivers a revelation to Joseph Smith about what Mormons are allowed to eat. "Strong drinks" (which Mormons agree means alcoholic beverages) were expressly forbidden, and tobacco was banned unless used medicinally. But what was the meaning of the third prohibited item, "hot drinks"? Coffee and tea, literally hot, were removed from the Mormon diet, but this linguistic ambiguity incited a debate about whether or not caffeine was the offensive "hot" (i.e., stimulating) substance. Some Mormons avoid caffeine altogether and, until 2012, the sale of all caffeinated drinks, including sodas, was banned on the campus of the predominantly Mormon Brigham Young University. In the 1970s, Brigham Young University students hid a secret "black market" Coke machine in the theater department, which had to be moved regularly to avoid detection. Since then, the university has loosened its stance on soda, but the issue is far from resolved. During the 2012 US presidential election, Mormon candidate Mitt Romney caused a media stir when he drank a Diet Coke on camera and confessed to enjoying a scoop of coffee ice cream.

NAZIS: The Third Reich championed decaf coffee so heartily that you might think it was an Aryan health drink. The nonstimulant brew was the invention of Ludwig Roselius, a German national and aspiring Nazi. After his father's death, which he attributed to the overconsumption of coffee, the inventor figured out how to remove caffeine from coffee beans. (Many reports claim his discovery was accidental.) Roselius patented his invention in 1905 and marketed it as a luxury good and healthy coffee alternative.

The Nazis bit, and decaf drinks became state policy, served at Nazi festivals and Hitler Youth camps. Despite their fondness for his coffee, however, the Nazis twice denied Roselius membership in their party. But inventor and invention did just fine, with the drink soon hitting shelves across the world as Sanka, short for "sans caffeine."

OLYMPIC ATHLETES: Before 2004, if an Olympian tested positive for high levels of caffeine, they risked being ejected from competition. This was not an empty threat: In 1972, Mongolian judo silver medalist Bakaava Buidaa was stripped of his title for excessive caffeine. The World Anti-Doping Agency considers caffeine, at high levels, to be a performance enhancer that improves speed and stamina. As innocuous as coffee seems, studies have shown that caffeinated athletes do indeed perform better—showing about a 1 to 2 percent improvement, running slightly faster and jumping slightly higher. Throughout the years, the upper limit for caffeine has vacillated between 12 and 15 micrograms per liter of urine, which is a lot, approximately the equivalent of six to eight cups of coffee consumed within a few hours. A threshold this high, many argue, should separate the casual drinkers from the caffeine dopers, but it's still contentious territory because all bodies process the stimulant at different rates, making the line between cappuccinos and cheating a moving target.

FUTURISTIC CLIFF RESTAURANT

BEN ABEBA • ETHIOPIA

How to try it
Ben Abeba is open
from 7 a.m. to 10 p.m.
General manager
Habtamu Baye also
operates a local
transportation
company that can
arrange transfers
to the restaurant
from local hotels.

Lalibela is a holy city and a UNESCO World Heritage Site, famous for its 12th-century churches cut into the rock of the Earth. A short walk away you'll find another architectural stunner: Ben Abeba, a snail shell of a building that looks like a spaceship that landed on a rock. Perched high on a hill on the north side of town, the restaurant has been compared to everything from a bouquet of flowers to a futuristic amusement park ride.

Ben Abeba was the dream of owner Susan Aitchison, a retired home economics professor who came to Ethiopia from her native Scotland, initially to help a friend set up a school. Faced with leaving Lalibela, she opted to stay and open a restaurant with her Lalibelian business partner, Habtamu Baye. Aitchison worked with local architects to bring her vision to life. They built a central spiral staircase that leads to multiple levels of curved open-air decks, each of them offering unobstructed views of the breathtaking river valley below.

The award-winning restaurant serves a menu of traditional Ethiopian dishes and Western fare, sometimes combining the two. Ben Abeba prides itself on being eco-friendly and community-minded: The restaurant has planted 50,000 trees in the valley around the restaurant, trains young Ethiopians looking to become food service professionals, and sources local ingredients, many of which are grown in the garden on the premises.

ALL-OUT MEAT EXTRAVAGANZA

CARNIVORE RESTAURANT • KENYA

How to try it

Carnivore is near Nairobi's Wilson Airport on Langata Road. The "Beast of a Feast" dinner, which comes with unlimited meat and an array of accompaniments, costs 3,600 Kenyan shillings, or about $36.

Enter Carnivore, twice named one of the world's 50 best restaurants by *Restaurant Magazine,* and you'll be faced with a giant roasting pit, where traditional Maasai swords are laden with hunks of meaty goodness from just about every animal that's not on the endangered species list: beef, lamb, pork, chicken, turkey, camel, crocodile, ostrich, ox, and more.

After guests are seated and introduced to a double-decker revolving tray of sauces, servers swarm them, swords in hand, offering a cut of whatever strikes the customer's fancy. The meat is unlimited, and visitors are encouraged to eat until they can take no more, signaling their surrender by lowering a white flag provided for them in the center of the table. Servers will then bring around dessert and coffee to those who are up to the challenge.

Besides the meat extravaganza, Carnivore also offers a concert venue, gardens, a playground for children, an events area, an African heritage gallery, and believe it or not, a vegetarian menu. The decor is indoor/outdoor, with tropical plants and streams weaving around tables. For your birthday, the staff will even gather around your table with drums and sing the Kenyan song "Jambo Bwana," sometimes called "Hakuna Matata" (no relation to the song from *The Lion King*).

At Carnivore Restaurant, meat is roasted on Maasai swords.

FERMENTED RUNNER'S MILK

MURSIK • KENYA

How to try it

Mursik can be found in small restaurants around the high-elevation city of Eldoret (also known as the "home of heroes") in western Kenya.

Kenyans have a reputation for dominating long-distance footraces. When the heroes and heroines return to their villages after winning trophies and breaking world records, the first part of their congratulatory reception is often a sip of mursik, a traditional fermented milk.

Mursik is an integral part of the culture and heritage of the Kalenjin community, which has produced many of Kenya's renowned runners, and the tangy fermented milk has become synonymous with the country's athletics. With a history tracing back more than 300 years, the drink likely began as a way to preserve milk during times of surplus production. To make mursik, dairy farmers boil milk (typically from cows, but sometimes from goats or sheep) and, once it has cooled, pour it into a calabash gourd, known as a sotet, that has been lined with charcoal from local tannin-rich trees. (In the past, animal blood was also sometimes added to the milk.) The gourd is sealed and then stored in a cool, dry place for at least three days to allow the milk to ferment.

The charcoal in the sotet imparts a unique smoky flavor and a bluish color, which is of high aesthetic value to Kenyan connoisseurs of mursik. The fermented milk should be smooth and sour, but the flavor can vary significantly because it's heavily dependent on which tree bark is used and the quality of the original milk.

MILK

Whether produced by humans or barnyard animals, milk has earned a reputation for being nature's perfect food, which makes it an ideal substance for intrepid marketing, weird science, and unconventional applications.

Skim Milk

Before World War II, skim milk was nothing more than a pesky by-product of making butter. The cloudy liquid waste was fed to farm animals or cast into nearby creeks, where it would eventually clog the waterways, sour, and attract swarms of flies. By the 1920s, American dairy towns smelled like the spoiled contents of an unplugged refrigerator, or the preferred term at the time, "dairy air." Instead of investing in expensive industrial sanitation, dairy producers partnered with organic chemists to turn the by-product into something drinkable. The result: skim milk. First released as a powder, skim got a lucky break from a wartime contract that sent tons of powdered milk to the front lines. When the war ended, the former dairy waste got a second makeover. Fresh skim milk was repositioned as "diet milk," the best way to stay slim and healthy—a reputation that remains to this day.

Animal Wet Nurses

Mythological brothers Romulus and Remus are classically portrayed beneath a she-wolf, suckling at her teats. While the image is meant to bestow a kind of folkloric ferocity to the founding of Rome, animals nursing human babies is not hyperbole. When a mother in ancient Europe was short of milk, or a baby was abandoned by its mother, nursing was sometimes outsourced to a lactating animal. In southern Africa, the Khoikhoi people were known to strap their babies to the bellies of goats, where they would drink directly from the animal. In the 18th and 19th centuries, with the rise of syphilis, goats were sometimes more sanitary than people: European foundling hospitals of that era used skilled goats as wet nurses, training them to stretch above the infants in their cribs in order to bring milk straight to their mouths.

Milk, trusted and beloved for centuries, has become inherently good in the minds of many.

Kumiss

Even Genghis Khan was raised on milk. The storied horseman drank the traditional fermented milk of the Central Asian steppes called kumiss, made by agitating the sugar-rich milk of a mare until the liquid is acidified and slightly alcoholic, and tastes like a cross between sparkling wine and sour cream. Without this fermentation, mare's milk contains so much lactose that it is essentially a laxative. During Genghis's day, kumiss was often agitated in a horsehide container strapped to a galloping horse, but today's kumiss makers churn the milk in a vat or barrel, much like butter. In Central Asia, a bowl of kumiss is not only a gesture of hospitality but a cure for whatever ails you. This reputation

gave rise to "kumiss cure" resorts—medicinal lodges tucked high in the mountains, where visitors ranging from wellness vacationers to the terminally ill come to drink fresh kumiss by the gallon in the hope of purifying their bodies.

Competitive Milk Weight Gain

To celebrate their new year, the Bodi tribe of Ethiopia selects an unmarried man from each of their 14 clans to compete in the Ka'el Ceremony, or "Ceremony of Fat Men." The contestants seclude themselves for six months, gorging on a mixture of cow's milk and blood, in an attempt to gain as much weight as possible. The cow is sacred to the Bodi, and the mixture of the animal's vital secretions is a cherished food source. On the day of the competition, the men emerge from their huts, substantially heavier, prepared to compete in physical and acrobatic challenges. Naked and smeared with clay and ashes, the men run for hours under the watchful eye of the village elders. The most impressive man is crowned "Fat Man of the Year" and becomes a village hero.

Participants in the Ka'el Ceremony spend six months gaining weight before the big day.

THE OBSCURE LANGUAGE OF THE
Lake Kivu Fishermen

Most nights, just before sunset, a group of fishermen emerge from the green terraced hills of Kibuye, Rwanda, get in their boats, and paddle toward the center of Lake Kivu, an idyllic lake shared by Rwanda and the Democratic Republic of Congo. They set out in teams of three boats, attached by long eucalyptus rods that the fishermen cross like balance beams. Beneath the boats, they stretch a net for catching sambaza—a small fish similar in taste to tilapia but resembling a sardine—and light gas lanterns. The bright, winking light attracts the fish to the boats and creates a nightly spectacle on the horizon.

While working, some men sing in Amashi, the language that practically marks them as fishermen. The little-used language is spoken ubiquitously on Lake Kivu, where most everyone is a fisherman, and is taught Amashi by family members. (Rwanda's national language is Kinyarwanda, which is spoken by 93 percent of the population.) Most believe the language is a product of the shared border between Rwanda and the Democratic Republic of Congo. Amashi is a language from the Abashi people of Eastern Congo, historically located around Bukavu, a bustling Congolese city on the southern tip of Lake Kivu that borders Rwanda. Amashi, however, is no longer the predominant language in Bukavu, though it's alive and well on both sides of the border that divides Lake Kivu. The dialect changes around the lake, but if an outsider wants to learn the fishing trade, they must also learn some basic Amashi.

When the nets are set and the lanterns lit, the sun dips low and the fishermen relax. They have several hours until it is time to pull the nets—the first pull of several they make each night. When it's time to haul the catch, they communicate, of course, in Amashi.

Concerned about Amashi's potential disappearance, some fishermen have recorded amasare, or work songs of the fishermen. They use these songs most when paddling out, singing in unison as they set up. A different member of the crew leads each night, favoring their treasured melodies, some of which incorporate intricate harmonies and whistles. Although the lyrics change, "be mighty" features frequently, as does "may God watch over us." Some songs include exultations of God, and prayers for family and fish. When a fisherman slowly starts to sing, everyone quickly joins in.

DROPLET CHILI OIL

AKABANGA • RWANDA

Bright orange and flaming hot, Akabanga is so spicy that workers are required to wear face masks while making it. The Rwandan hot sauce is generally packaged in small plastic eyedropper bottles to keep dosages under tight control. With a heat rating of more than 150,000 Scoville units, a single drop is a good place to start. (For comparison, jalapeños score about 5,000 on the Scoville heat chart.)

In the past few decades, this fiery sauce has garnered a cult following, but its rise to fame was largely unintentional. In the early 1980s, a young Rwandan vendor named Sina Gerard was selling mandazi (fried savory doughnuts) from his roadside stand. To help his snacks stand out, he decided to make a condiment to serve with them: a chili oil made from local Scotch bonnet peppers, picked and pressed when ripe and yellow. Gerard named his creation Akabanga, roughly translated from the Kinyarwanda language to mean "secret," in reference to the beguiling hit of heat. Earthy, smoky, and painfully addictive, the chili oil soon had customers flocking to his stand. Today, Akabanga is Rwanda's iconic and ubiquitous spicy condiment, and the travel-size eyedropper bottles are commonly kept, at the ready, in purses and pockets.

How to try it
Akabanga is sold in convenience stores in Kigali, Rwanda's capital, or it can be ordered online.

····· FOOD PIONEER·····

SINA GERARD

b. 1963

Sina Gerard's first enterprise was a roadside stand where he sold bread and doughnuts he baked himself. He then expanded into fresh juice from his family's orchard. And then came Akabanga, the hot sauce that became a runaway hit and bankrolled the rest of his endeavors.

Today, the self-made millionaire is described as a "pig farmer, timber trader, bakery owner, supermarket owner, spice maker, and philanthropist." His myriad businesses are all run within Rwanda because he is devoted to building his country's economy. Self-taught and self-made, Gerard is known to apply eccentric methodology to his enterprises. At his piggery, for example, he plays music on speakers mounted to the wooden beams of the sty (a mix of R&B, rap, and local hits). He says the music keeps the pigs happy and makes them more productive. To prove it, he set up a control group of pigs without music, and indeed, those pigs did not feed, mate, or deliver piglets with the same ease and pace. Instead of staple crops, Gerard experiments with higher-earning produce like strawberries, apples, and grapes for wine. (He also makes banana wine.)

The hot-sauce millionaire circulates his money, knowledge, and agricultural innovations within the country that made him rich. His central objective is to help his fellow Rwandans, 75 percent of whom are engaged in farming. To that end, he gives out seeds and fertilizer to local farmers, teaches them to grow the crops, and then purchases what they grow. Much of this gets processed into higher-value products at his factories.

Gerard himself still lives in his hometown of Nyirangarama, having built his business headquarters on the same land where he once slung doughnuts from a stand. He constructed the town's first school, which is free, and hopes the students will come to work for him. Akabanga, his celebrity hot sauce, is still made in Nyirangarama—now in industrial quantities.

LAST OF THE INDEPENDENT MILK BARS

KURUHIMBI • RWANDA

How to try it

Kuruhimbi is located at KN 204 St. 14. The bar is cash only. The hours are inconsistent; typically, it's open every day from 6:30 a.m. to 9:00 p.m., but that is dependent on how many customers are in the bar at any given time.

Kuruhimbi is one of Kigali's most popular bars, and it doesn't serve a drop of liquor. Instead, milk is on tap. Located in the city's Kimisagara neighborhood, Kuruhimbi is a milk bar, a Rwandan stalwart, and one of the last of its kind.

Inside, frothy cups of milk are poured from a big metal drum and served hot or cold. Ikivuguto, a thick fermented milk similar to probiotic yogurt, is one of Kuruhimbi's specialties, and locals swear that the bar brews the best in the city. Condiments—honey, sugar, and cocoa powder—are readily available.

The bar seats no more than ten people at a time, but customers pop in and out quickly, just long enough to throw back a half liter of milk or fill up a jerry can for takeout. Kuruhimbi is one of the community watering holes, and many nearby residents spend late mornings and afternoons chatting in the shop. The owners have lived in the neighborhood for decades, and they source Kuruhimbi's milk from farms just outside Kigali's city limits.

Milk bars are unique to Rwanda. When rural citizens left their cows behind as they took up urban life, the milk bar was born as a way to keep Rwandans connected to their dairy heritage.

Independent Kigali milk bars, once ubiquitous, are slowly being replaced by Inyange Milk Zones, a sterile, government-backed chain. Kuruhimbi is one of just a few operational neighborhood milk bars still standing.

WEDDING CAMEL JERKY

MUQMAD • SOMALILAND

How to try it

Muqmad can be bought at the market in Hargeisa, the capital city of Somaliland, but to try your hand at the xeedho, you'll have to marry into a northern Somali family.

Muqmad is the Somali version of jerky, made by slicing meat into thin strips, hanging the strips out to dry in the sun, then chopping the meat into cubes and deep-frying them into salty, chewy morsels that can keep for more than a year. Typically made from camel (but sometimes beef), muqmad began as a preservation method for Somali nomad communities and is now a symbolic part of many northern Somali wedding ceremonies.

To dress up camel jerky for a wedding, muqmad is placed in a xeedho, a wood-and-leather container prepared by the bride's family. The vessel, which represents the bride, is then wrapped in white cloth, bound by intricately knotted rope, and given as a gift to the groom and his family. On the seventh day after the wedding, members of both families gather for the opening of the xeedho, and a relative of the groom is tasked with untying the knots. If the relative fails, the bride's family has the power to claim her back, and the reputation of the groom and his clan will suffer. If successfully opened, the xeedho reveals another, smaller container made of mashed and hardened dates, which in turn contains the muqmad. The jerky is distributed to the guests, along with parts of the date container, and only then can the marriage be truly celebrated.

BAOBAB SEED CANDY

UBUYU • TANZANIA

When you've been snacking on ubuyu, Zanzibar's favorite baobab candy, the evidence is left on your red-stained tongue, lips, and fingernails. To make the candy, the nutrient-rich seeds of the baobab tree, which have a natural citrus kick, are coated in red-dyed sugar syrup that's laced with salt, black pepper, cardamom, and vanilla. As you suck on the candies, the morsels give off alternating bursts of sour, spicy, and sweet. The ride is over when you reach the seed, which should be spit from your bright-red mouth.

How to try it
Babu Issa is a famous ubuyu producer that sells cups of candied seeds throughout the islands of Unguja and Pemba, as well as on mainland Tanzania. A 300-gram (10.5 oz.) serving goes for 1,000 Tanzanian shillings (about 44 cents).

HIGH TIDE ISLAND RESTAURANT

THE ROCK • TANZANIA

Once the site of a fisherman's post, The Rock restaurant sits perched atop its namesake, just off the eastern coast of Unguja Island in the Zanzibar archipelago. At low tide, the raised eatery hovers above the sand on Michamvi Pingwe beach. At high tide, water rushes beneath and the restaurant becomes an island. Depending on the time of day, guests arrive on foot or by boat.

A wooden staircase leads up to The Rock, a small structure with 12 cozy tables beneath a makuti (palm tree leaf) roof. Diners enjoy unobstructed views of the Indian Ocean; during high tide, the back patio is surrounded by turquoise water on three sides. The restaurant serves lunch and dinner, so visitors can time their meal reservations to match the desired tide level.

The menu is largely European-inspired, with local seafood and house-made pasta, but the restaurant also aims to impart the flavors of Zanzibar and the surrounding region in every dish. The fish carpaccio is served with coconut, lime, and chili pepper. Most desserts come topped with "Zanzibar spices" ice cream. The beef, spices, and vegetables are all farmed nearby.

While dining at The Rock is exponentially more expensive than dining elsewhere in Zanzibar, the restaurant sponsors the Kichanga Foundation, an organization that teaches community members to swim and focuses on sustainability programs like waste sorting and recycling.

How to try it
The Rock offers two lunch seatings (at noon or 2 p.m.) and two dinner seatings (at 4 p.m. or 6 p.m.), both by reservation only.

OVERSTUFFED CREPE BOAT

ZANZIBAR PIZZA • TANZANIA

How to try it
Prices range from
4,000 Tanzanian
shillings ($2.00) for
a basic vegetarian
pizza to up to 15,000
shillings ($7.50) for
a mixed seafood pizza.
The Forodhani Night
Market is a good place
to find them.

*A cook prepares Zanzibar
pizza in Stone Town's
Forodhani Gardens.*

Pizza purists may balk at a dish that veers so far from the original, but on the Tanzanian islands of Unguja and Pemba, "Zanzibar pizza" is a loose interpretation made with pride. More like a mash-up of a crepe and a savory pancake, these tasty fried pockets of dough house a dizzying array of fillings. Avocado with squid and tomatoes. Lobster with cheese. Vegetables with egg and mayo. Snickers with banana and Nutella. Anything is possible with a Zanzibar pizza.

Vendors flatten a ball of dough, layer on a second smaller piece of dough to reinforce it, and then pile on as many meats, sweets, spices, and vegetables as the customer desires. After folding up the

sides, they fry the pizza in clarified butter on a hot tava (a large flat or concave frying pan). When the fillings are hot and the crust crispy, the pizza is slid onto a paper plate and smothered with fresh, spicy mango-chili sauce.

You can find at least 30 Zanzibar pizza spots on Unguja and Pemba. It's a popular late-night snack said to have been invented nearly 30 years ago by a cook, Haji Hamisi, who traveled to Mombasa and was inspired by the Kenyan city's famous egg chapati (a stuffed, pan-fried meat omelet). Zanzibar pizza is also similar to Nairobi's mkate wa nyama (meat bread) and the mutabbaq (stuffed grilled pancakes) made in Saudi Arabia, Iraq, Yemen, and India—but Zanzibar's version sets itself apart with its local sauce, meshing of styles, and unrestricted stuffing combinations.

ROLLED EGGS

ROLEX • UGANDA

How to try it
The city of Kampala
holds an annual Rolex
Festival in August,
where thousands of
rolex fans gather to
enjoy rolled eggs of
all sizes and flavors.

Step up to a street stand in Uganda, say "roll eggs" as fast as you can, and you'll get a rolex—the ubiquitous omelet whose name arose from a misunderstanding. A rolex is exactly what the original name implies: a beaten egg cooked flat on a charcoal-heated skillet, rolled up in a freshly griddled chapati, and served blistering hot. The rolex vendor, often beneath a colorful umbrella, will have some omelet additions on hand, like onions, tomatoes, and cabbage. But if you're near a market and have something special, like an avocado, in your basket, obliging vendors will fold your shopping into the eggs and make a deluxe, personalized rolex. In Uganda, omelets are eaten throughout the day and into the night, and rolex is often available until dawn.

Reviving the Almost Lost Art of Bigwala Gourd Trumpets

Bigwala is the music of the Basoga kingdom, one of the traditional monarchies of Uganda. In the local Lusoga language, *Bigwala* is an all-encompassing term, referring to the dance that accompanies the music, the music itself, and the instruments—five differently sized trumpets fashioned from gourds that were nearly lost to history.

For centuries, Bigwala trumpets were considered royal instruments, their joyful sound played at any important event for the Basoga kingdom. But Bigwala was also a music for the people, and performances invited participation: Men thumped on drums, creating a beat for the smooth, deep blast of the trumpets as women danced in a circle around them.

But in 1966, Ugandan prime minister Milton Obote imposed a new constitution that, in an effort to unify the country, abolished the kingdoms and banned Bigwala. The traditional monarchs were demonized, and those playing the king's music were arrested. Bigwala performers went into hiding, and their music largely disappeared. By the time President Yoweri Museveni restored the kingdoms in the 1990s, royal musical traditions were on the brink of extinction.

In 2005, a Ugandan academic named James Isabirye made it his mission to revive the tradition among the younger generation. Isabirye won Bigwala a spot on UNESCO's List of Intangible Cultural Heritage in Need of Urgent Safeguarding. Working with elderly musicians, Isabirye set out to teach young people to play the trumpets, but he quickly ran into a problem: The seeds needed to grow the gourds to make the trumpets were lost.

Isabirye organized community leaders to search the country for the seeds. They looked and looked, farther and farther, traveling hundreds of miles by motorbike, until they found an old woman with a gourd on her fireplace—the exact type of gourd they were looking for. Inside were 36 seeds, which were planted and grew to produce the first new generation of trumpets.

As of 2013, only four master practitioners of Bigwala were still alive. But since 2015, with support from UNESCO, more than a hundred young people from different villages in the Busoga region have been trained in making gourd trumpets and performing Bigwala music. (Gourds are grown to maturity, gently dried above a fireplace for a month, and then glued to form trumpets of various lengths.) The new generation of Bigwala players has performed at coronation anniversaries and other events to mark Kyabazinga (King) Day. Against all odds, young Ugandans are taking up an ancient musical tradition that was once in danger of losing its instruments.

Musician James Lugolole (left) and friend with Bigwala gourd instruments.

THE WORLD'S LARGEST EDIBLE MUSHROOM

TERMITOMYCES TITANICUS • ZAMBIA

In Zambia, where mushroom gathering is a part of life, *Termitomyces titanicus* is especially beloved. *T. titanicus* is the world's largest edible mushroom, with a cap that can reach more than 3 feet (91 cm) in width. The genus name, *Termitomyces*, refers to where the mushroom grows—inside a termite hill. These fungi have a symbiotic relationship with the insects: They grow on termites' fecal matter and in turn break down plant material for the termites to eat. (Termites also chomp away at decayed mushroom tissue.) The colossal mushrooms have a savory, smoky flavor and meaty texture, and they flourish during the rainy season.

How to try it
The Mutinondo Wilderness Lodge in Kalonje offers mushroom-gathering expeditions, but keep in mind that the mushrooms grow only during the winter rainy season.

SOUTHERN AFRICA

INSECT NEST OVEN

TERMITE MOUND OVENS • BOTSWANA

Termites are prolific builders, constructing dirt mounds that can stand as high as 30 feet (9.1 m). The insects don't actually live inside these structures; the sturdy but porous towers serve as "lungs" for the colonies below, letting carbon dioxide out and oxygen in.

In parts of Africa, Australia, and South America, these impressive works of insect architecture double as outdoor ovens for baking bread and pizza. (In the past, they were used to cook meats, from emu to snake.) To turn a termite mound into an oven, first confirm that the mound has been fully abandoned. Then cut a hole at the base of the hill, stuff it with newspaper, light a fire, and wait about 10 minutes for the whole thing to heat up. Toss in a steak and cover up the hole, and in an hour you'll have dinner.

A fire-burning termite mound oven.

How to try it
African Horseback Safaris in Botswana's Okavango Delta lead horseback tours that include a stop for pizza made in a termite hill oven.

Hunt Like a San
A MARATHON BEFORE DINNER

On hot days in the Kalahari Desert, men of the San tribes will head out on runs of 20 miles (32 km) or more. They are the world's last persistence hunters, engaged in what is likely humanity's first form of hunting. Over the course of a day, they will chase an antelope on foot, literally exhausting their prey to death by covering more ground than a marathon.

The San have long lived in the Kalahari, where they hunt, gather, and live a traditionally seminomadic lifestyle largely governed by the scarcity of water. When San men go out on persistence hunts, they follow a millennia-old playbook:

TIMING: The right time to hunt is when the animal is at its weakest. The hunt always begins in the middle of hot days, when the heat will wear down the animal until it collapses in a panting heap. Other good times are after a full moon, when an animal may be tired from being up all night, or late in the dry season, when there is less to eat.

TRACKING: San hunters are expert trackers. When telltale signs such as a hoofprint or bent blade of grass are absent, they crouch down, imagine themselves as the antelope, and predict its actions.

TOOLS: Hunters carry enough supplies for a night in the bush, including a blanket, firesticks, and water vessels. Their small bows look diminutive, but the arrows are tipped with poison made from the larvae of a local beetle and can bring down a giraffe. Hunters also carry spears. Working in small groups and using hand signals, they usually select a lone hunter to make the final run and spear the exhausted animal after hours of pursuit.

Colonization and environmental neglect have changed the San way of life. Boreholes risk depleting the already limited water supply, ranchers have set up fences that disrupt the once-massive migrations of wildebeest and other animals, and the San have been banned from hunting in many areas. Most persistence hunters are middle aged or older, and they lament that young men are not learning the traditional skills.

WILD DESERT WATERMELON

TSAMMA • NAMIBIA

For the hunter-gatherer San tribe of southern Africa, hunting season is made infinitely better by the wild, desert-growing tsamma melon. It's said that between its nutritious seeds and the high water content of its flesh, a person could survive for six weeks, if not longer, on nothing but tsamma. (The 19th-century missionary and explorer David Livingstone wrote of desert-dwelling tribes he encountered in southern Africa who survived on tsamma for several months.)

The perennial fruit was first domesticated hundreds of years ago in Africa. It's typically pollinated by bees and flies and, once sown in the rainy season, can start to germinate within a week. From the outside, the tsamma looks like a watermelon—which it is. But inside, the flesh is the pale, cool green of a honeydew. Some tsammas taste vaguely sweet, but most are flavorless.

The San use all parts of the tsamma: The flesh is dried and cooked into stews, and the protein-packed seeds are roasted and eaten plain or ground into flour. The seeds are also pressed for their oil, which can be used for cooking and for moisturizing skin, and the melon's leaves can be cooked like spinach.

How to try it
The name *tsamma* refers to the species *Citrullus ecirrhosus*, or Namib tsamma, which grows wild in the Kalahari and Namib Deserts.

A BREAD LOAF STUFFED WITH CURRY

BUNNY CHOW • SOUTH AFRICA

Bunny chow, called a bunny for short, is a hollowed-out chunk of soft white bread filled to the brim with curry. The dish emerged from the large Indian community in Durban, South Africa, but the facts get a bit confused from there. Some say the inventors were the Indians known as banias, or merchants, and that "banias' chow" slipped linguistically into "bunny chow." Others believe Indian sugarcane laborers came up with the cheap, edible way to transport their lunch. Some think it was golf caddies who couldn't break for lunch.

Whichever story you believe, the dish dates back to the mid-20th century, a time when South Africa was racially segregated by apartheid. Beginning in 1948, both Indian and black South Africans were banned from entering many establishments, including restaurants, and bunny chow became a cheap meal that could be passed through a window and required no silverware. (Eating utensils were also segregated into sets for whites and nonwhites.) Over time, bunny chow transitioned into a food ordered out of desire rather than necessity, but its history remains rooted in a dark time of South African history.

Bunny chow is typically ordered based on the protein and the quantity of bread. A "quarter mutton," for example, will get you a quarter loaf filled with mutton curry. The hunk of bread that is scooped out so that the interior of the loaf can be filled with curry is served alongside the order and used for dipping. Using utensils is frowned upon, so these bunnies need to be eaten quickly before the bread becomes too soggy to handle.

How to try it
Canecutters in Durban is a popular bunny chow restaurant. You can order its bunnies by the quarter and half loaf, filled with mutton, chicken, prawn, or vegetarian curry.

MILK TART

MELKTERT • SOUTH AFRICA

When Dutch colonizers arrived on the Cape of Good Hope in the 17th century, many of them became dairy farmers. They used their milk to make a custard pie called melktert, a now quintessential South African dessert found at supermarkets, bakeries, bake sales, church events, and most every celebration. The combination is simple but timeless: silky, vanilla-scented milk custard poured into a shortcrust or puff pastry shell, chilled, and then dusted with cinnamon before serving. Most recipes are quick and straightforward, but even with such a simple preparation, everyone's family recipe is a little different.

Melktert

Makes 2 tarts

Crusts

5 ounces (142 grams) butter, at room temperature

½ cup (100 grams) sugar

2 eggs

2¼ cups (272 grams) flour

2 teaspoons (8 grams) baking powder

A pinch of salt

Filling

4½ cups (1 kilogram) milk

3 tablespoons (42 grams) butter

3 eggs

¾ cup (150 grams) sugar

3 tablespoons (21 grams) cornstarch

3 tablespoons (23 grams) flour

1 tablespoon (13 grams) vanilla extract

Topping

2 tablespoons (25 grams) sugar

1 teaspoon (2 grams) ground cinnamon

1. Preheat the oven to 400°F (204°C).

2. To make the crusts: Cream together the butter and sugar. Add the eggs and mix well. Add the flour, baking powder, and salt, and stir until the mixture forms a dough. Divide the dough in half and press each piece into a 9-inch (23-centimeter) pie plate. Prick the crusts all over with a fork. Bake for 10 minutes, then remove from the oven and set aside to cool.

3. To make the filling: Combine the milk and butter in a medium saucepan over medium heat, and heat until the butter melts, stirring often. Allow to cool for 10 minutes.

4. Combine the eggs with the sugar, cornstarch, flour, and vanilla in a large bowl and beat well. Whisking the egg mixture continuously, slowly drizzle in half a cup of the hot milk mixture. Add the rest of the hot milk

mixture in this way, half a cup at a time, never forgetting to whisk. (Whisking while slowly adding the hot milk tempers the eggs, allowing you to bring them up in temperature without scrambling them.)

5. Pour the custard mixture into the saucepan you used to heat the milk and set it over medium heat. Cook, whisking constantly, until the custard thickens, about 8 minutes.

6. Pour the thickened custard into the prebaked pie shells. Combine the sugar and cinnamon and sprinkle over the tart as a topping.

7. Allow to cool completely, and then refrigerate.

MOPANE WORMS

AMACIMBI • ZIMBABWE

ike many places in the world, bugs are a hot commodity in Zimbabwe. After the seasonal rains, which arrive between November and January, local families race to harvest the outbreak of mopane "worms"—which are not technically worms, but the caterpillar form of the emperor moth (*Gonimbrasia belina*). The worms spend nearly their entire lives on mopanes, trees with butterfly-shaped leaves that are native to parts of southern Africa. The insects lay their eggs on the tree's leaves, which the larvae gorge on from the moment they hatch. After literally eating until they burst (they molt their skin four or five times), the worms grow to about 4 inches (10 cm) and are ripe for the picking.

The flesh of the mopane worm contains up to three times the amount of protein as an equivalent mass of beef, and a skilled collector can gather between 55 and 110 pounds (25 and 50 kg) of worms each day. Once picked, the worms are pinched open at one end and squeezed to expel a vibrant green mass of half-digested leaves and innards. The empty bodies of the worms are dried and then smoked, roasted, pickled, or fried to the cook's taste. These protein-packed morsels last throughout the year and are vital to the country's economy and nutrition. The flavor varies slightly with the terroir, but the earthy, vegetal taste has a savory element some compare to that of a well-done steak. However, compared to beef, which is among the world's most resource-intensive proteins, mopane worms are exceedingly sustainable, requiring about 6 pounds (3 kg) of mopane leaves to bring 2 pounds (1 kg) of worms to edible maturity.

How to try it
Prepared mopane worms can be found throughout Zimbabwe, especially in the capital city of Harare, where vendors sell them from baskets. Mopane worms can also be ordered online.

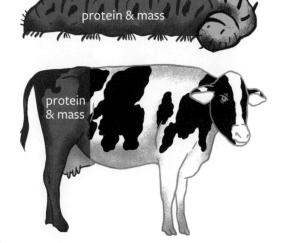

protein & mass

protein & mass

THE MASSIVE FORBIDDEN FRUIT

COCO DE MER • SEYCHELLES

The coco de mer, a most unusual palm tree, produces the largest seed of any plant in the world. Weighing up to 60 pounds (27 kg), the seed is also remarkable for its distinctive shape, which resembles a woman's shapely buttocks. In 1881, British general Charles Gordon encountered the sensuous seeds and concluded that the coco de mer was the tree of knowledge, and its seed the original forbidden fruit.

Coco de mer palms are incredibly rare, growing naturally on just two islands in the Seychelles, an archipelago off the coast of East Africa. The International Union for Conservation of Nature (IUCN) classifies the species as endangered. The government strictly monitors these trees, and anyone with a coco de mer palm growing on their land must follow certain rules: The seeds may be given as gifts, traded, or eaten, but money can't be exchanged for the unprocessed seed.

At its best, the coco de mer fruit contains a milky jelly that tastes like a sweet, slightly citrusy coconut with the texture of soft Turkish delight. Alas, this flavor manifests (and passes) before the interior seed reaches maturity, and harvesting the jelly from the young fruit means losing the potential to plant a new coco de mer tree. As a result, few have tasted the fresh natural jelly. Instead, the mature fruit is often hollowed out and sold as a decorative husk, and the mature flesh is dried and shipped abroad to places such as China and Hong Kong, where it's sold as herbal medicine. Over the centuries, the curvaceous seed has taken on something of a mythical status—its husk prized by Roman emperors and European royalty, and its flesh used around the world as an aphrodisiac, a skin whitener, and an ingredient in medicines like cough syrup.

Conservationists fear that treating the fruit as food will create a demand that will further devastate the sparse tree population, so for now it's better to enjoy the seeds with your eyes.

How to try it

Because the coco de mer is endangered, we don't recommend buying products containing it. The Seychelles government allows a small number of (nonedible) seeds to be sold to visitors as souvenirs—they go for hundreds of dollars each. The approved seeds have an anti-counterfeit holographic sticker and an export permit attached. Stores near Anse Lazio beach on the island of Praslin may have them.

The coco de mer grows exclusively on two islands in the Seychelles.

Oceania

AUSTRALIA · NEW ZEALAND

PACIFIC ISLANDS

AUSTRALIA

DINING ABOARD THE HISTORIC GHAN TRAIN

QUEEN ADELAIDE RESTAURANT • AUSTRALIA

The Ghan train serves local specialties throughout its 1,850-mile (3,000 km) journey across the middle of Australia.

How to try it

Voyages on the Ghan aren't cheap, with overnight trips starting at AU$1,099. Occasionally, while at a station, the Queen Adelaide opens for a pop-up, so travelers without the budget or time for a train journey can experience the restaurant.

The Queen Adelaide is a white-tablecloth restaurant aboard the Ghan, a train that traverses the Australian Outback from north to south. The menu, inspired by the country's native flora and fauna, includes dishes like crocodile sausage, kangaroo steak, grilled barramundi fish, bush tomatoes, and quandong (wild peach) pancakes.

To score a table at the Queen Adelaide, travelers must book a train journey, which can range from a quick overnight jaunt from Darwin to Alice Springs to a two-week transcontinental expedition from Adelaide to Darwin and back. The menu changes daily and often reflects the local offerings at each stage of the train's journey. While in the north, for example, the chefs serve curry made with buffalo, an animal that was introduced to the Northern Territory in the 19th century. In the south, diners feast on lamb from Kangaroo Island, a nature reserve southwest of Adelaide.

Depending on the train's route, travelers can stop for other regional food experiences, like a tour of a Top End cattle farm or an underground lunch with the opal miners of Coober Pedy.

A DELICIOUS, IMPRACTICAL STRAW

TIM TAM SLAM • AUSTRALIA

n 1958, a horse called Tim Tam won the Kentucky Derby. Six years later, the Australian biscuit manufacturer Arnott's named its (now) iconic cookie after the horse. Inspired by the British Penguin cookies, Tim Tams feature two biscuits, a creamy filling, and a chocolate coating. This structure, though seemingly unremarkable, gives Tim Tams the ability to become an edible straw.

After biting off opposite corners of the cookie, snackers can suck liquid—usually coffee or tea—through the center. The liquid dissolves the creamy filling and creates a straw-like passageway. This process happens quickly, so the molten cookie must be "slammed" before it falls apart. (Slamming means shoving the whole cookie—or biscuit, as Arnott's prefers—into your mouth.) The Tim Tam Slam has since spread internationally. According to astrophysicist Neil deGrasse Tyson, the sensation is "a moment in your life experience that you can chalk up and say, 'That was different from anything else I've ever experienced.'"

How to try it

The Tim Tam website has a handy Tim Tam locator to help you find retailers near you.

The Tim Tam cookie doubles as a straw—but only if bitten at both ends.

HOME OF THE LAST PUREBRED LIGURIAN BEES

KANGAROO ISLAND BEE SANCTUARY • AUSTRALIA

n the 1880s, a group of Italian queens moved to Kangaroo Island, about 10 miles (16 km) south of mainland Australia. With its Mediterranean-like climate and largely unspoiled wilderness, the sunny island was the perfect home for these Ligurian royalty, all of which were bees.

Today, Kangaroo Island is home to the last surviving purebred Ligurian bee population. The island's isolation, coupled with an 1885 act of Parliament that designated the land a bee sanctuary, has kept the bees from disease and interbreeding. Today, the Australian government prohibits outside bees, honey, pollen, and used beekeeping tools from entering the island to keep the bee lineage pure and the honey pristine.

The taste of the honey reflects the natural environment, changing with the season and the flowers the bees visit. On Kangaroo Island, the Ligurian bees that feed from eucalyptus flowers tend to produce intensely flavored, amber-hued honey. The sugar gum eucalyptus yields the island's most well-known variety, which is lighter in color, softer in flavor, and more floral than other eucalyptus honeys. In the spring, bees feed on flowers such as canola and capeweed and make more delicate honeys.

How to try it

Kangaroo Island is open to visitors, and there's no shortage of opportunities to taste Ligurian honey. Island Beehive, one of the biggest organic honey producers in Australia, offers beekeeping tours.

HONEY

Honey is one of the few known edible substances with an everlasting shelf life. Thanks to its high acidity, low moisture content, and naturally occurring hydrogen peroxide, honey has antibacterial properties that have been tapped to treat flesh wounds and embalm bodies since ancient times. Making honey, however, is punishing work. The typical honeybee lives for just six weeks, during which time it produces a literal drop of honey ($\frac{1}{12}$ of a teaspoon, or less than a gram). After flying miles to gather nectar, honeybees deposit the liquid, via a relay of bee-to-bee regurgitation, into a honeycomb within the hive. To thicken the fresh nectar, the bees must flap their wings like tiny fans, pulling water from the sugar syrup before it's sealed within the comb and ready to be harvested and enjoyed by humans around the world.

Bilbila Giyorgis

Ethiopia's holy honey church is occupied by bees that, according to local lore, took up residence shortly after the church was completed in the 5th century. Since then, the bees have been cared for by a continuous succession of priests. Their honey is considered holy by the congregation and is used to treat both physical and psychological ailments. Typically administered by the head clergy, the holy honey is either ingested or applied to the skin. Dark amber in color and studded with bits of grit, honeycomb, beeswax, and tiny dead bees, this honey is believed to help with conditions as serious as leprosy. The town of Lalibela, just south of Bilbila Giyorgis, is named after a king whose name means "the bees recognize his sovereignty."

White Kiawe Honey

Brought to the Big Island (also known as Hawaii) in 1823, the kiawe is a desert mesquite tree native to Ecuador and Peru. It grows up to 60 feet (18 m) tall and flowers throughout the year, providing year-round nourishment for the bees that make this smooth, creamy, rare white honey. The honey is 99 percent monofloral—which means the bees that make it feed almost exclusively off the kiawe flower. Some say that the aftertaste carries a hint of menthol, while others taste vanilla and almond.

Tupelo Honey

Tupelo honey hails from the wetlands of the Florida Panhandle, where Ogeechee tupelo gum trees grow. Their flowers are in bloom for just two to three weeks each year, during which time beekeepers scramble to bring their bees to the often-remote nectar collection sites. Some bring their hives in by truck; others transport them by boat or set them up on barges to reach the more secluded stands of trees in the swamps. Pure tupelo honey is fruity and buttery, with notes of pear and rose water, and a sweetness that inspired Van Morrison's song "Tupelo Honey."

Florida's Ogeechee tupelo trees are known for their high-maintenance honey, but they also produce limes.

Honeybee Fences

These fences are cropping up on farms in Africa and India as a humane way to keep elephants away from crops. Elephants are frightened by bees, whose stings can cause serious pain on the soft inside of their trunk. Even the sound of bees makes elephants retreat, so a wall of beehives makes an effective barrier against the otherwise unstoppable giants. The beehive fences are far cheaper than concrete or electric walls, and there is a massive added benefit: bees. The honeybees pollinate the crops and can produce enough honey for the farmers to sell as a cash crop.

Beehive fences in southern Kenya provide sweet protection from crop-eating elephants.

These towering, ancient trees once fed dinosaurs.

GIANT PINE CONE NUT

BUNYA • AUSTRALIA

Bunya pines are the stuff of legend. Roaming dinosaurs likely snacked on these towering evergreens, and the trees have been an Aboriginal food source for centuries. Native to Queensland, where they thrive in the state's wet, tropical soils, these pines can grow to more than 150 feet (46 m) tall, with a trunk that is more than 4 feet (1.2 m) in diameter. Every few years, they produce pine cones the shape of an egg and the size of a football. Each one weighs as much as 22 pounds (10 kg) and is filled with anywhere from 30 to 100 husk-covered edible nuts.

Traditionally, Aboriginal Australians threw massive celebrations every three years when the bunya nuts were ripe. Groups would put aside their differences to gather together and trade, arrange marriages, and, of course, feast on the bunya nut, which can be eaten raw, roasted, boiled, or ground into flour and baked. These festivals—and bunya-eating culture itself—faded away in the early 20th century as European colonizers relocated Aboriginal people to government settlements and started logging bunya pine timber.

Today, Queensland's Bunya Mountains are still home to the country's largest stand of these enormous ancient trees, and the bunya nut is making a slow culinary comeback. You can often find it at food markets featuring Indigenous foods (or "bush tucker," as it's called), and there's talk of reviving the traditional Aboriginal bunya nut festival.

How to try it
Something Wild, an Aboriginal foods purveyor in Adelaide Central Market, carries bunya nuts when they're ripe.

Bunya nuts are dry and crunchy with a taste similar to chestnuts.

FIELD RATION EATING DEVICE

FRED • AUSTRALIA

The "field ration eating device," a multipurpose gadget distributed to members of the Australian military, is either a great invention or utterly useless depending on whom you ask. Those who fall in the latter camp have been known to call it a "fucking ridiculous eating device." In either case, the acronym FRED is the tool's common moniker.

Introduced in the early 1940s, FRED has three functions: can opener, bottle opener, and spoon. On one end, a small blade is engineered to puncture the lid of a can and then saw around the perimeter until the top is liberated. (This function is considered FRED's best feature.) In the center, a hook-shaped opening works as a bottle opener, and the opposite end serves as a spoon. The spoon is where things get controversial: It's so shallow that using it to get food to your mouth is a perilous undertaking. Users agree that FRED opens rations with military precision, but using it to eat what's in the can is where FRED falls apart.

As of 2020, FRED was still standard issue in ration packs for the Australian military.

How to try it
FREDs are sold online, but genuine military-issue models are prized possessions earned through military service, so many owners are reluctant to part with them.

Try eating a bowl of soup with this.

Bush Tucker

The word *aboriginal* comes from the Latin *ab* and *origine*, which together mean "from the beginning." The Aboriginal people, along with the Torres Strait Islanders, were Australia's first people and have lived off the land and its incredible array of Indigenous resources for an estimated 65,000 years. For those who know where to look, the Australian bush can be a wonderland of obscure and edible delights, many of which have natural health benefits.

WITCHETTY GRUBS

These thick, white, thumb-size worms—the larvae of the cossid wood moth—are harvested from inside the woody roots of the witchetty bush. The grubs are about 15 percent protein and 20 percent fat, with a nutty flavor and crunchy skin when skewered and barbecued.

Crushed into a paste, witchettty grubs are used topically as a treatment for burns and wounds.

DEAD FINISH

The name of this spiky acacia tree refers to its most impressive trait, which is its ability to withstand a drought until the "dead finish"—the very end. As the last tree standing in times of scarcity, it's a highly valued bush food. Aboriginal Australians use its seeds to make seedcakes.

The tree's needles have antiseptic properties; when inserted into a wart, they can cause it to shrivel up and dry, making it easy to remove.

MACADAMIA NUT

While Hawaii produces about 70 percent of the world's macadamia nuts, a 2019 study revealed that all Hawaiian macadamia plants are likely the descendants of a single tree in the nut's native Queensland. This remarkable lack of genetic diversity makes macadamia crops vulnerable to disease and climate change. But Australia's wild macadamia population remains relatively robust, providing a genetic safety net for the crumbly, buttery nuts.

Macadamia nuts are packed with the mineral manganese.

FINGER LIME

Inside this oblong microcitrus are tiny, caviar-like bubbles that pop when chewed, releasing a tart explosion of lime juice. Native to the rain forests of South East Queensland, these elegant fruits have provided folate, potassium, and vitamins C and E to Aboriginal groups for thousands of years. Finger limes reach an average length of 3 inches (7 cm) and grow in shades of green, red, yellow, purple, and pink.

Finger limes are rich with antioxidants, which help fend off disease, and contain three times more vitamin C than a mandarin orange.

WATTLESEED

An edible type of acacia—a bush with hundreds of varieties—the wattleseed produces small, flat pods containing seeds that taste like a mix of chocolate, hazelnut, and coffee. Typically cooked in the pod or ground into powder (and then baked into "bush bread"), the seeds have been an Aboriginal staple food for at least 40,000 years.

Wattleseed is considered a superfood of the bush; it's loaded with protein, potassium, calcium, iron, and zinc. It also has a low glycemic index.

EDWARD ABBOTT

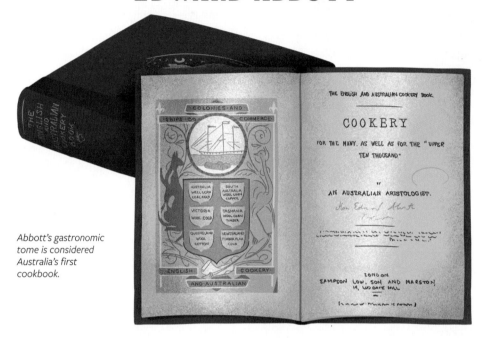

Abbott's gastronomic tome is considered Australia's first cookbook.

When Europeans colonized Australia's shores, many were wary of the island's native foods. Local ingredients were often seen as novelties or last resorts; most colonizers preferred to cook familiar dishes from home. Edward Abbott, an Australian of Canadian parentage, wanted to change that. In 1864, Abbott anonymously published *The English and Australian Cookery Book*, the world's first Australian cookbook. The byline read simply, "by an Australian aristologist," or an expert in cooking and fine dining.

At more than 300 pages, the book was an impressive tome with a big promise: "cookery for the many, as well as for the 'upper ten thousand.'" (The "upper ten thousand" is a 19th-century term for high society, coined by American writer Nathaniel Parker Willis in reference to the 10,000 wealthiest residents of New York City.)

Born in Sydney in 1801, Abbott lived most of his life on the island of Tasmania. He worked as a clerk for his father, a deputy judge advocate, before eventually becoming a newspaper publisher and landowner. An eccentric man, Abbott famously spent 30 years squabbling with colonial authorities over the land rights to a swamp and was notorious for having attacked the premier of Tasmania with an umbrella. It was only in his final years that Abbott turned to writing the cookbook that would become his greatest legacy.

The English and Australian Cookery Book is crammed full of European preparations, but Abbott also lovingly lays out recipes that make good use of often-overlooked native Australian ingredients. There's roast wombat and fricassee of kangaroo tail. There's also Slippery Bob, or breaded kangaroo brains fried in emu fat. There are recipes that call for echidna, turtle, ibis eggs, and "kangaroo ham."

Abbott's long and strange love letter to food includes quotes from Shakespeare, advice on smoking, musings on the British Empire, and multiple pages of advertisements. It is also practical and includes many recipes that might appeal to the modern chef. Fewer than 3,000 copies were printed, and while Abbott planned more books, he died in 1869. His cookbook was largely forgotten until its recent sesquicentennial, when it was reprinted and found a new generation of admirers.

AN INNOVATIVE INDIGENOUS MARKET

SOMETHING WILD • AUSTRALIA

How to try it

Something Wild is stall 55 at the Adelaide Central Market, open Tuesday through Saturday.

Within Adelaide's lively Central Market is Something Wild, one of Australia's premier purveyors of Indigenous Australian foods and beverages. The company supplies its food to restaurants, caters events, and, at their outpost in the Central Market, sells their Indigenous goods straight to the consumer.

In the meat case, there's kangaroo, emu, and camel. As an alternative protein, there are green ants, sold either dried or in a bottle of Green Ant Gin. Beyond sourcing Indigenous ingredients, Something Wild excels at giving these traditional foods a contemporary twist. Wattleseed lager, for example, is made from the seeds of Australian acacia plants, while recipes for Wallaby Stroganoff and Kangaroo Chili con Carne can be found on the company's website.

Part-owner and General Manager Daniel Motlop, himself Aboriginal and Torres Strait Islander, makes a priority of hiring Aboriginal employees. He hopes that in spreading Indigenous cuisine, he can also deliver economic benefits to Australia's Indigenous community.

A WHIMSICAL FRUIT PLAYGROUND

BUNDABERG BOTANIC GARDENS • AUSTRALIA

How to try it

The town of Bundaberg is a 4.5-hour train ride, or 1-hour flight, north of Brisbane, Queensland's capital. Bundaberg is also famous for its rum and (non-alcoholic) ginger beer.

The Bundaberg Botanic Gardens are an incredible, edible playground. Visitors to these grounds, located on Australia's Queensland coast, are welcome to roam and pluck freely from the offerings—including some impressive and unusual fruits.

Among the bounty is the fabled peanut butter tree, or *Bunchosia glandulifera*. During the Australian winter (June–August), these trees yield bright red-orange fruit that tastes and smells like peanut butter, and even has a similar texture.

Other garden residents include the fruit of the rain forest plum tree, the prickly and citrusy soursop fruit, the bulburin nut, and the panama berry—whose taste has been likened to "fairy floss," otherwise known as cotton candy. Those up for a taste adventure should seek out the miracle berry. This West African fruit contains a protein called miraculin that makes sour foods taste sweet: To experience the science, simply eat a berry, then bite a lemon.

WORM-FILLED, COCONUT-FLAVORED TREE TUMOR

BUSH COCONUT • AUSTRALIA

This "coconut" is neither coco nor nut—it's technically a tree tumor.

A grub-like coccid insect, usually *Cystococcus pomiformis*, settles on the branch of a desert bloodwood tree. She—and it's always a she—irritates the tree until it defends itself by sprouting a knobby tumor known as a gall. The gall grows around the grub, who spends the rest of her life within the fortress, drinking tree sap and mating with male grubs via a tiny air hole.

How to try it

Alice Springs Desert Park in the Northern Territory is a great place to see (and taste) a bush coconut.

Together, the gall and the worm form the bush coconut, sometimes called the less appetizing "bloodwood gall." Lumpy and small, this faux coconut is named for the gall's coconut-flavored flesh. Foragers typically eat both gall and worm, which has a sweet, juicy taste. In the northern savanna woodlands, the bush coconut has long been a source of nutrition for Aboriginal Australians.

WATERMELON ATHLETICS

MELON FESTIVAL • AUSTRALIA

How to try it

The Chinchilla Melon Festival takes place every other year in February.

Watermelon skiers get pulled down a slippery track at the 2015 Chinchilla Melon Festival.

Watermelon skiing is the main event at Chinchilla's biennial Melon Festival. Aspiring fruit athletes don a helmet, slip each foot into a hollowed-out watermelon, and hold on tight. The rope they grasp is held on either end by volunteers, who pull the skiers down a long, slippery tarp strewn with smashed melons until they belly flop (common) or make it to the end of the line (rare). Those who are truly ambitious can attempt the Melon Iron Man, which includes four events: watermelon skiing, pip spitting, watermelon bungee (four people struggling within a big elastic band to retrieve melons in competing directions), and a watermelon race (a 984-feet/300-m race while holding a 17-pound/8-kg watermelon).

The Curious Case of August Engelhardt, Leader of a Coconut Cult

In 1902, 26-year-old August Engelhardt set sail from Germany with a suitcase full of books and a peculiar mission: to establish a new Edenic order on the sunbaked shores of Papua New Guinea. Engelhardt's formula for happiness was simple: abandon earthly possessions, move to a tropical island, become a nudist, and eat only coconuts.

From his newly purchased island home, Engelhardt established a cult called Sonnenorden, or the Order of the Sun, a religion that worshipped the sun, which he saw as the ultimate giver of life, and coconuts, which he believed to be the tropical transubstantiation of God's very flesh. The principles of Sonnenorden are meticulously outlined in Engelhardt's collection of writings, *A Carefree Future: The New Gospel*. The obsessive text contains page after page of wild theories that extol the virtues of the coconut and adoring, devotional poems with titles like "The Coconut Spirit" and "How to Become a Coconut Palm."

Engelhardt's coconut obsession was rooted in a thin theory. The coconut, with its spherical shape and furry shell, is the fruit that most resembles the human head, and therefore the most ideal fruit for man's consumption. According to Engelhardt, coconuts are "vegetal human heads, and they alone are the proper human nourishment." But despite his devotion, Engelhardt's cult attracted no more than 15 disciples, all of whom were German. Together, in their quiet life of island devotion, they sunbathed for hours, swam in the cool waters of the Pacific, and ate their holy fruit.

Alas, paradise was not without its perils, and Engelhardt's cult was short-lived. Unaccustomed to the warm climate and stringent coconut diet, several of his followers died, and others contracted malaria. Engelhardt himself grew seriously ill, and despite his recovery, the remaining cult members disbanded and returned to Germany. Engelhardt blamed his followers' illnesses on their deviation from the coconut diet.

In response to the cult's ruinous outcome, the German government issued a stern warning banning anyone else from joining Engelhardt on the island. Engelhardt was left alone, scribbling lengthy treatises on the healing powers of plants and studying the dietary habits of the island's natives. An emaciated nudist, he was treated as something of a sideshow by visiting tourists who would occasionally ask him to pose for photographs.

Little is known about the eventual fate of Engelhardt. It is widely assumed that he died in his mid-40s, nearly 17 years after setting foot on the island. While no trace of a gravesite or memorial remains, his body is believed to have been discovered on the shores of Papua New Guinea in May 1919, his legs riddled with ulcers.

August Engelhardt believed coconuts were the secret to everlasting health and communion with the divine.

THE WORLD'S MOST STUNNING

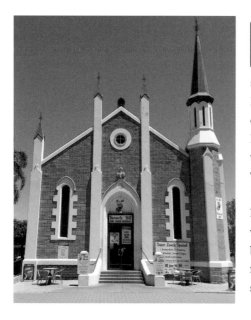

In the coastal city of Port Pirie, housed within a 19th-century stone church, is a most glorious outpost of Barnacle Bill—a popular South Australian seafood chain. Outside, the church spires loom over Barnacle Bill's logo: a portly sailor balancing a tray of fish on one hand and a ship's wheel on the other. Inside, the pulpit is now a deep-frying counter, and the pews have been replaced by tables and a salad bar. The former Congregational church, which opened in 1879, shut its doors around 1991, and the building lay abandoned for five years. It was about to be razed when the current owners, Kevin and Kym Spirou, bought the building and turned it into a Barnacle Bill franchise—entering it into the pantheon of the most stunning fast-food restaurants in the world.

STARBUCKS NINENZAKA YASAKA CHAYA (KYOTO, JAPAN): Within this two-story, 100-year-old town house is a Starbucks with tatami floor seating, where visitors must remove their shoes before they caffeinate.

LINDA MAR TACO BELL (PACIFICA, CALIFORNIA): This 1960s wooden building is now a beachfront Taco Bell with surfboard parking, an indoor-outdoor fireplace, and pristine ocean views.

Fast-Food Restaurants

MCDONALD'S IMPERIAL (PORTO, PORTUGAL): Imperial, once an iconic 1930s Portuguese coffeehouse, now houses an art deco McDonald's with vaulted ceilings, a soaring stained-glass window, and crystal chandeliers.

MCDONALD'S (BATUMI, GEORGIA): The winner of an architecture award, this futuristic McDonald's is covered in 460 glass panels and surrounded by a reflective pool.

Delicious Diaspora

CHINESE IN AUSTRALIA

The Chinese have a long history of immigration to Australia. While some historians believe that Chinese contact with the continent predated Captain Cook's 18th-century arrival, it was the gold rushes of the 1850s and '60s that brought an estimated 40,000 Chinese to Australia's shores. Largely indentured and contract laborers, the goldfield-bound men were met with European resentment and racism. The Chinese formed enclave-like camps, where they tended small plots of fruits and vegetables to feed themselves and supplement their income. European miners, who had little access to fresh food, bought the produce, and when the gold rush ended, many Chinese immigrants found their next opportunity in market gardening—growing produce on a small scale for sale at local markets.

By the late 19th century, Chinese-owned market gardens had spread across Australia, especially in the growing suburbs. The Chinese cornered much of the produce market and opened restaurants and green grocery stores. In 1901, when Australia became a federation, the government passed the White Australia Policy, which discriminated against all non-European immigrants. But there was a loophole—Chinese cooks were allowed into the country. Australia, while fostering a deep-seated racism against the Chinese, had developed a fondness for their cooking, and by the turn of the 20th century, approximately one in every three cooks in Australia was from China.

These days, Chinese food remains one of the most popular cuisines in Australia. While traditional Chinese market gardens are now largely lost to time and industrialization, one historic garden remains in La Perouse, a suburb of Sydney. Here, Chinese farmers have been cultivating the land since the 1870s, and for the last 80 years, it has been passed generationally through three families. They work the crops by hand as they have since the beginning. The heritage-listed site has been under threat, most recently from a cemetery expansion project, but locals have fought hard to protect this historical plot.

Melbourne's Chinatown, established in the 1850s, is considered the oldest Chinatown in the southern hemisphere.

THE WORLD'S OLDEST EMU FARM

FREE RANGE EMU FARM • AUSTRALIA

When Australia began granting licenses to raise emus commercially in 1987, Kip and Charmian Venn received one of the first and used it to open Free Range Emu Farm. Endemic to Australia and valued for millennia by Aboriginal Australians, the enormous flightless birds were an exciting new industry that promised lean meat, healthy oil, and eggs eight times larger than a hen's. Emu farms sprang up across the country, but demand for emu products did not keep pace, and many farms closed.

Today, emus are making a commercial comeback. Chefs covet their dark, glossy eggs for their impressive size, rich flavor, and deep-orange yolks. Raising emus for their meat, which many say tastes like beef, is a far more sustainable enterprise than raising cows. (Emus are rapid breeders, laying multiple clutches of six to ten eggs throughout the breeding season.) But it's emu oil, made from the bird's fat, that's driving the growth. Emu oil has long been used by Aboriginal people to treat skin conditions. Although modern clinical testing is still in early stages, emu oil has gained fandom across the world thanks to its purported ability to moisturize skin, protect against sun damage, and treat burns, scars, and wounds.

At Free Range Emu Farm, now the oldest emu farm in Australia, visitors can see a hundred or so emus at any given time. The birds breed and lay eggs from April to August, hatch from July to October, and run through acres of pasture land all year long.

How to try it

Free Range Emu Farm is located at 681 Clackline Road in Toodyay, Western Australia. It is open to the public every day from 10 a.m. to 4 p.m., and visitors can purchase emu meat, eggs, oil, feathers, and even live chicks.

Emus are the second tallest bird in the world, outranked only by the ostrich.

How Australia Came to Have the Largest Feral Camel Population in the World

In the 19th century, British colonists were stumped by the desert expanse of Australia's vast interior. Was it flat or mountainous? Dry or a giant inland sea? European modes of transportation, like horses, weren't suited to the new terrain and early expeditions were unsuccessful. But a solution arrived from elsewhere in the empire: Camels, which the British encountered in colonial India, were an ideal solution for traversing the dry, rugged island.

In 1858, the Victorian Exploration Committee tasked horse dealer George Landells with recruiting camels and their drivers from India and bringing them to Australia. Over the next few decades, an estimated 20,000 camels were imported to the continent, along with about 3,000 camel handlers, who together enabled the settlement of Australia's interior. The hardy, steady animals could trek for hours under brutal sun with little water, and they became integral to the overland network of goods, labor, and infrastructure. But the Muslim migrants—dubbed "Afghan cameleers" by white Australians, despite not always being from Afghanistan—were the target of rampant discrimination.

On January 1, 1901, Australia became an independent country and enacted a set of new, decidedly racist immigration laws. Collectively called the White Australia policy, these laws halted almost all nonwhite immigration, and by the 1920s, the vast majority of cameleers had fled the country. Left behind, some of the camels were shot under the South Australian Camels Destruction Act of 1925. Others were released into the wild, where their descendants continue to live today.

Australia is now home to the largest feral camel population in the world, with estimates around one million. Left to roam, the animals pose a threat to delicate native ecosystems and water supplies. The Australian government has sponsored aerial camel culls in which feral camels are shot down by helicopter. But many argue for another solution: use the animals as food.

The Australian market for camel meat is growing, but its success hinges on capturing the camels and transporting them to processing facilities, which is expensive. The lean meat, which many people liken to a cross between lamb and beef, is sold to many Middle Eastern and North African countries and their diaspora communities. The animals are typically processed at an abattoir, and the meat is distributed to butchers both domestic and international.

Indian camels and their drivers were brought to Australia for work in the late 19th century, but when the drivers fled the country, the remaining camels ran wild.

WILD RICE CONSERVATION ART

MOMI-2010 • AUSTRALIA

Wander into a certain part of the Australian bush and you'll encounter enormous carvings blasted into the terrain. Lizards and insects crawl along the sides of granite boulders and below, carved into the floodplain, is a gigantic 269-foot-long (82 m) stalk of wild rice.

Found in the Mount Bundey area of the Northern Territory, this is the work of Mitsuaki Tanabe, a Japanese sculptor who dedicated much of his art to the importance of wild rice. (He called his wild rice sculptures "Momi.") Tanabe's works dot the globe, often depicting seeds or other organisms that help raise awareness about biodiversity. While working in Australia in the 1990s and early 2000s, he dreamed up a new project.

With the cooperation of the Australian government, Tanabe began work on these carvings in 2010. For ten years, he traveled to Australia during the dry season to work on the project. Tragically, Tanabe passed away before he could finish the work, but his son, Takamitsu Tanabe, along with some sculptor friends, completed the pieces in 2016.

How to try it
The carvings are located to the north of the Arnhem Highway. The wetlands are flooded for several months of the year, so check the ground condition before planning a visit.

NEW ZEALAND

LAMB MASQUERADING AS GOOSE

COLONIAL GOOSE • NEW ZEALAND

A plump goose with its elegant neck, roasted until golden brown, was a hallmark of the English holiday table. When homesick 19th-century British colonizers in New Zealand found themselves craving goose dinner, they had to get creative. With the island's lack of geese and preponderance of sheep, inspiration struck: Why not make a goose from a sheep?

Colonial goose, now a classic New Zealand dish, is a stuffed and marinated leg of lamb that's trussed up to look like a goose. While most recipes tell you to debone the shoulder, cooks serious about faking poultry leave in a length of shank bone to approximate the goose's neck and head. Stuffed with a mixture of breadcrumbs, herbs, onions, and honey, the lamb is tied up tight and marinated in a red wine mixture, which makes the outside glossy and goose-like. Goose on the outside, lamb on the inside, this wacky roast is sliced like a loaf of bread and is every bit as delicious as it is confusing.

How to try it
Colonial goose is served at restaurants during New Zealand's midwinter festivities, which take place in June and often feature English-inspired spreads.

UNDERGROUND MAORI OVEN

HĀNGI • NEW ZEALAND

How to try it

Whakarewarewa is a living Maori village located in the geothermal area of Rotorua. Open to visitors every day from 8:30 a.m. to 5 p.m., the village heats its hāngi with geothermal power. Residents also harness the heat of the mineral pool to boil vegetables and seafood.

The Maori people landed on the shores of New Zealand around the 13th century, likely hailing from central-eastern Polynesia. With them came a method of underground cooking known as hāngi.

This traditional fire pit technique requires digging a large hole, heating volcanic stones in a large fire, and placing the hot stones in the bottom. Early hāngi masters would set kai (food) that they'd foraged, hunted, or grown on top of the stones and then cover everything in foliage and soil to trap the steam inside. A few hours later, they had tender, smoked meat and vegetables that emanated an earthy, almost ashen aroma. In areas of New Zealand rife with geothermal activity, such as Rotorua, a region now known for Maori culture, hāngi masters employed natural springs to heat their stones.

Historically, the Maori people roasted fish, shellfish, chicken, and turtle alongside banana, sweet potato, and other starches in the hāngi. (When they arrived in New Zealand and encountered its enormous flightless birds, their ovens grew larger.) Today, hāngi masters also include pork, lamb, pumpkin, cabbage, and stuffing.

The centuries-old hāngi method of fire cooking uses volcanic stones.

When the Maori First Settled New Zealand, They Hunted Flightless, 500-Pound Birds

Before the arrival of humans, New Zealand was a land of birds. With no large carnivores on the island, an avian hierarchy flourished, from the burrowing muttonbirds to the gigantic but now extinct Haast's eagle, which perched at the top of the food chain. And then there were the moas: nine species of flightless birds, the smallest the size of turkeys, the largest 10 feet (3 m) tall and more than 500 pounds (227 kg). During its time, the giant moa was the tallest bird to walk the earth, and moa species proliferated across New Zealand, inhabiting different ecosystems suited to their size and diets.

The hierarchy was upended in the 13th century with the arrival of the early Polynesians, now known as Maori. Starting in Asia, most likely Taiwan, they traveled across the Pacific by canoe for thousands of years, populating islands along the way. New Zealand was the final stop, and as the last major uninhabited landmass to be settled by humans, it proved to be fertile hunting grounds.

Without wing bones, moas couldn't fly from their new foes. But they did have large leg bones, which has led to speculation that they were fast runners with a powerful kick. The newly arrived Maori had yet to develop bows, and so researchers have used archaeological and anthropological findings to piece together how these birds were hunted. Some believe that the Maori used snares to snag their prey, while others think they had help from dogs that either hunted moas themselves or drove the birds to locations where they could be cornered and killed.

After a successful hunt, Maori base camps functioned as butchering sites. (Enormous quantities of leftover bones have been found buried with the trash from these campsites.) While smaller moas could be carried away whole, hunters dealt with the 500-pounders by separating and carrying away only their meat-heavy legs. Researchers believe that the meat was cooked underground, likely in a hāngi fire pit, using koromiko wood as kindling.

Before the arrival of the Polynesians, an estimated 160,000 moas roamed New Zealand. Within 150 years, they were gone—annihilated in what a University of Missouri study calls "the most rapid, human-facilitated megafauna extinction documented to date." The moas had few natural predators (other than the giant eagles), and it's possible they weren't very afraid of humans. The birds laid few eggs—only one or two every breeding season—and took a long time to reach maturity. Hunted faster than they could reproduce, the moas were soon extinct.

When British naturalist Richard Owen confirmed the existence of moas in 1839 from a single bone, his revelation sparked something of a moa craze. The birds were as unique as the kiwi, as extinct as the dodo, and more monumental than any other avian species. Twenty years later, a workman unearthed the largest moa egg ever known: the Kaikoura egg, which had been nestled next to a body in a Maori grave. It likely weighed almost 9 pounds (4 kg) when fresh, and it is now on display at the Te Papa museum in Wellington, New Zealand.

The largest eagle known to exist once hunted the moose-sized moa in New Zealand.

A feral pig messes with the nest of a white-capped albatross on Auckland Island.

The Livestock Living at the End of the World

In the spring of 1866, the USS *General Grant* struck the western cliffside of Auckland Island, a remote, subantarctic mass of rocky land in the middle of the South Pacific. Trapped inside a rocky cavern, the ship began its fateful plunge into the frigid water, dragging most of its passengers down with it. Things looked bleak for the few who survived, but on the island, the castaways found a surprising resource that helped keep them alive for 18 months: a herd of long-haired, narrow-faced pigs.

The origin story of the strange swine begins in the early 19th century, when whalers and sealers sailed to the Auckland Islands—more than 360 miles (579 km) south of the mainland of New Zealand—to hunt the fur seals, sea lions, and whales drawn to its cold shores. According to lore, the whalers and sealers intentionally mischarted the islands to keep their hunting grounds secret. That cartographical distortion had devastating effects. Within the span of a century, sailors on at least nine ships, believing themselves to be in open seas, ended up smashing into the islands' cliffs.

In 1806, when British mariner Abraham Bristow happened upon the archipelago, he worried about the well-being of future castaways. A year later, he returned with a shipful of pigs and released them on the island. More pigs were plopped ashore in 1843, and again in the 1890s. By the end of the 19th century, the feral pig population was thriving. And while they did indeed feed a few castaways, the pigs also scarfed down plant roots, albatross eggs, and penguins, and generally began to wreak havoc on the island's flora and fauna. According to New Zealand's Department of Conservation (DOC), they're largely responsible for the disappearance of more than 30 native bird species.

Following the pigs, goats were released in multiple locations, then a colony of rabbits and a small herd of cattle. For nearly two centuries, the stranded animals lived in isolation with few natural predators, running completely unchecked until the DOC decided to intervene. In 1991, a sharp-shooting crew was deployed to kill cattle, and by 1992, goats had been eradicated from the main Auckland Island. To get rid of rabbits, they dropped poison pellets in the grazing areas.

But eradication efforts then paused in deference to another type of conservation: livestock biodiversity. In the face of climate change, maintaining a diversity of breeds able to adapt to different weather, temperatures, soil compositions, and overall environments is critical. As agriculture increasingly prioritizes size, yield, and productivity, the number of minority breeds grows smaller and smaller. The Auckland Island animals, which developed in relative isolation, showed incredible adaptive behaviors. The Auckland Island goat is among the largest in New Zealand, while the pigs are small and markedly athletic. When the rabbits ate most of the grass on the island, cattle were driven to higher ground and steep cliff faces in pursuit of vegetation. (Some claim they even ate seaweed.)

The most valuable trait of some of these animals, however, isn't one they've acquired but one they lack. Thanks to 200 years of seclusion, the Auckland Island pigs had never been exposed to the viruses and bacteria common in modern pigs—pathogens that could potentially be transmitted to humans and have been a major obstacle to xenotransplantation, or the grafting of cells from animals for use in human therapies. On the mainland of New Zealand, biotechnology firm Living Cell Technologies (LCT) retrieved a small herd of the feral pigs and began breeding them in a secure, high-tech quarantine facility. These pigs are worth hundreds of thousands of dollars.

As of 2019, most of the Auckland Islands are free of the nonnative pests, but the main island continues to bear feral pig and cat populations. In 2018, conservation minister Eugenie Sage pledged NZ$2 million to complete plans for restoring the vast, rugged island to its predator-free status. If all goes according to plan, within the next decade the pigs will disappear—from the Auckland Islands, but not from the world—and the albatross will be left to safely nest, the penguins to roam, and the plants to grow.

NEW ZEALAND'S FINEST BIVALVE

BLUFF OYSTER • NEW ZEALAND

How to try it

Beginning in March, Bluff oysters are everywhere around New Zealand, until they run out. Bluff's festival is held in May, but be sure to check for the exact dates—and to make sure that the year's harvest went well.

You'd be hard-pressed to find the famed wild Bluff oysters outside their native New Zealand. The big, sweet, minerally mollusks are available only between March and August, when they're harvested from the ice-cold Foveaux Strait between the town of Bluff and Stewart Island—a perilous stretch of rough, unpredictable waters that has taken many lives over the years. The annual harvest, which is about ten million oysters, falls short of the tremendous demand. (Helicopter couriers are not uncommon.) To guarantee a taste of the hyper-local, hard-won oyster, many people travel to the tiny town of Bluff for its annual oyster festival.

Bluff is the southernmost port town on mainland New Zealand, and its citizens are the hearty descendants of whalers, traders, and missionaries. They speak with uncommon Southland accents that feature a strong Scottish burr, and only about 2,000 of them live in the town. On oyster festival day in May, well-heeled Aucklanders arrive by morning flight, gorge themselves on the seasonal bounty, and depart in the evening. Adhering to the town's heritage, the festival kicks off with the oysters being "piped in" (brought in on a platter, serenaded by bagpipes). Next, a man in a tam-o'-shanter and tartan trews performs the traditional "Ode to the Oyster," exclaiming, "We put you on a pedestal, O Oyster from the Sea." What follows is a quirky mix of oyster eating (regular and competitive), a maritime-themed fashion show, and liters and liters of beer and wine.

Plates of New Zealand's prized shellfish at the Bluff Oyster and Food Festival.

AN ODE TO 16TH-CENTURY LIQUOR PROOFING

GUNPOWDER RUM • NEW ZEALAND

In the 18th century, when sailors in the British Royal Navy wanted to test the potency of their daily allotment of rum, they employed a 16th-century technique: Mix a pinch of gunpowder into a small amount of liquor and strike a match. If the wet gunpowder still caught flame, it was "proof" that the spirit had sufficient levels

of alcohol. If it didn't, the sailor knew that it was watered-down swill. (The liquor term *proof* comes from this practice.) "Navy strength" is generally defined as 57 percent alcohol by volume (ABV), which is the dividing line between booze that will and will not burn gunpowder.

In New Zealand, this fiery practice inspired the Smoke & Oakum Manufactory's Gunpowder Rum, made from a secret recipe that incorporates the three main elements of traditional gunpowder: saltpeter (potassium nitrate), sulfur, and charcoal. Blended with nicotine-free tobacco and chili peppers, the dark rum has notes of smoke and chocolate, and flavors of spice and molasses. (It should be noted that potassium nitrate, which is occasionally used as a preservative, is dangerous when consumed in large quantities.)

Smoke & Oakum's Gunpowder Rum is an homage to the dark, full-bodied rums consumed by most sailors—be they navy men, pirates, or smugglers—centuries ago. These rums were produced without standardization and bottled in whatever was available, which is why Smoke & Oakum's Gunpower Rum comes in a motley crew of bottle shapes, all wrapped in brown paper. At 51.6 percent ABV, however, this rum is just shy of navy strength.

How to try it

Smoke & Oakum's Gunpowder Rum is released in limited batches. Check the store locator on the company's website to find a retail location, then contact that store to be sure the rum is in stock.

PACIFIC ISLANDS

FIJI ASPARAGUS

DURUKA • FIJI

In the swampy marshes of Fiji, a nation comprised of hundreds of islands, you'll find the tall, grassy stems of *Saccharum edule*, a cane shoot closely related to sugarcane. Peel back the slim green sheaths and you'll find duruka. Nicknamed Fiji asparagus for its resemblance to the slender vegetable, duruka is actually the flower of the cane shoot. It has a sweet flavor, reminiscent of corn.

Duruka is a favorite ingredient in curries. About 40 percent of Fiji's population is of Indian ancestry, descendants of the indentured Indian laborers who worked the sugar plantations in the late 19th century. The fleshy seasonal flower holds up well in soups and stews but is also excellent roasted over charcoal or simmered in coconut milk.

How to try it

Duruka season is in April and May. Vendors at the Suva Municipal Market, in Fiji's capital, sell it in huge wrapped bundles.

YAM HOUSES

BWEMA • PAPUA NEW GUINEA

How to try it

Yam houses can be found throughout the Trobriand Islands. The harvest takes place from June through August and is traditionally accompanied by a festival, called Milamala (though the festival is contingent upon the success of the harvest).

Off the coast of Papua New Guinea is Kiriwina, the largest of the Trobriand Islands, where yams represent wealth, prestige, and power. The tubers lie at the heart of Trobriand cultural life, and are so important that they're given houses of their own. Known as bwema, these stylized wooden structures are arranged in concentric circles, with the innermost houses typically decorated with intricate carvings etched into logs painted red, white, and black.

Nearly every Trobriand household has a yam house, as well as a garden, called a kaymata, used exclusively for growing yams. Yams are not easy to cultivate. They require frequent thinning and can be grown only once a year. Trobriand Islanders sometimes call on the help of yam-growing spells performed by a towosi, or a professional gardening magician. The local culture revolves around a traditional system of giving and receiving, so the yams are always grown for someone else in the community. When they're ready, they are transported, sometimes in a parade accompanied by a dance, to the recipient's yam house.

There is little life the tuber does not touch: yams pay land rents, celebrate weddings, bless births, and structure the calendar year, which revolves around the yam harvest. When someone dies, family members save up yams for months, in yam houses, and give them out during mortuary feasts.

Climate change has made Trobriand yam-collecting on the island of Kiriwina more difficult, and more meaningful, than ever.

The tall, skinny storage houses are built of logs and raised high above the ground. Their walls have plenty of open space to optimize air circulation, allowing the yams inside to stay fresh for months. In a show of power, village chiefs have the biggest, most decorated yam houses.

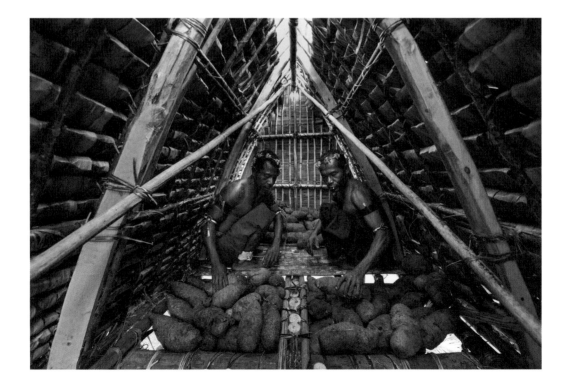

VOLCANIC EGG INCUBATOR

EGG FIELDS OF SAVO • SOLOMON ISLANDS

From Honiara, the capital of the Solomon Islands, Savo Island is reached by a 90-minute boat ride across Iron Bottom Sound—so named for the dozens of ships and planes that sank in it during World War II. The 11-square-mile (28-sq-km) island is home to an active, steaming volcano that attracts megapodes—chicken-size black birds that make use of the volcanic heat to incubate their eggs.

In the sand fields surrounding the nearby village of Panueli, megapodes arrive at dawn to lay and bury their eggs. The volcanic earth keeps the eggs warm, which frees the mother birds of their brooding duties. But when the mothers leave, men from the village arrive, digging more than three feet down to unearth the birds' nests. They dig by hand, taking care not to damage the eggs, and wrap them in banana leaves for safekeeping. Afterward, women fill in the holes and level the sand.

Megapode eggs are relatively large—about the size of duck eggs—and each one is worth about $2 in the local economy. They were once abundant around Panueli, but overharvesting has led to an unsustainable system. As of 2017, only one egg-laying sand field remains in the area, and the yield is sparse. Visitors can still come at dawn to witness the incredible egg-laying scene, but they should abstain from purchasing or eating the eggs.

How to try it

The most common way to get to Savo Island is by boat from Visale, a town at Guadalcanal's northern tip. From there, the trip takes about 30 minutes, so day-trippers eager to see megapodes lay their eggs should depart before dawn. Those who would rather arrive the night before can stay at the Sunset Lodge, which is the main accommodation on the vehicle-less island.

Megapode eggs are buried deep in the sand so they can be warmed by the volcanic heat of Savo Island.

GIANT *Egg-Shaped* WONDERS

WINLOCK EGG (WINLOCK, WASHINGTON, USA)

Named the "World's Largest Egg" in 1989 by Ripley's Believe It or Not!, this colossal structure has been built four times. In the 1920s, to celebrate the area's booming egg industry, the egg was constructed out of canvas stretched over a wooden frame. That egg was replaced by a plastic version in the 1940s and a fiberglass model in the 1960s. The current edition, made of cement, was built in 1991. It is 12 feet (3.7 m) long and weighs 1,200 pounds (544 kg).

THE EGGS OF MERRY BAY (VIKURLAND, ICELAND)

In 2009, Icelandic artist Sigurður Guðmundsson created 34 enormous granite eggs in honor of the 34 species of native bird that nest in eastern Iceland. Perched atop a slab of concrete, each stone specimen accurately depicts the shape, patterns, and colors of the bird egg that it represents.

RIVERSIDE ROUNDABOUT (LOS ANGELES, CALIFORNIA, USA)

In the Cypress Park neighborhood of LA is a traffic roundabout filled with granite egg sculptures, each containing a human face. The 2017 installation is not only a visually engaging art piece but was also designed as a stormwater retention landscape. Each face is sculpted from the image of an actual member of the local community, randomly selected from hundreds of applicants.

SOLAR EGG (KIRUNA, SWEDEN)

In one of the northernmost towns in
Sweden, a 15-foot (4.5-m) golden egg
stands in the middle of a field of snow,
reflecting the white expanse from
69 panes of glass. Inside, the egg is a
sauna where local residents can bask
in the heat, relax, and talk. Heated by
wood, it seats eight people and is free
of charge. The egg sauna was a gift from
the Swedish government as repayment
for massive sinkholes they left in the
area while extracting iron ore. Beginning
in 2017, the Solar Egg embarked on an
extended tour with stops in Copenhagen,
Paris, and Minneapolis.

DALÍ THEATRE-MUSEUM (FIGUERES, SPAIN)

From the outside, this museum looks like
a dream-logic breakfast castle, complete
with giant eggs on the parapets and loaves
of bread decorating the walls. Designed
by Salvador Dalí himself, the egg fortress
is home to the world's largest collection
of the Spanish artist's work.

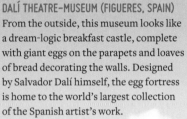

SHRUB-BASED TINGLE TEA

KAVA TEA • VANUATU

How to try it

Port-Vila, Vanuatu's capital, is filled with kava bars. El Manaro is a rustic option, with open-air thatch-roofed seating areas and a communal atmosphere. A recommended dose for newcomers is three to four coconut shells. (Locals might have twice this.)

Kava is typically served in a coconut shell.

t's just after dusk on the island of Espiritu Santo in the Melanesian archipelago of Vanuatu. Before grabbing dinner in the stalls of the Luganville marketplace, local men, expats, and visiting divers walk into a thatched hut on the hillside above. Inside, there's a wooden counter next to a large, sink-like basin and behind the counter, a length of stretched pantyhose with a giant lump in the bottom dripping gray fluid into a bowl below.

One by one people line up, chug some of the gray liquid from half a coconut shell, rinse their mouths with water, and spit a few times into the basin. Then they all take seats on benches, lean back, and start to tingle. This is the nightly Vanuatu ritual for kava, a mildly psychoactive drink made from the root of the *Piper methysticum* shrub. It creates a warm anesthetic feeling, starting at the lips and radiating outward, enlivened by little spikes of euphoria. Kava contains 15 or more active compounds, known as kavalactones, and Vanuatu is known for having the most potent varieties.

Kava has a long history across the Pacific—from Hawaii to Tonga to Micronesia—though some consider Vanuatu its spiritual home. Its usage ranges from casual relaxation to medicinal and ceremonial purposes. Modern purveyors prepare fresh kava root by grinding it against a rough coral cone, though traditionally it was prepared by women who chewed pieces before spitting them into a woven sieve.

Canada

WESTERN CANADA · EASTERN CANADA

WESTERN CANADA

A TOWERING FIBERGLASS DUMPLING

THE WORLD'S LARGEST PYROGY • ALBERTA

How to try it

Take Highway 28 to Glendon, about two hours northeast of Edmonton. It's located in Pyrogy Park, which is on Pyrogy Drive.

n the small village of Glendon, a 27-foot (8.2-m) dumpling weighing 6,000 pounds (2,721 kg) stands in the middle of a community park, a mammoth fork stabbed through the filling. The Giant Pyrogy, as it's known, is one of the "Giants of the Prairies," a collection of massive sculptures scattered across western Canada (among them "Giant Potato" in Vauxhall and "World's Largest Mushroom" in Vilna). Unveiled in 1991, the sculpture is Glendon's tribute to the eastern European

THE EXPANSIVE WORLD OF

Scottish Clootie Dumpling

Vietnamese Bánh Bao

Uzbek Chuchvara

Bolivian Salteña

Chinese Shumai

Indian Modak

dumpling—one of the most popular imported foods in Canada. According to Johnnie Doonanco, who dreamed up the sculpture when working as the town's mayor, the original design needed a little help. "People went by and they responded that it looked like a cow pie or something," Doonanco said, so he added a fork to let them know it was a pyrogy.

Next to the Giant Pyrogy sculpture is a café (one of two restaurants in Glendon) serving smaller, edible versions of the fiberglass dumpling.

Dumplings

American Baked Apple Dumpling

Russian Pelmeni

Italian Raviolo Gigante

Georgian Khinkali

Turkish Manti

West African Kenkey

DRINKABLE SPAGHETTI ALLE VONGOLE

CAESAR • ALBERTA

How to try it

The Calgary Inn is now the Westin, but they still serve a Caesar (with cherrywood-smoked tomato puree).

Alle vongolle (spaghetti with clams) is a traditional Italian preparation that Walter Chell, manager of the Calgary Inn, ate in Venice and never forgot. In 1969, when asked to create a signature drink for the inn's new Italian restaurant, Chell made a clam spaghetti–inspired cocktail. He began with a base of mashed "clam nectar," then added tomato juice, vodka, lime, spices, Worcestershire sauce, and hot sauce. He named his invention the Caesar, and although Chell was not the first person to put clams in a cocktail (recipes exist from as early as 1900), it was his blend that really took off.

Around the same time, a drink called Clamato (a portmanteau of clam and tomato) hit the market, invented by Californians who, like Chell, found their muse in a seafood meal: Manhattan clam chowder. When word reached Canada that the United States had a shortcut for mixing Caesars, the country clamored for Clamato. By the mid-1990s, cases of Clamato poured into western Canada, 70 percent of which was being poured into Caesars. Since then, the beverage has become a vital part of Canadian bar culture. Three hundred and fifty million Caesars are imbibed each year, making it the country's favorite mixed drink. (And in 2009, it became the official cocktail of Canada.)

Comparisons to the American Bloody Mary are inevitable, but Canadians insist their beloved Caesar is far tastier and more complex, as Americans remain stubbornly squeamish about drinking clams. What researchers call "the clam barrier" is real. Clamato sales are still meager among Americans, but Canadians are happy to absorb all the extra bottles.

A REVIVAL OF FLUORESCENT SOCKEYES

OSOYOOS LAKE SALMON • BRITISH COLUMBIA

For thousands of years, the Sylix, or Okanagan, people of the Pacific Northwest have eaten the sockeye salmon of Osoyoos Lake. The fish are known for their bright red skin, which appears as they prepare to spawn, and their distinct taste, which is light yet rich with buttery flavors, thanks to a diet rich in plankton and crustaceans.

How to try it

Okanagan Select Tasting Room (105-3535 Old Okanagan Highway) is a store affiliated with the Okanagan Nation Alliance. They sell salmon from Indigenous fishing groups and take orders online.

Alas, due to overfishing and climate change, the local sockeye population took a major downturn. In 2003, the Okanagan Nation Alliance launched a repopulation initiative dubbed Kt cp'elk' stim' (Sylix for "cause to come back"). Through the program, they re-outfitted dams to allow the sockeyes' passage, cleaned up the water, and incorporated Indigenous cultural practices such as feeding the local eagles and owls. By 2010, their efforts had paid off: For the first time in more than 75 years, the sockeye population was deemed sustainable and measured in the hundreds of thousands.

Osoyoos Lake sockeye season is fleeting—from July through part of September—but for those who can't get it fresh, the fish are also candied with sugar, salt, and syrup.

Delicious Diaspora

RICHMOND NIGHT MARKET

Starting in the 19th century, Chinese immigrants, mainly from Guangdong Province, began arriving in western Canada to mine for gold and work on the Canadian Pacific Railway. Despite the racist legislation and sentiment of the time, many chose to stay, establishing a Chinese Canadian community that developed and flourished over the next century. Today, the population of Richmond is more than 50 percent ethnic Chinese, and the city is home to the largest Asian night market in North America.

From May to October, when the sun goes down, some 300 vendors at the Richmond Night Market sell snacks, clothing, and trinkets in a setting modeled after the bustling night markets of Asia. Steam billows from food stands selling fish balls, crab claws, pork hocks, dumplings, bubble tea, and countless other snacks from around the world such as Mexican churros, Japanese takoyaki, and Filipino sisig. Each night the market plays host to 5,000–8,000 visitors, all eating their way through some of Asia's finest midnight munchies.

How to try it

Richmond Night Market sets up at 8351 River Road and is open for business Friday, Saturday, and Sunday nights, from May to October.

THE BATTLE FOR BISON ENERGY BARS

PEMMICAN WARS • MANITOBA

How to try it
Canadian Prairie Bison
makes pemmican
(original, and varieties
with sunflower seeds and
berries) at the University
of Saskatchewan. You
can buy it at Canadian
supermarkets such as
Safeway.

For more than 200 years, spanning the 17th to 19th centuries, European powers battled for prime fur-trading territory in northwestern Canada. But in order to push operations into the subarctic regions, Europeans faced a significant nutritional challenge. A single man needed 4,000 to 6,000 calories every day, and the weevil-infested flour and spoiled meat coming from Europe wasn't nearly enough to sustain an expedition. They turned to pemmican—the energy bar of the Indigenous North Americans.

Pemmican is made from dried, finely ground animal meat that's mixed with the animal's rendered fat. It's nutritionally dense, lightweight, shelf-stable, and contains about 3,500 calories per pound. Although any meat (or even fish) can get the pemmican treatment, bison fueled the fur trade. The Métis, an aboriginal group descended from First Nations people, and Europeans from the colonial era produced much of the pemmican. After a big bison hunt, they made the dried meat and fat mixture, and then stuffed it into buffalo skin bags, a concoction they called a taureau. One taureau contained 300,000 calories and could keep, unrefrigerated, for as long as a decade. Pemmican was sold to trading posts around the region and became pivotal in the expansion of Europe's commercial beaver hunting empire—so much so that it started a war.

In the early 1800s, a new colony connected to the British fur traders (the Hudson's Bay Company) attempted to pass a law stating that all provisions, including pemmican, could not be taken out of the region. This cut off the supply to their rivals, North West Company, and incited two years of pemmican-related fighting, ending with the burning of two forts and dozens of deaths. But the Pemmican Wars weren't the most devastating consequence of the compacted meat-and-fat business: Pemmican became so essential to commercial beaver hunting that it nearly wiped out the Canadian bison herds north of the Missouri River.

Beyond Indigenous North Americans and European fur trappers, pemmican found its way into the packs of explorers in the Antarctic, and Robert Peary carried it to the North Pole. He later proclaimed his appreciation for the food, saying that "Too much cannot be said of the importance of pemmican to a polar expedition."

Buffalo meat being dried over an open fire, later to be ground and used in pemmican.

New Iceland

....

Traditional Culture Frozen in Canada

In the late 19th century, Sigtryggur Jónasson led a group of Icelandic immigrants to the remote shores of Manitoba's Lake Winnipeg. The expedition hoped to find a suitable place in Canada to begin a new settlement, abundant with farmland and natural resources, and not so different from the Nordic landscape of Iceland. Over the next few decades, following an Icelandic volcano eruption that devastated the local economy, some 20 percent of Iceland's population emigrated to North America. In Manitoba, newcomers faced brutal winters and many perished in the early years. But those who survived—largely thanks to help from First Nations people—were determined to build the community now known as New Iceland.

In New Iceland, it's often easier to find traditional Icelandic foods than it is on the Nordic island. Rúllupylsa, a dish of pounded lamb flank rolled into a log, is rare in Iceland but relatively abundant in the Canadian region, sold at general stores and supermarket chains. The potent Icelandic liqueur brennivin flows freely at bars, and the shelves of local stores are stocked with dried fish, homemade slátur (a kind of Icelandic haggis), and crepe-like ponnukokur.

There is an intriguing disconnect between New Iceland and Iceland. After World War II, Iceland entered into a relationship with NATO and the United States that modernized the country very quickly, while New Iceland maintained a largely traditional way of life. This is especially evident in the region's food culture. Vínarterta, for example, is a multilayered prune jam and cardamom cake that was at the height of fashion in 1875, when the first wave of immigrants arrived to Lake Winnipeg. In Iceland, making vínarterta is a fading practice, but in New Iceland, bakeries, gift shops, and most every amma (grandma) bakes the old-style treat.

Iceland and New Iceland share a friendly fascination with each other. The Icelandic prime minister makes a point of flying over for the annual Icelandic festival each year. The Canadian settlement attracts busloads of curious Icelandic tourists and visitors from the country's diaspora, all looking to experience their traditional culture, set in a place that feels preserved in amber—stuck in a time closer to the 19th-century volcanic explosion than to modern Iceland.

A 15-foot Viking statue in Gimli, Manitoba, pays tribute to the area's large Icelandic population.

Vínarterta, an Icelandic cake popular in the 19th century, is still handmade at shops like the Hnausa General Store in New Iceland.

PERMAFROST COLD STORAGE

TUKTOYAKTUK ICE HOUSE • NORTHWEST TERRITORIES

How to try it
The Ice House is
no longer open to
the public, but the
village is conducting
a feasibility study in
hopes of reopening
with additional safety
precautions.

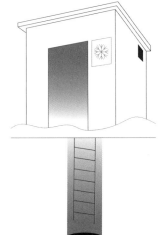

The village of Tuktoyaktuk sits in the extreme north, a place so cold it's not uncommon to see locals taking a snowmobile to the store. Families rely on hunting, fishing, and trapping to sustain themselves, and must work with the weather to survive. In the summer, they fish. In the fall, they hunt caribou. All year round, they use an underground labyrinth of rooms dug from permafrost as their freezer.

Looking at the small, outhouse-like structure, it seems unlikely this building could lead to much. But go inside and look down: Cut from the floor is a square opening like a trapdoor, the walls fuzzy with ice, descending into frozen darkness. To store your meat, you must carry it into that hole and lower yourself, step by step, carefully down a wooden ladder. At the bottom, the space opens dramatically, revealing a catacomb-like passageway caked in frost and crystals. This is the Tuktoyaktuk Ice House, the village's communal cold storage.

Dug in 1963, the Ice House is carved 30 feet (9 m) deep into the permafrost. Three hallways lead to 19 separate rooms where locals stash their excess meat after a hunt. The rooms hold at a fairly steady 5°F (–15°C), making them perfect freezers.

Before electricity, most northern villages had ice houses of their own. In recent years, many have shut down in favor of modern refrigeration, but Tuktoyaktuk chose to preserve theirs, adding the small entrance structure to protect it. Each year, as ice falls from the ceiling to the floor, the passage gets smaller, and locals must duck a little lower to get to their reserves.

HOCKEY ARENA COMMUNITY GARDEN

INUVIK GREENHOUSE • NORTHWEST TERRITORIES

How to try it
Members pay $25 a year
and must volunteer for
ten hours. Visitor tours
are $5.

The climate of Inuvik, located 120 miles (193 km) above the Arctic Circle, is extreme in every way. Temperatures swing between –40 and 80°F (–40 and 27°C) throughout the year. During the summer, the days are literally endless, with more than 50 days of 24-hour sunlight. Harnessing this brief yet powerful season, Inuvik residents rescued an old hockey arena from demolition in 1998 and turned it into Canada's northernmost commercial greenhouse.

The semicircular, glass-windowed structure is divided into two distinct sections: A 4,000-square-foot (370-sq-m) commercial greenhouse uses half the space and funds the second half, a community garden. About 180 individual plots are tended by residents of the town. They grow spinach, lettuce, tomatoes, strawberries, squash, and many other plants that wouldn't otherwise survive in the Arctic. A portion of the raised beds is allocated for groups such as town elders, children, and local charities. The growing season is short, just May to September, but the seasonal abundance brings valuable nutrition and food security to the far-flung community.

THE FRANKLIN EXPEDITION'S EERIE LEFTOVERS

BEECHEY CAN CAIRN INDENTATION • NUNAVUT

On the rocky shore of Beechey Island, high above the Arctic Circle in Nunavut, there is a circular depression covered in patchy moss, roughly 12 feet (3.7 m) in diameter. This is all that remains of what was once a 7-foot-tall (2 m) pyramid of tin food cans, and among what little remains of the arctic expedition that stacked them there.

This indentation was left by a "can cairn," built by the explorers of the 1845 Franklin Expedition. The crew of 129 men sailed from England in two ships, hoping to be first to find the Northwest Passage. Instead, no one returned, leaving behind very few clues about their fate. One of the most significant findings was the can cairn, a towering stack of empty food tins. Franklin and his men brought more than 8,000 cans of food on their voyage, including 33,000 pounds (14,969 kg) of canned meat and 8,900 pounds (4,037 kg) of canned vegetables. When they stopped on Beechey Island for their first winter, they left their hollowed-out tins (along with the first three of their crew to die).

When Franklin's crew still hadn't returned to England three years later, numerous search parties were sent to find them. In 1851, teams landed on Beechey Island and discovered the cans and the three graves. At the time, preserving food in metal tins was new technology, and the tins Franklin and his crew ate from were thin and soldered closed with lead. For years, these tins were implicated in the crew's downfall, many believing the men suffered from lead poisoning. Since then, science has largely debunked lead as the main cause of death, and most research now points to a combination of malnutrition, hypothermia, tuberculosis, and starvation.

The cans have since disintegrated into the earth below them. In their wake is a verdant patch of moss, thriving on the minerals the cans left behind. The circular depression is all that's left of the Franklin Expedition can cairn, but not far away you can see another cairn with sturdier food tins, left behind by the search parties who came to rescue them.

How to try it
You can now fly across the Northwest Passage to Beechey Island.

A woodcut illustration of the McClintock Arctic Expedition of 1857, one of several search and rescue missions to find Franklin and his explorers.

INUIT BLUBBER CUBES

MUKTUK • NUNAVUT

According to Inuit legend, the whales, seals, and walruses that swim the northern waters were once the fingers of Sedna, goddess of the sea. By some accounts, Sedna's father panicked in the face of an oncoming storm and threw his daughter overboard, severing her fingers as she tried to hold on to the edge of the kayak. It's generally believed that Sedna is a vengeful goddess (in part because of the severed fingers) and that respect for the ocean's animals—once pieces of the goddess herself—is key to appeasing her. This respect often means using the entire animal as either food or tools.

How to try it
Muktuk, usually shared among Inuit people, has recently become available at country food markets in Nunavut, where hunters sell traditional Inuit foods.

Muktuk is one such dish that makes use of the whole animal. A traditional Inuit food, muktuk consists of the skin and blubber of a whale, usually a bowhead, beluga, or narwhal. It's typically served raw in tiny cubes, but it can also be deep-fried, pickled, or stewed.

Depending on the type of whale, muktuk may look like a black cap of skin with soft, pinkish-white blubber or striated layers of gray, white, and pink—similar to pork belly. The skin is frustratingly elastic, but it's often scored to make chewing somewhat easier. The blubber, however, melts gently as you chew, giving off an essence of the ocean without being overly fishy or briny.

Inuit tribes have been snacking on narwhal blubber for centuries.

WILD BERRIES FOR BARTERING AND PIE

SASKATOONS • SASKATCHEWAN

How to try it

Nine miles (15 km) north of downtown Saskatoon is the Wanuskewin Heritage Park—an active archaeological site and museum dedicated to preserving and celebrating the culture of the Northern Plains First Nations people. They also serve a mean saskatoon berry pie.

In River Landing, Saskatoon, there's a statue of the city's founder, John Lake, crouched beside Chief Whitecap of the Dakota First Nation tribe. With his arm outstretched, Chief Whitecap gestures to the land before him—an expanse that was once so full of saskatoon berries, they named the city after them.

Saskatoons (*Amelanchier alnifolia*) are small purple berries with a sweet almond flavor. They grow wild in North America and played a key role in the diets of Indigenous peoples and early colonizers, who pounded them into cakes and used them as a sweetener. According to an account from 1900, the berries were once so valuable that ten saskatoon cakes could be traded for one large buckskin.

Like other berries, saskatoons are great in jam, wine, and beer, but the most iconic application is pie. A filling of saskatoons tossed with a little lemon juice, sugar, and flour is a common preparation. But as humans encroach on saskatoon habitats, the berries are becoming harder to find, which means a pie packed with saskatoons is a precious, labor-intensive commodity.

Since the 1990s, attempts to domesticate the saskatoon have been underway in both Canada and the United States. This dual cultivation has caused a bit of a cultural conflict because American farmers felt that saskatoon, as a word, would not work in the US market and rebranded it the Juneberry. In Canada, the *saskatoon* remains the saskatoon.

Country Food Markets:
The Untraditional Way to Save Traditional Food

Walking into a country food market in Nunavut, Canada, you'll find a display of caribou heads and hearts, chunks of narwhal fat with the skin still attached, Arctic char (smoked, frozen, or made into dried chips called pitsi), igunaq (fermented seal meat), ground umingmak (musk ox), and frozen flatfish called turbot—among the most asymmetric vertebrates to ever live, with both eyes mashed on one side of its head. Known as "country food," this high-fat, vitamin-rich fare has sustained the Nunavummiut people for thousands of years. But until recently, it couldn't be bought at a store.

Country food is the Nunavummiut way of life: hunted, fished, or foraged, then shared within the community. In an inhospitable climate like the Canadian north, this lifestyle has always been precarious, and insufficient hunts have led to conditions like "rabbit starvation," a deadly protein poisoning that occurs when the body is deprived of fats. Today, the region is changing. Previously semi-nomadic communities have settled into permanent towns, and Nunavummiut children are spending less time learning migration patterns and reading sea ice. On top of everything, global warming is changing and shortening hunting seasons, which means country food is growing rare, and 70 percent of children in Nunavut live in food-insecure households.

In less remote regions, losing the ability to hunt might be remedied by the grocery store. But in Nunavut, where all commercial goods must be flown in, a single bunch of celery can cost a staggering nine dollars. Commercial food prices are two to three times more in Nunavut than in the rest of Canada, and local families simply can't afford it.

In an attempt to encourage hunting and create an economic incentive for country food, nonprofits such as Project Nunavut and Feeding Nunavut stage pop-up markets where hunters and fishers can come and sell their meat to the public. The creators of Project Nunavut were unsure if the concept would work, but at their first country market in 2010, they sold out in less than ten minutes. A few years later, permanent shops have opened in the area, selling whatever meat has been hunted that day at reasonable prices.

Traditional food markets are not unique to Nunavut. Nearby Greenland has had them for more than 150 years, but in Nunavut, the concept has been controversial because country food is meant to be shared, creating bonds and mutual reliance across the community. Selling seal or whale or char is still, to some extent, seen as a betrayal of traditional values.

Other attempts to revive country food include government-subsidized hunts, programs for teaching traditional hunting methods, and community freezers open to all. But as locals work to bolster time-honored pathways to food and nutrition, the country food market gives the Nunavummiut community a way to keep their traditional foods alive and accessible in a rapidly modernizing Canada.

Huntsmen in Nunavut transport a shot musk ox on a sledge.

A STORIED APPENDAGE SERVED IN A GLASS

SOURTOE COCKTAIL · YUKON

The Sourtoe, the city of Dawson's signature cocktail, is served every night at the Sourdough Saloon. It can consist of any liquor your heart desires and has just one nonnegotiable ingredient: a human toe that's dropped into the glass and must touch your lips as you tip the drink back. The same toe, pickled by time and alcohol into a sterile human appendage, goes into each cocktail. The enduring practice is the life's work of a self-proclaimed bastard, asshole, and professional wolf-poisoner named Captain Dick Stevenson, a man who once toured the country for 80 days with his sourtoe.

Captain Dick first encountered a stand-alone human toe when cleaning out a cabin once owned by Prohibition rum runners, the Linken brothers—one who froze his toe while bootlegging and one who cut the frozen toe off. Captain Dick was a fan of boozing himself, and one night he decided to drop the toe into a beer glass of champagne and try to get people to drink it. The Sourtoe Cocktail Club was born, admittance given to anyone willing to touch their lips to the toe.

Over the years, toes have been lost to hijinks. The first was accidentally ingested by a miner attempting to set a record by drinking 13 beer glasses filled with champagne and the toe. On the thirteenth glass, he fell over backward, hit his head on the deck, and swallowed the toe. As Captain Dick searched for a new toe, he substituted a pickled bear's testicle and used the "pecker bone" as a swizzle stick. (He named this the "Better Bitter Bear Ball Highball," which was used intermittently as a stand-in between lost toes.)

For admission into the Sourtoe Cocktail Club, intrepid drinkers must let this severed human toe touch their lips.

The second toe came from a foot with an inoperable corn, but it vanished shortly after. Captain Dick ran newspaper ads offering $300 for a new toe, while imploring Canadian police to search for the old one. After administering a polygraph test to ensure the lost toe wasn't a publicity stunt, police received a tip that the toe was being served in Memphis, Tennessee. They tracked it to Texas, recovered it, and eventually returned it to Canada. A third toe, donated by another frostbite victim, was briefly in service until swallowed by a baseball player. Then, in an unexpected windfall, a miner lost a leg and gave all five toes to Captain Dick. With the new wealth of toes, he started the SourFoot Club, for those willing to put all five nubs in their cocktail.

In 2009, Captain Dick wrote an "au'toe'biography" detailing his experience sourtoeing around the country. He never made much money off his antics (which included "the first nude beauty contest north of the 60th parallel" and a failed business trying to sell pet rocks), but his legacy lives on in the blackened, mummified toe that regularly touches the lips of those looking to join his senseless, yet exclusive, club. In 2019, Captain Dick died at the age of 89.

Klondike Supply List
A TON OF GOODS

When gold was discovered in the region of Klondike in the summer of 1896, prospectors from around the country scrambled to the Yukon to make their fortune. To get there, they sailed hundreds, sometimes thousands of miles in overloaded boats, typically in conjunction with brutal stretches of mountainous terrain they traversed by foot.

With a stampede of people rushing toward a barren landscape, Canadian law required anyone entering Yukon territory to bring a year's supply of food. Added to their camping gear, the average prospector (man or woman) was responsible for hauling about 2,000 pounds (907 kg). The majority of explorers couldn't afford pack animals or the services of locals, so they carried the goods in 50–80 pound (23–36 kg) loads, trekking back and forth between their personal stockpile and the next frontier. Often, they walked a thousand miles to move their supplies 30 miles (48 km) away.

The packing list for a year of groceries, opposite, was published by the T. Eaton Company, once Canada's largest department store chain, in an 1898 catalog.

Prospectors at Chilkoot Pass in 1898, bound for the Klondike gold fields.

500 lbs flour	$12.00
200 lbs bacon	$19.00
75 lbs sugar	$3.00
10 lbs coffee	$3.00
10 lbs tea	$2.50
10 lbs baking powder	$1.00
12 lbs soap	$.40
3 doz yeast cakes	$1.44
1 lb mustard	$.40
25 lbs candles	$2.50
100 lbs beans	$1.67
10 lbs barley	$.25
10 lbs split peas	$.25
25 lbs rice	$1.05
15 lbs evaporated apples	$1.43
12 lbs evaporated vegetables	$2.16
1 doz beef extract	$3.00
1 doz condensed milk	$1.50
5 tins assorted soup	$3.00
20 lbs salt	$.20
1 lbs pepper	$.15
50 lbs rolled oats	$1.04
20 lbs corn meal	$.29
21 lbs baking soda	$.63
1/2 gal lime juice	$2.49
5 boxes matches	$.50
10 lbs prunes	$.63
20 lbs evaporated apricots	$2.20

EASTERN CANADA

AN OBSCURE PIECE OF COD

COD TONGUES • NEWFOUNDLAND AND LABRADOR

How to try it

Nanny's Root Cellar Kitchen in Elliston serves fried cod tongues topped with scrunchions—bits of crispy fried pork eaten across Newfoundland.

Although "cod tongues" may not sound all that appetizing, this misnomer is more charming than what they actually are: small, meaty muscles extracted from the back of a cod's neck. The two-pronged morsels are a Labrador delicacy. They have a flavor similar to scallops, a slightly rubbery texture, and when floured and fried, they make a pricey dish served throughout the coastal province.

Back when the Labrador Sea was packed with cod, most fishermen didn't bother scooping out the neck muscle from their fish. It was often enterprising children who would parse through the piles of discarded cod heads and remove the fleshy bits to sell for pocket money. But by the early 1990s, rampant overfishing led to the near-extinction of local cod, and the Canadian government placed a moratorium on commercial fishing off Labrador's shores. The new law left thousands jobless and even more cod-less.

Though several small fisheries have been established in recent years, cod is no longer the free-flowing food it once was. Now every part matters and must be treated with respect, even the small, gelatinous muscle from the back of the throat.

When Labrador was overflowing with cod, children would sift through piles of fish, cutting out the "tongues" to sell for pocket money.

A VERSATILE BAG OF PUDDING

BLUEBERRY DUFF • NEWFOUNDLAND AND LABRADOR

How to try it

There are many recipes for blueberry duff online; assemble the ingredients, grab a pillowcase, and get started.

The word *pudding* has described an array of dishes across history, from sausage and haggis to steamed cake and custard. The term has evolved to signify primarily desserts, but blueberry duff plays by nobody's rules: The Newfoundland pudding is interchangeably lunch and dessert.

A blueberry duff is the classic accompaniment to a traditional midday Sunday meal called "Jiggs dinner," made by boiling salt beef and root vegetables in a big pot. As the meat and vegetables simmer, the duff comes together much like a cake batter, with flour, eggs, sugar, and blueberries. The mixture is poured into a cotton bag (a pillowcase will do in a pinch), the bag is tied, and the whole thing is dropped into the Jiggs dinner pot to cook. The result is a pale, spongy cake that's sweet from the batter and savory from the beef-laced liquid.

Once cooked, the duff can be taken in two directions. As a side dish for the Jiggs dinner, the cake is simply sliced and plated with the stewed meat and vegetables. To serve the duff as dessert, top it with rum sauce and serve it with tea.

PICKLES WORTH PANICKING OVER

MUSTARD PICKLES • NEWFOUNDLAND AND LABRADOR

Sitting down for Sunday dinner in Newfoundland, you'll likely be asked, multiple times, to pass the mustard pickles: big chunks of cucumber, onion, and cauliflower, brined and mixed together in a thick yellow sauce. They're sweet, they're spicy, and you'd better not say anything bad about them, because in this province, mustard pickles are under perpetual protection from slander.

How to try it
Bick's Sweet Mustard Pickles are available online and in Canadian grocery stores.

The pickles' popularity is the result of Newfoundland's often cold and always rocky climate. Without the benefit of grocery stores, the island province's early residents relied on preserved foods—salted meats, puddings, and root vegetables—to get through the long winters. On a plate like that, a dollop of mustard pickles was a ray of zesty, welcome sunshine. (The traditional Newfoundland Sunday meal, the Jiggs dinner, is still served with mustard pickles.)

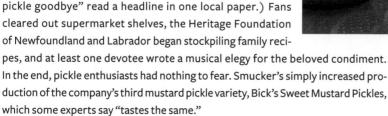

The brined vegetables are so entrenched in the local cuisine that a recent hiccup in their production caused immediate grief and panic. In 2016, Smucker Foods of Canada announced the company would end production of two of their mass-produced mustard pickle brands—the acidic Zest and the more robust Habitant. The news precipitated a wave of mourning across Newfoundland. ("Kiss your pickle goodbye" read a headline in one local paper.) Fans cleared out supermarket shelves, the Heritage Foundation of Newfoundland and Labrador began stockpiling family recipes, and at least one devotee wrote a musical elegy for the beloved condiment. In the end, pickle enthusiasts had nothing to fear. Smucker's simply increased production of the company's third mustard pickle variety, Bick's Sweet Mustard Pickles, which some experts say "tastes the same."

PICKLES

Not only do pickles taste amazing and last years without refrigeration, they are nutritional wonders. Celebrated Roman senator Cato the Elder recommended pickled cabbage first thing in the morning to remedy joint disease. Second-century Greek physician Galen believed eating brined olives and fermented fish sauce before a meal cleaned and reinforced the digestive system. These early pickle advocates weren't wrong. Fermented pickles are packed with vitamins and are an incredible source of probiotics, which have helped keep people alive and healthy throughout history.

Ancient luminaries like Greek physician Galen of Pergamon touted the benefits of pickled foods.

Sauerkraut

Popularized in Europe around the 18th century, sauerkraut was one of the Dutch navy's methods for preventing scurvy. When salted, pressed, and allowed to ferment, the pickled cabbage retained its high vitamin C content. British captain James Cook adopted the sauerkraut supplement on his ship, but at first his crew refused to eat it. To increase the cachet of the sour cabbage, Cook served it to just the high-ranking officers. Afterward, his crewmen agreed to eat it, too, and all of them were spared from scurvy.

Umeboshi

The prized Japanese dried and pickled plum umeboshi has been used to nourish the nation's fighters for centuries. Rich in acids and minerals, umeboshi is used to combat fatigue, stomachaches, dehydration, and hangovers. The mysterious assassins we now call ninjas ate "thirst balls" made from umeboshi pulp. Samurai took the salted fruit on long crusades and, since the 16th century, an umeboshi comes standard issue in the military rations of Japanese soldiers.

Naem

Thailand's sour sausage is made by fermenting seasoned pork, pork skin, and sticky rice for up to a week, until it develops its signature tang. The sticky rice, which becomes a breeding ground for lactic acid bacteria and yeast, acts as the souring agent, while the salt keeps the pork from going too sour. The result is spicy, sour, garlicky, and often eaten raw.

Pickle Juice

At least in America, pickle juice is no throwaway liquid. Americans use the briny, après-pickle fluid to relieve cramping and muscle ache after a strenuous workout. Packed with sodium and potassium, pickle juice helps replenish electrolytes much like commercial sports drinks. In 2000, when the Philadelphia Eagles beat the Dallas Cowboys in punishing 109°F (42.8°C) heat, the victors called upon pickle juice to keep them in optimum form.

Kimchi

These spicy fermented vegetables at the heart of the Korean diet may be what saved the country from severe acute respiratory syndrome (SARS). In 2003, SARS broke out in China and spread rapidly, killing 774 people across seven countries. Yet South Korea, whose citizens regularly travel to China, did not experience a single fatality. Many South Koreans, including doctors and scientists, believe the scores of healthy bacteria in a kimchi-rich diet are responsible for killing the SARS microbes and keeping the Korean public from infection.

In 2016, the average South Korean ate about 80 pounds of kimchi.

A RUM AND COD INITIATION

SCREECH-IN • NEWFOUNDLAND AND LABRADOR

How to try it
Christian's Pub on
George Street in
St. John's is known
for its educational and
moving screech-ins
led by Keith Vokey, the
son of the ceremony's
"inventor."

An English captain once wrote that the cod around Newfoundland were "so thick by the shore that we hardly have been able to row a boat through them." Starting in the 16th century, European sailors came by the thousands to fish for cod, salting the abundance and then selling it to Europe and its colonies. The British West Indies became an important buyer: Plantation owners needed protein to feed their enslaved workers, and salt cod provided a cheap, nonperishable solution. In return, Jamaica sent barrels of their local specialty: rum.

"Screech" is the name for rum in Newfoundland. While no one knows exactly why, legend goes it was named for the screeching sound emitted by an American GI after taking a shot of the 80-proof rum. Screech has become so ingrained in Newfoundland life that locals created an elaborate, tongue-in-cheek ritual known as a "Screech-In" that welcomes newcomers to their province.

To become an honorary Newfoundlander (or "Newfie") and be inducted to the Royal Order of the Screechers, you must first introduce yourself and allow the locals to mock you. Next you kiss a cod (salted, frozen, or fresh), eat some bologna (known as Newfie steak and nearly as popular as Screech), and when asked, "Is ye a Screecher?" answer proudly, "Deed I is, me old cock, and long may your big jib draw!" Although this response may sound uncouth, it is simply Newfie slang for "Yes, indeed, my friend, may your big sail always catch the wind." The inductee then takes a shot of Screech, and the deal is done.

*Kissing a cod is the
only way to become
an honorary Newfie.*

INDIGENOUS COMFORT FOOD

SEAL FLIPPER PIE • NEWFOUNDLAND AND LABRADOR

How to try it
Flipper pie is often
available during
the Lenten season
(which coincides with
seal-hunting season).
Bidgood's Market in
Goulds bakes meat
pies all year, including
flipper.

The meat of a seal flipper is rich, dark, and delicate. The flavor is simultaneously gamey and fishy, akin to duck, and when slowly braised in a gravy studded with vegetables, seal flippers make a filling to rival any potpie.

The Indigenous and maritime cultures of Canada have long relied on seals for their livelihood. Seal pelts provided waterproof material for coats and boots, seal oil was used for lamps, and seal meat contained valuable iron and vitamins that fended off scurvy. The flippers, however, had no obvious commercial value, and so they became pie.

Flipper eating has its detractors. Animal rights groups criticize the traditional seal hunt that takes place every spring, calling the ritual inhumane. Those who support the practice cite the strict regulations of the hunt and the growing seal

population. Seals are not endangered in Canada, and in many parts, the number is actually on the rise. Although seals are unlikely to be adopted as pie filling outside of Newfoundland, many argue that within the region, seal meat is one of the most sustainable meat sources available.

PREHISTORIC COCKTAIL COOLER

ICEBERG ICE • NEWFOUNDLAND AND LABRADOR

Newfoundland sits in Iceberg Alley, the famed stretch of the Atlantic Ocean known for ushering icy monoliths, calved from Greenland glaciers, southbound to the open sea. Starting in the early spring, when the icebergs begin rolling through, many locals get out their tools to begin harvesting the frozen, seasonal slabs.

While larger companies often use cranes, boats, and nets to do the job, smaller ice harvesters get creative when wrangling up "bergie bits." (One technique is shooting the ice with a rifle.) After the chunks are brought ashore, they're broken into smaller bits using a hammer or a mallet and a thin pin, which shapes the pieces into tiny icebergs.

Iceberg ice is used just like freezer ice. It's often coupled with alcoholic beverages, perhaps to kill off any sneaky prehistoric pathogens that might be inside. Aside from the fact that chilling a drink with a 12,000-year-old specimen is undeniably cool, people love iceberg ice for its taste—or rather, lack thereof. Many claim that pre–Industrial Revolution water and air, free of modern pollutants, give the ice its highly coveted tastelessness.

How to try it
If you're not into harvesting your own bergie bits, general stores (like B.J.'s General Store in Fogo) often sell it by the bag.

For these fishermen in Bonavista Bay, the big catch of the day is an iceberg chunk.

ACADIAN GATHERING PIE

RAPPIE PIE • NOVA SCOTIA

How to try it

Some Acadian restaurants, such as La Cuisine Robicheau in Saulnierville, Nova Scotia, serve rappie pies. To make it at home, there's an abundance of traditional recipes online, with fillings from poultry to seafood.

Rappie pie is no everyday food. The recipe calls for 20 pounds (9 kg) of potatoes, which must be peeled, grated ("râpé" in French), and wrung out in small batches to remove their liquid. Once dry, the potatoes are rehydrated with hot stock, which generally comes from a pot where a chicken's been boiling for hours. Once the liquid transplant is complete, the chicken-infused potatoes are poured into a casserole dish, topped with shredded chicken, more grated potatoes, hunks of salt pork, and dollops of butter, then crisped in an oven. Processing 20 pounds of potatoes requires time and teamwork, both in the making and the eating, which is precisely the point of a rappie pie. This casserole is an exercise in fellowship—a way to gather the dwindling Acadian community.

The Acadians are descendants of the early French colonists who settled in what is now Nova Scotia, New Brunswick, and Prince Edward Island starting in the 17th century. As the decades passed, Acadians formed a close-knit community largely independent from European influence. But in 1713, France ceded control of Acadia to the British, who feared the Acadians would remain loyal to France. In 1754, the two European powers went to war, and when France lost, the Brits forced out the Acadians in a violent series of events called the Great Expulsion.

More than 10,000 Acadians, many of whom died along the way, were forced from their homes. They took refuge in Louisiana, the Caribbean, and the English colonies along the Atlantic seaboard. Some went back to France. When the Acadians were permitted to return to Canada in 1764, they were given new land that was rocky and difficult to farm. The resettled community began to grow potatoes, which bore the tradition of making a dish with 20 pounds of potatoes and a lot of kinship.

Rappie pie has become a symbol of the Acadian plight. It's a dish that represents adversity, resilience, and ingenuity, while displaying French technique in a deceivingly humble presentation. And while rappie pie is delicious, the real importance lies in its ability to connect generations of displaced people.

SOAP-FLAVORED GUM

THRILLS GUM • ONTARIO

How to try it

Thrills is still sold in candy stores and online.

If you're tired of coworkers, friends, and family always asking you for a piece of gum, try handing them a purple nugget of Thrills. Canadians say the retro, rosewater-flavored chewing gum tastes like soap, and the company agrees. The box bears the reassuring slogan: "It still tastes like soap!" Fans cite not having to share as a major plus of chewing it.

For much of the 20th century, the O-Pee-Chee Gum Company, which also sold trading cards, provided Canadians with Thrills. In the 1950s and '60s, perfumed flavors like teaberry and violet were common at the candy store, and rosewater-flavored Thrills fit in perfectly. Although floral gum is less desirable these days, if you're lucky enough to like it you'll likely get the whole pack to yourself.

SAM PANOPOULOS
(1934–2017)

Sam Panopoulos, inventor of the notorious Hawaiian pizza, left Greece on a boat bound for Canada in 1954. Along the way, the boat stopped in Naples, where Panopoulos encountered pizza for the first time. When he arrived in the small Ontario town of Chatham, he opened the Satellite Restaurant and began serving the kind of food people ate in midcentury Canada: pancakes in the morning, burgers and fries for lunch, and liver and onions for dinner. But Panopoulos was eager to delight his customers with new dishes. First, he hired an Asian cook and put American Chinese food on his menu. Then, he checked out Detroit and Windsor's up-and-coming pizza scene and began his own experiments.

Pizza was still totally foreign to most Canadians. (A 1962 recipe from the *Toronto Star* includes a recipe for "Spanish pizza," made with yellow rice and Vienna sausages piled on a dough made from biscuit mix.) At the time, pizza boxes didn't exist, so Panopoulos cut circles out of cardboard boxes from a furniture seller next door, placed the pizza on top, and wrapped the whole thing in aluminum foil.

He mixed and matched toppings to see what worked. And although some of his discoveries, such as olives and anchovies, were simultaneously discovered by other pizza pioneers, the use of pineapple was something entirely his own.

In the 1960s, Hawaii loomed large in the fantasy of North Americans, fueled by the tales of returning soldiers who had seen the South Pacific paradise. Tiki culture became hugely popular, and canned pineapple, which was advertised extensively in Ontario's newspapers, became a staple of Canadian households. According to Panopoulos, sweet and sour was a rare flavor, available only in Chinese dishes. With the Satellite already serving Chinese food, he thought his customers might appreciate a sweet and savory pizza. In 1962 he opened a can of pineapple, drained it, and threw the pieces of fruit on a pie. He named his creation the "Hawaiian pizza," and amazingly, the ham and pineapple combination caught on.

Panopoulos passed away in 2017, but he never stopped loving his signature pie. When asked, at the age of 81, if he still ordered it, Panopoulos said, "Yeah, I do. I still like it."

Hawaiian pizza is neither Hawaiian nor Italian.

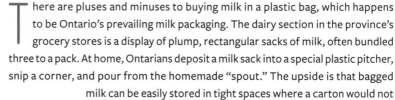

A PLASTIC BAG OF MILK

BAGGED MILK • ONTARIO

How to try it

In Ontario, milk bags are available in every grocery store and are commonly called "milk bladders."

There are pluses and minuses to buying milk in a plastic bag, which happens to be Ontario's prevailing milk packaging. The dairy section in the province's grocery stores is a display of plump, rectangular sacks of milk, often bundled three to a pack. At home, Ontarians deposit a milk sack into a special plastic pitcher, snip a corner, and pour from the homemade "spout." The upside is that bagged milk can be easily stored in tight spaces where a carton would not fit, and the minimal packaging reduces waste and transportation costs. The downside is that the bag cannot be resealed and so must be drunk relatively quickly, and the flimsy, makeshift spout is prone to accidents. Canada is far from the only nation with this system (other milk-bagging regions include eastern Europe, South America, India, and China), but the Canadian practice emerged almost by accident, when transitioning from British weights and measures.

Debuted in the late 1960s, milk bags weren't truly embraced until the 1970s, when Canada switched to the metric system. Redesigning machinery to manufacture glass bottles and cardboard cartons in liters, rather than gallons, was costly and time-consuming—but resizing plastic bags was simple. Milk companies started offering free plastic pitchers to entice Canadians to switch to bags, and many did. Today, Canadians drink about half their milk from a bag, and in the province of Ontario, it jumps to around 80 percent.

A POTATO TRUCKER'S THEME SONG

"BUD THE SPUD" • PRINCE EDWARD ISLAND

How to try it

The Canadian Potato Museum is located on Prince Edward Island. Their café serves everything PEI potato, from french fries to potato fudge.

Folk and country artist Stompin' Tom Connors made a long, distinguished career with his Canadian-centric music, crooning about union strikes, gold mining in the Yukon, and hockey. From the 1960s on, Connors wrote more than 300 tunes, among them the 1969 breakout hit "Bud the Spud," featuring a truck driver named Bud who hauls "the best dog-gone potatoes that's ever been growed" from Prince Edward Island. He travels the country, meeting people and delivering his spuds. The Ontario police chase him down the highway, but Bud is just a fun-loving potato hero doing important work: bringing the PEI potato to tables across the country. The song became so popular it inspired a children's book and cemented the PEI potato's place in Canadian life.

Canada's smallest province, Prince Edward Island, is known for its serene, pastoral landscape of rolling hills, woodland, and windswept coastline. The lush island grows more than a hundred potato varieties, which make up 25 percent of the Canadian crop. Local farmers say their weather (warm summers, cool winters, plenty of rain) coupled with their signature soil (deep red and iron-rich) makes the potatoes uniquely delicious. It's also an island of small family plots, with relatives passing their hard-won knowledge generationally. (Only about 300 farmers manage the entire crop.) In the words of the great Stompin' Tom Connors:

> Now I know a lot of people from east to west
> And they like the spuds from the island best
> Cause they stand up to the hardest test –
> Right on the table;
> So when you see that big truck rollin' by
> Wave your hand or kinda wink your eye
> Cause that's Bud the Spud, from old PEI.
> With another big load of potatoes!

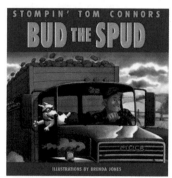

A BETTER WAY TO SEASON LIVER

MONTREAL STEAK SPICE • QUEBEC

I f you've ever enjoyed the peppery-sweet taste of a ribeye seasoned with Montreal steak spice, you can thank a Canadian grill cook known as the Shadow.

Like many cured-meat seasonings, the popular blend has its roots in eastern European cooking. Montreal steak spice features pepper, garlic, coriander, and dill—all common in recipes from Romania. It makes sense, then, that most accounts trace the origin of the spice blend to Schwartz's, a deli founded by a Romanian immigrant that's now the oldest, and arguably the most famous, deli in all of Canada.

According to *Schwartz's Hebrew Delicatessen: The Story* by Bill Browstein, every deli employee was allowed to eat their fill of only one item: cooked liver. It was perhaps this limited diet that made a cook named Morris Sherman so thin that he earned the nickname the Shadow. (His coworkers joked that if he turned sideways, only his shadow would be visible.) One day, according to Canadian deli legend, Sherman used a new blend of spices to make the liver more appealing, and customers liked it so much, they started requesting it on other items, especially steak. Montreal steak spice quickly became a seasoning classic, and Schwartz's, known for its smoked meat sandwiches, rose to Jewish deli fame. (In 2012, Céline Dion became a part owner.)

How to try it

For those who want to try Montreal steak spice at the source, the lines at Schwartz's can be long. Otherwise, it can easily be found in the grocery store and online.

Schwartz's was established in 1928 by Reuben Schwartz, a Jewish immigrant from Romania.

How to try it

In Rigaud, about an hour west of Montreal, the Sucrerie de la Montagne is open all year. After a heavy night of syrup, you can sleep in one of the sugar shack cabins.

MAPLE SYRUP HOGWARTS

SUCRERIE DE LA MONTAGNE • QUEBEC

Maple syrup runs through the veins of the Quebecois. They produce more than 90 percent of Canada's golden liquid supply, which makes up more than 70 percent of the world's maple syrup. To extract 150 million pounds of syrup from trees, much of the process has become high-tech: Computer-controlled vacuum tubes connect trees to reverse osmosis machines, before the syrup is cooked down in huge evaporators to a precise 66 percent sugar content. Much of the natural beauty has been lost to automation, but tucked in the woods about an hour west of Montreal is Sucrerie de la Montagne, an authentic sugar shack making syrup as it was done by early French arrivals, using tree taps, buckets, and a wood-fired evaporator.

Think of Sucrerie de la Montagne—with its log cabins and rural, whimsical setting—as a Maple Syrup Hogwarts. After a tour of the syrup production, you are welcomed into an immense banquet hall built of stone and massive wooden beams. A sugar shack feast arrives at the long communal tables. It's an all-you-can-eat spread of crusty bread, pea soup, maple-smoked ham, wood-fire baked beans, omelet soufflé, sausage, meatball stew, crispy-fried pork rinds, mashed potatoes, tourtière (a Canadian meat pie), homemade fruit ketchup, and pickles. On the table, you'll find jugs of maple syrup that are constantly refilled, to pour over anything your heart desires. For dessert, there is maple taffy, made by pouring syrup over fresh snow.

The Sucrerie de la Montagne even has its own Dumbledore, founder Pierre Faucher, who with his enormous white beard, wide-brimmed field hat, flowing flannel layers, and antique wool sash (known as a ceinture fléchée), and accompanied by his three-quarters wolf, one-quarter husky Louploup, seems like the human embodiment of maple syrup.

Pierre Faucher's sugar refinery collects sap for maple syrup the old-fashioned way, with buckets attached to maple trees.

|||||||||||||||||||||||||||||||||||||||||||||||||||||||||||||||||||||||||||||||||||||||||||||||||||||||||||||||||

The Great Canadian Maple Syrup Heist

It was a nearly perfect crime. Replacement barrels were painted the exact same shade of white. Replica stickers were printed. A specialized forklift was rented. Under the cover of night, dozens, then hundreds, then thousands of 600-pound (272-kg) barrels were extracted, drained, refilled, and brought back, neatly replaced into the towering six-barrel stacks. For months, this process happened over and over, undetected. Then someone realized maple syrup doesn't sweat.

The Canadian Maple Syrup Reserve, spread across multiple rural Quebec towns, is a string of huge warehouses that hold the country's excess supply of syrup. The reserve is controlled by the Federation of Quebec Maple Syrup Producers, an organization that oversees every aspect of the Quebec syrup business, including supply and price. (Some compare the federation to OPEC, the organization of oil-producing countries, others to the Mafia.) In July 2012, a federation representative was climbing stacks of 600-pound barrels inside the syrup reserve when one nearly slipped from under his feet. The barrel, he realized, was empty. He began inspecting other barrels and found rust, along with rings of condensation. (Maple syrup never sweats.) Suspicious, he opened the barrels. They were full of water.

Two hundred fifty investigators arrived to check every barrel in the reserve. They found nearly 10,000 barrels filled with water, which meant 18 million Canadian dollars' worth of syrup was missing. The Great Canadian Maple Syrup Heist, as the theft is commonly known, was the largest robbery in Quebec history.

Established to protect the industry from price swings and bankruptcy, the federation dictates how much syrup each producer can make, whom they can sell it to, and for how much. All syrup produced in excess is put into the Maple Syrup Reserve, also controlled by the federation. If a syrup producer refuses, or sells directly to the buyer, they are fined or have their syrup seized. This restricted system prompted a maple syrup black market, where smugglers known as "barrel rollers" are tasked with moving syrup into places such as the United States and Europe, beyond the reach of the Federation.

In 2017, after an extensive investigation, three major guilty sentences were finally obtained. Avik Caron, whose wife owned the property on which the reserve warehouse was rented, was fined $1.2 million CAD and sentenced to five years in prison. The barrel roller was Richard Vallières, a hotshot in the world of syrup smuggling, who took the barrels to a small sugar shack and siphoned the syrup. He was fined $9.4 million CAD and sentenced to eight years in prison. Étienne St-Pierre, who received the syrup in New Brunswick and sold it abroad, was sentenced to two years home imprisonment and fined more than a million dollars.

Shockingly, about two thirds of the "hot" syrup was recovered. The other third remains missing, likely poured over pancakes or otherwise enjoyed by unsuspecting diners across New England. After the arrests, tensions between the federation and the rebels only intensified. In a country where marijuana is legal, and even hard drugs are decriminalized, an increasing number of producers want to know why selling maple syrup is a crime.

THE FROZEN APPLE LIBATION

ICE CIDER • QUEBEC

When apples freeze, their juice becomes concentrated, and when that sugary, golden liquid is painstakingly pressed from the fruit then slowly fermented, it becomes ice cider, Quebec's gift to the world of libations. The amber liquor is made using one of two techniques. The first, which is riskier and more labor-intensive, leaves the apples in the orchard until about January, waiting for them to reach a temperature of −10°C (14°F). The apples grow gradually shriveled and hard as they dry out, then the frozen apples are pressed (a process that can take

How to try it
Ice cider is generally served as an aperitif or paired with a dessert course. Bottles of Montreal's finest can be ordered online.

hours) and the extracted juice is fermented. The second method juices fresh apples, then puts the juice outside in the cold, allowing the water to crystalize and separate from the sugary liquid. Then, with the water removed, the concentrated juice is fermented.

Both methods require huge amounts of apples: Nearly 10 pounds (4.5 kg) goes into every 375 ml bottle of ice cider, or about five times what's needed for regular hard apple cider. The taste is a rich distillation of apples coupled with the warmth of alcohol, sweet without being saccharine, sharp with a velvety texture.

The Beaver Club's Extravagant Dinners

In 1785, the Fur Barons of Montreal, a group of early European settlers in the beaver pelt industry, established a notoriously opulent dining club. The objective of the Beaver Club, according to their official rules, was "to bring together, at stated periods during the winter season, a set of men highly respectable in society, who had passed their best days in a savage country and had encountered the difficulties and dangers incident to a pursuit of the fur trade of Canada."

All dinners commenced at 4 p.m. with the passing of a calumet, an American Indian ceremonial pipe, followed by five toasts: to Mary Mother of All Saints, to the king, to the fur trade, to the voyagers and their families, and to absent members. From there, there was typically a Highland piper to play out the servants carrying a flaming boar's head on a velvet dais. Then the feasting and imbibing would begin in earnest with a table overflowing with country food and enough wine to drown each man. (Some meals ended in a final course of "a cheque for a sum of money" served on a plate.)

The Beaver Club was known to get rowdy as they danced on tables and broke china and crystal engraved with the club's insignia. In the wee hours,

Founder Joseph Frobisher (bottom left) allowed only the most "respectable" fur traders to join his decadent Beaver Club.

they often sat single file on the floor and pretended to row an imaginary canoe in a tradition called "The Grand Voyage." They sang voyageur songs and used fire pokers and walking sticks as paddles—while dressed in ruffled gold lace, gold-clasped garters, and silver-buckled shoes.

One night in 1808, 31 members and guests went out for dinner and racked up the following bill:

32 dinners

29 bottles of Madeira

19 bottles of Port

14 bottles of Porter

12 quarts ale

7 suppers

Brandy and gin

Cigars, pipes, tobacco

Three wine glasses broken

Total.................. £28.15

The exclusive club was both picky and formal about who they let in. When auditioning a new member, they invited him to dinner, got him drunk, and when he left, they voted (also drunk). If the prospective member earned a unanimous yes, he was let in. Over four decades, they inducted about a hundred members, but never exceeded 55 men at a time.

The United States

WEST COAST, ALASKA, AND HAWAII
FOUR CORNERS AND THE SOUTHWEST
GREAT PLAINS • THE MIDWEST • THE SOUTHEAST
THE MID-ATLANTIC • NEW ENGLAND

WEST COAST, ALASKA, AND HAWAII

THE NOAH'S ARK FOR CITRUS

CITRUS VARIETY COLLECTION • CALIFORNIA

How to try it

The Citrus Variety Collection hosts occasional public education events featuring tastings of hybrid fruits and their "parents."

The citrus collection at the University of California, Riverside, is the largest in America, containing more than a thousand different citrus varieties across 22 acres. And like the animals on Noah's Ark, they keep two of each species.

The thousands of specimens on display exhibit the staggering diversity of citrus, remarkable given that most modern citrus stems from just three ancient varieties: the Malaysian pomelo, the North Indian citron, and the Chinese mandarin. The sweet supermarket orange, for example, was produced through multiple crosses between a pomelo and a mandarin. The grapefruit was made by crossing a pomelo and a sweet orange.

When breeders want to create a new type of citrus or experiment with multiple varieties, they come to UC Riverside to play with the genetic material. Yellow-and-green-striped lemons, football-size pomelos, heart-shaped grapefruits with deep red veins, and fruits so small they look like peas—they all thrive in the orchard. When cut, some varieties ooze a mucosal slime. Others have tiny juice bubbles with a caviar-like pop. Whatever happens, it's all by design.

THAI FOOD IN A TEMPLE PARKING LOT

WAT THAI MARKET • CALIFORNIA

How to try it

Wat Thai market, located at 8225 Coldwater Canyon Avenue, is open on Saturdays and Sundays from 8 a.m. to 5 p.m. To purchase food, you must exchange cash for tokens, which are accepted by the vendors.

Since the 1980s, Wat Thai market in Los Angeles has sold some of the best Thai food outside of Thailand. Located in the parking lot of a Buddhist temple, these outdoor food stalls were conceived by a handful of Thai grandmothers who wanted to share their family recipes. Today, this weekend-only market has transformed into a bustling Thai street scene with a devout following of Californians. Make your way through the thick, sweet-and-smoky air to find classics like pad thai and papaya salad, as well as the lesser-known but equally delicious crispy mussel pancake, sour Isaan sausage, meaty larb, and sweet coconut fritters.

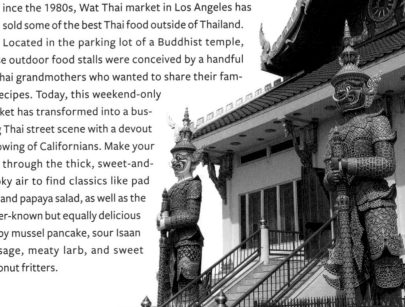

BROWNIE MARY

(1921–1999)

The *New York Times* compared Mary Jane Rathbun to American domestic goddesses Betty Crocker, Mrs. Field, and Sara Lee—with one big difference. Rathbun's signature baking ingredient was cannabis.

Born in 1921, Mary Jane—her real name—Rathbun spent 50 years working as a waitress. In the early 1970s she started selling pot brownies on the side. Her homemade flyers, decorated with squiggles and stars, advertised her "magically delicious" brownies. The marketing tactic brought police to her door, which she opened only to reveal dozens of brownies in her kitchen. Rathbun's first words to the cops were: "Oh, shit." At 57, she already had a sweet, elderly appearance, and reporters thrilled at the idea of a grass-slinging granny (Rathbun liked to smoke marijuana as well as bake it). Her arrest made national headlines.

Brownie Mary wearing her signature marijuana leaf button as she shows off her healing baked goods.

Charged with possession and sale of illegal drugs, Rathbun was sentenced to hundreds of hours of community service and became a fixture on the volunteering scene. In the 1980s, when San Francisco was hit hard by AIDS, Rathbun spent her time at San Francisco General Hospital, caring for AIDS and cancer patients. She called them her "kids," and to help alleviate their pain and nausea and stimulate their appetites, she baked them her signature pot brownies. In 1982, Rathbun was arrested again for bringing brownies to a cancer patient, but that didn't stop her—it's said that she baked some 1,500 brownies a month for patients. In 1986, the hospital named her "Volunteer of the Year."

Her third arrest, in 1992, also made the news, but this time headlines portrayed her as an AIDS activist who worked intimately with patients. Rathbun was ultimately acquitted of the charges, and August 25, 1992, was officially declared Brownie Mary Day.

Rathbun never gave up her signature brownie recipe. "When and if they legalize it, I'll sell my brownie recipe to Betty Crocker or Duncan Hines," she told a reporter, "and take the profits and buy an old Victorian for my kids with AIDS."

When Brownie Mary, the "angel of mercy," died of a heart attack in 1999, hundreds of people showed up to a vigil in her honor, hailing her as a social justice hero and a totally tubular baker.

INDIGENOUS CUISINE IN A BOOKSTORE

CAFE OHLONE • CALIFORNIA

Cafe Ohlone, a restaurant resurrecting local Indigenous American cuisine, was founded by two members of the Ohlone tribe whose ancestors hunted and gathered in the area centuries ago. Vincent Medina and Louis Trevino met at a 2014 conference on native languages and bonded while listening to records of tribal-elder interviews from the 1930s. Struck by the detailed information on disappearing culinary techniques, Medina and Trevino set out to re-create the recipes themselves. In 2018, they served their first meal on a patio behind Berkeley's University Press Books, where Cafe Ohlone still operates today.

How to try it

University Press Books closed in 2020 and Cafe Ohlone is looking for a new home in the Bay Area. In the meantime, they offer takeaway dinner boxes that contain prepared meals as well as ingredients you can use to make some of their dishes at home. You can reserve your box at makamham.com.

Founders Louis Trevino (left) and Vincent Medina (right) plating traditional Ohlone food at their café in Berkeley.

The Cafe Ohlone experience offers a glimpse into a little known Indigenous culture. Each meal begins with a solemn prayer in the Chochenyo language and a brief history of the native peoples of the East Bay Area, who preserved their culture despite persecution from successive Spanish, Mexican, and American governments. At each meal, Medina and Trevino introduce the dishes, which are based on wild ingredients gathered locally by native people. The menu changes seasonally, but it might include a cress, sorrel, and amaranth salad, venison meatballs with local mushrooms, an acorn flour brownie, and plenty of tea made from local herbs. Many meals close with songs or a fast-moving round of an ancient gambling game.

Cafe Ohlone's menu and hours are dependent on how much wild food they can sustainably source, so the restaurant updates their hours and offerings about three to four weeks in advance.

ENCRYPTED INEBRIATION

THE ZOMBIE • CALIFORNIA

How to try it

For an old-school experience, go to the tiny, cash-only Tiki-Ti in Los Angeles, which opened in the '60s. For the 21st-century spin, visit Jeff Berry's Latitude 29 in New Orleans, open since 2014.

The Zombie has a reputation for subduing its victims. The rum-based cocktail, invented at Hollywood restaurant Don the Beachcomber in 1934, packed such a punch that customers were cut off after two. And, for decades, proprietor Donn Beach—Zombie inventor and "father" of tiki—was the only person who knew what was in them.

Beach kept his liquors, elixirs, and proprietary mixes unlabeled behind the Beachcomber's bar. Each mystery bottle was given a number. The bartenders knew which bottles to pour and in what amount, but not what was in them. In other establishments, bartenders cobbled together fruit juices, syrups, and rum in a loose approximation of the original.

In 2007, tiki cocktail connoisseur and author Jeff "Beachbum" Berry solved the mystery. After finding a black book of coded recipes from Beach's restaurant, he worked with former Beachcomber staff to reverse engineer the cocktails. He published the decrypted Zombie recipe, nearly two decades after Donn Beach died, in the book *Sippin' Safari: In Search of the Great "Lost" Tropical Drink Recipes . . . and the People Behind Them.*

The Talented Groceries of
HOLLYWOOD POST-PRODUCTION

In the 1920s, when Universal Studios was transitioning from silent movies to sound, crewman Jack Foley showed them the way. His technique, now called "Foley art," was to lay an audio track over the film in post-production, adding sound effects like footsteps and slamming doors. Foley used unconventional methods to create convincing sounds, and today Foley artists reach for anything and everything to simulate the crunches, splashes, and thuds in the movies, which means food has been tapped to play some serious Hollywood roles.

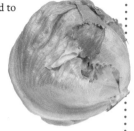

When freezing a wig and ripping Velcro didn't work, Foley artists turned to frozen lettuce to engineer the sound of Rose's ice-covered hair breaking as she clung to the headboard, waiting to be rescued after the shipwreck in **Titanic**.

The Foley artists working on **Fight Club** tried out many ways to mimic the sound of a physical brawl. One of the winners was punching a raw chicken stuffed with walnuts. The movie nabbed an Oscar for Best Sound Editing.

Terminator 2: Judgment Day opens with a postapocalyptic shot of Los Angeles in 2029, after a nuclear fire has killed three billion people. Shells of cars and human remains litter the ravaged landscape. From above the frame, a robotic foot crashes down, smashing a skull with a shattering succession of fractures and cracks. It sounds eerily like human bone. How did they do it? Pistachios.

Steven Spielberg wanted **E.T.** to sound "liquidy and friendly" when he moved, which inspired a Foley artist to wander a grocery store scouting for slippery, cheerful sounds. She found that packaged liver fit the bill, which, when mixed with the sound of jelly swishing in a wet towel and popcorn shifting gently in a bag, became the sound of the alien's movements.

When John Goodman lifts Jeff Bridges from his wheelchair in **The Big Lebowski**, Lebowski's back cracks audibly and he screams in pain—but it's just celery. Stalks of the green stuff are twisted and snapped to simulate breaking bones.

In **Jurassic Park**, a velociraptor hatches from its shell to the sound of an ice-cream cone being crumbled. The subsequent sound, of the baby dino emerging from its egg, was made by two gloved hands covered in liquid soap squishing the flesh of a melon.

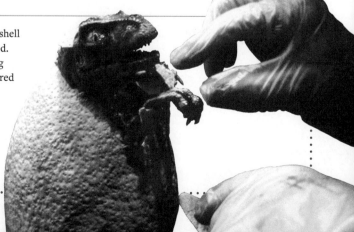

OREGON'S
Mysterious Mycology

O regonians hunt for mushrooms on vacation, take mushroom-cultivating classes at mushroom schools, attend fungus festivals, and occasionally ascend to the vocation of professional mushroom hunter. For the amateur aficionado or mycology maven, Oregon forests supply a buffet of unusual fungus ready to be identified, picked, and sautéed with brown butter.

BEAR'S HEAD TOOTH (*HERICIUM AMERICANUM*) is a mushroom that resembles a white, dripping mass of wax. The easily identified mushroom sprouts from trees and often takes up residence in recent cuts or wounds to the wood. When cooked, the soft spines are tender and sweet and taste vaguely of seafood.

CAULIFLOWER MUSHROOMS (*SPARASSIS CRISPA*) have curly, leafy lobes that grow into big spongy bushes. Once you've found a cauliflower mushroom, remember the place because they tend to grow in the same spot. After a meticulous cleaning, they're great simmered in flavorful liquid or broth, which brings out their lasagna noodle–like texture.

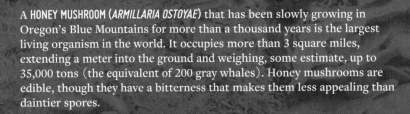

A HONEY MUSHROOM (*ARMILLARIA OSTOYAE*) that has been slowly growing in Oregon's Blue Mountains for more than a thousand years is the largest living organism in the world. It occupies more than 3 square miles, extending a meter into the ground and weighing, some estimate, up to 35,000 tons (the equivalent of 200 gray whales). Honey mushrooms are edible, though they have a bitterness that makes them less appealing than daintier spores.

LOBSTER MUSHROOMS (*HYPOMYCES LACTIFLUORUM*)
are not technically mushrooms but rather a
parasitic fungus that grows on mushrooms.
They appear after a heavy rain, often under
hemlock trees. Prized for their cooked-
lobster color and lobster-like flavor and
aroma, they pair well with seafood dishes.

BLACK TRUMPETS (*CRATERELLUS CORNUCOPIOIDES*)
are hollow, funnel-shaped mushrooms
with a dusty black-gray exterior. Finding
them can be tricky because they blend
into the forest floor, but their rich,
buttery, and woodsy flavor makes them
them a darling of the wild mushroom
world. When dried, they emit notes of
black truffle.

SAFFRON MILK CAPS (*LACTARIUS DELICIOSUS*)
are convex orange-capped mushrooms
with delicate gills. When they're sliced
open, the flesh excretes a milky, sunset-
colored latex liquid. When bruised,
they turn green. Milk caps are loved
around the world for their firm, almost
crunchy texture, and have been eaten
in Europe for millennia. Russians like
to preserve them in salt, while the
Spanish panfry them in garlic and olive
oil. Find them in pine forests or near
other conifers.

APRICOT JELLY (*GUEPINIA HELVELLOIDES*) is a bright, salmon-
colored, ear-shaped mushroom with a smooth,
gelatinous texture. Find it on the ground, generally
near a conifer tree. The thin, petal-like flesh is tasty
when raw in salads, as well as pickled or candied.

A GIANT PHALLIC CLAM

GEODUCK • WASHINGTON

Geoducks are harvested along coasts in the Pacific Northwest and have shells that can grow up to 8 inches (20 cm) long.

The geoduck (pronounced "gooey-duck") is the world's largest burrowing clam, found only in the coastal waters around Washington, British Columbia, and Alaska. The appearance of the hulking, wrinkled mollusk draws plenty of suggestive comparisons, but that doesn't deter its adoring international fan base.

By weight, geoducks are worth more than foie gras. Many characterize the clams as the ideal seafood: The meat is sweet and briny (without being fishy) and has a clean, snappy bite that's much crisper than other clams. Much of Washington's live geoduck is exported to restaurants in Asia. In China, geoducks are a prized hot pot ingredient, while in Japan they're eaten as sashimi. What stays in Washington is bought up quickly by locals, who make it into anything from chowder to carpaccio.

The area's Indigenous American Salish tribes gave the clam its name, which derives from gweduc, meaning "dig deep" in the Lushootseed language. As the geoduck grows, it uses its tiny foot to burrow into the seafloor, leaving only its neck above ground. With few natural predators, geoducks are one of the longest-living animals in the world. (The oldest phallic clam recorded was 168 years old.) Recently, scientists have been using the shells to study climate change. Much like trees, geoducks grow a ring each year and the width of that ring chronicles the temperature of the year.

How to try it
You can order a fresh 2-pound (1-kg) geoduck from the Washington company Taylor Shellfish Farms for $70.

AN OPEN-ACCESS EDIBLE PARK

BEACON FOOD FOREST • WASHINGTON

How to try it
Beacon Food Forest is located at 15 Avenue South and South Dakota Street. The Sound Transit Link Light Rail and the King County Metro routes #50, #60, and #36 are within walking distance of the forest.

The Seattle neighborhood of Beacon Hill is home to seven acres of public land teeming with trees, perennials, and annuals—a forest that provides the community with unlimited free access to fresh produce.

The Beacon Food Forest, among the largest public edible permaculture gardens in America, grows more than 350 species of plants and vegetables. Food forests are meant to mimic the natural, plant-based food production cycle of woodland ecosystems. All plants are positioned in a way that helps create harmony in growth. The canopy from large fruit trees, for example, shades smaller berry bushes, while root vegetables provide mulch. The plants are "layered," which means that vertical space is maximized. Ground vegetables grow beneath shrubs, which grow beneath dwarf trees, which grow beneath large trees. This diversity and density of plants ensures rich soil and copious amounts of food.

Anyone is allowed to forage in the Beacon Food Forest. Historically, residents of Beacon Hill have struggled with access to affordable local produce, and the open-door policy of the food forest is meant to remedy this nutritional deficit. There is no prerequisite for harvesting and eating, and no responsibilities in the form of gardening or volunteering. In this way, Beacon is distinguished from community gardens, where yields are often accessible only to those who manage the crops. Those who do work in the forest are given small plots of land for personal gardens, which cannot be bought, only worked for.

Food forests exist across the world, from Canada to Morocco to Vietnam, and have fed communities for thousands of years. Depending on the geography and climate, they all look a little different, but each design follows the basic rules of density, diversity, and layering in their pursuit of sustainable food security.

Beacon Food Forest breaking ground in 2012.

ESKIMO ICE CREAM

AKUTAQ • ALASKA

After a successful hunt, groups of Native Alaskan women gather to vigorously stir bowls of fat (generally from moose or caribou) and oil (usually from a seal) into akutaq, also known as Eskimo ice cream. From the Inupiaq word for "mixed together," akutaq is made by beating the fat and oil—and sometimes a bit of water or fresh snow—into a texture similar to whipped frosting.

Akutaq is made in two varieties. Savory meat-based akutaqs contain dried fish or ground caribou, which gives it a salty, often gamey taste. Berry-based versions, classically made with salmonberries or blueberries, are sweet yet briny, from the oil base. What goes into akutaq is dictated by the flora and fauna of the nearby terrain. In the North, there might be hints of caribou, bear, and musk-ox fat, while coastal akutaqs might use saltwater fish, and Southwestern akutaqs might include candlefish—an oily smelt that, when mixed with oil and fresh snow, creates an ephemeral frozen treat that lasts just minutes before collapsing.

How to try it
Check with the Yupiit Piciryarait Cultural Center in Bethel, Alaska, which is known to serve akutaq at events. The Alaska Native Medical Center offers the ice cream to patients as a part of the room-service menu. It can be ordered with or without fish.

RESCUING HIGHWAY MOOSE MEAT

ROADKILL SALVAGE PROGRAM • ALASKA

How to try it

Salvaging roadkill for human consumption is currently legal in 28 US states, although many require permits. Confer with local state laws before doing any highway harvesting.

n a state with nearly 200,000 roaming moose and high-speed roadways running through their habitat, vehicular moose collision is inevitable, especially during the coldest months when roads are icy and sunlight scarce. About 800 moose die in these impacts every year, along with the occasional bear, mountain goat, or caribou. Conservatively speaking, that leaves a million pounds of animal meat scattered across the state, which locals do not want to go to waste.

Alaska's solution was the Roadkill Salvage Program, launched in the 1970s and still thriving today. Every time a state trooper finds a big animal dead on the road, they report it to dispatchers who contact citizens and charities who have expressed interest in collecting moose cadavers and turning them into food (the lean red meat can be used like beef in stews, sausage, and burgers). Whoever can come fastest, usually with a flatbed truck and a winch, gets to salvage the animal and reap the spoils.

Kenai Peninsula has one of the highest rates of moose-vehicle collisions in Alaska; signs like this are updated regularly.

For institutions like food banks, where protein is difficult to come by, the roadkill program is a blessing. Alaskans also happen to love moose meat. Hunting moose for personal consumption is a popular Alaskan pastime, so eating an animal freshly slaughtered on the road is hardly a radical prospect. Many locals are also versed in recognizing a dead moose that's been corrupted by heat, time, or damage to internal organs—which keeps things safe and sanitary.

Although many states could benefit from a roadkill salvage program, Alaska's system likely isn't replicable elsewhere. In more populous areas, deer strikes happen in the tens of thousands, spread across road systems far more extensive than Alaska's. The biggest hurdle is that eating roadkill is a difficult sell in the lower 48 states, and perhaps for good reason: Deer and other big game outside Alaska have higher disease rates, and the weather is not as reliably frigid to prevent spoilage.

UNDERWATER PRODUCE

SEA PEACHES • ALASKA

How to try it

Sea peaches are found in the northern Pacific Ocean, from the Arctic Sea to the Puget Sound, 130–330 feet (40–100 m) below the surface. They're farmed commercially in Japan.

uspended in the Bering Sea, Saint Lawrence Island experiences powerful fall storms that churn the deep surrounding waters, gathering the sea's contents and heaving it onto the shoreline. For the Yupik people, Indigenous Alaskans who have lived on the island for centuries, autumn is a delicious time of year because the beach becomes blanketed with salty edibles. The Yupik call them sea foods or sea vegetables, but many of them are technically animals:

spineless invertebrates called tunicates that look like colorful organs and live on the sea floor.

The most popular "vegetable" is perhaps the sea peach, which looks like a human heart with two open valves and tastes like salty ocean with a rubbery chew. Sea peaches live stationary lives, attached to rocks, so it takes a good storm to dislodge the creatures and send them flying. When there isn't enough shoreline treasure to go around (the beach tends to be crowded after a squall), serious fans tie a long rope to a rake and either comb the water from the shoreline or get in a boat and drop the rake into the sea.

Other Underwater Produce

SEA PINEAPPLES

These oblong, sunset-colored creatures are covered with pointy knobs that squirt water when squeezed. Sea pineapples attach to rocks and grow rubbery shells to protect a soft, oozy meat that resembles an oyster but tastes briny and bitter with a slightly metallic aftertaste. Sea pineapples are popular in Korea and Japan, where they're eaten raw with vinegar-based sauces. The sea pineapple's agriculture was developed in the 1980s and has since become big business: About 21 tons are collected every year.

These so-called fruits and vegetables have a devoted following on dry land.

SEA GRAPES

Nicknamed "green caviar," these tiny verdant pearls pop in the mouth, releasing a burst of saline and seaweed. In Asia, where they're primarily eaten, the algae clusters are mixed into salads and used as a topping for sushi, rice bowls, and noodles. The residents of Okinawa, Japan, are especially fond of what they call umi-budō. They eat the green orbs in abundance and live longer than most people on Earth, which correlates with the food's other nickname: longevity seaweed.

SEA CUCUMBERS

A $60 million market, most sea cucumbers are harvested by hand, dried, and sold as a delicacy to Asian countries. There are more than a thousand species of the bottom-dwelling brainless hermaphrodites, but only a few are commercially valuable. Sea cucumbers are used in traditional Chinese medicine to treat everything from impotence to kidney issues. The mild-flavored, fishy-smelling critter has a slippery texture that takes some getting used to, but many have and are willing to pay up to $1,000 per kilo to eat them.

SPICED HAM STREET PARTY

SPAM JAM • HAWAII

Every April, Spam fans from across the globe make their way to the island of Oahu to pay homage to the beloved mystery meat. The Waikiki Spam Jam, a massive food festival and the largest Spam celebration in the world, has been delivering Spam fantasies since 2002, and it's only getting hammier.

Invented in the Midwest, Spam was brought to Hawaii during World War II by American soldiers, where it found its most enthusiastic fan base. Hawaiians eat seven million cans every year, and a typical grocery store may carry a dozen varieties including Turkey Spam, Chorizo Spam, and Hickory Smoke Spam.

With a population this devoted, the Spam Jam is a big deal. Spread along Waikiki's posh Kalakaua Avenue, flanked by high-end shopping and luxury hotels, the festival is a big event on the local social calendar. Larger-than-life Spam cans walk the street, waving happily at festivalgoers who stand in line for Spam musubi (a kind of Spam sushi), Spam pizza, buttery Spam pastries, Spam fries, macadamia nuts covered in powdered Spam, coconut Spam custard, and chocolate-covered Spam. Live music and hula dancers take the stage with Spam-loving celebrities. This is a festival with no tipping point: The more Spam T-shirts, Spam tattoos, and Spam animal mascots, the better.

The Hawaiian love for Spam is true, unironic, and deeply felt. Despite its reputation elsewhere, there is no social stigma against Spam in Hawaii, and the over-the-top festival, which attracts 35,000 people each year, feels like a natural expression of the islands' reverence for the delicious, versatile, inimitable canned meat.

A PERFECT PINEAPPLE

SUGARLOAF PINEAPPLE • HAWAII

If a tangy, juicy, yellow pineapple has any flaws, it's the unpalatable core and the prickly feeling left in your mouth after eating too much. In both cases, bromelain is the culprit. The enzyme is known to irritate the mouth, and aside from the stem, the highest concentration is found in the pineapple's core.

But the issues that plague the traditional pineapple are nonexistent in the sugarloaf, a variety that grows on the islands of Hawaii. The white, creamy flesh is unfathomably sweet with almost no acid, the core is edible, and no matter how much you eat, the aftertaste is clean. The variety also grows in South America and West Africa, but Hawaii is the sugarloaf's main stage. The rich, volcanic soil and long history of pineapple cultivation make the islands, and the islanders, especially adept at coddling the finicky fruit. A new plant requires 18 to 24 months to bear its first fruit, and because pineapples produce no seeds, they can only be grown through hard-won propagation material.

Delicious Diaspora

HAWAII'S PLATE LUNCH

Hawaiian cuisine is easily misunderstood. Outsiders tend to think of pineapple-glazed meats and flaming cocktails. Traditionally, Hawaiian food means pounded taro and coconut pudding, smoked octopus, and earthen ovens. But contemporary Hawaiian food, known colloquially as local food, is something quite different.

Since the 1850s, when migrant workers began arriving from around the world to work the sugarcane and pineapple plantations, the cuisine of Hawaii has evolved into a distinctive mishmash of foreign influence—and the plate lunch is the ultimate expression of how locals really eat.

The Hawaiian plantations of the 19th century were a hotbed of cultural exchange. Chinese, Japanese, Koreans, Filipinos, Puerto Ricans, and Portuguese lived in migrant communities where shops and grocery stores catered to the multitude of ethnicities. The Japanese bento, the traditional portable meal, is believed to be the foundation for the Hawaiian plate lunch. Because the workers were predominantly Asian, rice was the cheap and comforting starch of choice that accompanied a main dish from their home countries. With time, the patchwork community began to exchange recipes and a distinct cuisine emerged. Korean kimchi was served alongside Japanese chicken katsu, Chinese chow mein beside Filipino pork adobo and native Hawaiian kalua pork. The options continued to evolve: After World War II and leading up to Hawaii's statehood, Spam became a standard addition, followed by continental American classics like chili and hamburger steak.

The plantation work eventually came to an end, but plate lunches stuck around, becoming the default lunch of day laborers and construction workers before establishing itself as arguably the island's favorite meal. Thanks to lunch wagons and restaurants, a universal format took shape. Plate lunch, to this day, always includes a protein, two scoops of white rice, and one scoop of macaroni salad. (Ice-cream scoops are standard operating equipment.)

Plate lunch, with its many cuisines sharing a limited space, provides an easy metaphor for contemporary Hawaiian culture. Hawaii is an island—a collision of cultures in a finite area—working to form a unified community while remaining distinct and honoring the cultures' separate identities. Unlike fusion food, plate lunch keeps recipes and traditions intact. The idea is to make room on the plate for everyone.

Though the foods span many cultures, they all find a home on the plate.

FOUR CORNERS AND THE SOUTHWEST

GIANT ORGAN PIZZERIA

ORGAN STOP PIZZA • ARIZONA

How to try it

Find Organ Stop Pizza at 1149 E. Southern Ave. in Mesa.

Each night in Mesa, Arizona, the largest theater pipe organ ever created rises on a rotating hydraulic elevator above a 700-seat dining room filled with patrons enjoying pizza, pasta, and sandwiches. Played by a virtuoso theater organist, the 276-key instrument is linked to a mind-boggling series of xylophones, glockenspiels, gongs, and cymbals.

The landmark attraction was the brainchild of the late William P. Brown, a real-estate developer, pizza enthusiast, and accomplished theater organist. The original Organ Stop Pizza opened in Phoenix in 1972 and was so popular, Brown opened a second, larger outpost in Mesa. Today, the eccentric Mesa pizzeria is owned by longtime employee Mike Everitt, who has expanded the organ so much that the show had to be moved to its current largest location in 1995.

While diners sup below, four industrial blowers pump pressurized air through the 6,000 pipes of the 1927 Wurlitzer organ, which is insured for $5 million. The performance hall restaurant serves 300,000 visitors each year, while the organ plays classics like "The Flight of the Bumblebee," "The Hills Are Alive" from *The Sound of Music*, "Under the Sea" from *The Little Mermaid*, and the theme from *Star Wars*.

A COMPETITIVE DISPOSAL OF TERRIBLE CAKE

THE GREAT FRUITCAKE TOSS • COLORADO

How to try it

The event is held in late January. Entrance costs one nonperishable food item for a local charity. Those who ate their holiday fruitcake can throw a "rental" for a dollar.

There is an American Christmas tradition of gifting a fruitcake, which endures despite the other American tradition of disliking fruitcake. All too often, the sweet, dense, and artificially flavored loaf gets tossed in the trash—which gave the residents of Manitou Springs a brilliant idea.

In 1996, a group of fruitcake haters gathered in a public park to dispose of their unloved Christmas cakes. Instead of the trash, they launched them across the park, which sparked a local competition that's been going strong for two decades. The

annual January celebration has grown to include a slew of events. In addition to the classic hand toss, there has been a fruitcake slingshot (with robotic, mechanical, and three-man divisions) and a pneumatic weapon launch. In 2007, a team of Boeing engineers shot a cake 1,420 feet (433 m) using a mock artillery piece. (By comparison, the hand toss winner that year clocked 124 feet / 38 m.) Children have their own division complete with targets, as well as speed and balance games. Those less athletically inclined can enter the fruitcake costume competition or the "Too Good to Toss" bake-off.

ELVIS PRESLEY'S CROSS-COUNTRY INDULGENCE

FOOL'S GOLD SANDWICH • COLORADO

Elvis Presley once ate a sandwich made with a whole jar of blueberry jam, a whole jar of peanut butter, and an entire pound of bacon. The novelty item, served at the now-defunct Colorado Mine Company in Denver, was known as the Fool's Gold. It cost $49.95 and was served in an entire hollowed-out loaf of bread.

The King never forgot the sandwich. On February 1, 1976, he went back for a second round. Rather than re-create the Fool's Gold at Graceland (his home in Memphis, Tennessee), he took his private jet to Denver and back in one night. The owners of the Colorado Mine Company recall bringing 30 gargantuan loaves directly to the plane. Elvis and his comrades ate and drank from the comfort of the Combs hangar at Stapleton International Airport (also defunct), then flew back home.

How to try it
Nick's Café in Golden, Colorado, is run by a chef who cooked for Elvis as a teenager, then went on to open this Elvis-themed diner where you can order the Fool's Gold.

Nick Andurlakis served the King a Fool's Gold sandwich in 1976, and now he whips them up in his diner in Golden.

AN OLD WEST EATERY ON THE PONY EXPRESS

MIDDLEGATE STATION • NEVADA

How to try it

Middlegate Station is located at 42500 Austin Highway. They open daily at 7 a.m. and serve until 9 or 10 p.m.

Alongside a stretch of the historic Lincoln Highway, US Route 50, dubbed the Loneliest Road in America, is an isolated Wild West–style saloon announced by a wooden sign that (accurately) describes its location as "in the middle of nowhere."

This rustic restaurant in the heart of the Nevada desert, decorated with bull skulls, a neon "BAR" sign, and an antique wagon, is Middlegate Station, a historic eatery created in the 19th century as a stop on the Pony Express. Founded in 1857 by James Simpson, the restaurant that stands today was once an active station and rest stop along the historic trail. When the Pony Express ceased operations in October 1861, Middlegate Station stayed open, serving as a stage and freight stop for gold and silver mines. Since then, the outpost has survived as the only gas station for nearly 50 miles (80 km) in either direction and a rare roadside eatery along the Lincoln Highway. Their Middlegate Monster Burger is legendary, so big that anyone who finishes it wins a T-shirt.

Another attraction of Middlegate Station is the ceiling covered in cash, where you can leave a donation of your own. According to the owner, the cash ceiling started because there was no bank nearby. Regulars would attach dollar bills to the ceiling, write their names on them, and leave the cash to spend on another visit.

Middlegate, an unincorporated Nevada community, has a population of 17.

THE WORLD'S ONLY HOT PEPPER SCHOOL

CHILE PEPPER INSTITUTE • NEW MEXICO

New Mexicans are known to put chile sauce on anything. Made from one of the state's official vegetables (despite technically being a fruit), chile sauce is suitable for sandwiches, pizza, stew, pasta, and even wine. New Mexico chiles are roasted and pureed into green sauce or dried and reconstituted into red sauce and ladled on everything from burgers to enchiladas. New Mexico was the first state to adopt an official state question: red or green? When asking for both types of chile sauce, the answer is "Christmas."

This abundance and fervor for chile sauce is largely thanks to the Chile Pepper Institute at New Mexico State University. Mexican-born horticulturalist Fabian Garcia, a member of the first graduating class in 1894, was appointed director of the Agricultural Experimentation Station in 1913. He dedicated much of his work to breeding chiles, and successfully cultivated the first pepper with a standard pod and heat level, which he called "New Mexico 9." This pepper became the catalyst for the state's booming chile industry, which now grows on about 8,000 acres. The Science Center, where the Chile Pepper Institute is located and peppers from around the world are researched and bred, is named after the pioneering pepper maven.

The Chile Pepper Institute is a nonprofit program whose objective is to educate the public about chiles—from growing and picking to tasting, cooking, and extinguishing a burning mouth. The world's largest pepper, the foot-long Numex Big Jim, was developed at NMSU in the 1970s; in 2001, NMSU tested the hard-to-find Bhut Jolokia pepper from northeastern India and declared it the world's hottest pepper. Outside, in the Teaching Garden, the program grows more than 150 varieties of peppers. It not only showcases beautiful, flourishing peppers from classic green to vibrant violet, it's a teaching ground for how to fight against disease and treat prevailing problems. The institute also sells obscure chile pepper seeds, offers chile sauce tastings, and hawks Bhut Jolokia brownie mix and frozen bags of roasted peppers.

How to try it

The institute is located in room 265 of Gerald Thomas Hall. The Teaching Garden can be found at 113 West University Avenue, Las Cruces. To visit, call to make a reservation. You can also shop their online store, which ships chiles across the United States.

Paul Bosland, longtime director of the Chile Pepper Institute, oversaw experiments like creating a "spiceless" jalapeño.

TRADITIONAL FOOD OF TAOS PUEBLO

TIWA KITCHEN • NEW MEXICO

How to try it
Tiwa Kitchen serves
lunch from 11 a.m. to
4 p.m. and is closed on
Tuesdays.

The Indigenous American Taos people have continuously inhabited the legend-ary Taos Pueblo, a collection of multistoried adobe buildings, for more than 1,000 years. Located just off the highway en route to this UNESCO World Heritage Site, Tiwa Kitchen is as close as it gets to being invited for lunch at a local family's table.

Owners Ben and Debbie Sandoval began constructing the Pueblo adobe build-ing by hand in 1992. Out back, they constructed an adobe oven, called a horno, for baking traditional breads, cookies, and pies. A rare outpost for home-style Pueblo and New Mexican comfort food, Tiwa Kitchen serves dishes that have been passed from generation to generation—taught to Ben by his grandmothers.

Phien-tye is a dish of blue corn fry bread stuffed with buffalo and covered in chili.

Ben, who grew up in Taos Pueblo, incorporates local ingredients into the menu. The Pueblo's bison herd supplies meat for their burgers, served on buns baked out back in the horno. Homegrown blue corn adds a crisp coating to local trout and appears in hard-to-find specialties such as Phien-tye (pictured to the left) and steaming mugs of grits-like, periwinkle atole. Even popular New Mexican dishes, such as the restau-rant's heirloom red chile stew, are crafted using crops harvested from Pueblo land.

24-HOUR FULL-SIZE PIES

PECAN PIE VENDING MACHINE • TEXAS

How to try it
Berdoll Pecan Candy &
Gift Company is located
at 2626 TX-71, where
the vending machine is
always open.

If you're driving through Texas down Highway 71, keep an eye out for a sign pointing the way to a giant squirrel statue holding a pecan. Once you've seen the 14-foot (4.3 m) squirrel (her name is Ms. Pearl), make your way to the less flashy but equally glorious landmark beside her: a vending machine stocked with full-size homemade pecan pies.

Both Ms. Pearl and the pie vending machine belong to the nearby Berdoll Pecan Farm. Their pecan pies are in such high demand that the business put in a 24-hour vending machine to satisfy pie lovers around the clock. The pecan pie machine—the only one of its kind in the United States—is located out front of the Berdoll Pecan Candy & Gift Company shop. It's restocked every day with freshly baked pies and other pecan treats, with even more frequency during the holiday season. Those visiting during business hours can do their shopping inside the store.

To find an all-night pecan pie machine, look for the squirrel as tall as a house.

COW'S HEAD BARBECUE

BARBACOA DE CABEZA • TEXAS

In northern Mexico, the word *barbacoa*, or barbecue, still typically refers to goat's meat. Central Mexicans associate the word with lamb, while the people of the Yucatàn prefer barbecue pork. And in Texas, where the Mexican culinary influence runs deep, barbacoa often means barbacoa de cabeza, or cow's head barbecue.

Borrowing from the traditional Mexican technique, cows' heads are wrapped in water-soaked burlap and maguey leaves, then buried in pozos, or wells, heated by wood embers. The pit is covered with more maguey leaves, and the swaddled head is left to cook for hours until the meat is tender and glistening with fat.

Almost every piece of meat on a cow's head is edible. The lengua (tongue) is fatty and luscious. The cachete, or cheeks, are tender and beefy. The brain is creamy. The eyes are gelatinous. The gristle and cartilage counter the soft, silky bits, and the head as a whole—when chopped up and nestled in a warm tortilla, as is the fate of all proper barbacoa—is brightened and balanced by a topping of salsas, cilantro, and onions.

How to try it

Vera's Backyard Bar-B-Que in Brownsville makes barbacoa de cabeza using the old-fashioned pit technique. They go through about 65 heads every weekend.

THE POTATO DOUGHNUT

SPUDNUTS • UTAH

During the 1930s, brothers Al and Bob Penton were living in California, working unfulfilling jobs, and dreaming up ways to reinvent the doughnut. Bob, who had served in the navy as a baker, had a German doughnut recipe that called for potatoes. The brothers began experimenting with spuds—adding potato water to the doughnut dough, mixing in mashed potatoes—before landing on a mix with dehydrated potatoes. The brothers returned home to Utah and set up shop.

Spudnuts, as the brothers named them, were large, fluffy doughnuts fried in shortening and glazed. The potatoes in the mix absorbed moisture, which kept them tender, while their starchy consistency held air and made them light. Instead of giving up their secret formula, the Pentons decided to franchise by selling their dry doughnut mix, and by the end of the 1940s, there were more than 200 Spudnut shops across the country.

Spudnut was the first doughnut chain in America and, for many years, it was also the largest. (At its peak, there were more than 300 stores across the United States, Canada, and Japan.) But their decline came almost as quickly as their success.

How to try it

Spudnut shops now use various dough recipes because the mix became unavailable when Bake-N-Serv went under. In Utah, try Johnny O's Spudnuts, which has outposts in Layton and Logan.

In 1968, the Penton brothers sold their company to Vancouver-based Pace Industries, and in 1973, Pace sold the company to North Dakota–based Bake-N-Serv. When the Bake-N-Serv owner was convicted of fraud and conspiracy in 1979, the company closed and all the Spudnut franchises were orphaned.

Spudnuts, made with dehydrated potato, were all the rage in mid-century America.

A CASSEROLE FOR MORMONS IN MOURNING

FUNERAL POTATOES • UTAH

How to try it

No one has to die for you to eat funeral potatoes. The Hoof & Vine steakhouse in Salt Lake City serves them at dinner Monday through Saturday.

A death in the Mormon community is eased with a warm, comforting casserole of potatoes (shredded or cubed), canned cream soup (chicken or mushroom), butter, sour cream, and grated cheddar cheese. On top, there is always a crunchy sprinkling of corn flakes.

While no one's exactly sure where funeral potatoes originated, most sources attribute their spread to the Relief Society, a women's organization within the Church of Jesus Christ of Latter-day Saints. Society members attend to the needs of the bereaved, including meals, and the ingredients of funeral potatoes were almost always stocked in a Mormon pantry. Mormons are urged to maintain a three-month food supply at all times. The stockpile is intended to hedge against hard times, which could be a layoff, a natural disaster, or a funeral.

Funeral potatoes—with their creamy starchiness—provide a soothing hit of comfort. But this dish isn't just for Mormons, and the recipe has spread throughout Utah. In 2002, when Salt Lake City hosted the Winter Olympics, the official pins featured little casseroles of funeral potatoes.

Anti-Masturbatory Food

Presbyterian minister Sylvester Graham was one of the leading voices of the anti-alcohol temperance movement of the early 19th century—but his real passion was vegetarianism, which he hoped would cure Americans of "self-abuse" (more formally known as masturbation). His Graham Diet eschewed all foods that provided pleasure or could be associated with indulgence. He called these foods "excitants" because he believed they fired the blood, and they included all spices (even salt and pepper), condiments (like vinegar and mustard), candy, eggs, and most dairy. To combat these thrilling foods, he invented the graham cracker— a coarse unbleached flour, bran, and wheat germ biscuit meant to dull the senses and keep people from touching themselves. Graham died in 1851, at the age of 57, before his graham cracker was commercially processed with sugar and used as a vessel for chocolate and marshmallows.

One of Graham's most fervent followers was John Harvey Kellogg, anti-masturbation health activist and actual medical doctor. Kellogg, who spent most of his life as a Seventh-day Adventist, also believed a bland vegetarian diet would curb sexual urges and keep people pure. He ran a sanitarium in Battle Creek, Michigan, where he experimented with recipes for bland breakfast food. Around 1877 he baked a wheat, oat, and corn dough that he crumbled and sold as "granula." But Kellogg's biggest break was in cereal flakes, a process he and his brother discovered when they ran a sheet of stale dough through the rolling machine. Cereal became a health trend, a cold plain food in direct opposition to the era's standard morning meal of meat, potatoes, cake, and pie. Kellogg believed eating his cereal would keep the public from carnal impulses, and it might have worked had not his brother, Will Kellogg, insisted on adding sugar to the flakes and advertising them as fun, tasty food. (It was Will, not John, behind the Kellogg Company that brought sugary cereals mainstream.)

GREAT PLAINS

IDAHO STURGEON ROE

WHITE STURGEON CAVIAR • IDAHO

How to try it

White sturgeon is now being farmed in other states such as California and Maine. For the Idaho variety, get in touch with the Fish Breeders of Idaho, who take orders by phone and email.

daho caviar is something of an industry secret. Most of the world still associates the luxury product with Beluga sturgeon, which was severely overfished in the 20th century and is now critically endangered. In 1988, Idaho fishermen found their rivers made a prime habitat for white sturgeon, a species native to North America, and set out to farm the fish sustainably. Like Beluga, white sturgeon is enormous and commonly grows to 7 feet (2 m) and more than 1,000 pounds (454 kg). The impressive size means impressive eggs: large, shiny globules that pop clean, sweet, and briny in the mouth.

Idaho now boasts a number of caviar farms, each with their own technique. At Leo Ray's in Hagerman, the sturgeon live in a pool that is perpetually refreshed with cold mountain streams and warm geothermal water, impeding the growth of unwanted algae that muddies the flavor. The egg harvest is timed just before the fish would lay them herself (harvest too early and the flavor is undeveloped; too late and the eggs lose their taut, poppable quality). In the days leading up to the harvest, the fish is biopsied using a plastic tube, so a small sample of eggs can be examined. Patience and accuracy is of the essence because the sturgeon must be killed to harvest its eggs. When the time comes, the sacs are removed by hand from the belly and the eggs gently separated from the membrane, rinsed, salted, and canned. The rest of the fish is also sold.

Researchers tag a great white sturgeon in the Snake River in Hells Canyon.

Delicious Diaspora

BASQUES IN IDAHO

The Basques, who occupy a small autonomous region on the border of France and Spain, are thought to be the oldest civilization of Europe. (Their language, Euskera, is the oldest European language.) The Romans report contact with them as early as 200 BCE, but the Basques did not keep written records, so their origins are cloaked in almost impenetrable obscurity. It's also difficult to track their diaspora because most censuses don't differentiate between Basque and Spanish. But in Idaho, where Basques began to settle in the late 1800s, their presence is well known, and the state is now the unlikely home to the most concentrated Basque population outside of Basque country—with around 15,000 in Boise alone.

Drawn to Idaho as sheepherders and silver miners, early Basque immigrants cultivated a community, bringing over wives and workers to help develop the sheep industry. The first Basque boardinghouses opened in 1900, offering rooms to

shepherds. As the life of a shepherd was solitary, these houses became lively, social places for Basques to gather and speak their language, eat their foods, and drink the wines of their home country. The Basque American style of large-format, family-style meals originated in these boardinghouses.

Along downtown Boise's Basque Block, the glory of the cuisine is on full display. Bar Gernika specializes in chicken croquetas and classic sandwiches like solomo (marinated pork loin with pimento peppers), beef tongue, and chorizo. Along with cooking classes, the Basque Market offers pintxos (Basque for tapas) and a tasting flight of the region's best wines. Leku Ona is where you'll find the family-style platters that hearken back to the boardinghouse days, featuring lamb stew, meatballs, and fried cod. Perhaps the most Basque of all is the kalimotxo, which is easily found in every bar along the street and delivers a perfect combination of Basque and American influence: half red wine, half Coca-Cola.

The Oinkari Basque Dancers perform at the Trailing of the Sheep Festival in Hailey, Idaho.

THE FIRST
American Fireworks

Long before Americans celebrated Independence Day by lighting up the night sky, the earliest European colonizers gathered to watch nocturnal displays of pyrotechnics. "Such a fire is a splendid sight when one sails on the rivers at night while the forest is ablaze on both banks," wrote Adriaen van der Donck, a prominent early resident of New York. These weren't modern fireworks—they were annual burns set by local Indigenous American tribes to transform the surrounding landscape on an epic scale.

Across the continent, different tribes set fires for different reasons. Fires warded off rattlesnakes and mosquitoes, cleared land for homes, and denied enemy tribes cover they could use in an attack. Fire also played a key role in North America's food system.

BISON HABITATS

Early American colonizers were astonished by the abundance of buffalo roaming the stretch of land that came to be called the Great Plains. The Plains Indians used fire to increase the buffalo's habitat, essentially creating a man-made game park.

HUNTING

Annual burns cleared out undergrowth, making American forests as pleasant and easy to walk through as planned parks. This increased the number of deer, bison, and other prey. But fire was used in the hunt itself, too. Whether pursuing moose, alligators, rabbits, or grasshoppers, tribes could cut off their prey's escape with fire.

BERRIES AND NUTS

Burning created the conditions to gather huckleberries, strawberries, blackberries, and raspberries. It also increased the availability of nuts, especially acorns. Fires cleared way for oak trees that produced nuts that could be gathered each fall to make porridge and bread.

FARMING

North America is one of the most wooded places on Earth, which made fire an essential tool for clearing land to plant crops such as squash, beans, or maize, the dominant grain of the Americas. Fires on existing fields also killed pests and weeds, while providing ash that acted as fertilizer for the next crop.

European artist Karl Bodmer's painting Bison Hunting on the Prairie *depicts Indigenous American hunters in the 19th century.*

NATURE'S SPICE RACK

AMERICAN SPICEBUSH • KANSAS

Bite into a berry from the American spicebush and experience a spice rack exploding in your mouth: The small, round fruit contains notes of mace, pink peppercorn, sassafras, and the seasoning known as allspice. But the berry is not the only flavorful part of the North American plant—the bark and leaves, once used by Indigenous Americans to flavor meat and brew medicinal teas, have a peppery taste with a warm kick of cinnamon.

With its collision of familiar flavors, the versatile spicebush has also served as a handy seasoning substitute. During the Revolutionary War, when reserves of the Caribbean-derived allspice ran low, home cooks simply plucked the fruit growing in their backyards, ground it into a powder, and swapped it into their recipes.

How to try it

In Kansas, the spicebush is native to the southeast, growing in moist soil along riverbanks and in wetlands. Outside of Kansas, it can be found in similar conditions from the East Coast to Texas. The plant blooms in early spring.

THE HISTORICAL VACATION BERRY

HUCKLEBERRIES • MONTANA

Huckleberries, the blueberry's wild doppelgänger, have never been commercially farmed. The tart, sometimes bitter fruit with crunchy seeds thrives on steep slopes among heavy brush. The huckleberry plant requires a finicky balance of sunlight, warmth, and moisture in order to bear fruit during its fleeting two-month season.

Montana huckleberry yields are some of the highest in the country. Indigenous tribes drew the connection between productive harvests and intermittent burning. After a fire, the huckleberries would go fallow, but eventually the ashy, nutrient-rich soil would bring an explosive crop. For centuries, Indigenous Americans burned areas and then reaped the fruit, relying on the berries as a staple of their diet. Using the backbones of salmon, they made combs to cull the fruit from the bush and stockpiled the berries in massive quantities, drying them and mashing them into cakes.

In 1910, an enormous wildfire blazed through northern Montana. Two decades later, the area reaped massive huckleberry returns. Indigenous Americans set up camp on one side of the land, erecting hundreds of tepees, while other locals grouped together and pitched tents across the way. When the season opened, the buzzy atmosphere was compared to the California Gold Rush.

These days, huckleberry picking is still a competitive sport. Most seasons there aren't enough berries to go around, and so the huckleberry's value resets every year.

While huckleberries are mostly used in the same way as blueberries (in pancakes, muffins, pies, jams), fans of the huck say they pack more flavor, texture, and character than the standard blue supermarket variety. For the devoted, the inaccessibility is part of the huckleberry's charm.

How to try it

Around midsummer, you can start picking huckleberries in the Flathead Valley in northwest Montana. Picking in the Flathead National Forest is free and does not require a permit, unless you plan to pick more than 10 gallons a person.

Agriculture That Changes the Weather

Corn Belt Climate Change

The American "Corn Belt"—the Midwest's unfathomable expanse of cornfields—is the world's most productive agricultural region. In recent years, corn yields have been explosive: From 1950 to 2010, production increased from 3 billion to about 10 billion bushels each year.

Nebraska farmers have since sensed shifts in the weather. Summers have been wetter and 100°F (37°C) days fewer than before—observations that contradict many predictions of global warming.

The new weather patterns have to do with what farmers call "corn sweat." As plants open their pores to let in carbon dioxide, they also release water. This process, called transpiration, cools the plant and the air surrounding it, while also increasing the amount of water in the air, which will eventually return as rainfall. More corn means more transpiration, which accounts for the cooler, wetter weather.

By studying observed data and modeling the region's climate, MIT researchers found that the intensified corn production has increased the region's summer rainfall by 5 to 15 percent, and decreased the temperature by as much as 33°F (1°C). While temperatures around the world have risen, the study confirmed that eastern Nebraska has gotten cooler thanks to the heavy agriculture, which has counteracted the effects of greenhouse gas emissions. (In China, similar effects have been observed in rice-growing regions.)

The region's explosive agricultural growth is unsustainable. Only so much corn can grow on the limited amount of land, and greenhouse gas emissions have no real limit. Eventually, the mitigatory effects produced by agriculture will be overtaken. For some farmers, knowing this helps them prepare for the future, which likely includes the return of droughts. Until then, many are working on reducing fuel consumption and increasing efficiency during the window of favorable weather.

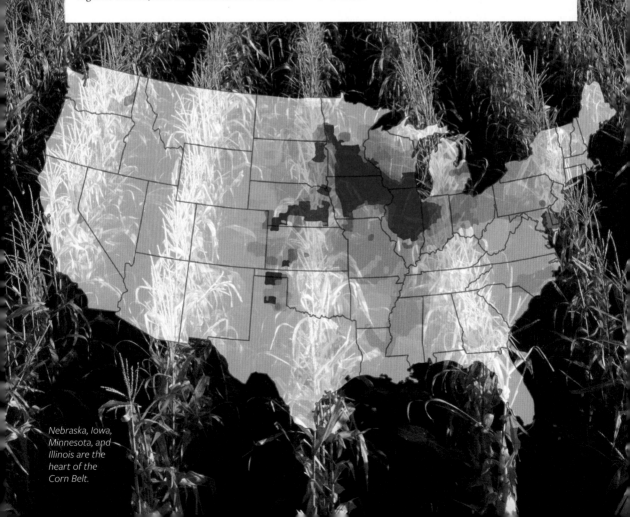

Nebraska, Iowa, Minnesota, and Illinois are the heart of the Corn Belt.

THE INTERNATIONAL ART OF
Corn on the Cob

Corn, known as maize in most of the world, was domesticated 10,000 years ago by the Indigenous people of modern Mexico. It was revered as a gift from the gods, a motherly substance, and even life itself. Corn was uniquely Mesoamerican until the 15th century, when the plant caught the attention of European voyagers. Columbus brought corn back to Spain, where it slowly spread north. Around the same time, Portuguese traders carried the plant east to Africa and Asia. In each place, corn kept moving. By the end of the 16th century, the Ottoman army was eating maize, China was drawing pictures of it, and it was growing in Germany, India, and Thailand.

Corn flourished almost everywhere it went. While some, namely Europeans, first mistrusted the new plant as food, corn found an essential place in diets across the globe. The versatile, resilient vegetable-cum-starch was adopted and transformed by countless culinary traditions, which is apparent in the myriad ways an ear of corn is eaten around the world.

TAIWANESE

Basted with garlic soy paste and sweet chili sauce, blackened on the grill, then slathered with lard.

PERUVIAN

Giant kernel white corn (choclo) boiled and served with a slab of fresh cheese and an herbaceous sauce called huacatay.

KENYAN

Grilled and doused in lime, rolled in ground salt and chilies, and served in its own husk as a carrying case.

KOREAN

Glutinous waxy corn steamed or boiled in salted, sugared water until the texture is sticky and chewy.

AMERICAN SOUTH

Whole ear pushed onto a stick, dipped in cornmeal batter, and fried until crispy.

PERSIAN

Blistered on a grill, then dunked in hot salt water to season.

Corn on the cob is a popular street food worldwide, from the Shilin Night Market in Taipei, Taiwan (left), to the chocolo vendors in Cusco, Peru (right).

NEBRASKA'S BEEFY HAND WARMER

RUNZA • NEBRASKA

How to try it

Runzas are readily available in Nebraskan bakeries. Runza the restaurant chain uses scratch-made dough and local beef sourced primarily from Nebraska. Their flavors include Swiss and mushroom, BBQ bacon, and BLT (bacon, lettuce, and tomato).

Runza history begins with Catherine the Great, a German princess who married into the Russian royal family in 1745. During her three-decade reign as empress of Russia, she invited Germans to move to her adopted country, enticing them with the promise of autonomy. No men would serve in the army, no family would pay taxes for 30 years, and all immigrants would have full governmental control of their villages and schools. Many Germans accepted her offer and came to farm the Volga River Valley. They began making something called bierok, a yeast dough filled with meat, which became the portable meal of choice for field workers. The Volga River Germans stayed for about a century, until Alexander II came to power and repealed his great-grandmother Catherine's law. Throughout the 1870s, Russian Germans were stripped of their special privileges. Rather than bend to the new regime, the Germans sent scouts out into the world to find a new place, similar to the Volga River Valley, to live. When the scouts returned, they recommended Nebraska.

The German word *runza* means "bun shape" and became the Nebraskan term for bieroks. Members of the Russian German Nebraskan community opened small shops dedicated to the handheld spiced meat pocket, which grew so popular that it spawned a chain. The first Runza store opened in 1949. Today, there are about 85. Locals eat runzas regularly, but they are especially abundant at football games, where they're used as edible hand warmers.

A COWBOY DATE NIGHT

PITCHFORK FONDUE • NORTH DAKOTA

How to try it

Medora, a city in the Badlands of North Dakota, does outdoor Pitchfork Fondue dinners during the summer months.

If you're familiar with Swiss fondue, the cowboy style can be made with a few simple adjustments. Instead of a quart-size ceramic pot suspended above a tiny flame, use a 30-quart metal cauldron on an outdoor gas burner. The cowboy version requires no cheese sauce, just a lot of oil poured into the cauldron. Heat up the oil and it's time to dip. And in country fondue, there's only beef. Steaks get skewered onto a pitchfork, then plunged into the hot oil. A rare steak with a dark crunchy exterior will be ready in three minutes. Medium takes about five.

When Eating Crow Was an Oklahoma Food Trend

In the 1930s, there were too many crows in Tulsa, Oklahoma. Hordes of the birds were raiding fields and covering the town in their droppings. To combat the aggressive flocks, former county health superintendent Dr. T. W. Stallings decided to promote crows as a food. The doctor began holding banquets where he peddled the main ingredient as quail. By the time locals developed a taste for "quail," they didn't mind Stallings's big reveal. Even as crow, they carried on eating it. One of the most outspoken fans was the governor of Oklahoma, who founded the Statehouse Crow Meat Lovers Association.

Stallings's winning recipe involved rubbing lard on the plucked crows to combat their dryness, cooking them in a sealed cast-iron pan with celery, then finishing them off with lots of gravy.

Stallings's passion for eating crow caused a craze. In 1935, the *Pittsburgh Post-Gazette* reported that a "wave of enthusiasm for crow" had swept Oklahoma. In the trailing days of the Great Depression, eating crow provided both a welcome source of protein and a way for farmers to rid their fields of serious predators. For many, the dark meat was pleasantly gamey and relatively tasty. Cultivating this sentiment was no easy battle because scavenging crows are liable to eat meat and garbage—but people pressed on. Crows were plentiful and easy to hunt, and for years, the "black partridge" stayed on the Oklahoma dinner menu. Luckily for the crows, the trend eventually fizzled, likely because times got less desperate.

A QUAPAW TRIBE FARM-TO-TABLE RESTAURANT

RED OAK STEAKHOUSE ○ OKLAHOMA

The Quapaw Indigenous American tribe has a reputation for agricultural excellence. Settling in the junction of the Arkansas and Mississippi rivers (in modern-day Arkansas), they developed a special relationship with the area's fertile soil, perfecting agricultural techniques over centuries to yield prodigious amounts of flavorful produce. As guardians of the region's breadbasket, the Quapaw strengthened their ties with neighboring tribes and later earned military support from the French. Their crucial role in the early American food economy helped them survive to modern day with their traditions intact—traditions you can still taste in the tribe's very own casino in Oklahoma.

While the US government forced the Quapaw from their ancestral homeland after the Louisiana Purchase, the menu at Downstream River Casino's Red

How to try it
Red Oak Steakhouse is nestled within the tribe's casino, Downstream River Casino, in Quapaw, Oklahoma.

The restaurant's produce is grown in on-site greenhouses.

Oak Steakhouse is a tribute to their agricultural legacy. Meat from the tribe's 1,000-strong herd of cattle and bison is prepared in their own on-site processing plant. Greens, herbs, and spices are sourced from the tribe's five greenhouses, just a short walk from the kitchen. Honey is produced by the tribe's own bee colony, and it makes its way into cocktails and salad dressings. The tribe roasts its own coffee and brews its own beer, too—all available in the adjacent steakhouse. True to nature, the dishes on Red Oak's menu rotate to suit each ingredient's peak season.

FREE PHEASANT FOR SOLDIERS

PHEASANT SALAD SANDWICH • SOUTH DAKOTA

South Dakota's Game, Fish, and Parks website claims the state is known for two things: pheasants and Mount Rushmore—in that order. Their headliner, Pheasants, were introduced to the United States from their native China in 1908. By the 1940s, the bird's population had boomed in South Dakota. So much so that the city of Aberdeen made use of the teeming bird population and began giving away pheasant salad sandwiches by the thousand. They dubbed themselves the World's Standout for a Handout.

Throughout World War II, soldiers traveling toward training or deployment on the Chicago, Milwaukee, and St. Paul Railroad all passed through Aberdeen, where the local canteen became known for its free pheasant salad sandwiches. Volunteers, most of them housewives, operated the facility every day from 8 a.m. to midnight, even on holidays. Their signature filling contained carrots, onions, celery, sweet pickle relish, hard-boiled eggs, and mayonnaise, but it was the pheasant that made the sandwich a standout. Industrialized farming had yet to mass-produce chicken, and so America was still smitten with poultry, which was expensive and considered the lavish alternative to red meat.

The Aberdeen canteen closed in 1946, but the pheasant salad sandwich remains a South Dakota specialty. In the city of Brookings, the aptly named Pheasant Restaurant still serves the dish, and because the sandwich is no longer a handout, it's been upgraded with apple, dried cranberries, and roasted pecans.

How to try it

Pheasant Restaurant, established just three years after the Aberdeen canteen closed its doors, features live music and pheasant salad sandwiches.

AN IMMERSIVE BISON EXPERIENCE

TERRY'S BISON RANCH • WYOMING

Have you ever dreamed of boarding an old-fashioned dining train and enjoying a leisurely Sunday lunch while chugging through open pastures of bison? At Terry's Bison Ranch in Cheyenne, this dream could be yours. Established in 1993 as a bison farm, their property has a history that extends much further: In 1910, when the land was owned by F. E. Warren, Wyoming's first territorial governor, bison enthusiast Theodore Roosevelt came to dine. The menu from Bison meal, which included game broth and trout, is on display at the ranch's steakhouse.

Today, Terry's Bison Ranch is a working farm with interactive bison experiences and award-winning bison ribs. Custom-built trains take visitors through bison country, meandering past ostriches and camels before the main event: petting and feeding bison. You can also see the sights on horseback or on an ATV, then head inside for a bison burger.

Feeding the bison, then feeding on bison, may seem like an incongruous experience, but the practice of raising bison like cattle was a key factor in keeping the species from extinction. At the end of the 19th century, the American bison was nearly wiped out and conservation efforts, which focused on finding protected habitats, moved slowly. But around the 1970s, American ranchers made a concerted push to raise the animals like cattle, and today the number of bison raised for food is about 20 times the number being traditionally conserved.

American bison (scientific name: *Bison bison*) have lived in North America for hundreds of thousands of years and are the national mammal of the United States. Growing up to 6 feet (1.8 m) tall and 2,000 pounds (907 kg), they are majestic to behold, especially in their native land, and at Terry's Bison Ranch, you can do it all from the comfort of a slow-moving train.

How to try it

Terry's Bison Ranch is located at 51 I-25 Frontage Road. The regular train tour takes about 90 minutes and runs multiple times a day. The lunch train departs at 12 p.m. on Sundays and requires a reservation.

THE MIDWEST

ONE OF THE WORLD'S WORST LIQUORS

JEPPSON'S MALÖRT • ILLINOIS

How to try it

Ninety percent of Jeppson's Malört is consumed in Chicago. The traditional way is to take a shot, but wormwood cocktails are cropping up around the city.

In the early 1930s, Swedish immigrant, cigar shop owner, and heavy smoker Carl Jeppson peddled a homemade alcohol called Jeppson's Malört—an astringent, foul-flavored spirit, and one of the only things Jeppson's tobacco-dulled mouth could actually taste.

In Swedish, *malört* means "wormwood"—a bitter herb used to treat worms. It is the alcohol's only flavoring, and it is appalling. During Prohibition, law enforcement allowed Jeppson to continue selling it because they couldn't conceive that something so terrible-tasting could be anything but medicinal.

CULINARY GIFTS FROM THE
Chicago World's Fair

In 1893, the city of Chicago hosted the World's Columbian Exposition—an ambitious, staggering showcase of culture and innovation—to commemorate the 400th anniversary of Christopher Columbus's arrival in the New World. Over six months, more than 27 million people came to stroll the promenades of the newly erected fairground city while inventors, entrepreneurs, scientists, and artists showed off their newfangled goods and ideas—a few of which went on to become seminal products of 20th-century America.

Lore has it that the beer, Pabst Select, was renamed **PABST BLUE RIBBON** after the company won a first-place award at the Chicago fair. By the time of the fair, the Milwaukee-born company had already won numerous awards for its beer and had been tying blue silk ribbons—at great expense—around every bottle. Whether they really took the top prize in Chicago is uncertain, but Pabst launched the prizewinning name, and after the fair, it became one of America's most popular beers. (Until the silk shortage of World War I, Pabst churned through more than a million feet of ribbon every year.)

SHREDDED WHEAT also made its public debut at the Chicago fair. The inventor, Ohio lawyer Henry Perky, was a man plagued by diarrhea. He conceived of the nourishing, wholesome food after seeing a man eat boiled wheat with cream. He pitched the idea to a machinist friend and

together they invented a machine that could churn out "little whole wheat mattresses." The pair came to the Columbian Exposition to sell the shredded wheat machine, but the public was far more interested in the wheat snack itself. After the fair, Perky moved east and started the Shredded Wheat Company, which he sold to Nabisco in 1928.

Austrian-Hungarian immigrants Emil Reichel and Sam Ladany brought their then-novel

The taste, which has become sport to describe, is almost universally hated. Bug spray, gasoline, and burnt vinyl are often used as comparisons. For many years, the back of the bottle read: "Most first-time drinkers of Jeppson Malört reject our liquor . . . Our liquor is rugged and unrelenting (even brutal) to the palate." And yet it's one of Chicago's most distinguished libations, served ubiquitously at bars across the city.

The most common reaction is "Malört face," wrinkled, stunned, and disgusted. But as Jeppson's marketing goes: "For the braggart who stays the first few rounds . . . odds are he'll be Jeppson's forever." The citizens of Chicago (and only Chicago) have developed a fondness for the hard stuff. The astringent libation is used as both a rite of passage for out-of-towners and a way for locals to prove their ability to take a shot like a champion.

Josephine Cochrane with a later version of her dishwasher.

of a machine that would do the job gently and efficiently and set out to build it with a mechanic. Her invention was the first successful hand-powered **DISHWASHER**, which she presented at the Chicago fair. Her dishwashing contraption (called Lavadora, then Lavaplatos) won an award for design and durability. The Lavaplatos were primarily sold to restaurants and hotels until the 1950s, when housewives began to bite. Eventually, Cochrane's machines became known under a different name: KitchenAid.

Milton **HERSHEY** was also in attendance—but at the time, he was a caramel maker. At the fair, he encountered a German chocolate-making machine so impressive he eventually sold his thriving caramel business, Lancaster Caramel Company, for the incredible price of one million dollars (the equivalent of about $30 million today) and poured all his resources into chocolate.

(to American audiences) all-beef hot dogs to the Chicago fair and, to their surprise, sold millions of sausages from their street cart. With their profits, they opened the first **VIENNA BEEF** shop a year later, then began distributing their hot dogs to vendors all over the city. In the 1930s, some Vienna Beef stands started advertising a hot dog with "salad on top," which led to the famous Chicago-style hot dog: mustard, onion, sweet pickle relish, a dill pickle spear, tomato, sport peppers, and celery salt.

Josephine Cochrane, a wealthy Illinois socialite who liked to entertain, was fed up with her servants breaking her very nice china when they washed it by hand. In 1887, she conceived

William Wrigley Jr. came to Chicago as a salesman for the Wrigley family business, which at the time was known for soap and baking powder. To drum up sales, he started throwing in a free stick of gum with each purchase and soon found his customers were more excited by chewing gum than household supplies. In 1893, he brought his own line of gum to the Columbian Exposition, where he gave the public their first taste of **JUICY FRUIT**.

THE BURMESE COMMUNITY CENTER

CHIN'S GROCERY • INDIANA

How to try it

Chin Brothers is located at 2318 E Stop 11 Road, on the south side of Indianapolis, and is open nearly every day.

In Myanmar (or Burma, as it was known before 1989), most socializing happens in tea shops, but there were none to be found in Indiana when Than Hre arrived in 2002. He was part of the first wave of Chin people—a Burmese Christian ethnic group—to arrive in Indianapolis. Many Chin followed in his steps, fleeing religious persecution in Myanmar. Today, there are so many Chin in Indianapolis it's earned the nickname "Chindianapolis.'

In 2007, after working for five years and saving his money, Hre decided the burgeoning Chin community needed a space of their own. Despite having no business experience, he bought a grocery store and set out to fill it with food from his home country. But in 2007, Myanmar was undergoing sanctions and nothing could be imported. With great trouble and expense, Hre sourced Burmese products packaged in Thailand, Vietnam, or Cambodia and managed to stock his store with things like lahpet (fermented tea leaves), rakhine noodles, ngapi (dried shrimp powder), and htoe mont (glutinous rice cake). Chin people came to shop, and within a year and a half, Hre added a restaurant.

With Chin chefs in the back and Hre's wife out front, Chin Brothers Restaurant caters to a largely Burmese clientele. In the morning, they serve the traditional breakfast pe pyot, a sprouted yellow bean boiled with turmeric and fried onion, eaten with ei kya kway (Chinese fried dough sticks), or with breads like naan or paratha. Later in the day, there's the Chin specialty sabuti (ground white corn that's stewed with beef or pork bones, offal, and split peas), vok ril (Chin pork blood sausage), and mohinga (fish soup with noodles). At one table, there might be a family from Hre's tiny village in Chin State, and beside them, a Midwestern couple eating Chin food for the first time. At breakfast, it often looks like a Burmese community center.

The name Hre gave his business, Chin Brothers, was decided on a whim at the registration office. He hadn't thought about a name, but coming from a country with painful divisions along religious and ethnic lines, he wanted to make a statement about inclusivity. "We are all brothers and sisters," Hre explains. "We are all Chin."

Than and Biak Hre spread Chin culture with their grocery store and restaurant.

AN HEIRLOOM SEED SANCTUARY

SEED SAVERS EXCHANGE • IOWA

How to try it

Seed Savers Exchange sells hundreds of seeds on their website, seedsavers.org. When possible, Heritage Farm welcomes visitors, but call ahead to make sure.

The Seed Savers Exchange—one of the largest non-governmental seed banks in the United States—is dedicated to preserving and exchanging seeds in order to protect and perpetuate plants that might otherwise be lost. Headquartered on Heritage Farm, an 890-acre organic farm, the exchange houses more than 20,000 plant varieties. Each year they work to regenerate rare plant species, keeping a detailed directory and historical record of every seed they've conserved. Plants grown from the seeds are kept in a refrigerated central collection,

while seeds themselves are frozen in an underground vault. The apple orchid is perhaps the best representation of the exchange's mission: More than a thousand heirloom apple varieties grow side by side in what is essentially a living collection of apple heritage.

Seed Savers Exchange regenerates rare plant species.

AMERICA'S LAST NIGHT LUNCH WAGON

THE OWL • MICHIGAN

In the late 1800s, most restaurants closed at 8 p.m., which left all manner of hungry people wandering the street. Sensing an opportunity, a Rhode Island man named Walter Scott began peddling sandwiches and coffee from a basket, then a pushcart, and finally, once business began to boom, from a horse-drawn wagon. His idea caught on and soon the "night lunch wagon" swept the country.

The wagons averaged about 8 by 14 feet (2.4 by 4.3 m) in size, allowing just enough space for a small counter with cooking equipment and a handful of patrons. Many lunch wagons were lavishly designed with murals and elegant carvings, and attracted a diverse clientele. (The fancy interiors did not match the menus, which typically consisted of humble sandwiches, pies, and coffee.) Many wagons could not withstand the wear and tear of moving around town, so the wagons began to stay put, evolving into what we now know as diners.

The last known surviving wagon is the Owl Night Lunch Wagon. Henry Ford, who was once an Owl Night customer, purchased the wagon in 1927 when Detroit banned lunch wagons (restaurants lobbied against the roving entrepreneurs) and installed it at Greenfield Village, an outdoor historical village that is part of the Henry Ford museum. Ford put the Owl to its former use, and for years it was the only place to buy food in Greenfield Village's sprawling grounds.

In the 1980s, the Owl underwent a full renovation. Gigantic red-and-blue letters now decorate the sides, and etched-glass windows depict owls perched atop crescent moons, an ode to the nighttime eateries of the past.

How to try it

The Henry Ford Museum is located in the Detroit suburb of Dearborn, Michigan. Greenfield Village is open seven days a week, from 9:30 a.m. to 5 p.m.

Before roadside diners, night lunch wagons like the Owl fed late-night appetites.

Instant Salads of the Midwest

I n the American heartland, the term *salad* adheres to regional vernacular and often has nothing to do with vegetables. These iconic preparations hail from the retro era of processed foods, when recipes were passed from friend to neighbor on handwritten cards. While the glory days may be over, these salads still make appearances at summer potlucks, church basements, and holiday gatherings around the Midwest.

COOKIE SALAD was invented in Minnesota, where the cookie of choice is the Keebler Fudge Stripe—a thin, tire-shaped shortbread with a chocolate drizzle. The crushed cookies get bathed in buttermilk, vanilla instant pudding, and whipped cream topping, followed by a can of mandarin oranges and, if you're feeling fancy, a sliced banana.

WATERGATE SALAD has nothing to do with the Nixon scandal, except perhaps that the pistachio pudding is meant to "cover up" the other ingredients. The recipe, published by General Foods in 1975, mixes bright green pistachio instant pudding with whipped cream topping, which makes an excellent disguise for the canned pineapple, pecans, and miniature marshmallows.

JELL-O SALAD rose to prominence as an easy, affordable way for housewives to prepare something new and stylish—marketed as a refined preparation derived from the aspics of the Victorian era. Using a packet of instant Jell-O, these molded salads could contain almost anything, sweet or savory, from shrimp and olives in lime Jell-O to cottage cheese in orange Jell-O.

GLORIFIED RICE can still be found in deli counters across the upper Midwest. Cooked white rice becomes glorified when anointed with whipped cream and canned crushed pineapple, stirred, then topped with the popular regional garnish of marshmallows and maraschino cherries.

THE CASSEROLES OF MINNESOTA LAWMAKERS

CONGRESSIONAL HOTDISH COMPETITION • MINNESOTA

How to try it

The hotdish competition, held in Washington, D.C., isn't open to the public, probably because people would become overwhelmed with excitement. After the winner is declared each year, authenticated recipes are posted on an official government website.

I n 2010, then Minnesota senator Al Franken challenged the ten members of his state's congressional delegation to a hotdish cook-off. Six members answered his call, gathering with homemade, Minnesota-style casseroles in a bid to prove their talents beyond the realm of politics. Trash talk ensued. Casserole rivalry was established.

The hotdish—a Depression-era, easy, and thrifty way to feed a crowd—has become one of Minnesota's most emblematic foods. The one-baking-dish meal combines a starch, a meat, a canned or frozen vegetable, and a can of creamy soup. Canned tuna, frozen peas, egg noodles, and mushroom soup, for example, is a classic tuna hotdish. Another standard, Tater Tot hotdish, is made with ground beef, canned corn, frozen tater tots, and cheddar cheese soup.

On competition day, congressional members turn all their legislative energy toward casserole. In 2013, Representative Michelle Bachmann told Al Franken: "I will smoke you."

The event has quickly become a Capitol Hill favorite. Along with the classic components, the entries must include an ingredient from their home state, so the hotdishes remain decidedly Minnesotan, from Senator Amy Klobuchar's I Can't Believe It's Not Spam Pepperoni Pizza hotdish (Spam hails from Minnesota) to Representative Tim Walz's Hermann the German hotdish, with local bratwurst and Schell's beer.

The grand prize is a personalized Pyrex dish, which comes with a year's worth of showboating privileges. Walz, who has won three times, entered the 2018 competition trailed by three staffers holding up the baking dish trophies from his previous victories.

WINNERS OF THE CONGRESSIONAL HOTDISH COMPETITION

2012: A tie between Senator Al Franken's Mom's Mahnomen Madness hotdish and Rep. Chip Cravaack's Minnesota Wild Strata hotdish

2013: Representative Tim Walz's Hermann the German hotdish

2014: Representative Tim Walz's Turkey Trot Tater Tot hotdish

2015: Representative Betty McCollum's

Turkey, Sweet Potato, and Wild Rice hotdish

2016: Representative Tim Walz's Turkey Taco Tot hotdish

2017: Representative Collin Peterson's Right to Bear Arms hotdish

2018: Representative Tom Emmer's Hotdish of Champions

2019: Representative Betty McCollum's Among Friends hotdish

Senators Amy Klobuchar and Tina Smith and Representative Angie Craig sample entries from the 2019 Hotdish Competition.

A BUTTER SCULPTURE FOR A DAIRY PRINCESS

PRINCESS KAY OF THE MILKY WAY • MINNESOTA

How to try it

The Minnesota State Fair takes place in the Falcon Heights suburb of St. Paul from late August to early September. Engrossing butter sculpture action happens every day.

Each spring, nearly a hundred aspiring Dairy Princesses from around Minnesota vie to be crowned Princess Kay of the Milky Way. The women (all unwed and under the age of 24) must be hometown dairy ambassadors, either working in the industry or the direct kin of dairy-producing people. Twelve finalists are interviewed and give speeches before the crowning, and the winner becomes the state's traveling dairy diplomat for the next year. But this is a competition with no losers because all finalists receive the honor of having their likenesses carved from 90-pound (41-kg) blocks of Grade A butter.

For more than 40 years, Linda Christensen has been the resident butter sculptress. During her residency, she's carved more than 500 sculptures from 32,000 pounds (14,515 kg) of butter. For the 12 days of the Minnesota State Fair, Christensen sits in a glass-walled booth and carves the women, one by one, producing a "butter head" each day. Princess Kay goes first. Dressed in warm layers, she sits for 6 to 8 hours in the 40°F (4.4°C) showroom, posing for her sculpture as spectators watch from outside the glass. Christensen uses knives and other sculpture tools to slowly coax the princess's features from the block of fat.

Each finalist gets to keep her butter head. Some choose to preserve and care for them as art, while others like to eat them, donating their heads to big community meals like pancake breakfasts and corn feeds.

2008 Princess Kay of the Milky Way Kristy Mussman poses for her official butter sculpture at the state fair.

CAROLINE SHAWK BROOKS

(1840–1913)

In November 1877, about 2,000 spectators gathered in an auditorium in Des Moines, Iowa, to watch a unique demonstration. Onstage a woman in her mid-30s perched on a stool. She held several wooden paddles and a straw brush. Before her was an easel and a metal milk pan filled completely with butter. Next to her was a full brass band.

The show began, and the musicians struck up "La Marseillaise," the national anthem of France. The woman scraped and brushed with her paddle, creating the wide cheekbones and distinct forelock of Napoleon. When the band switched to a more American song, the artist quickly reshaped the face with the furrowed brows and strong nose of George Washington. A sudden low note from the tuba rattled the easel and Washington's shoulder began to slide off. The artist calmly caught it, stuck it back on, and the room erupted in applause.

Brooks carves butter at a Boston exhibition in 1877.

Caroline Shawk Brooks, aka the Butter Woman, was the world's premiere butter sculptor. From the mid-19th through the early 20th century, her unusual talent brought her widespread renown.

Brooks had always shown a knack for unorthodox materials—as a kid in Ohio, she sculpted a bust of Dante out of mud from a nearby creek. When she married and moved to a farm in Arkansas, she took up butter sculpting out of economic necessity. Women farmers were often responsible for making and selling butter while their husbands worked the fields. In 1867, when her farm's cotton crop failed, Brooks distinguished her butter by carving it into intricate animals, shells, and faces. A grand departure from the premade molds used by the other farm wives, neighbors were eager to buy Brooks's elegant butter shapes.

In 1873, Brooks found the character that would become her lasting muse: Iolanthe, the blind princess at the center of a popular play titled *King Rene's Daughter*. The play moved Brooks, and for the first time, she took up her butter tools solely out of inspiration. *Dreaming Iolanthe* was put on display in a local Cincinnati art hall where 2,000 visitors paid 25 cents each to see it. The piece also attracted the attention of the *New York Times*, who called it "a face that may yet make [Brooks] famous."

Lucy Webb Hayes, the future first lady and a big fan of Brooks, commissioned her to carve a *Dreaming Iolanthe* for the Women's Pavilion at the 1876 Centennial Exposition in Philadelphia. The sculpture drew such large crowds that Brooks was asked to demonstrate her techniques for an audience. Under the gaze of reporters and judges, Brooks carved her 12-pound (5.4-kg) block of butter into a relief bust, shuffling the piece back and forth to the refrigerator to restore the desired texture.

Over the years, as Brooks gained fame and popularity, critics urged her to switch to what they viewed as "real" material. And while she did eventually try new mediums, even spending seven years with marble-cutting artisans in Italy, she never gave up butter. "I had previously modeled in everything workable, in clay, sea sand, mashed potatoes, putty and so on," she told the *Akron Daily Democrat* in 1893. "[But] I began my best work in butter, and with butter I shall end."

THE BREAKOUT DESIGNER APPLE

HONEYCRISP • MINNESOTA

How to try it

During the fall, the Applehouse store at the University of Minnesota sells honeycrisps as well as rare and experimental apples grown at the university.

When you bite into a honeycrisp apple, the flesh bursts with sweet, tart juice—all by design. The scientists at the University of Minnesota apple breeding program engineered larger cells that act as liquid capsules, delivering maximum mouth-watering apple flavor. They also endowed the honeycrisp with a thin skin, a vibrant blushing color, and a long shelf life. The result was what many consider to be the world's first celebrity apple.

The honeycrisp apple took 30 years to get ready for market. When it came on to the 1990s apple scene, Americans went crazy for the designer fruit. They learned

to call it by name and grew accustomed to paying three to four times more than they would for a standard supermarket apple. The taste for honeycrisp spread quickly, and soon it was the most glamorous apple in the country, with orchards, farm stands, and markets setting up big seasonal displays of the fruity jewels.

The success of the honeycrisp ushered in a new era of apple branding. While bananas and blueberries remained bananas and blueberries, apples grew identities. Pink Ladies were bright, tart, and effervescent. Jazz apples were firm, snappy, and juicy. Apples have long been America's most popular fruit (each person eats about 16 pounds/7 kg a year), but the honeycrisp set a new bar for what a humble apple could do in the marketplace.

A GOLF-CART BAR IN A BAT-FILLED CAVE

BAT BAR • MISSOURI

How to try it

Carts are available for rent from 8:00 a.m. until 45 minutes before sunset. Drivers are permitted alcohol, but not before signing a liability waiver.

Top of the Rock, a mountaintop bluff in the Ozarks, is the entry point into the area's finest watering hole—a bat-filled bar that's accessible only by golf cart. After renting a two- or four-person vehicle, visitors make their way through a 2.5-mile (4-km) woodland path over streams and bridges, with the option of stopping at a butterfly garden and a scenic outlook. Shortly into the trip, the trail dips into the Lost Canyon Cave, which contains this one-of-a-kind bar.

While everyone on the journey must stay in the golf cart, the ride is filled with surprises: The lantern-lit cave contains a natural waterfall, a live bat colony, and skeletons of both a saber-tooth tiger and a short-faced bear. When it's time for a drink, park beside the wooden bar and order up a Bat's Bite (strawberry and peach lemonade) or a John L's Lemonade (vodka, grapefruit, lemonade, and grenadine), then go for a loop around the waterfall pool.

Missouri's premier mountaintop cave bar is accessible only by golf cart.

Depressing Dishes of the Great Depression

Penny restaurants offered a dignified alternative to breadlines during the Great Depression.

When the stock market crashed in 1929 and the economy nosedived, sourcing regular meals became a grim and perpetual challenge. To aid the hungry masses, "penny restaurants," where humble foods like pea soup and bread could be had for a cent, began popping up across the country. These restaurants were charitable projects, intended to restore dignity to people growing accustomed to waiting in endless breadlines. In New York, weightlifter and fitness pioneer Bernarr MacFadden opened a four-story penny restaurant with health-conscious offerings like prunes and whole wheat bread. In California, Clifton's Cafeteria made it a mission to feed penniless diners in accordance with their slogan "Dine free unless delighted." In its first three months, Clifton's (which is still open in Los Angeles today) served 10,000 people for free. The service was formidable and a welcome supplement to the scrappy, unconventional home-cooked meals born out of scarcity.

MOCK APPLE PIE was an apple pie made without apples. Instead of fruit, butter crackers were boiled in a sugar syrup, mixed with cinnamon and lemon juice, and baked in a crust. The sweet, spiced crackers made a surprisingly moist and satisfying apple replacement, although they provided no vitamins or minerals.

PEANUT BUTTER AND MAYONNAISE SANDWICHES were once as popular as PB&Js, valued for the high-calorie combination of protein and fat that provided incredible nutritional density for little money. By the 1960s, Hellmann's Mayonnaise was advertising ways to jazz up the classic PB&M. A "double crunch" added bacon and pickles, while a "Crazy Combo" meant salami, sliced eggs, and onions.

POUDING CHÔMEUR, or "unemployed person pudding," was created by women factory workers in the French-speaking province of Quebec. They took stale bread, soaked it in brown sugar sauce, and baked it until golden and caramelized. Despite its belittling name, the dish provided a bowl of comfort; and pouding chômeur remains a popular dessert, although it's now more often made with a batter than with stale bread.

NORTH AMERICA'S MANGO

PAWPAW FRUIT • OHIO

Native to the central and eastern half of the United States, pawpaws are a little bigger than an avocado and comparably heavy. A ripe pawpaw has an almost liquid texture with a pungent, sweet smell and a taste reminiscent of tropical fruits like mangoes and bananas. (They're sometimes referred to as the poor man's banana or hillbilly mangoes.) Advocates praise pawpaws' creamy, tropical taste, while detractors find their puckery flavor more suitable for those with blunted palates.

Pawpaws are the largest edible fruit native to North America—millennia ago, they fed mastodons. Fruits and vegetables such as corn, strawberries, and carrots were small and bitter before humans tediously grafted and bred them for size and flavor. But wild pawpaws were large and one of the most nutritious fruits, providing a good source of potassium, several amino acids, vitamin C, iron, and copper. Pawpaws were a staple of many Indigenous American diets, and Lewis and Clark were content to live off them during a leg of their 1804–1806 journey across America. George Washington was also an enthusiast.

But the pawpaw is persnickety in its own way. The trees are harvestable only from late August to mid-October, and if kept at room temperature, the fruit ripens to the point of fermentation within three days. Pawpaws bruise easily, and the only effective way to ship them is frozen. Once the shortcomings of apples and strawberries were bred away, the pawpaw fell out of favor.

That doesn't mean there aren't still fans. Every year, the Ohio city of Albany hosts a Pawpaw Festival, where the pawpaw flows freely and growers enter their fruit for awards.

How to try it
The Pawpaw Festival happens in September near Albany's Lake Snowden. Otherwise, finding pawpaws requires persistent seasonal hunting at farmers' markets.

THE WORLD'S MOST BITTER ISLAND

WASHINGTON ISLAND • WISCONSIN

How to try it

Nelsen's Hall Bitters Pub is located at 1201 Main Road on Washington Island. It's open seven days a week.

The standard way to enjoy bitters is in moderation—a dash or two in a Manhattan or a Sazerac for a sharp, earthy tang. But on Washington Island, a remote islet in Wisconsin's share of Lake Michigan, locals prefer to drink it straight, as they have for a hundred years. Their brand of choice is Angostura—the yellow-capped bottle found in nearly every bar in the world—and they drink so much of it that tiny Washington Island (population 700) has acquired the title of world's largest consumer of bitters. According to an Angostura representative, they do upward of 10,000 shots every year.

The tradition began with Tom Nelsen, a Danish immigrant who arrived on the island in the late 1800s. After traversing the northernmost reaches of Wisconsin and surviving the choppy, treacherous stretch of water known as the Death's Door Strait (for the many shipwrecks that occur there), Nelsen decided to settle down and open a dance hall and bar, where he sold drinks until Prohibition made it illegal in 1920. At first, Nelsen despaired. Then, he got a pharmaceutical license.

Bitters, despite containing alcohol, could be classified and sold as "stomach tonic for medicinal purposes." With a pharmaceutical license, Nelsen could legally sell bitters without a doctor's prescription, and so he began pouring shots of the 90 proof "medical tincture" for his "patients." The tonic was extremely popular, unearthing hundreds of previously undiagnosed stomach ailments. Patients kept coming, Nelsen kept pouring, and Nelsen's Hall Bitters Pub stayed open all through Prohibition—making it the oldest continuously operating tavern in Wisconsin.

When Prohibition was repealed in 1933 and the pub resumed normal operations, locals didn't give up bitters. Angostura shots become a local drinking tradition and remained one of the best-selling items on the menu. (Nelsen himself is said to have consumed up to a pint of bitters, or about 16 shots, every day until he passed at the ripe age of 90.)

In the mid-20th century, Nelsen's pub was passed on to his nephew, Gunnar, and Gunnar's wife, Bessie, who founded the Bitters Club. To join, you must take a shot. First-timers to the island often make Nelsen's a priority because the shot comes with an official Bitters Club card that states you are "now considered a full-fledged islander and entitled to mingle, dance, etc. with all the other islanders." The card is notarized by the bartender, who sticks a thumb in the dregs of the empty shot glass, then stamps a thumbprint on the card and writes the new club member's name in a ledger.

THE SOUTHEAST
THE SUMMER SEAFOOD WINDFALL

MOBILE BAY JUBILEE • ALABAMA

Each summer, on a sultry, full moon night, residents around the coastal region of Mobile Bay are roused from sleep by news of a wondrous natural phenomenon. Along a 15-mile (24 km) stretch of Alabama coast, a bounty of seafood rises from the Mobile Bay floor. Catfish, shrimp, and flounder wash onto the sand, still alive, writhing at the water's edge while eels and crabs scuttle around them. This exodus of sea life provides residents with as much seafood as they can gig, net, or scoop, and the atmosphere is so celebratory they call it a jubilee.

Jubilees have a legendary quality to them, but science backs the annual windfall. Estuaries contain layers of water with different densities and salinities. Jubilees occur when the bottom layer of water, which is salty and low in oxygen, gets pushed by easterly winds into the shallow shoreline area of Mobile Bay. In response to the movement and increased summer salinity of this inhabitable water, sea creatures flee in front of it, toward the shoreline, where they eventually wash up.

The oldest records of jubilee dates back to the 1860s, and after so many years, residents say they can feel them coming. They tailgate after midnight at the dock when signs suggest one might manifest. If they're lucky enough to be right, locals alert their neighbors, and hundreds of people, along with flocks of sweeping pelicans and gulls, arrive in their pajamas to sweep the shoreline of its seafood. Jubilees are the only time of year fishing quotas go unpoliced. Employers and schools are also known to be more lenient the day after a jubilee, when the town is busy steaming fish, cracking crab, peeling shrimp, and generally enjoying the free onslaught of good eating.

How to try it

Time magazine, CNN, *National Geographic*, and other outlets have come to Mobile Bay over the years, trying but failing to document the event. But those willing to wait out a summer will likely be rewarded—years without a jubilee are extremely rare.

Locals make the most of each seafood jubilee, like this harvester during a recent bounty in Point Clear in 2012.

A CELEBRATION OF GOOBERS

NATIONAL PEANUT FESTIVAL • ALABAMA

When the National Peanut Festival debuted in 1938, the guest speaker was celebrity peanut heavyweight George Washington Carver, famous for his sensational 1918 agricultural bulletin, *How to Grow the Peanut and 105 Ways of Preparing It for Human Consumption*. Carver played a significant role in reviving Alabama's agricultural economy. Cotton, the state's historic cash crop, had depleted the region's soil and was being ravaged by boll weevils. At Carver's advice, Alabama farmers switched to peanuts and now the booming industry produces 400 million pounds (181 million kg) of peanuts annually.

The National Peanut Festival—a ten-day peanut party for 200,000 people—is about as American as it gets. There's a cheerleading competition, a gun show,

How to try it

The National Peanut Festival takes place every fall, typically in November, as a way to honor the farmers and welcome the harvest season. General admission is $7. A cup of boiled peanuts is $3.

A mural in Alabama's Dothan Historic District commemorates the local peanut industry and festival.

a demolition derby, a professional chainsaw sculptor, army helicopter rides, a "greased pig scramble" where students must catch a pig in an arena and coerce it across a finish line, a parade of peanut-themed people atop peanut-themed floats, and an abundance of foods celebrating the mighty peanut. The most serious competition is perhaps the Miss National Peanut beauty pageant, whose contestants must hail from peanut-producing states like Alabama, Florida, or Georgia. The women compete on the large civic center stage where they're judged, according to the official rules, on "Appearance, Poise, Communication Skills, Personal Interview, and of course, Knowledge of Peanuts."

PERFECT PORK FROM A FAMILY HOME

JONES BAR-B-Q DINER • ARKANSAS

The Jones family has been perfecting barbecue for more than 100 years.

Jones Bar-B-Q, a two-table eatery in the town of Marianna, is one of only two restaurants in Arkansas to ever receive a prestigious James Beard Award. The owners, James and Betty Jones, hadn't even heard of the award before winning the "America's Classics" category in 2012.

The small diner takes up the ground floor of the couple's home. The sign out front reads "since 1964," but the family operation dates back to at least 1910. James Jones's recipes are the same ones that his grandfather used when he sold barbecued meat out of his home and that his father used when he opened up an earlier iteration of the restaurant, known as the Hole in the Wall (so-called because his father served everything through a window).

Today, James runs the pit and restaurant, while a man named Sylvester chops wood and operates the attached smokehouse, which is a shed. Oak and hickory logs burn in a cinderblock barbecue pit, where pork shoulders—the only meat Jones sells—smoke for 12 hours at a time. The menu includes pork by the pound and sandwiches: pork dressed in a slightly sweet vinegar sauce and served between slices of white bread. Beyond slaw, sides are nonexistent. But with smoked pork this perfect, they're also unnecessary.

How to try it
Jones Bar-B-Q is located at 219 W. Louisiana Street. The restaurant opens at 7 a.m. and closes when it sells out. This could happen at 10 a.m., so plan to eat pork for breakfast.

GEORGIA GILMORE

(1920–1990)

Before Rosa Parks was arrested on a segregated bus in December 1955, sparking a citywide bus boycott by African Americans, Montgomery native Georgia Theresa Gilmore had begun a protest of her own. Two months earlier, a white driver had kicked her off a bus for using the front door, then drove away with her fare. "I decided right then and there I wasn't going to ride the buses anymore," Gilmore said.

When the city's bus boycott began in earnest, the organizers (known as the Montgomery Improvement Association, or MIA) needed money. Hundreds of cars, trucks, and wagons were required to transport protestors across the city. To support the cause, Gilmore assembled a group of women who pooled together $14 to buy chicken, bread, and lettuce, then sold sandwiches at a rally. When the sandwiches were a hit, they expanded into pound cakes, sweet potato pies, fried fish, and greens, which they sold door-to-door.

Georgia Gilmore's living room restaurant became a clubhouse for civil rights leaders.

The MIA threw biweekly rallies, and Gilmore's fund-raising updates were one of the highlights. Twice a week for more than a year, she sauntered down the aisle singing "Shine on Me" or "I Dreamt of a City Called Heaven," then emptied the club's earnings into the collection plate, announcing the amount to jubilant applause and stomping feet. Her food raised $125 to $200 each week, or the equivalent of $1,100 to $1,800 today. She is believed to have raised more money for the boycott than any other person in Montgomery.

Gilmore eventually testified against the white driver who kicked her off the bus—an act that cost Gilmore her job at the National Lunch, a segregated restaurant. But a fan of her cooking stepped in to help: Dr. Martin Luther King Jr. lived a couple blocks away and encouraged Gilmore to open a restaurant. With his financial support, she transformed her dining room into a makeshift restaurant, which served as a clubhouse for civil rights leaders.

Every morning, Gilmore woke around 3 or 4 a.m. to prepare a rotating menu of ham hocks, stuffed pork chops, potato salad, collard greens, candied yams, bread pudding, and black-eyed peas. By noon, her house was crowded with customers. About a dozen people could squeeze around her dining room table, but everyone else had to eat standing up in her living room or kitchen. "Georgia House" became the unofficial office and social club of Dr. King, who held clandestine meetings around her table.

Between her no-nonsense attitude and notorious sense of humor, Gilmore became as much of an attraction as her food. She often greeted her guests by calling from the kitchen, using nicknames like "heifer" (for Dr. King) and "whore" (for the Reverend Dixon). In response, Dr. King affectionately called the large woman "Tiny."

Gilmore remained active in the civil rights movement for the rest of her life, using her food to fuel social change. She died on March 7, 1990—the 25th anniversary of the Selma to Montgomery march. Against doctor's orders, she had risen early to prepare chicken and potato salad for the people marching in commemoration. Instead, her family served the food to people who came to mourn her. Years later, Gilmore's sister Betty remembered: "Lots of people brought food to the house, too, but everybody ate Georgia's chicken and potato salad first. Nobody could fix it better."

HORSE-DRAWN KITCHEN GALLOP

CHUCKWAGON RACES • ARKANSAS

How to try it

Admission to the Chuckwagon Race grounds is $20–35/day, but once you're in there's free camping, roping clinics, rodeos, karaoke, cowboy mounted shooting, barrel racing, horseshoeing, and "cowboy church service." The party lasts eight days, with three days of chuckwagon racing.

Scattered across America is a collection of preserved chuckwagons—the portable "field kitchens" used in the 19th century to feed traveling workers or pioneering settlers. Strapped to horses, the wooden wagons transported pantry items and cooking equipment, and while they're still used on occasion for their original purpose, the chuckwagon at its core is a four-wheeled vehicle. And where there are vehicles, eventually there will be a race.

On Labor Day weekend in Clinton, Arkansas, chuckwagons from near and far gather to compete in America's premiere wagon race. What began as an impromptu competition between friends in 1986 has blossomed into a weeklong outdoor blowout for some 30,000 people and hundreds of racers. In Arkansas, chuckwagon racing involves teams of three: a driver, a cook, and an outrider. The cook and the outrider begin on the ground, while the driver is in the wagon. With a signal from a judge, the cook loads the stove into the wagon and hops in. With a gunshot, the outrider loads the tent into the wagon, then mounts his horse (the racers are almost exclusively men). The driver and the cook take off in the kitchen, galloping around a grassy field while the outrider tries to overtake them on his horse. The outrider must pass his teammates before they cross the finish line, and the chuckwagon must retain its stove and tent in order to receive a qualifying time.

Chuckwagon racing was born in Canada in 1923, where the sport remains a huge draw at the Calgary Stampede—a ten-day rodeo that draws a million people. The high-speed competitions have drawn criticism from animal welfare groups, as the intense courses and unwieldy kitchen equipment have ended in the injury and death of horses. Those arguing for the sport's survival claim that losses are a part of ranching, farming, and keeping horses.

Fourche Mountain Rough Riders racing in the 1994 National Championships.

A MASSIVE TROPICAL FRUIT EMPORIUM

ROBERT IS HERE • FLORIDA

In 1959, Robert Moehling's father, a Florida farmer, tasked his son with selling his surplus cucumbers on the side of the road. Robert was six years old, and the cars speeding past took no notice. To draw attention to the makeshift operation, his father spray-painted a message on a hurricane shutter and placed it beside the cucumbers: "Robert Is Here."

More than 60 years later, that statement remains true, but what was once a ramshackle stand is now the Disney World of tropical fruit. Just off US 1, this kitschy, massive shop features produce, jams, souvenirs, animals (including goats, emu, iguanas, and birds), a picnic area, and live music on the weekends. The barn-like emporium has become a local landmark for those visiting the Everglades or traveling the long stretch of highway to Key West and the Florida Turnpike. Robert, now well into his 60s, still works there alongside his immediate family and grows much of the fruit himself.

The stand specializes in unique fruit varieties, like egg fruit, dragonfruit, *Monstera deliciosa*, and sugar apples. Whimsical descriptions accompany each product, such as soursop, which is described as tasting like "pineapple cotton candy." But the most beloved offering might be the milkshakes, made from Robert's fresh fruit, milk, yogurt, and soft-serve ice cream. During peak season, they sell about 1,400 shakes each day.

How to try it
Robert Is Here is located at 19200 SW 344th Street in Homestead.

Robert Moehling is still here, arranging the produce at his eponymous fruit stand.

Florida Grows the Most Diverse Fruit in the United States

The South Florida city of Homestead is hot, humid, and just two degrees north of the Tropic of Cancer, making it the perfect climate for growing tropical fruit. The land is farmed by an international community of people—from Latin America to Africa, the Caribbean to Asia—that has turned Homestead into a global fruit lovers paradise. Within the patchwork of farms, you'll find dozens of varieties of mangoes and avocados, as well as lychees, longans, jackfruits, green papayas, sapotes, tamarinds, starfruits, and guavas.

THE WORLD'S LARGEST COLLECTION OF METAL-SIDED NOSTALGIA

LUNCH BOX MUSEUM • GEORGIA

The original children's metal lunch pail was plain and utilitarian, modeled after the cheerless vessels of the workingman. In 1935, all that changed when Mickey Mouse debuted on the side of a lunch box, and other brands followed suit. Licensed characters began to appear on lunch box sides, exploding with the 1950s television boom. Suddenly there were hundreds of choices, from Snoopy to

A vintage Flintstones lunch box and thermos, ca. 1962.

How to try it

The Lunch Box Museum is open Monday–Saturday, 10 a.m. to 6 p.m. Woodall takes pride in the hands-on aspect of his museum: All the lunch boxes are meant to be picked up, unfastened, and played with.

Annie Oakley to the Beatles. But by 1985, metal lunch boxes were largely replaced by cheaper plastic or vinyl versions, leaving a legacy of some 450 old metal boxes with distinctive character designs.

Collector Allen Woodall, who operates the Lunch Box Museum in Columbus, Georgia, has all 450. Now the world's largest collection of lunch boxes, the museum contains more than 3,000, many of which are accompanied by their matching thermoses. Archie & Friends, Arthur & Friends, the Avengers, Pac-Man, Cabbage Patch Kids, the Smurfs, the Beatles, King Kong, and Knight Rider—Woodall has them all. Some of the rarest pails are valued at more than $10,000. He's perpetually culling his main collection, which he organizes alphabetically.

With so many lunch boxes, many of them are duplicates or replicas. Woodall keeps a "barter room," where he'll sell certain pails to the public, or trade lunch boxes with other aficionados.

THE CHEESE SANDWICH SCANDAL OF THE MASTERS TOURNAMENT

PIMENTOGATE • GEORGIA

How to try it

WifeSaver restaurants still sell their secret-recipe pimento cheese. The Junior League of Augusta, Georgia, published the included recipe in their cookbook, *Par 3 Tea-Time at the Masters,* which many hail as the closest to the original.

Pimento cheese—the heady blend of cheese, mayonnaise, and pimento peppers—is a thick, spreadable delicacy that's known as the paté of the American South. And though the main draw to the Masters Tournament is arguably golf, the pimento cheese sandwich is a quintessential part of the experience. The tradition began in the mid-1950s, when South Carolina caterer Nick Rangos began selling his sandwiches to hungry attendees, gradually cultivating a fan base that came to associate the golf tournament with his signature sandwich. His pimento cheese reign lasted nearly half a century, until 1998, when the tournament gave the sandwich contract to local restaurant WifeSaver. Rangos, jilted from his position, refused to give up his beloved recipe (in fact, he took it to his grave), and so WifeSaver set out to reconstruct it. Recipe testers ordered dozens of cases of cheeses for experimentation and delivered attempts to the tournament's concession committee—all were rejected. Eventually, a woman who worked for the Masters stepped forward. She had been saving a batch of the original recipe in her freezer, and with this sample (and some tips from Rangos's suppliers), WifeSaver was able to reverse engineer a pimento cheese that satisfied the golf fans.

But in 2013, the tournament brought the sandwich-making in house. WifeSaver, like Rangos, refused to surrender its formula, and this time, without a frozen sample, the tournament was out of luck. The pimento cheese sandwich, while still $1.50 and sold in the iconic green plastic sack, is decidedly different: more heavily spiced, some say looser with mayo. Fans were shaken by the abrupt end to an era. An ESPN article covering this final change quoted one disgruntled fan, who said "I am fine with adding the female members, and I am tolerating the belly putters, but changing the pimento cheese recipe is taking change too damn far."

Masters-Style Pimento Cheese Sandwich

Makes 8 sandwiches

3 cups shredded white cheddar cheese

2 cups shredded yellow sharp cheddar cheese

4 ounces crumbled blue cheese

1 cup shredded parmesan cheese

1 (4-ounce) jar sliced pimentos, drained

1 cup light mayonnaise

2 tablespoons dijon mustard

1 loaf white bread

Combine cheeses, pimentos, mayonnaise, and mustard in a food processor and process until smooth. Cover and chill. Spread on bread slices.

A DEGREE IN DISTILLATION

MOONSHINE UNIVERSITY • KENTUCKY

Back in the day, when bootleggers wanted to sell their moonshine, they might put jars of the illegal homemade hooch in a hollowed-out tree stump in the woods. Within a day or two, they'd come back to find the shine gone and their money waiting in the stump. The unregulated liquor, distilled across the homes and backwoods of the American South, was a centuries-old game of production and evasion. Moonshine developed a dangerous reputation, which was only aided by the practice of using dicey machinery like car radiators as condensers and harmful additives like lye. Rebellion runs deep in whiskey-making history: In 1791, when distillers in Pennsylvania (the birthplace of American whiskey) were slapped with a liquor tax, they revolted against the tax collectors, tarring and feathering them and attacking the home of a prominent inspector in what's now known as the Whiskey Rebellion.

But in 2010, moonshine—now a term that refers to clear, unaged whiskey—was legalized in the United States, and in Louisville, Kentucky, there's a school to teach you how to make it.

How to try it

The six-day Distiller Course, held at the Distilled Spirits Epicenter in Louisville, is offered four times a year and costs $6,250.

Moonshine University is intended for people looking to get into the distilling business. Students study the science and business side of the industry, then get immersed in the production: milling grain, cooking mash, measuring, tasting, and smelling. After an intensive six-day course, graduates come away with a body of knowledge meant to prepare them for starting a distillery of their own. As the state that produces 95 percent of the world's bourbon and exports more than a billion dollars of whiskey every year, many consider Kentucky the whiskey capital of the world. Now that moonshine is legal, Moonshine University is a crash course in what promises to be a much bigger business than wads of cash in hollowed-out tree stumps.

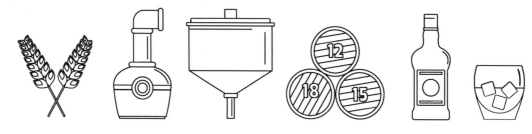

THE ARM WORKOUT COCKTAIL

RAMOS GIN FIZZ • LOUISIANA

How to try it

New Orleans's Sazarac Bar serves a supremely fluffy Ramos Gin Fizz.

In 1888, Henry C. Ramos purchased the Imperial Cabinet saloon in New Orleans and a year later introduced the world to the New Orleans Gin Fizz. His namesake version, the Ramos Gin Fizz, graced the menu of his next saloon: the Stag. Located near the popular St. Charles Hotel, it became a New Orleans destination and the Ramos Gin Fizz an emblem of the city.

The Ramos Gin Fizz takes the standard combination of gin, sugar, lemon juice, and club soda and adds egg whites, orange flower water, lime juice, cream, and powdered sugar (in place of cane sugar). In drink lore, the subsequent step was 12 minutes of cocktail shaking, although experts agree 5 minutes was probably more accurate. Nonetheless, his namesake drink wasn't perfect until it reached a near-whipped state.

With a process so laborious and time-consuming, Ramos hired several full-time "shaker boys" to help prepare his gin fizzes. Especially around Mardi Gras, dozens of shaker boys would shake continuously, for hours on end, trying to keep up with the demand.

Despite the craze, Ramos did not tolerate drunken tomfoolery. He enforced a policy against drunkards and a strict 8 p.m. closing time. The saloon was a calm space and a stage for fine cocktails—not a place for late-night debauchery and disorder. Ramos followed the rules, and with the ratification of the 18th Amendment, he shut down the bar for good in 1919. He died before Prohibition ended.

A 1928 issue of the *New Orleans Item-Tribune* published advice from the late Ramos, who insisted that the key to the cocktail was care, patience, and quality ingredients. Readers were instructed to "shake and shake and shake until there is not a bubble left, but the drink is smooth and snowy white and of the consistency of good rich milk. The secret in success lies in the good care you take and in your patience, and be certain to use good material."

A FRENCH TRADITION IN LOUISIANA

GIANT OMELETTE CELEBRATION • LOUISIANA

The land that makes up Abbeville, Louisiana, was purchased for $900 by a French priest named Father Antoine Désiré Mégret in 1843. With the help of the Acadians—descendants of the French Canadian colonists who settled in Louisiana in the 18th century—Mégret set out to design a rural, French-style village, gathered around a main place he called Magdalen Square. For nearly two centuries, Mégret's square has served as a gathering place for the community and, in the last few decades, as the location of a new French tradition called the Giant Omelette Celebration.

Every November, the Confrérie d' Abbeville ("Brotherhood of Abbeville") gathers to crack and scramble 5,000 eggs, which get poured into a 12-foot (3.7 m) pan over a blazing wood fire and fed to anyone who shows up to celebrate. This French tradition dates back to Napoleon Bonaparte, who was said to have eaten such a delicious omelet while traveling through the south of France, he ordered one the next day large enough to feed his army. In the town of Bessières, where Napoleon fell for the omelet, the Confrérie Mondiale des Chevaliers de l'Omelette Géante ("World Brotherhood of Knights of the Giant Omelette") puts on a 15,000-egg spectacle every Easter. Confreries of foreign chapters around the world also appoint their own "omelette knights" every year.

In 1984, three Abbeville natives attended the Bessières celebration and decided to bring the tradition to Louisiana. While the Abbeville chefs still uphold the primary practices of making the omelet in the town square and sharing it among the townspeople, the Abbeville omelet is distinctly Cajun (as the Louisiana Acadian descendants are known). The Southern version is made with 50 pounds (23 kg) of onions, 75 pounds (34 kg) of bell peppers, and 15 pounds (7 kg) of Louisiana crawfish tails. And while the base is still scrambled eggs, those eggs are spiked with a healthy dose of Tabasco, Louisiana's signature hot sauce.

How to try it

The Giant Omelette Celebration takes place every November in Abbeville's Magdalen Square. With each new celebration, they add one egg to the original 5,000. In 2018, they cracked 5,034.

Abbeville chefs were inspired by the Knights of the Giant Omelette of Bessières, France, shown here.

How to try it
Notable venues still in
business include the
Apollo in New York City,
the Howard Theater in
Washington, D.C., and
Southern Whispers in
Greenville, Mississippi,
which is also a stop on
the Mississippi Blues
Trail.

ENTERTAINMENT SAFE HOUSES IN JIM CROW AMERICA

THE CHITLIN CIRCUIT • MISSISSIPPI

Pig intestines, or chitlins, were a staple for enslaved African Americans. Chitlins required intense cleaning, and slaveowners preferred the choicest cuts that required little work, like the upper portions of the leg and the back (hence the affluence-denoting phrase "high on the hog").

West Africans were particularly accustomed to eating every part of the animal, so intestines were nothing new. Chitlins were deep fried, simmered in soup, and paired with cornbread and collard greens—all recipes that belong to the culinary tradition of soul food, a confluence of Indigenous American, African, European, and Southern cooking developed by African Americans during the time of slavery.

Under Jim Crow, from about 1930 to 1950, chitlins gained a new significance. For black performers traveling through the country, the hog intestines became a kind of insider code, as they knew that establishments serving chitlins would welcome them. This collection of restaurants, music venues, and nightclubs became known as the Chitlin Circuit. Stretching from Texas to Massachusetts, it functioned as a touring route for black performers. Big-name acts occasionally made the rounds, but the establishments were mostly mom-and-pop places, often in small towns, that offered an informal stage for aspiring performers.

With so much talent traveling along the same route and appearing in the same rooms, the Chitlin Circuit was fertile ground for promoters and managers, who began to champion their favorite acts. Some performers, like Louis Jordan and Roy Brown, had so much success that they climbed the Billboard charts. Today, America's love for blues, swing, and rock and roll is largely thanks to the black performers who came up through the soul food circuit.

Performers like Floyd Smith (top) and Dick Wilson (bottom) graced the stage of the Howard Theater in the 1940s.

Arnett Cobb and Walter Buchanan, Apollo Theatre, New York, NY, ca. Aug. 1947

Music and the warm welcome of soul food drew crowds from Texas to Massachusetts.

KOOL-AID BRINED PICKLES

KOOLICKLES • MISSISSIPPI

The quirky combination of dill pickles and Kool-Aid, America's iconic beverage powder, hails from the Mississippi Delta, where the psychedelic spears are sold at community and convenience stores for a dollar. Known locally as koolickles, the sweet and vinegary pickles are generally loved and widely eaten. Cherry is the classic flavor, but koolickles are limited only by the assortment of Kool-Aid on hand: The line includes pink lemonade, watermelon, peach mango, and strawberry kiwi.

To make a batch of koolickles, drain the brine from a jar of pickles into a bowl.

How to try it

The Mississippi-based convenience store chain Double Quick sells them as "Pickoolas."

Into the brine, mix a package of unsweetened Kool-Aid powder and some sugar, then pour it back into the jar. Soaking whole pickles creates a corona of color around the circumference of the pickle. Slicing pickles lengthwise before curing allows the Kool-Aid to dye the interior a bright jewel tone. Either way, devotees recommend leaving pickles in their Kool-Aid bath for at least a week.

ALL-YOU-CAN-EAT DEPRESSION BURGERS

SLUGBURGER EATING CHAMPIONSHIP • MISSISSIPPI

How to try it

The Slugburger Festival is held every July in downtown Corinth. First prize is $1,500. Participants must be 18 or older and abide by the rules of the MLE.

During the lean days of the Great Depression, "meat extending" was a necessary practice. Burger joints in Mississippi began cutting their ground meat patties with potato flour, deep-frying them, and sliding them into buns laced with mustard and onion. It was a surprisingly satisfying burger that was crispy on the outside and soft on the inside. The slugburger, which sold for a nickel, was so popular that even after the Depression, Mississippians kept extending their meat out of sheer pleasure.

Since 1987, the town of Corinth has been throwing the Slugburger Festival, a three-day event to honor the divine union of beef, starch (now soybean meal), and a hot vat of fat. There's a Slug Idol singing competition and a cornhole throwing contest, but the glitziest draw is the World Slugburger Eating Championship.

Since the contest debuted in 2012, celebrity eaters ranked by the Major League Eating (MLE) association have arrived in Corinth to compete for the international title of Slugburger Champ. Matt "the Megatoad" Stonie from San Jose took

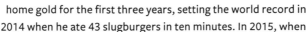

home gold for the first three years, setting the world record in 2014 when he ate 43 slugburgers in ten minutes. In 2015, when Stonie took a year off, first place went to the eminent Joey "Jaws" Chestnut, the reigning king of the Nathan's Hot Dog Eating Contest (in 2018, he set the world record with 74 hot dogs in ten minutes). Chestnut, who ate his first slugburger during competition in 2013, said he enjoyed the burger but had more trouble swallowing than anticipated. While signing autographs, he apologized to fans, saying, "Next year I'll come back and know what I'm getting into and eat more." (He did; in 2014 he ate 42, a dozen more than the previous year.)

The Great Eater of Kent

Before competitive eating was rife with bigwigs and fanfare, there was Nicholas Wood, the Great Eater of Kent.

Wood's career, which spanned the early 17th century, was mostly chronicled by the English poet John Taylor, who was so taken by Wood he later became his manager. Taylor's awe is embodied in his pamphlet, *The Great Eater, of Kent, or Part of the Admirable Teeth and Stomach Exploits of Nicholas Wood, of Harrisom in the County of Kent His Excessive Manner of Eating Without Manners, In Strange and True Manner Described.*

The story goes that Taylor first encountered Wood at an inn in Kent, where he watched him devour 60 eggs, a good portion of lamb, and a handful of pies, before declaring himself still hungry. Wood, who was a farmer by trade, had a local reputation as a superhuman feaster and was known to perform at town festivals and take dares and wagers from nobles. While he had emerged victorious from many feats (he once ate seven dozen rabbits in a single sitting), Wood was far from invincible. During a challenge with a man named Sir William Sedley, Wood ate so much he fell over, passed out, and was put in the stocks—a punishment for his failure. In another instance, a man named

John Dale fed him 12 loaves of bread that he'd soaked in ale, and Wood got so drunk, he passed out and was humiliated once again.

Despite these losses, Wood was a kind of celebrity in Kent. The poet Taylor made Wood an offer, reasoning that they could both make money if they took his talents to London. Taylor would provide payment, lodging, and massive amounts of food, and Wood, in return, would perform daily feats of overeating at the city's Bear Gardens, which at the time hosted animal fights. (Suggested meals included a wheelbarrow full of tripe, and as many puddings as would stretch across the Thames.)

But Wood declined. He was reaching the end of his youth and with it, the end of his intensive eating career. He'd recently eaten an entire mutton shoulder—bones and all—and the experience had left him with only one tooth. He wasn't confident he could perform, so he turned down the enterprising poet.

Though Taylor never got his shot at big city fame, his admiration for Wood never wavered. In his writings, he compares Wood's monumental feats of gluttony to the achievements of Charlemagne and Alexander the Great, declaring he "doth well deserve the title of Great."

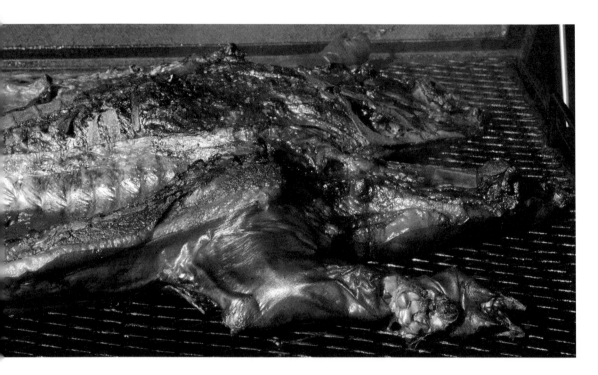

WHOLE HOG HOEDOWN

PIG PICKIN' • NORTH CAROLINA

How to try it

The annual Jamestown pig pickin' event is open to the public. Past themes include Swine & Shakespeare, Cork & Pork, and Hammin' & Jammin'.

n North Carolina, the word *barbecue* is a noun and it always means pork. *Pig pickin'* is also a noun, and in this state it means a party featuring a succulent, slow-cooked whole hog with meat so soft, guests can pick it right off the pig.

Before the Civil War, Southerners ate 5 pounds of pork for every pound of beef. Pigs were left to live in the forest until one was needed for food, when it would be hunted, butchered, and cooked on an open fire. Often, at the helm of these cook-outs was an enslaved African, who expertly tended to meat and fire in a technique their masters would claim as their own. In West and Central Africa, smoking and roasting animals was a common practice, and the knowledge enslaved Africans brought to the American South is what made North Carolina pig pickin' what it is today.

By the 19th century, pig pickin's were adopted by politicians as a way to gather big crowds to listen to their speeches. Politicians vied for popularity by bringing the most food to a pig pickin', which led to the phrase "going whole hog." In North Carolina especially, pigs and politics became fully entrenched, and attending a rally became synonymous with feasting on pork.

These days, pig pickin's still draw crowds. They also draw a lot of opinions. Cooking a whole hog requires teamwork, about eight hours, and agreement over several major issues. Some pit masters prefer the even cooking heat of propane, while others like the smoky flavor of charcoal or the aroma of wood. In the Piedmont region of North Carolina, hogs are basted with a tomato sauce. To the east, locals use a thin vinegar and pepper sauce. And though state can't always agree on what to put on or around the pig, the pig itself remains an almost holy facet of North Carolina's culinary heritage, shaped by centuries of European, African, and political influence.

A TIMES SQUARE ALTERNATIVE

NEW YEAR'S EVE PICKLE DROP • NORTH CAROLINA

At the corner of Cucumber and Vine street, hundreds of revelers gather to ring in the New Year outside the Mt. Olive Pickle Company. At the stroke of 7 p.m., they cheer as a 3-foot-long (1-m) fluorescent pickle drops from a 45-foot (14-m) flagpole into a redwood pickle tank. The tank sprays a delicate fountain of liquid as the pickle hits and the crowd goes wild, blowing on noisemakers and applauding the spectacle.

Since 1999, the Mt. Olive Pickle Company has been dropping the massive celebratory pickle. The event attracts families, older adults, and anyone else wanting to line dance to live music under the glow of a magnificent pickle while also getting to bed at a reasonable time. Seven p.m. Eastern Standard Time happens to be midnight Greenwich Mean Time, which makes the countdown official and justifies the early bedtime.

How to try it

The pickle party starts at 5:30 p.m. at 1 Cucumber Boulevard in Mount Olive. Part of the event is a canned food drive, where all participants are entered to win an inflatable pool pickle.

AFRICAN SESAME COOKIES

BENNE WAFERS • SOUTH CAROLINA

Benne (pronounced "benny") means "sesame seed" in Bantu, a family of languages spoken in sub-Saharan Africa. In the 1700s, when slave traders brought Africans to work the fields of South Carolina, they loaded the ships' cargo holds with African crops intended to feed the captives during the long transatlantic passage. Among these crops was sesame—a buttery, protein-rich seed that the Africans later planted in South Carolina and pressed into cooking oil.

While plantation owners explored sesame's potential as an alternative to imported olive oil, sesame-based substitutes gained little traction until the

How to try it

Olde Colony Bakery in Mount Pleasant uses a 100-year-old recipe, which they claim is the original recipe for benne wafers.

19th century. Instead, South Carolinians developed a fondness for benne wafers, a light and crispy cookie made by toasting sesame seeds, mixing them with brown sugar, butter, and small amounts of flour, and baking them into small nutty discs. Over the last two centuries, benne wafers have become a Low Country staple, tied to the regional cuisine of South Carolina and sold at bakeries and gift shops around the state. Yet many never realize the sweet and salty snack is a vestige of slavery, a tradition owed to those who planted, tended, and popularized the sesame seed.

Benne Wafers from the historic Charleston City Market, established in the 1790s.

CORNMEAL MUSH ENTRAPMENT COMPETITION

ROLLING IN THE GRITS · SOUTH CAROLINA

How to try it

There are two age divisions for Rolling in the Grits: 12 to 16, and 17 or older. Prospective rollers can register at the festival. It's advisable to book your accommodations early because the town's population increases to 45,000 people during festival days.

The small hamlet of St. George has a population of 2,000 and one big claim to fame: They eat more grits per capita than any other place on Earth. To celebrate their town's passion for the Southern dish, St. George hosts the annual World Grits Festival and invites honored members of the community to roll around in an inflatable pool with 3,000 pounds (1,361 kg) of grits.

The object of the competition, called Rolling in the Grits, is to trap as many grits on your body as possible. Participants have taken to wearing grits-catching clothes: sweatshirts with big hoods worn backward, sleeves rolled and duct-taped into pockets, and baggy sweatpants that cinch at the ankle. Contestants are weighed before and after diving into the grits, and the largest weight gain wins. In the pool, they have ten seconds to do their best work, swimming, rolling, and scooping. (The rules state: "Once ten seconds is up, roller must stand up slowly with their arms upward and no grabbing the pants.") In 2015, the world record was set when Tiffany McGirr gained 66 pounds (30 kg) of grits.

Preparing the grits for competition is a challenge in itself. Twenty-seven cases of grits are cooked until just thick enough to hold a paddle upright. Each year, depending on the weather, the recipe is adjusted. (Hot weather, for example, dries out the grits, and they require extra time for cooling.) Since the inaugural contest in 1986, the competition has always used plain grits. But the cook, a man named Philip Ranck, who's been preparing the grits since 2001, recently expressed interest in trying a shrimp base.

With only ten seconds per attempt, contestants try to maximize their grits hoarding ability with baggy clothes.

A REPLICA OF THE FIRST MODERN GROCERY STORE

PIGGLY WIGGLY AT PINK PALACE MUSEUM • TENNESSEE

Before 1916, shopping for groceries was a time-consuming, social endeavor: A clerk served customers one by one, pulling their items from the shelves. Nothing was marked with prices and tallying the bill was done by hand. Clarence Saunders, a flour and grain salesman, conceived of a self-service grocery store where customers would shop autonomously. In 1916, he opened the first Piggly Wiggly. Saunders advertised in newspapers and on billboards, telling the public that grocery shopping was about to change forever. On opening day 487 customers bought groceries—an impossible feat in a clerk-serviced store. Within a year, eight more stores opened in Memphis and by 1923, there were 1,200 stores across the country and countless copycats. Although Saunders's prophecy was right that his self-service concept would change grocery shopping in the United States forever, it's unlikely that he foresaw his own financial ruin. In 1923, with Piggly Wiggly public on the stock exchange, Saunders made some risky trades and lost the company along with millions of dollars.

At the time Saunders lost his grocery-store fortune, he was building a palatial mansion outside Memphis, faced with pink marble. Plans included a ballroom, shooting gallery, and indoor pool, but the unfinished house was taken by his creditors and later donated to the city of Memphis. Now the Pink Palace Museum, visitors to the house can see a replica of Saunders's early Piggly Wiggly stores and step back into a time when grabbing groceries off the shelf (and knowing their price) was a novelty.

How to try it

The Pink Palace Museum is located at 3050 Central Avenue, Memphis, TN. Piggly Wigglys still operate in the southern and midwestern United States.

BEER STEIN HOME-MUSEUM

STEINS UNLIMITED • VIRGINIA

How to try it

From the road, the museum is entirely nondescript, but GPS will get you there. Although technically open every day from 8 a.m. to 5 p.m., Adams is a one-man show, so it's best to call ahead.

Located just outside Pamplin, a tiny 200-person village along an isolated stretch of Virginia's US 460, the Steins Unlimited home-museum is advertised by two hand-painted signs—one hanging from the mailbox, the other rising from the edge of the yard.

Visitors step into a large two-room outdoor shed and are greeted by an array of floor-to-ceiling shelves brimming with some of the most ornate and historically significant drinking vessels ever made. The collection of 10,000-plus rare beer steins is George Adams's lifelong obsession, which took more than 50 years to compile.

Adams uses his formidable collection to tell the story of beer drinking from 1350 to modern day. He's the museum's only host, and quick to offer a "bottomless pint" of America's oldest beer, Yuengling, from an on-site kegerator. (Beer and admission are free, though donations are welcomed.) For about an hour, Adams guides guests down a rabbit hole of German and American beer history. A tour typically covers the institutionalization of the stein via 15th-century sanitation laws (following the Black Death), the ensuing "golden era" of European beer drinking, the rise of beautifully crafted steins as status symbols, American prohibition, the drinking habits of the Third Reich, and much more.

Adams's finest treasures are displayed within his home, a four-bedroom brick rancher. The keystone of the collection is a room containing about 500 vessels that include hand-carved wooden steins, silver steins, and even gold-lidded steins, many of which are hundreds of years old.

THE MID-ATLANTIC

AN INSIDER'S JAM

BEACH PLUM JELLY • DELAWARE

To get your hands on some beach plum jelly, chances are you'll have to forage for beach plums, which requires climbing windy sand dunes and combing through the jagged leaves of gnarled bushes to find the elusive, burgundy-colored fruit. Beach plums, which never make it to the grocery store, are growing increasingly hard to source from the wild. But those who find them are rewarded with a zesty, highly coveted jelly ingredient.

Beach plum jelly wasn't always so hard to find. Explorers have written about the presence of beach plums since 1524. Farmers cultivated the plant in the 1800s, and Ocean Spray even sold beach plum jelly back in the 1930s. But in recent years, coastal developments have taken over much of the beach plum's natural habitat. Some have taken to domesticating the plums in backyard gardens for the sole purpose of jelly-making, but purists say the garden variety is less flavorful than the wild one. Among those who still forage, the sites of known remaining bushes often become well-kept secrets, even within families.

How to try it

Delaware company Backyard Jams and Jellies makes a much-loved beach plum jelly. From late spring to early fall, the jams are sold at Delaware's Rehoboth, Milton, and Historic Lewes farmers' markets, and year-round in specialty stores listed on the company's website.

Tart like plums but bite-size like cherries, beach plums grow in sand dunes.

EVER-EVOLVING HEAT

FISH PEPPERS • MARYLAND

Fish peppers begin life a pale milky color, and then slowly transform into light then darker green, then orange with brown, then finally red, when the pepper is at its hottest.

The Caribbean pepper is believed to have arrived in North America around the 19th century. It was embraced by African Americans living in the Chesapeake Bay area, where it became a favored secret ingredient in the kitchens of crab and oyster

How to try it

The Seed Savers Exchange sells fish pepper seeds on its website, where it's listed as an "All-Time Favorite."

houses (giving the fish pepper its name). The young, pale-colored pepper melted discreetly into the white creamy sauces they used on fish, giving them an invisible kick that no one could name. The trick was passed down orally, rarely recorded in written recipes, which meant in the 20th century, when the pepper fell out of favor, its whispered existence nearly led to extinction.

In the 1940s, a Pennsylvania painter named Horace Pippin was treating his arthritis with an old folk remedy that required being stung by bees. To acquire the bees, he traded seeds with a beekeeper, and among those seeds was the forgotten fish pepper. The beekeeper, H. Ralph Weaver, passed the seeds down through his family and in 1995, his grandson made the fish pepper seed publicly available through the Seed Savers Exchange in Iowa.

Fish peppers taste a lot like fresh serranos—bright, crisp, decisively spicy—and can be used similarly. What makes them distinctive is their vibrant, ornamental appearance. Not only are the peppers on the plant perpetually in varying stages of color and ripeness, each leaf is marbled and flecked by a unique mix of green and white. No two leaves, and no two peppers, are quite the same, making the fish pepper especially suited for landscaped gardens.

Fish peppers ripen through several stages of colors and reach maximum heat when red.

A TINY EDIBLES COMPETITION

SMALL FOODS PARTY • MARYLAND

Baltimore locals have been shrinking wontons, crab cakes, banana splits, and other conventional-size dishes since 2006, when a group of artists began the tradition at a holiday party. Since then, their small-food obsession has morphed into an annual competition that now draws more than 500 people.

Participants of the Small Foods Party compete for everything from the Bad Idea award (where food is charmingly unappealing, like mini Tide Pods made with coconut gelée) to the International award (for food that originates outside the United States). The most innovative contestant takes home the Bright Idea award, while the chef with the best reproduction of a full meal claims the Blue Plate Special. Fingertip-size cupcakes and tiny sub sandwiches are among the past winners of the Golden Toothpick, which praises the most impressive proportional accuracy between full-size original and mini re-creation. The Yummo! award (honoring the party's decree, "Thou shalt not compromise taste for smallness") has gone to a Caesar salad atop a piece of fried parmesan. To earn the grand prize, the tiny food must capture the "heart, mind, and stomachs of the people." One winning team performed as an assembly line of uniformed employees cranking out miniature "Crappy Meals," complete with a burger, fries, and lidded drink. In addition to becoming a small-food legend, the grand prize comes with a giant decorated can of mini corn and the chance to host the next year's showdown.

How to try it

The Small Foods Party is held at the American Visionary Art Museum. The event benefits Moveable Feast, an organization that brings nutritious food to Maryland people with life-threatening or chronic illnesses. Anyone can enter the competition, or simply attend, but no one should arrive hungry.

CONTROVERSIALLY KNOWN AS TAYLOR HAM

PORK ROLL • NEW JERSEY

Every morning, locals all over the Garden State start their day with the same sandwich: two eggs, American cheese, and pork roll—a processed meat that graces nearly every diner and deli menu. Pork roll is endemic to New Jersey and about as old school as it gets. In 1856, a state senator by the name of John Taylor started making the hefty roll of sliceable tube meat that exists somewhere on the spectrum between sausage, bologna, and Canadian bacon. He called it "Taylor's Prepared Ham," but was forced to change the name in 1906, when the Pure Food and Drug Act decreed that hams had to be actual hams.

Here begins a divisive New Jersey debate. People from the southern part of the state took to the name change. When Taylor renamed his product "John Taylor's Original Taylor Pork Roll," they went along with the changing times and began calling it pork roll. But up north, locals stuck with Taylor Ham—for more than a hundred years. The small state is still divided on terminology, and how someone refers to the porcine delicacy immediately gives away their New Jersey provenance and continues to be a source of friendly ire. But pork roll or Taylor ham, the way to enjoy it is not up for debate: slice the meat, cut slits in the sides to prevent curling in the pan, crisp it up, eat it for breakfast.

How to try it

Trenton, New Jersey, throws a Pork Roll Festival in May. Phillipsburg, New Jersey, throws a Pork Roll Palooza in October. For all months in between, check out any local bagel shop or deli.

THE GOLDEN AGE OF

I n the early 20th century, newly industrialized America was eager for places to eat, and prefab, shippable diners were the perfect solution for entrepreneurs looking to fill the demand. Diners—designed to resemble train dining cars—were built in factories and transported, fully assembled, to their permanent locations around the country.

Starting in 1912, thousands of shiny metal restaurants were built and shipped from New Jersey. Although the diner manufacturing industry is all but gone today, some of New Jersey's original handiwork is still standing and operating across America.

WHITE MANNA, Hackensack, NJ. Opened in 1946, manufactured in 1939 by Paramount Diners of Oakland, NJ.

AGAWAM DINER, Rowley, MA. Opened in 1970, manufactured in 1954 by Fodero Dining Car Company of Newark and Bloomfield, NJ.

PEARL DINER, Manhattan, NY. Opened in the early 1960s, manufactured by Kullman Dining Car Company of Lebanon, NJ.

MICKEY'S DINING CAR, Saint Paul, MN. Opened in 1939, manufactured by Jerry O'Mahony Diner Company of Elizabeth, NJ.

NEW JERSEY DINERS

DAVIE'S CHUCK WAGON DINER, Lakewood, CO. Opened in 1957, manufactured by Mountain View Diners Company of Singac, NJ.

FRANK'S DINER, Kenosha, WI. Opened in 1926, manufactured by Jerry O'Mahony Diner Company of Elizabeth, NJ.

DAVIES' chuck wagon DINER

OPEN

PANCAKES

STEAKS

FRIED CHICKEN

The Lost Language of
NEW YORK SODA JERKS

Throughout the 1930s and 1940s, soda jerks across the country were known for a kind of esoteric slang. Behind the counter that was their stage, the soda jerks' responsibilities were manifold: breaking and draining eggs with one hand, carving chicken, remembering orders, pulling the correct spigots and spindles on the drugstore fountain, and, perhaps most important, juggling a beguiling linguistic shorthand for all the orders. Especially in New York City, where the density of candy stores, pharmacies, and customers kept soda jerks working at a quick-witted pace, the counter workers became a show in themselves.

An order of a simple float might yield a shout of "burn it and let it swim!" A more complex chocolate malted milk with chocolate ice cream: "Burn one all the way." If you nixed the ice cream and added an egg, your server would "twist it, choke it, and make it cackle." Coca-Cola flavored with cherry might be "shoot one in the red." Drinks without ice "held the hail." Big drinks were "stretched"; small ones were "short." But a term in one drugstore might not hold in another. In fact, most expressions didn't travel beyond one or two soda fountains, and there was a certain amount of pressure to keep mixing them up. A simple glass of milk might variously be called "cow juice," "bovine extract," or "canned cow," while water went by everything from "aqua pura" to "city cocktail" to the deeply unappetizing "Hudson River ale."

Alas, the era of razzle-dazzle soda jerks came to an end when decorum-minded owners started enforcing notepads and cracking down on shouting. While most of the slang and hijinks are forgotten, here are a few phrases from the heyday of the soda jerk.

In the world of soda jerks, you might start your day with a mug of murk and end it with a glob.

ADD ANOTHER: Coffee

ALL BLACK: Chocolate soda with chocolate ice cream

BABY: Glass of fresh milk

BLACK BOTTOM: Chocolate sundae with chocolate syrup

BLACK COW: Chocolate milk

C. O. COCKTAIL: Castor oil prepared in soda

CANARY ISLAND SPECIAL: Vanilla soda with chocolate cream

CHOC IN: Chocolate soda

CHOKER HOLES: Doughnuts

COFFEE AND: Cup of coffee and cake

COWCUMBER: Pickle

DRAW SOME MUD: Coffee

GIVE: Large glass of fresh milk

GLOB: Plain sundae

IN THE HAY: Strawberry milkshake

MAIDEN'S DELIGHT: Cherries

MUG OF MURK: Cup of coffee without cream

NINETY-FIVE: Customer walking out without paying

OH GEE: Orangeade

ONE ON THE CITY: Water

POP BOY: Soda man who doesn't know his business

RHINELANDER: Chocolate soda with vanilla ice cream

SALTWATER MAN: Ice-cream mixer

SCANDAL SOUP: Tea

YUM-YUM: Sugar

ORGANIC URBAN ROOFTOP FARMING

BROOKLYN GRANGE ROOFTOP • NEW YORK

Set against the Manhattan skyline is Brooklyn Grange, an expansive urban farm covering three rooftops and spanning a lush 5.6 acres (2.3 ha). The largest rooftop soil farm in the world, it produces almost 100,000 pounds (45,360 kg) of organic produce every year.

Started by a few New Yorkers, Brooklyn Grange was born in 2010 when a small team of workers craned 3,000 sacks of soil up seven stories and began laying down the farm over two weeks. The farm's foundation is comprised of a drainage layer and filter fabric, which protects the roof and acts like a giant sponge on rainy days, holding stormwater in the system and then draining it out slowly. Surprisingly, even while holding tens of thousands of gallons of stormwater, the farm weighs less than what the building's roof can hold. The farm's strategic positioning high above the road traffic also means less pollution: Heavy metal contaminants, which are denser than air, have a hard time reaching the vegetables.

Brooklyn Grange grows dozens of leafy greens and 40 varietals of tomatoes, as well as eggplants, peppers, turnips, beans, carrots, and herbs, which are sold at markets, via CSA membership, and used in restaurant kitchens around the city. They also operate an apiary, maintaining more than 30 honey-producing beehives.

In line with their mission of growing organic produce in a local, sustainable system, Brooklyn Grange doubles as an educational space in a city with little access to farming. Thousands of kids and adults come to the farm each year for workshops, and to bring home bundles of some seriously elevated veggies.

How to try it
The Brooklyn Grange holds a free open house on Saturdays, May through October. Private guided tours are available with advanced booking, as well as yoga classes, beekeeping workshops, and jam-making classes.

NEW YORK'S HIDDEN EATERIES

Secreted away in other establishments, some of New York City's tastiest spots are hard to find, open for limited hours, and known by multiple names. But for those who know where to find them, these hidden eateries offer a delicious portal to the world of the culinary cognoscenti.

NANO BILLIARD CAFÉ (185 E. 167TH STREET, BRONX): In the basement of a nondescript residential building is a fluorescent-lit pool hall, and in that pool hall is a lunch counter serving some of the city's best Dominican food. Before the pool players arrive at night, the mostly takeout spot slings home-style island classics like locrio de pollo (chicken and rice) and sancocho (meat and veggie soup) that people drive across state lines to eat.

5 DE MAYO FOOD MARKET (81–06 ROOSEVELT AVENUE, QUEENS): During the week, this market is a typical Roosevelt Avenue grocery store stocked with fruit and candy. But come during the weekend, head past the groceries, and you'll find a beloved taco stand with knockout lamb and goat barbacoa. Slow cooked for hours, the meat is folded into a fresh, warm tortilla and topped with onion, cilantro, and salsa verde.

STREECHA (33 EAST 7TH STREET, NEW YORK): Spot the Cyrillic sign and head downstairs into Streecha, a lace-curtained room with plastic tablecloths that serves top-notch, traditional Ukrainian food. The restaurant raises money for the nearby St. George's Ukrainian Catholic Church, and the cooks are all volunteers, which gives the place a homey, church basement feel.

GOVINDA'S VEGETARIAN LUNCH (305 SCHERMERHORN STREET, BROOKLYN): In the basement of a Hare Krishna temple is this meatless cafeteria serving a rotating assortment of (mostly) Indian food. The portions are large, chanting and hymns play from the speakers, and the clientele is businesspeople, bankers, bureaucrats, and monks.

MATRYOSHKA (88 FULTON STREET, NEW YORK): Descend into the Russian bathhouse in Manhattan's Financial District to find Matryoshka, the restaurant in this three-story underground spa. (Fittingly, matryoshka is the term for a Russian nesting doll.) Dine on pickle platters, beef tongue, pelmeni, borscht, and copious amounts of vodka—all made even more delightful by dining in a bathrobe.

TAOIST PURVEYORS OF MOCK MEATS

MAY WAH VEGETARIAN MARKET • NEW YORK

How to try it
May Wah is located at 213 Hester Street. It's open every day from 9:30 a.m. to 8 p.m.

One of the most unassuming landmarks in New York's Chinatown is a 25-year-old grocery store with a bright green awning. Inside, the shelves are crammed with chicken wings, pork belly, and spot prawns—all entirely animal-free. Although mock meats may seem like a modern phenomenon, they're actually a centuries-old tradition popularized by the Buddhist and Taoist principle of doing no harm to living things, and May Wah Vegetarian Market is a prime destination for impressively analogous meat substitutes.

In 1994, May Wah was started by two Taoist Taiwanese immigrants, Lee Mee Ng and her daughter Lily, who were homesick for mock meat. (In Taiwan, restaurants commonly offer mock meat versions of every dish they serve.) In the early years, the plant-based meat was hard to sell, but as vegetarianism grew increasingly popular, their store took off.

The Ngs work with a Taiwan-based manufacturing company called Chin Hsin Foods, which ensures the mock meat they're getting is as good as back home. Their chicken nuggets are made with soy protein and have chicken-like fibers when pulled apart. Their shark fin is made with plant-based gelatin. Their shrimp, made from the Japanese yam flower konjac, gets its fishy flavor from seaweed. Then there's jerky, ham, bacon, mutton, scallops, barbecue ribs, crab, and duck—all lovingly formed without harming a single animal.

LEGENDARY EEL SMOKEHOUSE

DELAWARE DELICACIES • NEW YORK

Ray Turner's smoked eels—which he catches in the Delaware River, smokes himself, and sells out of a wooden shack in the woods of Hancock, New York—are the stuff of local legend. Turner brines his eels in salt and dark honey before smoking them over applewood, resulting in a sweet and savory and hyper-local delicacy.

Getting these eels requires a pilgrimage: First follow the signs for "Delaware Delicacies Smoke House" on Route 17, then turn onto a dirt road, head past the quarry, and keep going until you hit the small store and smokehouse. Inside you'll find Ray with his long white beard presiding over his case of smoked goods, which includes not just eels but shrimp, trout, salmon, bacon, and Gouda.

How to try it
Delaware Delicacies is located at 420 Rhodes Road in Hancock. Eel season is in the fall and supplies are limited, so call ahead before venturing into the woods.

To find Ray Turner and his legendary smoked goods, follow the signs that say "EEL" nailed to trees along a dirt road.

A FOUNDING FATHER'S PARTY STARTER

BENJAMIN FRANKLIN'S MILK PUNCH • PENNSYLVANIA

How to try it

The good old internet hosts many contemporary spins on Benjamin Franklin's signature recipe. If your batch turns out clear rather than cloudy, you've done it right—the straining process really is clarifying.

Eighteenth-century England was rife with harsh liquors and devoid of refrigerators. Clarification solved both problems. In 1711, homemaker Mary Rockett recorded the earliest-known clarified milk punch recipe. Brandy was combined with lemon juice, sugar, and water, then mixed with a big glug of hot milk. After sitting for an hour, the mixture was strained through a flannel bag to produce a clear, silky-smooth, shelf-stable elixir that lasted for months, no refrigerator necessary.

Benjamin Franklin was a big clarified milk punch fan. He even had his own recipe, which he enclosed in a letter to the future governor of Massachusetts, James Bowdoin, in 1763. (He and the governor were pen pals for 40 years.) Franklin included in the note: "Herewith you have the Receipt you desired," implying this wasn't the first time the men had talked punch.

Ben Franklin's Milk Punch Recipe

Take 6 quarts of Brandy, and the Rinds of 44 Lemons pared very thin; Steep the Rinds in the Brandy 24 hours; then strain it off. Put to it 4 Quarts of Water, 4 large Nutmegs grated, 2 quarts of Lemon Juice, 2 pound of double refined Sugar. When the Sugar is dissolv'd, boil 3 Quarts of Milk and put to the rest hot as you take it off the Fire, and stir it about. Let it stand two Hours; then run it thro' a Jelly-bag till it is clear; then bottle it off.

The secret to clarified milk punch is the curdling, which makes it possible to strain out dairy solids through a cheesecloth or fine mesh until the beverage is clear. Since this can take hours, clarified milk punch can't be "made to order." But the process is cheap, requires little equipment, and makes milk punch essentially nonperishable. (When Charles Dickens died, they found milk punch in his cellar that had outlived him.)

THEMED FEASTS IN A 19TH-CENTURY UNDERGROUND BREWERY

BUBE'S BREWERY AND CATACOMBS • PENNSYLVANIA

How to try it
Bube's is located in the town of Mount Joy. An unbelievable lineup of events is posted on its website.

At least once a month, Bube's Brewery throws a pirate-themed dinner party in their 19th-century basement restaurant, called Catacombs, located 43 feet (13 m) underground. Actors in period costumes rub elbows with swashbuckling guests dining in candlelight, beside enormous wooden beer-aging barrels. On non-pirate-themed nights, Bube's Brewery looks like a cross between a Renaissance faire (which it becomes during monthly medieval festivals) and a Victorian haunted house (which it becomes during regular ghost tours).

This historic brewery was established in 1876 by a German immigrant named Alois Bube. At the time, Lancaster County, where Bube's is located, was known as the "Munich of America" for its thriving German beer scene. Capitalizing on the American love of lagers, Bube slowly built a beer institution, complete with a bar, the "catacombs," and an inn that featured the town's first flushing toilet. Today, Bube's still makes its own microbrews, which are brewed in what was once the icehouse.

AFRICAN AMERICAN HERITAGE CAFETERIA

SWEET HOME CAFÉ • WASHINGTON, DC

How to try it
Passes are required to enter the Smithsonian National Museum of African American History and Culture, where Sweet Home Café is located. While the dishes offered rotate, visitors recommend the Brunswick Stew and the Gospel Bird Family Platter.

In 19th-century New York City, African American restaurateur Thomas Downing ran an elite oyster bar known for its seafood specialties. While customers ate upstairs, Downing used the restaurant's basement to house people fleeing slavery, as a stop on the Underground Railroad. Today, you can order an oyster pan roast celebrating Downing at the Sweet Home Café, located inside the Smithsonian's National Museum of African American History and Culture.

Divided into four regions (the Agricultural South, the Creole Coast, the North States, and the Western Range), the cafeteria pays homage to the rich African, Indigenous American, Caribbean, Latin American, and European influences in African American cooking. From a Gullah take on Hoppin' John (a Southern New Year's staple) to Western-style pan-roasted rainbow trout with cornbread and mustard green stuffing, diners can sample dishes that demonstrate the breadth of African American cuisine.

The café's décor seeks to educate visitors about the importance of African American food, including the political struggle it has nourished: A photograph of the 1960 Greensboro Woolworth's Lunch Counter sit-in spans the length of the cafeteria, reminding diners of the people who fought to grant African Americans equal access to public spaces, like the one they're in.

RECLAIMING ROAD MEAT

ROADKILL COOK-OFF • WEST VIRGINIA

How to try it
The Roadkill Cook-Off is part of Pocahontas County's Autumn Harvest Festival, which usually takes place in September.

Since 1991, the 1,000 people who call Marlinton their home have been reclaiming the word *hillbilly*. The small town, which has suffered from poverty and scarce resources for decades, especially after the collapse of the coal industry, has amplified their redneck reputation to bring life and resources to the local economy. Each year, they set up shop in a big grassy field and welcome thousands of visitors, TV crews, and reporters to their town, all of them lured by the promise of eating roadkill.

Technically speaking, the featured meat does not have to be roadkill. The competition rules state that dishes must feature an animal "commonly found dead on the road," but they do not stipulate that it must have died there. Acceptable meats include groundhog, opossum, crow, snake, bear, and squirrel, and each is inspected before competition to ensure it's safe to eat. Not knowing the provenance of the meat, some say, also adds to the excitement of the day.

After the health inspection, it's time to cook. Following the spirit of the festival, many of the dishes have overtly redneck, tongue-in-cheek names. "Fender Fried Fawn Smothered in Vulture Vomit," for example, contains no vomit, but a reduction of apples, jalapeños, and onions. Other names, like "Ma, them hogs are runnin' wild in the pineapple!" are self-explanatory. Over the years, the competition has attracted rural cooks from all over America. In 2014, a team drove from California to prepare iguana tacos.

Festivalgoers pay $5 to run wild through the roadkill offerings, which are doled out in manageable two-ounce portions. Pots of bubbling turtle stew and plates of biscuits with squirrel gravy are classic offerings, but flavors can get international, too, with fried venison wontons and deer—and alligator—Solomon Gundy (a Jamaican paté). First-prize winners are awarded $1,200 by a panel of judges who "have been tested for cast-iron stomachs and have sworn under oath to have no vegetarian tendencies." Each year, the festival brings in tens of thousands of dollars for the town of Marlinton.

Cooking isn't the only title on offer at the festival. Each year, local girls compete in a beauty pageant for multiple age-specific crowns: Miss Roadkill, Miss Teen Roadkill, Miss Pre-Teen Roadkill, Little Miss Roadkill, and Tiny Miss Roadkill.

NEW ENGLAND

A FEMINIST VEGETARIAN CAFETERIA

BLOODROOT KITCHEN • CONNECTICUT

Inside one of America's last remaining feminist restaurants.

Founded by a small women's collective in 1977, Bloodroot Kitchen is one of America's last remaining eateries of the feminist restaurant movement. The cozy dining room has no wait staff, the walls are decorated with political posters, and there are plenty of discount books on offer. The space hearkens back to an earlier era, between the 1970s and early 1990s, when hundreds of feminist restaurants opened their doors. Often run by lesbian collectives, these spaces were a place for second-wave feminists to gather, relax, and organize.

At Bloodroot, like at many feminist restaurants, the self-service food is purely vegetarian. They offer a rotating menu of seasonal, often vegan, specials that include Thai vegetarian "chicken," chilled zucchini soup, and okra gumbo. There is also a popular chocolate dessert called the "devastation" cake made with sourdough, which you can enjoy beneath a bulletin board featuring slogans like "I'll be post-feminist in the post-patriarchy," and "The road to health is paved with good intestines."

How to try it

Bloodroot is run by lifelong feminists Selma Miriam and Noel Furie. The restaurant is located at 85 Ferris Street in Bridgeport.

SPECTACLE OF BONY FISH

SHAD BAKE • CONNECTICUT

A successful shad bake begins with the skillful use of a boning knife. A single filet contains about a thousand tiny bones, which must be removed before the filets are nailed to planks planted in a circle around hot coals. Angling the planks just right allows the shad to release excess oil, while the planks—which are usually hickory, oak, or cedar—impart smoky flavor and cook the shad in a way that doesn't require flipping. When the fish is ready, a grillmaster shouts "Board!"

How to try it

Although the shad is not as abundant as it used to be, it's still available in New England seafood markets from May through roughly mid-June. The town of Essex, Connecticut, throws a huge shad bake every year in late spring.

Shad strapped to their planks with bacon seatbelts.

which means it's time to remove the planks from the fire and feast.

This cooking method is hundreds of years old—at least—likely taught to colonial New Englanders by Indigenous Americans. Back then shad was so plentiful, with schools migrating each year from the North Atlantic to mating areas upriver, that prisoners revolted against being fed the bony fish every day. (One 19th-century story describes the shad as the devil's creation.)

In the late 1800s, the shad underwent a major rebranding. Appealing to the burgeoning middle class's interest in travel and Americana, marketers advertised the shad bake as a quintessential springtime event. Shad bakes took off across the Northeast, but the residents of Connecticut have been most vocal about claiming them as their own.

THE LUCRATIVE BUSINESS OF BABY EELS

ELVERS • MAINE

How to try it
Most American baby eels are raised and eaten in Japan, but some Maine restaurants have the local delicacy on their menu. Try Sammy's Deluxe or North Beacon Oyster, both in Rockland.

In 2011, a massive tsunami hit Japan, wiping out many eel farms. And, around the same time, Europe began tightening restrictions on eel exports. A gap opened in the lucrative international eel market, and importers turned to the United States.

In Maine, where teeny eels known as elvers wash up in rivers and streams, the sudden overseas need for eels has changed lives. The demand comes mostly from Asia, where elvers are farmed to adulthood and then sold into the Japanese food market. In 2018, a pound of the tiny, glassy eels fetched as much as $2,700 and the state allowed fishermen to harvest 9,688 pounds (4,394 kg). Apart from South Carolina, where the industry is small, Maine is the only US state that permits elver fishing. Government-restricted fishing permits have kept the eel population healthy, but the inflated price has ushered in a new wave of illegal eel traffickers.

Fishermen catch elvers at night, in quiet solitude, their nets cast into shallow fresh water. The already furtive technique made it fairly easy for gun-wielding poachers to come in and harvest illegally, cutting or stealing nets under nightfall, threatening legal fishermen, and selling their catch for cash on the elver black market.

An undercover federal investigation called Operation Broken Glass (after the glassy appearance of the elvers) led to the conviction of several eel bandits. Among them was Bill Sheldon, the so-called Grandfather of Eels, who was charged with seven counts of "conspiracy to smuggle eels." Sheldon was something of a celebrity in the Maine elver business. He played a central role in establishing the state's fishery and was considered a pioneer in the fledgling industry. (He even drove a truck with the license plate "EEL WGN.") In 2018, he pled guilty to buying 281 pounds (127 kg) of elvers valued at about $545,000 from states where the practice is illegal, then transporting them in his EEL WGN, and flying them to Asia.

International Food Crime

Cheese is the most stolen food in the world. According to a 2011 UK study, about 4 percent of the world's cheese gets lifted each year, which is reflected in the fromage heists of the last few decades: $875,000 worth of Parmigiano-Reggiano from Italy, 700 blocks of Saint-Nectaire from France, two prizewinning wheels of English cheddar, and dozens of loaded-up cheese trucks gone mysteriously missing. Cheese stealing may get a lot of attention, but there are so many more types of comestible crimes.

BAKED BEANS HEIST (WORCESTERSHIRE, ENGLAND): In 2013, the driver of a Heinz truck slept as thieves cut a hole in the curtain-walled vehicle and made off with 6,400 cans of baked beans with sausages worth about $10,000. A police spokesperson said they were "appealing for information, especially about anyone trying to sell large quantities of Heinz baked beans in suspicious circumstances," but the bean thieves were never caught.

WINE FRAUD (SILICON VALLEY, CALIFORNIA, USA): Rudy Kurniawan spent the early 2000s passing himself off as a Burgundy expert, repackaging bottles of red wine in his basement and then selling them as rare and expensive vintages to auction houses and wealthy wine buyers. He sold millions of dollars of forged wine before he was caught. In 2009, he was sued by billionaire art and wine collector William Koch, who'd bought Kurniawan's fake wine. Kurniawan was sentenced to ten years in a California prison and his personal wine collection was sold to help repay his debts.

AVOCADO KIDNAPPING (TANCITARO, MEXICO): The town of Tancitaro exports more than $1 million worth of avocados every day, a number that caught the attention of Mexican drug cartels. Gangs began kidnapping farmers, extorting landowners, and terrorizing those who refused to cooperate. Tancitaro became a site of violence and fear, until its citizens banded together to form an avocado police force. Since 2014, a team of trained officers in armored patrol trucks and bulletproof vests have been setting up checkpoints, patrolling farms, and generally protecting avocados and those who work with them. Half the force's funding comes from the government, and half from the avocado producers, who report that the new militia is keeping crime down.

TRUFFLE DOG SABOTAGE (ITALY & FRANCE): Hunting down Europe's elusive white truffle often requires the help of a dog, typically a pointer, hound, or setter trained to sniff out the expensive mushroom. In recent years, the truffle trade has become so cutthroat that truffle dogs have become the target of warring foragers. Dozens of dogs are sabotaged every year, taken from their homes or otherwise ensnared. In the Italian city of Celano, poisoned meatballs were hidden in bushes to eliminate dogs in prime truffle territory. These dogs are trained for multiple years, worth up to $9,000, and loved by their owners—their loss is not taken lightly, which means truffle season is also the time to see newspaper ads seeking missing pups and owners leading their dogs in circles, trying to lose anyone who might be following. (Miraculously, many missing truffle dogs turn back up when truffle season is over.)

AMISH CHARCUTERIE

CHARCUTERIE • MAINE

A decade ago, Matthew Secich was working in the kitchen of a Michelin-starred restaurant. That was before he left the high-stress world behind, converted to the Amish faith, and opened a small charcuterie shop in Unity, Maine.

How to try it
Charcuterie is open only Wednesday, Friday, and Saturday, along Leelyn Road in Unity.

Today, you'll find Secich at the end of a long road in the middle of a pine wood, beard down to his chest, hand-grinding meat to make sausages. In line with his faith, Secich's small shop is lit by oil lamps and heated by a wood stove. His meat is kept cool in a pine room stocked with 80 tons of ice that's hand-cut each winter after being harvested from a local lake. The low-tech kitchen produces high-quality charcuterie such as maple-tarragon kielbasa, smoked duck sausage, sweet bologna, and smoked cheddar—all marked by the finesse of an elite chef.

THE SITE OF A TERRIBLE MOLASSES ACCIDENT

THE GREAT MOLASSES FLOOD PLAQUE • MASSACHUSETTS

How to try it
The plaque is located at an entrance to the Harborwalk, at the intersection of Commercial Street and Copps Hill Terrace.

At 12:45 on the afternoon of January 15th, 1919, Boston Police patrolman Frank McManus shouted into his transmitter: "Send all available rescue vehicles and personnel immediately! There's a wave of molasses coming down Commercial Street!" A five-story-tall cylindrical metal tank, 90 feet (27 m) in diameter, had burst—and a two-story-tall wave containing 2.3 million gallons (8.7 million L) of molasses was surging in all directions.

The molasses spread across the city at an estimated 35 miles per hour. The tank itself was also deadly: It had torn into sharp projectiles, and metal bolts shot from its sides like bullets. As the wave and debris crashed down Commercial Street, buildings were smashed to bits or else floated away whole in the tide of

molasses. Electrical poles keeled over, exposing live wires. A steel elevated train support beam was torn to smithereens. Molasses covered everything. According to a *Boston Post* article, "Horses died like so many flies on sticky fly paper." And it wasn't just horses: The great Boston molasses flood killed 21 people.

After many years of litigation, the tank company was found culpable for the disaster and forced to pay settlement of $8 million in today's money. Cleanup required more than 87,000 man-hours, and the area was said to be sticky-feeling and sweet-smelling for years afterward.

Standing in Boston's North End, you'd never know a deadly molasses flood once destroyed a neighborhood—save for an easily missed plaque at the scene of the crime. The small green sign, while unremarkable, is worth seeking out if only to stand and contemplate how terrifying two stories of molasses moving at 35 miles per hour really is.

A Brief History of Presidential Cheese

The United States government has a centuries-long tradition of unloading tremendous amounts of cheese onto the American public. The practice of gifting, mismanaging, and partying with big cheese goes back to Thomas Jefferson—and although the meaning of cheese has evolved throughout the years, there has consistently been way too much.

THOMAS JEFFERSON: In July 1801, the residents of Cheshire, Massachusetts, milked every cow in town and made an enormous 1,200-pound (544-kg) wheel of cheese in support of presidential candidate Thomas Jefferson. Local pastor Elder John Leland, who led the cheesemaking in a giant cider press, conceived of the cheese as a way to praise Jefferson's support of religious and civil liberty. Leland insisted that "no federal cow" (owned by a federalist farmer) be allowed to contribute milk, and that only free people be allowed to make it "without the assistance of a single slave." On the hulking cheddar, he stamped the words "Rebellion to tyrants is obedience to God."

Ronald Reagan shows off the block of cheese he received after a tax reform speech.

Too large for conventional transportation, the 4-foot-wide (1.2-m) cheese was pulled by Leland by sleigh to the Hudson River, where he and his cheese took a boat to Baltimore, then a horse-drawn wagon to Washington, DC. After a three-week, 500-mile (805-km) journey, Leland presented the cheese to President Jefferson on January 1, 1802. By then, much of America had heard about the celebrity cheese.

ANDREW JACKSON: Supporters of Andrew Jackson couldn't let their president be outshined by Jefferson's cheese. The task became competitive, and in 1835, dairy farmer Thomas S. Meacham crafted a 1,400-pound (635-kg) cheddar that was heavier and thicker than Jefferson's and wrapped in a belt inscribed with political slogans. Jackson's cheese was featured (with nine other cheeses) at a patriotic party in Oswego, New York, then went on a multicity publicity tour before landing at the White House.

Jackson, however, was less excited about his cheese and had no idea what to do with it. The hulking cheddar sat on display for nearly two years,

but in 1837, his last year in office, he needed to get rid of it. During the final party of his presidency, Jackson invited the public to come and eat his cheese, which led to a greasy, smelly free-for-all that dismantled the 1,400 pounds in two hours. According to Jackson's successor, Martin Van Buren, the cheese room had to be aired out for many days, the curtains removed, and the walls painted.

RONALD REAGAN: Government cheese, as we know it, is the result of the government pouring too much money into the dairy industry. In 1977, with the dairy industry floundering, a $2 billion subsidy was created to stabilize milk prices and the income of farmers. To take advantage of the new money, dairy farmers began producing as much milk as possible, which led to a massive milk surplus. Whatever the farmers couldn't sell (which was a lot) the government bought and turned into cheese, adding it to a growing, self-perpetuating stockpile. By the 1980s, the supply had grown to a staggering 500 million (227 million kg) pounds of cheese, or 2 pounds of cheese for every American.

The government's bright yellow cheddar was distributed across the country to low-income citizens until the 1990s, when the dairy industry stabilized. Today, sentiments about government cheese are mixed. Some recall a moldy, inedible cheese and the shame of having to eat it. Others grew a fondness for it and insist the processed stuff made exceptional grilled cheese sandwiches and macaroni and cheese.

BARACK OBAMA: Big Block of Cheese Day was added to the presidential cheese canon by Barack Obama. Three years in a row (2014–2016), the Obama administration hosted an event inspired by Jackson's big cheese blowout. Big Block of Cheese Day, although less grotesque than Jackson's open house, was also a political event used to gather Capitol Hill VIPs and answer questions from the public. While the emphasis was more on policy than cheese, Obama served plenty of it, along with cheese-based puns. As stated on the White House website, "Excited? So are brie."

HUTS OF THE WHITE MOUNTAINS

MOUNTAIN HUT CROO • NEW HAMPSHIRE

How to try it

The huts are run by the Appalachian Mountain Club. While full service is available only during the summer, guests can use the kitchen facilities year-round.

Along New Hampshire's rugged White Mountains, which cover 87 miles (140 km) and contain the highest peak in the Northeast, are a string of eight outposts known as high mountain huts. These strategically placed lodges, modeled after huts in the Alps, allow hikers to sleep and refuel along their journey. From late May to mid-fall, a group of devoted staff called "croo" prepare 2,300 family-style meals for hikers.

While croo members are rarely professional chefs, a rich oral tradition ensures newbies learn tricks of the backcountry-cooking trade. Before the season starts, croos attend a five-day training, including six or so hours on cooking and baking. In May, helicopters airlift about 16,000 pounds (7,257 kg) of the heaviest supplies—including propane, flour, and canned goods—to each hut, after which deliveries are made by the croo. Twice a week, each of the roughly 50 staffers lugs trash and recycling out of the shelters and brings back 40 to 60 pounds (18 to 27 kg) of vegetables, frozen meat, butter, and cheese—all in a contraption made of wood, canvas, and leather called a packboard.

Today, the huts host 36–90 guests at capacity and are run by 5–11 croo members. Home-cooked meals are the main attraction, and hut binders display well-loved recipes: lentil soup, dijon mustard chicken, lasagna, garlic-cheddar bread, and vegan chocolate cake. To ensure hut-hopping backpackers eat varied meals along the way, each hut cooks a similar entrée on the same night of the week—stuffed shells on Sunday, beef on Monday, and so on.

According to croo members, hiking food in and trash out gets easier over the course of the summer. Many say the twice-a-week-supply sojourns put them in the best shape of their lives, providing a sense of strength and empowerment when the treks became enjoyable.

Greenleaf Hut, located near Mount Lafayette, is one of eight refueling outposts for White Mountains hikers.

FIRE POKER COCKTAIL TORCH

LOGGERHEAD • RHODE ISLAND

When British settlers in colonial America needed to boil cocktails, cauterize wounds, and ignite the occasional cannon, the loggerhead was their multi-tool of choice.

Fashioned by attaching a long iron rod to a short wooden handle, loggerheads were pole-shaped tools whose metal end was left to heat on an open flame. When red-hot, the loggerhead could melt solids and seal up flesh. Bartenders were big fans of the blistering rod, which helped them create hot and splashy cocktails. By plunging the heated metal into an earthenware pitcher or large pewter mug, they could caramelize, boil, and froth boozy concoctions into all kinds of steamy drinks. Before central heating, patrons warmed up with the help of hot beverages like toddies, hot punches, and the most popular colonial cocktail of all, the flip, made from frothed ale, rum, and sweetener.

In England, loggerheads were so ubiquitous that British people used the term as an insult, suggesting their target had a piece of iron for a head. The fights that arose after a night of many flips begot the idiom "at loggerheads," which means to be at odds with someone; on the pub circuit, the phrase came to imply a disagreement that escalated into physical violence. Some accounts of these bar brawls cite the dueling parties pulling the loggerheads from the fire and brandishing them against each other, which points to the clearest etymology of all.

How to try it
Loggerheads are no longer used, but fire pokers made from metal are still common household objects. Please enjoy responsibly.

THE OLDEST STILL-OPERATING TAVERN IN AMERICA

WHITE HORSE TAVERN • RHODE ISLAND

In 1673, a tavern opened in Newport with a sign depicting a white steed—the universal symbol of a public house (useful at a time when many were illiterate), and the image that would eventually give the establishment its official name.

William Mayes Jr., a notorious pirate, returned to Newport with pillaged bounty and inherited the tavern from his father in 1702. He ran the White Horse until the British pressured him to hand the reins to his sister and her husband. Pirate-run management reflected poorly on the establishment, which had become the official meeting place for Rhode Island politicians.

Until the 1730s, when the state built its Colony House, the White Horse hosted Rhode Island's General Assembly, Criminal Court, and City Council. Many say the business lunch began here, as politicians would charge their food and drink to the public treasury.

During the Revolutionary War, the British housed Hessian mercenaries in the building, forcing the owner, Walter Nichols, and his family out. When the war was over and the colonies won their independence, Nichols returned and refurbished his tavern.

How to try it
The White Horse Tavern is located at 26 Marlborough Street in Newport. The restaurant has a "business casual" dress code for dinner, when collared shirts for men are required.

But the centuries of wear and tear took a toll on the White Horse. By 1954, the building was in desperate need of repair. The Preservation Society of Newport took on the job of meticulously restoring the building, and it reopened in 1957 when the work was complete. Today, the architecture remains faithful to the 17th century: Candles and oil lamps burn beneath the thick beams of the roof. During the winter, a fire burns in the massive hearth. The cuisine is still classic New England, the flag on display still has just 13 stars, and the tavern ghost is alive and well, lurking just to the right of the dining room fireplace.

The storied 17th-century White Horse Tavern was once owned by a pirate.

COLONIAL SPORTS DRINK

SWITCHEL • VERMONT

How to try it

Vermont Switchel Company ships their immune-boosting elixir around the country. It's great on its own or mixed into cocktails. Recipes are also available online.

From the 1700s to the 1900s, it was common to see ceramic jars placed throughout fields—below the shade of trees or tucked alongside a stream—and filled with America's thirst-quenching, electrolyte-boosting sweetheart: switchel.

Made with ginger, apple cider vinegar, sweetener, and water, switchel had a flavor profile similar to lemonade—tangy, refreshing, and sweet. Farmers noted multiple health benefits to drinking the liquid, among them its ability to clear the throat and sinuses, provide energy, and fight off sickness. At the time, no one understood exactly how switchel worked, but science now points to the anti-inflammatory power of ginger, the potassium in molasses, and the microbial gut benefits of raw apple cider vinegar. Aside from the water, every ingredient in switchel contains potassium, which is an electrolyte—but electrolytes weren't understood until the late 19th century.

Beyond switchel's healthy properties, people really liked to drink it. The vinegar gave off the throat-warming heat of alcohol without any alcohol, which made it a favorite among temperance advocates. And while it tasted a good bit like lemonade, switchel required no citrus, which was much harder to procure than vinegar.

Latin America

MEXICO • CENTRAL AMERICA

THE CARIBBEAN ISLANDS • SOUTH AMERICA

MEXICO

MUSHROOM-FLAVORED CORN FUNGUS

HUITLACOCHE • MEXICO

How to try it

Fresh huitlacoche is available at markets in Mexico City, particularly the Central de Abastos. Throughout Mexico and beyond, it can be purchased canned or jarred in specialty markets.

When Aztec farmers found blue-black spores overtaking their corn, they didn't worry—they rejoiced! It was huitlacoche, corn infected by the pathogenic fungus *Ustilago maydis*, which bestows a rich, mushroom-like flavor, and makes an excellent quesadilla filling.

The name *huitlacoche* derives from the Aztec language, Nahuatl, and most believe it translates best to "sleeping excrescence" because the fungus grows around the kernels and impedes their growth. In the United States, farmers use a less poetic name: corn smut.

Although technically a plant disease, corn smut is a prized ingredient in Mexican cuisine, and an infected cob is worth significantly more than a regular one. The bulbous spores retain much of the corn's flavor, while contributing a nutty, mushroomy taste that makes it distinctly fungal. Sautéed with onions and chilies, the resulting inky mixture enriches everything from tacos to omelets.

Now a much-sought-after delicacy (some menus describe it as "Mexican truffles"), huitlacoche is a testament to the ingenuity of the Aztecs, who turned a scourge on their staple crop into a culinary blessing.

Baskets of the prized fungus at Mexico City's wholesale market.

LOVE POTION NUMBER DIE

TOLOACHE • MEXICO

Smoke a leaf of the nightshade *Datura innoxia*, and you might hallucinate. Drink a potion made from its seeds, and it's possible you'll fall in love. Steep a handful of the plant in hot liquid, and beware of death—a lethal dose is said to be about 5 ounces (150 g).

The perennial shrub, which produces a white, trumpet-like flower and prickly, bulbous fruit, has many names across the Americas. In Mexico, it's known as toloache, from the Nahuatl words for "bow the head" and "reverential." Elsewhere, the names are less affectionate: The Navajos call it ch'oxojilghei, or "crazy maker."

The plant is categorized as a "deliriant"—a hallucinogen that leads the mind away from the lucid world, triggering feelings of insanity and a loss of control over the physical self. For centuries, Mexican shamans have smoked cigars rolled with its leaves or eaten its seeds during divination rituals. In northwestern Mexico, the Tarahumara still prepare a ceremonial drink of sprouted corn and toloache to encourage visions.

In small quantities, toloache operates as a pain reliever. Ancient Aztecs wrote of a fever remedy based on a weak toloache infusion, while Uto-Aztecan oral histories describe midwives making a toloache brew to help ease childbirth pains. Modern practitioners of witchcraft (or *brujería* as it's known in Spanish) in Mexico make toloache love potion. Folklore suggests that mixing small doses into the food or tobacco of the person you desire will make them yours.

How to try it
Mercado de Sonora in Mexico City carries toloache products along with other powders, potions, and plants.

AUTO REPAIR SHOP TAQUERÍA

EL VILSITO • MEXICO

Visit El Vilsito during the day and you'll find mechanics working on cars. Stop by the humble garage after 8 p.m., and you'll find one of Mexico City's best taquerías.

How to try it
Check El Vilsito's Facebook page for taco-serving hours. Don't show up outside those times unless you need to get your car repaired.

Wielding giant knives, servers carve slices off hulking, spinning spits of al pastor—Mexico's beloved achiote-marinated pork. The juicy meat cylinder is formed by stacking thin slices of pork onto a vertical spit, a technique learned from Lebanese immigrants who brought shwarma to Mexico. The succulent, lightly charred meat falls into a warm tortilla, and is topped with a slice of pineapple (kept at the top of the rotisserie), and a sprinkling of onions, cilantro, salsa, and lime. Addictively sweet, savory, fatty, and acidic, there's a reason tacos al pastor are considered one of the most iconic dishes of the Mexican capital.

This rotating spit of al pastor is set up nightly in an auto body shop.

EGGS

The chicken egg is one of the most nutritious foods on the planet, packed with nearly every vitamin the human body requires. But not all eggs are created equal. Only a few varieties are more nutritionally potent than the hen's, and many are near nutritionless—which, incidentally, doesn't stop us from going to tremendous lengths to eat them.

Crocodile Eggs

Fiercely protected by their mothers, crocodile eggs are dangerous to harvest in the wild. The safest way to procure them is from crocodile farms in places like Southeast Asia, where the harvest is so abundant, locals hold crocodile-egg-eating contests. In Pattaya, on Thailand's southeast coast, the fastest person to eat ten hard-boiled crocodile eggs wins. The taste is described as strong, salty, and fishy.

Gull Eggs

Seagull eggs of the black-headed gull variety can be found only four to six weeks a year in the wetlands of England. A small group of licensed "eggers" have permission to forage for them, but the practice is highly regulated. Only one egg may be removed from each nest, and the nest locations are kept secret. After an egger removes an egg, they mark the remaining eggs with an X, so that the next egger will know to move along. When hard-boiled, the gull eggs' flavor is subtle but rich—rich being the key word here because a single gull's egg costs about $7.

Snail Eggs

These tiny, white, and glossy orbs are prized among European gourmands with a big egg budget. Snails, notorious for their leisurely pace, take two to three years to produce eggs. But Sicilian producers have found a way to make snails pump out eggs in about eight months using an accelerated maturing technique. The crunchy caviar has an earthy, woodsy taste often compared to baked mushrooms or asparagus, and sells for about $100 for 50 grams (roughly 2 tablespoons).

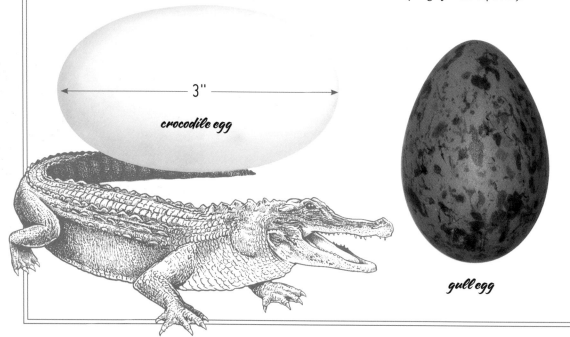

3"

crocodile egg

gull egg

Octopus Eggs

An octopus mother cares for her eggs for up to six grueling months. Nesting in dark underwater dens, typically found in the crevices of rocks, the mother hovers over her eggs, circulating them with fresh aerated water. During this brooding period, she usually does not leave the nest or eat, preferring to starve rather than abandon her young. Often, the mother dies when her job is done. Octopus eggs are sometimes found in Japanese sushi preparations, where the milky sacs are eaten raw. In nature they look like translucent teardrops, and as they mature, you can see the tiny octopus developing inside.

octopus eggs

Turtle Eggs

Eating the offspring of the endangered sea turtle is illegal in most of the world, but they're still considered a delicacy in many countries. In Nicaragua, where turtle-eating dates back to pre-Columbian times, turtle eggs are considered an aphrodisiac, and there remains a robust and largely unregulated black market trade. Under nightfall, poachers find nests in the sand and net up to 100 eggs with each sweep. For the unaccustomed palate, the soft shell and slimy, musty taste are reason enough to leave the eggs alone—but tradition keeps the practice alive.

Quail Eggs

For centuries, these mini eggs have been revered around the world for their extensive healing properties. In Chinese medicine, quail eggs are used to strengthen yin, the feminine, dark, and negative counterpart to yang. Yin can slow down the aging process, and so quail eggs are mixed into beauty products. They are also eaten to treat allergies, blood impurities, and skin conditions.

quail eggs

turtle egg

THE BARS SERVING GODLY ELIXIR

PULQUERÍAS • MEXICO

How to try it
Fresh pulque has a short shelf life, usually just a couple of days, so it rarely makes it out of Mexico except in canned form. In Mexico City, Las Duelistas is a small, beloved pulquería that's always sweaty and packed with a lively clientele. As is the case for many shops in the country, their pulque comes in an assortment of rotating flavors including mango, celery, and red wine.

Aztec goddess Mayahuel is often depicted with 400 breasts, each one pouring agave sap. According to ancient myth, the first agave plant sprouted at the site of Mayahuel's burial, and the sweet liquid is thought to be her divine blood.

Aguamiel ("honey water") is produced in the stalk of the agave. When the stalk is opened, the aguamiel can be scooped from the cavity like water from a well. Distill aguamiel, and you'll get tequila or mezcal. Ferment it, and within a couple of hours you'll get pulque, a thousand-year-old elixir that was once so sacred, it was held in reserve for priests, nobles, and a few of the sick and elderly and as the final treat for victims of ritual sacrifice. When Spanish Christian colonialists arrived in the 16th century, pulque fell out of favor because the colonists looked to eradicate local religions and customs.

Today, pulque is experiencing a revival. "Neo-pulquerías" are attracting a new, younger following, with some modern spins on the conventional brew (cookies-and-cream pulque, anyone?). In a pulquería, expect to drink a lot and to be judged by the size of your serving. The biggest, glasses, which hold 2 liters, are called macetas (flowerpots), followed by cañones (cannons), chivitos (little goats), catrinas (dandies), and tornillos (screws).

Sour, with a foamy, saliva-like texture, pulque's primary appeal is not its taste. The milky beverage has an ancient reputation for treating diabetes, stomach pains, and infertility. And while it is indeed alcoholic (2 to 8 percent ABV), drinkers describe a wide and eclectic array of sensations—from mysterious paralysis to chatty, blissful elation—that keep the pulquerías in brisk business.

A man draws "honey water" from the stalk of the agave.

SMOKED BOOZE WITH THE ESSENCE OF MEAT

MEZCAL DE PECHUGA • MEXICO

Traditional mezcal is made from the core of the agave plant, known as the piña. After roasting the piñas to give the drink its signature smoky essence, mezcaleros blend the piñas with fruits, nuts, and spices, then ferment and distill the mix three times. It's in this third round of distillation that mezcal de pechuga gets a special addition: a piece of raw chicken dangled over the top.

Suspended over the open clay or copper still, the chicken breast (pechuga means "breast" in Spanish) mingles with the vapors, and its meaty essence helps counterbalance the alcohol's bracing flavor. Some liquor historians believe that this tradition began as a way to mask the taste of subpar mezcal.

In Mexico, mezcal de pechuga is commonly consumed during special occasions, such as quinceañeras and weddings, but it's also gaining popularity in the United States, where it's stocked alongside bottles of more traditional, poultry-free mezcals.

Although the flavor of the chicken is subtle at best, the meat-dangling remains important. Some versions of mezcal de pechuga feature other types of meat, including rabbit, iguana, or Ibérico ham.

How to try it

Most mezcal is produced in Oaxaca. Head to the mezcal shop Mezcalillera, which doubles as a tasting room.

DESERT CAVIAR

ESCAMOLES • MEXICO

Ant pupae and larvae, an opulent treat in Mexico, resemble pine nuts, taste like butter, and have a texture akin to cottage cheese. To retain their delicate flavor, escamoles are often prepared simply, fried in butter with onion and chilies, then wrapped in corn tortillas.

This prized egg is produced by *Liometopum apiculatum*, or the velvety tree ant, but locals prefer a different name. *La hormiga pedorra* means "the farty ant," nicknamed after the sulfuric odor that wafts from their nests.

Escamoles are collected from the high plains desert of central Mexico, where the velvety tree ant tunnels its home among the roots of agave plants. Escamoleros, the people who track down these tiny eggs in the wild, are up against incredible demand, and although many carefully scrape away the tops of nests and use sieves to separate ants from their larvae, others are not so diligent, and the desert delight (which sells for up to $100 for 2.2 pounds/1 kg) is at risk of being overharvested.

Centuries before the larvae were trendy, before the Spanish arrived in what we now call Mexico, escamoles were favored among the Indigenous elite: Ancient menus tell us that Aztec emperors hosted elaborate banquets and feasted on this desert caviar.

Ant eggs are a delicate, buttery Mexican delicacy.

How to try it

Escamoles cannot be brought across the border, so interested parties must get to Mexico, where the eggs grace the menus of many restaurants. Try El Cardenal in Mexico City for upscale ant pupae tacos. Those looking for volume can go to the Mercado San Juan, where they sell the eggs by the kilo.

A SUMPTUOUS SHOWCASE OF CAKES

PASTELERÍA IDEAL • MEXICO

How to try it

Pastelería Ideal is located at Calle 16 de Septiembre 18, in Mexico City's Centro Histórico.

A wonderland of model cakes above Mexico City's iconic bakery.

On the second floor of the bakery institution Pastelería Ideal is a massive cake showroom featuring a dazzling array of custom confections that can be ordered downstairs at the shop. Towering multitiered cakes, advertised to weigh more than 200 pounds (90.7 kg), drip icicles of frosting from tiers that can reach 8 feet (2.4 m) in the air. Favorite cartoon heroes and movie princesses are represented in sugar, along with thousands of piped flowers and perfect fondant cutouts of everything from clowns to skulls. The cakes on display are for visual consumption only, so eat a snack at the bakery before taking the trip upstairs to wander among Supreme Cakedom.

SWEET-AND-SOUR CANDY PASTA

SALSAGHETI • MEXICO

How to try it

Taste the spicy tang of Salsagheti at corner stores in Mexico, or order up a bulk supply from online candy distributors.

Salsagheti, which combines the word *salsa* ("sauce" in both Spanish and Italian) with a misspelling of the latter half of the word *spaghetti*, might sound like a marinara-slathered Italian pasta dish, but it's actually a heap of spicy Mexican candy straws.

These tubular, sour watermelon–flavored gummies are coated in a refined mix of chili-tamarind powder and sugar crystals. A packet of tamarind sauce—the salsa—has a runny, gravy-like consistency. Squeeze the packet onto the 'gheti and enjoy a meal with almost no nutritional value.

✳✳✳ Mexican Candy ✳✳✳

The addictive union of sweet, salty, sour, and spicy is the hallmark of Mexico's whimsical world of candy. These confections sound like they sprang from the mind of a mad scientist with a sweet tooth: candy salsas, powdered candy that doubles as food seasoning, candy shaped like corn but flavored like strawberries. The surprising, explosive flavor combinations are made for the country's vibrant, chili-loving palate—and are like nothing else in the world.

SALSAGHETI

Squeezable sweet-and-sour tamarind gel

Pineapple suckers that foam like beer

Watermelon lollipops with a hard chili powder shell

Sweet-and-sour salted apricots showered in chili powder

Individual doses of powdered citrus and salt

Banana bubble gum with a liquid banana core

Cucumber meets chili for a spicy vegetal confection

Liquid spicy pickled fruit

Like Avocados?
Thank This Extinct Giant Sloth.

Mexico is the avocado capital of the world, with two central states (Michoacán and State of Mexico, aka the Avocado Belt) supplying nearly half of the global market. An Aztec symbol of love and fertility turned cosmopolitan salad ingredient, the trendy green fruit has been a hit since prehistoric times, when it got its first big break from an unwitting benefactor.

Though lestodons might sound like toothy, scaly dinosaurs, these Cenozoic-era creatures were sloths. They are the direct ancestors of the sloths still around today, but lestodons were enormous, putting the "mega" in "megafauna." Weighing from 2 to 4 tons, lestodons, along with other "ground sloths," roamed grassy plains in South America. Their diet consisted of grass and foliage and, occasionally, a more nutritious treat: the early avocado.

Giant sloths, along with megafauna such as gomphotheres and glyptodonts, feasted on whole avocados and spread their seeds over South America. These enormous creatures' digestive systems could process large seeds, and avocados

benefited. When pooped out, far from their parent trees, the seeds could sprout and grow without competition for water and sunlight. It was a good deal all around, and it likely resulted in avocados as we know them: fatty and large-pitted, all the better to attract huge sloths.

Enormous prehistoric sloths spread avocados by eating them and pooping out their seeds.

Near the end of the Pleistocene Ice Age (about 11,000 years ago), a fluctuating climate wiped out many megafauna. (Some survived, such as the much-bigger-than-you-think moose.)

The avocado might have survived only in a valley or two as a small, obscure fruit if a new propagator hadn't come along: us. Humans weren't swallowing the fruits whole, but they did plant them widely over South and Central America.

CINNAMON-FLAVORED BUGS

JUMILES • MEXICO

In the town of Taxco, the traditional way to eat jumiles is while they're alive. Harvested from their mountain homes, these ancient stinkbugs are commonly doused with lime, wrapped in tortillas, and consumed while the bug still has full capacity of its scuttling legs. The flavor is a medicinal blend of cinnamon and mint, and the smell is as pungent as the name "stinkbug" suggests.

Reports from the 1930s and 1940s describe Indigenous Mexicans using the insects to treat kidney, liver, and stomach ailments. They're also rumored to be aphrodisiacs.

Taxco holds an annual Jumil Day to honor the multipurpose bugs. It takes place on the Monday after the Day of the Deceased because many locals believe the insects are the reincarnation of their ancestors. It's not uncommon to hear locals ask, *Are you carrying family?* What they're really asking is if you have jumiles.

How to try it
You need to eat the bugs alive to experience their full mouth-numbing properties, but they're a tasty (and much tamer) experience when cooked. Jumiles are a favorite taco filling in Taxco, where you can buy them by the bagful at the local market.

THE 16TH-CENTURY HOT CHOCOLATE FROTHER

MOLINILLO • MEXICO

The molinillo is one of history's greatest unitaskers. Its one job: whipping hot chocolate into foamy perfection.

The wooden whisk's roots lie in colonization. When Spaniards arrived in Mexico in the 16th century, they didn't care for the local chocolate drink. Hernán Cortés and his conquistadores initially refused to drink it, and in 1590, a Jesuit writing about the sweet beverage compared its foamy consistency to feces.

But in recognition of chocolate's value as an Aztec status symbol, the Spanish kept it around and eventually developed a taste for it. Historians even suspect that the molinillo was a Spanish innovation because the Mesoamerican style of making the beverage was pouring molten chocolate from one pot to another.

Both functional and beautiful, the molinillo—often carved from a single piece of wood—has a long handle with a ball or square at the end with notched rings that speed up the agitation process. To use the molinillo, submerge the bulbous end into the liquid chocolate, press the handle between two palms, and twist back and forth until the drink is sufficiently foamy.

The cocoa-based confection, long considered an aphrodisiac, also influenced matters outside the kitchen. Legend goes that in some regions of Mexico, the key to finding a husband was a young woman's ability to impress with perfectly frothed hot chocolate.

How to try it
To make Mexican hot chocolate, melt semisweet chocolate into a pot of warm milk, add sugar, a cinnamon stick, a pinch of salt and cayenne, and twist away.

CENTRAL AMERICA

AN INTOXICATING CHRISTMAS TRADITION

BLACK FRUITCAKE • BELIZE

I t's hard not to love a recipe that begins with a pound of butter, a pint of stout, and a quart of rum—which is why black fruitcake is the crown jewel of Belizean Christmas. In Belize, making Christmas fruitcake is (practically) mandatory. As is the inclusion of rum. Sure, some recipes say you can substitute grape juice for the hard stuff, but what kind of fruitcake would that be? Not a black fruitcake.

The origins of this particular cake date back to the 17th century, when English colonizers brought their sweet puddings to the Caribbean. Over the years, locals adapted the recipe to their own tastes, substituting rum for the English brandy and incorporating spices from the islands. The very best black fruitcakes start months, even a year, in advance. (A week, locals say, is the absolute minimum time needed to see a real transformation, but the longer the better.) A quart of rum is poured over a bounty of dried fruits such as raisins, currants, dates, and citrus peels. The fruit soaks in the rum along with some brown sugar throughout the summer and fall, expanding into juicy, potent morsels, while the rum thickens into a syrup.

The Belizean cake gets its black color from the pint of stout. The stout goes into a batter of flour, sugar, eggs, butter, allspice, and nutmeg. Then the soaked fruit is added. The rum syrup is reserved for pouring over the top of the baked and cooled cake.

Black fruitcake should be packed with fruit. It should have a dense, moist texture, and a rich, boozy taste. In Belize, where dried fruits are expensive, the gift of a fruitcake is a serious token of affection and respect. And with fruit soaking since summer, this is no last-minute gift.

How to try it

Black fruitcake isn't complete without a glass of rum popo, a creamy cocktail made with milk and eggs, because what goes better with rum than more rum? To the same effect: If the cake gets dry from sitting on the counter, locals suggest hitting it with a bit more rum.

THE CORN DRINK DANCE SONG

ATOL DE ELOTE • EL SALVADOR

A tol de elote is a warm, sweet, and corn-packed drink that's often so thick it's eaten with a spoon. The beverage is such a cultural institution, the band Los Flamers recorded a hit dance song called "Atol de elote." The chorus encourages listeners to dance three easy steps: Everybody should start by moving and getting low (moviendo agachadito), then moving the hips (moviendo las caderas), and moving the corn drink (moviendo el atol de elote). The corn drink is almost certainly a euphemism for butt. In the music video, dancers groove with the large wooden spoons traditionally used to stir atol de elote, while drums and horns sound euphorically around them.

Rich and silky, atol de elote gets its delightful texture from pulverizing fresh corn against a grinding stone. After mixing in milk, sugar, and spices such as cinnamon and vanilla, vendors heat the concoction in a giant pot until it's thickened, usually without the assistance of a dance track.

How to try it

Check out San Salvador's Mercado Central, where a piping-hot ladle of atol de elote sells for about a quarter. You can also make it at home in a blender.

LIME-CURED BULL'S TESTICLES

CEVICHE DE CRIADILLAS • GUATEMALA

Ceviche de criadillas, or bull testicle ceviche, can be just as tasty and refreshing as the seafood variety. Some say it tastes like a cross between two ceviche classics: tuna and octopus. After curing the testicles in citrus, a cook cuts up the testicles into slices or small chunks and tosses them with chopped onions, chilies, cilantro, and tomato. The spicy, tangy mixture is served cold or at room temperature. If you do acquire a taste for it, be careful about going nuts—Guatemalans say it's an aphrodisiac.

How to try it

Antigua, Guatemala, and Cajamarca, Peru, are known for ceviche de criadillas. Although some cevicherias stock fresh testicles, you may have to track down the raw materials yourself, from either a butcher or marketplace stall. Keep in mind that curing animal flesh with acid won't kill bacteria the way heat does, so make sure to use fresh, clean meat.

CHEESE AND CHARCUTERIE FOR THE DEAD

FIAMBRE • GUATEMALA

Every November 1, on All Saints' Day, Guatemalan families and friends unite at the grave sites of their loved ones to celebrate the lives of the departed. They tell stories, recite prayers, and adorn the grave with flowers and candles, and in the evening, the living share a meal—always making sure to leave food and drink behind for souls who have worked up an appetite.

Fiambre generally refers to cold cuts in Spanish, but in Guatemala, it's the signature dish of All Saints' Day. Made with an average of 50 ingredients, this giant colorful salad often includes shrimp, hard-boiled eggs, salami, cheese, pickles, pacaya flowers, sardines, and beef tongue. Families come together days in advance to purchase, pickle, grill, and dice, then make a cohesive dish by mixing and marinating everything in vinaigrette for at least a day.

Guatemalans pass down their own family recipes, and the massive salad is designed to give the deceased a smattering of options. Common variations include a vegetarian version, an unmixed style called divorciado (literally "divorced"), and rojo ("red") or blanco ("white")—renditions made with or without beets. Locals know it's tricky to surmise exactly what the dead are craving, so with fiambre, they give them an array of choices.

How to try it

Guatemalan fiambre is a homemade meal prepared only for All Saints' Day. In other Spanish-speaking countries, fiambre simply denotes cold food, such as platters of charcuterie and cheese.

A beautiful spread for snacking in the afterlife.

IT'S RAINING FISH

LLUVIA DE PESCES • HONDURAS

How to try it

The fish arrive with the first major rainfall, so those hoping to witness the phenomenon should arrive before May and prepare to be patient until July.

The residents of Yoro, a town in Honduras, have described the same annual phenomenon for more than a century: torrential rains, thunder and lightning, a biblical storm that keeps everyone indoors. After so many years, the locals know the drill well. They wait eagerly for the weather to clear, then go outside to collect their feast.

Every spring, the residents say, this blessed rain covers their town with hundreds of small silver fish—they writhe in the streets, so fresh they're still alive. And yet the closest body of water is the Atlantic Ocean, nearly 124 miles (200 km) away. Many believe the fish are a gift from God, and one popular theory credits 19th-century Catholic priest Father José Manuel Subirana, who prayed to God for sustenance to feed the town's hungry people, and at the end of his prayer, it rained fish.

Meteorologists offer a second opinion. They point to waterspouts, which have the capacity to pull small creatures, like sardines, from bodies of water and deposit them elsewhere. Another theory suggests there may be subterranean water beneath Yoro. Flash flooding could push fish to the surface and leave them stranded. But even experts admit it's pretty miraculous that these weather patterns could happen with such regularity.

As most residents believe the fish are a holy blessing, it's illegal to profit from the downpour, and the excess is distributed throughout the community during Yoro's annual festival.

The Original Food from Heaven?

According to the book of Exodus, after Moses led the Israelites out of slavery in Egypt, they endured two weeks in the desert before complaining of hunger. The Lord heard their murmurs and with the morning dew, manna appeared—"thin flakes like frost on the ground" (Exodus 16:14). The heavenly substance was "white like coriander seed and tasted like wafers made from honey" (Exodus 16:31) and would feed the Israelites for the 40 years they spent wandering the desert.

Some scientists believe that manna occurs naturally, then and now, in the Sinai Desert. The most popular explanation points to the tamarisk tree, a plant native to dry areas in Eurasia, which produces a sticky resin similar to wax that melts in the sun and is made mostly of sugar—just as the Bible describes. There is also an insect that feeds off the tamarisk tree's sap and secretes from its butt a sweet liquid called honeydew that loses its moisture quickly and turns into a sticky solid rich with carbohydrates that could, conceivably, be pounded into nourishing cakes as depicted in the book of Numbers. Many cultures eat honeydew, from Europe to the Middle East.

But this is no perfect science. Religious scholars believe there may have been as many as two million Jews in Moses's flock, a population that would require an ungodly amount of tamarisk trees and insect secretions to sustain. Additionally, the trees and their insect life choices produce the sweet stuff only seasonally, from May to July, while the manna in the Bible fell six days a week for 40 years.

A more scandalous theory cites Exodus 16:7, which reads, "and in the morning you will see the glory of the Lord because he has heard your grumbling against him." Several researchers who study the historical and societal impact of fungi believe manna may have come from a species of psychedelic mushroom. *Psilocybe cubensis* produces molecules that resemble frost and has been shown to incite spiritual and religious experiences. The scholars draw parallels between the mushroom's mind-altering effects (including heightened senses that, they argue, abetted the group's unlikely survival) and the Bible's warning that the Israelites would eat the manna and "see the glory of the Lord."

The Israelites Gathering Manna *by Ercole de' Roberti, ca. 1490s* (National Gallery, London).

THE CRAZY WOMAN'S SIGNATURE DISH

VIGORÓN • NICARAGUA

Vigorón, the official dish of the city of Granada, Nicaragua, is a street food made with soft-boiled yucca, crispy fried chicharrón (pork skin), and curtido, a vinegar-and-chili-soaked salad of cabbage and a tangy local fruit called mimbro. The three crunchy, salty, sour layers are served on a banana leaf and always eaten with your hands.

The street snack was the invention of Maria Luisa Cisnero Lacayo, nicknamed La Loca ("the Crazy Woman"). In 1914, Lacayo was a vendor at the local baseball stadium and came up with the dish as a way to stand out from the typical offerings of boiled corn and sweet tamales. After seeing a poster for a health tonic called "Vigorón," she took the name for her game-day snack. A century later, her creation has become the most iconic food of her city. Locals say it's so addictive, you can't help but suck every last bit from your fingers.

How to try it
Granada may have lost La Loca, but it's found a worthy successor in La Pelona (the Bald Woman), who dishes out top-notch vigorón in the city's Municipal Market.

A DELICIOUS MONSTER

MONSTERA DELICIOSA • PANAMA

How to try it

Even when ripe, Monstera deliciosa still contains small amounts of oxalate and should be avoided by those who are sensitive to it. You may also notice some black specks in the fruit. These are edible but can irritate the mouth.

Monstera deliciosa should come with an instruction manual. Unripe fruits are chock-full of oxalate crystals, which, in oxalic acid form, is a substance strong enough to bleach wood and clean rust off metal. Those who make the mistake of biting into an unripe monstera experience severe throat and skin irritation. When ripe, however, this monster of a fruit is indeed delicious.

The fully ripe monstera offers a wonderful combination of strong tropical flavors like pineapple, coconut, and banana. When not eaten on its own, the fruit is most often prepared into jams or monstera-based desserts.

Unlocking that flavorful potential—and avoiding any painful toxicity—is all a matter of timing. To ripen the fruit, set it inside a jar or glass and cover it with a brown bag. In time, the green hexagonal scales that make up the outer skin will slowly fall off from one end to another. You can nudge the scales off gently with a finger, but should stop if you find yourself using force.

When the green scales fall off, the fruit is ripe.

A woman from the Emberá tribe, an Indigenous people of Panama, ceremonially decorated with jagua bodypaint.

THE NATURAL FRUIT INK

JAGUA TATTOOS • PANAMA

Centuries before anyone was peeling the plastic from stick-on temporary tattoos, isolated tribes across Central and South American jungles were making jet-black body art that would disappear within 20 days, using nothing but a fruit called jagua.

The unripe jagua produces a colorless juice that, when exposed to air, oxidizes and transforms from light brown to blue black to onyx. Applied to the surface of the skin, the fruit ink can create sharp, delicate tattoos that look every bit as real as the permanent kind. Among these remote tribes, painting the body still has countless functions, from looking fierce in battle to discerning one tribe from another to general beautification. The fruit also boasts medicinal properties, chiefly as an antibiotic, so applying the juice to the skin was considered a way to fend off parasites.

In modern tattoo culture, jagua is often mixed with henna to create a richer color, or as a way to test-drive a tattoo design before forever inking it to the body. Apart from its capacity to dye things profoundly black (not just skin but utensils, baskets, and fabric), jagua, of course, is an edible fruit. The fruit ranges in size from kiwi to grapefruit, and when ripe, it tastes like dried apple or quince. Those more excited by fruit than tattoos can opt for jagua sweets, wine, and syrup.

How to try it

Panama's Indigenous Emberá are among those who use jagua for tattoos. Some traditional Emberá villages, such as Ella Drua north of Panama City, welcome visitors and invite them to be tattooed.

FESTIVAL OF THE CHEESE CURL

FESTIVAL DEL ALMOJÁBANO CON QUESO • PANAMA

The fritter is rolled by hand, first into a tube, then pinched in two places to make the customary curl, which mimics the shape of Panama.

Variations of almojábano, or cheese bread, abound in Latin America, from fluffy baked buns to rice flour fritters. But only in Panama is there a four-day festival celebrating the snack, which in this country is shaped like an *S* and eaten all day long.

Technically, the festival celebrates almojábanos con queso, which in Panama means the national salty white cheese. Crumbled by hand, the cheese goes into a bright yellow dough made from milled corn, water, sugar, and salt. Hot from the fryer, the cheese should be supple when the crispy exterior is broken.

Every January or February, thousands of people flock to the tiny mountain town of Dolega to indulge in the traditional cheese curl, which is sold by dozens of vendors pumping out huge quantities of their unique family recipes. Over the years, the festival has incorporated a dynamic folklore component, with groups arriving from across the country to play Panamanian music, perform traditional dances, and ride in a parade with ox-pulled floats to the sound of tamborito, the country's vibrant percussion-filled, call-and-response song and dance.

How to try it

The closest airport to Dolega is in the city of David, 12 miles (19 km) away. A regional bus runs between the two towns, and the trip takes about 20 minutes.

THE CARIBBEAN ISLANDS

THE JEWEL OF ANTIGUA'S COAT OF ARMS

BLACK PINEAPPLE • ANTIGUA

How to try it

Roadside stalls selling Antigua black pineapples are sprinkled throughout the island, but for the best variety head south to an area called Old Road, also known as the fruit basket of Antigua.

Antigua's coat of arms is a gathering of the island's signature elements—the blue and white sea, two stately deer, bright red hibiscus, and the stars of their local produce. A yucca plant, the culinary staple of Antigua, stands parallel to a stalk of sugarcane, the historic cash crop. At the top, perched like a glistening crown, is Antigua's illustrious black pineapple, said to be the world's sweetest.

Brought to Antigua from South America by the Arawak people, the black pineapple has been cultivated on the island's southern coast for centuries. Black pineapples still grow on small farms, almost exclusively for local consumption.

Crisp in texture, low in acid, and high in sugar, black pineapples are delectable to the core, which is almost always eaten. Despite the name, the fruit is never black. The skin remains green, even when ripe, so picking the perfect orb relies heavily on smell and touch. Local farmers say the island's rich soil, moderate rainfall, and copious sunshine create an ideal growing climate that cannot be replicated anywhere else.

EACH ENDEAVOURING ALL ACHIEVING

Fidel Castro's state-run ice-cream parlor can accommodate 1,000 people.

FIDEL CASTRO'S ICE-CREAM PARLOR

COPPELIA ∘ CUBA

Fidel Castro, insatiable dairy enthusiast, brought ice cream to his people with Coppelia, a sprawling, retro-modern helado complex. Commissioned in the 1960s by Castro himself, this grandiose ice-cream cathedral was erected on the site of an old hospital and designed to look like a UFO, with long concrete spokes radiating from the top of the structure and surrounded by a park that spans an entire city block. The enterprise was named after the favorite ballet of Celia Sánchez, Castro's secretary and close confidante, who was in charge of the project.

Determined to serve more ice-cream flavors than the parlors in the United States, Castro ordered 28 containers of ice cream from Howard Johnson's, then the largest American hotel and restaurant chain, and tasted every flavor they made. In those early days, Coppelia offered 26 ice-cream flavors and flavor combinations, with whimsical names such as Turquoise Special, Indian Canoe, and Chocolate Soldier. Today, patrons are lucky to find three flavors on offer.

Still, Coppelia continues to serve long lines of customers every day. Cubans eat ice cream in tremendous quantities, with amorous devotion. In the 1990s, when trade fluctuations meant the country had to decide between dairy resources for butter or ice cream, the people chose ice cream.

How to try it

Coppelia is located on Calle 23 in Havana's bustling Vedado district. The popular en salada is five scoops of ice cream and a sprinkling of cookies for about a quarter.

AN ILLEGAL TONIC TURNED CURE-ALL APHRODISIAC

MAMA JUANA • DOMINICAN REPUBLIC

How to try it

Available in most bars and markets in the Dominican Republic, Mama Juana can be tailored to what ails you. If it's virility you're after, ask for more mariscos, or "seafood," in the tonic (especially miembro de carey, or "turtle penis"). If you're trying to get pregnant, look for an ingredient called uña de gato, or "cat's claw."

The Taíno Indians—native to the island that is now home to the Dominican Republic—were remarkably resourceful. By the 15th century, they could remove cyanide from yucca, make balls out of natural rubber, and tap the medicinal potential of the abundant local flora. They brewed teas from barks and leaves to relieve everything from common colds to respiratory, circulatory, and digestive diseases. It wasn't until after 1492, when Christopher Columbus and his men landed on their island, that alcohol was added to the recipe, resulting in what is now known as Mama Juana.

Derived from the French term *Dame Jeanne*, which refers to a large squat bottle, Mama Juana is made by filling a jug with tree barks and herbs (think star anise, clove, basil, and agave), then adding rum, red wine, and honey. The taste of the liquor, which is woody and sweet, gets stronger with time and is sometimes compared to port wine, and other times to cough syrup.

In the 1950s, Mama Juana experienced a boost in popularity and reputation when a man named Jesus Rodriguez began selling the elixir as a medicinal tonic and aphrodisiac. It was a hit, and aspiring entrepreneurs jumped into the game, peddling all manner of potions and touting their alleged medicinal benefits. Rafael Trujillo, the country's president-turned-dictator, put a stop to the craze by declaring the sale of Mama Juana illegal unless dispensed by someone with a medical license. While this law put an end to the rogue vending, it also gave credence to the idea that Mama Juana was indeed medication.

Nowadays, Mama Juana is both legal and abundant. It's often referred to by Dominicans as the "baby maker" or El Para Palo, which translates to "The Stick Lifter." It's commonly made at home, and almost always consumed at room temperature as a shot. When the liquor is drained, simply add more rum and wine. The process, locals say, can be repeated for up to a decade.

A COLLABORATIVE BEACH DAY FEAST

OIL DOWN • GRENADA

Grenadians love to lime, the island's expression for relaxing. Liming in cafés and along the marina is a favorite national pastime. When liming on the beach, it's only natural to bring a big pot, light a fire in the sand, and start an oil down.

Grenada's national dish is an all-day social endeavor. The enormous pot gets fired up early in the morning and slowly filled throughout the day. The women helm this operation, and although the dish is meant for a lazy beach day, the preparation requires some serious work. A ripe breadfruit must be chopped and soaked, along with green bananas, taro, and yams. Salt fish must be soaked and rinsed, leafy greens washed and chopped. Dumplings must be kneaded from flour and rolled into the customary shape of logs. Pig snouts and tails—a vestige from the sugarcane plantations, when these scraps were passed down from the plantation house—must be washed, broken down, and soaked.

Every cook has their own way of packing the pot, but a common method is meat and starchy stuff on the bottom, veggies in the middle, and fish and dumplings on top. Everything is boiled in coconut milk with spices such as turmeric, nutmeg, and ginger. The name *oil down* comes from the process of letting the ingredients soak up the coconut milk, until there's nothing left on the bottom but oil. The breadfruit and dumplings have a soft, spongy consistency that pairs well with the salty fish and leafy greens. It's customary for every guest to bring an ingredient to contribute, and so each creamy, steaming pot is uniquely enhanced by the people who will eat it.

Grenada's St. George market carries all the fresh produce for an oil down.

How to try it

Thursday is Oil Down Day at the Coconut Beach restaurant in St. George's, where you can enjoy your meal with your feet in the sand.

A HISTORIC CARIBBEAN SOUP HOUSE

AN CHODYÈ LA • GUADELOUPE

How to try it

An Chodyè La is located at 59 Rue Gilbert de Chambertrand. The café is also known locally as "Kaz a Soup."

On a small Pointe-à-Pitre street is a café housed within a bright-turquoise building. Called An Chodyè La, it specializes in hearty, flavorful soups that tell a story about Guadeloupe—from its dark colonial past to the resilience of its people.

According to Jean-Claude Magnat, the restaurant's chef, his soups are deeply rooted in the island's history of slavery. Enslaved families were forced to survive on their masters' leftovers, which they boiled with water into soup. Over time, cooks infused their own heritage flavors and techniques to make new recipes. Magnat's soups are re-creations of dishes originally made by his great-great-grandmother Lucille Deris. The turquoise building that contains his restaurant was once her home, which she purchased with money she earned from washing clothes.

The café's menu is conveyed verbally and features a rotation of soups such as traditional Caribbean lambi, oxtail soup, sea-snail soup, lobster bisque, and ouassous giraumon, a pumpkin soup with freshwater shrimp.

SPAGHETTI WITH HOT DOGS FOR BREAKFAST

ESPAGETI • HAITI

No one can explain exactly why Haitians eat spaghetti for breakfast, and yet it's a morning staple, ingrained in their cuisine as a national comfort food. There are two essentials to Haitian espageti: There must be processed tube meat (typically hot dogs, but Vienna sausage is also good), and there must be ketchup. It's a noodle dish that exists happily in a vacuum, with no reverence for Italy, so conventional pasta rules do not apply.

Americans, not Italians, were responsible for influencing the creation of this dish and the result is audaciously un-European. During the time when the United States invaded Haiti in 1915, they brought their processed foods. Dried spaghetti was introduced to the local diet alongside ketchup and salty, shelf-stable meats. Cross two oceans to another former US territory, the Philippines, and you'll find an entirely disparate cuisine that also loves hot dogs with their spaghetti—a dish they call spags.

For people pressed for time or on the go, Haitians have developed a workaround that still allows them to eat their espageti—or rather drink it. Vendors are happy to throw noodles and sauce into a blender and blitz until the meal can be pulled through a straw.

How to try it
Spicing the pasta is up to the whimsy of the chef, but a drizzle of ketchup over the top is de rigueur.

PEANUT BUTTER WITH SCOTCH BONNET PEPPERS

MAMBA • HAITI

When made by hand, mamba—a spicy peanut butter—starts with a giant cauldron over an open fire, often in a backyard. Locals roast the peanuts, keeping them moving against the hot cauldron walls, then pour them into a woven winnowing tray. The process of separating the peanuts from their shells is a practiced maneuver, a rhythmic tossing and catching, tossing and catching, until the peanuts are rendered shiny and skinless. The batch of nuts then takes a ride through a grinder, gets swirled with hot peppers like Scotch bonnets or habaneros, and is then ready to be spread onto its preferred partner, cassava crackers. The spice doesn't show itself right away. It creeps up at the end, cutting into the creamy richness.

Beyond the island's backyard production, Haiti boasts a few commercial labels, supplied by a budding peanut farming industry. Haitians abroad often complain that the peanut butters of other nations don't satisfy their cravings, so it's not uncommon to see suitcases leaving the island packed with jars of the spicy stuff.

How to try it
Brands Rebo and Compa Direct are 100 percent Haitian. The brand Manba is made from Haitian peanuts but is produced in Montreal. On the streets of Port-au-Prince, you can find street vendors selling mamba on cassava crackers.

PEANUT BUTTER

Fresh on the tree, ackee is chock-full of poison.

SAVORY DEATH-INDUCING FRUIT

ACKEE • JAMAICA

How to try it

Jamaica exports canned ackee around the world, but you're unlikely to find it fresh unless you're on the island. For best results, visit during the fruit-bearing season, which spans January to March, and June to August.

Ackee and salt fish, Jamaica's cherished national dish, is a combination of salted cod and a savory yellow fruit that contains so much poison, it's generally illegal to export when fresh. Still, Jamaicans find every excuse to remove the poison and dig in. The fruit contains hypoglycin A, a poison that, according to the FDA, can cause "vomiting with profound hypoglycemia, drowsiness, muscular exhaustion, prostration, and possibly coma and death." Boiling the ripe fruit leaches out the toxins and renders ackee safe to eat. Native to West Africa, the toxic fruit was brought to the island by slavers in the 1770s.

Jamaicans grow ackee in two varieties: the yellow-tinged, soft "butter ackee" and the cream-colored, hard "cheese ackee." Both types turn yellow when exposed to heat and have a mild taste many compare to hearts of palm or scrambled eggs, which makes them especially popular at breakfast time.

CRACK AN EGG, SEE THE FUTURE

EGG SETTING • JAMAICA

How to try it

Play it safe by cracking half a dozen eggs before going to bed; they can't all be caskets.

When the sun rises on Good Friday, many Jamaicans can be found looking into a glass of water, trying to divine their futures. Eggs, symbolic of new life, have always played a part in the Christian holiday, but in Jamaica, they're not just for painting and baskets. The much older, local tradition is to drop an egg white into a glass of water before Good Friday, then to study the form it takes when the sun comes up. An airplane or ship means there will be travel in the coming year, while a long dress foretells a marriage. Some islanders avoid the superstition altogether, warned off by tales of people seeing caskets and then dying shortly after.

Pantry Alternatives to Tarot Cards

Divining the future is all fun and games until someone gets arrested, which was surprisingly common in the psychic tea rooms of 1930s New York City. Fortune-tellers reading tea leaves for profit were busted by police sting operations. The women, serving a mostly female clientele, were accused by the *New York Times* in a 1931 editorial of causing "a wave of melancholia among women" because of their startling prophecies. But tea was just the beginning of the food prophecy racket: While the tea leaf readers were being chased, the onion oracles and the coconut clairvoyants were free to roam.

APPLES have been used to make love predictions for centuries: A 1714 English poem depicts a country maiden flinging an apple peel over her head and being thrilled by the "L" shape it forms because she's in love with a shepherd named Lubberkin. In Europe and the Middle East, the fruit has long been a mythological symbol of female fertility and youth. An apple peel thrown over a shoulder is still a common way to predict a lover's initial, but you can also recite the alphabet while peeling, stopping when the ribbon breaks from the fruit. Apple seeds come in handy when making more specific prophecies. If you're torn between lovers, assign them each a seed, then moisten the seeds and stick them to your face. The last seed standing is your true love.

COCONUTS are the best for answering yes/no questions. In Obeah fortune-telling—a West African divination practice—four pieces of coconut, with husk on one side and flesh on the other, are held in a diviner's hand. After a quick prayer over the question, the pieces are tossed like dice to the ground. All four pieces white side up is the strongest yes, while four dark sides is an absolute no, along with the implication that the asker needs some serious spiritual cleansing. An equal split means yes. Three whites is a maybe. Three darks is a no. In Yoruba culture, kola nuts were the original divining medium, but after the diaspora, coconuts replaced the hard-to-find nut, and the tropical fruit is now widely accepted as a suitable mouthpiece of the divine.

GASTROMANCY was a popular ancient Greek divination technique that involved listening to the gurgling of a human belly, believed to be voices of the dead who had taken up residence in the stomach. The keepers of these mystic bellies would interpret the voices and use them to communicate with the departed, in addition to predicting the future. This was a popular after-dinner activity, where even the marks on the outside of the belly were considered clues. Pythia, more widely known as the Oracle of Delphi, was one of the earliest prophets to use gastromancy and was known to communicate with Apollo through her stomach. During the Middle Ages, the practice was considered a form of witchcraft. By the 18th century, these belly prophets were revealed to be the world's first ventriloquists, simply manipulating their voices to project through their guts. With their spiritual credibility shot, they moved their act to the stage.

ONIONS, with their quick-growing sprouts, were the go-to veggie for divination in ancient Europe, Africa, and Siberia. To mine the depths of a person's soul, their name was inscribed onto an onion, then the onion was placed on an altar. Sprouting had a positive correlation: Depending on the question, a fast-sprouting onion could mean a person was happy, healthy, or suitable for marriage. In a German tradition, 12 pieces of onion, each representing a month of the year, are laid on a table and left out overnight with a grain of salt on each piece. In the morning, the onion pieces with the most liquid foretell the rainiest months.

How to try it

Irish moss can be found in cafés and bars. As of recently, there is also a canned version sold commercially as "Big Bamboo," in case anyone was unclear about the desired effect.

ROADSIDE APHRODISIAC SLINGERS

PUNCH MEN • JAMAICA

Imagine the texture of melted ice cream, add the briny flavor of algae, take a long, viscous gulp, and ask yourself: Are you feeling sexy? The men of Jamaica are saying yes.

Across the island, vendors called Punch Men sling liquid aphrodisiacs along the side of the road. Their erotic elixirs feature a red algae called Irish moss, touted for its abilities to moisturize skin, revitalize the mind, and, most notably, increase libido. To prepare the drink, the Punch Men wash the moss, then boil it, which releases an extract called carrageenan. A natural thickener—dairy producers often add it to yogurt—carrageenan provides the drink's signature gluey viscosity. Milk, vanilla, cinnamon, and nutmeg spice up the brew, which is left to cool before being dispensed to men (and some women) seeking a boost in the bedroom.

Native to Ireland, the red algae is packed with nutrition—10 percent protein and 15 percent mineral matter. During the Irish potato famine of the mid-1800s, the algae helped nourish the country's starving population. Irish immigrants to Jamaica brought their miracle moss, and it now grows on the island's rocks.

A PROCESSED, SPREADABLE EASTER CHEESE

TASTEE CHEESE • JAMAICA

How to try it

Tastee Cheese is easy to find in Jamaican stores, bakeries, and cafés. It's harder to find everywhere else, but it is sold in the US, in the UK, and on other Caribbean islands.

What does it take to make Jamaican Tastee Cheese? New Zealand cheddar cheese.

The dairy corporation Fonterra (formerly the New Zealand Dairy Board) grinds, pasteurizes, and cans their cheddar before shipping it off to Jamaica. Despite the involvement of around 10,500 Kiwi dairy farmers, Tastee Cheese is distinctly Jamaican—produced in flavors such as jerk (a Caribbean spice blend) and Solomon Gundy (a Jamaican pickled fish pâté).

Tastee Cheese is also an essential half of a classic Jamaican Easter food pairing, "Bun and Cheese." A Caribbean twist on the British hot cross bun, Tastee Cheese is spread inside a Jamaican spiced bun. Locals made a few tweaks to the recipe, shaping the dough into a loaf, swapping out honey for molasses, and adding dried fruit.

A CHICKEN TECHNIQUE PIRATED BY PIRATES

POULET BOUCANÉ • MARTINIQUE

During the 17th and 18th centuries, the island of Martinique was the site of relentless battles. The French, who arrived with ships of enslaved Africans, fought ruthlessly to displace the Indigenous Carib in order to grow sugarcane.

Pirates added to the violence, preying on European ships traveling to the island. It was off the coast of Martinique, in 1717, that the pirate Blackbeard commandeered a French slave ship, which became his infamous flagship the *Queen Anne's Revenge*.

Long before the French knew Martinique existed, the Indigenous islanders had honed a technique for smoking and preserving food, usually involving salt, wood, and fragrant plants. The invaders appropriated this method, and poulet boucané, or "buccaneer's chicken," was born.

How to try it

To find poulet boucané, look for smoke wafting off a hot barbecue. It's almost always served with sauce chien. Literally, "dog sauce," the parsley, chive, and chili blend gets its name from the French idiom *avoir du chien*, or "to have spunk."

After a long soak in onion, garlic, chili pepper, lime juice, thyme, and oil, a whole chicken is dried and placed in a smoker, which is often constructed from a metal drum cut in half lengthwise. Cooks place burning sugarcane at the bottom of the metal drum and chicken on a grate in the middle, then close the drum and let the smoke work its magic. The result is tender, zesty, and herbaceous chicken that can be taken on long and gruesome warring crusades, or eaten as a simple lunch

THE CARIBBEAN'S ONLY PIZZA BOAT

PIZZA PI ○ ST. THOMAS, US VIRGIN ISLANDS

One of the highest rated, most beloved restaurants in the US Virgin Islands has no official address and is best accessed by chartered boat, dinghy, or swimming. The floating pizzeria, called PiZZA Pi, is the Caribbean's only "food truck boat," specially fitted with a commercial kitchen that cranks out New York–style pizzas. The restaurant takes orders by boat radio, phone, or email, but collecting your pie is a little harder because the restaurant anchors about a mile off the shore of St. Thomas's Christmas Cove.

PiZZA Pi is the whimsical invention of Sasha Bouis, a MIT-educated mechanical engineer turned boat captain, and Tara Bouis, a teacher turned award-winning yacht chef. The American couple spent two years restoring an abandoned boat, adding a double-brick-lined pizza oven, hood ventilation, a water production system, and solar panels.

In 2018, Sasha and Tara sold their pizza boat to new owners Heather and Brian Samelson, another expat couple whose daughter worked aboard the PiZZA Pi. Throughout the day, boats pull up to the floating pizzeria, tie up, and enjoy the freshly made pizza passed from the kitchen window. The restaurant also offers delivery via their dinghy, which doubles as a small dining area when the occasional swimmer arrives.

How to try it

PiZZA Pi moors off the shore of Christmas Cove, on the east end of St. Thomas. They are open every day from 11 a.m. to 6 p.m. Order ahead by calling +1 340 643 4674, or getting on marine radio VHF 16.

THE INTERNATIONAL ART OF

How to try it

La Casita Blanca, a homey San Juan institution located in a small white house, doles out pegao to those smart enough to request it.

STRATEGICALLY BURNED RICE

PEGAO • PUERTO RICO

In Puerto Rico, burning rice is an art.

Pegao means "stuck," as the rice is meant to stick to the bottom of a cast-aluminum pot called a caldero. According to Puerto Rican chef Jose Santaella, who dedicated an entire page of his cookbook *Cocina Tropical* to the crunchy layer, "the rice, the pot, the method, and the finishing are all crucial." The method involves cooking the rice until it's just done, then strategically raising the heat in the final few minutes to scorch the bottom of the pot. This finishing blast is tricky to get right because there's no way to see what's happening at the bottom. There's a fine line between rice that's chewy, nutty, and crunchy, and rice that's bitter and acrid. The technique takes practice, a developed sense of smell, and an intimate familiarity with pot and stove.

In Puerto Rico, there is etiquette to sharing a pot of rice. Diners should scoop a portion of the top, fluffy rice, then top the mound with a couple of scrapes of pegao. Ratios must be respected: To take more than a bite or two is considered rude.

guoba

nurungji soup

Burning Rice

Most every rice-eating culture has discovered the delectable magic of scorching their grains. Dominicans call it concon and make their rice in a seasoned aluminum pot. In Costa Rica, the term is a crunchy onomatopoeia: corroncho. In Colombia, cucayo is so sought after, there's a Barranquilla restaurant that specializes in crusty rice. A 1973 Peruvian song called "Arroz con Concolón" is still popular and sung widely today.

On the other side of the globe, burnt rice is just as tied to Asian culinary traditions. The Korean dish bibimbap is commonly served in a hot stone bowl called a dolsot that sears the rice at the table. In China, guoba is an all-purpose block of brittle rice that's a popular snack and starchy base for many dishes, a favorite being sweet-and-sour shrimp. Okoge is an important part of the traditional Japanese kaiseki meal, which is charred rice moistened with water, soup, or tea.

The Persians make scorched rice look glamorous: After the grains have formed a hard golden layer in the pot—called tahdig—it's overturned onto a plate so that it looks almost like a cake. The Iraqis break their layer into pieces to make sharing easier.

Then there's the international superstar paella, whose socarrat is cultivated carefully with a final blast of heat, creating a caramelized crust just before serving.

bibimbap

paella

okoge

tahdig

THE SECRET SAUCE OF CARIBBEAN COOKING

BROWNING • TRINIDAD AND TOBAGO

In Trinidad and Tobago, most dishes begin with something called browning, the little-known secret behind their cuisine's complex taste. While browning can be bought in a bottle, you'll rarely see one in a Caribbean kitchen, as it's simple to prepare.

Heat oil, add brown sugar, and allow it to—you guessed it—brown. When the sugar and oil have cooked for a few minutes and turned the color of coffee, Trini cooks can take the sauce in countless directions. Chunks of meat can be swirled in the sticky sauce to start a stew, or the browning can be added to cake batters for a distinctive toffee undertone. Simple but essential, browning is the elusive flavor note of Trinidad and Tobago's cuisine. The dark caramel flavor adds balance and depth to a cuisine that is typically spicy and intensely flavored.

The secret ingredient in rice and peas is often browning.

How to try it
Browning creates the base in popular recipes such as pelau (the country's rice-based dish), oxtail stew, rice and peas, and black cake. If you can't be bothered to caramelize sugar yourself, there are many commercial brands, such as Uncle Panks and Grace Browning, that will do it for you.

THE QUINTESSENTIAL TRINIDADIAN MEAL

RED SOLO, ROTI, AND DOUBLES • TRINIDAD AND TOBAGO

How to try it
Every local has their favorite spot, but try Amin's The Buss Up Shut King or Mona's Roti Shop, where you can watch them hand-making the flatbread. For doubles, use the Trinidad & Tobago Doubles Directory app to point you in the direction of more than 400 doubles shops. When ordering, keep in mind that doubles are always plural; even a single doubles is ordered as "one doubles."

Beginning in 1845, more than 100,000 Indians migrated to Trinidad to work as indentured laborers, and when their contracts ended, many chose to make the island their home. Indian flavors were absorbed readily into the local cuisine. Roti and doubles, two of the island's most iconic dishes, paired with a soda invented by the son of an indentured migrant, is often what homesick Trinis cite as the meal that transports them back to their island.

Roti, a Hindi word for bread, bends to a Caribbean sensibility in the style locals call "Buss Up Shut." Named for its resemblance to a tattered shirt, the roti is shredded on a griddle and then dipped in curry. "Dhalpuri" roti, the alternate style, is used like a pita, filled with a ground split pea mash. Then there's "doubles," two fried flatbreads called baras filled with curried chickpeas and a slew of fruit and hot pepper chutneys. These Indo-Trinidadian creations are acceptable fodder for breakfast, lunch, and dinner, and especially good for late nights and early Saturday mornings.

There is a correct accompaniment to roti and doubles. Locals call it Red Solo, a super-sweet soda made from the herbaceous sorrel plant, with a taste some compare to kiwi fruit or sour wild strawberries. For a truly Trinidadian experience, the Red Solo must be ice cold and served in a glass bottle.

····· FOOD PIONEER ·····

JOSEPH CHARLES

(SERJAD MAKMADEEN, 1910–1965)

The story of Trinidad's beloved Red Solo soda begins with a young Indo-Caribbean boy named Serjad Makmadeen. The youngest of eight children, Makmadeen quit school at the age of ten to help support his family. As a teenager, he quickly became the top salesman at his local bakery. The young entrepreneur knew to spend money to make money, offering a free loaf of bread to anyone who bought 12 or more.

Years later, Makmadeen borrowed $250, combined it with his savings, and bought the small, hand-cranked soda factory down the road. With the help of his wife, he began cooking small batches of syrup and manually carbonating the soda. He started peddling his drinks to the customers on his bakery route, alongside his bread, with great success. At the same time, he sent letters off to soft drink producers in Britain, soliciting advice on how to make his budding business more efficient. All his letters went unanswered. On a hunch, Makmadeen wrote again, this time using the English pseudonym, Joseph Charles. Advice from England started coming in.

Business steadily ramped up, but the arrival of World War II brought a bottle shortage that threatened to slow production. The newly christened Joseph Charles caught wind of a Montreal-based soda company going out of business and selling off its equipment. He bought their bottles sight unseen, and when they arrived in Trinidad branded with the name "Solo," alongside the image of a pilot and an airplane, Charles made yet another bold move. He commandeered the ready-made logo and gave the name to his bootstrapped soda. Two thousand miles (3,219 km) from Canada, under Charles's direction, the Solo label got a second life with a devoted island following.

By the time Charles died in 1965 and was succeeded by his sons, most every local knew the catchphrase "a roti and a Red Solo." The sweet, cherry-red drink found an irrefutable soul mate in the spicy and savory flavors of roti and doubles, cementing a place in the cultural vocabulary of Trinidad and Tobago. Many islanders believe the Trinidadian fast food isn't complete without the soda in the heavy glass bottle, homegrown by the scrappy, tenacious entrepreneur who surmounted an illiterate childhood, flagrant racism, and two decades of hawking bread to build a soda empire.

The chicken roti at Hott Shoppe in Port of Spain.

LOST CARGO OF THE HMS *BOUNTY*

BREADFRUIT • TRINIDAD AND TOBAGO

How to try it

Breadfruit salad, a dish that closely resembles American potato salad, is a popular restaurant side dish in Trinidad. Cheap in the Caribbean and expensive abroad, breadfruit is best produced locally.

n 1787, Captain William Bligh departed England for Tahiti with a single directive—collect breadfruit, known for its bread-like texture and potato-like taste. The Royal Society had selected the green fruit as the ideal cheap food for the thousands of enslaved Africans in the West Indies. Bligh's ship—the infamous HMS *Bounty*—spent ten grueling months at sea, followed by five months of collecting breadfruit in Tahiti. When the ship finally set sail for the West Indies, the commander's cabin was filled with 1,015 breadfruit plants.

Anyone familiar with the novel *Mutiny on the Bounty* knows things quickly fell apart from here. About 1,300 miles (2,092 km) west of Tahiti, the ship's crew rebelled against their captain. Often remembered as cruel and pompous, Bligh's personality is typically blamed for the uprising. But the men also missed Tahitian island life and were reportedly quite dehydrated, as Bligh was hoarding water for his breadfruits. Bligh and a handful of loyal men were set adrift in a tiny boat. The mutineers also took issue with their arrogant captain's treasured breadfruits, which were thrown overboard.

After reaching the island of Timor—3,600 miles (5,794 km) from where the crew cast off—Bligh made his way back to England. Undeterred, in 1791 he launched a second expedition to Tahiti, where he gathered breadfruit seedlings and successfully delivered them to the Caribbean. But in the end, no one liked breadfruit. The enslaved workers preferred bananas and plantains, and the breadfruit was fed mostly to pigs.

Breadfruit has since become a beloved staple starch across the islands, where it's treated much like a potato. Many of the trees that descended from Bligh's plants still stand in the Caribbean today. The next time you're eating on the island, there's a decent chance their progeny will end up on your plate.

SOUTH AMERICA

AN ENTIRE COW

VACA ENTERA • ARGENTINA

In Argentina, beef is a way of life, and a stroll down most any street will yield a parillero (a grill cook) hawking freshly barbecued steaks and other prime meaty bits. It makes sense that a country this passionate about beef would mastermind the vaca entera—a whole cow freshly splayed and suspended over an open fire.

Grilling an entire cow begins with a massive grilling rack. A dozen people heave the enormous cow into the apparatus, strap it in tight, and light four wood fires in the corners of the pit beneath. The first half of the 24-hour process is all about controlling the fire. Grill masters typically won't even touch the cow until the second half, when they must use brute strength to manually rotate the grilling cage like a rotisserie. With scalding fat dripping from the flesh, a blazing fire, and searing metal grates, it's a job that requires concentration, strength, and finesse.

The shopping list for vaca entera is brief: a butterflied cow and a pound (0.45 kg) of salt. A gallon of chimichurri, the Argentinian green herb sauce, is nice but not entirely necessary. The nonedible supplies are far more involved: two cords of wood—a stack of logs 16 feet wide, 4 feet high, and 4 feet deep (4.9 x 1.2 x 1.2 m); a pulley system set in concrete; a two-sided truss; and a 9-foot (3 m) sheet of corrugated metal to tent the cow like a massive piece of foil. Lastly, and arguably most tactically difficult, vaca entera requires a dozen loyal and robust insomniacs willing to wait out the night while fending off packs of wild foxes and coddling a raging, tempestuous fire, all for the love of beef.

How to try it

Los Talas del Entrerriano, in northwest Buenos Aires, is a locally beloved rustic steakhouse where you can watch whole cows being grilled as you await your meal.

THE WORLD'S ONLY BAR MADE FROM GLACIAL ICE

GLACIOBAR • ARGENTINA

The Argentine city of El Calafate is the gateway to Los Glaciares National Park, a trekking and climbing hot spot that contains an incredible array of glaciers, including the 121-square-mile Perito Moreno. For those looking to learn more about glaciers, there is Glaciarium, a center with multimedia exhibitions explaining how ice is formed and how glaciers move and shape their surroundings. If all this sounds a little too serious, Glaciarium is also home to Glaciobar, the world's only bar built entirely from glacial ice.

The Glaciobar is so cold, you can only enter after donning the capes, gloves, and boots provided. Inside, everything is made of ice, including the seats, tables, and glasses. Even with proper attire, you can only stay for 20 minutes—just long enough for a cocktail on the frozen couch.

How to try it

Entrance to the Glaciarium is 480 Argentine pesos ($11 US). It's an additional 300 pesos ($7) to enter the Glaciobar, which includes a drink and warm clothing rental. (RP11, Z9405 El Calafate, Santa Cruz, Argentina)

VOLCANIC ROCK SOUP

K'ALAPURKA • BOLIVIA

How to try it
From Potosí's city center, take a $1 taxi over to Doña Eugenia, a k'alapurka institution serving bubbling crocks of the breakfast soup to the town's locals. A bowl typically costs around 35 bolivianos ($5) and should be paired with a dark and malty morning beer.

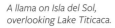

The city of Potosí is home to Cerro Rico, or "Rich Mountain," which once produced 80 percent of the world's silver—a fortune that, between the 16th and 18th centuries, bankrolled the Spanish Empire. That bounty came at an enormous cost to human life. Hundreds of thousands of miners, predominantly conscripted native Peruvians and enslaved Africans, perished in the treacherous, disease-ridden mines. A bowl of k'alapurka, or volcano soup, was often what they ate for breakfast before descending into uncertain doom.

Hearty and blistering hot, this soup is a cauldron of comfort. An earthen bowl is brought to the table and a scorching volcanic rock is dropped, tableside, into the yellow corn-flour broth, creating a steaming ripple and violent bubbles that appear in the stone's wake. Long before Cerro Rico was the world's source of silver, the mountain was a volcano, and the rocks in k'alapurka are chips off that ancient block.

K'alapurka is considered by many visitors to be one of Bolivia's tastiest dishes. It packs sweetness and spice, with chili pepper, oregano, ají sauce, and aromatic chachacoma leaves. Potatoes, vegetables, and a savory meat—often beef jerky or fried pork—soften the spices and add heft to the meal. Perfectly paired with 13,000 feet (3,962 m) of rugged elevation, harsh winds, and frigid temperatures, k'alapurka is a dish that bears a dark history and happens to be delicious.

SLOW DINING ON THE ISLAND OF THE SUN

LAS VELAS • BOLIVIA

On the streets of Isla del Sol, a small island suspended in the middle of Lake Titicaca, there is no motorized traffic: Everything moves at the pace of your feet. To get to the restaurant Las Velas ("The Candles"), located at the top of a rocky peak, you must hike 30 minutes from the southern pier, uphill through

A llama on Isla del Sol, overlooking Lake Titicaca.

a eucalyptus forest. Just when you think you might be lost, a stunning view of the water will open before you, and you will have arrived.

Located in a thatched-roof cottage and run entirely by Chef Pablo and his wife, Las Velas has no electricity. During the day, Pablo cooks using natural light, and at night, he lights candles and sometimes straps on a headlight. The signature dish is quinoa and baked trout, pulled straight from the lake below. Pablo uses a wood oven and cooks alone. He makes everything from scratch and to order, so be prepared to hang out for a couple of hours, if not three. There are Bolivian wine and decks of cards to keep you entertained, but the view is more than enough: Blue during the day and inky silver at night, it's easy to see why Lake Titicaca is the setting of the Incan creation myth, which says the Sun God was born on this island, followed by the first Incas.

How to try it

Las Velas is open daily from 9 a.m. to 10:30 p.m., but keep in mind these hours are subject to island time. Although most people make the trek by foot, it's possible to rent a donkey.

THE WORLD'S FIRST FREEZE-DRIED FOOD

CHUÑOS • BOLIVIA

Freeze-drying, the food preservation technique famously used by NASA, was purportedly invented in a Parisian laboratory in 1906. But mention that fact around the Andean highland and prepare to be corrected, because in these parts, people have been freeze-drying potatoes for millennia.

Chuños, as the preserved tubers are called, start off as freshly harvested potatoes. Farmers leave them outside in freezing mountain temperatures for several nights until they are frosted over. During the warmer daytime hours, farmers trample the potatoes underfoot, flattening them and pushing out as much liquid as possible.

The routine continues for several days, stomping during the daytime and refreezing at night, before the chuños are ready to be fully dehydrated. If left out in the sun, they become chuños negros, or black chuños. If washed and protected from sun exposure while drying outside, they're known as chuños blancos, or white chuños.

Chuños can be stored for years without degrading. They are a blessing in the harsh Andean climate, where the tubers are often rehydrated in soups or pulverized into flour and used in baked goods. This ultra-stable spud was conceived as a cunning way to feed many people during periods of drought and scarcity. In the pre-Columbian era, centuries before spacemen required portable meals, Incan armies marched into battle on chuños, the world's first freeze-dried food.

Farmers freeze-dry potatoes, naturally, at extreme elevation.

How to try it

Although produced in June and July, when the day and night temperatures are most extreme, the preserved tubers are available at markets and restaurants year-round. Try them as the traditional accompaniment to sajta, a Bolivian chicken stew, or in black potato soup.

◆ ◆ ◆ ◆ ◆ ◆ ◆ ◆ ◆ ◆ ◆ ◆ ◆ ▸ **REGION OF WONDER** ◂ ◆ ◆ ◆ ◆ ◆ ◆ ◆ ◆ ◆ ◆ ◆ ◆

La Paz

Flying into the city of La Paz is an experience you're not likely to forget. Perched in the Andes and set against a towering range of snowcapped mountains, La Paz is the highest capital city in the world, with the highest international airport. Brick buildings cling to the sides of cliffs, descending down into a basin. The weather is nicer down below, which is where you'll find the technicolor markets, street vendors, and untold restaurants that take most visitors by surprise. Here's the best of La Paz:

Salteñas are sold all over Bolivia, but in La Paz they're the traditional midmorning snack. A cross between an empanada and a soup dumpling, the half-moon pastry contains a meat-and-potato filling seasoned with olives and raisins, and a lot of sauce. For clean handling, take a bite out of the top and sip out the sauce first.

Sanduíche de chola is the city's signature sandwich, made with slow-cooked, crispy-skinned pork topped with pickled onions and spicy chili sauce. They're named after the Indigenous Aymara women (cholitas) who sell them, and the best of these vendors have been selling the same sandwich, from the same spot, for half a century. The bread, a light crunchy roll called marraqueta, is also a La Paz specialty.

Seafood is abundant in La Paz, as Lake Titicaca is about 50 miles (80.5 km) north. Unlike in other cities, here salteñas come in shrimp and fish varieties, and ceviche is fresh and abundant. Look for ispi, a small lake fish, which is fried and eaten whole.

Llajwa de mani, the unsung national peanut sauce, deserves a lot more attention considering the peanut originated in ancient Bolivia. The thick, spicy, and garlicky sauce tops the ubiquitous street food anticuchos—a skewer of grilled beef heart that makes a good entry point into offal.

BRAZIL'S WINE CHURCH

CAPELA NOSSA SENHORA DAS NEVES • BRAZIL

At the heart of Brazil's winemaking region is a chapel called the Capela Nossa Senhora das Neves, or the Chapel of Our Lady of the Snow, a small and unassuming historic building constructed out of wine.

Brazil's Vale de Vinhedos (Valley of Vineyards) was settled in the late 1800s by Italian immigrants, who began growing grapes and making wine as they had in Italy. In 1904, 20 local families began work on Nossa Senhora das Neves, but a terrible drought struck and halted their progress. With water scarce, the community decided to tap their stores of wine. Each family donated 300 liters, which was kneaded with clay and wheat straw to make mortar, and the chapel was completed in 1907.

The chapel's appearance is also a nod to its unusual building material, from the exterior paint accents (a wine-red) to the altar made of wine barrels. These days, the wine church no longer holds services and is undergoing a restoration, but visitors are very much welcome.

How to try it

The wine church is located in the southern town of Bento Gonçalves, which is considered a center of winemaking and Italian immigration to Brazil.

When a drought halted construction of this church, residents made mortar out of wine.

CACAO'S TANGY COUSIN

CUPUAÇU • BRAZIL

Overshadowed by its hyped-up chocolate-making cousin, cacao, cupuaçu has some tricks of its own. When ripe, the large, oblong fruit has a dreamy, tropical smell before it even leaves the tree: a mix of pineapple, chocolate, and, some say, bubble gum. Beneath its hard brown exterior, the taste is even more complex. People have compared it to pears, bananas, coconuts, and chocolate.

Cupuaçu can perform some of cacao's tricks, too. Rich in fatty acids, cupuaçu butter (pressed from the seeds of the fruit) has a similar consistency to cocoa butter. Slathered on hair, lips, and skin, cupuaçu works as a natural moisturizer, sunscreen, and anti-inflammatory. Studies show the antioxidant-packed fruit helps the immune system and lowers blood pressure when ingested.

Recently, the easy-to-grow jungle fruit is attracting new attention as a serious contender to displace Brazil's reigning "superfruit," the acai. Scientists have found that pound for pound, cupuaçu outmatches the trendy berry in antioxidants, vitamins, and affordability.

How to try it

Outside the Amazon jungle, cupuaçu can be found on the internet's Amazon in whole fruit, capsules, powders, drinks, and butter.

THE COFFEE VERSION
OF THE NEW YORK STOCK EXCHANGE

BOLSA OFFICIAL DE CAFÉ • BRAZIL

How to try it

The port city of Santos is 43 miles (70 km) south of São Paulo and easily accessible by plane, bus, and car.

In the early 20th century, coffee was Brazil's main export, and Bolsa Official de Café (Portuguese for the "official coffee exchange") was where the money was made.

Built in 1922, this opulent building was where the captains of the industry haggled over the price of coffee. To take part in these discussions, merchants had to buy a chair, which could cost as much as a house. Until the trading floor closed in the 1960s, it was the financial epicenter of Brazil.

The wealth generated by coffee is evident in the palace's grandeur. The building is topped with a 130-foot-tall clock tower, while Ceres, goddess of agriculture, and Mercury, god of commerce, look out from either side of the entrance. Inside, the opulence continues with a massive stained glass ceiling, marble floors, and a jacaranda wood table in the traders' room.

Food Currencies

Bringing Home the Bacon, Making the Cheddar, Raking in the Clams

In 2014, a Russian farmer named Mikhail Shlyapnikov petitioned to create, print, and use a currency of his own invention, called kolions, which would be pegged to the price of potatoes. Each kolion would be worth 10 kilograms (22 lbs) of potatoes and would be used to trade for goods within his rural farming community. In his town, where access to rubles was extremely limited, a potato-pegged currency would insulate against external economic turmoil. Although a Moscow court ruled against Shlyapikov and eventually declared his kolions illegal, history favors the farmer's ingenuity. For centuries, food has doubled as a popular and effective currency, selected for its inherent value, relative stability, and ability to keep people alive when markets tank.

CHOCOLATE

During the reign of the Aztecs in Mesoamerica, cacao was considered a spiritual, even mystical substance. The Mayans, who had been growing it for hundreds of years, traded the beans with the newly arrived Aztecs, who in turn developed an obsession with cacao, conquered the Mayans, and took over their beans. The Aztecs couldn't get enough: They demanded taxes in the form of cacao and pegged the price of goods to their magical crop. In the 1500s, a turkey hen was worth 200 cacao beans, while one of its eggs went for three beans.

PEPPERCORNS

During the Roman Empire, pepper was considered a precious commodity, so valuable it was stockpiled in the treasury. By the time the Roman Empire fell, the city's invaders—including Attila the Hun—demanded the city's ransoms not in gold, but in pepper.

The building now houses the Coffee Museum, which names Francisco de Melo Palheta as the man who brought coffee to Brazil. Palheta, a Portuguese lieutenant colonel in the Brazilian army, was sent to French Guiana in 1727 under the guise of settling a land dispute between the French and Dutch colonies. His real mission was to bring back a coffee plant. The French governor refused to share the lucrative crop. As the 300-year-old story goes, Palheta seduced the governor's wife, and on his last evening in Guiana, she gifted him a bouquet of flowers with cuttings of a coffee plant.

This building was once exclusively open to wealthy coffee tycoons.

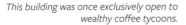

PARMESAN CHEESE

It's not easy to get a loan in Italy, but if you happen to have a massive spare wheel of Parmigiano-Reggiano, your chances just got a lot higher. Italy's Credito Emiliano, a regional bank locally known as Credem, has been accepting wheels of cheese as collateral for loans since 1953. At last count, it has 360,000 wheels in its possession, stacked 20 shelves high. Credem charges between 2 and 3 percent interest on the loans, depending on the quality of the cheese, plus a fee for maintaining the cheese vault, where they care for the wheels as the cheese makers would, lovingly cleaning and rotating their investment.

AFRICAN POTATO MASHER

In the area now known as Cameroon, the Bafia people used rare and heavy iron potato mashers called ensubas, which weighed around 11 pounds, to bring muscle to a serious financial transaction. In the 19th century, a Bafian wife would cost about 30 potato mashers.

TEA BRICKS

Compressed bricks of tea were the preferred currency in parts of Asia for more than a thousand years, from the 9th to the 20th century. Tea leaves, ground or whole, were compacted into various sizes, using herbs to add flavor and occasionally animal manure to hold them together. A value was stamped on the brick, which corresponded with the quality of the mixture. In Tibet, the price of horses and swords was set in tea bricks. In China, taxes could be paid to the emperor in tea.

A traditionally dressed woman from Bahia stuffs an acarajé.

THE FLUFFIEST BEAN FRITTERS IN BAHIA

ACARAJÉ DA CIRA • BRAZIL

How to try it

Acarajé da Cira is located on Largo da Mariquita, a small square in the neighborhood of Rio Vermelho. The shrimp are meant to be eaten whole, so don't let the locals catch you peeling them.

The first stop for many visitors to Salvador is the restaurant Acarajé da Cira, the holy grail of Brazilian bean fritters.

It's not an easy trek: The 5-mile (8 km) trip south of the city will take half an hour on a local bus. But once there, you will be greeted by women called baianas, dressed in traditional skirts and headdresses, presiding over an elaborate series of silver pots in the open air.

You, like the rest of the hungry crowd, are here for the acarajé, a bean fritter made from black-eyed peas and stuffed with a variety of tidbits from those silver pots. To make the bean batter, the baianas individually peel each black-eyed pea, which helps give the fritter its fluffy, cloud-like consistency. The batter is fried in dendê palm oil. Cira's trademark is that the oil is used only once, so the fritters will never be tainted by less-than-perfect oil. Hot from the fryer, the acarajé is split open and stuffed with a fresh tomato salad, a spicy coconut and peanut paste called vatapá, and whole, unpeeled shrimp.

Originally from West Africa, acarajé was brought to Brazil with the Atlantic slave trade. When slavery was abolished in the late 19th century, acarajé was a vital source of income for the newly freed Africans. The baianas have since become a cultural touchstone. Between 1993 and 1994, the back of the short-lived 50,000 cruzeiro real note displayed a baiana assembling an acarajé, which may or may not be as delicious as the ones at Cira's.

Other Enticing Bean Fritters

INDIA	MYANMAR	TURKEY
Mangodae, made with mung beans ground with ginger, green chilies, cumin, and garam masala	Baya kyaw, made by blending yellow split peas, onion, cilantro, turmeric, and garlic	Fasulye mucveri, made with fresh green beans, scallions, and dill in an egg-and-flour batter

STUFFED GOAT'S STOMACH

BUCHADA DE BODE • BRAZIL

Northeast Brazil is goat country, so it makes sense that one of the region's traditional dishes focuses on making the most of every last bit of the bode, the Portuguese word for "goat." Buchada, whose name comes from *bucho*, or "stomach," can be made out of any animal stomach, but goat is the most common in the Brazilian states of Pernambuco and Ceará.

The overall concept will sound familiar to anyone who's ever tried haggis: The stomach is stuffed with whatever entrails or organs are on hand (blood, intestines, liver, lungs), seasoned, and then sewn up and cooked. Restaurants will often serve buchada inside a larger stew. When plated as a main dish, the distinctive pattern of the stomach lining is clearly visible.

Buchada doesn't have many fans outside Brazil, but inside the country, especially in the northeast, it's not uncommon for politicians running for office to feel they must publicly consume one to prove they can relate to everyday people.

How to try it
Bode do Nô restaurant in Recife serves its buchada as a whole, intact stomach.

AIR-BREATHING MONSTER FISH

PAICHE • BRAZIL

Chuck a line into the Amazon River and you might pull out a convulsing, prehistoric leviathan twice the length of an adult human.

The paiche, also known as arapaima or pirarucu, is one of the largest freshwater fish in the world. Fully grown, it can reach up to 15 feet (4.6 m) from tip to tail. Weightwise, paiche can reach anywhere from 200 to 400 pounds (90.7 to 181 kg).

This fish has been around for so long it's considered a living fossil, dating back to the Miocene epoch (5.3 million to 23 million years ago).

This prehistoric relic has some strange traits, including the need to surface for air. In addition to gills, the fish has a lung-like organ. The ability to breathe air is helpful in the oxygen-deprived waters of the Amazon basin but leaves the paiche vulnerable. When the fish surfaces, it often sucks in air with a loud, distinctive gulp that local fishermen can identify from some distance away, making the paiche easy to catch. Amazonian fishermen have long prized the fish for its large size and tasty meat, netting or spearing the fish in such large numbers that its future was in doubt by the beginning of the 21st century.

Conservation efforts and an increase in farmed paiche have ensured that this ancient fish will not disappear anytime soon. And that's a great thing for Amazonian cuisine, as paiche is a delectable and meaty fish, with a firm fillet that stays succulent in most preparations, whether roasted, grilled, or steamed. It's also a fantastic fish for ceviche.

How to try it
You can find fresh paiche at the Mercado Municipal in Manaus.

Paiche is considered a living fossil.

Delicious Diaspora

JAPANESE IN BRAZIL

In 1908, the first boat of Japanese immigrants arrived in Brazil to work in the expanding coffee industry. Japan's feudal system had recently collapsed, leaving many rural citizens hungry and desperate for work. Seven hundred and eighty-one Japanese workers, mostly farmers, came over on the first boat from Kobe to São Paulo. By the 1990s, more than 200,000 of their countrymen had followed.

For nearly 50 years, life was hard for the Japanese in Brazil. Ostracized from Brazilian society, they lived in enclaves on meager wages, treated as a cheap source of labor. But the Japanese strengthened the Brazilian farming industry and eventually earned a reputation as skilled agriculturists. In the 1970s, as

Japan rose to economic power, Japanese Brazilians gained newfound prestige, wealth, and respect. Today, Brazil is home to 1.5 million people of Japanese descent, the largest population outside of Japan.

Collaboration and intermarriage between the nations has led to a culture uniquely its own. Brazilian jujitsu, where strength meets cleverness, is a joint endeavor. In Japanese Brazilian homes, sticky short-grain rice is eaten alongside feijoada, the Brazilian bean stew, and sushi can be made with churrasco instead of fish. But Japanese Brazilian cuisine is not just the typical mash-up of a dish from one culture fused with a dish from another: It's a blending of lifestyles, techniques, and preferences.

Japanese rodízio is Japanese cuisine served in the popular Brazilian steakhouse style (rodízio) that includes an all-you-can-eat buffet. In Japan, buffets are a rare spectacle, but in Brazil almost every barbecue-meat-slinging restaurant has one. The Japanese style means sushi and sashimi, along with tempura, gyoza, and yakisoba, in unlimited quantities until you say stop.

Temakerias are fast-casual sushi restaurants making elaborate hand rolls (temaki). While the concept, in theory, is Japanese, the execution is definitively Brazilian. Mangoes and kiwis are common additions to hand rolls, which are astoundingly huge. In Japan, a hand roll is just a few bites; in Brazil, it's more like a meal. A popular Brazilian variety is deep-fried temaki, filled with cream cheese and salmon.

Pastéis are the omnipresent street snacks of Brazil, made of paper-thin dough filled with meat, fish, or cheese, then deep-fried. Like an empanada but lighter and crispier, the pastéis is believed to be an invention of Japanese migrants, who riffed on

the Chinese recipe for fried wontons.

Sakerinhas are caipirinhas—Brazil's national cocktail—made with sake instead of cachaça.

Persimmon, Fuji apples, and ponkan oranges are among the fruits developed by early Japanese farmers. The introduction of new fruit as well as sustainable farming practices changed the Brazilian diet and brought more fresh produce to the table, laying the groundwork for the extensive fruit industry of today.

Cashew apples

Cashew nut

THE APPLE JUICE OF BRAZIL

SUCO DE CAJU • BRAZIL

The beloved, buttery cashew grows from a false fruit called a cashew apple, which often goes to waste once the nut is harvested. Recently, industrial drink producers such as PepsiCo have been devising ways to transform this cashew by-product into something delicious, drinkable, and lucrative. The Brazilians, one of the top producers of cashews, have been doing exactly that for years.

Cashew apple juice, known locally as suco de caju, is a popular Brazilian beverage that can be bought ubiquitously, from supermarket shelves to roadside stalls. The liquid is sour and bright, with hints of raw green pepper and subtle citrus. Often sold in concentrated form, cashew apple juice has become a mainstay at large gatherings and birthday parties and reminds many Brazilians of childhood.

How to try it

A few cashew juices are bottled and sold internationally, most notably the Brazilian brand Maguary. You can press your own, but beware that the apples are highly perishable and must be processed within 24 hours of falling from the tree.

BEER MADE FROM FOG

ATRAPANIEBLA • CHILE

The Atacama Desert, in the northern reaches of Chile, is the world's driest non-polar desert, with less than 0.004 inch (0.102 mm) of rain each year. In coastal communities such as Peña Blanca, the main source of fresh water comes in the form of thick cloud banks, known as camanchaca, that roll inland off the Pacific Ocean.

Set up along hillsides in prime fog areas, fog-catching nets capture the condensation. Droplets drip down the nets into piping that sends the water to barrels and reservoirs. The project, which began in the 1950s, has been a huge success, revolutionizing modern desert water collection. It also gave two local brewers an idea.

How to try it

Bars and restaurants in Chile's Coquimbo region serve Atrapaniebla beer in bottles and on tap.

Brothers Miguel and Marco Carcuro started the Atrapaniebla brewery, which produces the world's first beer made from fog water. Atrapaniebla ("fog catcher" in Spanish) currently produces 24,000 liters each year that are distributed around Chile. The Carcuro brothers say that the water from the camanchaca gives their beers a wholly unique taste, and that the fresh purity of the fog water adds clarity and depth that's unrivaled by other brews. The taste, drinkers say, is crisp and refreshing with just the slightest hint of atmospheric salt.

Shape-Shifting Strawberries

ANTIFREEZE STRAWBERRIES

Much speculation surrounds the creation of this fishy frankenberry, which began as an attempt to give the soft, fragile fruit a longer shelf life during the winter months. To do this, scientists in Thailand injected the seeds of the garden variety red strawberry with a gene found naturally in arctic flounder: antifreeze. The antifreeze gene—discovered and isolated in the late 1960s—increases tolerance to cold while mitigating damage caused by freezing. Addressing public concern, experts assure that the gene does not make its subjects taste like fish. While further experimentation is still required before antifreeze strawberries hit the market (the gene is being tested on everything from frozen foods to therapy for hypothermia), the future looks promising for winter produce.

SEA STRAWBERRIES

This crab-claw-shaped fruit grows along the saltwater coasts of California, Mexico, and Chile, where it hides in grassy tufts sprouting from black rocks and sand. While *Carpobrotus aequilaterus* is not technically a strawberry, it earned the name "sea strawberry" because it tastes just like one, albeit very salty. The claws are filled with a sugary red goop that resembles the inside of a soft fig and is extremely perishable. The fruit is ripe for just two to three weeks a year, after which it turns to mush.

PINEBERRIES

Strawberries that taste like pineapples may seem like genetically modified fruit. But pineberries are simply strawberries that have been slowly and selectively bred for their appearance and taste. Due to their tiny size (smaller than an inch) and low yields, pineberries are both expensive to buy and not especially profitable to grow. For a few weeks each summer, you might find them at American farmers' markets or high-end grocery stores, but pineberries are unlikely to be mass distributed anytime soon.

Pineberries have been bred to taste like pineapples.

THE MOTHER OF ALL STRAWBERRIES

PURÉN WHITE STRAWBERRY • CHILE

How to try it
Get to Purén during the summer harvest and find a local market, where the berries will be sold directly by the small collective of farmers.

The DNA of the pale, lightly floral Chilean strawberry exists in every supermarket in the United States, most of Europe, and anywhere large red strawberries are sold. The modern strawberry, or garden strawberry, is a hybrid of two species. Growing side by side in an 18th-century French garden, a strawberry from Virginia bred with a strawberry from the Chilean mountain town of Purén, and voilà, the contemporary variety was born.

The Chilean berry was originally prized for its impressive size, but its colorless appearance and delicate flavor are now its most distinctive traits. The pigment is

what gives red strawberries their signature tartness, and so Chile's berries are light on acid and their taste is surprisingly floral—almost like eating strawberry perfume.

Fewer than 30 farmers work the strawberry fields in the small town of Purén, where the berries grow on steep, terraced hillsides facing the sea. Without any mechanized equipment, the farmers till 14 hectares (34.6 acres) of clay terrain and harvest strawberries by hand during the short two-month season.

White strawberries have a light, floral flavor.

BLUE EGG HENS

ARAUCANA • CHILE

Every now and then, chicken farmers will find an anomaly in the coop: nestled among regular white and brown eggs, a bright blue orb. There's no predicting when or how often a chicken's eggs will come out looking like Easter, which is what makes the Araucana chicken so special. The domesticated Chilean breed lays a dazzling aquamarine egg every single time.

No one knows exactly where Araucana chickens originated, as their history was undocumented until the Spanish observed them in the early 20th century. Some believe they are a serendipitous hybrid of native Chilean birds, while others credit foreign influence. Araucanas are a rumpless chicken, meaning they lack a last vertebra and have no tails, which points to Asian chickens as their ancestors—specifically the Balinese breed carried to Chile by Dutch traders. But Balinese chickens don't produce blue eggs, and so theories of their heritage remain roundly debated among poultry historians.

In order to lay these enchanted eggs, Araucanas require one thing: the outdoors. The chickens can't survive in industrial chicken farms, and so the shell's blue hue has unwittingly become an indicator of a happy chicken with a free-range life.

How to try it

Araucanas have been bred with many other chicken varieties, whose blue-egg-laying offspring now live throughout the world. Before eating, enjoy the aesthetic as much as you can because the taste is exactly like a normal egg.

The Araucana chicken lays Easter eggs.

A STONY SEA CREATURE WITH A GORY INTERIOR

PIURE • CHILE

Anyone swimming by this unassuming rock-like sea creature might not give it a second glance. But slice into its bumpy carapace and you'll find little orifices filled with swollen masses of tomato-red flesh, oozing clear blood.

Chilean fishermen harvest and sell the creature, known as piure, to local vendors, who remove the vibrant innards and hang the fresh or dehydrated meat from strings. Locals compare the taste to sea urchin but are quick to add that piure's

How to try it

Piure live off the coast of both Chile and Peru but are primarily eaten in Chile. Santiago's Mercado Central is sure to carry it. In Valparaíso, try the Caleta Portales ("Fisherman Cove"), where the local catch is brought each day.

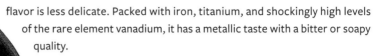

flavor is less delicate. Packed with iron, titanium, and shockingly high levels of the rare element vanadium, it has a metallic taste with a bitter or soapy quality.

Along the coast, locals enjoy fresh piure in ceviche with onion, coriander, and lemon juice. They also slice and boil it for a rice-and-salad pairing or incorporate it into a traditional seafood stew called paila marina.

Piure belongs to the class of immobile, invertebrate filter feeders known as "sea squirts," all of which are hermaphrodites. Born male, piure becomes a hermaphrodite at puberty and can reproduce, alone or with others, by shooting out eggs and sperm that then mingle together in a cloud.

Perhaps the creature's versatile sexual abilities are why piure has also been touted as an aphrodisiac.

THE WORLD'S OLDEST CLAMBAKE

CURANTO • CHILE

How to try it

Chile's spring and summer (dry season) is the only time to take part in a traditional curanto feast. For those just wanting to eat it, head to Dalcahue and look behind the local crafts market for the food stalls being run by a team of grandmothers.

On a Chilean archipelago of lush islands called Chiloé, archaeologists discovered a 6,000-year-old cooking pit. It contained skeletal remains of nutrias, sea lions, birds, fish, and whales, along with shells from scallops, snails, abalone, mussels, and clams. These were the vestiges of an early curanto, one of the most ancient recipes still prepared today.

The word *curanto* means "hot rock" or "stony ground," and it begins with a 3-foot (1-m) hole lined with stones that have been heated in a bonfire. After the rocks, ingredients go in, and while the components vary from century to century, pit to pit, it's typically an assortment of shellfish, smoked meat, chicken, longaniza (sausage), and potatoes.

The last ingredient is where the curanto really shines. Chilotés are masters of the potato, cultivating hundreds of varieties on their islands. A proper curanto showcases the bounty and variety of these tubers with chapaleles (potato pancakes), milcaos (potato dumplings), and whole steam-roasted potatoes.

After loading ingredients into the cavity, the cook covers the hole with wild rhubarb leaves, damp sacks, and packed dirt. As the shellfish cook, the shells open and release juices that sizzle on the hot rocks and help steam the rest of the food, while also imparting a distinct smoky flavor. The formidable feast emerges several hours later, slicked in briny juices and meaty oils, offering a delicious glimpse into a more primal past.

A FRESH BLOOD GELATIN SNACK

ÑACHI • CHILE

Making ñachi means moving fast. As soon as butchers slaughter the animal (typically a pig, lamb, or goat), they immediately collect the hot blood and mix it with lemon juice, salt, cilantro, and smoked pepper. After a setting period, the blood coagulates with the lemon's acid and forms a solid jelly. Chileans typically cut the jelly into cubes and serve it with bread, but ñachi can also be eaten while still soup-like.

The word *ñachi* means "blood" in Mapudungun, an Indigenous Chilean language. Ñachi is a dish of Chile's Mapuche people that is now enjoyed countrywide. Blood has long been consumed in the region for its nutritional value, but experts caution that eating raw blood comes with a pathogen risk. For the initiated, a glass of wine or chicha (a spit-fermented drink) is the stomach sterilization method of choice.

How to try it

To find ñachi, head out to Chile's countryside. Blood in small doses is typically safe to ingest, but don't overindulge. Too much blood can cause hemochromatosis, an iron buildup that leads to liver, lung, and nervous system disorders.

BRIGHT YELLOW CHICKENS

GALLINAS CAMPESINAS • COLOMBIA

An hour north of Bogotá is the town of Ubaté, so renowned for its dairy industry that an imposing metal cow statue presides high above the main traffic circle. Visitors to Ubaté are typically drawn to the row of small specialty cheese shops. Others skip the cheese, heading straight for the gallinas campesinas and stuffed chicken necks.

On the outside, the most striking detail about gallinas campesinas is their color: The chickens are a bright, unnatural yellow. Looking at them, stacked on top of each other and lit beneath a heat lamp, you can't tell that each of these birds died an expectant mother, their necks swiftly broken when their eggs reached the embryo stage. They are a regional dish found only in Ubaté and are prized for their soft, luscious texture. The birds are slowly braised over a charcoal stove with aromatics and spices such as onions, thyme, and bay leaves. Right before being served, the whole bird is split down the middle, exposing the eggs and the tender flesh. The best-tasting eggs are very young. They're mostly yolk, have no shell, and make for decadent chicken broth–infused bites. Stuffed hen necks, or gallinas rellenas, are often found nearby: A chicken's head, severed from the base of the neck, is stuffed with a mixture of potatoes, rice, peas, and chicken blood. Sewn shut, the chicken-head sausage is roasted over an open flame. The flavor is so rich and earthy, the small portion is plenty for a single sitting.

How to try it

The Ubaté town square is surrounded by food stalls, one of which is La Chata, where you'll find the town's favorite chickens and stuffed chicken necks.

THE DISAPPEARING HOT SAUCE

AJÍ NEGRO • COLOMBIA

How to try it

Ají negro is in danger of disappearing from Amazonian communities. Colombian chefs, however, have taken an interest in the preservation of traditional recipes, and ají negro is making appearances on the menus of high-end restaurants like El Panóptico in Bogotá.

South American cooking is teeming with recipes that find a way around the poisonous nature of cassava, the starchy tuber that fills out the diet of nearly half a billion people. Ají negro, a hot sauce that requires several days to detoxify, is one example of such ingenuity.

Traditionally a product of northwest Amazonia, ají negro begins with cassava that's been peeled, washed, diced, and left to soak in a stream for several days.

A hollowed-out tree is the customary vessel for the next step, which involves pounding the cassava in the giant arboreal mortar until it becomes a pulp. Transferred to a woven sack, the pulp undergoes hours of twisting to extract the juice, which is then filtered to remove the starch and simmered for half a day until it becomes dark and thick. Only then can cooks use the starchless juice to make the hot sauce.

Recipes vary significantly between ethnic groups. Along with hot peppers, the sauce can include fish, meat, ants, vegetables, flowers, and seeds.

The smoked chicken with cassava and ají negro at Bogotá restaurant El Panóptico.

EASTER SOUP TOPPED WITH A BUFFET

FANESCA • ECUADOR

How to try it

When spring rolls around, Ecuadorian restaurants start competing for the brisk fanesca business, and the establishment that serves the best bowl is a source of infinite debate. In Quito, Casa Gangotena serves the general manager's great-grandmother's recipe in an upscale setting; a few blocks away, El Criollo is a family-run favorite. In Cuenca, the kiosks in El Centro market are a good place to sample a variety of bowls.

The ingredient list for fanesca, Ecuador's Easter potage, sounds more like an elaborate buffet spread than a recipe for soup—the garnishes alone (fried plantains, hard-boiled eggs, peppers, mini empanadas, and fresh cheese) cover all five food groups. It's no wonder this Holy Week indulgence takes two days to prepare.

Fanesca's thick base begins with salt cod cooked in milk and thickened with pumpkin seeds or peanuts. Then chefs add a dozen different beans, vegetables, and grains—one, some say, for each of Jesus's twelve apostles (Jesus himself is represented by the cod). Each fanesca maker has a unique veggie-and-legume lineup, but popular choices include peas, pumpkin, lupini beans, and hominy. When the soup's finished, it's time to add the garnishes, which float on the surface of the dense, sunset-colored soup.

Why the onslaught of ingredients? One story traces the tradition to the pre-Columbian Andes, where people celebrated a bountiful harvest by throwing the abundance into a single soup.

While fanesca is especially popular for lunch on Good Friday, Ecuadorians feast on the soup throughout Lent and Holy Week. After all, the memory has to last for the rest of the year.

Fanseca is the official Good Friday lunch of Ecuador.

INTELLIGENT DREAMING

GUAYUSA · ECUADOR

t's just before sunrise in the Ecuadorian rain forest. Members of the Kichwa community boil leaves from the guayusa (pronounced "gwai-yoo-sa") tree in a large metal pot. When the brew is ready, they sit around the fire, sip the tea, and discuss their dreams.

This is how the Indigenous tribe begins each day. They believe that guayusa facilitates dream interpretation, which is essential to decision-making in the community. One Kichwa legend tells of twins who went in search of a plant that would teach them how to dream. After they fell asleep, they dreamed of meeting their ancestors, who gifted them guayusa leaves. When they awoke, they were still clutching the plants in their hands. The Kichwa believe that dreams show a glimpse of the future, and they use their nocturnal visions to guide how they approach the day's work, especially hunting.

How to try it

Tips for lucid dreaming include reading fiction before bed, setting random alarms throughout the night, and waking up with your eyes closed. Guayusa may be the easiest entry point, available from tea distributors online.

The slightly bitter, caffeine-and-antioxidant-packed tea is now a popular natural stimulant. It's earned the nickname "the night watchman" for the calm wakefulness it provides, which allows for a second application: lucid dreaming. Those in the practice of cogent dreaming tap into the subconscious mind, effectively allowing them awareness in the realm of sleep. Some lucid dreamers claim guayusa guides them into a shallow sleep while still keeping them sharp enough to participate in their dreams.

SPIT-FERMENTED LIQUOR

MASATO • PERU

How to try it
Traditional, spit-made drinks can carry hepatitis B, but if you're brave and immunized, some small shops in Peru still carry it.

Masato, an ancient Amazonian drink made from boiled yuca, starts its fermentation process in the mouths of village women. They chew the tuber, which mixes with enzymes in their saliva that break the starch down into sugar, then spit the mash into a pitcher, where it ferments, over several days, into a fruity, sour-tasting drink with enormous nutritional value.

Their husbands, who typically skip lunch, rely on this carb-heavy, lightly alcoholic brew to power them through their workday. It's essential to their diet and livelihood, and so the ancient spit drink has become a kind of bargaining chip for the village wives, who dispense their masato strategically, depending on whether they are rewarding or punishing.

On its own, masato has a tart, almost vinegary taste, but it's often infused with warm spices such as cloves or cinnamon, then mixed with fresh fruit, which gives the drink a more refreshing, cocktail-like quality. Refusing a glass of masato is considered deeply offensive, so if you enter the jungle and find a circle of women munching on yuca, be prepared to partake in this intimate ritual.

FESTIVAL OF THE BABY BREAD

FESTIVAL DEL PAN WAWA • PERU

How to try it
The Festival of the Baby Bread is held annually, around the Day of the Dead, in Cusco's Plaza Túpac Amaru.

On the Day of the Dead, Peruvians believe the souls of their loved ones visit the Earth. To welcome them, they prepare pan wawa, bread baked into the shape of a swaddled baby. The loaves were originally presented as gifts at the tombs of children, but now the bread is enjoyed by all ages, both living and dead.

At Cusco's annual Festival of the Baby Bread, a titanic toddler is constructed by some of the city's best bakers. In 2012, 22 bakers joined forces in an attempt to set the record for the largest ever made: They built a pan wawa 72 feet long and 26 feet wide (22 x 8 m).

How the Colombian Government Killed Spit-Fermented Drinks

Outside the Amazon, South American spit-fermented libations go by the name chicha.

Colombian chicha had been ritually consumed by the pre-Columbian Muisca people since 3000 BCE. When the Spanish colonists arrived in 1499, the mouth-made brew grew popular among the working classes. By the 19th century, Bogotá alone had more than 800 chicherías—bars dedicated to the cheap brew—whose primary clientele were artisans, farmers, and those whose schedules didn't adhere to typical work hours. Patrons came to socialize over dice and cards, eat a meal, buy groceries, or slip into a room to sleep. Chicherías were deeply communal, with one large bowl of chicha generally passed among tablemates.

Between the years 1910 and 1920, Colombians were suffering from extreme poverty, and Colombian politicians found a scapegoat in chicha. Chicherías came under fire as hotbeds of public disorder and the sole impediment to Colombia's rise as an industrialized economy. The bulk of Colombia's poor were Indigenous people, who were considered a drag on progress. Chicha—with its ancient heritage, association with unstructured days, and production method of chewing and spitting—made a convenient symbol for the country's problems.

But chicherías, inextricable from the daily lives of the lower classes, were too popular to eradicate neatly. The government needed more muscle, so they turned to German immigrant Leo Kopp and his new beer operation, Bavaria Brewery. Founded in 1889, Bavaria Brewery quickly established dominance in the Colombian beer market, positioning itself as the spiritual opposite of chicha and chicherías. The brewery buildings were industrial and modern, production was efficient, and the beer was served in individual, sterilized glass bottles. To the Colombian government, Bavaria Brewery represented European progress—a model they badly wanted to emulate.

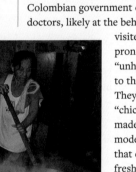

For thousands of years, chicha has been brewed over an open fire.

Colombia's bourgeoisie latched on to Bavaria, but most Colombians didn't have cash to burn on beer. Chicherías remained everywhere, but the Colombian government did not relent. Prominent doctors, likely at the behest of politicians, visited poor neighborhoods, pronouncing the drink "unhygienic" and a hazard to the country's well-being. They even invented an illness—"chichism"—which purportedly made its sufferers insane. (Many modern, unbribed doctors agree that chicha's alcohol content and freshness would render most versions safe to drink.)

Bavaria doubled down on the government's efforts, giving its beer shameless names such as "No Mas Chicha," "Consum Bier," and "Hygienic," alongside images of robust, healthy-looking ladies and children happily drinking beer. Meanwhile, the government launched an aggressive propaganda campaign. "Chicha begets crime," read one political poster, along with a filthy hand clutching a bloody knife. "The jails are filled with people who drink chicha," read another, which featured a nun weeping over a man peering out from behind bars. The government also hiked taxes and enacted strict, arbitrary rules for chicherías. Unable to comply, establishments shuttered or moved underground.

With chicha already on life support, the plug was abruptly pulled on April 9, 1948, when Jorge Eliécer Gaitán, a liberal presidential candidate, was murdered on a Bogotá street. Gaitán was widely regarded by the working class as the country's populist savior, and his death set off a ten-year period of brutal unrest known now simply as La Violencia.

While bloody riots swept through the city, President Ospina Pérez signed a law declaring that all fermented beverages had to be industrially produced in individual glass containers—a de facto ban on the centuries-old tradition.

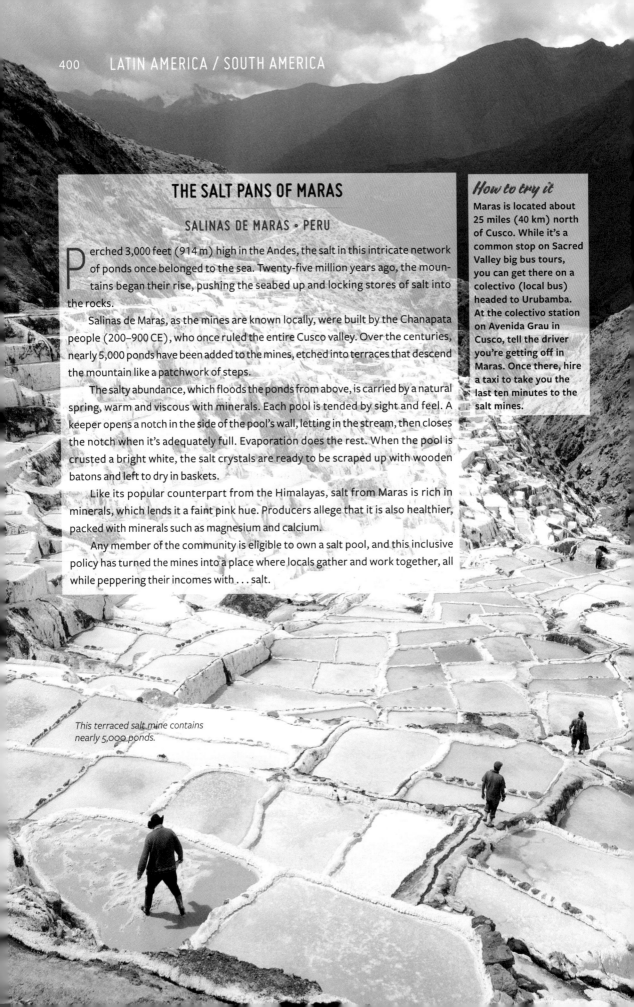

THE SALT PANS OF MARAS

SALINAS DE MARAS • PERU

Perched 3,000 feet (914 m) high in the Andes, the salt in this intricate network of ponds once belonged to the sea. Twenty-five million years ago, the mountains began their rise, pushing the seabed up and locking stores of salt into the rocks.

Salinas de Maras, as the mines are known locally, were built by the Chanapata people (200–900 CE), who once ruled the entire Cusco valley. Over the centuries, nearly 5,000 ponds have been added to the mines, etched into terraces that descend the mountain like a patchwork of steps.

The salty abundance, which floods the ponds from above, is carried by a natural spring, warm and viscous with minerals. Each pool is tended by sight and feel. A keeper opens a notch in the side of the pool's wall, letting in the stream, then closes the notch when it's adequately full. Evaporation does the rest. When the pool is crusted a bright white, the salt crystals are ready to be scraped up with wooden batons and left to dry in baskets.

Like its popular counterpart from the Himalayas, salt from Maras is rich in minerals, which lends it a faint pink hue. Producers allege that it is also healthier, packed with minerals such as magnesium and calcium.

Any member of the community is eligible to own a salt pool, and this inclusive policy has turned the mines into a place where locals gather and work together, all while peppering their incomes with . . . salt.

How to try it

Maras is located about 25 miles (40 km) north of Cusco. While it's a common stop on Sacred Valley big bus tours, you can get there on a colectivo (local bus) headed to Urubamba. At the colectivo station on Avenida Grau in Cusco, tell the driver you're getting off in Maras. Once there, hire a taxi to take you the last ten minutes to the salt mines.

This terraced salt mine contains nearly 5,000 ponds.

BIG-ASS ANTS

SIQUI SAPA • PERU

Large as a cockroach and curvy as a pinup, the siqui sapa (literally "big butt" in the Quechua language) are coveted by gourmands around the world—but they're not easy to procure.

The big-butt ants that make for good eating are dominated by the females. They live up to 20 feet (6 m) underground and are protected by a rigid caste system. Worker ants build the anthill; soldier ants defend it. The princesses, as the females are known, are tasked solely with reproduction. After mating with prince ants in a ritual called chamuscada, a term that refers to passion, the males die and the princesses fly off to each start a new anthill where they'll become queen.

The mating season, October to November, is the only time to harvest siqui sapa. If hunters can move swiftly enough to get past the soldier ants that attack with bites that draw blood, they will be rewarded with females that fetch $15 a pound (0.45 kg) during peak season and up to $40 when supplies are scarce.

In South America, the bugs are soaked in salted water, roasted, and eaten like peanuts At first, the flavor is reminiscent of pork rinds, but it quickly evolves into something earthier and more bitter. They are sometimes compared to caviar, which seems an unlikely match until you realize their "butts" are so well endowed because they're swollen with eggs.

How to try it
You can find big-butt ants in markets in the Amazon region of Peru. Vendors in the main square in the city of Tarapoto sell small bags of the ants for just a few soles.

ICE-CREAM BEAN

INGA EDULIS • PERU

Money may not grow on trees, but in tropical swaths of Central and South America, you can find king-size candy bars dropping from tree branches.

A foot-long confection produced by inga trees, ice-cream beans are actually legumes. Split open the pod and you'll find seeds wrapped in white fluff that looks like cotton candy and tastes like vanilla ice cream. Eat the fluff, spit out the seed, and within a year it's likely a new tree will stand where you were snacking.

As far as vending machines go, inga trees are generous. They grow with velocity and ease up to 60 feet (18 m) and are commonly used as shade for other crops. Farmers have found pods that hold an impressive 6 feet (2 m) of fluff.

In countries such as Peru, Ecuador, and Colombia, locals eat ice-cream beans raw, as do monkeys, birds, and other animals that enjoy the treat. But only humans can roast the otherwise inedible seeds as a snack and mix ice-cream beans into chocolate, coffee, or cream.

How to try it
Pick up some inga edulis at Mercado Nº 1 de Surquillo in Lima, a market full of fruit vendors. Or, if you're feeling ambitious, you can purchase a starter plant online for $100.

WE WERE EATING HERE FIRST
The Inca Empire

The Incas (1438–1533 CE) developed the most sophisticated food supply chain in pre-Columbian history, feeding millions of subjects across steep, mountainous terrain that ran along the western coast of South America. Here's how they did it.

TERRACED FARMING

The Andes mountain range lay at the heart of the Inca Empire. The largely vegetarian, agriculture-focused kingdom had to adapt to a multitude of extreme climates. They cut flat terraces into the Andes, working from the valley upward, and built stone retaining walls around each field, which absorbed the sun's heat during the day and released it at night, keeping crops from freezing at high elevation.

The Incas built cisterns and irrigation systems that collected rainwater and melting glacial ice, to carry it through the fields and down the mountains. Their plots were fertilized with guano (seabird poop), so prized that anyone caught killing a guano-producing bird was sentenced to death.

The Incas' three staple crops were potatoes, corn, and quinoa, each developed for resiliency at specific elevations ranging from sea level to 14,000 feet (4,267 m). Between these elevations, farmers traded crops with one another and also grew a rotating variety of produce to hedge their bets against failure each season.

QULLQAS (COLLCAS)

The Incas prioritized food security and deliberately grew excess crops, to store in tens of thousands of qullqas, or storehouses.

Qullqas were built near every city, farm, and crop-producing estate. For the best ventilation, qullqas were mostly built on the

LABOR FORCE

sides of hills, where wind would keep the temperature cool and the moisture low. Channels below the buildings acted as drainage canals, whisking away moisture and minimizing rot. Fresh crops could last up to two years; freeze-dried products lasted four.

Circular qullqas stored corn and rectangular qullqas stored potatoes. Both crops were held in ceramic pots to deter rodents. Often a layer of herbs, straw, or gravel was laid as the storehouse's foundation, which allowed air to circulate and kept worms out.

Inventory of the qullqas was kept by state officials using a quipu, an accounting device of colored strings and knots.

THE ROYAL HIGHWAY

The Incan road system included two major north-south roads with many offshoots, extending 25,000 miles (40,234 km), known as the Royal Highway. Ordinary civilians were not allowed to use the road—it was only for the transportation of goods.

Most everything was carried by herds of llamas and alpacas, whose nimble feet could handle steep mountainous terrain.

LABOR FORCE

Chaski (or chasqui) were the most skilled messengers of the Inca Empire. Chosen as boys, the chaski trained in speed and endurance, running at grueling altitudes, which helped strengthen their lungs and splay their feet. The chaskis transported important messages and perishable foods, such as fish and fruit, between cities as fast as possible using a relay system. They ran at top speed between refueling stations called tampus, where they would blow on a conch shell trumpet to alert the next runner who would sprint to receive the package and run the next leg. If the emperor in Cusco had a desire for fresh seafood, it could be run from the coast, 250 miles (402 km) away, in about two days.

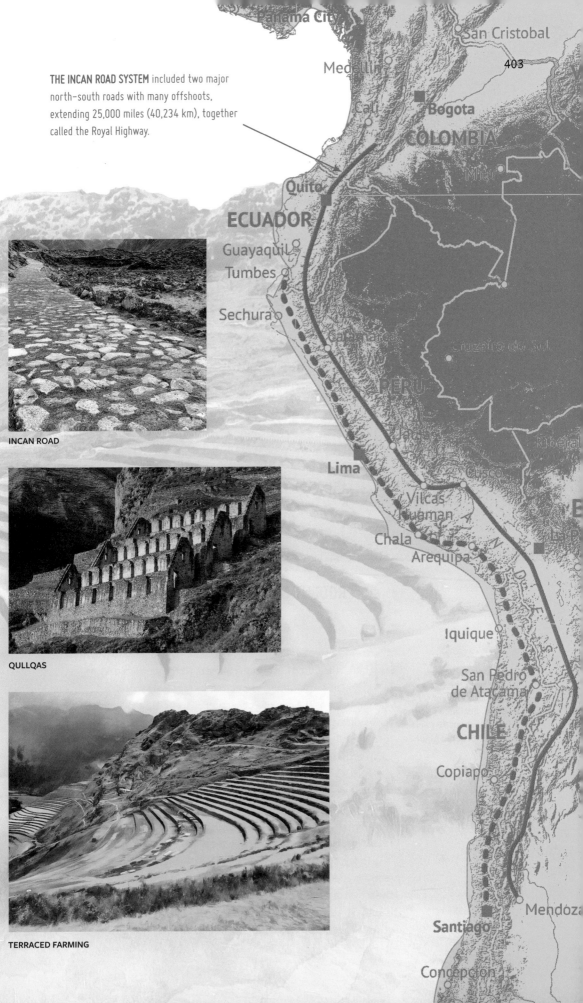

THE INCAN ROAD SYSTEM included two major north–south roads with many offshoots, extending 25,000 miles (40,234 km), together called the Royal Highway.

Panama City

San Cristobal

Medellín

Cali

Bogota

COLOMBIA

Mitu

Quito

ECUADOR

Guayaquil

Tumbes

Cruzeiro do Sul

Sechura

Cajamarca

PERU

Jauja

Riberal

Lima

Cusco

Vilcas
Huaman

Chala

La P

Arequipa

Iquique

San Pedro
de Atacama

CHILE

Copiapo

Mendoza

Santiago

Concepción

INCAN ROAD

QULLQAS

TERRACED FARMING

Instead of bread and wine, Jesus and his disciples ate guinea pig and chicha.

A RODENT STARS IN CATHOLIC CONVERSION ART

GUINEA PIG LAST SUPPER • PERU

How to try it

The Cusco Cathedral is located in the Plaza de Armas in the center of town. Entrance costs 25 soles (about $8) and includes an audio guide.

Da Vinci's *Last Supper* displayed a classic menu of unleavened bread and wine—but in the Cusco Cathedral, guinea pig is the centerpiece.

The Last Supper, as painted by Marcos Zapata, in 1753, is an obvious standout among the massive collection of art and archaeological relics housed in the basilica. Lying paws-up on a golden serving tray, the cooked guinea pig sits right in front of Jesus. Instead of wine on the table, the disciples are drinking chicha, the local Peruvian libation.

It's surprising that this painting was tolerated by the Catholic Church, especially during the time of the Inquisition, but Zapata was a big deal in his day—as were guinea pigs. It is possible church officials felt that the painting, featuring two home-town heroes, could be pardoned as a populist conversion technique. Whatever the reasoning, his painting was hung in the newly built Cusco Cathedral.

Today, cuy, as Peruvians call the domesticated rodent, is typically reserved for festivals and holidays, when the guinea pig is baked, fried, or spit-roasted. Before the arrival of cattle, eating cuy was synonymous with eating meat, and the practice is still going strong. Peruvians consume 65 million guinea pigs a year, and the furry critters have become something of a cultural icon.

Mitterand's Last Supper

A last meal is a final, impossible attempt at pleasure and comfort before being swept away by certain death. It demands a deep scrutiny of desires, and the underlying question: What and how much should a person consume when there is literally no tomorrow?

In December 1995, former French president François Mitterrand knew he was about to die. He had been battling prostate cancer for years, a fact that he and his doctors hid for the majority of his presidency. When faced with the reality and urgency of his condition, Mitterrand chose to hold a feast for 30 people on New Year's Eve. He was so weak, he had to be carried to his chair where he began the voracious but anguished consumption of three dozen Marennes oysters, foie gras, crusty bread, capon (a castrated rooster bred for fatness), and enough wine to keep him occupied for four hours. The grand finale came as a surprise—not for Mitterrand, but for his guests. A man appeared holding a tray of tiny songbirds called ortolans, a dish that was once a rite of passage for macabre gourmands and was now illegal (and prohibitively expensive) to consume in France.

The pale brown, palm-size birds are caught in southwest France and kept in pitch dark, which disorients them and compels the birds to gorge themselves until their tiny bodies stretch like balloons (Roman emperors used to blind them to achieve the same effect). The swollen creatures are then drowned in Armagnac, a French brandy that acts as a marinade, roasted for exactly eight minutes, then plucked.

While not all of Mitterrand's guests consented to eat an ortolan, some did. The modest way to consume the bird is with a cloth over your head, shielding the shameful act from view. The bird goes feet first into the diner's mouth, the head is bitten off, and the ortolan is consumed whole: a sodden mouthful of tiny bones and guts and liquor. On this night, Mitterrand ate two. He passed away eight days later.

THE LENT–APPROVED AQUATIC RODENT

CAPYBARA ∘ VENEZUELA

In the 18th century, local clergy in Venezuela wrote to the Vatican with a special request. They had discovered a local animal that lived in water, had webbed feet, and resembled a fish. With Lent and Holy Week approaching, they asked the Vatican to grant the animal the status of fish, so they might eat it during the meat-free religious holiday. By letter, the Catholic Church agreed, and the capybara—the largest living rodent in the world—became the favorite "fish" of Venezuelan Lent.

Locals quickly developed a taste for the giant aquatic rodent. The demand grew to a fever pitch, and illegal poaching threatened to wipe out the population. With the help of government regulation and speedy reproduction, capybaras are no longer endangered, but there is still a robust black market trade. Capybara is considered an essential holiday extravagance, and Venezuelans happily shell out twice the amount they pay for beef.

The flavor, locals say, is more fish than meat because capybaras survive mostly on aquatic grasses. Capybara is almost always dried, salted, and shredded. The prepared "fish" goes into everything from soup to casseroles to empanadas.

How to try it

Venezuela's national dish is pabellón criollo: shredded beef, rice, black beans, and fried plantains. During Lent, capybara often replaces the beef. In Caracas, try traditional Venezuelan restaurants such as La Cocina de Francy and La Gorda.

Glorious Lent Cheating

In 1522, Zurich pastor Ulrich Zwingli was arrested for attending a sausage dinner during the Lenten fast. To be clear, the pastor had not actually eaten any sausage—simply witnessing the act was crime enough.

Zwingli defended his behavior by citing the Bible, which never actually prohibits meat during Lent. Meat fasting was a 4th-century invention of the Catholic Church, a tradition with a long and elaborate history of loopholes, fishy interpretations, and freewheeling bishops. Here are some Catholic Church–sanctioned meat alternatives that keep the faithful from being arrested or shamed.

MOCK EGG

In the Middle Ages, all animal products including dairy were forbidden during Lent. On these days, chefs had to get creative, channeling the power of almonds to bind pastry, thicken sauces, and make an eerie approximation of a hard-boiled egg. A 1430 recipe book instructed chefs to fill an empty chicken's egg with a mixture of almond-milk-based jelly and a crunchy almond center, dyed yellow with saffron and ginger. By most accounts they were nearly inedible.

DOLPHINS

The medieval German word for dolphin is merswin, or "pig of the ocean." The term was likely a way to excuse the fact that dolphins are warm-blooded, like God himself, and therefore probably prohibited on days of meat abstinence. But they came from the sea, so for a while, they were Lent-approved. Dolphin sausages were a trendy choice year-round for posh British families, as were dolphin roasts.

BARNACLE GEESE

This black-and-white goose, which breeds above the arctic circle and migrates to Europe for the winter, confused bird-watchers of the 13th century, who never saw a nest. Unaware of seasonal migration, they hatched a theory that the geese were born not from eggs but from barnacles that fell into the ocean off driftwood or rocks. And a goose that hatched in the ocean? Well, that was definitely a fish.

ALLIGATOR

In New Orleans, where alligator is a popular protein, the Catholic community hoped they could still enjoy their gator sausage, gumbo, and jambalaya during the Lenten fast. To be sure, in 2010 a parishioner wrote to the archbishop of New Orleans, who assured them: "God has created a magnificent creature that is important to the state of Louisiana, and it is considered seafood."

BEAVER

When the Europeans arrived in North America, two of their primary objectives were to collect as many beaver pelts as possible and to convert the local population to Catholicism. The locals liked to eat the beaver meat, which was convenient for the Europeans, who only cared for the skin. In a colonialist two-for-one, the 17th-century bishop of Quebec granted Lent keepers permission to eat the semiaquatic rodent, hereby a fish, to make the religious holiday more accommodating to new converts. Some modern-day Missourians still eat beaver as a meat substitute.

CORNED BEEF

In Ireland and Irish-heavy parts of America, when Saint Patrick's Day falls during Lent, certain exceptions must be made. The traditional meal of corned beef is difficult to reclassify, as cows spend so little time in the ocean. But a benevolent God, many countrymen argue, would never dream of keeping the Irish from their national celebration meal, and the archbishop of Ireland agrees. Depending on how the calendar falls, sometimes beef is allowed during the meatless fast.

Antarctica

W hen explorer Ernest Shackleton's crew ventured across Antarctica in the early 1900s, they dined on old army biscuits soaked with seawater and meat-and-fat energy bars (page 246). Today, an Antarctic researcher can tuck into seared scallops with black pudding at the British Rothera Research Station, snag some nagashi somen (page 133) at Japan's Shōwa Station, or grab a Crown Royal cocktail at the American Amundsen-Scott South Pole Station.

With approximately 4,400 summer residents and 1,100 winter residents, representing 31 countries and spread across 40 active permanent research stations, Antarctica is an increasingly busy place. And for the researchers scattered across the continent, from geologists at India's Maitri Station to ecologists at Italy's Zucchelli Station, food is a point of pride—and a way to break the monotony of life at an icebound research facility.

Because most stations get their entire supply of "freshies" only once a year (supplemented by a few occasional greenhouse veggies), creative and careful supply management is a must for Antarctic chefs. For example, by using the age-old technique of oiling the shells of fresh eggs, creating a protective barrier to contamination, chefs can make their precious supply last all year.

Lucky stations are quite close to one another, just a brisk walk away. At the Chilean Villa Las Estrellas base and craving Chinese food? Throw on a parka and dash over to China's Great Wall Station for the best peppery chicken on the continent.

BASE STATION *Cuisine*

1 ZUCCHELLI STATION • ITALY

At Zucchelli Station, time is measured not in weeks, but in pizzas. Antarctica is a land without day or night, so the passage of time becomes difficult to track. But at Zucchelli, you know it's Saturday when it's pizza day. So don't be surprised when a researcher tells you they've been stationed at Zucchelli for "seven pizzas."

2 MCMURDO STATION'S SOUTHERN EXPOSURE BAR • UNITED STATES

For the best party on Antarctica, join the people who keep McMurdo Station running at Southern Exposure. A bar with an interior indistinguishable from that of a Wisconsin dive, this watering hole is a mixing pot of carpenters, ice tractor drivers, and scientists who need a drink after a long, cold day. Smoking is allowed here, since stepping outside for a cigarette isn't recommended.

3 GREAT WALL STATION • CHINA

The Chinese Great Wall Station has a reputation for incredible food, so much so that researchers from other stations will gear up and venture out across the ice just to eat there. Just a short walk (less than a mile!) or snowmobile ride from the Argentinian, Brazilian, Chilean, Polish, Russian, South Korean, Uruguayan, and other Chinese stations, the Great Wall outpost has something no other station can boast: a team of culinary professors and students who have been returning for years to cook for the researchers posted there—and a hydroponic greenhouse that provides the Chinese chefs with fresh vegetables

China's Great Wall Station boasts a hydroponic greenhouse.

long after the other stations have run out.

4 CONCORDIA STATION EUROPEAN UNION

Run by Italian and French agencies, Concordia Station has a serious culinary reputation to uphold. While its researchers are testing Martian travel conditions, its chef is busy making foie gras, Yorkshire pudding, and chicken Parmesan, all served with a side of French wine. To become the chef at Concordia Station, candidates enter a lottery. Incredible chefs from around the world apply, and the winner gets the chance to go work day and night, with limited ingredients, in the most remote place on the planet. Of course, few other chefs can claim that Lonely Planet called

Concordia Station

their food the best cuisine on an entire continent.

5 SHŌWA STATION • JAPAN

At the Japanese Shōwa Station, the meal marking the end of an expedition is often held outdoors. What better meal to serve than nagashi somen, or cold noodles served in flowing water? Normally plucked with chopsticks as they flow by in a bamboo water slide, in Antarctica the noodles are served flowing through a channel cut right into the ice. Picture an Olympic luge track, only with noodles in place of athletes. It wasn't the only inventive food served at Shōwa Station. Akuma no onigiri, or "devil's rice balls," a mixture of edible algae, fried tempura batter, and rice, was invented by the station's chef before becoming a popular convenience store snack back in Japan.

6 VILLA LAS ESTRELLAS • CHILE

One of the stations built closest to the tip of South America, Villa Las Estrellas is part research station, part military base, and part town. It's the largest of two civilian settlements on Antarctica and home to most of the very few children who live on the continent. Like most other kids, the 21 youngsters who live with their families at Villa Las Estrellas go to school, play games, and enjoy the kid-friendly meals of mashed potatoes, chicken, and Fanta soda that the chef offers up.

7 DAVIS STATION • AUSTRALIA

Each person at Australia's Davis Station is allocated more than a pound of Vegemite per year. It may be just a tad more than is needed; visiting researchers often leave with an extra jar of the thick, salty, dark brown spread in their luggage.

8 ROTHERA RESEARCH STATION UNITED KINGDOM

On Saturday evenings, white tablecloths and candles elevate the normally mundane dining room at Rothera Research Station. Wine, bread baskets, and cheese plates are part of the impressive food offered by the chef. Dinner can stretch up to 12 courses and includes dishes such as seared scallops with black pudding and apple. As the kitchen pantry starts to thin out over the year, the chef haggles with other stations, trading British staples for a broader range of ingredients, such as antelope meat from the South Africans or peanut butter from the Americans.

9 HENRYK ARCTOWSKI STATION POLAND

Arctowski Station prides itself on serving a traditional Polish Easter breakfast, complete with a pot of schmaltz (rendered chicken fat), bread, cold cuts, plates of sausages (including wurst-like links and blood sausages), head cheese, mustard, and borscht and featuring the exchange of elaborately decorated pisanka eggs.

10 MAITRI STATION • INDIA

Maitri's 24/7 convenience store, well stocked with sweet and salty snacks (including namkeen, papads, and other goodies from famous Indian snack manufacturer Haldiram), means researchers can satisfy their cravings at any hour of the day. No money is required—it's all on the house.

11 JANG BOGO STATION SOUTH KOREA

The brand-new Jang Bogo Station came with hot-plate stations ready to serve up piping-hot Korean pork and BBQ prawns. International researchers with a high tolerance for spicy food preferred.

12 VERNADSKY STATION • UKRAINE

Originally the British Faraday Station, this research base was taken over by Ukraine in 1996. The Ukrainians renamed it Vernadsky (in honor of one of that country's most distinguished scientists), redecorated the station's bar, and made three-dollar vodka the signature drink.

ACKNOWLEDGMENTS

Bringing this book to life required incredible orchestration of teamwork and wizardry. Luckily, we were blessed with a highly skilled team of magicians at Workman Publishing, who helped us transform a concept about wonder and food into a big, beautiful book. Thank you to Suzie Bolotin, Maisie Tivnan, Janet Vicario, and Dan Reynolds for their unwavering support, enthusiasm, and wisdom. For introducing this book to the world, we are thankful to the inimitable marketing team of Rebecca Carlisle, Chloe Puton, and Moira Kerrigan. Many thanks as well to the keen eyes and creative minds of Amanda Hong, Kate Karol, Barbara Peragine, Claire McKean, Anne Kerman, Sophia Reith, Aaron Clendening, Doug Wolff, Sun Robinson-Smith, Analucia Zepeda, Eric Wiley, Alan Berry Rhys, and Rachel Krohn.

Gastro Obscura is the creation of countless talented and curious people, many of whom we get to call colleagues. Thank you to Alex Mayyasi, Sam O'Brien, Anne Ewbank, and Rachel Rummel, whose fingerprints are on every page of this book. To the unflappable Marc Haeringer, who kept this project on a years-long tightrope: You are the unsung hero of all Atlas Obscura books.

We are grateful to everyone at Atlas Obscura who tracked down a remarkable food and contributed to this book: Reina Gattuso, Leigh Chavez Bush, Rohini Chaki, Abbey Perreault, Luke Fater, Natasha Frost, Kerry Wolfe, Eric Grundhauser, Meg Neal, Cara Giaimo, Matt Taub, Paula Mejia, Josh Foer, Samir Patel, Sarah Laskow, Vittoria Traverso, Ike Allen, Michael Inscoe, Abi Inman, Samantha Chong, Larissa Hayden, Michael Harshman, Anika Burgess, David Plotz, Ella Morton, Tyler Cole, Tao Tao Holmes, and Sommer Mathis. To Lisa Gross, Alexa Harrison, and Kit Sudol: Thank you for being Gastro Obscura's champions.

Most important, this book would not be possible without the writers, users, and contributors who make Atlas Obscura the treasure trove it is. We are inspired each day by what you find and share with us.

CECILY: Dylan, your magnetic energy, creativity, and genuine sense of wonder has left a huge stamp on my brain and heart: Thank you for being our inexhaustible buoy. Marc, thank you for keeping me sane and fed, for supporting me when I needed it most, and for being simply the best; know that I will forever think of this book as our child. Alex, thank you for your tenacious vision and care, your steady hand, and your emergency supply of squid ink. Thank you to Sam for the heroic guidance, to Rachel for throwing me perfect sentences like alley-oops, and to Anne, who pulls astonishing things from the internet like no one I've ever met. Thank you also to Ella for showing me the way. Finally, thank you, Read, for patiently listening to all my obscure food knowledge for the last two years and remaining married to me.

DYLAN: Like *Atlas Obscura* that came before it, this book is the product of many people. First and foremost the users and contributors of Atlas Obscura and Gastro Obscura: It is your unending curiosity that inspires us to keep exploring the world. To Reina Gattuso, Leigh Chavez Bush, Rohini Chaki, Abbey Perreault, Luke Fater, Natasha Frost, Paula Mejia, and many more, you are all immensely talented writers and editors, and you have shared culinary wonders with us that I could scarcely have imagined. We wouldn't have been able to serve this dish without Rachel Rummel, Annie Ewbank, Sam O'Brien, and Alex Mayyasi—you are all head chefs of this restaurant, and your dedication to making *Gastro Obscura* into something great shines through this book. Sommer Mathis and Lisa Gross, thank you both for your sage advice and for help guiding this project. Josh Foer, none of this would exist without you. Marc Haeringer, you are everyone's rock. To everyone at Workman: Susan, Dan, Maisie, Rebecca, Janet, thank you for taking a chance on us in the first place and for doing it again with *Gastro*. Saving the best for last: Cecily, you bring joy, delight, and brilliance to all that you do, and this book is the epitome of that generous spirit. I count myself extremely lucky to have my name on a book next to yours.

Thank you to the following writers who wrote entries for *Gastro Obscura*: Tatiana Harkiolakis, Susan van Allen, James Rudd, Susie Armitage, Jared Rydelek, Awanthi Vardaraj, Sarah Corsa, James Jeffrey, Shannon Thomson, Elphas Ngugi, Amanda Leigh Lichtenstein, Ximena Larkin, Tony Dunnell, Zoe Baillageon, Leah Feiger, Richard Collett, Mariellen Ward, Tiffany Ammerman, Jennifer Walker, Jennifer Nalewicki, Megan Iacobini de Fazio, Faith Roswell, Jacob Wallace, and Karissa Chen.

We are grateful to our entire community of users, in particular: AaronNetsky, Max Cortesi, mjespuiva, sarahcorsa, Rob, trevorxtravesty, Rachel, giraffe1541, capemarsh, jessemiers, Annetta Black, lewblank, cnkollbocker, Dr Alan P Newman, hovpl, Dampo, hrnick, Tawsam, moroccanzest, ewayte, meganjamer, canuck, Gastropod, hfritzmartinez, CPilgrim, Megan8777, GizzysMama, Leslie McIntyre, Michelle Enemark, e1savage, rebeccaclara, Dana Stabenow, and Chris Kudrich.

The following stories were first published on Gastro Obscura's website, then adapted for the book. We are immensely grateful to these talented writers.

EUROPE:
- "The Club Devoted to Celebrating Great Britain's Great Puddings" by Lottie Gross
- "How a Special Diet Kept the Knights Templar Fighting Fit" by Natasha Frost
- "The Worst Freelance Gig in History Was Being the Village Sin Eater" by Natalie Zarrelli
- "Inside the World's Only Sourdough Library" by Anne Ewbank

- "Remembering When Runners Drank Champagne as an Energy Drink" by Katherine Alex Beaven
- "The Strange History of Royals Testing Food for Poison with Unicorn Horn" by Anne Ewbank
- One of Florence's Wine Windows Is Open Once More" by Lisa Harvey
- "Gladiator Diets Were Carb-Heavy, Fattening, and Mostly Vegetarian" by Ryleigh Nucilli
- "The Ancient Walled Gardens Designed to Nurture a Single Citrus Tree" by Kristan Lawson
- "When the Soviet Union Paid Pepsi in Warships" by Anne Ewbank
- "Why the World's Greatest Toasts Happen in Georgia" by Pesha Magid
- "The Brief, Wondrous, High-Flying Era of Zeppelin Dining" by Natasha Frost
- "On Restaurant Day in Helsinki, Anyone Can Open an Eatery, Anywhere" by Karen Burshtein
- "A Banana Grows in Iceland" by Kasper Friis

ASIA:
- "America's Pistachio Industry Came from a Single Seed" by Anne Ewbank
- "How Bootleg Fast Food Conquered Iran" by Sarra Sedghi
- "The Prickly Symbolism of Cactus Fruit in Israel and Palestine" by Miriam Berger
- "For Thousands of Years, People Have Been Obsessed with Fat-Tailed Sheep" by Anne Ewbank
- "The Festival Where Millions of Women Prepare a Feast for a Goddess" by Jessica Gingrich
- "How Mumbai's Dabbawalas Deliver 200,000 Homemade Meals a Day" by Akanksha Singh
- "The Restaurant Reconstructing Recipes That Died with the Ottoman Empire" by Jen Rose Smith
- "The Chinese City Famous for Eggs with Two Yolks" by Anne Ewbank
- "The Mandatory Canteens of Communist China" by Hunter Lu
- "At Sea on Taiwan's Last Fire-Fishing Boats" by Leslie Nguyen-Okwu
- "The Special Stew at the Heart of Sumo Wrestling" by Natasha Frost
- "The Hidden History of the Nutmeg Island That Was Traded for Manhattan" by Mark Hay
- "How Building Churches out of Egg Whites Transformed Filipino Desserts" by Richard Collett

AFRICA:
- "The Egyptian Egg Ovens Considered More Wondrous Than the Pyramids" by Vittoria Traverso
- "In 1930s Tunisia, French Doctors Feared a 'Tea Craze' Would Destroy Society" by Nina Studer
- "The Language Used Only by Lake Kivu's Fishermen" by Leah Feiger
- "To Revive This Royal Music, Ugandans Had to Grow New Instruments" by Natalia Jidovanu

OCEANIA:
- "After Decades of Being Ignored, a Nut from 20-Pound Pine Cones Is Back on Australian Menus" by Laura Kiniry
- "The Curious Case of August Engelhardt, Leader of a Coconut-Obsessed Cult" by Zoë Bernard
- "Australia's Growing Camel Meat Trade Reveals a Hidden History of Early Muslim Migrants" by Reina Gattuso
- "A Japanese Sculptor's Tribute to Wild Rice Covers an Australian Floodplain" by Selena Hoy
- "When the Māori First Settled New Zealand, They Hunted Flightless, 500-Pound Birds" by Anne Ewbank
- "The Livestock Living at the End of the World" by Abbey Perreault

CANADA:
- "The Canadian Towns That Icelanders Visit for a Taste of Their Past" by Karen Burshtein
- "Meet the 81-Year-Old Greek-Canadian Inventor of the Hawaiian Pizza" by Dan Nosowitz

USA:
- "Remembering 'Brownie Mary,' San Francisco's Marijuana Pioneer" by Anne Ewbank
- "Indigenous Cuisine Is Being Served in the Back of a Berkeley Bookstore" by Richard Foss
- "How Alaska's Roadkill Gets a Second Life as Dinner" by Mark Hay
- "Americans Have Planted So Much Corn That It's Changing the Weather" by Eric J. Wallace
- "When Eating Crow Was an American Food Trend" by Anne Ewbank
- "The Burmese Restaurant at the Heart of 'Chindianapolis'" by Mar Nwe Aye and Charlotte Chadwick
- "America's First Butter Sculptor Was an Artist and a Celebrity" by Cara Giaimo
- "How a Tiny Wisconsin Island Became the World's Biggest Consumer of Bitters" by Leigh Kunkel
- "The Mysterious Bounty of Mobile Bay's Midnight Jubilees" by Anna Marlis Burgard
- "The Underground Kitchen That Funded the Civil Rights Movement" by Jessica Gingrich
- "Competitive Eating Was Even More Gluttonous and Disgusting in the 17th Century" by Eric Grundhauser
- "Drink Up at the Home-Museum Displaying over 10,000 Beer Steins" by Eric J. Wallace
- "The Family That's Sold New York Mock Meats for Decades" by Priya Krishna
- "The Lost Lingo of New York City's Soda Jerks" by Natasha Frost
- "The Scholar Mapping America's Forgotten Feminist Restaurants" by Reina Gattuso
- "The 'Croos' That Haul 50-Pound Packs to Feed Hungry Hikers" by Courtney Hollands

LATIN AMERICA
- "Like Avocados? Thank This Giant Extinct Sloth" by Anne Ewbank
- "Inside a Brazilian Chapel Made out of Wine" by Danielle Bauter
- "How a Brewer and the Government Killed Colombia's Ancestral Drink" by Lauren Evans

COVER CREDITS

Front Cover Credits (In Clockwise Order): (Pigeon Houses) mauritius images GmbH/Alamy Images; (Donut) Elena Milenova/Alamy Images; (Filipina Dancer) Mariano Sayno/Moment/Getty Images; (Black-headed Gull) Nature Photographers Ltd/Alamy Images; (Bird Pie) Donna LeBel /Atlas Obscura; (Australian Emu) Anan Kaewkhammul/ Alamy Images; (Bunya Pine Cone) downunder/Alamy Images; (The Ghan Passenger Train) MMphotos/Alamy Images; (Steaks with Pitchfork) Layne Kennedy/Corbis NX/Getty Images; (Goldfish Candy "Amezaiku") Ayumi H/ Shutterstock.

Back Cover Credits (In Clockwise Order): (Honey) RTimages/Alamy Images; (Yakut Woman) Tatiana Gasich/ Shutterstock; (Dhow Boat) Robert Harding/Alamy Images; (Breakfast Sandwich) Aaron Bastin/Alamy Stock Photo; (Ukadiche Modak) RBB/Moment/Getty Images; (Antique Print) Antiqua Print Gallery/Alamy Images; (Horse Rider) ZUMA Press, Inc./Alamy Images; (Bottle Cap) Jpbarrass at English Wikipedia/Public domain.

EUROPE

AGE fotostock america, Inc: Picture-Alliance/dpa p. 79 (right). **Alamy:** Mauricio Abreu p. 32 (top); ACORN 1 p. 23 (top); agefotostock 76 (top); Agencja Fotograficzna Caro p. 48 (bottom); ams images p. 42 (top); Yi Ci Ang p. 52 (top); Arco Images GmbH p. 67 (bottom right and top); Chronicle p. 66 (bottom left); COMPAGNON Bruno/SAGAPHOTO.COM p. 72; Contraband Collection p. 21 (top); Guy Corbishley p. 61 (left); Luis Dafos p. 50 (top); Design Pics Inc p. 74 (top); Bertie Ditch p. 16 (top); Anton Eine p. 45; David R. Frazier Photolibrary, Inc. p. 44 (bottom); Nick Gammon p. 16 (bottom); Clive Helm p. 20; L A Heusinkveld p. 35; imageBROKER pp. 25, 57 (bottom); INTERFOTO p. 56 (bottom left & bottom right); ITAR-TASS News Agency p. 62 (top); Andrey Khrobostov p. 58 (bottom); Dorling Kindersley p. 55 (bottom); kpzfoto p. 46 (top); Josef Kubes p. 46 (bottom); Andrew Lockie p. 2; Lordprice Collection p. 3 (top left & top middle); Marcin Marszal p. 52 (bottom); Steven McAuley p. 13 (top); David L. Moore—ISL p. 75 (top); Jeff Morgan 11 p. 40 (bottom left); Niday Picture Library p. 39 (bottom); Nordicphotos pp. 66–67 (background); OlegMit p. 63; PA Images p. 15 (top); Panther Media GmbH p. 22 (bottom); Massimo Parisi p. 41 (top middle); Amir Paz p. 65 (bottom); Photononstop p. 21 (bottom); PicoCreek p. 69; Pictorial Press Ltd pp. 3 (top right), 11 (bottom); Picture Partners pp. 76 (bottom), 80 (middle right); Graham Prentice p. 8; Prisma by Dukas Presseagentur GmbH p. 5; Kay Roxby p. 14; Russell p. 6 (bottom left); Neil Setchfield p. 9; Dmytro Synelnychenko p. 67 (bottom left); The Advertising Archives p. 41 (bottom left); Marc Tielemans p. 1; Trinity Mirror/Mirrorpix p. 19; Lillian Tveit p. 79 (left); unknown 56–57 (background); Martin Williams p. 10 (top left); Naci Yavuz (fogbird) p. 66 (top); Michael Zech p. 71; ZUMA Press, Inc. pp. 27 (bottom), 74 (bottom); Yurii Zushchyk p. 61 (right). **Can Stock Photo:** Olga Berlet p. 22 (top); drstokvektor p. 57 (top); santi0103 p. 28. **Dreamstime:** Lenutaidi p. 54 (top); Aleksandra Suzi p. 68 (top). **Getty Images:** Franco Banfi/WaterFrame

p. 31; Bettmann/Contributor p. 48 (top); coldsnowstorm/ iStock p. 53 (bottom left); Denis Doyle/Getty Images News p. 44 (top); Denis Doyle/Stringer p. 18; Alexander Farnsworth/iStock p. 75 (bottom left); Katie Garrod/ AWL Images p. 53 (top); Dorling Kindersley p. 56 (top); Peter Lewis/Stone p. 7; Xurxo Lobato/Getty Images News p. 43; Pronina_Marina/iStock p. 53 (bottom right); New York Daily News Archive/Contributor p. 24; Stefano Oppo/Cultura Exclusive/Publisher Mix p. 29; photovs/ iStock p. 51; Yelena Strokin/Moment Open p. 59; SVF2/ Universal Images Group p. 55 (top); vandervelden/iStock Unreleased p. 66 (bottom right); Alvaro German Vilela p. 32 (bottom); Horacio Villalobos/Corbis News p. 40 (bottom right); Peter Williams p. 6 (bottom right). **Shutterstock.com:** Ismael Silva Alves p. 38 (top); Anna_ Andre p. 47; bonchan p. 38 (bottom); Bruno Tatiana Chekryzhova p. 41 (bottom right); Formatoriginal p. 39 (top); Tatiana Gasich p. 60 (bottom); Toni Genes p. 40 (bottom right above); Dimitris Legakis p. 80 (bottom); Hanna Loban p. 62 (bottom); Natalia Mylova p. 37; nelen p. 49; Korea Panda p. 75 (middle); ronstik p. 57 (middle).

Wikimedia Commons: The following images are used under a Creative Commons Attribution CC BY-SA 4.0 License (https://csreativecommons.org/licenses/by-sa/4.0/deed.en) and belong to the following Wikimedia Commons users: Cholbon p. 60 (top); Raimond Spekking p. 68 (bottom); Sergei Frolov p 54 (bottom). The following image is used under a Creative Commons Attribution CC BY-SA 3.0 (https://creativecommons.org/licenses/by-sa/3.0/deed.en) and belongs to the following Wikimedia Commons user: Holger Ellgaard p. 78. **Public Domain**: pp. 13 (bottom), 23 (bottom).

Courtesy of Atlas Obscura Contributors:
Jennifer Adhya p. 42 (bottom); Anja Bbarte Telin, Produktionskollektivet p. 80 (top right); HaliPuu p. 69 (top); Capemarsh p. 4; Deutsches Zusatzstoff Museum p. 80 (middle left); Finnmark Sauna/finnmarksauna.com p. 65 (top); Lisa Harvey p. 27 (top left and top right); Frank Schuiling p. 36 (top and bottom); Jesse Miers/ Jessemiers p. 10 (top right); Andrea Fernández @lvfoodgasm p. 75 (bottom right); Emiliano Ruprah p. 30; Karl De Smedt p. 17 (bottom); Starkenberger p. 17 (top); Trinenp23 p. 64.

ASIA

Adobe Stock: milosk50 p. 99. **Alamy:** agefotostock p.158 (top); Kiekowski Anton/Hemis Fr. p. 161; Burhan Ay p. 110; Walter Bibikow/Danita Delimont Creative p. 95 (top right); Frank Bienewald pp. 102–103 (spread); Nattanai Chimjanon p. 148; Chronicle p. 137 (bottom); Robert Cicchetti p. 154; Zaneta Cichawa p. 115; Iconic Cornwall p. 125 (top); Samantha Crimmin p. 127; Dar1930/Panther Media GmbH p. 157 (bottom); Michele Falzone/Jon Arnold Images Ltd p. 93; Oleg Fedotov p. 84 (top); Guenter Fischer/Alamy Stock Photo p. 95 (top left); Fotosearch/Unlisted Images Inc. p. 131 (bottom); Stephen Frost p. 121 (top); Biswarup Ganguly p. 90 (top right); Rania Hamed p. 91 (top); Hemis pp. 113, 125 (bottom); Historic Collection p. 162 (bottom); Historical image collection by Bildagentur-online p. 87 (bottom); Jim Hubatka p. 101 (top); Janny2 p. 91 (bottom); Peter

Jordan p. 94 (bottom left); Evgeniy Kalinovskiy p. 119 (top); Sergii Koval pp. 137 (top), 139 (bottom left); Eric Lafforgue p. 86 (bottom); Loop Images Ltd pp. 126–127 (spread); Volodko Marina p. 92 (top); Jenny Matthews p. 107 (top); Maria Medvedeva p. 81; Trevor Mogg p. 135 (bottom); Tuul and Bruno Morandi pp. 82 (top), 87 (top), 117 (top); Frederick Morbe p. 130; Kirrily Morris p. 89 (top); Arthur Mustafa p. 88; National Geographic Image Collection p. 132 (bottom); Niday Picture Library p. 138 (bottom); Araya Pacharabandit p. 140 (inset); Panther Media GmbH p. 94 (bottom right); Pictorial Press Ltd p. 122 (bottom); Picture Partners p. 97 (bottom); Premaphotos p. 157 (top); Paul Quayle pp. 106, 107 (bottom); RealyEasyStar/Daniele Bellucci p. 144 (bottom); Realy Easy Star/Tullio Valente p. 105 (top); Simon Reddy p. 139 (top); Frederic Reglain p. 136 (bottom); Karla Rosenberg p. 158 (bottom); Neil Satcherfield p. 169; Juergen Schonnop p. 111; searagen p. vi; dave stamboulis p. 149 (top); Maxim Tatarinov p. 92 (bottom); Top Photo Corporation p. 118; Leisa Tyler p. 156; Leisa Tyler p. 156 (inset); Nopadol Uengbunchoo p. 139 (bottom right); Lucas Vallecillos p. 104; World Discovery p. 134; YAY Media AS p. 152; ZUMA Press, Inc pp. 120, 168. **Can Stock Photo:** kaiskynet p. 101 (bottom); Stasevich p. 126. **Depositphotos:** Postnikov p. 108. **Dreamstime:** Jasmina p. 85 (inset); Phloenphoto p. 160. **Getty Images:** bonchan/iStock p. 83 (bottom left); Buena Vista Images/Photodisc p. 95(bottom); enviromantic/E+ p. 167 (bottom); gyro/iStock p. 155 (bottom); Jethuynh/Moment p. 170 (bottom); Kaveh Kazemi/Getty Images News p. 84 (bottom); Junko Kimura/Getty Images News p. 142; Kyodo News p. 141; Jordan Lye/Moment p. 165 (top); Douglas MacDonald/Moment p. 153; John Moore/Getty Images News p. 85; Nastasic/DigitalVision Vectors p. 121 (bottom); Zhang Peng/LightRocket p. 122 (top); Andrey Pozharskiy/Moment p. 124; Andrew Rowat/The Image Bank p. 170 (top); Mariano Sayno/Moment p. 163; Pankaj & Insy Shah p. 94 (top); Morten Falch Sortland/Moment Open p. 133; Jasen Yang/500px p. 129 (top); zhouyousifang/Moment p. 116. **Pexels.com:** Ali Yasser Arwand p. 96. **Shutterstock.com:** AP/Shutterstock p. 147 (top); dapperland p. 129 (bottom); Vladimir Goncharenko p. 83 (top); Ayumi H pp. 135 (top left & top right); inforim p. 150; Attila Jandi p. 86 (top); Budimir Jevtic p. 90 (top left); Melvin Jong p. 155 (top); jreika p. 139 (middle); milestone p. 140; Dolly MJ p. 159; Elena Moiseeva p. 109 (top); Myibean p. 97 (top); Prabhas Roy p. 109 (bottom).

Wikimedia Commons: The following images are used under a Creative Commons Attribution CC BY 2.0 (https://creativecommons.org/licenses/by/2.0/deed.en) and belong to the following Wikimedia Commons users: Dirtsailor2003/Flickr p. 151; Kerri-Jo Stewart p.114; sam.romilly p. 165 (bottom). The following image is used under a Creative Commons Attribution CC BY 2.5 (https://creativecommons.org/licenses/by/2.5 /deed.en) and belongs to the following Wikimedia Commons user: wjlee4284 p. 146. The following image is used under a Creative Commons Attribution CC BY-SA 3.0 (https://creativecommons.org/licenses/by-sa/3.0/deed.en) and belongs to the following Wikimedia Commons user:

Ramon FVelasquez p.164. **Public Domain:** 123, Jpbarrass at English Wikipedia/Public domain p. 147 (bottom).

Courtesy of Atlas Obscura Contributors: Ariunna p. 145 (bottom); Asitane Restaurant p. 112; Richard Collett p. 162 (top); Beth Dixson p. 83 (bottom right); Emilieknss p. 119 (bottom); ESSI p. 131 (top); Tony Lin p. 117 (bottom); Jasmine Minori p. 166; SHOPINISTA206 p. 130 (middle left); Tsatsral p. 145 (top); Wara art festival p. 144 (top).

AFRICA
Alamy: Oriol Alamany p. 192 (bottom); Artokoloro Quint Lox Limited p. 173 (top and bottom); BonkersAboutTravel p. 171; Charles O. Cecil p. 202 (top); François-Olivier Dommergues p. 189 (top); dpa picture alliance p. 184 (bottom); Oscar Espinosa p. 198; Hemis 210; Peter Horree p. 195 (top); Images of Africa Photobank p. 206; Sergii Koval p. 191 (bottom); Eric Lafforgue pp. 188 (bottom right), 189 (bottom), 197 (bottom); Lanmas p. 174; mauritius images GmbH pp. 172, 175 (bottom); Andrew McConnell p. 188 (top right); Ville Palonen p. 179 (bottom); Simon Reddy p. 208; Edwin Remsberg p. 209; robertharding p. 201; Grant Rooney p. 194; Grant Rooney Premium p. 190 (bottom right and bottom left); Surachet Shotivaranon p. 187 (bottom); Friedrich Stark p. 187 (top); Sklifas Steven pp. 176–177 (spread); Leon Swart p. 207; The Advertising Archives p.193 (bottom); The Yarvin Kitchen p. 188 (top left); V&A Images p.175 (top); Ivan Vdovin p. 200 (bottom); John Warburton-Lee Photography p. 205; World History Archive p. 197 (top); Vladimir Zuev p. 180. **Can Stock Photo:** Icefront p. 196 (bottom). **Getty Images:** Dark_Eni/iStock p. 176 (bottom left); Education Images/Universal Images Group; Frances Linzee Gordon/Lonely Planet Images p. 188 (bottom left); Isaac Kasamani p. 202 (bottom). **Matteo Bertolino:** p.185.

Wikimedia Commons: The following images are used under a Creative Commons Attribution CC BY-SA 4.0 (https://creativecommons.org/licenses/by-sa/4.0/deed.en) and belong to the following Wikimedia Commons users: Blimeo p. 204 (top); Kwameghana p. 186. The following images are used under a Creative Commons Attribution CC BY-SA 3.0 (https://creativecommons.org/licenses/by -sa/3.0/deed.en) and belong to the following Wikimedia Commons users: John Hill p. 177 (bottom); Kgjerstad p. 183; Library of Congress/LC-DIG-PPMSC-06041 p. 181; MiracleFruitFarm p.182; Stephenwanjau p.195 (bottom).

Courtesy of Atlas Obscura Contributors: African Horseback Safaris p. 204 (bottom); Leah Beth Feiger p. 200 (top); Natalia Jidovanu p. 203; Rachel Rummel pp. 178, 179 (top).

OCEANIA
Alamy: Sergio Azenha p. 225 (bottom); Susanna Bennett p. 222 (top); Blue Pebble p. 213 (top); Pat Canova p. 215 (plant); Clearviewimages RF p. 217 (top); Danler pp. 214–215 (background); David Tipling Photo Library p. 237 (top and bottom); EB Images p. 225 (top); Kevin Hellon p. 226; Hemis p. 236; imageBROKER

p. 239 (bottom); Anan Kaewkhammul pp. 227 (top, bottom left, bottom right); Steve Lindridge p. 211; MMphotos p. 212 (inset top, inset bottom); Ozimages p. 221 (bottom); Graham Prentice p. 225 (middle spot); RTimages p. 215 (honey); Dan Santillo NZ p. 230 (top and bottom), Steve Taylor ARPS p. 215 (bottom); TGB p. 228; Wendy White p. 238 (top left); Ray Wilson pp. 218–219 (background); Szefei Wong p. 235 (bottom). **Getty Images:** HomoCosmicos/iStock Editorial pp. 238–239 (background); Dianne Manson/Getty Images Entertainment p. 234; Newspix p. 222 (bottom); Alex Wang/iStock p. 216; www.bensmethers.co.uk/Moment Open p. 240. **Roving Tortoise Photos:** Tui De Roy pp. 232–233 (spread).

Wikimedia Commons: The following images are used under a Creative Commons Attribution CC BY-SA 3.0 (https://creativecommons.org/licenses/by-sa/3.0/deed.en) and belong to the following Wikimedia Commons users: Bidgee p. 212 (main); Mark McIntosh p. 217 (bottom).

Courtesy of Atlas Obscura Contributors: Courtesy of Mr Takamitsu Tanabe p. 229; Freyja Bardell p. 238 (top right); Jean-Baptiste p. 239 (top); Kanesue p. 224 (middle); Olga Skomorokhova p. 223; Courtesy of Something Wild p. 221 (top); Courtesy of Taco Bell p. 224 (bottom); Allen Tiller p. 224 (top).

CANADA
Alamy: Barrett & MacKay/All Canada Photos p. 247 (bottom left); Luis Fernandez p. 242 (middle left); First Collection/Alamy Stock Photo p. 254 (top); john t. fowler p. 254 (bottom); Elena Glushchenko p. 243 (top left); Mamuka Gotsiridze p. 243 (middle left); Historical Images Archive p. 249 (top); Chris Howes/Wild Places Photography p. 253; INTERFOTO/Personalities p. 256 (top); JoeFoxBerlin/Radharc Images p. 247 (top); Brian Light p. 265 (Canadian leaf); Elena Maltenieks p. 257 (bottom right); Stephen Mcsweeny p. 244 (bottom); Jill Morgan p. 262; Panther Media GmbH p. 264; Laschon Robert Paul pp. 242, 243 (flags); Norman Pogson p. 241; Denio Rigacci p. 261 (bottom); Rick Rudnicki pp. 243 (sculpture), 246; Aleksandrs Samuilovs p. 256 (bottom left); SeaTops p. 251; SOTK2011 p. 259 (top); Petr Štepánek p. 243 (middle right); Egmont Strigl/imageBROKER p. 248; The Picture Art Collection p. 266 (bottom); Carrie Vonderhaar/Ocean Futures Society/National Geographic Images Collection p. 250 (top); Chester Voyage p. 252 (top and bottom); Evgenii Zadiraka p. 250 (bottom); Zoonar GbmH/MYCHKO p. 260; Zoonar GmbH p. 243 (top right); Denis Zubchenko pp. 242–243 (spread), 247 (fish). **Can Stock Photo:** 3dalia p. 249 (bottom); Djvstock p. 265 (inset); VasikO p. 244 (top). **Dreamstime:** Meunierd p. 263 (bottom); Sarawuth Wannasathit p. 257 (top). **Getty Images:** alpaksoy/iStock p. 243 (bottom left); Jason Gallant p. 245 (top and bottom right); Norio Kitagawa/Aflo p. 256 (bottom right); laughingmango/iStock p. 266 (top); Jordan Lye/Moment p. 242 (bottom right); Michael Powell/Photolibrary p. 242 (top left); RBB/Moment p. 242 (bottom left); semenovp/iStock p. 257 (bottom left); TG23/iStockphoto p. 243 (bottom right); Veronique de Viguerie/Reportage Archive p. 259 (bottom); Ned White, Inc./Moment p. 258.

Shutterstock.com: Darryl Brooks p. 245 (bottom); Barbara MacDonald p. 242 (top left); Ratov Maxim p. 242 (middle right); TonyNg p. 242 (top right).

Atlas Obscura Contributors: Micah Grubert Van Iderstine p. 247 (bottom right); Melissa May Thomas @melissamaythomas p. 255 (top); Felicity Roberts p. 255 (bottom).

THE UNITED STATES
Adobe Stock: lefebvre_jonathan p. 278 (bottom). **Alamy:** Roman Adamjan p. 288 (top); AF Archive p. 271 (bottom right & top left); Aaron Bastin p. 331 (bottom); Felix Choo p. 299 (gum); B Christopher p. 316; Chronicle p. 287 (bottom left); Citizen of the Planet p. 321 (bottom); David Cobb p. 273 (top left); Ian Dagnall p. 348 (top); Srdjan Draskovic p. 328 (top right); Richard Ellis pp. 325 (bottom), 326; David R. Frazier Photolibrary, Inc. p. 289 (bottom); Hector p. 287 (bottom right); Grant Helman Photography p. 292; HHelene p. 272 (bottom left); Historic Images p. 323 (bottom); Brent Hofacker pp. 286 (bottom), 302 (top); Keith Homan pp. 287 (top), 299 (bottom), 310 (bottom left); Hum Images p. 321 (top); D. Hurst p. 281 (top); IFMC p. 271 (middle right); Image Professionals GmbH pp. 302 (bottom), 342 (bottom); Jamie Pham Photography p. 330 (top); Jeffrey Isaac Greenberg 5 p. 312 (top); Christopher Jones/Alamy Stock Photo p. 340 (bottom); Volodymyr Krasyuk p. 290 (top); Ekaterina Kriminskaya p. 271 (top right); Len Collection pp. 332–333 (spread); Y. Levy p. 293 (bottom right); LianeM pp. 272–273 (background); Charles Lytton p. 324; Olekcii Mach p. 338 (Franklin); Werner Meidinger/imageBROKER p. 272 (top right); Moviestore collection Ltd p. 271 (middle left); myViewPoint p. 279; National Geographic Image Collection p. 291 (top), 204, 315; North Wind Picture Archives pp. 298–299 (background); Boyd Norton p. 288 (bottom); Ockra p. 293 (top); Steve Oehlenschlager p. 296 (bottom); George Ostertag/age footstock pp. 291 (bottom), 309; Lesley Pardoe p. 328 (bottom left); Don Paulson p. 274; Pixel-shot pp. 315 (bottom), 338 (bottom); Norbert Probst/imageBROKER p. 277 (bottom); Paul Quayle p. 293 (bottom left); Jim Richardson/National Geographic Image Collection p. 301 (top); Pierre Rochon photography p. 346; Joel Sartore/National Geographic Image Collection p. 276 (bottom); Neil Setchfield p. 277 (top left) Hakan Soderholm p. 273 (middle right); studiomode p. 271 (bottom left); suwinai sukanant p. 277 (top right); Maxim Tatarinov p. 273 (bottom right); The Picture Art Collection p. 305; Terry Thomas p. 276 (top); trekandshoot p. 267; Universal Images Group North America LLC/DeAgostini p. 286 (top); LFrank Vetere p. 329; Weizhong/www.truphotos.com p. 337 (top); Christine Whitehead p. 273 (middle left); Jonathan Yonan p. 301 (bottom), 332 (top left & top middle); Zoonar GmbH p. 271 (walnuts); ZUMA Press, Inc. p. 320 (inset). **AP/Wide World Photos:** Associated Press p. 313. **Brooklyn Grange Rooftop Farm:** p. 335; **Can Stock Photo:** anatolir p. 318 (top). **Getty Images:** Bettmann p. 299 (top); Camerique/ClassicStock p. 334; Donaldson Collection/Michael Ochs Archive p. 320 (top); Remy Gabalda/AFP p. 319; Karl Gehring/Denver Post p. 281 (bottom); Jeff Greenberg/Universal Images

Group Editorial pp. 332 (top right), 333 (waitress); Dirck Halstead/The LIFE Images Collection p. 345; Historical Picture Archive/Corbis Historical p. 290 (bottom); Phil Huber/Sports Illustrated p. 314; Layne Kennedy/Corbis NX p. 294 (bottom); Kohjiro Kinno/Sports Illustrated p. 317; Robert Landau/Corbis Historical p. 298; John Preito/Denver Post p. 333 (b/w); Joe Raedle/Hulton Archive p. 283; George Rinhart/Corbis Historical p. 308; Chip Somodevilla/Staff p. 303 (bottom); The Washington Post p. 320 (bottom); University of Southern California/ Corbis Historical p. 327. **Shutterstock.com:** Stephen Albi p. 306; Dan4Earth p. 272 (top left); Keith Homan p. 325 (top) Purplexsu p. 282; tishomir p. 268. **The Pocahontas County Chamber of Commerce:** The Pocahontas County Chamber of Commerce p. 340 (top).

Wikimedia Commons: The following images are used under a Creative Commons Attribution CC BY 2.0 (https://creativecommons.org/licenses/by/2.0/deed.en) and belong to the following Wikimedia Commons users: CGP Grey p. 297; Diçdoco p. 322 (bottom); K. Shuyler p. 275 (middle). **Public Domain:** Boston Public Library p. 344 (bottom).

Courtesy of Atlas Obscura Contributors: Patrick Lehnherr p. 312 (bottom); Auntie_Nadine p. 278 (top); Big Cedar Lodge p. 307; makam-'ham/Cafe Ohlone p. 270 (top); Chin Brothers LLC p. 300; Michael Clifton Tran@cliftontran_ p. 342 (top); Spencer Darr/spencerdarr.com p. 284 (bottom); Dani Bittner p. 280; Jennifer Souers Chevraux p. 284 (top); Door County Visitor Bureau p. 310 (bottom right); Downstream Casino Resort p. 296 (top); Jon Hauge p. 311; Rick Heineman and Washington Island History p. 310 (bottom); Farrell Parker, D.C.-based artist p. 337 (bottom left); Mike Mehlhorn p. 344 (top); WhiskeyBristles p. 282 (inset); Pam Jarrin p. 341; Scott Sommerdorf/San Francisco Chronicle/Polaris p. 269; Stephanie Eng p. 337 (bottom right); Teakwoods p. 339.

LATIN AMERICA
AGE fotostock america, Inc: Eric Lafforgue p. 365; Helene Rogers/Art Directors & Trips Photo p. 374 (top). **Alamy:** 19th era 2 p. 353 (middle right); AGB Photo Library p. 349; Album p. 354; Antiqua Print Gallery p. 389 (bottom); Jennika Argent p. 384 (top); Lee Avison p. 361 (top); Suzanne Bosman p. 380; Marc Bruxelle p. 375 (top); Olena Danileiko p. 386 (bottom right); dbimages p. 379 (bottom); Adam Eastland p. 367 (bottom); Foto Arena LTDA p. 385 (bottom); Tim Gainey p. 392; Nicholas Gill p. 396; Vladislav Gudovskiy p. 363 (bottom); Hemis p. 364 (bottom); Andrii Hrytsenko p. 353 (bottom left); Tommy Huynh p. 367 (top left); Iconotec p. 369 (top); Idea studio pp. 402–403 (Background and inset); JG Photography p. 359 (top); Jesse Kraft p. 403 (top); Jason Langley p. 400; Y.Levy p. 404; Lordprice Collection p. 367 (top right); Tatsiana Mastabai p. 364 (top); Anamaria Mejia p. 401 (top); Cathyrose Melloan p. 356; Raquel Mogado p. 376 (bottom left); Carlos Mora p. 399; MsFong/Stockimo p. 382; National Geographic Image Collection p. 402 (top); Nature Photographers Ltd p. 352 (bottom right); olneystudio p. 359 (bottom); Panther Media GmbH p. 387 (middle left); Pulsar Imagens p. 387 (top);

Ievgen Radchenko p. 381 (top); Simon Reddy p. 378; Ewart Rennalls p. 372 (top); Ed Rooney p. 358 (top); Andriy Sarymsakov p. 387 (bottom right); Wei Seah p. 363 (bottom); Neil Setchfield p. 355; Anton Starikov p. 371 (top); Kyoko Uchida p. 377 (bottom right); Wisnu Haryo Yudhanto p. 377 (top). **Can Stock Photo:** anatolir p. 371 (bottom); buriy p. 372 (bottom); Danler p. 366 (top); ican pp. 376–377 (background); nebojsa78 p. 395; stargatechris p. 371 (pepper). **Dreamstime:** Adolfolazo p. 361 (bottom); Jaboticaba Fotos p. 390 (middle). **Getty Images:** bonchan/iStock p. 393 (top); John Bulmer/Popperfoto p. 383; dexph119_066 p. 376 (middle); Donyanedomam/iStock p. 368; GI15702993/iStock p. 377 (bottom left); Hermsdorf/iStock p. 366 (bottom); jmillard37/iStock p. 401 (bottom); George Kalaouzis/Moment p. 384 (bottom); Dorling Kindersley p. 377 (middle); MCT/Tribune News Service p. 350; Luiz Henrique Mendes/iStock p. 390 (bottom right); Eiichi Onodera/Emi Kimata p. 376 (top); Layla Pujol/500px p. 397 (top); Jaime Razuri/AFP p. 398 (bottom); rchphoto/iStock p. 403 (middle) Alex Robinson/AWL Images p. 388; Danilo Saltarelli/iStock p. 390 (bottom left); ToprakBeyBetmen/iStock p. 393 (bottom); ullstein bild Dtl. P. 394 (bottom); Iara Venanzi/DigitalVision p. 386 (bottom left). **Shutterstock.com:** 365FOOD p. 376 (bottom right); Larisa Blinova p. 394 (top); Chai Chaiyo p. 353 (bottom right); FINNARIO p. 371 (top); Erika Kirkpatrick p. 353 (top left); Re Metau p. 369 (bottom); MicroOne p. 360 (top); Moriz p. 352 (bottom left); photomaster p. 405 (top); Pictures_for_You p. 352 (top); pixpenart p. 353 (bottom middle); rukxstockphoto p. 352 (bottom middle); Anny Ta p. 391 (top).

Wikimedia Commons: The following image is used under a Creative Commons Attribution CC BY-SA 2.0 License (https://creativecommons.org/licenses/by-sa/2.0/) and belongs to the following Wikimedia Commons user: penelope_134 p.381 (bottom). The following image is used under a Creative Commons Attribution CC BY-SA 4.0 License (https://csreativecommons.org/licenses /by-sa/4.0/deed.en) and belongs to the following Wikimedia Commons user: Koen Adams p. 401. **Public Domain**: gallerix.ru p. 363 (top).

Courtesy of Atlas Obscura Contributors: Andrew Reilly p. 375 (bottom); Danielle Bauter p. 385 (top); brunomichauxvignes p. 370 (top and bottom); Tony Dunnell p. 398 (top); Samantha O'Brien p. 351; Tastee Cheese p. 374 (bottom).

ANTARCTICA
Alamy: Imaginechina Limited p. 408 (top); Terence Mendoza pp. 410–411 (spread); Niebrugge Images p. 407; B.O'Kane p. 410 (inset); David Parker p. 409; Science History Images p. 408 (bottom); Graeme Snow pp. 408–409 (background).

Wikimedia Commons: The following images are used under a Creative Commons Attribution CC BY-SA 4.0. (https://creativecommons.org/licenses/by-sa/4.0) and belongs to the following Wikimedia Commons user: Σρτ p. 409.

INDEX

ABOUT THE AUTHORS

CECILY WONG is a writer for Atlas Obscura and the author of two novels. Her debut, *Diamond Head*, was a Barnes and Noble Discover Great New Writers Selection, received an *Elle* Readers' Prize, and was voted a best debut of the 2015 Brooklyn Book Festival. Her second novel, *Kaleidoscope*, will be published in 2022. Her work has appeared in the *Wall Street Journal*, the *LA Review of Books*, *Self* magazine, Bustle, Atlas Obscura, and elsewhere. She lives in Portland, Oregon, with her husband and daughter. Visit Cecily online at @cecilyannwong.

DYLAN THURAS is the cofounder and creative director of Atlas Obscura. Coauthor of the #1 *New York Times* bestseller *Atlas Obscura: An Explorer's Guide to the World's Hidden Wonders* and the *New York Times* bestselling kids' book *An Explorer's Guide for the World's Most Adventurous Kid*, he is also the host of the *Atlas Obscura* podcast. He lives in New York State's Hudson Valley with his family. Visit him online at @dylanthuras.

ABOUT GASTRO OBSCURA

Gastro Obscura's mission is to inspire wonder and curiosity about the world through food and drink. Launched in 2017 as part of the travel and media company Atlas Obscura, our articles, videos, recipes, and global guide to places to eat and drink, as well as the experiences and trips we run around the world, allow readers, travelers, and curious people to explore what food and drink reveal about the places where they're made and the people who make them.

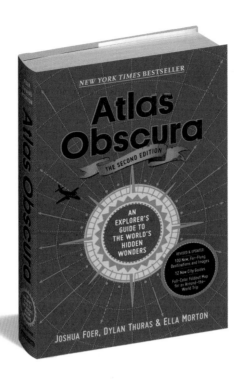